fodors 05

GERMANY

Where to Stay and Eat
for All Budgets

Must-See Sights
and Local Secrets

Ratings You Can Trust

Fodor's Travel Publications   New York, Toronto, London, Sydney, Auckland
www.fodors.com

FODOR'S GERMANY 2005
Editor: Amanda Theunissen

Editorial Production: Jenna L. Bagnini
Editorial Contributors: Kerry Brady, Uli Ehrhardt, Tim Howe, Christina Knight, Heather Phibbs, Marton Radkai, Jürgen Scheunemann, Ted Shoemaker
Maps: David Lindroth, *cartographer;* Bob Blake and Rebecca Baer, *map editors*
Design: Fabrizio La Rocca, *creative director;* Moon Sun Kim, *cover design;* Guido Caroti, *art director;* Melanie Marin, *senior picture editor*
Production/Manufacturing: Robert B. Shields
Cover Photo (Dinkelsbuhl Annual Children's Festival): Robert Harding World Imagery

ISBN 1–4000–1433–6

ISSN 1525–5034

SPECIAL SALES
This book is available for special discounts for bulk purchases for sales promotions or premiums. Special editions, including personalized covers, excerpts of existing books, and corporate imprints, can be created in large quantities for special needs. For more information, write to Special Markets/Premium Sales, 1745 Broadway, MD 6-2, New York, New York 10019, or e-mail specialmarkets@randomhouse.com.

AN IMPORTANT TIP & AN INVITATION
Although all prices, opening times, and other details in this book are based on information supplied to us at press time, changes occur all the time in the travel world, and Fodor's cannot accept responsibility for facts that become outdated or for inadvertent errors or omissions. So **always confirm information when it matters,** especially if you're making a detour to visit a specific place. Your experiences—positive and negative—matter to us. If we have missed or misstated something, **please write to us.** We follow up on all suggestions. Contact the Germany editor at editors@fodors.com or c/o Fodor's at 1745 Broadway, New York, New York 10019.

DESTINATION GERMANY

E very epoch has left its mark on Germany's landscape of fertile river valleys, rolling vineyards, and lofty peaks. Roman relics keep company with medieval castles, baroque palaces with half-timber farmhouses, and Renaissance patrician homes with communist-era high rises. From the days of Charlemagne through the Reformation, two world wars, and 40 years of division it has been a tumultuous ride for this country that only became a nation in 1871. Though its history is a heavy one, Germany is just as well known for its lighter diversions such as oompah music, cuckoo clocks, beer gardens, and one-liter beer steins. Germans have a tradition of easygoing hospitality and friendliness—whether you visit the terraced hills along the Rhine, the snow-covered Alps, or the boisterous beer halls in Munich, you're sure to feel right at home. Have a fabulous trip!

Tim Jarrell, Publisher

CONTENTS

ON THE ROAD WITH FODOR'S

A trip takes you out of yourself. Concerns of life at home completely disappear, driven away by more immediate thoughts—about, say, what marvels will beguile the next day or where you'll have dinner. That's where Fodor's comes in. We make sure that you know all your options, so that you don't miss something around the next bend just because you didn't know it was there. With Fodor's at your side, serendipitous discoveries are never far away.

Our success in showing you every corner of Germany is a credit to our extraordinary writers. Although there's no substitute for travel advice from a good friend who knows your style, our contributors are the next best thing—the kind of people you would poll for travel advice if you knew them.

Kerry Brady was born in St. Louis, Missouri, and now lives in Wiesbaden. After working at the German Wine Information Bureau in New York, she moved to Germany in 1981 to coordinate the activities of the European and overseas press services of the German Wine Institute, Mainz. Today she runs Fine Lines, a public relations agency specializing in wine, food, and travel. Her latest books are *The Hungry Traveler: Germany,* and *A Traveller's Wine Guide to Germany.*

Uli Ehrhardt, a native German, has had a long career in the travel and tourism fields. He began as an interpreter and travel consultant in the United States and then for 20 years served as director of the State Tourist Board Bodensee–Oberschwaben (Lake Constance–Upper Swabia). He now makes his home in the city of Ulm as a tourism consultant, writer, and teacher at a state college for tourism.

Tim Howe taught German in his native England before catching the travel bug and taking off to earn a living (but not a fortune) as an itinerant teacher of English in and around Europe. When he arrived in Munich three years ago, Tim liked the area too much to move on. When he's not writing travel features or translating, Tim can be found touring Bavaria by foot, bicycle, or on skis.

Christina Knight, a former Fodor's editor, spent years editing guides to Germany before gathering up her notes and moving to Berlin. She currently writes for the city's English-language monthly, the *Ex-Berliner,* and other publications.

Heather Phibbs moved to Frankfurt in early 2002, pursuing a long-held desire to live in Europe. A native of Richmond, Virginia, she studied journalism at the University of North Carolina. She has also lived in Washington, D.C., South Carolina, New York City, and Sydney, Australia. Heather works as an advertising copywriter and freelance travel writer.

Marton Radkai is a native New Yorker of Bavarian-Hungarian descent and lives in Munich. Since 1985 he has worked as a travel photographer, translator, editor, and writer for radio and print media in Germany and Austria.

Jürgen Scheunemann grew up in Hamburg and fell in love with Berlin 15 years ago. He has written, published, and translated several history and travel books on U.S. and German cities, including *Fodor's Berlin,* First Edition (2002), and has been an editor at Berlin's leading daily, *Der Tagesspiegel,* and an associate producer for BBC Television. Today his award-winning articles are also published in U.S. magazines such as *Hemispheres.*

Ted Shoemaker settled in Germany more than 40 years ago when, as a U.S. Army officer, he married a German. He has been editor of three English-language magazines in Germany and a correspondent for many American publications. He lives in Frankfurt.

ABOUT THIS BOOK

The best source for travel advice is a like-minded friend who's just been where you're headed. But with or without that friend, you'll be in great shape to find your way around your destination once you learn to find your way around your Fodor's guide.

SELECTION

Our goal is to cover the best properties, sights, and activities in their category, as well as the most interesting communities to visit. We make a point of including local food-lovers' hot spots as well as neighborhood options, and we avoid all that is touristy unless it's really worth your time. You can go on the assumption that everything in this book is recommended wholeheartedly by our writers and editors. Flip to On the Road with Fodor's to learn more about who they are. It goes without saying that no property pays to be included.

RATINGS

Orange stars ★ denote sights and properties that our editors and writers consider the very best in the entire book. These, the best of the best, are listed in the Fodor's Choice section in the front of the book. Black stars ★ highlight the sights and properties we deem Highly Recommended, the don't-miss sights within any region. In cities, sights pinpointed with numbered map bullets ❶ in the margins tend to be more important than those without bullets.

SPECIAL SPOTS

Pleasures & Pastimes and text on chapter title pages focus on experiences that reveal the spirit of the destination. Also watch for Off the Beaten Path sights. Some are out of the way, some are quirky, and all are worthwhile. When the munchies hit, look for Need a Break? suggestions.

TIME IT RIGHT

Check On the Calendar up front and chapters' Timing sections for weather and crowd overviews and best days and times to visit.

SEE IT ALL

Use Fodor's exclusive Great Itineraries as a model for your trip. Either follow those that begin the book, or mix regional itineraries from several chapters. In cities, Good Walks guide you to important sights in each neighborhood; ▶ indicates the starting points of walks and itineraries in the text and on the map.

BUDGET WELL

Hotel and restaurant price categories from ¢ to $$$$ are defined in the opening pages of each chapter—expect to find a balanced selection for every budget. For attractions, we always give standard adult admission fees; reductions are usually available for children, students, and senior citizens. Look in Discounts & Deals in Smart Travel Tips for information on destination-wide ticket schemes.

BASIC INFO

Smart Travel Tips lists travel essentials for the entire area covered by the book; city- and region-specific basics end each chapter. To find the best way to get around, see the Transportation section; see individual modes of travel ("By Car," "By Train") for details.

ON THE MAPS	Maps throughout the book show you what's where and help you find your way around. Black and orange numbered bullets ❶ ❶ in the text correlate to bullets on maps.
BACKGROUND	We give background information within the chapters in the course of explaining sights as well as in CloseUp boxes and in Understanding Germany at the end of the book. German Vocabulary and the Menu Guide can be invaluable.
FIND IT FAST	Within the book, chapters are arranged geographically in a clockwise direction starting with Munich, in the southeastern part of the country. All city chapters begin with exploring information, with a section for each neighborhood (each recommending a good tour and listing sights alphabetically). All regional chapters are divided geographically; within each area, towns are covered in logical geographical order and with attractive routes, and interesting places between towns are flagged as En Route. Heads at the top of each page help you find what you need within a chapter.
DON'T FORGET	Restaurants are open for lunch and dinner daily unless we state otherwise; we mention dress only when there's a specific requirement and reservations only when they're essential or not accepted— it's always best to book ahead. Unless we say otherwise, hotels have private baths, phone, TVs, and air-conditioning and operate on the European Plan (aka EP, meaning without meals). We always list facilities but not whether you'll be charged extra to use them, so when pricing accommodations, find out what's included.
SYMBOLS	

Many Listings

★ Fodor's Choice
★ Highly recommended
⊠ Physical address
✢ Directions
⬠ Mailing address
☎ Telephone
🖷 Fax
⊕ On the Web
✉ E-mail
🎫 Admission fee
◷ Open/closed times
► Start of walk/itinerary
Ⓤ U-bahn/S-bahn stations
▭ Credit cards

Hotels & Restaurants

🏨 Hotel
◇ Number of rooms
♨ Facilities
⦿ Meal plans
✗ Restaurant
⌂ Reservations
🏛 Dress code
⊻ Smoking
✗🏨 Hotel with restaurant that warrants a visit

Other

♨ Family-friendly
🛈 Contact information
⇨ See also
⊠ Branch address
☞ Take note

Germany

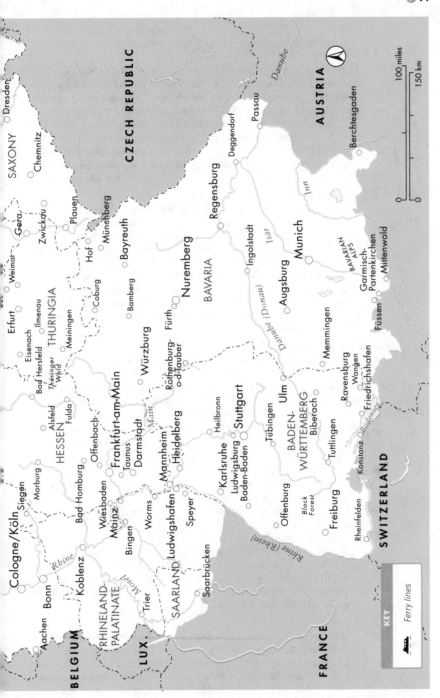

BELGIUM

Aachen

Cologne/Köln

Bonn

Siegen

Marburg

Rhine

Koblenz

RHINELAND-
PALATINATE

LUX.

Trier

Mosel

Bad Homburg

Wiesbaden

Mainz

Bingen

Worms

SAARLAND

Saarbrücken

Ludwigshafen

Speyer

FRANCE

Alsfeld

Fulda

HESSEN

Offenbach

Frankfurt-am-Main

Taunus

Darmstadt

Mannheim

Heidelberg

Main

Karlsruhe

Ludwigsburg

Baden-Baden

Offenburg

*Black
Forest*

Freiburg

Rheinfelden

SWITZERLAND

Heilbronn

Stuttgart

BADEN-
WÜRTTEMBERG

Tübingen

Biberach

Tuttlingen

Konstanz

Bodensee

Friedrichshafen

Wangen

Ravensburg

Ulm

Memmingen

Rhine (Rhein)

Marburg

Weimar

Erfurt

Eisenach

Bad Hersfeld

Ilmenau

THURINGIA

*Thüringer
Wald*

Meiningen

Coburg

Würzburg

Rothenburg-
o-d-Tauber

Bamberg

Fürth

Nuremberg

BAVARIA

Ingolstadt

Isar

Augsburg

Danube (Donau)

Munich

BAVARIAN
ALPS

Garmisch-
Partenkirchen

Füssen

Mittenwald

Gera

Weimar

Zwickau

Plauen

Münchberg

Hof

Bayreuth

Regensburg

Deggendorf

Passau

Inn

AUSTRIA

Berchtesgaden

SAXONY

Dresden

Chemnitz

CZECH REPUBLIC

Danube

100 miles

150 km

0   0

WHAT'S WHERE

1 Munich

Hands and beer steins down, the easygoing and fun-loving capital of Bavaria is the favorite city of both natives and visitors from abroad. Class and kitsch coexist amicably here—the former embodied in the glorious city palaces of the art-loving Wittelsbach dynasty and the latter the stuff of Oktoberfest, a fortnight-long tribute to beer and its consequences. The city's fashionable burghers support some of the best restaurants in the country, but the *Gemütlichkeit* is nowhere stronger than in the city's many beer halls. A much more tranquil refuge is the Englischer Garten, where you can cross-country ski or sunbathe nude, depending on the season.

2 The Bavarian Alps

Majestic peaks, rocky pastures, and frescoed houses further brightened by window boxes overflowing with geraniums make for Germany's most photogenic region. Year-round you can find the country's finest skiing in Garmisch-Partenkirchen and scenic hikes above mountain lakes such as Tegernsee, Schliersee, or the pristine Königsee, near Berchtesgaden. "Mad" King Ludwig let loose his architectural fantasies on the island palace Schloss Herrenchiemsee, modeled on Versailles. Craftsmanship continues in towns such as Mittenwald, where violin makers have worked since the 17th century, and in Oberammergau, where many residents are wood-carvers.

3 The Bavarian Forest

Hikers, anglers, and nature lovers head to this idyllic mountainous retreat on the border of the Czech Republic. The region is part of Europe's largest and densest forest and had long been inaccessible to outsiders. People living here have their own distinctive accent and, unlike southern Germans, a quiet reserve. They take great pride in their handicrafts such as glassmaking. The region's only large and well-known city is Passau, almost Mediterranean in its appearance. A gateway city to the west of the forest is the wonderfully medieval Regensburg.

4 The Romantic Road

Picturesque beyond words, the Romantische Strasse (Romantic Road) is more than 355 km (220 mi) of castles, walled villages, half-timber houses, and imposing churches, all set in pastoral countryside. The Rivers Tauber, Lech, and Main are never distant. Though it looks like a fairy-tale version of a medieval town, Rothenburg-ob-der-Tauber is authentic and one of Europe's best-preserved. A total fantastical construction of a castle is King Ludwig II's Schloss Neuschwanstein, which even Walt Disney looked to for inspiration. The baroque era still lives in the city of Würzburg where powerful prince-bishops spared little expense in creating astonishing opulence.

5 Franconia

The region of Franconia is rich in ancient and cultural cities, making it a small but immensely interesting area. The countryside is dotted with old villages and a few historic and very prosperous cities that have played a significant role in German cultural history. The former imperial city of Nürnberg, in the heart of hilly Franconia, greets visitors with one of Europe's most beautiful medieval downtowns. Bamberg, Coburg, and Krombach are little-known villages with quiet streets and breathtaking churches or cloisters. Bayreuth is a national shrine, where Germany's elite come each year to applaud the dramatic operas of Richard Wagner, who once lived here.

6 The Bodensee

The Bodensee, or Lake Constance, is the warmest area in Germany, and though it's a popular vacation area, no tourist developments have spoiled its historic atmosphere. The scenery is enchanting, especially when viewed from the shoreline promenades or from ferries traveling between towns like terraced Meersburg and beautifully preserved Konstanz. Formal gardens of tulips, hyacinths, and narcissi thrive on the colorful island of Mainau. The maze of streets in the island town of Lindau carries a history that takes you back to Roman Gaul. Bike routes circle the lake; pedal long enough and you'll cross into Switzerland or Austria.

7 The Black Forest

The Black Forest is synonymous with cuckoo clocks and primeval woodland: certainly thousands of acres are cloaked in pines, and at least one entire town, little Triberg, goes all atwitter every hour. The area also gave its name to one of Germany's most favorite cakes. For many Germans, the Black Forest is the epitome of a healthy vacation filled with hikes and fresh mountain air. A world apart from the quaint villages is the stately spa and casino resort Baden-Baden. Westward through the deep Hell Valley gorge is the beautifully restored university town of Freiburg, the region's largest city.

8 Heidelberg & the Neckar Valley

For most tourists, good old Heidelberg is quintessential Germany—the medieval town is full of cobblestone alleys, half-timber houses, vineyards, castles, and Germany's oldest university. The Castle Road makes its way through the Neckar Valley, passing fortresses and villages all the way south to the Schwabenländle, the German nickname for the Swabian cities of Stuttgart, Heilbronn, and Tübingen. It's the home of hardworking people, speaking with one of the country's most distinctive dialects, a singing and soft version of southern German. It's also one of the most affluent areas in Europe. The area's largest employer is DaimlerChrysler, headquartered in Stuttgart. The Swabians are also famous for their pasta mania: everything here is served with curly egg noodles called *spätzle*.

9 Frankfurt

With its skyline of skyscrapers, Frankfurt is home to Germany's leading stock exchange, the Börse; host to many international trade fairs; and the seat of the new European Central Bank, which controls the euro. Prosperity here has left the art museums flush with works by Dürer, Vermeer, Rembrandt, Rubens, Monet, and Renoir, among others. The city has Germany's oldest jazz cellar and an annual jazz festival. But not everything is modern here. Römerberg Square is lined with historic buildings, and writer Goethe's home is a popular attraction. Frankfurters relax in traditional ways—they head for the nearby Taunus Hills for a hike or stop for *Apfelwein* (hard cider) at taverns in the district of Sachsenhausen, on the south bank of the Main River.

⑩ The Pfalz & Rhine Terrace

Wine reigns supreme here. Bacchanalian festivals pepper the calendar between May and October, and wineries welcome drop-ins for tastings year-round. Once you've had your fill of looking at the bottom of a wine glass, head for Worms, whose streets were ancient even when Charlemagne and Luther walked them. Its Jewish cemetery has been in use for more than a millennium. Three great cathedrals are found in Worms, Speyer, and Mainz. Mainz is also where Johannes Gutenberg printed the first Bible and where Germany's powerful public television station ZDF is headquartered. The region's most famous son is former German chancellor Helmut Kohl, the longest-reigning German head of state in the 20th century.

⑪ The Rhineland

Although it's part of westernmost Germany, the Rhineland is the country's spiritual heart. Stories that originated here—of the Nibelungen and the Loreley—have become national legends, and tourists have been enthralled for centuries by the mighty Rhine River and the Mosel, the tributary with improbable twists and turns. Cruises on either river last anywhere from a few hours to a week, passing riverbanks terraced with castles, villages, and vineyards (the world's best Rieslings are produced here). Rüdesheim, the region's unofficial wine capital, has plenty of cozy wine taverns and the entire area has castle hotels. Ancient Trier, on the Mosel, was 1,300 years old when Caesar's legions arrived. Wiesbaden, on the Rhine, was founded by Roman soldiers who discovered its hot springs. Farther north, in vibrant Köln (Cologne), a certain 18th-century eau de cologne is still for sale on Glockengasse at the address for which it is named, No. 4711. However, the city may be most famous as the site of the country's largest and finest Gothic cathedral and for the German version of Mardi Gras, the Karneval, in February.

⑫ The Fairy-Tale Road

The Märchenstrasse (Fairy-Tale Road), stretching 370 mi between Hanau and Bremen, is also the road less traveled (all the better for those who choose it). This is Brothers Grimm country, the area that the great compilers of folklore mined for their sometimes-dark tales of magic and miracles. The Grimms' imaginations were nourished during a childhood in Steinau an der Strasse, a medieval beauty of a town where their stories delight children today at the Steinauer Marionettentheater. In Hameln (Hamelin), sculptures, plaques, and even rat-shape pastries recall the tale of the Pied Piper. Bremen is fabled to have been saved by a quartet of animal musicians. Their statues can be seen against the backdrop of a medieval downtown, a historic reminder of Bremen's proud membership in the Hanseatic League. All along the Fairy-Tale Road, misty woodlands and small towns full of half-timber houses look as if they have mysterious and compelling tales to tell.

(13) Hamburg

With its international port, rusty brick warehouses, fish market, and Reeper-bahn red-light district, Hamburg is undeniably gritty. But its downtown is truly elegant, laced with canals spanned by small bridges. The Inner and Outer Alster Lakes, bordered with parks and shopping arcades and big enough for sailing, form the city's heart, and a 14½-km (9-mi) foot-path lines the Elbe's riverbanks. The city's architecture is diverse, en-compassing the neo-Renaissance Rathaus, on a square not unlike Venice's Piazza San Marco, and turn-of-the-20th-century art nouveau buildings.

(14) Schleswig-Holstein & the Baltic Coast

Schleswig-Holstein and the former East Germany's Baltic coast share a windswept landscape scattered with medieval towns, fishing villages, long white beaches, and summer resorts. The Ahlbeck pier dates from the 19th century, and charming Stralsund has a 14th-century redbrick Rathaus (town hall). Schwerin, the area's second-largest town after Ro-stock, has an amazing castle, and striking chalk cliffs edge remote, quiet Rügen island. In Schleswig-Holstein, major draws are chic Sylt island and medieval Lübeck.

(15) Berlin

By night this capital is saucy, and culture thrives in its opera houses, con-cert halls, and theaters. Two cities' worth of world-class museums com-pete for your daylight hours, as do the shops along 2-mi Kurfürstendamm, which ends at a sobering World War II memorial, the Kaiser-Wilhelm-Gedächtniskirche. One can't forget modern history at other landmarks such as the Brandenburger Tor, which stood alone in divided Berlin's no-man's-land. Originally the capital of Prussia, the city displays its royal finery and grand collections at Schloss Charlottenburg and at Pots-dam's magnificent palace of Sanssouci, the most beautiful and largest palace complex east of Versailles.

(16) Saxony, Saxony-Anhalt & Thuringia

Much of Germany's cultural contributions to the world stem from these eastern states. Weimar was home to the poets Goethe and Schiller. The Bach family home and the Thomaskirche, where Johann Sebastian served as choirmaster for 27 years, are in Leipzig, where Richard Wag-ner was born. Both he and Richard Strauss had premieres at the Sem-per Opera House in Dresden, whose Brühlsche Terrasse above the Elbe River was once called "Europe's balcony." It was in Meissen that an 18th-century alchemist discovered how to make fine porcelain. And Mar-tin Luther nailed his 95 Theses to the door of Wittenberg's Schlosskirche, inching closer to a break with Rome.

Highlights of Germany
12 to 18 days

Germany offers everything from opera houses to oompah bands and from seaside villages to snowcapped mountains. For a parade of early German architecture, cruise the steeply banked, vineyard-terraced Rheingau between Mainz and Koblenz, full of riverside castles. The Romantic movement, a product of this evocative setting, flourished in the university town of Heidelberg. Munich, Germany's most laid-back city and the capital of Bavaria and of beer, is the gateway to the Alps and foothill lakes. In Nürnberg, relics of the Holy Roman Empire coexist with ruins of the Third Reich. Leipzig and Dresden are the pearls of what was East Germany, and just to the north of these is the racy capital of Berlin.

RHINE VALLEY FROM MAINZ TO KOBLENZ

3 to 4 days. From Frankfurt take the short train ride over the Rhine to see Mainz's Dom, one of Europe's greatest Romanesque cathedrals. Continue by train through Rheingau vineyards to Bingen and stay in a castle hotel. In the morning take a leisurely river cruise as far as Koblenz, breaking up your journey to stay overnight in a riverside inn. Allow a day for exploring Koblenz, setting aside an hour to visit the scenic Deutsches Eck, the point where the Mosel flows into the Rhine, and the site of monuments to Germany's unity and division.

HEIDELBERG

1 to 2 days. Generations of artists, composers, writers, and romantics have crossed the Alte Brücke, spanning the Neckar River, and climbed up the steep, winding Schlangenweg to the aptly named Philosophers' Path. At the top, you'll have a view of Germany's

archetypal university city and its ruined Renaissance castle. Don't leave Heidelberg without eating (and drinking) in a centuries-old student tavern.

MUNICH & THE ALPS

3 to 4 days. Visit the Wittelsbach palaces Schloss Nymphenburg and Residenz, reminders that Bavaria once was the second-most-powerful kingdom in Germany. Follow that with an evening in a beer hall, which will confirm everything you've ever heard about beer, pork, and potato consumption in Bavaria. Relax on the morning train to Berchtesgaden, the Bavarian Alps a soothing cyclorama beyond the window. Not far away from Berchtesgaden, Hitler's Obersalzberg retreat takes priority, but find time for the most beautiful

corner of Germany, the mountain-ringed Königsee.

NÜRNBERG

1 to 2 days. In Nürnberg you'll see the full spectrum of German history. The city's massive fortress, dating from 1050, was the residence of successive Holy Roman Emperors. The former home of Renaissance artist Albrecht Dürer is now a fascinating museum. Ride the S-2 suburban rail line to the Zeppelinfeld, the enormous parade grounds where Hitler addressed the Nürnberg rallies.

LEIPZIG & DRESDEN

2 to 3 days. To understand the enormous political and social changes brought about by German reunification, you have to visit Leipzig or Dresden—both, if possi-

Berlin

POLAND

SPREEWALD

190 km

A13

111 km

Leipzig · A14 · Dresden

SAXONY

A9

A9

270 km

Bayreuth

A9

Nürnberg

BAVARIA

A9

175 km

A9

Munich

A8

162 km · A8

AUSTRIA

Berchtesgaden

ble. Deteriorated after nearly a half century of Communism, they have returned to commercial and cultural prominence. A choral concert in Leipzig's Thomaskirche, where Johann Sebastian Bach was choirmaster, or a walk high above the Elbe River along Dresden's Brühlsche Terrasse is completely enchanting.

BERLIN

2 to 3 days. Reunited and rebuilt, Berlin races forward. The German parliament is back in the Reichstag, and world-renowned architects have changed the city's face. Hip restaurants and bars fill the courtyards and alleyways of Mitte, which is also home to many museums. Sights recalling World War II and the Cold War are everywhere, and antiquities steal the spotlight on Museum Island. The Zoologischer Garten, Tiergarten, and Ku'-damm cafés offer the relaxation you'll need after being swept up in this city's energy.

BY PUBLIC TRANSPORTATION

Mainz is a 30-minute train ride from Frankfurt, and Bingen is 40 minutes farther by train or bus. Cruise boats leave Bingen daily for the Rhine journey to Koblenz. Catch an InterCity train in Koblenz for the return trip south, changing at Mannheim for Heidelberg (3 hrs). Return to Mannheim by a local train (10 min) and change to an InterCity or Eurocity train to Munich (about 3 hrs). InterCity Express and Eurocity services link Munich and Nürnberg (1 hr, 45 min). InterCity and InterRegio services link Nürnberg and

Leipzig (3 hrs, 40 min) and Leipzig and Dresden (1 hr). There are hourly InterCity and other express services from Dresden to Berlin (1 hr). Return from Berlin to Frankfurt by InterCity Express (3 hrs) or fly back (1 hr).

Castles in Wine Country
7 to 10 days

Centuries of German culture unfold on a medieval castle tour through the valleys of the Rhine and its tributaries. Today castle guest rooms and restaurants provide panoramic views as well as glasses of crisp Riesling and velvety Spätburgunder (Pinot Noir), Germany's finest white and red wines. Wine estates often post signs near their entrances that announce WEINVERKAUF (wine for sale) or HEUTE WEINPROBE (wine tastings today). Come in summer or autumn, when the wine-festival season is in full swing and many a castle courtyard hosts theater and concerts.

MITTELRHEIN & MOSEL

3 to 4 days. The Mittelrhein wine town of St. Goar is an ideal base for excursions into the Rhine and Mosel valleys. The terrace of the hotel-restaurant opposite Burg Rheinfels, the Rhine's largest fortress ruin, is a superb vantage point. Ferry across the river to catch a train to Rüdesheim, the liveliest town in the Rheingau wine region. Return to St. Goar on a KD Rhine steamer, and savor a glass of delicate Mosel wine or its fuller-bodied Rhine counterpart. Set aside a full day to tour the Rhine's only impregnable castle, the Marksburg, followed by a jaunt through the lower Mosel valley from Koblenz to the fairy-tale cas-

NECKAR VALLEY

2 to 3 days. Spend one day exploring Heidelberg's Old Town and massive castle ruins, but beware of summer crowds. The town straddles the Hessische Bergstrasse and northern Baden wine regions. The white varietals Riesling, Grauburgunder (Pinot Gris), and Weissburgunder (Pinot Blanc) yield the finest wines. On the Burgenstrasse (Castle Road), have lunch on the castle terrace in Hirschhorn. Neckarzimmern's Burg Hornberg, residence of a celebrated 16th-century knight, is the perfect stopover. Atop its own terraced vineyards in the Württemberg wine region, the 12th-century castle includes guest rooms with splendid views of the Neckar Valley as well as good food and wine (try the spicy white varietals Traminer and Muskateller). There's a museum and falconry at Burg Guttenberg, and medieval Bad Wimpfen has a former imperial palace and a Benedictine monastery.

tle Burg Eltz. En route, you'll pass breathtakingly steep vineyards and dozens of wine estates.

TAUBER & MAIN VALLEYS

2 to 3 days. The Baden, Württemberg, and Franken wine regions converge in the peaceful Tauber Valley. Foremost are the earthy, robust, dry white Silvaner and Rivaner (Müller-Thurgau) wines, often bottled in the flagon-shape Bocksbeutel. Bad Mergentheim, a pretty spa and former residence of the Knights of the Teutonic Order, lies in the heart of the valley. In neighboring Weikersheim, tour the Renaissance hunting palace of the counts of Hohenlohe, after which you can sample the local

wines in the shop at the gateway. Follow the course of the Tauber to its confluence with the Main River at Wertheim, also known as "little Heidelberg" because of its impressive hilltop castle ruins. In Würzburg, your next stop, you'll see many Gothic and baroque masterpieces plus the Marienberg fortress and its successor, the opulent Residenz. Three first-class wine estates here have wine pubs and shops.

BY PUBLIC TRANSPORTATION

Fast, frequent train service from Frankfurt to St. Goar, Koblenz, Heidelberg, or Würzburg, supplemented by local train and bus

service, gets you to the above destinations within two hours. The Deutsche Touring company's Europabus travels the Burgenstrasse, including Heidelberg and the Neckar Valley, as well as the Romantic Road, serving Würzburg, Bad Mergentheim, and Weikersheim. Sights are open and boats cruise the Rhine, Mosel, Neckar, and Main rivers from Easter through October.

The Great German Outdoors
7 to 10 days

Germans love the outdoors, and the autobahns are often jammed with families on their way to the countryside. News of a cold front on its way from Russia sets Germans to dusting off their skis, and the prediction of a high-pressure zone moving up from the Mediterranean fills the beds in hiking retreats. The mountains and lakes of Bavaria are southern Germany's playground. The Black Forest and Bodensee (Lake Constance), also in the south, are popular spa and recreation destinations. The gateway to all of them is Munich.

BAVARIAN ALPS & LAKES
3 to 4 days. The Ammersee, ringed by cycling paths and walking trails, is a short ride from Munich. Most of the lakes in the Alps are warm enough for swimming in summer, and boatyards rent small sailboats and windsurfing boards. There are hiking trails in the mountains above Tegernsee; for more challenging walking, head to Garmisch-Partenkirchen. It's one of Bavaria's three leading ski centers, with skiing virtually year-round on the glacier atop the Zugspitze, Germany's highest mountain. From here, wind your way down to the warmer clime of the Bodensee via the Deutsche Alpenstrasse.

BODENSEE
2 to 3 days. The Bodensee area is great for bicycling. An uninterrupted cycle path follows the shore of the lake, which you and your bike can cross via ferries. Bikes are rented at shops and some hotels. The climate here is unusually warm for Germany. Vineyards and orchards fill the hillsides, and rare and exotic plants decorate the tiny island of Mainau. On the rural island Reichenau, you can hike or pedal between Romanesque churches dating back to the year 816. Bird-watchers should head to the Mettnau Peninsula.

THE BLACK FOREST
2 to 3 days. The Black Forest has wide-open spaces for walking, horseback riding, cycling, and even golfing. In winter, meadows become ski slopes, and forest paths are meticulously groomed as cross-country ski trails. This is also spa country, where you can rest your weary limbs in hot springs in Baden-Baden while rubbing elbows with high society.

BY PUBLIC TRANSPORTATION
The lakes near Munich are easily accessible both by S-bahn suburban services and local trains that run hourly between Munich and Garmisch-Partenkirchen. The Bodensee towns are all within three hours of Munich by train, and local buses and trains travel the north shore of the lake. Baden-Baden is about 6½ hours from Munich by train via Stuttgart or Karlsruhe and 3–4 hours from Friedrichshafen. Local buses and trains link Baden-Baden with most Black Forest resorts.

Munich

Ammersee · A96 · 40 km · A8 · 50 km · 318 · Tegernsee · 207 km · A95 · 90 km · Zugspitze · Garmisch-Partenkirchen

MAP KEY
Castles in Wine Country
The Great German Outdoors

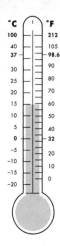

The tourist season in most of Germany runs from May through October, when the weather is at its best. Prices are generally higher in summer, so **consider visiting during the off-season to save money** (but be aware that the weather is often cold and some attractions are closed or have shorter hours in winter). Most resorts offer between-season (*Zwischensaison*) and edge-of-season (*Nebensaison*) rates, and tourist offices can provide lists of hotels that offer low-price inclusive weekly packages (*Pauschal-angebote*). It's wise to **avoid cities at times of major trade fairs,** when attendees commandeer all hotel rooms and prices soar. You can check trade fair schedules with the German National Tourist Office.

Climate

Germany's climate is temperate, although cold spells can drop temperatures well below freezing, particularly in the Alps, the Harz region of Lower Saxony and Saxony-Anhalt, the Black Forest, and the higher regions of northern Franconia. Summers are usually warm, though you should **be prepared for a few rainy days,** especially in the north. As you get nearer to the Alps, the summers get shorter, with warm weather often not beginning until the end of May. Fall can be spectacular in the south. Germans measure temperature in Celsius.

▶ Forecasts **Weather Channel Connection** ☎ 900/932–8437 95¢ per minute from a Touch-Tone phone ⊕ www.weather.com.

The following are the average daily maximum and minimum temperatures for Berlin, Frankfurt, and Munich.

BERLIN

Jan.	35F	2C	May	66F	19C	Sept.	68F	20C
	26	– 3		47	8		50	10
Feb.	37F	3C	June	72F	22C	Oct.	56F	13C
	26	– 3		53	12		42	6
Mar.	46F	8C	July	75F	24C	Nov.	45F	7C
	31	0		57	14		36	2
Apr.	56F	13C	Aug.	74F	23C	Dec.	38F	3C
	39	4		56	13		29	– 1

FRANKFURT

Jan.	39F	4C	May	69F	20C	Sept.	69F	21C
	30	– 1		49	9		52	11
Feb.	43F	6C	June	74F	23C	Oct.	57F	14C
	31	1		55	13		44	7
Mar.	51F	11C	July	75F	24C	Nov.	45F	7C
	37	3		58	15		37	3
Apr.	59F	15C	Aug.	76F	24C	Dec.	40F	4C
	41	5		57	14		32	0

MUNICH

Jan.	35F	1C	May	64F	18C	Sept.	67F	20C
	23	– 5		45	7		48	9
Feb.	38F	3C	June	70F	21C	Oct.	56F	14C
	23	– 5		51	11		40	4
Mar.	48F	9C	July	74F	23C	Nov.	44F	7C
	30	– 1		55	13		33	0
Apr.	56F	14C	Aug.	73F	23C	Dec.	36F	2C
	38	3		54	12		26	– 4

ON THE CALENDAR

Germany ranks number one in the world for the number of foreign visitors attending fairs and exhibitions. Top seasonal events include Carnival festivities in January and February, spring festivals around Easter and Pentecost, Bayreuth's Richard Wagner Festival in August, wine festivals throughout the southern half of the country in late summer and fall, the Oktoberfest in Munich in late September and early October, the Frankfurt Book Fair in October, and December's Christmas markets. For event listings, see the German National Tourist Office's Web site (⊕ www.germany-tourism.de).

ONGOING

Dec.

Christmas Markets, outdoor festivals of light, choral and trumpet music, handcrafted gift items, and mulled wine (*Gluhwein*), are held in just about every German city. Nürnberg's is the most famous.

New Year's Eve is a noisy, colorful event in Berlin, where fireworks are set off from nearly every neighborhood street.

Jan.

Ostensibly a 10-day farm show, Internationale Grüne Woche (Green Week; ☎ 030/30380 ⊕ www.gruenewoche.com) draws thousands to Berlin's convention center with its produce and fine edibles.

Feb.

Fasching season. The Rhineland is Germany's capital of Carnival events. Some of the main Carnival cities are Koblenz, Köln, Mainz, Bonn, and Düsseldorf, although there's also plenty of activity in Munich and southern Germany. Festivities always run through February, finishing on Fasching Dienstag (Shrove or Fat Tuesday).

Frankfurt International Fair is a major consumer-goods trade fair.

International Filmfestspiele Berlin (☎ 030/259–200) is one of Europe's leading film festivals.

The International Toy Fair takes place in Nürnberg.

Mar.

ITB (☎ 030/30380), one of Europe's largest international tourism fairs, takes place in Berlin.

Strong Beer Season in Munich brings out the bands and merrymaking in all the beer halls.

Apr.

Walpurgis festivals. Towns in the Harz Mountains celebrate with spooky, Halloween-like goings-on the night before May Day.

May

Medieval Festival. By downing a huge tankard of wine in one gulp, a 17th-century mayor of Rothenburg-ob-der-Tauber saved the town from sacking. On Pentecost weekend his Meistertrunk is reenacted.

Religious processions, featuring hundreds of horses, giant candles, and elaborate statues, are particularly spectacular in Catholic east-

	ern Bavaria during Pentecost weekend. The best ones are at Bogen, Sankt Englmar, and Kötzting.
May–Sept.	**Rhine in Flames** highlights the river with fireworks, floodlighted castles, and a fleet of illuminated boats; it's held around Bonn (May), Rüdesheim (July), Koblenz (August), and St. Goar (September).
June	**Kiel Week** is an international sailing regatta and cultural festival in the town of Kiel in Schleswig-Holstein.
June–Sept.	**Castle Illuminations,** with spectacular fireworks, are presented in Heidelberg in June, July, and September.
	The **Schleswig-Holstein Music Festival** takes place over six weeks in July and August. World-famous and young musicians perform in cities and towns throughout Schleswig-Holstein.
	Several hundred **Wine Festivals** held throughout the 13 German wine-growing regions, celebrate local wine from early summer until the harvest in late autumn.
July	**Kinderzeche** is Dinkelsbühl's medieval pageant and festival. It reenacts an incident from the Thirty Years' War in which the children stood at the gate and pleaded with the conquerors to spare their homes.
Aug.	**Kulmbach Beer Festival** takes place in Franconia.
	Richard Wagner Festival unfolds the Wagner operas in Bayreuth.
	The Student Prince, the noted Sigmund Romberg operetta set in Heidelberg, is performed in English in Heidelberg's castle courtyard.
Sept.	**Berlin Festival Weeks** feature classical music concerts, exhibits, and many other special events.
	Folk and Beer Festival at Stuttgart/Bad Cannstatt is said to be just as big and raucous as Munich's Oktoberfest.
	Oktoberfest (late September–early October) in Munich draws millions of visitors to cavernous beer tents and fairgrounds.
	Wurstmarkt, the world's largest wine festival, is held next to a giant cask in Bad Dürkheim.
Oct.	**Jazz Fest Berlin** is an international jazz festival held each autumn.
	Bremen Freimarkt is a centuries-old folk festival and procession in Bremen.
	Frankfurt Book Fair is a famous annual literary event and a browser's paradise.
Nov.	**St. Martin's Festival** includes children's lantern processions and is celebrated throughout the Rhineland and Bavaria.

PLEASURES & PASTIMES

Beer & Wine Germany is the world's largest producer and consumer of beer. Each of its high-quality brands is brewed in accordance with the strict German *Reinheitsgebot* (legislation governing purity of ingredients). Drinking beer, even in public and at any time of the day, is socially quite acceptable. North Germans favor *Pils,* a light lagerlike beer. *Alt* is a dark, bitter, English-style ale popular in the northwest. Bavaria prefers the rather heavy *Bockbier* (a type of malt beer) and the typical summer beer *Hefeweizen,* brewed with yeast, also called *Weissbier.* These are usually served in tall ½-liter (16-ounce) glasses.

Germany is also home to the world's finest Riesling wines—inimitable for their refreshing acidity and extraordinary spectrum of aromas and flavors. Other traditional white grape varieties in Germany are Silvaner, Rivaner (Müller-Thurgau), and members of the Pinot family, such as Weissburgunder (Pinot Blanc) and Grauburgunder (Pinot Gris). The red Pinot Spätburgunder (Pinot Noir) is the most important red wine grape. Dornfelder, Portugieser, and Trollinger are also popular reds. Wines labeled Classic or Selection or labels that include the words *trocken* (dry) or *halbtrocken* (off-dry) are drier-style, food-compatible wines. At the other end of the scale are the lusciously sweet dessert wines, labeled as *Auslese,* or longer variations thereof, and *Eiswein* (ice wine). The latter are world-renowned rarities and come at a price. The heart of German wine country lies in the Rhine River Valley and its tributaries, such as the Mosel, Ahr, Nahe, Main, and Neckar rivers. There are also two small regions in the east: in the Elbe River Valley in Saxony and along the Saale and Unstrut rivers in Saxony-Anhalt.

Castles & Palaces Watching over nearly any town that ends in "-burg" is a medieval fortress or Renaissance palace, often now serving the populace as a museum, restaurant, or hotel. Grand 18th- and 19th-century palaces are the pride of almost every *Residenzstadt,* a city that was once a king's, duke's, or bishop's seat, such as Würzburg. Holy Roman Emperors made their home in Nürnberg's Kaiserburg, and renegade Martin Luther spent most of the year 1521 within the hulking Wartburg in Eisenach, hiding from the pope. The castle ruins along the Rhine River are the result of ceaseless fighting with the French, but even their remains were picturesque enough to inspire 19th-century Romantic poets and painters. Other fine castles can be found lurking along the Burgenstrasse (Castle Road) in the Neckar Valley and in mountainous Saxony. The north and northwest are dotted with Renaissance-style *Wasserschlösser* (water palaces), a peculiar variety rarely seen outside Germany. They're built in the middle of a lake or surrounded by an ingenious canal system. Some palaces, such as Ludwig II's Neuschwanstein in Bavaria, are not really castles but were built for show. Berlin, Potsdam, Dresden, Meissen, Schwerin, Munich, and Regensburg have some of the finest palaces in Germany.

Museums

Germans value education more highly than wealth or social status and regularly bring their children to museums to glean some appreciation of art, history, and the world's achievements. Cities such as Stuttgart, Dresden, Frankfurt, and Berlin have nurtured a *Museumslandschaft* (museum landscape), presenting expansive complexes of museums at a single location. Berlin's Museum Island holds monuments of antiquity from around the world and is probably the most amazing museum complex you will ever see. Among the finest German art museums are those in Hamburg, Munich, Frankfurt, and Cologne. Other museums typical for Germany are those showcasing technological inventions, such as the Deutsche Museum in Munich and the Zeppelin Museum on the shore of the Bodensee. Even small towns have *Heimatmuseen* (local museums), which detail the history and cultural contributions of a particular region. Another quirky sort of museum in Germany is the tiny one that exposes Germans' peculiar and often amusing *Sammelleidenschaft* (passion for collecting things)—such as a thimble, crèche, or miniature-toy-soldier museum.

Music

Germany has a lively and centuries-old musical tradition. Though the country is primarily known for its love of classics by Bach, Mozart, Beethoven, Brahms, Haydn, Händel, Wagner, and others, there's also a legion of modern classical composers. Masters such as Schönberg, Richard Strauss, Mahler, Orff, and Stockhausen are hugely popular. Germans don't just listen carefully at classical concerts (avoid any opportunity for your neighbor or the whole row to shush you), they also like to perform. Practically every small town has a music school or *Musikverein* (music association) that regularly presents concerts. This tradition has formed some of the world's leading orchestras, such as the Berlin Philharmonic, and opera houses, as in Berlin, Munich, and Hamburg. Equally important in daily life (just check the local newspapers) are choral societies, mainly church or folk choirs, which appear on stage more often than complete orchestras. The German label Deutsche Grammophon is the leading producer of classical music.

Walks & Hikes

German history, literature, and folk songs are full of *Wanderlust*, the passion for hiking and walking. From the leisurely Sunday afternoon stroll to the more strenuous ramble, walks and hikes are a favorite national pastime in this densely populated land. A retreat into nature is never far off, as an expansive network of trails crisscrosses the whole country. Many towns, communities, and states have carefully laid out their hiking trails to connect points of natural or historic interest. Most paths lead through forests or mountain ranges, but there are also numerous trails along the coast and marshlands. Tourist-information offices are a good source for getting maps and arranging trips in which you can hike from inn to inn while someone else transports your luggage.

FODOR'S CHOICE

The sights, restaurants, hotels, and other travel experiences on these pages are our editors' top picks—our Fodor's Choices. They're the best of their type in the area covered by the book—not to be missed and always worth your time. In the destination chapters that follow, you will find all the details.

WHERE TO STAY

$$$$	**Brenner's Park Hotel & Spa**, Baden-Baden. Luxury abounds at this stately hotel, which claims to be one of the best in the world.
$$$$	**Hotel Brandenburger Hof**, Berlin. The clean, timeless Bauhaus style of this Relais & Chateaux hotel is breathtaking.
$$$$	**Kempinski Atlantic Hotel Hamburg**, Hamburg. A gracious Edwardian palace houses one of Germany's most sumptuous hotels.
$$$$	**Kempinski Grand Hotel**, Heiligendamm. Arguably the finest hotel on the Baltic Coast, the Kempinski is nestled in five meticulously restored, gleaming white structures on a secluded beach.
$$$$	**Nassauer Hof**, Wiesbaden. This elegant hotel on the site of a Roman fortress is renowned for its luxuriously appointed rooms, topflight service, and restaurants.
$$$$	**Raffles Vier Jahreszeiten**, Hamburg. Antiques accentuate the stylish bedrooms, and rare oil paintings adorn the walls of this handsome 19th-century town house.
$$$$	**Schloss Reinhartshausen**, Eltville. A palace in every sense of the word, this hotel and wine estate majestically overlooks beautifully landscaped gardens and the Rhine River.
$$$-$$$$	**Hotel Elephant**, Weimar. The historic Elephant, dating from 1696, is famous for its timeless blend of art deco and Bauhaus styles.
$$$-$$$$	**Hotel Fürstenhof Leipzig**, Leipzig. Impeccable service and stunning 19th-century grandeur make this Leipzig's grandest hotel.
$$$-$$$$	**Opera**, Munich. In a quiet residential district, the Opera offers elegant rooms and perhaps the best service in Munich.
$$$-$$$$	**Park Hotel Bremen**, Bremen. This palatial lakeside hotel has the atmosphere of an exclusive country mansion.
$$$-$$$$	**Steigenberger Insel-Hotel**, Konstanz. This former 16th-century monastery, with its original cloisters, offers luxurious lodging in the Bodensee region.
$$-$$$$	**Admiral**, Munich. On a quiet side street, the Admiral has warm, simple rooms, many with a balcony overlooking the garden.

$$–$$$$	**Hotel Die Hirschgasse,** Heidelberg. A stunning castle view and country home–style suites mark this historic inn.
$$–$$$$	**Johann Lafer's Stromburg,** Stromberg. This luxurious castle hotel and restaurant overlooking Stromberg is run by prolific chef Johann Lafer.
$$–$$$$	**Steigenberger Hotel Frankfurter Hof,** Frankfurt. Old-fashioned, formal elegance is updated with modern services at the Steigenberger, one of Frankfurt's oldest hotels.
$$–$$$$	**Waldhotel Sonnora,** Dreis. Experience one of Germany's finest dining and wining experiences in this elegant country inn set within the forested Eifel Hills in the Rhineland.
$$$	**Bischoff am See,** Tegernsee. Each room in this small hotel in the Bavarian Alps is individually designed with an Asian touch. The restaurant and common rooms have a splendid view of the lake.
$$$	**Hotelrestaurant Jörg Müller,** Westerland. Situated in an old thatch-roof farmhouse, this hotel has a handful of lovely rooms combining Frisian-style designs with classical elegance.
$$–$$$	**Burghotel Auf Schönburg,** Oberwesel. Located in a 12th-century castle, this romantic hotel offers guests an unforgettable stay in the Rhineland.
$$–$$$	**Grand Hotel Russischer Hof,** Weimar. Tolstoy, Liszt, Schumann, and others once stayed at this former Russian city palace in the eastern state of Thuringia.
$$–$$$	**Hotel Deidesheimer Hof,** Deidesheim. A favorite among celebrities, this hotel is known for its country charm and friendly service.
$$–$$$	**Hotel Eisenhut,** Rothenburg-ob-der-Tauber. This is one of the prettiest small hotels in Germany. The rooms are charming, and the restaurant is one of the best along the Romantic Road.
$$–$$$	**Hotel Krone Assmannshausen,** Rüdesheim. This elegant, antiques-filled hotel and restaurant offers first-class service and fine wining and dining.
$$–$$$	**Romantik Hotel Victoria,** Bad Mergentheim. You'll find an elegant lounge, luxurious bedrooms, and a top-notch restaurant at this charmer along the Romantic Road.
$$	**Hotel-Restaurant St. Nepomuk,** Bamberg. This half-timber house seems to float over the Regnitz River in Franconia, offering guests a serene atmosphere and inspiring views.
$$	**Hotel–Restaurant Zur Krone,** Herxheim-Hayna. The simple facade belies this upscale inn that offers modern facilities, tasteful interiors, and an outstanding restaurant.

$$	**Kronenschlösschen,** Eltville-Hattenheim. This stylish art nouveau house boasts individually designed rooms with antique furnishings and marble baths. The two restaurants are excellent.
$$	**Parkhotel Luisenbad,** Bad Reichenhall. If you fancy spoiling yourself in a fin-de-siècle spa hotel, this is *the* place.
$–$$	**Hotel-Restaurant Luther,** Freinsheim. This elegant country inn provides modern comfort amid refined decor; the restaurant is one of the best along the German Wine Road.
$–$$	**InterCity Hotel,** Frankfurt. For convenience and comfort, come to this elegant old-world hostelry, right across the street from Frankfurt's main train station.

BUDGET LODGING

$	**Charlottenburger Hof,** Berlin. No-fuss travelers will find great value in this low-key hotel.
$	**Parkhotel Cham,** Cham. You'll find far-reaching rural views, good service, and outstanding sports facilities at this small hotel outside Cham.
$	**Miethaner Landhotel,** Viechtach. Cozy and child-friendly, this peaceful hotel in the Bavarian Forest boasts stunning views over the surrounding countryside.

RESTAURANTS

$$$$	**Capricorn i Aries,** Köln. Indulge in truly heavenly French cuisine at one of the four tables in this intimate fine-dining establishment.
$$$$	**Endtenfang,** Celle. Chef Hans Sobotka has turned this elegant restaurant along the Fairy-Tale Road into one of the culinary magnets of northern Germany.
$$$$	**Residenz Heinz Winkler,** Aschau. This sturdy village inn is one of Germany's most extraordinary hotel-restaurant complexes. A grand piano and a harp add harmony to the sophisticated scene.
$$$$	**Seehotel Siber,** Konstanz. The major attraction in this small turn-of-the-20th-century villa is its restaurant—the most elegant in the Bodensee region.
$$$$	**Seven Seas,** Hamburg. On a small hill along the River Elbe, this traditional "getaway restaurant" is run by one of Europe's premier chefs.
$$$$	**VAU,** Berlin. This trendsetter defined hip in the Mitte district years ago, and remains a favorite even as it ages. The German fish and game dishes have earned endless praise and awards.
$$$–$$$$	**Hans Thoma Stube,** Freiburg. Innovation meets tradition at this restaurant located in two 18th-century farmhouse rooms, lavishly furnished and decorated with Black Forest antiques.

$$–$$$$	**Waldhorn,** Bebenhausen. Stop for an extraordinary meal here before or after a visit to the Zisterzienzerkloster (Cistercian Monastery).
$$$	**Essigbrätlein,** Nürnberg. Built in 1550, this tiny but elegant restaurant caters to the distinguishing gourmet with a taste for spices.
$$$	**Gargantua,** Frankfurt. Enjoy modern versions of German classics and French-accented dishes in this laid-back dining room.
$–$$$	**PianPolvere,** Düsseldorf. Witness the nightly see-and-be-seen ballet at this ultrastylish and delicious Italian restaurant.
$–$$	**Landgasthaus Schuster,** Freyung. Noted for its excellent local cooking, this tiny restaurant is a good place to sample the cuisine of the Bavarian Forest.
$–$$	**Paeffgen,** Köln. This is the best spot in Köln to taste Kölsch, the city's home brew. The typical German fare is excellent.
$–$$	**Weilachmühle,** Munich. Behind the old, dark wooden door of this restored farmhouse outside Munich, you'll find a restaurant–cum–beer garden–cum–stage and exhibition room serving faultless food.
¢–$$	**Künstlerklause,** Coburg. Excellent cuisine with a surprising exotic touch is served in this little warren of rooms with dark-wood paneling and comfortable leather seats.
¢–$$	**Vitus,** Regensburg. A mixture of modern and classic cuisine is served under Gothic vaulted ceilings at this French favorite.

BUDGET RESTAURANTS

¢–$	**Prinz Myshkin,** Munich. This sophisticated vegetarian restaurant spices up antipasti, homemade gnocchi, tofu, and other dishes by mixing Italian and Asian influences.

CASTLES & PALACES

Burg Eltz (Eltz Castle), Alken. A genuine medieval castle, Burg Eltz merits inclusion on any itinerary.

Schloss, Heidelberg. One of Germany's most memorable sights, the Schloss mesmerizes with its Gothic turrets, Renaissance walls, and abandoned gardens.

Schloss Herrenchiemsee, Chiemsee. King Ludwig II modeled this castle after Louis XIV's Versailles. Though never completed, what remains is impressive.

Schloss Neuschwanstein, Schwangau. Walt Disney modeled Sleeping Beauty's castle after this spectacular palace along the Romantic Road.

Schloss Salem, Salem. Once a palace for the Baden princes, this stunning complex of buildings houses an array of museums and workshops.

Wartburg, Eisenach. Begun in 1067 and expanded through the centuries, this mighty castle has hosted a parade of German historical celebrities, including Frederick the Wise and Martin Luther.

Zwinger, Dresden. This magnificent baroque palace is a riot of garlands, nymphs, ornamentation, and sculpture.

CHURCHES & OTHER BUILDINGS OF INTEREST

Dom (Cathedral), Köln. Köln's landmark embodies one of the purest expressions of the Gothic spirit in Europe.

Frauenkirche (Church of Our Lady), Dresden. Germany's greatest Protestant church is undergoing reconstruction but is still worth a visit.

Kaiserdom (Imperial Cathedral), Frankfurt. Magnificent, original Gothic carvings and a panoramic view from the tower are highlights here.

Kaiserdom, Speyer. With its four towers and 100-foot-high portal, this is one of the finest Romanesque cathedrals in the world.

Kloster Eberbach, Eltville. The Romanesque and Gothic buildings of this former Cistercian monastery in the Rhineland look untouched by time.

Rathaus (Town Hall), Hamburg. A pompous neo-Renaissance affair, this immense building, with its imposing central clock tower and opulent interior, is the symbolic heart of Hamburg.

Schlosskirche (Castle Church), Wittenberg. In 1517 the indignant Martin Luther affixed his 95 Theses to these church doors.

St. Michaeliskirche (St. Michael's Church), Hamburg. This is northern Germany's finest baroque-style ecclesiastical building. Its tower bears the largest tower clock in Germany.

Thomaskirche (St. Thomas's Church), Leipzig. Johann Sebastian Bach was choirmaster at this Gothic church for 27 years and is now buried here.

Vierzehnheiligen, Lichtenfels. The fanciful interior of this august yellow-sandstone edifice represents one of the great examples of rococo decoration in Franconia.

Zisterzienzerkloster (Cistercian Monastery), Bebenhausen. This is a rare example of an almost perfectly preserved medieval monastery dating from the late 12th century.

MUSEUMS

Alte Pinakothek (Old Picture Gallery), Munich. This massive museum exhibits a collection of old masters including works by Dürer, Titian, Rembrandt, Rubens, and Murillo.

Deutsches Museum, Munich. Filled with aircraft, locomotives, and other machinery, this museum is an engineering student's dream.

Festung Rosenberg (Rosenberg Fortress), Kronach. The mighty walls of this fortress in Franconia now house a youth hostel and a gallery featuring works of art from the Middle Ages and the Renaissance.

Goethe Nationalmuseum (Goethe National Museum), Weimar. Explore the life and works of Goethe, one of Germany's greatest writers and poets.

Lutherhalle (Luther Hall), Wittenberg. A museum dedicated to Martin Luther and the Reformation, this is the Augustinian monastery where Luther lived as a teacher-monk.

Museumsinsel (Museum Island), Berlin. This unique complex, including four state museums, houses some of the world's most outstanding art collections.

Naturkundemuseum Senckenberg (Natural History Museum), Frankfurt. Children and adults alike will enjoy the collection here, which includes the famous diplodocus dinosaur.

Neues Museum (New Museum), Nürnberg. Behind the slick, modern edifice of this museum is a remarkable collection devoted to international design.

Staatsgalerie (State Gallery), Stuttgart. This complex, which includes the Neue Staatsgalerie designed by British architect James Stirling, is home to one of the finest art collections in Germany.

OUTDOOR ATTRACTIONS

Bavarian Forest National Park. Known as Europe's Green Roof, this is a 32,000-acre stretch of protected forest. Visitors can hike, view wildlife, learn about the history of the area, and enjoy picnics.

Europa Park, Gengenbach. On 160 acres, this amusement park offers endless shows, rides, dining, shops, and two hotels.

TOWNS & VILLAGES

Bad Wimpfen, Neckar Valley. Once an ancient Celtic settlement, this is one of the most strikingly attractive towns in the Neckar Valley.

Lübeck, Schleswig-Holstein. Lübeck dates to the 12th century and has one of Europe's largest Old Towns.

Rothenburg-ob-der-Tauber, Bavaria. This walled town on the Romantic Road is a treasure of medieval towers and turrets.

Rügen Island, Vorpommern. Rügen's diverse and awe-inspiring landscapes have inspired poets and painters for more than a century.

Sylt Island, Schleswig-Holstein. Famous for its clean air and white-sand beaches, Sylt is the hideaway for the jet set of Germany.

SMART TRAVEL TIPS

Finding out about your destination before you leave home means you won't squander time organizing everyday minutiae once you've arrived. You'll be more streetwise when you hit the ground as well, better prepared to explore the aspects of Germany that drew you here in the first place. The organizations in this section can provide information to supplement this guide; contact them for up-to-the-minute details, and consult the A to Z sections that end each chapter for facts on the various topics as they relate to Germany's many regions. Happy landings!

ADDRESSES

In this book the words for street (*Strasse*) and alley (*Gasse*) are abbreviated as -str. or Str., and g. within italicized information. Brüdergasse will appear as Brüderg., for example.

AIR TRAVEL

BOOKING

When you book, look for nonstop flights and remember that "direct" flights stop at least once. Try to avoid connecting flights, which require a change of plane. Two airlines may operate a connecting flight jointly, so ask whether your airline operates every segment of the trip; you may find that the carrier you prefer flies you only part of the way. To find more booking tips and to check prices and make online flight reservations, log on to www.fodors.com.

CARRIERS

Lufthansa is Germany's leading carrier and has shared mileage plans and flights with Air Canada and United, among other airlines.

Germany's internal air network is excellent, with flights linking all major cities in little more than an hour. A handful of smaller airlines compete with low-fare flights within Germany and to other European cities. These companies are reliable, do most of their business over the Internet, and often beat the fares offered by the railway. The earlier you book, the cheaper the fare.

▶ To & From Germany Air Canada ☎ 888/247-2262. **American** ☎ 800/433-7300. **Continental** ☎ 800/525-0280. **Delta** ☎ 800/241-4141. **LTU** ☎ 866/266-5588. **Lufthansa** ☎ 800/645-3880. **Northwest** ☎ 800/225-2525. **United** ☎ 800/241-6522. **US Airways** ☎ 800/428-4322.

▶ Within Germany Air Berlin ☎ 01801/737-800 ⊕ www.airberlin.com. **Deutsche BA** ☎ 01805/932-322 ⊕ www.flydba.com. **Germanwings** ☎ 01805/955-855 ⊕ www.germanwings.com. **Hapag-Lloyd Express** ☎ 01805/093-509 ⊕ www.hlx.com. **Lufthansa** ☎ 0180/380-3803 or 0180/5838-42672 ⊕ www.lufthansa.com.

▶ From the U.K. British Airways ☎ 0345/222-111. **EasyJet** ☎ 0871/7500-100 in U.K., 01803/654321 in Germany ⊕ www.easyjet.com. **Lufthansa** ☎ 0345/737-747. **Ryanair** ☎ 0871/246-0000, 0190/669-900 in Germany ⊕ www.ryanair.com.

CHECK-IN & BOARDING

Always **find out your carrier's check-in policy.** Plan to arrive at the airport about two hours before your scheduled departure time for domestic flights and 2½ to 3 hours before international flights. You may need to arrive earlier if you're flying from one of the busier airports or during peak air-traffic times. In Germany, be at your gate with boarding pass in hand 30 minutes before an internal flight. For international flights, arrive at the airport 1½ hours in advance; allow an extra half-hour to claim V.A.T. taxes back at customs.

To avoid delays at airport-security checkpoints, try not to wear any metal. Jewelry, belt and other buckles, steel-toe shoes, barrettes, and underwire bras are among the items that can set off detectors.

Assuming that not everyone with a ticket will show up, airlines routinely overbook planes. When everyone does, airlines ask for volunteers to give up their seats. In return, these volunteers usually get a several-hundred-dollar flight voucher, which can be used toward the purchase of another ticket, and are rebooked on the next flight out. If there are not enough volunteers, the airline must choose who will be denied boarding. The first to get bumped are passengers who checked in late and those flying on discounted tickets, so get to the gate and check in as early as possible, especially during peak periods.

CUTTING COSTS

The least expensive airfares to Germany are priced for round-trip travel and must usually be purchased in advance. Airlines generally allow you to change your return date for a fee; most low-fare tickets, however, are nonrefundable. Fares from the British Isles to Germany through the "no-frills" Irish airline, Ryanair, range from €15 to €35. Lufthansa, by contrast, might charge €432 from London (Heathrow).

It's smart to call a number of airlines and check the Internet; when you are quoted a good price, book it on the spot—the same fare may not be available the next day, or even the next hour. Always check different routings and look into using alternate airports. Also, price off-peak flights, which may be significantly less expensive than others. Travel agents, especially low-fare specialists (⇨ Discounts & Deals), are helpful.

Consolidators are another good source. They buy tickets for scheduled flights at reduced rates from the airlines, then sell them at prices that beat the best fare available directly from the airlines. (Many also offer reduced car-rental and hotel rates.) Sometimes you can even get your money back if you need to return the ticket. Carefully read the fine print detailing penalties for changes and cancellations, purchase the ticket with a credit card, and confirm your consolidator reservation with the airline.

▶ Consolidators AirlineConsolidator.com ☎ 888/468-5385 ⊕ www.airlineconsolidator.com, for international tickets. **Best Fares** ☎ 800/880-1234 or 800/576-8255 ⊕ www.bestfares.com; $59.90 annual membership. **Cheap Tickets** ☎ 800/377-1000 or 800/652-4327 ⊕ www.cheaptickets.com. **Expedia** ☎ 800/397-3342 or 404/728-8787 ⊕ www.expedia.com. **Hotwire** ☎ 866/468-9473 or 920/330-9418 ⊕ www.hotwire.com. **Now Voyager Travel** ✉ 45 W. 21st St., Suite 5A, New York, NY 10010 ☎ 212/459-1616 🖷 212/243-2711 ⊕ www.nowvoyagertravel.com. **Onetravel.com** ⊕ www.onetravel.com. **Orbitz** ☎ 888/656-4546 ⊕ www.orbitz.com. **Priceline.com** ⊕ www.priceline.com. **Travelocity** ☎ 888/709-5983, 877/282-2925 in Canada, 0870/876-3876 in U.K. ⊕ www.travelocity.com.

ENJOYING THE FLIGHT

State your seat preference when purchasing your ticket, and then repeat it when you confirm and when you check in. For more legroom, you can request one of the few emergency-aisle seats at check-in, if you're capable of moving obstacles comparable in weight to an airplane exit door (usually between 35 pounds and 60 pounds)—a Federal Aviation Administration requirement of passengers in these seats. Seats behind a bulkhead also offer more legroom, but they don't have under-seat storage. Don't sit in the row in front of the emergency aisle or in front of a bulkhead, where seats may not recline.

Ask the airline whether a snack or meal is served on the flight. If you have dietary concerns, request special meals when booking. These can be vegetarian, low-cholesterol, or kosher, for example. It's a good idea to pack some healthful snacks and a small (plastic) bottle of water in your carry-on bag. On long flights, try to maintain a normal routine, to help fight jet lag. At night, get some sleep. By day, eat light meals, drink water (not alcohol), and **move around the cabin** to stretch your legs. For additional jet-lag tips consult *Fodor's FYI: Travel Fit & Healthy* (available at bookstores everywhere).

Smoking policies vary from carrier to carrier. Many airlines prohibit smoking on all of their flights; others allow smoking only on certain routes or certain departures. Ask your carrier about its policy.

FLYING TIMES

Flying time to Frankfurt is 1½ hours from London, 7½ hours from New York, 10 hours from Chicago, and 12 hours from Los Angeles.

HOW TO COMPLAIN

If your baggage goes astray or your flight goes awry, complain right away. Most carriers require that you **file a claim immediately.** The Aviation Consumer Protection Division of the Department of Transportation publishes *Fly-Rights,* which discusses airlines and consumer issues and is available online. You can also find articles and information on mytravelrights.com, the Web site of the nonprofit Consumer Travel Rights Center.

🛂 Airline Complaints **Aviation Consumer Protection Division** ✉ U.S. Department of Transportation, Office of Aviation Enforcement and Proceedings, C-75, Room 4107, 400 7th St. SW, Washington, DC 20590 ☎ 202/366-2220 ⊕ airconsumer.ost.dot.gov. **Federal Aviation Administration Consumer Hotline** ✉ for inquiries: FAA, 800 Independence Ave. SW, Washington, DC 20591 ☎ 800/322-7873 ⊕ www.faa.gov.

RECONFIRMING

Check the status of your flight before you leave for the airport. You can do this on your carrier's Web site, by linking to a flight-status checker (many Web booking services offer these), or by calling your carrier or travel agent. Always confirm international flights at least 72 hours ahead of the scheduled departure time.

AIRPORTS

Frankfurt is Germany's air hub. The large airport has the convenience of its own long-distance train station, but if you're simply transfering between flights, don't dawdle or you could miss your connection. There are a few direct connections from North America to Munich and Düsseldorf but none to Berlin.

🛂 Airport Information Berlin: **Flughafen Tegel** (TXL), **Tempelhof** (THF), **Schönefeld** (SXF) ☎ 01805/000-186, €.12 per minute ⊕ www.berlin-airport.de. Düsseldorf: **Flughafen Düsseldorf** (DUS) ☎ 0211/4210 ⊕ www.duesseldorf-international.de. Frankfurt: **Flughafen Frankfurt Main** (FRA) ☎ 01805/372-4636, 069/6900 from outside Germany ⊕ www.frankfurt-airport.de. Hamburg: **Fuhlsbüttel International Airport** (HAM) ☎ 040/50750 ⊕ www.ham.airport.de. Köln: **Flughafen Köln/Bonn** (CGN) ☎ 02203/404-001 ⊕ www.airport-cgn.de. Munich: **Flughafen München** (MUC) ☎ 089/97500 ⊕ www.munich-airport.de. Stuttgart: **Flughafen Stuttgart** (STR) ☎ 0711/948-2790 ⊕ www.stuttgart-airport.de.

BIKES IN FLIGHT

Most airlines accommodate bikes as luggage, provided they are dismantled and boxed; check with individual airlines about packing requirements. Some airlines sell bike boxes, which are often free at bike shops, for about $20 (bike bags can be considerably more expensive). International travelers often can substitute a bike for a piece of checked luggage at no charge; otherwise, the cost is about $100. Most U.S. and Canadian airlines charge $40–$80 each way.

DUTY-FREE SHOPPING

You can purchase duty-free goods when traveling between any EU country, such as Germany, and a non-EU country. The big sellers at duty-free (also called tax-free) shops are perfumes and cosmetics, liquor, tobacco products, and chocolates.

BOAT & FERRY TRAVEL

Eurailpasses and German Rail Passes (⇨ Train Travel) are valid on all Rhine River services of the Köln-Düsseldorfer Deutsche Rheinschiffahrt (KD Rhine Line) and on the Mosel River between Trier and Koblenz (if you use the fast hydrofoil, a supplementary fee is required). The railroad follows the Rhine and Mosel rivers most of their length, meaning you can go one way by ship and return by train. Cruises generally operate between April and October (⇨ Cruise Travel).

The MS *Duchess of Scandinavia* carries passengers and cars three times a week for the 18½-hour run between Cuxhaven, Germany and Harwich, England.

🚗 Car Ferry **MS *Duchess of Scandinavia*** ☎ 040/389-0371 DFDS Seaways ⊕ www.dfdsseaways.co.uk.

BUSINESS HOURS

Business hours are consistent throughout the country. Many smaller visitor information offices close by 4 during the week and might not be open on weekends. Catholic areas of the country in the south, primarily Bavaria, may have more closings for religious holidays than in other parts of Germany.

BANKS & OFFICES

Banks are generally open weekdays from 8:30 or 9 to 3 or 4 (5 or 6 on Thursday), sometimes with a lunch break of about an hour at smaller branches. Some banks close by 2:30 on Friday afternoon. Banks at airports and main train stations open as early as 6:30 AM and close as late as 10:30 PM. Some offices start picking up the phone as early as 8 AM and nearly all close by 5 PM. Automated telephone menus and even voice mail and answering machines are not a given in Germany, which means you shouldn't count on leaving a message after hours. *See* Mail & Shipping for post office hours.

GAS STATIONS

Along the autobahn and major highways as well as in major cities, gas stations and their small convenience shops are often open late, if not around the clock.

MUSEUMS & SIGHTS

Most museums are open from Tuesday to Sunday 10–6. Some close for an hour or more at lunch. Many stay open until 8 or later one day a week.

PHARMACIES

Most pharmacies are open 9–6 weekdays and 9–1 on Saturday. Those in more prominent locations often open an hour earlier and/or close an hour later. A list of pharmacies in the vicinity that are open late or on Sunday is posted on the door.

SHOPS

All stores are closed on Sunday, with the exception of those in or near train stations. Department stores and larger stores are generally open from 9 or 9:30 to 8 weekdays and Saturday. Shops in cities might open at 10 and close between 6 and 7. Smaller shops and some department stores in smaller towns close at 6 or 6:30 on weekdays and as early as 4 on Saturday. These shops may also close for two to three hours at lunchtime.

BUS TRAVEL

Germany has good local bus service but no nationwide network, other than the few cities served by BerlinLinien Bus. Deutsche Touring, a subsidiary of the railroad that has offices and agents countrywide, travels from Germany to other European destinations. Its domestic service consists of one-day tours along the Romantic Road, between Würzburg (with connections to and from Frankfurt) and Füssen (with connections to and from Munich, Augsburg, and Garmisch-Partenkirchen). With a regular Deutsche Bahn rail ticket, Eurailpass, or German Rail Pass you get a 60% discount on this route. Buses, with an attendant on board, travel in each direction between April and October.

All towns of any size have local buses, which often link up with trams (streetcars) and electric railway (S-bahn) and subway (U-bahn) services. Fares sometimes vary according to distance, but a ticket usually allows you to transfer freely between the various forms of transportation. Most cities issue 24-hour tickets at special rates.

⚑ Intercity Buses **BerlinLinien Bus** ✉ Masurenallee 4-6 Berlin ☎ 030/301-0380 for reservations ⊕ www.berlinlinienbus.de. **Deutsche Touring** ✉ Am Römerhof 17, D-60486 Frankfurt am Main ☎ 069/790-350 🖷 069/790-3219 ⊕ www.deutsche-touring.de.

CAMERAS & PHOTOGRAPHY

The *Kodak Guide to Shooting Great Travel Pictures* (available at bookstores everywhere) is loaded with tips.

⚑ Photo Help **Kodak Information Center** ☎ 800/242-2424 ⊕ www.kodak.com.

EQUIPMENT PRECAUTIONS

Don't pack film or equipment in checked luggage, where it is much more susceptible to damage. X-ray machines used to view checked luggage are extremely powerful and therefore are likely to ruin your film. Try to ask for hand inspection of film, which becomes clouded after repeated exposure to airport X-ray machines, and keep videotapes and computer disks away from metal detectors. Always keep film, tape, and computer disks out of the sun. Carry an extra supply of batteries, and be prepared to turn on your camera, camcorder, or laptop to prove to airport security personnel that the device is real.

VIDEOS

The German standard for video is VHS–PAL, which is not compatible with the U.S. VHS–NTSC standard.

CAR RENTAL

Rates with the major car-rental companies begin at about €55 per day and €300 per week, including value-added tax, for an economy car with a manual transmission

and unlimited mileage. Volkswagen, Opel, and Mercedes are some standard brands of rentals; most rentals are manual, so if you want an automatic, be sure to **request one in advance.** If you're traveling with children, don't forget to **arrange for a car seat** when you reserve. The agency Sixt is affiliated with Lufthansa. Note that in some major cities, even automobile-producing Stuttgart, rental firms are prohibited from placing signs at major pickup, drop-off locations, such as the main train station. If dropping a car off in an unfamiliar city, you might have to guess your way to the station's underground parking garage and once there, look for a generic sign such as *Miet Wagen* (rental cars).

⚑ Major Agencies **Alamo** ☎ 800/522-9696 ⊕ www.alamo.com. **Avis** ☎ 800/331-1084, 800/879-2847 in Canada, 0870/606-0100 in U.K., 02/9353-9000 in Australia, 09/526-2847 in New Zealand ⊕ www.avis.com. **Budget** ☎ 800/527-0700, 0870/156-5656 in U.K. ⊕ www.budget.com. **Dollar** ☎ 800/800-6000, 0800/085-4578 in the U.K. ⊕ www.dollar.com. **Hertz** ☎ 800/654-3001, 800/263-0600 in Canada, 0870/844-8844 in U.K., 02/9669-2444 in Australia, 09/256-8690 in New Zealand ⊕ www.hertz.com. **National Car Rental** ☎ 800/227-7368, 0870/600-6666 in U.K. ⊕ www.nationalcar.com.

⚑ Local Agencies **Sixt** ☎ 01805/252-525, €.12 per minute ⊕ www.sixt-europe.com.

CUTTING COSTS

For a good deal, book through a travel agent who will shop around.

Do look into wholesalers, companies that do not own fleets but rent in bulk from those that do and often offer better rates than traditional car-rental operations. Prices are best during off-peak periods. Rentals booked through wholesalers often must be paid for before you leave home.

⚑ Wholesalers **Auto Europe** ☎ 207/842-2000 or 800/223-5555 🖷 207/842-2222 ⊕ www.autoeurope.com. **Destination Europe Resources** (DER) ✉ 9501 W. Devon Ave., Rosemont, IL 60018 ☎ 800/782-2424 🖷 800/282-7474 ⊕ www.der.com. **Europe by Car** ☎ 212/581-3040 or 800/223-1516 🖷 212/246-1458 ⊕ www.europebycar.com. **Kemwel** ☎ 877/820-0668 or 800/678-0678 🖷 207/842-2147 ⊕ www.kemwel.com.

INSURANCE

When driving a rented car, you are generally responsible for any damage to or loss of the vehicle. Collision policies that car-rental companies sell for European rentals typically do not cover stolen vehicles. Before you rent—and purchase collision or theft coverage—see what coverage you already have under the terms of your personal auto-insurance policy and credit cards.

REQUIREMENTS & RESTRICTIONS

In Germany your own driver's license is acceptable, but an International Driver's Permit is a good idea; it's available from the American or Canadian Automobile Association and, in the United Kingdom, from the Automobile Association and Royal Automobile Club. These international permits are universally recognized, and having one in your wallet may save you a problem with the local authorities. In Germany you usually must be 21 to rent a car. Nearly all agencies will allow you to drive the car to Germany's neighboring countries, and it's frequently possible to return the car in another West European neighbor. East European neighbors, like Poland and the Czech Republic, are more of a problem. You can usually drive to them, but it's rarely possible to return there.

SURCHARGES

Before you pick up a car in one city and leave it in another, ask about drop-off charges or one-way service fees, which can be substantial. Also inquire about early-return policies; some rental agencies charge extra if you return the car before the time specified in your contract while others give you a refund for the days not used. To avoid a hefty refueling fee, fill the tank just before you turn in the car, but be aware that gas stations near the rental outlet may overcharge. It's almost never a deal to buy the tank of gas that's in the car when you rent it; the understanding is that you'll return it empty, but some fuel usually remains.

CAR TRAVEL

Entry formalities for motorists are few: all you need is proof of insurance, an international car-registration document, and a U.S., Canadian, Australian, or New Zealand driver's license. If you or your car is from an EU country, Norway, or Switzerland, all you need is your domestic license and proof of insurance. *All* foreign cars must have a country sticker. There are no toll roads in Germany, except for a few Alpine mountain passes.

Your driver's license may not be recognized outside your home country. International driving permits (IDPs) are available from the American and Canadian automobile associations and, in the United Kingdom, from the Automobile Association and Royal Automobile Club. These international permits, valid only in conjunction with your regular driver's license, are universally recognized; having one may save you a problem with local authorities.

EMERGENCY SERVICES

The German automobile clubs ADAC and AvD operate tow trucks on all autobahns. NOTRUF signs every 2 km (1 mi) on autobahns (and country roads) indicate emergency telephones. By picking up the phone, you'll be connected to an operator who can determine your exact location and get you the services you need. The official road-side assistance number is 01802/222–222. If you have a mobile phone, just dial 222–222. Help is free (with the exception of materials).

GASOLINE

Gasoline (petrol) costs are around €1.10 per liter—which is higher than in the United States. Most German cars run on lead-free fuel. Some models use diesel fuel, so if you're renting a car, **find out which fuel the car takes.** Some older vehicles cannot take unleaded fuel. German filling stations are highly competitive, and bargains are often available if you shop around, but *not* at autobahn filling stations. Self-service, or *SB-Tanken*, stations are cheapest. Pumps marked *Bleifrei* contain unleaded gas.

PARKING

Daytime parking in cities and small, historic towns is difficult to find. Restrictions are not always clearly marked and can be hard to understand when they are.

Rental cars come with a "time wheel," which you can leave on your dashboard when parking signs indicate free, limited-time allowances. Larger parking lots have parking meters (*Parkautomaten*). After depositing enough change in a meter, you will be issued a timed ticket to display on your dashboard. Parking-meter spaces are free at night. In German garages you must **pay immediately on returning to retrieve your car**, not when driving out. Put the ticket you got on arrival into the machine and pay the amount displayed. Retrieve the ticket, and upon exiting the garage, insert the ticket in a slot to get the barrier raised.

ROAD CONDITIONS

Roads are generally excellent. *Bundesstrasse* are two-lane highways, abbreviated "B," as in B–38. Autobahns are high-speed thruways abbreviated with "A," as in A–7.

ROAD MAPS

The best-known road maps of Germany are put out by the automobile club ADAC, by Shell, and by the Falk Verlag. They're available at gas stations and bookstores.

RULES OF THE ROAD

Germans **drive on the right** and cars coming from the right have right-of-way at intersections. Road signs give distances in kilometers. There *are* posted speed limits on autobahns, and drivers are advised to keep below 130 kph (80 mph). Speed limits on country roads vary from 70 kph to 100 kph (43 kph to 62 mph) and are usually 50 kph (30 mph) through small towns. The blood-alcohol limit for driving in Germany is very low (.05%). Note that **seat belts must be worn at all times by front- *and* backseat passengers.** Passing is permitted on the left side only. Headlights, not parking lights, are required during inclement weather. Don't enter a street with a signpost bearing a red circle with a white horizontal stripe—it's a one-way street. Blue *EINBAHNSTRASSE* signs indicate you're headed the right way down a one-way street. A right turn on a red light is permitted only if there's also a green arrow.

SCENIC ROUTES

Germany has many specially designated tourist roads. The longest is the Deutsche Ferienstrasse, the German Holiday Road, which runs from the Baltic to the Alps, a distance of around 1,720 km (1,070 mi). The most famous, however, is the Romantische Strasse (Romantic Road; ⇨ Chapter 4), which runs from Würzburg to Füssen in the Alps, covering around 355 km (220 mi).

Among other notable touring routes are the Strasse der Kaiser und Könige (Route of Emperors and Kings), running from Frankfurt to Passau (and on to Vienna and Budapest); the Burgenstrasse (Castle Road), running from Mannheim to Bayreuth; the Deutsche Weinstrasse (German Wine Road; ⇨ Chapter 10), running through the Palatinate wine country; and the Deutsche Alpenstrasse (German Alpine Road; ⇨ Chapter 2), running the length of the country's Alpine southern border from near Berchtesgaden to Bodensee. Less well-known routes are the Märchenstrasse (Fairy-Tale Road; ⇨ Chapter 12), the Weser Renaissance Strasse, and the Deutsche Fachwerkstrasse (German Half-Timber Road).

CHILDREN IN GERMANY

Almost every city in Germany has its own children's theater, and the country's puppet theaters rank among the best in the world. Playgrounds are around virtually every corner, and there are about a half-dozen major theme parks around the country. Many tourist offices have booklets for younger visitors.

If you're renting a car, don't forget to arrange for a car seat when you reserve. For general advice about traveling with children, consult *Fodor's FYI: Travel with Your Baby* (available in bookstores everywhere).

BABYSITTING

For recommended local sitters, **check with your hotel desk.** Updated lists of well-screened babysitters are also available from most local tourist offices. Rates are usually between €8 and €13 per hour.

FLYING

If your children are two or older, ask about children's airfares. As a general rule, infants under two not occupying a seat fly at greatly reduced fares or even for free. But if you want to guarantee a seat for an infant, you have to pay full fare. Consider flying during off-peak days and times; most airlines will grant an infant a seat without a ticket if there are available seats. When booking, confirm carry-on allowances if you're traveling with infants. In general, for babies charged 10% to 50% of the adult fare you are allowed one carry-on bag and a collapsible stroller; if the flight is full, the stroller may have to be checked or you may be limited to less.

Experts agree that it's a good idea to use safety seats aloft for children weighing less than 40 pounds. Airlines set their own policies: if you use a safety seat, U.S. carriers usually require that the child be ticketed, even if he or she is young enough to ride free, because the seats must be strapped into regular seats. And even if you pay the full adult fare for the seat, it may be worth it, especially on longer trips. Do **check your airline's policy about using safety seats during takeoff and landing.** Safety seats are not allowed everywhere in the plane, so get your seat assignments as early as possible.

When reserving, request children's meals or a freestanding bassinet (not available at all airlines) if you need them. But note that bulkhead seats, where you must sit to use the bassinet, may lack an overhead bin or storage space on the floor.

WHERE TO STAY

Many hotels in Germany allow children under a certain age to stay in their parents' room at no extra charge. Beyond that age they may be charged half price or even be considered extra adults; be sure to **find out if the cutoff age applies.** If your room has a TV, be aware that sex-talk phone lines are advertised on television as early as 9 PM and that late-night pornographic programs are carried on normal networks.

SIGHTS & ATTRACTIONS

Places that are especially appealing to children are indicated by a rubber-duckie icon (🐤) in the margin.

SUPPLIES & EQUIPMENT

Supermarkets and drugstores (not pharmacies) carry disposable diapers (*Windeln*). Baby formula is available in powder form and comes in two types: *Anfangsmilch/nahrung* is labeled with a big number 1 and is suitable for infants ages 0–4 months; *Folgemilch/nahrung* is labeled with a big number 2 and is suitable for infants from 4 months. *Dauermilch/nahrung* is suitable for all ages. Coloring books (*Malbücher*) and crayons (*Buntstifte*) are widely available, as is modeling clay (*Knetmasse*).

COMPUTERS ON THE ROAD

Nearly all hotels in cities have in-room data ports, but you may have to purchase, or borrow from your hotel, a cable with an end that matches German phone jacks. Most notebooks with a modem or single modems will have a plug-in to match the German Telekom socket. If you're plugging into a phone line, you'll need a local access number for a connection. Small pensions may not even have a phone in the room, or a jack that will match modem connections. Internet cafés are prevalent in German cities. Often they're smoky basement shops that sell a few soft drinks and snacks. In smaller towns, try the library for Internet use.

CONSUMER PROTECTION

Whether you're shopping for gifts or purchasing travel services, **pay with a major credit card** whenever possible, so you can cancel payment or get reimbursed if there's a problem (and you can provide documentation). If you're doing business with a particular company for the first time, contact your local Better Business Bureau and the attorney general's offices in your state and (for U.S. businesses) the company's home state as well. Have any complaints been filed? Finally, if you're buying a package or tour, always consider travel insurance that includes default coverage (⇨ Insurance).

📰 BBBs **Council of Better Business Bureaus** ✉ 4200 Wilson Blvd., Suite 800, Arlington, VA 22203 ☎ 703/276-0100 🖷 703/525-8277 ⊕ www.bbb.org.

CRUISE TRAVEL

The American-owned Viking River Cruises company tours the Rhine, Main, Elbe, and Danube rivers, with 4- to 8-day itineraries. The longer cruises (18 days) on the Danube (Donau, in German), which go to the Black Sea and back, are in great demand, so **reserve six months in advance.** The company normally books American passengers on ships that cater exclusively to Americans. The ships are no-smoking, and English is the only language on board. If you prefer to travel on a European ship, specify so when booking. Köln–Düsseldorfer Deutsche Rheinschiffahrt (KD Rhine Line) offers trips of one day or less on the Rhine and Mosel. Between Easter and October there's Rhine service between Köln and Mainz, and between May and October, Mosel service between Koblenz and Cochem. You'll get a free trip on your birthday, if you bring a document verifying your date of birth.

To learn how to plan, choose, and book a cruise-ship voyage, consult *Fodor's FYI: Plan & Enjoy Your Cruise* (available in bookstores everywhere).

🚢 Cruise Lines **KD Rhine Line** ✉ Frankenwerft 35, D-50667 Köln ☎ 0221/208-8318 🖷 0221/208-8345 ⊕ www.k-d.com. **Viking River Cruises** ✉ Hohe Strasse 68-82, D-50667 Köln ☎ 0800/258-4667 toll-free or 0221/258-209 in Germany, 0207/752-0000 or 01372/742033 in U.K. ⊕ www. vikingrivercruises.com ✉ 21820 Burbank Blvd., Woodland Hills, CA 91367 ☎ 818/227-1234.

CUSTOMS & DUTIES

When shopping abroad, keep receipts for all purchases. Upon reentering the country, **be ready to show customs officials what you've bought.** Pack purchases together in an easily accessible place. If you think a duty is incorrect, appeal the assessment. If you object to the way your clearance was handled, note the inspector's badge number. In either case, first ask to see a supervisor. If the problem isn't resolved, write to the appropriate authorities, beginning with the port director at your point of entry.

IN AUSTRALIA

Australian residents who are 18 or older may bring home A$400 worth of souvenirs and gifts (including jewelry), 250 cigarettes or 250 grams of cigars or other tobacco products, and 1,125 ml of alcohol (including wine, beer, and spirits). Residents under 18 may bring back A$200 worth of goods. Members of the same family traveling together may pool their allowances. Prohibited items include meat products. Seeds, plants, and fruits need to be declared upon arrival.

🛂 **Australian Customs Service** ⌕ Regional Director, Box 8, Sydney, NSW 2001 ☎ 02/9213-2000 or 1300/363263, 02/9364-7222 or 1800/020-504 quarantine-inquiry line 🖷 02/9213-4043 ⊕ www. customs.gov.au.

IN CANADA

Canadian residents who have been out of Canada for at least seven days may bring in C$750 worth of goods duty-free. If you've been away fewer than seven days but more than 48 hours, the duty-free allowance drops to C$200. If your trip lasts 24 to 48 hours, the allowance is C$50. You may not pool allowances with family members. Goods claimed under the C$750 exemption may follow you by mail; those claimed under the lesser exemptions must accompany you. Alcohol and tobacco products may be included in the seven-day and 48-hour exemptions but not in the 24-hour exemption. If you meet the age requirements of the province or territory through which you reenter Canada, you may bring in, duty-free, 1.5 liters of wine *or* 1.14 liters (40 imperial ounces) of liquor *or* 24 12-ounce cans or bottles of beer or ale. Also, if you meet the local age requirement for tobacco products, you may bring in, duty-free, 200 cigarettes and 50 cigars. Check ahead of time with the Canada Customs and Revenue Agency or the Department of Agriculture for policies regarding meat products, seeds, plants, and fruits.

You may send an unlimited number of gifts (only one gift per recipient, however) worth up to C$60 each duty-free to Canada. Label the package UNSOLICITED GIFT—VALUE UNDER $60. Alcohol and tobacco are excluded.

🛂 **Canada Customs and Revenue Agency** ✉ 2265 St. Laurent Blvd., Ottawa, Ontario K1G 4K3 ☎ 800/

461–9999 in Canada, 204/983–3500, 506/636–5064 ⊕ www.ccra.gc.ca.

IN GERMANY

Since a single, unrestricted market took effect within the European Union (EU) early in 1993, there have no longer been restrictions for persons traveling among the 15 EU countries. However, there are restrictions on what can be brought in without declaration. For example, if you have more than 800 cigarettes, 90 liters of wine, or 10 liters of alcohol, it is considered a commercial shipment and is taxed and otherwise treated as such.

For anyone entering Germany from outside the EU, the following limitations apply: (1) 200 cigarettes or 100 cigarillos or 50 cigars or 250 grams of tobacco; (2) 2 liters of still table wine; (3) 1 liter of spirits over 22% volume or 2 liters of spirits under 22% volume (fortified and sparkling wines) or 2 more liters of table wine; (4) 50 grams of perfume and 250 milliliters of eau de toilette; (5) 500 grams of roasted coffee or 200 grams of instant coffee; (6) other goods to the value of €175.

Tobacco and alcohol allowances are for visitors age 17 and over. Other items intended for personal use can be imported and exported freely. If you bring in cash, checks, securities, precious metals, or jewelry with a value of more than €15,000, you must tell the customs people where you got it and what you intend to do with it. This is a new measure for fighting money laundering.

If you have questions regarding customs or bringing a pet into the country, contact the Zoll-Infocenter, preferably by mail or e-mail.

⚑ **Zoll-Infocenter** ⊠ Hansaallee 141, D–60320 Frankfurt am Main ☎ 069/4699–7600 🖷 069/4699–7699 ✍ info@zoll-infocenter.de.

IN NEW ZEALAND

All homeward-bound residents may bring back NZ$700 worth of souvenirs and gifts; passengers may not pool their allowances, and children can claim only the concession on goods intended for their own use. For those 17 or older, the duty-free allowance also includes 4.5 liters of wine or beer; one 1,125-ml bottle of spirits; and either 200 cigarettes, 250 grams of tobacco, 50 cigars, *or* a combination of the three up to 250 grams. Meat products, seeds, plants, and fruits must be declared upon arrival to the Agricultural Services Department.

⚑ **New Zealand Customs** ⊠ Head office: The Customhouse, 17–21 Whitmore St., Box 2218, Wellington ☎ 09/300–5399 or 0800/428–786 ⊕ www.customs.govt.nz.

IN THE U.K.

If you are a U.K. resident and your journey was wholly within the European Union, you probably won't have to pass through customs when you return to the United Kingdom. If you plan to bring back large quantities of alcohol or tobacco, check EU limits beforehand. In most cases, if you bring back more than 200 cigars, 3,200 cigarettes, 400 cigarillos, 10 liters of spirits, 110 liters of beer, 20 liters of fortified wine, and/or 90 liters of wine, you have to declare the goods upon return. Prohibited items include unpasteurized milk, regardless of country of origin.

⚑ **HM Customs and Excise** ⊠ Portcullis House, 21 Cowbridge Rd. E, Cardiff CF11 9SS ☎ 0845/010–9000 or 0208/929–0152 advice service, 0208/929–6731 or 0208/910–3602 complaints ⊕ www.hmce.gov.uk.

IN THE U.S.

U.S. residents who have been out of the country for at least 48 hours may bring home, for personal use, $800 worth of foreign goods duty-free, as long as they haven't used the $800 allowance or any part of it in the past 30 days. This exemption may include 1 liter of alcohol (for travelers 21 and older), 200 cigarettes, and 100 non-Cuban cigars. Family members from the same household who are traveling together may pool their $800 personal exemptions. For fewer than 48 hours, the duty-free allowance drops to $200, which may include 50 cigarettes, 10 non-Cuban cigars, and 150 ml of alcohol (or 150 ml of perfume containing alcohol). The $200 allowance cannot be combined with other individuals' exemptions, and if you exceed it, the full value of all the goods will be taxed. Antiques, which U.S. Customs and Border Protection defines as objects more than 100 years old, enter duty-free, as do original works of art done entirely by hand, including paintings, drawings, and sculptures. This doesn't apply to folk art or handicrafts, which are in general dutiable.

You may also send packages home duty-free, with a limit of one parcel per addressee per day (except alcohol or tobacco products or perfume worth more than $5). You can mail up to $200 worth of goods for personal use; label the package PERSONAL USE and attach a list of its contents and their retail value. If the package contains your used personal belongings, mark it AMERICAN GOODS RETURNED to avoid paying duties. You may send up to $100 worth of goods as a gift; mark the package UNSOLICITED GIFT. Mailed items do not affect your duty-free allowance on your return.

To avoid paying duty on foreign-made high-ticket items you already own and will take on your trip, register them with Customs before you leave the country. Consider filing a Certificate of Registration for laptops, cameras, watches, and other digital devices identified with serial numbers or other permanent markings; you can keep the certificate for other trips. Otherwise, bring a sales receipt or insurance form to show that you owned the item before you left the United States.

For more about duties, restricted items, and other information about international travel, check out U.S. Customs and Border Protection's online brochure, *Know Before You Go*.

🔳 **U.S. Customs and Border Protection** ✉ For inquiries and equipment registration, 1300 Pennsylvania Ave. NW, Washington, DC 20229 ⊕ www.cbp. gov ☎ 877/287-8667 or 202/354-1000 ✉ For complaints, Customer Satisfaction Unit, 1300 Pennsylvania Ave. NW, Room 5.2C, Washington, DC 20229.

DISABILITIES & ACCESSIBILITY

Many cities and towns issue special guides for visitors with disabilities, which offer information, usually in German, about how to get around destinations and suggestions for places to visit.

WHERE TO STAY

All the major hotel chains have special facilities for guests with disabilities. Some privately owned hotels also cater to travelers with disabilities; local tourist offices can provide lists of these hotels and additional information.

RESERVATIONS

When discussing accessibility with an operator or reservations agent, ask hard questions. Are there any stairs, inside *or* out? Are there grab bars next to the toilet *and* in the shower–tub? How wide is the doorway to the room? To the bathroom? For the most extensive facilities meeting the latest legal specifications, opt for newer accommodations. If you reserve through a toll-free number, consider also calling the hotel's local number to confirm the information from the central reservations office. Get confirmation in writing when you can.

TRAIN TRAVEL

The Deutsche Bahn (⇨ Train Travel) provides a complete range of services and facilities for travelers with disabilities. All InterCity Express (ICE), InterRegio, and DB Night trains and most EuroCity and InterCity trains have special areas and toilets for wheelchair users, and the larger stations have a portable device for lifting wheelchairs aboard. Reservations for wheelchair users and a travel companion are free of charge. A free service called the Bahnhofs-Mission (Railway Station Mission) has support facilities at all major and many smaller regional stations. It assists with boarding, leaving, and changing trains and also helps with reservations. Local trams and buses often have sections that can accommodate a wheelchair and entrances that are, if not flush with the platform, at least quite low to the ground.

Deutsche Bahn issues a booklet, with an English section, detailing its services. For access to train platforms that are not wheelchair accessible, to temporarily borrow a wheelchair, and for other services, **call Deutsche Bahn's mobility service line at least 24 hours before your trip.**

🔳 Complaints **Aviation Consumer Protection Division** (⇨ Air Travel) for airline-related problems.

Departmental Office of Civil Rights ✉ For general inquiries, U.S. Department of Transportation, S-30, 400 7th St. SW, Room 10215, Washington, DC 20590 ☎ 202/366-4648 📠 202/366-9371 ⊕ www.dot. gov/ost/docr/index.htm. **Disability Rights Section** ✉ NYAV, U.S. Department of Justice, Civil Rights Division, 950 Pennsylvania Ave. NW, Washington, DC 20530 ☎ ADA information line 202/514-0301, 800/ 514-0301, 202/514-0383 TTY, 800/514-0383 TTY ⊕ www.ada.gov. **U.S. Department of Transportation Hotline** ☎ For disability-related air-travel problems, 800/778-4838 or 800/455-9880 TTY.

TRAVEL AGENCIES

In the United States, the Americans with Disabilities Act requires that travel firms serve the needs of all travelers. Some agencies specialize in working with people with disabilities.

🚹 Travelers with Mobility Problems **Access Adventures/B. Roberts Travel** ✉ 206 Chestnut Ridge Rd., Scottsville, NY 14624 ☎ 585/889-9096 ⊕ www.brobertstravel.com ✍ dltravel@prodigy. net, run by a former physical-rehabilitation counselor. **CareVacations** ✉ No. 5, 5110-50 Ave., Leduc, Alberta, Canada, T9E 6V4 ☎ 780/986-6404 or 877/ 478-7827 📠 780/986-8332 ⊕ www.carevacations. com, for group tours and cruise vacations. **Flying Wheels Travel** ✉ 143 W. Bridge St., Box 382, Owatonna, MN 55060 ☎ 507/451-5005 📠 507/451-1685 ⊕ www.flyingwheeltravel.com.

DISCOUNTS & DEALS

Several German cities sell discount passes that grant free or reduced admission to major attractions and discounts on public transportation. The passes are usually available at tourist offices or participating museums.

Be a smart shopper and compare all your options before making decisions. A plane ticket bought with a promotional coupon from travel clubs, coupon books, and direct-mail offers or purchased on the Internet may not be cheaper than the least expensive fare from a discount ticket agency. And always keep in mind that what you get is just as important as what you save.

DISCOUNT RESERVATIONS

To save money, look into discount reservations services with Web sites and toll-free numbers, which use their buying power to get a better price on hotels, airline tickets (➪ Air Travel), even car rentals. When booking a room, always **call the hotel's local toll-free number** (if one is available) rather than the central reservations number—you'll often get a better price. Always ask about special packages or corporate rates.

When shopping for the best deal on hotels and car rentals, look for guaranteed exchange rates, which protect you against a falling dollar. With your rate locked in, you won't pay more, even if the price goes up in the local currency.

🚹 Airline Tickets **Air 4 Less** ☎ 800/AIR4LESS; low-fare specialist.

🚹 Hotel Rooms **Accommodations Express** ☎ 800/444-7666 or 800/277-1064 ⊕ www.acex. net. **Hotels.com** ☎ 800/246-8357 ⊕ www.hotels. com. **International Marketing & Travel Concepts** ☎ 800/790-4682 ⊕ www.imtc-travel.com. **Steigenberger Reservation Service** ☎ 800/223-5652 ⊕ www.srs-worldhotels.com. **Turbotrip.com** ☎ 800/473-7829 ⊕ www.turbotrip.com.

PACKAGE DEALS

Don't confuse packages and guided tours. When you buy a package, you travel on your own, just as though you had planned the trip yourself. Fly–drive packages, which combine airfare and car rental, are often a good deal. In cities, ask the local visitor's bureau about hotel and local transportation packages that include tickets to major museum exhibits or other special events. If you **buy a rail/drive pass,** you may save on train tickets and car rentals. All Eurailpass holders get a discount on Eurostar fares through the Channel Tunnel and often receive reduced rates for buses, hotels, ferries, sightseeing cruises, and car rentals. A German Rail Pass is also good for travel aboard some KD German Rhine Line steamers and on certain ferries to Finland, Denmark, and Sweden (if the pass includes those countries). Discounts are available on some Deutsche Touring/Europabus routes.

EATING & DRINKING

Almost every street in Germany has its *Gaststätte,* a sort of combination diner and pub, and every village its *Gasthof,* or inn. The emphasis in either is on *gutbürgerliche Küche,* or good home cooking—simple food at reasonable prices. A *Bierstube* (pub) or *Weinstube* (wine cellar) may also serve light snacks or meals. Italian restaurants are about the most popular of all ethnic restaurants in Germany.

Service can be slow, but you'll never be rushed out of your seat. Something else that may seem jarring at first: people can, and do, join other parties at a table in a casual restaurant if seating is tight. It's common courtesy to ask first, though.

Regional specialties are given in the dining sections of individual chapters. The restaurants we list are the cream of the crop in each price category. Properties indicated by a ✕🗔 are lodging establishments with worthwhile restaurants.

BUDGET EATING TIPS

Imbiss (snack) stands can be found in almost every busy shopping street, in parking lots, train stations, and near markets. They serve *Würste* (sausages), grilled, roasted, or boiled, and rolls filled with cheese, cold meat, or fish. Prices range from €1.50 to €2.50 per portion. It's acceptable to bring sandwich fixings to a beer garden and order a beer there.

Butcher shops, known as *Metzgerei,* often serve warm snacks or very good sandwiches. Try *Warmer Leberkäs mit Kartoffelsalat,* a typical Bavarian specialty, which is a sort of baked meat loaf with sweet mustard and potato salad. In northern Germany try *Bouletten,* small meatballs, or *Currywurst,* sausages in a piquant curry sauce.

Restaurants in department stores are especially recommended for appetizing and inexpensive lunches. Kaufhof, Karstadt, Wertheim, and Horton are names to note. Germany's vast selection of Turkish, Italian, Greek, Chinese, and Balkan restaurants are often inexpensive.

MEALS & SPECIALTIES

Most hotels serve a buffet-style breakfast (*Frühstück*) of rolls, cheese, cold cuts, eggs, cereals, yogurt, and spreads, which is often included in the price of a room. Cafés offer a similar choice, but don't expect a refillable coffee. By American standards, a cup (*Tasse*) of coffee in Germany is very petite. Order a *Pot* or *Kännchen if you want a larger portion of the brew.*

For lunch (*Mittagessen*), you can get sandwiches from most cafés and bakeries, and many fine restaurants have special lunch menus that make the gourmet experience much more affordable.

Dinner (*Abendessen*) is usually accompanied by a potato or Spätzle side dish. A salad sometimes comes with the main dish.

MEALTIMES

Gaststätte normally serve hot meals from 11:30 AM to 9 PM; many places stop serving hot meals between 2 PM and 6 PM, although you can still order cold dishes. Unless otherwise noted, the restaurants listed in this guide are open daily for lunch and dinner.

PAYING

Credit cards are generally accepted only in moderate to expensive restaurants, so check before sitting down. You will need to ask for the bill in order to get it from the waiter, the idea being that the table is yours for the evening. Round up the bill 5%–10% and pay the waiter directly rather than leave any money or tip on the table.

RESERVATIONS & DRESS

Reservations are always a good idea; we mention them only when they're essential or not accepted. Book as far ahead as you can, and reconfirm as soon as you arrive. (Large parties should always call ahead to check the reservations policy.) We mention dress only when men are required to wear a jacket or a jacket and tie.

Note, though, that even when Germans dress casually, their look is generally crisp and neat.

SMOKING

For such an otherwise health-conscious nation, Germans smoke a lot. When warm weather doesn't allow for open windows and terraces, bars can become uncomfortably smoky. No-smoking sections in restaurants are almost unheard of, although in summer, this problem is alleviated by outdoor seating. A smoker would find it intrusive if you requested him or her to refrain.

WINE, BEER & SPIRITS

Chapter 10, which follows the German Wine Road, and Chapter 11, which covers the Rhine and Mosel valleys, have the most information regarding wines and wine estates. The German Wine Information Bureau (GWIB) promotes the wines of all 13 German wine regions and can supply you with general background information and such invaluable free brochures as the German wine-festivals schedule and *Vintners to Visit* (a roster of visitor-friendly wineries).

Germany holds its brewers to a "purity law" that dates back to 1516, and though there are cheaper brands and more expensive ones, across the board, German beer is good. The drink is nearly as commonly seen on the streets as soft drinks are. It's legal to drink from open containers in public and having a beer at one's midday break is nothing to raise an eyebrow at.

⚑ Wine Information **German Wine Information Bureau** ✉ 245 Park Ave., 39th fl., New York, NY 10167 ☎ 212/792-4134 📠 212/792-4001 ⊕ www. Germanwineusa.org. **Deutsches Weininstitut** ✉ Gutenbergpl. 3-5, 55116 Mainz, ☎ 06131/282-933 ⊕ www.germanwines.de.

ELECTRICITY

To use electric-power equipment purchased in the United States or Canada, **bring a converter and adapter.** The electrical current in Germany is 220 volts, 50 cycles alternating current (AC); wall outlets take Continental-type plugs, with two round prongs.

If your appliances are dual-voltage, you'll need only an adapter. Most laptops operate equally well on 110 and 220 volts and so require only an adapter.

EMBASSIES

⚑ Australia ✉ Wallstr. 76-79, D-10179 Berlin ☎ 030/880-0880 📠 030/8800-88210 ⊕ www. australian-embassy.de

⚑ Canada ✉ Friedrichstr. 95, 12th fl., D-10117 Berlin ☎ 030/203-120 📠 030/203-12121 ⊕ www. canada.de

⚑ Ireland ✉ Friedrichstr. 200, D-10117 Berlin ☎ 030/220-720 📠 030/220-72299 ⊕ www. botschaft-irland.de

⚑ New Zealand ✉ Friedrichstr. 60, D-10117 Berlin ☎ 030/206-2110 📠 030/206-21114 ⊕ www. nzembassy.com

⚑ South Africa ✉ Tiergartenstr. 18, D-10785 Berlin ☎ 030/220-730 📠 030/2207-3202 ⊕ www. suedafrika.org

⚑ United Kingdom ✉ Wilhelmstr. 70-71, D-10117 Berlin ☎ 030/204-570 ⊕ www.britischebotschaft.de

⚑ United States ✉ Neustädtische Kirchstr. 4-5, D-10117 Berlin ☎ 030/83050, 030/832-9233 for American citizens 📠 030/8305-1215 ⊕ www. usembassy.de

EMERGENCIES

Throughout Germany call ☎ 110 for police, ☎ 112 for an ambulance or the fire department, and ☎ 11880 for medication needs.

ENGLISH-LANGUAGE MEDIA

NEWSPAPERS & MAGAZINES

The *International Herald Tribune* is widely available at newsstands. On Friday it includes a translated insert of the week's highlights as reported in the German daily *Frankfurter Allgemeiner Zeitung.* To find American publications such as *USA Today, Time,* or *Newsweek* and British publications such as the *Daily Mail, Daily Telegraph,* or *Times,* go to a central newspaper shop, at a place such as a major train station.

RADIO & TELEVISION

In Frankfurt, the American Forces Network presents American news, sports, and music. Its AM broadcast (primarily talk) is at 873; the FM signal (primarily music) is at 98.7. You can pick up the BBC World Service in Berlin at 90.2 FM, and local station Rock Star FM (at 87.9 FM) has regular news bulletins, current affairs reports, and music programs from American networks.

Most hotels have a range of American cable TV channels on offer, including CNN and MTV. BBC World broadcasts free.

ETIQUETTE & BEHAVIOR

Being on time for appointments, even casual social ones, is very important. Germans are more formal in addressing each other than Americans. Always address acquaintances as Herr (Mr.) or Frau (Mrs.) plus their last name; do not call them by their first name unless invited to do so. The German language has an informal and formal pronoun for "you": formal is "*Sie*," and informal is "*du*." Even if adults are on a first-name basis with one another, they may still keep the *Sie* form between them.

Germans are less formal when it comes to nudity: a sign that reads FREIKÖRPER or FKK indicates a park or beach that allows nude sunbathing.

GAY & LESBIAN TRAVEL

Though only a few of the German states have laws banning discrimination on the basis of sexual orientation, the German people are very tolerant. The law recognizes gay marriages and property rights, and it is unlikely that same-sex couples will have trouble at hotel front desks, even in rural areas.

🖪 Gay- & Lesbian-Friendly Travel Agencies **Different Roads Travel** ⊠ 8383 Wilshire Blvd., Suite 520, Beverly Hills, CA 90211 ☎ 323/651-5557 or 800/429-8747 (Ext. 14 for both) 🖶 323/651-5454 ✉ lgernert@tzell.com. **Kennedy Travel** ⊠ 130 W. 42nd St., Suite 401, New York, NY 10036 ☎ 212/840-8659 or 800/237-7433 🖶 212/730-2269 ⊕ www.kennedytravel.com. **Now, Voyager** ⊠ 4406 18th St., San Francisco, CA 94114 ☎ 415/626-1169 or 800/255-6951 🖶 415/626-8626 ⊕ www.nowvoyager.com. **Skylink Travel and Tour/Flying Dutchmen Travel** ⊠ 1455 N. Dutton Ave., Suite A, Santa Rosa, CA 95401 ☎ 707/546-9888 or 800/225-5759 🖶 707/636-0951, serving lesbian travelers.

HOLIDAYS

The following national holidays are observed in Germany: January 1; January 6 (Epiphany—Bavaria, Saxony-Anhalt, and Baden-Württemberg only); Good Friday; Easter Monday; May 1 (Workers' Day); Ascension; Pentecost Monday; Corpus Christi (southern Germany only); Assumption Day—Bavaria and Saarland only; October 3 (German Unity Day); November 1 (All Saints' Day—Baden Württemberg, Bavaria, North Rhine-Westphalia, Rhineland-Pfalz, and Saarland only); December 24–26 (Christmas).

Pre-Lenten celebrations in Cologne and the Rhineland are known as Carnival, and for several days before Ash Wednesday, work grinds to a halt as people celebrate with parades, banquets, and general debauchery. Farther south, in the state of Baden Württenburg, the festivities are called Fasching and tend to be more traditional. In either area, expect businesses to be closed both before and after "Fat Tuesday."

INSURANCE

The most useful travel-insurance plan is a comprehensive policy that includes coverage for trip cancellation and interruption, default, trip delay, and medical expenses (with a waiver for preexisting conditions).

Without insurance you'll lose all or most of your money if you cancel your trip, regardless of the reason. Default insurance covers you if your tour operator, airline, or cruise line goes out of business—the chances of which have been increasing. Trip-delay covers expenses that arise because of bad weather or mechanical delays. Study the fine print when comparing policies.

If you're traveling internationally, a key component of travel insurance is coverage for medical bills incurred if you get sick on the road. Such expenses aren't generally covered by Medicare or private policies. U.K. residents can buy a travel-insurance policy valid for most vacations taken during the year in which it's purchased (but check preexisting-condition coverage). British and Australian citizens need extra medical coverage when traveling overseas.

Always **buy travel policies directly from the insurance company**; if you buy them from a cruise line, airline, or tour operator that goes out of business, you probably won't be covered for the agency or operator's default, a major risk. Before making any purchase, review your existing health and homeowner's policies to find what they cover away from home.

🖪 Travel Insurers In the U.S.: **Access America** ⊠ 2805 N. Parham Rd., Richmond, VA 23294 ☎ 800/284-8300 🖶 804/673-1491 or 800/346-9265 ⊕ www.accessamerica.com. **Travel Guard International** ⊠ 1145 Clark St., Stevens Point, WI 54481 ☎ 715/345-0505 or 800/826-1300 🖶 800/955-8785 ⊕ www.travelguard.com.

In the U.K.: **Association of British Insurers** ✉ 51 Gresham St., London EC2V 7HQ ☏ 020/7600-3333 🖷 020/7696-8999 ⊕ www.abi.org.uk. In Canada: **RBC Insurance** ✉ 6880 Financial Dr., Mississauga, Ontario L5N 7Y5 ☏ 800/668-4342 or 905/816-2400 🖷 905/813-4704 ⊕ www.rbcinsurance.com. In Australia: **Insurance Council of Australia** ✉ Insurance Enquiries and Complaints, Level 12, Box 561, Collins St. W, Melbourne, VIC 8007 ☏ 1300/780808 or 03/9629-4109 🖷 03/9621-2060 ⊕ www.iecltd.com.au. In New Zealand: **Insurance Council of New Zealand** ✉ Level 7, 111-115 Customhouse Quay, Box 474, Wellington ☏ 04/472-5230 🖷 04/473-3011 ⊕ www.icnz.org.nz.

LANGUAGE

English is spoken in most hotels, restaurants, airports, stations, museums, and other places of interest. However, English is not widely spoken in rural areas; this is especially true of the eastern part of Germany.

Unless you speak fluent German, you may find some of the regional dialects hard to follow, particularly in Saxony and Bavaria. However, most Germans can speak "high," or standard, German.

LANGUAGES FOR TRAVELERS

A phrase book and language-tape set can help get you started. *Fodor's German for Travelers,* (available at bookstores everywhere) is excellent.

LODGING

The standards of German hotels are very high, down to the humblest inn. You can nearly always **expect courteous and polite service and clean and comfortable rooms.** In addition to hotels proper, the country has numerous *Gasthöfe* or *Gasthäuser,* which are country inns that serve food and also have rooms, and pensions, or *Fremdenheime* (guesthouses). Most hotels have restaurants, but those listed as *Garni* provide breakfast only. At the lowest end of the scale are *Fremdenzimmer,* meaning simply "rooms," normally in private houses. (Look for the sign reading ZIMMER FREI or ZU VERMIETEN on a green background, meaning "to rent"; a red sign reading BESETZT means there are no vacancies.)

The hotels in our listings are divided by price into five categories: $$$$, $$$, $$, $,

and ¢. The lodgings we list are the cream of the crop in each price category. Properties are assigned price categories based on the range from their least-expensive standard double room at high season (excluding holidays) to the most expensive. Properties marked ✕🏨 are lodging establishments whose restaurants are recommendable. We always list the facilities that are available—but we don't specify whether they cost extra. **Ask about breakfast and bathroom facilities** when booking. All hotels listed have a private bath or shower unless otherwise noted. A generous continental breakfast buffet is often included in the rate, but be careful to inquire, particularly in upscale city hotels. Breakfast spreads at some hotels can run between 9€–15€.

Room rates are by no means inflexible and depend very much on supply and demand. You can save money by inquiring about reductions: many resort hotels offer substantial discounts in winter, except in the Alps, where rates often rise then. Likewise, many $$$$ and $$$ hotels in cities cut their prices dramatically on weekends and when business is quiet. If you have booked and plan to arrive late, let the hotel know. And if you have to cancel a reservation, inform the hotel as soon as possible; otherwise you may be charged the full amount for the unused room.

Tourist offices will also make bookings for a nominal fee, but they may have difficulty doing so after 4 PM in high season and on weekends, so **don't wait until too late in the day to begin looking for your accommodations.** If you do get stuck, ask someone—like a mail carrier, police officer, or waiter, for example—for directions to a house renting a Fremdenzimmer or a Gasthof.

The Deutsche Hotel- und Gaststättenverband (DEHOGA), Germany's hotel and gastronomy federation, publishes a yearly tome of more than 10,000 lodgings listings. The more than 1,200-page book (€12) is sold at bookstores, and although it has English instructions on how to use the guide, you're better off doing a free search of the guide online at its bilingual Web site, which includes links to properties. Hotels that have volunteered to be rated by DEHOGA receive one- to five-star ratings based on amenities offered.

🏠 Lodging Listings Deutsche Hotel- und Gaststättenverband ⊕ www.hotelguide.de.

APARTMENT & HOUSE RENTALS

If you want a home base that's roomy enough for a family and comes with cooking facilities, consider a furnished rental. These can save you money, especially if you're traveling with a group. Home-exchange directories sometimes list rentals as well as exchanges.

🏠 International Agents Drawbridge to Europe ✉ 98 Granite St., Ashland, OR 97520 ☎ 541/482-7778 or 888/268-1148 🖷 541/482-7779 ⊕ www.drawbridgetoeurope.com. **Hideaways International** ✉ 767 Islington St., Portsmouth, NH 03801 ☎ 603/430-4433 or 800/843-4433 🖷 603/430-4444 ⊕ www.hideaways.com, annual membership $145. **Interhome** ✉ 1990 N.E. 163rd St., Suite 110, North Miami Beach, FL 33162 ☎ 305/940-2299 or 800/882-6864 🖷 305/940-2911 ⊕ www.interhome.us. **Villas International** ✉ 4340 Redwood Hwy., Suite D309, San Rafael, CA 94903 ☎ 415/499-9490 or 800/221-2260 🖷 415/499-9491 ⊕ www.villasintl.com.

CAMPING

Campsites are scattered across the length and breadth of Germany. The DCC, or German Camping Club, produces an annual listing of 8,000 sites Europe-wide, of which 5,500 are in Germany. It also lists a number of sites where you can rent trailers and mobile homes. The Web site is in German only.

The majority of sites are open year-round, and most are crowded during high season. Prices at ordinary campsites range from around €10 to €25 for a car, tent, or trailer and two adults, though prices at fancier ones, with pools, sports facilities, and entertainment, can be considerably more. If you want to camp elsewhere, you must **get permission from the landowner beforehand;** ask the police if you can't track him or her down. Drivers of mobile homes may park for a limited time on roadsides and in autobahn parking-lot areas but may not set up camping equipment there.

🏕 Campsites DCC (German Camping Club) ✉ Mandlstr. 28, D-80802 Munich ☎ 089/380-1420 🖷 089/334-737 ⊕ www.camping-club.de.

CASTLE-HOTELS

Germany's historic castle-, or *Schloss,* hotels are all privately owned and run. The simpler ones may lack some amenities, but the majority combine four-star luxury with valuable antique furnishings, four-poster beds, stone passageways, and a baronial atmosphere. Some offer full resort facilities. Nearly all are in the countryside (⇨ Chapters 8 and 11, in particular, have several castle-hotel reviews). Euro-Connection has a brochure listing about 26 castle-hotels in Germany and can advise you on castle-hotel packages, including four- to six-night tours.

🏰 Euro-Connection ✉ 7500 212th St. SW, Suite 103, Edmonds, WA 98026 ☎ 800/645-3876 ⊕ www.euro-connection.com. **Gast im Schloss Marketing** ✉ Box 1428, D-65527 Niedernhausen ☎ 06127/999098 🖷 06127/920822 ⊕ www.gast-im-schloss.de.

FARM VACATIONS

Almost every regional tourist office has a brochure listing farms that offer bed-and-breakfasts, apartments, and entire farmhouses to rent (*Ferienhöfe*). The German Agricultural Association provides an illustrated brochure, *Urlaub auf dem Bauernhof* (Vacation Down on the Farm), that covers more than 2,000 inspected and graded farms, from the Alps to the North Sea. It costs €9.90 and is also sold in bookstores.

🚜 German Agricultural Association DLG Reisedienst, Agratour (German Agricultural Association) ✉ Eschborner Landstr. 122, D-60489 Frankfurt am Main ☎ 069/247-880 🖷 069/2478-8110 ⊕ www.landtourismus.de.

HOME EXCHANGES

If you would like to exchange your home for someone else's, join a home-exchange organization, which will send you its updated listings of available exchanges for a year and will include your own listing in at least one of them. It's up to you to make specific arrangements.

🏠 Exchange Clubs HomeLink International ✉ Box 47747, Tampa, FL 33647 ☎ 813/975-9825 or

800/638-3841 🖶 813/910-8144 ⊕ www.homelink.
org; $110 yearly for a listing, online access, and cata-
log; $70 without catalog. **Intervac U.S.** ✉ 30 Corte
San Fernando, Tiburon, CA 94920 ☎ 800/756-4663
🖶 415/435-7440 ⊕ www.intervacus.com; $125
yearly for a listing, online access, and a catalog; $65
without catalog.

HOSTELS

No matter what your age, you can save on
lodging costs by staying at hostels—rates
average €13.30 for people under 27 and
€13.30–€19 for those older (breakfast included). Accommodations can range from
single-sex, dorm-style beds to rooms for
couples and families. Germany's more
than 600 *Jugendherbergen* (youth hostels)
are among the most efficient and up-to-
date in Europe, and many are in castles.
There's an age limit of 26 in Bavaria; elsewhere, there are no age restrictions,
though those under 20 take preference if
space is limited. The DJH Service GmbH
provides a complete list of German hostels
and has information on regional offices
around the country. Hostels must be reserved well in advance for midsummer, especially in eastern Germany. To book a
hostel, you can go on DJH's Web site or
call a lodging directly; it's helpful to be a
member of a national hosteling association
or Hostelling International (HI), the um-
brella group for a number of national
youth-hostel associations. Without membership, there's an extra charge, but with
each overnight stay you receive a "welcome stamp." Six welcome stamps will
grant you full membership in HI.

Membership in any HI national hostel association, open to travelers of all ages, allows
you to stay in HI-affiliated hostels at member rates; one-year membership in the U.S.
is about $28 for adults (C$35 for a two-
year minimum membership in Canada, £4
in U.K., A$52 in Australia, and NZ$40 in
New Zealand); hostels charge about
$10–$30 per night. Members have priority
if the hostel is full; they're also eligible for
discounts around the world, even on rail
and bus travel in some countries.

🏠 In Germany **DJH Service GmbH** ✉ Bismarkstr.
8, D-32754 Detmold ☎ 05231/74010 🖶 05231/740-
149 ⊕ www.jugendherberge.de.

🏠 Organizations **Hostelling International–USA**
✉ 8401 Colesville Rd., Suite 600, Silver Spring, MD
20910 ☎ 301/495-1240 🖶 301/495-6697 ⊕ www.
hiusa.org. **Hostelling International–Canada**
✉ 205 Catherine St., Suite 400, Ottawa, Ontario
K2P 1C3 ☎ 613/237-7884 or 800/663-5777 🖶 613/
237-7868 ⊕ www.hihostels.ca. **YHA England and
Wales** ✉ Trevelyan House, Dimple Rd., Matlock,
Derbyshire DE4 3YH, U.K. ☎ 0870/870-8808, 0870/
770-8868, 0162/959-2600 🖶 0870/770-6127
⊕ www.yha.org.uk. **YHA Australia** ✉ 422 Kent St.,
Sydney, NSW 2001 ☎ 02/9261-1111 🖶 02/9261-1969
⊕ www.yha.com.au. **YHA New Zealand** ✉ Level 1,
Moorhouse City, 166 Moorhouse Ave., Box 436,
Christchurch ☎ 03/379-9970 or 0800/278-299
🖶 03/365-4476 ⊕ www.yha.org.nz.

HOTELS

There are many European chain hotels in
Germany. The Accor Hotel group is preva-
lent and includes the respectable chains
Ibis, Mercure, Novotel, and Sofitel. Major
American hotel chains—Hilton, Sheraton,
Holiday Inn, Best Western, Marriott—are
represented in cities.

Most hotels in Germany do not have air-
conditioning, nor do they need it given the
climate and the German style of building
construction that uses thick walls and re-
cessed windows to help keep the heat out.
Smaller hotels do not provide much in
terms of bathroom amenities. Except in
four- and five star hotels, you won't find a
washcloth. Hotels often have no-smoking
rooms or even no-smoking floors, so it's always worth asking for one when you reserve. All hotels listed have private bath
unless otherwise noted. Specify your preference for a shower or bathtub; though
bathtubs come with a handheld shower
nozzle, standing with free hands under a
mounted spray is usually not possible. Beds
in double rooms often consist of two twin
mattresses placed side by side within a
frame. When you arrive, if you don't like
the room you're offered, ask to see another.

RESERVING A ROOM

Most hotels can process a letter or fax asking for a reservation in English, but here
are sample phrases in German:

Sehr geehrte Damen und Herren! (Dear
Sir/Madam).

Ich möchte ein Doppelzimmer/Zweibettzimmer mit Bad reservieren (I would like to reserve a double/twin room with bath).

und zwar von. bis. (from. until.; dates are written day/month/year).

Ich hätte gern ein Zimmer auf der oberen Etage/auf der unteren Etage/mit Ausblick/in ruhiger Lage (I would like a room on a high floor/a low floor/with a view/a quiet room).

Könnten Sie mir bitte weitere Informationen auf Englisch über Ihr Hotel zuschicken (Please send me more information in English about your hotel).

Mit freundlichen Grüssen (Kind regards).

⛶ Toll-Free Numbers Best Western ☎ 800/528-1234 ⊕ www.bestwestern.com. **Choice** ☎ 800/424-6423 ⊕ www.choicehotels.com. **Clarion** ☎ 800/424-6423 ⊕ www.choicehotels.com. **Comfort Inn** ☎ 800/424-6423 ⊕ www.choicehotels.com. **Four Seasons** ☎ 800/332-3442 ⊕ www.fourseasons.com. **Hilton** ☎ 800/445-8667 ⊕ www.hilton.com. **Holiday Inn** ☎ 800/465-4329 ⊕ www.ichotelsgroup.com. **Hyatt Hotels & Resorts** ☎ 800/233-1234 ⊕ www.hyatt.com. **Inter-Continental** ☎ 800/327-0200 ⊕ www.ichotelsgroup.com. **Marriott** ☎ 800/228-9290 ⊕ www.marriott.com. **Le Meridien** ☎ 800/543-4300 ⊕ www.lemeridien.com. **Nikko Hotels International** ☎ 800/645-5687 ⊕ www.nikkohotels.com. **Quality Inn** ☎ 800/424-6423 ⊕ www.choicehotels.com. **Radisson** ☎ 800/333-3333 ⊕ www.radisson.com. **Ramada** ☎ 800/228-2828, 800/854-7854 international reservations ⊕ www.ramada.com or www.ramadahotels.com. **Renaissance Hotels & Resorts** ☎ 800/468-3571 ⊕ www.renaissancehotels.com/. **Ritz-Carlton** ☎ 800/241-3333 ⊕ www.ritzcarlton.com. **Sheraton** ☎ 800/325-3535 ⊕ www.starwood.com/sheraton. **Westin Hotels & Resorts** ☎ 800/228-3000 ⊕ www.starwood.com/westin.

ROMANTIK HOTELS

Among the most delightful places to stay—and eat—in Germany are the aptly named Romantik Hotels and Restaurants. The Romantik group has 185 establishments throughout Europe, with 86 in Germany. All are in atmospheric and historic buildings—a condition for membership—and are personally run by the owners, with the emphasis on excellent food and service. Prices vary considerably but in general represent good value, particularly the special weekend and short-holiday rates. A three- or four-day stay, for example, with one main meal, is available at about €150–€250 per person. A detailed brochure listing all Romantik Hotels and Restaurants is available by mail.

⛶ Romantik Hotels and Restaurants ⊠ Lyoner Stern, Hahnstr. 70, D-60528 Frankfurt/Main ☎ 069/661-2340 ⓑ 069/6612-3456 ⊠ C/o tma target market america 505 Majorca Ave., Coral Gables FL 33134 ☎ 305/447-1222 or 800/650-8018 ⓑ 305/574-7769 ⊕ www.romantikhotels.com.

SPAS

Taking the waters in Germany, whether for curing the body or merely pampering it, has been popular since Roman times. More than 300 health resorts, mostly equipped for hot mineral, mud, or brine treatments, are set within pleasant country areas or historic communities. The word *Bad* before or within the name of a town usually means it's a spa destination.

There are four main groups of spas and health resorts: the mineral and moorland spas, where treatments are based on natural warm-water springs; those on the Baltic and North Sea coasts; hydropathic spas, which use an invigorating cold-water process developed during the 19th century; and climatic health resorts, usually in the mountains, which depend on their climates and fresh air for their health-giving properties.

Saunas, steam baths, and other hot-room facilities are often used "without textiles" in Germany—in other words, naked. Wearing a bathing suit is sometimes even prohibited in saunas, but sitting on a towel is always required (you may need to bring your own towels). The Deutsche Heilbäderverband has information in German only.

⛶ Deutsche Heilbäderverband (German Health Resort and Spa Association) ⊠ Schumannstr. 111, D-53113 Bonn ☎ 0228/201-200 ⓑ 0228/201-2041 ⊕ www.deutscher-heilbaederverband.de.

MAIL & SHIPPING

Post offices (*Deutsche Post*) are recognizable by the postal symbol, a black bugle on a yellow background. Stamps (*Briefmarken*) can also be bought at some news agencies and souvenir shops. Letters take approximately 3–4 days to the United Kingdom, 5–7 days to the United States, and 7–10 days to Australia and New Zealand. Post offices are generally open weekdays 8–6, Saturday 8–noon.

OVERNIGHT SERVICES

The Deutsche Post has an express international service that will deliver your letter or package the next day to countries within the EU, within one to two days to the United States, and slightly longer to Australia. A letter or package to the United States weighing less than 200 grams costs €48.57. You can drop off your mail at any post office, or it can be picked up for an extra fee. Deutsche Post works in cooperation with DHL. International carriers tend to be slightly cheaper (€35–€45 for the same letter) and provide more services.

🖪 Major Services **Deutsche Post Express International** ☎ 08105/345-2255 ⊕ www.deutschepost. de. **DHL** ☎ 0800/225-5345 ⊕ www.dhl.de. **FedEx** ☎ 0800/123-0800 ⊕ www.fedex.com. **UPS** ☎ 0800/882-6630 ⊕ www.ups.com.

POSTAL RATES

Airmail letters to the United States, Canada, Australia, and New Zealand cost €1.55; postcards, €1. All letters to the United Kingdom cost €.55; postcards, €.45.

RECEIVING MAIL

You can arrange to have mail sent to you in care of any German post office; **have the envelope marked "Postlagernd."** This service is free, and the mail will be held for 14 days. Or you can have mail sent to any American Express office in Germany. There's no charge to cardholders, holders of American Express traveler's checks, or anyone who has booked a vacation with American Express.

SHIPPING PARCELS

Most major stores that cater to tourists will also ship your purchases home. You should check your insurance for coverage of possible damage. The companies listed under ⇨ Overnight Services also have international shipping services, although these are quite expensive.

MONEY MATTERS

Payment by credit card is not as frequent an option as in the United States, so be sure to have cash handy at all times. A good way to budget is to seek lodging in local pensions rather than hotels and to visit lesser-known cities and towns. All along the Main and Neckar rivers, for example, you'll find small towns that are as charming as, but significantly less expensive than, the likes of Rothenburg and Heidelberg. Wine lovers can explore the Pfalz and Rhine Terrace areas of the German Wine Road instead of the classic Rhine-Mosel tour.

The five states (Brandenburg, Mecklenburg-Vorpommern, Saxony, Saxony-Anhalt, and Thuringia) of the former East Germany still have a lower standard of living than does the former West Germany, but prices in leading hotels and restaurants in Dresden and Leipzig match rates in Frankfurt and Munich.

Prices throughout this guide are given for adults. Substantially reduced fees are almost always available for children, students, and senior citizens. For information on taxes, *see* Taxes.

ATMS

Twenty-four-hour ATMs (*Geldautomaten*) can be accessed with Plus or Cirrus credit and banking cards. Some German banks exact €3–€5 fees for use of their ATMs. Your PIN should be set for four digits; if it's longer, change it at your bank before the trip. Since some ATM keypads show no letters, know the numeric equivalent of your password.

CREDIT CARDS

All major U.S. credit cards are accepted in Germany. If you have a four-digit PIN for your card, you can use it at German ATMs.

Throughout this guide, the following abbreviations are used: **AE,** American Express; **DC,** Diners Club; **MC,** MasterCard; and **V,** Visa.

🖪 Reporting Lost Cards **American Express** ☎ 069/97970. **Diners Club** ☎ 069/6616-6123. **MasterCard** ☎ 0800/819-1040. **Visa** ☎ 0800/811-8440.

CURRENCY

Germany shares a common currency, the euro (€), with 11 other countries: Austria, Belgium, Finland, France, Greece, Ireland, Italy, Luxembourg, Netherlands, Portugal, and Spain. The euro is divided into 100 cents. There are bills of 5, 10, 20, 50, 100, and 500 euros and coins of €1 and €2, and 1, 2, 5, 10, 20, and 50 cents.

CURRENCY EXCHANGE

At press time, you could get €.81 for a U.S. dollar, €.61 for a Canadian dollar, €1.50 for a British pound, €.59 for an Australian dollar, €.53 for a New Zealand dollar, and €.13 for a South African rand.

For the most favorable rates, **change money through banks.** Although ATM transaction fees may be higher abroad than at home, ATM rates are excellent because they're based on wholesale rates offered only by major banks. You won't do as well at exchange booths in airports or rail and bus stations, in hotels, in restaurants, or in stores. To avoid lines at airport exchange booths, get a bit of local currency before you leave home.

🖪 Exchange Services **International Currency Express** ✉ 427 N. Camden Dr., Suite F, Beverly Hills, CA 90210 ☎ 888/278-6628 orders ⊟ 310/278-6410 ⊕ www.foreignmoney.com. **Travel Ex Currency Services** ☎ 800/287-7362 orders and retail locations ⊕ www.travelex.com.

TRAVELER'S CHECKS

Do you need traveler's checks? It depends on where you're headed. If you're going to rural areas and small towns, go with cash; traveler's checks are best used in cities. Lost or stolen checks can usually be replaced within 24 hours. To ensure a speedy refund, buy your own traveler's checks—don't let someone else pay for them: irregularities like this can cause delays. The person who bought the checks should make the call to request a refund.

PACKING

What you pack depends more on the time of year than on any particular dress code. Winters can be bitterly cold; summers are warm but with days that suddenly turn cool and rainy. In summer **take a warm jacket or heavy sweater** for the Bavarian

Alps, where the nights can be chilly even after hot days.

For cities, **pack as you would for an American city**: dressy outfits for formal restaurants and nightclubs, casual clothes elsewhere. Jeans are as popular in Germany as anywhere else and are perfectly acceptable for sightseeing and informal dining. In the evening men will probably feel more comfortable wearing a jacket and tie in more expensive restaurants, although it's almost never required. Many German women wear stylish outfits to restaurants and the theater, especially in the larger cities.

To discourage purse snatchers and pickpockets, **carry a handbag with long straps** that you can sling across your body bandolier style and with a zippered compartment for money and other valuables.

For stays in budget hotels, **take your own soap.** Many provide no soap at all or only a small bar.

In your carry-on luggage, pack an extra pair of eyeglasses or contact lenses and enough of any medication you take to last a few days longer than the entire trip. You may also ask your doctor to write a spare prescription using the drug's generic name, as brand names may vary from country to country. In luggage to be checked, **never pack prescription drugs, valuables, or undeveloped film.** And don't forget to carry with you the addresses of offices that handle refunds of lost traveler's checks. Check *Fodor's How to Pack* (available at online retailers and bookstores everywhere) for more tips.

To avoid customs and security delays, carry medications in their original packaging. Don't pack any sharp objects in your carry-on luggage, including knives of any size or material, scissors, nail clippers, and corkscrews, or anything else that might arouse suspicion.

To avoid having your checked luggage chosen for hand inspection, don't cram bags full. The U.S. Transportation Security Administration suggests packing shoes on top and placing personal items you don't want touched in clear plastic bags.

CHECKING LUGGAGE

You're allowed to carry aboard one bag and one personal article, such as a purse or a laptop computer. Make sure what you carry on fits under your seat or in the overhead bin. Get to the gate early, so you can board as soon as possible, before the overhead bins fill up.

Baggage allowances vary by carrier, destination, and ticket class. On international flights, you're usually allowed to check two bags weighing up to 70 pounds (32 kilograms) each, although a few airlines allow checked bags of up to 88 pounds (40 kilograms) in first class. Some international carriers don't allow more than 66 pounds (30 kilograms) per bag in business class and 44 pounds (20 kilograms) in economy. On domestic flights, the limit is usually 50 to 70 pounds (23 to 32 kilograms) per bag. In general, carry-on bags shouldn't exceed 40 pounds (18 kilograms). Most airlines won't accept bags that weigh more than 100 pounds (45 kilograms) on domestic or international flights. Expect to pay a fee for baggage that exceeds weight limits. Check baggage restrictions with your carrier before you pack.

Airline liability for baggage is limited to $2,500 per person on flights within the United States. On international flights it amounts to $9.07 per pound or $20 per kilogram for checked baggage (roughly $640 per 70-pound bag), with a maximum of $634.90 per piece, and $400 per passenger for unchecked baggage. You can buy additional coverage at check-in for about $10 per $1,000 of coverage, but it often excludes a rather extensive list of items, shown on your airline ticket.

Before departure, itemize your bags' contents and their worth, and label the bags with your name, address, and phone number. (If you use your home address, cover it so potential thieves can't see it readily.) Include a label inside each bag and **pack a copy of your itinerary.** At check-in, make sure each bag is correctly tagged with the destination airport's three-letter code. Because some checked bags will be opened for hand inspection, the U.S. Transporta-

tion Security Administration (TSA) recommends that you leave luggage unlocked or use the plastic locks offered at check-in. TSA screeners place an inspection notice inside searched bags, which are resealed with a special lock.

If your bag has been searched and contents are missing or damaged, file a claim with the TSA Consumer Response Center as soon as possible. If your bags arrive damaged or fail to arrive at all, file a written report with the airline before leaving the airport.

🔁 Complaints **U.S. Transportation Security Administration Contact Center** ☎ 866/289-9673 ⊕ www.tsa.gov.

PASSPORTS & VISAS

When traveling internationally, carry your passport even if you don't need one (it's always the best form of ID) and **make two photocopies of the data page** (one for someone at home and another for you, carried separately from your passport). If you lose your passport, promptly call the nearest embassy or consulate and the local police.

U.S. passport applications for children under age 14 require consent from both parents or legal guardians; both parents must appear together to sign the application. If only one parent appears, he or she must submit a written statement from the other parent authorizing passport issuance for the child. A parent with sole authority must present evidence of it when applying; acceptable documentation includes the child's certified birth certificate listing only the applying parent, a court order specifically permitting this parent's travel with the child, or a death certificate for the nonapplying parent. Application forms and instructions are available on the Web site of the U.S. State Department's Bureau of Consular Affairs (⊕ travel.state.gov).

ENTERING GERMANY

U.S., Canadian, Australian, New Zealand, and British citizens need only a valid passport (even those that have been expired up to five years are considered valid) to enter Germany for stays of up to 90 days.

PASSPORT OFFICES

The best time to apply for a passport or to renew is in fall and winter. Before any trip, check your passport's expiration date, and, if necessary, renew it as soon as possible.

Australian Citizens Passports Australia Australian Department of Foreign Affairs and Trade ☎ 131-232 ⊕ www.passports.gov.au.

Canadian Citizens Passport Office ✉ To mail in applications: 200 Promenade du Portage, Hull, Québec J8X 4B7 ☎ 819/994-3500 or 800/567-6868 ⊕ www.ppt.gc.ca.

New Zealand Citizens New Zealand Passports Office ☎ 0800/22-5050 or 04/474-8100 ⊕ www.passports.govt.nz.

U.K. Citizens U.K. Passport Service ☎ 0870/521-0410 ⊕ www.passport.gov.uk.

U.S. Citizens National Passport Information Center ☎ 877/487-2778, 888/874-7793 TDD/TTY ⊕ travel.state.gov.

RESTROOMS

It's customary to leave a €.20–€.30 gratuity in a restroom if it has an attendant.

SAFETY

Don't wear a money belt or a waist pack, both of which peg you as a tourist. Distribute your cash and any valuables (including your credit cards and passport) between a deep front pocket, an inside jacket or vest pocket, and a hidden money pouch. Do not reach for the money pouch once you're in public.

Germany has one of the lowest rates of violent crime in Europe. The best advice is to take normal precautions. Put valuables in the hotel safe. Don't carry a shoulder bag or purse in such a way that it can be easily snatched. Avoid remote areas late at night. And then, don't worry too much.

WOMEN IN GERMANY

If you carry a purse, choose one with a zipper and a thick strap that you can drape across your body; adjust the length so that the purse sits in front of you at or above hip level. (Don't wear a money belt or a waist pack.) Store only enough money in the purse to cover casual spending. Distribute the rest of your cash and any valuables between deep front pockets, inside jacket or vest pockets, and a concealed money pouch.

SENIOR-CITIZEN TRAVEL

Senior citizens qualify for some discounts in Germany, such as on the railways and in museums. For €11, the German Railroad's ReisePacket service (⇨ Train Travel) includes help boarding and getting off trains, transfer of luggage, and other small services.

To qualify for age-related discounts, mention your senior-citizen status up front when booking hotel reservations (not when checking out) and before you're seated in restaurants (not when paying the bill). Be sure to have identification on hand. When renting a car, ask about promotional car-rental discounts, which can be cheaper than senior-citizen rates.

Educational Programs Elderhostel ✉ 11 Ave. de Lafayette, Boston, MA 02111-1746 ☎ 877/426-8056, 978/323-4141 international callers, 877/426-2167 TTY 🖷 877/426-2166 ⊕ www.elderhostel.org. Interhostel ✉ University of New Hampshire, 6 Garrison Ave., Durham, NH 03824 ☎ 603/862-1147 or 800/733-9753 🖷 603/862-1113 ⊕ www.learn.unh.edu.

SPORTS & OUTDOORS

Germans are very active and constantly organize themselves into sports teams and clubs. Hiking trails abound throughout the country.

BIKING

There are many long-distance bicycle routes in Germany. Among the best river bike paths are those along the Danube River (*Donau* in German), which you can join at Regensburg or Passau, and along the Weser River, which you can join at Hannoversch-Münden. Another route, somewhat rugged, is along the Baltic Coast, mainly in the state of Mecklenburg-Vorpommern. The *Radfährerkarten,* issued by the Bielefelder Verlaganstalt and by Haupka Verlag, are good bike travel maps available at bookstores.

The Call-a-Bike rental service Deutsche Bahn is available in Berlin, Frankfurt, Köln, and Munich. Solidly built silver bikes cost €.05 per minute, not to exceed €15 for 24 hours. First register online or by phone (credit card information is necessary). The bikes are left electronically locked at major intersections, and by calling in the bike's code number, the bike is yours to roll away. When you're done using it, return it to a major intersection and call in to report you're finished. Most bike shops have rentals for about €10 per day or €25 a week.

Bikes cannot be transported on InterCity Express trains. Trains that do carry them have a little bicycle symbol on the timetable. Bike transportation costs €3 on local trains (RB, RE, IRE). On all other trains **you must make advance reservations** and pay €8. Bikes can usually be transported on municipal suburban trains, trams, and buses, but an extra ticket for your bike is often required.

🚲 Clubs Allgemeiner Deutscher Fahrrad-Club (German Cycle Club) ⏏ Postfach 107747, D-28077 Bremen ☎ 0421/346-290 🖷 0421/346-2950 ⊕ www.adfc.de. **Deutsche Bahn bicycle hotline** ☎ 01805/151-415 information, 0700/0522-5522 call-a-bike ⊕ www.callabike.de.

HIKING

Tourist offices in all Bavarian Alpine resorts have details on mountaineering schools offering weeklong courses. Most town tourist offices will have details on local hiking areas. The Deutscher Alpenverein maintains more than 50 mountain huts and about 15,000 km (9,300 mi) of Alpine paths. In addition, it can provide courses in mountaineering and route suggestions. The organization is not a tour-planner and does not make hut reservations. It can report on weather and trail conditions. Foreigners may become members.

🚲 Deutscher Alpenverein ⊠ Haus der Alpinismus, Praterinsel 5, Munich ☎ 089/294-940 🖷 089/140-0312 ⊕ www.alpenverein.de.

SKIING

The Black Forest has many marked and groomed cross-country ski trails (*Loipe*). Ask about ski and boot rentals in any town, as well as how to get to the local trail. Downhill (*Alpin*) is most popular in the Bavarian Alps.

STUDENTS IN GERMANY

Most museums and modes of transportation have reduced prices for students, so have your student ID card handy. EurAide offers help with travel plans at Munich's

main train station and at Berlin's Zoologischer Garten train station. *See* Lodging for hosteling information.

🚲 IDs & Services STA Travel ⊠ 10 Downing St., New York, NY 10014 ☎ 212/627-3111, 800/777-0112 24-hr service center 🖷 212/627-3387 ⊕ www.sta.com. **Travel Cuts** ⊠ 187 College St., Toronto, Ontario M5T 1P7, Canada ☎ 800/592-2887 in U.S., 416/979-2406 or 866/246-9762 in Canada 🖷 416/979-8167 ⊕ www.travelcuts.com.

TAXES

VALUE-ADDED TAX

Most prices you see on items already have Germany's 16% value-added tax (V.A.T.) included. When traveling to a non-EU country, you are entitled to a refund of the V.A.T. you pay (multiply the price of an item by .138 to find out how much V.A.T. is embedded in the price). Some goods, such as books and antiquities, carry a 7% V.A.T. as a percentage of the purchase price. An item must cost at least €25 to qualify for a V.A.T. refund.

When making a purchase, **ask for a V.A.T. refund form** and find out whether the merchant gives refunds—not all stores do, nor are they required to. Have the form stamped like any customs form by customs officials when you leave the country or, if you're visiting several European Union countries, when you leave the EU. Be ready to show customs officials what you've bought (pack purchases together, in your carry-on luggage); budget extra time for this. After you're through passport control, take the form to a refund-service counter for an on-the-spot refund, or mail it to the address on the form (or the envelope with it) after you arrive home.

A service processes refunds for most shops. You receive the total refund stated on the form. Global Refund is a Europe-wide service with 210,000 affiliated stores and more than 700 refund counters—located at major airports and border crossings. Its refund form is called a Tax Free Check. The service issues refunds in the form of cash, check, or credit-card adjustment. If you don't have time to wait at the refund counter, you can mail in the form instead.

If you're departing from Terminal 1 at Frankfurt Airport, bring your purchases to one of two areas, depending on how you've packed the goods. Bring items packed in check-in luggage to the customs office in the baggage claim areas of Arrivals Halls A, B, and C (access through the Terminal Supervisor Desk); or bring your baggage to Level 3 near the Sky Line Station, Hall B. For goods you are carrying on the plane with you, go to the customs office at Gates A 15/17, Transit Area B, near the passport control; or baggage claim area, Hall C. If you're departing from Terminal 2, bring goods in luggage to be checked to the customs office in Hall D, Level 2 (opposite the Delta Airlines check-in counters). For goods you are carrying on the plane with you, go to the customs office in Hall E, Level 3 (near security control).

At Munich's airport, the Terminal 2 customs area is on the same level as check-in. If your V.A.T. refund items are in your luggage, check in first, then bring your bags to the customs office. From here, your bags will be sent to your flight and you can go to the Global Refund counter around the corner. If your refund items are in your carry-on, go to the customs area on level 05. A Global Refund office is there as well.

🚩 **V.A.T. Refunds Global Refund** ✉ **99 Main St., Suite 307, Nyack, NY 10960** ☎ **800/566-9828** 🖷 **845/348-1549** ⊕ **www.globalrefund.com.**

TELEPHONES

AREA & COUNTRY CODES
The country code for Germany is 49. When dialing a German number from abroad, drop the initial "0" from the local area code. When making international calls from Germany, the country code is 001 for the United States and Canada, 0061 for Australia, 0064 for New Zealand, 0044 for the United Kingdom, 00353 for Ireland, and 0027 for South Africa. When dialing within a local area code, drop the exchange number.

Many companies have service lines beginning with 0180. The cost of these calls averages €.12 per minute. Numbers that begin with 0190 can cost €1.85 per minute and more.

DIRECTORY & OPERATOR ASSISTANCE
The German telephone system is fully automatic, and it's unlikely you'll have to employ the services of an operator unless you're seeking information. If you have difficulty reaching your number, call 0180/ 200–1033. You can book collect calls through this number to the United States but not to other countries. For information in English dial 11837 for numbers within Germany and 11834 for numbers elsewhere. But first **look for the number in the phone book or on the Web** (⊕ www. teleauskunft.de), because directory assistance is costly. Calls to 11837 and 11834 cost at least €.50, more if the call lasts more than 30 seconds.

INTERNATIONAL CALLS
International calls can be made from just about any telephone booth in Germany. It costs only €.13 per minute to call the United States, day or night, no matter how long the call lasts. Use a phone card. If you don't have a good deal with a calling card, there are many stores that offer international calls at rates well below what you will pay from a phone booth. At a hotel, rates will be at least double the regular charge, so **avoid making international calls from your room.**

LOCAL CALLS
A local call from a telephone booth costs €.10 per minute. You can drop the local area code.

LONG-DISTANCE CALLS
Dial the "0" before the area code when making a long-distance call within Germany. German newspapers often print a column with prefix telephone numbers that offer discounted rates. Dial the prefix, often five digits, before the phone number you call. This can save you as much as .08¢ per minute.

LONG-DISTANCE SERVICES
AT&T, MCI, and Sprint access codes make calling long-distance relatively convenient, but you may find the local access

number blocked in many hotel rooms. First ask the hotel operator to connect you. If the hotel operator balks, ask for an international operator, or dial the international operator yourself. One way to improve your odds of getting connected to your long-distance carrier is to travel with more than one company's calling card (a hotel may block Sprint, for example, but not MCI). If all else fails, call from a pay phone.

☎ Access Codes **AT&T Direct** ☎ 0800/225-5288. **Sprint International Access** ☎ 0800/888-0013. **WorldPhone** ☎ 0800/888-8000.

MOBILE PHONES

The standard mobile phones used in the United States and Canada are *not* compatible with Germany's GSM digital mobile phone network. Because public phones are not nearly as ubiquitous as in North America, you should seriously consider renting a GSM cell phone if you intend to make calls regularly. You can rent a cell phone at the Airport Communications Service at Frankfurt's airport. It's in the Frankfurt Airport Center 1 and near the Sheraton Hotel. They can also deliver to you at a prearranged meeting point. At the Munich Airport Center, the Nokia Shop at Terminal 2 rents cell phones.

☎ Phone Rentals **Airport Communications Service** ☎ 069/6959-1163 ☎ 069/6959-1165 ⊕ www.aircom.de. **Nokia Shop** ☎ 089/9758-4550 ⊕ www.rentacell.com.

PHONE CARDS

Post offices, newsstands, and exchange places sell cards with €5, €10, or €20 worth of credit to use at public pay phones (*Zelle*), and cards to use from home or mobile phones. An advantage of a card: it charges only what the call costs. A €5 card with a good rate for calls to the United States, United Kingdom, and Canada is EuroExtra.

PUBLIC PHONES

Telephone booths are not a common feature on the streets, so be prepared to ask locals where to find one; you might have to walk a bit out of your way. Most phone booths have instructions in English as well as German. Most telephone booths in Germany are card-operated, so **buy a phone card.** Coin-operated phones, which take €0.10, €0.20, €0.50, €1, and €2 coins, don't make change.

TIME

Germany is on Central European Time, which is six hours ahead of Eastern Standard Time and nine hours ahead of Pacific Standard Time. Germans use military time (1 PM is indicated as 13:00) and write the date before the month, so October 3 will appear as 03.10.

TIPPING

The service charges on bills are sufficient for most tips in your hotel, though you should **tip bellhops and porters**; €1 per bag or service is ample. It's also customary to leave a small tip (a euro or so per night) for the room-cleaning staff. Whether you tip the desk clerk depends on whether he or she has given you any special service.

Service charges are included in all restaurant checks (listed as *Bedienung*), as is tax (listed as *MWST*). Nonetheless, it is customary to **round up the bill to the nearest euro or to leave about 5–10%** (give it to the waiter or waitress as you pay the bill; don't leave it on the table, as that's considered rude). Bartenders don't expect, but appreciate tips. Those who bring drinks to your table do expect a small tip.

In taxis, **round up the fare about a euro** as a tip. Give more only if you have particularly cumbersome or heavy luggage.

TOURS & PACKAGES

Because everything is prearranged on a prepackaged tour or independent vacation, you spend less time planning—and often get it all at a good price.

BOOKING WITH AN AGENT

Travel agents are excellent resources. But it's a good idea to collect brochures from several agencies, as some agents' suggestions may be influenced by relationships with tour and package firms that reward them for volume sales. If you have a special interest, find an agent with expertise in that area; the American Society of Travel Agents (ASTA; ⇨ Travel Agencies) has a database of specialists worldwide. You can log on to the group's Web site to find an ASTA travel agent in your neighborhood.

Make sure your travel agent knows the accommodations and other services of the place being recommended. Ask about the hotel's location, room size, beds, and whether it has a pool, room service, or programs for children, if you care about these. Has your agent been there in person or sent others whom you can contact?

Do some homework on your own, too: local tourism boards can provide information about lesser-known and small-niche operators, some of which may sell only direct.

BUYER BEWARE

Each year consumers are stranded or lose their money when tour operators—even large ones with excellent reputations—go out of business. So check out the operator. Ask several travel agents about its reputation, and try to **book with a company that has a consumer-protection program.** (Look for information in the company's brochure.) In the United States, members of the United States Tour Operators Association are required to set aside funds ($1 million) to help eligible customers cover payments and travel arrangements in the event that the company defaults. It's also a good idea to choose a company that participates in the American Society of Travel Agents' Tour Operator Program; ASTA will act as mediator in any disputes between you and your tour operator.

Remember that the more your package or tour includes, the better you can predict the ultimate cost of your vacation. Make sure you know exactly what is covered, and beware of hidden costs. Are taxes, tips, and transfers included? Entertainment and excursions? These can add up.

⧉ Tour-Operator Recommendations American Society of Travel Agents (⇨ Travel Agencies). **National Tour Association (NTA)** ⊠ 546 E. Main St., Lexington, KY 40508 ☎ 859/226-4444 or 800/682-8886 ⎙ 859/226-4404 ⊕ www.ntaonline.com. **United States Tour Operators Association (USTOA)** ⊠ 275 Madison Ave., Suite 2014, New York, NY 10016 ☎ 212/599-6599 ⎙ 212/599-6744 ⊕ www.ustoa.com.

TRAIN TRAVEL

Deutsche Bahn (DB—German Rail) is a very efficient, privatized railway. Its high-speed InterCity Express (ICE), InterCity (IC), and EuroCity (EC) trains make journeys between the centers of many cities—Munich–Frankfurt, for example—faster by rail than by air. It's also possible to sleep on the train and save a day of your trip. There are CityNightLine (CNL) trains to distant locations, and many overnight D-Class trains also have sleepers. The high-speed trains have a first-class service that includes breakfast in bed. All InterCity and InterCity Express trains have restaurant cars and trolley service. RE, RB, and IRE trains are regional trains.

With the high-speed expresses, you often have to cross to the other side of the station platform only to change trains. Special train maps on platform notice boards give details of the layout of trains arriving on that track, showing the locations of first- and second-class cars and the restaurant car, as well as where they will stop along the platform. Large railroad stations have English-speaking staff handling information inquiries.

Tickets that you purchase online over Deutsche Bahn's Web site can be retrieved from their vending machines. Always **check that your ticket is valid for the type of train you are planning to take.** If you have the wrong type of ticket, you will have to pay the difference on the train, in cash.

BAGGAGE SERVICE

Most major train stations have luggage lockers (in four sizes). By inserting coins into a storage unit, you release the unit's key. Prices range from €1 for a small locker to €3 for a "jumbo" one. Smaller towns' train stations may not have any storage options.

Throughout Germany you can use the Deutsche Bahn *KurierGepäck* service to deliver your baggage from a private residence or hotel to any of six large airports. Buy a *KurierGepäck* ticket at any DB ticket counter and call 01805/4884 to schedule a pickup. The service costs €14.90 for each of the first two suitcases (with a valid ticket). Delivery to the airports at Berlin, Frankfurt, Leipzig-Halle, Munich, Hamburg, and Hannover is guaranteed on the second weekday following pickup.

German railway's ReisePacket service is for travelers who are inexperienced, elderly, disabled, or just appreciative of extra help. It costs €10 and provides, among other things, help boarding, disembarking, and transferring on certain selected trains that serve the major cities and vacation areas. It also includes a seat reservation and a voucher for an onboard snack.

CLASSES

The difference between first- and second-class seats is that first-class passengers pay approximately 1.5% more for a bit more legroom and the convenience of having meals delivered directly to their seats. Most people find second class entirely adequate.

CUTTING COSTS

To save money, **look into rail passes.** But be aware that if you don't plan to cover many miles, you may come out ahead by buying individual tickets. If you plan to travel by train within a day after your flight arrives, **purchase a heavily discounted "Rail and Fly" ticket for DB trains at the same time you book your flight.** Trains connect with 14 German airports and two airports outside Germany (Basel and Amsterdam).

Deutsche Bahn offers many discount options with specific conditions, so do your homework on its Web site before simply walking to a counter and paying for a full-price ticket. For round-trip travel you can save 25% if you book at least three days in advance, and 50% if you book at least seven days in advance. However, there's a limited number of seats sold at any of these discount prices, so **book as early as possible** to get the savings. If you change your travel plans after booking, you will have to pay a fee. The surcharge for tickets bought on board is 10% of the ticket cost, or a minimum of €5.

The good news for families is that children under 15 travel free when accompanied by a parent or relative (**make sure the children are accounted for on your ticket**). For any group traveling together, the "Mitfahrer-Rabatt" gives up to four travelers a 50% discount (each person does pay a minimum of €15 for a second-class ticket). The *Schönes Wochenend Ticket* (Happy Weekend Ticket) provides unlimited travel on local trains, Saturday and Sunday for up to five persons for €30 (€28 if purchased online or at vending machine). Groups of six or more should inquire about "Gruppen & Spar" savings.

Of all the German train classes, InterCity Express trains are the most expensive. A €3.60 surcharge (€7.20 round-trip) is added to the ticket price on all InterCity and EuroCity journeys regardless of distance. The charge is €4.60 if paid on board the train.

🚆 **Deutsche Bahn Information** Deutsche Bahn (German Rail) ✉ Stephanstr. 1, D–60313 Frankfurt am Main ☎ 11861 for 24-hr hotline, roughly €0.60 per minute, 49/1805/996–633 from outside Germany, €0.12 per minute ⊕ www.bahn.de. **German Rail Passenger Services** ☎ 08702/435–363 in U.K.

RAIL PASSES

If Germany is your only destination in Europe, **consider purchasing a German Rail Pass,** which allows 4–10 days of unlimited first- or second-class travel within a one-month period on any DB train, up to and including the ICE. A Twin Pass saves two people traveling together 50% off one person's fare. A Youth Pass, sold to those 12–25, is also much the same but for second-class travel only. You can also **use these passes aboard KD Rhine Line** (⇨ Cruise Travel) along certain sections of the Rhine and Mosel rivers. Prices begin at $180 for a single traveler in second class. Twin Passes begin at $270 in second class, and Youth Passes begin at $142. Additional days may be added to either pass.

Rail 'n Drive combines train travel and car rental. For instance, two people pay $159 each for two rail travel days and two car rental days within a month. You can add up to three more rail days, and each additional car rental day is $49.

Germany is one of 17 countries in which you can **use Eurailpasses,** which provide unlimited first-class rail travel in all participating countries for the duration of the pass. Two adults traveling together can pay either $498 each for 15 consecutive days of travel, or $592 each for 10 days of travel within two months. The Youth fare is $414 for 15 consecutive days and $488 for 10 days within two months.

Eurailpasses and some of the German Rail passes **must be purchased before you leave** for Europe. You can purchase a German Rail pass at a higher cost at an aid office at Frankfurt airport and at some aid offices in German train stations. When you buy your pass, consider purchasing Railpass insurance in case you lose it during your travels.

In order to comply with the strict rules about validating tickets before you begin travel, **read the instructions carefully.** Some tickets require that a train official validate your pass, while others require you to write in the first date of travel.

📶 **Information & Passes DER Travel Services** ✉ 9501 W. Devon Ave., Rosemont, IL 60018 ☎ 800/782-2424 📠 800/860-9944 to request a brochure, 888/337-8687 fax-on-demand service ⊕ www.der.com. **Europe On Rail** ✉ 725 Day Ave., Suite 1, Ridgefield, NJ 07657 ☎ 201/255-2898 📠 866/329-7245 ⊕ www.europeonrail.com. **German Rail Passenger Services** ☎ 08702/435-363 in U.K.

FARES & SCHEDULES

Fare and schedule information on the Deutsche Bahn 0190 information phone line costs roughly .06¢ per seven seconds, and you may have to wait a few moments before someone can help you in English. The automated number 0800/150-7090 is toll-free. On the DB Web site, click on "Int. Guests" and then "Travel Service" to enter your departure and arrival points.

FROM THE U.K.

There are several ways to reach Germany from London on British Rail. Travelers coming from the United Kingdom should **take the Channel Tunnel to save time, the ferry to save money.** Fastest and most expensive is the route via the Channel Tunnel on Eurostar trains. They leave at

two-hour intervals from Waterloo and require a change of trains in Brussels. Roundtrip tickets from London to Köln cost between €122 and €198. Cheapest and slowest are the 8–10 departures daily from Victoria using the Ramsgate–Ostend ferry, jetfoil, or SeaCat catamaran service.

📶 **Train & Pass Information Eurostar** ☎ 0870/518-6186.

RESERVATIONS

Many travelers assume that rail passes guarantee them seats on the trains they wish to ride. Not so. You need to **book seats ahead even if you are using a rail pass**; seat reservations are required on some European trains, particularly high-speed trains, and are a good idea during summer and on popular routes. If you board the train without a reserved seat, you take the chance of having to stand. You'll also need a reservation if you purchase sleeping accommodations. Reservations are free if you make them online at the Deutsche Bahn Web site or at the time of ticket purchase at a vending machine. Otherwise, seat reservations on InterRegion Express and InterCity trains cost €3, and a reservation is absolutely necessary for the ICE-Sprinter trains (€10 for second class). There are no reservations on regional trains.

TRANSPORTATION AROUND GERMANY

The Deutsche Bahn, Germany's privatized railway, is an efficient way to travel around the country, though long-distance round-trip travel is often cheaper on discount airlines than by train. Day-of-travel train-ticket prices are not cheap, but an advance purchase can reduce a ticket price by as much as half. The carefully structured network of services—from the super-high-speed InterCity Express to regional trains—ensures fast connections between cities and good access to rural areas; very few towns are more than 10 km (6 mi) or so from a railroad station. Rural bus lines connect villages to the nearest train station.

The Deutsche Bahn "Sprinter" business special gets its passengers between Frankfurt and Munich or Berlin faster than a plane, by the time city-to-airport travel and check-in requirements are taken into account. The Frankfurt–Munich "Sprinter" stops only in Mannheim; the Frankfurt–Berlin one doesn't stop at all.

The only long-distance bus service in Germany is BerlinLinien Bus. Other buses that cross the country are either tourist services covering routes such as the Romantic Road or long-distance companies that pick up in German cities but sell tickets only to other European cities.

The autobahn network makes for good car travel, and though the recommended speed limit (130 kph [78 mph]) lets you cover distances quickly, school vacation times can jam the autobahn with traffic. All major German cities have multistructure urban transportation systems, incorporating subway (U-bahn) and metropolitan suburban (S-bahn) trains, trams, and buses. Public transportation in cities is invariably fast, clean, and efficient.

TRAVEL AGENCIES

A good travel agent puts your needs first. Look for an agency that has been in business at least five years, emphasizes customer service, and has someone on staff who specializes in your destination. In addition, **make sure the agency belongs to a professional trade organization.** The American Society of Travel Agents (ASTA)—the largest and most influential in the field with more than 20,000 members in some 140 countries—maintains and enforces a strict code of ethics and will step in to help mediate any agent-client disputes involving ASTA members if necessary. ASTA (whose motto is "Without a travel agent, you're on your own") also maintains a Web site that includes a directory of agents. (If a travel agency is also acting as your tour operator, *see* Buyer Beware *in* Tours & Packages.)

🖪 Local Agent Referrals **American Society of Travel Agents** (ASTA) ✉ 1101 King St., Suite 200, Alexandria, VA 22314 ☎ 703/739–2782 or 800/965–2782 24-hr hotline 🖷 703/684–8319 ⊕ www. astanet.com. **Association of British Travel Agents** ✉ 68–71 Newman St., London W1T 3AH ☎ 020/7637–2444 🖷 020/7637–0713 ⊕ www.abta.com. **Association of Canadian Travel Agencies** ✉ 130 Al-

bert St., Suite 1705, Ottawa, Ontario K1P 5G4 ☎ 613/237–3657 🖷 613/237–7052 ⊕ www.acta.ca. **Australian Federation of Travel Agents** ✉ Level 3, 309 Pitt St., Sydney, NSW 2000 ☎ 02/9264–3299 or 1300/363–416 🖷 02/9264–1085 ⊕ www.afta.com. au. **Travel Agents' Association of New Zealand** ✉ Level 5, Tourism and Travel House, 79 Boulcott St., Box 1888, Wellington 6001 ☎ 04/499–0104 🖷 04/499–0786 ⊕ www.taanz.org.nz.

VISITOR INFORMATION

Learn more about foreign destinations by checking government-issued travel advisories and country information. For a broader picture, consider information from more than one country.

Local tourist offices are listed in the A to Z sections of the individual chapters. Staff at the smaller offices, especially in eastern Germany, might not speak English. Many offices keep shorter hours than normal businesses, and you can expect some to close during weekday lunch hours and as early as noon on Friday. The German National Tourist Office's Web site in the U.S. is www.cometogermany.com.

🖪 German National Tourist Office **U.S.** ✉ 122 E. 42nd St., 52nd fl., New York, NY 10168–0072 ☎ 212/661–7200 or 800/651–7010 🖷 212/661–7174 ✏ gntonyc@d–z–t.com ✉ 8484 Wilshire Blvd., Suite 440, Los Angeles, CA 90211 ☎ 323/655–6085 🖷 323/655–6086 ✏ gntolax@d–z–t.com ⊕ www. cometogermany.com. ++tk canada confirm++**Canada** ☎ 480 University Ave., Suite 1410, Toronto, Ontario M5G 1V2, Canada ☎ 416/968–1685 🖷 416/968–0562 ✏ info@gnto.ca ⊕ www. cometogermany.com. **U.K.** ☎ Box 2695, London W1A 3TN ☎ 020/7317–0908 🖷 020/7317–0917 ✏ infogntolon@d–z–t.com ⊕ www.germany-tourism.co.uk. ++tk australia confirm++**Australia** ☎ GPO Box 1461, Sydney, NSW 2001 ☎ 02/8296–0488 🖷 2/8296–0487 ✏ gnto@germany. org.au. **Germany** ✉ Beethovenstr. 69, D-60325 Frankfurt 🖷 069/751–903 ✏ info@d–z–t.com ⊕ www.germany-tourism.de.

🖪 Government Advisories **U.S. Department of State** ✉ Overseas Citizens Services Office, 2100 Pennsylvania Ave. NW, 4th fl., Washington, DC 20520 ☎ 202/647–5225 interactive hotline, 888/407–4747 ⊕ www.travel.state.gov. **Consular Affairs Bureau of Canada** ☎ 800/267–6788 or 613/944–6788 ⊕ www.voyage.gc.ca. **U.K. Foreign and Commonwealth Office** ✉ Travel Advice Unit, Consular Division, Old Admiralty Bldg., London SW1A 2PA ☎ 0870/606-0290 or 020/7008-1500 ⊕ www.fco.gov.uk/travel. **Australian Department of Foreign Affairs and Trade** ☎ 300/139-281 travel advice, 02/6261-1299 Consular Travel Advice Faxback Service ⊕ www.dfat.gov.au. **New Zealand Ministry of Foreign Affairs and Trade** ☎ 04/439-8000 ⊕ www.mft.govt.nz.

WEB SITES

Do check out the World Wide Web when planning your trip. You'll find everything from weather forecasts to virtual tours of famous cities. Be sure to visit Fodors.com (⊕ www.fodors.com), a complete travel-planning site. You can research prices and book plane tickets, hotel rooms, rental cars, vacation packages, and more. In addition, you can post your pressing questions in the Travel Talk section. Other planning tools include a currency converter and weather reports, and there are loads of links to travel resources.

One site that goes in-depth regarding international telephone systems and modem hookup trouble-shooting is ⊕ www.kropla.com.

Many German tourism-related Web sites have an English-language version, usually indicated by an icon of the American or British flag. For general information on Germany, visit ⊕ www.cometogermany.com or ⊕ www.germany-tourism.co.uk, which are the German National Tourist Office's sites. The first Web site is geared to Americans, the second to tourists from the United Kingdom. There are differences on these sites other than spelling; the U.K. site, for instance, lists more than twice as many scenic routes in Germany.

MUNICH

(1)

Updated by
Marton Radkai

IN THE RELAXED AND SUNNY SOUTH, Munich (München) is the proud capital of Bavaria. Even Germans come here to vacation, mixing the city's pleasures with those of the inviting landscapes surrounding it. The very likable city bills itself as *Die Weltstadt mit Herz* ("the cosmopolitan city with heart"), but in rare bouts of self-deprecatory humor, friendly Bavarians will remind you that Munich is hardly anything more than a world village. It's the overall feeling of *Gemütlichkeit*—loosely translated as conviviality—that makes the city so special, with an open-air market here, a park there, and beer halls everywhere.

The Innenstadt, or city center, is younger than some of the surrounding neighborhoods, such as Neuhausen or Haidhausen. Munich was created in the 12th century as a market town on the "salt road" connecting mighty Salzburg and Augsburg, and it has never lost its sense for business and marketing. It continues to exist between two poles, tradition and high-tech, or, as the locals say, "laptops and lederhosen." It's a city of ravishing baroque and smoky beer cellars, of grand 19th-century architecture and sleek steel-and-glass office buildings, of millionaires and farmers. Germany's favorite city is a place with extraordinary ambience, a vibrant lifestyle all its own, and a splendid setting within view—on a clear day—of the towering Alps. The city is the stomping grounds of all kinds of media, from traditional publishing houses to top-notch digital postproduction companies. The concentration of electronics and computer firms—Siemens, Microsoft, SAP, and the like—in and around the city has turned it into the Silicon Valley of Europe.

As you may know, Munich is the world capital of beer and beer culture. Between visits to the world-class museums, you should definitely try some of the local brew, either in one of the larger, noisier beer halls or in a smaller *Kneipe*, a bar where everyone meets for basic food and beer. As soon as the first spring rays of sun start warming the air, Müncheners flock outside to their beer gardens, where you can join them in the shade of huge chestnut trees. Munich's most famous festival, the beer-soaked Oktoberfest, started as an agricultural fair held on the occasion of a royal marriage and is now one of the biggest public festivals in the world, spawning imitators around the globe.

The *other* Munich is one of charm, refinement, and sophistication, populated by museumgoers who shop in high-fashion boutiques and dine in five-star restaurants. Various "long nights" throughout the year celebrate museum-going, books, and musical performances. The city's appreciation of the arts began under the kings and dukes of the Wittelsbach Dynasty, which ruled Bavaria for more than 750 years until 1918. The Wittelsbach legacy is alive and well in the city's fabulous art museums, the Opera House, the Philharmonic, and much more. A special event in 2005 is the *Bundesgartenschau*, the Federal Garden Show, which will be held on the trade fair grounds from mid-April to mid-October in Riem just east of the city where the former airport once stood. If you need horticultural inspiration or just balm for the eyes, this is the event to see.

Munich's cleanliness, safety, and comfortable pace give it an ever so slightly rustic feeling, despite the fact that it's a large, prosperous city. This, com-

If you have
3 days

Visit the tourist information office at the Hauptbahnhof (main train station) and then head for one of the cafés at the nearby pedestrian shopping zone to get your bearings (try the cafeteria at the Hertie department store on the square opposite the train station or at the Mövenpick in the beautiful Künstlerhaus on Lenbachplatz). You can see the highlights of the city center and royal Munich in one day. Plan an eastward course across (or rather under) Karlsplatz and into Neuhauserstrasse and Kaufingerstrasse, plunging into this busy center of commerce. You can escape the crowds inside one of the three churches that punctuate the route: the Bürgersaal, the Michaelskirche, or the Frauenkirche, a soaring Gothic cathedral. Try to arrive in the city's central square, Marienplatz, in time for the 11 AM performance of the glockenspiel in the tower of the neo-Gothic Neues Rathaus (New Town Hall). Proceed to the city market, the Viktualienmarkt, for lunch, and then head a few blocks north for an afternoon visit to the Residenz, the rambling palace of the Wittelsbach rulers. End your first day with coffee at Munich's oldest café, the Tambosi, or sip an early-evening cocktail at Käfer's, both on Odeonsplatz. Set aside Days 2 and 3 for Munich's leading museums in the Maxvorstadt district. Also take time for a stroll east to the Englischer Garten, Munich's city park, for an outdoor lunch or an evening meal at one of its beer gardens or in the Seehaus, on the northern shore of the Kleinhesseloher See (Lake).

If you have
5 days

For the first three days follow the itinerary described above. On the fourth day venture out to suburban Nymphenburg for a visit to Schloss Nymphenburg, the Wittelsbachs' summer residence. Allow a whole day to view the palace's buildings and its museums and to stroll through its lovely park, breaking for lunch at the restaurant in the botanical garden. On the fifth day, tour the Olympiapark in the morning. Ride to the top of the Olympic Tower for the best view of Munich and the surrounding countryside. Then either take a walk along the surprisingly quiet city banks of the Isar River or visit one of the two villa-museums, the Museum Villa Stuck or the Städtische Galerie im Lenbachhaus. The latter is huge and has a popular café.

bined with broad sidewalks, endless shops and eateries, views of the Alps, and a huge green heart, the English Garden, makes Munich one of Germany's most enjoyable cities.

EXPLORING MUNICH

Munich is a wealthy city—and it shows. Everything is extremely upscale and up-to-date. At times the aura of affluence may be all but overpowering. But that's what Munich is all about: a new city superimposed on the old; conspicuous consumption; a fresh coat of glitter along with the traditional rustic charms. Such are the dynamics and duality of this fascinating town.

The City Center

Munich's Old Town has been rebuilt so often over the centuries that it no longer has that homogeneous look of so many other German towns. Postwar developments often separate clusters of buildings that date back to Munich's origins—and not always to harmonious effect. The outer perimeter of this tour is defined more by your stamina than by ancient city walls.

Numbers in the text correspond to numbers in the margin and on the Munich map.

a good walk

Begin your walk through the city center at the **Hauptbahnhof** ❶ ▶, the main train station and site of the city tourist office, which is next to the station's main entrance. Pick up a detailed city map here. Cross Bahnhofplatz, the square in front of the station (or take the underpass), and walk toward Schützenstrasse, which marks the start of Munich's pedestrian shopping mall, the Fussgängerzone, 2 km (1 mi) of traffic-free streets. Running virtually the length of Schützenstrasse is Munich's largest department store, Hertie. At the end of the street, descend via the pedestrian underpass into a vast underground complex of boutiques, shops, and snack bars. Above you is the busy traffic intersection, **Karlsplatz** ❷, always referred to as Stachus after an inn and beer garden that stood here back in the 19th century. Its fountain area is a favorite place to hang out. Just make sure your wallet is in a safe place.

Ahead stands one of the city's oldest gates, the Karlstor, first mentioned in local records in 1302. Beyond it lies Munich's main shopping thoroughfare, Neuhauserstrasse, and its extension, Kaufingerstrasse. On your left as you enter Neuhauserstrasse is another attractive fountain: a late-19th-century figure of Bacchus. This part of town was almost completely destroyed by bombing during World War II. Great efforts were made to ensure that the designs of the new buildings harmonized with the old city, although some of the modern structures are little more than functional. Though this may not be an architectural showplace, there are some redeeming features to the area, such as Haus Oberpollinger, on Neuhauserstrasse—a department store hiding behind an imposing 19th-century facade. Notice the weather vanes of old merchant ships on its high-gabled roof.

Shopping is not the only attraction on these streets. Worldly department stores rub shoulders with a remarkable church, the **Michaelskirche** ❸. A Renaissance construction, the Michaelskirche was originally built in the 16th century and entirely redone after the war. The fountain in front of the church features Salome, in honor of the opera of the same name by Munich's famous son Richard Strauss. The massive building next to the Michaelskirche was once a 13th-century Augustine church. Today it houses the **Deutsches Jagd- und Fischereimuseum** (German Hunting and Fishing Museum) ❹. Opposite is one of Munich's famous brewery inns, the Augustiner Bierhalle. Behind its Renaissance and baroque facade—the establishment occupies two buildings—are vaulted ceilings and a delightful little courtyard decorated with frescoes.

Beer & Beer Gardens

Munich has more than 100 beer gardens, ranging from huge establishments that seat several hundred to small terraces tucked behind neighborhood pubs and taverns. Beer gardens are such an integral part of Munich life that a council proposal to cut down their hours provoked a storm of protest in 1995, culminating in one of the largest mass demonstrations in the city's history. They open whenever the thermometer creeps above 10°C (50°F) and the sun filters through the chestnut trees that are a necessary part of beer-garden scenery. Most—but not all—allow you to bring your own food, but if you do, don't defile this hallowed territory with something so foreign as pizza or a burger from McDonald's.

Music & Opera

Munich and music complement each other marvelously. The city has two world-renowned orchestras (one, the Philharmonic, is directed by the American conductor James Levine), the Bavarian State Opera Company (managed by an ingenious British director, Peter Jonas), wonderful choral ensembles, a rococo jewel of a court theater, and a modern Philharmonic concert hall of superb proportions and acoustics—and that's just for starters.

Shopping

Munich has three of Germany's most exclusive shopping streets. At the other end of the scale, it has flea markets to rival those of any other European city. In between are department stores, where acute German-style competition assures reasonable prices and often produces outstanding bargains. Artisans and artists bring their wares of beauty and originality to the Christmas markets. Collect their business cards—in summer you're sure to want to order another of those little gold baubles that were on sale in December.

Next on your tour is Munich's hallmark cathedral, the **Frauenkirche** ❺, whose twin onion domes can be seen from all over town. To reach it, turn left at the museum onto crescent-shape Augustinerstrasse, which opens onto Frauenplatz, a quiet square with a shallow, sunken fountain. From the cathedral, follow any of the alleys heading east, and you'll reach the Marienhof, a patch of green where the city's Jewish quarter once stood. To your right is **Marienplatz** ❻, which is surrounded by stores and dining spots. Marienplatz, the true heart of Munich, is dominated by the 19th-century **Neues Rathaus** ❼. The **Altes Rathaus** ❽, a rebuilt medieval building of assured charm, sits more modestly at the eastern entrance of the square. Its pretty tower houses a toy museum.

Hungry? Thirsty? Help is only a few steps away. From the Altes Rathaus, cross the street, passing the Heiliggeistkirche, an early Munich church with a rococo interior added between 1724 and 1730. Heiliggeiststrasse brings you to the jumble known as the **Viktualienmarkt** ❾, the city's open-air food market, where you can eat a stand-up lunch at any of the many stalls.

From the market, follow Rosental and turn left onto Sendlingerstrasse, one of the city's most interesting shopping streets. On the way you'll

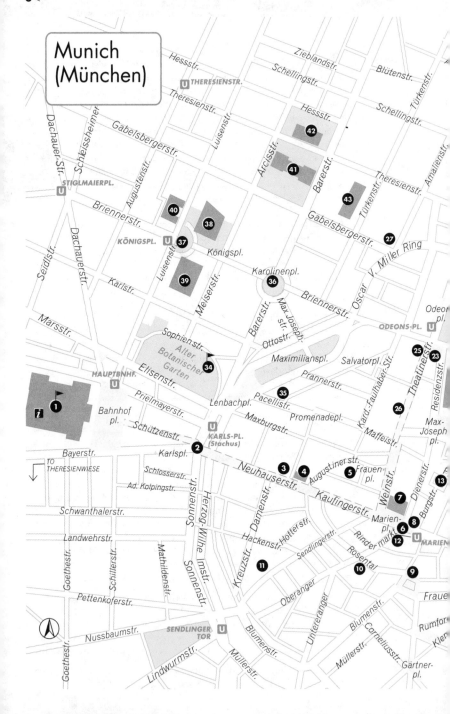

Munich (München)

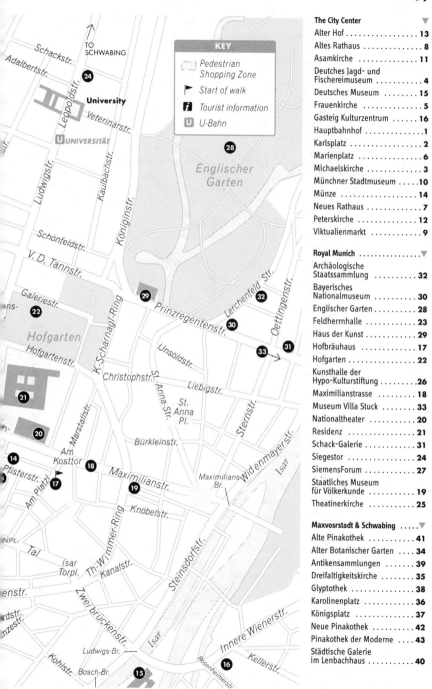

KEY

- Pedestrian Shopping Zone
- Start of walk
- 🛈 Tourist information
- Ⓤ U-Bahn

pass the rear of the **Münchner Stadtmuseum** (City Museum) ⑩ at the corner of Oberangerstrasse. As you head down Sendlingerstrasse, on your right is the remarkable **Asamkirche** ⑪. The exterior fits so snugly into the street's housefronts that you might easily overlook the church were it not for the somewhat incongruous rocks it was built upon. At the end of the street is Sendlinger Tor, a medieval brick gate.

Backtrack up Sendlingerstrasse and turn right onto Rindermarkt (the former cattle market) to the single, square tower of the **Peterskirche** ⑫, the city's oldest and best-loved parish church. From the Peterskirche, reenter Marienplatz and pass in front of the Altes Rathaus once again to step into Burgstrasse. You'll soon find yourself in the quiet, airy **Alter Hof** ⑬, the inner courtyard of the original palace of Bavaria's Wittelsbach rulers. A short distance beyond its northern archway, on the north side of Pfisterstrasse, stands the former royal mint, the **Münze** ⑭.

Return down Burgstrasse and make a left on Tal, once an important trading route that entered Munich at the Isartor, a massive brick gate with a tower attached, now restored to its original medieval appearance. A frieze on the Isator depicts the 1322 battle of Ampfing, during which Munich was saved from an Austrian attack. Cross Isartorplatz into Zweibrückenstrasse, and you'll come to the Isar River. There, on an island, is the massive bulk of the **Deutsches Museum** ⑮, with a gigantic thermometer and barometer on its tower showing the way to the main entrance. Budding scientists and young dreamers will be delighted by its many interactive displays with buttons to push and cranks to turn.

On a sunny day join the locals for ice cream and a stroll along the Isar River, where the more daring sunbathe nude on pebble islands. On a rainy day you can splash around in the Müllersches Volksbad, a restored art nouveau indoor swimming pool at Ludwigsbrücke, opposite the Deutsches Museum. The massive glass-and-brick facade on the hill above the Volksbad belongs to the **Gasteig Kulturzentrum** ⑯, home of the Munich Philharmonic Orchestra, the main city library, and multiple theaters, galleries, and cafés.

TIMING   Set aside at least a whole day for this walk, hitting Marienplatz when the Glockenspiel plays at 11 AM or noon. Prepare for a big spectator crowd, and try to avoid shopping in the pedestrian zone between noon and 2, when workers on lunch break make for the department stores.

What to See

⑬ **Alter Hof** (Old Palace). This palace was the original medieval residence of the Wittelsbachs, the ruling dynasty established in 1180. The palace now serves as local government offices. Don't pass through without turning to admire the oriel (bay window) that hides on the south wall, just around the corner as you enter the courtyard. The west wing has become home to the **Vinorant Alter Hof,** a fine restaurant and wine cellar. ✉ *Burgstr., City Center* Ⓤ *Marienplatz (U-bahn and S-bahn).*

🖑 ⑧ **Altes Rathaus** (Old Town Hall). Munich's first town hall was built in 1474. Its great hall—destroyed in 1944 but now fully restored—was the work of architect Jörg von Halspach. It's used for official receptions and is not normally open to the public. The tower provides a fairy-tale-like setting for the **Spielzeugmuseum** (Toy Museum), accessible via a winding staircase. Its toys and dolls are joined by quite a few Barbies visiting from the United States. ⊠ *Marienpl., City Center* ☎ *089/294–001* 🖃 *Museum €3* ☉ *Daily 10–5:30* Ⓤ *Marienplatz (U-bahn and S-bahn).*

★ ⓫ **Asamkirche** (Asam Church). Munich's most unusual church has a suitably extraordinary entrance, framed by raw rock foundations. The insignificant door, crammed between its craggy shoulders, gives little idea of the opulence and lavish detailing within the small 18th-century church (there are only 12 rows of pews). Above the doorway St. Nepomuk, a 14th-century Bohemian monk who drowned in the Danube, is being led by angels from a rocky riverbank to heaven. The church's official name is Church of St. Johann Nepomuk, but it's known as the Asamkirche for its architects, the brothers Cosmas Damian and Egid Quirin Asam, who lived next door. The interior of the church is a prime example of true southern German late-baroque architecture. Frescoes by Cosmas Damian Asam and rosy marble cover the walls. The sheer wealth of statues and gilding is stunning—there's even a gilt skeleton at the sanctuary's portal. ⊠ *Sendlingerstr., City Center* ☉ *Daily 9–5:30* Ⓤ *Sendlingertor (U-bahn).*

❹ **Deutsches Jagd- und Fischereimuseum** (German Museum of Hunting and Fishing). This museum contains the world's largest collection of fishhooks, some 500 stuffed animals (including a 6½-foot-tall North American grizzly bear), a 12,000-year-old skeleton of a deer found in Ireland, and a valuable collection of hunting weapons. You'll even find the elusive *Wolpertinger,* a legendary Bavarian animal. The museum also sells fine hunting equipment, from knives and rifles to sturdy clothing. ⊠ *Neuhauserstr. 2, City Center* ☎ *089/220–522* 🖃 *€3.50* ☉ *Fri.–Sun., Tues. and Wed. 9:30–5, Thurs. 9:30–8* Ⓤ *Karlsplatz (U-bahn and S-bahn).*

⓯ **Deutsches Museum** (German Museum). Within a monumental building on an island in the Isar River, this museum of science and technology— filled with aircraft, vehicles, locomotives, and machinery—is an engineering student's dream. The immense collection is spread out over 12 km (12 mi) of corridors, six floors of exhibits, and 30 departments. Children now have their own area, the **Kinderreich,** where they can learn about modern technology and science through numerous interactive displays (parents must accompany their child). The most technically advanced planetarium in Europe has up to six shows daily and includes a Laser Magic display. An IMAX theater—with a wraparound screen six stories high—shows nature and adventure films. The Internet café on the third floor is open daily 9–3. To arrange for a two-hour tour in English, call ☎ *089/217–9252* two weeks in advance. The Center for Transportation on the fairgrounds at the Theresienhöhe (where Oktoberfest is held) houses the museum's transportation exhibits. ⊠ *Museumsinsel 1, City Center* ☎ *089/21790, 089/2112–5180 to reserve tickets at planetarium and IMAX* ⊕ *www.deutsches-museum.de* 🖃 *Museum €5, Planetarium €6.25, IMAX €5.95; combined ticket for planetarium and IMAX €10.25, higher admission for some performances* ☉ *Daily 9 AM–11 PM* Ⓤ *Isartor (S-bahn).*

Fodor'sChoice ★

☺

> **off the beaten path**

FRANZISKANERKLOSTERKIRCHE ST. ANNA (Franciscan Monastery Church of St. Anne) – This striking example of the two Asam brothers' work is in the Lehel district. Though less opulent than the Asamkirche, this small Franciscan monastery church, consecrated in 1737, impresses visitors with its sense of movement and its heroic scale. It was largely rebuilt after wartime bomb damage. The ceiling fresco by Cosmas Damian Asam glows in all its original vivid joyfulness. The ornate altar was also designed by the Asam brothers. Towering over the delicate little church, on the opposite side of the street, is the neo-Romanesque bulk of the 19th-century church of St. Anne. ⊠ *St.-Anna-Str., Lehel* ☎ *089/212–1820* Ⓤ *Lehel (U-bahn).*

★ ❺ **Frauenkirche** (Church of Our Lady). Munich's *Dom* (cathedral) is a distinctive late-Gothic brick structure with two towers that are the city's chief landmark. Each is more than 300 feet high, and both are capped by onion-shape domes. The towers are an indelible feature of the skyline and a Munich trademark—some say because they look like overflowing beer mugs.

The main body of the cathedral was completed in 20 years (1474–94)—a record time in those days. The towers were added, almost as an afterthought, in 1524–25. Jörg von Halspach, the Frauenkirche's original architect, is buried here. The building suffered severe damage during Allied bombing and was restored between 1947 and 1957. Inside, the church combines most of von Halspach's original features with a stark, clean modernity and simplicity of line, emphasized by slender, white octagonal pillars that sweep up through the nave to the tracery ceiling. As you enter the church, look on the stone floor for the dark imprint of a large foot—the *Teufelstritt* (Devil's Footprint). According to lore, the devil challenged von Halspach to build a nave without windows. The architect accepted the challenge. When he completed the job, he led the devil to the one spot in the well-lit church from which the 66-foot-high windows could not be seen. The devil stomped his foot in rage and left the Teufelstritt. The cathedral houses an elaborate 15th-century black-marble tomb guarded by four 16th-century armored knights. It's the final resting place of Duke Ludwig IV (1302–47), who became Holy Roman Emperor Ludwig the Bavarian in 1328. The Frauenkirche's great treasure, however, is the collection of 24 carved wooden busts of the apostles, saints, and prophets above the choir, made by the 15th-century Munich sculptor Erasmus Grasser.

The observation platform high up in one of the towers offers a splendid view of the city. But beware—you must climb 86 steps to reach the tower elevator. ⊠ *Frauenpl., City Center* ☎ *089/290–0820* 🎫 *Cathedral free, Tower €2* ⊙ *Tower elevator Apr.–Oct., Mon.–Sat. 10–5* Ⓤ *Marienplatz (U-bahn and S-bahn).*

⓰ **Gasteig Kulturzentrum** (Gasteig Culture Center). Sitting high above the Isar River, this striking postmodern, brick cultural complex for music, theater, and film has an open-plan interior and a maze of courtyards and plazas. The center has two theaters, where plays in English are occasionally staged. ⊠ *Rosenheimerstr. 5, Haidhausen* ☎ *089/480–980* Ⓤ *Rosenheimerplatz (S-bahn).*

▶ ❶ **Hauptbahnhof** (Main Train Station). Traveling is not all you come here for. A host of rather fancy sandwich bars attracts people for a quick meal or snack at all times of the day and well into the night. On the underground level you'll find all sorts of shops that remain open even on Sunday and holidays. The city tourist office here has maps and helpful information on events around town. ⊠ *Bahnhofpl., Leopoldvorstadt* ☎ *089/2333–0256 or 089/2333–0257* Ⓤ *Hauptbahnhof (U-bahn and S-bahn).*

❷ **Karlsplatz.** In 1755 Eustachius Föderl opened an inn and beer garden here, which became known as the Stachus. The beer garden is long gone, but the name has remained—locals still refer to this busy intersection as the Stachus. One of Munich's most popular fountains is here, a circle of water jets that acts as a magnet on hot summer days when city shoppers and office workers seek a cool place to relax. In winter it makes way for an ice-skating rink. A semicircle of yellow buildings with tall windows and delicate, cast-iron balconies backs the fountain. Ⓤ *Karlsplatz (U-bahn and S-bahn).*

★ ❻ **Marienplatz.** Bordered by the Neues Rathaus, shops, and cafés, this square is named after the gilded statue of the Virgin Mary that has watched over it for more than three centuries. It was erected in 1638 at the behest of Elector Maximilian I as an act of thanksgiving for the city's survival of the Thirty Years' War, the cataclysmic religious struggle that devastated vast regions of Germany. When the statue was taken down from its marble column for cleaning in 1960, workmen found a small casket in the base containing a splinter of wood said to be from the cross of Christ. ⊠ *Bounded by Kaufingerstr., Rosenstr., Weinstr., and Dienerstr., City Center* Ⓤ *Marienplatz (U-bahn and S-bahn).*

❸ **Michaelskirche** (St. Michael's Church). A curious story explains why this sturdy Renaissance church has no tower. Seven years after the start of construction the principal tower collapsed. Its patron, pious Duke Wilhelm V, regarded the disaster as a heavenly sign that the church wasn't big enough, so he ordered a change in the plans—this time without a tower. Completed seven years later, the Michaelskirche was the first Renaissance church of this size in southern Germany. The duke is buried in the crypt, along with 40 other Wittelsbachs, including the eccentric King Ludwig II. A severe neoclassical monument in the north transept contains the tomb of Napoléon's stepson, Eugene de Beauharnais, who married one of the daughters of King Maximilian I and died in Munich in 1824. The church is the venue for free performances of church music. A poster to the right of the front portal gives the dates. ⊠ *Neuhauserstr. 52, City Center* ☎ *089/231–7060* 🎫 *€1* ⏱ *Daily 8–7, except during services* Ⓤ *Karlsplatz (U-bahn and S-bahn).*

❿ **Münchner Stadtmuseum** (City Museum). Wedged in by Oberanger, Rosental, and St.-Jakobsplatz, this museum is as eclectic within as the architecture is without. Though the entire complex was rebuilt in several stages after World War II, the original building dates to 1491 (the front on St.-

Jakobsplatz). Inside are instrument collections, international cultural exhibits, a film museum showing rarely screened movies, notably German silents, a photo and fashion museum, a puppet theater, and one of the liveliest cafés in town. ✉ *St.-Jakobspl. 1, City Center* ☎ *089/2332–2370* ⊕ *www.stadtmuseum-online.de* 🎟 *€2.50, free Sun.; special exhibitions €4* ⊙ *Tues.–Sun. 10–6* Ⓤ *Marienplatz (U-bahn and S-bahn).*

⓮ **Münze** (Mint). Originally the royal stables, the Münze was created by court architect Wilhelm Egkl between 1563 and 1567 and now serves as an office building. A stern neoclassical facade emblazoned with gold was added in 1809; the interior courtyard has Renaissance-style arches. ✉ *Pfisterstr. 4, City Center* 🎟 *Free* ⊙ *Mon.–Thurs. 8–4, Fri. 8–2* Ⓤ *Marienplatz (U-bahn and S-bahn).*

❼ **Neues Rathaus** (New Town Hall). Munich's present town hall was built between 1867 and 1908 in the fussy, turreted, neo-Gothic style so beloved by King Ludwig II. Architectural historians are divided over its merits, though its dramatic scale and lavish detailing are impressive. Perhaps the most serious criticism is that the Dutch and Flemish styles of the building seems out of place amid the baroque and rococo styles of so much of the rest of the city. The tower's 1904 glockenspiel (a chiming clock with mechanical figures) plays daily at 11 AM, noon, and 9 PM, with an additional performance at 5 PM June–October. As chimes peal out over the square, the clock's doors flip open and brightly colored dancers and jousting knights go through their paces. They act out two events from Munich's past: a tournament held in Marienplatz in 1568 and the *Schäfflertanz* (Dance of the Coopers), which commemorated the end of the plague of 1517. When Munich was in ruins after World War II, an American soldier contributed some paint to restore the battered figures, and he was rewarded with a ride on one of the jousters' horses, high above the cheering crowds. You, too, can travel up there, by elevator, to an observation point near the top of one of the towers. On a clear day the view is spectacular. ✉ *Marienpl., City Center* 🎟 *Tower €1.50* ⊙ *Mon.–Thurs. 9–4, Fri. 9–1* Ⓤ *Marienplatz (U-bahn and S-bahn).*

⓬ **Peterskirche** (St. Peter's Church). Munich's oldest and smallest parish church traces its origins to the 11th century and has been restored in various architectural styles. The rich baroque interior has a magnificent late-Gothic high altar and aisle pillars decorated with exquisite 18th-century figures of the apostles. In clear weather it's well worth the climb up the 300-foot tower—the view includes glimpses of the Alps. The Peterskirche has a Scottish priest who is glad to show English-speaking visitors around. ✉ *Rindermarkt, City Center* ☎ *089/ 260–4828* 🎟 *Tower €1.50* ⊙ *Mon.–Sat. 9–6, Sun. 10–6* Ⓤ *Marienplatz (U-bahn and S-bahn).*

off the beaten path

THERESIENWIESE – The site of Munich's annual beer festival—the notorious Oktoberfest—and of the very hip Christmas market (the Tollwood) is only a 10-minute walk from the Hauptbahnhof or a single stop away by subway (U-4 or U-5). The enormous exhibition ground is named after Princess Therese von Sachsen-Hildburghausen, who celebrated her marriage to the Bavarian crown prince Ludwig— later Ludwig I—here in 1810. The accompanying agricultural fair was such a success that it became an annual event. Beer was served then as now, but what began as a night out for the locals has become a 16-day international bonanza at the end of September and the beginning of October, attracting more than 6 million people each year (it qualifies as an *Oktober* fest by ending the first Sunday in October). Ⓤ *Theresienhöhe (U-bahn)*.

Overlooking the Theresienwiese is a 19th-century hall of fame featuring busts of numerous popular figures of the time—one of the last works of Ludwig I—and a monumental bronze statue of the maiden **Bavaria**, more than 100 feet high. The statue is hollow, and 130 steps take you up into the braided head for a view of Munich through Bavaria's eyes. 🎫 *€2.50* ⊗ *Dec.–Oct., Tues.–Sun. 10–noon and 2–4.*

★ ❾ **Viktualienmarkt** (Victuals Market). The city's open-air food market has a wide range of produce, German and international foodstuffs, and tables and counters for eating and drinking, which make the area a feast for the eyes as well as the stomach. All kinds of people come here for a quick snack at any number of stands, from well-heeled businesspeople and casual tourists to mortar- and paint-spangled workers. It's also the realm of the garrulous, sturdy market women who run the stalls with dictatorial authority. Whether here, or at a bakery, *do not* try to select your pickings by hand; ask for help. Ⓤ *Marienplatz (U-bahn and S-bahn)*.

> **off the beaten path**
>
> **ZAM.** Nestled in a passageway just off the Isartor, the ZAM (which stands for the German equivalent of Center for Unusual Museums) consists of the private collections belonging to the late Manfred Klauda, a Munich lawyer. There's no specific guiding theme, except perhaps the obsession of a single individual. Exhibitions include collections of chamber pots, *bourdalous* (a convenience for women in 17th- and 18th-century clothing), corkscrews, locks, Easter bunnies, pedal cars, perfume bottles, and ephemera relating to Empress Elisabeth of Austria (known as Sissi, the cousin of Ludwig II). ✉ *Westenriederstr. 41, City Center* ☎ *089/290–4121* ⊕ *www.zam-museum.de* 🎫 *€4* ⊗ *Daily 10–6* Ⓤ *Isartor (S-bahn)*.

Royal Munich

From the relatively modest palace of the Alter Hof, the Wittelsbachs expanded their quarters northward, away from the jumble of narrow streets in the old quarter. Three splendid avenues radiated outward from their new palace and garden grounds, and fine homes arose along them. One of them—Prinzregentenstrasse—marks the southern end of Munich's huge public park, the Englischer Garten, also the creation of a Wittelsbach ruler. Lehel is an upmarket residential neighborhood that also serves as Munich's museum quarter.

BAVARIA: A COUNTRY WITHIN A COUNTRY

F OR MOST VISITORS, Bavaria, with its traditional Gemütlichkeit, beer gardens, quaint little villages, and culturally rich cities, is often seen as the quintessence of Germany. In fact, nothing could be farther from the truth. Of the 16 German Länder, as the German federal states are called, none is more fiercely independent than Bavaria. In fact, it was an autonomous dukedom and later kingdom until 1871, when it was incorporated into the German empire.

For Bavarians, anything beyond the state's borders remains foreign territory. The state has its own anthem and its own flag, part of which, the blue-and-white lozenges in the center, has virtually become a regional trademark symbolizing quality and tradition. Bavarian politicians discussing the issue of Europe in speeches will often refer to Bavaria almost as if it were a national state. And they will inevitably call it by its full official name: Freistaat Bayern, or simply der Freistaat, meaning "the Free State." The term was coined by Kurt Eisner, Minister President of the socialist government who ridded the land of the Wittelsbach dynasty in 1918. It is simply a German way of saying republic—a land governed by the people. And it has an honorable place in the first line of the separate Bavarian constitution that was signed under the aegis of the American occupational forces in 1946.

Bavaria is not the only Freistaat in Germany, a fact not too many Germans are aware of. Thuringia and Saxony also sport that title. But the Bavarians are the only ones who make such a public point of it. As they say, clocks in Bavaria run differently. Now you know why . . .

a good walk

A good way to start this very long walk is with a Bavarian breakfast of Weisswurst, pretzels, and beer at the **Hofbräuhaus** ⑰ ☛, perhaps Munich's best-known beer hall, on Am Platzl. Turn right from the Hofbräuhaus for the short walk along Orlandostrasse to **Maximilianstrasse** ⑱, Munich's most elegant shopping street. Opposite you is a handsome city landmark: the Hotel Vier Jahreszeiten, a historic host to traveling princes, millionaires, and the expense-account jet set. Maximilianstrasse was named after King Maximilian II, whose statue you'll see far down on the right. This wide boulevard has many grand buildings, which contain government offices and the city's ethnological museum, the **Staatliches Museum für Völkerkunde** ⑲. The Maximilianeum, on a rise beyond the Isar River, is an impressive mid-19th-century palace where the Bavarian state parliament now meets.

Turn left on Maximilianstrasse and you'll arrive at Max-Joseph-Platz, a square dominated by the pillared portico of the 19th-century **Nationaltheater** ⑳, home of the Bavarian State Opera Company. The statue in the square's center is of Bavaria's first king, Max Joseph. Along the north side is the lofty and austere south wall of the **Residenz** ㉑, the royal palace of Wittelsbach rulers for more than six centuries.

Directly north of the Residenz, on Hofgartenstrasse, lies the former royal garden, the **Hofgarten** ㉒, which was started in the 16th century and eventually achieved its Italian Renaissance look. The plaza in front of the Hofgarten is Odeonsplatz. The monument on the southern end is the 19th-century **Feldherrnhalle** ㉓, modeled after the familiar Loggia dei Lanzi in Florence. Looking north up Ludwigstrasse, the arrow-straight avenue that begins at the Feldherrnhalle, you'll see the **Siegestor** ㉔, or victory arch, which marks the beginning of Leopoldstrasse. Completing this impressively Italianate panorama is the great yellow bulk of the former royal church of St. Kajetan, the **Theatinerkirche** ㉕, an imposing baroque structure across from the Feldherrnhalle. A few steps down Theatinerstrasse is the **Kunsthalle der Hypo-Kulturstiftung** ㉖. A left on Briennerstrasse and a right on Oskar-von-Miller-Ring will take you to the **Siemens-Forum** ㉗, which explores the long history of one of Germany's number one companies.

Now head north up Ludwigstrasse. Court architect Leo von Klenze designed this first stretch of the generous avenue to give the road to the village of Schwabing a look befitting what had become a kingdom after the Napoleonic wars. In much the same way that Baron Haussmann would later demolish many of the old streets and buildings in Paris, replacing them with stately boulevards, von Klenze swept aside the small dwellings and alleys that stood here and replaced them with severe neoclassical structures such as the Bayerische Staatsbibliothek (Bavarian State Library), the Universität (University), and the peculiarly Byzantine Ludwigskirche. Müncheners either love or hate the architect's formal buildings, which end just before Ludwigstrasse becomes Leopoldstrasse. Another leading architect, Friedrich von Gärtner, took over construction here with more delicate structures that are a pleasant backdrop to the busy street life in summer. Once the hub of the legendary artists' district of Schwabing, Leopoldstrasse still throbs with life from spring to fall, exuding the atmosphere of a Mediterranean boulevard, with cafés, wine terraces, and artists' stalls. In comparison, Ludwigstrasse is inhabited by ghosts of the past.

At the south end of Leopoldstrasse lies the great open quadrangle of the university. A circular area divides into two piazzas named after anti-Nazi resistance leaders: Geschwister-Scholl-Platz and Professor-Huber-Platz. From the university, Leopoldstrasse then continues into Schwabing itself, once Munich's bohemian quarter but now distinctly upscale and chic to the point of being monotonous. Explore the streets of old Schwabing around Wedekindplatz to get the feel of the place. Or enjoy the shops and cafés in the student quarter parallel to Leopoldstrasse. (Those in search of the bohemian mood that once animated Schwabing should head to Haidhausen, on the other side of the Isar River, though it is about to end there, too, owing to gentrification and high rents.)

Bordering the east side of Schwabing is the **Englischer Garten** ㉘. Five kilometers (3 mi) long and 1½ km (about 1 mi) wide, it's Germany's largest city park, stretching from Prinzregentenstrasse, the broad avenue laid out by Prince Regent Luitpold at the end of the 19th century, to the city's northern boundary, where the lush parkland is taken over by the rough embrace of open countryside. Dominating the park's southern border is one of the few examples of Hitler-era architecture still standing in Munich: the colonnaded **Haus der Kunst** ㉙, a leading art gallery and home to Munich's most fashionable nightclub, the P 1.

A few hundred yards farther along Prinzregentenstrasse are two other leading museums, the **Bayerisches Nationalmuseum** ㉚ and the **Schack-Galerie** ㉛, and around the first left-hand corner, on Lerchenfeldstrasse, is a museum of prehistory, the **Archäologische Staatssammlung** ㉜, in a modern concrete building appropriately covered with rusting steel Cor-Ten plates.

On a hill at the eastern end of Prinzregentenstrasse, just across the Isar River from the Schack-Galerie, is Munich's well-loved Friedensengel (Angel of Peace), a gilt angel crowning a marble column. Beyond the Friedensengel is another historic home that became a major Munich art gallery—the **Museum Villa Stuck** ㉝, an art nouveau fantasy wrapped in a sober, neoclassical shell.

TIMING   You'll need a day (and good walking shoes) for this stroll. Set aside at least two hours for a tour of the Residenz. If the weather is good, return to the southern end of the Englischer Garten at dusk—you'll be treated to an unforgettable silhouette of the Munich skyline, black against the retreating light.

What to See

㉜ **Archäologische Staatssammlung** (State Archaeological Collection). This is Bavaria's principal record of its prehistoric, Roman, and Celtic past. The perfectly preserved body of a ritually sacrificed young girl, recovered from a Bavarian peat moor, is among the more spine-chilling exhibits. Head down to the basement to see the fine Roman mosaic floor. ⊠ *Lerchenfeldstr. 2, Lehel* ☎ *089/211–2402* ✑ *€4.50, free Sun.* ◷ *Tues.–Sun. 9–4:30* Ⓤ *Lehel (U-bahn).*

㉚ **Bayerisches Nationalmuseum** (Bavarian National Museum). Although the museum places emphasis on Bavarian cultural history, it has art and artifacts of international importance and regular exhibitions that attract worldwide attention. The highlight for some will be the medieval and Renaissance wood carvings, with many works by the great Renaissance sculptor Tilman Riemenschneider. Tapestries, arms and armor, a unique collection of Christmas crèches (the *Krippenschau*), and Bavarian and German folk art compete for your attention. ⊠ *Prinzregentenstr. 3, Lehel* ☎ *089/211–2401* ⊕ *www.bayerisches-nationalmuseum.de* ✑ *€3, special exhibitions €5* ◷ *Tues.–Sun. 9:30–5* Ⓤ *Lehel (U-bahn).*

★ ㉘ **Englischer Garten** (English Garden). This virtually endless park, which melds into the open countryside at Munich's northern city limits, was designed for the Bavarian prince Karl Theodor by Benjamin Thompson, later Count Rumford, from Massachusetts, who fled America after having taken the wrong side during the War of Independence. The open, informal nature of the park—reminiscent of the rolling parklands with which English aristocrats of the 18th century liked to surround their country homes—gave the park its name. It has a boating lake, four beer gardens, and a series of curious decorative and monumental constructions, including the Monopteros, a Greek temple designed by Leo von Klenze for King Ludwig I and built on an artificial hill in the southern section of the park. In the center of the park's most popular beer garden is a Chinese pagoda erected in 1789. It was destroyed during the war and then reconstructed. The Chinese Tower beer garden is world famous, but the park has prettier places for sipping a beer: the Aumeister, for example, along the northern perimeter. The Aumeister's restaurant is in an early-19th-century hunting lodge. At the Seehaus, on the shore of the Kleinhesseloher *See* (lake), choose between a smart restaurant or a cozy *Bierstube* (beer tavern).

The Englischer Garten is a paradise for joggers, cyclists, musicians, soccer players, sunbathers, dog owners, and, in winter, cross-country skiers. The Munich Cricket Club grounds are in the southern section—and spectators are welcome. The park has designated areas for nude sunbathing—the Germans have a positively pagan attitude toward the sun—so don't be surprised to see naked bodies bordering the flower beds and paths. ⊠ *Main entrances at Prinzregentenstr. and Koniginstr., Schwabing and Lehel.*

need a break? For lunch, wander across the Ludwigstrasse to the heart of the student quarter. Light vegetarian food with a definite Asian touch is served to those on the fly at **S. M. Vegetarisch** (⊠ Amalienstr. 45 ☎ 089/281–882). The prices are perfect for those on a budget.

㉓ Feldherrnhalle (Generals' Hall). This open-sided, pavilionlike building was modeled after the 14th-century Loggia dei Lanzi in Florence and honors three centuries' worth of Bavarian generals. Two huge Bavarian lions are flanked by the larger-than-life statues of Count Johann Tserclaes Tilly, who led Catholic forces in the Thirty Years' War, and Prince Karl Philipp Wrede, hero of the 19th-century Napoleonic Wars. The imposing structure was turned into a militaristic shrine in the 1930s and '40s by the Nazis, who found it significant because it marked the site of Hitler's abortive coup, or putsch, which took place in 1923. All who passed it had to give the Nazi salute. Viscardigasse, a tiny alley behind the Feldherrnhalle linking Residenzstrasse and Theatinerstrasse and now lined with exclusive boutiques, was used by those who wanted to dodge the tedious routine, hence its nickname Heil Hitler Street. ⊠ *South end of Odeonspl., City Center* Ⓤ *Odeonsplatz (U-bahn).*

㉙ Haus der Kunst (House of Art). This colonnaded, classical-style building is one of Munich's few remaining examples of Hitler-era architecture and was officially opened by the führer himself. In the Hitler years it showed only work deemed to reflect the Nazi aesthetic. One of its most successful postwar exhibitions was devoted to works banned by the Nazis. It hosts exhibitions of art, photography, and sculpture, as well as theatrical and musical happenings. The survival-of-the-chicest disco, P 1, is in the building's west wing. ⊠ *Prinzregentenstr. 1, Lehel* ☎ *089/211–270* ⊕ *www.hausderkunst.de* 🎫 *Varies* ⊙ *Daily 10–10* Ⓤ *Odeonsplatz (U-bahn).*

▶ ⓲ **Hofbräuhaus.** Duke Wilhelm V founded Munich's most famous brewery in 1589. Hofbräu means "court brewery," and the golden beer is poured in king-size liter mugs. If the cavernous downstairs hall is too noisy for you, try the quiet restaurant upstairs. Americans, Australians, and Italians far outnumber Germans, and the brass band that performs here most days adds modern pop and American folk music to the traditional German numbers. ✉ *Am Platzl 9, City Center* ☎ *089/290–136* Ⓤ *Marienplatz (U-bahn and S-bahn).*

㉒ **Hofgarten** (Royal Garden). The formal garden was once part of the royal palace grounds. It's bordered on two sides by arcades designed in the 19th century by the royal architect Leo von Klenze. On the east side of the garden stands the new state chancellery, built around the ruins of the 19th-century Army Museum and incorporating the remains of a Renaissance arcade. Its most prominent feature is a large copper dome. Bombed during World War II air raids, the museum stood untouched for almost 40 years as a grim reminder of the war. It's now known as Palazzo Prozzi, an untranslatable joke referring to the huge sums that went into rebuilding it and its ostentatious look.

In front of the chancellery stands one of Europe's most unusual—some say most effective—war memorials. Instead of looking up at a monument, you are led down to a **sunken crypt** covered by a massive granite block. In the crypt lies a German soldier from World War I. The crypt is a stark contrast to the **memorial** that stands unobtrusively in front of the northern wing of the chancellery: a simple cube of black marble bearing facsimiles of handwritten wartime manifestos by anti-Nazi leaders, including members of the White Rose movement. ✉ *Hofgartenstr., north of Residenz, City Center* Ⓤ *Odeonsplatz (U-bahn).*

㉖ **Kunsthalle der Hypo-Kulturstiftung** (Hall of the Hypobank's Cultural Foundation). Chagall, Giacometti, Picasso, and Gauguin were among the artists featured in the past at this exhibition hall in the midst of the commercial pedestrian zone. Other exhibits have included art ranging from antiquity to the most modern studios. The foundation's success over the years has led to its expansion, designed by the Swiss architect team Herzog and de Meuron, who also designed London's Tate Modern. ✉ *Theatinerstr. 8, City Center* ☎ *089/224–421* ⊕ *www.hypo-kunsthalle.de* 🎫 *Varies* 🕙 *Daily 10–8* Ⓤ *Odeonsplatz (U-bahn).*

Ludwigskirche (Ludwig's Church). Planted halfway along the severe, neoclassical Ludwigstrasse is this curious neo-Byzantine–early-Renaissance–style church, built at the behest of Ludwig I to provide his newly completed suburb with a parish church. It's worth a stop to see the fresco of the *Last Judgment* in the choir. At 60 feet by 37 feet, it's one of the world's largest. ✉ *Ludwigstr. 22, Maxvorstadt* ☎ *089/288–334* 🕙 *Daily 7–7* Ⓤ *Universität (U-bahn).*

⓳ **Maximilianstrasse.** Munich's sophisticated shopping street was named after King Maximilian II, who wanted to break away from the Greek-influenced classical style of city architecture favored by his father, Ludwig I. With the cabinet's approval, he created this broad boulevard and lined its central stretch with majestic buildings. It culminates on a rise beyond the Isar River in the stately outlines of the **Maximilianeum,** a lavish 19th-century arcaded palace built for Maximilian II and now home to the Bavarian state parliament. Only the terrace can be visited.

㉝ Museum Villa Stuck. This neoclassical villa is the former home of one of Munich's leading turn-of-the-20th-century artists, Franz von Stuck (1863–1928). His work, which is at times haunting, at times erotic, and occasionally humorous, covers the walls of the ground-floor rooms, along with various special exhibitions. Renovation of the upstairs rooms, the artist's former quarters, is expected to last until 2005. ⊠ *Prinzregentenstr. 60, Haidhausen* ☎ *089/4555–5125* ⊕ *www.villastuck.de* ⊠ *Free* ⊙ *Tues.–Sun. 10–6* Ⓤ *Prinzregentenplatz (U-bahn).*

⑳ Nationaltheater (National Theater). Built in the late 19th century as a royal opera house with a pillared portico, this large theater was bombed during the war but is now restored to its original splendor and has some of the world's most advanced stage technology. ⊠ *Max-Joseph-Pl., City Center* ☎ *089/2185–1920* Ⓤ *Odeonsplatz (U-bahn).*

★ ㉑ Residenz (Royal Palace). Munich's royal palace began as a small castle in the 14th century. The Wittelsbach dukes moved here when the tenements of an expanding Munich encroached upon their Alter Hof. In succeeding centuries the royal residence developed according to the importance, requirements, and interests of its occupants. It came to include the Königsbau (on Max-Joseph-Platz) and then (clockwise) the Alte Residenz; the Festsaal (Banquet Hall); the Altes Residenztheater/Cuvilliés-Theater; the newly restored Allerheiligenhofkirche (All Souls' Church), a venue for cultural events; the Residenztheater; and the Nationaltheater.

Building began in 1385 with the **Neuveste** (New Fortress), which comprised the northeast section. Most of it burned to the ground in 1750, but one of its finest rooms survived: the 16th-century **Antiquarium,** which was built for Duke Albrecht V's collection of antique statues (today it's used chiefly for state receptions). The throne room of King Ludwig I, the **Neuer Herkulessaal,** is now a concert hall. The accumulated Wittelsbach treasures are on view in several palace museums. The **Schatzkammer** (Treasury; ⊠ €6, combined ticket with Residenzmuseum €7 ⊙ Apr.–Oct., Tues., Wed., Fri.–Sun. 9–6, Thurs. 9–8; Nov.–Mar., Tues.–Sun. 9–4) has a rather rich centerpiece—a small Renaissance statue of St. George, studded with 2,291 diamonds, 209 pearls, and 406 rubies. Paintings, tapestries, furniture, and porcelain are housed in the **Residenzmuseum** (⊠ €4 ⊙ Apr.–Oct., Tues., Wed., Fri.–Sun. 9–6, Thurs. 9–8; Nov.–Mar., Tues.–Sun. 9–4). Antique coins glint in the **Staatliche Münzsammlung** (⊠ €2, free Sun. ⊙ Tues., Wed., Fri.–Sun. 10–5, Thurs. 10–6:45). Egyptian works of art make up the **Staatliche Sammlung Ägyptischer Kunst** (⊠ Hofgarten entrance ⊠ €2.50, free Sun. ⊙ Tues. 9–9, Wed.–Fri. 9–4, weekends 10–5).

In summer, chamber-music concerts take place in the inner courtyard. Also in the center of the complex is the small, rococo **Altes Residenztheater/Cuvilliés-Theater** (⊠ Residenzstr. ⊠ €2 ⊙ Tues.–Sun. 10–4). It was built by François Cuvilliés between 1751 and 1755, and performances are still held here. The French-born Cuvilliés was a dwarf who was admitted to the Bavarian court as a decorative "bauble." Prince Max Emanuel recognized his innate artistic ability and had him trained as an architect. The prince's eye for talent gave Germany some of its richest rococo treasures. ⊠ *Max-Joseph-Pl. 3, entrance through archway at Residenzstr. 1, City Center* ☎ *089/290–671* ☉ *Closed a few days in early Jan.* Ⓤ *Odeonsplatz (U-bahn).*

㉛ Schack-Galerie. Those with a taste for florid and romantic 19th-century German paintings will appreciate the collections of the Schack-Galerie, originally the private collection of Count Schack. Others may find the gallery dull, filled with plodding and repetitive works by painters who now repose in well-deserved obscurity. ⊠ *Prinzregentenstr. 9, Lehel* ☎ *089/2380–5224* ▨ *€2.50, free Sun.* ☉ *Wed.–Mon. 10–5* Ⓤ *Lehel (U-bahn).*

㉔ Siegestor (Victory Arch). Marking the beginning of Leopoldstrasse, the Siegestor has Italian origins—it was modeled after the Arch of Constantine in Rome—and was built to honor the achievements of the Bavarian army during the Wars of Liberation (1813–15). The writing on the gable facing the inner city reads: DEDICATED TO VICTORY, DESTROYED BY WAR, ADMONISHING PEACE. ⊠ *Leopoldstr., Schwabing* Ⓤ *Unversität (U-bahn).*

㉗ SiemensForum. Siemens corporation has been one of Germany's major employers and technological innovators for more than 150 years. This company museum, housed in a spaceshiplike building, shows visitors the many areas in which Siemens has been active, from old-fashioned telegraph systems to hypermodern dentist chairs and fuel cells. Hands-on displays such as video telephones spice up the experience. ⊠ *Oskar-von-Miller-Ring* ☎ *089/6363–2612* ⊕ *www.siemesforum.de* ▨ *Free* ☉ *Sun.–Fri. 9–5, 1st Tues. in month 9–9* Ⓤ *Odeonsplatz (U-bahn).*

⑲ Staatliches Museum für Völkerkunde (State Museum of Ethnology). Arts and crafts from around the world are displayed in this extensive museum. There are also regular special exhibits. ⊠ *Maximilianstr. 42, Lehel* ☎ *089/2101–3610* ⊕ *www.voelkerkundemuseum-muenchen.de* ▨ *€3, free Sun.* ☉ *Tues.–Sun. 9:30–5:15* Ⓤ *Lehel (U-bahn).*

㉕ Theatinerkirche (Theatine Church). This mighty baroque church owes its Italian appearance to its founder, Princess Henriette Adelaide, who commissioned it in gratitude for the birth of her son and heir, Max Emanuel, in 1663. A native of Turin, the princess distrusted Bavarian architects and builders and thus summoned a master builder from Bologna, Agostino Barelli, to construct her church. Barelli worked on the building for 11 years but was dismissed before the project was completed. It was another 100 years before the Theatinerkirche was finished. Its lofty towers frame a restrained facade capped by a massive dome. The superb stucco work on the inside has a remarkably light feeling owing to its brilliant white color. The gaping space before the Feldherrnhalle and Theatinerkirche is often used for outdoor stage events. ⊠ *Theatinerstr. 22, City Center* Ⓤ *Odeonsplatz (U-bahn).*

need a break? Munich's oldest café, **Tambosi** (⊠ Odeonspl., Maxvorstadt ☎ 089/ 224–768), borders the street across from the Theatinerkirche. Watch the hustle and bustle from an outdoor table or retreat through a gate in the Hofgarten's western wall to the café's tree-shaded beer garden. If the weather is cool or rainy, find a corner in the cozy, eclectically furnished interior.

DenkStätte Weisse Rose (Memorial to the Weisse Rose Resistance Group). Siblings Hans and Sophie Scholl, fellow students Alexander Schmorell and Christian Probst, and Kurt Huber, Professor of Philosophy, founded the short-lived resistance movement against the Nazis in 1942–43 known as the Weisse Rose (White Rose). All were executed. A small exhibition about their work is in the inner quad of the university, where the Scholls were caught distributing leaflets and denounced by the janitor. ⊠ *Geschwister-Scholl-Pl. 1, Maxvorstadt* ☎ *089/2180–3053* ✑ *Free* ⊙ *Mon.–Thurs. 10–4, Fri. 10–3* Ⓤ *Unversität (U-bahn).*

Schwabing & Maxvorstadt

Most of the city's leading art galleries and museums are congregated in Schwabing and neighboring Maxvorstadt, making this area the artistic center of Munich. Schwabing, the old artists' quarter, is no longer the bohemian area where such diverse residents as Lenin and Kandinsky were once neighbors, but the solid cultural foundations of the Maxvorstadt, where you'll find Munich's largest and most important museums, are immutable. Where the two areas meet (in the streets behind the university), life hums with a creative vibrancy that is difficult to detect elsewhere in Munich.

a good walk Begin with a stroll through the city's old botanical garden, the **Alter Botanischer Garten** ㉞ ▶. The grand-looking building opposite the garden's entrance is the Palace of Justice, law courts built in 1897 in suitable awe-inspiring dimensions. On one corner of busy Lenbachplatz, you can't fail to notice one of Munich's most impressive fountains: the monumental late-19th-century Wittelsbacher Brunnen. Beyond the fountain, in Pacellistrasse, is the baroque **Dreifaltigkeitskirche** ㉟.

Leave the garden at its Meiserstrasse exit. On the right-hand side you'll pass two solemn neoclassical buildings closely associated with the Third Reich. The first served as the administrative offices of the Nazi Party in Munich. The neighboring building is the Music Academy, where, in 1938, Hitler, Mussolini, Chamberlain, and Daladier signed the prewar pact that carved up Czechoslovakia.

At the junction of Meiserstrasse and Briennerstrasse, look right to see the obelisk dominating the circular **Karolinenplatz** ㊱. To your left will be the expansive **Königsplatz** ㊲, bordered by two museums, the **Glyptothek** ㊳ and the **Antikensammlungen** ㊴, and closed off by the Propyläen, a colonnade framed by two Egyptian pylons.

After walking by the museums, turn right onto Luisenstrasse and you'll arrive at a Florentine-style villa, the **Städtische Galerie im Lenbachhaus** ㊵, which has an outstanding painting collection. Continue down Luisenstrasse, turning right on Theresienstrasse to reach Munich's three leading art galleries, the **Alte Pinakothek** ㊶; the **Neue Pinakothek** ㊷, opposite it; and the **Pinakothek der Moderne** ㊸. They are as complementary as their buildings are contrasting: the Alte Pinakothek, severe and serious in style; the Neue Pinakothek, almost frivolously Florentine; and the Pinakothek der Moderne, glass-and-concrete new.

After a few hours immersed in culture, end your walk with a leisurely stroll through the neighboring streets of Schwabing, which are lined with boutiques, bars, and restaurants. If it's a nice day, head for the **Elisabethmarkt,** Schwabing's permanent market.

TIMING   This walk may take an entire day, depending on how long you linger at the major museums en route. Avoid the museum crowds by visiting as early in the day as possible. All of Munich seems to discover an interest in art on Sunday, when admission to most municipal and state-funded museums is free; you might want to take this day off from culture and join the late-breakfast and brunch crowd at the Elisabethmarkt, a beer garden, or at any of the many bars and Gaststätten. Some have Sunday-morning jazz concerts. Many Schwabing bars have happy hours between 6 and 8—a relaxing way to end your day.

What to See

㊶ **Alte Pinakothek** (Old Picture Gallery). The long, massive brick Alte
Fodor'sChoice   Pinakothek was constructed by Leo von Klenze between 1826 and 1836
★   to exhibit the collection of old masters begun by Duke Wilhelm IV in the 16th century. It's now judged one of the world's great picture galleries. Among its many famous works are paintings by Dürer, Titian, Rembrandt, Rubens (the museum has one of the world's largest collections of works by Rubens), and two celebrated Murillos. ⊠ *Barerstr. 27, Maxvorstadt* ☎ *089/2380–5216* ⊕ *www.alte-pinakothek.de* ☒ *€5, combined day ticket with Neue Pinakothek and Pinakothek der Moderne €11; free Sun.* ⊙ *Tues., Wed., Fri.–Sun. 10–5, Thurs. 10–8* Ⓤ *Königsplatz (U-bahn).*

▶ ㉞ **Alter Botanischer Garten** (Old Botanical Garden). Munich's first botanical garden began as the site of a huge glass palace, built in 1853 for Germany's first industrial exhibition. In 1931 it shared the fate of a similarly palatial glass exhibition hall, London's Crystal Palace, when its garden burned to the ground; six years later it was redesigned as a public park. Two features from the 1930s remain: a small, square **exhibition hall,** still used for art shows, and the 1933 **Neptune Fountain,** an enormous work in the heavy, monumental style of the prewar years. At the international electricity exhibition of 1882, the world's first high-tension electrical cable was run from the park to a Bavarian village 48 km (30 mi) away. ⊠ *Entrance at Lenbachpl., Maxvorstadt* Ⓤ *Karlsplatz (U-bahn and S-bahn).*

**need a
break?**
Ideal for a quick lunch with either German, French, or Italian flair is the art deco **Brasserie Tresznjewski** (⊠ Theresienstrasse 72, at Barerstrasse, Maxvorstadt ☎ 089/282–349). It's a good spot especially if visiting the neighboring Pinakotheks . . . and it serves food well into the wee hours.

39 **Antikensammlungen** (Antiquities Collection). This museum has a collection of small sculptures, Etruscan art, Greek vases, gold, and glass. ⊠ *Königspl. 1, Maxvorstadt* ☎ *089/598–359* ☜ *€3, combined ticket to Antikensammlungen and Glyptothek €5; free Sun.* ☉ *Tues. and Thurs.–Sun. 10–5, Wed. 10–8* Ⓤ *Königsplatz (U-bahn).*

35 **Dreifaltigkeitskirche** (Church of the Holy Trinity). After a local woman prophesied doom for the city unless a new church was erected, this striking baroque exterior was promptly built between 1711 and 1718. It has frescoes by Cosmas Damian Asam depicting various heroic scenes. ⊠ *Pacellistr. 10, City Center* ☎ *089/290–0820* ☉ *Daily 7–7, except during services* Ⓤ *Karlsplatz (U-bahn and S-bahn).*

Elisabethmarkt (Elisabeth Market). Schwabing's permanent market is smaller than the popular Viktualienmarkt, but hardly less colorful. It has a pocket-size beer garden, where a jazz band performs every Saturday from spring to autumn. ⊠ *Arcistr. and Elisabethstr., Schwabing* Ⓤ *Giselastrasse (U-bahn).*

★ **38** **Glyptothek.** These Greek and Roman sculptures are among the finest collections in Munich. The small café that expands into the quiet courtyard is a favorite for visitors, which include budding artists practicing their drawing skills. ⊠ *Königspl. 3, Maxvorstadt* ☎ *089/286–100* ☜ *€3, combined ticket to Glyptothek and Antikensammlungen €5; free Sun.* ☉ *Tues., Wed., Fri.–Sun. 10–5, Thurs. 10–8* Ⓤ *Königsplatz (U-bahn).*

36 **Karolinenplatz** (Caroline Square). At the junction of Barerstrasse and Briennerstrasse, this circular area is dominated by an obelisk unveiled in 1812 as a memorial to Bavarians killed fighting Napoléon. **Amerikahaus** (America House) faces Karolinenplatz. It has an extensive library with many magazines to flip through and a year-round program of cultural events. ⊠ *Karolinenpl. 3, Maxvorstadt* ☎ *089/552–5370* Ⓤ *Königsplatz (U-bahn).*

37 **Königsplatz** (King's Square). This expansive square is lined on three sides with the monumental Grecian-style buildings by Leo von Klenze that gave Munich the nickname Athens on the Isar. The two templelike structures are now the Antikensammlungen and the Glyptothek museums. Although a busy road passes through it, the square has maintained the dignified appearance intended by Ludwig I thanks to the broad green lawns sprawling in front of the museums. Ⓤ *Königsplatz (U-bahn).*

42 **Neue Pinakothek** (New Picture Gallery). This exhibition space opened in 1981 to house the royal collection of modern art left homeless and scattered after its building was destroyed in the war. The exterior of the modern building mimics an older one with Italianate influences. The interior offers a magnificent environment for picture gazing, at least partly owing to the natural light flooding in from skylights. French Impressionists—Monet, Degas, Manet—are all well represented. The 19th-century German and Scandinavian paintings—misty landscapes predominate—are only now coming to be recognized as admirable products of their time. ⊠ *Barerstr. 29, Maxvorstadt* ☎ *089/2380–5195*

⊕ *www.neue-pinakothek.de* ✉ *€5, combined day ticket with Alte Pinakothek and Pinakothek der Moderne €11; free Sun.* ⊙ *Wed. and Fri.–Mon. 10–5, Thurs. 10–8* Ⓤ *Königsplatz (U-bahn).*

㊽ Pinakothek der Moderne. Munich's latest cultural addition is also Germany's largest museum for modern art, architecture, and design. The striking glass-and-concrete complex holds four outstanding art and architectural collections, including modern art, industrial and graphic design, the Bavarian State collection of graphic art, and the Technical University's architectural museum. ✉ *Barerstr. 40, Maxvorstadt* ☎ *089/2380–5360* ⊕ *www.pinakothek-der-moderne.de* ✉ *€9, combined day ticket with Neue Pinakothek and Pinakothek der Moderne €11* ⊙ *Tues. and Wed. and weekends 10–5, Thurs. and Fri. 10–8* Ⓤ *Königsplatz (U-bahn).*

㊿ Städtische Galerie im Lenbachhaus (Municipal Gallery). This delightful late-19th-century Florentine-style villa is the former home and studio of the artist Franz von Lenbach (1836–1904). Inside you'll find renowned works from the Gothic period to the present, including an exciting assemblage of art from the early-20th-century *Blaue Reiter* (Blue Rider) group: Kandinsky, Klee, Jawlensky, Macke, Marc, and Münter. The chambers of Lenbach are on view as well. The adjoining **Kunstbau** (art building), a former subway platform of the Königsplatz station, hosts changing exhibitions of modern art. ✉ *Luisenstr. 33, Maxvorstadt* ☎ *089/233–32000* ⊕ *www.lenbachhaus.de* ✉ *€6 (may vary)* ⊙ *Tues.–Sun. 10–6* Ⓤ *Königsplatz (U-bahn).*

Outside the Center

Ⓒ **Bavaria Filmstadt.** Munich is Germany's leading moviemaking center, and the local Hollywood-like neighborhood, Geiselgasteig, is on the southern outskirts of the city. The Filmexpress transports you on a 1½-hour tour of the sets of *Das Boot* (*The Boat*), *Die Unendliche Geschichte* (*The Neverending Story*), and other productions. Stunt shows are held at 11:30, 1, and 2:30, and action movies are screened in Showscan, the super-wide-screen cinema. The *Erlebniskino* (experience cinema) is a computer-animated thriller where you sit in a chair that moves with five-channel audio to really get you into the picture. Take U-bahn 1 or 2 from the city center to Silberhornstrasse and then change to Tram 25 to Bavariafilmplatz. The Munich transit authority (MVV) offers its own combined ticket for two adults plus three other people under 18 for €29.50, including travel. ✉ *Bavariafilmpl. 7, Geiselgasteig* ☎ *089/6499–2000* ⊕ *www.filmstadt.de* ✉ *€10, stunt show €5, Showscan €4, combined ticket €17* ⊙ *Nov.–Feb., daily 10–3, tours only on the hr; Mar.–Oct., daily 9–4, tours every 10 min.*

BMW Museum Zeithorizonte. Munich is the home of the famous BMW car firm. Its museum, a circular tower that looks as if it served as a set for *Star Wars*, contains not only a dazzling collection of BMWs old and new but also items and exhibitions relating to the company's social history and its technical developments. It adjoins the **BMW factory** (☎ 089/3895–3308 ⊙ weekdays 10–1) on the eastern edge of the Olympiapark.

You can see the factory as well, but only with a tour that begins at the museum's box office. Call ahead of time to reserve a spot. ⊠ *Petuelring 130, Milbertshofen* ☎ *089/3822–3307* ⊕ *www.bmwmobiletradition. com* 🖃 *€3* ⊙ *Daily 9–5; last entry at 4* Ⓤ *Petuelring (U-bahn).*

Deutsches Museum–"Flugwerft Schleissheim." Connoisseurs of fine airplanes and of the art of flying in general will appreciate this magnificent offshoot of the Deutsches Museum, some 20 km (12 mi) north of the city center off A–9. Old flying machines from the earliest days to a Soviet MiG fighter jet share the space with countless other exhibits that tell the fascinating tale of how humans have taken to the air over the past 100 years. It's an ideal complement to a visit to Schloss Schleissheim. Take S-bahn 1 to Oberschleissheim, and then Bus 292 (which doesn't run on weekends). If you're planning to visit the Deutsches Museum as well, ask for a combination ticket. ⊠ *Effnerstr. 7, Oberschleissheim* ☎ *089/315–7140* ⊕ *www.deutsches-museum.de* 🖃 *€3.50, combined ticket with the Deutsches Museum €7* ⊙ *Daily 9–5* Ⓤ *Oberschleissheim (S-bahn) and Bus No. 292.*

☺ **Hellabrunn Zoo.** There are many parklike enclosures but a minimum of cages at this attractive zoo. Some of the older buildings are in typical art nouveau style. Care has been taken to group animals according to their natural and geographical habitats. One of the latest additions is the **Urwaldhaus** (Rain-Forest house), which offers guided tours at night (call ahead of time). The 170 acres include restaurants and children's areas. Take Bus 52 from Marienplatz or U-bahn 3 to Thalkirchen, at the southern edge of the city. ⊠ *Tierparkstr. 30, Harlaching* ☎ *089/625–080* ⊕ *www.zoo-munich.de* 🖃 *€6* ⊙ *Apr.–Sept., daily 8–6; Oct.–Mar., daily 9–5* Ⓤ *Thalkirchen (U-bahn).*

☺ **Olympiapark** (Olympic Park). On the northern edge of Schwabing, undulating circus-tent-like roofs cover the stadiums built for the 1972 Olympic Games. The roofs are made of translucent tiles that glisten in the sun and act as amplifiers for the rock concerts held here. A €25 fee lets you climb the roofs with rubber-sole shoes in good weather. Tours of the park are conducted on a Disneyland-style train throughout the day. An elevator will speed you up the 960-foot **Olympia Tower** (€2.50) for a view of the city and the Alps; there's also a revolving restaurant near the top. Take U-bahn 3 to the park. ☎ *089/3067–2414, 089/ 3066–8585 restaurant* ⊕ *www.olympiapark-muenchen.de* 🖃 *Adventure tour €7, stadium tour €4* ⊙ *Main stadium daily 9–4:30; Olympia Tower daily 9* AM*–midnight. Tours Apr.–Nov.; grand tour at 2* PM*, stadium tour at 11* AM Ⓤ *Olympiazentrum (U-bahn).*

★ **Schloss Nymphenburg.** This glorious baroque and rococo palace is the largest of its kind in Germany, stretching more than 1 km (½ mi) from one wing to the other. The palace grew in size and scope over a period of more than 200 years, beginning as a summer residence built on land given by Prince Ferdinand Maria to his beloved wife, Henriette Adelaide, on the occasion of the birth of their son and heir, Max Emanuel, in 1663. The princess hired the Italian architect Agostino Barelli to build both the Theatinerkirche and the palace, which was completed in 1675 by his successor, Enrico Zuccalli. Within the original building, now the central axis of the palace complex, is a magnificent hall, the **Steinerner Saal,** extending over two floors and richly decorated with stucco and grandiose frescoes. In summer, chamber-music concerts are given here. One of the surrounding royal chambers houses the famous **Schönheitsgalerie** (Gallery of Beauties). The walls are hung from floor to ceiling with portraits of women who caught the roving eye of Ludwig I, among them a butcher's daughter and an English duchess. The most famous portrait is of Lola Montez, a sultry beauty and high-class courtesan who, after a time as the mistress of Franz Liszt and later Alexandre Dumas, so enchanted King Ludwig I that he almost bankrupted the state for her sake and was ultimately forced to abdicate.

The palace is in a park laid out in formal French style, with low hedges and gravel walks extending into woodland. Among the ancient tree stands are three fascinating structures. The **Amalienburg** hunting lodge is a rococo gem built by François Cuvilliés, architect of the Altes Residenztheater. The silver-and-blue stucco of the little Amalienburg creates an atmosphere of courtly high life, making clear that the pleasures of the chase did not always take place outdoors. In the lavishly appointed kennels you'll see that even the dogs lived in luxury. The **Pagodenburg** was built for royal tea parties. Its elegant French exterior disguises a suitably Asian interior in which exotic teas from India and China were served. Swimming parties were held in the **Badenburg,** Europe's first post-Roman heated pool.

Nymphenburg contains so much of interest that a day hardly provides enough time. Don't leave without visiting the former royal stables, now the **Marstallmuseum** (Museum of Royal Carriages; ☜ €2.50). It houses a fleet of vehicles, including an elaborately decorated sleigh in which King Ludwig II once glided through the Bavarian twilight, postilion torches lighting the way. On the walls hang portraits of the royal horses. Also exhibited are examples of Nymphenburg porcelain, produced here between 1747 and the 1920s.

A popular museum in the north wing of the palace has nothing to do with the Wittelsbachs but is one of Nymphenburg's major attractions. ☺ The **Museum Mensch und Natur** (Museum of Man and Nature; ☎ 089/ 171–382 ☜ €1.50, free Sun. ☉ Tues.–Sun. 9–5) concentrates on three areas of interest: the variety of life on Earth, the history of humankind, and our place in the environment. Main exhibits include a huge representation of the human brain and a chunk of Alpine crystal weighing half a ton. Take Tram 17 or Bus 41 from the city center to the Schloss Nymphenburg stop. ✉ *Notburgastr. at bridge crossing Nymphenburg Canal, Nymphenburg* ☎ *089/179–080* ☜ *Schloss Nymphenburg complex, combined ticket, including Marstall Museum but not Museum Mensch und Natur, €7.50, €6.50 in winter, when parts of complex are closed* ☉ *Apr.–Sept., daily 9–6; Oct.–Mar., daily 10–4; all except Amalienburg and gardens closed Mon.*

Schloss Schleissheim (Schleissheim Palace). In 1597 Duke Wilhelm V decided to look for a peaceful retreat outside Munich and found what he

ALL ABOUT GERMAN BEER

HOWEVER MANY FINGERS you want to hold up, just remember the easy-to-pronounce Bier (beer) Bit-te (please) when ordering a beer. The tricky part is, Germans don't just produce one beverage called beer; they brew more than 5,000 varieties. Germany has about 1,300 breweries, 40% of the world's total. The hallmark of the country's dedication to beer is the purity law, das Reinheitsgebot, unchanged since Duke Wilhelm IV introduced it in Bavaria in 1516. The law decrees that only malted barley, hops, yeast, and water may be used to make beer, except for specialty Weiss- or Weizenbier (wheat beers, which are a carbonated, sharp, and sour brew, often with floating yeast particles).

Most taverns have several drafts in addition to bottled beers. The type available depends upon the region you're in, and in southern Germany the choice can also depend on the time of year. The alcohol content of German beers also varies. At the weaker end of the scale is the light Munich Helles (3.7% alcohol by volume); stronger brews are the bitter-flavored Pilsner (around 5%) and the dark Doppelbock (more than 7%).

Germany's biggest breweries are in the city of Dortmund, which feeds the industrial Ruhr region. Popular northern beers are Export Lagers or the paler, more pungent Pilsners. Köln and Düsseldorf breweries in the Rhine region produce "old-fashioned" beers similar to English ales. But Bavaria is where the majority of breweries—and beer traditions—are found. The Bavarians and the Saarlanders consume more beer per person than any other group in the country.

In Munich you'll find the most famous breweries, the largest beer halls and beer gardens, the biggest and most indulgent beer festival, and the widest selection of brews. Even the beer glasses are bigger: a Mass is a 1-liter (almost 2-pint) serving; a Halbe is half a Mass and the standard size. The Hofbräuhaus is Munich's most well-known beer hall, but its oompah band's selections are geared more to Americans and Australians than to your average Münchener. You'll find the citizenry in one of the English Garden's four beer gardens.

Not even the widest Bavarians can be held wholly responsible for the staggering consumption of beer and food at the annual Oktoberfest, which starts at the end of September and ends in early October. Typically, 5 million liters (1,183,000 gallons) of beer, as well as 750,000 roasted chickens and 650,000 sausages, are put away by revelers of many nationalities. To partake, book lodging by April, and if you're traveling with a group, also reserve bench space in one of the 14 tents. See Munich's Web site, ⊕ www.muenchen-tourist.de, for beer-tent contacts. The best time to arrive at the grounds is lunchtime, when it's easier to find a seat—by 4 PM it's packed. The beer tents are actually huge pavilions, heaving and pulsating with thousands of beer-swilling, table-pounding "serious" drinkers, animated by brass bands pounding out their music on boxing-ring-style stages. The grounds close by 11:30 PM. Take advantage of an hour or two of sobriety to tour the fairground rides, which are also an integral part of Oktoberfest. Under no circumstances attempt any of these rides—all of which claim to be the world's most dangerous—after a liter or two of the Oktoberfest beer. The disgrace of throwing up on the figure eight is truly Germanic in scale.

–Robert Tilley

wanted at this palace, then far beyond the city walls but now only a short ride on a train and a bus. The large ballroom where concerts are sometimes held is quite a sight. A later ruler, Prince Max Emanuel, added a second, smaller palace, the **Lustheim.** Separated from Schleissheim by a formal garden and a decorative canal, the Lustheim houses Germany's largest collection of Meissen porcelain. To reach the palace, take the suburban S-bahn 1 line to Oberschleissheim station and then walk about 15 minutes to the palace, or take Bus 292 (which doesn't run on weekends). ⊠ *Maximilianshof 1, Oberschleissheim* ☎ *089/315–5272* 🎟 *Combined ticket for palaces and porcelain collection* €*2.50* ☉ *Tues.–Sun. 10–5.*

WHERE TO EAT

Munich claims to be Germany's gourmet capital. It certainly has an inordinate number of very fine restaurants, some with chef-owners who honed their skills under such Gallic masters as Paul Bocuse. For connoisseurs, wining and dining at Tantris or the Königshof could well turn into the equivalent of a religious experience; culinary creations are accorded the status of works of art on a par with a Bach fugue or a Dürer painting, with tabs equal to a king's ransom. Epicureans are convinced that one can dine as well in Munich as in any other city on the Continent.

However, genuine Munich cuisine is to be experienced in those rustic places that serve simple, robust Bavarian specialties in ample portions. Gradually, too, the smoky and boisterous beer hall has been giving way to chic, well-ventilated restaurants done up in traditional style where the food is just as original as ever.

Many Munich restaurants serve sophisticated cuisine, and they require their patrons to dress for the occasion. Less expensive restaurants will serve you regardless of what you wear.

WHAT IT COSTS In Euros				
$$$$	**$$$**	**$$**	**$**	**¢**
AT DINNER	over €25	€21–€25	€16–€20	€9–€15	under €9

Restaurant prices are per person for a main course at dinner.

City Center

$$$$ ✕ **Am Marstall.** The exciting menu of this celebrated restaurant combines the best of French and German cuisines—lamb bred on the salt-soaked meadows of coastal Brittany, for instance, or venison from the hunting grounds of Lower Bavaria. Book a window seat so you can while away the time between courses by watching Bavaria's well-heeled shoppers promenading on Maximilianstrasse. ⊠ *Maximilianstr. 16, City Center* ☎ *089/2916–5511* ⌦ *Reservations essential* 🍴 *Jacket and tie* 🖃 *AE, MC, V* ☉ *Closed Sun. and Mon.* Ⓤ *Marienplatz (S-bahn and U-bahn).*

$$$$ ✕ **Königshof.** This reliable old hotel restaurant is among Munich's finest and most traditional dining rooms. The outstanding menus created by

chef Götz Rothacker are French influenced, the surroundings elegant—
and if you book a window table, you'll have a view of Munich's busiest square, the Stachus, an incandescent experience at night. ⊠ *Karlspl.
25, City Center* ☎ *089/5513–6142* ⚞ *Reservations essential* 🏛 *Jacket
and tie* ⊟ *AE, DC, MC, V* ⊗ *Closed Sun. No lunch in Aug.* Ⓤ *Karlsplatz (U-bahn and S-bahn).*

$$$ ✕ **Halali.** The Halali is an old-style Munich restaurant—polished wood
paneling and antlers on the walls—which is *the* place to try traditional
dishes of venison and other game. Save room for the homemade vanilla
ice cream. ⊠ *Schönfeldstr. 22, City Center* ☎ *089/285–909* 🏛 *Jacket
and tie* ⊟ *AE, MC, V* ⊗ *Closed Sun. No lunch Sat.* Ⓤ *Odeonsplatz
(U-bahn and S-bahn).*

$$–$$$ ✕ **Hunsinger's Pacific.** Werner Hunsinger, one of Germany's top restau-
rateurs, has brought Munich a reasonably priced restaurant serving
eclectic cuisine, borrowing from the Pacific Rim of East Asia, Australia,
and North and South America. The restaurant's clam chowder is the
best in the city, while another praised specialty is the Chilean-style steak
fillet, wrapped in a mantle of onion and eggplant-flavor maize. The many
"small dishes" will give you a good panoramic taste of the place. At lunch,
two-course meals cost around €12. ⊠ *Maximiliansplatz 5, City Cen-
ter* ☎ *089/5502–9741* ⊟ *AE, DC, MC, V* ⊗ *No lunch weekends*
Ⓤ *Karlsplatz (U-bahn and S-bahn).*

★ **$–$$$** ✕ **Dukatz.** A literary and business crowd mixes at this smart bar and
restaurant in the Literaturhaus, a converted city mansion where regu-
lar book readings are presented. Food includes German nouvelle cuisine, but there's a strong Gallic touch with dishes such as calves' head
and lamb tripe. Note the verbal art, some of it by New York artist Jen-
nifer Holzer, such as the statement at the bottom of your cup saying:
"More eroticism, gentlemen!" ⊠ *Salvatorpl. 1, City Center* ☎ *089/291–
9600* ⊟ *No credit cards* Ⓤ *Odeonsplatz (U-bahn).*

$–$$$ ✕ **Hackerhaus.** The cozy, upscale restaurant belonging to the Hacker brew-
ery (founded in the 15th century) has three floors of wood-panel rooms.
In summer you can order a cheese plate and beer in the cool, flower-
bedecked inner courtyard; in winter you can snuggle in a corner of the
Ratsstube and warm up on thick homemade potato broth, followed by
schnitzel and *Bratkartoffein* (pan-fried potatoes), or take a table in the
Bürgerstube and admire its proud centerpiece, the world's largest beer
mug. ⊠ *Sendlingerstr. 14, City Center* ☎ *089/260–5026* ⊟ *AE, DC,
MC, V* Ⓤ *Sendlinger Tor (U-bahn).*

★ **$–$$$** ✕ **Spatenhaus.** A view of the opera house and the royal palace comple-
ments the Bavarian mood of the wood-panel and beamed Spatenhaus.
The menu is international, with everything from artichokes to *zuppa Ro-
mana* (alcohol-soaked, fruity Italian cake-pudding). But since you're in
Bavaria, try the Bavarian plate, an enormous mixture of local meats and
sausages. Make reservations if you want to go after a concert or opera.
⊠ *Residenzstr. 12, City Center* ☎ *089/290–7060* ⊟ *AE, MC, V*
Ⓤ *Odeonsplatz (U-bahn).*

$–$$ ✕ **Ganga.** The upholstery is becoming worn at the Ganga, but this, and
the friendly service, only contributes to the warm atmosphere. So do
the curry and tandoori dishes, which are among the best in Munich, and

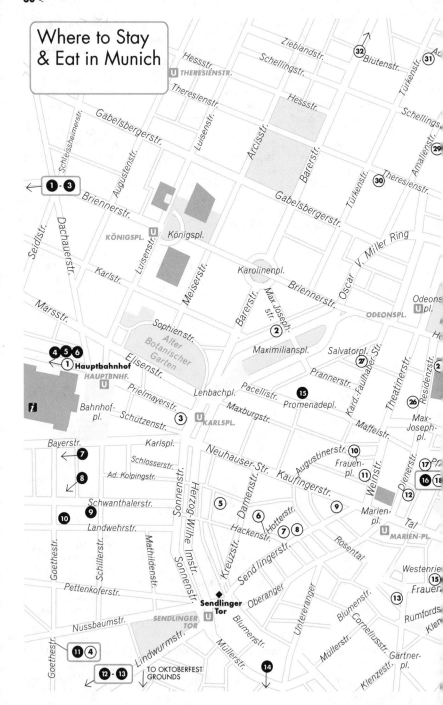

Where to Stay & Eat in Munich

Restaurants ▼

Am Marstall	**20**
Andescher am Dom	**10**
Augustiner Keller	**1**
Bistro Cezanne	**32**
Buxs, City Center	**15**
Buxs, Maxvorstadt	**29**
Café am Beethovenplatz	**4**
Cohen's	**30**
Due passi	**18**
Dukatz	**27**
Dürnbräu	**22**
Gandl	**24**
Ganga	**14**
Gasthaus Isarthor	**23**
Hackerhaus	**8**
Halali	**28**
Hofbräuhaus	**21**
Hofer	**12**
Hundskugel	**6**
Hunsinger's Pacific	**2**
Königshof	**3**
Max-Emanuel-Brauerei	**31**
Monaco	**13**
Nürnberger Bratwurst Glöckl am Dom	**11**
Orlandohaus	**19**
Pfälzer Weinprobierstube	**25**
Prinz Myshkin	**7**
Spatenhaus	**26**
Spöckmeier	**9**
Tantris	**33**
Weinhaus Neuner	**5**
Weisses Bräuhaus	**16**
Vinorant Alter Hof	**17**

Hotels ▼

Admiral	**19**
Adria	**23**
Advokat	**20**
ArabellaSheraton Grand Hotel	**26**
Bayerischer Hof	**15**
Biederstein	**28**
Brack	**12**
Cortiina	**24**
Creatif Hotel Elephant	**5**
Eden-Hotel Wolff	**4**
Erzgiesserei Europe	**3**
Gästehaus am Englischen Garten	**27**
Hotel Amba	**6**
Hotel Concorde	**17**
Hotel Mirabell	**10**
Hotel Pension Am Siegestor	**25**
Hotel-Pension Schmellergarten	**13**
Hotel-Pension Beck	**21**
Hotel-Pension Mariandl	**11**
Jagdschloss	**7**
Kempinski Hotel Vier Jahreszeiten München	**22**
Kriemhild	**1**
Kurpfalz	**9**
Olympic	**14**
Opera	**29**
Park-Hotel Theresienhöhe	**8**
Platzl	**16**
Rotkreuzplatz	**2**
Torbräu	**18**

the price is right. Remember that what is mild for an Indian may send you through the roof! ⊠ *Baaderstr. 11* ☎ *089/201–6465* ▤ *AE, MC, V* ⊙ *No lunch weekends* Ⓤ *Isartor (U-bahn).*

★ **$–$$** ✕ **Hundskugel.** This is Munich's oldest tavern and also one of the city's smallest. You'll be asked to squeeze together and make room for late-comers looking for a spot at one of the few tables that clutter the hand-kerchief-size dining room. The tavern dates from 1440 and in many ways doesn't appear to have changed much over the centuries. Even the menu is medievally basic and a bit hit-and-miss, although any combination of pork and potatoes or sauerkraut can be recommended. ⊠ *Hotterstr. 18, City Center* ☎ *089/264–272* ▤ *No credit cards* Ⓤ *Sendlinger Tor (U-bahn).*

$–$$ ✕ **Monaco.** One of the nicest additions to the Italian scene, the Monaco makes its guests feel at home right away, ensuring returning customers. The decor is simple and unpretentious. Excellent wines on the menu are backed by a serendipitous selection; ask your waiter for recommendations. ⊠ *Reichenbachstr. 10, City Center* ☎ *089/268–141* ▤ *MC, V* Ⓤ *Sendlinger Tor (U-bahn).*

$–$$ ✕ **Nürnberger Bratwurst Glöckl am Dom.** Munich's most original beer tavern is dedicated to the delicious *Nürnberger Bratwürste* (finger-size sausages), a specialty from the rival city of Nürnberg. They're served by a busy team of friendly waitresses dressed in Bavarian dirndls, who flit between the crowded tables with remarkable agility. In summer, tables are placed outside under a bright awning and in the shade of the nearby Frauenkirche. In winter the mellow dark-panel dining rooms provide relief from the cold. ⊠ *Frauenpl. 9, City Center* ☎ *089/220–385* ▤ *DC, MC, V* Ⓤ *Marienplatz (U-bahn and S-bahn).*

$–$$ ✕ **Spöckmeier.** This rambling Bavarian beer restaurant spread over three floors, including a snug *Keller* (cellar), is famous for its homemade Weiss-wurst. If you've just stopped in for a snack and don't fancy the fat breakfast sausage, order coffee and pretzels or, in the afternoon, a wedge of cheesecake. The menu changes daily and offers more than two dozen hearty main-course dishes and a choice of four draft beers. The house *Eintopf* (a rich broth of noodles and pork) is a meal in itself. The Spöckmeier is only 50 yards from Marienplatz; on sunny summer days tables are set outside in the car-free street. ⊠ *Rosenstr. 9, City Center* ☎ *089/268–088* ▤ *AE, DC, MC, V* Ⓤ *Marienplatz (U-bahn and S-bahn).*

$–$$ ✕ **Weinhaus Neuner.** Munich's oldest wine tavern serves good food as well as superior wines in its three nooks: the wood-panel restaurant, the Weinstübe, and the small bistro. The choice of food is remarkable, from nouvelle German to old-fashioned country. Specialties include home-smoked beef and salmon. ⊠ *Herzogspitalstr. 8, City Center* ☎ *089/260–3954* ▤ *AE, MC, V* ⊙ *Closed Sun.* Ⓤ *Marienplatz (U-bahn and S-bahn).*

¢–$$ ✕ **Andechser am Dom.** The vaulted frescoed ceiling and the old stone floor recall the Andechs monastery. The boldly Bavarian food—blood sausage with potatoes, Weisswurst in champagne—and fine selection of Andechs beers will quickly put you at ease. The covered terrace with a view of the Frauenkirche is a favorite meeting place, rain or shine, for shoppers, local businesspeople, and even the occasional VIP. ✉ *Weinstr. 7a* ☎ *089/ 298–481* ⊟ *AE, MC, V* Ⓤ *Marienplatz (U-bahn and S-bahn).*

¢–$$ ✕ **Buxs.** This self-service vegetarian place has a full range of salads, excellent entrées, freshly pressed juices and smoothies, and desserts that are worth the caloric splurge. On warm days you can sit outside and watch the Viktualienmarkt activities. It closes daily at 8 PM, so only early dinners are possible. ✉ *Frauenstr. 9, City Center* ☎ *089/291–9195* ⊟ *No credit cards* ⊘ *Closed Sun. No dinner Sat.* Ⓤ *Marienplatz (U-bahn and S-bahn).*

¢–$$ ✕ **Dürnbräu.** A fountain plays outside this picturesque old Bavarian inn. Inside, it's crowded and noisy, and you should expect to share a table (the 21-foot table in the middle of the place is a favorite). Your fellow diners will range from businesspeople to students. The food is resolutely traditional—try the cream of spinach soup and the boiled beef. ✉ *Dürnbräug. 2, City Center* ☎ *089/222–195* ⊟ *AE, DC, MC, V* Ⓤ *Isartor (S-bahn).*

$ ✕ **Vinorant Alter Hof.** If you don't make it to Franconia, then you can at least get a taste of the region's food and wine in this simply decorated restaurant nestled in the old vaulted cellar and first floor of Munich's castle. The wine bar in the cellar serves hearty Franconian snacks along with Franconian wines, which can be ordered in small amounts, allowing you to let your taste buds travel among Franconia's vineyards. It's the perfect place to recover after a concert at the nearby national theater or the Residenz. ✉ *Alter Hof 3, City Center* ☎ *089/2424–3733* ⊘ *Closed Sun.* ⊟ *AE, DC, V* Ⓤ *Marienplatz (U-bahn and S-bahn).*

¢–$ ✕ **Due passi.** This former dairy shop, now an Italian specialty shop, offers excellent Italian meals for a quick, stand-up lunch. There's a small but fine selection of fresh antipasti, pasta, and desserts such as the white chocolate mousse. You can eat at the high marble tables and counters, or take your food to go. Menus change daily. ✉ *Ledererstr. 11* ☎ *089/ 224–271* ⊟ *No credit cards* ⊘ *Closed Sat. afternoon and Sun.* Ⓤ *Isartor (S-bahn).*

¢–$ ✕ **Hofbräuhaus.** The pounding oompah band draws the curious into this father of all beer halls, where singing and shouting drinkers contribute to the earsplitting din. This is no place for the fainthearted, although a trip to Munich would be incomplete without a look. Upstairs is a quieter restaurant. In March, May, and September ask for one of the special, extra-strong seasonal beers (Starkbier, Maibock, Märzen), which complement the heavy, traditional Bavarian fare. ✉ *Am Platzl 9, City Center* ☎ *089/221–676 or 089/290–1360* ⌖ *Reservations not accepted* ⊟ *V* Ⓤ *Isartor (S-bahn).*

¢–$ ✕ **Hofer.** In this restaurant, in the old scribe's house (Schreiberhaus), oak-plank floors and a red color scheme recall old Munich without the heaviness. The cuisine is influenced by Austrian home cooking with such dishes as fried potatoes with spinach and fried eggs, several dumpling specialties, Angus steak, or irresistible apricot dumplings for dessert. A small selection of so-called retrofood is also available: a fake crabmeat sandwich, for example, is typical 1960s Germany. The inner courtyard is perfect for a meal on a hot summer day, and the vaulted cellar hosts live music

ON THE MENU

Snacks

Munich's snacking tradition is centuries old, and a tempting array of food is available almost any time of day or night. The generic term for snacks is Imbiss, and thanks to growing internationalism, these come in all shapes, sizes, and flavors, from the generic Wiener (hot dog) to the Turkish Döner sandwich (pressed and roasted lamb, beef, or turkey). Virtually every butcher offers some sort of Brotzeit snack, which can range from a modest sandwich to a steaming plate of goulash with potatoes and salad.

Some edibles come with social etiquette attached. Before noon, during what is sometimes called Frühschoppen ("early mug"), one eats Weisswurst, a tender minced-veal sausage—made fresh daily, steamed, and served with sweet mustard, a crisp roll or a pretzel, and Weissbier (wheat beer). As legend has it, this white sausage was invented in 1857 by a butcher who had a hangover and mixed the wrong ingredients. A plaque on a wall in Marienplatz marks where the "mistake" was made. Some people use a knife and fork to remove the edible part from the skin; the rougher crowd might indulge in auszuzeln, using tooth and jaw to suck the innards out of the Weisswurst.

Another favorite Bavarian specialty is Leberkäs—literally "liver cheese," although neither liver nor cheese is among its ingredients. It's a spicy meat loaf baked to a crusty turn each morning and served in succulent slabs throughout the day. A Leberkäs Semmel—a wedge of the meat loaf between two halves of a crispy bread roll slathered with a slightly sharp mustard—is the favorite Munich on-the-go snack.

Good Home Cooking

Old Munich inns feature solid regional specialties and gutbürgerliche Küche, loosely translated as good home cooking. The settings for such victuals include boisterous brewery restaurants, beer halls, beer gardens, rustic cellars, and Kneipen, restaurant-pubs serving any manner of food depending on the owner's fancy. The crowd here is generally a mix of students, white-collar workers, and chic artist-types.

A Real Meal

Typical, more substantial dishes in Munich include Tellerfleisch, boiled beef with freshly grated horseradish and boiled potatoes on the side, served on wooden plates (there is a similar dish called Tafelspitz). Among roasts, sauerbraten (beef) and Schweinebraten (roast pork) are accompanied by dumplings and sauerkraut. Hax'n (ham hocks) are roasted until they're crisp on the outside and juicy on the inside. They are served with sauerkraut and potato puree. Game in season (venison or boar, for instance) and duck are served with potato dumplings and red cabbage. As for fish, the region has not only excellent trout, served either smoked as an hors d'oeuvre or fried or boiled as an entrée, but also the perchlike Rencke from Lake Starnberg.

You'll also find soups, salads, casseroles, hearty stews, and what may well be the greatest variety and the highest quality of baked goods in Europe, including pretzels. And for dessert, indulge in a bowl of Bavarian cream, apple strudel, or Dampfnudel, a fluffy leavened-dough dumpling usually served with vanilla sauce.

on Friday and Saturday evenings. ⊠ *Burgstr. 5, City Center* ☎ *089/242–10445* ⊟ *AE, DC, MC* Ⓤ *Marienplatz (U-bahn and S-bahn).*

¢–$ ✕ **Orlandohaus.** The Orlandohaus is located next to the famous Hofbräuhaus on the bustling Platzl square. This large, airy establishment with richly gilded walls, vaulted ceilings, and a cozy beer cellar in the evening was named after composer Orlando di Lasso (1532–94), who once lived here. The specialty of the house is all-you-can-eat buffets, offering a large number of dishes, usually with a theme: Bavarian, international, brunch, and so on. Prices are moderate: lunch €13, afternoon coffee and cakes €3.10, Sunday brunch €15.95. ⊠ *Platzl 4, City Center* ☎ *089/2423–8030* ⊟ *AE, MC, V* Ⓤ *Isartor (S-bahn).*

¢–$ ✕ **Pfälzer Weinprobierstube.** A maze of stone-vaulted rooms, wooden tables, flickering candles, dirndl-clad waitresses, and a long list of wines add up to a storybook image of a timeless Germany. The wines are mostly from the *Pfalz* (Palatinate), as are many of the specialties on the limited menu. You'll find former chancellor Kohl's favorite dish, *Saumagen* (meat loaf, spiced with herbs and cooked in a pig's stomach). Beer drinkers, take note—beer is not served here. ⊠ *Residenzstr. 1, City Center* ☎ *089/225–628* ⌫ *Reservations not accepted* ⊟ *No credit cards* Ⓤ *Odeonsplatz (U-bahn).*

¢–$ ✕ **Prinz Myshkin.** This sophisticated vegetarian restaurant spices up pre-
Fodor'sChoice dictable cuisine by mixing Italian and Asian influences. You have a choice
★ of antipasti, homemade gnocchi, tofu, stir-fried dishes, and excellent wines. If you're not very hungry, you can request half portions. The airy room has a majestically vaulted ceiling, and there's always some art exhibited to feed the eye and mind. ⊠ *Hackenstr. 2, City Center* ☎ *089/265–596* ⊟ *MC, V* Ⓤ *Sendlinger Tor (U-bahn).*

¢–$ ✕ **Weisses Bräuhaus.** If you have developed a taste for Munich's Weissbier, this is the place to enjoy it. The flavorful Weisse (from the Schneider brewery) is served with hearty Bavarian dishes, mostly variations of pork and dumplings or cabbage. Some of Munich's friendlier waitresses work here—good-humored women in crisp black dresses, who appear to match the art nouveau style of the restaurant's beautifully restored interior. ⊠ *Tal 7, City Center* ☎ *089/299–875* ⊟ *No credit cards* Ⓤ *Isartor (S-bahn).*

Maxvorstadt

¢–$$ ✕ **Buxs.** A smaller version of the Buxs on Vitualienmarkt, this branch offers self-service of the same fare: salads, warm dishes, and excellent cakes. It's a good place to watch Munich's chic student crowd while taking a break from the nearby art museums. ⊠ *Amalienstr. 38, Maxvorstadt* ☎ *089/2802–9940* ⊟ *No credit cards* ⊗ *Closed Sat. afternoon and Sun.* Ⓤ *Theresienstrasse (U-bahn).*

$ ✕ **Cohen's.** Reviving the old Jewish Central European tradition of good, healthy cooking together with hospitality and good cheer seems to be the underlying principle at Cohen's. Dig into a few hearty latkes, a steaming plate of Chulend stew, or a standard gefilte fish doused with excellent Golan wine from Israel. The kitchen is open from 12:30 PM to about 10:30 PM, and if the atmosphere is good, patrons may hang out chattering until the wee hours. Klezmer singers perform on Friday evenings.

✉ *Theresienstr. 31, Maxvorstadt* ☎ *089/280–9545* 🖃 *AE, MC, V* Ⓤ *Theresienstrasse (U-bahn).*

Lehel

$-$$ ✕ **Gandl.** This Italian specialty shop, where you can buy various staples from vinegar to coffee, doubles as a very comfortable, relaxed restaurant during the day. Seating is a little crowded inside, but chairs and tables have a homelike feel and the service is excellent. It's just the place for a quick pastry or excellent antipasto misto before proceeding with the day's adventures. ✉ *St.-Anna-Pl. 1, Lehel* ☎ *089/2916–2525* 🖃 *V* ⊘ *Closed Sun. No dinner* Ⓤ *Lehel (U-bahn).*

¢-$ ✕ **Gasthaus Isarthor.** The old-fashioned *Wirtshaus,* where the innkeeper keeps his patrons in sight and the mood going, lives on in this old, wedge-shape dining room. For Rainer Menne, who comes from Salzburg, Austria, having a social mix at his simple wooden tables is the secret of a good establishment—actors, government officials, apprentice craftspersons, journalists, and retirees sit side by side. Besides pork roasts, roast beef with onions, boiled beef, and the like, the house specialty is the Augustiner beer from a wooden barrel, tapped once a day around 6 PM. When the barrel is empty, that's it for the day. ✉ *Kanalstr. 2, Lehel* ☎ *089/ 227–753* 🖃 *No credit cards* Ⓤ *Isartor (S-bahn).*

Schwabing

★ $$$$ ✕ **Tantris.** Chef Hans Haas, named the country's best chef by Germany's premier food critics in the past, has kept this restaurant among the top five dining establishments in Munich. You, too, will be impressed by the exotic nouvelle cuisine on the menu, including such specialties as shellfish and creamed potato soup, or roasted wood pigeon with scented rice. But you may wish to ignore the bare concrete surroundings and the garish orange-and-yellow decor. ✉ *Johann-Fichte-Str. 7, Schwabing* ☎ *089/361–9590* 🍴 *Reservations essential* 🎩 *Jacket and tie* 🖃 *AE, DC, MC, V* ⊘ *Closed Sun.* Ⓤ *Münchener Freiheit (U-bahn).*

$$ ✕ **Bistro Cezanne.** You're in for French-Provençal dining at this truly Gallic bistro-restaurant in the heart of Munich's former bohemian quarter. Owner-chef Patrick Geay learned his craft from some of Europe's best teachers. His regularly changing blackboard menu offers the freshest market products, with vegetables prepared as only the French can do. Among the fish dishes, the scallops melt in the mouth, while the coq au vin will conquer the greatest hungers. Reservations are advised. ✉ *Konradstr. 1, Schwabing* ☎ *089/391–805* 🖃 *AE, DC, MC, V* Ⓤ *Giselastrasse (U-bahn).*

¢-$ ✕ **Max-Emanuel-Brauerei.** This historic old brewery tavern is a great value, with Bavarian dishes rarely costing more than €10; at lunchtime that amount will easily cover the cost of an all-you-can-eat buffet including a couple of beers. The main dining room has a stage, and there's often a cabaret or jazz concert during dinner. In summer take a table outside in the secluded little beer garden tucked amid the apartment blocks. ✉ *Adalbertstr. 33, Schwabing* ☎ *089/271–5158* 🖃 *AE, MC* Ⓤ *Josephsplatz (U-bahn).*

Leopoldvorstadt

¢–$ ✕ **Augustiner Keller.** This 19th-century establishment is the flagship beer restaurant of one of Munich's oldest breweries. The menu changes daily and offers Bavarian specialties, but try to order *Tellerfleisch* (boiled beef with horseradish), served on a big wooden board. Follow that with a *Dampfnudel* (yeast dumpling served with custard), and you probably won't feel hungry again for the next 24 hours. ✉ *Arnulfstr. 52, Leopold-vorstadt* ☎ *089/594–393* ▭ *AE, MC* Ⓤ *Hauptbahnhof (U-bahn and S-bahn).*

¢–$ ✕ **Café am Beethovenplatz.** Live music accompanies excellent fare every evening. An international breakfast menu is served daily (on Sunday with live classical music), followed by suitably creative lunch and dinner menus. The pork is supplied by a farm where the free-range pigs are fed only the best natural fodder—so the *Schweinsbraten* (roast pig) is recommended. Reservations are advised as a young and intellectual crowd fills the tables quickly. ✉ *Goethestr. 51 (at Beethovenpl.), Leopoldvorstadt* ☎ *089/5440–4348* ▭ *AE, MC, V* Ⓤ *Goetheplatz (U-bahn).*

WHERE TO STAY

Though Munich has a vast number of hotels in all price ranges, many are fully booked year-round; this is a major trade and convention city as well as a prime tourist destination. If you're visiting during any of the major trade fairs such as the ispo (sports, fashion) in February, the IHM (crafts) in mid-March, or Oktoberfest at the end of September, make reservations at least six months in advance.

Some of the large, very expensive hotels that cater to expense-account business travelers have very attractive weekend discount rates—sometimes as much as 50% below normal prices. Conversely, regular rates can go up during big trade fairs.

Munich's two tourist information offices—at the main railway station and in the city center (Marienplatz, in the Rathaus)—make hotel bookings. Telephone lines are often busy, so your best bet is to visit one of the offices in person.

	WHAT IT COSTS In Euros			
	$$$$	**$$$**	**$$**	**$**	**¢**
FOR 2 PEOPLE	over €225	€175–€225	€100–€175	€50–€100	under €50

Hotel prices are for two people in a standard double room, including tax and service.

City Center

$$$$ ▦ **Bayerischer Hof.** Germany's most respected family-owned hotel, the Bayerischer Hof began its rich history by hosting Ludwig I's guests. To this day, it still plays host to VIPs and international political confabs. Public rooms are grandly laid out with marble, antiques, and oil paintings. Laura Ashley–decorated rooms look out to the city's skyline of tow-

ers. Nightlife is built into the hotel, with Trader Vic's bar, and dancing at the Night Club. ✉ *Promenadepl. 2–6, City Center, D–80333* ☎ *089/ 21200* 🖷 *089/212–0906* ⊕ *www.bayerischerhof.de* ⟿ *337 rooms, 58 suites* ⚒ *3 restaurants, cable TV with movies and video games, pool, hair salon, massage, sauna, bar, nightclub, Internet, meeting rooms, parking (fee), some pets allowed (fee), no-smoking rooms* ⊟ *AE, DC, MC, V* ⊺⊙⊦ *BP* Ⓤ *Karlsplatz (U-bahn and S-bahn).*

★ **\$\$\$\$** ⊞ **Kempinski Hotel Vier Jahreszeiten München.** The Kempinski has been playing host to the world's wealthy and titled for more than a century. It has an unbeatable location on Maximilianstrasse, Munich's premier shopping street, only a few minutes' walk from the heart of the city. Elegance and luxury set the tone throughout; many rooms have handsome antique pieces. The Vier Jahreszeiten Eck restaurant is on the main floor. The afternoon tea in the poshly decorated foyer is a special treat. ✉ *Maximilianstr. 17, City Center, D–80539* ☎ *089/21250, 516/794– 2670 Kempinski Reservation Service* 🖷 *089/2125–2000* ⊕ *www. Kempinski-Vierjahreszeiten.de* ⟿ *268 rooms, 48 suites* ⚒ *Restaurant, cable TV with movies, pool, health club, massage, sauna, piano bar, meeting rooms, car rental, parking (fee), some pets allowed (fee), no-smoking rooms* ⊟ *AE, DC, MC, V* ⊺⊙⊦ *BP* Ⓤ *Odeonsplatz (U-bahn).*

\$\$–\$\$\$\$ ⊞ **Cortiina.** Munich's latest designer hotel, built and run by Rudi Krull, Munich's top design guru, and Albert Weinzierl, follows the minimalist gospel. The reception is in sleek gray stone, with indirect green-tinted lighting. Along one wall a high-tech gas fireplace can be switched on and off like a TV. For guests, the emphasis is on subtle luxury—fresh flowers, mattresses made from natural rubber, sheets made of untreated cotton. The rooms are paneled in dark moor oak and come with all the amenities. The hotel has no fitness center, but the Elixir, 15 minutes away on foot at Lenbachplatz, gives special discounts for hotel guests. ✉ *Ledererstr. 8, City Center, D–80331* ☎ *089/242–2490* 🖷 *089/2422–49100* ⊕ *www.cortiina.com* ⟿ *54 rooms* ⚒ *In-room data ports, cable TV, bar, parking (fee), some pets allowed (fee), no-smoking rooms* ⊟ *AE, DC, MC, V* ⊺⊙⊦ *BP* Ⓤ *Isartor (S-bahn).*

\$\$–\$\$\$\$ ⊞ **Platzl.** The Platzl, a privately owned enterprise, has won awards and wide recognition for its ecologically aware management, which uses heat recyclers in the kitchen, environmentally friendly detergents, recyclable materials, waste separation, and other ecofriendly practices. It stands in the historic heart of Munich, near the famous Hofbräuhaus beer hall and a couple of minutes' walk from Marienplatz and many other landmarks. Its Pfistermühle restaurant, with 16th-century vaulting, is one of the area's oldest and most historic establishments. ✉ *Sparkassenstr. 10, City Center, D–80331* ☎ *089/237–030, 800/448–8355 in U.S.* 🖷 *089/2370–3800* ⊕ *www.platzl.de* ⟿ *167 rooms* ⚒ *Restaurant, cable TV with movies, gym, sauna, steam room, bar, parking (fee), some pets allowed (fee), no-smoking rooms; no a/c in some rooms* ⊟ *AE, DC, MC, V* ⊺⊙⊦ *BP* Ⓤ *Marienplatz (U-bahn and S-bahn).*

\$\$–\$\$\$\$ ⊞ **Torbräu.** In this snug hotel you'll sleep under the shadow of one of Munich's ancient city gates—the 14th-century Isartor. The location is excellent, as it's midway between the Marienplatz and the Deutsches Museum (and around the corner from the Hofbräuhaus). The hotel has been run by the same family for more than a century. Comfortable rooms are decorated in a plush and ornate Italian style. Its Italian restaurant, La Famiglia, is one of the best in the area. ✉ *Tal 41, City Center, D–80331* ☎ *089/242–340* 🖷 *089/2423–4235* ⊕ *www.torbraeu.de* ⇥ *89 rooms, 3 suites* ⚐ *Restaurant, café, in-room data ports, cable TV, Internet, business services, meeting rooms, some pets allowed (fee), no-smoking rooms* ▤ *AE, MC, V* ⧉ *BP* Ⓤ *Isartor (S-bahn).*

Isarvorstadt

$$–$$$$ 🏨 **Admiral.** The small, privately owned Admiral enjoys a quiet side-street
location and its own garden, close to the Isar River and Deutsches Mu-
★ seum. Many of the simply furnished and warmly decorated bedrooms have a balcony overlooking the garden. Bowls of fresh fruit are part of the friendly welcome awaiting guests. The breakfast buffet is a dream, complete with homemade jams, fresh bread, and Italian and French delicacies. ✉ *Kohlstr. 9, Isarvorstadt, D–80469* ☎ *089/216–350* 🖷 *089/293–674* ⊕ *www.hotel-admiral.de* ⇥ *33 rooms* ⚐ *In-room data ports, cable TV, bar, parking (fee), some pets allowed, no-smoking rooms; no a/c* ▤ *AE, DC, MC, V* ⧉ *BP* Ⓤ *Isartor (S-bahn).*

$$–$$$$ 🏨 **Advokat.** If you value the clean lines of modern taste over plush luxury, this is the hotel for you. It's within a residential neighborhood that's an easy walk from the Marienplatz and a shorter one from the subway. Between outings you can snack on the fruit plate that welcomes you upon arrival. ✉ *Baaderstr. 1, Isarvorstadt, D–80469* ☎ *089/216–310* 🖷 *089/216–3190* ⊕ *www.hotel-advokat.de* ⇥ *50 rooms* ⚐ *In-room data ports, cable TV, parking (fee), some pets allowed, no-smoking rooms; no a/c* ▤ *AE, DC, MC, V* ⧉ *BP* Ⓤ *Isartor (S-bahn).*

$$ 🏨 **Olympic.** The English-style lobby, with its leather easy chairs and mahogany fittings, is an attractive introduction to this friendly small hotel, a beautifully converted turn-of-the-20th-century mansion, amid the bars and boutiques of the colorful district between Sendlinger Tor and Isartor. Most of the rooms look out over a quiet interior courtyard. Do not expect constant and fawning care: the style of the hotel is casual; the idea is to make the guest feel really at home. ✉ *Hans-Sachs-Str. 4, Isarvorstadt, D–80469* ☎ *089/231–890* 🖷 *089/2318–9199* ⊕ *www. olympic.de* ⇥ *38 rooms, 3 apartments* ⚐ *In-room data ports, cable TV, parking (fee), some pets allowed (fee); no a/c* ▤ *AE, DC, MC, V* ⧉ *BP* Ⓤ *Sendlinger Tor (U-bahn).*

Maxvorstadt

$$–$$$ 🏨 **Erzgiesserei Europe.** Though this hotel is in a residential section of the city, the nearby subway whisks you in five minutes to Karlsplatz, convenient to the pedestrian shopping area and the main railway station. Rooms in this attractive, modern hotel are particularly bright, decorated in soft pastels with good reproductions on the walls. The cobblestone garden café is a haven of peace. ✉ *Erzgiessereistr. 15, Maxvorstadt, D–80335* ☎ *089/126–820* 🖷 *089/123–6198* ⊕ *www.top-hotels.de/ erzeurope* ⇥ *105 rooms, 1 suite* ⚐ *Restaurant, café, in-room data ports, cable TV with movies, bar, parking (fee), some pets allowed (fee),* *no-smoking rooms; no a/c* ⊟ *AE, DC, MC, V* |◎| *BP* Ⓤ *Stiglmaierplatz (U-bahn).*

$–$$ 🏢 **Hotel Amba.** The Amba, which is right next to the train station, has clean, bright rooms, good service, no expensive frills, and everything you need to plug and play. The lobby, with a small bar, invites you to relax in a Mediterranean atmosphere of wicker sofas with bright-color upholstery. No sooner have you enjoyed a solid breakfast at the buffet (with sparkling wine) on the first floor overlooking the station than you'll be out on the town visiting the nearby sights on foot. Budget travelers should ask for rooms without bathrooms. ⊠ *Arnulfstr. 20, Maxvorstadt, D–80335* ☎ *089/545–140* 🖷 *089/5451–1555* ⊕ *www.hotel-amba.de* 📞 *86 rooms* ♨ *Cable TV with movies, some pets allowed (fee), no-smoking rooms; no a/c* ⊟ *AE, DC, MC, V* |◎| *BP* Ⓤ *Hauptbahnhof (U-bahn and S-bahn).*

★ $ 🏢 **Hotel Pension Am Siegestor.** This modest but very appealing pension takes up three floors of a fin-de-siècle mansion between the Siegestor monument, on Leopoldstrasse, and the university. An ancient elevator with a glass door brings you to the fourth-floor reception desk. Most of the simply furnished rooms face the impressive Arts Academy across the street. Rooms on the fifth floor are particularly cozy, tucked up under the eaves. ⊠ *Akademiestr. 5, Maxvorstadt, D–80799* ☎ *089/399–550 or 089/ 399–551* 🖷 *089/343–050* 📞 *20 rooms* ♨ *No room phones; no TV in some rooms, no a/c* ⊟ *No credit cards* |◎| *CP* Ⓤ *Universität (U-bahn).*

Schwabing

$$–$$$ 🏢 **Biederstein.** This hotel is not the prettiest from the outside—a modern, uninspired block—but it seems to want to fit into its old Schwabing surroundings. At the rim of the Englischer Garten, the Biederstein has many advantages: peace and quiet; excellent service; and comfortable, well-appointed rooms that were carefully renovated. Guests are requested to smoke on the balconies, not inside. ⊠ *Keferstr. 18, Schwabing, D–80335* ☎ *089/389–9970* 🖷 *089/3899–97389* 📞 *34 rooms, 7 suites* ♨ *Cable TV, bar, free parking, some pets allowed (fee); no a/c* ⊟ *AE, DC, MC, V* |◎| *BP.*

★ $–$$ 🏢 **Gästehaus am Englischen Garten.** Reserve well in advance for a room at this popular converted water mill, more than 200 years old, adjoining the Englischer Garten. The hotel is only a five-minute walk from the bars, shops, and restaurants of Schwabing. Be sure to ask for one of the 12 nostalgically old-fashioned rooms in the main building, which has a garden on an island in the old millrace; a modern annex down the road has 13 apartments, all with cooking facilities. In summer, breakfast is served on the terrace of the main house. ⊠ *Liebergesellstr. 8, Schwabing, D–80802* ☎ *089/383–9410* 🖷 *089/3839–4133* ⊕ *www. hotelenglischergarten.de* 📞 *12 rooms, 6 with bath or shower; 13 apartments* ♨ *Cable TV, in-room data ports, free parking, some pets allowed (fee); no a/c* ⊟ *AE, DC, MC, V* |◎| *BP.*

Leopoldvorstadt

$$–$$$$ 🏢 **Eden-Hotel Wolff.** Chandeliers and dark-wood paneling in the public rooms contribute to the old-fashioned elegance of this downtown favorite. It's directly across the street from the train station and near the Theresienwiese fairgrounds. The rooms are well furnished with large comfortable beds, and the colors are relaxing pastels. You can dine on excellent Bavarian specialties in the intimate wood-panel Zirbelstube restaurant. ⊠ *Arnulfstr. 4, Leopoldvorstadt, D–80335* ☎ *089/551–150* 🖷 *089/5511–5555* ⊕ *www.ehw.de* ⟿ *209 rooms, 7 suites* △ *Restaurant, café, cable TV with movies, gym, bar, Internet, meeting rooms, parking (fee), some pets allowed (fee); no a/c in some rooms* ⊟ *AE, DC, MC, V* ▮❍▮ *BP* Ⓤ *Hauptbahnhof (U-bahn and S-bahn).*

$–$$$$ 🖭 **Creatif Hotel Elephant.** Tucked away on a quiet street near the train station and a 10-minute walk to the city center, this hotel appeals to a wide range of travelers, from businesspeople on the fly to tourists on a budget. The rooms are simple, clean, and quiet. A bright color scheme in the reception and breakfast room creates a cheery atmosphere. Note that prices skyrocket during Octoberfest. ⊠ *Lämmerstr. 6, Leopoldvorstadt, D–80335* ☎ *089/555–785* 🖷 *089/550–1746* ⟿ *40 rooms* △ *Cable TV, some pets allowed; no a/c* ⊟ *AE, MC, V* ▮❍▮ *BP* Ⓤ *Hauptbahnhof (U-bahn and S-bahn).*

$–$$$ 🖭 **Brack.** Oktoberfest revelers value the Brack's proximity to the beer festival grounds, and its location—on a busy, tree-lined thoroughfare just south of the city center—is handy for city attractions. Rooms are furnished in light, friendly veneers and are soundproof (a useful feature during Oktoberfest) and have amenities such as hair dryers. The buffet breakfast will set you up for the day. ⊠ *Lindwurmstr. 153, Leopoldvorstadt, D–80337* ☎ *089/747–2550* 🖷 *089/7472–5599* ⊕ *www.hotelbrack.de* ⟿ *50 rooms* △ *In-room data ports, cable TV with movies, free parking, some pets allowed; no a/c* ⊟ *AE, DC, MC, V* ▮❍▮ *BP* Ⓤ *Poccistrasse (U-bahn).*

★ $–$$ 🖭 **Hotel Mirabell.** This family-run hotel is used to American tourists who appreciate the friendly service, central location (between the main railway station and the Oktoberfest fairgrounds), and reasonable room rates. Three apartments are for small groups or families. Rooms are furnished in modern light woods and bright prints. Breakfast is the only meal served, but snacks can be ordered at the bar. Prices are much higher during trade fairs and Oktoberfest. ⊠ *Landwehrstr. 42, entrance on Goethestr., Leopoldvorstadt, D–80336* ☎ *089/549–1740* 🖷 *089/550–3701* ⊕ *www.hotelmirabell.de* ⟿ *65 rooms, 3 apartments* △ *In-room data ports, cable TV with movies, bar, some pets allowed (fee), no-smoking rooms* ⊟ *AE, MC, V* ▮❍▮ *BP* Ⓤ *Hauptbahnhof (U-bahn and S-bahn).*

$–$$ 🖭 **Hotel-Pension Mariandl.** The American armed forces commandeered this turn-of-the-20th-century neo-Gothic mansion in May 1945 and established Munich's first postwar nightclub, the Femina, on the ground floor (now the charming café-restaurant Café am Beethovenplatz). Most rooms are mansion size, with high ceilings and large windows overlooking a leafy avenue. The Oktoberfest grounds and the main railway station are both a 10-minute walk away. ⊠ *Goethestr. 51, Leopoldvorstadt, D–80336* ☎ *089/534–108* 🖷 *089/5440–4396* ⊕ *www.hotelmariandl.*

com 🛏 *28 rooms* ⚄ *Restaurant, some pets allowed; no a/c, no room phones, no room TVs* ▭ *AE, DC, MC, V* ⑩ *BP* Ⓤ *Hauptbahnhof (U-bahn and S-bahn).*

$–$$ 🏨 **Kurpfalz.** Visitors have praised the friendly welcome and service they receive at this centrally placed and affordable lodging. Rooms are comfortable, if furnished in a manner only slightly better than functional, and all are equipped with satellite TV. Breakfast is included. The main train station and Oktoberfest grounds are both within a 10-minute walk, and the area is rich in restaurants, bars, and movie theaters. ✉ *Schwantalerstr. 121, Leopoldvorstadt, D–80339* ☎ *089/540–9860* 🖷 *089/5409–8811* ⊕ *www.kurpfalz-hotel.de* 🛏 *44 rooms with shower* ⚄ *In-room data ports, cable TV, bar, some pets allowed, no-smoking rooms; no a/c* ▭ *AE, MC, V* ⑩ *BP* Ⓤ *Hackerbrücke (S-bahn).*

Isarvorstadt

★ **$–$$** 🏨 **Hotel-Pension Schmellergarten.** This genuine family business will make you feel right at home and is very popular with young budget travelers. The little place is on a quiet street just off Lindwurmstrasse, a few minutes' walk from the Theresienwiese. The Poccistrasse subway station is around the corner to take you into the center of town. ✉ *Schmellerstr. 20, Isarvorstadt, D–80337* ☎ *089/773–157* 🖷 *089/725–6886* 📧 *milankuhn@web.de* 🛏 *14 rooms* ⚄ *Some pets allowed; no a/c* ▭ *No credit cards* ⑩ *CP* Ⓤ *Poccistrasse (U-bahn).*

Lehel

$$–$$$$ 🏨 **Hotel Concorde.** The privately owned Concorde is right in the middle of Munich and yet very peaceful owing to its location on a narrow sidestreet. The nearest S-bahn station (Isartor) is only a two-minute walk away. Rooms in one tract are done in pastel tones and light woods; in the other tract they tend to be somewhat darker and more rustic. Fresh flowers and bright prints add a colorful touch. A large breakfast buffet is served in a stylish, mirrored dining room. ✉ *Herrnstr. 38, Lehel, D–80539* ☎ *089/224–515* 🖷 *089/228–3282* ⊕ *www.concorde-muenchen.de* 🛏 *67 rooms, 4 suites* ⚄ *In-room data ports, cable TV, parking (fee), some pets allowed (fee), no-smoking rooms; no a/c* ▭ *AE, DC, MC, V* ⑩ *BP* Ⓤ *Isartor (S-bahn).*

$$–$$$$ 🏨 **Opera.** In the quiet residential district of Lehel (St.-Anna-Strasse is a
Fodor'sChoice cul-de-sac accessed through the neo-Renaissance arcades of the Ethno-
★ graphic Museum), the Opera offers rooms decorated in an elegant style—lots of Empire, some art deco. Some rooms have glassed-in balconies. The service is perhaps the best in Munich. Instead of having mini-bars, guests can order room service round the clock. Enjoy summer breakfast in the little back courtyard decorated with orange and lemon trees. ✉ *St. Anna-Strasse 10, City Center, D–80331* ☎ *089/210–4940* 🖷 *089/2104–9477* ⊕ *www.hotel-opera.de* 🛏 *25 rooms* ⚄ *In-room data ports, cable TV, bar, some pets allowed, no-smoking rooms; no a/c* ▭ *AE, DC, MC, V* ⑩ *BP* Ⓤ *Lehel (U-bahn).*

$$–$$$ 🏨 **Adria.** This modern, comfortable hotel is ideally set in the middle of Munich's museum quarter. Rooms are large and tastefully decorated, with old prints on the pale-pink walls, Oriental rugs on the floors, and flowers beside the double beds. A spectacular breakfast buffet (including a glass of sparkling wine) is included in the room rate. There's no hotel restaurant, but the area is rich in good restaurants, bistros, and bars. ☒ *Liebigstr. 8a, Lehel, D–80538* ☎ *089/242–1170* 🖷 *089/ 2421–17999* ⊕ *www.adria-muenchen.de* ↩ *43 rooms* 🛆 *In-room data ports, cable TV, some pets allowed (fee), no-smoking rooms; no a/c* ☰ *AE, MC, V* ⦿ *BP* Ⓤ *Lehel (U-bahn).*

★ **$** 🏠 **Hotel-Pension Beck.** American and British visitors receive a particularly warm welcome from the Anglophile owner of the rambling, friendly Beck (she and her pet canary are a regular presence). Bright carpeting, with matching pinewood furniture, gives rooms a cheerful touch. The pension has no elevator but does have a prime location convenient to the museums on Prinzregentenstrasse and to the Englischer Garten. ☒ *Thierschstr. 36, Lehel, D–80538* ☎ *089/220–708 or 089/225–768* 🖷 *089/220–925* ⊕ *www.bst-online.de/pension.beck* ↩ *44 rooms, 7 with shower* 🛆 *Some in-room data ports, cable TV, some pets allowed; no a/c* ☰ *MC, V* ⦿ *CP* Ⓤ *Lehel (U-bahn).*

Nymphenburg

$–$$ 🏠 **Kriemhild.** If you're traveling with children, you'll appreciate this welcoming, family-run pension in a quiet western suburb near parks and gardens. It's a 10-minute walk from Schloss Nymphenburg and around the corner from the Hirschgarten Park, site of one of the city's best beer gardens. The tram ride (No. 16 or 17 to Kriemhildenstrasse stop) from the train station is 10 minutes. The buffet breakfast is included in the rate. ☒ *Guntherstr. 16, Nymphenburg, D–80639* ☎ *089/171–1170* 🖷 *089/1711–1755* ⊕ *www.kriemhild.de* ↩ *18 rooms* 🛆 *In-room data ports, cable TV, bar, free parking, some pets allowed; no a/c* ☰ *AE, MC, V* ⦿ *BP.*

Outer Munich

$$–$$$$ 🏠 **ArabellaSheraton Grand Hotel.** The building itself may raise a few eyebrows. It stands on a slight elevation and is not the most shapely on the Munich skyline. What goes on inside, however, is sheer five-star luxury. Guests are greeted with a glass of champagne, and snacks and drinks are available round the clock in the Towers Lounge. The excellent restaurant Ente vom Lehel has come to roost here as well. And if you'd like to add a special Bavarian flavor to your stay, book one of the 60 "Bavarian rooms." ☒ *Arabellastr. 5, Bogenhausen, D–81925* ☎ *089/ 92640* 🖷 *089/9264–8699* ⊕ *www.arabellasheraton.de* ↩ *644 rooms, 31 suites* 🛆 *2 restaurants, cable TV with movies, pool, hair salon, sauna, steam room, bars, Internet, business services, meeting rooms, free parking, some pets allowed (fee), no-smoking rooms* ☰ *AE, DC, MC, V* ⦿ *BP* Ⓤ *Richard-Strauss-Strasse (U-bahn).*

$$–$$$$ 🏠 **Park-Hotel Theresienhöhe.** The Park-Hotel claims that none of its rooms are less than 400 square feet. Suites are larger than many luxury apartments, and some of them come with small kitchens. The sleek, modern rooms are mostly decorated with light woods and pastel-color fabrics and carpeting; larger rooms and suites get a lot of light, thanks to the floor-to-ceiling windows. Families are particularly welcome, and a baby-sitting service is provided. There's no in-house restaurant, but you can order in. ⊠ *Parkstr. 31, Westend, D–80339* ☎ *089/519–950* 🖷 *089/5199–5420* ↪ *35 rooms* ⚐ *Some in-room data ports, cable TV, bar, baby-sitting, some pets allowed, no-smoking rooms; no a/c* ☰ *AE, DC, MC, V* ⫯⊙⫯ *BP* Ⓤ *Theresienwiese (U-bahn).*

$$ ⊡ **Jagdschloss.** This century-old hunting lodge in Munich's leafy Obermenzing suburb is a delightful hotel. The rustic look has been retained with lots of original woodwork and white stucco. Many of the comfortable pastel-tone bedrooms have wooden balconies with flower boxes bursting with color. In the beamed restaurant or sheltered beer garden you'll be served Bavarian specialties by a staff dressed in traditional lederhosen (shorts in summer, breeches in winter). ⊠ *Alte Allee 21, D–81245 München-Obermenzing* ☎ *089/820–820* 🖷 *089/8208–2100* ⊕ *www. weber-gastronomie.de* ↪ *22 rooms, 1 suite* ⚐ *Restaurant, cable TV, beer garden, playground, free parking, some pets allowed; no a/c* ☰ *MC, V* ⫯⊙⫯ *BP.*

$$ ⊡ **Rotkreuzplatz.** This small, family-run business on lively Rotkreuzplatz is five minutes by subway (U-1 and U-7) from the main train station. Breakfast in the neighboring café is included in the price. There are no grand amenities, but a pleasant stay is guaranteed. The café and many rooms look out over one of Munich's most original squares, Rotkreuzplatz, where people from all walks of life meet around a modern fountain. ⊠ *Rotkreuzpl. 2, Neuhausen, D–80634* ☎ *089/139–9080* 🖷 *089/ 166–469* ⊕ *www.hotel-rotkreuzplatz.de* ↪ *56 rooms* ⚐ *In-room data ports, cable TV, free parking, some pets allowed, no-smoking rooms; no a/c* ☰ *AE, DC, MC, V* ⫯⊙⫯ *BP* Ⓤ *Rotkreuzplatz (U-bahn).*

NIGHTLIFE & THE ARTS

The Arts

Bavaria's capital has an enviable reputation as an artistic hot spot. Details of concerts and theater performances are listed in *Vorschau* and *Monatsprogramm,* booklets available at most hotel reception desks, newsstands, and tourist offices. The English-language magazine *Munich Found* is also a good source. Otherwise, just keep your eye open for advertising pillars and posters especially on church walls. Some hotels will make ticket reservations, or you can book through ticket agencies in the city center, such as **Max Hieber Konzertkasse** (⊠ Liebfrauenstr. 1, City Center ☎ 089/2900–8014). Two **Zentraler Kartenverkauf** (⊠ City Center ☎ 089/264–620) ticket kiosks are in the underground concourse at Marienplatz. The **Abendzeitung Schalterhalle** (⊠ Sendlingerstr. 10, City Center ☎ 089/267–024) is a ticket service offered by one of Munich's two rags, the *Abendzeitung.* It's open weekdays 8:30–7, Saturday 10–4. The **Residenz Bücherstube** (⊠ Residenzstr. 1, City Center ☎ 089/220–868) sells only concert tickets. Tickets for performances at the Altes Residenztheater/Cuvilliés-Theater, Bavarian State Theater–New Residence Theater, Nationaltheater, Prinzregententheater, and Staatheater am Gartnerplatz are sold at the **central box office** (⊠ Maximilianstr. 11, City Center ☎ 089/2185–1920). It's open weekdays 10–6, Saturday 10–1, and one hour before curtain time. One ticket agency, **München Ticket** (☎ 089/5481–8181 ⊕ www.muenchenticket.de), has a German-language Web site where tickets for most Munich theaters can be booked.

Concerts

Munich and music go together. The first Saturday in May, the **Long Night of Music** (⊠ €10 ☎ 089/5481–8181) is devoted to live performances through the night by untold numbers of groups, from heavy-metal bands to medieval choirs, at more than 100 locations throughout the city. One ticket covers everything, including transportation on special buses between locations.

Munich's world-class concert hall, the **Gasteig Culture Center** (⊠ Rosenheimerstr. 5, Haidhausen ☎ 089/480–980), is a lavish brick complex standing high above the Isar River, east of downtown. Its Philharmonic Hall is the permanent home of the Munich Philharmonic Orchestra. The city has three other principal orchestras, and the leading choral ensembles are the Munich Bach Choir, the Munich Motettenchor, and Musica Viva, the last specializing in contemporary music. The choirs perform mostly in city churches.

The Bavarian Radio Symphony Orchestra performs at the **Bayerischer Rundfunk** (⊠ Rundfunkpl. 1, Maxvorstadt ☎ 089/558–080) and also at other city venues. The box office is open Monday–Thursday 9–noon and 2–4, Friday 9–noon.

The Bavarian State Orchestra is based at the **Nationaltheater** (Also called the Bayerische Staatsoper; ⊠ Opernpl., City Center ☎ 089/2185–1920). The Kurt Graunke Symphony Orchestra performs at the romantic art nouveau **Staatstheater am Gärtnerplatz** (⊠ Gärtnerpl. 3, Isarvorstadt ☎ 089/2185–1960).

Herkulessaal in der Residenz (⊠ Hofgarten, City Center ☎ 089/2906–7263) is a leading orchestral and recital venue. Free concerts featuring conservatory students are given at the **Hochschule für Musik** (⊠ Arcisstr. 12, Maxvorstadt ☎ 089/128–901).

Munich's major pop-rock concert venue is the **Olympiahalle** (⊠ U-3 Olympiazentrum stop, Georg-Brauchle-Ring ☎ 089/3061–3577). The box office, at the ice stadium, is open weekdays 10–6 and Saturday 10–3. You can also book by calling **München Ticket** (☎ 089/5481–8181).

Opera, Ballet & Musicals

Munich's Bavarian State Opera Company and its ballet ensemble perform at the **Nationaltheater** (⊠ Opernpl., City Center ☎ 089/2185–1920). The **Staatstheater am Gärtnerplatz** (⊠ Gärtnerpl. 3, Isarvorstadt ☎ 089/2185–1960) presents a less ambitious but nevertheless high-quality program of opera, ballet, operetta, and musicals.

Theater

Munich has scores of theaters and variety-show venues, although most productions will be largely impenetrable if your German is shaky. Listed here are all the better-known theaters, as well as some of the smaller and more progressive spots. Note that most theaters are closed during July and August.

Altes Residenztheater/Cuvilliés-Theater (⊠ Max-Joseph-Pl., entrance on Residenzstr., City Center ☎ 089/2185–1940). This is an intimate stage for compact opera productions such as Mozart's *Singspiele* and classic and contemporary plays (Arthur Miller met with great success here).

Amerika Haus (America House; ⊠ Karolinenpl. 3, Maxvorstadt ☎ 089/343–803). A very active American company, the American Drama Group Europe presents regular English-language productions here.

Bayerisches Staatsschauspiel/Neues Residenztheater (Bavarian State Theater–New Residence Theater; ⊠ Max-Joseph-Pl., City Center ☎ 089/2185–1940). This is Munich's leading stage for classic playwrights such as Goethe, Schiller, Lessing, Shakespeare, and Chekhov.

Deutsches Theater (⊠ Schwanthalerstr. 13, Leopoldvorstadt ☎ 089/5523–4444). Musicals, revues, balls, and big-band shows take place here. The box office is open weekdays noon–6 and Saturday 10–1:30.

Feierwerk (⊠ Hansastr. 39, Westend ☎ 089/743–1340) has four venues that present a wide range of musical fare, cabaret, and experimental art shows.

The Carl-Orff Saal and the Black Box theaters, in the **Gasteig Culture Center,** occasionally present English-language plays. The box office is open weekdays 10:30–6 and Saturday 10–2.

The **Komödie im Bayerischen Hof** (⊠ Bayerischer Hof Hotel, Promenadenpl., City Center ☎ 089/292–810) offers light theatrical fare. The box office is open Monday–Saturday 11–8 and Sunday 3–8.

Münchner Kammerspiele-Schauspielhaus (⊠ Maximilianstr. 26, City Center ☎ 089/2333–7000). A city-funded rival to the nearby state-backed Staatliches Schauspiel, this theater of international renown presents the classics as well as new works by contemporary playwrights.

For a spectrum of good jazz, chánsons, and café theater, check out the **Pasinger Fabrik** (⊠ August-Exter-Str. 1, Pasing ☎ 089/8292–9079), which also offers live music with breakfast, lunch, dinner ($–$$), or late-night drinks. To get there, take any S-bahn out to Pasing (exit the station to the north). The box office is open Thursday–Saturday 4:30–8:30 PM.

Prinzregententheater (⊠ Prinzregentenpl. 12, City Center ☎ 089/2185–2899). Munich's art nouveau theater, an audience favorite, presents not only opera but musicals and musical gala events.

CHILDREN'S
THEATER
Munich has several theaters for children. Because pantomime plays such a strong part in the repertoire, the language problem tends to disappear. Munich is the winter quarters of the big-top **Circus Krone** (⊠ Zirkus-Krone-Str. 1–6, Leopoldvorstadt ☎ 089/545–8000), which performs from Christmas until the end of March. The **Münchner Marionettentheater** (⊠ Blumenstr. 32, City Center ☎ 089/265–712) lets its puppets chew on highbrow material, notably works of Carl Orff. The

Münchner Theater für Kinder (✉ Dachauerstr. 46, Neuhausen ☎089/595–454) will keep the young ones happy with fairy tales and traditional pieces such as *Pinocchio*. The puppet shows at **Otto Bille's Marionettenbühne** (✉ Bereiterangerstr. 15, Au ☎089/150–2168) are for young children. The **Schauburg Theater der Jugend** (✉ Franz-Joseph-Str. 47, Schwabing ☎089/2333–7171) appeals to older youth and adults.

Nightlife

Munich's nocturnal attractions vary with the seasons. The year starts with the abandon of Fasching, the Bavarian carnival time, which begins quietly in mid-November with the crowning of the King and Queen of Fools, expands with fancy-dress balls, and ends with a great street party on Fasching Dienstag (Shrove Tuesday) in early March. Men should forget wearing neckties on Fasching Dienstag: women posing as witches make a point of cutting them off. From spring until late fall the beer garden dictates the style and pace of Munich's nightlife. When it rains, the indoor beer halls and taverns absorb the thirsty like blotting paper.

The beer gardens and most beer halls close at midnight, but there's no need to go home: some bars and nightclubs are open until 6 AM. A word of caution about bars: most are run honestly, but a few may intentionally overcharge, especially the seedier ones near the main train station. Stick to beer or wine if you can, and pay as you go.

Clubs, discos, and the like can be a bit of a problem in Munich: the bouncers outside are primarily there to add to the often specious exclusivity of the inside. Bouncers are usually rude, crude, and somewhat thick and as such have achieved dubious notoriety throughout Germany. They are in charge of picking who is "in" and who is "out," and there's no use trying to warm up to them.

Bars

Alter Simpl (✉ Turkenstr. 57 ☎089/272–3083) turned 100 in 2002. Media types drink Guinness and Kilkenny at its square bar and German pub food is served throughout the day and night. **Bar Centrale** (✉ Ledererstr. 23 ☎089/223–762) has a retro-looking back room with leather sofas and is very Italian—the waiters don't seem to speak any other language. The coffee is excellent; small fine meals are served as well.

Eisbach (✉ Marstallstr. 3, Lehel ☎089/2280–1680) occupies a corner of the Max Planck Institute building opposite the Bavarian Parliament. The bar is among Munich's longest and is overlooked by a mezzanine restaurant area where you can choose from a limited but ambitious menu. Outdoor tables nestle in the expansive shade of huge parasols. The nearby Eisbach Brook, which gives the bar its name, tinkles away like ice in a glass. The Bayerischer Hof's **Night Club** (✉ Promenadepl. 2–6, City Center ☎089/212–00) has live music, from jazz to reggae to hip-hop; a small dance floor; and a very lively bar. On fashionable Maximilianstrasse, **O'Reilly's Irish Cellar Pub** (✉ Maximilianstr. 29, City Center ☎089/293–311) offers an escape from the German bar scene as it pours genuine Irish Guinness. At the English, nautical-style **Pusser's**

New York Bar (✉ Falkenturmstr. 9, City Center ☎ 089/220–500), great cocktails and Irish-German black and tans (Guinness and strong German beer) are made to the sounds of live jazz. The pricey sandwiches are about the only "New York" in Pusser's.

The incredibly modern **Scalar** (✉ Seitzstr. 12, Lehel ☎ 089/2157–9636) attracts a fairly mixed crowd of fashionable people. Its cellar is home to the Blue Oyster Club, where dancing is encouraged. The bartenders are busy shaking cocktails at **Schumann's** (✉ Maximilianstr. 36, City Center ☎ 089/229–060) after the curtain comes down at the nearby opera house (the bar is closed on Saturday). Exotic cocktails are the specialty at **Trader Vic's** (✉ Promenadenpl. 4, City Center ☎ 089/226–192), a smart cellar bar in the Hotel Bayerischer Hof. The bar is popular among out-of-town visitors and attracts Americans. The **Kempinski Vier Jahreszeiten** (✉ Maximilianstr. 17, City Center ☎ 089/21250) offers piano music until 9 and then dancing to recorded music or a small combo.

Beer Gardens

Everybody in Munich has at least one favorite beer garden, so you're in good hands if you ask someone to point you in the right direction. You do not need to reserve. No need to phone either: if the weather says yes, then go. Note, however, that Munich has very strict noise laws, so beer gardens tend to close around 11. The famous **Biergarten am Chinesischen Turm** (☎ 089/383–8730) is at the five-story Chinese Tower in the Englischer Garten. The Englischer Garten's smaller beer garden, **Hirschau** (☎ 089/369–945), has minigolf to test your skills after a few beers. It's about 10 minutes north of the Kleinhesselohersee. The **Seehaus im Englischen Garten** (☎ 089/381–6130) is on the banks of the artificial lake Kleinhesselohersee, where all of Munich converges on hot summer days (bus line 44, exit at Osterwaldstrasse; you can't miss it). Surprisingly large and green for a place so centrally located is the **Hofbräukeller** (✉ Innere Wiener Str. 19, tramway 18 to Wiener-Pl. or U-bahn 4 or 5 to Max-Weber-Pl., Haidhausen ☎ 089/459–9250), which is a beer relative of the Hofbräuhaus. Some evenings you can move into the spacious cellar for live jazz. Out in the district of Laim is the huge **Königlicher Hirschgarten** (☎ 089/172–591), where the crowd is somewhat more blue-collar and foreign. To get there, take any S-bahn toward Pasing, exit at Laim, walk down Wotanstrasse, take a right on Winifriedstrasse and then a left into De-la-Paz-Strasse. The crowd at the **Taxisgarten** (☎089/156–827) in the Gern district (U-bahn Gern, Line 1 toward "Westfriedhof") is more white collar and tame, hence less chance of communicating with the natives, but the food is excellent, and while parents refresh themselves, children can enjoy a nice playground.

Dance Clubs

Schwabing claims more than a dozen dance clubs and live-music venues between its central boulevard, Leopoldstrasse, and the area around its central square, the Münchner-Freiheit. Two streets—Feilitzstrasse and Occamstrasse—are lined with clubs, discos, and pubs. Haidhausen is Munich's other "in" area. A former factory hosts the city's largest rave scene: the **Kultfabrik** (✉ Grafingerstr. 6, Haidhausen Ⓤ Ostbahnhof [S-bahn]) ☎ 089/4900–9070), has no fewer than 17 "entertainment areas," including a Latin dance club among others, bars, and a huge slot-machine and computer-game hall. Kunstpark Ost may be migrating toward the north of Munich. The **Backstage** (⊠ Friedenheimerbrücke 7, Laim Ⓤ Friedenheimerbrücke [S-bahn] ☎ 089/126–6100) is very relaxed, with several areas for either dancing or enjoying drinks. Old Bavarian thrillers are screened in summer as a backdrop to the nocturnal beer garden. The crowd ranges from 18-year-olds to thirtysomethings. **Muffathalle** (⊠ Rosenheimerstr. 1, behind the Müllersche Volksbad, Haidhausen ☎ 4587–5010) usually posts orange-and-purple schedules on advertising pillars. Hodgepodge is the only way to describe the events, but the people here are relaxed, young, and nonchalant. The **Skyline** (⊠ Münchner-Freiheit, Schwabing ☎ 089/333–131) is at the top of the Hertie department store and focuses mainly on Latin American sounds and salsa. Bordering the Englischer Garten, **P 1** (⊠ Prinzregentenstr., on west side of Haus der Kunst, Lehel ☎ 089/294–252) is allegedly the trendiest club in town; find out for yourself, if you can make it past the bouncer. The **Parkcafé** (⊠ Sophienstr. 7, Maxvorstadt ☎ 089/598–313) is one of those fashionable places where you'll have to talk your way past the doorman to join the chic crowd inside.

The **Feierwerk** (⊠ Hansastr. 39, Westend ☎ 089/7248–8109) has that ramshackle old factory look to it, but it's a genuine institution in the musical scene. Many local bands were launched to fame—and back—here. The big FEST festival in July is one of the city's better alternatives in the night scene. **Nachtwerk** (⊠ Landsbergerstr. 185, Westend ☎ 089/570–7390), in a converted factory, blasts the sounds of punk and avantgarde nightly between 8 PM and 4 AM. Live bands also perform here regularly. Just a few buildings down the street from the Nachtwerk is the latest industrial-size dance palace **4004** (⊠ Landsbergerstr. 169, Westend ☎ 0171/154–8038), with four different clubs on two floors, three bars, and so forth. The real ravers ride the S-bahn to Munich's Franz-Josef-Strauss Airport, alighting at the Besucherpark station for techno and other beats until dawn at **Nightflight** (☎ 089/9759–7999). The **Nachtgalerie** (⊠ Arnulfstr. 17, Leopoldvorstadt ☎ 089/3245–5595) offers nights with solid disco, 1970s fare for a plain old fun night of dancing. The **Schlachthof** (⊠ Zenettistr. 8, Thalhausen ☎ 089/765–448) is, as the name suggests, at the slaughterhouse. The mixed crowd is not overly hip, and the music usually includes excellent jazz and soul.

Gay & Lesbian Bars

Munich's growing gay scene stretches between Sendlingertorplatz and Isartorplatz. For an overview check ⊕ www.munich-cruising.de. The **Nil** (⊠ Hans-Sachs-Str. 2, Isarvorstadt ☎ 089/265–545) is famous for its decent prices and its schnitzel. The **Fortuna** (⊠ Maximilianstr. 5, Isarvorstadt ☎ 089/554–070) is more than just a bar and disco for women; it's also an events venue and organizer (skiing excursions, rafting on the Isar, for example). **Fred's Pub** (⊠ Reisingerstr. 15, Isarvorstadt ☎ 089/2602–2809) shows gay movies on a large screen. The upscale **Morizz** (⊠ Klenzestr. 43, Isarvorstadt ☎ 089/201–6776) fills with a somewhat ritzy crowd. The **Ochsengarten** (⊠ Müllerstr. 47, Isarvorstadt ☎ 089/266–446) is Munich's leather bar. **Old Mrs. Henderson** (⊠ Rumfordstr.

2, Isarvorstadt ☎ 089/263–469) puts on the city's best transvestite cabaret for a mixed crowd and has various other events.

Jazz

Munich likes to think it's Germany's jazz capital, and some beer gardens have taken to replacing their brass bands with funky combos. Jazz musicians sometimes accompany Sunday brunch at pubs, too. One top club is the tiny **Mr. B's** (⊠ Herzog-Heinrich-Str. 38, Isarvorstadt ☎ 089/534–901), run by New Yorker Alex Best, who also mixes great cocktails and, unlike so many barkeeps, usually sports a welcoming smile. Equally tiny is **Alfonso's** (⊠ Franzstrasse 5, Schwabing ☎ 089/338–835), where the nightly live music redefines the concept of intimacy. The city's longest bar is in Schwabing at the **Coccodrillo** (⊠ Hohenzollernstrasse 11, Schwabing ☎ 089/336–639), which has to be accessed through the Caffè Florian (where you can eat as well). From September to May the old brick vaulting resounds to the sounds of live jazz and rock three times a week. The **Unterfahrt** (⊠ Einsteinstr. 42, Haidhausen ☎ 089/448–2794) is the place for the serious jazzologist, though hip-hop is making heavy inroads into the scene. A haunt with nondescript furnishings rather than chic dilapidation is **Nachtcafé** (⊠ Maximilianpl. 5, City Center ☎ 089/595–900). Food (costly) is served all night, and there's no dancing. Sunday is set aside for jazz at **Waldwirtschaft Grosshesselohe** (⊠ Georg-Kalb-Str. 3, Grosshesselohe ☎ 089/795–088) in a southern suburb. If it's a nice day, the excursion is worth it.

SPORTS & THE OUTDOORS

The **Olympiapark** (Ⓤ Olympiazentrum [U-bahn]), built for the 1972 Olympics, is one of the largest sports and recreation centers in Europe. For general information about sports in and around Munich contact the sports emporium **Sport Scheck** (⊠ Sendlingerstr. 6, City Center ☎ 089/21660). The big store not only sells every kind of equipment but is very handy with advice.

Ice-Skating

In winter, depending on weather conditions, there's outdoor skating on the lake in the Englischer Garten and on the Nymphenburger Canal, where you can also go curling (*Eisstockschiessen*). Rental equipment is available at the little wooden huts, which also sell hot drinks. Players rent sections of machine-smoothed ice on the canal. Watch out for signs reading GEFAHR (danger), warning you of thin ice. Additional information is available from **Bayerischer Eissportverband** (⊠ Georg-Brauchle-Ring 93, Moosach ☎ 089/157–9920). In winter the fountain on **Karlsplatz** is turned into a public rink with lots of music, an outdoor bar for drinks, and a rowdy crowd. The **Eissportstadion** (⊠ Spiridon-Louis-Ring 3, Schwabing ☎ 089/6301–9147) in Olympiapark has an indoor rink. For outdoor rinks use the **Prinzregentenstadion** (⊠ Prinzregentenstr. 80, Haidhausen ☎ 0180/179–6223). In the west is another outdoor rink, the **Eisbahn West** (⊠ Agnes-Bernauer-Str. 241, Laim ☎ 089/8968–9007).

Jogging

The best place to jog is the **Englischer Garten** (Ⓤ Münchner-Freiheit or Universität [U-bahn]), which is 11 km (7 mi) around and has dirt and asphalt paths amid its lakes. You can also jog through **Olympiapark** (Ⓤ Olympiazentrum [U-bahn]). The 500-acre park of **Schloss Nymphenburg** (⊕ Take Tramway 12 to Romanplatz) is ideal for running. The banks of the **Isar River** are also a favorite spot. For a longer jog along the river, take the S-bahn to Unterföhring and pace yourself back to Münchner-Freiheit—a distance of 6½ km (4 mi).

Swimming & Spas

You can try swimming outdoors in the Isar River at Maria-Einsiedel, but because the water comes from the Alps, it's frigid even in summer. Warmer lakes near Munich are the **Ammersee** and the **Starnbergersee**. A very relaxing experience is swimming at one of the metropolitan spas. There are pools at the **Cosima Bad** (⊠ Englschalkingerstr. and Cosimastr., Bogenhausen), with man-made waves. The **Dantebad** (⊠ Dantestr. 6, Gern) has a huge lawn and is very popular in summer. The **Müllersche Volksbad** (⊠ Rosenheimerstr. 1, Haidhausen ☎ 2361–3434) is in a grand art nouveau building right on the Isar. Tuesday and Thursday are reserved for women only in the wellness section. And remember: if you use the saunas and steam baths in these spas, the rules say it's in your birthday suit. The **Nordbad** (⊠ Schleissheimerstr. 142, Schwabing) has a small, pleasant wellness center. The **Olympia-Schwimmhalle** (⊠ Olympiapark, Schwabing) has not only an Olympic-size pool but also a sauna area with a "steam cavern" as an extra delight.

SHOPPING

Shopping Districts

Munich has an immense central shopping area, a 2-km (1-mi) *Fussgängerzone* (pedestrian zone) stretching from the train station to Marienplatz and north to Odeonsplatz. The two main streets here are Neuhauserstrasse and Kaufingerstrasse, the sites of most major department stores. For upscale shopping, Maximilianstrasse, Residenzstrasse, and Theatinerstrasse are unbeatable and contain classy and tempting stores that are the equal of any in Europe. Schwabing, north of the university, has several of the city's most intriguing and offbeat shopping streets—Schellingstrasse and Hohenzollernstrasse are two to try.

Antiques

Bavarian antiques—from a chipped pottery beer mug to a massive farmhouse dresser—are found in the many small shops around the Viktualienmarkt, including on Westenriederstrasse, just south of the market. Number 8 Westenriederstrasse houses three antiques shops packed from floor to ceiling with curios, including a great collection of ancient dolls and toys. Also try the area north of the university—Türkenstrasse, Theresienstrasse, and Barerstrasse are all filled with antiques stores.

Strictly for window-shopping—unless you're looking for something really rare and special and money's no object—are the exclusive shops lining Prannerstrasse, at the rear of the Hotel Bayerischer Hof. Inter-

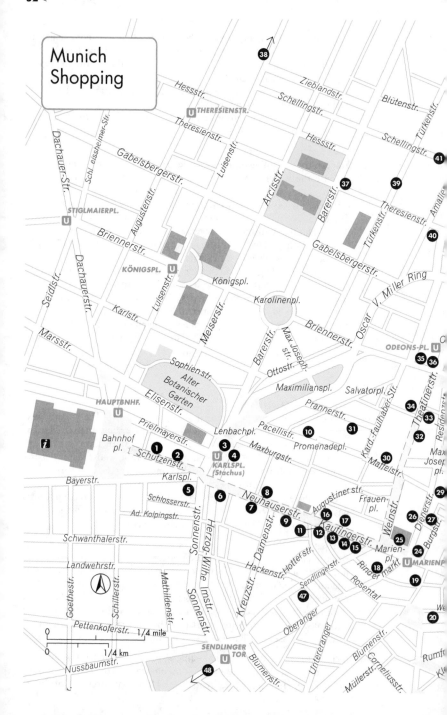

Munich
Shopping

KEY

- Pedestrian Shopping Zone
- **i** Tourist information
- **U** U-Bahn

esting and inexpensive antiques and assorted junk from all over eastern Europe are laid out at the weekend flea markets beneath the Donnersberger railway bridge on Arnulfstrasse (along the northern side of the Hauptbahnhof).

In **Antike Uhren Eder** (⊠ Hotel Bayerischer Hof, Prannerstr. 4, City Center ☎ 089/220–305), the silence is broken only by the ticking of dozens of highly valuable German antique clocks and by discreet negotiation over the high prices. Old, beautiful beer steins are the specialty of **Ulrich Schneider** (⊠ Am Radlsteg 2, City Center ☎ 089/292–477). Nautical items or antiquated sports equipment fill the **Captain's Saloon** (⊠ Westenriederstr. 31, City Center ☎ 089/221–015). German antique silver and jewelry are the specialty of **Roman Odesser** (⊠ Westenriederstr. 21, City Center ☎ 089/226–388). For Munich's largest selection of dolls and marionettes, head to **Die Puppenstube** (⊠ Luisenstr. 68, Maxvorstadt ☎ 089/272–3267).

Department Stores & Malls

★ **Hertie** (⊠ Bahnhofpl. 7, Leopoldvorstadt ☎ 089/55120 ✉ Karstadt am Nordbad, Münchner-Freiheit, Schwabing ☎ 089/381–060), commanding an entire city block between the train station and Karlsplatz, is the largest and, some claim, the best department store in the city. The basement has a high-class delicatessen with a champagne bar and stand-up bistro that offers a menu that changes daily and puts many high-price Munich restaurants to shame. Hertie's Schwabing branch is a high-gloss steel-and-glass building. **Karstadt** (⊠ Neuhauserstr. 18, City Center ☎ 089/290–230 ✉ Schleissheimerstr. 93, Schwabing ☎ 089/13020), in the 100-year-old Haus Oberpollinger, at the start of the Kaufingerstrasse shopping mall, is another upscale department store, with Bavarian arts and crafts. Karstadt also has a Schwabing branch, **Karstadt am Nordbad. Kaufhof** (⊠ Karlspl. 21–24, City Center ☎ 089/51250 ✉ At Kaufingerstr. and Marienpl., City Center ☎ 089/231–851) offers goods in the middle price range. The end-of-season sales are bargains.

For a classic selection of German clothing, including some with a folk touch, and a large collection of hats, try Munich's traditional family-run **Breiter** (⊠ Kaufingerstr. 23, City Center ☎ 089/599–8840 ✉ Stachus underground mall, City Center ☎ 089/599–8840 ✉ Schützenstr. 14, Maxvorstadt ☎ 089/599–8840 ✉ Zweibrückenstr. 5–7, Isarvorstadt ☎ 089/599–8840).

Ludwig Beck (⊠ Marienpl. 11, City Center ☎ 089/236–910) is considered a step above other department stores by Müncheners. It's packed from top to bottom with highly original wares—from fine feather boas to roughly finished Bavarian pottery. In December a series of booths, each delicately and lovingly decorated, are occupied by craftspeople, who turn out traditional German toys and decorations. The collection of CDs on the upper floor is one of the finest in the city. **Hirmer** (⊠ Kaufingerstr. 28, City Center ☎ 089/236–830) has Munich's most comprehensive collection of German-made men's clothes, with a markedly friendly and knowledgeable staff. **Hallhuber** (⊠ Kaufingerstr. 9, City Center ☎ 089/260–4862) dresses men and women in toned-down elegance and at good value for the quality. Hallhuber has a branch farther down the road on Marienplatz.

The main pedestrian area has two malls. The aptly named **Arcade** (⊠ Neuhauserstr. 5, City Center) is where the young find the best designer jeans and chunky jewelry. **Kaufinger Tor** (⊠ Kaufingerstr. 117, City Center) has several floors of boutiques and cafés packed neatly together under a high glass roof. For a more uppercrust and upper-price shopping experience, visit the many shops, boutiques, galleries, and cafés of the **Fünf Höfe,** a vast and modern arcade carved into the block of houses between Theatinerstrasse and Kardinal-Faulhaber-Strasse. The modern architecture of the passages and courtyards is cool and elegant, in sharp contrast to the facades of the buildings.

Folk Costumes

If you want to deck yourself out in lederhosen or a dirndl, or acquire a green loden coat and little pointed hat with feathers, you have a wide choice in the Bavarian capital. Much of the fine loden clothing on sale at **Lodenfrey** (⊠ Maffeistr. 7–9, City Center ☎ 089/210–390) is made at the company's own factory, on the edge of the Englischer Garten. **Wallach** (⊠ Residenzstr. 3, City Center ☎ 089/220–8710) has souvenirs downstairs and shoes and clothing upstairs (though no children's wear). The tiny **Lederhosen Wagner** (⊠ Tal 2, City Center ☎ 089/225–697), right up against the Heiliggeist Church, carries lederhosen, woolen sweaters called *Walk* (not loden), and children's clothing.

Gift Ideas

Munich is a city of beer, and items related to its consumption are obvious choices for souvenirs and gifts. Munich is also the home of the famous Nymphenburg Porcelain factory. **Dallmayr** (⊠ Dienerstr. 014–15, City Center ☎ 089/21350) is an elegant gourmet-food store, with delights ranging from the most exotic fruits to English jams, served by efficient Munich matrons in smart blue-and-white-linen costumes. The store's famous specialty is coffee, with more than 50 varieties to blend as you wish. There's also an enormous number of breads and a temperature-controlled cigar room. Visit **Ludwig Mory** (⊠ Marienpl. 8, City Center ☎ 089/224–542) for items relating to beer, from mugs of all shapes and sizes and in all sorts of materials, to warmers for those who don't like their beer too cold. Check out **Sebastian Wesely** (⊠ Rindermarkt 1, at Peterspl., City Center ☎ 089/264–519) for beer-related vessels and schnapps glasses (*Stampferl*), walking sticks, scarves, and napkins with the famous Bavarian blue-and-white lozenges. If you've been to the Black Forest and forgot to equip yourself with a clock, or if you need a good Bavarian souvenir, try **Max Krug** (⊠ Neuhauserstr. 2, City Center, ☎ 089/224–501) in the pedestrian zone.

The **Nymphenburg store** (⊠ At Odeonspl. and Briennerstr., Maxvorstadt ☎ 089/282–428) resembles a drawing room of the Munich palace, with soft dove-gray furnishings and delicate, expensive porcelain safely locked away in bowfront cabinets. You can buy directly from the factory on the grounds of **Schloss Nymphenburg** (⊠ Nördliches Schlossrondell 8, Nymphenburg ☎ 089/1791–9710). For Dresden and Meissen ware, go to **Kunstring Meissen** (⊠ Briennerstr. 4, Maxvorstadt ☎ 089/281–532).

Bavarian craftspeople have a showplace of their own, the **Bayerischer Kunstgewerbe–Verein** (✉ Pacellistr. 6–8, City Center ☎ 089/290–1470); here you'll find every kind of handicraft, from glass and pottery to textiles. **Kunst und Spiel** (✉ Leopoldstr. 49, Schwabing ☎ 089/381–6270) has a fine selection of toys and clothing for children and various other handcrafted items. Germany is known for its work ethic, so you are bound to find excellent work clothing, shirts, aprons, boots, jackets, and even dishrags made to last at **Berufsbekleidung Neubert** (✉ Sendlingerstr. 11, City Center ☎ 089/260–9076).

Lehmkuhl (✉ Leopoldstr. 45, Schwabing ☎ 089/3801–5013), one of Munich's finest bookshops, also sells beautiful cards. In an arcade of the Neues Rathaus is tiny **Johanna Daimer Filze aller Art** (✉ Dienerstr., City Center ☎ 089/776–984), a shop selling every kind and color of felt imaginable. For an unusual gift of genuine art made of "alternative materials," try **Galerie Biro** (✉ Zieblandstr. 19, Schwabing ☎ 089/273–0686). The works are by no means inexpensive, but they are crafted by top artists working with unusual materials, from Bakelite to plywood. The gallery is closed from Sunday through Tuesday.

A little way outside the center to the south is **tragbar** (Ⓤ Poccisstrasse [U-bahn]), where you can find handcrafted jewelry and home-made noodles, chocolates, and other edibles (✉ Zenettistr. 33, Thalkirchen ☎ 089/7670–3974).

All sorts of lighters, little statues, fine Bavarian snuff boxes, and many other quality gifts to bring home are available at the **Münchner Feuerzeugzentrale** (✉ Karlspl. 3, City Center ☎ 089/591–885). **Otto Kellnberger's Holzhandlung** (✉ Heiliggeiststr. 7–8, City Center ☎ 089/226–479) specializes in wooden crafts. **Obletter's** (✉ Karlspl. 11–12, City Center ☎ 089/5508–9510) has two extensive floors of toys, many of them handmade playthings of great charm and quality. From the end of November until December 24, the open-air stalls of the **Christkindlmarkt** (✉ Marienpl., City Center) are a great place to find gifts and warm up with mulled wine. Two other perennial Christmas-market favorites are those in Schwabing (Münchner-Freiheit Square) and at the Chinese Tower, in the middle of the Englischer Garten.

Markets

Munich's **Viktualienmarkt** is *the* place to shop and to eat. Just south of Marienplatz, it's home to an array of colorful stands that sell everything from cheese to sausages, from flowers to wine. A visit here is more than just collecting picnic makings; it's central to an understanding of the Müncheners' easy-come-easy-go nature. If you're in the Schwabing area, the daily market at **Elisabethplatz** is worth a visit—it's much, much smaller than the Viktualienmarkt, but the range and quality of produce are comparable.

SIDE TRIPS FROM MUNICH

Munich's excellent suburban railway network, the S-bahn, brings several quaint towns and attractive rural areas within easy reach for a day's excursion. The two nearest lakes, the Starnbergersee and the Ammersee, are popular year-round. Dachau attracts overseas visitors, mostly because of its concentration-camp memorial site, but it's a picturesque and historic town in its own right. Landshut, north of Munich, is way off the tourist track, but if it were the same distance south of Munich, this jewel of a Bavarian market town would be overrun. All these destinations have a wide selection of restaurants and hotels, and you can bring a bike on any S-bahn train. German railways, DB, often has weekend specials that allow a family or group of five to travel for as little as €17.50 during certain times. (Inquire at the main train station for the *Wochenendticket*.)

Starnbergersee

20 km (12 mi) southwest of Munich.

The Starnbergersee was one of Europe's first pleasure grounds. Royal coaches were already trundling out from Munich to the lake's wooded shores in the 17th century. In 1663 Elector Ferdinand Maria threw a shipboard party at which 500 guests wined and dined as 100 oarsmen propelled them around the lake. Today, pleasure steamers provide a taste of such luxury for the masses. The lake is still lined with the small baroque palaces of Bavaria's aristocracy, but their owners now share the lakeside with public parks, beaches, and boatyards. The Starnbergersee is one of Bavaria's largest lakes—20 km (12 mi) long, 5 km (3 mi) wide, and 406 feet at its deepest point—so there's plenty of room for swimmers, sailors, and windsurfers. The water is of drinking quality (as with most other Bavarian lakes), a testimony to stringent environmental laws.

The Starnbergersee is named after its chief resort, **Starnberg**, the largest town on the lake and the nearest to Munich. Pleasure boats set off from the jetty for trips around the lake. The resort has a tree-lined lakeside promenade and some fine turn-of-the-20th-century villas, some of which are now hotels. There are abundant restaurants, taverns, and chestnut-tree-shaded beer gardens.

On the lake's eastern shore, at the village of Berg, you'll find the **King Ludwig II Memorial Chapel.** A well-marked path leads through thick woods to the chapel, built near the point in the lake where the drowned king's body was found on June 13, 1886. He had been confined in nearby Berg Castle after the Bavarian government took action against his withdrawal from reality and his bankrupting castle-building fantasies. A cross in the lake marks the point where his body was recovered.

The castle of **Possenhofen,** home of Ludwig's favorite cousin, Sisi, stands on the western shore, practically opposite Berg. Local lore says they used to send affectionate messages across the lake to each other. Sisi married the Austrian emperor Franz Joseph I but spent more than 20 summers in the lakeside castle, now a luxury hotel, the **Kaiserin Elisabeth.** ✉ *Tutzingerstr. 2–6, Feldafing* ☎ *08157/93090* ⊕ *www.kaiserin-elisabeth.de.*

Buchheim Museum. The Buchheim Collection is one of the finest private collections of German expressionist art in the form of paintings, drawings, watercolors, and prints. Among the artists represented are Otto Dix, Max Beckmann, Ernst Ludwig Kirchner, Karl Schmitt-Rotluff, and other painters of the so-called Brücke movement (1905–13). The museum is housed in an impressive modern building on the lakeside. Some areas of the museum are reserved for African cultic items and Bavarian folk art. The nicest way to get to the museum from Starnberg is by ship. Ask for a combined ticket (€16). ☒ *Am Hirschgarten 1* ☏ *08158/ 997–060* ⊕ *www.buchheimmusem.de* ☒ *€7.80* ☉ *Apr.–Oct., weekdays 10–6, weekends 10–8; Nov.–Mar., Tues.–Sun. 10–6.*

Just offshore is the tiny **Roseninsel** (Rose Island), where King Maximilian II built a summer villa. You can swim to its tree-fringed shores or sail across in a dinghy or on a Windsurfer (rentals are available at Possenhofen's boatyard and at many other rental points along the lake).

Where to Stay & Eat

$–$$ ✕ **Seerestaurant Undosa.** This restaurant is only a short walk from the Starnberg railroad station and boat pier. Most tables command a view of the lake, which provides some of the best fish specials on the international menu. This is the place to try the mild-tasting *Renke,* a perch-type fish. The Undosa also has jazz evenings and a large café, the Oberdeck, also overlooking the lake. ☒ *Seepromenade 1* ☏ *08151/998– 930* ⌆ *Reservations not accepted* ☰ *AE, MC, V* ☉ *Closed Mon. and Tues., most of Jan., and half of Feb.*

¢–$ ✕ **Königswasser.** A large, airy atrium welcomes you to this comfortable spot. You can enjoy coffee and cakes or a meal ranging from fresh salad to an Argentinean steak drowned in pepper sauce. The Königswasser has a shelf full of photography books and travel guides that invite you to just sit, relax, and enjoy some time off your feet. It's open past midnight from Wednesday through Saturday, and until 6 PM the rest of the week. ☒ *Maximilianstr. 2b, 82319 Starnberg* ☏ *08151/444–086* ☰ *MC, V.*

$$ ✕▥ **Hotel Seehof.** This small hotel right next to the train station has several rooms with a view of the lake. Rooms are simply done, with light colors and flower prints hanging on the walls. The Italian restaurant attached, Al Gallo Nero ($–$$$), has dishes ranging from low-price pizzas to high-price fish items that will satisfy any palate. ☒ *Bahnhofpl. 6, D–82319 Starnberg* ☏ *08151/908–500* ☐ *08151/28136* ⊕ *www.hotel-seehof-starnberg.de* ⌂ *38 rooms* ⌆ *Restaurant, in-room data ports, cable TV, some pets allowed (fee); no a/c* ☰ *AE, DC, MC, V* ⍟ *BP.*

$$–$$$ ✕▥ **Forsthaus am See.** The handsome, geranium-covered Forsthaus faces the lake, and so do most of the large, pinewood-furnished rooms. The excellent restaurant ($$$) has a daily changing international menu, with lake fish a specialty. The hotel has its own lake access and boat pier, with a chestnut-shaded beer garden nearby. ☒ *Am See 1, D–82343 Possenhofen* ☏ *08157/93010* ☐ *08157/4292* ⊕ *www.forsthaus-am-see. de* ⌂ *21 rooms, 1 suite* ⌆ *Restaurant, beer garden, Internet, some pets allowed (fee); no a/c* ☰ *AE, MC, V* ⍟ *BP.*

Starnbergersee A to Z

TRANSPORTATION TO & FROM STARNBERGERSEE

Starnberg and the north end of the lake are a 25-minute drive from Munich on the A–95 autobahn. Follow the signs to Garmisch and take the

Starnberg exit. Country roads then skirt the west and east banks of the lake, but most are closed to the public.

The S-bahn 6 suburban line runs from Munich's central Marienplatz to Starnberg and three other towns on the lake's west bank: Possenhofen, Feldafing, and Tutzing. The journey from Marienplatz to Starnberg takes 35 minutes. The east bank of the lake can be reached by bus from the town of Wolfratshausen, the end of the S-bahn 7 suburban line.

VISITOR INFORMATION

The quickest way to visit the Starnbergersee area is by ship. On Saturday evenings, the good ship *Seeshaupt* has dancing and dinner.
📍 Tourist-Information **Seeshaupt** ☎ 08151/12023. **Tourismusverband Starnberger Fünf-Seen-Land** ✉ Wittelsbacher Str. 2c, D–82319 Starnberg ☎ 08151/906–00 🖨 08151/906–090 ⊕ www.starnberg.de.

Ammersee

40 km (25 mi) southwest of Munich.

The Ammersee, the "peasant lake," is the country cousin of the better-known, more cosmopolitan Starnbergersee ("the prince lake"), and, accordingly, many Bavarians (and tourists, too) like it all the more. Munich cosmopolites of centuries past thought it too distant for an excursion, not to mention too rustic, so the shores remained relatively free of villas and parks. Though some upscale holiday homes claim some stretches of the eastern shore, the Ammersee still offers more open areas for bathing and boating than the larger lake to the west. Bicyclists circle the 19-km-long (12-mi-long) lake (it's nearly 6 km [4 mi] across at its widest point) on a path that rarely loses sight of the water. Hikers can spread out the tour for two or three days, staying overnight in any of the comfortable inns along the way. Dinghy sailors and windsurfers zip across in minutes with the help of the Alpine winds that swoop down from the mountains. A ferry cruises the lake at regular intervals during summer, stopping at several piers. Board it at Herrsching.

Herrsching has a delightful promenade, part of which winds through the resort's park. The 100-year-old villa that sits so comfortably there seems as if it were built by Ludwig II; such is the romantic and fanciful mixture of medieval turrets and Renaissance-style facades. It was actually built for the artist Ludwig Scheuermann in the late 19th century and became a favorite meeting place for Munich and Bavarian artists. It's now a municipal cultural center and the scene of chamber-music concerts on some summer weekends.

The Benedictine monastery of **Andechs,** one of southern Bavaria's most famous pilgrimage sites, lies 5 km (3 mi) south of Herrsching. You can reach it on Bus 951 (which also connects Ammersee and Starnbergersee). This extraordinary ensemble, surmounted by an octagonal tower and onion dome with a pointed helmet, has a busy history going back more than 1,000 years. The church, originally built in the 15th century, was entirely redone in baroque style in the early 18th century. The **Heilige Kapelle** contains the remains of the old treasure of the Benedictines in

Andechs, including Charlemagne's "Victory Cross," and a monstrance containing the three sacred hosts brought back from the crusades by the original rulers of the area, the Counts of Diessen-Andechs. One of the attached chapels contains the remains of composer Carl Orff, and one of the buildings on the grounds has been refurbished as a concert stage for the performance of his works. The church is being renovated completely in preparation for the 550th anniversary of the monastery in 2005. Crowds of pilgrims are drawn not only by the beauty of the hilltop monastery but also by the beer brewed here (600,000 liters [159,000 gallons] annually). The monastery makes its own cheese as well, and it's an excellent accompaniment to the rich, almost black beer. You can enjoy both at large wooden tables in the monastery tavern or on the terrace outside. ⊕ *www.andechs.de* ☉ *Daily 7–7.*

The little town of **Diessen** at the southwest corner of the lake has one of the most magnificent religious buildings of the whole region: the **Augustine abbey church of St. Mary.** No lesser figure than the great Munich architect Johann Michael Fischer designed this airy, early rococo structure. François Cuvillié the Elder, whose work can be seen all over Munich, did the sumptuous gilt-and-marble high altar. Visit in late afternoon, when the light falls sharply on its crisp gray, white, and gold facade, etching the pencil-like tower and spire against the darkening sky over the lake. Don't leave without at least peeping into neighboring St. Stephen's courtyard, its cloisters smothered in wild roses. But Diessen is not all church. It has attracted artists and craftspeople since the early 20th century. Among the most famous who made their home here was the composer Carl Orff, author of numerous works inspired by medieval material, including the famous *Carmina Burana.* His life and work—notably the pedagogical Schulwerk instruments—are exhibited in the **Carl-Orff-Museum** (⊠ Hofmark 3, Diessen ☎ 08807/91981 ☉ Weekends 2–5).

Where to Stay & Eat

$$ ✕🖭 **Ammersee Hotel.** This very comfortable, modern resort hotel has views from an unrivaled position on the lakeside promenade. Rooms overlooking the lake are more expensive and in demand. The Artis restaurant ($–$$) has an international menu with an emphasis on fish. You can enjoy a spicy bouillabaisse or catfish from the Danube. ⊠ *Summerstr. 32, D–82211 Herrsching* ☎ *08152/96870, 08152/399–440 restaurant* 🖷 *08152/5374* ⊕ *www.ammersee-hotel.de* ✍ *40 rooms* ♤ *Restaurant, in-room data ports, cable TV, gym, hot tub, sauna, some pets allowed (fee); no a/c* ⊟ *AE, DC, MC, V* ⊺◯⊦ *BP.*

$ 🖭 **Hotel Garni Zur Post.** Families feel particularly at home here where children can amuse themselves at the playground and small deer park. Rooms are Bavarian country style, with solid pine furnishings, and are clean and functional. A delicious breakfast buffet will prepare you for a long day of touring. ⊠ *Starnberger Str. 2, D–82346 Andechs* ☎ *08152/3433* 🖷 *08152/2303* ⊕ *www.zur-post-herrsching.de* ✍ *17 rooms* ♤ *Cable TV, playground, Internet, some pets allowed (fee); no a/c* ⊟ *MC* ⊺◯⊦ *CP.*

Ammersee A to Z

TRANSPORTATION TO & FROM AMMERSEE

Take A–96, follow the signs to Lindau, and 20 km (12 mi) west of Munich take the exit for Herrsching, the lake's principal town.

Herrsching is also the end of the S-bahn 5 suburban line, a 47-minute ride from Munich's Marienplatz. From the Herrsching train station, Bus 952 runs north along the lake, and Bus 951 runs south and continues on to Starnberg in a 40-minute journey.

Getting around on a boat is the best way to visit. Each town on the lake has an *Anlegestelle* (pier).

VISITOR INFORMATION

🔝 Tourist-Information Verkehrsbüro ⊠ Bahnhofspl. 2, Herrsching ☎ 08152/5227 ⊘ Weekdays 8:30–noon.

Dachau

20 km (12 mi) northwest of Munich.

Dachau predates Munich, with records going back to the time of Charlemagne. It's a handsome town, too, built on a hilltop with views of Munich and the Alps. A guided tour of the town, including the castle and church, leaves from the Rathaus on Saturday at 10:30, from May through mid-October. Dachau is better known worldwide as the site of the first Nazi concentration camp, which was built just outside it. Dachau preserves the memory of the camp and the horrors perpetrated there with deep contrition while trying, with commendable discretion, to signal that the town has other points of interest.

To get a history of the town, drop in on the **Bezirksmuseum,** the district museum, which displays historical items, furniture, and traditional costumes from Dachau and its surroundings ⊠ *Augsburgerstr. 3* ☎ *08131/ 567–511* 🖾 *€2* ⊘ *Wed.–Fri. 11–5, weekends 1–5.*

The site of the infamous camp, now the **KZ-Gedenkstätte Dachau** (Dachau Concentration Camp Memorial), is just outside town. Photographs, contemporary documents, the few remaining cell blocks, and the grim crematorium create a somber and moving picture of the camp, where more than 30,000 of the 200,000-plus prisoners lost their lives. A documentary film in English is shown daily at 11:30 and 3:30. The former camp has become more than just a grisly memorial: it's now a place where people of all nations meet, to reflect upon the past and on the present. Several religious shrines and memorials have been built to honor the dead, who came from Germany and all occupied nations. To reach the memorial by car, leave the center of the town along Schleissheimerstrasse and turn left into Alte Römerstrasse; the site is on the left. By public transport take Bus 724 or 726 from the Dachau S-bahn train station or the town center. Both stop within a two-minute walk from the site (ask the driver to let you out there). If you are driving from Munich, turn right on the first country road (marked B) before entering Dachau and follow the signs. ⊠ *Alte Römerstr. 75* ☎ *08131/669–970* ⊕ *www.kz-*

gedenkstaette-dachau.de ☜ *Free* ⊙ *Tues.–Sun. 9–5. Guided English tour June–Aug., Tues.–Sun. at 12:30; Sept.–May, weekends at 12:30.*

Schloss Dachau, the hilltop castle, dominates the town. What you'll see is the one remaining wing of a palace built by the Munich architect Josef Effner for the Wittelsbach ruler Max Emanuel in 1715. During the Napoleonic Wars the palace served as a field hospital and then was partially destroyed. King Max Joseph lacked the money to rebuild it, so all that's left is a handsome cream-and-white building, with an elegant pillared and lantern-hung café on the ground floor and a former ballroom above. About once a month the grand Renaissance hall, with a richly decorated and carved ceiling, covered with painted panels depicting figures from ancient mythology, is used for chamber concerts. The east terrace affords panoramic views of Munich and, on fine days, the distant Alps. There's also a 250-year-old *Schlossbrauerei* (castle brewery), which hosts the town's beer and music festival each year in the first two weeks of August. ☒ *Schlosspl.* ☎ *08131/87923* ☜ *€1, tour €2.50* ⊙ *May–Sept., weekends 10–6; tour of town and Schloss May–mid-Oct., Sat. at 10:30.*

St. Jacob, Dachau's parish church, was built in the early 16th century in late-Renaissance style on the foundations of a 14th-century Gothic structure. Baroque features and a characteristic onion dome were added in the late 17th century. On the south wall you can admire a very fine 17th-century sundial. A visit to the church is included in the guided tour of the town. ☒ *Konrad-Adenauer-Str. 7* ⊙ *Daily 7–7.*

An artists' colony formed here during the 19th century, and the tradition lives on. Picturesque houses line Hermann-Stockmann-Strasse and part of Münchner Strasse, and many of them are still the homes of successful artists. The **Gemäldegalerie** displays the works of many of the town's 19th-century artists. ☒ *Konrad-Adenauer-Str. 3* ☎ *08131/567–516* ☜ *€2* ⊙ *Wed.–Fri. 11–5, weekends 1–5.*

Where to Eat

$–$$
Fodor'sChoice
★
✕ **Weilachmühle.** You have to drive a ways for this absolute gem of a restaurant–cum–beer garden–cum–stage and exhibition room in the little village of Thalhausen. It's in a farmhouse that was restored the way it should be, the old dark wooden door opening onto a generous dining area paneled in simple light pine. The food is faultless, beginning with the benchmark Schweinsbraten. To get to the Weilachmüle, drive 26 km (16 mi) north of Dachau toward Aichach; when you reach the village of Wollomoos, take a right toward Thalhausen. (Thalhausen is 2 km [1 mi] from Wollomoos.) ☒ *Am Mühlberg 5, Thalhausen* ☎ *08254/1711* ⊕ *www.weilachmuehle.de* ☐ *No credit cards* ⊙ *Closed Mon.–Wed.*

¢–$
✕ **Gasthof drei Rosen** In a 19th-century building at the foot of Dachau's old town, this little inn caters primarily to locals. Among the inexpensive and filling Bavarian specialties on the menu is *Hendl à la Parkvilla*, chicken marinated in milk and deep fried. You can order it to go as well. ☒ *Schlossstr. 8* ☎ *08131/354–515* ☐ *No credit cards* ⊙ *Closed Mon. and Tues.*

¢–$
✕ **Zieglerbräu.** Dachau's leading beer tavern, once a 17th-century brewer's home, is a warren of cozy wood-panel rooms where you'll prob-

ably share a table with a party of locals on a boys' night out. The food consists of pork, potato, and sausages prepared in various ways. In summer the tables spill out onto the street for a very Italian feeling. The restaurant runs the neighboring nightclub. ✉ *Konrad-Adenauer-Str. 8* ☎ *08131/ 454–396* ▭ *No credit cards.*

Dachau A to Z

TRANSPORTATION TO & FROM DACHAU

Take the B–12 country road or the Stuttgart autobahn to the Dachau exit from Munich. Dachau is also on the S-bahn 2 suburban line, a 20-minute ride from Munich's Marienplatz.

VISITOR INFORMATION

🚺 Tourist-Information **Verkehrsverein Dachau** ✉ Konrad-Adenauer-Str. 1 ☎ 08131/ 75286 🖷 08131/84529 ⊕ www.dachau-info.de.

Landshut

64 km (40 mi) north of Munich.

If fortune had placed Landshut south of Munich, in the protective folds of the Alpine foothills, instead of the same distance north, in the subdued flatlands of Lower Bavaria—of which it is the capital—the historic town would be teeming with tourists. Landshut's geographical misfortune is the discerning visitor's good luck, for the town is never overcrowded, with the possible exception of the three summer weeks when the *Landshuter Hochzeit* (Landshut Wedding) is celebrated. The next celebration is June 25 to July 17, 2005, and is well worth attending. The festival commemorates the marriage in 1475 of Prince George of Bavaria-Landshut, son of the expressively named Ludwig the Rich, to Princess Hedwig, daughter of the king of Poland. Within its ancient walls, the entire town is swept away in a colorful reconstruction of the event. The wedding procession, with the "bride" and "groom" on horseback accompanied by pipes and drums and the hurly-burly of a medieval pageant, is held on three consecutive weekends while a medieval-style fair fills the central streets throughout the three weeks.

Landshut has two magnificent cobblestone market streets. The one in **Altstadt** (Old Town) is one of the most beautiful city streets in Germany; the other is in **Neustadt** (New Town). The two streets run parallel to each other, tracing a course between the Isar River and the heights overlooking the town. A steep path from Altstadt takes you up to **Burg Trausnitz**. This castle was begun in 1204 and accommodated the Wittelsbach dukes of Bavaria-Landshut until 1503. ☎ *0871/924–110* ⊕ *www. burgtrausnitz.de* ✑ *€2.50, including guided tour* ☉ *Apr.–Sept., daily 9–6; Oct.–Mar., daily 10–4.*

The **Stadtresidenz** in Altstadt was the first Italian Renaissance building of its kind north of the Alps. It was built from 1536 to 1537 but was given a baroque facade at the end of the 19th century. The Wittelsbachs lived here during the 16th century. The facade of the palace forms an almost modest part of the architectural splendor and integrity of the Altstadt, where even the ubiquitous McDonald's has to serve its hamburgers behind a baroque exterior. The Stadtresidenz includes exhibitions on the history of Landshut. ⊠ *Altstadt 79, Altstadt* ☎ *0871/22638* 🖭 *€2.50* ⊗ *Apr.–Sept., daily 9–6; Oct.–Mar., daily 10–4.*

The **Rathaus** (Town Hall) stands opposite the Stadtresidenz, an elegant, light-color building with a typical neo-Gothic roof design. It was originally a set of 13th-century burgher houses, taken over by the town in the late 1300s. The famous bride and groom allegedly danced in the grand ceremonial hall during their much-celebrated wedding in 1475. The frescos here date to 1880, however. The tourist information bureau is on the ground floor. ⊠ *Altstadt 315* ☎ *0871/922–050* 🖭 *Free* ⊗ *Weekdays 2–3, and on official tours.*

The **Martinskirche** (St. Martin's Church), with the tallest brick church tower (436 feet) in the world, soars above the other buildings with its bristling spire. The church, which was elevated to the rank of *basilica minor* in 2002, contains some magnificent late-Gothic stone and wood carvings, notably a 1518 Madonna by the artist Martin Leinberger. It's surely the only church in the world to contain an image of Hitler, albeit in a devilish pose. The führer and other Nazi leaders are portrayed as executioners in a 1946 stained-glass window showing the martyrdom of St. Kastulus. In the nave of the church is a clear and helpful description of its history and treasures in English. Every first Sunday of the month, a tour is conducted between 11:30 and 12:30 that will take you up the tower and to the **Schatzkammer,** the church's treasure chamber. ⊠ *At Altstadt and Kirchg.* ☎ *0871/922–1780* ⊗ *Apr.–Sept., Tues.–Sun. 7–6:30; Oct.–Mar., Tues.–Sun. 7–5.*

Built into a steep slope of the hill crowned by Burg Trausnitz is an unusual art museum, the **Skulpturenmuseum im Hofberg,** containing the entire collection of the Landshut sculptor Fritz Koenig. His own work forms the permanent central section of the labyrinthine gallery. ⊠ *Kolpingstr. 481* ☎ *0871/89021* 🖭 *€3* ⊗ *Tues.–Sun. 10:30–1 and 2–5.*

off the beaten path

FREISING – This ancient episcopal seat, 35 km (22 mi) southwest of Landshut, houses a cathedral and Old Town well worth visiting. The town is also accessible from Munich (at the end of the S-bahn 1 line, a 45-minute ride from central Munich).

Where to Stay & Eat

There are several attractive Bavarian-style restaurants in Altstadt and Neustadt, most of them with beer gardens. Although Landshut brews a fine beer, look for a *Gaststätte* offering a *Weihenstephaner,* from the world's oldest brewery, in Freising. Helles (light) is the most popular beer variety.

$$ ✕🖭 **Hotel Goldene Sonne.** The steeply gabled Renaissance exterior of the "Golden Sun" fronts a hotel of great charm and comfort. It stands in the center of town, near all the sights. Its dining options are a paneled, beamed restaurant ($–$$); a vaulted cellar; and a courtyard beer garden, where the service is friendly and helpful. The menu follows the seasons and tows the "quintessential Bavarian" line, with pork roast, steamed or smoked trout with horseradish, asparagus in the spring (usually accompanied by potatoes or ham), and venison in the fall. ✉ *Neustadt 520, D–84028* ☎ *0871/92530* 🖷 *0871/925–3350* ⊕ *www.goldenesonne.de* ⤶ *53 rooms* ◔ *Restaurant, in-room data ports, cable TV, beer garden, pub, some pets allowed (fee), no-smoking rooms; no a/c* ⊟ *AE, DC, MC, V* ⅋ *BP.*

$–$$ ✕🖭 **Romantik Hotel Fürstenhof.** This handsome Landshut city mansion, located a few minutes on foot from the center of town, had no difficulty qualifying for inclusion in the Romantik group of hotels—it just breathes romance, from its plush gourmet restaurant ($$$), covered in wood paneling, to the cozy bedrooms. A vine-covered terrace shadowed by a chestnut tree adds charm. ✉ *Stethaimerstr. 3, D–84034* ☎ *0871/92550* 🖷 *0871/925–544* ⊕ *www.romantikhotels.com/landshut* ⤶ *24 rooms* ◔ *Restaurant, cable TV, sauna, Internet, no-smoking rooms; no a/c in some rooms* ⊟ *AE, DC, MC, V* ⅋ *BP* ⊗ *Restaurant closed Sun.*

$–$$ ✕🖭 **Schloss Schönbrunn.** This country mansion is now a luxurious hotel, with many of its original features intact. Rooms in the most historic part of the building are particularly attractive, with huge double beds, and represent excellent value. The handsome house stands in the Schönbrunn district of Landshut, about 2 km (1 mi) from the center. The journey is worthwhile even for the excellent restaurant ($$–$$$), where the menu includes fish from the hotel's own pond, or for a romantic evening at the beer garden. ✉ *Schönbrunn 1, D–84036* ☎ *0871/95220* 🖷 *0871/952–2222* ⊕ *www.hotel-schoenbrunn.de* ⤶ *33 rooms* ◔ *Restaurant, café, in-room data ports, cable TV, bar, beer garden, some pets allowed (fee), no-smoking rooms; no a/c* ⊟ *AE, DC, MC, V* ⅋ *BP.*

Landshut A to Z

TRANSPORTATION TO & FROM LANDSHUT

Landshut is a 45-minute drive northwest of Munich on either the A–92 autobahn—follow the signs to Deggendorf—or the B–11 highway. The Plattling–Regensburg–Passau train line brings you from Munich in about 50 minutes. A round-trip costs about €20.

VISITOR INFORMATION

🛈 Tourist-Information **Landshut Wedding 2005 celebration** ☎ 0871/22918 🖷 0871/274–653. **Verkehrsverein** ✉ Altstadt 315 ☎ 0871/922–050 ⊕ www.landshut.de.

MUNICH A TO Z

To research prices, get advice from other travelers, and book travel arrangements, visit www.fodors.com.

AIRPORTS

Munich's International Airport is 28 km (17 mi) northeast of the city center, between the small towns of Freising and Erding. When departing from Munich for home, you can claim your V.A.T. refund (for purchases made during your stay) at a counter either between areas B and C, or between C and D.

🛈 **Flughafen München** ☎ 089/97500 ⊕ www.munich-airport.de.

A fast train service links the airport with Munich's main train station. The S-1 and S-8 lines operate from a terminal directly beneath the airport's arrival and departure halls. Trains leave every 10 minutes, and the journey takes around 40 minutes. Several intermediate stops are made, including the Ostbahnhof (convenient for lodgings east of the Isar River) and such city-center stations as Marienplatz. A one-way ticket costs €8, or €7.20 if you purchase a multiple-use "strip" ticket (you will have two strips left at the end). A family of up to five (two adults and three children under 15) can make the trip for €15 by buying a *Tageskarte* (which allows travel until 6 AM the next morning). The bus service is slower than the S-bahn link (€9 one-way, €14.50 round-trip). A taxi from the airport costs around €50. During rush hours (7 AM–10 AM and 4 PM–7 PM), allow up to an hour of traveling time. If you're driving from the airport to the city, take route A–9 and follow the signs for MÜNCHEN STADTMITTE (downtown). If you're driving from the city center, head north through Schwabing, join the A–9 autobahn at the Frankfurter Ring intersection, and follow the signs for the airport (FLUGHAFEN).

BIKE TRAVEL

Munich and its environs are easily navigated on two wheels. The city is threaded with a network of bike paths, and bikes are allowed on the S-bahn (except from 6 AM to 9 AM and from 4 PM to 6 PM). Bicycles on public transportation cost either one strip on a multiple ticket, or €2.50 for a day ticket, €0.90 for a single ticket. A free map showing all bike trails is available at all city tourist offices.

Bikes can be rented from April through October at the Hauptbahnhof and at some S-bahn and main-line stations around Munich. A list of stations that offer the service is available from the Deutsche Bahn. The cost is €3.80–€12.50 a day depending on the type of bike.

Aktiv-Rad ⊠ Hans-Sachs-Str. 7, Isarvorstadt ☎ 089/266-506. **the bike and walk company GmbH** ⊠ Tal 31, City Center ☎ 089/5895-8930. **Hauptbahnhof** ⊠ Radius Touristik, opposite platform 31, Leopoldvorstadt ☎ 089/596-113. **Spurwechsel** ⊠ Steinstr. 3, Haidhausen ☎ 089/692-4699. **Will Fahrradverleih** ⊠ Kleinhesselohe 4, at Kleinhesselohe Lake in Englischer Garten, Schwabing ☎ 089/338-353.

BUS TRAVEL TO & FROM MUNICH

Long-distance buses arrive at and depart from an area to the west of the main train station. The actual office of the bus company, Touring GmbH, is in the northern section of the train station itself, an area referred to as the Starnberger Bahnhof.

Zentraler Busbahnhof ⊠ Arnulfstr., Leopoldvorstadt ☎ 089/545-8700.

CAR RENTAL

All Hauptbahnhof (train station) branches are in the mezzanine-level gallery above the Deutsche Bahn information and ticket center. Airport branches are in the central area, Zentralbereich.

Avis ⊠ Airport ☎ 089/9759-7600 ⊠ Hauptbahnhof, Leopoldvorstadt ☎ 089/550-2251 ⊠ Nymphenburgerstr. 61, Maxvorstadt ☎ 089/1260-0020 ⊠ Balanstr. 74, Haidhausen ☎ 089/403-091. **Europcar** ⊠ Airport ☎ 089/973-5020 ⊠ Kreillerstr. 56a, Berg am Laim ☎ 089/696-950. **Hertz** ⊠ Airport ☎ 089/978-860 ⊠ Hauptbahnhof,

Leopoldvorstadt ☎ 089/550-2256 ✉ Nymphenburgerstr. 81, Maxvorstadt ☎ 089/129-5001. **Sixt** ✉ Airport ☎ 089/526-2525 ✉ Hauptbahnhof, Leopoldvorstadt ☎ 089/550-2447 ✉ Seitzstr. 9, Lehel ☎ 089/223-333.

CAR TRAVEL

From the north (Nürnberg or Frankfurt), leave the autobahn at the Schwabing exit. From Stuttgart and the west, the autobahn ends at Obermenzing, Munich's most westerly suburb. The autobahns from Salzburg and the east, Garmisch and the south, and Lindau and the southwest all join the Mittlerer Ring (city beltway). When leaving any autobahn, follow the signs reading STADTMITTE for downtown Munich.

PARKING Parking in Munich is nerve-racking and not cheap. There are several parking garages throughout the center, but your best bet is to use public transportation, which is exemplary.

CONSULATES

🛂 Canada **Canadian Consulate** ✉ Tal 29, City Center ☎ 089/219-9570.
🛂 United Kingdom **British Consulate General** ✉ Bürkleinstr. 10, Lehel ☎ 089/211-090.
🛂 United States **U.S. Consulate General** ✉ Königinstr. 5, Maxvorstadt ☎ 089/28880.

EMERGENCIES

Police (☎ 110).

Fire department, ambulance, and medical emergencies (☎ 112).

ENGLISH-LANGUAGE MEDIA

The monthly English-language magazine *Munich Found* is sold at most newspaper stands and in many hotels. It contains excellent listings, reviews restaurants and shows, and generally gives an idea of life in the city.

The Anglia English Bookshop is the leading English-language bookstore in Munich, although the shop is in incredible disorder and the books are very expensive. Hugendubel has a good selection geared more toward novels. The Internationale Presse store is at the main train station. Words'worth is a well-kept shop with books in English. If you're just looking for some light literature or inexpensive German-language coffee-table books, try texxt; the English-language section is in the basement.

🛂 Bookstores **Anglia English Bookshop** ✉ Schellingstr. 3, Schwabing ☎ 089/283-642. **Hugendubel** ✉ Marienpl. 22, 2nd fl., City Center ☎ 089/23890 or 01803/484-484 ✉ Karlspl. 3, City Center ☎ 089/552-2530. **Internationale Presse** ☎ 089/13080. **texxt** ✉ Sendlinger-Str. 24, City Center ☎ 089/2694-9503. **Words'worth** ✉ Schellingstr. 21a, Schwabing ☎ 089/280-9141.

PHARMACIES

Internationale Ludwigs-Apotheke and Europa-Apotheke, both open weekdays 8–6 and Saturday 8–1, stock over-the-counter medications. Munich pharmacies stay open late on a rotating basis, and every pharmacy has a schedule in its window.

🛂 **Europa-Apotheke** ✉ Schützenstr. 12, near the Hauptbahnhof, Leopoldvorstadt ☎ 089/595-423. **Internationale Ludwigs-Apotheke** ✉ Neuhauserstr. 11, City Center ☎ 089/260-3021.

TAXIS

Munich's cream-color taxis are numerous. Hail them in the street or phone for one (there's an extra charge of €1 if you call). Rates start at €2.40. Expect to pay €8–€10 for a short trip within the city. There's a €0.50 charge for each piece of luggage.

🚕 **Taxi** ☎ 089/21610 or 089/19410.

TOURS

For the cheapest sightseeing tour of the city center on wheels, board Streetcar 19 outside the Hauptbahnhof on Bahnhofplatz and make the 15-minute journey to Max Weber Platz. Explore the streets around the square, part of the old Bohemian residential area of Haidhausen (with some of the city's best bars and restaurants, many on the villagelike Kirchenstrasse), and then return by a different route on Streetcar 18 to Karlsplatz. A novel way of seeing the city is to hop on one of the bike-rickshaws. The bike-powered two-seater cabs operate between Marienplatz and the Chinesischer Turm in the Englischer Garten. Just hail one—or book ahead by calling Rikscha-Mobil. Cost is €37 per hour.

The tourist office offers individual guided tours for fees ranging between €100 and €250. Bookings must be made at least 10 days in advance. Taxi tours with specially trained drivers are offered by IsarFunk Taxizentrale GmbH. These are a good alternative for groups of up to four people. Cost is €68 per trip for the first hour and €18 for each subsequent half-hour. Cityhopper Touren offers daily escorted bike tours March–October. Bookings must be made in advance, and starting times are negotiable. Radius Touristik has bicycle tours from May through the beginning of October at 10:15 and 2; the cost, including bike rental, is €7.70. Mike's Bike Tours is run by a young American who hires native English speakers to take visitors on a two- to three-hour spin through Munich. The tours start daily at the Old Town Hall, the Altes Rathaus, at 11:20 and 3:50. They cost €22, including bike rental. Mike also organizes walking tours for €9.

🚲 **Cityhopper Touren** ☎ 089/272–1131. **IsarFunk Taxizentrale GmbH** ☎ 089/450–540. **Mike's Bike Tours** ☎ 089/2554–3988. **Munich Tourist Office** ☎ 089/2333–0234. **Radius Touristik** ✉ Arnulfstr. 3, opposite Platforms 30–36 in Hauptbahnhof, Leopoldvorstadt ☎ 089/596–113. **Rikscha-Mobil** ☎ 089/129–4808.

BUS TOURS Bus excursions to the Alps, to Austria, to the royal palaces and castles of Bavaria, or along the Romantic Road can be booked through DER. Next to the main train station, Panorama Tours operates numerous trips, including the Royal Castles Tour (Schlösserfahrt) of "Mad" King Ludwig's dream palaces; the cost is €41, excluding entrance fees to the palaces. Bookings for both companies can also be made through all major hotels in the city. The tours depart from the front of the Hauptbahnhof outside the Hertie department store.

City bus tours are offered by Panorama Tours. The blue buses operate year-round, departing from the Hertie department store on Bahnhofplatz. A one-hour tour of Munich highlights leaves daily at 10, 11, 11:30, noon, 1, 2:30, 3, and 4. The cost is €11. A 2½-hour city tour departs daily at 10 AM and includes brief visits to the Alte Pinakothek, the Peterskirche, and Marienplatz for the glockenspiel. An afternoon tour, also 2½ hours and starting at 2:30 PM, includes a tour of Schloss Nymphenburg. The cost of each tour is €19. Another 2½-hour tour, departing Saturday, Sunday, and Monday at 10 AM, includes a visit to the Bavaria film studios. The cost is €23. A four-hour tour, starting daily at 10 AM and 2:30 PM, includes a visit to the Olympic Park. The cost is €19. The München bei Nacht tour provides 4½ hours of Munich by night and includes dinner and a show at the Hofbräuhaus, a trip up the Olympic Tower to admire the lights of the city, and a final drink in a nightclub. It departs April through November, Friday and Saturday at 7:30 PM; the cost is €60.

Yellow Cab Stadtrundfahrten has a fleet of yellow double-decker buses, in which tours are offered simultaneously in eight languages. They leave hourly between 10 AM and 4 PM from the front of the Elisenhof shopping complex on Bahnhofplatz. Tours cost €9.

🔒 **DER** ✉ Hauptbahnhofpl. 2, in main train-station bldg., Leopoldvorstadt ☎ 089/5514-0100. **Panorama Tours** ✉ Arnulfstr. 8, Leopoldvorstadt ☎ 089/323-040. **Yellow Cab Stadtrundfahrten** ✉ Sendlinger-Tor-Pl. 2, Isarvorstadt ☎ 089/303-631.

WALKING TOURS Downtown Munich is only a mile square and is easily explored on foot. Almost all the major attractions in the city center are on the interlinking web of pedestrian streets that run from Karlsplatz, by the main train station, to Marienplatz and the Viktualienmarkt and extend north around the Frauenkirche and up to Odeonsplatz. The two tourist information offices issue a free map with suggested walking tours.

Two-hour tours of the Old City center are given daily in summer (March–October) and on Friday and Saturday in winter (November–February). Tours organized by the visitor center start at 10:30 and 1 in the center of Marienplatz. The cost is €8. Munich Walks conducts daily tours of the Old City and sites related to the Third Reich era. The cost is €10. Tours depart daily from the Hauptbahnhof, outside the EurAide office by Track 11, and also pick up latecomers outside the McDonald's at Karlsplatz.

🔒 **The Original Munich Walks** ☎ 089/5502-9374 ⊕ www.radius-munich.com.

TRAIN TRAVEL

All long-distance rail services arrive at and depart from the Hauptbahnhof; trains to and from some destinations in Bavaria use the adjoining Starnbergerbahnhof, which is under the same roof. The high-speed InterCity Express (ICE) trains connect Munich, Augsburg, Frankfurt, and Hamburg on one line; Munich, Nürnberg, Würzburg, and Hamburg on another. Regensburg can be reached from Munich on Regio trains. Call for information on train schedules; most railroad information employees speak English. For tickets and travel information, go to the station information office or try the ABR-DER travel agency, right by the station on Bahnhofplatz.

🔒 **ABR-DER** ✉ Bahnhofpl., Leopoldvorstadt ☎ 089/5514-0200. **Hauptbahnhof** ✉ Bahnhofpl., Leopoldvorstadt ☎ 089/2333-0256 or 089/2333-0257, 01805/996-633 train schedules.

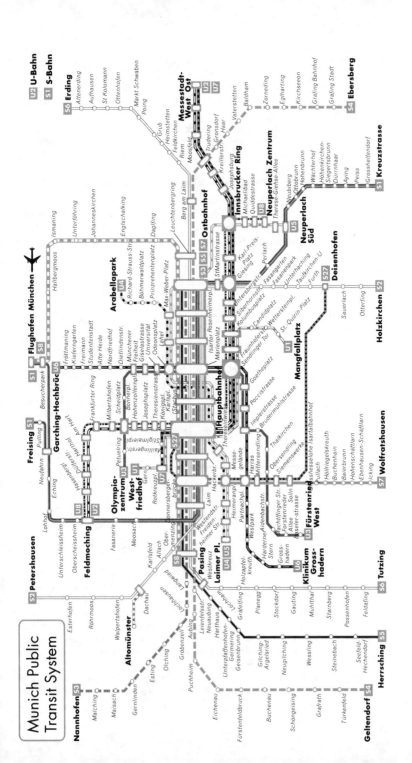

Munich Public Transit System

TRANSPORTATION AROUND MUNICH

Munich has an efficient and well-integrated public transportation system, consisting of the U-bahn (subway), the S-bahn (suburban railway), the Strassenbahn (streetcars), and buses. Marienplatz forms the heart of the U-bahn and S-bahn network, which operates from around 5 AM to 1 AM. An all-night tram and bus service operates on main routes within the city. For a clear explanation in English of how the system works, pick up a copy of *Rendezvous mit München,* free at all tourist offices.

Fares are uniform for the entire system. As long as you are traveling in the same direction, you can transfer from one mode of transportation to another on the same ticket. You can also interrupt your journey as often as you like, and time-punched tickets are valid for up to four hours, depending on the number of zones you travel through. Fares are constantly creeping upward, but a basic *Einzelfahrkarte* (one-way ticket) costs €2 for a ride in the inner zone and €1 for a short journey of up to four stops. If you're taking a number of trips around the city, save money by buying a *Mehrfahrtenkarte,* or multiple-strip ticket. Red-strip tickets are valid for children under 15 only. Blue strips cover adults—€9 buys a 10-strip ticket. All but the shortest inner-area journeys (up to four stops) cost two strips (one for young people between 15 and 21), which must be validated at one of the many time-punching machines at stations or on buses and trams. For two to five people on a short stay the best option is the *Partner-Tageskarte,* which provides unlimited travel for one day (maximum of two adults, plus three children under 15). It's valid anytime except 6 AM to 9 AM on weekdays. The costs are €7.50 for an inner-zone ticket and €15 for the entire network. The day card exists in single version for €4.50 for the inner city, €9 for the whole network. A three-day card is also available, costing €11 for a single and €17.50 in the partner version.

The *Welcome Card* covers transport within the city boundaries and includes up to 50% reductions in admission to many museums and attractions in Munich and in Bavaria (lifts up to the Zugspitze in Garmisch-Partenkirchen, for example). The card, obtainable from visitor information offices, costs €6.50 for one day and €15.50 for three days. A three-day card for two people costs €22.50. You can also get a partner card that includes airport transport fare for €38.

All tickets are sold at the blue dispensers at U- and S-bahn stations and at some bus and streetcar stops. Bus drivers have single tickets (the most expensive kind). There are ticket-vending machines in trams, but they don't offer the strip cards. Otherwise tourist offices and Mehrfahrtenkarten booths (which display a white K on a green background) also sell tickets. Spot checks are common and carry an automatic fine of €30 if you're caught without a valid ticket. Holders of a EurailPass, a Youth Pass, or an Inter-Rail card can travel free on all suburban railway trains (S-bahn).

TRAVEL AGENCIES

DER, the official German travel agency, has outlets all over Munich. The two most central ones are in the main train-station building and at the Münchner-Freiheit Square, in Schwabing.

🖼 **American Express** ⊠ Promenadenpl. 6, City Center ☎ 089/290–900. **DER** ⊠ Bahn-hofpl. 2, Leopoldvorstadt ☎ 089/5514–0100 ⊠ Münchner-Freiheit 6, Schwabing ☎ 089/336–033.

VISITOR INFORMATION

The Hauptbahnhof tourist office is open Monday–Saturday 9–8 and Sunday 10–6; the Info-Service in the Rathaus is open weekdays 10–8 and Saturday 10–4.

For information on the Bavarian mountain region south of Munich, contact the Tourismusverband München-Oberbayern.

🖼 **Hauptbahnhof** ⊠ Bahnhofpl. 2, next to DER travel agency, Leopoldvorstadt ☎ 089/2333–0123 ⊕ www.munich-tourist.de. **Info-Service** ⊠ Marienpl., City Center ☎ 089/2332–8242. **Tourismusverband München-Oberbayern** (Upper Bavarian Regional Tourist Office) ⊠ Bodenseestr. 113, Pasing D-81243 ☎ 089/829–2180.

THE BAVARIAN ALPS

2

Updated by
Marton Radkai

OBERBAYERN, OR UPPER BAVARIA, a region of fir-clad mountains, comes closest to what most of us envision as "Germany." Quaint towns full of half-timber houses—fronted by flowers in summer and snowdrifts in winter—pop up among the mountain peaks, as do the creations of "Mad" King Ludwig II. Shimmering Alpine lakes abound, and the whole area has sporting opportunities galore, making this Germany's favorite year-round vacationland.

This part of Bavaria fans south from Munich to the Austrian border, and as you follow this direction, you'll soon find yourself on a gently rolling plain leading to lakes fed by rivers and streams and surrounded by ancient forests. In time the plain merges into foothills, which suddenly give way to jagged Alpine peaks. In places such as Königsee, near Berchtesgaden, snowcapped mountains seem to rise straight up from the gemlike lakes.

Continuing south, you'll encounter cheerful villages with richly frescoed houses, churches and monasteries filled with the especially voluble and sensuous Bavarian baroque and rococo styles, and several minor spas where you can "take the waters" and tune up your system. Sports possibilities are legion: downhill and cross-country skiing, snowboarding, and ice-skating in winter; tennis, swimming, sailing, golf, and, above all (sometimes literally), hiking, paragliding, and ballooning in summer.

EXPLORING THE BAVARIAN ALPS

The Bavarian Alps comprise a fairly small region. You can easily stay in one spot and make day trips to specific sights. The A–8 autobahn is the region's great traffic artery.

About the Restaurants

You can still find many old *Gasthöfe* with geraniums gushing off balconies and a wood-panel dining area with simple tables and benches, or beer gardens in the region. The mood at these spots is casual; you may even be asked to share a table with strangers. The more upscale places also try to maintain a feeling of familiarity, although you may feel more comfortable at the truly gourmet restaurants if you dress up a bit. Note that many restaurants take a break between 2:30 PM and 6 PM. If you want to eat during these hours, look for the magic words *Durchgehend warme Küche,* meaning warm food served throughout the day, possibly snacks during the off-hours.

About the Hotels

With few exceptions, a hotel or *Gasthof* in the Bavarian Alps and lower Alpine regions has high standards and is traditionally styled, with balconies, pine woodwork, and gently angled roofs upon which the snow sits and insulates. Check out the seven-day packages in the larger resort towns. Private homes all through the region offer Germany's own version of bed-and-breakfasts, indicated by signs reading ZIMMER FREI (rooms available). Their rates may be less than €25 per person. As a general rule, the farther from the popular and sophisticated Alpine resorts you go, the lower the rates. Note, too, that many places

Numbers in the text correspond to numbers in the margin and on the Bavarian Alps map.

2

If you have

3 days

Consider basing yourself in one spot and exploring the immediate area—you'll still experience just about everything the Bavarian Alps have to offer. Choose between the western (Garmisch-Partenkirchen) area and the eastern (Berchtesgaden) corner. If busy little ⊞ **Garmisch-Partenkirchen ❶** ⌐ is your base, devote a couple of days to exploring the magnificent countryside. Wait for good weather to take the cable car or cog railway to the summit of Germany's highest mountain, the Zugspitze. A comfortable day trip takes in the monastery at ⊞ **Ettal ❷** and **Schloss Linderhof ❸**. Also worth a visit is **Oberammergau ❹**, where villagers stage the famous Passion Play every 10 years (the next performance is in 2010). Allow a third day to visit **Mittenwald ❺** and its violin museum, taking in the village of Klais (with Germany's highest-altitude railroad station) on the way. If you devote your three days to ⊞ **Berchtesgaden ⍟**, allow one of them for **Obersalzberg ㉑**, site of Hitler's retreat, called Eagle's Nest, and a second for a boat outing on Königsee, deep in the mountains' embrace. On the third day choose between a trip down into Berchtesgaden's salt mine, the Salzbergwerk, or a cross-border run into the Austrian city of Salzburg.

If you have

5 days

Spend a day or two in ⊞ **Garmisch-Partenkirchen ❶** ⌐, and then head for Bavaria's largest lake, ⊞ **Chiemsee ⍟** (about a two-hour trip via the autobahn). Spend the night in one of the several villages on its western shore (Prien has a mainline railway station and a boat harbor) and take boat trips to **Schloss Herrenchiemsee** island and to the smaller and utterly enchanting **Fraueninsel.** Round off the journey with two days in ⊞ **Berchtesgaden ⍟** and the surrounding countryside.

If you have

7 days

Begin with a day or two based in ⊞ **Garmisch-Partenkirchen ❶** ⌐ for excursions to **Schloss Linderhof ❸** and **Oberammergau ❹**. Next, strike out east along the well-signposted Deutsche Alpenstrasse. Leave the route after 20 km (12 mi), at Wallgau, to relax for an hour or two on the southern shore of picturesque Walchensee. Then dodge in and out of Austria on a highland road that snakes through the tree-lined Aachen Pass to ⊞ **Tegernsee ⍟**, where hills dip from all sides into the lake. Book two or three nights at one of the nearby, moderately priced Gasthöfe, or spoil yourself at one of the luxurious hotels in upscale Rottach-Egern. A day's walk (or a 20-minute drive) takes you to Tegernsee's neighboring lake, the shimmering **Schliersee ⍟**. From there the road becomes a switchback (one stretch is a privately maintained toll road), climbing from narrow valleys to mountain ski resorts and finally plunging to the Inn River valley. Consider leaving the Alpine route here for a stay on the shores of the ⊞ **Chiemsee ⍟**, where King Ludwig's Schloss Herrenchiemsee stands on one of the three islands. Back on the Alpine route, you'll inevitably head back into the mountains, dropping down again into elegant ⊞ **Bad Reichenhall ⍟**, another overnight stop. From here it's only 20 km (13 mi) to ⊞ **Berchtesgaden ⍟**, where you conclude your stay in the Alps viewing the town, its castle museum, Hitler's mountaintop retreat, and the beautiful Königsee.

offer a small discount if you stay more than one night. By the same token, at some places you will harvest a frown if you are staying only one night, especially during the high seasons, in summer, at Christmas, and on winter weekends. In spas and many mountain resorts a "spa tax" is added to the hotel bill. It amounts to no more than €3 per person per day and allows free use of spa facilities and entry to local attractions and concerts.

WHAT IT COSTS In Euros				
	$$$$	**$$$**	**$$**	**$**	**¢**
RESTAURANTS	over €25	€21–€25	€16–€20	€9–€15	under €9
HOTELS	over €225	€175–€225	€100–€175	€50–€100	under €50

Restaurant prices are per person for a main course at dinner. Hotel prices are for two people in a standard double room, including tax and service.

Timing

This mountainous region is a year-round holiday destination. Snow is promised by most resorts from December through March, although there's year-round skiing on the glacier slopes at the top of the Zugspitze. Spring and autumn are ideal times for mountain walking. November is a between-seasons time, when many hotels and restaurants close down or attend to renovations. Note, too, that many locals take a vacation after January 6, and businesses may be closed for anywhere up to a month.

Garmisch-Partenkirchen

▶ ❶ *90 km (55 mi) southwest of Munich.*

Garmisch, as it's more commonly known, is the undisputed capital of Alpine Bavaria, a bustling, year-round resort and spa. Once two separate communities, Garmisch and Partenkirchen fused in 1936 to accommodate the Winter Olympics. Today, with a population of 28,000, the area is large enough to offer every facility expected from a major Alpine resort without being overwhelming. Garmisch is walkable but spread out, and the narrow streets and buildings of smaller Partenkirchen hold snugly together. In both parts of town pastel frescoes of biblical and bucolic scenes decorate facades.

Partenkirchen was founded by the Romans, and you can still follow the road they built between Partenkirchen and neighboring Mittenwald, which was part of a major route between Rome and Germany well into the 17th century. In the early 18th century the region experienced an economic boom thanks to the discovery of iron ore.

Winter sports rank high on the agenda here. There are more than 99 km (62 mi) of downhill ski runs, 40 ski lifts and cable cars, and 180 km (112 mi) of *Loipen* (cross-country ski trails). One of the principal stops on the international winter-sports circuit, the area hosts a week of races every January. You can usually count on good skiing from December through April (and into May on the Zugspitze).

Biking & Hiking

With its lakeside and mountain trails, this region is a mountain biker's paradise. Sports shops rent mountain bikes for around €15 a day. Well-marked and well-groomed hiking trails lead from the glorious countryside, along rivers and lakes, through woods, and high into the Alps. If you just want an afternoon stroll, head for the lower slopes. If you're a serious hiker, make for the mountain trails of the Zugspitze, in Garmisch-Partenkirchen; the heights above Oberammergau, Berchtesgaden, or Bad Reichenhall; or the lovely Walchensee. Well-marked trails near the Schliersee or Tegernsee (lakes) lead steadily uphill and to mountaintop inns. A special treat is a hike to the Tatzelwurm Gorge near Bayrischzell.

Boating & Sailing

All the Bavarian Alpine lakes have sailing schools that rent sailboards as well as various other types of boats. At Tegernsee you can hire motorboats at the pier in front of the Schloss Cafe, in the Tergensee town center. Chiemsee, with its wide stretch of water whipped by Alpine winds, is a favorite for both sailing enthusiasts and windsurfers. There are boatyards all around the lake and a very good windsurfing school at Bernau.

On the Menu

Designed to pack in the calories after a day's walking or skiing, the food in Bavaria's mountainous areas is understandably hearty and filling. Portions are usually huge, whether they're great wedges of roast pork, dumplings big enough to fire from a cannon, or homemade *Apfelstrudel* (apple-filled pastry), which is a meal in itself. In lakeside inns and restaurants the day's catch might be plump perch (*Renke*) or freshwater trout (*Forelle, Lachsforelle,* or *Bachsaibling*). Many inns have pools where the trout grow even fatter, although they lack the mountain-water tang. Most districts in the Alps distill their own brand of schnapps from mountain herbs, and you can quaff what is arguably the region's best beer on the banks of the Tegernsee.

Skiing & Snowboarding

Garmisch-Partenkirchen was the site of the 1936 Winter Olympics and remains Germany's premier winter-sports resort. The upper slopes of the Zugspitze and surrounding mountains challenge the best ski buffs and snowboarders, and there are also plenty of runs for intermediate skiers and families. The slopes above Reit im Winkl (particularly the Winklmoosalm) are less crowded, but the skiing is comparable to that of the Zugspitze area. Hotels in the region offer skiing packages.

Garmisch-Partenkirchen isn't all sporty, however. In Garmisch, beautiful examples of Upper Bavarian houses line Frühlingstrasse, and a pedestrian zone begins at Richard-Strauss-Platz. Off Marienplatz, at one end of the car-free zone, is the 18th-century parish church of **St. Martin.** It contains some significant stucco work by the Wessobrunn artists Schmutzer, Schmidt, and Bader. The chancel is by another fine 18th-century artist from Austria, Franz Hosp. Across the Loisach River, on Pfarrerhausweg, stands another **St. Martin** church, dating from

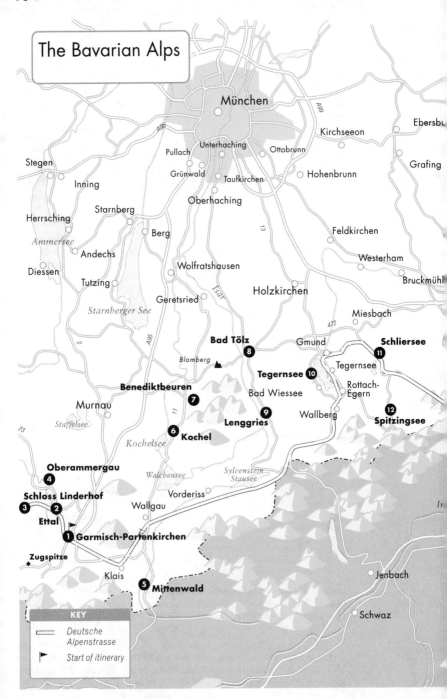

The Bavarian Alps

1280, whose Gothic wall paintings include a larger-than-life-size figure of St. Christopher.

Objects and exhibitions on the region's history can be found in the excellent **Werdenfelser Museum,** which is itself housed in a building dating back to around 1200. The museum is spread over five floors and explores every aspect of life in the Werdenfels region, which was an independent county for more than 700 years (until 1802). ⊠ *Ludwigstr. 47, Partenkirchen* ☎ *08821/2134* ⊠ *€1.50* ⊙ *Tues.–Fri. 10–1 and 3–6, Sat. 10–1.*

On the eastern edge of Garmisch, at the end of Zöppritzstrasse, stands the **villa of composer Richard Strauss,** who lived here until his death in 1949. It's the center of activity during the *Richard-Strauss-Tage,* an annual music festival held in mid-June that features concerts and lectures on the town's most famous son.

The number one attraction in Garmisch is the **Zugspitze,** the highest mountain (9,731 feet) in Germany. There are two ways up the mountain: a leisurely 75-minute ride on a cog railway from the train station in the town center, combined with a cable-car ride up the last stretch; or a 10-minute hoist by cable car, which begins its giddy ascent from the Eibsee, 10 km (6 mi) outside town on the road to Austria. There are two restaurants with sunny terraces at the summit and another at the top of the cog railway. A round-trip combination ticket allows you to mix your mode of travel up and down the mountain. Prices are lower in winter than in summer, even though they include use of all the ski lifts on the mountain. You can rent skis at the top. ⊠ *Cog railway leaves from Olympiastr. 27* ☎ *08821/7970* ⊕ *www.zugspitze.de* ⊠ *Funicular or cable car €43 in summer, €34 in winter, round-trip; parking €3.*

A four-seat cable car goes to the top of one of the lesser peaks: the **Wank** or the **Alpspitze,** some 2,000 feet lower than the Zugspitze. You can tackle both mountains on foot, provided you're properly shod and physically fit.

Where to Stay & Eat

For information about accommodation packages with ski passes, call the **Zugspitze** (☎ 08821/7970 ⊠ 08821/797–901 ⊕ www.zugspitze. de) or get in touch with the tourist office in Garmisch.

$–$$$$ ✕ **Riessersee.** On the shores of a small, green tranquil lake—a 3-km (2-mi) walk from town—this café-restaurant is an ideal spot for lunch or afternoon tea (on weekends there's live zither music from 3 to 5). House specialties are fresh trout and local game (which fetches the higher prices on the menu). ⊠ *Riess 5* ☎ *08821/95440* ⊟ *AE, MC, V* ⊙ *Closed Mon. and Dec. 1–15.*

★ **$$–$$$$** ✕⊡ **Reindl's Partenkirchner Hof.** Owner Karl Reindl ranks among the world's top hoteliers. His award-winning hotel is a real family concern, with daughter Marianne in charge of the kitchen, which cooks up excellent Bavarian specialties and international gastronomical goodies. The light-filled bistro annex serves meals, coffee, and cake in an atmosphere that contrasts sharply with the heavier, wood-and-velvet main building.

Each guest room has pinewood furniture and a balcony or patio. Some of the double rooms are huge. If you're planning to stay for several days, ask about specials. ⊠ *Bahnhofstr. 15, D–82467* ☎ *08821/943–870* 🖶 *08821/9438–7250* ⊕ *www.Reindls.de* ⟿ *65 rooms, 23 suites* ♿ *Restaurant, cable TV with movies, pool, gym, sauna, bicycles, bar, no-smoking rooms; no a/c in some rooms* ⊟ *AE, DC, MC, V* ⦿ *BP.*

$–$$ ✕🏨 **Post-Hotel Partenkirchen.** What makes the Post-Hotel a delight to the eye and a unique spot in the region is the original old furnishings, beginning with the reception area's 20-foot oak refectory table. The rooms continue in the same style, with wood paneling, heavy drapes, and comfortable chairs. The elegant, 500-year-old vaulted cellar restaurant offers a menu that changes daily, with dishes such as leg of lamb in rosemary sauce. The café boasts opulently carved paneling and delicious cakes. ⊠ *Ludwigstr. 49, D–82467* ☎ *08821/93630* 🖶 *08821/9363–2222* ⟿ *56 rooms* ♿ *Restaurant, café, cable TV, some pets allowed (fee); no a/c* ⊟ *AE, DC, MC, V* ⦿ *BP.*

$ ✕🏨 **Gasthof Fraundorfer.** You can sled your way to dreamland in this beautiful old Bavarian Gasthof—some of the beds are carved like old-fashioned sleighs; others take the form of antique automobiles. The colorfully painted facade is covered with geraniums most of the year. The tavern-restaurant, its walls covered with pictures and other ephemera, presents "Bavarian evenings" of folk entertainment. ⊠ *Ludwigstr. 24, D–82467* ☎ *08821/9270* 🖶 *08821/92799* ⊕ *www.gasthof-fraundorfer. de* ⟿ *20 rooms, 7 suites* ♿ *Restaurant, in-room data ports, cable TV, sauna, steam room, some pets allowed (fee); no a/c* ⊟ *AE, MC, V* ⊘ *Closed late Nov.–early Dec.* ⦿ *BP.*

$ ✕🏨 **Hotel-Gasthof Drei Mohren.** In the Partenkirchen village you'll find all the simple, homey comforts you'd expect of a 150-year-old Bavarian inn. All rooms have mountain views, and most are furnished with farmhouse-style painted beds and cupboards. A free bus to Garmisch and the cable-car stations will pick you up right outside the house. The restaurant ($–$$) serves solid fare, including a series of *Pfanderl*, large portions of meat and potatoes in various guises: fried, roasted, or in sauce. ⊠ *Ludwigstr. 65, D–82467* ☎ *08821/9130* 🖶 *08821/18974* ⊕ *www. dreimohren.de* ⟿ *21 rooms, 2 apartments* ♿ *Restaurant, cable TV, bar, Internet, some pets allowed (fee); no a/c* ⊟ *AE, MC, V* ⦿ *BP.*

★ $$ 🏨 **Wittelsbacher Hof.** Dramatic mountain vistas from bedroom balconies and a spacious garden terrace make this hotel especially attractive. Public rooms are elegantly Bavarian, and the restaurant has graceful art nouveau features. The bedrooms are spacious, with corner lounge areas and mahogany or cherrywood furniture. Ask for a room facing south for Zugspitze views. ⊠ *Von-Brug-Str. 24, D–82467* ☎ *08821/53096* 🖶 *08821/57312* ⊕ *www.wittelsbacher-hof.com* ⟿ *60 rooms, 2 suites* ♿ *Restaurant, cable TV, pool, sauna, spa, piano bar, Internet, some pets allowed (fee), no-smoking rooms; no a/c* ⊟ *AE, DC, MC, V* ⦿ *BP.*

$–$$ 🏨 **Edelweiss.** Like its namesake, the "eternally white" Alpine flower of *Sound of Music* fame, this small downtown hotel has plenty of mountain charm. Inlaid with warm pinewood, it has Bavarian furnishings and individually decorated rooms. ⊠ *Martinswinkelstr. 15–17, D–82467* ☎ *08821/4849* 🖶 *09621/2458* ⊕ *www.hoteledelweiss.de* ⟿ *31 rooms*

    ⚘ *Cable TV, some pets allowed (fee), no-smoking rooms; no a/c* ⊟ *V* ⦿ *BP.*

$ ☷ **Hotel Hilleprandt.** The Hilleprandt, 500 yards from the train station, is a family enterprise, priding itself on friendliness and good service. A small garden and warmly decorated rooms, most with a balcony, welcome you—as does a small drink on the house. What you gain during the three-course evening meal (€16) you can attempt to undo in the first-class wellness center. ✉ *Riffelstr. 17, D–82467* ☎ *08821/943–040* 📠 *08821/74548* ⊕ *www.hotel-hilleprandt.de* ⇆ *13 rooms, 3 suites* ⚘ *In-room data ports, cable TV, hot tub, sauna, some pets allowed; no a/c* ⊟ *MC, V* ⦿ *BP.*

Sports & the Outdoors

HIKING &
WALKING
There are innumerable spectacular walks on 300 km (186 mi) of marked trails through the lower slopes' pinewoods and upland meadows. If you have the time and good walking shoes, try one of the two trails that lead to striking gorges. The **Höllentalklamm** route starts at the **Zugspitze Mountain railway terminal** (✉ Olympiastr. 27) in town and ends at the mountaintop (you'll want to turn back before reaching the summit unless you have mountaineering experience). The **Partnachklamm** route is quite challenging and takes you through a spectacular, tunneled water gorge (entrance fee), past a pretty little mountain lake, and far up the Zugspitze; to do all of it, you'll have to stay overnight in one of the huts along the way. Ride part of the way up in the **Eckbauer cable car** (€7.50 one-way, €10 round-trip), which sets out from the Skistadion off Mittenwalderstrasse. The second cable car, the **Graseckbahn,** takes you right over the dramatic gorges (€3.50 one-way, €5 round-trip). There's a handy inn at the top, where you can gather strength for the hour-long walk back down to the Graseckbahn station. Horse-drawn carriages also cover the first section of the route in summer; in winter you can skim along it in a sleigh. The carriages wait near the Skistadion. Or you can call the local coaching society, the **Lohnkutschevereinigung** (☎ 08821/942–920), for information. Contact **Deutscher Alpenverein** (German Alpine Association; ✉ Von-Kahr-Str. 2–4, D–80997 Munich ☎ 089/140–030 ⊕ www.alpenverein.de) for details on hiking and on staying in mountain huts.

SKIING &
SNOWBOARDING
Garmisch-Partenkirchen's principal draw in winter is skiing. The local mountains are crisscrossed with slopes for all skill levels. The area is divided into two basic regions. The **Riffelriss** with the **Zugspitzplatt** is Germany's highest skiing area, with snow guaranteed from November to May. Access is with the **Zugspitzbahn** funicular. Cost for a day pass is €34, for a 2½-day pass €68 (valid from noon on the first day). The **CLASSIC-Gebiet,** or classical area, offers a total of 17 lifts in the **Alpspitz, Kreuzeck** and **Hausberg** region. Day passes cost €28, a two-day pass €48. You can also use the three cable cars individually. The town has a number of ski schools and tour organizers. The best place for information for all your snow-sports needs is the Alpine office at the tourist information office, **Alpine Auskunftstelle** (✉ Richard-Strauss-Pl. 2, Garmisch ☎ 08821/180–744 ☉ Mon.–Thurs. 4–6). Skiers looking for instruction can try the **Skischuke Alpin** (✉ Reintalstr. 8, Garmisch ☎ 08821/945–676). Cross-country skiers should check with the **Erste Skilanglaufschule**

Garmisch-Partenkirchen (☎ 08821/1516) at the eastern entrance of the Olympic stadium in Garmisch. For snowboarders, there's the **Snowboardschule Erwin Gruber** (⊠ Mittenwalderstr. 47d, Garmisch ☎ 08821/76490). Telemark skiing is also popular in these rugged mountains. For information, contact the **Telemark Schule Leismüller** (⊠ Waldeckstr. 7, Garmisch ☎ 08821/752–696).

Nightlife & the Arts

In season there's a busy **après-ski scene.** Many hotels have dance floors, and some have basement discos that pound away until the early hours. Bavarian folk dancing and zither music are regular features of nightlife. In summer there's entertainment every Saturday evening at the **Bayernhalle** (⊠ Brauhausstr. 19). Wednesday through Monday the cozy tavern-restaurant **Gasthof Fraundorfer** (⊠ Ludwigstr. 24 ☎ 08821/9270) hosts lots of yodeling and folk dancing. Concerts are presented from Saturday to Thursday, mid-May through September, in the park bandstand in Garmisch, and on Friday in the Partenkirchen park. Tickets are available at **Garmisch-Partenkirchen-Ticket** (⊠ Richard-Strauss-Pl. 2 ☎ 08821/752–545 ⊟ 08821/752–547 ⊘ Weekdays 9–1 and 2–7, Sat. 9–1).

The **casino** (⊠ Am Kurpark 10 ☎ 08821/95990) is open daily 3 PM–2 AM and Saturday 3 PM–3 AM, with more than 100 slot machines, roulette, blackjack, and poker tables.

Ettal

★ ❷ *16 km (10 mi) north of Garmisch-Partenkirchen, 85 km (53 mi) south of Munich.*

The village of Ettal is presided over by the massive bulk of **Kloster Ettal,** the great monastery founded in 1330 by Holy Roman Emperor Ludwig the Bavarian for a group of knights and a community of Benedictine monks. The abbey was replaced with new buildings in the 18th century and now serves as a school. The original 10-sided church was brilliantly redecorated in 1744–53, becoming one of the foremost examples of Bavarian rococo. The church's chief treasure is its enormous dome fresco (83 feet wide), painted by Jacob Zeiller, circa 1751–52. The mass of swirling clouds and the pink-and-blue vision of heaven are typical of the rococo fondness for elaborate and glowing illusionistic ceiling painting.

Ettaler, a liqueur made from a centuries-old recipe, is still distilled at the monastery. It's made with more than 70 mountain herbs and has legendary health-giving properties. The ad tells it best: "Two monks know how it's made, 2 million Germans know how it tastes." You can buy bottles of the libation from the gift shop and bookstore outside the monastery. This is the largest Benedictine monastery in Germany; approximately 55 monks live here, including one from Compton, Los Angeles. ☎ 08822/740 *for guided tour of church* ☒ *Free* ⊘ *Daily 8–6.*

Where to Stay & Eat

¢–$ ✕ **Edelweiss.** This friendly café and restaurant next to the monastery is an ideal spot for a light lunch or coffee and homemade cakes. ⊠ *Kaiser-Ludwig-Pl. 3* ☎ *08822/4509* ⊟ *No credit cards.*

$ ✕🏨 **Blaue Gams.** This family-run inn is large but well fitted to the landscape around it. At lunch, a terrace draws diners outside for a breath of fresh air; at dinner, Bavarian specialties are served indoors, either in the pleasant Klause dining room ($–$$$) or the little Stübchen, where a tile oven warms the spirit. Note that the lunch menu has lower prices. Some of the rooms have attractive antique furnishing. ⊠ *Vogelherdweg 12, D–82488* ☎ *08822/6449* 🖷 *08822/869* ⊕ *www.blaue-gams.de* 🛏 *51 rooms* ⚲ *Restaurant, cable TV, some pets allowed (fee); no a/c* ▤ *No credit cards* ❙⦿❙ *BP.*

$ ✕🏨 **Hotel Ludwig der Bayer.** Backed by mountains, this fine old hotel is run by the Benedictine order. There's nothing monastic about it, except for the exquisite religious carvings and motifs that adorn the walls. Most come from the monastery's own carpentry shop, which also made much of the sturdy furniture in the comfortable bedrooms. The hotel has two excellent restaurants ($–$$) with rustic, Bavarian atmosphere and a vaulted tavern that serves sturdy fare and beer brewed at the monastery. The entire wellness area was rebuilt in 2004. ⊠ *Kaiser-Ludwig-Pl. 10, D–82488* ☎ *08822/9150* 🖷 *08822/74480* 🛏 *70 rooms, 32 apartments* ⚲ *2 restaurants, cable TV, tennis court, pool, gym, sauna, bicycles, bowling, 2 bars, some pets allowed (fee); no a/c* ▤ *MC, V.*

$ ✕🏨 **Posthotel.** Families are warmly welcomed at this traditional Gasthof in the center of town. There's a playground in the shady garden, and the Bavarian restaurant ($–$$), which is covered in warm wood paneling, has a children's menu. ⊠ *Kaiser-Ludwig-Pl. 18, D–82488* ☎ *08822/ 3596* 🖷 *08822/6971* ⊕ *www.posthotel-ettal.de* 🛏 *21 rooms, 4 apartments* ⚲ *Restaurant, cable TV, gym, sauna, steam room, playground, some pets allowed (fee), no-smoking rooms; no a/c, no room phones* ▤ *MC, V* ◷ *Closed Oct. 26–Dec. 18* ❙⦿❙ *BP.*

Schloss Linderhof

➌ *10 km (6 mi) west of Ettal on B–23, 95 km (59 mi) south of Munich.*

Built between 1870 and 1879 on the grounds of his father's hunting lodge, Schloss Linderhof was the only one of Ludwig II's royal residences to have been completed during the monarch's short life and in which he spent much time. Linderhof was the smallest of this ill-fated king's castles and his favorite country retreat. Set in sylvan seclusion, between a reflecting pool and the green slopes of a gentle mountain, the charming, French-style, rococo confection is said to have been inspired by the Petit Trianon at Versailles. From an architectural standpoint it's a whimsical combination of conflicting styles, lavish on the outside, somewhat overdecorated on the inside. But the main inspiration came from the Sun King of France, Louis XIV, who is referred to in numerous reliefs, mosaics, paintings, and stucco pieces. Ludwig's bedroom is filled with brilliantly colored and gilded ornaments, the Hall of Mirrors is a shimmering dream world, and the dining room has a clever piece of 19th-century engineering—a table that rises from and descends to the kitchens below.

The formal gardens contain still more whimsical touches. There's a Moorish pavilion—bought wholesale from the 1867 Paris Universal Exposition—and a huge artificial grotto in which Ludwig had scenes from

Wagner operas performed, with full lighting effects. It took the BASF chemical company much research to develop the proper glass for the blue lighting Ludwig desired. The gilded Neptune in front of the castle spouts a 100-foot water jet. According to hearsay, while staying at Linderhof the eccentric king would dress up as the legendary knight Lohengrin to be rowed in a swan boat on the grotto pond; in winter he took off on midnight sleigh rides behind six plumed horses and a platoon of outriders holding flaring torches (in winter be prepared for an approach road as snowbound as in Ludwig's day—careful driving is called for). ☎ *08822/92030* 🖅 *Summer €6, winter €4.50; grounds alone in summer €3* ☉ *Fri.–Wed. 9–6, Thurs. 9–8; pavilion and grotto closed Nov.–Mar.*

Oberammergau

❹ *20 km (12 mi) northwest of Garmisch-Partenkirchen, 4 km (2½ mi) northwest of Ettal, 90 km (56 mi) south of Munich.*

Its location alone, in an Alpine valley beneath a sentinel-like peak, makes this small town a major attraction (allow a half hour for the drive from Garmisch). Its main streets are lined with frescoed houses (such as the 1784 Pilatushaus on Ludwig-Thoma-Strasse), and in summer the village bursts with color as geraniums pour from every window box. Many of these lovely houses are occupied by families whose men are highly skilled in the art of wood-carving, a craft that has flourished here since the early 12th century.

Oberammergau, however, is best known for its **Passion Play**, first presented in 1634 as an offering of thanks after the Black Death stopped just short of the village. In faithful accordance with a solemn vow, it will next be performed in the year 2010 as it has every 10 years since 1680. Its 16 acts, which take 5½ hours, depict the final days of Christ, from the Last Supper through the Crucifixion and Resurrection. It's presented daily on a partly open-air stage against a mountain backdrop from late May to late September. The entire village is swept up in the production, with some 1,500 residents directly involved in its preparation and presentation. Men grow beards in the hope of capturing a key role; young women have been known to put off their weddings—the role of Mary went only to unmarried girls until 1990, when, amid much local controversy, a 31-year-old mother of two was given the part.

You'll find many wood-carvers at work in town, and shop windows are crammed with their creations. From June through October a workshop is open free to the public at the **Pilatushaus** (✉ Ludwig-Thoma-Str. 10 ☎ 08822/92310 tourist office); working potters and painters can also be seen. Pilatushaus was completed in 1775, and the frescoes—considered among the most beautiful in town—were done by Franz Seraph Zwinck, one of the greatest *Lüftlmalerei* painters. The house is named for the fresco over the front door depicting Christ before Pilate. Contact the tourist office to sign up for a weeklong course in wood carving (classes are in German), which costs between €330 and €460, depending on whether you stay in a bed-and-breakfast or a hotel.

The **Heimatmuseum** (Natural History Museum) has historic examples of the wood craftsman's art and an outstanding collection of Christmas crèches, which date from the mid-18th century. Numerous exhibits also document the wax and wax-embossing art, which also flourishes in Oberammergau. ⊠ *Dorfstr. 8* ☎ *08822/94136* 🖃 *€2.50* ⊗ *Mid-May–Oct., Tues.–Sun. 2–6; Nov.–mid-May, Sat. 2–6.*

The immense theater, the **Oberammergau Passionsspielhaus,** in which the Passion Play is performed every 10 years, can be toured. Visitors are given a glimpse of the costumes, the sceneries, the stage, and even the auditorium. ⊠ *Passionstheater, Passionswiese* ☎ *08822/32278* 🖃 *€2.50* ⊗ *Summer daily 9:30–5, winter daily 10–4.*

The 18th-century **St. Peter and St. Paul Church** is regarded as the finest work of rococo architect Josef Schmutzer and has striking frescoes by Matthäus Günther and Franz Seraph Zwinck (in the organ loft). Schmutzer's son, Franz Xaver Schmutzer, did a lot of the stucco work. ⊠ *Pfarrpl. 1* ☎ *08824/553* ⊗ *Daily 9 AM–dusk.*

Where to Stay & Eat

¢–$ ✕ **Ammergauer Stubn.** A homey restaurant with pink tablecloths and a lot of wood, the Stubn has a comprehensive menu that serves both Bavarian specialties and international dishes. You can expect nice roasts and some Swabian dishes, such as *Maultaschen,* a large meat-filled ravioli. ⊠ *Wittelsbach Hotel, Dorfstr. 21* ☎ *08822/92800* 🖃 *AE, DC, MC* ⊗ *Closed Tues. and Nov.–mid-Dec. No lunch.*

$ ✕🖼 **Alte Post.** You can enjoy carefully prepared local cuisine ($–$$) on the original pine tables in this 350-year-old inn. There's a special children's menu, and in summer, meals are also served in the beer garden. If it weren't for the steady automobile traffic groaning through Oberammergau, the front terrace of this delightful old building would be something close to paradise. The rooms are simply appointed, with tasteful rustic furniture. ⊠ *Dorfstr. 19 D–82487* ☎ *08822/9100* 🖃 *08822/ 910–100* ⊕ *www.altepost.ogau.de* ⤶ *31 rooms* ⚴ *Restaurant, cable TV, Internet café, some pets allowed (fee), no-smoking rooms; no a/c* 🖃 *DC, V* ⊗ *Closed Nov.–mid-Dec.* ⁑⊙⁑ *BP.*

$ ✕🖼 **Gasthaus zum Stern.** This is a traditional old place (around 500 years old), with coffered ceilings, thick walls, an old Kachelofen that heats the dining room beyond endurance on cold winter days, and smiling waitresses in dirndls. The food ($–$$) is hearty, traditional Bavarian. For a quieter dinner or lunch, reserve a space in the Bäckerstube. ⊠ *Dorfstr. 33, D–82487* ☎ *08822/867* 🖃 *08822/7027* ⤶ *12 rooms* ⚴ *Some pets allowed; no a/c, no room phones* 🖃 *AE, DC, MC, V* ⊗ *Restaurant closed Wed.* ⁑⊙⁑ *BP.*

$ ✕🖼 **Hotel Landhaus Feldmeier.** This quiet family-run hotel, idyllically set just outside the village, has mostly spacious rooms with modern pinewood furniture. All have geranium-bedecked balconies, with views of the village and mountains. The rustic restaurant ($$–$$$) is one of the region's best. You can dine on the sunny, covered terrace in summer. Only hotel guests can use credit cards in the restaurant. ⊠ *Ettalerstr. 29, D–82487* ☎ *08822/3011* 🖃 *08822/6631* ⊕ *www.hotel-feldmeier.de* ⤶ *22 rooms,*

4 apartments ♿ *Cable TV, gym, hot tub, sauna, steam room, Internet, some pets allowed (fee), no-smoking rooms; no a/c* ▤ *MC, V* ⊗ *Closed mid-Nov.–mid-Dec.* ⦿ *BP.*

★ $ ✕⊡ **Hotel Turmwirt.** Rich wood paneling reaches from floor to ceiling in this transformed 18th-century inn, set in the shadow of Oberammergau's mountain, the Kofel. The hotel's own band presents regular folk evenings in the restaurant ($–$$). The *Ammergauer Pfanne,* a combination of meats and sauces, will take care of even industrial-size hunger. Rooms have corner lounge areas, and most come with balconies and sweeping mountain views. ✉ *Ettalerstr. 2, D–82487* ☎ *08822/92600* 🖷 *08822/1437* ⊕ *www.turmwirt.de* ⟿ *44 rooms* ♿ *Restaurant, cable TV, recreation room, Internet, some pets allowed (fee), no-smoking rooms; no a/c* ▤ *AE, DC, MC, V* ⊗ *Closed Jan. 7–Jan. 21* ⦿ *BP.*

$$ ⊡ **Parkhotel Sonnenhof.** Away from the sometimes crowded town center, the modern Sonnenhof provides a balcony with every guest room, so you can sun yourself and soak up the Alpine view. There's also a children's playroom. ✉ *König-Ludwig-Str. 12, D–82487* ☎ *08822/9130* 🖷 *08822/3047* ⊕ *www.parkhotel-sonnenhof.de* ⟿ *51 rooms, 10 suites* ♿ *Restaurant, some in-room data ports, cable TV, pool, sauna, billiards, bowling, bar, some pets allowed (fee); no a/c* ▤ *AE, DC, MC, V* ⦿ *BP.*

The Arts

Though the Passion Play theater was traditionally not used for anything other than the Passion Play (the next Passion Play will be done in 2010), Oberammergauers decided that using it for opera during the 10-year pause between the religious performances might be a good idea. The first stagings of Verdi's *Nabucco* and Mozart's *Magic Flute* in 2002 established a new tradition. Ticket prices are between €34 and €69. For reservations, call 08822/923–158.

Mittenwald

➎ *20 km (12 mi) southeast of Garmisch, 105 km (66 mi) south of Munich.*

Many regard Mittenwald as the most beautiful town in the Bavarian Alps. It has somehow avoided the architectural sins found in other Alpine villages by maintaining a balance between conservation and the needs of tourism. Its medieval prosperity is reflected on its main street, which has splendid houses with ornately carved gables and brilliantly painted facades. Goethe, Germany's greatest author and thinker, called it "a picture book come alive," and it still is. The town has even re-created the stream that once flowed through the market square, and the main road was detoured around Mittenwald, markedly raising the quality of life in town.

In the Middle Ages, Mittenwald was the staging point for goods shipped from the wealthy city-state of Venice by way of the Brenner Pass and Innsbruck. From Mittenwald, goods were transferred to rafts, which carried them down the Isar River to Munich. In the mid-17th century, however, the international trade route was moved to a different pass, and the fortunes of Mittenwald declined.

In 1684 Matthias Klotz, a farmer's son turned master violin maker, returned from a 20-year stay in Cremona, Italy. There, along with Antonio Stradivari, he had studied under Nicolo Amati, who gave the violin its present form. Klotz taught the art of violin making to his brothers and friends; before long, half the men in the village were crafting the instruments using woods from neighboring forests. Mittenwald became known as the Village of a Thousand Violins, and stringed instruments—violins, violas, and cellos—were shipped around the world. In the right weather—sunny, dry—you may even catch the odd sight of laundry lines hung with new violins out to receive their natural dark hue. The violin has made Mittenwald a small cultural oasis in the middle of the Alps. Not only is there an annual violin- (and viola-, cello-, and bow-) building contest each year in June, with concerts and lectures, but also an organ festival in the church of St. Peter and St. Paul held from the end of July to the end of September. The town also boasts a violin-making school.

The **Geigenbau und Heimatmuseum** (Violin and Local Museum) describes in fascinating detail the history of violin making in Mittenwald. Ask the museum curator to direct you to the nearest of several violin makers—they'll be happy to demonstrate the skills handed down to them. ⊠ *Ballenhausg. 3* ☎ *08823/2511* 🖾 *€2.50* ☉ *Mid-Dec.–Oct., Tues.–Fri. 10–1 and 3–6, weekends 10–1.*

On the back of the altar in the 18th-century **St. Peter and St. Paul Church** (as in Oberammergau, built by Josef Schmutzer and decorated by Matthäus Günther), you'll find Matthias Klotz's name, carved there by the violin maker himself. Note that on some of the ceiling frescoes, the angels are playing violins, violas da gamba, and lutes. In front of the church, Klotz is memorialized as an artist at work in a vivid bronze sculpted by Ferdinand von Miller (1813–79), creator of the mighty Bavaria monument in Munich. The church, with its elaborate and joyful stuccowork coiling and curling its way around the interior, is one of the most important rococo structures in Bavaria. Note its Gothic choir loft, added in the 18th century. The bold frescoes on its exterior are characteristic of *Lüftlmalerei,* a style that reached its height in Mittenwald. Images, usually religious motifs, were painted on the wet stucco exteriors of houses and churches. On nearby streets you can see other fine examples on the facades of three famous houses: the Goethehaus, the Pilgerhaus, and the Pichlerhaus. Among the artists working here was the great Franz Seraph Zwinck. ⊠ *Ballenhausg., next to Geigenbau und Heimatmuseum.*

Where to Stay & Eat

★ **$$–$$$$** ✕ **Arnspitze.** Get a table at the large picture window and soak in the towering Karwendel Mountain range as you ponder a menu that combines the best traditional ingredients with international touches. Chef and owner Herbert Wipfelder looks beyond the edge of his plate all the way to Asia, if need be, to find inspiration. The fish pot-au-feu has a Mediterranean flare; the jugged hare in red wine is truly Bavarian. ⊠ *Innsbrucker Str. 68* ☎ *08823/2425* 🖃 *AE* ☉ *Closed Nov.–mid-Dec. No lunch Tues. and Wed.*

$–$$ ✕▥ **Post.** Stagecoaches carrying travelers and mail across the Alps stopped here as far back as the 17th century. The hotel has changed a lot since then, but it still retains much of its historic charm. The elegant rooms come in various styles, from modern to art nouveau to Bavarian rustic. The lounge-bar, with its dark woods and green velvet upholstered armchairs, lightens up when the open fire is crackling and live music gets you on the dance floor. You can have dinner here, in the wine tavern or at the low-beam Postklause ($–$$). The food in each is excellent, with an emphasis on Bavarian fare such as roasts and great *Semmelknödel* (bread dumplings). ✉ *Obermarkt 9, D–82481* ☎ *08823/938–2333* 🖷 *08823/938–2999* ⊕ *www.posthotel-mittenwald.de* ➯ *74 rooms, 7 suites* ♻ *2 restaurants, in-room data ports, cable TV, pool, sauna, Ping-Pong, bar, some pets allowed (fee), no-smoking rooms; no a/c* ☰ *MC, V* ⊙ *BP.*

$ ✕▥ **Alpenrose.** Once part of a monastery and later given one of the town's most beautiful painted baroque facades, the Alpenrose is one of the area's handsomest hotels. The typical Bavarian bedrooms and public rooms have lots of wood paneling, farmhouse cupboards, and finely woven fabrics. The restaurant ($–$$) devotes the entire month of October to venison dishes, for which it has become renowned. In winter the hotel organizes sleigh rides for its guests. A zither player strums away most evenings in the Josefi wine cellar. ✉ *Obermarkt 1, D–82481* ☎ *08823/92700* 🖷 *08823/3720* ➯ *16 rooms, 2 apartments* ♻ *Restaurant, cable TV, sauna, bar, Internet, some pets allowed (fee); no a/c* ☰ *AE, DC, MC, V* ⊙ *BP.*

$ ✕▥ **Gasthof Stern.** This white house with brilliant blue shutters is right in the middle of Mittenwald. The painted furniture is not antique but reminiscent of old peasant Bavaria, and the featherbeds are incredibly soft. Locals meet in the dining room for loud conversation, folk music dribbles quietly from the speakers, and the beer garden is a pleasant, familial place to while away the hours with a *Bauernschmaus,* a plate of sausage with sauerkraut and homemade liver dumplings. ✉ *Fritz-Plössl-Pl. 2, D–82481* ☎ *08823/8358* ⊕ *www.stern-mittenwald.de* 🖷 *08823/94322* ➯ *5 rooms* ♻ *Restaurant, beer garden, some pets allowed; no a/c, no room phones* ☰ *No credit cards* ⊙ *BP.*

$ ▥ **Bichlerhof.** Carved oak furniture gives the rooms of this Alpine-style hotel a solid German feel. A breakfast buffet is served until 11 AM and will keep the hardiest hiker going all day. Although the restaurant serves only breakfast, there's no shortage of taverns in the area. Most guest rooms have mountain views. ✉ *Adolf-Baader-Str. 5, D–82481* ☎ *08823/9190* 🖷 *08823/4584* ⊕ *www.bichlerhof-mittenwald.de* ➯ *30 rooms* ♻ *In-room data ports, cable TV, pool, gym, sauna, steam room, some pets allowed (fee), no-smoking rooms; no a/c* ☰ *AE, DC, MC, V* ⊙ *BP.*

Sports & the Outdoors

Mittenwald lies literally in the shadow of the mighty **Karwendel** Alpine range, which rises to a height of nearly 8,000 feet. The **Dammkar** run is nearly 5 mi long and offers some of the best free-riding skiing, telemarking, or snowboarding in the German Alps. A **cable car** (☎ 08823/8480 🚡 €12.50 one-way, €20 round-trip, day pass €25 ⊙ Dec.–Oct., daily 8:30–5) carries hikers and skiers to a height of 7,180 feet, the beginning of numerous trails down, or farther up into the Karwendel range. You can book a guide with **Bergerlebnis und Wanderschule Oberes Isartal** (☎ 08651/5835). Skiers, cross-country and downhill, and snowboarders can find all they need including equipment and instruction at the **Erste Schischule Mittenwald** (✉ Bahnhofsparkplatz, parking next to train station ☎ 08823/3582 or 08823/8548).

Shopping

It's not the kind of gift every visitor wants to take home, but if you'd like a violin, a cello, or even a double bass, the Alpine resort of Mittenwald can oblige. There are more than 30 craftsmen whose work is coveted by musicians throughout the world. If you're buying or even just curious, call on **Anton Maller** (✉ Professor-Schreyögg-Pl. ☎ 08823/5865). He's been making violins and other stringed instruments for more than 25 years. The **Geigenbau Leonhardt** (✉ Mühlenweg 53a ☎ 08823/8010) is another good place to purchase one of the town's famous stringed instruments. For traditional Bavarian costumes—dirndls, embroidered shirts and blouses, and lederhosen—try **Trachten Werner** (✉ Hochstr. 1 ☎ 08823/3785). **Trachten Werner-Leichtl** (✉ Dekan-Karl-Pl. 1 ☎ 08823/8282) has a large selection of dirndls and other traditional wear for women.

> **en route** One of the most beautiful stretches of the Deutsche Alpenstrasse follows the course of the fast-flowing Isar River and is lined by fir-clad slopes and rocky peaks. The first 15 km (9 mi) of this stretch from Wallgau (7 km [4½ mi] north of Mittenwald at the junction of the road north to Benediktbeuren) to Vorderiss is a toll road (€2 per vehicle, though the booths at each end are not always manned). Vorderiss is at the western end of the Sylvenstein dam-lake, a mysterious sliver of water whose dark surface covers a submerged village. Halfway along the lake the road divides, east to the Achen Pass, which cuts through Austria (there is no official border, but make sure you have your passport just in case) and on to Tegernsee, and north to the Alpine resort of Lenggries and Bad Tölz.

Walchensee

20 km (12 mi) north of Mittenwald, on B–11 85 km (53 mi) south of Munich.

The first of the truly Alpine lakes north of Mittenwald and Garmisch is the beautiful Walchensee, whose deep blue waters are ringed by fir-clad mountains and the twin peaks of the Benediktenwand and **Herzogstand.** Many VIPs have been attracted to the lake's shores, from the painter Lovis Corinth to King Ludwig II of Bavaria. A memorial was placed at the top of the mountain on the 100th anniversary of the "Mad King's" death. Hiking trails lead off from the town of Walchensee, and the rapidly changing winds make this stretch of water a surfer's paradise. A chairlift climbs to the summit of the 5,539-foot-high Herzogstand (€12 round-trip; open daily 9–4:15, longer in summer if the weather is good).

Where to Stay & Eat

$ ✕🏨 **Karwendelblick.** This friendly establishment stands on a promontory with a magnificent, sunny view of the Karwendel range and the lake. History buffs may be interested to know the place was built in 1884 by Sir Georg Vollmar, one of the founding fathers of Social Democracy in Bavaria, and its walls saw such grand and radical figures as Karl Liebknecht and Rosa Luxemburg. The restaurant ($–$$) serves excellent Bavarian specialties and fish from the lake. ⊠ *Urfeld 15, D–82432* ☎ *08851/410* 🖷 *08851/615–514* ⇄ *3 rooms* ⌂ *Restaurant, in-room data ports, cable TV, some pets allowed; no a/c* ▤ *No credit cards* ☽ *Restaurant closed Mon.* 🍽 *BP.*

Kochel

❻ *35 km (22 mi) north of Mittenwald, on B–11 60 km (37 mi) south of Munich.*

The serpentine mountain road leading to the spectacular lake, **Kochelsee,** was hammered out of the original path in 1492, when Mittenwald became a stop on the road to Venice, an important port for trade. Duke Albrecht VI decided that the rest of the region should have access to the goods and benefits. The hero of the attractive little lakeside town of Kochel is the Schmied von Kochel, or Blacksmith of Kochel, Balthasar Mayer. His fame stems from his role—and eventual death—in the 1705 peasants' uprising against the Austrians, who occupied Bavaria in the wake of the Spanish War of Succession (1701–04). You can see his statue in the town center. The lake is a longtime favorite for summer water sports and mountain walks.

The Kochelsee and the nearby gentler and less dramatic Staffelsee provided the inspiration for the bohemian artists who called themselves the *Blauer Reiter* (Blue Rider). Russian painters Wassily Kandinsky and Alfred Kubin and French artist Franz Marc founded the group in 1911 and were later joined by artists such as Paul Klee and August Macke. (The best collection of Blauer Reiter works are in Munich, at the Städtische Galerie im Lenbachhaus.) After living in various villages in Upper Bavaria, Marc purchased a house in Ried, north of Kochel, in 1914. Shortly after, in 1916, he became one of the millions to die in World War I. Kochel's **Museum Franz Marc,** in a house to the south of town, has a small but fine collection of more than 150 of his works. ⊠ *Herzogstandweg 43* ☎ *08851/7114* ⊕ *www.franz-marc-museum.de* 🖾 *€4* ☽ *Mar.–mid-Jan., Tues.–Sun. 2–6.*

off the beaten path

FREILICHTMUSEUM AN DER GLENTLEITEN (Glenleiten Open-Air Museum) – This open-air museum functions just as a Bavarian village did centuries ago, complete with cobbler, blacksmith, and other craftsmen who would have kept such a community self-sufficient. The houses were collected from around Bavaria and rebuilt here. Various items and foodstuffs are for sale in the original shops, but best of all, architectural purists can find all the elements that make up the authentic Alpine style. The museum is more than a mile to the south of Grossweil, a little village known for its potters. ⊠ *Grossweil, near*

Kochelsee, off Munich-Garmisch autobahn ☎ *08851/1850* ⊕ *www. glentleiten.de* ⌫ *€4.50* ⊙ *Apr.–Oct., Tues.–Sun. 9–6.*

Where to Stay & Eat

$–$$ ✕⊞ **Seehotel Grauer Bär.** The friendly atmosphere at this hotel on the shore of the Kochelsee has much to do with the family that has owned and managed it since 1905. Ask for one of the spacious rooms overlooking the lake, where the hotel also has its own stretch of private beach. Lake-fish entrées often appear on the extensive menu of the airy pavilion-style restaurant ($–$$), where you should try to book a table with a water view. The hotel also has a small wellness area that opens onto the shore. ⊠ *Mittenwalderstr. 82–86, D–82431* ☎ *08851/92500* ⊟ *08851/925–015* ⊕ *www.grauer-baer.de* ⛵ *26 rooms, 3 apartments* ♿ *Restaurant, café, some in-room data ports, cable TV, sauna, beach, boating, bicycles, some pets allowed (fee); no a/c* ⊟ *AE, DC, MC, V* ⦿ *BP.*

$ ⊞ **Landhotel Herzogstand.** The white walls, red roof, green shutters, and geraniums spell pure Bavaria, while the hospitality and friendliness guarantee a very agreeable stay. You can wake up in the morning at the foot of the Herzogstand mountain, enjoy a solid breakfast on the terrace, and weather permitting, you'll be ready for a day's activity. If requested, the hotel will also serve a meal at the end of the day. ⊠ *Herzogstandweg 3, D–82431* ☎ *08851/324* ⊟ *08851/1066* ⊕ *www. herzogstand.de* ⛵ *26 rooms, 2 apartments* ♿ *Cable TV, some pets allowed (fee), no-smoking rooms; no a/c* ⊟ *MC, V* ⦿ *BP.*

Sports & the Outdoors

Solid hiking boots, a parka, water, sunscreen, a walking stick, and about six to eight hours are all you need to explore some of the local mountains. The Herzogstand and Jochberg hikes have refuges to duck into in case of bad weather. Take the cable car up the **Herzogstand** (5,539 feet) and follow signs back to Walchensee on the path marked AV 441. The **Jochberg** (5,014 feet) can be accessed by bus from the Blacksmith statue in Kochel. You can get close to the Kesselberg pass and hike along path number AV 451 to get back down to Kochel. The **Hirschhörndlkopf** (4,848 feet, AV 451 and 483a) and the Rabenkopf (4,677 feet, AV 452, then 451 and 454) hikes begin in Kochel at the Zimmermoos Bridge. The 5,400-foot-high **Benediktenwand,** east of Kochel, is a challenge for mountaineers.

⊙ On the shores of Kochelsee, the lido **Trimini** is one of the largest and most spectacular in Bavaria, with a collection of indoor and outdoor pools, water slides, and enough other amusements to keep a family busy the whole day. ⊠ *Trimini* ☎ *08851/5300* ⌫ *3-hr ticket €6.50, all-day family ticket €21.50* ⊙ *Daily 9–8:30.*

Murnau

16 km (10 mi) west of Kochel; follow unmarked country road skirting northern shore of Staffelsee.

This pretty market town on the shore of Staffelsee is well worth a detour, especially since traffic has been at least partially banned from the center. You may even want to stay here for a while since it's within easy reach of the Alps and Munich and has a number of sights in its own right. Murnau attracted an artistic crowd early in the 20th century. Blauer Reiter group members Wassily Kandinsky and his German wife, Gabriele Münter, lived in Murnau for five years, and playwright Ödön von Horváth (1901–38) also spent time here. The house Münter and Kandinsky inhabited drew artists such as the painter Franz Marc and the composer Arnold Schönberg. The **Münter Haus–das "Russenhaus"** (Russian House) provides insight into the lives of the artist couple—including furniture that they decorated to their own highly individual, colorful tastes, and, of course, paintings. ☒ *Kottmüllerallee 6* ☎ *08841/628–880* ☒ *€2.50* ☉ *Tues.–Sun. 2–5.*

The permanent collection at the **Schlossmuseum** (Castle Museum) is devoted to Münter, von Horváth, and reverse glass painting, which is used as decoration in many restaurants and hotels. The building itself is worth a closer look. The sliding medieval windows in one of the rooms are unique in Germany. ☒ *Schlosshof 4–5* ☎ *08841/476–207* ⊕ *www. schlossmuseum-murnau.de* ☒ *€3.50* ☉ *Oct.–June, Tues.–Sun. 10–5; July–Sept., Tues.–Fri. 10–5, weekends 10–6.*

Where to Stay & Eat

$$–$$$ ✕▦ **Alpenhof Murnau.** All the luxurious rooms at this sprawling yet discreet hotel enjoy views over meadows to the Alps beyond. They're furnished in rich dark woods and colors such as wine red and forest green. The softly lit restaurant ($$$–$$$$), with two rustically furnished rooms, rightly claims to be one of the area's best and has won awards to prove it. Window tables have sweeping Alpine views. The breakfast buffet is perhaps one of the most extensive in Germany. Should adverse weather prevent any excursions, you may find the wellness and beauty spa to be an adequate distraction. ☒ *Ramsachstr. 8, D–82418* ☎ *08841/ 4910* 🖷 *08841/5438* ⊕ *www.alpenhof-murnau.com* 🛏 *60 rooms, 17 suites* ⚭ *Restaurant, in-room data ports, cable TV, pool, gym, sauna, steam room, wine bar, some pets allowed (fee), no-smoking rooms; no a/c in some rooms* ▤ *AE, DC, MC, V* ⦿❙ *BP.*

Benediktbeuren

❼ *45 km (28 mi) north of Mittenwald, 52 km (32 mi) south of Munich.*

The village of Benediktbeuren has a great mid-8th-century **monastery** thought to be the oldest Benedictine institution north of the Alps. It was a flourishing cultural center in the Middle Ages; paradoxically, it also kept record of the most profane poems and songs of those times, the *carmina burana* (also known as the Goliardic songs). In summer these songs are performed using Bavarian composer Carl Orff's 1937 orchestration, in the monastery where the original work was compiled in the 12th century. The frescoes of the monastery's 17th-century church were painted by the father of the Asam brothers, whose church building and artistic decoration made them famous far beyond the borders of Bavaria. Cosmas Damian Asam, the eldest son, was born in Benediktbeuren. The monastery has a delightful beer garden that fills with hikers and day-trippers in summer. ☎ *08857/880 for concert information* 🖃 *€3* ☉ *Monastery church daily 8–6. Guided tour of monastery July–Sept., daily at 2:30; Oct.–mid-May, weekends at 2:30; mid-May–June, Wed. and Sat. at 2:30, Sun. at 10:30 and 2:30.*

Bad Tölz

❽ *16 km (10 mi) northeast of Benediktbeuren, 48 km (30 mi) south of Munich.*

If you can, visit Bad Tölz on a Wednesday morning—market day—when stalls stretch along the main street to the Isar River, the dividing line between the old and new towns. The latter, dating from the mid-19th century, sprang up with the discovery of iodine-laden springs, which allowed the locals to call their town *Bad* (bath or spa) Tölz. You can take the waters, either by drinking a cupful from the local springs or going all the way with a full course of health treatments at a specially equipped hotel.

Bad Tölz clings to its ancient customs more tightly than does any other Bavarian community. Folk costumes, for example, are worn regularly. The town is also famous for its painted furniture, particularly farmhouse cupboards and chests. Several local shops specialize in this type of *Bauernmöbel* (farmhouse furniture, usually hand-carved from pine) and will usually handle export formalities.

If you're in Bad Tölz on November 6, you'll witness one of the most colorful traditions of the Bavarian Alpine area: the Leonhardiritt equestrian procession, which marks the anniversary of the death in 559 of St. Leonhard, the patron saint of animals, specifically horses. The procession ends north of town at an 18th-century chapel on the Kalvarienberg, above the Isar River.

★ The **Alpamare**, Bad Tölz's very attractive spa complex, pumps spa water into its pools, one of which is disguised as a South Sea beach complete with surf. Its five water slides include a 1,082-foot-long adventure run. Another—the Alpa-Canyon—has 90 degree drops, and only the hardiest swimmers are advised to try it. A nightmarish dark tunnel is aptly named the Thriller. ⊠ *Ludwigstr. 13* ☎ *08041/509–999* ⊕ *www. alpamare.de* 🖃 *4-hr ticket €20 weekdays, €23 weekends; 9 AM–11 AM and after 4 PM price is €17* ☉ *Mon.–Thurs. 9–9, Fri.–Sun. 9 AM–10 PM.*

The **Heimatmuseum**, in the Altes Rathaus (Old Town Hall), has many fine examples of Bauernmöbel, as well as a fascinating exhibit on the history of the town and its environs. ⊠ *Marktstr. 48* ☎ *08041/504–688* 🖃 *€2.50* ☉ *Tues.–Wed. and Fri. 10–noon and 2–4, Thurs. 10–noon and 2–6, Sat. 10–4, Sun. 10–6.*

☼ Bad Tölz's local mountain, the **Blomberg**, 3 km (2 mi) west of town, has moderately difficult ski runs and can also be tackled on a toboggan in winter and in summer. The winter run of 5 km (3 mi) is the longest in Bavaria, although the artificial concrete channel used in summer snakes only 3,938 feet down the mountain. A ski-lift ride to the start of the run and toboggan rental are included in the price. ☎ *08041/3726* 🖃 *€7* *per toboggan ride* ⊘ *Jan.–Oct., daily 9–4; Nov.–Dec., hrs depend on weather conditions.*

Where to Stay & Eat

★ **$$–$$$$**   ╳✎ **Hotel Jodquellenhof-Alpamare.** The *Jodquellen* are the iodine springs that have made Bad Tölz wealthy. You can take advantage of these revitalizing waters at this luxurious spa, where the emphasis is on fitness. Vegetarian and low-calorie entrées are served in the restaurant ($$$–$$$$). The imposing 19th-century building, with private access to the Alpamare Lido, contains stylish rooms, with granite and marble bathrooms. The room price includes full use of the spa facilities. There are discounts for children. ⊠ *Ludwigstr. 13–15, D–83646* ☎ *08041/5090* 📠 *08041/509–441* ⊕ *www.jodquellenhof.com* ⟿ *71 rooms* △ *Restaurant, in-room data ports, cable TV, pool, hot tubs, sauna, spa, steam room; no a/c* ⊟ *AE, DC, MC, V* ¡⊙¡ *BP.*

$–$$ ✎ **Hotel Kolbergarten.** Located right near the old town and surrounded by a quiet garden with old trees, this hotel offers comfortable rooms, each carefully done in a particular style such as baroque or biedermeier. The restaurant ($$) offers gourmet food at affordable prices and a wine list that will take you around the world. ⊠ *Fröhlichgasse 5, D–83646* ☎ *08041/78920* 📠 *08041/9069* ⊕ *www.hotel-kolbergarten.de* ⟿ *13 rooms, 2 suites* △ *Cable TV, Internet, some pets allowed, no-smoking rooms; no a/c* ⊟ *AE, DC, MC, V* ¡⊙¡ *BP.*

Nightlife & the Arts

Bad Tölz is world renowned for its outstanding **boys' choir** (☎ 08041/78670 for program details from Städtische Kurverwaltung). When it's not on tour, the choir gives regular concerts in the Kurhaus.

The town has four discos; **Arena** (⊠ Demmeljochstr. 42) is considered the best.

Shopping

Looking for a typical piece of Bavarian farmhouse furniture to ship home? Bad Tölz and the surrounding villages provide a rich hunting ground. Try the **Scheune** (⊠Miesbacherstr. 33 ☎09041/83240), an old barn stacked high with pine and oaken cupboards, tables, chairs, and carved bedsteads.

Lenggries

❾ *10 km (6 mi) south of Bad Tölz, 12 km (7 mi) north of Sylvenstein Lake, 55 km (34 mi) south of Munich.*

Lenggries is a small but popular ski resort, wedged into a narrow valley between the towering Benediktenwand Mountain and the peaks of the Tegernsee Alps. There are fine walks into the Brauneck mountain range and along the Isar River, and the skiing is the best in the region.

Where to Stay & Eat

$ ╳✎ **Altwirt.** The history of this former tavern stretches back to the 15th century. The house is under preservation order and is one of the sights to see in Lenggries. Rooms are a little old-fashioned, but comfortable. Guests are given a discount for staying more than one night. Its restaurant ($–$$) serves such regional specialties as venison with cranberry sauce and dumplings, depending on the season. Note that the kitchen closes at 8:30 PM. ⊠ *Marktstr. 13, D–83661* ☎ *08042/8085* 🖷 *08042/5357* ⊕ *www.altwirt-lenggries.de* 🛏 *20 rooms* ⟁ *Restaurant, cable TV, sauna, Internet, some pets allowed (fee), no-smoking rooms; no a/c* ☰ *MC, V* ⊙ *Restaurant closed Mon.* ¶◎¶ *BP.*

¢ ✕🏨 **Draxlhof.** At the foot of the Brauneck mountain range in the village of Wegscheid, this is the place for anyone wanting to get out in the fresh air for hikes or skiing. The old farmhouse has pretty rooms, simply decorated. For more space, there are three apartments available at extremely reasonable rates. The terrace offers basic Bavarian food to hungry skiers and hikers. ⊠ *Untermurbach 24, D–83661 Lenggries-Wegscheid* ☎ *08042/5020* 🖷 *08042/4224* ⊕ *www.draxlhof.de* 🛏 *7 rooms, 3 apartments* ⟁ *Restaurant, cable TV, billiards, some pets allowed; no a/c* ☰ *No credit cards* ¶◎¶ *BP.*

Tegernsee

★ ➓ *16 km (10 mi) east of Bad Tölz, 50 km (31 mi) south of Munich.*

The beautiful shores of the Tegernsee are among the most expensive property in all Germany. The interest in the region shown by King Maximilian I of Bavaria at the beginning of the 19th century attracted VIPs and artists, leading to a boom that has never really faded. Most hotels have sensible rates. Tegernsee's wooded shores, rising gently to scalable mountain peaks of no more than 6,300 feet, invite hikers, walkers, and picnicking families (the tourist office in the town of Tegernsee has hiking maps). The lake itself draws swimmers and yachters. In fall the russet-clad trees provide a colorful contrast to the snowcapped mountains.

On the eastern shore of the lake, the town of Tegernsee is home to a large Benedictine monastery (⊠ *Schlosspl.*). Founded in the 8th century, this was one of the most productive cultural centers in southern Germany; the Minnesänger (musician and poet) Walther von der Vogelweide (1170–1230) was a welcome guest. Not so welcome were Hungarian invaders who laid waste to the monastery in the 10th century. During the Middle Ages the monastery made a lively business producing stained-glass windows thanks to a nearby quartz quarry, and in the 16th century it became a major center of printing. It was secularization that sealed its fate at the beginning of the 19th century: almost half of the buildings were torn down. Maximilian I bought the surviving ones and had Leo von Klenze redo them for use as a summer retreat.

The late-Gothic **church** was refurbished in Italian baroque style in the 18th century. The frescoes are by Hans Georg Asam, whose work also graces the Benediktbeuren monastery. The property houses a beer tavern, a brewery, a restaurant, and a high school. Students in what was the monastery write their exams beneath inspiring baroque frescoes.

Olaf Gulbransson Museum. This museum is housed in a discreet modern building set back from the main lakeside road of Tegernsee. It's devoted to the Norwegian painter Olaf Gulbrannson, who went to Munich in 1902 and worked as a caricaturist for the satirical magazine *Simplicissimus.* His light, almost transparent works depict noisy politicians and snooty social upper-crusters as well as other subjects. ⊠ *Im Kurgarten, Tegernsee* ☎ *08022/3338* ⊕ *www.olaf-gulbransson-museum.de* ⌦ *€3* ⊙ *Tues.–Sun. 11–5.*

Maximilian showed off this corner of his kingdom to Czar Alexander I of Russia and Emperor Franz I of Austria during their journey to the Congress of Verona in October 1821. You can follow their steps through the woods to one of the loveliest lookout points in Bavaria, the **Grosses Paraplui.** A plaque marks the spot where they admired the open expanse of the Tegernsee and the mountains beyond. The path starts opposite Schlossplatz and is well marked.

Rottach-Egern is the fashionable and upscale resort at the southern end of the lake. Its classy shops, chic restaurants, and expensive boutiques are as well stocked and interesting as many in Munich; its leading hotels are world-class. Rottach-Egern's church, **St. Laurentius,** is worth seeing for its baroque influences.

While at the Rottach-Egern tourist office (*Kuramt*), have a look at the collection of horse-drawn vehicles at the adjoining **Kutschen-, Wagen- und Schlittenmuseum.** It contains beautifully restored coaches, sleds, oxcarts, and all the implements of the wagondriver's trade. ⊠ *Nördliche Hauptstrasse 9* ☎ *08022/671–341* ⌦ *€2* ⊙ *Tues.–Sun. 2–5.*

Where to Stay & Eat

$$–$$$$ ✕ **Freihaus Brenner.** Proprietor Josef Brenner has brought a taste of nouvelle cuisine to the Tegernsee. His attractive restaurant commands fine views from high above Bad Wiessee. Try any of his suggested dishes, ranging from roast pheasant in wine sauce to fresh lake fish. ⊠ *Freihaushöhe 4, Bad Wiessee* ☎ *08022/82004* ☰ *MC, V* ⊙ *Closed Tues. and Wed.*

$–$$ ✕ **Weinhaus Moschner.** You're pretty much expected to drink wine in this dark, old tavern on the edge of ritzy Rottach-Egern, though beer from the monastery brewery is also served. The menu has a wide range of options, from sturdy smoked pork to homemade ravioli filled with grilled salmon. But nobody comes here just to eat. You are welcome to join the locals at a rough wooden table in the log-wall tavern taproom, order a glass of ale or Franconian wine, and leave the fine dining until tomorrow. ⊠ *Kisslingerstr. 2, Rottach-Egern* ☎ *08022/5522* ☰ *AE, DC, MC, V* ⊙ *Closed Mon. and Tues.*

¢–$ ✕ **Herzogliches Bräustüberl.** Once part of Tegernsee's Benedictine monastery, then a royal retreat, the Bräustüberl is now an immensely popular beer hall and brewery. Only basic Bavarian snacks (sausages, pretzels, all the way up to steak tartare) are served in this crowded place, but hearty meals can be had in the adjoining **Schlossgaststätte** ($–$$). In summer, quaff your beer beneath the huge chestnuts and admire the delightful view of the lake and mountains. ⊠ *Schlosspl. 1, Tegernsee* ☎ *08022/4141* ⌦ *Reservations not accepted* ☰ *No credit cards* ⊙ *Closed Nov.*

$$–$$$ ✕⌂ **Bischoff am See.** Owners Petra and Markus Bischoff have their **Fodor's**Choice heart in their hotel, and it shows in every detail. Each room is individ-★ ually designed in understated yet warm style with an Asian touch. The bar, breakfast room, restaurant, and terrace have a splendid view of the lake. This top-of-the-line hideaway has four suites, two of which have their own sauna, and the others have whirlpool tubs. The restaurant ($$$–$$$$; closed Mon. and Tues.) prepares international specialties and has 950 wines on its wine list. Every fourth Thursday in the month is sushi night. ⊠ *Schweighofstr. 53, D–83684* ☎ *08022/3966* 🖷 *08022/ 1720* ⊕ *www.bischoff-am-see.de* 🗬 *7 rooms, 5 suites* ᗷ *Restaurant, cable TV with movies, bar, some pets allowed (fee), no-smoking rooms; no a/c in some rooms* 🖃 *MC, V* ❢◯❢ *BP.*

$$–$$$ ✕🖭 **Hotel Bayern.** The elegant, turreted Bayern and its two spacious annexes sit high above the Tegernsee, backed by the wooded slopes of Neureuth Mountain. Rooms overlooking the lake are in big demand despite their relatively high cost, so book early. All guests can enjoy panoramic views of the lake and mountains from the extensive terrace fronting the main building. You can dine in the hotel's stylish little restaurant ($$$–$$$$) or the cozy tavern. The extensive Bayern spa includes a heavenly musical tub and a colored light and aroma solarium. ⊠ *Neureuthstr. 23, D–83684* ☎ *08022/1820* 🖷 *08022/3775* ⊕ *www. hotel-bayern.de* 🗬 *63 rooms, 10 suites* ᗷ *2 restaurants, in-room data ports, cable TV, pool, hair salon, spa, bowling, bar, some pets allowed (fee), no-smoking rooms; no a/c* 🖃 *AE, MC, V* ❢◯❢ *BP.*

$$ ✕🖭 **Seegarten.** This lakeside hotel, with pinewood paneling and matching furniture, has cheerful rooms in the bright primary colors typical of Bavarian country-farmhouse style. Ask for a room with a balcony overlooking the Tegernsee. The Seegarten's kitchen ($–$$) is famous for its cakes, made by the in-house pastry chef. In winter a log fire and hot, spiced wine welcome you in the cozy vestibule. ⊠ *Adrian-Stoop-Str. 4, D–83707 Bad Wiessee* ☎ *08022/98490* 🖷 *08022/85087* 🗬 *18 rooms* ᗷ *Restaurant, cable TV, Internet, some pets allowed; no a/c* 🖃 *AE, MC, V* ❢◯❢ *BP.*

$–$$ ✕🖭 **Seehotel Zur Post.** The lake views from most rooms are somewhat compromised by the main road outside, but a central location and a winter garden and terrace are pluses. The restaurant ($–$$), with a panoramic view of the mountains and the lake, serves fresh fish, and there are also special venison weeks worthy of a long detour. ⊠ *Seestr. 3, D–83684* ☎ *08022/66550* 🖷 *08022/1699* ⊕ *www.seehotel-zur-post.de* 🗬 *43 rooms, 39 with bath or shower* ᗷ *Restaurant, cable TV, some pets allowed (fee), no-smoking rooms; no a/c* 🖃 *DC, MC, V* ❢◯❢ *BP.*

Nightlife & the Arts

Every resort has its **spa orchestra**—in the summer they play daily in the music-box-style bandstands that dot the lakeside promenades. A strong Tegernsee tradition is the summerlong program of **festivals,** some set deep in the forest. Tegernsee's lake festival in August, when sailing clubs deck their boats with garlands and lanterns, is an unforgettable experience.

Bad Wiessee has a lakeside **casino** (☎ 08022/82028) that's open daily 3 PM–2 AM and sets the tone for a surprisingly lively after-dark scene. The **Bischoff am See** (⊠ Schweighoferstr. 53 ☎ 08022/3966), on the lake shore in Tegernsee, has a sensational terrace bar with prices to match one of Bavaria's finest views.

Shopping

In Bad Tölz, you'll find all the region can offer at **Schöttl** (✉ 61a Mark-tstr.). To get there, follow the lovely Marktstrasse up from the river and watch for the oversize top hat at the corner of Hindenburgstrasse. **Greif** (✉ Nördliche Hauptstr. 24, Rottach-Egern ☎ 08022/5540) has a fine selection of tastefully modern Bavarian fashions and a large stock of hand-woven fabrics that you can either buy or have a costume fitted from. At her workshop just outside Gmund, **Marianne Winter-Andres** (✉ Mies-bacherstr. 88, Gmund ☎ 08022/74643) creates a wide and attractive range of high-quality pottery at sensible prices.

Sports & the Outdoors

GOLF Besides swimming, hiking, and skiing, the Tegernsee area has become a fine place for golfing. The **Tegernseer GOLFCLUB e. V** (✉ 83707 Bad Wiessee ☎ 08022/8769), has an 18-hole course overlooking the lake with a clubhouse and excellent restaurant. It also has fine apartments for rent.

> **off the beaten path**
>
> **WALLBERG** – For the best vista in the area, climb this 5,700-foot mountain at the south end of the Tegernsee. It's a hard four-hour hike, though anyone in good shape should be able to make it since it involves no rock climbing. A cable car makes the ascent in just 15 minutes and costs €8 one-way, €13 round-trip. At the summit are a restaurant and sun terrace and several trailheads; in winter the skiing is excellent.

Schliersee

⓫ *20 km (12 mi) east of Tegernsee, 55 km (34 mi) southeast of Munich.*

Schliersee is smaller, quieter, and less fashionable than Tegernsee, but hardly less beautiful. The different histories of the two lakes are made clear in the names local people have long given them: the Tegernsee is *Herrensee* (Masters' Lake), while the Schliersee is *Bauernsee* (Peasants' Lake), although today Schliersee is more for the well-heeled. There are walking and ski trails on the mountain slopes that ring its placid wa-ters. The lake is shallow and often freezes over in winter, when the tiny island in its center is a favorite hiking destination.

Schliersee was the site of a monastery, built in the 8th century by a group of noblemen. It subsequently became a choral academy, which eventu-ally moved to Munich. Today only the restored 17th-century **Schliersee church,** in the middle of town, recalls this piece of local history. The church has some frescoes and stucco work by Johann Baptist Zimmermann.

Where to Stay & Eat

¢–$ ✕ **Zum Hofhaus am See.** What better place to enjoy a meal than in a small beer garden on the shore? The Hofhaus radiates a kind of friendly in-timacy—even if the waitress doesn't crack a smile. Down-to-earth food, such as hocks or fresh forest mushrooms in cream with an herbed dumpling, is the order of the day. In winter the Hofhaus offers fondue as a specialty. ✉ *Mesnerg. 2* ☎ *08026/94499* ▭ *No credit cards.*

★ **$–$$** ✕⊡ **Hotel Gasthof Terofal.** This handsome, steep-eaved, flower-filled inn is in the center of Schliersee town. In the coziest rooms, carved and painted four-poster beds are part of the traditional Bavarian furnishings. The beamed tavern-restaurant ($–$$) serves a wide range of fare, and every Thursday there is a special "medieval" meal, for those wanting a genuine flavor of old Bavaria. Comedies are performed regularly at the inn's own theater. ⊠ *Xaver-Terofal-Pl. 2, D–83727* ☎ *08026/923–5400* 🖶 *08026/923–5300* ⊕ *www.hotel-schliersee.de* ↩ *23 rooms* ⟋ *Restaurant, in-room data ports, cable TV with movies, beer garden, theater, some pets allowed (fee), no-smoking rooms; no a/c* ☼ *Closed mid-Jan.–mid-Feb.* ▭ *No credit cards* ℟⬤❙ *BP.*

$ ⊡ **Gästehaus Franke am See.** Light, clean rooms with simple no-nonsense furniture can be very pleasant as a change from all the heavy dark beams and wood paneling you may have seen on your journey. The house's garden is a few steps from the lake. The Franke is small, giving it a nice family feel. ⊠ *Seestr. 8, D–83727* ☎ *08026/4097* 🖶 *08026/4098* ⊕ *www.gaestehaus-franke-schliersee.de* ↩ *7 rooms, 2 suites* ⟋ *Cable TV, some pets allowed; no a/c* ▭ *No credit cards* ℟⬤❙ *CP.*

Shopping

If at the end of your Upper Bavarian tour you're still looking for *something,* stop at the busy market town of Miesbach (north of Schliersee) and climb the stairs to **Cilly's Gschirrladn** (⊠ Stadtpl. 10, Miesbach ☎ 08025/1705). A warren of rooms is stocked ceiling high with every variety of item for the home, from embroidered tablecloths to fine German porcelain.

Spitzingsee

⑫ *10 km (6 mi) south of Schliersee, 65 km (40 mi) southeast of Munich.*

Arguably the most beautiful of this group of Bavarian lakes, the Spitzingsee is cradled 3,500 feet up between the Taubenstein, Rosskopf, and Stumpfling peaks, and the drive there is spectacular. The lake is usually frozen over in winter and almost buried in snow. In summer it's warm enough for a swim. Walking in this area is breathtaking in every season and in every sense. The skiing is very good, too. The only downside is the overrun town of Spitzingsee, whose modern architecture violates almost every rule of aesthetics.

Where to Stay & Eat

¢–$ ✕ **Alte Wurzhütte.** If you can't sit outside on the terrace and enjoy a dreamy view of the lake, then you'll have to make due with the cozy, Bavarian log-cabin atmosphere inside. Dishes here, such as Bavarian duck with red cabbage and a monster potato dumpling, are nice and heavy and come at excellent prices. ⊠ *Rosskopfweg 1* ☎ *08026/60680* ▭ *No credit cards.*

$$–$$$ ✕⊡ **Arabella Sheraton Alpenhotel.** For an out-of-the-way break in the mountains, head for this luxurious hotel on the shore of the Spitzingsee—even though its architecture is an eyesore. Rooms meet the high standards of comfort expected from the hotel chain that runs the establishment. If you can't stay overnight, come for a leisurely lunch

($$–$$$) at the **König Ludwig Stuben**, or for a fondue night or theme buffet. Try the lake fish or the venison, in-season. For lighter Italian fare, you can enjoy **Osteria L'Oliva** with a menu of pasta, salads, and dishes from the grill. ⊠ *Seeweg 7, D–83727* ☎ *08026/7980* 🖷 *08026/798–879* ⊕ *www.arabellasheraton.de* ⊰ *120 rooms, 13 suites ⚭ 2 restaurants, some in-room data ports, cable TV, 2 tennis courts, pool, gym, sauna, steam room, boating, bowling, bar, library, some pets allowed (fee), no-smoking rooms; no a/c* ▤ *AE, DC, MC, V* ⵔ *BP.*

Bayrischzell

🔞 *10 km (6 mi) east of Schliersee, 65 km (40 mi) southeast of Munich.*

Bayrischzell is in an attractive family-resort area, where many a Bavarian first learned to ski. The wide-open slopes of the Sudelfeld Mountain are ideal for undemanding skiing; in summer and fall you can explore countless upland walking trails. Access to the Sudelfeld area costs €1.50 per car.

The town sits at the end of a wide valley overlooked by the 6,000-foot **Wendelstein** Mountain, which draws expert skiers. At its summit is a tiny stone-and-slate-roof chapel that's much in demand for wedding ceremonies. The cross above the entrance was carried up the mountain by Max Kleiber, who designed the 19th-century church. An instructive **geopark**, laid out beneath the summit, explains the 250-million-year geological history of the area on 36 graphic signboards. You can reach the summit from two directions: The cable car sets out from Osterhofen on the Bayrischzell-Munich road and costs €17 round-trip, €10 one-way (its last descent is at 4 PM). The historic cog railway leaves from Brannenburg, on the north side of the mountain, between Bayrischzell and the Inn Valley autobahn. A round-trip costs €23.50, a single trip €14.50; it's closed November and the first three weeks of December. The cable car closes for two weeks in mid-April.

Where to Stay & Eat

$–$$ ✕▥ **Hotel Feuriger Tatzelwurm.** This archetypal old Bavarian inn (with a modern wing) is named after the nearby Tatzelwurm Gorge and is ideally placed for hikes or ski trips. The inn sits in isolated splendor above a forest pond, some 980 feet from the main Oberaudorf-Bayrischzell road. Bavarian dishes (also vegetarian) are served in the warren of paneled dining rooms ($–$$$$), one of which is dominated by a historic tile stove. The two-person *Jadgherrenplatte Brünnstein* will let you sample the game of the area (both people need to be ravenous to finish off this plate). The spa area has everything anyone could desire. ⊠ *Am Tatzelwurm, D–82080 Oberaudorf/Bayrischzell* ☎ *08034/30080* 🖷 *08034/7170* ⊰ *45 rooms ⚭ Restaurant, in-room data ports, cable TV, spa, bicycles, Ping-Pong, some pets allowed (fee), no-smoking rooms; no a/c* ▤*DC, MC, V* ⵔ *BP.*

$ ✕▥ **Wendelstein.** This large restaurant ($) in the middle of Bayrischzell fills up quickly on winter evenings. On warm summer days, there's always the beer garden, shaded by old chestnut trees. The generous portions come at reasonable prices. If you are not into slabs of meat, you can try some of the vegetarian dishes such as a schnitzel of celery. Rooms here are simple but comfortable. ✉ *Ursprungstr. 1* ☎ *08023/ 80890* 🖷 *08023/808–969* ➳ *18 rooms* ⚒ *Restaurant, cable TV, beer garden, Internet, some pets allowed (fee), no-smoking rooms; no a/c* 🖃 *AE, MC, V* ☉ *Restaurant closed Nov.–mid-Dec. and Mon.* ¶⊙¶ *BP.*

 en route

A few miles east of Bayrischzell on the Sudelfeld Road is the **Tatzelwurm** gorge and waterfall, named for a winged dragon that supposedly inhabits these parts. Dragon or not, this can be an eerie place to drive at dusk. A hiking trail is signposted. From the gorge, the road drops sharply to the valley of the Inn River, leading to the busy ski resort of Oberaudorf.

The Inn River valley, an ancient trade route, is the most important road link between Germany and Italy. The wide, green Inn gushes here, and in the parish church of St. Bartholomew, at **Rossholzen** (16 km [10 mi] north of Oberaudorf), you can see memorials and naively painted tributes to the local people who have lost their lives in its chilly waters. The church has a baroque altar incorporating vivid Gothic elements. A simple tavern adjacent to the church offers an ideal opportunity for a break on the Alpine Road.

Rosenheim

14 *34 km (21 mi) north of Bayrischzell, 55 km (34 mi) east of Munich.*

Bustling Rosenheim is a medieval market town that has kept much of its character despite the onslaught of industrial development. The arcaded streets of low-eaved houses are characteristic of Inn Valley towns. Lake Chiemsee is nearby, and the area has a handful of rural lakes of its own (Simssee, Hofstättersee, and Rinssee). Leisure activities and culture at lower prices than in Munich have made the area very popular.

The old restored locomotive shed, the **Lokschuppen** (✉ Rathausstr. 24 ☎ 08031/365–9036), attracts crowds from as far away as Salzburg and Munich to its special exhibitions (mostly of art).

The Inn River was a major trade artery that bestowed a fair amount of wealth onto Rosenheim, especially in the Middle Ages. It not only served the purpose of transportation but also created jobs thanks to fishing, shipping, bridge-building, shipbuilding, and the like. The **Inn Museum** tells the story of the river, from geology to business. ✉ *Innstr. 74* ☎ *08031/31511* 💶 *€2* ☉ *May–Oct., Fri. 9–noon, weekends 10–4.*

Wood is another traditional big business around Rosenheim. **Das Holztechnische Museum** documents how it's grown and how it's used, for example in interior decoration, transportation, architecture, and art. ✉ *Max-Josephs-Pl. 4* ☎ *08031/16900* 💶 *€2* ☉ *Tues.–Sat. 9–1 and 2–5.*

need a break?

The **aran coffeehouse** (✉ Kaiserstr. 16 ☎ 08031/357–673 ☉ Closed weekend afternoons), on the main square, makes the best coffee and tea in the region, as well as sandwiches made of freshly home-baked bread, and sweets. You can also purchase coffee beans to go, or other gifts, such as books and large candles.

Where to Stay & Eat

$ ✕▦ **Fortuna.** This modern hotel at the entrance of Rosenheim (when arriving from the autobahn) has its focus on comfort and good value. Rooms are done in minimalist style, in contrast perhaps to the restaurant. A large Italian menu with everything from simple pizza to grilled fish is a nice change in the Pork-Roast Belt of Germany. ✉ *Hochplattenstr. 42, D–83026* ☎ *08031/616–363* 📠 *08031/6163–6400* ⊕ *www. hotel-fortuna.de* 🛏 *18 rooms* ♿ *Restaurant, in-room data ports, cable TV, some pets allowed (fee)* ▭ *MC, V* ❢❢ *BP.*

$$ ▦ **Panorama Cityhotel.** The Panorama is a modern, convenient hotel in the middle of town offering comfortable rooms. It even has two nicely furnished apartments at reasonable rates. Note that prices are lower on weekends, but rise during Oktoberfest (Rosenheim is 45 minutes by train from Munich) and the big trade fairs in Munich. ✉ *Brixstr. 3, D–83022* ☎ *08031/3060* 📠 *08031/306–415* ⊕ *www.panoramacityhotel.de* 🛏 *89 rooms* ♿ *In-room data ports, minibars, cable TV with movies, bar, parking (fee), some pets allowed, no-smoking rooms; no a/c* ▭ *AE, DC, MC, V* ❢❢ *BP.*

Chiemsee

⑮ *20 km (12 mi) east of Rosenheim, 80 km (50 mi) east of Munich.*

Chiemsee is north of the Deutsche Alpenstrasse, but it demands a detour, if only to visit King Ludwig's huge palace on one of its idyllic islands. It's the largest Bavarian lake, and although it's surrounded by reedy flatlands, the nearby mountains provide a majestic backdrop. The town of **Prien** is the lake's principal resort. The tourist offices of Prien and Aschau offer an €18 transportation package covering a boat trip, a round-trip rail ticket between the two resorts, and a round-trip ride by cable car to the top of Kampen Mountain, above Aschau.

Despite its distance from Munich, the beautiful Chiemsee drew Bavarian royalty to its shores. Its dreamlike, melancholy air caught the imagination of King Ludwig II, and it was on one of the lake's three islands FodorsChoice that he built his third and last castle, sumptuous **Schloss Herrenchiem-** ★ **see.** The palace was modeled after Louis XIV's Versailles, but this due to more than simple admiration: Ludwig, whose name was the German equivalent of Louis, was keen to establish that he, too, possessed the absolute authority of his namesake, the Sun King. As with most of Ludwig's projects, the building was never completed, and Ludwig only spent nine days in the castle. Moreover, Herrenchiemsee broke the state coffers and Ludwig's private ones as well. The gold leaf that seems to cover more than half of the rooms is especially thin. Nonetheless, what remains is impressive—and ostentatious. Regular ferries out to the island depart from Stock, Prien's harbor. If you want to make the journey in style, board the original 1887 steam train from Prien to Stock to pick up the ferry. A horse-drawn carriage takes you to the palace itself.

Most spectacular is the Hall of Mirrors, a dazzling gallery where candlelighted concerts are held in summer. Also of interest are the ornate bedrooms Ludwig planned, the "self-rising" table that ascended from the kitchen quarters, the elaborately painted bathroom with a small pool for a tub, and the formal gardens. The south wing houses a **museum** containing Ludwig's christening robe and death mask, as well as other artifacts of his life. While the palace was being built, Ludwig stayed in a royal suite of apartments in a former monastery building on the island, the Alten Schloss. Germany's postwar constitution was drawn up here in 1948, and this episode of the country's history is the centerpiece of the museum housed in the ancient building, the **Museum im Alten Schloss** (⊠ €1.50) ☎ 08051/68870 palace ⊠ Palace, including Museum im Alten Schloss €6.50 ☉ Apr.–Sept., daily 9–6; Oct., daily 9:40–5, Nov.–Mar., daily 9:40–4; English-language palace tours daily at 11:45 and 2:25.

Boats going between Stock and Herrenchiemsee Island also call at the small retreat of **Fraueninsel** (Ladies' Island). The **Benedictine convent** there, founded 1,200 years ago, now serves as a school. One of its earliest abbesses, Irmengard, daughter of King Ludwig der Deutsche, died here in the 9th century. Her grave in the convent chapel was discovered in 1961, the same year that early frescoes there were brought to light. The chapel is open daily from dawn to dusk. Otherwise, the island has just a few private houses, a couple of shops, and a hotel.

off the
beaten
path

AMERANG – There are two interesting museums in this town, northwest of Chiemsee. In the **Museum für Deutsche Automobilgeschichte** (Museum of German Automobile History), 220 automobiles begin with an 1886 Benz and culminate in contemporary models. The world's largest small-gauge model-railway panorama is spread out over nearly 6,000 square feet. ⊠ Wasserburger Str. 38 ☎ 08075/8141 ⊕ www.efa-automuseum.de ⊠ €6.50 ☉ Mar.–Oct., Tues.–Sun. 10–6; last entry at 5.

The **Bauernhausmuseum** (Farmhouse Museum) consists of four beautiful farm houses with a bakery, bee hives, saw mill, and blacksmith's workshop. It's worth seeing to find out more about everyday life in the Chiemgau. Every Sunday afternoon an 85-year-old roper shows off his craft, as does a lace maker. On alternate Sundays, spinning, feltmaking, and blacksmithing are demonstrated. You can take in the idyllic surroundings from the beer garden. ⊠ Im Hopfgarten ☎ 08075/915–090 ⊕ www.bauernhausmuseum-amerang.de ⊠ €3 ☉ Mid-Mar.–mid-Nov., Tues.–Sun. 9–6; last entry at 5.

Where to Stay & Eat

★ ¢–$$ ✕ **Wirth von Amerang.** Theme restaurants are an up-and-coming business in Bavaria, and the Wirth is the spearhead. The interior design comes very close to medieval, with brick stoves of handmade bricks, dripping candles, and a floor resembling packed clay. The food is definitely Bavarian, with Knödels (dumplings) and pork roast, hocks, and a top-notch potato soup. Reservations are recommended. You may want to purchase the pumpkinseed oil or a homemade schnapps. ⊠ *Postweg 4, Amerang* ☎ *08075/185–918* ▤ *No credit cards* ⊘ *No lunch Nov.–Mar.*

$$ ✕⚏ **Inselhotel zur Linde.** Catch a boat to this enchanting inn on the car-free Fraueninsel: but remember, if you miss the last connection to the mainland (at 9 PM), you'll have to stay the night. The island is by and large a credit-card-free zone, so be sure to bring cash. Rooms are simply furnished and decorated with brightly colored fabrics. The Linde is one of Bavaria's oldest hotels, founded in 1396 as a refuge for pilgrims. Artists have favored the inn for years, and one of the tables in the small Fischerstüberl dining room ($–$$) is reserved for them. ⊠ *Fraueninsel im Chiemsee 1, D–83256* ☎ *08054/90366* ▤ *08054/7299* ⊕ *www. inselhotel-zurlinde.de* ⇆ *14 rooms* ♿ *Restaurant, bar, Internet; no a/c* ▤ *MC, V* ⊘ *Closed mid-Jan.–mid-Mar.* ⏀ *BP.*

$–$$ ✕⚏ **Hotel Luitpold am See.** Boats to the Chiemsee islands tie up right outside your window at this handsome old Prien hotel, which organizes shipboard disco evenings as part of its entertainment program. Rooms have traditional pinewood furniture, including carved cupboards and bedsteads. Fish from the lake is served at the pleasant restaurant ($–$$). ⊠*Seestr. 110, D–83209 Prien am Chiemsee* ☎*08051/609–100* ▤*08051/ 609–175* ⊕ *www.luitpold-am-see.de* ⇆ *51 rooms* ♿ *Restaurant, café, cable TV, Internet, some pets allowed (fee), no-smoking rooms; no a/c* ▤ *AE, DC, MC, V* ⏀ *BP.*

$ ✕⚏ **Schlosshotel Herrenchiemsee.** This handsome mansion on the island of Herrenchiemsee predates King Ludwig's palace, which is a 15-minute walk through the woods. The rooms aren't palatial but are comfortable. A big plus is the pavilionlike restaurant ($–$$), which serves fresh fish. If you're just here to eat, make sure to catch the last boat to the mainland (9 PM)—otherwise you'll be sleeping on this traffic-free island. ⊠ *Herrenchiemsee, D–83209* ☎ *08051/1509* ▤ *08051/1509* ⇆ *12 rooms, 6 with bath or shower* ♿ *Restaurant, some pets allowed; no a/c, no room phones* ▤ *AE, DC, MC, V* ⊘ *Hotel closed Oct.–Easter* ⏀ *CP.*

Sports & the Outdoors

There are boatyards all around the lake and several windsurfing schools. The **Mistral-Windsurfing-Center** (⊠ Waldstr. 20 ☎ 08054/909–906), at Gdstadt, has been in operation for decades. From its boatyard the average windsurfer can make it with ease to the next island. The gentle hills of the region are ideal for golf. **Chiemsee Golf-Club Prien e.V** (☎08051/ 62215), in Prien, has a year-round, 9-hole course. **SportLukas** (⊠ Hauptstr. 3, D–83259 Schkeching ☎ 08649/243) provides equipment for any kind of sport imaginable, from skiing to kayaking, climbing to curling, and it organizes tours.

Aschau

⓰ *10 km (6 mi) south of Chiemsee, 75 km (46 mi) east of Munich.*

Aschau is an enchanting red-roof village nestled in a wide valley of the Chiemgauer Alps. Its **Schloss Hohenaschau** is one of the few medieval castles in southern Germany to have been restored in the 17th century in baroque style. Chamber-music concerts are presented regularly in the

Rittersaal (Knights Hall) during the summer. Parts of the castle can be visited—the rest of the rooms are used as a vacation home for Germany's federal tax officials! The **Prientalmuseum** (Museum of the Prien Valley), with historical documents on the region, is in the former deacon's house. Exhibitions by contemporary international artists are also on display. ☎ 08052/904–937 ✉ Castle €2.50 ⊙ May–Sept., Tues.–Fri. tours at 9:30, 10:30, and 11:30; Apr. and Oct., Thurs. at 9:30, 10:30, and 11:30; museum during tour times and Sun. 1:30–5.

Where to Stay & Eat

$$–$$$$
Fodor'sChoice
★

✕🔲 **Residenz Heinz Winkler.** Star chef Heinz Winkler has turned a sturdy village inn into one of Germany's most extraordinary hotel-restaurant complexes. Rooms in the main house are noble in proportions and furnishings, and the maisonette-style suites in the annexes are cozy and romantic. All have views of the mountains. The restaurant ($$$$) has kept with ease the awards that Winkler won when in charge of Munich's Tantris. A grand piano and a harp add harmony to this deliciously sophisticated scene. ✉ Kirchpl. 1, D–83229 ☎ 08052/17990 🖷 08052/179–966 ⊕ www.residenz-heinz-winkler.de ➷ 19 rooms, 13 suites ♨ Restaurant, in-room data ports, cable TV, pool, sauna, spa, steam room, bar, some pets allowed (fee); no a/c ▭ AE, DC, MC, V ⦿I BP.

$–$$

🔲 **Hotel Bonnschlössl.** This turreted country palace is set in its own park studded with centuries-old trees. In good weather breakfast is served on the balustraded terrace. The hotel is 6 km (4 mi) north of Aschau and has a similarly enchanting sister property in the nearby village of Bernau, the Gasthof Alter Wirt. Both the Schloss and the Gasthof are protected by preservation orders. Emperor Maximilian I stayed overnight at the Gasthof in 1503 on his way to besiege the castle of Marquartstein. ✉ Kirchpl. 9, D–83233 Bernau ☎ 08051/89011 🖷 08051/89103 ⊕ www.alter-wirt-bernau.de ➷ 22 rooms ♨ Restaurant, cable TV, sauna, spa, beer garden, Weinstube, some pets allowed, no-smoking rooms; no a/c ▭ MC, V ⊙ Closed Mon. ⦿I BP.

en route

At Aschau you'll join the most scenic section of the Deutsche Alpenstrasse as it passes through a string of villages—Bernau, Rottau, Grassau, Marquartstein, and Oberwössen. In summer the farmhouses of Rottau are covered with flowers. The houses of Grassau shrink beside the bulk of the 15th-century Church of the Ascension, worth visiting for its rich 17th-century stucco work. For those interested in technical things, stop at the **Klaushäusl** (☎ 08641/5467 ✉ €2 ⊙ May–Oct., Tues.–Sat. 2–5, Sun. 10–5), between Rottau and Grassau. The little stone house is home to one of the many pumps that used to carry brine from Berchtesgaden and Bad Reichenhall all the way to Rosenheim. It operated from 1810 to 1957.

Reit im Winkl

⓱ 16 km (10 mi) south of Chiemsee, 100 km (62 mi) east of Munich.

Reit im Winkl has produced at least two German ski champions who trained on the demanding runs high above the village. The intensity of tourism here means crowds and the usual automobile traffic. Many of the quickly built houses are often disproportionately large, and though meant to be "Alpine," they somehow don't quite cut it. A nice way to tour the town is by **horse-drawn cart** (☎ 08641/5657 or 0171/698–0504) or sled in winter. The ski area, **Winklmoosalm,** can be reached by bus or chairlift, and it's a great place for bracing upland walks in summer and fall.

The **Heimatmuseum** (Museum of Local History, also called Hausenhäusl) is one of Reit im Winkl's last intact "small houses" in which people lived and worked in the mountains. It exhibits a weaver's and a shoemaker's workshop and has reconstructed the living space of a typical family of so-called *Kleinhäusler* (literally, "small-house residents"). ✉ *Weitseestr. 10* ☎ *08640/80020* 🎫 *€1.50* ⏲ *June–Sept., daily 2–4.*

Where to Stay & Eat

$–$$ ✕ **Kupferkanne.** Outside, a garden surrounds the building; inside, you could be in an Alpine farmstead. The food is good country fare enhanced by Austrian specialties and spicy concoctions from the Balkans. Try the *Salzburger Brez'n,* a thick, creamy bread-based soup. ✉ *Weitseestr. 18* ☎ *08640/1450* 💳 *No credit cards* ⏲ *Closed Sat. and Nov.*

$–$$ ✕🏨 **Landgasthof Rosi Mittermaier.** Rosi Mittermaier, skiing star of the 1976 Innsbruck Olympics, owns this charming Gasthof with her husband, Christian Neureuther, a champion skier himself. During their frequent visits to the inn, they're always ready with advice about the ski runs or mountain trails. In the rustic Café Olympia, which has a brand-new terrace for warm days, or in the cozy, pine-panel tavern-restaurant ($–$$) you'll find a mix of Bavarian and Tyrolian dishes and a rather Mediterranean buffet for a change in fare. It's essential to book in advance. ✉ *Chiemseestr. 2a, D–83242* ☎ *08640/1011* 📠 *08640/1013* 🛏 *8 rooms* 🛎 *Restaurant, café, some in-room data ports, cable TV, sauna, some pets allowed (fee), no-smoking rooms; no a/c* 💳 *No credit cards* 🍽 *BP.*

en route

Between Reit im Winkl and Ruhpolding is the **Holzknechtmuseum** (Forester Museum), devoted to the sylvan lives and tribulations of the forest workers. The parklike grounds show how skilled these fellows were with their axes and saws and how they arranged their working lives outdoors: the huge hand-built waterwheel that drove a pump is particularly impressive. ✉ *Laubau* ☎ *08663/639* 🎫 *€3* ⏲ *Tues.–Sat. 1–5.*

Ruhpolding

18 *24 km (15 mi) east of Reit im Winkl, 125 km (77 mi) east of Munich.*

The history of this valley goes back to the 10th century, when people came here to avoid attacks by pillaging Magyar tribes. In the 16th century the Bavarian rulers journeyed to Ruhpolding to hunt. In fact, the Renaissance-style hunting lodge of Prince Wilhelm V still stands (it's now used as the offices of the local forestry service). The hilltop 18th-century **Pfarrkirche St. Georg** (Parish Church of St. George) is one of the finest baroque and rococo churches in the Bavarian Alps and has a magnificent view of the town. In one of its side altars stands a rare 12th-century carving, the Ruhpoldinger Madonna. Note also the crypt chapel in the quiet churchyard.

Youngsters are encouraged to play with many of the fine exhibits at the **Ruhpoldinger Modellbahnschau** (Model Railway Museum), which has a small-gauge track. There's a high-tech Märklin-made panorama with nearly 200 feet of track and roads with moving cars and trucks. This is the model railway raised to high art. A true work of art as well is the 20-foot "winter mountains" landscape. ⊠ *Schulg. 4* ☎ *08663/ 5613* 🔲 *€4* ⊙ *Weekends 9:30–5:30.*

Two priests, the late Max Weidenauer and Alois Gantenhammer, spent years collecting the exhibits for the **Museum für bäerliche und sakrale Kunst** (Museum of Peasant and Religious Art). Antique Bavarian peasant furniture, closets, trunks, beds, pipes, pitchers, and jewelry are displayed in almost flea-market manner on the ground floor of the former parish house. The first floor is devoted to one of Europe's finest collections of paraments, liturgical garments, and brocade fabrics. ⊠ *Roman-Friesinger-Str. 1* ☎ *08663/5078* 🔲 *€1* ⊙ *May–Sept., Tues.–Sat. 9:30–noon and 2–4, Sun. 9:30–noon; Oct.–Apr., weekends 9:30–noon.*

off the beaten path

BRAND – In this village just north of Ruhpolding, you can visit a 300-year-old bell foundry, now a fascinating museum of the ancient crafts of the foundry man and blacksmith. In the Middle Ages, thanks to local iron ore and water power, no fewer than 40 blacksmiths plied their trade here, making everything from church bells to goat bells. Tyrenia Ullrich, who watches over the museum, is the daughter of the last smith to work here. The museum is signposted from the main road. A half-hour hike through the forest is needed to reach the place. ☎ *08663/2309* 🔲 *€3* ⊙ *Mid-May–June and mid-Sept.–mid-Oct., weekdays 10–noon and 2–4; July–mid-Sept., weekdays 10–4.*

Where to Stay & Eat

$–$$ ✕ **Gasthof zur Alten Säge.** About 10 minutes' walk from the center of town behind the train station, this former sawmill will offer all the *Gemütlichkeit* you need in its airy dining room or on the sunny patio. Some days are "all-you-can-eat" days: Monday it's stew, Thursday potato pancakes, and on Friday evenings live music accompanies the generous buffet. ⊠ *Miesenbacher Str. 8* ☎ *08663/5993* ▤ *MC, V.*

$–$$ ✕▦ **Hotel zur Post.** A Zur Post sign in any Bavarian town or village indicates a good place to find solid local fare ($–$$). In business since 1424, Ruhpolding's inn has been in the hands of the same family for 150 years. Call in advance for room reservations. For families, the hotel keeps very comfortable apartments in somewhat traditional style with those pretty tile stoves (*Kachelofen*) that are an Alpine trademark. Off-season, the hotel has excellent deals that include discounts on greens fees for the local golf course, entrance to the wellness spa, a ride on the cable car, and a meal a day in addition to breakfast. ⊠ *Hauptstr. 35, D–83324* ☎ *08663/5430* 🖶 *08663/1483* ⊕ *www.hotel-post-ruhpolding.de* ⬎ *56* *rooms, 19 apartments* ⚘ *Restaurant, cable TV, some pets allowed (fee), no-smoking rooms; no a/c* ☰ *MC, V* ⊙ *Restaurant closed Wed.* ⫷Ⓞⵏ *BP.*

$ ✕⊞ **Hotel Gasthof zum Fuchs.** Just a few minutes from the center of town, this family-run inn-hotel has a friendly feel to it, and it's quiet. Rooms are comfortably appointed, if a little staid. The restaurant serves hearty food for those with a day of hiking behind them. ⊠ *Brandstätterstr. 38a, D–83324* ☏*08663/88000 or 0800/880–055* ⤶*08663/880–040* ⊕*www. ruhpolding.de* ⟿ *18 rooms* ⚘ *Restaurant, cable TV, some pets allowed (fee); no a/c* ☰ *MC, V* ⊙ *Restaurant closed Mon.* ⫷Ⓞⵏ *CP.*

Bad Reichenhall

⑲ *30 km (19 mi) east of Ruhpolding, 20 km (12 mi) west of Salzburg.*

Bad Reichenhall is remarkably well located, near the mountains for those who want to hike and ski, and near Salzburg in Austria for visitors who wish to enjoy a lively cultural scene. The town shares a remote corner of Bavaria with another prominent resort, Berchtesgaden. Although the latter is more famous, Bad Reichenhall is older, with saline springs that made the town rich. Salt is so much a part of the town that you can practically taste it in the air. Europe's largest source of brine was first tapped here in pre-Christian times; salt mining during the Middle Ages supported the economies of cities as far away as Munich and Passau. Tourism gave the local economy an additional boost and another use for the salt, namely for its healing properties, starting in the early 20th century.

In the early 19th century, King Ludwig I built an elaborate saltworks and spa house—the **Alte Saline und Quellenhaus**—in vaulted, pseudomedieval style. Their pump installations, which still run, are astonishing examples of 19th-century engineering. A "saline" **chapel** is part of the spa's facilities and was built in exotic Byzantine style. An interesting museum in the same complex looks at the history of the salt trade. The Alte Saline also houses a small **glass foundry** (☏ 08651/69738 ⊕ www.riedl-glaskunst.de ⊡ Free ⊙ Weekdays 9–6, Sat. 9–2), run by the famous company Riedl, makers of fine tableware. Glassblowers and engravers display their art in a small self-service restaurant, and children can try their mouths, so to speak, at glassblowing. The showroom has many articles for sale, notably glass globes used to ensure your potted plants are being slowly watered while you are away. There are tours through the whole salt complex, including visits to the museum. ⊠ *Salinen Str.* ☏ *08651/700–2146* ⊕ *www.suedsalz.de* ⊡ *€5.20, combined ticket with Berchtesgaden salt mine €14.50* ⊙ *May–Oct., daily 10–1:30 and 2–4; Nov.–Apr., Tues. and Thurs. 2–4.*

The pride and joy of the Reichenhallers is the steep, craggy mountain appropriately named the **Predigtstuhl** (Preaching Pulpit), which stands at 5,164 feet, southeast of town. A ride to the top offers a splendid view of the area. You can hike, ski in winter, or just enjoy a meal at the **Berhotel Predigtdstuhl** ($–$$). The cable-car ride costs €9.50 one-way up, €8 one-way down, and €15 round-trip. Departures begin at 9:30 AM and continue (as needed) until the last person is off the mountain. ⊠ *Südtiroler Platz 1* ☏ *08651/1719* ⊕ *www.predigtstuhl-bahn.de.*

Hotels here base spa treatments on the health-giving properties of the saline springs and the black mud from the area's waterlogged moors. The waters can also be taken in the elegant, pillared **Wandelhalle** pavilion of the attractive spa gardens throughout the year. Breathing salt-laden air is a remedy for various lung conditions. All you need to do is walk along the 540-foot Gradierwerk, a massive wood-and-concrete construction that produces a fine salty mist by trickling brine down a 40-foot wall of dense blackthorn bundles. ⊠ *Salzburgerstr.* ⊘ *Mon.–Sat. 8–12:30 and 3–5, Sun. 10–12:30.*

The ancient church **St. Zeno** is dedicated to the patron saint of those imperiled by floods and the dangers of the deep, an ironic note in a town that flourishes on the riches of its underground springs. This 12th-century basilica, one of the largest in Bavaria, was remodeled in the 16th and 17th centuries, but some of the original Romanesque cloisters remain, although these can be seen only during services and from 11 to noon on Sunday and holidays. ⊠ *Kirchpl. 1* ☎ *08651/4889.*

Where to Stay & Eat

$$$–$$$$ ✕🏨 **Steigenberger-Hotel Axelmannstein.** Ludwig would have enjoyed the palatial air that pervades this hotel—and he would have been able to afford the price, which rivals that of top hotels in Germany's most expensive cities but does include a meal. Luxurious comfort is found in rooms ranging in style from rustic to demure. The fine restaurant ($$–$$$$) always has a range of interesting creations, from goosefish and angler to delicate lamb roasts. ⊠ *Salzburgerstr. 2–6, D–83435* ☎ *08651/7770* 🖷 *08651/5932* ⊕ *www.bad-reichenhall.steigenberger. de* ➱ *143 rooms, 8 suites ⌂ 2 restaurants, cable TV, tennis court, pool, gym, hair salon, sauna, spa, bowling, bar, babysitting, some pets allowed (fee), no-smoking rooms; no a/c* ⊟ *AE, DC, MC, V* ❙❃❙ *BP.*

$$ ✕🏨 **Parkhotel Luisenbad.** If you fancy spoiling yourself in a typical German fin-de-siècle spa hotel, this is *the* place—a fine porticoed and pillared building whose imposing pastel-pink facade promises luxury within. Rooms are large, furnished in deep-cushioned, dark-wood comfort, most with flower-filled balconies or loggias. The elegant restaurant ($$–$$$) serves international and traditional Bavarian cuisines with an emphasis on seafood (lobster Thermidor, for example), and a pine-panel tavern, Die Holzstubn'n, pours excellent local brew. ⊠ *Ludwigstr. 33, D–83435* ☎ *08651/6040* 🖷 *08651/62928* ⊕ *www.parkhotel. de* ➱ *70 rooms, 8 suites ⌂ Restaurant, cable TV, pool, gym, hot tub, sauna, bicycles, bar, beer garden, recreation room, Internet, some pets allowed (fee); no a/c* ⊟ *DC, MC, V* ❙❃❙ *BP.*

FodorsChoice
★

$ ✕🏨 **Bürgerbräu.** Each dining area in this old brewery inn reflects the social class that once met here: politicos, peasants, burghers, and salt miners. Reichenhallers from all walks of life still meet here to enjoy good conversation, hearty beer, and excellent food. Rooms at the inn are simple but airy and modern, and best of all, you're in the middle of town. ⊠ *Am Rathausplatz, D–83435* ☎ *08651/6089* 🖷 *08651/608–504* ➱ *32 rooms ⌂ Restaurant, cable TV, some pets allowed (fee); no a/c* ⊟ *AE, DC, MC, V* ❙❃❙ *BP.*

$ 🏨 **Villa Erika.** This four-story villa, painted a staid red, has been family-run since 1898, and it shows in the best sense. Everything radiates comfort, from the light-filled dining room to the generous garden, which supplies the kitchen with herbs. Owner Anton Oberarzbacher cooks the dinner options ($) himself, tapping a repertoire that includes French and Italian cuisines. The pedestrian zone in town is a minute away. ⊠ *Adolf-Schmid-Str. 3, D–83435* ☎ *08651/95360* ⊠ *08651/953–6200* ⊕ *www.hotel-pension-erika.de* ⇦ *32 rooms, 1 suite* ⚹ *Restaurant, in-room data ports, cable TV, some pets allowed; no a/c* ⊟ *AE, MC, V* ⊗ *Closed Nov.–Feb. Restaurant closed Sun.* ⧠ *BP.*

★ ¢–$ ☒ **Pension Hubertus.** This delightfully traditional family-run lodging stands on the shore of the tiny Thumsee, 5 km (3 mi) from the town center. The Hubertus's private grounds lead down to the lake, where guests can swim or boat (the water is bracingly cool). Rooms, some with balconies overlooking the lake, are furnished with hand-carved beds and cupboards. Excellent meals or coffee can be taken at the neighboring rustic **Madlbauer** ($–$$). There are special rates in the off-season (October–April). ⊠ *Am Thumsee 5, D–83435* ☎ *08651/2252* ⊠ *08651/63845* ⇦ *18 rooms* ⚹ *Cable TV, gym, boating, paddle tennis, some pets allowed (fee), no-smoking rooms; no a/c, no phones in some rooms* ⊟ *AE, DC, MC, V* ⧠ *CP.*

Nightlife & the Arts

Bad Reichenhall is proud of its long musical tradition and of its orchestra, founded more than a century ago. It performs six days a week throughout the year in the chandelier-hung Kurgastzentrum Theater or, when weather permits, in the open-air pavilion, and at a special Mozart Week in March. Call the **Orchesterbüro** (☎ 08651/8661 ⊠ 08651/710–551) for program details. As a spa town and winter resort, Bad Reichenhall is a natural for night haunts. The big draw is the elegant **casino** (⊠ Wittelsbacherstr. 17 ☎ 08651/95800 ⊠ €2.50, free with a Kurkarte; ask for one at your hotel ⚹ Jacket and tie), open daily 3 PM–1 or 2 AM depending on business.

Shopping

Using flowers and herbs grown in the Bavarian Alps, the **Josef Mack Company** (⊠ Ludwigstr. 36 ☎ 08651/78280) has made medicinal herbal preparations since 1856. **Leuthenmayr** (⊠ Ludwigstr. 27 ☎ 08651/2869) is a youngster in the business, selling its "cure-all" dwarf-pine oil since 1908. Your sweet tooth will be fully satisfied at the confection emporium of **Paul Reber** (⊠ Ludwigstr. 10–12 ☎ 08651/60030), makers of the famous chocolate and marzipan *Mozartkugel,* and many other dietary bombs. Candle-making is a local specialty, and **Kerzenwelt Donabauer** (⊠ Reichenhaller Str. 15, Piding ☎ 08651/8143), just outside Bad Reichenhall, has a selection of more than 1,000 decorative items in wax. It also has a free wax museum depicting fairy-tale characters.

Berchtesgaden

⑳ *18 km (11 mi) south of Bad Reichenhall, 20 km (12 mi) south of Salzburg.*

Berchtesgaden's reputation is unjustly rooted in its brief association with Adolf Hitler, who dreamed besottedly of his "1,000-year Reich" from the mountaintop where millions of tourists before and after him drank in only the superb beauty of the Alpine panorama. Below those giddy heights of his retreat is a historic old market town and mountain resort of great charm. In winter it's a fine place for skiing and snowboarding; in summer it becomes one of the region's most popular (and crowded) resorts. An ornate palace and working salt mine make up some of the diversions in this heavenly setting.

Salt—or "white gold," as it was known in medieval times—was once the basis of Berchtesgaden's wealth. In the 12th century Emperor Barbarossa gave mining rights to a Benedictine abbey that had been founded here a century earlier. The abbey was secularized early in the 19th century, when it was taken over by the Wittelsbach rulers. Salt is still important today because of all the local wellness centers. The entire area has been declared a "health resort region" (*Kurgebiet*) and was put on the UNESCO biosphere list. Not surprisingly, salt is celebrated in the *Salzsaga* (the Salt Saga), a musical by Klaus Ammann based on a story by the Bavarian author Ludwig Ganghofer. This love story full of romance, passion, betrayal, and politics is performed at the Königsee Lake at the **Theater am Königsee** (⊠ Seestr. 3 ☎ 01805/588–775 ⊕ www. theateramkoenigsee.com).

The last royal resident of the Berchtesgaden abbey, Crown Prince Rupprecht (who died here in 1955), furnished it with rare family treasures that now form the basis of a permanent collection—the **Königliches Schloss Berchtesgaden Museum.** Fine Renaissance rooms exhibit the prince's sacred art, which is particularly rich in wood sculptures by such great late-Gothic artists as Tilman Riemenschneider and Veit Stoss. You can also visit the abbey's original, cavernous 13th-century dormitory and cool cloisters. ⊠ *Schlosspl. 2* ☎ *08652/947–980* ⊕ *www.haus-bayern. com* ⊠ *€7 with tour* ☉ *Easter–Oct. 15, Sun.–Fri. 10–noon and 2–4; Oct. 16–Easter, weekdays 11–2; last entry and tour at 2.*

The **Heimatmuseum,** in the Schloss Adelsheim, displays examples of wood carving and other local crafts. Wood carving in Berchtesgaden dates to long before Oberammergau established itself as the premier wood-carving center of the Alps. ⊠ *Schroffenbergallee 6* ☎ *08652/4410* ⊠ *€2* ☉ *Tues.–Sun. 10–4, guided tours at 3.*

★ The **Salzbergwerk** (salt mine) is one of the chief attractions of the region. In the days when the mine was owned by Berchtesgaden's princely rulers, only select guests were allowed to see how the source of the city's wealth was extracted from the earth. Today, during a 90-minute tour, you can sit astride a miniature train that transports you nearly 1 km (½ mi) into the mountain to an enormous chamber where the salt is mined. Included in the tour are rides down the wooden chutes used by miners to get from one level to another and a boat ride on an underground saline lake the size of a football field. You may wish to partake in the special four-hour **brine dinners** down in the mines (€65). ⊠ *2 km (1 mi) from center of Berchtesgaden on B–305 Salzburg Rd.* ☎ *08652/600–220* ⊕ *www.salzbergwerk-berchtesgaden.de* ⊠ *€12.50, combined ticket with Bad Reichenhall's saline museum €14.50* ☉ *May–mid-Oct., daily 9–5; mid-Oct.–Apr., Mon.–Sat. 11:30–3:30.*

㉑ The **Obersalzberg**, site of Hitler's luxurious mountain retreat, is part of the north slope of the Hoher Goll, high above Berchtesgaden. It was a remote mountain community of farmers and foresters before Hitler's deputy, Martin Bormann, selected the site for a complex of Alpine homes for top Nazi leaders. Hitler's chalet, the Berghof, and all the others were destroyed in 1945, with the exception of a hotel that had been taken over by the Nazis, the Hotel zum Türken. Beneath the hotel is a section of the labyrinth of tunnels built as a last retreat for Hitler and his cronies; the macabre, murky **bunkers** (🖼 €2.50 ⊙ May–Oct., Tues.–Sun. 9–5; Nov.–Apr., daily 10–3) can be visited. Nearby, the **Dokumentation Obersalzbergmuseum** (✉ Salzbergstr. 41 ☎ 08652/947–960 ⊕ www.obersalzberg.de 🖼 €2.50 ⊙ Apr.–Oct., Tues.–Sun. 9–5; Nov.–Mar., Tues.–Sun. 10–3; last entry at 2) documents the Third Reich's history in the region.

Beyond Obersalzberg, the hairpin bends of Germany's highest road come to the base of the 6,000-foot peak on which sits the **Kehlsteinhaus** (☎ 08652/2969), also known as the Adlerhorst (Eagle's Nest), Hitler's personal retreat and his official guesthouse. It was Martin Bormann's gift to the führer on Hitler's 50th birthday. The road leading to it, built in 1937–39, climbs more than 2,000 dizzying feet in less than 6 km (4 mi). A tunnel in the mountain will bring you to an elevator that whisks you up to what appears to be the top of the world (you can walk up in about a half hour). There are refreshment rooms and a restaurant. The round-trip from Berchtesgaden's post office by bus and elevator costs €16.20 per person. The bus runs mid-May through September, daily from 9 to 4:50. By car you can travel only as far as the Obersalzberg bus station. From there the round-trip fare is €12.50. The full round-trip takes one hour. From July through September the tourist office organizes Eagle's Nest by Night tours, including a cocktail and three-course dinner accompanied by live Bavarian music.

Where to Stay & Eat

$–$$ ✕🖼 **Alpenhotel Denninglehen.** Nonsmokers appreciate the special dining room set aside just for them in this mountain hotel's restaurant. The house was built in 1981 in Alpine style, with lots of wood paneling, heavy beams, and wide balconies with cascades of geraniums in summer. Skiers enjoy the fact that the slopes are about 200 yards away. The restaurant's menu is regional (the usual schnitzels and roasts) with a few items from the French repertoire (a fine steak in pepper sauce, for example). ✉ *Am Priesterstein 7, D–83471 Berchtesgaden-Oberau* ☎ *08652/ 97890* 🖷 *08652/64710* ⊕ *www.denninglehen.de* ♨ *Restaurant, pool, sauna, some pets allowed (fee), no-smoking rooms; no a/c* ▤ *MC* ⊙ *Closed last 2 wks in Jan.* ⧖❙ *BP.*

$ ✕🖼 **Hotel Grünberger.** Only a few strides from the train station in the town center, the Grünberger overlooks the River Ache—it even has a private terrace beside the river you can relax on. The cozy rooms have farmhouse-style furnishings and some antiques. The wellness area has in-house acupuncture and traditional Chinese medicine treatments. The hotel restaurant focuses on German fare with some international dishes to lighten the load. ✉ *Hansererweg 1, D–83471* ☎ *08652/4560*

🏛 *08652/62254* ⊕ *www.hotel-gruenberger.de* 🛏 *65 rooms* 🏃 *Restaurant, cable TV, pool, sauna, beer garden, Internet, no-smoking rooms; no pets, no a/c, no room phones, no TV in some rooms* ☰ *MC, V* ⊘ *Closed Nov.–mid-Dec.* ⦿| *BP.*

$ ✕🍴 **Hotel Post.** This central and reliable hostelry offers fine Bavarian food, with some lighter Italian fare—pastas, salmon, flounder—for anyone needing a break from hocks and pork roast. If trout from the nearby Königsee is available, order it. In summer you can eat in the beer garden. The rooms are basic but clean and pleasant. ⊠ *Maximilianstr. 2, D–83471* ☎ *08652/5067* 🏛 *08652/64801* ⊕ *www.hotel-post-bgd.de* 🏃 *Restaurant, cable TV, some pets allowed (fee); no a/c* ☰ *MC, V* ⦿| *BP.*

$–$$ 🍴 **Hotel Wittelsbach.** This is one of the oldest (built in 1892) and most traditional lodgings in the area. The small rooms have dark pinewood furnishings and deep red and green drapes and carpets. Ask for one with a balcony. ⊠ *Maximilianstr. 16, D–83471* ☎ *08652/96380* 🏛 *08652/66304* ⊕ *www.hotel-wittelsbach.com* 🛏 *26 rooms, 3 apartments* 🏃 *Cable TV, Internet, some pets allowed; no a/c* ☰ *AE, DC, MC, V* ⦿| *BP.*

$–$$ 🍴 **Stoll's Hotel Alpina.** Set above the Königsee in the delightful little village of Schönau, the Alpina offers rural solitude and easy access to Berchtesgaden. Families are catered to with apartments, a resident doctor, and a playroom. ⊠ *Ulmenweg 14, D–83471 Schönau* ☎ *08652/65090* 🏛 *08652/61608* ⊕ *www.stolls-hotel-alpina.de* 🛏 *52 rooms, 8 apartments* 🏃 *Restaurant, some in-room data ports, cable TV, pool, hair salon, sauna, some pets allowed (fee); no a/c* ☰ *AE, DC, MC, V* ⊘ *Closed early Nov.–mid-Dec.* ⦿| *BP.*

$ 🍴 **Hotel zum Türken.** The view alone is worth the 10-minute journey from Berchtesgaden to this hotel. Confiscated during World War II by the Nazis, the hotel is at the foot of the road to Hitler's mountaintop retreat. Beneath it are remains of Nazi wartime bunkers. There's no restaurant, although evening meals can be ordered in advance. ⊠ *Hintereck 2, D–83471 Obersalzberg-Berchtesgaden* ☎ *08652/2428* 🏛 *08652/4710* ⊕ *www.hotel zum tuerken.de* 🛏 *17 rooms, 12 with bath or shower* 🏃 *Some pets allowed, no-smoking rooms; no a/c, no phones in some rooms* ☰ *AE, DC, MC, V* ⊘ *Closed Nov.–Dec. 20* ⦿| *BP.*

---

off the beaten path

SCHELLENBERG EISHÖHLEN – Germany's largest ice caves lie 10 km (6 mi) north of Berchtesgaden. By car take B–305, or take the bus (€4) from the Berchtesgaden post office to the village of Marktschellenberg. From there you can reach the caves on foot by walking 2½ hours along the clearly marked route. A guided tour of the caves takes one hour. On the way to Marktschellenberg watch for the **Almbachklamm,** a narrow valley good for hikes. At its entrance is an old (1683) mill for making and polishing marble balls. 🎫 €4 ☎ *08650/352* ⊘ *Mid-June–mid-Oct., daily 10–5.*

Shopping

The **Berchtesgadener Handwerkskunst** (⊠ Schlosspl. 1½, D–83471 ☎ 08652/979–790 ⊘ Mon.–Sat. 9–noon, weekdays 2–6) offers handicrafts—such as wooden boxes, woven tablecloths, woodcarvings, and Christmas-tree decorations—from Berchtesgaden, the surrounding region, and other parts of Bavaria.

Sports & the Outdoors

Germany's highest course, the **Berchtesgaden Golf Club** (✉ Salzbergstr. 33 ☏ 08652/2100), is on a 3,300-foot plateau of the Obersalzberg. Only fit players should attempt the demanding 9-hole course. Seven Berchtesgaden hotels offer their guests a 30% reduction on the €25 greens fee—contact the tourist office or the club for details.

Whatever your mountain-related needs, whether it's climbing and hiking in summer or cross-country tours in winter, you'll find it at the **Erste Bergschule Berchtesgadenerland** (✉ Silbergstr. 25, Strub ☏ 08652/2420 May–Oct., 08652/5371 Nov.–Apr. 🖷 08652/2420).

At the sleek and classy **Watzmann Therme** you'll find fragrant steam rooms, saunas with infrared cabins for sore muscles, an elegant pool, whirlpools, and more. If you happen to be staying a few days, you might catch a tai chi course, enjoy a bio-release facial massage, or partake in an evening of relaxing underwater exercises. ✉ *Bergwerkstr.* ☏ *08652/94640* 🗠 *4 hrs €12.80, day including sauna €14.30* ☉ *Daily 10–10.*

Berchtesgaden National Park

5 km (3 mi) south of Berchtesgaden.

The deep, mysterious, and fabled Königsee is the most photographed panorama in Germany. Together with its much smaller sister, the Obersee, it's nestled within the Berchtesgaden National Park, 210 square km (82 square mi) of wild mountain country where flora and fauna have been left to develop as nature intended. No roads penetrate the area, and even the mountain paths are difficult to follow. The park administration organizes guided tours of the area from June through September. *Nationalparkhaus* ✉ *Franziskanerpl. 7, D–83471 Berchtesgaden* ☏ *08652/ 64343* ⊕ *www.nationalpark-berchtesgaden.de.*

★ One less strenuous way into the Berchtesgaden National Park is by boat. A fleet of 21 excursion boats, electrically driven so that no noise disturbs the peace, operates on the **Königsee** (King Lake). Only the skipper of the boat is allowed to shatter the silence—his trumpet fanfare demonstrates a remarkable echo as notes reverberate between the almost vertical cliffs that plunge into the dark green water. A cross on a rocky promontory marks the spot where a boatload of pilgrims hit the cliffs and sank more than 100 years ago. The voyagers were on their way to the tiny, twin-tower baroque chapel of St. Bartholomä, built in the 17th century on a peninsula where an early Gothic church once stood. The princely rulers of Berchtesgaden built a hunting lodge at the side of the chapel; a tavern and restaurant now occupy its rooms.

Smaller than the Königsee but equally beautiful, the **Obersee** can be reached by a 15-minute walk from the second stop (Salet) on the boat tour. The lake's backdrop of jagged mountains and precipitous cliffs is broken by a waterfall, the Rothbachfall, that plunges more than 1,000 feet to the valley floor.

Boat service (☏ 08652/963–618 ⊕ www.bayerische-seenschifffahrt.de) on the Königsee runs year-round, except when the lake freezes. A round-trip to St. Bartholomä and Salet, the landing stage for the Obersee, lasts almost two hours, without stops, and costs €14. A round-trip to St. Bartholomä lasts a little over an hour and costs €11. In summer, the Berchtesgaden tourist office organizes evening cruises on the Königsee, which includes a concert in St. Bartholomä Church and a four-course dinner in the neighboring hunting lodge.

THE BAVARIAN ALPS A TO Z

To research prices, get advice from other travelers, and book travel arrangements, visit www.fodors.com.

AIRPORTS

Munich, 95 km (59 mi) northwest of Garmisch-Partenkirchen, is the gateway to the Bavarian Alps. If you're staying in Berchtesgaden, consider the closer airport in Salzburg, Austria, although it has fewer international flights.

BOAT TRAVEL

Passenger boats operate on all the major Bavarian lakes. They're mostly excursion boats, and many run only in summer. However, there's year-round service on the Chiemsee. Eight boats operate year-round on the Tegernsee, connecting the towns of Tegernsee, Rottach-Egern, Bad Wiessee, and Gmund.

BUS TRAVEL

The Alpine region is not well served by long-distance buses. There's a fairly good network of local buses, but they tend to run at commuter times. Inquire at any local train station, travel agent, or at your hotel, or log onto the German railways' itinerary planning site, ⊕ www.bahn. de. Larger resorts operate buses to outlying areas. The Wendelstein region, for example, is serviced by the Wendelstein Ringlinie, offering fares from a simple €7 per day to more complex ones involving skiing tickets. It connects the skiing areas of Sudelfeld with Bayrischzell, the Tatzelwurm Gorge, Bad Aibling near Rosenheim, and other towns and areas. Garmisch-Partenkirchen runs night buses to and from Murnau, Oberammergau, Mittenwald, and Krün. Night buses also run between Murnau and Oberammergau. The cost is €2.50.

CAR RENTALS

🚗 **Avis** ⊠ Königseerstr. 47, Berchtesgaden ☎ 08652/69107 ⊠ St.-Martin-Str. 17, Garmisch-Partenkirchen ☎ 08821/934-242. **Hertz** ⊠ Isarstr. 1d, Rosenheim ☎ 08031/609-666. **Sixt** ⊠ Bahnhofstr. 31, Garmisch-Partenkirchen ⊠ Hauptbahnhof, main railway station, Rosenheim ☎ 08031/43004, 01805/252-525 for national reservations.

CAR TRAVEL

Three autobahns reach into the Bavarian Alps: A–7 comes in from the northwest (Frankfurt, Stuttgart, Ulm) and ends near Füssen in the western Bavarian Alps; A–95 runs from Munich to Garmisch-Partenkirchen; take A–8 from Munich for Tegernsee, Schliersee, and Chiemsee and for Berchtesgaden. All provide speedy access to a network of well-paved country roads that penetrate high into the mountains. (Germany's highest road runs above Berchtesgaden at more than 5,000 feet.) Note that on weekends and at the start and end of national holidays, A–8 can become a long parking lot heading toward Austria or Munich. The two major climbs around the Irschenberg and Bernau are particularly affected. Weekend traffic also jams up the end of A–95 near Garmisch-Partenkirchen.

EMERGENCIES
🚩 **Police and ambulance** ☎ 110. **Fire and emergency medical aid** ☎ 112.

TOURS
BERCHTESGADEN In Berchtesgaden, the Schwaiger bus company runs tours of the area and across the Austrian border as far as Salzburg. An American couple runs Berchtesgaden Mini-bus Tours out of the local tourist office, opposite the railroad station.
🚩 **Schwaiger** ☎ 08652/2525. **Berchtesgaden Mini-bus Tours** ☎ 08652/64971.

GARMISCH-PARTENKIRCHEN Bus tours to King Ludwig II's castles at Neuschwanstein and Linderhof and to the Ettal Monastery, near Oberammergau, are offered by DER travel agencies. Local agencies in Garmisch also run tours to Neuschwanstein, Linderhof, Ettal, and into the neighboring Austrian Tyrol.

The Garmisch mountain railway company, the Bayerische Zugspitzbahn, offers special excursions to the top of the Zugspitze, Germany's highest mountain, by cog rail and/or cable car.
🚩 **Bayerische Zugspitzbahn** ☎ 08821/7970. **DER** ✉ Garmisch-Partenkirchen ☎ 08821/55125. **Dominikus Kümmerle** ☎ 08821/4955. **Hans Biersack** ☎ 08821/4920. **Hilmar Röser** ☎ 08821/2926. **Weiss-Blau-Reisen** ☎ 08821/3766.

TRAIN TRAVEL
Most Alpine resorts are connected with Munich by regular express and slower services. Trains to Garmisch-Partenkirchen depart hourly from Munich's Hauptbahnhof. Garmisch-Partenkirchen and Mittenwald are on the InterCity Express network, which has regular direct service to all regions of the country. (Klais, just outside Garmisch, is Germany's highest-altitude InterCity train station.) A train from Munich also connects to Gmund on Tegernsee. Bad Reichenhall, Berchtesgaden, Prien, and Rosenheim are linked directly to north German cities by long-distance express service. If you're making a day trip to the Zugspitze from Munich, Augsburg, or any other southern Bavarian center, take advantage of an unbeatable deal offered by Deutsche Bahn that includes rail fare and a day pass to all the Garmisch-Partenkirchen mountains, including the Zugspitze.

VISITOR INFORMATION
The Bavarian regional tourist office in Munich, Tourismusverband München Oberbayern, provides general information about Upper Bavaria and the Bavarian Alps.
🚩 **Aschau** ✉ Verkehrsamt, Kampenwandstr. 38, D–83229 ☎ 08052/904–937 ⊕ www.aschau.de. **Bad Reichenhall** ✉ Kur-und-Verkehrsverein, im Kurgastzentrum, Wittelsbacherstr. 15, D–83424 ☎ 08651/606–303 ⊕ www.bad-reichenhall.de. **Bad Tölz** ✉ Kurverwaltung, Ludwigstr. 11, D–83646 ☎ 08041/78670 ⊕ www.bad-toelz.de. **Bad Wiessee** ✉ Kuramt, Adrian-Stoop-Str. 20, D–837004 ☎ 08022/86030 ⊕ www.

Bad-Wiessee.de. **Bayrischzell** ✉ Kirchpl. 2, Kurverwaltung ⌂ Postfach 2, Kurverwaltung D–83735 ☎ 08023/1034 ⊕ www.bayrischzell.de. **Berchtesgaden** ✉ Kurdirektion, D–83471 ☎ 08652/9670 ⊕ www.berchtesgadener-land.com. **Chiemsee** ✉ Tourismusverband Chiemsee, Kurverwaltung, Alte Rathausstr. 11, D–83209 Prien ☎ 08051/69050 ⊕ www.chiemsee.de. **Ettal** ✉ Verkehrsamt, Kaiser-Ludwig-Pl., D–82488 ☎ 08822/3534. **Garmisch-Partenkirchen** ✉ Verkehrsamt der Kurverwaltung, Richard-Strauss-Pl. 2, D–82467 ☎ 08821/180–420 ⊕ www.garmisch-partenkirchen.de. **Kochel am See** ✉ Kalmbachstr. 11, D–82431 ☎ 08851/338 ⊕ www.kochel.de. **Mittenwald** ✉ Kurverwaltung, Dammkarstr. 3, D–82481 ☎ 08823/33981 ⊕ www.mittenwald.de. **Murnau** ✉ Verkehrsamt Murnau, Kohlgruber Strasse 1, D–82418 ☎ 08841/61410 ⊕ www.murnau.de. **Oberammergau** ✉ Verkehrsamt, Eugen-Papst-Str. 9a, D–82487 ☎ 08822/92310 🖷 08822/923–190 ⊕ oberammergau.de. **Prien am Chiemsee** ✉ Alter Rathausstr. 11, D–83209 ☎ 08051/69050 ⊕ www.prien.chiemsee.de. **Reit im Winkl** ✉ Verkehrsamt, Rathauspl. 1, D–83242 ☎ 08640/80020 ⊕ www.reit-im-winkl.de. **Rottach-Egern/ Tegernsee** ✉ Kuramt, Nördliche Hauptstr. 2, D–83684 ☎ 08022/180–149 ⊕ www.tegernsee.de. **Ruhpolding** ✉ Kurverwaltung, Hauptstr. 60, D–83324 ☎ 086638806–0 ⊕ www.tegernsee.de. **Tourismusverband München Oberbayern** ✉ Bodenseestr. 113, D–81243 Munich ☎ 089/829–2180.

THE BAVARIAN FOREST

3

TRY BAVARIA'S BEST DUMPLING
at Dampfnudel Uli ⇨*p.128*

TEST YOUR SKILL AT BLOWING GLASS
in the Kunstglasbläserei Seeman
(Seeman Artistic Glass Foundry) ⇨*p.139*

SAY HELLO TO MOTHER NATURE
in the Bavarian Forest National Park ⇨*p.141*

GET A DANUBE VIEW WITH DINNER
at Passauer Wolf restaurant ⇨*p.148*

SLEEP LIKE ROYALTY
at the Hotel Wilder Mann ⇨*p.148*

Updated by
Tim Howe

LOW-KEY, UNDERSTATED, AND AFFORDABLE, the Bayerischer Wald (Bavarian Forest) is a welcome alternative to Germany's hyped-up, overcrowded tourist regions. For years this picturesque, wooded region of Lower Bavaria (Niederbayern) was an isolated part of western Europe, its eastern boundary flanked by the Iron Curtain and the impenetrable, dark density of the Czech Republic's Bohemian Forest. The flavor of Lower Bavaria is vastly different from the popular concept of Bavaria (that world supposedly populated by men in lederhosen and funny feathered green hats and buxom women in flowing dirndls, who sing along with oompah bands and knock back great steins of beer). People here are reserved; even their accent is gentler than that of their southern countrymen. Farming and forestry are the chief economic bases of this rural land, where the flat grainfields south of the Danube rise to wooded heights.

Taken together, the Bavarian and Bohemian forests form the largest area of protected closed woodland in central Europe, earning them the nickname "Europe's Green Roof." Villages of jumbled red roofs and oniondome churches dot the vast forest, which has largely buffered communities from further development. Cut off for centuries from the outside world, the small towns of the Bavarian Forest developed a tough self-sufficiency, which is evident today in a kind of cultural independence. Ancient, even heathen traditions are kept alive, and each community boasts its own natural history museum or collections of local curiosities (snuffboxes, for instance).

The collapse of Communism in Czechoslovakia and the formation of the Czech Republic made possible the renewal of old contacts between Germans and Bohemian Czechs. The ancient trading route between Deggendorf and Prague—the Böhmweg—has been revived for hikers. No visit to the Bavarian Forest would be complete without at least a day trip across the border; bus trips into the Bohemian region of the Czech Republic, as far as Prague and Plsen, are organized by every local tourist office.

The Bavarian Forest has long been a secret of Germans who enjoy relaxing, affordable holidays at mountainside lodges or country inns, but tourism is growing. In some parts of the forest the concentration of small hotels, pensions, and holiday apartments is the highest in Germany, but their presence doesn't overwhelm the natural surroundings, since that's what people are coming to explore. All those in search of peace and quiet—hikers, nature lovers, anglers, horseback riders, skiers looking for uncrowded slopes, and golfers distressed by steep greens fees at more fashionable courses—will find their niche here.

Exploring the Bavarian Forest

The Bavarian Forest is a compact area between the Danube River and the borders of Austria and the Czech Republic. The region has three major towns, Regensburg, Deggendorf, and Passau, all good bases for day trips into the forest or for longer outings. Many of the larger country hotels are ideal for a family vacation, as they usually offer a very wide range

If you have
3 days

Numbers in the text correspond to numbers in the margin and on the Bavarian Forest, Regensburg, and Passau maps.

Start in ⊡ **Regensburg** ❶–⓭ ► and spend a day exploring the historic sites of the city. On the second day take a leisurely two-hour drive to ⊡ **Bodenmais** ⓲ and the nearby silver mine at **Silberberg.** On your third day, head out to Grafenau and the **Bavarian Forest National Park** ㉑.

If you have
5 days

Spend one day touring ⊡ **Regensburg** ❶–⓭ ► before traveling down to ⊡ **Deggendorf** ⓴ and the nearby abbey in **Metten.** On Day 3 head north to the **Grosser Arber,** overnighting in ⊡ **Bodenmais** ⓲, ⊡ **Zwiesel** ⓳, or ⊡ **Viechtach** ⓱, all famous for fine glass. From Zwiesel, follow the course of the Regen River as far as Frauenau and head into the ⊡ **Bavarian Forest National Park** ㉑ to stay in the resort town of Grafenau. From Grafenau, follow the Ilz River down to ⊡ **Passau** ㉓–㉚.

3

of leisure and sports facilities. You could spend a week or two at such a resort and enjoy everything the Bavarian Forest has to offer without venturing beyond the village boundaries.

About the Restaurants

While the lack of large towns in far southeast Germany generally means you have to travel much farther to find a place to eat, restaurants in the Bavarian Forest certainly compensate by offering a wide selection of regional food at reasonable prices. As in many rural areas of the country, many *Gaststätten* (informal restaurants that are usually inexpensive) serve hot meals only between 11:30 AM and 2 PM, and 6 PM and 9 PM.

About the Hotels

Prices here are among the lowest in Germany. Many hotels offer special 14-day packages for the price of a 10-day stay, and 10 days for the price of 7. There are also numerous sports packages. All local tourist offices can supply lists of accommodations; most can help with reservations.

WHAT IT COSTS In Euros				
	$$$$	**$$$**	**$$**	**$**	**¢**
RESTAURANTS	over €25	€21–€25	€16–€20	€9–€15	under €9
HOTELS	over €225	€175–€225	€100–€175	€50–€100	under €50

Restaurant prices are per person for a main course at dinner. Hotel prices are for two people in a standard double room, including tax and service.

Timing

Summer is the time to visit the Bavarian Forest. Although local tourist offices do their best to publicize events spread throughout the calendar year, only winter-sports fans and other hardy types venture deep into

Rhanwalting

16 Cham Haidstein Grosser Bayerisch-Eisenstein

Arber

CZECH REPUBLIC GERMANY

Silberberg ◆ Frauenau

Pfahl

17 Viechtach **18** **19 Zwiesel** **Bodenmais** Lusen

Schwarzer Rachel

Patersdorf Regen Rinchnach

Regensburg 1 - 13 see detail map Regen **21 Mauth**

Burg **Bavarian Forest**

Bischofsmais Weissenstein **National Park** Philippsreut

14 Walhalla Grafenau

Metten Schönberg Freyung Haidmühle

Danube

15 Weltenburg **20 Deggendorf** Saldenburg

Dreiburgensee

Englburg **22** Tittling

Passau 23 - 30 see detail map

Osterhofen **AUSTRIA**

Vilshofen Danube

The Bavarian Forest

Isar

KEY

► Start of itinerary

0 _____ 20 miles
0 _____ 30 km

the forest in the months between late fall and early spring. The cold continues through February, and snow lies deep in the ski resorts from December through March.

REGENSBURG

► *120 km (74 mi) northwest of Munich.*

Few visitors to Bavaria venture this far off the well-trod tourist trails, and even Germans are surprised when they discover medieval Regensburg. Because it escaped World War II with no major damage, the capital of the Oberpfalz (Upper Palatinate) is one of the best-preserved medieval cities in Germany, as well as an excellent base for excursions into the Bavarian Forest.

The key to Regensburg is the Danube. Before the Rhine-Main-Danube Canal was completed in the 1990s, the great river was not navigable a few miles to the west, and this simple geographic fact allowed Regensburg to control trade along the Danube between Germany and central Europe for centuries. The Danube was a conduit of ideas as well. It was from Regensburg that Christianity spread across much of central Europe in the 7th and 8th centuries. By the Middle Ages Regensburg had

3

On the Menu

The region has given Germany one of its most popular dishes, the *Pichelsteiner Eintopf,* a delicious broth of vegetables and pork. Sausages come in all varieties—the best are *Regensburger* (short, thick, spicy sausages, rather like the bratwurst of Nürnberg) and *Bauernseufzer* (literally, "farmer's sigh") sausage. Dumplings, made out of anything and everything, appear on practically every menu. Try *Deggendorfer Knödel* (bread dumplings) if you fancy something really local. The Danube provides a number of excellent types of fish, particularly *Donauwaller* (Danube catfish) from Passau, served *blau* (poached) or *gebacken* (breaded and fried). Radishes are a specialty, especially *Weichser Rettiche* (a large white radish), and are a good accompaniment to the many local beers.

Hiking & Biking

The Bavarian Forest is prime hiking country, crisscrossed with trails of varied difficulty, including three officially recognized and marked hiking trails. The longest, the Pandurensteig, runs nearly 167 km (104 mi), from Waldmünchen, in the northwest, to Passau, in the southeast, and across the heights of the Bavarian Forest National Park. It follows an old trading route, and the towns of Schönberg, Regen, and Bayerisch-Eisenstein have close access to the trail. The Pandurensteig can be covered in stages with the aid of a tourist package that transfers hikers' luggage from one stop to the next.

Resorts between Deggendorf and Bayerisch-Eisenstein on the Czech border have remapped the centuries-old Böhmweg trading route, which connected the Danube and Moldau rivers. It can be comfortably covered in three or four days, with accommodations at village taverns on the way. Like the Böhmweg, the Gunterweg strikes deep into the Czech Republic, following the 1,000-year-old wanderings of the missionary St. Gunter.

Skiing & Snowboarding

Advanced downhill skiers make for the World Cup slopes of the Grosser Arber. The summit is reached by chairlifts from Bayerisch-Eisenstein and from just outside Bodenmais. Other ski areas in the Bavarian Forest are not as demanding, and many resorts are ideal for families. Cross-country skiing trails are everywhere; a map of 22 of the finest and a separate list of resorts offering all-inclusive ski holidays can be obtained free of charge from the Tourismusverband Ostbayern.

---

become a political, economic, and intellectual center. For many centuries it was the most important city in southeast Germany, serving as the seat of the Perpetual Imperial Diet from 1663 until 1806, when Napoléon ordered the dismemberment of the Holy Roman Empire.

Regensburg's story begins with the Celts around 500 BC. They called their little settlement Radasbona. In AD 179, as an original marble inscription in the Historisches Museum proclaims, it became a Roman military post called Castra Regina. The Porta Praetoria, or gateway, built by the Romans, remains in the Old Town, and whenever you see huge ashlars incorporated into buildings, you are looking at bits of the old Roman settlement. When Bavarian tribes migrated to the area in the 6th century, they occupied what remained of the Roman town and, apparently on the basis of its Latin name, called it Regensburg. Anglo-Saxon missionaries led by St. Boniface in 739 made the town a bishopric before heading down the Danube to convert the heathen in even more far-flung lands. Charlemagne, first of the Holy Roman Emperors, arrived at the end of the 8th century and incorporated Regensburg into his burgeoning domain.

Today, the ancient and hallowed walls of Regensburg continue to buzz with life. Students from the university fill the restaurants and pubs, and locals do their daily shopping and errand-running in the inner city, where small shops and stores have managed to keep international consumer chains out. Any serious tour of Regensburg includes an unusually large number of places of worship. If your spirits wilt at the thought of inspecting them all, you should at least see the Dom (cathedral), famous for its Domspatzen (boys' choir—the literal translation is "cathedral sparrows").

a good walk

Begin your walk in the very center of Regensburg, on medieval Rathausplatz. At the tourist office you can book a tour of the adjacent **Altes Rathaus** (Old Town Hall) ❶ ► and pick up maps and brochures. Head east along Goliathstrasse; turn left on Bruckstrasse to take a short detour down to the bank of the Danube and the **Steinerne Brücke** (Stone Bridge) ❷, which was key to the city's rise to medieval trading power. Walk to the bridge's center for an unforgettable view of Regensburg's Old Town center, with the ancient tower, now the **Brückturm Museum** (Bridge Tower Museum) ❸, acting as a gate leading to the jumble of cobblestone streets and steeply eaved houses. From the tower follow Residenzstrasse south, and within a few minutes you'll reach Domplatz, dominated by Regensburg's soaring cathedral, **Dom St. Peter** ❹. Behind the cathedral square is the quieter Alter Kornmarkt, bordered on three sides by historic churches: the **Alte Kapelle** ❺, the adjoining **Karmelitenkirche** ❻, and the **Niedermünster** ❼. At the northern exit of Alter Kornmarkt is a reminder of Regensburg's Roman past, the **Porta Praetoria** ❽, a former gateway to the Roman camp. Other Roman remains can be viewed in Regensburg's city museum, the **Historisches Museum** ❾, on Dachauplatz, just south of the Alter Kornmarkt. Regensburg's oldest church, **St. Kassian** ❿, is 200 yards west of Dachauplatz and Alter Kornmarkt, at the southern edge of another ancient city square, **Neupfarrplatz** ⓫, where you'll also find the city's first Protestant church, the Neupfarrkirche. Leave Neupfarrplatz at its southern edge and a short stroll brings you to the great bulk of Regensburg's extraordinary palace, **Schloss Emmeram** ⓬. Across from the palace is the church of **St. Emmeram** ⓭. To complete your walk, continue westward along Obermünsterstrasse, turning right into Obere Bachgasse. This street becomes Untere Bachgasse and will take you back within minutes to your starting point, Rathausplatz.

Regensburg

KEY

▶ Start of walk

i Tourist information

0   220 yards
0   200 meters

TIMING Regensburg is compact; its Old Town center is about 1 square mi. All of its attractions lie on the south side of the Danube, so you won't have to cross it more than once—and then only to admire the city from the north bank. Try to time your tour so that you arrive at lunchtime at the ancient Historische Wurstküche, a tavern nestling between the river and the bridge. You'll need about two hours or more to explore Schloss Emmeram and St. Emmeram Church. Schedule at least another hour to visit the cathedral.

What to See

5 **Alte Kapelle** (Old Chapel). The Carolingian structure was erected in the 9th century. Its dowdy exterior gives little hint of the joyous rococo treasures within—extravagant concoctions of sinuous gilt stucco, rich marble, and giddy frescoes, the whole illuminated by light pouring in from the upper windows. ⊠ *Alter Kornmarkt 8* ☎ *No phone* ☉ *Daily 9–dusk.*

▶ **1** **Altes Rathaus** (Old Town Hall). The picture-book complex of medieval buildings, with half-timber, windows large and small, and flowers in tubs, is one of the best preserved town halls in the country, as well as one of the most historically important. It was here, in the imposing Gothic **Reichssaal** (Imperial Hall), that the Perpetual Imperial Diet met from 1663 to 1806. This parliament of sorts consisted of the emperor, the electors (seven or eight), the princes (about 50), and the burghers, who assembled to discuss and determine the affairs of the far-reaching German lands. The hall is sumptuously appointed with tapestries, flags, and heraldic designs. Note the wood ceiling, built in 1408, and the different elevations for the various estates. The Reichssaal is occasionally used for concerts. The neighboring **Ratsaal** (Council Room) is where the electors met for their consultations. The cellar holds the actual torture chamber of the city; the **Fragstatt** (Questioning Room); and the execution room, called the **Armesünderstübchen** (Poor Sinners' Room). Any prisoner who withstood three degrees of questioning without confessing was considered innocent and released—which tells you something about medieval notions of justice. ⊠ *Rathauspl.* ☎ *0941/507–4411* ⊠ *€2.50* ☉ *Daily 9–4; tours in English May–Sept., Mon.–Sat. at 3:15.*

need a break? Just across the square from the Altes Rathaus is the **Prinzess Confiserie Café** (⊠ Rathauspl. 2 ☎ 0941/595–310), Germany's oldest coffeehouse, which first opened its doors to the general public in 1686. The homemade chocolates are highly recommended, as are the rich cakes.

❸ **Brückturm Museum** (Bridge Tower Museum). With its tiny windows, weathered tiles, and pink plaster, this 17th-century tower stands at the south end of the Steinerne Brücke. The tower displays a host of items relating to the construction and history of the old bridge. It also offers a gorgeous view of the Regensburg roof landscape. The brooding building, with a massive roof to the left of the Brückturm, is an old salt warehouse that now houses the Salzstadel Wirtshaus, where you can try your first Regensburger sausage. ⊠ *Steinerne Brücke* ☎ *0941/565–746* ⊠ *€2* ☉ *Apr.–Oct., daily 10–5; call ahead to ask about English tours.*

★ ❹ **Dom St. Peter** (St. Peter's Cathedral). Regensburg's transcendent cathedral, modeled on the airy, vertical lines of French Gothic architecture, is something of a rarity this far south in Germany. Begun in the 13th century, it stands on the site of a much earlier Carolingian church. Remarkably, the cathedral can hold 6,000 people, three times the population of Regensburg when building began. Construction dragged on for almost 600 years until Ludwig I of Bavaria, then ruler of Regensburg, finally had the towers built. These had to be replaced in the mid-1950s. Behind the Dom is a little workshop where a team of 15 stonecutters is busy full-time during the summer recutting and restoring parts of the cathedral.

Before heading into the Dom, take time to admire the intricate and frothy carvings of its facade. Inside, the glowing 14th-century stained glass in the choir and the exquisitely detailed statues of the archangel Gabriel and the Virgin in the crossing (the intersection of the nave and the transepts) are among the church's outstanding features. ⊠ *Dompl.* ☎ *0941/597–1002* ⊠ *Tour, only in German; for tours in English call ahead, €2.50* ☉ *Cathedral tour May–Oct., weekdays at 10, 11, and 2, Sun. at noon and 2; Nov.–Apr., weekdays at 11, Sun. at noon.*

Be sure to visit the **Kreuzgang** (Cloisters), reached via the garden. There you'll find a small octagonal chapel, the Allerheiligenkapelle (All Saint's Chapel), a Romanesque building that is all sturdy grace and massive walls, a work by Italian masons from the mid-12th century. You can barely make out the faded remains of stylized 11th-century frescoes on its ancient walls. The equally ancient shell of St. Stephan's Church, the Alter Dom (Old Cathedral), can also be visited. The cloisters, chapel, and Alter Dom can be seen only on a guided one-hour tour. 📷 €2.50 ⊙ *Tour mid-May–Oct., daily at 10, 11, and 2; Nov.–Mar., weekdays at 11, Sun. at noon; Apr.–mid-May, daily at 11 and 2.*

The **Domschatzmuseum** (Cathedral Museum) contains valuable treasures going back to the 11th century. Some of the vestments and the monstrances, which are fine examples of eight centuries' worth of the goldsmith's trade, are still used during special services. The entrance is in the nave. ⊠ *Dompl.* 📷 *0941/57645* 📷 *€1.50* ⊙ *Apr.–Oct., Tues.–Sat. 10–5, Sun. noon–5; Dec.–Mar., Fri. and Sat. 10–4, Sun. noon–4.*

need a break?

The restaurant **Haus Heuport** (⊠ Dompl. 7 📷 0941/599–9297), opposite the entrance of the Dom, is in one of the old and grand private ballrooms of the city. The service is excellent, all dishes taste good, and the tables at the windows have a wonderful view of the Dom. For snack fare, such as sandwiches and salads, head for the bistro area.

★ ⑨ **Historisches Museum** (Historical Museum). The municipal museum vividly relates the cultural history of Regensburg. It's one of the highlights of the city, both for its unusual and beautiful setting—a former Gothic monastery—and for its wide-ranging collections, from Roman artifacts to Renaissance tapestries and remains from Regensburg's 16th-century Jewish ghetto. The most significant exhibits are the paintings by Albrecht Altdorfer (1480–1538), a native of Regensburg and, along with Cranach, Grünewald, and Dürer, one of the leading painters of the German Renaissance. His work has the same sense of heightened reality found in that of his contemporaries, in which the lessons of Italian painting are used to produce an emotional rather than a rational effect. His paintings would not have seemed out of place among those of 19th-century Romantics. Far from seeing the world around him as essentially hostile, or at least alien, he saw it as something intrinsically beautiful, whether wild or domesticated. Altdorfer made two drawings of the old synagogue of Regensburg, priceless documents that are on exhibit here. ⊠ *Dachaupl. 2–4* 📷 *0941/507–2448* 📷 *€2* ⊙ *Tues.–Sun. 10–4.*

⑥ **Karmelitenkirche** (Church of the Carmelites). This lovely church, in the baroque style from crypt to cupola, stands next to the Alte Kapelle. It has a finely decorated facade designed by the 17th-century Italian master Carlo Lurago. ⊠ *Alter Kornmarkt.*

⑪ **Neupfarrplatz.** This oversize open square was once a Jewish ghetto. The Regensburg Jews had lived in fair harmony with the town's citizens, but hard economic times and superstition led to their eviction by decree in 1519. While the synagogue was being torn down, one worker survived a very bad fall. A church was promptly built to celebrate the miracle and before long a pilgrimage began. The **Neupfarrkirche** (New Parish Church) was built as well to accommodate the flow of pilgrims. During the Reformation, the Parish Church was given to the Protestants, hence its bare-bones interior. In the late 1990s, excavation work (for the power company) on the square uncovered well-kept cellars, and to the west of the church, the old synagogue, including the foundations of its Romanesque predecessor. Archaeologists salvaged the few items they could from the old stones (including a stash of 684 gold coins) and, not knowing what to do with the sea of foundations, ultimately carefully reburied them. Recovered items were carefully restored and are on exhibit in the Historisches Museum. Only one small underground area to the south of the church, the **Document**, accommodates viewing of the foundations. In a former cellar, surrounded by the original walls, visitors can watch a short video reconstructing life in the old Jewish ghetto. Over the old synagogue, the Israeli artist Dani Karavan designed a stylized plaza where people can sit and meet. Call the educational institution VHS for a tour of the Document (reservations are requested). For spontaneous visits, tickets are available at Tabak Götz on the western side of the square, at Neupfarrplatz 3. ✉ *Neupfarrpl.* ☎ *0941/507–2433 for tours led by VHS* ⊕ *www.vhs-regensburg.de* ✆ *Document €2.50* ☉ *Church daily 9–dusk, document tour Thurs.–Sat. at 2:30.*

---

need a break?

Dampfnudel is a kind of sweet yeast-dough dumpling that is tasty and filling. The best in Bavaria can be had at **Dampfnudel Uli** (✉ Watmarkt 4), a little establishment in a former chapel. The decoration is incredibly eclectic, from Bavarian crafts to a portrait of Ronald Reagan inscribed "To Uli Deutzer, with best wishes, Ronald Reagan." It's open Tuesday–Friday 10–6 and Saturday 10–3.

---

❼ Niedermünster. This 12th-century building with a baroque interior was originally the church of a community of nuns, all of them from noble families. For a quarter hour beginning at 12:05 PM daily, concerts are given by students of the church music school. ✉ *Alter Kornmarkt 5* ☎ *0941/597–1002.*

❽ Porta Praetoria. The rough-hewn former gate to the old Roman camp, built in AD 179, is one of the most interesting relics of Roman times in Regensburg. Look through the grille on its east side to see a section of the original Roman street, about 10 feet below today's street level. ✉ *North side of Alter Kornmarkt.*

⓭ St. Emmeram. The family church of the princely Thurn und Taxis family stands across from their ancestral palace, the Schloss Emmeram. The foundations of the church date to the 7th and 8th centuries. A richly decorated baroque interior was added in 1730 by the Asam brothers. St. Emmeram contains the graves of the 7th-century martyred Regensburg bishop Emmeram and the 10th-century saint Wolfgang. ✉ *Emmeramspl. 3* ☎ *0941/51030* ☉ *Mon.–Thurs. and Sat. 10–4:30, Fri. 1–4:30, Sun. noon–4:30.*

10 **St. Kassian.** Regensburg's oldest church was founded in the 8th century. Don't be fooled by its dour exterior; inside, it's filled with delicate rococo decoration. ⊠ *St. Kassianpl. 1* ☎ *No phone* ☉ *Daily 9–5:30.*

12 **Schloss Emmeram** (Emmeram Palace). Formerly a Benedictine monastery, this is the ancestral home of the princely Thurn und Taxis family, who made their fame and fortune after being granted the right to carry official and private mail throughout the empire and Spain by Emperor Maximilian I (1493–1519) and by Philip I, king of Spain, who ruled during the same period. Their business extended over the centuries into the Low Countries (Holland, Belgium, and Luxembourg), Hungary, and Italy. The little horn that still symbolizes the post office in several European countries comes from the Thurn und Taxis coat of arms. For a while Schloss Emmeram was heavily featured in the gossip columns thanks to the wild parties and somewhat extravagant lifestyle of the young dowager Princess Gloria von Thurn und Taxis. After the death of her husband, Prince Johannes, in 1990, she had to auction off belongings in order to pay inheritance taxes. Ultimately a deal was cut, allowing her to keep many of the palace's treasures as long they were put on display.

The **Thurn und Taxis Palace,** with its splendid ballroom and throne room, allows you to witness the eloquent setting of courtly life in the 19th century. A visit usually includes the fine **Kreuzgang** (cloister) of the former Benedictine abbey of St. Emmeram. The items in the **Thurn und Taxis Museum,** which is part of the Bavarian National Museum in Munich, have been carefully selected for their fine craftsmanship—be it dueling pistols, a plain marshal's staff, a boudoir, or a snuffbox. The palace's **Marstallmuseum** (former royal stables) holds the family's coaches and carriages as well as related items. ☎ *0941/504–8133* 🖾 *Palace and cloisters €8; Marstallmuseum €4.50; Marstall plus Thurn und Taxis Museum €4.50; Thurn und Taxis Museum alone €3.50* ☉ *Weekdays 11–5, weekends 10–5; Marstallmuseum closed Nov.–Mar.*

★ **2** **Steinerne Brücke** (Stone Bridge). This impressive old bridge resting on massive pontoons is Regensburg's most celebrated sight. It was completed in 1146 and was rightfully considered a miraculous piece of engineering at the time. As the only crossing point over the Danube for miles, it effectively cemented Regensburg's control over trade. The significance of the little statue on the bridge is a mystery, but the figure seems to be a witness to the legendary rivalry between the master builders of the bridge and those of the Dom.

Where to Stay & Eat

¢–$$ ✕ **Vitus.** A mixture of modern and classic cuisine, Vitus feels just like Fodor'sChoice the "Grande Nation" in miniature. Sip traditional *soupe oignon* or ★ tuck into mouth-watering *boeuf bourgignon* soaked in roast pears and served under Gothic vaulted ceilings. ⊠ *Hinter der Grieb 8* ☎ *0941/52646* 🖃 *AE, MC, V.*

¢–$ ✕ **Felix.** Awash with arty chandeliers, torches, and large framed mirrors, this trendy all-age meeting place initially feels more like a castle than a café-bar. Felix offers everything from sandwiches to steaks and literally buzzes with activity from breakfast until the early hours. ⊠ *Fröhliche-Türkenstr. 6* ☎ *0941/59059* ⊟ *AE, DC, MC, V.*

¢–$ ✕ **Leerer Beutel.** Excellent international cuisine—from antipasti to solid pork roast—is served in a pleasant vaulted room supported by massive rough-hewn beams. The restaurant is in a huge warehouse that's also a venue for concerts, exhibitions, and film screenings, so this is an ideal place to spend the evening. ⊠ *Bertoldstr. 9* ☎ *0941/58997* ⊟ *AE, DC, MC, V.*

¢–$ ✕ **Lokanta.** With a mixed crowd at the tables and a pastel-orange color scheme, this lively restaurant serves simple and excellent Kurdish-Turkish dishes. A few plates of the *amuse-gueules* (cocktail snacks) will be just the thing before or after a concert. ⊠ *Wollwirkerg.* ☎ *0941/53321* ⊟ No credit cards.

¢ ✕ **Historische Wurstküche.** Succulent Regensburger sausages—the best in town—are prepared right before your eyes on an open beech-wood charcoal grill in this tiny kitchen. If you eat them inside in the tiny dining room, you'll have to squeeze past the cook to get there. Inside are plaques recording the levels the river reached in the various floods that have doused the restaurant's kitchen in the past 100 years. ⊠ *Thundorferstr. 3* ☎ *0941/59098* ⊟ No credit cards.

$$ ✕▥ **Hotel-Restaurant Bischofshof am Dom.** This is one of Germany's most historic hostelries, a former bishop's palace where you can sleep in an apartment that includes part of a Roman gateway. Other chambers are only slightly less historic, and some have seen emperors and princes as guests. The hotel's restaurant (¢–$) serves fine regional cuisine (including the famous Regensburger sausages) at reasonable prices. The beer comes from a brewery founded in 1649. ⊠ *Krauterermarkt 3, D–93047* ☎ *0941/58460* ⊞ *0941/5941–01171* ⊕ *bischofshof-am-dom.de* ⤙ *55 rooms, 3 suites* ⟑ *Restaurant, cable TV, bar, beer garden, some pets allowed (fee); no a/c* ⊟ *AE, DC, MC, V.*

$–$$ ✕▥ **Hôtel Orphée.** This protected monument hotel offers a special experience with theme rooms. The first floor is devoted to the upcoming bourgeoisie of the 19th century (the Sigmund Freud room, for example); the second floor gives you a feel for how the aristocracy lived. The reception and breakfast room are in the dark wood-panel Orphée Restaurant on the next street. The menu is mostly French ($$–$$$), with a selection of crepes, salads, and heavier meat dishes. ⊠ *Untere Bachgasse, D–93047* ☎ *0941/596–020* ⊞ *0941/5960–2222* ⊕ *www.hotel-orphee.de* ⤙ *15 rooms* ⟑ *Restaurant, bar, some pets allowed (fee); no a/c, no TV in some rooms* ⊟ *MC, V.*

$–$$ ▥ **Held.** Quietly located and family-oriented, the Held hotel offers a wide range of facilities at a reasonable price. Sizable rooms are rustically furnished with carpet or parquet floor. Specify whether you require a smoking or no-smoking room. Enjoy international cuisine in the cozy restaurant or relax in the wellness center. ⊠ *Irl 11, D–93055* ☎ *09401/9420* ⊞ *09401/7682* ⊕ *www.Hotel-Held.de* ⤙ *150 rooms* ⟑ *Restaurant, in-room data ports, cable TV, indoor pool, sauna, steam room, bowling, bar, parking (fee), some pets allowed (fee)* ⊟ *AE, MC, V* ⫟ *BP.*

$–$$ ▥ **Kaiserhof am Dom.** Renaissance windows punctuate the green facade of this historic city mansion. The rooms are 20th-century modern, with perks such as under-floor heating and cable TV. Try for one with a view of the cathedral, which stands directly across the street. Breakfast is served beneath the high-vaulted ceiling of the former 14th-century chapel, and there's also a smart brasserie. ☒ *Kramgasse 10–12, D–93047* ☎ *0941/ 585–350* 🖷 *0941/585–3595* ⊕ *www.kaiserhof-am-dom.de* ☞ *30 rooms* ⚴ *Café, cable TV, Internet, some pets allowed (fee); no a/c* ▤ *AE, DC, MC, V.*

$–$$ ▥ **Parkhotel Maximilian.** A handsome 18th-century palace between the railway station and the Old Town is home to the most elegant and sophisticated hotel in Regensburg. Rooms are well-appointed, generous in size, and luxurious. Breakfast, meals, or drinks can be had on a pretty terrace in the back of the hotel. ☒ *Maximilianstr. 28, D–93047* ☎ *0941/56850* 🖷 *0941/52942* ⊕ *www.maximilian-hotel.de* ☞ *52 rooms, 5 suites* ⚴ *Café, in-room data ports, cable TV with movies, hair salon, 2 bars, recreation room, some pets allowed (fee), no-smoking rooms; no a/c* ▤ *AE, DC, MC, V.*

$ ▥ **Hotel Münchner Hof.** In this little hotel, in a block near the Neupfarrkirche, the rooms are big and tastefully decorated. In some, the original arches of the ancient building are visible. The restaurant is quiet and comfortable, serving Bavarian specialties and good Munich beer. The bottom line: you get top service at a good price, and Regensburg is at your feet. ☒ *Tändlergasse 9, D–93047* ☎ *0941/58440* 🖷 *0941/561– 709* ⊕ *www.muenchner-hof.de* ☞ *53 rooms* ⚴ *Restaurant, some in-room data ports, cable TV, some pets allowed (fee), no-smoking rooms; no a/c* ▤ *AE, DC, MC, V.*

¢ ▥ **Am Peterstor.** The recently renovated rooms of this popular hotel in the heart of the Old Town represent unbeatable value. The emphasis here is decidedly more on practical fittings than luxury frills, but the rooms are neat and clean. The many local eateries, including the excellent "Felix" a few doors away, more than compensate for the lack of an in-house restaurant. ☒ *Fröhliche-Türken-Str. 12, D–93047* ☎ *0941/ 54545* 🖷 *0941/54542* ⊕ *www.hotel-am-peterstor.de* ☞ *36 rooms* ⚴ *No a/c, no room phones* ▤ *AE, MC, V.*

Shopping

Regensburg is a shopper's paradise. The winding alleyways of the Altstadt are packed with small boutiques, ateliers, jewelers, and other small shops offering a vast array of arts and crafts. You may also want to visit the daily market (Monday through Saturday, 9–4) at the Neupfarrplatz, where you can buy regional specialities such as *Radi* (juicy radish roots), which local people love to wash down with a glass of wheat beer.

Nightlife & the Arts

Regensburg offers a range of musical experiences, though none so moving as a performance by the famous boys' choir, the Regensburger Domspatzen, at the cathedral. The best-sung mass is held on Sunday at 9 AM. It can be a remarkable experience, and it's worth scheduling your visit to the city to hear the choir. If you're around in summer, look out for the Citizens Festival (Bürgerfest) and the Bavarian Jazz Festival (Bayreisches Jazzfest) (www.bayernjazz.de) in July, both in the Old Town.

The kind of happy-go-lucky, friendly, mixed nightlife that has become hard to find in some cities is alive and well in this small university city in the many *Kneipen*, bar-cum-pub-cum-bistros or -restaurants, such as the Leerer Beutel. It's good to ask around for what happens to be hopping at any given time. The **Jenseits** (⊠ Keplerstr. 15 ☎ 0941/54944) puts on a mix of jazz and classical music and even exhibitions. The trendsetting disco **Scala** (⊠ Gesandtenstr. 6 ☎ 0941/54944) has three bars and some of the best dance music in town.

Regensburg A to Z

BOAT TRAVEL

The most popular excursions are boat trips on the Danube River from Regensburg to Ludwig I's imposing Greek-style Doric temple of Walhalla or to the monastery at Weltenburg. There are daily sailings to Walhalla from Easter through October. The round-trip costs €8 and takes three hours. To reach Weltenburg from Regensburg, change boats at Kelheim. The Regensburg–Kelheim ride takes 2½ hours; Kelheim to Weltenburg takes 30 minutes (the fare is €5.50). Daylong upstream cruises from Regensburg, which take in Weltenburg via the valley of Altmühltal, are also possible. Regensburg boats depart from the Steinerne Brücke.
🛈 **Regensburg departures** ☎ 0941/55359. **Kelheim departures** ☎ 09441/3402 or 09441/8290 ⊕ www.renate.de.

CAR RENTAL

Regensburg is 120 km (74 mi) north of Munich and 332 km (206 mi) southeast of Frankfurt.
🛈 **Avis** ⊠ Prüfeningerstr. 98, Regensburg ☎ 0941/396–090. **Sixt** ⊠ Im Gewerbepark C38, Regensburg ☎ 0941/401–035.

TRAIN TRAVEL

Regular InterCity services connect Nürnberg and Regensburg with Frankfurt and other major German cities. There are hourly trains from Munich direct to Regensburg.

VISITOR INFORMATION

English-language guided walking tours of Regensburg are conducted May–September, Wednesday and Saturday at 1:30. They cost €6 and begin at the tourist office. Eichstätt offers walking tours of the city for €3, Saturday and Wednesday at 1:30 at the tourist information office.
🛈 **Office of Tourism** ⊠ Altes Rathaus, D-93047 ☎ 0941/507–4410 ⊕ www.regensburg.de/tourismus/international.

Walhalla

★ *11 km (7 mi) east of Regensburg.*

Walhalla is an excursion from Regensburg you won't want to miss, especially if you have an interest in the wilder expressions of 19th-century German nationalism. Danube River cruises stop here for the town's incongruous Greek-style Doric temple. To get to the temple from the river, you'll have to climb 358 marble steps. There is, however, a parking lot near the top. To drive to it, take the Danube Valley country road (unnumbered) east from Regensburg 8 km (5 mi) to Donaustauf. The Walhalla temple is 1 km (½ mi) outside the village and well signposted. Walhalla—a name resonant with Nordic mythology—was where the god Odin received the souls of dead heroes. This monumental temple was erected in 1840 for Ludwig I to honor important German personages through the ages. In the neoclassic style then prevailing, it's actually a copy of the Parthenon, in Athens. Even if you consider the building more a monument to kitsch, it remains a supremely well-built structure, and its expanses of costly marble are evidence of both the financial resources and the craftsmanship at Ludwig's command. If you're around in late October, look out for the free spectacular classical music firework display held between the Walhalla and the Danube.

Weltenburg

★ ⑮ *25 km (15 mi) southwest of Regensburg.*

In Weltenburg you'll find the great **Stiftskirche Sts. Georg und Martin** (Abbey Church of Sts. George and Martin), on the bank of the Danube River. The most dramatic approach to the abbey is by boat from Kelheim, 10 km (6 mi) downstream. On the stunning ride the boat winds between towering limestone cliffs that rise straight up from the tree-lined riverbanks. The abbey, constructed between 1716 and 1718, is commonly regarded as the masterpiece of the brothers Cosmas Damian and Egid Quirin Asam, two leading baroque architects and decorators of Bavaria. Their extraordinary composition of painted figures whirling on the ceiling, lavish and brilliantly polished marble, highly wrought statuary, and stucco figures dancing in rhythmic arabesques across the curving walls is the epitome of Bavarian baroque. Note especially the bronze equestrian statue of St. George above the high altar, reaching down imperiously with his flamelike, twisted gilt sword to dispatch the winged dragon at his feet. ☉ *Daily 9–dusk.*

THE BAVARIAN FOREST

One of the most sparsely populated regions in Germany, the Bavarian Forest stretches between the Danube River and the Czech border. Although the forest has no recognized boundaries, it can be said to end in the west where the upland, wooded slopes drop to the Franconian flatlands north of Regensburg. Wherever you start your journey, you will soon find yourself driving miles on end through virtually unspoiled rolling countryside of brooks, lakes, meadows, and tree-clad mountain slopes.

Cham

⑯ *58 km (36 mi) northeast of Regensburg via A–3 and B–20; 58 km (36 mi) northwest of Deggendorf.*

Beautifully set on the Regen River, Cham regards itself as the gateway to the forest and is further distinguished by its intact sections of 14th-century town walls, including the massive Straubinger Turm (tower) and the Biertor (gate). Every day at five minutes past noon a glockenspiel in the 15th-century **Rathaus** tower plays the French national anthem, the "Marseillaise." It's a municipal commemoration of the town's most famous son, Count Nikolaus von Luckner, who rose through the ranks of various armies to become a French marshal to whom French troops dedicated their most famous song.

Where to Stay & Eat

¢–$ ✕ **Bürgerstuben.** The Stuben is in Cham's central Stadthalle (City Hall), where card-playing, beer-swilling regulars add some local color to the evening. Tasty regional dishes and an appealingly simple atmosphere round out the authentic Bavarian experience. ⊠ *Fürtherstr. 11* ☎ *09971/1707* ▭ *No credit cards* ⊘ *Closed Mon.*

¢–$ ✕ **Italia.** This popular Italian restaurant on the main square serves pizza and pasta, delicious homemade bread, and a wide choice of wines. Reasonable prices make it more affordable for families than the neighboring Bürgerstuben. ⊠ *Marktpl. 6, D–93413 Cham* ☎ *09971/803–801* ▭ *No credit cards* ⊘ *Closed Tues.*

$ ▥ **Parkhotel Cham.** This peacefully located hotel in a village just outside
Fodor'sChoice Cham offers far-reaching rural views and good all-around service at a
★ reasonable price. Sports enthusiasts are catered to with a fitness room, indoor and outdoor tennis facilities, beach volleyball, gliding, and bicycle rental. The staff also organizes carriage rides, canoe trips, visits to local sights, and excursions to the nearby Czech Republic. The simple bistro-style restaurant serves regional and international dishes, and the breakfast buffet, included in the room price, is excellent. ⊠ *Prälat-Wolker-Str. 5, D–93413 Cham-Altenmarkt* ☎ *09971/3950* 📠 *09971/395–120* ⊕ *www.parkhotel-cham.de* ↵ *67 rooms* ⚴ *Restaurant, 16 tennis courts, gym, hot tub, sauna, steam room, bicycles, volleyball* ▭ *AE, V* ⬧○⬧ *BP.*

¢–$ ▥ **Hotel am Stadtpark.** This popular lodging is an unbeatable value, with comfortable rooms costing as little as €46—including a forest view and a large breakfast. The house stands on the edge of Cham's resort park. Families are especially welcome, and the hotel has three large apartments and a huge suite that can accommodate up to eight people. There's no restaurant, but Cham has no shortage of cheap and cheerful eateries. ⊠ *Tilisiterstr. 3, D–93413* ☎ *09971/2253* 📠 *09971/79253* ⊕ *www.hotel-am-stadtpark-cham.de* ↵ *10 rooms, 1 suite, 3 apartments* ⚴ *No a/c; no room TVs* ▭ *No credit cards.*

Nightlife & the Arts

Germany's oldest street **folk festival** (☎ 09973/50980 or 09973/19433), dating from medieval times, takes place in Furth im Wald (20 km [12 mi] north of Cham). Dressed in period costume, townsfolk participate in the ritual slaying of a fire-breathing "dragon" that stalks the main street. The weeklong festival takes place between the second and third Sundays of August.

Sports & the Outdoors

Hoher Bogen Sport und Freizeitzentrum. Attractions at this year-round sports and leisure center include skiing, summer and winter tobogganing, roller skating, and in-line skating. You can also hike from the top of a chairlift on the 3,540-foot mountain. ☒ *Liftstr. 2, D–93453 Neukirchen bei Hl. Blut (about 33 km [21 mi] NE of Cham)* ☎ *09947/464* ⊕ *www. hoher-bogen.de* ✉ *Prices vary depending on activity, call for info* ⊙ *Daily 9:30–5.*

Cyclists can explore the countryside by choosing from the bike excursions offered by **Travel agents Baumgartner** (☒ Schwanenestr. 8, Cham ☎ 09971/858–080 🖷 09971/858–088 ⊕ www.baumgartner-reisen. de). One-day trips start from €30.

| en route | As you head southeast of Cham on B–85, watch on the left for the ruins of a medieval castle perched on the 2,500-foot-high **Haidstein Peak.** Around the year 1200 it was home to the German poet Wolfram von Eschenbach, author of the metrical romance *Parzival.* On the mountain slopes is a 1,000-year-old linden tree known as Wolframslinde (Wolfram's Lime Tree). With a circumference of more than 50 feet, its hollow trunk could easily shelter 50 people. Continuing on B–85, you'll pass villages with trim streets and gardens and see two sinuous lakes created by the dammed Regen River. From here, the Weisser (white) Regen soon becomes the Schwarzer (black) Regen. |

Between the village of Prackenbach and the little town of Viechtach you'll see a dramatic section of the **Pfahl,** one of Europe's most extraordinary geological phenomena. The ridge of glistening white quartz shoots out of the ground in an arrow-straight spur that extends more than 100 km (62 mi) through the Bavarian Forest. Here the quartz rises in folds to heights of 100 feet or more.

Viechtach

⑰ *30 km (19 mi) southeast of Cham, 29 km (18 mi) north of Deggendorf.*

This little market town in the folds of the Bavarian Forest is a center of glassmaking and a must-stop along the Glass Route. Before stocking up on fragile produce, you may like to call at the spectacularly decorated rococo church of **St. Augustin.** Dominating Viechtach's central market square, its severe white-and-yellow west front contrasts colorfully with the surrounding high-gable Renaissance and baroque buildings.

Among the most unusual museums of the Bavarian Forest is the ★ **Ägayrischen Gewölbe** (Ägarian Vaults), a collection of 400 replicas of Egyptian antiquities spanning 4,000 years. The originals are in some of the world's leading museums. Owner and artist Reinhard Schimd uses the adjacent chapel (1580) to exhibit his own art. ☒ *Spitalg. 5* ☎ *09942/ 6891* ⊕ *www.ge-woelbe.de* ✉ *€2.50* ⊙ *Apr.–June, Sept. and Oct., Tues.–Sun. 10–4; July and Aug., daily 10–4..*The unusual **Gläserne Scheune** (Glazed Barn), decorated on the outside with colorful paintings, houses a variety of exhibitions in glass, including glass walls painted with historic local scenes. ☒ *Raubühl 3* ☎ *09942/8147* ⊕ *www.glaeserne-scheune.de* ✉ *€3.50* ⊙ *Apr.–Sept., daily 10–5; Oct., daily 10–4.*

Four centuries of glassmaking are documented in Viechtach's **Kristall-museum** (Crystal Museum), which also has a vivid exhibition on the Pfahl, together with samples of more than 1,000 crystals and minerals and replicas of the world's most famous diamonds. ⊠ *Linprunstr. 4* ☎ *09942/ 5497* ✉ *€2* ☉ *Dec., Jan., Mar.–Oct., Mon.–Sat. 9–6, Sun. 10–4; Feb. and Nov. Mon.–Sat. 9–6.*

Where to Stay & Eat

$–$$ ✕🏠 **Hotel Schmaus.** Run by the same family for 13 generations, this former stagecoach inn is for the energetic. The kitchen ($–$$) turns out meals on the assumption that every guest has just finished a 40-km (25-mi) hike through the forest, although the all-weather sports facilities could make you equally hungry. In summer dine in the grill garden. Ask to stay in the older section—some of the modern rooms are somewhat plain. ⊠ *Stadtpl. 5, D–94234* ☎ *09942/94160* 🖶 *09942/941–630* ⊕ *www. hotel-schmaus.de* ➥*40 rooms* ♨ *Restaurant, 2 tennis courts, pool, sauna, Weinstube, Internet, meeting rooms; no a/c* ⊟ *AE, DC, MC, V* ☉ *Closed last 3 wks in Jan.*

$ ✕🏠 **Miethaner Landhotel.** Cozy and child-friendly, this family-run hotel
Fodor'sChoice boasts stunning views over the surrounding countryside. Much of the
★ food in the hotel's excellent restaurant is based on weekly thematic menus including Bavarian, Scandinavian, and Italian "specials." For typical Bavarian fare, try the *Leberkäs* (meat loaf), *Knödel* (potato dumplings), or *Schweinshaxe* (knuckle of pork). ⊠ *Höllenstein 13, D–94234* ☎ *09941/9530* 🖶 *09941/9530* ⊕ *www.landhotel-miethaner.de* ➥ *70 rooms* ♨ *Restaurant, massage, sauna* ⊟ *V.*

Nightlife & the Arts

A **Theater Festival** with roots in the Middle Ages is held from mid-July to early August in Neunussberg Castle, just outside Viechtach. Call the Viechtach tourist office for details.

Shopping

Günther Götte's **Pegasus-Studio** (⊠ Kandlbach 3 ☎ 09942/2729) has a wide range of local pottery. For glass objects and other arts and crafts, try the **Viechtacher Kunststube** (⊠ Stadtpl. 1 ☎ 09942/2441), in the Altes Rathaus.

Bodenmais

⑱ *24 km (15 mi) east of Viechtach, 34 km (21 mi) north of Deggendorf.*

This resort is in a valley below the Bavarian Forest's highest mountain, the Grosser Arber. A nearby silver mine helped Bodenmais prosper before tourism reached this isolated part of the country. Bodenmais's long tradition of glassmaking includes Bavaria's largest glassworks, the **Joska Waldglashütte,** which welcomes visitors at its foundry and showrooms in the Am Moosbach industrial zone. The foundry also has a restaurant. ⊠ *Am Moosbach 1* ☎ *09924/7790* ✉ *Free* ☉ *Weekdays 9–6, Sat. 9–2.*

You can watch glassblowers at the foundry **Austen Glashütte** and buy goods at very reasonable prices. ⊠ *Bahnhofstr. 57* ☎ *09924/7006* ✉ *Free* ☉ *Weekdays 10–6, Sat. 10–4.*

off the beaten path

SILBERBERG – The 600-year-old silver mine closed in 1962, but you can still view its workings near the summit of the 3,000-foot-high Silberberg. The air within the mine is so pure that one of the side shafts is used to treat asthmatics and people with chronic bronchial complaints. You can walk from Bodenmais to the entrance of the mine or take the chairlift from Arbersee Road, about 2 km (1 mi) north of Bodenmais. ☎ 09924/304 *guided tours* ⊕ *www.silberberg-online.de* ☎ €5.20 ☉ *Apr.–June, Sept., and Oct., daily 10–4; July and Aug., daily 9–4:45; Nov.–late Dec., Wed. only for one tour at 1; late Dec.–early Jan., daily 10–3; early Jan.–Mar., Tues., Wed., Fri., and Sat. 1–3.*

Where to Stay & Eat

$ ✕🏠 **Bodenmaiser Hof.** The maisonette rooms in this expansive and meticulously run hotel are large and luxurious, with galleried sleeping areas and living rooms beneath. Ordinary double rooms are also generous in size, and most have terraces or balconies with forest views. The winter-garden restaurant (¢–$$) and a tavern are warm retreats on cold days, and a glass-roof terrace beckons in summer. The hotel produces its own bread and meat and even has an in-house distillery that creates a fine schnapps. ⊠ *Risslochweg 4, D–94249* ☎ *09924/9540* 🖷 *09924/9540* ⊕ *www.bodenmaiser-hof.de* 🛏 *20 rooms, 10 suites* ⚘ *Restaurant, café, gym, hair salon, sauna; no a/c* ⊟ *No credit cards.*

$–$$ 🏠 **Feriengut-Hotel Böhmhof.** The Böhmhof estate on the edge of the forest has been owned by the Geiger family for more than three centuries. Their long tradition of hospitality can be felt from the friendly reception to the comfortable, spacious rooms, several of which are "country-house suites" with separate living areas. One estate building provides farmhouse-style accommodations, ideal for families. The outdoor and indoor pools allow for year-round swimming; walking and cross-country ski trails start at the front door. ⊠ *Böhmhof 1, D–94249* ☎ *09924/94300* 🖷 *09924/943–013* ⊕ *www.feriengut-boehmhof.de* 🛏 *22 rooms, 15 suites* ⚘ *Restaurant, café, cable TV, 2 pools (1 indoor), gym, hot tub, sauna, recreation room, Internet; no a/c* ⊟ *No credit cards* ☉ *Closed mid-Nov.–mid-Dec.*

Sports & the Outdoors

Bodenmais is 13 km (8 mi) south of the **Grosser Arber,** the highest mountain (4,800 feet) in both the Bavarian Forest and the Czech Republic's Bohemian Forest. Several hiking trails lead to the summit; in winter it offers challenging alpine and cross-country skiing. A bus service runs from Bodenmais to the base of the mountain, where a chairlift (€8) makes the 10-minute trip to the summit. Alternatively, there's a one-hour walk starting at the bottom of the lift that circles the mountain summit. There's a great view of the central European stretch of woodland from here. Short walks from the bottom of the lift lead to two woodland lakes, the **Grosser Arbersee** and the smaller **Kleiner Arbersee,** both ideal for summer swimming and boating. Beside the Grosser Arbersee, children can wander through the **Märchenwald** (Fairy-Tale Wood), which has a collection of colorful model scenes from famous stories. You can rent boats from the Gaststätte Arbersee across from the Märchenwald en-

THE GLASS ROUTE

YOU DON'T NEED TO BE *a passionate collector of cut glass to appreciate a trip along the Glasstrasse (Glass Route), one of the region's official tourist routes. The 250-km (165-mi) route offers fascinating insight into the centuries-old glassblowing tradition, which is still practiced today. Running north to south, the route connects Neustadt an der Waldnaab with Passau and passes through some of the loveliest countryside in southeast Germany.*

Local glass production dates back to the 14th century, when glass makers settled in the Bavarian Forest, lured by its rich supply of wood, which was required as fuel for glass melting. While modern-day glassworks are largely automated, they still play a key role in the local economy, particularly in the northeast part of the forest.

One of the best places to join the Glass Route is in the town of Zwiesel, which has 18 firms and more than 2,000 townspeople involved in shaping, engraving, or painting glass using traditional methods. Mostly hidden in backyards and private houses, the workshops and galleries sell a wide range of vases, goblets, and figurines. Zwiesel is also home to Schott-Zwiesel, Germany's largest drinking glass manufacturer. Factory products are sold in Theresienthal, north of the town, where you can also visit the Zum Schlössl glass museum (Castle glass museum). At the Kunstglasbläserei Seemann (Seemann Artistic Glass Foundry) in the nearby village of Rabenstein, you can try your own skill at blowing glass.

Some 10 km (6 mi) east lies Frauenau, where glass has been melted since around 1400. This tradition is kept alive by the von Poschinger family, which has been linked to glass production for 14 generations. The crystal glass factory of Baron von Poschinger still produces refined consumer glass using traditional artisan techniques. Tours of the factory are offered throughout the year. For more information on the factory and the local Glasmuseum, currently under renovation, contact the Tourist-Information Office at Frauenau (09926/94100).

No tour of the Glass Route would be complete without a side trip to the picturesque town of Viechtach, half way between Cham and Regen, and home to the Kristallmuseum and the Gläserne Scheune, two of the most fascinating museums in the Bavarian Forest.

To combine your interest in glass making with an invigorating trek through the Bavarian Forest, leave the Glass Route at Lam (roughly halfway between Zwiesel and Fürth im Wald), to hike along the "Glass Path." Beginning at Lahmer Winkel, this 40-km (25-mi) trail includes the sites of past and present-day glass works and leads to Bayerisch-Eisenstein bordering the Czech Republic. The complete official path continues 60 km (37 mi) farther to Grafenau. The local Verkehrsamt (09925/327) offers "Hiking without luggage" packages.

Passau, the 2,000-year-old city where glassblowing began in the 16th century, marks the end of the Glass Route. Don't miss a visit to the Glasmuseum (Passau's Glass Museum). For more information about the Glass Route, log onto www. germany-tourism.de.

trance. ✉ *Arberseestr. 42* 🎫 *Marchenwald €2* ⊙ *Marchenwald May–Oct., daily 10–5.*

off the beaten path

BAYERISCH-EISENSTEIN – Travelers who can't resist quirky sights should detour to this little town on the Czech Republic border. The frontier actually cuts the local train station in half. More than 20 historic old steam locomotives are housed in one of the ancient engine sheds, and some of them regularly roll back into service for outings into the Czech Republic. ✉ *Bahnhofstr. 44* ☎ *09925/1376* 🎫 *Half-day excursion €10* ⊙ *Apr.–Oct. and late Dec.–early Jan., Tues.–Sat. 10–12:30 and 2–5; Nov.–late Dec. and early Jan.–Mar., weekends 10–2.*

REGENHÜTTE – You can see glassblowers at work at the **Alte Kristallglashütte,** in this village, just outside Bayerisch-Eisenstein. ✉ *Arberseestr.* ☎ *09925/1231* 🎫 *Free* ⊙ *Foundry weekdays 9–3, Sat. 9–noon; showroom and shop weekdays 9–5, weekends 9–4.*

Zwiesel

⑲ *15 km (9 mi) south of Bayerisch-Eisenstein, 40 km (25 mi) northeast of Deggendorf, 70 km (43 mi) northwest of Passau.*

As the region's glassmaking center, Zwiesel has 18 firms and more than 2,000 townspeople involved in shaping, engraving, or painting glass. Most open their foundries to visitors. At **Kunstglasbläserei Seemann** (Seemann Artistic Glass Foundry; ✉ Stormbergerstr. 36 ☎ 09922/6999), in the village of Rabenstein, you can try your own skill at blowing glass on Thursday from 10 to noon and often on Friday from 9 AM to 11 AM (but please call in advance). Take home the result of your efforts for a €5 fee.

Just 2 km (1 mi) north of Zwiesel, in the village of Theresienthal, the **Glasmuseum zum Schlössl** (Castle Glass Museum) is part of a glass park that includes two of Europe's oldest glass foundries, as well as showrooms, shops, and a restaurant. ✉ *Glaspark Theresienthal* ☎ *09922/1030* 🎫 *€3, including guided tour* ⊙ *Weekdays 10–2.*

Where to Stay

$ 🏨 **Hotel Sonnenhof.** This large, friendly pension is set in rolling countryside on the edge of Zwiesel, with panoramic views of the Bavarian Forest. It's an ideal base for exploring the area, and special rates apply for stays of a week or more. Families are warmly welcome. ✉ *Ahornweg 10, D-94227* ☎ *09922/9005* 🖷 *09922/60521* ⊕ *www.sonnenhof-zwiesel.de* 🛏 *23 rooms* ⚭ *Restaurant, cable TV, pool, sauna, bicycles, paddle tennis; no a/c* ▤ *AE, DC, MC, V* ⊙ *Closed mid-Nov.–late Dec.*

$ 🏨 **Hotel zur Waldbahn.** The great-grandfather of the current owner, assisted by 13 children, built the Hotel zur Waldbahn more than 100 years ago to accommodate train passengers traveling to Bohemia. Today the emphasis is still on making the traveler feel at home. After dining at the restaurant, lay your weary head on snowy-white pillows in rooms furnished in a blend of modern and traditional styles. ✉ *Bahnhofpl. 2,*

D–94227 ☎ *09922/8570* 🖷 *09922/3001* ⊕ *www.zurwaldbahn.de*
🛏 *28 rooms* ⚴ *Restaurant, indoor pool, gym, hot tub, sauna, Ping-
Pong; no a/c* ▭ *V* ⊘ *Closed mid-Mar.–mid-Apr.*

Deggendorf

 *37 km (23 mi) southwest of Zwiesel, 140 km (87 mi) northeast
of Munich.*

Between the Danube and the forested hills that rise in tiers to the Czech
border, Deggendorf justifiably regards itself as the Bavarian Forest's southern gateway. The town was once on the banks of the Danube, but repeated flooding forced its inhabitants to higher ground in the 13th
century. You can still see a 30-yard stretch of the protective wall built
around the medieval town.

Deggendorf is unique in Lower Bavaria for its specially developed "cultural quarter," created from a section of the Old Town. Lining the leafy,
traffic-free square are the city museum; a public library; a handicrafts
museum—the only one of its kind in the Bavarian Forest; and the Ka-
puzinerstadl, a warehouse converted into a concert hall and theater venue.

The 16th-century **Rathaus,** in the center of the wide main street, the Marktstrasse, has a central tower with a tiny apartment that traditionally housed
the town watchman and lookout. The rooms remain much as they were
centuries ago, and from their windows you can get a fine view. The tower
can be visited only as part of a guided tour of the town, offered
June–September, daily at 9:30. ⊠ *Oberer Stadtpl.* ☎ *0991/296–0169*
🖷 *€20.*

★ The **Heilig Grabkirche** (Church of the Holy Sepulchre) was originally built
as a Gothic basilica in the 14th century. Its lofty tower—regarded as the
finest baroque church tower in southern Germany—was added 400 years
later by the Munich master builder Johann Michael Fischer. ⊠ *Michael-
Fischer-Pl.* ⊘ *Daily 9–dusk.*

Exhibits at the **Handwerksmuseum** (Museum of Trades and Crafts) focus
on typical regional handicrafts such as glassmaking and wood carving.
⊠ *Maria-Ward-Pl. 1* ☎ *0991/296–0555* 🖷 *Combined ticket with
Stadtmuseum €2* ⊘ *Tues.–Sat. 10–4, Sun. 10–5.*

> off the
> beaten
> path

ST. MARGARETHA KIRCHE – This church contains important work
by baroque artists, including a series of large, ornate frescoes and
altar paintings by Cosmas Damian Asam, as well as elaborate
sculptures of angels and cherubs by Egid Quirin Asam and Johann
Michael Fischer. The three worked here in a rare partnership between
1728 and 1741. Cosmas Damian's self-portrait is amid the
extravagant decor. To get here, cross the Danube just outside
Deggendorf, or take the ferry at Winzer, and then the Passau road
(B–15) to the village of Osterhofen. ⊠ *Osterhofen* ⊘ *Daily 9–7,
except during Sun. services. Free guided tours, Tues. and Thurs. at 3;
for tours in German, meet at main church door; call ahead for
English tours.*

Where to Stay & Eat

¢–$ ✕ **Ratskeller.** In the vaulted rooms of the Rathaus, you could easily find yourself sharing a table with a town councillor, perhaps even the mayor. The menu includes both Bavarian and modern German cuisine; the beer flows freely. ⊠ *Oberer Stadtpl. 1* ☎ *0991/31453* ▤ *No credit cards.*

¢–$ ✕ **Zum Grafenwirt.** In winter ask the host for a table near the fine old tile stove that sits in the dining room. Try such filling dishes as roast pork and Bavarian dumplings. In summer watch for Danube fish on the menu. ⊠ *Bahnhofstr. 7* ☎ *0991/8729* ▤ *AE, MC, V* ☉ *Closed Tues.*

★ $ ✕▥ **Donauhof.** This lovely 19th-century stone warehouse has spotless rooms with modern Scandinavian furniture. The Wintergarten Café ($–$$) is a local favorite for its delicious cakes and coffee. ⊠ *Hafenstr. 1, D–94469* ☎ *0991/38990* 🖷 *0991/38990* ⊕ *www.hotel-donauhof. de* ➱ *60 rooms, 3 suites* ♨ *Restaurant, café, cable TV, sauna, meeting rooms; no a/c* ▤ *AE, DC, MC, V.*

$ ✕▥ **Schlosshotel Egg.** The "Egg" doesn't stand for something you might eat in this castle-hotel's excellent restaurant ($–$$$); it's derived from Ekke, the name of the 12th-century owner. Today the hotel, 13 km (8 mi) northwest of Deggendorf, is a memorable place to stay. A vaulted dining room, the Burgstall, and a paved courtyard garden maintain the medieval mood of the ivy-covered old building. There are just a few comfortable apartment-size suites, so it's essential to book ahead. ⊠ *Schloss Egg, D–94505 Bernried* ☎ *09905/289* 🖷 *09905/8262* ⊕ *www. schlosshotel-egg.de* ➱ *8 suites* ♨ *Restaurant, cable TV, beer garden; no a/c* ▤ *V* ☉ *Closed Jan. and Feb.*

en route | **Metten.** This village along the Danube holds two outstanding examples of baroque art within the white walls and quiet cloisters of its **Benedictine monastery,** founded in the 9th century by Charlemagne. The 18th-century **library** has a collection of 160,000 books whose gilt leather spines are complemented by the heroic splendor of their surroundings—Herculean figures support the frescoed, vaulted ceiling, and allegorical paintings and fine stuccowork identify different categories of books. In the **church** is Cosmas Damian Asam's altarpiece Lucifer Destroyed by St. Michael; created around 1720, it has vivid coloring and a swirling composition that are typical of the time. E 7 km (4 1/2 mi) west of Deggendorf P 0991/91080 A e2 C Guided tours daily at 10 and 3.

Bavarian Forest National Park

❷❶ *51 km (32 mi) northeast of Deggendorf; main entrance at Neuschönau,*
Fodor'sChoice *50 km (31 mi) north of Passau.*
★

The roughly 1.5-million-acre Bavarian Forest National Park was the very first national park to be founded in Germany (1970) and is one of the last remaining primeval forests in Europe. Substantial efforts have been made to reintroduce bears, wolves, lynx, and other animals to the park, though today the 32 species of animals are restricted to large enclosures. Seven kilometers (4½ miles) of well-marked paths lead to points where wildlife can best be seen. Vigorous walks also take you through the thickly wooded terrain to the two highest peaks of the park, the 4,350-foot **Rachel** and the 4,116-foot **Lusen.** Specially marked educational trails trace the geology and botany of the area, and picnic spots and playgrounds abound. In winter, park wardens will lead you through the snow to where wild deer from the mountains feed. A visitor center—the **Hans-Eisenmann-Haus** (☎ 08558/96150)—is at the main entrance to the park, on the edge of the village of Neuschönau. It's open daily 9–5. Slide shows and English-language brochures provide introductions to the area. There's no entrance fee to the park, but expect to pay €1 per hour for parking.

Free tours of the national park are organized between 9 and 4 by the **Grafenau Verkehrsamt** (✉ Tourist office, Rathausg. 1, Grafenau ☎ 08552/962–343). For as little as €157, the Verkehrsamt at nearby Freyung offers a five-day "without baggage" hike, including five nights at B&Bs, a map and route description, and a video of the Bavarian Forest National Park.

There are several glass foundries in the villages bordering the national park. You can watch glassblowers at work and buy products at their source at the **Kristallglasfabrik** (✉ Hauptstr. 2–4, Spiegelau ☎ 08553/2400). Workshop demonstrations are offered weekdays 9:15–1:45. At the **Glasmacherhof** (✉ Birkenweg 21, Mauth ☎ 08557/96140 ⊕ www.glassmacherhof-mauth.com) you not only can shop but are also encouraged to try glassblowing yourself.

The town of **Grafenau** (☎ 08552/3318) has two unusual and interesting museums. The **Bauernhausmuseum,** in the resort's spa-park, consists of two restored Lower Bavarian farmhouses containing furnishings and implements from the 18th and 19th centuries. The **Schnupftabak-Museum** (Snuff Museum; ✉ Spitalstr.), in a historic almshouse, depicts (and attempts to explain) the habit of sniffing snuff. Snuffboxes from several countries disprove the theory that only Bavarians are addicted. Both museums are open mid-December–October, daily 2–5, and cost €1.50 each.

Where to Stay & Eat

$–$$$ ✕ **Adalbert Stifter.** Named after a popular 19th-century novelist, this friendly country restaurant at the foot of the Dreisessel Mountain is at its best turning out the sort of time-honored dishes Stifter knew. Try one of the Bohemian-style roasts, served with fresh dumplings. ✉ *Frauenberg 32, 94145 Haidmühlet* ☎ *08556/355* ▤ *No credit cards* ☉ *Closed Nov.*

$–$$ ✕ **Landgasthaus Schuster.** Noted for its excellent local cooking, this small

Fodor'sChoice family-run restaurant offers a wide range of meat and fish dishes with

★ seasonal trimmings. If it's available, be sure to try the juicy wild duck or the tureen of herbs, or scampi. ✉ *Ort 19, D–94078 Freyung* ☎ *08551/7184* ⊕ *www.landgasthaus-schuster.de* ▤ *No credit cards* ☉ *No lunch Tues.; closed Mon. and Aug.–early Sept.*

★ **$–$$** ✕▥ **Säumerhof.** The Bavarian Forest isn't known for haute cuisine, but here in Grafenau, one of the prettiest resorts has a restaurant ($–$$$) that bears comparison with Germany's best. It's part of a small country hotel run by the Endl family. Gebhard Endl's territory is the kitchen, where he produces original dishes using local ingredients. Try the pheasant on champagne cabbage or the roast rabbit in herb-cream sauce. ⊠ *Steinberg 32, D–94481 Grafenau* ☎ *08552/408–990* 🖶 *08552/408–9950* ⊕ *www.saeumerhof.de* ⌂ *10 rooms* ⚐ *Restaurant, cable TV, sauna; no a/c* ⊟ *AE, DC, MC, V.*

¢–$ ✕🏠 **Gasthöf-Restaurant Bärnriegel** On the edge of the Bavarian Forest National Park, this family-run restaurant (¢–$$) caters to those made hungry by a day's walking. Sauerbraten is one of the best dishes on the menu; local lake fish is also a specialty. Fresh vegetables and herbs come from the Bärnriegel's own garden. The weary will also be provided for here with a stay in one of the inexpensive but comfortable pinewood-furnished rooms. ⊠ *Halbwaldstr. 32, D–94151 Finsterau* ☎ *08557/96020* 🖶 *08557/960–249* ⊕ *www.baernriegel.de* ⌂ *24 rooms* ⚐ *Cable TV, gym, hot tub; no a/c* ⊟ *No credit cards* ⊘ *Closed early Nov.–early Dec.*

$ 🏠 **Mercure Hotel Sonnenhof.** If you're traveling with children, this is the hotel for you: during high season the staff includes a *Spieltante* (playtime auntie) who keeps youngsters amused. The ultramodern hotel is on extensive grounds, and there's lots to do—even horse-drawn sleigh rides in winter. You can choose between two room styles: country house, with light woods and pastel tones, or rustic, with dark furnishings and brightly colored fabrics. ⊠ *Sonnenstr. 12, D–94481 Grafenau* ☎ *08552/4480* 🖶 *08552/4680* ⊕ *www.accor-hotels.com* ⌂ *147 rooms, 3 suites* ⚐ *2 restaurants, cable TV, miniature golf, 6 tennis courts, pool, gym, hair salon, sauna, bowling, bar; no a/c* ⊟ *AE, DC, MC, V.*

★ $ 🏠 **Romantik Hotel Die Bierhütte.** The name means "beer hut," and this was once a royal brewery. Now a member of the select Romantik hotel group, the elegant 18th-century building has its own quiet grounds beside a lake, near the village of Hohenau. The rooms are furnished with rustic pinewood beds and flowered fabrics. ⊠ *Bierhütte 10, D–94545, Hohenau* ☎ *08558/96120* 🖶 *08558/961–270* ⊕ *www.romantikhotels.com* ⌂ *37 rooms, 6 suites, 4 apartments* ⚐ *Restaurant, cable TV, hair salon, sauna; no a/c* ⊟ *AE, DC, MC, V.*

Sports & the Outdoors

The **B.u.S. Schneesportschule und Eventtouristik** (⊠ Grund 2, D–92237, Sulzbach-Rosenberg ☎ 09661/906–9999) is a snow sports school, which rents out winter sports equipment. Call for details of special events and excursions.

Dreiburgenland

On the Ostmarkstrasse (B–85) between Schönberg and Passau.

Fürstenstein, Englburg, and Saldenburg are the three castle-rich villages that make up Dreiburgenland, or Land of the Three Castles. Unfortunately none of the castles are open to visitors, but the area is wonderful for hiking, and local shops sell maps called *Wanderkarten*, which suggest walking tours.

㉒ On the shore of the **Dreiburgensee** in Tittling, 20 km (12 mi) north of Passau, you'll find the **Museumsdorf Bayerischer Wald** (Open-Air Museum), which consists of 50 reconstructed Bavarian Forest houses. In summer you can sit on the benches of a 17th-century schoolhouse, drink schnapps in an 18th-century tavern, or see how grain was ground in a 15th-century mill. Although the buildings are closed in winter, you can still take a stroll through the grounds for €1. ⊠ *Next to Hotel Dreiburgensee, Tittling* ☎ *08504/8482* 🖼 *€2.50* ☉ *Mid-Mar.–Oct., daily 8–5; Nov.–mid Mar., daily 9–5.*

Where to Stay & Eat

$ ✕🛏 **Hotel Dreiburgensee.** The hotel primarily books extended vacations, but it's also convenient for an overnight stop if you're visiting the nearby open-air museum. All the hotel's rooms have balconies with views of the Dreiburgensee or the forest. Some have Bavarian-style four-poster beds with painted headboards and large, fluffy goose-down covers. Children love the sturdy bunk beds in the spacious family rooms. ⊠ *Am Dreiburgensee, D–94100 Tittling/Passau* ☎ *08504/2092* 🖶 *08504/1094* 🛏 *100 rooms* 🍴 *Restaurant, café, miniature golf, pool, gym, sauna, boating, bicycles, playground; no a/c* ▭ *No credit cards* ☉ *Closed Nov.–Apr.*

Passau

66 km (41 mi) southeast of Deggendorf, 179 km (111 mi) northeast of Munich.

Flanking the borders of Austria and the Czech Republic, Passau boasts a history dating back over 2,500 years. Originally settled by the Celts, then by the Romans, Passau later passed into the possession of prince-bishops whose domains stretched into present-day Hungary. At its height, the Passau episcopate was the largest in the entire Holy Roman Empire.

Passau's location is truly unique. Nowhere else in the world do three rivers—the Ilz from the north, the Danube from the west, and the Inn from the south—meet. Wedged between the Inn and the Danube, the Old Town is a maze of narrow cobble-stone streets lined with beautifully preserved burgher and patrician houses and riddled with churches. Many streets have been closed to traffic, giving the town an almost Venetian feel and making it a pedestrian's paradise.

For 45 post-war years Passau was a backwater in a "lost" corner of West Germany. The collapse of the Iron Curtain opened nearby frontiers, putting the historic city back on the central European map. Despite its small size, Passau has a stately, grand-dame atmosphere.

a good walk

Begin your walk at the tourist office on the west side of Rathausplatz, where you can pick up brochures and maps. Passau's 14th-century **Rathaus** ㉓ ☞ forms one side of the square and faces the Danube and its landing stages. Before leaving the square in the direction of the city center, stop by the **Glasmuseum** ㉔, in the Hotel Wilder Mann. Next, turn right at the end of the short street, Schrottgasse, and you're on Residenzplatz, dominated by the baroque bulk of the Neue Bischöfliche Residenz, where religious treasures from the city's illustrious episcopal past are housed in the **Domschatz- und Diözesanmuseum** ㉕. A flight of steps leading up from the Domschatz- und Diözesan Museum brings you to the **Domplatz** ㉖ and Passau's towering **Dom** ㉗. Descend the steps in the square's southwest corner and you'll arrive at the Inn River. A 15-minute stroll east will take you to the gardens of the **Dreiflusseck** ㉘, the confluence of the Danube, Inn, and Ilz rivers. Continue along the southern bank of the Danube upstream to the Luitpoldbrücke; cross this bridge to reach the northern bank, where a steep path leads you to the **Veste Oberhaus** ㉙; you can also catch a bus to this fortress from Rathausplatz. Now make your way back to Rathausplatz to explore Passau's attractive pedestrian shopping zone (an area of eight streets). If time permits and you're in museum mode, walk south along the Heilig Geist Gasse and cross the Inn River by its pedestrian bridge to the outstanding **Römermuseum Kastell Boiotro** ㉚, which holds remnants of Passau's Roman past.

TIMING   Passau can be toured leisurely in the course of one day. Try to visit the Dom at noon to hear a recital on its great organ, the world's largest. Early morning is the best time to catch the light falling from the east on the old town walls and the confluence of the three rivers. Passau shrouded in the dank river fogs of winter rivals even Venice for its brooding atmosphere.

What to See

㉗ **Dom** (St. Stephan's Cathedral). Passau's mighty cathedral rises majestically on the highest point of the earliest-settled part of the city. A baptismal church stood here in the 6th century. Two hundred years later, when Passau became a bishop's seat, the first basilica was built. It was dedicated to St. Stephan and became the original mother church of St. Stephan's Cathedral in Vienna. A fire reduced the medieval basilica to smoking ruins in 1662; it was then rebuilt by Italian master architect Carlo Lurago. What you see today is the largest baroque basilica north of the Alps, complete with an octagonal dome and flanking towers. Little in its marble- and stucco-encrusted interior reminds you of Germany, and much proclaims the exuberance of Rome. Beneath the dome is the largest church organ assembly in the world. Built between 1924 and 1928 and enlarged in 1979–80, it claims no fewer than 17,774 pipes and 233 stops. The church also houses the most powerful bell chimes in southern Germany. ⊠ *Dompl.* 🏛 *Free; concerts midday €3, evening €5* ☉ *May–Oct., daily 8–11 and 12:30–6; Nov.–Apr., daily 8–dusk. Tours May–Oct. weekdays 12:30, assemble at cathedral's front right-hand aisle; Nov.–Apr., Mon.–Sat. noon, assemble under the cathedral organ; concerts May–Oct. and Dec. 20–25, Mon.–Wed. and Fri. noon, Thurs. noon and 7:30 PM.*

㉖ **Domplatz** (Cathedral Square). This large square in front of the Dom is bordered by sturdy 17th- and 18th-century buildings, including the **Alte Residenz**, the former bishop's palace and now a courthouse. The fine statue depicts Bavarian king Maximilian Joseph I.

㉕ **Domschatz- und Diözesanmuseum** (Cathedral Treasury and Diocesan Museum). The cathedral museum houses one of Bavaria's largest collections of religious treasures, the legacy of Passau's rich episcopal history. The museum is part of the **Neue Residenz**, which has a stately

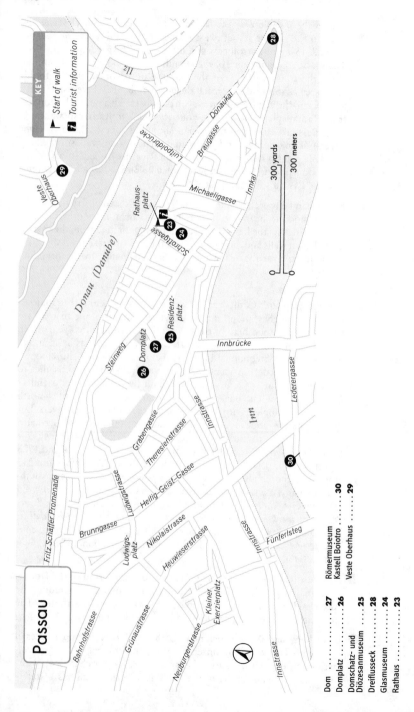

Passau

KEY

▲ Start of walk

ℹ Tourist information

300 yards

300 meters

baroque entrance opening onto a magnificent staircase—a scintillating study in marble, fresco, and stucco. ⊠ *Residenzpl.* 🖫 *€1.50* ⊙ *Apr.–Oct., Mon.–Sat. 10–4.*

㉘ Dreiflusseck (Junction of the Three Rivers). At this tongue of land at the eastern extremity of Passau, the Danube, Inn, and tiny Ilz rivers join together in an embrace that, thanks to a phenomenon of nature, leaves each of them with a distinct identity until they all flow out of Passau's grip and into Austria, where their waters merge into the Danube, bound for the Black Sea. For the best perspective, climb to the Veste Oberhaus to see how the Inn's chalky green water, typical of a mountain river, slowly gives way to the darker hues of the Danube, more brown than blue, and how the almost black Ilz adds its small contribution. It's the end of the journey for the Inn—which flows here from the mountains of Switzerland—and the much shorter Ilz, which rises in the Bavarian Forest.

㉔ Glasmuseum (Glass Museum). The world's most comprehensive collection of Bohemian glass is housed in the lovely Hotel Wilder Mann. The history of central Europe's glassmaking is captured in 30,000 items, from baroque to art deco, spread over 35 rooms. ⊠ *Am Rathauspl.* 🖀 *0851/ 35071* 🖫 *€5* ⊙ *Daily 1–5.*

▶ **㉓ Rathaus.** Passau's 14th-century city hall sits like a Venetian merchant's house on a small square fronting the Danube. It was the home of a wealthy German merchant before being declared the seat of city government after a 1298 uprising. Two assembly rooms have wall paintings depicting scenes from local history and lore, including the (fictional) arrival in the city of Siegfried's fair Kriemhild, from the Nibelungen fable. The Rathaus tower has Bavaria's largest glockenspiel, which plays daily at 10:30, 2, and 7:25, with an additional performance at 3:30 on Saturday. ⊠ *Rathauspl.* 🖀 *0851/3960* 🖫 *€1.50* ⊙ *Apr.–Oct. and late Dec.–early Jan., daily 10–4.*

㉚ Römermuseum Kastell Boiotro (Roman Museum). A stout fortress with five defense towers and walls more than 12 feet thick came to light as archaeologists excavated the site of a 17th-century pilgrimage church on a hill known as Mariahilfberg, on the south bank of the Inn. The Roman citadel Boiotro was discovered along with a Roman well, its water still plentiful and fresh. Pottery, lead figures, and other artifacts from the area are housed in this museum at the edge of the site. ⊠ *Ledererg. 43* 🖀 *0851/34769* 🖫 *€2* ⊙ *Mar.–May and Sept.–Nov., Tues.–Sun. 10–noon and 2–4; June–Aug., Tues.–Sun. 10–noon and 1–4.*

㉙ Veste Oberhaus (Upper House Stronghold). The powerful fortress and summer castle commissioned by Bishop Ulrich II in 1219 looks over Passau from an impregnable site on the other side of the river, opposite the Rathaus. Today the Veste Oberhaus is Passau's most important museum, containing exhibits that illustrate the city's 2,000-year history. From the terrace of its café-restaurant (open Easter–October), there's a magnificent view of Passau and the convergence of the three rivers. ⊠ *Oberhausleitenstiege* 🖀 *0851/493–3512* 🖫 *Museum €4* ⊙ *Mar.–Oct., weekdays 9–5, weekends 10:30–6* 🚌 *Bus from Rathauspl. to museum Apr.–Oct. every ½ hr 10:30–5.*

Where to Stay & Eat

★ **$-$$** ✕ **Passauer Wolf.** The owner, Richard Kerscher, is master of his own kitchen, and restaurant guides crown his efforts with the highest praise. Kerscher's stylish dining room, which commands views of the Danube from its snug window seats, is considered Passau's best. His delicacies, all based on traditional German recipes, are also served in the vaulted 16th-century wine bar. ⊠ *Rindermarkt 6–8* ☎ *0851/931–5110* ⊕ *www. passauerwolf.de* ⊟ *AE, DC, MC, V* ⊙ *Closed Sun. No lunch Sat.*

¢-$$ ✕ **Blauer Bock.** This is one of Passau's oldest houses (first mentioned in city records in 1257) and has been welcoming travelers since 1875. The Danube flows by the tavern windows, and in summer you can watch the river traffic from a beer garden. The food is traditional; you'll find pork and potatoes in every variety. The tavern also offers accommodation in tastefully fitted rooms. ⊠ *Höllg. 20* ☎ *0851/34637* ⊟ *MC, V.*

¢-$$ ✕ **Peschl Terrasse.** The beer you sip on the high, sunny terrace overlooking the Danube is brought fresh from the Old Town brewery below, which, along with this traditional Bavarian restaurant, has been in the same family since 1855. ⊠ *Rosstränke 4* ☎ *0851/2489* ⊟ *AE, DC, MC, V* ⊙ *Closed Mon.*

¢-$ ✕ **Hacklberger Bräustüberl.** Shaded by magnificent old trees, locals sit in this famous brewery's enormous beer garden (seating more than 1,000), sipping a Hacklberger and tucking into a plate of sausages. In the winter they simply move to the wood-panel interior, where beer has been on tap from the brewery next door since 1618. ⊠ *Bräuhauspl. 7* ☎ *0851/58382* ⊟ *MC, V.*

★ **$-$$$$** ▣ **Hotel Wilder Mann.** Passau's most historic hotel dates from the 11th century and shares prominence with the ancient city hall on the waterfront market square. Empress Elizabeth of Austria and American astronaut Neil Armstrong have been among its guests. On beds of carved oak you'll sleep beneath chandeliers and richly stuccoed ceilings. For sheer indulgence, ask for either the King Ludwig or Sissi (Empress Elisabeth) suite. The esteemed Glasmuseum is within the hotel. ⊠ *Am Rathauspl. 1, D–94032* ☎ *0851/35071* 🖷 *0851/31712* ⊕ *www.rotel-tours.de* 🛏 *48 rooms, 5 suites* ♨ *Restaurant, cable TV; no a/c* ⊟ *AE, DC, MC, V.*

$-$$ ▣ **Hotel König.** Though built in 1984, the König blends successfully with the graceful Italian-style buildings alongside the elegant Danube waterfront. Rooms are large and airy; most have a fine view of the river. ⊠ *Untere Donaulände 1, D–94032* ☎ *0851/3850* 🖷 *0851/385–460* ⊕ *www.hotel-koenig.de* 🛏 *61 rooms* ♨ *In-room data ports, cable TV, sauna, steam room, bar, meeting room; no a/c* ⊟ *AE, DC, MC, V.*

$-$$ ▣ **Schloss Ort.** This 13th-century castle's large rooms have views of the Inn River, which flows beneath the hotel's stout walls. The rooms are decorated in a variety of styles with old-fashioned four-poster beds or modern wrought-iron details. The restaurant is closed in winter, but the kitchen will always oblige hungry hotel guests. In summer the garden terrace is a delightful place to eat and watch the river. ⊠ *Ort 11, D–94032* ☎ *0851/34072* 🖷 *0851/31817* ⊕ *www.schlosshotel-passau. de* 🛏 *18 rooms* ♨ *Restaurant, cable TV; no a/c* ⊟ *D, MC, V.*

¢ ▣ **Rotel Inn.** "Rotels" are usually hotels on wheels, an idea developed by a local entrepreneur to accommodate tour groups in North Africa and Asia. The first permanent Rotel Inn is on the banks of the Danube in central Passau and resembles an ocean liner. Its rooms are truly ship-shape—hardly any wider than the bed inside—but they're clean, decorated in a pop-art style, and amazingly cheap. The building's unique design—a red, white, and blue facade with flowing roof lines—has actually been patented. It's definitely for young travelers but also fun for families. ⊠ *Am Hauptbahnhof/Donauufer, D–94032* ☎ *0851/95160* 🖨 *0851/951–610* ⊕ *www.rotel-tours.de* 🛏 *100 rooms* 👃 *No a/c* ▤ *No credit cards* ⊙ *Closed Oct.–Mar.*

Sports & the Outdoors

If you're looking for sports equipment, **Big Point** (⊠ Neuburgerstr. 108, 94032 Passau ☎ 0851/720–2450) is a well-stocked chain store, which sells and rents a wide selection of sports clothes and equipment, including ski gear.

CYCLING Cyclists can choose between eight (!) long-distance paths along the rivers Danube (as far as Vienna) and Inn (tracing the river to its source in the Swiss Engadine). Bikes are permitted on most Danube boats and local trains, so you can cover part of the journey by river or rail. **Fahrrad-Laden Passau** (⊠ Rosstränke 12, 94032 Passau ☎ 0851/722–26) is the best address in Passau for renting and repairing bicycles.

Nightlife & the Arts

Passau is the cultural center of Lower Bavaria. Its **Europäische Wochen** (European Weeks) festival—featuring everything from opera to pantomime—is a major event on the European music calendar. Now into its 53rd year, the festival runs from June to July. For program details and reservations, write the **Kartenzentrale der Europäischen Wochen Passau** (⊠ Dr.-Hans-Kapfinger-Str. 22, D–94032 Passau ☎ 0851/560–960 ⊕ www.europaeische-wochen-passau.de).

Live jazz programs are regularly presented at **Theater im Scharfrichterhaus** (⊠ Milchg. 2 ☎ 0851/35900), home of the city's nationally famous cabaret company. The company hosts a cabaret festival every fall from October through December.

Passau's **Christmas fair**—the Christkindlmarkt—is the biggest and most spectacular of the Bavarian Forest. It's held in and around the Nibelungenhalle from late November until just before Christmas.

off the
beaten
path

MT. DREISESSEL – You can't get much more off the beaten track than in the remote corner of the country north of Passau, where the German frontier bobs and weaves along the Czech Republic and Austria. It's possible to walk in and out of a virtually forgotten corner of the Czech Republic—a feat that was possible even when the border was guarded everywhere else by heavily armed soldiers—in the area where the border cuts across the summit of Mt. Dreisessel, west of Altreichenau. *Dreisessel* means "three armchairs," an apt description of the summit and its boulders, which are shaped like the furniture of a giant's castle. If you're driving to the Dreisessel, take B–12 to Philippsreut, just before the frontier, and then follow the well-marked country road. The mountain is about 67 km (42 mi) from Passau. Several bus operators in Passau and surrounding villages offer tours. There are no visitor facilities within the forest.

THE BAVARIAN FOREST A TO Z

To research prices, get advice from other travelers, and book travel arrangements, visit www.fodors.com.

AIRPORTS

The nearest airports are in Munich and Nürnberg. Each is about 160 km (100 mi) from the western edge of the Bavarian Forest.

BOAT & FERRY TRAVEL

Cruises on Passau's three rivers begin and end at the Danube jetties on Fritz-Schäffer Promenade. Ludwig Wurm has a range of small cruise-ship services upriver between Passau and Regensburg, taking in Deggendorf, Metten, Straubing, and Walhalla. Wurm & Köck runs 45-minute trips daily on the Danube, Inn, and Ilz from March through October, in the last week of December, and on weekends from mid-November to Christmas Eve. Prices begin at €6.50. A two-hour Danube cruise aboard the *Sissi* costs €9; cruises run daily at 11:15 and 2:45 from early May to the end of October. There's also a trip to Linz, Austria (it's possible to stay overnight in Linz, but you can return on the same day), for €72. If it's luxury you're looking for, you can take the 225-foot day-cruise vessel, *Regina Danubia,* which travels between Passau and Engelhartszell, Austria, every Sunday and includes a buffet lunch.

DDSG offers two-day cruises to Vienna for around €130 per person one-way and Danube cruise connections via Budapest all the way to the Black Sea.

An Austrian shipping operator, M. Schaurecker, runs a daily service on the Inn River from Tuesday through Sunday, mid-March through October, between Passau and the enchanting Austrian river town of Schärding. The round-trip fare is €8.

🚢 **DDSG** ✉ Im Ort 14a, D–94032 Passau ☎ 0851/33035 ⊕ www.ddsg-blue-danube. at. **Ludwig Wurm** ✉ Donaustr. 71, D–94342 Irlbach ☎ 09424/1341. **M. Schaurecker** ✉ A.-Stifterstr. 34, A–4780, Schärding ☎ 0043/7712-3231. **Wurm & Köck** ✉ Höllg. 26, D–94032 Passau ☎ 0851/929-292 ⊕ www.donauschiffahrt.at.

CAR TRAVEL

The principal autobahns that link to the Bavarian Forest are A–3 from Regensburg and A–92 from Munich. Traffic on both roads is always relatively light. Regensburg is 120 km (74 mi) north of Munich and 77 km (47 mi) west of Deggendorf. Passau is 120 km (75 mi) southeast of Regensberg and 179 km (111 mi) northeast of Munich.

B–85 runs the length of the Bavarian Forest from Passau to Cham, and its designation as a scenic route (the Ostmarkstrasse) extends northward to Bayreuth.

EMERGENCIES
🚺 Police and ambulance ☎110. Fire and emergency medical aid ☎112.

TOURS
Many town tourist offices (including Freyung, Furth im Wald, Grafenau, and Tittling) organize bus tours of the region and day trips to the Czech Republic. The Freyung tourist office has weekly half-day trips to the Bavarian Forest National Park and to Dreisessel Mountain. In Tittling the Hötl bus company has daily forest excursions in summer. From Zwiesel, Lambürger operates regional bus tours, as well as a tour three times a week to Prague, with a supper stop on the way home in the Plsen brewery tavern. There's a weekly tour to the Czech spas Marienbad and Karlsbad (Karlovy Vary) and another to the original home of Budweiser beer, Budweis.

The Passau tourist office leads tours of Passau from April through October. There are two tours (at 10:30 and 2:30) on weekdays and one (at 2:30) on weekends. Tours start at the Maximilian Joseph statue in the Domplatz (Cathedral Square) and last one hour. Day tours of the Bavarian Forest (€7.50) are offered every Monday by the Verkehrsamt Lalling, the tourist office of a town near Passau. The Wolff Ost-Reisen bus company, in Furth im Wald, runs one- and two-day excursions to Prague twice a week May–October, as well as trips to the Czech spa town of Karlsbad.

Major visitor-information offices have details on hiking packages. Typical is a €115 five-day tour along the Böhmweg, which includes overnight accommodations, full breakfasts, and a schnapps reception by one of the tourist offices en route. Luggage is transported for you. Deutsche Bahn, the German railway, sends hikers out on its three-day tour of the Bavarian Forest National Park with a bottle of Bärwurz schnapps. The €97 cost of the tour includes three nights' accommodations in a pension, breakfast, and luggage transfer.

🚺 **Deutsche Bahn** ✉ Bahnhofspl., D-94227 Zwiesel ☎01805/996-633. **Hötl** ☎08504/4040. **Lambürger** ✉Stadtpl. 37, Zwiesel ☎09922/84120. **Passau Tourist Office** ☎08551/955-980. **Verkehrsamt Lalling** ☎09904/374. **Wolff Ost-Reisen** ☎09973/5080.

TRAIN TRAVEL
Two main rail lines cross the region: one runs west–east via Nürnberg, Regensburg, Passau, and Vienna; the other runs south–north via Munich, Landshut, and Straubing. This latter route slices right through the heart of the Bavarian Forest, making stops in Deggendorf, Plattling, and Bayerisch-Eisenstein on its way to the Czech Republic (if you're going on to Prague, this is the train to take). Deutsche Bahn runs a special holiday express daily from Hamburg to Bavarian Forest resorts, with Zwiesel as its final destination. The express links up with train services from Berlin and Frankfurt International Airport. Plattling, just south of Deggendorf, and Cham are the main rail junctions for the area. Passau is the principal rail gateway between southeast Germany and Austria.

VISITOR INFORMATION
For information on the whole region, contact Tourismusverband Ostbayern.

🚺 **Bodenmais** ✉Kur-Verkehrsamt, Bahnhofstr. 56, D-94249 ☎09924/778-135 ⊕www.bodenmais.de. **Cham** ✉Fremdenverkehrsverein Cham, Propsteistr. 46, D-93413 ☎09971/

803–493. **Deggendorf** ✉ Kultur- und Verkehrsamt, Oberer Stadtpl. 4, D–94469 ☎ 0991/296–0535 ⊕ www.deggendorf.de. **Freyung** ✉ Touristinformation/Kurverwaltung, Rathauspl. 2, D–94078 ☎ 08551/58850 ⊕ www.freyung.de. **Furth im Wald** ✉ Tourist-Information Furth im Wald, Schlosspl. 1, D–93437 ☎09973/50980 ⊕www.furth.de. **Grafenau** ✉ Verkehrsamt Grafenau, Rathausg. 1, D–94481 ☎ 08552/962–343 ⊕ www.grafenau.de. **Passau** ✉ Tourist-Information Passau, Rathauspl. 3, D–94032 ☎ 0851/955–980 ⊕ www.passau.de. **Regensburg** ✉ Altes Rathaus, D–93047 ☎ 0941/507–4410 ⊕ www.regensburg.de. **Spiegelau** ✉ Touristinformation Spiegelau, Konrad-Wilsdorf-Str. 5, D–94518 ☎ 08553/960–017 ⊕ www.spiegelau.de. **Tittling** ✉ Verkehrsamt Tittling, Marktpl. 10, D–94104 ☎ 08504/40114 ⊕ www.tittling.de. **Tourismusverband Ostbayern** ✉ Luitpoldstr. 20, D–93047 Regensburg ☎0941/585–390 ⊕www.ostbayern-tourismus.de. **Viechtach** ✉ Tourismusverband, Rathaus, Stadtpl. 1, D–94234 ☎ 09942/1661 ⊕ www.viechtach.de. **Zwiesel** ✉ Kurverwaltung, Stadtpl. 27, D–94227 ☎ 09922/840523 ⊕ www.zwiesel.de.

THE ROMANTIC ROAD

4

Updated by Uli
Ehrhardt

OF ALL THE TOURIST ROUTES that crisscross Germany, none rivals the aptly named Romantische Strasse, or Romantic Road. The scenery is more pastoral than spectacular, but the route is memorable for the medieval towns, villages, castles, and churches that anchor its 355-km (220-mi) length. Many of these are tucked away beyond low hills, their spires and towers just visible through the greenery.

The road runs south from Würzburg, in northern Bavaria, to Füssen, on the border of Austria. You can, of course, follow it in the opposite direction, as a number of bus tours do. Either way, among the major sights you'll see are one of Europe's most scintillating baroque palaces, in Würzburg, and perhaps the best-preserved medieval town on the Continent, Rothenburg-ob-der-Tauber. Then there's the handsome Renaissance city of Augsburg. Finally the fantastical highlight will be Ludwig II's castle, Neuschwanstein.

The Romantic Road concept developed as West Germany rebuilt its tourist industry after World War II. A public-relations wizard coined the catchy title for a historic passage through Bavaria and Baden-Württemberg that could be advertised as a unit. In 1950 the Romantic Road was born. The name itself isn't meant to attract lovebirds but, rather, uses the word *romance* as meaning wonderful, fabulous, and imaginative. And, of course, the Romantic Road started as a road on which the Romans traveled.

Along the way, the road crosses centuries-old battlefields. The most cataclysmic conflict, the Thirty Years' War, destroyed the region's economic base in the 17th century. The depletion of resources prevented improvements that would have modernized the area—thereby assuring the survival of the historic towns' now charmingly quaint infrastructures.

As you travel the Romantic Road, two names crop up repeatedly: Walther von der Vogelweide and Tilman Riemenschneider. Walther von der Vogelweide, who died in Würzburg in 1230, was the most famous of the German *Minnesänger,* poet-musicians who wrote and sang of courtly love in the age of chivalry. Knights and other nobles would hire them to help win the favors of fair ladies. Von der Vogelweide broke with this tradition by writing love songs to maidens of less-than-noble rank. He also accepted commissions of a political nature, producing what amounted to medieval political manifestos. His work was romantic, lyrical, witty, and filled with a sighing wistfulness and philosophical questioning. Medieval sculptor Tilman Riemenschneider spent his most creative and esteemed years in Würzburg. Owing to his support of farmers and guildsmen during the 1524–25 Peasants' War, he also ended his life in Würzburg as a pauper and outcast.

Exploring the Romantic Road

The Romantic Road runs from the vineyard-hung slopes of the Main River valley at Würzburg to the snow-covered mountains overlooking Füssen in the Allgäuer Alps. For much of its route it follows two enchanting rivers, the Tauber and the Lech, and at one point crosses the

4

Although a long-distance bus covers the Romantic Road daily during summer in less than 12 hours, it's difficult to resist an overnight stay. Würzburg and Augsburg are each worth two or three days of exploration, and such attractions as the minster of Ulm are time-consuming but rewarding diversions from the recognized Romantic Road.

Numbers in the text correspond to numbers in the margin and on the maps in this chapter.

If you have 3 days

Spend the first day in **Würzburg** ①–⑯ ⌐, where you can stroll through the streets and enjoy the splendor of the city. The next morning, head south and stop in **Bad Mergentheim** ⑰, once the home of the Teutonic Knights. Next, head east for a few miles to visit the castle of the counts of Hohenlohe in **Weikersheim** ⑱. Continue east to **Creglingen** ⑲, where you can admire the Tilman Riemenschneider altar in the **Herrgottskirche** ⑳. Continue toward Rothenburg but do not drive into the town; rather follow the signs to Ansbach. You'll pass under the autobahn and continue for 18 km (11 mi) toward **Castle Colmberg,** where you can stay for the night and dine like a duke in medieval settings. The next morning, venture into **Rothenburg-ob-der-Tauber** ㉑–㉘ before the crowds arrive. In the afternoon drive back to Würzburg.

If you have 5 days

Tackle the entire length of the Romantic Road by just hitting the highlights: Spend a night and day in 🏛 **Würzburg** ①–⑯ ⌐, with all its baroque splendor. The next afternoon, head south toward **Bad Mergentheim** ⑰, making a short stop before continuing on to 🏛 **Rothenburg-ob-der-Tauber** ㉑–㉘. Try to arrive in the early evening, when the tourist buses have left. Spend the evening roaming the streets, and the next morning—before the daily crowds arrive—look at the highlights. Spend the rest of the day exploring the towns of **Dinkelsbühl** ㉛, **Nördlingen** ㉜, and 🏛 **Augsburg** ㉟–㊲. The next morning, continue south toward **Landsberg am Lech** ㊽. After a stop here, continue south for about 40 km (25 mi) until, at the small town of Steingaden, you see road signs to the rococo **Wieskirche,** which stands in a heavenly Alpine meadow (*Wiese*). Next, head to 🏛 **Füssen** ㊼ at the end of the Romantic Road. You can spend your last nights here while you explore **Schloss Neuschwanstein** ㊼ and **Schloss Hohenschwangau** ㊱ during the day.

If you have 7 days

Devote two days to 🏛 **Würzburg** ①–⑯ ⌐ before heading south. Take Day 3 to investigate **Bad Mergentheim** ⑰ and 🏛 **Rothenburg-ob-der-Tauber** ㉑–㉘, overnighting in **Castle Colmberg** 18 km (11 mi) east of Rothenburg. Spend the fourth day visiting two other exquisitely preserved medieval towns, **Dinkelsbühl** ㉛ and **Nördlingen** ㉜. Continue on to 🏛 **Ulm** ㉞ to look at the mighty cathedral and the old city. The next day, head back to the Romantic Road to 🏛 **Augsburg** ㉟–㊲, where you can explore and shop. On the sixth day continue south to **Landsberg am Lech** ㊽ and to the lovely **Wieskirche.** Spend the night in 🏛 **Füssen** ㊼, and use your last day for a day trip to **Schloss Neuschwanstein** ㊼ and **Schloss Hohenschwangau** ㊱.

great Danube, still a surprisingly narrow river this far from the end of its journey in the Black Sea. The city of Augsburg marks the natural halfway point of the Romantic Road. South of Augsburg, the road climbs gradually into the Alpine foothills, and the landscape changes from the lush green of Franconian river valleys to mountain-backed meadows and forests.

About the Restaurants

During peak season, restaurants along the Romantic Road tend to be crowded, especially in the larger towns. You may want to plan your mealtimes around visits to smaller villages, where there are fewer people and the restaurants are pleasant and clean. The food will be more basic Franconian or Swabian, but it will also be generally less expensive than in the well-known towns. You may find that some of the small, family-run restaurants close around 2 PM, or whenever the last lunch guests have left, and open again at 5 or 5:30 PM. Some serve cold cuts or coffee and cake during that time, but no hot food.

About the Hotels

With a few exceptions, the Romantic Road hotels are quiet and rustic, and you'll find high standards of comfort and cleanliness. Make reservations as far in advance as possible if you plan to visit in summer. Hotels in Würzburg, Rothenburg, and Füssen are often full year-round. Augsburg hotels are in great demand during trade fairs in nearby Munich. Tourist information offices can usually help with accommodations, especially if you arrive early in the day.

WHAT IT COSTS In Euros				
$$$$	**$$$**	**$$**	**$**	**¢**
RESTAURANTS over €25	€21–€25	€16–€20	€9–€15	under €9
HOTELS over €225	€175–€225	€100–€175	€50–€100	under €50

Restaurant prices are per person for a main course at dinner. Hotel prices are for two people in a standard double room, including tax and service.

Timing

Late summer and early autumn are the best times to travel the Romantic Road, when the grapes ripen on the vines around Würzburg and the geraniums run riot on the medieval walls of towns such as Rothenburg and Dinkelsbühl. You'll also miss the high-season summer crush of tourists. Otherwise, consider visiting the region in the depths of December, when Christmas markets pack the ancient squares of the Romantic Road towns and snow gives turreted Schloss Neuschwanstein a final magic touch.

NORTHERN ROMANTIC ROAD

The northern section of the Romantic Road skirts the wild, open countryside of the Spessart uplands before heading south through the plains of Swabia and along the lovely Tauber and Lech rivers.

Bicycling

One of the most interesting ways to get to know the Romantic Road is by bicycle, especially because the route, which mostly follows rivers, is relatively flat. Even if you pedal all the way from Würzburg to Füssen, you won't have to climb any mountains. In the Alpine foothills you'll have a few longer inclines, but even those can be managed by an average cyclist. Of course, if you'd rather avoid inclines altogether, start in Füssen and then roll back down in the opposite direction, following the River Lech.

There are three ways to explore the Romantic Road by bicycle. One is to venture out with as little baggage as possible, finding places to stay along the way. Another possibility is to have a tour operator book rooms for you and your group and transport your luggage. Or, you can do day trips. Most tourist offices and good hotels along the Romantic Road will supply bicycles, maps, and information for local and regional bike trips.

The Romantic Road office in Dinkelsbühl has a booklet with detailed maps for cycling, and signs mark the Romantic Road bicycle path (all 420 km [260 mi] of it) from beginning to end. In any town on the Romantic Road you can board the Deutsche Touring bus (with a trailer for bicycles), which travels the length of the Romantic Road daily.

On the Menu

The best Franconian and Swabian food combines hearty regional specialties with nouvelle elements. Various forms of pasta are common. *Schupfnudeln* (little potato dumplings) are eaten either with a sweet or savory accompaniment, and spaetzle (small tagliatellelike ribbons of rolled dough) is often served with *Rinderbraten* (roast beef), the traditional Sunday lunchtime dish. One of the best regional dishes is *Maultaschen,* a Swabian version of ravioli, usually served floating in broth strewn with chives. Würzburg is one of the leading wine-producing areas of Germany, and the many Franconian beers range from *Räucherbier* (literally, "smoked beer") to the lighter ales of Augsburg.

Würzburg

▶ *115 km (71 mi) east of Frankfurt.*

The baroque city of Würzburg, the pearl of the Romantic Road, is a heady example of what happens when great genius teams up with great wealth. Beginning in the 10th century, Würzburg was ruled by powerful (and rich) prince-bishops, who created the city with all the remarkable attributes you see today.

The city is at the junction of two age-old trade routes in a calm valley backed by vineyard-covered hills. Festung Marienberg, a fortified castle on the steep hill across the Main River, overlooks the town. Constructed between 1200 and 1600, the fortress was the residence of the prince-bishops for 450 years.

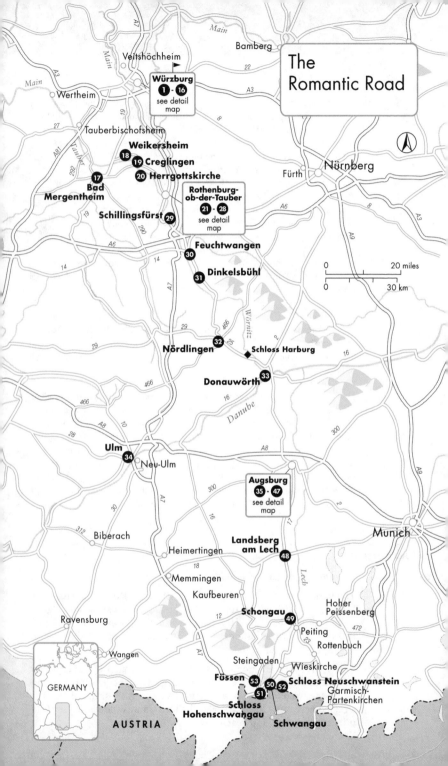

Present-day Würzburg is by no means completely original. On March 16, 1945, seven weeks before Germany capitulated, Würzburg was all but obliterated by Allied saturation bombing. The 20-minute raid destroyed 87% of the city and killed at least 4,000 people. Reconstruction has returned most of the city's famous sights to their former splendor. Except for some buildings with modern shops, it remains a largely authentic restoration.

a good walk

No two sights are more than 2 km (1 mi) from each other. Begin your tour on Marktplatz (Market Square) at the city tourist office, in the mansion **Haus zum Falken** ❶ ▶. Collect the handy English-language tour map with a route marked out. Red signs throughout the city point the way between major sights. Next door to the Haus zum Falken is one of the city's loveliest churches, the delicate **Marienkapelle** ❷. Leave the square at its eastern exit and you'll find yourself on Würzburg's traffic-free shopping street, **Schönbornstrasse** ❸, named after the city's greatest patron, the prince-bishop Johann Philipp Franz von Schönborn. Head north, passing the **Augustinerkirche** ❹, a former Dominican church, and you'll arrive within a few minutes at the broad Juliuspromenade, dominated by the impressive baroque **Juliusspital** ❺, an infirmary. Follow Juliuspromenade eastward; it will become Heinestrasse, and you'll come to the first baroque church built in Franconia, the **Stift Haug** ❻. Next, retrace your steps along Heinestrasse and make a left on Theaterstrasse. After one block, you'll pass the Gothic **Bürgerspital** ❼, another charitable institution. At the end of Theaterstrasse stands the mighty **Residenz** ❽ of the Würzburg prince-bishops, built for Schönborn by the great baroque-era architect Balthasar Neumann.

From the Residenz, walk down Domerschulstrasse and turn left onto Schönthalstrasse for the **Alte Universität** ❾. The southern section of the building is taken up by the Neubaukirche, a fine Renaissance church. Next, head north on Schönthalstrasse to Plattnerstrasse; where this street becomes Schönbornstrasse, you'll find Würzburg's cathedral, the **Dom St. Kilian** ❿, and the nearby **Neumünster** ⓫ church. From the cathedral take Domstrasse westward, and you'll see the high tower of the 14th-century **Rathaus** ⓬; beyond this the **Alte Mainbrücke** ⓭ crosses the Main River. Before you cross the bridge, stroll north along the riverbank to one of Würzburg's familiar landmarks, the **Alter Kranen** ⓮, a wharf crane. To conclude your walk, retrace your steps, cross the Alte Mainbrücke to the other side of the river, and climb the vineyard-covered hill to the great brooding fortress, the **Festung Marienberg** ⓯. Within its massive walls are two very interesting museums. You can ride back into central Würzburg on the bus that stops in front of the main entrance.

TIMING You need two days to do full justice to Würzburg. The Residenz alone demands several hours of attention. If time is short, head for the Residenz as the doors open in the morning, before the first crowds assemble, and aim to complete your tour by lunchtime. Then continue to the nearby Juliusspital Weinstuben or one of the many traditional taverns in the area for lunch. In the afternoon explore central Würzburg and cross the Main River to visit the Festung Marienberg and the Mainfränkisches Museum.

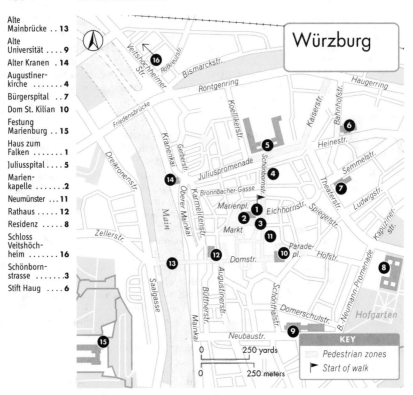

Würzburg

KEY

⬜ Pedestrian zones
▶ Start of walk

0 ─── 250 yards
0 ─── 250 meters

What to See

⓭ Alte Mainbrücke (Old Main Bridge). Construction on this ancient structure, which crosses the Main River, began in 1473. Twin rows of infinitely graceful statues of saints line the bridge. They were placed here in 1730, at the height of Würzburg's baroque period. Note the *Patronna Franconiae* (commonly known as the Weeping Madonna). There's a beautiful view of the Marienberg Fortress from the bridge.

❾ Alte Universität (Old University). Founded by Prince-Bishop Julius Echter and built in 1582, this rambling institution is one of Würzburg's most interesting Renaissance structures. ✉ *Neubaustr. 1–9.*

⓮ Alter Kranen (Old Crane). Near the Main River and north of the Old Main Bridge, the crane was erected in 1772–73 by Balthasar Neumann's son, Franz Ignaz Michael. It was used to unload boats; notice the old customs building right beside it.

❹ Augustinerkirche (Church of St. Augustine). This baroque church, a work by Balthasar Neumann, was a 13th-century Dominican chapel. Neumann retained the soaring, graceful choir and commissioned Antonio Bossi to add colorful stuccowork to the rest of the church. ✉ *Dominikanerpl. 2* ☎ *0931/30970* ☯ *Daily 7–6.*

❼ Bürgerspital (Almshouse). Wealthy burghers founded this refuge for the city's poor and needy in 1319; it now sells wine. The arcade courtyard is baroque in style. From mid-March through October there's a weekly tour (Saturday at 2), which includes a glass of wine. ⊠ *Theaterstr. 19* ☎ *0931/35030* ⊕ *www.buergerspital.de* ⊠ *Tour €5.*

❿ Dom St. Kilian (St. Kilian Basilica). Würzburg's Romanesque cathedral, the fourth largest of its kind in Germany, was begun in 1045. Step inside and you'll find yourself, somewhat disconcertingly, in a shimmering rococo treasure house. Prince-Bishop von Schönborn is buried here. His tomb is the work of his architect and builder Balthasar Neumann. Tilman Riemenschneider carved the tombstones of two other bishops at the cathedral. ⊠ *Paradepl., south end of Schönbornstr.* ☎ *0931/ 321–1830* ⊠ *Tour €2* ⊙ *Easter–Oct., daily 8–6; Nov.–Easter, daily 8–noon and 2–6; guided tours May–Oct., Mon.–Sat. at 12:20, Sun. at 12:30.*

⓯ Festung Marienberg (Marienberg Fortress). This complex was the original home of the prince-bishops, beginning in the 13th century. The oldest buildings—note especially the **Marienkirche** (Church of the Virgin Mary)—date from around 700, although excavations have disclosed evidence that there was a settlement here in the Iron Age, 3,000 years ago. In addition to the rough-hewn medieval fortifications, there are a number of Renaissance and baroque apartments. To reach the hilltop Marienberg, you can make the fairly stiff climb on foot through vineyards or take the bus from the Residenz. It runs every 40 minutes from February to October, starting at 9:45 AM.

★ The highlight is the remarkable collection of art treasures in the **Main-fränkisches Museum** (Main-Franconian Museum; ☎ 0931/205–940 ⊕ www.mainfraenkisches-museum.de ⊠ €3 ⊙ Apr.–Oct., Tues.–Sun. 10–5; Nov.–Mar., Tues.–Sun. 10–4), which traces the city's rich and varied history. Be sure to visit the gallery devoted to Würzburg-born sculptor Tilman Riemenschneider, who lived from the late 15th to the early 16th century. Also on view are paintings by Tiepolo and Cranach the Elder, as well as exhibits of porcelain, firearms, antique toys, and ancient Greek and Roman art. Other exhibits include enormous old winepresses and exhibits about the history of Franconian wine making. From April through October, tours around the fortress are offered for €2 per person, starting from the Scherenberg Tor.

The Marienberg collections are so vast that they spill over into another outstanding museum that is part of the fortress, the **Fürstenbaumuseum** (Princes' Quarters Museum), which traces 1,200 years of Würzburg's history. The holdings include breathtaking exhibits of local goldsmiths' art. ⊠ *Combined ticket for Mainfränkisches and Fürstenbau museums €4* ⊙ *Apr.–Sept., Tues.–Sun. 9–5; Oct.–Mar., Tues.–Sun. 10–4.*

▶ ❶ **Haus zum Falken.** The city's most splendid baroque mansion, formerly a humble inn, now houses the city tourist office. Its colorful rococo facade was added in 1751. ⊠ *Am Marktpl. 9* ☎ *0931/372–398* ⊙ *Jan.–Mar., weekdays 10–6, Sat. 10–1; Apr.–Oct., weekdays 10–6, weekends 10–2.*

GERMANY'S MASTER SCULPTOR

TILMAN *Riemenschneider, Germany's master of late-Gothic sculpture (1460–1531), lived an extraordinary life. His skill with* wood and stone was recognized at an early age, and he soon presided over a major Würzburg workshop. Riemenschneider worked alone, however, on the life-size figures that dominate his sculptures. Details such as the folds of a robe or wrinkles upon a face highlight his grace and harmony of line.

At the height of his career Riemenschneider was appointed city councillor; later he became mayor of Würzburg. In 1523, however, he made the fateful error of siding with the small farmers and guild members in the Peasants' War. He was arrested and held for eight weeks in the dungeons of the Marienberg Fortress, above Würzburg, where he was frequently tortured. Most of his wealth was confiscated, and he

returned home a broken man. He died in 1531.

For nearly three centuries he and his sculptures were all but forgotten. Only in 1822, when ditchdiggers uncovered the site of his grave, was Riemenschneider once again included among Germany's greatest artists. Today Riemenschneider is recognized as the giant of German sculpture. The richest collection of his works is in Würzburg, although other masterpieces are on view in churches and museums along the Romantic Road as well as in other parts of Germany; for example, the renowned Windsheim Altar of the Twelve Apostles is in the Palatine Museum in Heidelberg.

⑤ Juliusspital. Founded in 1576 by Prince-Bishop Julius Echter as a home for the poor, the elderly, and the sick, this enormous edifice now houses an impressive restaurant serving wine from the institution's own vineyards. It also sells wineglasses. All profits from the restaurant are used to run the adjacent home for the elderly. A glass of wine is included in a weekly tour of the wine cellars. ⊠ *Juliuspromenade 19* ☎ *0931/393–1400* ☜ *Tour €5* ⊙ *Daily 10 AM–midnight; tours Apr.–Oct., Fri. at 3.*

② Marienkapelle (St. Mary's Chapel). This tranquil Gothic church (1377–1480) tucked modestly away at one end of Würzburg's market square is almost lost amid the historic old facades. Balthasar Neumann lies buried in the church. ⊠ *Marktpl.* ☎ *0931/321–1830* ⊙ *Daily 8–6:30.*

⑪ Neumünster (New Minster). Next to the Dom St. Kilian, this 11th-century Romanesque basilica was completed in 1716. The original church was built above the grave of the early Irish martyr St. Kilian, who brought Christianity to Würzburg and, with two companions, was put to death here in 689. Their missionary zeal bore fruit, however—17 years after their death a church was consecrated in their memory. By 742 Würzburg had become a diocese, and over the following centuries 39 flourishing churches were established throughout the city. ☒ *Schönbornstr.* ☎ *0931/321–1830* ☉ *Daily 7–6.*

⑫ Rathaus. The Gothic town hall, once headquarters of the bishop's administrator, has been the center of municipal government since 1316. A permanent exhibition in the tower documents Würzburg's destruction by Allied bombs, some examples of which are on display. ☒ *Marktpl.* ☎ *0931/370* ☒ *Free* ☉ *Weekdays 9–5; tours May–Oct., Sat. at 10.*

★ ⑧ Residenz (Residence). The line of Würzburg's prince-bishops lived in this glorious baroque palace after moving down from the hilltop Festung Marienberg. Construction started in 1719 under the brilliant direction of Balthasar Neumann. Most of the interior decoration was entrusted to the Italian stuccoist Antonio Bossi and the Venetian painter Giovanni Battista Tiepolo. It's the spirit of the pleasure-loving prince-bishop Johann Philipp Franz von Schönborn, however, that infuses the Residenz. Now considered one of Europe's most sumptuous palaces, this dazzling structure is a 10-minute walk from the railway station, along pedestrians-only Kaiserstrasse and then Theaterstrasse.

As you enter the building, the largest baroque staircase in the country, the **Treppenhaus**, greets you. Halfway up, the stairway splits and peels away 180 degrees to the left and to the right. Soaring above on the vaulting is Tiepolo's giant fresco *The Four Continents,* a gorgeous exercise in blue and pink, with allegorical figures at the corners representing the four continents known at the time (take a careful look at the elephant's trunk). Tiepolo immortalized himself and Balthasar Neumann as two of the figures—they're not too difficult to spot. The fresco, which survived a devastating wartime bombing raid, is being restored bit by bit, so don't be surprised to find a small section covered by scaffolding.

Next, make your way to the **Weissersaal** (White Room) and then beyond to the grandest of the state rooms, the **Kaisersaal** (Throne Room). Tiepolo's frescoes show the 12th-century visit of Emperor Frederick Barbarossa, when he came to Würzburg to claim his bride. If you take part in the guided tour, you'll also see private chambers of the various former residents.

The **Hofkirche** (chapel; ☉ Apr.–Oct., daily 9–noon and 1–5; Nov.–Mar., daily 9–noon and 1–4) demonstrates the prince-bishops' love of ostentation. Among the lavish marble, rich gilding, and delicate stuccowork, note the Tiepolo altarpieces, ethereal visions of *The Fall of the Angels* and *The Assumption of the Virgin.* Finally, tour the **Hofgarten**; the entrance is next to the chapel. The 18th-century formal garden has stately gushing fountains and trim ankle-high shrubs outlining geometric flower beds and gravel walks. ☒ *Residenzpl.* ☎ *0931/355–170* ☒ €4, *including guided tour* ☉ *Apr.–Oct., daily 9–5:30; Nov.–Mar., daily 10–4.*

⑯ Schloss Veitshöchheim. This first summer palace of the prince-bishops is 8 km (5 mi) north of Würzburg, at Veitshöchheim. The palace cannot be visited because of renovations, but the gardens remain open. A bus service to the palace runs from Würzburg's Kirchplatz. From mid-April to mid-October a boat service operates between Würzburg and the palace daily 10–4. The 40-minute trip costs €8 round-trip. ☎ *0931/355–170* ⊠ *Gardens free* ☉ *Gardens daily 7–dusk.*

❸ Schönbornstrasse. Würzburg's main pedestrian mall is filled with shops, cafés, and not-so-posh eateries.

❻ Stift Haug. Franconia's first baroque church, designed by the Italian architect Antonio Petrini, was built between 1670 and 1691. Its elegant twin spires and central cupola make an impressive exterior. The altarpiece is a 1583 Crucifixion scene by Tintoretto. ⊠ *Bahnhofstr. at Heinestr.* ☎ *0931/54102* ☉ *Daily 8–6:30.*

Where to Stay & Eat

$–$$$ ✕ **Ratskeller.** The vaulted cellars of Würzburg's Rathaus shelter one of the city's most popular restaurants. Beer is served, but Franconian wine is what the regulars drink. The food is staunch Franconian fare. ⊠ *Beim Grafeneckart, Langg. 1* ☎ *0931/13021* ▭ *AE, DC, MC, V.*

★ $–$$$ ✕ **Wein- und Speisehaus zum Stachel.** On a warm spring or summer day take a bench in the ancient courtyard of the Stachel, which is shaded by a canopy of vine leaves and enclosed by tall ivy-covered walls. The entrées are satisfyingly Franconian, from lightly baked onion cake to hearty roast pork. Excellent fish from their own pond is a specialty. Another reason to come here is to sample the wine, some made from the tavern's own grapes. ⊠ *Gresseng. 1* ☎ *0931/52770* ⊕ *www.weinhaus-stachel.de* ▭ *No credit cards* ☉ *Closed Sun.*

¢–$$ ✕ **Backöfele.** More than 400 years of tradition are sustained by this old tavern. Hidden away behind huge wooden doors in a back street, the Backöfele's cavelike interior is a popular meeting and eating place for regulars and newcomers alike. The menu includes local favorites such as suckling pig and marinated pot roast as well as some good fish dishes. ⊠ *Ursulinerg. 2* ☎ *0931/59059* ⊕ *www.backoefele.de* ▭ *AE, MC, V.*

¢–$$ ✕ **Juliusspital Weinstuben.** This tavern serves wine from its own vineyard and good portions of basic Franconian fare. In summer you can enjoy your food and drinks on a quiet terrace in the courtyard. ⊠ *Juliuspromenade 19* ☎ *0931/54080* ▭ *No credit cards.*

$$ ✕▥ **Hotel Greifensteiner Hof.** The modern Greifensteiner offers comfortable, individually furnished rooms in a quiet corner of the city, just off the market square. The cheaper doubles are small but lack no comforts or facilities. The hotel restaurant, the Fränkische Stuben ($–$$), has excellent cuisine—mostly Franconian specialties. ⊠ *Dettelbacherg. 2, D–97070* ☎ *0931/35170* 📠 *0931/57057* ⊕ *www.greifensteiner-hof. de* ⇌ *42 rooms* ⌂ *Restaurant, cable TV, meeting room; no a/c* ▭ *AE, DC, MC, V.*

$$ ✕▥ **Hotel Walfisch.** Guest rooms are furnished in solid Franconian style with farmhouse cupboards, bright fabrics, and heavy drapes. You'll breakfast in a dining room on the banks of the Main with views of the vineyard-covered Marienberg. For lunch and dinner try the hotel's cozy Walfisch-Stube restaurant ($$–$$$). ⊠ *Am Pleidenturm 5, D–97070* ☎ *0931/35200* 📠 *0931/352–0500* ⊕ *www.hotel-walfisch.com* ⇌ *40 rooms* ⌂ *Restaurant, cable TV, meeting room; no a/c* ▭ *AE, DC, MC, V* ⦿ *CP.*

$–$$ ✕▦ **Hotel Zur Stadt Mainz.** This traditional Franconian inn dates from the early 15th century. The cuisine ($–$$$) is based on its own historic recipe book. Eel from the Main River and locally caught carp and pike are specialties. Homemade apple strudel is served with afternoon coffee; the breakfast buffet is enormous. Rooms are comfortably furnished, with old-fashioned touches such as gilt mirrors and heavy drapes. ✉ *Semmelstr. 39, D–97070* ☎ *0931/53155* 🖷 *0931/58510* ⊕ *www. hotel-stadtmainz.de* 🗲 *15 rooms* ♨ *Restaurant, shops; no a/c* ▤ *AE, MC, V* ☉ *Closed 2 wks in Jan. Restaurant closed Sun. evening* ⎮◎⎮ *CP.*

$–$$ ✕▦ **Ringhotel Wittelsbacher Höh.** Most of the cozy rooms in this historic redbrick mansion offer views of Würzburg and the vineyards. The restaurant's wine list embraces most of the leading local vintages, and Franconian and Italian dishes ($$–$$$) pack the menu. In summer take a table on the terrace and soak up the view. ✉ *Hexenbruchweg 10, D–97082* ☎ *0931/453–040* 🖷 *0931/415–458* ⊕ *www.ringhotels.de* 🗲 *73 rooms, 1 suite* ♨ *Restaurant, cable TV, sauna; no a/c* ▤ *AE, DC, MC, V* ⎮◎⎮ *CP.*

★ $$–$$$ ▦ **Hotel Rebstock zu Würzburg.** This hotel's rococo facade has welcomed guests for centuries. The spacious lobby, with its open fireplace and beckoning bar, sets the tone, and there's an attractive winter garden where you can enjoy a cup of coffee. All rooms are individually decorated and furnished in English country-house style. ✉ *Neubaustr. 7, D–97070* ☎ *0931/30930* 🖷 *0931/309–3100* ⊕ *www.rebstock.com* 🗲 *63 rooms, 9 suites* ♨ *Restaurant, cable TV, bar, meeting rooms, no-smoking rooms; no a/c in some rooms* ▤ *AE, DC, MC, V* ⎮◎⎮ *CP.*

$ ▦ **Spehnkuch.** What was once a large apartment with high-ceiling rooms is today a small, spotlessly clean, very price-worthy pension. It's just opposite the main railway station. The only possible drawback is that the shower and toilet are located down the hall. ✉ *Röntgenstr. 7, 97070* ☎ *0931/54752* 🖷 *0931/54760* ⊕ *www.pension-spehnkuch.de* 🗲 *7 rooms* ♨ *No room phones, no room TVs, no a/c* ▤ *No credit cards* ⎮◎⎮ *CP.*

$ ▦ **Strauss.** Close to the river and the pedestrians-only center, the pink-stucco Strauss has been in the same family for more than 100 years. Rooms are simply furnished in light woods; those on the top floor are particularly cozy. The beamed Würzburg restaurant serves Franconian cuisine, as well as international dishes, complemented by excellent Franconian wines. ✉ *Juliuspromenade 5, D–97070* ☎ *0931/30570* 🖷 *0931/305–7555* ⊕ *www.hotel-strauss.de* 🗲 *75 rooms, 3 suites* ♨ *Restaurant, cable TV, bicycles; no a/c* ▤ *AE, DC, MC, V* ☉ *Restaurant closed late Dec.–Feb.* ⎮◎⎮ *EP.*

Festivals

Würzburg's cultural year starts with the International Film Weekend in January and ends with a Johann Sebastian Bach Festival in November. Its annual Mozart Festival, between May and June, attracts visitors from all over the world. Most concerts are held in the magnificent setting of the Residenz. The annual jazz festival is in November. The town hosts a series of wine festivals from May to August.

Sports & the Outdoors

Visitors are welcome to play the 9-hole course at the **Würzburg Golf Club** (✉ Am Golf Pl. 2 ☎ 0931/67890 ⊕ www.golfclub-wuerzburg.de). Take

B–19 out of town in the direction of Bad Mergentheim. There's a sign marking the exit for the golf club on the right.

If you're interested in bicycling, turn left as you leave the main railway station and walk 100 feet to **Fahrradstation** (⊠ Bahnhofplatz 4 ☎ 0931/57445), a bicycle shop that rents bikes for €10 a day or €45 a week. You can also get professional advice here on the best places to cycle along the Romantic Road.

Shopping

Würzburg is the true wine center of the Romantic Road. Visit any of the vineyards that rise from the Main River and choose a *Bocksbeutel,* the distinctive green, flagon-shape wine bottle of Franconia. It's claimed that the shape came about because wine-guzzling monks found it the easiest to hide under their robes. The old **Bürgerspital** and **Juliusspital** both sell fine wines.

The **Haus des Frankenweins** (House of Franconian Wine; ⊠ Kranenkai 1 ☎ 0931/390–110) has wine tastings for individual visitors. Some 100 Franconian wines and a wide range of wine accessories are sold.

Die Murmel (⊠ Augustinerstr. 7 ☎ 0931/59349) is the place to go if you're looking for a special toy. **Ebinger** (⊠ Karmelitenstr. 23 ☎ 0937/59449) sells fine antique jewelry, clocks, watches, and silver. At the **Eckhaus** (⊠ Langgasse 8, off the Marktpl. ☎ 0931/12001) you'll find high-quality gifts. In summer the selection consists mostly of garden and terrace decorations; from October through December the store is filled with delightful Christmas ornaments and candles. In the **tourist information office** (⊠ Falkenhaus am Markt ☎ 0931/372–398) you'll not only get excellent advice in German or English, but you can also buy good wines, steins, and Würzburg platters.

en route From Würzburg, follow the Romantic Road through Bavarian Franconia and Swabia and into the mountains of Upper Bavaria. For the first stretch, to Bad Mergentheim, B–19 takes you through the open countryside of the Hohenloher Plain.

Bad Mergentheim

 38 km (23 mi) south of Würzburg.

Between 1525 and 1809 Bad Mergentheim was the home of the Teutonic Knights, one of the most successful medieval orders of chivalry. In 1809 Napoléon expelled them as he marched toward his ultimately disastrous Russian campaign. The expulsion seemed to sound the death knell of the little town, but in 1826 a shepherd discovered mineral springs on the north bank of the river. They proved to be the strongest sodium sulfate and bitter-salt waters in Europe, with health-giving properties that ensured the town's future prosperity.

The **Deutschordensschloss**, the Teutonic Knights' former castle, at the eastern end of the town, has a museum that follows the history of the order. ⊠ *Schloss 16* ☎ *07931/52212* 🖾 *€3.50, guided tour €1.50* ☉ *Tues.–Sun. 10–5; tours Thurs. and Sun. at 3.*

The **Wildpark Bad Mergentheim,** just outside Bad Mergentheim, is a wildlife park with Europe's largest selection of European species, including wolves and bears. ⊠ *B–290* ☎ *07931/41344* ⊕ *www.wildtierpark.de* ⊠ €7 ⊙ *Mid-Mar.–Oct., daily 9–6; Nov.–mid-Mar., weekends 10:30–4.*

---

off the beaten path

STUPPACH – This village, 11 km (7 mi) southeast of Bad Mergentheim, has a **chapel** guarding one of the great Renaissance German paintings, the *Stuppacher Madonna,* by Matthias Grünewald (circa 1475–1528). It was only in 1908 that experts finally recognized it as the work of Grünewald; repainting in the 17th century had turned it into an unexceptional work. Though Grünewald was familiar with the developments in perspective and natural lighting of Italian Renaissance painting, his work remained resolutely anti-Renaissance in spirit: tortured, emotional, dark. ⊙ *Chapel Mar. and Apr., daily 10–5; May–Oct., daily 9–5:30; Nov.–Feb., daily 11–4.*

Where to Stay & Eat

¢–$ ✕ **Klotzbücher.** You can order 10 different kinds of beer—4 from the tap— at the long wooden bar in this renovated Franconian brewery tavern. In the other room, paneled with dark wood, you can have the obligatory bratwurst on heavy wooden tables, but why not try the trout on sauerkraut or a good steak? In summer, head for the beer garden. ⊠ *Boxbergerstr. 6* ☎ *07931/562–928* ⊕ *www.victoria-hotel.de* ☐ *No credit cards* ⊙ *No lunch.*

$$–$$$ ✕▥ **Romantik Hotel Victoria.** As you enter this hotel, you'll find yourself
Fodor'sChoice in an elegant lounge, with a library and open fireplace. The bedrooms
★ are large and luxurious, and most have both a bath and shower. The restaurant Zirbelstube ($$$$) is open only for dinner but is known as one of the best in the region. In the Vinothek ($$), open all day, you can eat at the bar and watch the chefs prepare your next dish behind a huge glass partition. The hotel very conveniently has its own wine shop. ⊠ *Poststr. 2–4, D–97980* ☎ *07931/5930* ☐ *07931/593–500* ⊕ *www. victoria-hotel.de or www.romantikhotels.com* ⌁ *75 rooms, 3 suites* ⌂ *Restaurant, cable TV, hair salon, massage, sauna, steam room, bar, pub; no a/c* ☐ *AE, DC, MC, V* ⊙ *Restaurant Zirbelstube closed Jan. and Sun.* ⏿ *CP.*

Weikersheim

⓲ *10 km (6 mi) east of Bad Mergentheim, 40 km (25 mi) south of Würzburg.*

The Tauber River town of Weikersheim is dominated by the **castle** of the counts of Hohenlohe. Its great hall is the scene each summer of an international youth music festival. The **Rittersaal** (Knights' Hall) contains life-size stucco wall sculptures of animals, reflecting the counts' love of hunting. In the cellars you can drink a glass of wine drawn from the huge casks that seem to prop up the building. Outside, stroll through the gardens and enjoy the view of the Tauber River. ☎ *07934/8364* ⊠ *€4, gardens only €1.50* ⊙ *Apr.–Oct., daily 9–6; Nov.–Mar., daily 10–noon and 1:30–4:30.*

Where to Stay & Eat

$ ✕⊞ **Flair Hotel Laurentius.** This traditional hotel on Weikersheim's market square is a good stopover on the Romantic Road. You can avoid the crowds and the relatively high prices of nearby Rothenburg and visit that town the next morning. Rooms are comfortable and individually furnished, some with German antiques. The vaulted ground floor has a wine tavern as well as a good restaurant ($$–$$$; dinner only). The brasserie ($–$$), served by the same excellent kitchen, is open all day. ✉ *Marktpl. 5, D–97990* ☎ *07934/91080* 🖷 *07934/910–818* ⊕ *www. hotel-laurentius.de* ⟳ *13 rooms* ⌕ *Restaurant, café, cable TV, Weinstube; no a/c* ⊟ *AE, DC, MC, V* ⟲ *CP.*

Creglingen

⑲   *20 km (12 mi) east of Weikersheim, 40 km (25 mi) south of Würzburg.*

The village of Creglingen has been an important pilgrimage site since the 14th century, when a farmer had a vision of a heavenly host plow-
★ **⑳** ing his field. The **Herrgottskirche** (Chapel of Our Lord) is in the Herrgottstal (Valley of the Lord), 3 km (2 mi) south of Creglingen; the way there is well signposted. The chapel was built by the counts of Hohenlohe, and in the early 16th century Tilman Riemenschneider carved an altarpiece for it. This enormous work, 33 feet high, depicts in minute detail the life and ascension of the Virgin Mary. Riemenschneider entrusted much of the background detail to the craftsmen of his Würzburg workshop, but he allowed no one but himself to attempt its life-size figures. Its intricate detail and attenuated figures are a high point of late-Gothic sculpture. ☎ *07933/508* 🖸 *€1.50* ⊙ *Apr.–Oct., daily 9:15–5:30; Nov.–early Jan. and Mar., Tues.–Sun. 10–noon and 1–4.*

The **Fingerhutmuseum** is opposite the Herrgottskirche. *Fingerhut* is German for "thimble," and this delightful, privately run museum has thousands of them, some dating from Roman times. ☎ *07933/370* 🖸 *€1.50* ⊙ *Apr.–Oct., daily 9–6; Nov.–Mar., daily 1–4.*

The fascinating **Feuerwehrmuseum** (Firefighting Museum), with an impressive collection of old fire engines, lies 8 km (5 mi) north of Creglingen, within the stout castle walls of Schloss Waldmannshofen. ✉ *Waldmannshofen* ☎ *09335/674* 🖸 *€2.50* ⊙ *Daily 10–noon and 2–5.*

Where to Stay

¢   ⊞ **Heuhotel Ferienbauernhof.** For a truly off-the-beaten-track experience, book a space in the hayloft of the Stahl family's farm at Creglingen. Guests bed down in freshly turned hay in the farmhouse granary. Bed linen and blankets are provided. The overnight rate of €16 includes a cold supper and breakfast. For €21 you can swap the granary for one of three double rooms or even an apartment. Children are particularly well catered to, with tours of the farmyard and their own playground. ✉ *Frauental-Weidenhof 1, D–97993* ☎ *07933/378* 🖷 *07933/7515* ⊕ *www.ferienpension-heuhotel.de* ⌕ *Bicycles; no a/c, no room TVs* ⊟ *No credit cards* ⟲ *CP.*

Rothenburg-ob-der-Tauber

Fodor's Choice   *20 km (12 mi) southeast of Creglingen, 75 km (47 mi) west of Nürnberg.*
★

Rothenburg-ob-der-Tauber (literally, "red castle on the Tauber") is the kind of medieval town that even Walt Disney might have thought too picturesque to be true, with half-timber architecture galore and a wealth of fountains and flowers against a backdrop of towers and turrets. As late as the 17th century it was a small but thriving market town that had grown up around the ruins of two 12th-century churches destroyed by an earthquake. Then it was laid low economically by the havoc of the Thirty Years' War, and with its economic base devastated, the town slumbered until modern tourism rediscovered it. It's undoubtedly something of a tourist trap but genuine enough for all the hype. There really is no place quite like it. Whether Rothenburg is at its most appealing in summer, when the balconies of its ancient houses are festooned with flowers, or in winter, when snow lies on its steep gables, is a matter of taste. Few people are likely to find this extraordinary little survivor from another age anything short of remarkable.

a good walk

Sights are dotted around town, and the streets don't lend themselves to a particular route. However, the **Rathaus** ㉑ ►, on Rathausplatz, is a logical place to begin a tour. The **Herterichbrunnen** ㉒ is just steps away, on Marktplatz. Continue walking south on Schmiedgasse until you come to the **Plönlein**, a small square that is an excellent spot for taking pictures of a small half-timber house in the foreground and a city gate on each side. Go back along Schmiedgasse and turn left on Burggasse to visit the **Mittelalterliches Kriminalmuseum** ㉓. Opposite the museum walk up the Hofbronnengasse, to the **Puppen und Spielzeugmuseum** ㉔ on your left. Continue back to the Marktplatz. Turn left along Herrengasse and right into the small Kirchgasse, which leads you to the **Stadtpfarrkirche St. Jakob** ㉕, where you'll find a magnificent Riemenschneider altar. From the church, follow Klingengasse north to the church of **St. Wolfgang** ㉖, built into the defenses of the town. On the outside it blends into the forbidding **Stadtmauer** ㉗ (city wall). If you stay inside the city wall and turn left, you'll reach the **Reichsstadtmuseum** ㉘. If you turn right, you can continue along the wall for nearly a mile.

TIMING   Crowds will affect the pace at which you can tour the town. Early morning is the only time to appreciate the place in relative calm. The best times to see the mechanical figures on the Rathaus wall are in the evening, at 8, 9, or 10.

What to See

㉒ **Herterichbrunnen** (Herterich Fountain). A *Schäfertanz* (Shepherds' Dance) was performed around the ornate Renaissance fountain on the central Marktplatz whenever Rothenburg celebrated a major event. The dance is still done, though it's now for the benefit of tourists. It takes place in front of the Rathaus several times a year, chiefly at Easter, on Whitsunday, and in September. ✉ *Marktpl.*

㉓ **Mittelalterliches Kriminalmuseum** (Medieval Criminal Museum). The gruesome medieval implements of torture on display here are not for the faint-

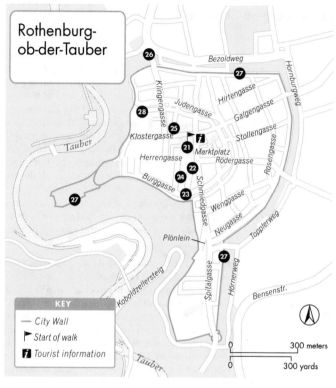

Rothenburg-
ob-der-Tauber

KEY
— City Wall
► Start of walk
🛈 Tourist information

hearted. The museum, the largest of its kind in Europe, also soberly documents the history of German legal processes in the Middle Ages. ⊠ *Burgg. 3* ☎ *09861/5359* 🎫 *€3.20* ⊙ *Apr.–Oct., daily 9:30–6; Nov. and Jan.–Mar., daily 2–4; Dec., daily 10–4.*

🐾 **㉔ Puppen und Spielzeugmuseum** (Doll and Toy Museum). This complex of medieval and baroque buildings houses more than 1,000 dolls, the oldest dating from 1780, the newest from 1940, as well as a collection of dollhouses, model shops, and theaters guaranteed to charm every youngster. ⊠ *Hofbronneng. 13* ☎ *09861/7330* 🎫 *€4* ⊙ *Jan. and Feb., daily 11–5; Mar.–Dec., daily 9:30–6.*

► **㉑ Rathaus.** Half of the town hall is Gothic, begun in 1240; the other half is neoclassic, started in 1572. Below the building are the **Historiengewölbe** (Historic Vaults; 🎫 *€2* ⊙ *Apr.–Oct., daily 9:30–5:30; Christmas market season, daily 1–4*), housing a museum that concentrates on the Thirty Years' War.

Great prominence is given to an account of the *Meistertrunk* (Master Drink), an event that will follow you around Rothenburg. It came about when the Protestant town was captured by Catholic forces. During the victory celebrations, the conquering general was embarrassed to find himself unable to drink a great tankard of wine in one go, as his manhood demanded. He volunteered to spare the town further destruction if any of the city councillors could drain the mighty 6-pint draft. The mayor took up the challenge and succeeded, and Rothenburg was preserved. The tankard itself is on display at the Reichsstadtmuseum. On the north side of the main square is a fine clock, placed there 50 years after the mayor's feat. A mechanical figure acts out the epic Master Drink daily on the hour from 11 to 3 and in the evening at 8, 9, and 10. The feat is also celebrated at two annual pageants, when townsfolk parade through the streets in 17th-century garb. The Rathaus tower offers a good view of the town. ⊠ *Rathauspl.*

28 **Reichsstadtmuseum** (Imperial City Museum). This city museum is two attractions in one. Its artifacts illustrate Rothenburg and its history. Among them is the great tankard, or *Pokal,* of the Meistertrunk. The setting of the museum is the other attraction; it's in a former Dominican convent, the oldest parts of which date from the 13th century. Tour the building to see the cloisters, the kitchens, and the dormitory; then see the collections. ⊠ *Klosterhof 5* ☎ *09861/939–043* ⊠ €3 ☉ *Apr.–Oct., daily 10–5; Nov.–Mar., daily 1–4.*

26 **St. Wolfgang.** A historic parish church of Gothic origins with a baroque interior, St. Wolfgang's is most notable for the way it blends into the forbidding city wall. ⊠ *Klingeng.* ☎ *09861/40492* ⊠ €1 ☉ *Mid-Mar.–Oct., daily 10–1 and 2–5.*

27 **Stadtmauer** (City Wall). Rothenburg's city walls are more than 2 km (1 mi) long and provide an excellent way of circumnavigating the town from above. The walls' wooden walkway is covered by eaves. Stairs every 200 or 300 yards provide ready access. There are superb views of the tangle of pointed and tiled red roofs and of the rolling country beyond.

25 **Stadtpfarrkirche St. Jakob** (Parish Church of St. James). The church has some notable Riemenschneider sculptures, including the famous *Heiliges Blut* (Holy Blood) altar. Above the altar a crystal capsule is said to contain drops of Christ's blood. There are three 14th- and 15th-century stained-glass windows in the choir, and the Herlin-Altar is famous for its 15th-century painted panels. ⊠ *Klosterg. 15* ☎ *09861/700–620* ⊠ €1.50 ☉ *Jan.–Mar. and Nov., daily 10–noon and 2–4; Apr.–Oct., daily 9–5:30; Dec., daily 10–5.*

Where to Stay & Eat

$$–$$$
Fodor'sChoice
★
✕▦ **Hotel Eisenhut.** It's fitting that the prettiest small town in Germany should have one of the prettiest small hotels. Every one of the 79 rooms is different—each with its own charming color scheme, most with antique furniture. Try for one on the top floor toward the back overlooking the old town and the Tauber River valley. The restaurant ($$$–$$$$), one of the region's best, offers impeccable service along with delicious food and a lovely view of the garden. In summer you'll want to eat on the terrace, surrounded by flowers. ⊠ *Herrng. 3–5, D–91541* ☎ *09861/ 7050* 🖷 *09861/70545* ⊕ *www.eisenhut.com* ⇖ *77 rooms, 2 suites* ⚘ *Restaurant, café, cable TV, piano bar; no a/c* ▭ *AE, DC, MC, V* ☉ *Closed early Jan.–early Mar.* ❙❶❙ *EP.*

★ **$–$$** ✕▣ **Hotel-Restaurant Burg Colmberg.** East of Rothenburg in Colmberg, this castle turned hotel maintains a high standard of comfort within its original medieval walls. As you enter the hotel, logs are burning in the fireplace of the entrance hall, illuminating an original Tin Lizzy from 1917. The restaurant Zur Remise ($–$$$) serves venison from the castle's own hunting grounds. ⊠ *Burg 1–3, D–91598 Colmberg, 18 km (11 mi) east of Rothenburg* ☎ *09803/91920* 🖷 *09803/262* ⊕ *www.burgcolmberg.de* ⇝ *24 rooms, 2 suites* ⌂ *Restaurant, cable TV, 9-hole golf course, bicycles, Weinstube, playground, no-smoking rooms; no a/c* ⊟ *AE, MC, V* ☾ *Closed Feb.* ¶Ol *CP.*

$$ ▣ **Romantik-Hotel Markusturm.** The Markusturm began as a 13th-century custom house, an integral part of the city defense wall, and has since developed over the centuries into an inn and staging post and finally into a luxurious small hotel. Some rooms are beamed, others have Laura Ashley decor or gaily painted bedsteads, and some have valuable antiques from the Middle Ages. ⊠ *Röderg. 1, D–91541* ☎ *09861/94280* 🖷 *09861/ 113* ⊕ *www.markusturm.de* ⇝ *23 rooms, 2 suites* ⌂ *Restaurant, cable TV, no-smoking rooms; no a/c* ⊟ *AE, DC, MC, V* ¶Ol *CP.*

$$ ▣ **Burg-Hotel.** This exquisite little hotel abuts the town wall and was once part of a Rothenburg monastery. Most rooms have a view of the Tauber Valley. All have plush furnishings, with antiques or fine reproductions. Ask for a room with a four-poster bed. Breakfast is served in good weather on a terrace adjoining the wall. ⊠ *Klosterg. 1–3, D–91541* ☎ *09861/94890* 🖷 *09861/948–940* ⊕ *www.burghotel.rothenburg.de* ⇝ *17 rooms* ⌂ *Cable TV, laundry service, Internet; no a/c* ⊟ *AE, DC, MC, V* ¶Ol *CP.*

$–$$ ▣ **Hotel-Gasthof Zum Rappen.** Close to the Würzburger Tor (a town gate) and first mentioned in town records in 1603, this tavern offers a surprisingly high standard of comfort. Guest rooms have a colorful, airy touch, with light woods and floral fabrics. Those in the more modern Hotel Zum Rappen just beside the Gasthof Zum Rappen have balconies overlooking a quiet courtyard and are a bit higher priced. ⊠ *Würzburger Tor 6 and 10, D–91541* ☎ *09861/95710* 🖷 *09861/6076* ⊕ *www.hotel-rappen.com* ⇝ *35 rooms* ⌂ *Restaurant, beer garden, Weinstube; no a/c* ⊟ *AE, DC, MC, V* ¶Ol *CP.*

$–$$ ▣ **Hotel Reichs-Küchenmeister.** Master chefs in the service of the Holy Roman Emperor were the inspiration for the name of this historic hotel-restaurant, one of the oldest trader's houses in Rothenburg. For five generations it's been run by the same energetic family. Rooms are furnished in a stylish mixture of old and new; light veneer pieces share space with heavy oak bedsteads and painted cupboards. ⊠ *Kirchpl. 8–10, D–91541* ☎ *09861/9700* 🖷 *09861/970–409* ⊕ *www.reichskuechenmeister.com* ⇝ *45 rooms, 2 suites, 3 apartments* ⌂ *Restaurant, cable TV, hot tub, sauna, pub, no-smoking rooms; no a/c* ⊟ *AE, MC, V* ¶Ol *CP.*

$ ▣ **Hotel-Gasthof Post.** This small family-run hotel, two minutes on foot from the eastern city gate, must be one of the friendliest in town. The rooms are simple but clean, and all have shower or bath. The Dreyer family is happy to help with questions about sights in and around Rothenburg. ⊠ *Ansbacherstr. 27, D–91541* ☎ *09861/6058* 🖷 *09861/ 7896* ⊕ *www.post-rothenburg.com* ⇝ *18 rooms* ⌂ *Restaurant, cable TV; no a/c* ⊟ *DC, MC, V* ¶Ol *CP.*

¢–$ ⊞ **Gasthof Klingentor.** This sturdy old staging post is outside the city walls but still within a 10-minute walk of Rothenburg's historic center. Rooms are spacious and furnished in the local rustic style. Its inexpensive restaurant serves substantial Franconian fare. A well-marked path for hiking or biking starts outside the front door. ⊠ *Mergentheimerstr. 14, D–91541* ☎ *09861/3468* ♨ *09861/3492* ⊕ *www.hotel-klingentor.de* ⊲ *20 rooms, 16 with bath* ⊜ *Restaurant, cable TV, beer garden, no-smoking rooms; no a/c, no TV in some rooms* ⊟ *MC, V* ⊚ *CP.*

Festivals

Highlights of Rothenburg's annual calendar are the **Meistertrunk Festival,** over the Whitsun weekend, celebrating the famous wager said to have saved the town from destruction in the Thirty Years' War, and the **Reichstadt-Festtage,** on the first weekend of September, commemorating Rothenburg's attainment of Free Imperial City status in 1274. Both are spectacular festivals, when thousands of townspeople and local horsemen reenact the events in period costume.

Sports & the Outdoors

At the **Golfclub Ansbach** (⊠ Rothenburgerstr. 35 ☎ 09803/600), in the nearby town of Colmberg, visitors are welcome to play the 9-hole golf course, just below the castle Burg Colmberg.

Happy Ballooning (☎ 09861/87888 ♨ 09861/86552 ⊕ www.happy-ballooning.de) conducts daily trips over Rothenburg and the countryside for €180.

Shopping

On the old and atmospheric premises of the **Kunstwerke Friese** (⊠ Grüner Markt 7–8, near the Rathaus ☎ 09861/7166) you'll find everything from cuckoo clocks and beer tankards to porcelain and glassware. If you are looking specifically for Hummel articles, try **Haus der Tausend Geschenke** (⊠ Obere Schmiedeg. 13 ☎ 09861/4801).

Käthe Wohlfahrt (⊠ Herrng. 1 ☎ 09861/4090) carries children's toys and seasonal decorations. The Christmas Village part of the store is a wonderland of mostly German-made toys and decorations. **Teddyland** (⊠ Herrng. 10 ☎ 09861/8904 ⊕ www.teddyland.de) has Germany's largest teddy bear population. More than 5,000 of them pack this extraordinary store. Children adore the place, but be prepared: these are pedigree teddies, and they don't come cheap.

Schillingsfürst

㉙ *20 km (12 mi) south of Rothenburg-ob-der-Tauber.*

The town's landmark is the **Schloss Schillingsfürst** (⊠ Schlossplatz 1 ☎ 09868/201), a baroque castle of the Princes of Hohenlohe-Schillingsfürst. Standing on an outcrop, it can be seen from miles away. If you visit the castle, try to arrive in time for one of the demonstrations of Bavarian falconry, held in the courtyard. You can watch eagles and falcons, on a single command, shoot down from the sky to catch their prey. The castle is open Tuesday–Sunday 10–6; the falconry show and guided tour of the castle (€7 for both) are March–October, daily at 11 and 3.

$ ✕⊡ **Die Post.** Stagecoaches carrying the mail—*Post* in German—used to stop here, giving this charming inn its name. Die Post has been owned by the same family since 1870. Rooms are comfortable and spacious. Enjoy lunch or dinner at the restaurant and try the fresh carp from the fish pond. They serve more than a dozen different kinds of spirits from their own distillery. ✉ *Rothenburger Str. 1, D–91583* ☎ *09868/9500* 🖷 *09868/950–250* ⊕ *www.rothenburg.de/hotel-post* ⇗ *14 rooms* ♿ *Restaurant, fishing, bicycles; no a/c* ▭ *DC, MC, V* ⦿⦿ *CP.*

$ ✕⊡ **Hotel Zapf An der Wörnitzquelle.** The Zapf family runs this pleasant country inn and its well-known restaurant ($–$$). Try the local specialty *Schillingsfürster Zigeuner Eintopf,* a delicious vegetable hot pot served with neck of pork. Ask for a room in the main house, a striking building with a stepped-gable Renaissance facade. Most rooms are in the less-lovely modern extension; they are nevertheless comfortable, well furnished, and have balconies. ✉ *Dombühlerstr. 9, D–91583 Schillingfurst* ☎ *09868/989–390* 🖷 *09868/5464* ⊕ *www.hotelzapf.de* ⇗ *17 rooms, 4 apartments* ♿ *Restaurant, café, cable TV, sauna, bicycles, beer garden; no a/c* ▭ *AE, DC, MC, V* ⦿⦿ *CP.*

Feuchtwangen

③⓪ *14 km (9 mi) south of Schillingsfürst.*

Feuchtwangen has a central market square with a fountain and an ideal ensemble of half-timber houses. Summer is the time to visit, when, from mid-June to mid-August, open-air theater productions are staged in the low, graceful cloisters next to the **Stiftskirche** (Collegiate Church; ✉ Kirchpl.). Inside the church is a 15th-century altar carved by Albrecht Dürer's teacher, Michael Wohlgemut.

The **Fränkisches Museum** has an excellent collection of Franconian folk arts and crafts, including more than 600 ceramics. ✉ *Museumstr. 19* ☎ *09852/2575* ⊕ *www.fraenkisches-museum.de* 🖃 *€2* ⦿ *Mar., Apr., Oct.–Dec., Wed.–Sun. 2–5; May–Sept., Wed.–Sun. 11–5.*

A state-run **casino** (✉ Am Casino 1 ☎ 09852/90060) has 12 roulette tables plus 4 tables for blackjack and 2 for poker. Admission is €2.50.

¢ ✕ **Ursel's Kleine Wirtschaft.** Ursel's "little tavern" is a typical Franconian establishment, cheap and cheerful, with a simple menu and a good selection of regional beers and wines. Friday is set aside for tripe dishes. ✉ *Herrenstr. 12* ☎ *09852/615–191* ⊕ *www.ukw-online.de* ▭ *No credit cards* ⦿ *No lunch.*

★ $–$$ ✕⊡ **Romantik Hotel Greifen Post.** The solid exterior of this historic house (formerly a staging post on the medieval route between Paris and Prague) gives little hint of the luxuries within. Ask for the 17th-century room with the four-poster bed. If that's taken, settle for the romantic Louis XVI–style room, the Biedermeier-style room, or the room designed in English country-house style. The indoor pool is within the original Renaissance walls of this ancient house. In the stylish gourmet restaurant ($–$$$) you can enjoy international specialties such as stuffed quail or delicate fish dishes. In the more intimate Kaminstube, you'll find more Franconian specialties on the menu. ⊠ *Marktpl. 8, D–91555* ☎ *09852/ 6800* 🖷 *09852/68068* ⊕ *www.greifen.de* ↔ *35 rooms* ♤ *Restaurant, cable TV, pool, sauna, bicycles, bar, meeting rooms, no-smoking rooms; no a/c* ⊟ *AE, DC, MC, V* |◎| *CP.*

Dinkelsbühl

★ ③ *12 km (7 mi) south of Feuchtwangen.*

Within the walls of Dinkelsbühl, a beautifully preserved medieval town, the rush of traffic seems a lifetime away. There's less to see here than in Rothenburg, and the mood is much less tourist-oriented. Like Rothenburg, Dinkelsbühl was caught up in the Thirty Years' War, and it also preserves a fanciful episode from those bloody times. Local lore says that when Dinkelsbühl was under siege by Swedish forces and in imminent danger of destruction, a young girl led the children of the town to the enemy commander and implored him in their name for mercy. The commander of the Swedish army is said to have been so moved by the plea that he spared the town. Whether or not it's true, the story is retold every year during the Kinderzech Festival, a pageant by the children of Dinkelsbühl during a 10-day festival in July. An annual open-air-theater festival takes place from mid-June until mid-August.

The **Stadtpfarrkirche St. Georg** (St. George's Parish Church) is the standout sight in town. At 235 feet in length it's large enough to be a cathedral, and it's among the best examples in Bavaria of the late-Gothic style. Note the complex fan vaulting that spreads sinuously across the ceiling. If you can face the climb, head up the 200-foot tower for amazing views over the jumble of rooftops. ⊠ *Marktpl.* ☎ *09851/2245* 🔁 *Tower €1.50* ⊙ *Church daily 9–noon and 2–6; tower May–Sept., Sat. 10–6, Sun. 1–6.*

⊙ The **Museum 3 Dimension** is the world's first museum of three-dimensional technology. Exhibits describe how its lifelike effects are achieved in photography, the cinema, and other art forms. Children enjoy the 3-D film run at various times during the day, as well as the 3-D art on display. ⊠ *Nördlinger Tor* ☎ *09851/6336* 🔁 *€7, family ticket €22* ⊙ *Apr.–Oct., daily 10–6; Nov.–late Dec. and early Jan.–Mar., weekends 11–4.*

Where to Stay & Eat

$$ ✕🖃 **Hotel Deutsches Haus.** This medieval inn, with a facade of half-timber gables and flower boxes, has many rooms fitted with antique furniture. One of them has a romantic four-poster bed. Dine beneath heavy oak beams in the restaurant (¢–$$), where you can try the local specialty, a type of grain called Dinkel. It's very nutritious and often served roasted with potatoes and salmon. ⊠ *Weinmarkt 3, D–91550* ☎ *09851/ 6058 or 09851/6059* 🖷 *09851/7911* ⊕ *www.deutsches-haus-dkb.de* ↔ *8 rooms, 2 suites* ♤ *Restaurant, cable TV, Internet, meeting rooms, no-smoking rooms; no a/c* ⊟ *AE, DC, MC, V* ⊙ *Closed 3 wks in Jan.* |◎| *CP.*

$–$$ ✕🖃 **Goldene Rose.** Since 1450 the inhabitants of Dinkelsbühl and their guests—among them Queen Victoria in 1891—have enjoyed good food and refreshing drinks in this half-timber house. Dark paneling in the restaurant creates the cozy atmosphere in which you can enjoy good regional cuisine, especially fish and game. Even in some of the modern bedrooms you will find half-timber walls. ✉ *Marktplatz 4, D–91550* ☎ *09851/57750* 📠 *09851/577–575* 🌐 *www.hotel-goldene-rose.com* 🛏 *31 rooms* 👍 *Restaurant, cable TV, Internet; no a/c* 💳 *AE, DC, MC* 🍽 *CP.*

$ ✕🏨 **Hotel Goldene Kanne.** This central hotel was built in 1690. Rooms are furnished with solid German oak; many have sitting-room corners with desks. It's particularly recommended for families (seven of the rooms have children's beds), although couples are also catered to with a special honeymoon suite. The cozy restaurant ($$–$$$) serves both local and international cuisine. ✉ *Segringerstr. 8, D–91550* ☎ *09851/57290* 📠 *09851/572–929* 🌐 *www.hotel-goldene-kanne.de* 🛏 *22 rooms, 2 suites* 👍 *Restaurant, cable TV, Internet; no a/c* 💳 *AE, DC, MC, V* 🍽 *CP.*

Shopping

Deleika (✉ Waldeck 33 ☎ 09857/97990) makes barrel organs to order, although it won't deliver the monkey! The firm also has a museum of barrel organs and other mechanical instruments. It's just outside Dinkelsbühl. Call ahead. At **Dinkelsbüler Kunst-Stuben** (✉ Segringer Str. 52 ☎ 08951/6750), the owner, Mr. Appelberg, sells his own drawings, paintings, and etchings of the town. **Jürgen Pleikies** (✉ Segringerstr. 53–55 ☎ 09851/7596) is doing his part to restore his town's former reputation for fine earthenware; he also offers courses at the potter's wheel. At **Weschcke und Ries** (✉ Segringerstr. 20 ☎ 09851/9439), Hummel porcelain figures share window space with other German porcelain and glassware.

Nördlingen

㉜ *32 km (20 mi) southeast of Dinkelsbühl, 70 km (43 mi) northwest of Augsburg.*

In Nördlingen the cry of "*So G'sell so*"—"All's well"—still rings out every night across the ancient walls and turrets. Sentries sound out the traditional message from the 300-foot tower of the central parish church of **St. Georg** at half-hour intervals between 10 PM and midnight. The tradition goes back to an incident during the Thirty Years' War, when an enemy attempted to slip into the town and was detected by a resident. You can climb the 365 steps up the tower—known locally as the Daniel—for an unsurpassed view of the town and countryside, including, on clear days, 99 villages. The ground plan of the town is two concentric circles. The inner circle of streets, whose central point is St. Georg, marks the earliest medieval boundary. A few hundred yards beyond it is the outer boundary, a wall built to accommodate expansion. Fortified with 11 towers and punctuated by five massive gates, it's one of the best-preserved town walls in Germany. ✉ *Marktpl.* 🎫 *Tower €1.50* ⏲ *Daily 9–dusk.*

Nördlingen lies in the center of a huge, basinlike depression, the **Ries,** that until the beginning of this century was believed to be the remains of an extinct volcano. In 1960 it was proven by two Americans that the 24-km-wide (15-mi-wide) crater was caused by a meteorite at least 1 km (½ mi) in diameter. The compressed rock, or *Suevit,* formed by the explosive impact of the meteorite was used to construct many of the town's buildings, including St. Georg's tower.

Nördlingen possesses one of Germany's largest steam railway engine museums, the **Bayerisches Eisenbahnmuseum,** adjacent to the railroad station. About a dozen times a year some of the old locomotives puff away on outings to Harburg. Call for a timetable. ⊠ *Am Hohen Weg 6* ☎ *09081/9808* ⊕ *www.bayerisches-eisenbahnmuseum.de* ☜ *€4* ☉ *Mar.–June, Sept., and Oct., Sun. 10–5; July and Aug., Tues.–Sat. noon–4, Sun. 10–5.*

Where to Stay & Eat

$–$$$ ✕ **Meyer's-Keller.** Choose between a table in the casual Stüble or in the fancier restaurant; in summer take a place under chestnut and plane trees in the beer garden. Prices in the excellent restaurant are higher, and the menu is suitably diverse and imaginative. The Rieser Surprise Menu, for €23, features only fresh products from local farms, while a gourmet menu for about double the price includes a glass of carefully selected wine with each of the four courses. Fish dishes include freshly delivered Atlantic specialties. ⊠ *Marienhöhe 8* ☎ *09081/4493* ⊕ *www.meyerskeller.de* ⊟ *AE, MC, V* ☉ *Closed Mon. and 2 wks in Feb. No lunch Tues.*

$–$$ ⊞ **Kaiserhof-Hotel-Sonne.** The great German poet Goethe stayed here, only one in a long line of distinguished guests starting with Emperor Friedrich III in 1487. The vaulted-cellar wine tavern is a reminder of those days. The three honeymoon suites are furnished in 18th-century style, with hand-painted four-poster beds. ⊠ *Marktpl. 3, D–86720* ☎ *09081/5067* ☷ *09081/29290* ⊕ *www.kaiserhof-hotel-sonne.de* ➪ *40 rooms* ♤ *Restaurant, cable TV, Weinstube; no a/c* ⊟ *AE, MC, V* ⦿I *CP.*

$ ⊞ **Braunes Ross.** This Gasthaus in the central square, directly opposite the city tower, was first mentioned in city archives in 1481 as "a place to eat and drink." The Haubner family bought the house 517 years later, in 1998, and renovated it from top to bottom. It now features modern rooms with cable TV, phones, and private baths; and a cozy, Bavarian-style restaurant. ⊠ *Marktplatz 12, D–86720* ☎ *09081/290–120* ☷ *0981/ 290–1228* ⊕ *www.hotel-braunes-ross.de* ➪ *14 rooms* ♤ *Restaurant, cable TV; no a/c* ⊟ *MC, V* ⦿I *CP.*

$ ⊞ **Hotel Goldene Rose.** This small, modern hotel is in the heart of town, ideal for those who wish to explore Nördlingen on foot. The in-house restaurant serves wholesome, inexpensive dishes. ⊠ *Baldingerstr. 42, D–86720* ☎ *09081/86019* ☷ *09081/24591* ⊕ *www.goldene-rose-noerdlingen.de* ➪ *17 rooms, 1 apartment* ♤ *Restaurant, cable TV, no-smoking rooms; no a/c* ⊟ *MC, V* ⦿I *CP.*

Festivals

From the end of June through July, an annual open-air **theater festival** takes place in front of the ancient walls of Nördlingen's Alter Bastei (Old Bastion).

Sports & the Outdoors

Ever cycled around a huge meteor crater? You can do just that in the **Nördlingen Ries,** the basinlike depression left by a meteor that hit the area in prehistoric times. The **Nördlingen tourist office** (☎ 09081/84116) has a list of 10 recommended bike routes, including one 47-km (29-mi) trail around the northern part of the meteor crater. **Radsport Boeckle** (⊠ Reimlingerstr. 19 ☎ 09081/801–040) rents bikes. For a spectacular view of the town and Ries crater, contact the local flying club, the **Rieser Flugsportverein** (☎ 09081/28963), for a ride in a light aircraft.

A traditional **horse race,** the Scharlachrennen, with medieval origins, is held annually in August. It's the central focus of an international show-jumping festival.

Shopping

Nördlingen has a **market** in the pedestrian shopping zone on Wednesday and Saturday. **Otto Wolf** (✉ Marktpl. ☎ 09081/4606) stocks a wide selection of Hummel figures at competitive prices.

en route At the point where the little Wörnitz River breaks through the Franconian Jura Mountains, 20 km (12 mi) southeast of Nördlingen, you'll find one of southern Germany's best-preserved medieval castles. **Schloss Harburg** was already old when it passed into the possession of the counts of Oettingen in 1295; before that time it belonged to the Hohenstaufen emperors. The ancient and noble house of Oettingen still owns the castle, and inside you can view treasures collected by the family. Among them are works by Tilman Riemenschneider, along with illuminated manuscripts dating as far back as the 8th century, and an exquisite 12th-century ivory crucifix. The castle is literally on B–25, which runs under it through a tunnel in the rock. ✉ *Harburg* ☎ *09080/96990* ⊕ *www.fuerst-wallerstein. de* ✉ *€4, including guided tour* ☉ *Apr.–Oct., Tues.–Sun. 10–5; Nov.–Mar., Tues.–Sun. 10–4.*

Donauwörth

③ *11 km (7 mi) south of Harburg, 41 km (25 mi) north of Augsburg.*

At the old walled town of Donauwörth, the Wörnitz River meets the Danube. If you're driving, pull off into the clearly marked lot on B–25, just north of town. Below you sprawls a striking natural relief map of Donauwörth and its two rivers. The oldest part of town is on an island. A wood bridge connects it to the north bank and the single surviving town gate, the Riederstor. North of the gate is one of the finest avenues of the Romantic Road: Reichsstrasse (Empire Street), so named because it was once a vital link in the Road of the Holy Roman Empire between Nürnberg and Augsburg. The Fuggers, a famous family of traders and bankers from Augsburg, acquired a palatial home here in the 16th century; its fine Renaissance-style facade, under a steeply gabled roof, stands proudly at the upper end of Reichsstrasse.

Donauwörth is the home of the famous Käthe Kruse dolls, beloved for their sweet looks and frilly, floral outfits. You can buy them at several outlets in town, and they have their own museum, where more than 130 examples dating from 1912 are displayed in a specially renovated monastery building, the **Käthe-Kruse-Puppen-Museum.** ✉ *Pflegstr. 21a* ☎ *0906/789–185* ✉ *€2* ☉ *May–Sept., Tues.–Sun. 11–5; Apr. and Oct., Tues.–Sun. 2–5; Nov.–Mar., Wed., and weekends 2–5.*

Where to Stay & Eat

$–$$ ⊞ **Parkhotel.** Members of the Landidyll chain of hotels have one feature in common: an idyllic location. This one qualifies with its position high above Donauwörth. Most rooms have floor-to-ceiling windows with panoramic views. All are decorated in bright pastel tones and have wicker chairs and sofas. ⊠ *Sternschanzenstr. 1, D–86609* ☎ *0906/706–510* 🖶 *0906/706–5180* ⊕ *www.parkhotel-donauwoerth.de* 🛏 *45 rooms* ⚘ *In-room data ports, cable TV, pool, bowling, Weinstube, no-smoking rooms; no a/c* ⊟ *AE, DC, MC, V* ⏐⊙⏐ *CP.*

Sports & the Outdoors

There's challenging canoeing on the four rivers (including the Danube) in and around Donauwörth. The **Kanu-Laden in Donauwörth** (⊠ Alte Augsburger Str. 12 ☎ 0906/8086) rents canoes and can provide professional advice and suggested routes.

Ulm

❸❹ *60 km (40 mi) west of Augsburg.*

Ulm isn't considered part of the Romantic Road, but it's definitely worth visiting, if only for one reason: its mighty Münster, which has the world's tallest church tower (536 feet). To get to Ulm from Donauwörth, take Highway B–16 west, connecting with B–28. Or, from Augsburg, take a 40-minute ride on one of the superfast ICE (Intercity Express) trains that run to Ulm every hour.

Ulm grew as a medieval trading city thanks to its location on the Danube River. Today the proximity of the Old Town to the river adds to Ulm's charm. In the Fisherman and Tanner quarters the cobblestone alleys and stone-and-wood bridges over the Blau (a small Danube tributary) are especially picturesque.

★ Ulm's **Münster,** the largest church in southern Germany, was unscathed by wartime bombing. It stands over the huddled medieval gables of Old Ulm, visible long before you hit the ugly suburbs encroaching on the Swabian countryside. Its single, filigree tower challenges the physically fit to plod 536 feet up the 768 steps of a giddily twisting spiral stone staircase to a spectacular observation point below the spire. On clear days the highest steeple in the world will reward you with views of the Swiss and Bavarian Alps, 160 km (100 mi) to the south. The Münster was begun in the late-Gothic age (1377) and took five centuries to build, with completion in the neo-Gothic years of the late 19th century. It contains some notable treasures, including late-Gothic choir stalls and a Renaissance altar. ⊠ *Münsterpl.* 🎫 *Tower €3, organ recitals €1.50* ⊙ *Daily 9–5; organ recitals May–Oct., daily at 11:30.*

The central **Marktplatz** is bordered by medieval houses with stepped gables. Every Wednesday and Saturday there's a market here. Summer or winter, farmers from the surrounding area arrive by 6 AM to erect their stands and unload their produce. Potatoes, vegetables, apples, pears, berries, honey, fresh eggs, poultry, homemade bread, and all kinds of other edible things are carefully displayed. Flowers of every color and variety are also available. If you plan to come, be sure to get here early; the market packs up around noon.

A reproduction of local tailor Ludwig Berblinger's flying machine hangs inside the elaborately painted **Rathaus.** In 1811 Berblinger, a tailor and local eccentric, cobbled together a pair of wings and made a big splash by trying to fly across the river. He didn't make it, but he grabbed a place in German history books for his efforts. ⊠ *Marktpl. 1.*

The **Ulmer Museum** (Ulm Museum), on the south side of Marktplatz, is an excellent natural history and art museum. Exhibits illustrate centuries of development in this part of the Danube Valley, and a modern art section has works by Kandinsky, Klee, Léger, and Lichtenstein. ⊠ *Marktpl. 9* ☎ *0731/161–4330* ⊠ *€2.50* ☉ *Tues., Wed., and Fri.–Sun. 11–5, Thurs. 11–8; guided tour Thurs. at 6.*

Einstein's home was a casualty of an Allied raid and was never rebuilt. The **Einstein Denkmal** (Einstein Monument; ⊠ Friedrich-Ebert-Str.), erected in 1979, marks the site opposite the main railway station.

German bread is world renowned, so it's not surprising that a national museum is devoted to bread making. The **Deutsches Brotmuseum** (German Bread Museum) is housed in a former salt warehouse, just north of the Münster. It's by no means as crusty or dry as some might fear, with some often-amusing tableaux illustrating how bread has been baked over the centuries. ⊠ *Salzstadelg. 10* ☎ *0731/69955* ⊕ *www. brotmuseum-ulm.de* ⊠ *€2.50* ☉ *Thurs.–Tues. 10–5, Wed. 10–8:30; guided tour Wed. at 7.*

Complete your visit to Ulm with a walk down to the banks of the Danube, where you'll find long sections of the **old city wall** and fortifications intact.

Where to Stay & Eat

★ **$–$$$** ✕ **Zur Forelle.** For more than 350 years, the aptly named Forelle, which means "trout," has stood over the small River Blau. The Blau flows through a large basin right under the restaurant, providing the perfect source for the amazingly fresh trout on the menu. If you're not a trout fan, there are 10 other fish dishes available, as well as excellent venison, in season. On a nice summer evening try to get a table on the small terrace. You'll literally sit over the small river, with a weeping willow on one side, half-timber houses all around you, and the towering cathedral in the background. ⊠ *Fischerg. 25* ☎ *0731/63924* ⊠ *0731/69869* ⊕ *www.zurforelle.com* ☰ *DC, MC, V.*

¢**–$$** ✕ **Zunfthaus der Schiffleute.** The sturdy half-timber Zunfthaus (Guildhall) has stood here for more than 500 years, first as a fishermen's pub and now as a charming tavern-restaurant. Ulm's fishermen had their guild headquarters here, and when the nearby Danube flooded, the fish swam right up to the door. Today they land on the menu. One of the "foreign" intruders on the menu is Bavarian white sausage, *Weisswurst.* The local beer is an excellent accompaniment. The minimum amount for credit cards is €25. ⊠ *Fischerg. 31* ☎ *0731/64411* ⊕ *www.zunfthaus-ulm. de* ☰ *AE, DC, MC, V.*

¢–$ ✕ **Barfüsser.** Ulm's leading brewery has two taverns, one just around the corner from the central Münsterplatz and the other across the river in Neu-Ulm (with a beer garden overlooking the Danube). The brewery's own Swabian pretzels are served in both taverns. ✉ *Lautenberg 1* ☎ *0731/602–1110* ✉ *Paulstr. 4* ☎ *0731/974–480* ▭ *AE, MC, V.*

$$ ✕▥ **Maritim.** Whether you come here to eat or stay, be prepared for incredible views. The elegant rooms and restaurants all offer breathtaking panoramas. In the main restaurant on the 16th floor, the international dishes are good and the view is amazing. Huge floor-to-ceiling windows reveal the Old Town of Ulm with the cathedral, the Danube, and the Swabian Alb all at your fingertips. The large, luxurious bar with cozy corners and live piano music every night has become a favorite with hotel and restaurant guests. Ask for weekend rates. ✉ *Basteistr. 40, D–89073* ☎ *0731/9230* ▤ *0731/923–1000* ⊕ *www.maritim.de* ➦ *287 rooms* ⌂ *2 restaurants, in-room data ports, cable TV with movies, pool, gym, massage, sauna, steam room, bar, meeting rooms, parking (fee), no-smoking rooms; no a/c* ▭ *AE, DC, MC, V* ▯❙ *EP.*

$ ▥ **Hotel am Rathaus/Reblaus.** The owner's love for antique paintings, furniture, and dolls is evident throughout this hotel. Some of the rooms have antique furniture. Part of the breakfast room is furnished like a private dining room with an antique settee and cupboard. In the annex, the half-timber Reblaus, most rooms have hand-painted cupboards. If you take a room toward the front, look up from your window and you'll see the cathedral with its huge spire a few hundred feet away. The hotel is behind the old historic Rathaus, on the fringe of the Old City, where you'll find more than a dozen restaurants and taverns. ✉ *Kronengasse 10, D–89073* ☎ *0731/968–490* ▤ *0731/968–4949* ⊕ *www.rathausulm.de* ➦ *34 rooms* ⌂ *Cable TV, no-smoking rooms; no a/c* ▭ *AE, DC* ▯❙ *CP.*

¢–$ ▥ **Zum Bäumle.** Hidden away in the little street just north of the mighty cathedral is this small half-timber hotel. The rooms are nice, but simply furnished. Some have a private shower and toilet; others share. The cozy wood-panel Weinstube, where you'll get solid Swabian food, is a favorite with locals. ✉ *Kohlgasse 6, D–89073* ☎ *0731/62287* ▤ *0731/602–2604* ✉ *baeumle.ulm@t-online.de* ➦ *21 rooms* ⌂ *Restaurant; no room phones, no room TVs, no a/c* ▭ *MC* ☾ *Restaurant closed weekends* ▯❙ *CP.*

Nightlife & the Arts

The mighty organ of the **Münster** can be heard in special recitals every Sunday at 11:15 from Easter until November.

Ulm has a lively after-hours scene. The piano bar in the **Hotel Maritim** (✉ Basteistr. 40 ☎ 0731/9230) has nightly music. Jazz fans make for the **Jazzkeller** (✉ Prittwitzstr. 10 ☎ 0731/601–210).

Augsburg

41 km (25 mi) south of Donauwörth, 60 km (37 mi) west of Munich.

Augsburg is Bavaria's third-largest city, after Munich and Nürnberg. It dates to 15 years before the birth of Christ, when a son of the Roman emperor Augustus set up a military camp here on the banks of the Lech River. The settlement that grew up around it was known as Augusta, a name Italian visitors to the city still call it. It was granted city rights in 1156, and 200 years later was first mentioned in municipal records of the Fugger family, who were to Augsburg what the Medici family was to Florence.

a good
walk

A walking tour of Augsburg is easy because signs on almost every street corner point the way to the chief sights. The signs are integrated into three color-charted tours devised by the tourist office. There's an office at Bahnhofstrasse 7, near the Hauptbahnhof, and on the south side of the central Rathausplatz. Pick up tour maps and begin your walk at Rathausplatz; the walk described below covers several of the sights described in the "green" tour.

On the eastern side of Rathausplatz rises the impressive bulk of the city's 17th-century town hall, the **Rathaus** ③⑤ ☞. Even taller than the two onion domes of the Rathaus is the nearby **Perlachturm** ③⑥. Follow the green signs north along Schlachthausgasse to the **Brecht Haus** ③⑦, where the playwright Bertolt Brecht was born; it's now a museum. Cross the nearby brook via the small bridge leading to Auf dem Rain and turn left into Barfüsserstrasse, leading to Jakoberstrasse. After 300 feet you'll find on the right the **Fuggerei** ③⑧, a 16th-century housing project. Following the green signs, recross the brook (which follows the route of a Roman-built canal), pass the small alley Hinterer Lech, and turn left down Mittlerer Lech. This will lead you to the **Holbein Haus** ③⑨, the home of painter Hans Holbein the Elder (at Vorderer Lech).

Continue farther south, recrossing the brook onto Oberer Graben, and head south through the Vogeltor, a Gothic city gate, to the southern extremities of the medieval defense wall. The gate here, the **Rotes Tor** ④⑩, was the main entrance to Augsburg in earlier centuries. Now follow the green route north through a small park enclosed by the remains of the ancient bastion. Continue north and you'll soon see the soaring tower of the Gothic church of **Sts. Ulrich and Afra** ④①, on Ulrichsplatz. Ulrichsplatz leads directly north into **Maximilianstrasse**, Augsburg's main thoroughfare. At No. 46 stands the **Schaezler Palais** ④②, home of two impressive art collections. The Herkulesbrunnen, the fountain in the center of the street outside the palace, is a symbolic work by the Renaissance sculptor Adrian de Vries. You can see a second de Vries fountain farther north on the same street. Just steps away, at Maximilianstrasse 36, is the sturdy **Fuggerhäuser** ④③, former home of Jakob Fugger, founder of the Fuggerei.

Wend your way across Zeugplatz, Bürgermeister-Fischer-Strasse, and Martin-Luther-Platz to Anna-Strasse. If you have time and energy, stop at the **Maximilian-Museum** ④④, on Phillipine-Welser-Strasse. The exquisite **St. Annakirche** ④⑤ is on Anna-Strasse. Head north from here, cross busy Karlstrasse, and go through the Kesselmarkt and across Johannisgasse to the gardens of the city cathedral, **Dom St. Maria** ④⑥. A short walk north along Frauentorstrasse takes you to the **Mozart-Haus** ④⑦, birthplace of Mozart's father, Leopold. By retracing your steps to the cathedral, into Hoher Weg and then Karolinenstrasse, you'll arrive within a few minutes back at Rathausplatz.

Augsburg

KEY

▶ *Start of walk*

🛈 *Tourist information*

TIMING   You'll need a complete day if you linger in any of the museums. Set aside at least two hours for the Schaezler Palais and a half hour each for the churches of Sts. Ulrich and Afra and the Dom St. Maria. There are plenty of opportunities en route for lunch or a coffee break.

What to See

❸⑦ Brecht Haus. This modest artisan's house was the birthplace of the renowned playwright Bertolt Brecht (1898–1956), author of *Mother Courage* and *The Threepenny Opera*. ⊠ *Auf dem Rain 7* 🎫 €1.50 ⊘ *Tues.–Sun. 10–5.*

❹⑥ Dom St. Maria (Cathedral of St. Mary). Augsburg's cathedral stands out within the city's panorama because of its square Gothic towers, which were built in the 9th century. A 10th-century Romanesque crypt, built in the time of Bishop Ulrich, also remains from the cathedral's early years. The 11th-century windows on the south side of the nave, depicting the prophets Jonah, Daniel, Hosea, Moses, and David, form the oldest cycle of stained glass in central Europe. Five important paintings by Hans Holbein the Elder adorn the altar.

The cathedral's treasures are on display at the **Diözesan Museum St. Afra** (⊠ Kornhausg. 3–5 🎫 €2.50 ⊘ Tues.–Sat. 10–5, Sun. 2–5). A short walk from the cathedral will take you to the quiet courtyards and small raised garden of the former episcopal residence, a series of 18th-century buildings in baroque and rococo styles that now serve as the Swabian regional government offices ⊠ *Dompl.* ☉ *Daily 9–dusk.*

❸❽ Fuggerei. This neat little settlement is the world's oldest social housing project, established by the Fugger family in 1516 to accommodate the city's deserving poor. The 104 homes still serve the same purpose; the annual rent of "one Rhenish guilder" (€1) hasn't changed, either. Residents must be Augsburg citizens, Catholic, and destitute through no fault of their own—and they must pray daily for their original benefactors, the Fugger family. ⊠ *Jacoberstr.*

❹❸ Fuggerhäuser. The 16th-century former home and business quarters of the Fugger family now houses a restaurant in its cellar and offices on the upper floors. In the ground-floor entrance are busts of two of Augsburg's most industrious Fuggers, Raymund and Anton. Beyond a modern glass door is a quiet courtyard with colonnades, the Damenhof (Ladies' Courtyard), originally reserved for the Fugger women. ⊠ *Maximilianstr. 36–38.*

❸❾ Holbein Haus. The rebuilt 16th-century home of painter Hans Holbein the Elder, one of Augsburg's most famous residents, is now a city art gallery, with changing exhibitions. ⊠ *Vorderer Lech 20* ☜ *Varies* ☉ *May–Oct., Tues., Wed., and Fri.–Sun. 10–5, Thurs. 10–8; Nov.–Apr., Tues., Wed., and Fri.–Sun. 10–4, Thurs. 10–8.*

❹❹ Maximilian-Museum. Augsburg's main museum houses a permanent exhibition of Augsburg arts and crafts in a 16th-century merchant's mansion. ⊠ *Philippine-Welser-Str. 24* ☜ €4 ☉ *Tues.–Sun. 10–5.*

Maximilianstrasse. This main shopping street was once a medieval wine market. Most of the city's sights are on this thoroughfare or a short walk away. Two monumental and elaborate fountains punctuate the long street. At the north end is the **Merkur,** designed in 1599 by the Dutch master Adrian de Vries (after a Florentine sculpture by Giovanni da Bologna), which shows winged Mercury in his classic pose. Farther up Maximilianstrasse is another de Vries fountain: a bronze **Hercules** struggling to subdue the many-headed Hydra.

❹❼ Mozart-Haus (Mozart House). Leopold Mozart, the father of Wolfgang Amadeus Mozart, was born in this bourgeois 17th-century residence; he was an accomplished composer and musician in his own right. The house now serves as a Mozart memorial and museum, with some fascinating contemporary documents on the Mozart family. ⊠ *Frauentorstr. 30* ☎ *0821/324–3894* ☜ €1.50 ☉ *Tues.–Sun. 10–5.*

❸❻ Perlachturm (Perlach Tower). This 258-foot-high plastered brick bell tower has foundations dating to the 11th century. Although it's a long climb to the top of the tower, the view over Augsburg and the countryside is worth the effort. ⊠ *Rathauspl.* ☎ *No phone* ☜ €1 ☉ *May–mid-Oct., daily 10–6; Dec., weekends noon–7.*

▶ ❸❺ Rathaus. Augsburg's city hall was Germany's largest when it was built in the early 17th century; it's now regarded as the finest Renaissance secular structure north of the Alps. Its **Goldenener Saal** (Golden Hall) was given its name because of its rich decoration—a gold-based harmony of wall frescoes, carved pillars, and coffered ceiling. ⊠ *Rathauspl.* ☎ *0821/502–0724* ⬚ *€1.50* ⊙ *10–6 on days when no official functions take place.*

40 Rotes Tor (Red Gate). The city's most important medieval entrance gate once straddled the main trading road to Italy. It provides the backdrop to an open-air opera and operetta festival in June and July. ⊠ *Eserwallstr.*

45 St. Annakirche (St. Anna's Church). This site was formerly part of a Carmelite monastery, where Martin Luther stayed in 1518 during his meetings with Cardinal Cajetanus, the papal legate sent from Rome to persuade the reformer to renounce his heretical views. Luther refused, and the place where he publicly declared his rejection of papal pressure is marked with a plaque on Maximilianstrasse. You can wander through the quiet cloisters, dating from the 14th century, and view the chapel used by the Fugger family until the Reformation. ⊠ *Anna-Str., west of Rathauspl.* ⊙ *Tues.–Sat. 10–12:30 and 3–6, Sun. noon–6.*

41 Sts. Ulrich and Afra. Standing at the highest point of the city, this basilica was built on the site of a Roman cemetery where St. Afra was martyred in AD 304. The original structure was begun in the late-Gothic style in 1467; a baroque preaching hall was added in 1710 as the Protestant church of St. Ulrich. St. Afra is buried in the crypt, near the tomb of St. Ulrich, a 10th-century bishop who helped stop a Hungarian army at the gates of Augsburg in the Battle of the Lech River. The remains of a third patron of the church, St. Simpert, are preserved in one of the church's most elaborate side chapels. From the steps of the magnificent altar, look back along the high nave to the finely carved baroque wrought-iron and wood railing that borders the entrance. As you leave, look into the separate but adjacent church of St. Ulrich, the former chapter house that was reconstructed by the Lutherans after the Reformation. ⊠ *Ulrichspl.* ⊙ *Daily 9–dusk.*

42 Schaezler Palais. This elegant 18th-century city palace was built by the von Liebenhofens, a family of wealthy bankers. Schaezler was the name of a baron who married into the family. Today the palace rooms contain the **Deutsche Barockgalerie** (German Baroque Gallery), a major art collection that features works of the 17th and 18th centuries. The palace adjoins the former church of a Dominican monastery. A steel door behind the palace's banquet hall leads into another world of high-vaulted ceilings, where the **Staatsgalerie Altdeutsche Meister,** a Bavarian state collection, highlights old-master paintings, among them a Dürer portrait of one of the Fuggers. ⊠ *Maximilianstr. 46* ⬚ *€2* ⊙ *Tues.–Sun. 10–5.*

Where to Stay & Eat

★ **$$–$$$$** ✕ **Die Ecke.** Situated on an *Ecke* (corner) of the small square right behind Augsburg's city hall, the Ecke is valued for the imaginative variety of its cuisine and the scope of its wine list. In season, the venison dishes are among Bavaria's best. The fish, in particular the *Zander* (green pike) or the trout sautéed in butter and lightly dressed with herbs and lemon, is magnificent and complemented nicely by the Riesling Gimmeldinger Meersspinne, the house wine for 40 years. ⊠ *Elias-Holl-Pl.*

2 ☎ *0821/510–600* ⊕ *www.restaurantdieecke.de* ⌕ *Reservations essential* ⊟ *AE, DC, MC, V.*

★ **$$** ✕🏨 **Steigenberger Drei Mohren Hotel.** Kings and princes, Napoléon and the Duke of Wellington, have all slept here. Except the modern fourth- and fifth-floor rooms, all the rooms maintain a luxurious, traditional style. Ask for weekend rates. Dining options include the elegant, Mediterranean-style restaurant Maximilian's ($$$) and Bistro 3M ($$). The Sunday Jazz Brunch at Maximilian's has been a town favorite since the late '90s. If ever you loved Paris in the springtime, you'll enjoy Bistro 3M; the atmosphere is thoroughly French, the food is excellent, and the service is very efficient. ⊠ *Maximilianstr. 40, D–86150* ☎ *0821/50360* 🖷 *0821/157–864* ⊕ *www.steigenberger.com* ⮎ *106 rooms, 5 suites* ⌕ *2 restaurants, cable TV, bar, meeting rooms, no-smoking rooms; no a/c on some floors* ⊟ *AE, DC, MC, V* ⦿*| EP.*

$–$$ ✕🏨 **Privat Hotel Riegele.** The hotel is just opposite the main railway station. The tavern-restaurant ($$–$$$), the Bräustüble, is a local favorite. The food is good German cooking and the service is efficient and friendly. Public rooms and some bedrooms have plush armchairs, deep-pile rugs, and heavy drapes. ⊠ *Viktoriastr. 4, D–86150* ☎ *0821/509–000* 🖷 *0821/517–746* ⊕ *www.hotel-riegele.de* ⮎ *27 rooms, 1 apartment* ⌕ *Restaurant, cable TV, meeting rooms; no a/c* ⊟ *AE, DC, MC, V* ⊘ *Restaurant closed Sun. evening* ⦿*| CP.*

$–$$ ✕🏨 **Romantikhotel Augsburger Hof.** A preservation order protects the beautiful Renaissance facade of this charming old Augsburg mansion, but rather than remake an old-world atmosphere inside, the owners opted for a cheerful but classic look with natural wood finishes and flowered curtains. The restaurant ($–$$$) serves excellent Maultaschen and other Swabian dishes. In season, try the duck. The cathedral is around the corner; the town center is a five-minute stroll. ⊠ *Auf dem Kreuz 2, D–86152* ☎ *0821/343–050* 🖷 *0821/343–0555* ⊕ *www.augsburger-hof.de* ⮎ *36 rooms* ⌕ *Restaurant, cable TV, sauna, no-smoking rooms; no a/c* ⊟ *AE, DC, MC, V* ⦿*| CP.*

$–$$ 🏨 **Dom Hotel.** Just around the corner from Augsburg's cathedral, this snug establishment has personality. Ask for one of the attic rooms, where you'll sleep under beam ceilings and wake to a rooftop view of the city. Or try for one of the rooms on the top floor that have a small terrace facing the cathedral. Even if you have to settle for a room in the apartment-house extension, you'll lack no comforts. A garden terrace borders the old city walls, and there's also an indoor pool, sauna, and solarium. ⊠ *Frauentorstr. 8, D–86152* ☎ *0821/343–930* 🖷 *0821/ 3439–3200* ⊕ *www.domhotel-augsburg.de* ⮎ *44 rooms, 8 suites* ⌕ *Cable TV, pool, sauna; no a/c* ⊟ *AE, DC, MC, V* ⦿*| CP.*

$ 🏨 **Hotel-Garni Schlössle.** From the main railroad station, a 10-minute ride on tram number 3 to the end of the line at Stadtbergem brings you to this friendly, family-run hotel. Soccer fans will enjoy the cozy Bavarian restaurant *Lamm* on the ground floor. Rooms under the steep eaves are particularly cozy. The location offers fresh country air, walks, and sporting facilities (a golf course is within a good tee-shot's range). ⊠ *Bauernstr. 37, Stadtbergen D–86391* ☎ *0821/243–930* 🖷 *0821/437–451* ⮎ *14 rooms* ⌕ *Cable TV; no a/c, no smoking* ⊟ *MC, V* ⊘ *Restaurant closed Sat.* ⦿*| CP.*

The Arts

Augsburg has chamber and symphony orchestras, as well as ballet and opera companies. The city stages a Mozart Festival of international stature in September. The **Kongresshalle** (✉ Göggingerstr. 10 ☎ 0821/324–2348) presents music and dance performances from September through July.

Augsburg's annual open-air **opera and operetta** (☎ 0821/502–070 city tourist office) season takes place in June and July. Productions move to the romantic inner courtyard of the **Fugger Palace** for part of July and August. Phone the city tourist office for details.

Children love the city's excellent **Augsburger Puppenkiste** (Puppet theater; ✉ Spitalg. 15, next to Rotes Tor ☎ 0821/4503–4540).

en route Leaving Augsburg southward on B–17—the southern stretch of the Romantic Road—you'll drive across the Lech battlefield, where Hungarian invaders were stopped in 955. Rich Bavarian pastures extend as far as the Lech River, which the Romantic Road meets at the historic town of Landsberg.

TOWARD THE ALPS

South of Augsburg, the Romantic Road climbs gradually into the foothills of the Bavarian Alps, which burst into view between Landsberg and Schongau. The route ends dramatically at the northern wall of the Alps at Füssen, on the Austrian border.

Landsberg am Lech

48 *35 km (22 mi) south of Augsburg, 58 km (36 mi) west of Munich.*

The town was founded by the Bavarian ruler Heinrich der Löwe (Henry the Lion) in the 12th century and grew wealthy from the salt trade. You'll see impressive evidence of Landsberg's early wealth among the solid old houses packed within its turreted walls; the early 18th-century **Historisches Rathaus** (Old Town Hall) is one of the finest in the region. Today Landsberg is a lively and prosperous town, a good place to stop, look, eat, and sleep.

Where to Stay & Eat

¢–$ ✗**Gasthof zum Mohren.** Good Bavarian food at reasonable prices has been served at this restaurant on the left side of the Rathaus since 1436. Whereas at the beginning of the Romantic Road, in Franconia, wine is the focus, you are now definitely in beer country. Here, you can choose from 12 kinds of beer, 5 on tap. In summer take a seat in the Biergarten. ✉ *Hauptplatz 148* ☎ *08191/911–880* 🖷 *08191/32132* ⊕ *www.zum-mohren.de* ▭ *No credit cards.*

¢–$ ✗**Zederbräu.** This typical historic Bavarian restaurant is on the right side of the Rathaus. You have a choice of tasty food and wine from many countries, not just Bavaria. ✉ *Hauptplatz 155* ☎ *08191/42241* 🖷 *08191/ 944–122* ▭ *MC, V.*

$ 🏠**Hotel Goggl.** Overstuffed armchairs make you feel welcome as you enter this hotel, just off the central main square. The rooms are airy with light-brown furniture. If you want to feel like a duke, take the suite Fürsten-zimmer (Duke's Room), where you can have your breakfast served on a private terrace. A public garage is just behind the hotel. Book ahead, especially during trade fairs and the Oktoberfest, when many people stay here instead of in Munich, which is only 60 km (36 mi) away. ⊠ *Hubert von Herkomerstr. 19, D–86899* ☎ *08191/3240* 🖶 *08191/324–100* ⊕ *www.goggl.de* 🛏 *65 rooms* ⚲ *Cable TV, steam room, no-smoking rooms; no a/c* ☐ *AE, DC, MC, V* ⦿| *CP.*

Schongau

🟠 *28 km (17 mi) south of Landsberg, 70 km (43 mi) southwest of Munich.*

Schongau, founded in the 11th century at about the same time as Landsberg, has virtually intact wall fortifications, complete with towers and gates. In medieval and Renaissance times, the town was an important trading post on the route from Italy to Augsburg. The steeply gabled 16th-century Ballenhaus was a warehouse before it was elevated to the rank of Rathaus.

☺ A popular **Märchenwald** "fairy-tale forest" lies 1½ km (1 mi) outside Schongau, suitably set in a clearing in the woods. It comes complete with mechanical models of fairy-tale scenes, deer enclosures, and an old-time miniature railway. ⊠ *Diessenerstr. 6* ☎ *08861/7527* ⊕ *www.schongauer-maerchenwald.de* 🎫 *€3.50* ⦿ *Apr. and Oct., daily 9–6; May–Sept., daily 9–7.*

Where to Stay & Eat

$ ✕🗔 **Hotel Holl.** The Alpine-style hotel, on wooded slopes, is a 10-minute stroll from the town center. If you are looking for peace and quiet, this is the place to come. The rooms have great views, and the restaurant ($–$$) features regional specialties including light and tasty fish dishes, using the catch from local rivers and lakes in season. ⊠ *Altenstädter-str. 39, D–86956* ☎ *08861/23310* 🖶 *08861/233–112* ⊕ *www.hotel-holl-schongau.de* 🛏 *21 rooms, 1 suite* ⚲ *Restaurant, cable TV, meeting rooms, no-smoking rooms; no a/c* ☐ *AE, DC, MC, V* ⦿ *Restaurant closed Fri.–Sun., and late Dec. and Jan.* ⦿| *CP.*

Sports & the Outdoors

The rolling meadowlands that form the foothills of the Bavarian Alps are ideal for hikers and cyclists. Tour operators focus on five main routes, providing luggage transport and arranging for accommodations. The **Schongau Verkehrsamt** (☎ *08861/7216*) has details.

---

off the
beaten
path

Fodor'sChoice
★

WIESKIRCHE – This church—a glorious example of German rococo architecture—stands in an Alpine meadow just off the Romantic Road near the village of Steingaden, 9 km (5½ mi) east of Rottenbuch, on the Steingaden road. Its yellow-and-white walls and steep red roof are set off by the dark backdrop of the Trauchgauer Mountains. The architect Dominicus Zimmermann, former mayor of Landsberg and creator of much of that town's rococo architecture, built the church in 1745 on the spot where six years earlier a local woman claimed to have seen tears running down the face of a picture of Christ. Although the church was dedicated as the Pilgrimage Church of the Scourged Christ, it's now known simply as the Wieskirche (Church of the Meadow). Visit it on a bright day if you can, when light streaming through its high windows displays the full glory of the glittering interior. A complex oval plan is animated by brilliantly colored stuccowork, statues, and gilt. A luminous ceiling fresco completes the decoration. Concerts are presented in the church from the end of June through the beginning of August. Contact the **VERKEHRSAMT** (☎ 08861/7216) in Schongau for details. A Free C Daily 8–dusk.

Schwangau

50 *18 km (11 mi) south of Steingaden, 105 km (65 mi) southwest of Munich.*

The lakeside resort town of Schwangau is an ideal center from which to explore the surrounding mountains. Here you'll encounter the heritage of Bavaria's famous 19th-century King Ludwig II. Ludwig spent much of his youth at Schloss Hohenschwangau; it's said that its neo-Gothic atmosphere provided the primary influences that shaped his wildly romantic Schloss Neuschwanstein, the fairy-tale castle he built across the valley after he became king.

The two castles are 1 km (½ mi) from each other and about 2 km (1 mi) from the center of Schwangau. To visit them, follow the road signs toward KONIGSCHLÖSSER (King's castles). After 2 mi you come to Hohenschwangau, a small village consisting of a few houses, some good hotels, and five clearly marked spacious parking lots (parking fee €4). You have to park here. Buy your entrance tickets for one or both castles at the ticket center in the village.

To get to Schloss Neuschwanstein, you can walk up one of the clearly marked paths (about a 25-minute uphill walk); you can use one of the horse-drawn carriages that leave from Hotel Müller (uphill €5, downhill €2.50); or you can take the small bus that leaves from the Hotel Lisl (uphill €1.80, downhill €1), and takes you halfway up the hill to an outlook called Aussichtspunkt Jugend. From there it's a 10-minute walk to the castle.

To get to Schloss Hohenschwangau you can take a 15-minute walk up either of two clearly marked paths; or you can take one of the horse drawn carriages that leave from Hotel Müller (uphill €3.50, downhill €1.50).

★ **51** **Schloss Hohenschwangau** was built by the knights of Schwangau in the 12th century. It was remodeled later by Ludwig's father, the Bavarian crown prince (and later king) Maximilian, between 1832 and 1836. Unlike Ludwig's more famous castle across the valley, Neuschwanstein, the somewhat garishly yellow Schloss Hohenschwangau has the feeling of a noble home, where comforts would be valued as much as outward splendor. It was here that the young Ludwig met the composer Richard Wagner. Their friendship shaped and deepened the future king's interest in theater, music, and German mythology—the mythology Wagner

THE FAIRY-TALE KING

KING LUDWIG II (1845–86), the enigmatic presence indelibly associated with Bavaria, was one of the last rulers of the Wittelsbach dynasty, which ruled Bavaria from 1180 to 1918. Though his family had created grandiose architecture in Munich, Ludwig II disliked the city and preferred isolation in the countryside, where he constructed monumental edifices born of fanciful imagination and spent most of the royal purse on his endeavors. Although he was also a great lover of literature, theater, and opera (he was Richard Wagner's great patron), it is his fairy-tale-like castles that are his legacy.

Ludwig II reigned from 1864 to 1886, all the while avoiding political duties whenever possible. By 1878 he had completed his Schloss Linderhof retreat and immediately began Schloss Herrenchiemsee, a tribute to Versailles and Louis XIV (⇨ Chapter 2). The grandest of his extravagant projects is Neuschwanstein, one of Germany's top attractions and concrete proof of the king's eccentricity. In 1886, before Neuschwanstein was finished, members of the government became convinced that Ludwig had taken leave of his senses. A medical commission declared the king insane and forced him to abdicate. Within two days of incarceration in the Berg Castle, on Starnbergersee (⇨ Side Trips from Munich in Chapter 1), Ludwig and his doctor were found drowned in the lake's shallow waters. Their deaths are still a mystery. A poor leader, but still a visionary, Ludwig II is memorialized in a musical based in Füssen, Ludwig II—Longing for Paradise.

---

drew upon for his *Ring* cycle of operas. 🎫 €8, including guided tour ☎ 08362/930–830 🖨 08362/930–8320 ⊕ www.hohenschwangau.de ☾ Apr.–Sept., daily 9–6; Oct.–Mar., daily 10–4.

❺❷ **Schloss Neuschwanstein** was conceived by a set designer instead of an ar-
Fodor'sChoice chitect, thanks to Ludwig's deep love of the theater. The castle soars from
★ its mountainside like a stage creation—it should hardly come as a surprise that Walt Disney took it as the model for his castle in the movie
Sleeping Beauty and later for the Disneyland castle itself.

The life of the proprietor of this spectacular castle reads like one of the great Gothic mysteries of the 19th century, and the castle symbolizes that life. Yet during the 17 years from the start of Schloss Neuschwanstein's construction until his death, the king spent less than six months in the country residence, and the interior was never finished. The Byzantine-style throne room is without a throne; Ludwig died before one could be installed. The walls of the rooms leading to Ludwig's bedroom are painted with murals depicting characters from Wagner's operas—Siegfried and the Nibelungen, Lohengrin, Tristan, and others. Ludwig's bed and its canopy are made of intricately carved oak. A small corridor behind the bedroom was made as a ghostly grotto, reminiscent of

Wagner's *Tannhäuser*. **Chamber concerts** (☎ 08362/81980) are held in September in the gaily decorated minstrels' hall—one room, at least, that was completed as Ludwig conceived it. On the walls outside the castle's gift shop are plans and photos of the castle's construction. There are some spectacular walks around the castle. The delicate **Marienbrücke** (Mary's Bridge) is spun like a medieval maiden's hair across a deep, narrow gorge. From this vantage point there are giddy views of the castle and the great Upper Bavarian Plain beyond. ⊠ *Neuschwansteinstr. 20* ☎ *08362/81035 or 08362/81801* ⊕ *www.neuschwanstein.com* ✉ *€8, including guided tour* ☉ *Oct.–Mar., daily 10–4; Apr.–Sept., daily 9–6.*

If you plan to visit Hohenschwangau or Neuschwanstein, bear in mind that more than 1 million people pass through the two castles every year. If you visit in summer, get there early. The best time to see either castle without waiting a long time is a weekday between January and April. The prettiest time, however, is in fall. Get your ticket at the center near the parking lot before going up to the castle. The average wait between buying a ticket and entering the castle is one hour. With a deposit or credit card number you can book your tickets in advance through **Verwaltung Hohenschwangau** (⊠ Alpseestr. 12, D–87645 Hohenschwangau ☎ 08362/930–830 ☎ 08362/930–8320 ⊕ www.hohenschwangau. de). If you book tickets in advance, there's a €1.60 processing fee per ticket; a written confirmation will follow. You can cancel or change entrance times up to two hours before the confirmed entrance time. The processing fee will not be returned.

Where to Stay & Eat

$$–$$$ ✕⌧ **Schlosshotel Lisl und Jägerhaus.** These jointly run 19th-century properties are across the street from one another, and both share views of the nearby castles. The intimate Jägerhaus has five suites and six double rooms, all decorated with floral wallpaper and drapery. The bathrooms have swan-motif golden fixtures. The Lisl's rooms have bright blue carpeting and fabrics. Lisl's restaurant, Salon Wittelsbacher, provides a view of Neuschwanstein as well as a tasty dish of *Tafelspitz* (boiled beef with horseradish). ⊠ *Neuschwansteinstr. 1–3, D–87643* ☎ *08362/ 8870* ☎ *08362/81107* ⊕ *www.lisl.de* ➳ *42 rooms, 5 suites* ⌂ *2 restaurants, cable TV, bar, lobby lounge; no a/c* ▭ *AE, MC, V* ❢⊙❢ *EP.*

$$ ✕⌧ **Hotel Müller.** Between the two Schwangau castles, the Müller fits beautifully into the stunning landscape, its creamy Bavarian baroque façade complemented by the green mountain forest. Inside, the baroque influence is everywhere, from the finely furnished bedrooms to the chandelier-hung public rooms and restaurant ($). The mahogany-paneled, glazed veranda (with open fireplace) provides a magnificent view of Hohenschwangau Castle. Round your day off with a local specialty such as the *Allgäuer Lendentopf* (sirloin) served with spaetzle. ⊠ *Alpseestr. 16, Hohenschwangau D–87643* ☎ *08362/81990* ☎ *08362/819–913* ⊕ *www.hotel-mueller.de* ➳ *39 rooms, 4 suites* ⌂ *2 restaurants, cable TV, bar; no a/c* ▭ *AE, DC, MC, V* ☉ *Closed Jan. and Feb.* ❢⊙❢ *CP.*

Sports & the Outdoors

Schwangau's mountain, the Tegelberg, offers challenging hiking in spring, summer, and fall and good skiing in winter. There's a cable car (€14 round-trip) and six ski lifts. A summer sledge-run snakes for 1 km (½ mi) down the lower slopes (six rides for €9.50). At the bottom of the run is a children's playground and beer garden. Hikers can combine a stiff mountain walk with a tour of the geographic, geological, zoological, and historical landscape of this region by following the **Kulturpfad Schutzengelweg,** a trail marked by placards explaining points of interest. The trail climbs to 5,670 feet and takes about 2½ hours to complete.

Füssen

🟢 *5 km (3 mi) southwest of Schwangau, 110 km (68 mi) south of Munich.*

Füssen is beautifully located at the foot of the mountains that separate Bavaria from the Austrian Tyrol. The Lech River, which accompanies much of the final section of the Romantic Road, embraces the town as it rushes northward. The town's **Hohes Schloss** (High Castle) is one of the best-preserved late-Gothic castles in Germany. It was built on the site of the Roman fortress that once guarded this Alpine section of the Via Claudia, the trade route from Rome to the Danube. Evidence of Roman occupation of the area has been uncovered at the foot of the nearby Tegelberg Mountain, and the **excavations** next to the Tegelberg cable-car station are open for visits daily. The Hohes Schloss was the seat of Bavarian rulers before Emperor Heinrich VII mortgaged it and the rest of the town to the bishop of Augsburg for 400 pieces of silver. The mortgage was never redeemed, and Füssen remained the property of the Augsburg episcopate until secularization in the early 19th century. The bishops of Augsburg used the castle as their summer Alpine residence. It has a spectacular 16th-century **Rittersaal** (Knights' Hall) with a carved ceiling, and a princes' chamber with a Gothic tile stove. ✉ *Magnuspl. 10* ☎ *08362/940–162* 🎫 *€2.50* 🕐 *Apr.–Oct., Tues.–Sun. 11–4; Nov.–Mar., Tues.–Sun. 2–4.*

The summer presence of the bishops of Augsburg ensured that Füssen received an impressive number of baroque and rococo churches. Füssen's **Rathaus** (✉ Lechalde 3) was once a Benedictine abbey, built in the 9th century at the site of the grave of St. Magnus, who spent most of his life ministering in the area. A Romanesque crypt beneath the baroque abbey church has a partially preserved 10th-century fresco, the oldest in Bavaria. In summer, chamber concerts are held in the high-ceiling baroque splendor of the former abbey's **Fürstensaal** (Princes' Hall). Program details are available from the tourist office.

Füssen's main shopping street, called **Reichenstrasse,** was, like Augsburg's Maximilianstrasse, once part of the Roman Via Claudia. This cobblestone walkway is lined with high-gabled medieval houses and backed by the bulwarks of the castle and the easternmost buttresses of the Allgäu Alps.

Where to Stay & Eat

¢–$ ✕ **Markthalle.** This is a farmers' market where you can grab a quick bite and drink at very reasonable prices. Try the fish soup. There are even a few tables. The building started in 1483 as the *Kornhaus* (grain storage) and then became the *Feuerhaus* (fire station). ⊠ *Schrannenplatz 1* 🗎 *No credit cards* ⊙ *Weekdays 8–6, Sat. 8–noon.*

$–$$ ✕🖭 **Alpen-Schlössle.** A Schlössle is a small castle, and although this comfortable, rustic hotel doesn't quite qualify, it does have a solitary, corner tower. The elegant little restaurant ($–$$$; closed Tuesday) is prized for its imaginative cuisine, which is based on local products such as beef and veal from the Allgäu region. For fine-weather dining there's a very attractive, sunny terrace. The small rooms are richly furnished with Russian pine, larch, and cherrywood. If you take the suite, you'll have your own large, sunny terrace. ⊠ *Alatseestr. 28, D–87629* 🕾 *08362/4017* 🖷 *08362/39847* ⊕ *www.hotel-alpenschloessle.com* 🖙 *11 rooms, 1 suite* ⅃ *Restaurant, cable TV; no a/c* 🗎 *MC, V* ⅈ⊙ⅈ *CP.*

$–$$ ✕🖭 **Hotel Hirsch.** A mother-and-daughter team provides friendly service at this traditional Füssen hotel. Outside the majestic building is its trademark stag (*Hirsch* in German); inside, the decor is Bavarian. You can stay in the King Ludwig room with his pictures on the walls and books about him to read, or stay with King Maximilian or with Spitzweg, a famous German painter who painted in Füssen. In both restaurants you'll be served an interesting variety of seasonal and local specialties. ⊠ *Kaiser-Maximilian-Pl. 7, D–87629* 🕾 *08362/93980* 🖷 *08362/939– 877* ⊕ *www.hotelhirsch.de* 🖙 *58 rooms* ⅃ *2 restaurants, cable TV, pub, meeting rooms, no-smoking rooms; no a/c* 🗎 *AE, DC, MC, V* ⅈ⊙ⅈ *CP.*

$ ✕🖭 **Altstadthotel Zum Hechten.** Geraniums flower most of the year on this comfortable inn's balconies. It's one of the town's oldest lodgings and is directly below the castle. In one of the two restaurants ($), which have sturdy, round tables and colorfully frescoed walls, vegetarian meals are served. ⊠ *Ritterstr. 6, D–87629* 🕾 *08362/91600* 🖷 *08362/916– 099* ⊕ *www.hotel-hechten.com* 🖙 *36 rooms, 30 with bath or shower* ⅃ *2 restaurants, cable TV, gym, sauna, bowling; no a/c* 🗎 *AE, MC* ⅈ⊙ⅈ *CP.*

Sports & the Outdoors

Pleasure boats cruise Forggensee lake mid-June–early October. Alpine winds ensure good sailing and windsurfing. The **Forgensee-Yachtschule** (⊠ Seestr. 10, Dietringen 🕾 08367/471 ⊕ www.segeln-info.de) offers sailing courses of up to two weeks' duration, with hotel or apartment accommodations. There are also boatyards and jetties with craft for rent at Waltenhofen.

There's good downhill skiing in the mountains above Füssen. Cross-country enthusiasts are catered to with more than 20 km (12 mi) of trails. Füssen's highest peak, the Tegelberg, has a ski school, **Skischule Tegelberg A. Geiger** (🕾 08362/8455 ⊕ www.skischule-tegelberg.de).

THE ROMANTIC ROAD A TO Z

To research prices, get advice from other travelers, and book travel arrangements, visit www.fodors.com.

AIRPORTS

The major international airports serving the Romantic Road are Frankfurt and Munich. Regional airports include Nürnberg and Augsburg.

BICYCLE TOURS

From April through September, Velotours offers a five-day trip from Würzburg to Rothenburg for €320 per person and a five-day trip from Rothenburg to Donauwörth for €320 per person. These two trips can be combined for a nine-day tour for €640. The tour operator Alpenland-Touristik offers several guided six- to eight-day bike tours starting from Landsberg am Lech into the Alpine foothills. Please call for exact dates.

🚲 **Velotours** ✉ Ernst-Sachsstr. 1, D–78467 Konstanz ☎ 07531/98280 📠 07531/982–898 ⊕ www.velotours.de. **Alpenland–Touristk** ✆ Box 10-13-13, D-86899 Landsberg ☎ 08191/308-620 📠 08191/4913 ⊕ www.radler-paradies.de.

BUS TRAVEL

From April through October daily bus service covers the northern stretch of the Romantic Road, leaving Frankfurt at 8 AM and arriving in Munich at 8 PM; daily buses in the opposite direction leave Munich at 9 AM and arrive in Frankfurt at 8:30 PM. A second bus covers the section of the route between Dinkelsbühl and Füssen. Buses leave Dinkelsbühl daily at 4:15 PM and arrive in Füssen at 8 PM. In the other direction, buses leave Füssen daily at 8 AM, arriving in Dinkelsbühl at 12:45 PM. All buses stop at the major sights along the road. A Frankfurt–Füssen ticket costs €69 (€137 round-trip). Deutsche Touring also operates six more extensive tours along the Romantic Road and along the region's other major holiday route, the Burgenstrasse (Castle Road), which ends at Rothenburg. The tours range from two to five days and cost from €256 to €770. Reservations are essential; contact Deutsche Touring. Local buses cover much of the route but are infrequent and slow.

🚌 **Deutsche Touring** ✉ Am Römerhof 17, D-60486 Frankfurt am Main ☎ 069/790-350 ⊕ www.touring-germany.com.

CAR RENTAL

🚗 **Avis** ✉ Proviantbachstr. 30, Augsburg ☎ 0821/38241 ✉ Nürnberger-Str. 90, Würzburg ☎ 0931/24043. **Europcar** ✉ Pilgerhausstr. 24, Augsburg ☎ 0821/346-510 ✉ Am Hauptbahnhof, Würzburg ☎ 0931/12060 ✉ Gattingerstr. 5, Würzburg ☎ 0931/200-480. **Hertz** ✉ Werner-Heisenstr. 11, Königsbrunn [near Augsburg] ☎ 08231/34930 ✉ Rottendorferstr. 40-42, Würzburg ☎ 0931/784-6913. **Sixt** ✉ Viktoriastr. 1 [in Hauptbahnhof], Augsburg ☎ 0821/349-8502 ✉ Bahnhofpl. 4 [in Hauptbahnhof], Würzburg ☎ 0931/465-1406.

CAR TRAVEL

Würzburg is the northernmost city of the Romantic Road and the natural starting point for a tour. It's on the Frankfurt–Nürnberg autobahn, A–3, and is 115 km (71 mi) from Frankfurt. If you're using Munich as a gateway, Augsburg is 60 km (37 mi) from Munich via A–8.

The Romantic Road is most easily traveled by car, starting from Würzburg as outlined above and following country highway B–27 south to meet Roads B–290, B–19, B–292, and B–25 along the Wörnitz River.

The roads are busy and have only two lanes, so figure on covering no more than 70 km (40 mi) each hour, particularly in summer. The 40-km (24-mi) section of the route that's the least "romantic," the A–2 between Augsburg and Donauwörth, is also heavily used by trucks and other large vehicles traveling to northern Bavaria, so expect delays. For route maps, with roads and sights highlighted, contact the Tourist-Information Land an der Romantischen Strasse or Touristik-Arbeitsgemeinschaft Romantische Strasse (⇨ Visitor Information).

TOURS

All the cities and towns on the Romantic Road offer guided tours, either on foot or by bus. Details are available from local tourist information offices. Following is a sample of the more typical tours.

AUGSBURG Augsburg has self-guided walking tours, with routes posted on color-coded signs throughout the downtown area. From mid-May to mid-October a bus tour (€9.50) starts from the Rathaus at 2, from Thursday through Sunday, and walking tours (€4.50) set out from the Rathaus daily at 10:30. From mid-October until May a walking tour takes place every Saturday at 2. All tours are conducted in German and English. The tourist office organizes morning and afternoon trips into the countryside north and south of Augsburg.

DINKELSBÜHL The watchman does a nightly round at 9 from April through October, and though he doesn't give official tours, he's always happy to answer questions (but don't expect a reply in fluent English). Daily guided tours of Dinkelsbühl in horse-drawn carriages (April–October) cost €4.

ROTHENBURG-OB-DER-TAUBER The costumed night watchman conducts a nightly tour of the town, leading the way with a lantern. From April to October and in December, tours in English begin at 8 and 9:30 and cost €3 (a daytime tour begins at 2).

ULM The tourist office's 90-minute tour includes a visit to the Münster, the Old Town Hall, the Fischerviertel (Fishermen's Quarter), and the Danube riverbank. From May through October there are tours at 10 and 2:30 Monday–Saturday, 11 and 2:30 Sunday; from November through April tours are at 10 on Saturday and 11 on Sunday. The departure point is the tourist office on Münsterplatz; the cost is €5. From May to mid-October you can view Ulm from on board the motor cruiser *Ulmer Spatz*. There are up to five 50-minute cruises daily (€5). The boats tie up at the Metzgerturm, a two-minute walk from the city hall.

WÜRZBURG Two-hour bus tours of the city start at the main railway station from April through October, Monday–Saturday at 2 and Sunday and holidays at 10:30. The fare is €8.50. Guided walking tours start at the Haus zum Falken tourist office from April through October, daily at 10:30. The two-hour tours cost €5 and include a visit to the Residenz. If you'd rather guide yourself, pick up a map from the same tourist office and follow the extremely helpful directions marked throughout the city by distinctive signposts.

Three shipping companies ply the Main River from Würzburg. The Fränkische Personenschiffahrt (FPS) and the Würzburger Personenschiffahrt Kurth & Schiebe operate excursions to vineyards; wine tasting is included in the price. Fränkische Personenschiffahrt also offers cruises of up to two weeks on the Main, Neckar, and Danube rivers and on the Main–Danube Canal. Kurth & Schiebe and Veitshöchheimer Personenschiffahrt offer daily service to Veitshöchheim, once the summer residence of the bishops of Augsburg. Views of Aschaffenburg and its mighty palace are part of the attraction of Main cruises offered by the Aschaffenburger Personenschiffahrt Sankt Martin.

🚢 **Aschaffenburger Personenschiffahrt Sankt Martin** ✉ Ruhlandstr. 5, D-63741 Aschaffenburg ☎ 06021/87288 ⊕ www.aschaffenburger-personenschiffahrt.de **Fränkische Personenschiffahrt (FPS)** ✉ Unterer Fuchsgraben 18, D-97318 Kitzingen ☎ 09321/91810 **Veitshöchheimer Personenschiffahrt** ✉ Obere Maing. 8, D-97209 Veitshöchheim ☎ 0931/91553. **Würzburger Personenschiffahrt Kurth & Schiebe** ✉ St.-Norbert-Str. 9, D-97299 Zell ☎ 0931/58573.

TRAIN TRAVEL

Infrequent trains link most major towns of the Romantic Road, but both Würzburg and Augsburg are on the InterCity and high-speed InterCity Express routes and have fast, frequent service to and from Berlin, Frankfurt, Munich, Stuttgart, and Hamburg. Deutsche Bahn offers special weekend excursion rates covering travel from most German railroad stations to Würzburg and hotel accommodations for up to four nights. Details are available at any train station.

VISITOR INFORMATION

A central tourist office based in Dinkelsbühl covers the entire Romantic Road: Touristik-Arbeitsgemeinschaft Romantische Strasse. Its color brochure describes all the attractions along the Romantic Road.

🚢 **Touristik-Arbeitsgemeinschaft Romantische Strasse** ✉ Marktpl., D-91550 Dinkelsbühl ☎ 09851/90271 🖶 09851/90281 ⊕ www.romantischestrasse.de. **Augsburg** ✉ Tourist-Information, Bahnhofstr. 7, D-86150 ☎ 0821/502-070 ⊕ www.regioaugsburg.de. **Bad Mergentheim** ✉ Städtisches Kultur-und Verkehrsamt, Marktpl. 3, D-96980 ☎ 07931/57135 ⊕ www.bad-mergentheim.de. **Dinkelsbühl** ✉ Tourist-Information, Marktpl., D-91550 ☎ 09851/90240 ⊕ www.dinkelsbuehl.de. **Donauwörth** ✉ Städtisches Verkehrs-und Kulturamt, Rathausg. 1, D-86609 ☎ 0906/789-151 ⊕ www.donauwoerth.de. **Feuchtwangen** ✉ Kultur-und Verkehrsamt, Marktpl. 1, D-91555 ☎ 09852/90444. **Füssen** ✉ Kurverwaltung, Kaiser-Maximilian-Pl. 1 D-87629 ☎ 08362/93850 ⊕ www.fuessen.de. **Harburg** ✉ Fremdenverkehrsverein, Schlossstr. 1, D-86655 ☎ 09080/96990. **Landsberg am Lech** ✉ Kultur-und Fremdenverkehrsamt, Hauptpl. 152, D-89896 ☎ 08191/128-245 ⊕ www.landsberg.de. **Nördlingen** ✉ Städtisches Verkehrsamt, Marktpl. 2, D-86720 ☎ 09081/4380. **Rothenburg-ob-der-Tauber** ✉ Tourist-Information, Rathaus, Marktpl. 2, D-91541 ☎ 09861/40492 ⊕ www.rothenburg.de. **Schillingsfürst** ✉ Info-Center Rothenburgerstr. 2, D-91583 ☎ 09868/222 ⊕ www.schillingsfuerst.de. **Schongau** ✉ Tourist-Information, Münzstr. 5, D-86956 ☎ 08861/7216 ⊕ www.schongau.de. **Schwangau** ✉ Information Schwangau, Münchenerstr. 2, D-87645 ☎ 08362/81980 ⊕ www.schwangau.de. **Ulm** ✉ Tourist-Information, Münsterpl. 50 [Stadthaus], D-89073 ☎ 0731/161-2830 ⊕ www.tourismus.ulm.de. **Weikersheim** ✉ Städtisches Kultur-und Verkehrsamt, Marktpl. 12, D-97990 ☎ 07934/10255 🖶 07934/10558. **Würzburg** ✉ Fremdenverkehrsamt, Am Congress-Centrum, D-97070 ☎ 0931/372-335 ⊕ www.wuerzburg.de.

FRANCONIA

5

BE A KID AGAIN
at the Museum der Deutschen
Spielzeugindustrie (Toymaking Museum) ⇨*p.206*

STORM THE BATTLEMENTS
of Festung Rosenberg
(Rosenberg Fortress) ⇨*p.207*

OPERA LOVERS UNITE
at the Wagner Festival ⇨*p.213*

GET THE REAL DEAL ON DENIM
at the Levi-Strauss Museum ⇨*p.218*

TRY NÜRNBERG'S BEST BRATWURST
at Historisches Bratwurst-Küche
Zum Gulden Stern p. ⇨*p.225*

Updated by
Marton Radkai

ALL THAT IS LEFT OF THE HUGE, ANCIENT kingdom of the Franks is the region known today as Franken (Franconia). The Franks were not only tough warriors but also hard workers, sharp tradespeople, and burghers with a good political nose. The name *frank* means bold, wild, and courageous in the old Frankish tongue. It was only in the early 19th century, following Napoléon's conquest of what is now southern Germany, that the area was incorporated into northern Bavaria. Modern Franconia stretches from the Bohemian Forest on the Czech border to the outskirts of Frankfurt. But its heart—and the focal point of this chapter—is an area known as the Fränkische Schweiz (Franconian Switzerland), bounded by Nürnberg (Nuremberg) in the south, Bamberg in the west, and the cultural center of Bayreuth in the east. Its rural appearance belies a solid economic backbone that is buttressed by a solid infrastructure of new businesses, electronics firms, call centers, and software.

Franconia is hardly an overrun tourist destination, yet its long and rich history, its diversified landscapes and leisure activities (including skiing, golfing, hiking, and cycling), and its gastronomic specialties place it high on the enjoyment scale.

Exploring Franconia

Although many proud Franconians would dispute it, this historic homeland of the Franks, one of the oldest Germanic peoples, is unmistakably part of Bavaria. Its southern border areas end at the Danube and merge into Lower Bavaria (Niederbayern) and the Bavarian Forest, while its northern border is marked by the Main River, which is seen as the dividing line between northern and southern Germany. Despite its extensive geographic spread, however, Franconia is a homogeneous region of rolling agricultural landscapes and thick forests climbing to the mountains of the Fichtelgebirge. Franconian towns such as Bayreuth, Coburg, and Bamberg are practically places of cultural pilgrimage, while rebuilt Nürnberg is the epitome of German medieval beauty.

About the Restaurants & Hotels

Many restaurants in this region serve hot meals only between 11:30 AM and 2 PM, and 6 PM and 9 PM. *Durchgehend warme Küche* means that hot meals are also served between lunch and dinner.

Make reservations well in advance for hotels in all the larger towns and cities if you plan to visit anytime between June and September. During the Nürnberg Toy Fair at the beginning of February rooms are rare and at a premium. If you're visiting Bayreuth during the annual Wagner Festival, in July and August, consider making reservations up to a year in advance. Remember, too, that during the festival, prices can be double the normal rates.

Numbers in the text correspond to numbers in the margin and on the Franconia and Nürnberg maps.

If you have 3 days

Make ⊞ **Nürnberg** ❻–❿ ▶ your base and take day trips on each of the three days to **Bayreuth** ❹ (an imperative visit whether or not it's Wagner Festival season); **Bamberg** ❺, once the seat of the most powerful ruling families in the country; and **Coburg** ❶, home of the Saxe-Coburg duchy. Each town is only a 50- to 70-minute drive away.

If you have 5 days

Spend one day in ⊞ **Nürnberg** ❻–❿ ▶, then take a day trip to **Bayreuth** ❹. On your third day settle in ⊞ **Coburg** ❶, visiting **Bamberg** ❺ on the way. On the fourth day take side trips to **Banz Abbey** and **Vierzehnheiligen,** two mighty churches that stand facing each other across the valley of the River Main. On the fifth day follow the Main upstream from Coburg to **Kulmbach** ❸, the beer capital of Germany. Among its several brands is reputedly the world's strongest brew.

5

	WHAT IT COSTS In Euros				
	$$$$	**$$$**	**$$**	**$**	**¢**
RESTAURANTS	over €25	€21–€25	€16–€20	€9–€15	under €9
HOTELS	over €225	€175–€225	€100–€175	€50–€100	under €50

Restaurant prices are per person for a main course at dinner. Hotel prices are for two people in a standard double room, including tax and service.

Timing

Summer is the best time to explore Franconia, though spring and fall are also fine when the weather cooperates. Avoid the cold and wet months of November, January, and February; many hotels and restaurants close, and no matter how pretty, many towns do seem quite dreary. If you're in Nürnberg in December, you're in time for one of Germany's largest and loveliest Christmas markets.

NORTHERN FRANCONIA

Three major German cultural centers lie within this region of Franconia: Coburg, a town with blood links to royal dynasties throughout Europe; Bamberg, with its own claim to German royal history and an Old Town area, which has been designated as a UNESCO World Heritage site; and Bayreuth, where composer Richard Wagner finally settled, making it a place of musical pilgrimage for Wagner fans from all over the world.

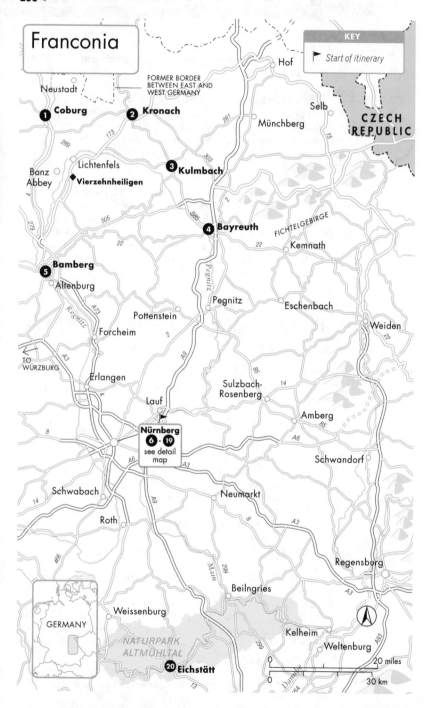

Franconia

KEY

► *Start of itinerary*

FORMER BORDER
BETWEEN EAST AND
WEST GERMANY

Neustadt

1 **Coburg**

2 **Kronach**

Hof

Selb

Münchberg

CZECH
REPUBLIC

Lichtenfels

Banz
Abbey

Vierzehnheiligen

3 **Kulmbach**

4 **Bayreuth**

FICHTELGEBIRGE

Kemnath

5 **Bamberg**

Altenburg

Pegnitz

Pottenstein

Eschenbach

Weiden

Forcheim

TO
WÜRZBURG

Erlangen

Lauf

Nürnberg
6 · **19**
see detail
map

Sulzbach-
Rosenberg

Amberg

Schwandorf

Schwabach

Neumarkt

Roth

GERMANY

Weissenburg

NATURPARK
ALTMÜHLTAL

Beilngries

Regensburg

Kelheim

Weltenburg

20 **Eichstätt**

0   20 miles

0   30 km

5

On the Menu Franconia is known for its good and filling food and for its simple and atmospheric *Gasthäuser*. Pork is a staple, served either as *Schweinsbraten* (a plain roast) or sauerbraten (marinated). Nürnberg has a unique shoulder cut called *Schäfele* (literally "little shovel"), served with *Knödel* (dumplings made from either bread or potatoes). Short sausages are also a specialty in Nürnberg, where they are eaten either grilled or heated in a stock of onions and wine (*saurer Zipfel*). The specialty in the Altmühltal is lamb.

Hiking & Walking The wild stretches of forest and numerous nature parks in northern Franconia make this ideal hiking country. There are more than 40,000 km (25,000 mi) of hiking trails, with the greatest concentration in the Altmühltal Nature Park, a wooded gorge, and in the Frankenwald.

Skiing & Snowboarding The highest peaks of Franconia's upland region, the Fichtelgebirge and Frankenwald, rarely pass the 3,200-foot mark, but their exposed location in central Germany near Bayreuth assures them good snow conditions most winters. Cross-country skiers also head to this region because of its lack of mass tourism.

Vineyards & Breweries Not to be missed are Franconia's liquid refreshments from both the grape and the grain. Franconian wines, usually white and sold in distinctive flagons called *Bocksbeutel*, are renowned for their special bouquet (Silvaner is the traditional grape). The region has the largest concentration of local breweries in the world (Bamberg alone has 10, Bayreuth 7), producing a wide range of brews, the most distinctive of which is the dark, smoky *Rauchbier*.

Coburg

❶ *105 km (65 mi) north of Nürnberg.*

Coburg is a surprisingly little-known treasure—whether it's glittering under the summer sky or frosted white with the snows of winter. The east-west border once isolated this area, but since Germany's reunification it has experienced a minor economic revolution. A taste of this dark era can be had at an exhibition of (mostly) photos at the **Thüringisch-Fränkische Begegnungsstätte** (⊠ Schützenplatz 1 ☎ 09568/81126 ☜ Free ⊙ Wed., Sat., and Sun. 2–4) in Neustadt, to the northeast of Coburg.

Coburg was founded in the 11th century and remained in the possession of the dukes of Saxe-Coburg-Gotha until 1918; the present duke still lives here. The remarkable Saxe-Coburg dynasty established itself as something of a royal stud farm, providing a seemingly inexhaustible supply of blue-blood marriage partners to ruling houses the length and breadth of Europe. The most famous of these royal mates was Prince

Albert, who married Queen Victoria, after which she gained special renown in Coburg. Their numerous children, married off to other kings, queens, and emperors, helped to spread the tried-and-tested Saxe-Coburg stock even farther afield. Despite all the history that sweats from each sandstone ashlar, Coburg is a modern and bustling town.

Coburg's **Marktplatz** (Market Square) has a statue of Prince Albert, the high-minded consort, standing proudly surrounded by gracious Renaissance and baroque buildings. The **Stadhaus,** former seat of the local dukes, begun in 1500, is the most imposing structure here. A forest of ornate gables and spires projects from its well-proportioned facade. Opposite is the **Rathaus** (Town Hall). Look at the statue of the **Bratwurstmännla** on the building's tympanum (it's actually St. Mauritius in armor); the staff he carries is said to be the official length against which the town's famous bratwursts are measured. These tasty specialties, roasted on pinecone fires, are available on the market square.

Prince Albert spent much of his childhood in **Schloss Ehrenburg,** the ducal palace. Built in the mid-16th century, it has been greatly altered over the years, principally following a fire in the early 19th century. Duke Ernst I invited Friedrich Schinkel from Berlin to redo the palace in the then-popular Gothic style. Some of the original Renaissance features were kept. The rooms of the castle are quite special, especially those upstairs, where the ceilings are heavily decorated with stucco and the floors have wonderful patterns of various woods. The Hall of Giants is named for the larger-than-life caryatids that support the ceiling; the favorite sight downstairs is Queen Victoria's flush toilet, which was the first one installed in Germany. Here, too, the ceiling is worth noting for its playful, gentle stuccowork. The baroque chapel attached to Ehrenburg is often used for weddings. ✉ *Schlosspl.* ☎ *09561/80880* 🌐 *www.sgvcoburg.de* 🎫 *€3, combined ticket with Schloss Rosenau €4.50* 🕐 *Tour Tues.–Sun. 10–5 on the hr; additional 4:30 tour Apr.–Sept.*

Near Schloss Ehrenburg, the **Puppenmuseum** (Doll Museum) contains a collection of more than 900 antique dolls and art dolls, and around 50 carefully furnished dollhouses arranged chronologically to represent lifestyles from the period between 1810 and 1950. The building was once home to the poet and orientalist Friedrich Rückert. The museum includes a doll and toy shop. ✉ *Rückertstr. 2–3* ☎ *09561/74047* 🎫 *€2* 🕐 *Apr.–Oct., Tues.–Sun. 9–5; Nov.–Mar., daily 10–5.*

The **Veste Coburg** fortress, one of the largest and most impressive in the country, is Coburg's main attraction. The brooding bulk of the castle guards the town from a 1,484-foot hill. Construction began around 1055, but with progressive rebuilding and remodeling, today's predominantly late Gothic–early-Renaissance edifice bears little resemblance to the original crude fortress. One part of the castle harbors the **Kunstsammlungen,** a grand set of collections including art, with works by Dürer, Cranach, and Hans Holbein, among others; sculpture from the school of the great Tilman Riemenschneider (1460–1531); furniture and textiles; magnificent weapons, armor, and tournament garb spanning four centuries (in the so-called **Herzoginbau,** or Duchess's Building); carriages and ornate sleighs; and more. The room where Martin Luther lived for six months in 1530 while he observed the goings-on of the Augsburg Diet has an especially dignified atmosphere. The **Jagdintarsien-Zimmer** (Hunting Marquetry Room), an elaborately decorated room that dates back to the early 17th century, has some of the finest woodwork in southern Germany. Inquire at the ticket office for tours and reduced family tickets. Finally, there's the **Carl-Eduard-Bau** (Carl-Eduard Building), which contains a valuable antique glass collection, mostly from the baroque age. Inquire at the ticket office for tours and reduced family tickets. ☎ 09561/8790 ⊕ www.kunstsammlungen-coburg.de ⊡ €3 ⊙ Museums Apr.–Oct., Tues.–Sun. 10–5; Nov.–Mar., Tues.–Sun. 1–4; castle Apr.–Oct., Tues.–Sun. 10–5; Nov.–Mar., Tues.–Sun. 2–5; castle grounds daily 6:30–6.

need a break?

The **Burgschänke** (⊠ Veste Coburg ☎ 09561/80980), Veste Coburg's own tavern, allows you to relax and soak up centuries of history while sampling a Coburg beer and one of the traditional dishes from the basic menu. The tavern is closed Monday and January–mid-February.

The **Naturkundemuseum** (Natural History Museum) is in the castle's former palace garden, the Hofgarten. This is the country's leading museum of its kind, with more than 8,000 exhibits of flora and fauna, geology, human history, and mineralogy. The museum is being revamped, a process that will still take a few years, but it can be visited nonetheless. ⊠ Veste Coburg ☎ 09561/808–120 ⊕ www.naturkunde-museum-coburg.de ⊡ €1.50 ⊙ Weekdays 9–1 and 1:30–5, weekends 9–5.

Perched on a hill 5 km (3 mi) to the west of Coburg is **Schloss Callenberg,** until 1231 the main castle of the Knights of Callenberg. In the 16th century it was taken over by the Coburgs. From 1842 on it served as the summer residence of the hereditary Coburg prince and later Duke Ernst II. It holds a number of important collections, including that of the Windsor gallery; arts and crafts from Holland, Germany, and Italy from the Renaissance to the 19th century; precious baroque, empire, and Biedermeier furniture; table and standing clocks from three centuries; a selection of weapons; and various handicrafts. The best way to reach the castle is by car via Baiersdorf or by Bus 5 from the Marktplatz. ⊠ Callenberg ☎ 09561/55150 ⊕ www.schloss-callenberg.de ⊡ €3.50 ⊙ Tour Apr.–Oct., daily at 10, 11, noon, 2, 3, and 4; Nov.–Mar., Tues.–Sun. at 2, 3, and 4; and by appointment. Closed last 3 wks of Jan.

off the beaten path

AHORN – This town 4 km (2½ mi) southwest of Coburg has a wonderful museum that gives close insight into the life and times of farmers in the region. The houses of the **Grätemuseum des Coburger Landes** (Museum of Farm Appliances of the Coburg Region) date to the early 18th century and are constructed of sandstone with harmonious half-timber superstructures. Exhibits depict estate life, with everything from farm implements to a smithy, while outside farm animals roam about. Snacks and drinks are available at the Schäferstuben (Shepherd's Room). ⊠ On Rte. B–303 *before Ahorn* ☎ *09561/1304* 🗺 *€2.50* ☉ *Apr.–Oct., Tues.–Sun. 2–5; Nov.–Mar., Sun. 2–5 and by appointment.*

☉ **Wildpark Schloss Tambach –** This old castle a few miles west of Ahorn off B–303 is still in private hands. Its grand collection of wild animals and birds includes boar, deer, eagles, condors, owls, falcons, and storks. Flight demonstrations are held March–August, daily at 11, 3, and 5. The **Jagd- und Fischereimuseum** (Museum of Hunting and Fishing), laid out on two floors, displays everything you have ever wanted to know about hunting, from clothing to weapons, stuffed animals, pennants, and tricks of the trade throughout the centuries. ✉ Schlossallee 1a, Tambach ☎ 09567/1861 ⊕ www. wildpark-tambach.de 🗺 e6.50 for the museum and park, e2.50 for the museum alone ☉ Mar.–Oct., Mon.–Sat. 10–5:30, Sun. 10–6; Nov.–early Jan., Sun. 10–5; early Jan.–Feb. by appointment.

Where to Stay & Eat

¢–$$ ✕ **Künstlerklause.** This little maze of rooms with dark-wood paneling,
Fodor'sChoice a fireplace, old photos, and comfortable leather seats welcomes a mixed
★ crowd, from businesspeople to artists. The upscale cuisine gets the occasional exotic touch through spices. You might find a standard turkey schnitzel with dumplings, or venison in aspic with diced and fried sweet potato, celery, and carrots in juniper sauce. The Sunday specialty is Omas Braten (Grandma's Roasts), traditional home cooking. ✉ *Theaterpl. 4a* ☎ *09561/90705* 🖚 *Reservations essential* ▭ *No credit cards* ☉ *Closed Mon.*

¢–$ ✕ **Ratskeller.** The local specialties taste better here beneath the old vaults and within earshot of the Coburg marketplace. Try the sauerbraten, along with a glass of crisp Franconian white wine. The prices become a little higher in the evening, and the menu adds a few more dishes. ✉ *Markt 1* ☎ *09561/92400* ▭ *No credit cards.*

★ $–$$ ✕▥ **Hotel Festungshof.** Duke Carl Eduard had this guest mansion built right outside the Veste in Coburg. This turn-of-the-20th-century building has comfortably (if not very imaginatively) furnished rooms. The restaurant ($–$$$) has solid Franconian cooking, with seasonal dishes— fish in the summer, venison in winter; the café has a generous terrace, and the beer garden seats 300. A bus will take you to the town center, or you can take a 20-minute walk through the castle garden and the wooded landscape to reach the market square. ✉ *Rosenauerstr. 30, D–96450* ☎ *09561/80290* 🗺 *09561/802–933* ⊕ *www.hotel-festungshof. de* 🖚 *14 rooms* ⚒ *Restaurant, café, cable TV, beer garden, Internet, some pets allowed (fee); no a/c* ▭ *MC, V* ⦿ *BP* ☉ *No dinner Sun.*

¢–$ ✕▥ **Goldene Rose.** One of the region's oldest, this agreeable inn is located about 5 km (3 mi) southeast of Coburg. The rustic interior carries its age well, with simple wooden paneling and floors. On a warm summer evening, however, the beer garden is the best place to enjoy traditional Franconian dishes, or a plate of homemade sausages, and meet some of the locals. Rooms are well appointed and comfortable—the wooden theme is continued but the style is definitely modern. ✉ *Coburgerstr. 31, D–96271* ☎ *09560/92250* 🗺 *09560/1423* ⊕ *www.goldene-*

rose.de ⤳ *14 rooms* ⟨ *Restaurant, cable TV, beer garden; no a/c* ⊟ *MC, V* ⊙| *BP* ⊗ *Restaurant closed Mon.*

$$ ⊞ **Hotel Mercure Coburg.** You can expect modern, clean, well-designed rooms that are airy and functional at the Mercure. In the morning, an excellent breakfast buffet gets you ready for a day of sightseeing. Friendly and very helpful staff will round out your stay. The Mercure is about 15 minutes, on foot, south of Coburg's center. ⊠ *Ketschendorfer Str. 86, D–96450* ☎ *09561/8210 or 0800/100–0048* 🖷 *09561/821–444* ⊕ *www.mercure.com* ⤳ *123 rooms* ⟨ *In-room data ports, cable TV with movies, some pets allowed, no-smoking rooms; no a/c* ⊟ *AE, DC, MC, V* ⊙| *BP.*

$$ ⊞ **Romantic Hotel Goldene Traube.** Book a room overlooking the square, and on summer evenings you can fall asleep to the splash of the fountain named after Queen Victoria. The hotel feels such a strong link with Britain's former queen and empress that it even named its bar after her. There's also a sauna complex with solarium. ⊠ *Am Viktoriabrunnen 2, D–96450* ☎ *09561/8760* 🖷 *09561/876–222* ⤳ *69 rooms, 1 suite* ⟨ *Restaurant, in-room data ports, cable TV, miniature golf, gym, sauna, steam room, bicycles, bar, some pets allowed (fee), no-smoking rooms; no a/c* ⊟ *AE, DC, MC, V* ⊙| *BP.*

Nightlife & the Arts

Coburg is home to Europe's only **Brazilian Samba Festival,** a wild three-day bacchanal held in mid-July (July 9–11, in 2005). Check the Coburg tourist office's Web site for this and other events.

Coburg's **Landestheater** (⊠ Schlosspl. 6 ☎ 09561/92742) opera season runs from October through mid-July. Call (9 AM–1 PM) for tickets.

Shopping

Coburg is full of culinary delights; its *Schmätzen* (gingerbread) and *Elizenkuchen* (almond cake) are famous. You'll find home-baked versions in any of the many excellent **patisseries** or at a Grossman store (there are three in Coburg). Rödental, northeast of Coburg, is the home of the world-famous M. I. Hummel figurines, made by the Göbel porcelain manufacturer. There's a **Hummel Museum** (⊠ Coburgerstr. 7, Rödental ☎09563/92303 ⊕www.goebel.de) devoted to them, and 18th- and 19th-century porcelain from other manufacturers. The museum is open Monday–Saturday 9–5. Besides the museum's store, there are several retail outlets in the village.

en route | Near the village of Rödental, 9 km (5½ mi) northeast of Coburg, the 550-year-old **Schloss Rosenau** sits in all its neo-Gothic glory in the midst of an English-style park. Prince Albert was born here in 1819, and one room is devoted entirely to Albert and his queen, Victoria. Much of the castle furniture was made especially for the Saxe-Coburg family by noted Viennese craftsmen. In the garden's Orangerie is the **Museum für Modernes Glas** (Museum for Modern Glass), which displays nearly 40 years' worth of glass sculptures (dating from 1950–90) that contrast sharply with the venerable architecture of the castle itself. ☎ *09563/4747 castle, 09563/1606 museum* ⊕ *www. kunstsammlungen-coburg.de* ⌑ *Castle* €4, *museum* €1, *free with* *entrance ticket to Veste in Coburg* ☉ *Tour Apr.–Oct., daily at 10, 11, noon, 2, 3, and 4; Nov.–Mar., Tues.–Sun. at 3 and 4; and by appointment. Closed last 3 wks of Jan.*

Neustadt

15 km (10 mi) northeast of Coburg.

★ ♺ The **Museum der Deutschen Spielzeugindustrie** (Museum of the German Toymaking Industry) in Neustadt is a must. All manner of toys and dolls, from wooden to plasticine, are included. Dolls model traditional German costumes in one room, and in another the craft of doll- and toy-making is revealed. A bevy of very sooty-looking teddy bears makes up part of the antiques collection, which stands in contrast to modern action figures, various ethnic dolls, and, of course, Barbie. Christmas decorations are also on display. In short, everything you ever wanted to know about toys is right here in a modern, barnlike building. A doll doctor in town will tend to your favorite doll, if it's sick. ✉ *Hindenburgpl. 1* ☎ *09568/5600* ⊕ *www.spielzeugmuseum-neustadt.de* ⊠ €3 ☉ *Daily 10–5; last entry at 4:15.*

Lichtenfels

21 km (13 mi) southeast of Coburg.

Rather than speed from Coburg to Bayreuth on the autobahn, take a detour along the small road (B–289) to Lichtenfels, just across the Main River. You might call the little town a basket case—it's known for its basket-weaving tradition. The basketwork market (☎ 09571/18283), on the third weekend in September, is one of a kind. All sorts of baskets are sold, and a German basket queen is chosen. To get a little closer to the tradition, climb up to the town's hallmark tower, the **Oberer Torturm,** and inspect the basket maker's workshop there.

Just south of Lichtenfels off the main road (B–173) to Bamberg are two religious gems, a church and an abbey, each proudly crowning the heights along the banks of the Main River. On the east side of the Main is **Vierzehnheiligen,** a tall, elegant yellow-sandstone edifice, whose interior represents one of the great examples of rococo decoration. The church was built by Balthasar Neumann (architect of the Residenz at Würzburg) between 1743 and 1772 to commemorate a vision of Christ and 14 saints—*vierzehn Heiligen*—that appeared to a shepherd in 1445. The interior, known as "God's ballroom," is supported by 14 columns. In the middle of the church is the Gnadenaltar (Mercy Altar) featuring the 14 saints. Thanks to clever play with light, light colors, and fanciful gold-and-blue trimmings, the interior seems to be in perpetual motion. Guided tours of the church are given on request; a donation is expected. ☎ *09571/95080* ⊕ *www.vierzehnheiligen.de* ☉ *Oct.–May, daily 8–4; June–Sept., daily 7–7.*

Fodor'sChoice
★

On the west bank of the Main is **Kloster Banz** (Banz Abbey), standing on what some call the "holy mountain of Bavaria." There had been a monastery here since 1069, but the present buildings—now a political-seminar center and think tank—date from the end of the 17th century. The highlight of the complex is the **Klosterkirche** (Abbey Church), the work of architect Leonard Dientzenhofer and his brother, the stuccoist Johann Dientzenhofer (1663–1726). Balthasar Neumann later contributed a good deal of work. Concerts are occasionally held in the church, including some by members of the renowned "Bamberger Symphoniker." To get to Banz from Vierzehnheiligen, drive south to Unnersdorf, where you can cross the river. From Lichtenfels, take the road via Seubelsdorf and Reuendorf. ☎ 09573/7311 or 09573/5092 ۞ May–Oct., daily 9–noon and 2–4; Nov.–Apr., daily 9–noon; call to request a tour.

A delightful basket museum, the **Deutsches Korb Museum Michelau**, in nearby Michelau, which calls itself the "cradle of German basketweaving," displays furniture, decoration, and household items from around the world. ✉ Bismarckstr. 4, Michelau ☎ 09571/83548 ☞ €2 ۞ Apr.–Oct., Tues.–Sun. 10–4:30; Nov.–Mar., Mon.–Thurs. 10–4:30, Fri. 9–noon.

Kronach

② 24 km (15 mi) northeast of Lichtenfels, 120 km (74 mi) north of Nürnberg.

Kronach is a charming little gateway to the natural splendor of the Frankenwald region. In its old medieval section, the **Obere Stadt** (Upper Town), harmonious sandstone houses are surrounded by old walls and surmounted by a majestic fortress. Kronach is best known as the birthplace of Renaissance painter Lucas Cranach the Elder (1472–1553), but there's a running argument as to which house he was born in—Am Marktplatz 1 or in the house called Am Scharfen Eck, at Lucas-Cranach-Strasse 38. The latter is now a meeting place for locals, where you can enjoy a good Franconian meal at a good price ($). A good time to be in Kronach is the last weekend in June, when the town celebrates its past with a medieval festival featuring authentic garb, food, troubadours, and more.

Fodor'sChoice **Festung Rosenberg** (Rosenberg Fortress) is a few minutes' walk from the
★ town center. As you stand below its mighty walls, it's easy to see why it was never taken by enemy forces. During World War I it served as a POW camp with no less a figure than Charles de Gaulle as a "guest." Today Rosenberg houses a youth hostel and, more importantly, the **Fränkische Galerie** (the Franconian Gallery), an extension of the Bavarian National Museum in Munich, featuring paintings and sculpted works from the Middle Ages and the Renaissance. Lucas Cranach the Elder and Tilman Riemenschneider are represented, as well as artists from the Dürer School and the Bamberg School. In July and August the central courtyard is an atmospheric backdrop for performances of Goethe's *Faust*. The grounds of the fortress are also used by wood sculptors in the summer. ☎ 09261/60410 ⊕ www.kronach.de ☞ €3.50 ۞ Fortress tours Apr.–Oct., Tues.–Sun. at 10, 11, 2, and 3:30; Nov.–Mar., Tues.–Sun. at 11 and 2; Galerie Apr.–Oct., Tues.–Sun. 9–6; Nov.–Mar., Tues.–Sun. 10–4.

Kulmbach

❸ *19 km (12 mi) southeast of Kronach, 32 km (20 mi) east of Lichtenfels.*

Kulmbach has a claim to fame that belies its size. In a country where brewing and beer drinking break all records, this town produces more beer per capita than anywhere else: 9,000 pints for each man, woman, and child. A quarter of Kulmbachers earn their living directly or indirectly from beer. A special local brew only available in winter and during the Lenten season is *Eisbock,* a dark beer that is frozen as part of the brewing process to make it stronger. The locals claim it's the sparkling-clear springwater from the nearby Fichtelgebirge hills that makes their beer so special.

Kulmbach celebrates its beer every year in a nine-day festival that starts on the last Saturday in July. The main festival site, a mammoth tent, is called the *Festspulhaus*—literally, "festival swill house"—a none-too-subtle dig at nearby Bayreuth and its tony *Festspielhaus,* where Wagner's operas are performed.

The **Kulmbacher Brewery** (⊠ Lichtenfelsstr. ☎ 09221/705–113), a merger of four of six Kulmbach breweries, produces among others the strongest beer in the world—the *Doppelbock* Kulminator 28—which takes nine months to brew and has an alcohol content of more than 11%. The brewery runs the **Bayerisches Brauereimuseum Kulmbach** (Kulmbach Brewery Museum) jointly with the nearby Mönchshof-Bräu brewery and inn. ⊠ *Hoferstr. 20* ☎ *09221/4264* 🖭 *Tour €2.50, €1.50 if you spend €5 in the brewery tavern* ☉ *Tues.–Sun. 10–5.*

☉ The **Plassenburg,** the town's castle and symbol, is the most important Renaissance castle in the country. It stands on a rise overlooking Kulmbach, a 20-minute hike from the Old Town. The first building here, begun in the mid-12th century, was torched by marauding Bavarians who were eager to put a stop to the ambitions of Duke Albrecht Alcibiades—a man who spent several years murdering, plundering, and pillaging his way through Franconia. His successors built today's castle, starting in about 1560. Externally there's little to suggest the graceful Renaissance interior, but as you enter the main courtyard, the scene changes abruptly. The tiered space of the courtyard is covered with precisely carved figures, medallions, and other intricate ornaments, the whole comprising one of the most remarkable and delicate architectural ensembles in Europe. Inside, the **Deutsches Zinnfigurenmuseum** (Tin Figures Museum), with more than 300,000 miniature statuettes and tin soldiers, holds the largest collection of its kind in the world. The figures are arranged in scenes from all periods of history. From April to October, casting of the tin figures is demonstrated daily from 2 to 5. The **Landschaftsmuseum Obermain** (Obermain Landscape Museum) here documents the history and culture of this region. ☎ *09221/947–505* 🖭 *€3* ☉ *Daily 10–5.*

off the beaten path

NEUENMARKT – In this "railway village" near Kulmbach, more than 25 beautifully preserved gleaming locomotives huff and puff in a living railroad museum. Every now and then a nostalgic train will take you to the Brewery Museum in Kulmbach. Or you can enjoy a round trip to Marktschorgast that takes you up the very steep "schiefe Ebene" stretch (literally, slanting level). The museum also has model trains set up in incredibly detailed replicas of landscapes. ⊠ *Birkenstr. 5* ☎ *09227/5700* ⊕ *www.dampflokmuseum.de* ☑ *€4* ⊗ *Tues.–Sun. 10–5.*

Where to Stay & Eat

$ ✕⊞ **Hotel zur Gondel.** It's well worth driving the few miles to Altenkunstadt, between Kulmbach and Lichtenfels, for a few nights at these two elaborate half-timber houses right on the main square. The restaurant serves an excellent candlelit meal of Franconian and international specialties in a stylized rustic setting or in the delightful inner courtyard. The Jahn family has made sure that well-appointed rooms welcome you for a well-deserved rest. ⊠ *Marktpl. 7, D–96264 Altenkunstadt* ☎ *09572/ 3661* 🖷 *09572/4596* ⇦ *36 rooms* ⚐ *Restaurant, cable TV, some pets allowed; no a/c* ▤ *MC, V* ¶⊙¶ *BP* ⊗ *No lunch Sat.*

$$ ⊞ **Hotel Kronprinz.** This old hotel tucked away in the middle of Kulmbach's old town, right in the shadow of Plassenburg Castle, covers all basic needs, though the furnishings are somewhat bland. The café serves snacks and cakes. ⊠ *Fischerg. 4–6, D–95326* ☎ *09221/92180* 🖷 *09221/ 921–836* ⊕ *www.kronprinz-kulmbach.de* ⇦ *19 rooms* ⚐ *Café, in-room data ports, cable TV, bar; no a/c* ▤ *AE, DC, MC, V* ¶⊙¶ *BP.*

Bayreuth

❹ *24 km (15 mi) south of Kulmbach, 80 km (50 mi) northeast of Nürnberg.*

Bayreuth is pronounced Bye-*roit,* though it might as well be called Wagner. This small Franconian town is where 19th-century composer and musical revolutionary Richard Wagner (1813–83) finally settled after a lifetime of rootless shifting through Europe. Here he built his great theater, the Festspielhaus, as a suitable setting for his grand operas on mythological Germanic themes. The annual Wagner Festival, first held in 1876, brings hordes of Wagner lovers who push prices sky high, fill hotels to bursting, and earn themselves much-sought-after social kudos in the process (to some, it's one of *the* places to be seen). The festival is held from late July until late August, so unless you plan to visit the town specifically for it, this is the time to stay away. But Wagner is not all there is to the town. You'll find street musicians of all kinds playing in the sun-drenched streets, rock concerts, the occasional sports event, museums and galleries, and one of the most luxurious spa–wellness havens south of the Main River, the Lohengrin Therme. The Bayreuth tourist office on Luitpoldplatz offers the Bayreuth Card for €9, giving you unlimited use of the bus system, a tour of the town, entrance to nine museums, and a daily paper, the *Nordbayrischer Kurier.*

Built by Wagner, Wahnfried, now the **Richard-Wagner-Museum,** was the only house he ever owned. It's a simple, austere neoclassic building built in 1874, whose name, "peace from madness," was well earned. The war left only the facade; the rest was carefully rebuilt. Wagner lived here with his wife, Cosima, daughter of pianist Franz Liszt; and here they are buried. King Ludwig II of Bavaria, the young and impressionable "Fairy-Tale

King," who gave Wagner so much financial support, is remembered in a bust before the entrance. The exhibits, arranged along a well-marked tour through the house, require a great deal of German-language reading. The thrill is in seeing Wagner's handwriting and the original scores of such masterpieces as *Parsifal, Tristan und Isolde, Lohengrin, Der Fliegende Holländer,* and *Götterdämmerung.* You can also see designs for productions of his operas, as well as his piano and huge library. A multimedia display lets you watch and listen to various productions of his operas. The little house where Franz Liszt lived and died is right next door and can be visited on the Wagner ticket, but be sure to express your interest in advance. It, too, is heavy on the paper, but the last rooms—with pictures, photos, and silhouettes of the master, his students, acolytes, and friends—is well worth the detour. ⊠ *Richard-Wagner-Str. 48* ☎ *0921/757–2816* ⊕ *www.wagnermuseum.de* ✆ €4, during festival €4.50 ☉ Apr.–Oct, Fri.–Mon. and Wed. 9–5, Tues. and Thurs. 9–8; Nov.–Mar., daily 9–5.

Right around the corner from the Richard-Wagner-Museum is the remarkable little **Deutsches Freimaurer-Museum** (German Freemasons Museum), founded in 1902, which explains the origins of the Freemasons and the ins and outs of the fraternal, humanist organization. Everyday items on exhibit bear the famous symbols of the order. Though the placards are not in English, the exhibits do in most cases speak for themselves. The library, with more than 16,000 volumes, is a center for research of freemasonry in Germany. ⊠ *Im Hofgarten 1* ☎ *0921/69824* ✆ €1.50 ☉ Tues.–Fri. 10–noon and 2–4, Sat. 10–noon; during festival 10–4.

The **Festspielhaus** (Festival Theater) is by no means beautiful. In fact, this high temple of the Wagner cult is surprisingly plain. The spartan look is explained partly by Wagner's desire to achieve perfect acoustics. The wood seats have no upholstering, for example, and the walls are bare. The stage is enormous, capable of holding the huge casts required for Wagner's largest operas. Performances take place only during the annual Wagner Festival, still masterminded by descendants of the composer. ⊠ *Festspielhügel 1* ☎ *0921/78780* ✆ €2.50 ☉ Tour Tues.–Sun. at 10, 10:45, 2:15, and 3; closed Nov., during rehearsals, and afternoons during festival.

The **Neues Schloss** (New Palace) is a glamorous 18th-century palace built by the Margravine Wilhelmine, sister of Frederick the Great of Prussia and a woman of enormous energy and decided tastes. Though Wagner is the man most closely associated with Bayreuth, his choice of this setting is largely due to the work of this woman, who lived 100 years before him. Wilhelmine devoured books, wrote plays and operas (which she directed and, of course, acted in), and had buildings constructed, transforming much of the town and bringing it near bankruptcy. Her distinctive touch is evident at the palace, built when a mysterious fire conveniently destroyed parts of the original palace. Anyone with a taste for the wilder flights of rococo decoration will love it. Some rooms have been given over to one of Europe's finest collections of faience. ⊠ *Ludwigstr. 21* ☎ *0921/759–6921* ✆ €4 ☉ Apr.–Sept., daily 9–6; Oct.–Mar., daily 9–4; call for English-language tour times.

Another great architectural legacy of Wilhelmine is the **Markgräfliches Opernhaus** (Margravial Opera House). Built between 1745 and 1748, it is a rococo jewel, sumptuously decorated in red, gold, and blue. Apollo and the nine Muses cavort across the frescoed ceiling. It was this delicate 500-seat theater that originally drew Wagner to Bayreuth; he felt that it might prove a suitable setting for his own operas. It's a wonderful setting for the concerts and operas of Bayreuth's "other" musical festivals, which in fact go on virtually throughout the year. Visitors are treated to a sound-and-light show. ⊠ *Opernstr.* ☎ *0921/759–6922* 🖃 *€5* ⊙ *Apr.–Sept., Tues., Wed., and Fri.–Sun. 9–6, last entry at 5:30, Thurs. 9–8, last entry at 7:30; Oct.–Mar., Tues.–Sun. 10–noon and 1:30–3:30. Sound-and-light shows Apr.–Oct., at 9:15; Nov.–Mar., at 10:15. Closed during performances, and on rehearsal days.*

It's wise to remember that Bayreuth is an industrious Franconian town and that there's a lot more to it than opera and Wagner. Visiting the **Historisches Museum Bayreuth** (Bayreuth Historical Museum) is like poking around a miraculous attic with 34 rooms. It's no wonder the museum won the Bavarian Museum Award. A wonderfully eclectic collection includes items from the life of the town, be they royal remnants, faience items from the 18th century, clothes, or odd sports equipment. ⊠ *Kirchpl. 6* ☎ *0921/764–0123* 🖃 *€1.53* ⊙ *Tues., Wed., and Fri.–Sun. 10–5, Thurs. 10–8, Mon. 10–5 during festival.*

Bayreuth's small but high-quality **Kunstmuseum** (Art Museum) houses several permanent collections donated or lent by private collectors. Works by Lyonel Feininger, Max Beckmann (lithographs from his *Berlin Journeys*), and woodcuts by Emil Schuhmacher are highlights. An unusual collection donated by the BAT tobacco company features paintings, sculptures, and ephemera relating to all aspects of tobacco, from cultivation to smoking. The museum lies within the generous rooms of the old Town Hall and shares space with an upscale restaurant called Oskar. ⊠ *Maximilianstr. 33* ☎ *0921/764–5310* 🖃 *€1.60* ⊙ *Tues., Wed., and Fri.–Sun. 10–5, Thurs. 10–8; Mon. 10–5 during festival.*

Near the center of town, in the 1887 Maisel Brewery building, the **Brauerei und Büttnerei-Museum** (Brewery and Coopers Museum) reveals the tradition of the brewing trade over the past two centuries with a focus on the Maisel's trade, of course. The brewery operated until 1981, when its much bigger home was completed next door. After the 90-minute tour in this museum that earned an accolade from the *Guinness Book of Records* for being the largest of its kind, you can quaff a cool, freshly tapped beer in the museum's pub, which has traditional Bavarian Weissbier. ⊠ *Kulmbacherstr. 40* ☎ *0921/401–234* ⊕ *www.maisel.com* 🖃 *€3.60* ⊙ *Tour Mon.–Thurs. at 10 AM; individual tours by prior arrangement.*

The **Altes Schloss Eremitage** (Old Palace and Hermitage), 5 km (3 mi) north of Bayreuth on B–85, makes an appealing departure from the sonorous and austere Wagnerian mood of much of the town. It's an early-18th-century palace, built as a summer palace and remodeled in 1740 by the Margravine Wilhelmine. Although her taste is not much in evidence in the drab exterior, the interior, alive with light and color, displays her guiding hand in every elegant line. The extraordinary **Japanischer Saal** (Japanese Room), filled with Asian treasures and chinoiserie furniture, is the finest room. The park and gardens, partly formal, partly natural, are enjoyable for idle strolling. Fountain displays take place at the two fake grottoes at the top of the hour, 10–5 daily. ☎ *0921/759–6937* ✉ *Schloss €3, park free* ☉ *Schloss Apr.–mid-Oct., Fri.–Wed. 9–6, Thurs. 9–8; guided tour every ½ hr; park daily.*

The **Lohengrin Therme** (Lohengrin Spa), on the way to Seulbitz, is a modern and exciting center of wellness and the ideal place to take a break from the travel schedule. The program includes a pool, hot tubs, Jacuzzis, a beautiful sauna area (including a hot-rock steam room, a snow room, and gentle saunas), massages, light therapy, and more. Tickets for entrance and services can range from €8.50 for the pool and Jacuzzi area to €49.50 for various massages. ✉ *Kurpromenade 5* ☎ *0921/792–400* ⊕ *www.lohengrin–therme.de* ☉ *Daily 8–10; sauna and wellness Sun.–Thurs. 10–10, Fri. and Sat. 10 AM–11 PM.*

Where to Stay & Eat

¢–$ ✕ **Kraftraum.** The crowd is young, the atmosphere is casual, and the music ranges from jazz to Latin. The vegetarian food—thick soups, lively salads, pastas, and grains—is tasty and filling. You can enjoy a hearty breakfast until the afternoon and occasionally musical events in the evenings. ✉ *Sophienstr. 16* ☎ *0921/800–2515* ▭ *No credit cards.*

¢–$ ✕ **Oskar.** This modern establishment in a glassed-in annex of the art museum serves up refined Franconian specialties and Continental dishes on large tables. The chef insists on fresh produce, mostly organic, and has banned the microwave from the kitchen. The service is extremely friendly. The Oskar fills up at night and during Sunday brunch, especially if a jazz band is playing in one of the alcoves. ✉ *Maximilianstr. 10* ☎ *0921/516–0553* ▭ *No credit cards.*

¢–$ ✕ **Wolffenzacher.** This self-described "nostalgic inn" harks back to the days when the local *Wirtshaus* (inn–pub) was the meeting place for everyone from the mayor's scribes to the local carpenters. Beer and hearty food are shared at wooden tables either in the rustic interior or out in the shady beergarden (in the middle of town!), weather permitting. The hearty Franconian specialties on the menu here are counterbalanced by a few lighter French and Italian dishes. ✉ *Sternenplatz. 5* ☎ *0921/64552* ▭ *MC, V.*

★ $$–$$$ ✕▤ **Goldener Anker.** No question about it, this is *the* place to stay in Bayreuth. The hotel is right next to the Markgräfliches Opernhaus and has been entertaining composers, singers, conductors, and players for more than 100 years. The establishment has been run by the same family since 1753. Rooms are small but individually decorated; many have antique pieces. The restaurant ($$$–$$$$) is justly popular. Book your room far in advance. ✉ *Opernstr. 6, D–95444* ☎ *0921/65051* 🖷 *0921/ 65500* ⊕ *www.anker-bayreuth.de* ⇱ *40 rooms* ⚘ *Restaurant, some in-room data ports, cable TV, some pets allowed; no a/c* ▭ *AE, DC, MC, V* ☉ *Restaurant closed Mon., Tues., and Dec. 20–Jan. 10* ⎪⎧⎪ *BP.*

$$–$$$ ✕▤ **Schlosshotel Thiergarten.** Staying at this 250-year-old former hunting lodge is like being at your favorite aunt's, if she were an elderly millionaire. Rooms are individually furnished and have a plush, lived-in feel. The

intimate Kaminhalle, with an ornate fireplace, and the Venezianischer Salon, dominated by a glittering 300-year-old Venetian chandelier, offer regional and nouvelle cuisine ($$–$$$$). Reservations and a jacket and tie are essential at both restaurants. The hotel is 8 km (5 mi) from Bayreuth in the Thiergarten suburb. ⊠ *Oberthiergärtenerstr. 36, D–95448* ☎ *09209/ 9840* 🖶 *09209/98429* ⊕ *www.schlosshotel-thiergarten.de* ⇄ *8 rooms, 1 suite* ♨ *2 restaurants, cable TV, pool, sauna, bar, some pets allowed (fee); no a/c* ⊟ *AE, DC, MC, V* ⊗ *Restaurants closed Mon.* �’⊘❘ *BP.*

$–$$ ╳🏨 **Hotel Lohmühle.** The old part of this hotel is in Bayreuth's only half-timber house, a former saw mill by a stream. It's just a two-minute walk to the town center. The rooms are rustic with visible beams; the newer, neighboring building has correspondingly modern rooms. Between the two is a gallery with a bar where you can enjoy a small aperitif before trying some of the restaurant's traditional, hearty cooking ($$–$$$), such as Schaüfele or carp. ⊠ *Badstr. 37, D–95445* ☎ *0921/53060* 🖶 *0921/ 530–6469* ⊕ *www.hotel-lohmuehle.de* ⇄ *42 rooms* ♨ *Restaurant, in-room data ports, cable TV, bar, some pets allowed (fee), no-smoking rooms; no a/c* ⊟ *AE, DC, MC, V* ⊗ *No dinner Sun.* ❘⊘❘ *BP.*

Nightlife & the Arts

Opera lovers swear that there are few more intense operatic experiences than those offered by the annual **Wagner Festival** in Bayreuth, held July and August. For tickets write to the **Bayreuther Festspiele Kartenbüro** (🖃 Postfach 100262, D–95402 Bayreuth ☎ 0921/78780), but be warned: the waiting list is years long! You'll do best if you plan your visit a couple of years in advance. Rooms can be nearly impossible to find during the festival, too. If you don't get Wagner tickets, console yourself with visits to the exquisite 18th-century **Markgräfliches Opernhaus** (⊠ Opernstr. ☎ 0921/251–416); performances are given most nights from May through September, and sporadicaly throughout the rest of the year. Check with the tourist office for details.

Shopping

The **Hofgarten Passage,** off Richard-Wagner-Strasse, is one of the fanciest shopping arcades in the region; it's crammed with smart boutiques selling anything from high German fashion to simple local artifacts.

en route   The B–22 highway west to Bamberg is part of the officially designated **Strasse der Residenzen** (Road of Residences), named for the many episcopal and princely palaces along the way—including Bamberg's stunning Neue Residenz. The road cuts through the Fränkische Schweiz—or Franconian Switzerland—which got its name from its fir-clad upland landscape. Just north of Hollfeld, 23 km (14 mi) west of Bayreuth, the Jurassic rock of the region breaks through the surface in a bizarre, craggy formation known as the Felsgarten (Rock Garden).

Bamberg

❺ *65 km (40 mi) west of Bayreuth, 80 km (50 mi) north of Nürnberg.*

Few towns in Germany survived the war with as little damage as Bamberg, which is on the Regnitz River. This former residence of one of Germany's most powerful imperial dynasties is on UNESCO's World Heritage Site list. Bamberg, originally nothing more than a fortress in the hands of the Babenberg dynasty (later contracted to Bamberg), rose to prominence in the 11th century thanks to the political and economic drive of its most famous offspring, Holy Roman Emperor Heinrich II. He transformed the imperial residence into a flourishing episcopal city. His cathedral, consecrated in 1237, still dominates the historic area. For a short period Heinrich II proclaimed Bamberg the capital of the Holy Roman Empire of the German nation. Moreover, Bamberg earned fame as the second city to introduce book printing, in 1460.

The simplest pleasure here is to stroll through the narrow, sinuous streets of Old Bamberg, past half-timber and gabled houses and formal 18th-century mansions. Peek into flower-filled cobblestone courtyards or take time out in a waterside café in "little Venice," watching the small steamers as they chug past the colorful row of fishermen's houses. Bamberg's historic core, the **Altes Rathaus** (Old Town Hall), is tucked snugly on a small island in the Regnitz. To the west of the river is the so-called Bishops' Town; to the east, Burghers' Town. This rickety, extravagantly decorated building was built in this unusual place so that the burghers of Bamberg could avoid paying real-estate taxes to their bishops and archbishops. The excellent collection of porcelain here is on permanent loan from the Ludwig estate. It contains a vast sampling of many 18th-century styles, from almost sober Meissens with bucolic Watteau scenes to simple but rare Haguenau pieces from Alsace and voluble Strasbourg faience. ⊠ *Obere Brücke 1* ☎ *0951/871–871* ✇ *€3.10* ☉ *Tues.–Sun. 9:30–4:30.*

need a break? Before heading up the hill to Bambergs' main sights in the Bishops' Town, take a break in the old **Rathaus-Schänke** (⊠ Obere Brücke 3 ☎ 0951/208–0890) overlooking the river on the Burghers' Town side of the Town Hall. Coffee, cake, small meals, and cocktails can be enjoyed in a beautifully restored old half-timber house.

The **Neue Residenz** (New Residence), Bamberg's contribution to the Road of Residences, is a glittering baroque palace that was once the home of the prince-electors. Their plans to extend the immense palace even further is evident at the corner on Obere Karolinenstrasse, where the ashlar bonding was left open to accept another wing. The most memorable room in the palace is the **Kaisersaal** (Throne Room), complete with impressive ceiling frescoes and elaborate stuccowork. Among the thousands of books and illuminated manuscripts in the **Staatsbibliothek** (State Library) are the original prayer books belonging to Heinrich and his wife, a 5th-century codex of the Roman historian Livy, and manuscripts by the 16th-century painters Dürer and Cranach. The rose garden behind the Neue Residenz offers an aromatic and romantic space to stroll with a view of Bamberg's roof landscape. ⊠ *Dompl. 8* ☎ *0951/519–390 Staatsbibliothek* ✇ *Neue Residenz €3, Staatsbibliothek free* ☉ *Neue Residenz by tour only, Apr.–Sept., daily 9–6; Oct.–Mar., daily 9–4; Staatsbibliothek Sept.–July, weekdays 9–5, Sat. 9–noon; Aug., weekdays 9–noon.*

★ Bamberg's great **Dom** (Cathedral) is one of the country's most important, a building that tells not only the town's story but that of Germany as well. The first building here was begun by Heinrich II in 1003, and it was in this partially completed cathedral that he was crowned Holy Roman Emperor in 1012. In 1237 it was destroyed by fire, and the present late-Romanesque–early-Gothic building was begun. The dominant features are the massive towers at each corner. Heading into the dark interior, you'll find one of the most striking collections of monuments and art treasures of any European church. The most famous piece is the **Bamberger Reiter** (Bamberg Rider), an equestrian statue carved—no one knows by whom—around 1230 and thought to be an allegory of chivalrous virtue or a representation of King Stephen of Hungary. Compare it with the mass of carved figures huddled in the tympana above the church portals. In the center of the nave you'll find another masterpiece, the massive tomb of Heinrich and his wife, Kunigunde. It's the work of Tilman Riemenschneider. Pope Clement II is also buried in the cathedral, in an imposing tomb beneath the high altar; he's the only pope to be buried north of the Alps. ⊠ *Dompl.* ☎ *0951/502–330* ⊙ *Nov.–Mar., daily 8–5, Apr.–Oct. 8–6, no visits during services.*

The **Diözesanmuseum** (Cathedral Museum), directly next to the cathedral, contains one of many nails and splinters of wood reputed to be from the cross of Jesus. The "star-spangled" cloak stitched with gold that was given to Emperor Heinrich II by an Italian prince is among the finest items displayed. More macabre exhibits in this rich ecclesiastical collection are the elaborately mounted skulls of Heinrich and Kunigunde. The building itself was designed by Balthasar Neumann (1687–1753), the architect of Vierzehnheiligen, and constructed between 1730 and 1733. ⊠ *Dompl. 5* ☎ *0951/502–325* ☐ *€2* ⊙ *Tues.–Sun. 10–5; tour in English by prior arrangement.*

On the north side of the Dom is the **Alte Hofhaltung,** the former imperial and episcopal palace. It's a sturdy and weatherworn half-timber Gothic building with a large, unruly Renaissance courtyard that's used for various events, notably theater in summer. Today it contains the **Historisches Museum** (Historical Museum), with a collection of documents and maps that will appeal most to history buffs who read German well. Over the next few years restoration work will increase the size of the museum and more exhibits will be on display. ⊠ *Dompl. 8* ☎ *0951/ 519–0746* ☐ *€2.10* ⊙ *May–Oct., Tues.–Sun. 9–5.*

Bamberg's wealthy burghers built no fewer than 50 churches. Among the very special ones is the Church of Our Lady, known simply as **Obere Pfarre** (Upper Parish), whose history goes back to around 1325. It's unusual because it's still entirely Gothic from the outside. Also, the grand choir, which was added at a later period, is lacking windows. And then there's the odd, squarish box perched atop the tower. This watchman's abode served to cut the tower short before it grew taller than the neighboring cathedral, thereby avoiding a great scandal. The interior is heavily baroque. Note the slanted floor, which allowed crowds of pilgrims to see the object of their veneration, a 14th-century Madonna. Don't miss the *Ascension of Mary* by Tintoretto at the rear of the church. Around

Christmas, the Obere Pfarre is the site of the city's greatest Nativity scene. Avoid the church during services, unless you're worshipping. ⊠ *Untere Seelg.* ☉ *Daily 7–7.*

St. Michael, a former Benedictine monastery, has been gazing over Bamberg since about 1015. After being overwhelmed by so much baroque elsewhere, entering this haven of simplicity is quite an experience. The entire choir is intricately carved, but the ceiling is gently decorated with very exact depictions of 578 flowers and healing herbs. The tomb of St. Otto is in a little chapel off the transept, and the stained-glass windows hold symbols of death and transfiguration. The monastery is now used as a home for the aged. One tract, however, was taken over by the **Franconian Brewery Museum,** which exhibits everything that has to do with beer, from the making of malt to recipes. ⊠ *Michelsberg 10f* ☎ *0951/ 53016* 🖾 *Museum €2* ☉ *Apr.–Oct., Wed.–Sun. 1–5.*

In an 18th-century university building, the **Holowood Museum** exhibits all sorts of works and installations involving holography. It's the largest museum of its kind in Germany. It's no exaggeration to say, you won't believe your eyes. ⊠ *Willy-Lessing-Str. 10 10f* ☎ *0951/208–0814* ⊕ *www.holographie.de* 🖾 *€3.10* ☉ *Daily 10–6.*

Laser technology, art, and photography meet at the **Naturkunde Museum** (Museum of Natural History). Located in a unique 18th-century university building, the museum covers a wide range of subjects, from fossils to volcanoes. The pride of the place is the collection of 800 stuffed birds in a magnificent room that also has a whale's jawbone casually lying on the floor. ⊠ *Fleischstr. 2* ☎ *0951/863–1248* ⊕ *www.uni-bamberg.de/NatMus* 🖾 *€ 1.50* ☉ *Apr.–Sept., daily 9–5; Oct.–Mar., daily 10–4.*

Where to Stay & Eat

¢–$ ✕ **Bischohsmühle.** It doesn't always have to be beer in Bamberg. The old mill, its grinding wheel providing a sonorous backdrop for patrons, specializes in wines from Franconia and elsewhere. The menu offers Franconian specialties such as the French-derived *Böfflamott,* or beef stew. ⊠ *Geyerswörthstr. 4* ☎ *0951/27570* 🖃 *No credit cards* ☉ *Closed Wed.*

¢–$ ✕ **Café Abseits.** "Abseits" means off the beaten path, but that's not truly the case here. This quietly chic eatery has a merry and mixed crowd of burghers and students. Light-color walls display large prints (for sale), and there's a steady flow of 30 types of beer, along with tasty specials and à la carte breakfast that can be ordered until 3 PM (5 PM on Sunday and holidays). ⊠ *Pödeldorferstr. 39* ☎ *0951/303–422* 🖃 *No credit cards.*

¢–$ ✕ **Klosterbräu.** This massive old stone–and–half-timber house has been standing since 1533, and some of the customers nursing their dark, smoky beer near the big stove seem as if they are just a few generations away from the original patrons. The cuisine is basic, robust, filling, and tasty, with such items as a bowl of beans with a slab of smoked pork, or marinated pork kidneys with boiled potatoes. ⊠ *Obere Mühlbrücke* ☎ *0951/ 52265* 🖃 *No credit cards* ☉ *Closed Wed.*

$$ ✕🔲 **Hotel-Restaurant St. Nepomuk.** This half-timber house seems to float
Fodor'sChoice over the Regnitz. Sitting in the dining room, with its podium fireplace,
★ discreet lights, serene atmosphere, and direct view of the river, you get
the feeling of being on board a ship. The Grüner family makes a spe-
cial effort to bring not only high-quality food to the restaurant ($$$)
but a world of excellent wines as well. The rooms are comfortable, and
many have quite a view of the river and the old town hall on the island.
Each is furnished individually in elegant style. ⊠ *Obere Mühlbrücke 9,
D–96047* ☎ *0951/98420* 🖷 *0951/984–2100* ⊕ *www.hotel-nepomuk.
de* 🛏 *47 rooms* � *Restaurant, cable TV, some pets allowed (fee), no-
smoking rooms; no a/c* ▤ *DC, MC, V* ⦿| *BP.*

$$ ✕🔲 **Romantik Hotel Weinhaus Messerschmitt.** Willy Messerschmitt of avi-
ation fame grew up in this beautiful late-baroque house with a steep-
eaved, green-shutter stucco exterior. The very comfortable hotel has
spacious and luxurious rooms, some with exposed beams and many of
them lighted by chandeliers. You'll dine under beams and a coffered ceil-
ing in the excellent Messerschmitt restaurant ($$–$$$), one of Bamberg's
most popular culinary havens for Franconian specialties in gourmet cloak.
The hotel is fitted for guests with disabilities. ⊠ *Langestr. 41, D–96047*
☎ *0951/27866* 🖷 *0951/26141* 🛏 *19 rooms* ⓑ *Restaurant, cable TV,
bar, no-smoking rooms; no a/c* ▤ *AE, DC, MC, V* ⦿| *BP.*

The Arts

The **Sinfonie an der Regnitz** (⊠ Muss-Str. 20 ☎ 0951/964–7200), a fine
riverside concert hall, is home to Bamberg's world-class resident sym-
phony orchestra. The **Hoffmann Theater** (⊠ Schillerpl. 5 ☎ 0951/871–
433) has opera and operetta from September through July. In June and
July open-air performances are given at the **Alte Hofhaltung** (⊠ Dompl.
8 ☎ 0951/519–0746). The city's first-class choir, **Capella Antiqua Bam-
bergensis,** concentrates on ancient music. Throughout the summer
organ concerts are given in the **Dom.** For program details and tickets
to all cultural events, call 0951/871–161. If you happen to be travel-
ing around Christmastime, make sure you keep an eye out for crèches,
a Bamberg specialty.

Shopping

Of the many shops in Bamberg, the **AGIL** (⊠ Schranne 14 ☎ 0951/519–
0389) may be the one you'll want to visit for an unusual souvenir. Jost
Lohmann sells replicas of medieval household utensils and other pecu-
liar items.

en route From Bamberg you can either take the fast autobahn (A–73) south to
Nürnberg, or the parallel country road (B–4) that follows the Main-
Danube Canal (running parallel to the Regnitz River at this point)
and joins A–73 just under 25 km (15 mi) later at Forchheim-Nord.
The canal, a mighty feat of engineering first envisioned by
Charlemagne but only completed in the 1990s, connects the North
Sea and the Black Sea by linking the Rhine and the Danube rivers via
the Main River. There's no tangible division between northern and
southern Franconia. You do, however, leave the thickly wooded
heights of the Fichtelgebirge and the Fränkische Schweiz behind, and

the countryside opens up as if to announce the imminent arrival of a more populated region.

Eighteen kilometers (11 mi) south of Bamberg in the village of Buttenheim is a little blue-and-white half-timber house where Löb Strauss was born—in egregious poverty—in 1826. Take the tape-recorded tour of the **Levi-Strauss Museum** (✉ Marktstr. 33 ☎ 09545/442–602 ✉ €2.60 ⊘ Tues.–Thurs. 2–6, weekends 11–5 and by appointment) and learn how Löb emigrated to the United States, changed his name to Levi, and became the first name in denim. One of the special exhibits is a pair of jeans dating to 1880 discovered in the Nevada desert (the jeans on display are actually a replica). The stone-washed color of the house's beams, by the way, is the original 17th-century color. The museum also hosts special exhibitions and other events, all revolving around jeans, of course.

NÜRNBERG

➤ Nürnberg (Nuremberg) is the principal city of Franconia and the second-largest city in Bavaria. With a recorded history stretching back to 1050, it's among the most historic of Germany's cities; the core of the Old Town, through which the Pegnitz River flows, is still surrounded by its original medieval walls. Nürnberg has always taken a leading role in German affairs. It was here, for example, that the Holy Roman Emperors traditionally held the first Diet, or convention of the estates, of their incumbency. And it was here, too, that Hitler staged the most grandiose Nazi rallies; later, this was the site of the Allies' war trials, where top-ranking Nazis were charged with—and almost without exception convicted of—crimes against humanity. The rebuilding of Nürnberg after the war was virtually a miracle considering the 90% destruction of the Old Town. As if putting an end to its difficult, violent history, Nürnberg, in 2001, became the world's first city to receive the UNESCO prize for Human Rights Education.

As a major intersection on the medieval trade routes, Nürnberg became a wealthy town. With prosperity came a great flowering of the arts and sciences. Albrecht Dürer (1471–1528), the first indisputable genius of the Renaissance in Germany, was born here in 1471. He married in 1509 and bought a house in the city where he lived and worked for the rest of his life. Other leading Nürnberg artists of the Renaissance include painter Michael Wolgemut (a teacher of Dürer), stonecutter Adam Kraft, and the brass founder Peter Vischer. The tradition of the Meistersinger also flourished here in the 16th century, thanks to the high standard set by the local cobbler Hans Sachs (1494–1576). The Meistersinger were poets and musicians who turned songwriting into a special craft with a wealth of rules and regulations. They were celebrated three centuries later by Wagner in his *Meistersinger von Nürnberg*. The Thirty Years' War and the shift to sea routes for transportation led to a long decline, which ended only in the early 19th century when the first railroad opened in Nürnberg. Among a great host of inventions associated with the city, the most significant are the pocket watch, gun casting, the clarinet, and the geographic globe (the first of which was made before Columbus discovered the Americas). Among Nürnberg's famous products are *Lebkuchen* (gingerbread of sorts) and Faber-Castell pencils.

Exploring

Nürnberg is 63 km (39 mi) south of Bamberg and rich in special events and celebrations. By far the most famous is the **Christkindlesmarkt** (Christ-Child Market), an enormous pre-Christmas fair that runs from the Friday before Advent to Christmas Eve. One of the highlights is the candle procession, held every second Thursday of the market season, during which thousands of children parade through the city streets.

a good walk

Start your walk at the **Hauptbahnhof** ☞, the main train station, whose tourist office offers maps and brochures. Enter the Old Town through the **Königstor,** the old King's Gate. The Old Town walls, finished in 1452, come complete with moats, sturdy gateways, and watchtowers. Year-round floodlighting adds to their brooding romance. Take a left on Luitpoldstrasse and note, on your left, the **Neues Museum** ⑥, Nürnberg's museum for contemporary art. Take a left on Vordere Sterngasse and then a right when you reach the old wall again. Take your second right onto Strasse der Menschenrechte (Human Rights Street), which has an installation of 30 columns inscribed with the articles from the Declaration of Human Rights. On the right is one of Germany's most extraordinary museums, the **Germanisches Nationalmuseum** ⑦. A few hours spent here examining the sections devoted to the city will prepare you for the step back in time you'll make during the rest of your walk through Nürnberg. Follow Kornmarkt east and turn left on Pfannenschmiedsgasse to reach the beautiful **St. Lorenz Kirche** ⑧.

Continue north on Königstrasse and cross the bridge over the Pegnitz River at its most photogenic point, where the former hospital **Heilig-Geist-Spital** broods over the waters, and soon you'll reach the city's central market square, the **Hauptmarkt** ⑨, with the delicate late-Gothic **Frauenkirche** ⑩ standing modestly on the east side and the handsome **Schöner Brunnen** ⑪ (fountain) in the northwestern corner. Just north of the Hauptmarkt is Rathausplatz, site of another Gothic masterpiece of church architecture, **St. Sebaldus Kirche** ⑫. The **Altes Rathaus** ⑬ faces the church; behind the town hall is another pretty fountain, the **Gänsemännchenbrunnen** ⑭. To the north of the Altes Rathaus on Burgstrasse stands the fine Renaissance Fembohaus, which contains the **Stadtmuseum** ⑮. Save some energy for the climb up Burgstrasse to the great **Kaiserburg** ⑯, whose shadow falls on the **Albrecht-Dürer-Haus** ⑰, at the top of Albrecht-Dürer-Strasse, just below the castle. Follow this street southward and you'll come to a delightful toy museum, the **Spielzeugmuseum** ⑱, on Karlstrasse. If you still have time or energy, it's about a 15-minute walk to the trains and stamps of the **Museum für Kommunikation** ⑲, on Lessingstrasse, just south of the Germanisches Nationalmuseum. You can then return to your starting point for that much-needed refreshment. The train station has an extensive mall of restaurants and bars.

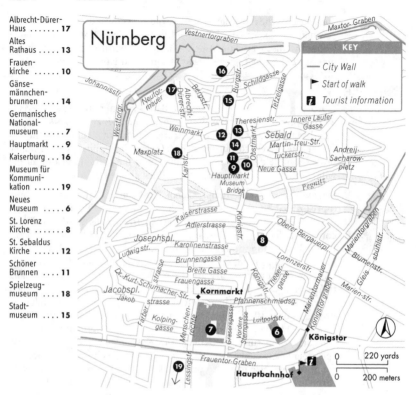

TIMING You'll need a full day to walk around Nürnberg, two if you wish to take more time at its fascinating museums. Most of the major sights are within a few minutes' walk of each other. Begin or end your day at the Kaiser-burg, whose ramparts offer a spectacular view over this medieval gem of a town.

What to See

★ ⓲ **Albrecht-Dürer-Haus** (Albrecht Dürer House). The great painter Albrecht Dürer lived here from 1509 until his death in 1528. This beautifully preserved late-medieval house is typical of the prosperous merchants' homes that once filled Nürnberg. Dürer, who enriched German art with Italianate elements, was more than a painter. He raised the woodcut, a notoriously difficult medium, to new heights of technical sophistication, combining great skill with a haunting, immensely detailed drawing style and complex, allegorical subject matter while earning a good living at the same time. A number of original prints adorn the walls, and printing techniques using the old press are demonstrated in the studio. An excellent opportunity to find out about life in the house is the Saturday 2 PM tour with a guide role-playing Agnes Dürer, Dürer's wife. ✉ *Albrecht-Dürer-Str. 39* ☎ *0911/231–2568* 🎟 *€5, with tour €7.50* ☉ *Tues., Wed., and Fri.–Sun. 10–5, Thurs. 10–8.*

⑬ Altes Rathaus (Old Town Hall). This ancient building on Rathausplatz abuts the rear of St. Sebaldus Kirche; it was erected in 1332, destroyed in World War II, and subsequently restored. Its intact medieval dungeons, consisting of 12 small rooms and one large torture chamber called the **Lochgefängnis** (or the Chapel, owing to the vaulted ceilings), provide insight into the gruesome applications of medieval law. ⊠ *Rathauspl.* ☎ *0911/231–2690* ☞ *€3, tours only beginning with 5 people* ☉ *Tues.–Sun. 10–5:30; during Christkindlesmarkt daily 10–5:30.*

⑩ Frauenkirche (Church of Our Lady). The fine late-Gothic Frauenkirche was built in 1350, with the approval of Holy Roman Emperor Charles IV, on the site of a synagogue that was burned down during a 1349 pogrom. The modern tabernacle beneath the main altar was designed to look like a Torah scroll as a kind of memorial to that despicable act. The church's real attraction is the **Männleinlaufen,** a clock dating from 1509, which is set in its facade. It's one of those colorful mechanical marvels at which Germans have long excelled. Every day at noon the seven electors of the Holy Roman Empire glide out of the clock to bow to Emperor Charles IV before sliding back under cover. It's worth scheduling your morning to catch the display. ⊠ *Hauptmarkt* ☉ *Mon.–Sat. 9–6, Sun. 12:30–6.*

⑭ Gänsemännchenbrunnen (Gooseman's Fountain). A work of rare elegance and great technical sophistication, this lovely Renaissance bronze fountain facing the Altes Rathaus was cast in 1550. ⊠ *Rathauspl.*

★ ❼ Germanisches Nationalmuseum (German National Museum). You could spend days visiting this vast museum, which showcases the country's cultural and scientific achievements, ethnic background, and history. It's the largest of its kind in Germany and perhaps the best arranged. The museum is in what was once a Carthusian monastery, complete with cloisters and monastic outbuildings. The extensions, however, are modern and sleek. The exhibition begins outside, with the tall, sleek pillars of the Way of Human Rights designed by Israeli artist Dani Karavan. There are few aspects of German culture, from the Stone Age to the 19th century, that are not covered by the museum, and quantity and quality are evenly matched. One highlight is the superb collection of Renaissance German paintings (with Dürer, Cranach, and Altdorfer well represented). Others may prefer the exquisite medieval ecclesiastical exhibits—manuscripts, altarpieces, statuary, stained glass, jewel-encrusted reliquaries—the collections of arms and armor, the scientific instruments, or the toys. Few will be disappointed. ⊠ *Kartäuserg. 1* ☎ *0911/13310* ⊕ *www.gnm.de* ☞ *€4, €5 for special exhibitions* ☉ *Tues. and Thurs.–Sun. 10–6, Wed. 10–9.*

need a break?

Opposite the Germanisches Nationalmuseum is a minimalist, Italian restaurant named **Vivere** (⊠ Kartäuserg. 12 ☎ 0911/133–1286). Al dente pasta or meat and fish dishes will bring you back to earth after the long hours spent in the museum. Entrées cost around €6–€14. Vivere is closed Monday.

❾ Hauptmarkt (Main Market). Nürnberg's central market square was at one time the city's Jewish Quarter. When the people of Nürnberg petitioned their emperor, Charles IV, for a big central market, the emperor happened to be in desperate need of money and, above all, political support. The Jewish Quarter was the preferred site, but as the official protector of the Jewish people, the emperor could not just openly take away their property. Instead, he instigated a pogrom that left the Jewish Quarter in flames and more than 500 dead. The next step of razing the ruins and resettling the remaining Jews thus appeared perfectly logical.

A market still operates here. Its colorful stands are piled high with produce, fruit, bread, homemade cheeses and sausages, sweets, and anything else you might need for a snack or picnic. It's here that the Christkindlesmarkt is held.

⑯ Kaiserburg (Imperial Castle). The city's main attraction is a grand yet playful collection of buildings standing just inside the city walls; it was once the residence of the Holy Roman Emperors. The complex comprises three separate groups. The oldest, dating from around 1050, is the **Burggrafenburg** (Castellan's Castle), with a craggy old pentagonal tower and the bailiff's house. It stands in the center of the complex. To the east is the **Kaiserstallung** (Imperial Stables), built in the 15th century as a granary and now serving as a youth hostel. The real interest of this vast complex of ancient buildings, however, centers on the westernmost part of the fortress, which begins at the **Sinwell Turm** (Sinwell Tower). The **Kaiserburg Museum** is here, a subsidiary of the Germanisches Nationalmuseum that displays ancient armors and has exhibits relating to horsemanship in the imperial era and to the history of the fortress. This section of the castle also has a wonderful Romanesque **Doppelkappelle** (Double Chapel). The upper part—richer, larger, and more ornate than the lower chapel—was where the emperor and his family worshipped. Also visit the **Rittersaal** (Knights' Hall) and the **Kaisersaal** (Throne Room). Their heavy oak beams, painted ceilings, and sparse interiors have changed little since they were built in the 15th century. ⊠ *Burgstr.* ☎ *0911/225–726* ▣ *€6* ⊙ *Apr.–Sept., Fri.–Wed. 9–6, Thurs. 9–8; Oct.–Mar., daily 10–4.*

⑲ Museum für Kommunikation (Communication Museum). Two museums have been amalgamated under a single roof here, the German Railway Museum and the Museum of Communication, in short, museums about how people get in touch. The first train to run in Germany did so on December 7, 1835, from Nürnberg to nearby Fürth. A model of the epochal train is here, along with a series of original 19th- and early-20th-century trains and stagecoaches. Philatelists will want to check out some of the 40,000-odd stamps in the extensive exhibits on the German postal system. You can also find out about the history of sending messages—from old coaches to optical fiber networks. ⊠ *Lessingstr. 6* ☎ *0911/219–2428* ▣ *€3* ⊙ *Tues.–Sun. 9–5.*

⑥ Neues Museum (New Museum). Anything but medieval, this museum opened in mid-2000 and is devoted to international design since 1945. The remarkable collection, supplemented by changing exhibitions, is in a slick, modern edifice that achieves the perfect synthesis between old and new. It's mostly built of traditional pink-sandstone ashlars, while the facade is a flowing, transparent composition of glass. The interior is a work of art in itself—cool stone, with a ramp that slowly spirals up to the gallery. Extraordinary things await, including a Joseph Beuys installation (*Ausfegen,* or Sweep-out) and *Avalanche* by François Morellet, a striking collection of violet, argon gas–filled fluorescent tubes. The café-restaurant adjoining the museum contains modern art, silver-wrapped candies, and video projections. ⊠ *Luitpoldstr. 5* ☎ *0911/240–200* 🖃 *€3.50* ☉ *Tues.–Fri. 10–8, weekends 10–6.*

❽ St. Lorenz Kirche (St. Laurence Church). In a city with several striking churches, St. Lorenz is considered by many to be the most beautiful. It was begun around 1250 and completed in about 1477; it later became a Lutheran church. Two towers flank the main entrance of the sizable church, which is covered with a forest of carvings. In the lofty interior, note the works by sculptors Adam Kraft and Veit Stoss: Kraft's great stone tabernacle, to the left of the altar, and Stoss's *Annunciation,* at the east end of the nave, are their finest works. There are many other carvings throughout the building, testimony to the artistic wealth of late-medieval Nürnberg. ⊠ *Lorenzer Pl.* ☎ *0911/209–287* ☉ *Mon.–Sat. 9–5, Sun. noon–4.*

⓬ St. Sebaldus Kirche (St. Sebaldus Church). Although St. Sebaldus lacks the quantity of art treasures found in its rival St. Lorenz, its nave and choir are among the purest examples of Gothic ecclesiastical architecture in Germany: elegant, tall, and airy. Veit Stoss carved the crucifixion group at the east end of the nave, while the elaborate bronze shrine, containing the remains of St. Sebaldus himself, was cast by Peter Vischer and his five sons around 1520. Not to be missed is the **Sebaldus Chörlein,** an ornate Gothic oriel that was added to the Sebaldus parish house in 1361 (the original is in the Germanisches Nationalmuseum). ⊠ *Albrecht-Dürer-Pl. 1* ☎ *0911/214–2500* ☉ *Jan.–Mar., daily 9:30–4, Apr., May, and Oct.–Dec., daily 9:30–6, June–Sept., daily 9:30–8.*

⓫ Schöner Brunnen (Beautiful Fountain). The elegant 60-foot-high Gothic fountain, carved around the year 1400, looks as though it should be on the summit of some lofty Gothic cathedral. It's adorned with 40 figures arranged in tiers—prophets, saints, local noblemen, sundry electors of the Holy Roman Empire, and one or two strays such as Julius Caesar and Alexander the Great. A gold ring is set into the railing surrounding the fountain, reportedly placed there by an apprentice carver. Stroking it is said to bring good luck. ⊠ *Hauptmarkt.*

☙ ⓲ Spielzeugmuseum (Toy Museum). Young and old are captivated by this playful museum, which has a few exhibits dating from the Renaissance; most, however, are from the 19th century. Simple dolls vie with mechanical toys of extraordinary complexity, such as a wooden Ferris wheel from the Erz Mountains adorned with little colored lights. The top floor displays Barbies and intricate Lego constructions. ⊠ *Karlstr. 13–15* ☎ *0911/231–3164* 🖃 *€5* ☉ *Tues. and Thurs.–Sun. 10–5, Wed. 10–9.*

need a break? Honoring Nürnberg's partnership with the French city of Nice, the **D'Azur** (⊠ Burgstr. 11 ☎ 0911/235–5355) has baguette sandwiches and other snacks with a Provençal touch. You can also purchase all sorts of delicacies here, such as ratatouille and fish soup in jars.

⑮ Stadtmuseum (City Museum). This city history museum is in the Fembohaus, a dignified patrician dwelling completed in 1598. It's one of the finest Renaissance mansions in Nürnberg. Each room explores another aspect of Nürnberg history, from crafts to gastronomy. The 50-minute multivision show provides a comprehensive look at the long history of the city. ⊠ *Burgstr. 15* ☎ *0911/231–2595* 🎟 *€4* ⊙ *Tues., Wed., and Fri.–Sun. 10–5, Thurs. 10–8.*

off the beaten path

TIERGARTEN NÜRNBERG – The well-stocked Nürnberg Zoo has a dolphinarium that children love; it's worth the extra admission fee. The zoo is on the northwest edge of town; reach it by taking the No. 5 streetcar from the city center. ⊠ *Am Tiergarten 30* ☎ *0911/54546* 🎟 *€6.50, dolphinarium €3* ⊙ *Zoo and dolphinarium Apr.–Sept., daily 8–7:30; Mar. and Oct., daily 8–5:30; Nov.–Feb., daily 9–5; dolphinarium display daily at 11, 2, and 4.*

JÜDISCHES MUSEUM FRANKEN – The Holocaust is not the focus of the Jewish Museum of Franconia; rather, items pertaining to the everyday life of the Jewish community in Franconia and Fürth are examined: books, Seder plates, coat hangers, old statutes concerning Jews, children's toys. Among the most famous members of the Fürth community was Henry Kissinger, born here in 1923. Changing exhibitions relate to contemporary Jewish life in Germany, and in the basement is the Mikwe, the ritual bath, which was used by the family who lived here centuries ago. A subsidiary to the museum, which houses special exhibitions, has been opened in the former synagogue in nearby Schnaittach. To get to the museum from Nürnberg, you can take the U1 U-bahn to the Rathaus stop. ⊠ *Königstr. 89, Fürth, 10 km (6 mi) west of Nürnberg* ☎ *0911/770–577* ⊕ *www.juedisches-museum.org* 🎟 *€3* ⊙ *Sun., Mon., and Wed.–Fri. 10–5, Tues. 10–8.*

ZEPPELINFELD – The enormous parade grounds where Hitler addressed his largest Nazi rallies lie on the city's eastern edge. Today it sometimes shakes to the amplified beat of pop concerts. The central stand area contains a remarkable museum with the **Ausstellung Faszination und Gewalt** (Fascination and Terror exhibition), which documents the political, social, and architectural history of the Nazi Party in Nürnberg. It's within one section of the horseshoe-shape Congressional Hall built by the Nazis to harbor a crowd of 50,000. Austrian architect Günther Domenig added a courageous glass corridor that adds light to the overwhelmingly solid construction. Tours of the grounds are offered by a private association called Geschichte für Alle (History for All). ☎ *0911/869–897 for Zeppelinfeld, 0911/332–735 for tour* 🎟 *Museum €1.50, tour €5* ⊙ *Museum mid-May–Oct., daily 10–6; Nov.–mid-May, by appointment. Tours Dec.–Mar., Sun. at 2; Apr.–Nov., weekends at 2. Meet at Luitpoldhain tram terminus (No. 9).*

Where to Stay & Eat

$$$ ✕ **Essigbrätlein.** Some rank this the top restaurant in the city and even
Fodor'sChoice among the best in Germany. As the oldest restaurant in Nürnberg, built
★ in 1550 and originally used as a meeting place for wine merchants, it's
unquestionably one of the most atmospheric. Today its tiny but elegant
period interior caters to the distinguishing gourmet with a taste for spe-
cial spice mixes (owner Andrée Köthe's hobby). The menu changes
daily. ⊠ *Weinmarkt 3* ☎ *0911/225–131* ⌖ *Reservations essential*
🗖 *AE, DC, MC, V* ☉ *Closed Sun. and Mon.*

★ $–$$$ ✕ **Heilig-Geist-Spital.** Heavy wood furnishings and a choice of more
than 100 wines make this more than 650-year-old wine tavern—built
as the refectory of the city hospital—a popular spot. The menu includes
grilled pork chops, pan-fried potatoes, and German cheeses. ⊠ *Spitalg.*
16 ☎ *0911/221–761* 🗖 *AE, DC, MC, V.*

★ ¢–$ ✕ **Barfüsser Kleines Brauhaus.** The huge cellar rooms of the old grain cus-
toms warehouse house this minibrewery and restaurant. Locals meet for
lunch or dinner to enjoy Franconian specialties or just plain home cooking along with fine beer brewed on the premises. The vaulted ceiling and
thick stone pillars are a simple but elegant backdrop. Try the carp, a regional specialty available only in months with an "r" in their name.
⊠ *Königstr. 60* ☎ *0911/204–242* 🗖 *AE, MC, V.*

★ ¢–$ ✕ **Historische Bratwurst-Küche Zum Gulden Stern.** This house, built in 1375,
survived the last war and holds the oldest bratwurst restaurant in the world.
The famous Nürnberg bratwursts are always freshly roasted on a beechwood fire; the boiled variation is prepared in a tasty stock of Franconian
wine and onions. This is where the city council meets occasionally to de-
cide upon the official size and weight of the Nürnberg bratwurst.
⊠ *Zirkelschmiedg. 26* ☎ *0911/205–9288* 🗖 *DC, MC, V.*

$–$$ ✕🖽 **Hotel-Weinhaus Steichele.** This skillfully converted former 19th-cen-
tury wine merchant's warehouse is part of the Flair hotel group but has
been managed by the same family for three generations. It's handily close
to the main train station, on a quiet street of the old walled town. The
cozy rooms are decorated in rustic Bavarian style. Two wood-panel, tra-
ditionally furnished taverns ($–$$$) serve Franconian fare with an ex-
cellent fish menu. ⊠ *Knorrstr. 2–8, D–90402* ☎ *0911/202–280* 🖨 *0911/*
221–914 ⊕ *www.steichele.de* 🛏 *56 rooms* ⌂ *Restaurant, cable TV,*
Weinstube, some pets allowed; no a/c 🗖 *AE, DC, MC, V* 🍽 *BP.*

$$–$$$ 🖽 **Agneshof.** This comfortable hotel is sandwiched north of the Old Town
between the fortress and St. Sebaldus Church. Interiors are very mod-
ern and tastefully done. The hotel also has a small wellness section that
will be welcome after a long day exploring. ⊠ *Agnesg. 10, D–90403*
☎ *0911/214–440* 🖨 *0911/2144–4144* ⊕ *www.agneshof-nuernberg.*
de 🛏 *72 rooms* ⌂ *In-room data ports, cable TV with movies, hot tub,*
sauna, some pets allowed (fee), no-smoking rooms; no a/c 🗖 *AE, DC,*
MC, V 🍽 *BP.*

★ $$–$$$ 🖽 **Hotel Drei Raben.** Legends and tales of Nürnberg form the leitmotiv run-
ning through the designer rooms at this hotel. One room celebrates the
local soccer team with a table-soccer game; in another room sandstone
decor recalls sights in the city. There are also standard rooms in the lower

price category. The reception, with its pods, is modeled after *2001: A Space Odyssey* yet doesn't seem overbearingly modern. You are three minutes from the train station, just within the Old Town walls. ✉ *Königstr. 63, D–90402* ☎ *0911/274–380* 📠 *0911/232–611* 🌐 *www.hotel-drei-raben.de* 🛏 *25 rooms* 👍 *In-room data ports, in-room fax, cable TV, bar, some pets allowed (fee), no-smoking rooms; no a/c* 💳 *AE, DC, MC, V* 🍴 *BP.*

$–$$ **Hotel Fackelmann.** This compact, convenient hotel near the Old Town is designed for giving quiet comfort to either the leisure or the business traveler. Clean and light rooms, a breakfast buffet, and a fitness area are all included. ✉ *Essenweinstr. 10, D–90443* ☎ *0911/206–840* 📠 *0911/2068–6460* 🌐 *www.hotel-fackelmann.de* 🛏 *34 rooms* 👍 *In-room data ports, cable TV, gym, sauna, some pets allowed (fee), no-smoking rooms; no a/c* 💳 *AE, MC, V* 🍴 *BP.*

$ **Albrecht Dürer Hotel Garni.** If all you're looking for is a place to sleep, this tiny hotel above a little bar near the Kaiserburg is a bargain and is still in a good location. Light pine cash-and-carry furniture, comfortable beds, a shower, and eight kinds of beer in the bar are what you can expect. Some of the rooms can open up to a suite for families. ✉ *Bergstr. 25, D–90403* ☎ *0911/204–592* 📠 *0911/204–104* 🛏 *9 rooms* 👍 *Cable TV, bar, Internet, some pets allowed (fee), no-smoking rooms; no a/c* 💳 *AE, DC, MC, V* 🍴 *CP.*

$ **Burghotel Stammhaus.** This little family-run hotel does all it can to make you feel at home. Accommodations are small but cozy, and the service is familial and friendly. If you need more space, ask about the wedding suite. The breakfast room with its balcony overlooking the houses of the Old Town has a charm all its own. A pool is in the basement. ✉ *Schildg. 14, D–90403* ☎ *0911/203–040* 📠 *0911/226–503* 🌐 *www.burghotel-stamm.de* 🛏 *22 rooms* 👍 *In-room data ports, cable TV, pool, some pets allowed; no a/c* 💳 *AE, DC, MC, V* 🍴 *BP.*

Nightlife & the Arts

Nürnberg has an annual summer festival, **Sommer in Nürnberg,** from May through September, with more than 200 events. Its international organ festival in June and July is regarded as Europe's finest. From May through August classical music concerts are given in the Rittersaal of the **Kaiserburg,** while regular pop and rock shows are staged in the dry moat of the castle. In June and July open-air concerts are given in the Kaiserburg's Serenadenhof. For reservations and program details, call ☎ 0911/225–726.

Shopping

Step into the **Handwerkerhof,** in the tower at the Old Town gate (Am Königstor) opposite the main railway station, and you'll think you're back in the Middle Ages. Craftspeople are busy at work in a "medieval mall," turning out the kind of handiwork that has been produced in Nürnberg for centuries: pewter; glassware; basketwork; wood carvings; and, of course, toys. The Lebkuchen specialist **Lebkuchen-Schmidt** has a shop here as well. The mall is open mid-March–December 24, weekdays 10–6:30, Saturday 10–4. December 1–24 the mall is also open Sunday 10–6:30.

The **Scherenschnittstudio** (✉ Albrecht-Dürer-Str. 13 ☎ 0911/443–025 ⊘ Tues.–Fri. 1–6 or by appointment) specializes in scissor-cut silhouettes. You can come and pose for owner Karin Dütz, send a picture (profile, do not smile), or just browse to pick up some items of this old and skilled craft.

ALTMÜHLTAL

The winding river valley, Altmühltal, stretches from Gunzenhausen in the west to Kelheim in the east, where the gentle Altmühl flows into the Danube River. It's ideal for a quiet holiday, since the valley hasn't really been discovered by tourist crowds. A relaxing getaway for canoe paddlers (the river flows, at times, through gorgelike landscapes), the Altmühltal first drew attention with its geology. In 1789 Alois Senefelder discovered that the limestone from the region around Solnhofen had special ink-retaining properties for lithography, which revolutionized the printing industry. The limestone is also a treasure trove of fossils, which are liberally exhibited in the region's museums. The park area, Naturpark Altmühltal, encompasses towns near the river's path—Weissenburg, Eichstätt, Beilngries, Dietfurt, and Riedenburg—and extends south to Ingolstadt and Neuburg on the Danube.

Eichstätt

⓴ *80 km (50 mi) south of Nürnberg via A–73 and A–9, exit Altmühltal, follow signs 20 km (13 mi) to Eichstätt.*

The main town of the Altmühltal is Eichstätt, a market town and bishopric rich in architectural monuments. The Marktplatz, with its curved line of houses and the episcopal residence, is one of the great baroque ensembles in Germany. The 1695 fountain features the local holy patron, St. Willibald. Although all the facades here are baroque, they are in fact built onto medieval structures. Only the tower of the Town Hall still reveals its ancient origins. The old fortress **Willibaldsburg** dominates Eichstätt but in palace garb. It was used first as a fort to defend the town and then, from the 14th to the 18th century, was used as a palace. Now it serves as the town hallmark and cultural center. The **Jura-Museum** here displays all sorts of items relating to local geology, geography, and topology, including many fossils. ☎ *08421/4730* 💶 *€3* ⊘ *Apr.–Sept., Tues.–Sun. 9–6; Oct.–Mar., Tues.–Sun. 10–4.*

The **Dom** (✉ Dompl.), a two-tower structure dating back to the 11th century, underwent a baroque face-lift in the early 18th century by Gabriel de Gabrieli, one of a fine school of masters hailing from the canton of Graubünden in Switzerland. Among the cathedral's treasures are the 16th-century stained-glass windows by Hans Holbein the Elder. The **Diocesan Museum** (☎08421/50279 ⊕www.bistum-eichstaett.de/dioezesanmuseum 💶€2, Sun. free ⊘Apr.–Oct., Wed.–Fri. 10:30–5, weekends 10–5; Nov.–Mar. by appointment only), accessible from the cathedral cloister, has a wealth of instructive exhibits documenting the construction of the cathedral, local people's religious customs, and the lives of the bishopprinces of Eichstätt as well as their vestments and monstrances.

Conveniently, the tourist office is in one of the town's finest baroque buildings, **Notre Dame de Sacre Coeur,** a former convent. The church is now used for exhibitions, concerts, and other events. It's also a work of Gabriel de Gabrieli (planned in 1719) and features frescoes by Johann Georg Bergmüller. ⊠ *Notre Dame 1* ☎ *08421/98760* ⊙ *Palm Sunday–Oct., Mon.–Sat. 9–5.*

The former prince-bishop's residence, by Gabriel de Gabrieli, is part of the cathedral complex and now used by the local administration. The **Spiegelsaal** (Hall of Mirrors) is one of the splendid rooms that can be seen on tour. The former chapel of the residence is now a small gallery devoted to the local painter Christian Otto Müller (1901–70), whose landscapes of the Eichstätt area led to his nickname Cézanne of the Altmühltal. ⊠ *Residenzpl. 1* ☎ *08421/70220* ⊙ *Tours Easter–Oct., Mon.–Thurs. at 11 and 3, Fri. at 11, weekends 10–11:30 and 2–3:30 every ½ hr.*

Where to Stay & Eat

$ ✕▦ **Waldgasthof Geländer.** Karl Feierle has turned his family's inn, located off the B–13 between Eichstätt and Weissenburg, into an experience: simple, well-appointed rooms, a large restaurant (specialty is local lamb) and beer garden, a private museum with dioramas showing the animal life of the region, and a marked path through the woods that gives visitors a complete taste of what makes the Altmühltal special. ⊠ *8 km (5 mi) west of Eichstätt, D–85132 Geländer bei Eichstätt* ☎ *08421/6761* ☒ *08421/2614* ⊕ *www.waldgasthof-gelaender.de* ⇆ *30 rooms* ⌂ *Restaurant, cable TV; no a/c* ⊟ *V* ⏐⊙⏐ *BP.*

$ ▦ **Hotel Adler.** White with pink trimmings, the centuries-old hostelry on the market square was so successful with renovations it earned itself the Bavarian Environmental Award in the process. Rooms are comfortable and spacious, especially the eight studio rooms, which are almost suite size. ⊠ *Marktpl. 22–24, D–85072* ☎ *08421/6767* ☒ *08421/8283* ⊕ *www.ei-online.de/adler* ⇆ *28 rooms* ⌂ *Cable TV, sauna, some pets allowed (fee), no-smoking rooms; no a/c* ⊟ *AE, DC, MC, V* ⏐⊙⏐ *BP.*

FRANCONIA A TO Z

To research prices, get advice from other travelers, and book travel arrangements, visit www.fodors.com.

AIRPORTS

The international airports near Franconia are at Frankfurt and Munich. Nürnberg and Bayreuth have regional airports; there are frequent flights between Frankfurt and Nürnberg. If there's fog in Munich, the Nürnberg airport serves as backup.

BIKE TRAVEL

The scenic Altmühltal Valley is particularly suitable for biking and is especially known for its rock formations. Otherwise the area consists of hills and landscapes dotted with pretty and sleepy villages. The tourist board for the Naturpark Altmühltal issues leaflets with suggested cycling tours and lists of rental outlets. Bicycles can also be rented from most major train stations. Cycling along the Danube is another favorite route. Ships let you take a bicycle along for a small fee (usually €1), so you can enjoy the scenery one way and get exercise on the other.

BOAT TRAVEL

A total of 15 different lines operate cruises on the Altmühl and Main rivers and the Main-Donau Canal from April through October. Contact the Franconia tourist board and ask for details on the Weisse Flotte cruises.

Several boats follow the Main River from Aschaffenburg to Würzburg and from Würzburg to Bamberg. These are worth considering if you plan to spend a lot of time in Franconia. For information contact Fränkische Personen-Schiffahrt or the Würzburg tourist office.

From March through October, Personenschiffahrt Kropf boats leave Bamberg daily beginning at 11 AM for short cruises on the Regnitz River and the Main-Danube Canal; the cost is €6.50.

Fränkische Personen-Schiffahrt ☎ 09321/91810. **Personenschiffahrt Kropf** ⊠ Kapuzinerstr. 5, Bamberg ☎ 0951/26679. **Würzburg Tourist Office** ⊠ Marktpl., Würzburg ☎ 0931/91810.

CAR RENTAL

Avis ⊠ Markgrafenallee 6, Bayreuth ☎ 0921/789-550 ⊠ Lossaustr. 6, main train station bldg., Coburg ☎ 09561/73075 ⊠ Allersbergerstr. 139, Nürnberg ☎ 0911/49696. **Bavaria Autovermietung** ⊠ Leiblstr. 23, Nürnberg ☎ 0911/311-718. **Europcar** ⊠ Nürnberg Airport off A-3, Nürnberg ☎ 0911/528-484. **Hertz** ⊠ Wasserg. 15, Coburg ☎ 09561/24135 ⊠ Nürnberg Airport, Nürnberg ☎ 0911/527-719. **Sixt** ⊠ Gleissbühlstr. 12-14, Nürnberg ☎ 0911/438-710.

CAR TRAVEL

Franconia is served by five main autobahns: A-7 from Hamburg, A-3 from Köln and Frankfurt, A-81 from Stuttgart, A-6 from Heilbronn, and A-9 from Munich. Nürnberg is 167 km (104 mi) north of Munich and 222 km (138 mi) southeast of Frankfurt. The Altmühltal can be accessed from A-9 (exit Beilngries north of Ingolstadt) or from Donauwörth on the Romantic Road (41 km [25 mi] to Treuchtlingen).

Some nearby scenic driving includes the eastern section of the Burgenstrasse (Castle Road), running from Heidelberg to Nürnberg; the Bocksbeutel Strasse (Franconian Wine Road), which follows the course of the Main River from Zeil am Main along the wine-growing slopes of the valley to Aschaffenburg; and the Strasse der Kaiser und Könige (Emperors' and Kings' Road), leading from Frankfurt to Vienna through Franconia via Aschaffenburg, Würzburg, and Nürnberg.

EMERGENCIES

Police & Ambulance ☎ 110. **Fire and emergency medical aid** ☎ 112.

TOURS

In Bamberg, guided walking tours set out from the tourist information office April–October, Monday–Saturday at 10:30 and 2 and Sunday at 11; November and December, Monday–Saturday at 2 and Sunday at 11; and January–March, Monday–Saturday at 2. The cost is €5. Bayreuth also offers walking tours beginning at Leopoldplatz at 10:30 daily from May to October. They cost €4.50. Guided walking tours of the historical center of Coburg depart at 3 every Saturday from the Albert statue in the market square. The cost is €2. Eichstätt offers walking tours of the city for €3, Saturday and Wednesday at 1:30 at the tourist information office.

In Nürnberg, English-language bus tours of the city are conducted May–October and December, daily at 9:30, starting at the Mauthalle, Hallplatz 2. The 2½-hour tour costs €11. An English-language tour on foot through the Old Town is conducted daily at 2:30; it departs from the tourist information office on Hauptmarkt. The tour costs €7.50 (plus entrance to the Kaiserburg €4.50). City tours are also conducted in gaily painted trolley buses April–October, daily at 45-minute intervals beginning at 10; November–March, weekends only, starting at 10 at the Schöner Brunnen. Tours are in German unless at least five participants request English. The cost is €5. For more information, call ☏ 0911/202–2910.

TRAIN TRAVEL

Regular InterCity services connect Nürnberg with Frankfurt and other major German cities. Trains run hourly from Frankfurt to Munich, with a stop at Nürnberg. The trip takes about three hours to Munich, two hours to Nürnberg. Nürnberg is a stop on the high-speed InterCity Express north–south routes, and there are hourly trains from Munich direct to Nürnberg. Some InterCity trains stop in Bamberg, which is most speedily reached from Munich. Local trains from Nürnberg connect with Bayreuth and areas of southern Franconia. In the Altmühltal, Treuchtlingen is on the Munich–Nürnberg line.

VISITOR INFORMATION

The principal regional tourist office for Franconia is Fremdenverkehrsverband Franken e.V. For information on resorts and snow conditions, call the Tourist-Information Fichtelgebirge.

🏛 **Bamberg** ⊠ Fremdenverkehrsamt, Geyerswörthstr. 3, D-96047 ☏ 0951/871-161 ⊕ www.bamberg.de/tourismus. **Bayreuth** ⊠ Fremdenverkehrsverein, Luitpoldpl. 9, D-95444 ☏ 0921/88588 🖶 0921/88555 ⊕ www.bayreuth.de. **Coburg** ⊠ Fremdenverkehrs- und Kongressbetrieb, Herrng. 4, D-96450 ☏ 09561/74180 ⊕ www.coburg-tourist.de. **Eichstätt** ⊠ Dompl. 8, D-85072 ☏ 08421/98800 🖶 08421/988-030 ⊕ www.eichstaett.de. **Fichtelgebirge Tourist-Information** ☏ 09272/969-030. **Franconia Tourist Board** ⊠ Fremdenverkehrsverband Franken e.V., Fürtherstr. 21, D-90429 Nürnberg ☏ 0911/264-202. **Kronach** ⊠ Marktpl., D-96317 ☏ 09261/97236 ⊕ w3www.kronach.de. **Kulmbach** ⊠ Fremdenverkehrsbüro, Stadthalle, Sutte 2, D-95326 ☏ 09221/95880. **Lichtenfels** ⊠ Am Marktpl. 1, D-96215 ☏ 09571/7950. **Naturpark Altmühltal Tourist Office** ⊠ Fremdenverkehrsamt, Notre Dame 1, D-85072 Eichstätt ☏ 08421/98760. **Nürnberg** ⊠ Congress- und Tourismus-Zentrale Frauentorgraben 3, D-90443 ☏ 0911/23360 ⊕ www.nuernberg.de.

THE BODENSEE

6

Updated by
Marton Radkai

LAPPING THE SHORES of Germany, Switzerland, and Austria, the Bodensee (Lake Constance), at 65 km (40 mi) long and 15 km (9 mi) wide, is the largest lake in the German-speaking world. Though called a lake, it's actually a vast swelling of the Rhine, gouged out by a massive glacier in the Ice Age and flooded by the river as the ice receded. The Rhine flows into its southeast corner, where Switzerland and Austria meet, and flows out at its west end. On the German side, the Bodensee is bordered almost entirely by the state of Baden-Württemberg (a small portion of the eastern tip, from Lindau to Nonnenhorn, belongs to Bavaria).

A natural summer playground, the Bodensee is ringed with little towns and busy resorts. It's one of the warmest areas of the country, not just because of its southern latitude but also owing to the warming influence of the water, which gathers heat in the summer and releases it in the winter like a massive radiator. The lake itself practically never freezes over—it has done so only once during the last two centuries. The climate is excellent for growing fruit, and along the roads you'll find stands and shops selling apples, peaches, strawberries, jams, juices, wines, and schnapps, much of it homemade.

The lake's natural attractions—including its abundance of fresh fish and its fertile soil—were as compelling several thousand years ago as they are today, making this one of the oldest continually inhabited areas of Germany. Highlights include the medieval island town of Lindau; Friedrichshafen, birthplace of the zeppelin; the rococo pilgrimage church in Birnau; and the town of Konstanz on the Swiss-German border. A day trip to Austria and Switzerland (and to little Liechtenstein) is easy to make, and border formalities are few.

Exploring the Bodensee

You can travel the entire length of the German shore of the Bodensee easily in a day—by car, train, or boat—but the enchanting towns along the way will deter any plan to rush through. Lindau is a pretty and unusual resort, close to Austria, Liechtenstein, and the mountains of the German Allgäu. Friedrichshafen is busier and sits at the head of a road inland to Ravensburg, Weingarten, and the extraordinary churches of the Baroque Road. Meersburg, built on a slope that slides down to the lakeside, is arguably the loveliest Bodensee town and is just a short ferry ride from the area's largest city, Konstanz, the regional gateway to Switzerland.

About the Restaurants & Hotels

In this area, international dishes are not only on the menu but on the map—you only have to drive a few miles to try the Swiss or Austrian dish you're craving in its own land. *Seeweine* (lake wines) from vineyards in the area include Müller-Thurgau, Spätburgunder, Ruländer, and Kerner.

The towns and resorts around the lake have a wide range of hotels, from venerable wedding-cake-style, fin-de-siècle palaces to more modest *Gasthöfe*. If you're visiting in July and August, make reservations in advance. For lower rates and a more rural atmosphere, consider staying a few miles away from the lake.

6

Numbers in the text correspond to numbers in the margin and on the Bodensee (Lake Constance) map.

If you have

3 days

Stroll around **Lindau** ❶ ☞ and then make for the next "town in the lake," **Wasserburg** ❷. Reserve a couple of hours for the Zeppelin Museum in **Friedrichshafen** ❹, which celebrates the airships once built there. Stay overnight in lovely ☒ **Meersburg** ❺, rising early to catch the sunrise over the lake and the ferry to ☒ **Konstanz** ❿, on the opposite shore. From here, there's a difficult choice—a day trip either to the Swiss Alps or to two Bodensee islands, **Mainau** ⓫ and **Reichenau** ⓬. After an overnight stay in Konstanz, go west to **Radolfzell** ⓭, rent a bike, and explore the **Höri** ⓮ peninsula.

If you have

5 days

Start your itinerary at **Lindau** ❶ ☞, continuing to **Wasserburg** ❷, **Langenargen** ❸ for a panoramic view of the lake from Montfort Castle, and **Friedrichshafen** ❹; then head inland via B–30 to medieval ☒ **Ravensburg** ❼, where you can find a number of historic hostelries. Although the great baroque pilgrimage church of **Weingarten** ❽ is only 5 km (3 mi) north of Ravensburg, allow a morning or an afternoon to do the magnificent structure justice. Return south to the lake for an overnight stay in ☒ **Meersburg** ❺. Catch the ferry to ☒ **Konstanz** ❿, on the opposite shore, and allow a full day and night to get to know this fascinating city. Devote the next day to the islands of **Mainau** ⓫ and eat at one of the ancient taverns of **Reichenau** ⓬; then head for **Radolfzell** ⓭, at the end of the peninsula that juts into the western end of the Bodensee. From there it's a short drive around the head of the lake to ☒ **Überlingen** ❻, where you can easily relax in its balmy clime. A visit to the nearby pilgrimage church of **Birnau**—a rococo masterpiece—is a marvelous finale to any Bodensee tour.

WHAT IT COSTS In Euros				
$$$$	**$$$**	**$$**	**$**	**¢**
RESTAURANTS over €25	€21–€25	€16–€20	€9–€15	under €9
HOTELS over €225	€175–€225	€100–€175	€50–€100	under €50

Restaurant prices are per person for a main course at dinner. Hotel prices are for two people in a standard double room, including tax and service.

Timing

The Bodensee's temperate climate makes for pleasant weather from April to October. In spring, orchard blossoms explode everywhere, and on Mainau, the "island of flowers," more than a million tulips, hyacinths, and narcissi burst into bloom. Holiday crowds come in summer, and autumn can be warm and mellow. Some hotels and restaurants in the smaller resort towns close for the winter.

THE NORTHERN SHORE

There's a feeling here, in the midst of a peaceful Alpine landscape, that the Bodensee is part of Germany and yet separated from it—which is literally the case in towns such as Lindau and Wasserburg, which sit in the lake tethered to land by causeways. At the northwestern finger of the lake, Überlingen, a beautiful resort beached on a small inlet of water, attracts many vacationers and spa goers. Clear days reveal the snowcapped mountains of Switzerland to the south and the peaks of the Austrian Vorarlberg to the east.

Lindau

▶ ❶ *180 km (112 mi) southwest of Munich.*

If not for the narrow causeway linking it with the mainland, ancient Lindau would be an island. On a hazy summer's day, the walls and roofs of Old Lindau seem to float on the shimmering lake. Lindau was made a Free Imperial City within the Holy Roman Empire in 1275. It had developed as a fishing settlement and then spent hundreds of years as a trading center along the route between the rich lands of Swabia and Italy. The Lindauer Bote, an important stagecoach service between Germany and Italy in the 18th and 19th centuries, was based here; Goethe traveled via this service on his first visit to Italy in 1786. The stagecoach was revived a few years ago, and every June it sets off on its 10-day journey to Italy. You can book a seat through the Lindau tourist office.

As the German empire crumbled toward the end of the 18th century, battered by Napoléon's revolutionary armies, Lindau fell victim to competing political groups. It was ruled by the Austrian Empire before passing into Bavarian control in 1805. Lindau's harbor was rebuilt in 1865. Its most striking landmark is a **seated lion,** the proud symbol of Bavaria. Carved from Bavarian marble and standing 20 feet high, the lion stares out across the lake from a massive plinth. Standing sentinel with the seated lion is the **Neuer Leuchtturm** (New Lighthouse), across the inner harbor's passageway. At the harbor's edge is the **Alter Leuchtturm** (Old Lighthouse), firmly based on the weathered remains of the 13th-century city walls. The third tower watching over the harbor is the old **Mangturm,** which was once the seat of the clothiers' guild.

A maze of ancient streets leading from the harbor makes up the **Altstadt.** Half-timber and gable houses line its main street, pedestrians-only Maximilianstrasse. The **Altes Rathaus** (Old Town Hall; ⊠ Maximilianstr.) is the finest of Lindau's handsome historical buildings. It was constructed between 1422 and 1436 in the midst of a vineyard and given a Renaissance face-lift 150 years later, though the original stepped gables remain. Emperor Maximilian I held an imperial diet here in 1496; a fresco on the south facade depicts a scene from this high point of local history. A part of the building that served as the town prison is identified by an ancient inscription enjoining the townsfolk "to turn aside from evil and learn to do good."

6

Bicycling

From spring through autumn, Germans pack their wheels and head for the scenic bike path that circles the entire lake. You can rent a bike as a guest at many hotels, at some tourist offices, from sports shops, and from bicycle tour operators. You can always save yourself some pumping by cutting across the lake on a ferry. Biking maps are available from newspaper stands, book shops, and tourist offices, and you can leave your baggage in the long-term storage available at the train stations in Konstanz, Überlingen, Friedrichshafen, and Lindau.

On the Menu

Fish specialties predominate around the Bodensee. There are 35 types of fish in the lake, with *Felchen* (a meaty white-fish) the most highly prized. Felchen belongs to the salmon family and is best eaten *blau* (poached in a mixture of water and vinegar with spices called *Essigsud*) or *Müllerin* (baked in almonds). Wash it down with a top-quality Meersburg white wine. If you venture north to Upper Swabia, *Pfannkuchen* and *spätzle*, both flour-and-egg dishes, are the most common specialties. Pfannkuchen (pancakes) are generally filled with meat, cheese, jam, or sultanas or chopped into fine strips and scattered in a clear consommé known as *Flädlesuppe*. Spätzle are roughly chopped, golden-color fried egg noodles that are the usual accompaniment to the Swabian Sunday roast-beef lunch of *Rinderbraten*. One of the best-known Swabian dishes is *Maultaschen*, a kind of ravioli, usually served floating in a broth strewn with chives.

Shopping

The Bodensee is artists' territory, and shopping means combing the many small galleries for watercolors, engravings, and prints. Local potters sell their wares directly from their shops. International goods are available in abundance. In Konstanz, if you must have Swiss chocolate or a Swiss watch, walk a few feet across the border into Kreuzlingen, the Swiss part of the twin-city. To do some serious shopping there are two cities within an hour's drive—St. Gallen, known for its textiles and embroidery, and Zurich, with its famous Bahnhofstrasse, Switzerland's most elegant and expensive shopping street. Across the bay from Lindau is the Austrian city of Bregenz, with some reputable Loden shops that carry fashionable alpine apparel.

The **Barfüsserkirche** (Church of the Barefoot Pilgrims; ⊠ Fischerg.), built from 1241 to 1270, is now Lindau's principal theater, and the Gothic choir is a memorable setting for concerts. Ludwigstrasse and Fischergasse lead to a watchtower, once part of the original city walls. Pause in the little park behind it, the **Stadtgarten** (City Park). If it's early evening, you'll see the first gamblers of the night making for the neighboring casino.

The **Peterskirche** (St. Peter's Church; ⊠ Schrannenpl.) is a solid Romanesque building, constructed in the 10th century and reputedly the oldest church in the Bodensee region. Step inside to see the frescoes by Hans Holbein the Elder (1465–1524) on the northern wall, some of which

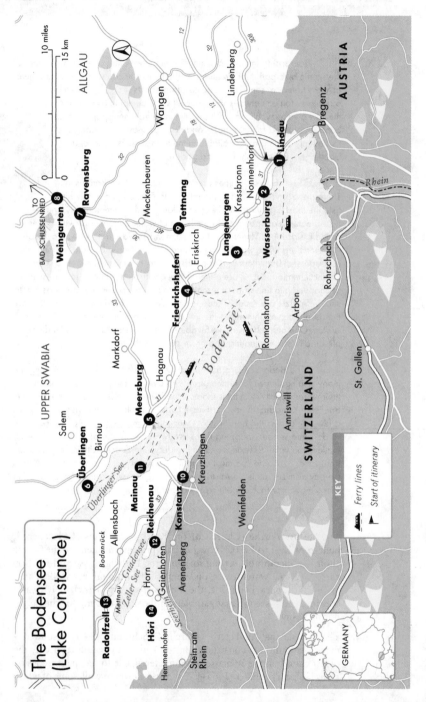

The Bodensee
(Lake Constance)

GERMANY

KEY

Ferry lines

Start of itinerary

AUSTRIA

SWITZERLAND

UPPER SWABIA

ALLGAU

Bodensee

Überlinger See

Gnadensee

Zeller See

Mettnau

Überlinger See

Rhein

10 miles

15 km

TO SCHUSSENRIED

TO BAD SCHUSSENRIED

1 Lindau
2 Wasserburg
3 Langenargen
4 Friedrichshafen
5 Meersburg
6 Überlingen
7 Ravensburg
8 Weingarten
9 Tettnang
10 Konstanz
11 Mainau
12 Reichenau
13 Radolfzell
14 Höri

Bregenz
Lindenberg
Lindenberg
Wangen
Meckenbeuren
Kressbronn
Nonnenhorn
Eriskirch
Markdorf
Hognau
Birnau
Salem
Allensbach
Bodanrück
Horn
Gaienhofen
Hemmenhofen
Stein am Rhein
Arenenberg
Kreuzingen
Weinfelden
Amriswill
St. Gallen
Rorschach
Arbon
Romanshorn

Rhein

depict scenes from the life of St. Peter, the patron saint of fishermen. Attached to the church is the old 16th-century bell foundry, now housing a pottery, where you can pick up plates, bowls, candleholders, and other household objects. Also worthy of note is the adjacent Unterer Schrannenplatz, where the bell-makers used to live. A 1989 fountain depicts five of the *Narren* (Fools) that make up the VIPs of the Alemannic Mardi Gras celebrations.

Lindau's **Marktplatz** (market square) is an almost austere place. It's lined by a series of sturdy and attractive old buildings. The Gothic **Stephanskirche** (St. Stephen's Church) is simple and sparsely decorated, as befits a Lutheran place of worship. It dates to the late 12th century but went through numerous transformations. One of its special features is the green-hue stucco ornamentation on the ceiling, which immediately attracts the eye toward the heavens. In contrast, the Catholic **Marienkirche** (St. Mary's Church), which stands right next to the Stephanskirche, is exuberantly baroque.

The **Haus zum Cavazzen** home dates to 1728. It belonged to a wealthy merchant and is now considered one of the most beautiful houses in the Bodensee region, owing to its rich decor of frescoes. Today it serves as a local history museum, with collections of glass and pewter items, paintings, and furniture from the last five centuries. ⊠ *Am Marktpl. 6* ☎ *08382/944–073* ✍ *€2.50* ☉ *Apr.–Oct., Tues.–Fri. and Sun. 11–5, Sat. 2–5.*

Where to Stay & Eat

★ $$$–$$$$ ✕ **Restaurant Hoyerberg Schlössle.** A commanding terrace view across the lake to Bregenz and the Alps combined with excellent nouvelle cuisine makes this one of the best dining experiences in Lindau. The specialties are fish and game, which change seasonally, and there are prix-fixe menus of four and six courses; one offers lobster, noodles with white truffles and goose liver, and roast breast of squab. Brick-trim arched windows, fresh flowers, and elegant high-back chairs complete the experience. ⊠ *Hoyerbergstr. 64* ☎ *08382/25295* ✍ *Reservations essential* ▤ *AE, DC, MC, V* ☉ *Closed Mon. and Feb. No lunch Tues.*

¢–$$ ✕ **Gasthaus zum Sünfzen.** This ancient inn was serving warm meals to the patricians, officials, merchants, and other good burghers of Lindau back in the 14th century. The chef insists on using fresh ingredients preferably from the region, such as fish from the lake, venison from the mountains, and apples—pressed to juice or distilled to schnapps—from his own orchard. The evening menu features specialties from the times of yore. Try either the herb-flavored *Maultaschen* (large raviolis), the excellent *Felchen* (whitefish) fillet in wine sauce, or the peppery Schübling sausage from the inn's butchershop. ⊠ *Maximilianstr. 1* ☎ *08382/5865* ▤ *AE, MC, V* ☉ *Closed Feb.*

$$–$$$$ ✕▥ **Hotel Bayerischer Hof/Hotel Reutemann.** This is *the* address in town, a stately hotel directly on the edge of the lake, its terrace lush with semitropical, long-flowering plants, trees, and shrubs. Most of the luxuriously appointed rooms have views of the lake and the Austrian and Swiss mountains beyond. Freshly caught pike perch is a highlight of the extensive menus in the stylish restaurants ($$–$$$$). Rooms at the

THREE-DAY BIKE TOUR

THE BEST WAY to experience the Bodensee area is by bike. In three days you can cross the borders of three nations, and the only burn your thighs will suffer on the flat landscape is from the sun. You could start anywhere, but this tour will begin in Lindau at the southeastern corner of the lake. Book a room in Meersburg or Konstanz for the first night; in Romanshorn, Switzerland, for the second night; and in Lindau for the third. Leave your baggage at your Lindau hotel, bringing with you only what you can comfortably carry on your back (don't forget your bathing suit). A sign displaying a bicyclist with a blue back wheel will be your guide for the bike paths through all three countries. Even without the signs or map, the water is an easy point of reference.

Once out of Lindau, turn left on the mainland and in 4 km (2½ mi) take a spin around Wasserburg. After, continue onward through meadows and marshland. You'll pass the charming villages of Nonnenhorn, Kressbronn, Langenargen, and Eriskirch.

After Langenargen, which is 8 km (5 mi) from Wasserburg, Friedrichshafen is another 18 km to the northwest. Once in town, reserve an hour or two for the Zeppelin Museum. After Friedrichshafen the bicycle path runs along the main road for a couple of miles. Follow the sign to Immenstaad to get away from the traffic. Pass through the village and continue toward Hagnau. After another 17 km (10½ mi), stay overnight in lovely Meersburg, rising early to catch the ferry to Konstanz.

When you come off the ferry, after approximately 110 yards, take a right turn into a small street that leads you along the shore to the flower island of Mainau. Return the same way past the ferry dock

and continue straight ahead into a street parallel to the lake. This way brings you into Konstanz through the scenic "back entrance." Basically keep as close to the water as you can—you'll cross a bridge over the Rhine, go through the old part of town, and head back to the harbor. If you spend some time in Konstanz, set out south in the early afternoon again. In two minutes you'll be in the Swiss city of Kreuzlingen.

After 23 km (14 mi) you'll arrive in Romanshorn to spend the night. It's not a tourist destination, but try one of its two nice hotels, the Inseli (⊕ www.inseli.ch) or the Schloss Hotel Garni (⊕ www. hotelschlossromanshorn.ch). If you need to return quickly to Lindau, take the ferry—the last one leaves Romanshorn at about 7:30 PM—to Friedrichshafen, where you can board a train for Lindau. The whole journey from Romanshorn to Lindau will take two to three hours. Assuming you're still game for biking, however, leave Romanshorn as early in the morning as possible. After 9 km (5½ mi) you'll pass Arbon, another 7 km (4½ mi) and you'll cycle through Rorschach, 9 km (5½ mi) more and you'll come to the small town of Rheineck on the border of Austria. After the border there are several paths to follow—keep as close to the lake as possible. After a while you'll cross the Rhine again.

Bregenz, the capital city of Vorarlberg, is 20 km (12 mi) from the border. There are plenty of attractions here, such as the cable car that ascends 3,870 feet to a marvelous view of the lake and the broad Rhine Valley. If you're too pooped to bike the 9 km (5½ mi) back to Lindau, you can board a train with your bicycle in Bregenz. You can also ferry across the bay—perhaps the nicest way to arrive in Lindau.

Reutemann are a little cheaper than those at the Bayerischer next door. ⊠ *Seepromenade, D–88131* ☎ *08382/9150* 🖷 *08382/915–591* ⊕ *www. bayerischerhof-lindau.de* ᗡ *98 rooms, 2 suites* ⌂ *Restaurant, café, cable TV, pool, massage, sauna, boating, bicycles, bar, meeting rooms; no a/c* ▭ *DC, MC, V* ⍩⍟ *BP.*

$ ✕▥ **Gasthof Engel.** The Engel traces its pedigree back to 1390. Tucked into one of the Old Town's ancient, narrow streets, the property creaks with history. Twisted oak beams are exposed inside and outside the terraced house. The bedrooms are simply furnished but comfortable. The restaurant (¢–$$) serves Swabian specialties with a few Swiss potato dishes (*Rösti*) for good measure. ⊠ *Schafg. 4, D–88131* ☎ *08382/5240* 🖷 *08382/5644* ᗡ *9 rooms, 7 with shower* ⌂ *Restaurant; no a/c, no room TVs* ▭ *No credit cards* ⊗ *Closed Nov.* ⍩⍟ *CP.*

$–$$ ▥ **Insel-Hotel.** What better place to wake up than in the middle of the pedestrian zone of Lindau? Rooms at this family-run enterprise are perhaps not the most modern, but the atmosphere is friendly. In good weather, breakfast can be taken on the sidewalk, where you can watch the town come alive. ⊠ *Maximilianstr. 42, D–88131* ☎ *08382/5017* 🖷 *08382/6756* ⊕ *www.insel-hotel-lindau.de* ᗡ *24 rooms* ⌂ *Restaurant, cable TV, some pets allowed (fee); no a/c* ▭ *AE, MC, V* ⍩⍟ *BP.*

$ ▥ **Landhotel Martinsmühle.** The old converted mill about 11 km (7 mi) northeast of Lindau stands in a quiet setting amid woods and fields and orchards. It's the ideal place to come back to after a day's sightseeing. Taste homemade jams at breakfast; put your day to bed with a shot of fragrant homemade schnapps. Rooms are in rustic style; some have traditional painted furniture. A meal is served if you request one (there's no menu); otherwise you can have hearty snacks, sandwiches, plates of wurst and cheese. ⊠ *Bechtersweiler 25, D–88131* ☎ *08382/5849* 🖷 *08382/6355* ⊕ *www.landhotel-martinsmuehle.de* ᗡ *98 rooms, 2 suites* ⌂ *Cable TV, café; no a/c* ▭ *MC, V* ⍩⍟ *BP.*

¢ ▥ **Jugendherberge.** This well-run youth hostel is open to travelers up to 26 years old and families with at least one child under 18. Rooms have one to six beds and a shower and toilet. There are also special family rooms. ⊠ *Herbergsweg 11, D–88131* ☎ *08382/96710* 🖷 *08382/967– 150* ⊕ *www.jugendherberge.de/jh/lindau* ᗡ *65 rooms* ⌂ *Café, cafeteria, recreation room, laundry facilities; no a/c, no room phones, no room TVs* ▭ *No credit cards* ⍩⍟ *CP.*

Nightlife & the Arts

You can play roulette, blackjack, poker, and slot machines at Lindau's modern and elegant **casino** (⊠ Chelles Alle 1 ☎ 08382/27740). It's open weekdays 3 PM–2 AM, weekends 3 PM–3 AM; the one-arm bandit room is open at noon. You can enjoy opera in the intimate setting at the **Lindauer Marionettentheater,** where puppets do the singing. Tickets are available at the **Stadttheater** (⊠ Fischerg. 37 ☎ 08382/944–650 ⊕ www.lindauer-mt.de ⊗ Weekdays 10–1:30). A dramatic floating stage supports orchestras and opera stars during the famous **Bregenzer Festspiele** (Bregenz Music Festival; ⊠ Bregenz ☎ 0043/5574–4076 ⊕ www.bregenzerfestspiele.com) from mid-July to the end of August. Make reservations well in advance. Bregenz is 13 km (8 mi) from Lindau, on the other side of the bay.

Sports & the Outdoors

BIKING   You can rent bikes at **Fahrradstation** (⊠ Im Hauptbahnhof ☎ 08382/ 21261). Bikes cost €10 per day, or €30 for four days.

BOATING &   The best way to see Lindau is from the lake. Take one of the pleasure
WINDSURFING   boats of the **Weisse Flotte** that leave Lindau's harbor five or six times a day for the 20-minute ride to Bregenz in Austria. These large boats carry up to 800 people on three decks. The round-trip costs €7.

The **Bodensee Yachtschule** (⊠ Christoph Eychmüller Schiffswerfte 3 ☎ 08382/944–588), in Lindau, charters yachts and has one-week camp sessions for children. You can rent windsurfing boards at **Windsurf-schule Kreitmeir** (⊠ Strandbad Eichwald ☎ 08382/23346 ⊕ www. bodensee-yachtschule.de).

Shopping

Biedermann (⊠ Maximilianstr. 2 ☎ 08382/944–913) carries the expensive Collections Femmes et Hommes from Italy, as well as custom-made clothing, cashmere sweaters, and Italian shoes. A find for interior decorators, **Böhm** (⊠ Maximilianstr. 21 and Krummg. 6 ☎ 08382/ 94880) consists of three old houses full of lamps, mirrors, precious porcelain, and elegant furniture. Böhm will deliver worldwide. Michael Zeller's reputable shop, the **Colony** (⊠ Binderg. 7 ☎ 08382/93020 ⊕ www.zeller.de), sells watercolors, engravings, prints, silver, and furniture. Michael Zeller also organizes the celebrated, twice-yearly Internationale Bodensee-Kunstauktion (art auction) in May and October. Smaller auctions are held during the Christmas season and in February and June.

Wasserburg

❷ *6 km (4 mi) west of Lindau.*

Wasserburg means "water castle," which describes exactly what this enchanting island town once was—a fortress, built by the St. Gallen Monastery in 924. The later owners, the counts of Montfort zu Tettnang, sold the fortress to the Fugger family of Augsburg to pay off mounting debts. The Fuggers in turn became so impoverished they couldn't even afford to maintain the drawbridge that connected the castle with the shore. Instead they built a causeway. In the 18th century the castle passed into the hands of the Habsburgs, and in 1805 the Bavarian government took it over.

Wasserburg has some of the most photographed sights of the Bodensee: the yellow, stair-gabled presbytery; the fishermen's St. Georg Kirche, with its onion dome; and the little Malhaus museum, with the castle, Schloss Wasserburg, in the background.

Where to Stay

$–$$ ✕🏨 **Hotel zum Lieben Augustin am See.** On the edge of the lake and just before the peninsula, five buildings make up this hotel, which has fine spa facilities and a beauty center. You can choose between lake or garden views. Breakfast is in a light-filled conservatory. The restaurant ($–$$)

serves a range of local, Italian, and light cuisine for the diet-conscious. The menu changes frequently in summer. The hotel has a private beach, with a new outdoor beer bar. Rental bicycles are available on request. ⊠ *Halbinselstr. 70, D–88142* ☎ *08382/9800* 🖷 *08382/887–082* ⮎ *40 rooms, 4 apartments, 4 suites* ⌂ *Restaurant, cable TV, pool, hot tub, sauna, spa, beach, bicycles, meeting rooms; no a/c* 🖃 *DC, MC, V* ☉ *Closed Jan. and Feb.* ⏵⊙⏴ *BP.*

Langenargen

❸ *8 km (5 mi) west of Wasserburg.*

The small, pretty town of Langenargen is a typical Bodensee summer resort, but because it's not as spectacular as nearby Wasserburg, there are practically no day-trippers in sight. If you walk along the shore, you'll come across the region's most unusual castle, Schloss Montfort.

Schloss Montfort (Montfort Castle)—named for the original owners, the counts of Montfort-Werdenberg—was a conventional medieval fortification until the 19th century, when it was rebuilt in pseudo-Moorish style by its new owner, King Wilhelm I of Württemberg. If you can, see it from a passenger ship on the lake; the castle is especially memorable in the early morning or late afternoon, when the softened, watery light gives additional mystery to its outline. These days the castle houses a café, restaurant, disco, and small concert hall that hosts classical chamber music concerts every Friday at 8 PM. Its tower is open to visitors. ⊠ *Untere Seestr. 5* ⌷ *Tower €1* ☉ *Mar. 1–Oct. 19., Mon.–Thurs. and Sat. 2–5, Fri. and Sun. 10–5.*

The parish church of **Martinkirche** (St. Martin; ⊠ Marktpl. 1) was built in 1718 by Anton III of Montfort and belongs to the great churches of the Barockstrasse. The ceiling paintings are by the baroque painter Franz Anton Maulbertsch (1684–1748), who was born in Langenargen but went on to a brilliant career in Vienna.

Friedrichshafen

❹ *10 km (6 mi) west of Langenargen.*

Named for its founder, King Friedrich I of Württemberg, Friedrichshafen is a young town (dating to 1811). In an area otherwise given over to resort towns and agriculture, Friedrichshafen played a central role in Germany's aeronautics tradition, which saw the development of the zeppelin airship before World War I and the Dornier seaplanes in the 1920s and '30s. The zeppelins were once launched from a floating hangar on the lake, and the Dornier water planes were tested here. The World War II raids on its factories virtually wiped the city off the map. The current layout of the streets is the same, but the buildings are all new and not necessarily pretty. The atmosphere, however, is good and lively, and occasionally you'll find a plaque with a picture of the old building that stood at the respective spot. The factories are back, too. Friedrichshafen is home to such international firms as EADS (airplanes, rockets, and helicopters) and ZF (gear wheels).

Graf Zeppelin (Ferdinand Graf von Zeppelin) was born across the lake in Konstanz, but Friedrichshafen was where, on July 2, 1900, his first "airship"—the LZ 1—was launched. The fascinating story of the zeppelin airships is told in the **Zeppelin Museum,** which holds the world's most significant collection of artifacts pertaining to airship history in its 43,000 square feet of exhibition space. In a wing of the restored Bauhaus **Friedrichshafen Hafenbahnhof** (harbor railway station), the main attraction is the reconstruction of a 108-foot-long section of the legendary *Hindenburg,* the LZ 129, which exploded at its berth in Lakehurst, New Jersey, on May 6, 1937. (The airships were filled with hydrogen, because the United States refused to sell the Germans helium, for political reasons.) Climb aboard the airship via a retractable stairway and stroll past the authentically furnished passenger room, the original lounges, and the dining room. The illusion of traveling in a zeppelin is followed by exhibits on the history and technology of airship aviation: propellers, engines, dining-room menus, and films of the airships traveling or at war. Car fans will appreciate the great Maybach standing on the ground floor; passengers once enjoyed being transported to the zeppelins in it. The museum's restaurant is a good place to take a break and enjoy lunch or dinner. ✉ *Seestr. 22* ☎ *07541/38010* ⊕ *www.zeppelin-museum.de* ▣ *€7.50* ◷ *May–Oct., Tues.–Sun. 10–6; Nov.–Apr., Tues.–Sun. 10–5.*

The **Deutsche Zeppelin Reederei GmbH** operates zeppelins in Friedrichshafen. You can board the *Zeppelin NT* (New Technology) for either an air journey or a tour of the zeppelin itself on its mooring mast at the airport. ✉ *Allmannsweilerstr. 132* ☎ *0700/937–72001* 🖷 *07541/590–0499* ⊕ *www.zeppelin-nt.com.*

Schloss Hofen (Hofen Castle), a short walk from town along the lakeside promenade, is a small palace that served as the summer residence of Württemberg kings until 1918. Today Duke Friedrich von Württemberg lives here with his family. The palace was formerly a priory—its foundations date from the 11th century. You can visit the adjoining priory **church,** a splendid example of regional baroque architecture. The swirling white stucco of the interior was executed by the Schmuzer family from Wessobrunn whose master craftsman, Franz Schmuzer, also created the priory church's magnificent marble altar. The church is open from 9 AM to 6 PM daily, from Easter to the end of October; otherwise only on Sunday.

From Friedrichshafen you can go directly to Romanshorn in Switzerland on a car ferry that leaves every hour from the harbor. The 40-minute trip offers an impressive view from the upper passenger deck: Swiss mountains ahead; Austrian mountains on your left; and the rolling green hills of Germany behind you. If you take your car, go one way by boat, and then return by driving from Romanshorn to Bregenz in Austria, then past Lindau, and back to Friedrichshafen. (If you take the highway in Austria, you will need a *Vignette* (available at most gas stations €7.60); avoid the Swiss autobahn, which also requires a toll sticker that costs €27. Car and driver one-way on the ferry costs between €14 and €20 depending on the length of the car; an extra person costs €6.

Where to Stay & Eat

$–$$$ ✕ **Zeppelin-Museumrestaurant.** The grand view of the harbor and the lake is only one of the attractions of this café and restaurant, in the Zeppelin Museum. You can enjoy cakes and drinks, or a wide range of Swabian specialties (such as lentils) or more Italianate dishes. ✉ *Seestr. 22* ☎ *07541/33306* ▤ *No credit cards.*

¢–$$ ✕ **Lukullum.** Students, businesspeople, and guests from the nearby top hotels rub elbows at this lively, novel restaurant. The friendly service keeps up with the pace of the socializing. Partitioned areas named after tourist regions allow privacy for groups or families. Other sitting arrangements are theme oriented: you sit in a beer barrel, in a bedroom, next to a waterwheel, etc. The dishes are good and basic, with surprising international touches. ✉ *Friedrichstr. 21* ☎ *07541/6818* ▤ *AE, DC, MC, V* ☽ *No lunch Mon.*

$–$$$ ✕▦ **Ringhotel Buchhorner Hof.** This traditional hotel near the train station, now part of the Ring group, has been run by the same family since it opened in 1870. Hunting trophies on the walls, leather armchairs, and Turkish rugs decorate the public areas; bedrooms are large and comfortable. The restaurant ($–$$$) is plush and subdued, with delicately carved chairs and mahogany-panel walls. It offers a choice of menus with dishes such as pork medallions, perch fillet, and lamb chops. ✉ *Friedrichstr. 33, D–88045* ☎ *07541/2050* 🖷 *07541/32663* ⊕ *www.buchhorn. de* ⇌ *87 rooms, 4 suites, 2 apartments* ⊙ *Restaurant, some in-room data ports, some in-room faxes, cable TV, miniature golf, gym, massage, sauna, bicycles, bar, meeting rooms, some pets allowed; no a/c in some rooms* ▤ *AE, DC, MC, V* ❑ *BP.*

$$ ✕▦ **Ringhotel Krone.** This Bavarian-theme hotel, made up of four buildings, is in the Schnetzenhausen district's semirural surroundings, 6 km (4 mi) from the center of town. You can roam the area on a bike rented from the hotel. All rooms have balconies. The restaurant ($$) specializes in game dishes and fish. ✉ *Untere Mühlbachstr. 1, D–88045* ☎ *07541/4080* 🖷 *07541/43601* ⊕ *www.ringhotel-krone.de* ⇌ *115 rooms* ⊙ *Restaurant, some in-room data ports, 4 tennis courts, pool, gym, hot tub, sauna, bicycles, bowling, bar, meeting rooms, some pets allowed; no a/c in some rooms* ▤ *AE, DC, MC, V* ❑ *BP.*

$ ▦ **Hotel Wohlwender.** If a hotel is simply a place for you to sleep, choose this small, clean, inexpensive one. You get the basics here. The restaurant serves Chinese and Vietnamese specialties. ✉ *Olgastr. 64, D–88046* ☎ *07541/70780* 🖷 *07540/707–828* ⊕ *hotel-wohlwender.de* ⇌ *14 rooms* ⊙ *Restaurant, some pets allowed; no a/c* ▤ *AE, MC, V* ❑ *CP.*

Nightlife & the Arts

College students and a mostly young crowd raise their glasses and voices above the din at **Cafebar Belushi** (✉ Montfortstr. 3 ☎ 07541/32531). A more mature crowd meets for music, food, dancing, and drinks at the **Halbhuber** (✉ Flughafen, P2 parking ☎ 07541/953–350), which is in the airport to the west of town.

Friedrichshafen's **Graf-Zeppelin-Haus** (✉ Olgastr. 20 ☎ 07541/72071) is a modern convention center on the lakeside promenade, a seven-minute walk from the train station. It's also a cultural center, where musicals, light opera, and classical as well as pop-rock concerts take place several times a week.

Shopping

Most of the town's shops line the pedestrian zone near the harbor. **Christina Teske** (✉ Seestr. 1 ☎ 07541/75356) carries women's and men's clothing. The gift shop **Ebe** (✉ Buchhornpl. ☎ 07541/26036) sells handmade candles, dolls, and postcards. Excellent chocolates, including a specialty in the shape of a zeppelin airship, are sold at **Weber & Weiss** (✉ Charlottenstr. 11 ☎ 07541/21771).

Meersburg

❺ *18 km (11 mi) west of Friedrichshafen.*

Meersburg is one of the most romantic old towns on the German shore of the lake. Seen from the water on a summer afternoon with the sun slanting low, the steeply terraced town looks like a stage set, with its bold castles, severe patrician dwellings, and a gaggle of half-timber houses arranged around narrow streets. It's no wonder that cars have been banned from the center: the crowds of people who come to visit the sights on weekends fill up the streets. The town is divided into the Unterstadt (Lower Town), which is joined by several steep streets and stairs to the Obere Stadt (Upper Town).

★ Majestically guarding the town is the **Altes Schloss** (Old Castle), the original Meersburg ("sea castle"). It's Germany's oldest inhabited castle, having been founded in 628 by Dagobert, king of the Franks. The massive central tower, with walls 10 feet thick, is named after him. The bishops of Konstanz used it as a summer residence until 1526, at which point they moved in permanently. They remained until the mid-18th century, when they built themselves what they felt to be a more suitable residence—the baroque Neues Schloss. Plans to tear down the Altes Schloss in the early 19th century were shelved when it was taken over by Baron Joseph von Lassberg, a man much intrigued by the castle's medieval romance. He turned it into a home for like-minded poets and artists, among them the Grimm brothers and his sister-in-law, Annette von Droste-Hülshoff (1797–1848), one of Germany's most famous poets. The Altes Schloss is still private property, but much of it can be visited, including the richly furnished rooms where Droste-Hülshoff lived and the chamber where she died, as well as the imposing knights' hall, the minstrels' gallery, and the sinister dungeons. The **Altes Schloss Museum** (Old Castle Museum) contains a fascinating collection of weapons and armor, including a rare set of medieval jousting equipment. ☎ 07532/80000 ⌑ €5.50 ☉ Mar.–Oct., daily 9–6:30; Nov.–Feb., daily 10–6:30.

The spacious and elegant **Neues Schloss** (New Castle) is directly across from its predecessor. It was built partly by Balthasar Neumann, the leading German architect of the 18th century, and partly by an Italian, Franz Anton Bagnato. Neumann's work is most obvious in the stately sweep of the grand double staircase, with its intricate grillwork and heroic statues. The interior's other standout is the glittering **Spiegelsaal** (Hall of Mirrors). In an unlikely combination of 18th-century grace and 20th-century technology, the first floor of the palace houses the **Dornier Museum**. Three rooms are devoted to Claude Dornier, the pioneer airplane builder, and his flying machines, which are exhibited in model form and pictures. Several videos are shown on request. ☎ *07532/440–4901* ✉ *€4, combined ticket that includes Weinbau Museum, Droste Museum and City Museum; available at the Tourist Information Office, €5* ⊙ *Apr.–Oct., daily 10–1 and 2–6.*

Sunbathed, south-facing Meersburg and the neighboring towns have been the center of the Bodensee wine trade for centuries. You can pay your respects to the noble profession in the **Weinbau Museum** (Vineyard Museum). A barrel capable of holding 50,000 liters (about the same number of quarts) and an immense wine press dating from 1607 are highlights of the collection. ✉ *Vorburg. 11* ☎ *07532/431–110* ✉ *€2* ⊙ *Apr.–Oct., Tues., Fri., and Sun. 2–6.*

An idyllic retreat almost hidden among the vineyards, the Fürstenhäusle was built in 1640 by a local vintner and later used as a holiday home by poet Annette von Droste-Hülshoff. It's now the **Droste Museum**, containing many of her personal possessions and giving a vivid sense of Meersburg in her time. ✉ *Stettenerstr. 9, east of Obertor, town's north gate* ☎ *07532/6088* ✉ *€3* ⊙ *Apr. 1–Oct. 26, weekdays 10–12:30 and 2–5, Sun. 2–5.*

Right next to the Meersburg Tourist Office is the **Stadtmuseum**, or City Museum, in a former Dominican priory. You can see an overview of the town's history that celebrates some of its famous residents, such as Franz Anton Mesmer, who developed the theory of "animal magnetism." (His name gave rise to the verb "to mesmerize.") ✉ *Kirchstr. 4* ☎ *07532/ 431–125* ✉ *€2* ⊙ *Apr.–Oct., Wed.–Thurs. and Sat. 2–6.*

Where to Stay & Eat

★ **$$–$$$** ✕ **Winzerstube zum Becher.** This traditional restaurant near the New Castle has been in the Benz family for three generations. If you want to try regional dishes and especially fresh fish from the lake, this is the place. A popular meat entrée is *badische Ente,* duck with bacon and apples in a wine-kirsch sauce. Do try the white wine from the restaurant's own vineyard. Reservations are recommended. ✉ *Höllg. 4* ☎ *07532/9009* ▤ *AE, DC, V* ⊙ *Closed Jan. and Mon.*

$$–$$$ ✕▦ **Romantik Hotel Residenz am See.** This tastefully modern hotel is one of the finest in town. Most of the elegant rooms face the lake, but the quieter ones look out onto a vineyard. The restaurant ($$$–$$$$) has earthy, terra-cotta-tone walls and floor-to-ceiling windows. Fish is the specialty—try the pike perch in season. The vegetarian menu is a pleasant surprise. Any guilt you feel at disturbing the form of your artfully composed dessert will quickly dissipate once you taste it. ✉ *Uferpromenade 11, D–88709* ☎ *07532/80040* 🖷 *07532/800–470* ⊕ *www. romantikhotels.com* ⇨ *23 rooms* ⚬ *Restaurant, cable TV, bar, meeting rooms; no a/c* ▤ *AE, DC, MC, V* �◖⬤ *BP.*

$–$$ ✕▦ **Löwen.** This centuries-old, ivy-clad tavern on Meersburg's market square is a local landmark. Its welcoming restaurant ($$–$$$), with pine paneling, serves regional and seasonal specialties, notably a tasty stew of local fish. Guest rooms are cozily furnished and have their own sitting corners, and some have genuine Biedermeier furniture. ☒ *Markt-tpl. 2, D–88709* ☎ *07532/43040* 🖷 *07532/430–410* ⊕ *www.hotel-loewen-meersburg.de* ➥ *21 rooms* ⚲ *Restaurant, cable TV, bicycles, Weinstube, meeting rooms, some pets allowed, no-smoking rooms; no a/c* ☰ *AE, DC, MC, V* ⦿| *BP.*

★ $–$$ ✕🎞 **See Hotel Off.** Colors, lots of glass, and a fantastic view of the lake from the balconies and terraces make this a place you will not want to leave. Owner Elisabeth Off has added little personal touches to the rooms that make you feel completely at home. Twelve rooms have been designed according to the laws of feng shui. In the restaurant, her husband, chef Michael Off, transforms local ingredients into gustatory adventures with a nod to nouvelle cuisine. The wellness area includes all sorts of alternative healing measures, from Reiki to aromatherapy. And you are only a few steps away from the lake if you feel like a swim. ☒ *Ufer-promenade 51, D–88709* ☎ *07532/44740* 🖷 *07532/447–444* ⊕ *www. hotel.off.mbo.de* ➥ *19 rooms* ⚲ *Restaurant, cable TV, spa, some pets allowed; no a/c* ☰ *AE, MC, V* ⦿| *BP.*

$ ✕🎞 **Zum Bären.** Built in 1605 and incorporating 13th-century Gothic foundations, the Bären was an important staging point for Germany's first postal service. The ivy-smothered facade, with its characteristic steeple, hasn't changed much over the centuries, but interior comforts certainly have. Some rooms are furnished with Bodensee antiques and brightly painted rustic wardrobes. If you have the chance, book Room 23 or 13. Both have semicircular alcoves with two overstuffed armchairs and six windows overlooking the marketplace. ☒ *Marktpl. 11, D–88709* ☎ *07532/43220* 🖷 *07532/432–244* ➥ *17 rooms* ⚲ *Restaurant, cable TV, some pets allowed; no a/c* ☰ *No credit cards* ⊙ *Closed Dec.–Feb.* ⦿| *BP.*

$ 🎞 **Gästehaus am Hafen.** This family-run, half-timber pension is in the middle of the Old Town, near the harbor. The rooms are small but have refrigerators and room for a child's bed, if needed. There's a place to store bikes as well. ☒ *Spitalg. 3* ☎ *07532/7069* 🖷 *07532/7789* ➥ *7 rooms* ⚲ *Refrigerators; no a/c, no room phones* ☰ *No credit cards* ⦿| *CP.*

Sports & the Outdoors

You can rent rowboats and paddle boats in the harbor, and just west of town are rocky beaches for swimming and sunbathing. The new, heavenly **Meersburg Thermen** (outdoor pool fed by hot springs) east of the harbor has lots of grass, a little sand, three pools, a thermal bath (33°C [91.4°F]), a sauna, minigolf, and a volleyball court. ☒ *Uferpromenade* ☎ *07532/4460–2850* 🖾 *€9.50* ⊙ *Weekdays 10–10, Sat. 10–8, Sun. 9–9.*

Shopping

Just at the entrance to Schlossplatz—the square in front of the Neues Schloss—are a few nice shops. **Ulmer** (☒ Schlosspl. 3 ☎ 07532/5788) has interesting gifts. Its specialty is children's clothes, including charming lederhosen for kids. If you can't find something at the incredible gift shop (toys, enamelware, books, dolls, model cars, and much more) called **Omas Kaufhaus** (☒ Marktpl. at Steigstr. ☎ 07532/5788), then at least you should see the exhibition of toy trains and tin boats on the first floor, the latter in a long canal filled with real water. **Benz** (☒ Höllg. 2 ☎ 07532/9965) sells handmade pottery.

en route

As you proceed northwest along the lake's shore, a settlement of **Pfahlbauten** ("pile dwellings")—a reconstructed village of Stone Age and Bronze Age dwellings built on stilts—sticks out of the lake. This is how the original lake dwellers lived, surviving off the fish that swam outside their humble huts. Real dwellers in authentic garb give you an accurate picture of prehistoric lifestyles. The nearby **Pfahlbauten Freilichtmuseum** (Open-Air Museum of German Prehistory) contains actual finds excavated in the area. ⊠ *Strandpromenade 6, Unteruhldingen* ☎ *No phone* ⊕ *www.pfahlbauten.de* ⊡ *€5* ⊙ *Apr.–Oct., daily 8–6; Nov.–Mar., daily 9–5.*

Just northwest of Unteruhldingen the **Wallfahrtskirche Birnau** (Pilgrimage Church) overlooks the lake from a small hill. The church was built by the master architect Peter Thumb between 1746 and 1750. Its simple exterior consists of plain gray-and-white plaster and a tapering clock-tower spire above the main entrance. The interior, by contrast, is overwhelmingly rich, full of movement, light, and color. It's hard to single out highlights from such a profusion of ornament, but seek out the *Honigschlecker* ("honey sucker"), a gold-and-white cherub beside the altar, dedicated to St. Bernard of Clairvaux, "whose words are sweet as honey" (it's the last altar on the right as you face the high altar). The cherub is sucking honey from his finger, which he's just pulled out of a beehive. The fanciful spirit of this dainty pun is continued in the small squares of glass set into the pink screen that rises high above the main altar; the gilt dripping from the walls; the swaying, swooning statues; and the swooping figures on the ceiling. ⊠ *Birnau* ⊙ *Daily 7–7.*

Überlingen

⊙ *13 km (8 mi) west of Meersburg, 24 km (15 mi) west of Friedrichshafen.*

This Bodensee resort has an attractive waterfront and an almost Mediterranean flair. It's midway along the north shore of the Überlingersee, a narrow finger of the Bodensee that points to the northwest. Überlingen is ancient—it's first mentioned in records dating back to 770. In the 13th century it earned the title of Free Imperial City and was known for its wines. No fewer than seven of its original city gates and towers remain from those grand days, as well as substantial portions of the old city walls. What was once the moat is now a grassy walkway, with the walls of the Old Town towering on one side and the Stadtpark stretching away on the other. The **Stadtgarten** (city garden), which opened in 1875, cultivates exotic plants and has a famous collection of cacti. The heart of the city is the Münsterplatz.

★ The huge **Nikolausmünster** (Church of St. Nicholas) was built between 1512 and 1563 on the site of at least two previous churches. The interior is all Gothic solemnity and massiveness, with a lofty stone-vaulted ceiling and high, pointed arches lining the nave. The single-most remarkable feature is not Gothic at all but opulently Renaissance—the massive high altar, carved by Jörg Zürn from lime wood that almost looks like ivory. The focus of the altar is the Christmas story. ⊠ *Münsterpl.*

Inside the late-Gothic **Altes Rathaus** (Old Town Hall) is a high point of Gothic decoration, the **Rathaussaal**, or council chamber. Its most striking feature amid the riot of carving is the series of figures representing the states of the Holy Roman Empire. There's a naïveté to the figures— their beautifully carved heads are all just a little too large, their legs a little too spindly—that makes them easy to love. ⊠ *Münsterpl.* 🎟 *Free* ⊙ *Apr.–mid-Oct., weekdays 9–noon and 2:30–5, Sat. 9–noon.*

The **Städtisches Museum** (City Museum) is in the Reichlin-von-Meldegg house, 1462, one of the earliest Renaissance dwellings in Germany. It displays exhibits tracing Bodensee history and a vast collection of antique dollhouses. ⊠ *Krummebergstr. 30* 🎟 *07531/991–079* 🎟 *€2* ⊙ *Apr.–Oct., Tues.–Sat. 9–12:30 and 2–5, Sun. 10–3.*

Where to Stay & Eat

¢–$$ ✕ **Restaurant Fischerstüble.** This small, simple place favors variety and quality over fancy decor. Owner-chef Friedemann Eberhard's specialty is fish, fish, fish! His menu includes fish dishes from the Bodensee and from the sea, various shellfish recipes, paella—you name it, he has it. And he prepares local specialties as well, such as lentil dishes, pork, freshly made french fries for the kids, and even some vegan dishes. ⊠ *Hafenstr. 6* 🎟 *07551/3347* 🖃 *MC, V.*

★ $–$$ ✕🏠 **Romantik Hotel Johanniter Kreuz.** The setting is a small village 3 km (2 mi) to the north of Überlingen. The old part of the hotel dates from the 17th century and is truly romantic—half-timber, with a huge fireplace in the center of the restaurant ($–$$$). In the modern annex you can relax on your room's balcony. An 18-hole golf course overlooking the lake is just 1½ km (1 mi) away. ⊠ *Johanniterweg 11, D–88662 Andelshofen* 🎟 *07551/61091* 🖷 *07551/67336* ⊕ *www.romantikhotels.com/ueberlingen* ⤳ *25 rooms* ⚭ *Restaurant, cable TV, some in-room data ports, hot tub, massage, sauna, bar, meeting rooms; no a/c* 🖃 *DC, MC, V* ¶ *BP.*

$ ✕🏠 **Landgasthof zum Adler.** You'll appreciate the unpretentiousness of this rustic country inn in a small village a few miles north of Überlingen. It has a blue-and-white half-timber facade, scrubbed wooden floors, maplewood tables, and thick down comforters on the beds. The food ($–$$) is simple and delicious; trout is a specialty. ⊠ *Hauptstr. 44, D–88662 Üb–Lippertsreute* 🎟 *07553/82550* 🖷 *07553/825–570* ⊕ *www.landgasthofadler.de* ⤳ *17 rooms* ⚭ *Restaurant, cable TV, meeting rooms, some pets allowed; no a/c* 🖃 *No credit cards* ⊙ *Closed 2 wks in Nov.* ¶ *BP.*

$ ✕🏠 **Schäpfle.** This ivy-covered hotel is in the center of town. The charm of the old house has been preserved and supplemented through time. In the hallways you'll find quaint furniture and even an old Singer sewing machine painted with flowers. The rooms are done with light, wooden Scandinavian farm furniture. Guests and Überlingen residents congregate in the comfortable taproom, where the regional and international dishes are reasonably priced ($–$$). If you need a lake view, the hotel has a second building a few steps away right on the lake. ⊠ *Jakob-Kessenringstr. 14, D–88662* 🎟 *07551/63494* 🖷 *07551/67695* ⤳ *32 rooms in 2 houses* ⚭ *Restaurant, cable TV, some pets allowed, no-smoking floor; no a/c* 🖃 *No credit cards* ¶ *BP.*

$–$$ ⊞ **Bad Hotel mit Villa Seeburg.** This stately hotel has the double advantage of being both on the lake and in the center of town. The spare, modern rooms are done in crisp whites and creams. Try to get a room looking toward the park and the lake, though they are a bit more expensive. ⊠ *Christophstr. 2, D–88662* ☎ *07551/8370* 🖷 *07551/837–100* ⊕ *www.bad-hotel-ueberlingen.de* ⇨ *62 rooms* ⌂ *Restaurant, cable TV, bar, meeting rooms; no a/c* ⊟ *AE, MC, V* ⊗ *Restaurant closed Jan.–Mar. 14* ℺ *BP.*

Shopping

The beauty and charm of Überlingen must attract artists to come, work, and live here, as there are more than 20 ateliers and artist shops in town (the tourist office has a brochure that lists them). **Galerie Tschirschky** (⊠ Turmg. 9 ☎ 07551/308–797) has a fine selection of exquisite china ware, all hand-painted by the proprietor and at reasonable prices. **Holzer** (⊠ Turmg. 8 ☎ 07551/61525) is the studio of a master craftsman of gold jewelry.

Salem

10 km (6 mi) north of Überlingen.

Salem is a tiny village in a sleepy valley away from the more trampled Bodensee paths. But it does have a major sight worth seeing, the huge **Schloss Salem** (Salem Castle), which began its existence as a convent and large church, the Münster. After many architectural permutations, it was transformed into a palace for the Baden princes, though traces of its religious past can still be seen. Today the complex of buildings is open to visitors. You can view the royally furnished rooms of the abbots and princes, a library, stables, and the church. The castle also houses an interesting array of museums, workshops, and activities, including a museum of firefighting, a potter, a musical instrument builder, a goldsmith shop, a glassblowing shop, pony farms, a golf driving range, and a fantasy garden for children. ⊠ *88682 Salem* ☎ *07553/81437* ⊕ *www.salem. de* 🖷 *€5.50* ⊗ *Apr.–Oct., Mon.–Sat. 9:30–6, Sun. 10:30–6.*

FodorśChoice
★

The **Affenberg** (Monkey Mountain), is a 50-plus-acre park with an old farm that serves as home to more than 200 Berber monkeys. A trail snakes through a well-kept forest where you'll find, among other things, a pond with a variety of aquatic birds, Fischreiher, Blässhühner, and ducks. Listen for the characteristic rattle of the storks which like to hover in the sky above. After a nice walk, you can sit down in the farm's beer garden and enjoy refreshments and snacks. There's also a gallery that explores some of the artistic views of monkeys. ⊠ *On road between Überlingen and Salem* ☎ *07583/381* ⊕ *www.affenberg-salem.de* 🖷 *€5.50* ⊗ *Mar. 15–Oct. daily 9–6; last entry at 5:30.*

THE UPPER SWABIAN BAROQUE ROAD

From Friedrichshafen, B–30 leads north along the valley of the little River Schussen and links up with one of Germany's less-known but most attractive scenic routes. The Oberschwäbische Barockstrasse

(Upper Swabian Baroque Road) follows a rich series of baroque churches and abbeys, including Germany's largest baroque church, the basilica in Weingarten.

Ravensburg

❼ *20 km (12 mi) north of Friedrichshafen.*

Ravensburg once competed with Augsburg and Nürnberg for economic supremacy in southern Germany. The Thirty Years' War put an end to the city's hopes by reducing it to little more than a medieval backwater. The city's loss proved fortuitous only in that many of its original features have remained much as they were built (in the 19th century, medieval towns usually tore down their medieval walls and towers, which were considered ungainly and constraining). Fourteen of Ravensburg's town gates and towers survive, and the Altstadt is among the best-preserved in Germany. An official tour of the city lets you climb some of those towers for a splendid view of Ravensburg and the surrounding countryside. Tours are available at the tourist office. ⊠ *Kirchstrasse 16* ☎ *0751/82324* ⊙ *Weekdays 9–5:30, Sat. 10–1.*

That ecclesiastical and commercial life were never entirely separate in medieval towns is evident in the former **Karmeliterklosterkirche** (Carmelite Monastery Church), once part of a 14th-century monastery. The stairs on the west side of the church's chancel lead to the meeting room of the Ravensburger Gesellschaft (Ravensburg Society), an organization of linen merchants established in 1400. After the Reformation, Catholics and Protestants shared the church, but in 1810 the Protestants were given the entire building. The neo-Gothic stained-glass windows on the west side, depicting important figures of the Reformation such as Martin Luther and Huldreich Zwingli, were sponsored by wealthy burghers.

Many of Ravensburg's monuments that recall the town's wealthy past are concentrated on **Marienplatz.** To the west is the 14th-century **Kornhaus** (Granary); once the corn exchange for all of Upper Swabia, it now houses the public library. The late-Gothic **Rathaus** is a staid, red building with a Renaissance bay window and imposing late-Gothic rooms inside. Next to it stands the 15th-century **Waaghaus** (Weighing House), the town's weighing station and central warehouse. Its tower, the **Blaserturm,** which served as the watchman's abode, was rebuilt in 1556 after a fire and now bears a pretty Renaissance helmet. It can be climbed for a delightful view of the town (weekdays 2–5, Saturday 12–4, €2). Finally there's the colorfully frescoed **Lederhaus,** once the headquarters of the city's leather workers, now home to a café. On Saturday morning the square comes alive with a large market.

One of Ravensburg's **defensive towers** is visible from Marienplatz: the **Grüner Turm** (Green Tower), so called for its green tiles, many of which are 14th-century originals. Another stout defense tower is the massive **Obertor** (Upper Tower), the oldest gate in the city walls. One of the city's most curious towers, the **Mehlsack,** or Flour Sack Tower (so called because of its rounded shape and whitewash exterior), stands 170 feet high and sits upon the highest point of the city. The Tourist- Information Of-

fice offers tours of the Mehlsack on Saturday from 10 to 1 for €2.
☏ *Tourist- Information Office: 0751/82324 or 0751/82326.*

Ravensburg's true parish church, the **Liebfrauenkirche** (Church of Our
Lady), is a 14th-century structure, elegantly simple on the outside but
almost entirely rebuilt inside. Among the church's finest treasures are
the 15th-century stained-glass windows in the choir and the heavily gilded
altar. In a side altar is a copy of a carved Madonna, the *Schutzmantel-
frau*; the late-14th-century original is in Berlin's Dahlem Museum.
✉ *Kirchstr. 18* ⊙ *Daily 7–7.*

Ravensburg is a familiar name to all jigsaw-puzzle fans, because its epony-
mous Ravensburg publishing house produces the world's largest selection
of puzzles, in addition to many other children's games. The company was
founded in 1883 by Otto Robert Maier. You can explore its history and
have a closer look at its games and puzzles at the **Verlagsmuseum.** Note
the neatly cut-out keyhole on the portal. ✉ *Markstr. 26* ☏ *0751/860* ⌨ *Free*
⊙ *Apr.–Oct., Thurs. 2–6, Sat. 10–1.*

Just to the west of town in the village of Weissenau stands the **Kirche St.
Peter und St. Paul.** It was part of a 12th-century Prémontré monastery
and now boasts a high baroque facade. The interior is a stupendous
baroque masterpiece, with ceiling paintings by Joseph Hafner that create the illusion of cupolas, and vivacious stucco work by Johannes
Schmuzer, one of the famous stucco artists from Wessobrunn. ✉ *Weissenau* ⊙ *Daily 9–6.*

Ravensburger Spieleland is an amusement park designed for small children, located 10 km (6 mi) from Ravensburg, in the direction of Lindau. Entrance is free to children on their birthday. ✉ *Liebenau–Am
Hangenwald 1, Meckenbeuren* ☏ *07542/4000 or 07542/400–101*
⊕ *www.spieleland.com* ⌨ *€17* ⊙ *Apr.–May and Sept.–early Nov.,
daily 10–5; June–Aug., daily 10–6.*

Where to Stay & Eat

★ ¢–$$ ✕ **Humpis.** When you first walk in, you may think you've been time-warped
to the Middle Ages, but the dark-wood panels are lightened up with chil-
dren's paintings. The restaurant attracts people from all walks of life
with its Swabian specialties—some given a vivacious Italian touch. Por-
tions are designed to satisfy big appetites. You may want to reserve a
seat if you're coming after 7:30 PM. ✉ *Marktstr. 47* ☏ *0751/25698* ⊟ *No
credit cards.*

¢–$ ✕ **Cafe-Restaurant Central.** This popular place, with two floors and a large
terrace on Marienplatz, has an international range of dishes, from ke-
babs and curries to pastas and local specialties. You can also enjoy cof-
fee, cakes, or an aperitif. ✉ *Marienpl. 48* ☏ *0751/32533* ⊟ *MC, V.*

★ $$ ✕☒ **Romantikhotel Waldhorn.** This historic hostelry has been in the Dres-
sel-Bouley family for more than 150 years. Suites and rooms in the main
building overlook the square. Rooms in the annex have views into the
gardens or a quiet street. The menu ($$–$$$$) is prepared by Albert
Bouley, fifth-generation proprietor and chef. In the dark-wood-panel din-
ing room you can enjoy the seven-course Waldhorn menu. Albert Bouley
also minds the kitchen of Rebleute, around the corner at Schulgasse 15.

The setting, an old guild hall with a beautiful *Tonnendecke* (barrel ceiling), serves more regional (and less expensive) specialties. ⊠ *Marienpl. 15, D–88212* ☎ *0751/36120* 🖷 *0751/361–2100* ⊕ *www.waldhorn.de* 🛏 *30 rooms, 3 suites, 7 apartments* ⬧ *Restaurant, in-room data ports, cable TV, bar, meeting rooms, some pets allowed; no a/c* 🖃 *AE, DC, MC, V* ⊗ *Restaurant closed Sun. and Mon.* ⦿ *BP.*

$ ✕�🖾 **Gasthof Ochsen.** The Ochsen is a typical, family-owned Swabian inn, and the personable Kimpfler family extends a warm welcome. If you have a choice, choose Room 2, which has three windows overlooking the lively scene (in summer, especially) of the Marktplatz. When checking in, reserve a table for dinner, as the restaurant ($–$$) can often book up. This is the place to try Maultaschen and *Zwiebelrostbraten* (roast beef with lots of onions). ⊠ *Eichelstr. 17, just off Marienpl., D–88212* ☎ *0751/25480* 🖷 *0751/352–5350* ⊕ *www.ochsen-rv.de* 🛏 *15 rooms* ⬧ *Restaurant, cable TV, meeting rooms, some pets allowed; no a/c, no room phones* 🖃 *MC* ⦿ *BP.*

Weingarten

❽ *5 km (3 mi) north of Ravensburg.*

Weingarten is famous Germany-wide for its huge and hugely impressive pilgrimage church, which you see up on a hill from miles away, long before you get to the town.

At 220 feet high and more than 300 feet long, **Weingarten Basilica** is the largest baroque church in Germany. It was built as the basilica of one of the oldest and most venerable convents in the country, founded in 1056 by the wife of Guelph IV. The Guelph dynasty ruled large areas of Upper Swabia, and generations of family members lie buried in the church. The majestic edifice was renowned because of the little vial it possesses, said to contain drops of Christ's blood. First mentioned by Charlemagne, the vial passed to the convent in 1094, entrusted to its safekeeping by the Guelph queen Juditha, sister-in-law of William the Conqueror. At a stroke Weingarten became one of Germany's foremost pilgrimage sites. To this day, on the Friday after Ascension, the anniversary of the day the relic was entrusted to the convent, a huge procession of pilgrims headed by 2,000 horsemen (many local farmers breed horses just for this occasion) wends its way to the basilica. It was decorated by leading early 18th-century German and Austrian artists: stuccowork by Franz Schmuzer, ceiling frescoes by Cosmas Damian Asam, and a Donato Frisoni altar—one of the most breathtakingly ornate in Europe, with nearly 80-foot-high towers on either side. The organ, installed by Josef Gabler between 1737 and 1750, is among the largest in the country. ⊗ *Daily 8–6.*

If you want to learn about early Germans—residents from the 6th, 7th, and 8th centuries whose graves are just outside town—visit the **Alemannenmuseum** in the Kornhaus, at one time a granary. Archaeologists discovered the hundreds of Alemannic graves in the 1950s. ⊠ *Karlstr. 28* 🖾 *Free* ⊗ *Mar.–Oct., Dec., and Jan., Tues.–Sun. 3–5, Thurs. 3–6.*

Bad Schussenried

29 km (17 mi) north of Weingarten on B–30.

If you have a half day after your visit to the Weingarten pilgrimage basil-ica, take an excursion to **Bad Schussenried,** a small spa resort with a large monastery. The main sight here is the library with its paintings and fres-coes. Particularly fun is the door with books cleverly painted on it. ⊠ *Off B–30, 13 km (7 mi) north of Bad Waldsee* ☎ *07583/331–001* ⊠ *€2.50* ☉ *Tues.–Thurs. 10–noon and 2–5, Fri.–Sun. 10–5.*

A local brewery in Bad Schussenried runs the **Schussenried Bierkrugmu-seum** (Beer-Mug Museum), with more than 1,000 exhibits of mugs spanning five centuries. On the second floor is a souvenir shop with per-fect gifts for beer drinkers back home. ⊠ *Wilhelm-Schussen-Str. 12* ☎ *07583/40411* ⊠ *€3* ☉ *Tues.–Sun. 10–5.*

★ Six kilometers (4 mi) northeast of Bad Schussenried, in the village of Steinhausen, is one of the finest examples of late-baroque religious ar-chitecture. The **pilgrimage church,** built between 1728 and 1733, is a har-monious white construction that dwarfs the houses of the village around it. Architect Dominikus Zimmermann designed the interior on an oval ground plan. Ten powerful pillars topped with elaborate stuccowork sup-port the roof. The transparent, almost pastel-hue ceiling painting, glo-rifying the life of the Virgin, is the work of Zimmermann's older brother Johann Baptist and his two sons. The stuccowork integrated into the edge of this masterpiece was done by a dozen Wessobrunn stucco artists. ⊠ *Dorfstr. 3* ☎ *07583/942710* ☉ *May–Oct., daily 7:30–7:30; Nov.–Apr., daily 7:30–dusk.*

Tettnang

❾ *13 km (8 mi) south of Ravensburg on B–467.*

Looking at Tettnang from the south, you see almost nothing of the small town but the Neues Schloss, former ancestral home of the counts of Mont-fort zu Tettnang. By 1780 the dynasty had fallen on such hard times that it ceded the town to the Habsburgs for hard cash, and 25 years later it passed to the Bavarian Wittelsbachs.

The **Neues Schloss** (New Castle) is an extravagant baroque palace that was built in the early 18th century, burned down in 1753, and then par-tially rebuilt before the Montfort finances ran dry. Enough remains, how-ever, to give some idea of the rulers' former wealth and ostentatious lifestyle. The palace is open only for tours. Call ahead to arrange for an English-speaking guide. ☎ *07542/953–839* ⊠ *€2.50* ☉ *Tours in Ger-man Apr.–Oct., daily at 10:30, 2:30, and 4.*

off the
beaten
path

HOPFENMUSEUM TETTNANG (Tettnang Hops Museum) – If you're a beer drinker, you've probably already tasted a product of the Tettnang area. Tettnang is the second-largest hops-growing area in Germany and exports most of its so-called "green gold" to the United States. This museum, dedicated to brewing, is in the tiny village of

Siggenweiler, 3 km (2 mi) northwest of Tettnang. ☒ *Siggenweiler*
☎ *07542/952–206* ⊕ *www.tettnanger-hopfenmuseum.de*
☉ *May–Oct., Tues.–Sun. 2–5.*

AROUND BODANRÜCK PENINSULA

The immense Bodensee owes its name to a small, insignificant town,
Bodman, on the Bodanrück Peninsula, at the northwestern edge of the
lake. The area's most popular destinations, Konstanz and Mainau, are
reachable by ferry from Meersburg. That's by far the most romantic
way to cross the lake, though a main road (B–31, then B–34, and finally B–33) skirts the eastern side of the Bodensee and ends its German journey at Konstanz.

Konstanz

🔟 *A ½-hr ferry ride from Meersburg.*

The university town of Konstanz is the largest on the Bodensee; it straddles the Rhine as it flows out of the lake, placing itself both on the Bodanrück Peninsula and the Swiss side of the lake. Konstanz is among
the best-preserved major medieval towns in Germany; during the war
the Allies were unwilling to risk inadvertently bombing neutral Switzerland. On the peninsula side of the town, east of the main bridge connecting Konstanz's two halves, runs **Seestrasse**, a stately promenade of
neoclassical mansions with views of the Bodensee. The old town center is a labyrinth of old narrow streets lined with restored half-timber
houses and dignified merchant dwellings and populated by a generally
youngish crowd of students. This is where you'll find eateries, hotels,
pubs, and much of the nightlife.

It's claimed that Konstanz was founded in the 3rd century by Emperor
Constantine Chlorus, father of Constantine the Great. The story is
probably untrue, though it's certain there was a Roman garrison here.
In the late 6th century, Konstanz was made a bishopric; in 1192 it became a Free Imperial City. What really put it on the map was the Council of Constance, held between 1414 and 1418 to settle the Great Schism
(1378–1417), the rift in the church caused by two separate lines of popes,
one leading from Rome, the other from Avignon. The Council resolved
the problem in 1417 by electing Martin V as the true, and only, pope.
The church had also agreed to restore the German Holy Roman Emperor's (Sigismund's) role in electing the pope, but only if Sigismund si-
lenced the rebel theologian Jan Hus of Bohemia. Even though Sigismund
had allowed Hus safe passage to Konstanz for the Council, he won the
church's favor by having Hus burned at the stake in July 1415.

In a historic satire, French author Honoré de Balzac created a character
called Imperia, a courtesan of great beauty and cleverness, who raised the
blood pressure of both religious and secular VIPs during the Council. No
one visiting the harbor today can miss the 28-foot statue of **Imperia** standing out on the breakwater. She is dressed in a most revealing and allur-
ing style. In her hands she is holding two dejected figures: one is the Emperor;

the other, the Pope. This hallmark of Konstanz, created by Peter Lenk, raised quite a controversy when it was unveiled in April 1993.

Most people enjoy Konstanz for its worldly pleasures—the elegant Altstadt, trips on the lake, walks along the promenade, the classy shops, the restaurants, the views. The heart of the city is the **Marktstätte** (Marketplace), near the harbor, with the simple bulk of the Konzilgebäude looming behind it. Erected in 1388 as a warehouse, the **Konzilgebäude** (Council Hall) is now a concert hall. Beside the Konzilgebäude are statues of Jan Hus and native son Count Ferdinand von Zeppelin (1838–1917). The Dominican monastery where Hus was held before his execution is still here, doing duty as a luxurious hotel, the Steigenberger Insel-Hotel.

The huge aquarium **Sealife** has gathered all the fish species that inhabit the Rhine and Lake Constance, from the river's beginnings in the Swiss Alps to its end in Rotterdam and the North Sea. If you're pressed for time, or the aquarium is crowded with schoolchildren, visit the **Bodensee Naturmuseum** at the side entrance, which gives a comprehensive overview of the geological history of the Bodensee and its fauna and flora right down to the microscopic creatures of the region. ⊠ *Hafenstr. 9* ☎ *07531/ 128–270* ⊕ *www.sealife.de* ☎ *€10* ⊘ *July and Aug., daily 10–7; May, June, and Sept., daily 10–6; Nov.–Apr., daily 10–5.*

The **Altes Rathaus** (Old Town Hall) was built during the Renaissance and painted with vivid frescoes—swags of flowers and fruits, shields, and sturdy knights wielding immense swords. Walk into the courtyard to admire its Renaissance restraint. Within the medieval guild house of the city's butchers, the **Rosgartenmuseum** (Rose Garden Museum) has a rich collection of art and artifacts from the Bodensee region. Highlights include exhibits of the life and work of the people around the Bodensee, from the Bronze Age through the Middle Ages and beyond. There's also a collection of sculpture and altar paintings from the Middle Ages. ⊠ *Rosgartenstr. 3–5* ☎ *07531/900–246* ☎ *€1.50* ⊘ *Tues.–Thurs. 10–5, Fri.–Sun. 10–4.*

Konstanz's cathedral, the **Münster,** was the center of one of Germany's largest bishoprics until 1827, when the seat was moved to Freiburg— where, ironically, the people never refer to their Münster as a cathedral. Construction on the cathedral continued from the 10th through the 19th centuries, resulting in today's interesting coexistence of architectural styles: the twin-tower facade is sturdily Romanesque; the elegant and airy chapels along the aisles are full-blown 15th-century Gothic; the complex nave vaulting is Renaissance; and the choir is severely neoclassic. The Mauritius Chapel behind the altar is a 13th-century Gothic structure, 12 feet high, with some of its original vivid coloring and gilding. It's studded with statues of the Apostles and figures depicting the childhood of Jesus. ⊠ *Münsterpl.*

The **Niederburg,** the oldest part of Konstanz, is a tangle of old, twisting streets leading to the Rhine. From the river take a look at the two city towers: the Rheintor (Rhine Tower), the one nearer the lake, and the aptly named Pulverturm (Powder Tower), the former city arsenal.

Where to Stay & Eat

$$$$

Fodor'sChoice

★

✕ **Seehotel Siber.** The major attraction in this small turn-of-the-20th-century villa is its restaurant—the most elegant in the region. The food, prepared by Bertold Siber, one of Germany's leading chefs, can be simply described as gourmet with regional touches. Try the lobster salad or bouillabaisse with local lake fish. The restaurant is divided into three rooms: one resembles a library; the other two are airy and spacious with bold modern paintings. ⊠ *Seestr. 25* ☎ *07531/996–6990* ⚭ *Reservations essential* 🏛 *Jacket and tie* ▭ *DC, MC, V* ☉ *Closed 2 wks in Feb.*

¢–$$$

✕ **Latinos.** Every university town needs one of these places where you can either snack, have coffee, enjoy a cocktail, or eat a full meal. Mexican cuisine is supplemented by various vegetarian dishes and, incongruously, a sushi bar (Tues.–Sun. 5–11). The crowd that meets within these adobe walls in the middle of Konstanz is young and dynamic. ⊠ *Fischmarkt* ☎ *07531/17399* ▭ *AE, MC, V.*

¢–$

✕ **Brauhaus J. Albrecht.** This small brewery with shiny copper cauldrons has a large dining room serving simple dishes such as fried eggs with home fries, and *Kassler* (smoked pork chops) with potato salad. If you're in a hurry, there are stand-up tables. ⊠ *Konradig. 2* ☎ *07531/25045* ▭ *No credit cards.*

¢–$

✕ **Hafenhalle.** You don't have to cross the Swiss border for Swiss *Rösti*—pan-fried potatoes and onions mixed with chopped smoked ham—and Bauernbratwurst; you can just take a seat at this warm-weather spot on the harbor. Sit outside on the terrace and watch the busy harbor traffic. The beer garden has a sandbox for children and a screen to watch sports events, and Sunday brunch is served to live Dixieland jazz. ⊠ *Hafenstr. 10* ☎ *07531/21126* ▭ *MC.*

¢

✕ **Sedir.** This little establishment in the house of the "Virgin of the silver moon" looks like an antiques store turned restaurant, with worn-out (but clean) tables, motionless old clocks hanging on the wall, 1970s upholstery on the benches, and an industrial woodstove for heat in winter. But it has charm, a good crowd, and above all, excellent Turkish food including kebabs, noodles, and vegetarian dishes. Luncheon specials go for €4.90. ⊠ *Hofhalde 11* ☎ *07531/29352* ▭ *No credit cards* ☉ *No lunch Sun.*

$$$–$$$$

Fodor'sChoice

★

✕🏨 **Steigenberger Insel-Hotel.** This former 16th-century monastery, with its original cloisters, offers the most luxurious lodging in town. Jan Hus was held prisoner here, and centuries later, Graf Zeppelin was born here. Bedrooms are spacious and stylish, more like those of a private home than a hotel, and many have lake views. The formal terrace restaurant has superb views of the lake. The Dominikanerstube is a smaller, more intimate restaurant. Both restaurants ($$$–$$$$) feature regional specialties, and there's the clubby, relaxed Zeppelin Bar. ⊠ *Auf der Insel 1, D–78462* ☎ *07531/1250* 🖷 *07531/26402* ⊕ *www.steigenberger. com* ⇥ *100 rooms, 2 suites* ☕ *2 restaurants, in-room data ports, cable TV, beach, bar, recreation room, babysitting, meeting rooms, some pets allowed; no a/c* ▭ *AE, DC, MC, V* ☉❙ *BP.*

$$–$$$

✕🏨 **Parkhotel am See.** This 19th-century villa, with a modern annex, offers its guests great comfort. Each room has a balcony or terrace where you can sit and enjoy the fresh air and silence of this wealthy part of

Konstanz. The restaurant ($$–$$$) has a small but fine menu prepared with the freshest local ingredients by chef Peter Walczak. The casino is right next door. ☒ *Seestr. 25a, D–78464* ☎ *07531/8990* 🖷 *07531/ 899–400* ⊕ *www.parkhotel-am-see.de* ➷ *39 rooms* ⌂ *Restaurant, in-room data ports, cable TV, sauna, some pets allowed; no a/c* ☰ *AE, DC, MC, V* ⏐◎⏐ *BP.*

$–$$ ✕⏍ **Barbarossa.** This stately old town house has been modernized in-side, but historic elements such as the huge wooden support beams are still visible. Rooms are comfortably furnished; several have been given special themes, such as Romeo and Juliet or Complete Harmony. The stained-glass windows and dark-wood paneling give the restaurant ($–$$$) a cozy, warm atmosphere. Fish and game in season are the spe-cialties. ☒ *Obermarkt 8* ☎ *07531/128–990* 🖷 *07531/128–99700* ⊕ *www.barbarossa-hotel.com* ➷ *55 rooms* ⌂ *Restaurant, in-room data ports, cable TV, some pets allowed, no-smoking rooms; no a/c* ☰*AE, D, MC, V* ⏐◎⏐ *BP.*

$–$$ ✕⏍ **Stadthotel.** This friendly hotel is a five-minute walk from the lake. Some rooms have a bath, others just a shower, but all have a TV. The Poseidon restaurant ($) draws locals and guests with its Greek cuisine. ☒ *Bruderturmg. 12, D–78462* ☎ *07531/90460* 🖷 *07531/904–646* ⊕ *www.stadthotel-konstanz.com* ➷ *24 rooms* ⌂ *Restaurant, in-room data ports, cable TV, some pets allowed; no a/c* ☰*AE, DC, MC, V* ⏐◎⏐ *CP.*

Nightlife & the Arts

The season of the **Bodensee Symphony Orchestra,** based in Konstanz, runs from October through April. Konstanz's international **summer music fes-tival** (☎ 07531/133–030) runs from mid-June to mid-July, including cel-ebrated organ concerts in the cathedral. Performances are held in the picturesque Renaissancehof (courtyard) of the town hall. The **Zeltfesti-val Konstanz** (Tent Festival; ☎ 01805/908–844) at the harbor draws in-ternational pop stars to Konstanz on weekends throughout the summer, concluding with the **Rock am See** event at the beginning of September. And if you're in Konstanz around August 9, you will experience the one-day city festival Konstanz shares with neighboring Kreuzlingen in Switzerland called **Seenachtfest** (Lake Night Festival), with street events, music, clowns, and magicians and ending with fireworks over the lake.

The **Stadttheater** (☒ Konzilstr. 11, D–78462 ☎ 07531/130–050 for fes-tival office, 07531/20070 for program details, 07532/82383 for Meers-burg program), Germany's oldest active theater, has staged plays since 1609 and has its own repertory company. The local season runs from September through June. From July through August the company moves to its summer theater in Meersburg.

The Bodensee nightlife scene is concentrated in Konstanz. The **casino** (☒ Seestr. 2 ☎ 07531/81570) is open 3 PM–3 AM. **Disco in Seehotel Siber** (☒ Seestr. 25 ☎ 07531/63044) is open Wednesday–Monday from 10 PM to 4 AM. **K 9** (☒ Obere Laube 71 ☎ 07531/16713) draws all ages with its dance club, theater, and cabaret in the former Church of St. Paul. Concerts and variously themed DJ nights are held at **Kulturladen** (☒ Joseph Belli Weg 5 ☎ 07531/52954).

An absolute must is the cozy and crowded **Seekuh** (⊠ Konzilstr. 1 ☎ 07531/27232), which features the occasional live jazz night. The very popular **Theatercafé** (⊠Konzilstr. 3 ☎07531/20243) draws a stylish crowd that's not too hip to dance when the mood strikes.

Shopping

Konstanz is a very good city for shopping, drawing even the Swiss from St. Gallen and Zurich, who have plenty of shops of their own. It's worthwhile to roam the streets of the old part of town where there are several gold- and silversmiths and jewelers. Elegant **Modehaus Jacqueline** (⊠ Hussenstr. 29 ☎ 07531/22990) has enough style for a city 10 times the size of Konstanz. The store gets most of its business from wealthy Swiss who come to Konstanz for what they consider bargain prices. Jacqueline deals in well-known names such as Rena Lange and Celine and has some unusual Italian lines such as Cavalli. Accessories from Moschino include handbags and exquisite shoes. **Oexle–China and Glassware** (⊠ Marktstätte 26 ☎07531/21307) carries not only famous china brands such as Meissen, Rosenthal, and Arzberg but also beautiful china and glass of lesser-known names such as Theresienthal and Royal Copenhagen. Among their quality gift items are Hummel figures, Kristallglass, and Swiss army knives.

The small but fine and not too expensive **pierre-moden** (⊠ Hussenstr. 3 ☎ 07531/22150) carries somewhat bold but always stylish men's fashions. You'll find well-known Carlo Colucci's imaginative knitwear, Signum shirts, Joker jeans, and items from Lacoste.

Sports & the Outdoors

BIKING Bike rentals generally cost €10 per day. You can book bicycle tours and rent bikes at **velotours** (⊠ Fritz Arnold-Str. 2d ☎ 07531/98280 ⊕ www.velotours.de). **Kultur-Rädle** (⊠Hauptbahnhof ☎07531/27310) rents bikes at the main train station. The longer you rent the bike, the cheaper the daily rate.

BOATING Sail and motor yachts are available at **Engert Yachtcharter** (⊠ Hafenstr. 8 ☎07531/16537 ⊕ www.bodensee-yachtzentrum.de). Small sailboats can be chartered from **Bodensee Segelschule Konstanz/Wallhausen** (⊠Zum Wittmoosstr. 10, Wallhausen ☎ 07533/4780).

Mainau

⓫ *7 km (4½ mi) north of Konstanz by road; by ferry, 50 min from Konstanz, 20 min from Meersburg.*

One of the most unusual sights in Germany, Mainau is a tiny island given over to the cultivation of rare plants and splashy displays of more than a million tulips, hyacinths, and narcissi. Rhododendrons and roses bloom from May to July; dahlias dominate the late summer. A greenhouse nurtures palms and tropical plants.

The island was originally the property of the Teutonic Knights, who settled here during the 13th century. In the 19th century Mainau passed to Grand Duke Friedrich I of Baden, a man with a passion for botany. He laid out most of the gardens and introduced many of the island's more exotic specimens. His daughter Victoria, later queen of Sweden, gave the island to her son, Prince Wilhelm, and it has remained Swedish ever since. Today it's owned by Prince Wilhelm's son, Count Lennart Bernadotte, who lives in the castle. In the former main reception hall are changing art exhibitions.

Beyond the flora, the island's other colorful extravagance is **Das Schmetterlinghaus,** Germany's largest butterfly conservatory. On a circular walk through a semitropical landscape with water cascading through rare vegetation, you'll see hundreds of butterflies flying, feeding, and mating. The exhibition in the foyer explains the butterflies' life-cycle, habitats, and ecological connections. Like the park, this oasis is open year-round.

At the island's information center, **Nature and Culture on Lake Constance,** you can view a multimedia show in which 14 projectors create a three-dimensional effect, capturing the beauty of the countryside around Lake Constance. The show also addresses environmental issues and ways to observe ecologically sound behavior on vacation and at home.

Ferries to the island from Meersburg and Konstanz depart approximately every 1½ hours between 9 and 5. The entrance fee to the island is €9.50.

Where to Eat
There are three restaurants on the island but no lodgings.

$$–$$$ ✕ **Schwedenschenke.** The lunchtime crowd gets what it needs here—fast and good service. At dinnertime (reservations essential) candlelight adds some extra style. The resident Bernadotte family is Swedish, and so are the specialties of the chef. Have your hotel reserve a table for you. In the evening your reservation will be checked at the gate, and you can drive onto the island without having to pay the admission fee. ⊠ *Insel Mainau* ☎ *07531/3030* ▤ *AE, D, MC, V.*

Reichenau

🕐 *10 km (6 mi) northwest of Konstanz, 50 min by ferry from Konstanz.*

Reichenau is an island rich in vegetation, but unlike Mainau, vegetables, not flowers, prevail here. In fact, 15% of its area (the island is 5 km [3 mi long and 1½ km [1 mi wide) is covered by greenhouses and crops of one kind or another. Though it seems unlikely amid the cabbage, cauliflower, lettuce, and potatoes, Reichenau has three of Europe's most beautiful Romanesque churches. This, and the warm microclimate, has earned the island a place on UNESCO's World and Nature Heritage list. Connected to the Bodanrück Peninsula by just a narrow causeway, Reichenau was a great monastic center of the early Middle Ages. Secure from marauding tribesmen on its fertile island, the monastic community blossomed from the 8th through the 12th century, in the process developing into a major center of learning and the arts. The churches are in each of the island's villages—**Oberzell, Mittelzell, and Niederzell,** which are separated only by 1 km (½ mi). Along the shore are pleasant pathways for walking or biking.

The **Stiftskirche St. Georg** (Collegiate Church of St. George), in Oberzell, was built around 900; now cabbages grow in ranks up to its rough plaster walls. Small round-head windows, a simple square tower, and massive buttresses signal the church's Romanesque origin from the outside. The interior is covered with frescoes painted by the monks around 1000. They depict the eight miracles of Christ. Above the entrance is a depiction of the Resurrection.

Begun in 816, the **Münster of St. Maria and St. Markus,** the monastery's church, is the largest and most important of the island's trio of Romanesque churches. Perhaps its most striking architectural feature is the roof, whose beams and ties are open for all to see. The monastery was founded in 725 by St. Pirmin and became one of the most important cultural centers of the Carolingian Empire. It reached its zenith around 1000, when 700 monks lived here. It was then probably the most important center of book illumination in Germany. The building is simple but by no means crude. Visit the **Schatzkammer** (Treasury) to see some of its more important holdings. They include a 5th-century ivory goblet with two carefully incised scenes of Christ's miracles and some priceless stained glass that is almost 1,000 years old. ⊠ *Münsterpl. 3, Mittelzell* ☎ *07534/999–5999 for guided tours* ⊗ *May–Sept., daily 11–noon and 3–4.*

Museum Reichenau, a museum of local history, in the Old Town Hall of Mittelzell lends interesting insights into life on the island over the centuries. ⊠ *Mittelzell* ☑ *€1* ⊗ *May–Sept., Tues.–Sun. 3–5.*

The **Stiftskirche St. Peter und St. Paul** (St. Peter and Paul Parish Church), at Niederzell, was revamped around 1750. The faded, Romanesque frescoes in the apse are now contrasted with strong rococo paintings on the ceiling and flowery stucco.

off the beaten path

WOLLMATINGER RIED – Just north of Konstanz on the Bodanrück Peninsula is the 1,000-acre Wollmatinger Ried, a moorland bird sanctuary. There are three-hour guided tours of the moor April through mid-October (Wednesday and Saturday at 4 PM) as well as other nature walks. Native breeding birds include the marsh harrier, hobby falcon, black kite, great reed warbler, and black-necked grebe. There are also remains of prehistoric pile houses. Bring sturdy, comfortable shoes and mosquito repellent. Binoculars can be rented. ⊠ *Kindlebildstr. 87* ☎ *07531/78870* ☑ *Donation requested* ⊗ *Apr.–Sept., weekdays 9–noon and 2–5, weekends 1–5; Oct.–Mar., weekdays 9–noon and 2–5.*

Where to Stay & Eat

$$ ✕ **Strandhotel Löchnerhaus.** The Strandhotel (Beach Hotel) stands commandingly on the water's edge, and about 80 yards from its own boat pier. Fresh lake fish figures prominently on the menu of the restaurant ($–$$). Most rooms have lake views; those that don't look out over a quiet, shady garden. ⊠ *An der Schiffslände 12, D–78479* ☎ *07534/8030* ☐ *07534/582* ⇨ *44 rooms* ⅙ *Restaurant, cable TV, beach, boating, meeting rooms, some pets allowed; no a/c* ➡ *MC, V* ⁑ *BP.*

Radolfzell

⓭ *22 km (14 mi) northwest of Konstanz.*

Radolfzell originally belonged to the Abbey of Reichenau, just a few miles away across the lake, until it became part of the Habsburg empire in the 15th century. In the old part of town are shops in half-timber houses and on the shore a long promenade with cafés, a boat rental place, and a small harbor for sailboats and the ships of the Weisse Flotte (White Fleet). In honor of the three local saints, the Hausherrenfest (Feast of the Patron Saints) is celebrated every third Sunday in July, with a water procession of decorated boats. The center of town is dominated by the Gothic **Münster unserer Lieben Frau** (Minster of Our Dear Lady). A farmers' market sets up every Wednesday and Saturday morning in the shadow of the cathedral.

Just east of Radolfzell is the small Mettnau Peninsula, which separates two fingers of the Bodensee, the Gnadensee from the Zeller See. The nature reserve **Naturschutzgebiet Mettnau** has free entry and guided tours of the reedy vegetation as well as bird-watching opportunities. You can spot many species of ducks, songbirds, curlews, lapwings, and cormorants. Tours depart from the **nature center,** which also has exhibits. ⊠ *Floerickeweg 2a* ☎ *07732/12339* ☜ *Free* ☉ *Reserve daily; nature reserve Mar.–Oct., weekends 2–6.*

Höri

⓮ *4 km (2½ mi) south of Radolfzell.*

Höri is a rural peninsula, settled with small villages, between the Zeller See and Seerhein portions of Bodensee. In the village of Horn, the beautiful setting of the church **St. Johannes und Veit of Horn** inspired a king of Württemberg to admit, "If I weren't king, I'd like to be the priest of Horn." From here you have a view of the reedy landscape; the Zeller See and the island of Reichenau; the silhouette of Konstanz; and, on a clear day, the snowcapped Alps.

In the early 1900s members of Dresden's artist group Die Brücke discovered the area. The most expressive paintings of the Bodensee landscape were created by Erich Heckel (1883–1970) and Otto Dix (1891–1969). Dix lived in the village of Hemmenhofen from 1936 until his death. You can see some of his landscapes in the **Otto Dix Haus.** ⊠ *Hemmenhofen* ☎ *07735/3151* ☜ *€2.50* ☉ *Apr.–Oct., Wed.–Sat. 2–5, Sun. 11–4.*

Two handsome half-timber houses in Gaienhofen, one a former schoolhouse, the other a farmhouse, have been turned into a multifunctional museum, the **Herrmann-Hesse-Höri Museum.** The Nobel laureate novelist and poet Hermann Hesse (1877–1962) lived in the farmhouse with his family from 1904 to 1908. His desk, his books, hundreds of pictures, and one of his typewriters are on exhibit. A few rooms are devoted to his friend the writer Ludwig Finck. A typical old Höri living room has been installed, while other rooms are used for special exhibitions and tableaux by local painters. ⊠ *Gaienhofen* ☎ *07735/81832* ☜ *€2.50* ☉ *Apr.–Oct., Tues.–Sat. 2–5, Sun. 11–5.*

Where to Eat

¢–$ ✕ **Schlössli.** After visiting the museums, this Renaissance castle turned restaurant and beer garden in Horn is an ideal place to muse about life and art while gazing out over the lake. Local dishes are served in the restaurant (fish in lemon sauce, for example), and typical beer-garden food is available out on the lawn: sausages, spare ribs, giant pretzels. ✉ *Hornstaaderstr.* ☎ *07735/2041* ▭ *No credit cards.*

THE BODENSEE A TO Z

To research prices, get advice from other travelers, and book travel arrangements, visit www.fodors.com.

AIRPORTS

The closest international airport to the Bodensee is in Zurich, Switzerland, 60 km (37 mi) from Konstanz, connected by the autobahn. There are also direct trains from the Zurich airport to Konstanz. There are several flights from Berlin, Düsseldorf, Frankfurt, London, and other destinations to the regional airport at Friedrichshafen.

BOAT & FERRY TRAVEL

Note that the English pronunciation of "ferry" sounds a lot like the German word *fähre,* which means car ferry. *Schiffe* is the term used for passenger ferries, which have different docking points from the car ferries in the various towns. The car ferries run all year; in summer you may have to wait in line. The passenger routes, especially the small ones, often do not run in winter, from November to March.

The Weisse Flotte line of boats, which is run by the BSB, or Bodensee-Schiffsbetriebe, links most of the larger towns and resorts. One of the nicest trips is from Konstanz to Meersburg and then on to the island of Mainau. The round-trip cost is €8.80. Excursions around the lake last from one hour to a full day. Many cross to Austria and Switzerland; some head west along the Rhine to the Schaffhausen Falls, the largest waterfall in Europe. Information on lake excursions is available from all local tourist offices and travel agencies.

The best deal for ferry travel is with the *BodenseeErlebniskarte* (Bodensee Card), available at all tourist offices, which gives the holder free use of passenger ships on the Bodensee (not car ferries!) and free access to 190 sights in Germany, Austria, Switzerland, and Liechtenstein, including the island of Maina, the Zeppelin Museum in Friedrichshafen, the old castle of Meersburg, and the Sealife center in Konstanz. A three-day card costs €54, a seven-day card €63, and a 14-day card €89. The Bodensee info line gives more information (☎ 07531/90940).

🚩 **Bodensee-Schiffsbetriebe** ✉ Hafenstr. 6, D–78462 Konstanz ☎ 07531/281–389 ⊕ www.bsb-online.com ✉ Friedrichshafen ☎ 07541/923–8389 ✉ Lindau ☎ 08382/944–416. In Überlingen, the BSB runs through **Schiffsbetriebe Alfons Heidegger** ✉ Im Guggenbül 3 ☎ 07551/66463. In Konstanz, it's **Ewald Giess** ✉ Seehorn 2 ☎ 07531/5261 who runs tours from the city, notably tours of the harbor.

BUS TRAVEL

Buses serve most smaller communities that have no train links, but service is infrequent. Along the shore there are buses that run every half hour during the day from Überlingen to Friedrichshafen, stopping in towns such as Meersburg, Hagnau, and Immenstaad (which have no train connections).

CAR RENTALS

Avis ✉ Friedrichshafen Airport ☎ 07541/930-705 ✉ Macairestr. 10, Konstanz ☎ 07531/99000 ✉ Kemptenerstr. 25, Lindau ☎ 08382/966-333. **Europcar** ✉ Eugenstr. 47, Friedrichshafen ☎ 07541/23053 ✉ Von Emmerichstr. 3, Konstanz ☎ 07531/52833. **Sixt** ✉ Zeppelinstr. 66, Friedrichshafen ☎ 07541/33066 ✉ Karl-Benz-Str. 14, Konstanz ☎ 07531/690-044.

CAR TRAVEL

Construction on the A–96 autobahn that runs from Munich to Lindau is ongoing. For a more scenic route, take B–12 via Landsberg and Kempten. For a scenic but slower route from Frankfurt, take B–311 at Ulm and follow the Oberschwäbische Barockstrasse (Upper Swabian Baroque Road) to Friedrichshafen. Lindau is also a terminus of the Deutsche Alpenstrasse (German Alpine Road). It runs east–west from Salzburg to Lindau.

Lakeside roads in the Bodensee area are scenic but experience occasional heavy traffic in summer. Stick to the speed limits in spite of the aggressive tailgaters: speed traps are frequent, especially in built-up areas. Formalities at border-crossing points are few. However, in addition to your passport you'll need insurance and registration papers for your car. For rental cars check with the rental company to make sure you are allowed to take the car into another country. Car ferries link Romanshorn, in Switzerland, with Friedrichshafen, as well as Konstanz with Meersburg. Taking either ferry saves substantial mileage. The fare depends on the size of the car; a one-way fare for a medium-size car including the driver costs €7.

TOURS

Most of the larger tourist centers have city tours with English-speaking guides, but call ahead to confirm availability.

AIRPLANE TOURS A fascinating way to view the lake is from a three-passenger Cessna operated by Slansky/Dussmann from Friedrichshafen's airport. They will also take you into the Alps, if you wish.
Slansky/Dussmann ☎ 07532/808-866 or 08388/1269.

BIKING TOURS The Bodensee is a paradise for bike travelers, with hundreds of miles of well-signposted paths that keep riders safe from cars. You can go on your own or enjoy the comfort of a customized tour with accommodations and baggage transport around the Bodensee (including a bike, if need be).
Bodensee-Radweg-Service GmbH ✉ Mainaustr. 34, Konstanz ☎ 07531/942-3640 ⊕ www.velotours.de. **Velotours** ✉ Fritz-Arnold-Str. 2d, Konstanz ☎ 07531/98280 ⊕ www.velotours.de.

WINE TOURS Wine-tasting tours are available in Überlingen, in the atmospheric Spitalweingut zum Heiligen Geist, as well as in Konstanz and Meersburg. Call the local tourist offices for information.

🏛 **Spitalweingut zum Heiligen Geist** ✉ Mühlbachstr. 115 ☎ 07551/65855.

TRAIN TRAVEL

From Frankfurt to Friedrichshafen and Lindau, take the ICE (InterCity Express) to Ulm and then transfer (total time 3½ hours). There are direct trains to Konstanz from Frankfurt every two hours (travel takes 4½ hours), which pass through the beautiful scenery of the Black Forest. From Munich to Lindau, the EC (Europe Express) train takes 2½ hours. From Zurich to Konstanz, the trip lasts 1½ hours. Local trains encircle the Bodensee, stopping at most towns and villages.

VISITOR INFORMATION

Information on the entire Bodensee region is available from the Internationaler Bodensee Tourismus.

🏛 **Bad Schussenried** ✉ Kultur-und Verkehrsamt, Klosterhof 5, on grounds of monastery, D-88427 ☎ 07583/940-171 ⊕ www.bad-schussenried.de. **Friedrichshafen** ✉ Tourist-Information, Bahnhofpl. 2, D-88045 ☎ 07541/30010 ⊕ www.friedrichshaven.de. **Internationaler Bodensee Tourismus** ✉ Insel Mainau, D-78465 Konstanz ☎ 07531/90940 🖶 07531/909-494 ⊕ www.bodensee-tourismus.com. **Konstanz** ✉ Tourist-Information, Konstanz, Fischmarkt 2, D-78462 ☎ 07531/133-030 ⊕ www.konstanz.de. **Langenargen** ✉ Langenargen Verkehrsamt, Obere Seestr. 2/2, D-88085 ☎ 07543/933-092 ⊕ www.langenargen.de. **Lindau** ✉ Verkehrsverein Lindau, Stadtpl., D-88103 ☎ 08381/80328 ⊕ www.lindau.de. **Meersburg** ✉ Verkehrsverwaltung, Kirchstr. 4, D-88709 ☎ 07532/431-110 ⊕ www.meersburg.de. **Radolfzell** ✉ Tourist-Information im Bahnhof, D-78315 ☎ 07732/81500 ⊕ www.radolfzell.de. **Ravensburg** ✉ Städtisches Verkehrsamt, Kirchstr. 16, D-88212 ☎ 0751/82324 ⊕ www.ravensburg.de. **Reichenau** ✉ Verkehrsbüro, Pirminstr. 145, D-78479 ☎ 07534/92070 ⊕ www.reichenau.de. **Tettnang** ✉ Verkehrsamt, Montfortpl. 1, D-88069 ☎ 07542/953-839 ⊕ www.tettnang.de. **Überlingen** ✉ Kurverwaltung, Landungspl. 14, D-88662 ☎ 07551/991-122 ⊕ www.ueberlingen.de. **Weingarten** ✉ Kultur- und Verkehrsamt, Münsterpl. 1, D-88250 ☎ 0751/405-125 ⊕ www.weingarten-info.de.

THE BLACK FOREST

7

BE DAZZLED BY GEMS & JEWELS
at the Schmuckmuseum
(Jewelry Museum) ⇨*p.271*

BUY THE BEST BLACK FOREST HAM
at Hermann Wein's ⇨*p.275*

RELAX IN THE ULTIMATE SPA TOWN
of Baden-Baden ⇨*p.277*

LET OFF STEAM
in a lavish thermal pool
at Caracalla-Therme ⇨*p.280*

GIVE YOUR KIDS A THRILL
at Europa Park,
a 160-acre amusement park ⇨*p.286*

GO CUCKOO BUYING A CLOCK
in Triberg ⇨*p.286*

Updated by
Ted Shoemaker

THE NAME CONJURES UP IMAGES OF A WILD, isolated place where time passes slowly. The dense woodland of the Black Forest—Schwarzwald in German—stretches away to the horizon, but this southwest corner of Baden-Württemberg (in the larger region known as Swabia) is neither inaccessible nor dull. Its distinctive characteristics include the cuckoo clock, the women's native costume with big red or black pom-poms on the hat, and the weird, almost pagan way the Carnival season is celebrated. The first travelers checked in here 19 centuries ago, when the Roman emperor Caracalla and his army rested and soothed their battle wounds in the natural-spring waters at what later became Baden-Baden.

Europe's upper-crust society discovered Baden-Baden when it convened nearby for the Congress of Rastatt from 1797 to 1799, which attempted to end the wars of the French Revolution. In the 19th century, kings, queens, emperors, princes, princesses, members of Napoléon's family, and the Russian nobility, along with actors, writers, and composers, flocked to the little spa town. Turgenev, Dostoyevsky, and Tolstoy were among the Russian contingent. Victor Hugo was a frequent visitor. Brahms composed lilting melodies in this calm setting. Queen Victoria spent her vacations here, and Mark Twain waxed poetic on the forest's beauty in his 1880 book *A Tramp Abroad,* putting the Black Forest on the map for Americans.

Today it's a favorite getaway for movie stars and millionaires, and you, too, can "take the waters," as the Romans first did, at thermal resorts large or small. The Black Forest sporting scene caters particularly to the German enthusiasm for hiking. The Schwarzwald-Verein, an outdoors association in the region, maintains no fewer than 30,000 km (18,000 mi) of hiking trails. In winter the terrain is ideally suited for cross-country skiing.

The Black Forest's enviable great outdoors is blessed with dependable snow in winter and sun in summer. Freudenstadt, at the center of the Black Forest, claims the greatest number of annual hours of sunshine of any town in Germany. You can play tennis, swim, or bike at most resorts, and some have golf courses of international standard.

The summer's warmth also benefits the vineyards of the Badische Weinstrasse (Baden Wine Road), which parallels, mainly to the east, the A-5 autobahn and the Rhine, using secondary roads to link up such places as Baden-Baden, Offenburg, Lahr, and Schliengen. Gutedel and Muskateller, two of the world's oldest grape varieties, are grown here. Baden cooperatives produce mostly dry wines that go well with the region's fine traditional food.

The Black Forest also happens to be the home of the cuckoo clock. It's still made (and sold) here, as it has been for centuries, along with hand-carved wood items and exquisite examples of glassblowing. Clock-making gave rise to a precision mechanics industry that is a guarantor of prosperity and employment throughout the region.

Despite its fame and the wealth of some of its visitors, the Black Forest doesn't have to be an expensive place to visit. It's possible to stay at a

Many first-time visitors to the Black Forest literally can't see the forest for the trees. Take time to stray from the beaten path and inhale the cool air of the darker recesses. Walk or ride through its shadowy corridors; paddle a canoe down the rippling currents of the Nagold and Wolf rivers. Then take time out to relax in a spa, order a dry Baden wine, and seek out the nearest restaurant for local specialties.

Numbers in the text correspond to numbers in the margin and on the Black Forest map.

7

If you have 3 days

Start at the confluence of three rivers in **Pforzheim** ❶ ►. Envy the glittering jewelry collection at the famous Schmuckmuseum, and then visit nearby Maulbronn's beautiful 12th-century Cistercian abbey. Spend a night in 🚂 **Bad Liebenzell** ❷, and on the second day soak up one of the Black Forest's oldest spas. After a visit to the ruined abbey in **Hirsau,** near **Calw** ❸, head south to 🚂 **Triberg** ⑬, site of Germany's highest waterfall and the lore of the cuckoo clock. On the last day go north to look at the farmhouses at the Open-Air Museum Vogtsbauernhof, near **Gutach** ⑫, before driving along the Schwarzwald-Hochstrasse (Black Forest Highway) from Mummelsee (with a stop at the lake) to **Baden-Baden** ❻. Save plenty of time for a walk around the fashionable spa.

If you have 5 days

Begin your trip by following the first two days of the three-day itinerary described above. On the third day continue directly south of Triberg to **Furtwangen** ⑭ to survey Germany's largest clock museum. The 🚂 **Titisee** ⑮, the jewel of the Black Forest lakes, is a good place to spend the third night. After taking some time to enjoy Titisee and the mountain-enclosed **Schluchsee** ⑰, head up the winding road northwest through the **Höllental.** End your day in 🚂 **Freiburg** ⑱ at the foot of the Black Forest; its Münster (cathedral) has the most perfect spire of any German Gothic church. On your fourth day, drive north from Freiburg on B–3 through the Baden vineyards to elegant 🚂 **Baden-Baden** ❻, where you can relax on the fifth day.

If you have 10 days

After visiting the attractions near **Pforzheim** ❶ ►, spend the first two nights in 🚂 **Bad Liebenzell** ❷. 🚂 **Freudenstadt** ❺ is a good base for the next two days; from here make excursions to the Schwarzwälder Freilichtmuseum Vogtsbauernhof in **Gutach** ⑫; the **Alpirsbach** ⑪ brewery; and Glaswaldsee (Glasswald Lake), near Schapbach. On the fifth day continue on to **Triberg** ⑬ to explore its waterfall and cuckoo-clock museum and then to **Furtwangen** ⑭. Spend the fifth and sixth nights near the shores of the 🚂 **Titisee** ⑮. From the lake, visit the Feldberg, the Black Forest's highest mountain, and the **Schluchsee** ⑰. Spend the following two days and nights in 🚂 **Freiburg** ⑱, allowing time for Schauinsland Mountain; the town of **Staufen** ⑲, where the legendary Dr. Faustus made his pact with the devil; and the vineyards on the slopes of the Kaiserstuhl. Finally, drive north through the Rhine Valley for two nights in 🚂 **Baden-Baden** ❻. Indulge in the city's attractions and take a trip to nearby Merkur Mountain.

modest family-run country inn or farmhouse where the enormous breakfast will keep you going for the better part of the day—all for not much more than the price of a meal in a city restaurant.

Exploring the Black Forest

The northern Black Forest is known for its broad ridges and thickly forested slopes; it contains the largest number of spas. The central region, Triberg in particular, is especially popular for its associations with folklore, cuckoo clocks, and the Schwarzwaldbahn (Black Forest Railway). The southern portion of the Black Forest has the most dramatic scenery and the most-frequented recreation areas. Two main attractions are the Titisee and the Schluchsee, two beautiful lakes created by glaciers.

About the Restaurants & Hotels

Restaurants in the Black Forest range from the well-upholstered luxury of Baden-Baden's chic eating spots to simple country inns. Old *Kachelöfen* (tile-heating stoves) are still in use in many area restaurants; try to sit by one if it's cold outside.

Accommodations in the Black Forest are varied and numerous, from simple rooms in farmhouses to five-star luxury. Some properties have been passed down in the same family for generations. *Gasthöfe* offer low prices and as much local color as you'll ever want.

WHAT IT COSTS In Euros				
	$$$$	**$$$**	**$$**	**$**	**¢**
RESTAURANTS	over €25	€21–€25	€16–€20	€9–€15	under €9
HOTELS	over €225	€175–€225	€100–€175	€50–€100	under €50

Restaurant prices are per person for a main course at dinner. Hotel prices are for two people in a standard double room, including tax and service.

Timing

The Black Forest is one of the most heavily visited mountain regions in Europe, so make reservations well in advance for the better-known spas and hotels. In summer the areas around Schluchsee and Titisee are particularly crowded. In early fall and late spring, the Black Forest scenery is less crowded (except during the Easter holidays) but just as beautiful. Some spa hotels close for the winter.

THE NORTHERN BLACK FOREST

This region is crossed by broad ridges that are densely wooded, with little lakes such as the Mummelsee and the Wildsee. The Black Forest Spa Route (270 km [167 mi]) links many of the spas in the region, from Baden-Baden (the best known) to Wildbad. Other regional treasures are the lovely Nagold River; ancient towns such as Bad Herrenalb and Hirsau; and the magnificent abbey at Maulbronn, near Pforzheim.

Bicycling

Bicycles can be rented in nearly all towns and many villages. The Deutsche Bahn, Germany's national railway, has excellent deals on bicycle rentals at train stations. Several regional tourist offices sponsor tours on which the biker's luggage is transported separately from one overnight stop to the next. Six- to 10-day tours are available at reasonable rates, including bed-and-breakfast and bike rental.

On the Menu

Don't pass up the chance to try *Schwarzwälder Schinken* (pinecone-smoked ham) and *Schwarzwälder Kirschtorte* (kirsch-soaked layers of chocolate cake with sour cherry and whipped cream filling). *Kirschwasser,* locally called *Chriesewässerle* (from the French *cerise,* meaning "cherry"), is cherry brandy, the most famous of the region's excellent schnapps varieties. If traveling in May or June, keep an eye out for white asparagus, the "king of vegetables."

Hiking & Walking

The Black Forest is ideal for walkers. The principal trails are well marked and cross the region from north to south, the longest stretching from Pforzheim to the Swiss city of Basel, 280 km (174 mi) away. Walks vary in length from a few hours to a week. As in many other German regions, the tourist office has gotten together with local inns to create *Wandern ohne Gepäck* (Hike Without Luggage) tours along the old clock carriers' route. Your bags are transported ahead by car to meet you each evening at that day's destination.

Spas & Health Resorts

There's an amazing variety of places to have a relaxing soak, from expensive spa towns to rustic places deep in the woods. Baden-Baden is stately and elegant. Bad Dürrheim has Europe's highest-brine spa. For a garden setting, head for Bad Herrenalb. Bad Liebenzell has an Olympic-size pool, and the spa town of Hinterzarten also provides opportunities to hike. Many of the spas offer special rates for stays lasting several days or even weeks.

Winter Sports

Despite Swiss claims to the contrary, the Black Forest is the true home of downhill skiing. In 1891 a French diplomat was sighted sliding down the slopes of the Feldberg, the Black Forest's highest mountain, on what are thought to be the world's first downhill skis. The idea caught on among the locals, and a few months later Germany's first ski club was formed. The world's first ski lift opened at Schollach in 1907. There are now more than 200 ski lifts in the Black Forest, but the slopes of the Feldberg are still the top ski area.

Pforzheim

▶ ❶ *35 km (22 mi) southeast of Karlsruhe, just off A–8 autobahn, the main Munich–Karlsruhe route.*

The Romans founded Pforzheim at the meeting place of three rivers, the Nagold, the Enz, and the Würm, and it's known today as the "gateway

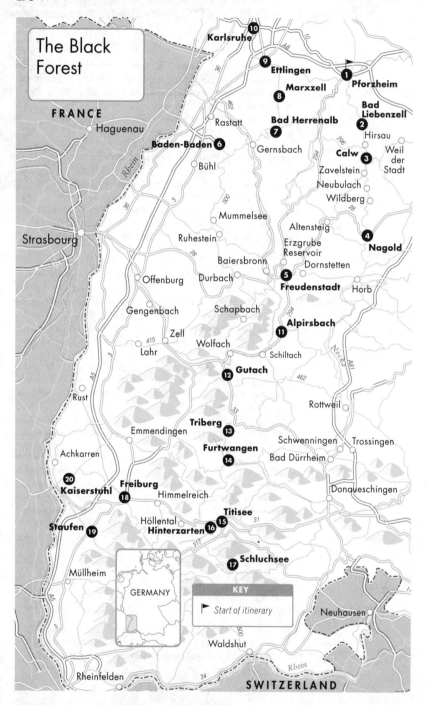

The Black Forest

FRANCE

Haguenau

Strasbourg

Rhein

Rust

Achkarren

Müllheim

Rheinfelden

Karlsruhe 10

Ettlingen 9

Marxzell 8

Bad Herrenalb 7

Baden-Baden 6

Rastatt

Gernsbach

Bühl

Mummelsee

Ruhestein

Baiersbronn

Durbach

Offenburg

Gengenbach

Zell

Lahr

Wolfach

Schapbach

Emmendingen

Gutach 12

Triberg 13

Furtwangen 14

Freiburg 18

Himmelreich

Kaiserstuhl 20

Staufen 19

Höllental

Hinterzarten 16

Titisee 15

Schluchsee 17

Pforzheim 1

Bad Liebenzell 2

Hirsau

Calw 3

Weil der Stadt

Zavelstein

Neubulach

Wildberg

Altensteig

Erzgrube Reservoir

Dornstetten

Freudenstadt 5

Horb

Nagold 4

Alpirsbach 11

Schiltach

Rottweil

Schwenningen

Bad Dürrheim

Trossingen

Donaueschingen

Neuhausen

Waldshut

GERMANY

KEY

► *Start of itinerary*

SWITZERLAND

to the Black Forest." The city was almost totally destroyed in World War II, which accounts for its not-so-attractive blocky postwar architectural style. Pforzheim owes its prosperity to its role in Europe's jewelry trade and its wristwatch industry. To get a sense of the "Gold City," explore the jewelry shops on streets around Leopoldplatz and the pedestrian area. The restored church of **St. Michael** (⊠ Schlossberg 10), near the train station, is the final resting place of the Baden princes. The original mixture of 13th- and 15th-century styles has been faithfully reproduced; compare the airy Gothic choir with the church's sturdy Romanesque entrance.

The Reuchlinhaus, the city cultural center, houses the **Schmuckmuseum** (Jewelry Museum). Its collection of jewelry from five millennia is one of the finest in the world. ⊠ *Jahnstr. 42* ☎ *07231/392–126* ⊕ *www. schmuckmuseum-pforzheim.de* ☜ *Free* ☾ *Tues.–Sun. 10–5.*

Pforzheim has long been known as a center of the German clock-making industry. In the **Technisches Museum** (Technical Museum), one of the country's leading museums devoted to the craft, you can see makers of watches and clocks at work; there's also a reconstructed 18th-century clock factory. ⊠ *Bleichstr. 81* ☎ *07231/392–869* ☜ *Free* ☾ *Wed. 9–noon and 3–6, 2nd and 4th Sun. of month 10–5.*

★ **Kloster Maulbronn** (Maulbronn Monastery), in the little town of Maulbronn, 18 km (11 mi) northeast of Pforzheim, is the best-preserved medieval monastery north of the Alps, with an entire complex of 30 buildings on UNESCO's World Heritage List. The main buildings were constructed between the 12th and 14th centuries. Next to the monastery's church is the cloister, with a fountain house and refectories for the monks and lay brothers. The monastery's fortified walls still stand, and its medieval water-management system, with its network of drains, irrigation canals, and reservoirs, remains intact. ⊠ *Off B–35* ☎ *07043/926–610* ⊕ *www. maulbronn.de* ☜ *€4.50* ☾ *Mar.–Oct., daily 9–5:30; Nov.–Feb., Tues.–Sun. 9:30–5; guided tour at 11:15 and 3.*

Where to Eat

$$–$$$ ✕ **Silberburg.** The Alsatian owners of this cozy restaurant outside the city center serve classic French cuisine. Try the duck with one of chef Gilbert Noesser's exquisite sauces. ⊠ *Dietlingerstr. 27* ☎ *07231/441– 159* ▤ *AE, DC, MC, V* ☾ *Closed Aug. No lunch Mon.–Tues.*

en route The road south of Pforzheim, B–463, follows the twists and turns of the pretty little Nagold River. Gardening enthusiasts should follow the signs to the **Alpine Garden** (on the left as you leave the city limits). The garden, on the banks of the Würm River, stocks more than 100,000 varieties of plants, including the rarest Alpine flowers. It has a pleasant café and florist shop. ☎ *07231/70590* ⊕ *www. alpengarten-pforzheim.de* ☜ *€2.50* ☾ *Mid-Apr.–Oct., daily 8–7.*

Bad Liebenzell

❷ *31 km (19 mi) south of Pforzheim on Highway 463.*

Bathhouses were built in Bad Liebenzell as early as 1403. Nearly six centuries later the same hot springs feed the more modern spas. Apart from medicinal baths (highly recommended for the treatment of circulatory problems), the town has the **Paracelsusbad lido complex,** with outdoor and indoor hot-water pools, and a steam grotto. There's also mixed nude bathing (except Thursday, which is reserved for women only) at the Sauna Pinea, whose little park complex outside affords beautiful panoramic views of wooded slopes. The nearby Kurpark has an interesting installation—a solar system model that lights up at night and lets you wander around the cosmos, so to speak. ⊠ *Reuchlinweg 1* 🕾 *07052/408–608* ⊕ *www.bad-liebenzell.de/mitteterme.htm* 🖃 *3 hrs in bath €7.50, 4 hrs in sauna €13* ⊙ *Bath Apr.–Oct., Mon.–Sat. 8 AM–9 PM, Sun. 8–8; Nov.–Mar., Mon.–Sat. 8:30 AM–9 PM, Sun. 8:30–8. Sauna Mon.–Thurs. 1–10, Fri. 1–11, Sat. 9 AM–11 PM, Sun. 9–8.*

Where to Stay & Eat

$$ ✕🏠 **Kronen Hotel.** At this member of the Wellness Hotels group, most of the functional rooms are in a large, rather bland modern wing. The Black Forest landscape is very close, however, and the Nagold River, teeming with fish, flows right in front of the hotel. There's a pool, a sauna, and a beauty spa, and one kitchen serves the three restaurants ($–$$$), one of which is no-smoking. The cuisine is called *Vitalkost,* meaning light, with plenty of fresh vegetables and herbs, good salads, and fruit. ⊠ *Badweg 7, D–75378* 🕾 *07052/4090* 🖷 *07052/409–420* ⊕ *www.kronenhotel. de* 🛏 *42 rooms* ♿ *3 restaurants, café, pool, sauna, some pets allowed (fee), no-smoking rooms; no a/c* ▤ *AE, DC, MC, V,* ⦿ *BP.*

en route
Weil der Stadt, a former imperial city, is in the hills 13 km (8 mi) west of Bad Liebenzell. This small, sleepy town of turrets and gables has only its well-preserved city walls and fortifications to remind you of its onetime importance. The astronomer Johannes Kepler, born here in 1571, was the first man to track and accurately explain the orbits of the planets. And, appropriately, the town now has a planetarium to graphically show you what he learned. The little half-timber house in which he was born is now the **Kepler Museum** (⊠ Keplerg. 2 🕾 07033/6586 ⊕ www.kepler-museum.de 🖃 €2, tour €10 ⊙ Tues.–Fri. 10–noon and 2–4, Sat. 11–noon and 2–4, Sun. 11–noon and 2–5) in the town center. It's devoted to his writings and discoveries.

Calw

❸ *8 km (5 mi) south of Bad Liebenzell on B–463.*

Calw, one of the Black Forest's prettiest towns, was the birthplace of Nobel prize–winning novelist Hermann Hesse (1877–1962). He was born at Marktplatz 6, now a private home inhabited by a gentleman who designs carpets. The town's market square, with its two sparkling fountains surrounded by 18th-century half-timber houses whose sharp gables pierce the sky, is an ideal spot for relaxing, picnicking, or people-watching, especially when it's market time.

The **Hermann Hesse Museum** recounts the life of the Nobel Prize–winning philosopher, author of *Steppenwolf* and *The Glass Bead Game,* who rebelled against his middle-class German upbringing to become a pacifist and the darling of the beat generation. The story of his life is told in personal belongings, photographs, manuscripts, and documents. (You can rent a recorder with earphones to guide you in English.) ⊠ *Marktpl. 30* ☎*07051/7522* ⊕*www.hermann-hesse.com* ⊠*€5* ⊗*Tues.–Wed. and Fri.–Sun. 11–5, Thurs. 11–7.*

Hirsau, 3 km (2 mi) north of Calw, has ruins of a 9th-century monastery, now the setting for the Klosterspiele Hirsau (open-air theater performances) in July and August. Buy advance tickets at the **Calw tourist office** (⊠ Marktbrücke 1 ☎ 07051/968–844).

Where to Stay & Eat

★ **$–$$** ✕▦ **Hotel Kloster Hirsau.** This hotel, a model of comfort and gracious hospitality, is just outside Calw in Hirsau, near the ruins of the monastery. The Klosterschenke restaurant ($–$$$) serves such regional specialties as *Flädelsuppe* (containing pieces of a special, very thin pancake) and *Schwäbischer Rostbraten* (panfried beefsteak topped with sautéed onions). ⊠ *Wildbaderstr. 2, D-75365* ☎ *07051/96740* ╝ *07051/967-469* ⊕ *www.hotel-kloster-hirsau.de* ⤸ *42 rooms* △ *Restaurant, in-room data ports, cable TV, tennis court, indoor pool, sauna, bowling, some pets allowed (fee), no-smoking rooms; no a/c* ⊟ *AE, MC, V* ⊦⊙⊧ *BP.*

$ ✕▦ **Ratsstube.** Most of the original features, including 16th-century beams and brickwork, are preserved at this historic house in the center of Calw. Rooms are small but half-timber like the exterior. The restaurant (¢–$) serves a selection of sturdy German and Greek dishes. A salad buffet will take care of smaller appetites, and lunchtime always has a special dish. ⊠ *Marktpl. 12, D-75365* ☎ *07051/92050* ╝ *07051/70826* ⊕ *www.hotel-ratsstube.de* ⤸ *13 rooms* △ *Restaurant, some pets allowed; no a/c, no TV in some rooms* ⊟ *MC, V* ⊦⊙⊧ *BP.*

Nagold

❹ *25 km (15 mi) south of Calw.*

This town of half-timber buildings has an elliptical street plan that was designed some 750 years ago when it was first established. The Romanesque **Remigiuskirche** (Remigius Church) and its few remaining frescoes dating from 1325, just outside of town, and the modest hilltop remains of a medieval castle are its historic highlights.

Where to Stay & Eat

$–$$ ✕▦ **Pfrondorfermühle.** This old mill with a modern annex is bordered on one side by the narrow Nagold River, and on the other by the road between Nagold and Wildberg. It offers family-style Black Forest comfort and hospitality. The elegant restaurant ($–$$$) has a delightful range of cuisine, from simple *Maultaschen* (a kind of large ravioli) to fine salmon in basil sauce. There are two luxurious suites for special occasions and a dance bar. ⊠ *On B–463, D-72202 Nagold* ☎ *07452/84000* ╝ *07452/840-048* ⊕ *www.pfrondorfer-muehle.de* ⤸ *21 rooms, 2 suites* △ *Restaurant, cable TV, tennis court, bar, playground, some pets allowed (fee); no a/c* ⊟ *AE, MC, V* ⊦⊙⊧ *BP.*

Freudenstadt

⑤ *40 km (25 mi) south of Nagold, 22 km (14 mi) southwest of Altensteig.*

At an altitude of 2,415 feet, Freudenstadt claims to be the sunniest German resort. The town was flattened by the French in April 1945, and it has since been rebuilt with painstaking care. It was founded in 1599 to house both silver miners and refugees from religious persecution in what is now the Austrian province of Carinthia (*Freudenstadt* means "city of joy").

The vast central square, more than 650 feet long and edged with arcaded shops, is Germany's largest marketplace. It still awaits the palace that was supposed to be built here for the city's founder, Prince Frederick I of Württemberg, who died before work could begin. When the fountains all spout on this vast expanse, it can be quite a sight, and a refreshing one as well. Don't miss Freudenstadt's Protestant **stadtkirche,** just off the square. Its lofty nave is L-shape, a rare architectural liberty in the early 17th century. It was constructed in this way so the sexes would be separated and unable to see each other during services.

> off the beaten path

SCHAPBACH – This town lies 22 km (14 mi) southwest of Freudenstadt, in the enchanting Wolfach River valley. From here, head up into the hills to **Glaswaldsee** (Glasswald Lake). You will probably find yourself alone with the tree-fringed lake. Parts of the neighboring Poppel Valley are so wild that carnivorous flowers number among the rare plants carpeting the countryside. In July and August the bug-eating *Sonnentau* is in full bloom in the **Hohlohsee** (Hohloh Lake) nature reserve, near Enzklösterle. Farther north, just off B–500 near Hornisgrinde Mountain, a path to the remote **Wildsee** passes through a nature reserve where rare wildflowers bloom in spring.

Where to Stay & Eat

★ **$$–$$$$** ✕ **Warteck.** The lead-pane windows with stained-glass work, flowers, and beautifully upholstered banquettes create a bright setting in the two dining rooms. The modern kitchen uses only natural products and spotlights individual ingredients. A popular dish is the oxtail. In season the *Spargel* (asparagus) is dressed in an aromatic hazelnut vinaigrette. ⊠ *Stuttgarterstr. 14* ☎ *07441/91920* ▭ *DC, MC, V* ⊗ *Closed Tues.*

¢–$$ ✕ **Ratskeller.** Though there's a modern cellar, this restaurant with a green marble bar and pine furnishings is more a modern bistro than traditional Ratskeller. An English-language menu will explain the Swabian dishes such as Zwiebelrostbraten, served with sauerkraut, and pork fillet with mushroom gravy. In season there's venison, and a specialty is the homemade trout roulade with crab sauce. ⊠ *Marktpl. 8* ☎ *07441/952–805* ▭ *AE, MC, V* ⊗ *Closed Tues. during Nov.–Mar.*

$ ✕▦ **Bären.** The Montigels have owned the sturdy old Gasthof Bären since 1878, and they strive to maintain tradition and personal service. Rooms are modern but contain such homey touches as farmhouse-style bedsteads and cupboards. The beamed restaurant ($–$$) is a favorite with the locals. Its menu includes Swabian dishes (roasts in heavy sauces, fried Maultaschen) and lighter international fare. The trout is caught locally. ✉ *Langestr. 33, D–72250* ☎ *07441/2729* 🖷 *07441/2887* ⊕ *www.hotel-baeren-freudenstadt.de* ⮂ *33 rooms* ♻ *Restaurant, some in-room data ports, cable TV, no-smoking rooms; no a/c* ▤ *DC, MC, V* ☺ *Restaurant closed Fri. No lunch except Sun.* ⦿️ *BP.*

$ ✕▦ **Hotel Adler.** This is a simple hotel just off the main square, but that doesn't mean it's uncomfortable. Some of the very affordable rooms even have a balcony so you can enjoy a view of behind-the-scenes Freudenstadt. The restaurant ($$) provides a square meal with local dishes. There are four Flammkuchen evenings a week. Flammkuchen is a specialty of neighboring Alsace, similar to a pizza but thinner, and with toppings such as sour cream, bacon, and onions. ✉ *Forststr. 15–17, D–72250* ☎ *07441/91520* 🖷 *07441/915–252* ⊕ *www.adler-fds.de* ⮂ *13 rooms* ♻ *Restaurant, cable TV; no a/c* ▤ *MC, V* ⦿️ *BP.*

$ ✕▦ **Zum Schwanen.** This bright, white building just a few steps from the main square now offers a special room with a water bed for those with allergies. Many locals come to enjoy fine regional specialties, not to mention giant pancakes, in the restaurant ($). The cakes are excellent during an afternoon coffee break on the warm terrace. ✉ *Forststr. 6, D–72250* ☎ *07441/91550* 🖷 *07441/915–544* ⊕ *www.schwanen-freudenstadt.de* ⮂ *17 rooms, 1 apartment* ♻ *Restaurant, in-room data ports, cable TV, some pets allowed (fee), no-smoking rooms; no a/c* ▤ *MC, V* ⦿️ *BP.*

Shopping

Germans prize Black Forest ham as an aromatic souvenir. You can buy one at any butcher shop in the region, but it's more fun to visit a *Schinkenräucherei* (smokehouse), where the ham is actually cured. **Hermann Wein's** (☎ 07443/2450 ⊕ www.schinken-wein.de) Schinkenräucherei, in the village of Musbach, near Freudenstadt, is one of the leading smokehouses in the area. If you have a group of people, call ahead to find out if the staff can show you around.

Baiersbronn

7 km (4½ mi) northwest of Freudenstadt.

The mountain resort of Baiersbronn has an incredible collection of hotels and bed-and-breakfasts providing rest and relaxation in beautiful surroundings. Most people come here to walk, ski, golf, and ride horseback. You may want to walk through the streets to preview the many restaurants. Near the town hall and church in the upper part of town is the little **Hauff's Märchenmuseum** (Fairy-Tale Museum), devoted to the crafts and life around Baiersbronn and the fairy-tale author Wilhelm Hauff (1802–27), who once lived here. ✉ *Rosenpl. 3* ☎ *07442/841–414* ▨ *€1.50* ☺ *Wed. and weekends 2–5.*

Where to Stay & Eat

★ **$$$$** ✕▦ **Bareiss.** This modern resort resembles a cruise ship moored on a hilltop above Baiersbronn. Inside, some guest rooms have dark-wood furniture and tapestry-papered walls, while others have a light and airy look. Its three restaurants range from the elegant Bareiss ($$$$), where you'll find 30 brands of champagne, to the Kaminstube ($$$–$$$$), which offers dining near the fireplace. There's also the rustic Dorfstube ($$). The hotel itself is among the most lavish and best equipped in the Black Forest. Suites start at €470 and one has its own sauna, solarium, and whirlpool bath. ⊠ *Gärtenbühlweg 14, D–07442 Mitteltal/Baiersbronn* ☎ *07442/470* 🖷 *07442/47320* ⊕ *www.bareiss.com* ⤳ *75 rooms, 42 apartments, 10 suites* ♨ *3 restaurants, some in-room data ports, in-room hot tubs, cable TV, tennis court, 9 pools (8 indoor), gym, hair salon, sauna, bicycles, bowling, bar, some pets allowed (fee), no-smoking rooms; no a/c in some rooms* ⊟ *AE, DC, MC, V* ⦿ *MAP.*

★ **$$$–$$$$** ✕⌨ **Traube Tonbach.** The luxurious Traube Tonbach hotel has three restaurants. If the classic French cuisine of the Schwarzwaldstube (menus begin at €74) is too expensive, try either the international fare of the Köhlerstube or the Bauernstube, renowned for its Swabian dishes. In the latter two you'll dine beneath beam ceilings at tables bright with fine silver and glassware. The hotel is a harmonious blend of old and new, and each room presents sweeping views of the Black Forest. A small army of extremely helpful and friendly staff nearly outnumbers the guests. ⊠ *Tonbachstr. 237, D–72270 Tonbach/Baiersbronn* ☎ *07442/4920* 🖷 *07442/492–692* ⊕ *www.traube-tonbach.de* ⤳ *108 rooms, 55 apartments, 12 suites* ♨ *3 restaurants, cafeteria, cable TV, tennis court, 3 pools (2 indoors), gym, hair salon, sauna, bowling, bar; no a/c in some rooms* ⊟ *AE, DC, MC, V in restaurants only; no credit cards in hotel* ⦿ *BP.*

$$ ✕⌨ **Hotel Lamm.** The steep-roofed exterior of this 200-year-old typical Black Forest building presents a clear picture of the traditional hotel within. Rooms are furnished with heavy oak fittings and some fine antiques. In winter the lounge's fireplace is a welcome sight when returning from the slopes (the ski lift is nearby). In its beamed restaurant ($–$$) you can order fish fresh from the hotel's trout pools. ⊠ *Ellbacherstr. 4, D–72270 Mitteltal/Baiersbronn* ☎ *07442/4980* 🖷 *07442/49878* ⊕ *www.lamm-mitteltal.de* ⤳ *48 rooms, 6 apartments* ♨ *Restaurant, cable TV, pool, sauna, billiards, some pets allowed (fee); no a/c* ⊟ *DC, MC, V* ⦿ *BP.*

en route | The back road from Baiersbronn, via Mitteltal and Obertal, enables you to join the Schwarzwald Hochstrasse at the little village of Ruhestein. From this little village, there's a well-marked back road to the west that leads to the **Allerheiligen** (All Saints) ruins. This 12th-century monastery was secularized in 1803, when plans were drawn up to turn it into a prison. Two days later lightning started a fire that burned the monastery to the ground. The locals claim it was divine intervention.

Bühl

On B–500, 3 km (2 mi) after the turnoff to the town of Bühl, which is 17 km (11 mi) north of Ruhestein, 16 km (10 mi) south of Baden-Baden.

Several of the finest hotels and restaurants in the Black Forest are on Bühlerhöhe, the thickly wooded heights above the town of Bühl. The Bühl Valley and the surrounding area have spas, ruins, quaint villages, and a legendary velvety red wine called *Affenthaler*.

Where to Stay & Eat

★ **$$$$** ✕▦ **Schlosshotel Bühlerhöhe.** This premier "castle-hotel" stands majestically on its own extensive grounds 15 km (9 mi) above Baden-Baden, with spectacular views over the heights of the Black Forest. Walking trails start virtually at the hotel door. Its restaurant, the Imperial ($$$$; closed Monday and Tuesday and January–mid-February), features French fare with international touches, such as lamb in feta cheese crust with ratatouille and gnocchi. In its Schlossrestaurant, overlooking the Rhine Valley, regional and international dishes are offered. ⊠ *Schwarzwaldhochstr. 1, D–77815 Bühl/Baden-Baden* ☎ *07226/550* 🖷 *07226/55777* ⊕ *www.buehlerhoehe.com* ⮌ *73 rooms, 17 suites* ♿ *2 restaurants, in-room safes, minibars, cable TV, tennis court, pool, health club, sauna, bar, Internet, some pets allowed (fee), no-smoking rooms; no a/c in some rooms* 🖃 *AE, DC, MC, V.*

$ ▦ **Cafe-Pension Jägersteig.** Magnificent views of the wide Rhine Valley as far as the French Vosges Mountains are included in the room rate at this spectacularly situated pension, high above the town of Bühl and its vineyards. ⊠ *Kappelwindeckstr. 95a, D–77815 Bühl/Baden-Baden* ☎ *07223/98590* 🖷 *07223/985–998* ⊕ *www.jaegersteig.de* ⮌ *14 rooms* ♿ *Restaurant, in-room data ports, cable TV, some pets allowed (fee); no a/c* 🖃 *MC, V* ⫴⦶⫴ *BP.*

Baden-Baden

★ ❻ *51 km (32 mi) north of Freudenstadt, 24 km (15 mi) north of Mummelsee.*

Baden-Baden, the famous and fashionable spa, is downhill all the way north on B–500 from the Mummelsee. The town rests in a wooded valley and is atop the extensive underground hot springs that gave the city its name. Roman legions of the emperor Caracalla discovered the springs and named the area Aquae. The leisure classes of the 19th century rediscovered the bubbling waters, establishing Baden-Baden as the unofficial summer residence of many European royal families. The spa tradition continues at the vast Caracalla Therme, where you might want to take a swim. The palatial homes and stately villas of the visiting aristocrats still grace the tree-lined avenues, evoking the feelings of a more unhurried age.

As Germany's ultimate high-fashion resort, the small city basks unabashedly in wealth and pleasure—it boasts Germany's highest concentration of millionaires. The spa concept is focusing on maintaining "wellness" (rather than curing ailments) these days, and the shops and eateries in town are gearing up for a younger crowd. The pop music scene is well established, and there are frequent ballet performances, plays, and concerts (by the excellent Southwest German Radio Symphony Orchestra). There's horse racing at the Iffezheim racetrack to the west of town and high-stakes action at Baden-Baden's renowned casino.

Sophienstrasse is a superb old-fashioned alley lined with trees that leads into the heart of town. The **Lichtentaler Allee,** right in the middle of town, is an extensive park with carefully groomed paths, occasional sculptures, and an extensive rose garden, the **Gönneranlage,** which contains more than 300 types of roses. Close by is the **Russian church** (✉ €.50 ⊙ Feb.–Nov. 10–6), identifiable by its golden onion dome. At the other end of the park the paths climb up the **Michaelsberg,** where the Black Forest brooks fall into bubbling rapids.

The Lichtentaler Allee ends at **Kloster Lichtenthal,** a medieval Cistercian abbey surrounded by thick defensive walls. The small royal chapel next to the church was built in 1288 and was used from the late 14th century onward as a final resting place for the Baden dynasty princes. ✉ *Hauptstr. 40* ☏ *07221/504–910* ✉ *Tours in groups of 7 or more €2* ⊙ *Tours Tues.–Sun. at 3.*

Baden-Baden is quite proud of its **casino**, Germany's largest and oldest, and some say most beautiful and traditional. It has, however, made an ever-so-slight concession to the times. You may wear your jeans! Gentlemen must, however, wear a jacket and tie with their jeans, and whatever you do, leave your sneakers at the hotel. The casino is part of the spa complex that includes a manicured park along the Oos River, the Kurhaus, the *Trinkhalle* (Drinking Hall), a theater, shops, hotels, and restaurants. It was in 1853 that a Parisian, Jacques Bénazet, persuaded the sleepy little Black Forest spa to build gambling rooms to enliven its evenings. The result was a series of richly decorated gaming rooms in which even an emperor could feel at home—and did. Kaiser Wilhelm I was a regular visitor, as was his chancellor, Bismarck. The Russian novelist Dostoyevsky, the Aga Khan, and Marlene Dietrich all patronized the place. The minimum stake is €2; maximum €10,000. Passports are necessary as proof of identity. Guided tours are offered. ✉*Kaiserallee 1* ☏*07221/30241* ✉*€3, tour €4* ⊙ *Sun.–Thurs. 2* PM*–2* AM, *Fri. and Sat. 2* PM*–3* AM. *Tours Apr.–Sept., daily 9:30–11:45* AM; *Oct.–Mar., daily 10–11:45* AM.

Where to Stay & Eat

$$$–$$$$ ✕ **Le Jardin de France.** This clean, crisp little French restaurant, whose owners are actually French, emphasizes elegant, imaginative dining in an elegant Victorian setting. The duck might be roasted with raisins, figs, and nuts at Christmastime; the Breton lobster is prepared with bouillon and ginger. ✉ *Lichtentalerstr. 13* ☏ *07221/300–7860* ▭ *AE, DC, MC, V* ⊙ *Closed Mon. No lunch Tues.*

$–$$ ✕ **Klosterschänke.** This rustic restaurant is a 10-minute drive from the center of Baden-Baden, and the food is well worth the trip, particularly on a summer evening, when you can dine outside on a tree-covered terrace. You'll probably share a rough oak table with locals; the Baden wine and locally brewed beer ensure conviviality. The menu is surprisingly imaginative, and it's the best place for venison when it's in season in fall and winter. ✉ *Landstr. 84* ☏ *07221/25854* ▭ *MC, V* ⊙ *Closed Mon. and 2 wks in Aug. No lunch Tues.*

¢–$ ✕ **Weinstube Zum Engel.** The Frölich family has been in charge of the Angel (in the suburb of Neuweier) for four generations. Eduard Frölich is responsible for the wine, Gerti Frölich for the kitchen. It's an ideal place for traditional German food such as sauerbraten or Wiener schnitzel. The selection of wines, served by the glass, does supreme justice to the fine local vintages. ✉ *Mauerbergstr. 62* ☏ *07223/57243* ▭ *No credit cards* ⊙ *Closed Mon., Tues., and 2 wks in Mar.*

★ **$$–$$$$** ✕▣ **Der Kleine Prinz.** Antoine de Saint-Exupéry's illustrations for his 1943 French children's classic, *Le Petit Prince*, are everywhere, from a multi-storied mural in the courtyard to the plates in the posh restaurant ($$$–$$$$). Owners Norbert Rademacher, a veteran of the New York Hilton and Waldorf Astoria, and his interior-designer wife, Edeltraud, have skillfully combined two elegant city mansions into a unique, antiques-filled lodging. ⊠ *Lichtentalerstr. 36, D–76530* ☎ *07221/346–600* 🖷 *07221/3466-059* ⊕ *www.derkleineprinz.de* ➬ *25 rooms, 15 suites* ♨ *Restaurant, in-room data ports, minibars, cable TV with movies, bar, laundry service, parking (fee), some pets allowed (fee)* ▤ *AE, MC, V* †◎† *BP.*

$$$$ ▣ **Brenner's Park Hotel & Spa.** With some justification, this stately hotel
Fodor'sChoice set in a private park claims to be one of the best in the world. Behind
★ it passes leafy Lichtentaler Allee, where Queen Victoria and Czar Alexander II, among others, strolled in their day. Luxury abounds in the hotel, and all the rooms and suites (the latter costing up to €680 a day) are sumptuously furnished and appointed. An extensive beauty and fitness program is offered. ⊠ *Schillerstr. 6, D–76530* ☎ *07221/9000* 🖷 *07221/ 38772* ⊕ *www.brenners-park.de* ➬ *68 rooms, 18 suites, 12 apartments* ♨ *2 restaurants, some in-room data ports, cable TV, pool (indoor), gym, hair salon, 2 saunas, spa, bar, some pets allowed (fee); no a/c in some rooms* ▤ *AE, DC, MC, V.*

$$$–$$$$ ▣ **Belle Epoque.** The heyday of Baden-Baden was during the decades prior to World War I, which the French refer to as the *belle époque* (beautiful era). This spacious two-story 1870s house, in its own garden behind wrought-iron gates, captures the gracious spirit of this period. The entire building, a sister hotel to Der Kleine Prinz, is under monument protection. Each of its suites and rooms, many with whirlpool baths, is furnished in a separate style, ranging from Henri II to art nouveau, and afternoon tea is included in the room price along with breakfast. Under the eaves are the Brahms or Mozart rooms, garrets of sheer luxury. In the garden is Baden-Baden's only California redwood. ⊠ *Maria-Victoria-Str. 2c, D–76530* ☎ *07221/300–660* 🖷 *07221/300–666* ⊕ *www. hotelbelleepoque.de* ➬ *4 rooms, 12 suites* ♨ *In-room data ports, cable TV* ▤ *AE, D, MC, V* †◎† *BP.*

$$ ▣ **Merkur.** The Merkur's large, comfortable rooms typify the high standards of German hospitality. A solid breakfast is served in the pleasant breakfast room. In the middle of Baden-Baden, the hotel's setting is quiet. If you stay for three, five, or seven days, ask for the special package, which includes cheaper rates, free admission to the casino and the Caracalla-Therme, a sumptuous meal, free parking, a glass of champagne, and a special cocktail at the bar. ⊠ *Merkurstr. 8* ☎ *07221/3030* 🖷 *07221/303–333* ⊕ *www.hotel-merkur.com* ➬ *44 rooms* ♨ *Restaurant, in-room data ports, cable TV with movies, bar, no-smoking rooms; no a/c* ▤ *AE, D, MC, V* †◎† *BP.*

$–$$ ▣ **Deutscher Kaiser.** This central, established hotel provides homey and individually styled rooms at comfortable prices. All the double rooms have balconies on a quiet street. The hotel is around the corner from the casino. ⊠ *Merkurstr. 9, D–76530* ☎ *07221/2700* 🖷 *07221/270–270* ⊕ *www.deutscher-kaiser-baden-baden.de* ➬ *28 rooms* ♨ *In-room* *data ports, cable TV, some pets allowed (fee); no a/c* ⊟ *AE, DC, MC, V* |◎| *BP.*

$ ▦ **Am Markt.** This 250-plus-year-old building houses a modest inn run (for more than 50 years) by the Bogner family. In the oldest part of town—a traffic-free zone, reached by pedestrians on a daunting flight of stone steps—it's close to such major attractions as the Roman baths. Some rooms overlook the city. ⊠ *Marktpl. 17–18, D–76530* ☎ *07221/27040* 📠 *07221/270–444* ⊕ *www.hotel-am-markt-baden.de* ⤳ *25 rooms, 14 with bath* ☖ *Some pets allowed; no a/c, no TV in some rooms* ⊟ *AE, DC, MC, V* |◎| *BP.*

Nightlife & the Arts

Nightlife revolves around Baden-Baden's elegant **casino,** but there are more cultural attractions as well. Baden-Baden has one of Germany's most beautiful performance halls, the **Theater** (⊠ Am Goethepl. ☎ 07221/932–700), a late-baroque jewel built in 1860–62 in the style of the Paris Opéra. It opened with the world premiere of Berlioz's opera *Beatrice et Benedict.* Today the theater presents a regular series of dramas, operas, and ballets.

The **Festspielhaus** (⊠ Beim Alten Bahnhof 2 ☎ 07221/301–3101) is a state-of-the-art concert hall superbly fitted onto the old train station. Each summer Baden-Baden holds a two-week **Philharmonischer Sommer Festival** (⊠ Schloss Solms, Solmsstr. ☎ 07221/932–791). Venues include the Kurhaus, the Kurgarten, Marktplatz, and the Brenner's Park Hotel. The **Kurhaus** hosts concerts year-round.

Baden-Baden tends to be a quiet place, but there is a nightclub in the Kurhaus, **Equipage** (⊠ Kaiserallee 1 ☎ 07221/32375). The Hotel Merkur has a small nightclub called the **Living Room** (⊠ Merkurstr. 8). For a subdued evening stop by the **Oleander Bar** (⊠ Schillerstr. 6 ☎ 07221/9000), in Baden-Baden's top hotel, the Brenner's Park.

Sports & the Outdoors

GOLF   The 18-hole Baden-Baden course is considered one of Europe's finest. Contact the **Golf Club** (⊠ Fremersbergstr. 127 ☎ 07221/23579).

HORSEBACK RIDING   The racetrack at nearby Iffezheim (☎ 07221/21120) still shows signs of Baden-Baden's elegant past. Its tradition dates back to 1858, and annual international meets take place in late May, late August, early September, and October. Those wishing to ride can rent horses and get instruction at the **Reitzentrum Baden-Baden** (⊠ Buchenweg 42 ☎ 07221/55920).

SWIMMING   The **Caracalla-Therme** is the most lavish thermal swimming pool complex in the Black Forest region. Built in the 1980s, it has one indoor and two outdoor pools, six saunas, a solarium, Jacuzzis, and several state-of-the-art fitness areas. ⊠ *Römerpl. 13* ☎ *07221/275–940* 🎫 *2 hrs €12, 3 hrs €14, 4 hrs €16* ☽ *Daily 8 AM–10 PM.*

The **Friedrichsbad** is a 19th-century bathing paradise. The sexes have different entrances but meet in the middle, so to speak. The swimming pool allows mixed nude bathing every day except Monday and Thursday. People who feel modest about such things should cross the Römerplatz to the Caracalla Pool. You must be 18 to enter the Friedrichsbad. ⊠ *Römerpl.*

1 ☎ 07221/275–920 ⊕ www.bad-bad.de/thermen/friedbad.htm ☎ 3 hrs €21; 3½ hrs, including massage, €29 ⊙ Mon.–Sat. 9 AM–10 PM, Sun. noon–8.

Shopping

Like everything else in Baden-Baden, the shops lean toward elegance. High-end antiques shops have great appeal for both collectors and browsers, but you will need a well-stuffed wallet.

The region's wines, especially the dry Baden whites and delicate reds, are highly valued in Germany. Buy them directly from any vintner on the Baden Wine Road. At Yburg, outside Baden-Baden, the 400-year-old **Nägelsförster Hof** vineyard (⊠ Nägelsförsterstr. 1 ☎ 07221/35550) has a shop where you can buy the product and sample what you buy (weekdays 8–6, Saturday 10–4).

en route | The road to Gernsbach, a couple of miles east of Baden-Baden, skirts the 2,000-foot-high mountain peak **Merkur,** named after a Roman monument to the god Mercury, which still stands just below the mountain summit. You can take the cable car to the summit, but it's not a trip for the fainthearted—the incline of close to 50% is one of Europe's steepest. ☎ *Round-trip €4 ⊙ Mar.–mid-Dec., daily 10–6.*

Bad Herrenalb

❼ *28 km (17 mi) northeast of Baden-Baden, 8 km (5 mi) south of Marxzell.*

The woodlands of the Alb River valley fold around the popular spa of Bad Herrenalb. The town has lots of amenities for relaxation, from an extensive park to shops, cafés, and, of course, the spa facilities, which address even cardiovascular and respiratory illnesses, rheumatism, and convalescing. The hills are crisscrossed with well-kept hiking paths. Neighboring Frauenalb (the *Frauen,* women, is the counterpart to *Herren,* men) has the ruins of a former cloister.

Where to Stay & Eat

$$–$$$ ✕⊡ **Mönchs Posthotel.** This half-timber building with an ornate turret is surrounded by beautiful gardens that include the ruins of an old monastery. The Locanda restaurant ($$–$$$$; closed Monday, Tuesday, and late December–February), in the park, offers Mediterranean fare, and the Kloster Schänke serves local dishes year-round. Guest rooms are comfortable and elegantly furnished, and no two are the same. ⊠ *Doblerstr. 2, D–76332 ☎ 07083/7440 🖷 07083/74422 ◁ 24 rooms, 1 suite, 6 apartments ⌂ 2 restaurants, cable TV, pool, some pets allowed (fee); no a/c ⊟ AE, DC, MC, V.*

Marxzell

❽ *8 km (5 mi) north of Bad Herrenalb on road to Karlsruhe.*

In the village of Marxzell a group of ancient locomotives and other old machines at the side of the road lure you into the **Fahrzeugmuseum** (Vehicle Museum). It looks more like a junkyard, with geese and ducks waddling freely about, but every kind of early engine is represented in this museum dedicated to the German automobile pioneer Karl Benz (1844–1929). Germans say it was he who built the first practical automobile, in 1888, a claim hotly disputed by the French. They assert a Frenchman constructed a steam-powered tricycle in 1769 that seated four and traveled for 20 minutes at 3.6 kph (2.25 mph). Items on display, many of them French, include motorcycles, Rolls-Royces, Mercedes, Alfa Romeos, Jaguars, and a vintage fire engine. ⊠ *Albtalstr. 2* ☎ *07248/6262* ⊕ *www.fahrzeugmuseum-marxzell.de* ✉ *€3* ⊘ *Daily 2–5.*

Ettlingen

❾ *12 km (7 mi) north of Marxzell.*

Ettlingen is a 1,200-year-old town that is now practically a suburb of its newer and much larger neighbor, Karlsruhe, just a streetcar ride away. Bordered by the Alb River, Ettlingen's ancient center is a maze of auto-free cobblestone streets. Come in summer for the annual Schlossberg theater and music festival in the beautiful baroque **Schloss.** The palace was built in the mid-18th century, and its striking domed chapel has been converted into a concert hall. Its ornate, swirling ceiling fresco is typical of the heroic, large-scale, illusionistic decoration of the period. ⊠ *Schlosspl. 3* ☎ *07243/101–273* ✉ *Free* ⊘ *Wed.–Sun. 10–5; tour weekends at 2.*

Where to Stay & Eat

$–$$ ✕ **Ratsstuben.** Originally used to store salt, these 16th-century cellars by the fast-flowing Alb River now welcome diners who come to enjoy international fare. There's also a pleasant terrace for summer dining on the marketplace. ⊠ *Kirchenpl. 1–3* ☎ *07243/76130* ▭ *AE, DC, MC, V.*

★ $$ ✕▦ **Hotel-Restaurant Erbprinz.** For many, the real reason for staying at this historic hotel is the top-rated restaurant's magnificent nouvelle German cuisine ($$$–$$$$)—though the rooms are also very comfortable. In summer dine in the charming garden, hidden away behind the hotel's green-and-gilt fencing. You might want to try apple pancakes flambéed with calvados for dessert. ⊠ *Rheinstr. 1, D–76275* ☎ *07243/3220* 🖨 *07243/322-322* ⊕ *www.hotel-erbprinz.de* ⚲ *81 rooms, 8 suites* ⚭ *Restaurant, in-room data ports, minibars, cable TV, gym, sauna, some pets allowed (fee); no a/c in some rooms* ▭ *AE, DC, MC, V* ☺ *BP.*

Rastatt

20 km (12 mi) southwest of Ettlingen.

The pink-sandstone, three-wing **Schloss,** the centerpiece of Rastatt, was built at the end of the 17th century by Margrave Ludwig Wilhelm of Baden (known as Ludwig the Turk for his exploits in the Turkish wars). It was the first baroque palace of such enormous proportions to be built in Germany. Its highlights include the chapel, gardens, and a pagoda. Inside the palace itself are museums of German history. ⊠ *Herrenstr., D–76437* ☎ *07222/34244* ✉ *€3* ⊘ *Guided tours Nov.–Mar., Fri.–Sun. 9:30-5; Apr.–Oct., Tues.–Sun. 9:30–5.*

Five kilometers (3 mi) south of Rastatt, in Förch, Ludwig the Turk's Bohemian-born wife, Sibylle Augusta, constructed her own charming little summer palace, **Schloss Favorite,** after his death. Inside, in an exotic, imaginative baroque interior of mirrors, tiles, and marble, her collection of miniatures, mosaics, and porcelain is strikingly displayed. ⊠ *Am Schloss Favorite 5* ☎ *07222/41207* 🎫 *€4.50* ⊙ *Mid-Mar.–Sept., Tues.–Sun. 10–5.*

Karlsruhe

🔟 *10 km (6 mi) north of Ettlingen.*

Karlsruhe, founded at the beginning of the 18th century, is a young upstart, but what it lacks in years it makes up for in industrial and administrative importance, sitting as it does astride a vital autobahn and railroad crossroads. It's best known as the seat of the German Supreme Court and has a high concentration of legal practitioners.

The town quite literally grew up around the former **Schloss** of the Margrave Karl Wilhelm, which was begun in 1715. Thirty-two avenues radiate from the palace, 23 leading into the extensive grounds, and the remaining nine forming the grid of the Old Town. The **Badisches Landesmuseum** (Baden State Museum), in the palace, has a large number of Greek and Roman antiquities and trophies that Ludwig the Turk brought back from campaigns in Turkey in the 17th century. Most of the other exhibits are devoted to local history. ⊠ *Schloss* ☎ *0721/926–6514* ⊕ *www.landesmuseum.de* 🎫 *€4* ⊙ *Tues. and Thurs. 10–5, Fri.–Sun. 10–6.*

★ One of the most important collections of paintings in the Black Forest region hangs in the **Staatliche Kunsthalle** (State Art Gallery). Look for masterpieces by Grünewald, Holbein, Rembrandt, and Monet and also for work by the Black Forest painter Hans Thoma. In the **Kunsthalle Orangerie,** next door, is work by such modern artists as Braque and Beckmann. ⊠ *Hans-Thoma-Str. 2* ☎ *0721/926–3355* ⊕ *www.kuntshalle-karlsruhe.de* 🎫 *Both museums €4* ⊙ *Tues.–Fri. 10–5, weekends 10–6.*

★ ⟳ In a former munitions factory, the vast **Zentrum für Kunst und Medientechnologie** (Center for Art and Media Technology), or simply ZKM, is an all-day adventure consisting of two separate museums. At the **Medienmuseum** (Media Museum) you can watch movies, listen to music, try out video games, flirt with a virtual partner, or sit on a real bicycle and pedal through a virtual New York City. The **Museum für Neue Kunst** (Museum of Modern Art; ☎ *0721/8100–1325*) is a top-notch collection of media art in all genres from the end of the 20th century. Take Bus 55 to Brauerstrasse to get here. ⊠ *Lorenzstr. 19* ☎ *0721/8100–1200* ⊕ *www.zkm.de* 🎫 *ZKM €5.10, Museum of Modern Art € 4.20, combined ticket €7.70* ⊙ *Both museums Wed. 10–8, Thurs. and Fri. 10–6, weekends ZKM 11–6, Museum of Modern Art 10–6.*

The Arts
One of the best opera houses in the region is Karlsruhe's **Badisches Staatstheater** (⊠ Baumeisterstr. 11 ☎ 0721/35570).

THE CENTRAL BLACK FOREST

The Central Black Forest takes in the Simonswald, Elz, and Glotter valleys as well as Triberg and Furtwangen, with their clock museums. The area around the Triberg Falls—the highest falls in Germany—is also renowned for pom-pom hats, thatch-roof farmhouses, and mountain railways. The Schwarzwaldbahn (Black Forest Railway; Offenburg–Villingen line), which passes through Triberg, is one of the most scenic in all of Europe.

Alpirsbach

⑪ *16 km (10 mi) south of Freudenstadt.*

The Kloster Alpirsbach monastery was built in flamboyant Gothic style and has had several restorations. The **Brauerei** (brewery) was once part of the monastery and has brewed beer since the Middle Ages. The unusually soft water gives the beer a flavor that is widely acclaimed. The brewery has a museum and souvenir shop. Tours are offered weekends at 3 PM, from April through October, and include two glasses of beer. At other times, call ahead to arrange a visit. ⊠ *Marktpl. 1* ☎ *01805/001–862* ⊕ *www.alpirsbach.de/infozentrum* ⊡ *€4.*

Where to Stay & Eat

¢–$ ✕ **Zwickel & Kaps.** That name is a highly sophisticated brewing term, describing the means by which the brewmaster samples the fermenting product. That should give you an idea of what this place is all about. Sit down at one of the massive wooden tables—next to the porcelaintile stove if it's a cold day—and order a bowl of *Flädelsuppe* (broth with pancake strips) and beef stewed in local wine. ⊠ *Marktstr. 3* ☎ *07444/51727* ⊟ *AE, MC, V* ☯ *Closed Mon., 2 wks after Carnival, and 2 wks late Aug.–early Sept.*

$$ ✕⊡ **Gasthof Waldhorn.** Just off the main road, the Waldhorn is where the locals come to enjoy a beer and discuss soccer or politics in a congenial atmosphere. The robust meals ($–$$$$), in portions fit for two, are served at family-size tables. The old half-timber hotel is remarkably large owing to a modern annex that is not visible from the outside. Rooms are clean and comfortable. ⊠ *Kreuzg. 4, D–72275* ☎ *07444/95110* ☐ *07444/951–155* ⊕ *www.alpirsbach.com/waldhorn* ↵ *24 rooms* ♨ *Minibars, cable TV, pub, some pets allowed; no a/c* ⊟ *AE, DC, MC, V* ⦿ *BP.*

Wolfach

25 km (15 mi) west of Alpirsbach.

This cobblestone town is known for its 600-year-old castle, the colorful facade of its town hall, and its market square edged with turreted and half-timber houses. The Wolfach and Kinzig rivers meet here, and a loggers' rafting festival is held each July.

en route | The **Dorotheenhütte** (Dorothea Blast Furnace) is one of the few remaining Black Forest factories where glass is blown using centuries-old techniques. You can watch the teams at work making vases or blowing and etching drinking glasses. The large sales room includes a Christmas display and has all kinds of items that make excellent souvenirs. ⊠ *Glashüttenweg 4* ☏ *07834/83980* ⊕ *www. dorotheenhuette.de* ⊒ *€3* ⊙ *Daily 9–4:30, shop 9–5* ⊙ *Closed Sun. during Jan.–Apr.*

Where to Stay & Eat

$ ✕⊞ **Gasthof Hecht.** There's a crisp, modern look to the rooms in this 300-year-old half-timber guest house on Wolfach's main street. The kitchen ($) serves such hearty fare as *Gamsbraten mit Steinpilzen* (chamois roast with cèpe mushrooms). ⊠ *Hauptstr. 51, D–77709* ☏ *07834/538* ☐ *07834/47223* ⊕ *www.hecht-wolfach.de* ⇌ *17 rooms* ⌂ *Restaurant, in-room data ports, cable TV, some pets allowed; no a/c* ▭ *AE, D, MC, V* ⊙ *Restaurant closed Tues. and 3 wks in Jan. No dinner Mon.* ⊙ *BP.*

Gutach

12 *8 km (5 mi) south of Wolfach, 17 km (11 mi) north of Triberg.*

Gutach lies in Gutachtal, a valley famous for the traditional costume, complete with pom-pom hats, worn by women on feast days and holidays. Married women wear black ones, unmarried women red ones. The village is one of the few places in the Black Forest where you can still see thatch roofs. However, escalating costs caused by a decline in skilled thatchers, and soaring fire insurance premiums, make for fewer thatch roofs than there were 20 years ago.

Near Gutach is one of the most appealing museums in the Black Forest, the **Schwarzwälder Freilichtmuseum Vogtsbauernhof** (Black Forest Open-Air Museum). Farmhouses and other rural buildings from all parts of the region have been transported here from their original locations and reassembled, complete with traditional furniture, to create a living museum of Black Forest building types through the centuries. Demonstrations ranging from traditional dances to woodworking capture life as it was in centuries past. ⊠ *B–33* ☏ *07831/93560* ⊕ *www. vogtsbauernhof.org* ⊒ *€5* ⊙ *Apr.–Oct., daily 9–6.*

off the beaten path | **SCHWARZWALDER TRACHTENMUSEUM** – Regional traditional costumes can be seen at this museum in a former Capuchin monastery in the village of Haslach, 10 km (6 mi) northwest of Gutach. Pom-pom-topped straw hats, bejeweled headdresses, embroidered velvet vests, and *Fasnet* (Carnival) regalia of all parts of the forest are on display. The town, which is somewhat secluded, still has an original and unpolished look and feel to it. ⊠ *Im Alten Kapuziner Kloster* ☏ *07832/706–172* ⊕ *www.trachtenmuseum-haslach.de.vu* ⊒ *€2.50* ⊙ *Apr.–Oct., Tues.–Sat. 9–5, Sun. 10–5; Nov.–Dec. and Feb.–Mar., Tues.–Fri. 9–noon and 1–5; Jan. by appointment.*

Gengenbach

27 km (17 mi) north of Gutach, 52 km (33 mi) west of Freudenstadt.

Walled, half-timber Gengenbach, with its splendidly restored market-place (home to a farmers' market), is sometimes called the Rothenburg of Baden, because of its wall and the brightly colored medieval houses on its narrow streets. In any season, the town is a charming sight to see.

The three-nave abbey church **St. Marien,** which adjoins the huge baroque Benedictine monastery behind the town hall, dates from the early 12th century. The Romanesque frescoes have been covered up by rather remarkable late-19th-century paintings by Carl Philipp Schilling. Note, especially, the coffered ceilings. ⊙ *Daily 9–7.*

Where to Stay & Eat

$ ✕🖫 **Pfeffermühle.** Few restaurants situated in ancient buildings truly succeed in modernizing while maintaining an authentic ambience within their ancient walls. The Pfeffermühle ($–$$), however, has managed it. It's easy to imagine the chalky officials from Gengenbach's beautiful Rathaus meeting here for the tasty *Pfeffersack,* a filet mignon steak drowned in pepper sauce. The Pfeffermühle maintains a separate hotel just outside the Old Town, but all reservations are made through the restaurant. ⊠ *Viktor-Kretzstr. 17, D–77723* ☎ *07803/93350* 🖷 *07803/6628* ⊕ *www.badenpage.de/pfeffermuehle* 🛏 *25 rooms* ⚭ *Restaurant, in-room data ports, minibars, cable TV, some pets allowed, no-smoking rooms; no a/c* ⊟ *AE, D, MC, V* ⊙ *Closed Thurs.* ⍑⊙⍑ *BP.*

Rust

20 km (12 mi) west of Gengenbach.

This town on the Rhine, about halfway between Freiburg and Strasbourg, boasts a castle dating from 1577 and painstakingly restored half-timber houses. But its big claim to fame is a huge amusement park, Germany's biggest, with its own autobahn exit.

FodorsChoice **Europa Park.** On an area of 160 acres, this park, drawing more than 3
★ million visitors a year, offers a great variety of shows, rides, dining, and shops, not to mention two hotels. Among many other things, it has the "Eurosat" to take you on a virtual journey past clusters of meteors and falling stars; the "Silver Star," Europe's biggest and highest roller coaster (80 mph, 240 feet); a Spanish jousting tournament; and a 4-D movie. ⊠ *Europa-Park-Str. 2, D–77977* ☎ *01805/776–688* ⊕ *www.europapark. de* 🖾 *€17.50* ⊙ *Apr.–Oct., daily 9–6; longer July–mid-Sept.*

Triberg

★ ⑬ *16 km (10 mi) south of Gutach.*

The cuckoo clock, that symbol of the Black Forest, is at home in the Triberg area. It was invented here, it's made and sold here, it's featured in two museums, and the town has "the world's largest cuckoo clock."

CUCKOO! FOR CUCKOO CLOCKS

"**S**WITZERLAND HAD BROTHERLY LOVE and five hundred years of democracy and peace. And what did they produce? The cuckoo clock."

So said Orson Welles in the classic 1949 film The Third Man. *He misspoke in two ways. First, the Swiss are an industrious, technologically advanced people. And second, they didn't invent the cuckoo clock. That was the work of the Germans living in the adjacent Black Forest.*

The first cuckoo clock was designed and built in 1750 by Franz Anton Ketterer in Schönwald near Triberg. He cleverly produced the cuckoo sound with a pair of wooden whistles, each attached to a bellows activated by the clock's mechanism.

Over the following years the making of carved wooden clocks developed rapidly in the Black Forest. The people on the farms needed ways to profitably occupy their time during the long snowbound winters, and the carving of clocks was the answer. Wood was abundant, and the early clocks were entirely of wood, even the works.

Come spring one of the sons would don a traditional smock and hat, mount the family's winter output on a big rack, hoist it to his back, and set off into the world to sell the clocks. In 1808 there were 688 clockmakers and 582 clock peddlers in the districts of Triberg and Neustadt.

The Uhrentrager (clock carrier) is an important part of the Black Forest tradition. Guides often wear his costume and a Triberg travel bureau arranges for hikers to travel the trails he knew.

The traditional cuckoo clock is made with brown stained wood with a gabled roof and some sort of woodland motif carved into it, such as a deer's head or a cluster of leaves. The works are usually activated by cast-iron weights, in the form of pinecones, on chains.

Today's clocks can be much more elaborate. Dancing couples in traditional dress automatically move to the sound of a music box, a mill wheel turns on the hour, a farmer chops wood on the hour, the Uhrentrager even makes his rounds. The cuckoo itself moves its wings and beak and rocks back and forth when calling.

The day is long past when the clocks were made entirely of wood. The works are of metal, and therefore more reliable and accurate. Other parts of the clock, such as the whistles, the face, and the hands, are usually of plastic now, but hand-carved wood is still the rule for the case.

The industry is still centered around Triberg. There are two museums in the area with sections dedicated to it, and clocks are sold everywhere, even in the kiosks. In Triberg itself, you can visit the "House of 1000 Clocks," located right at Germany's highest waterfall, or the firm of Hubert Herr, the only factory that continues to make cuckoo clocks practically from scratch.

At the head of the Gutach Valley, the Gutach River plunges nearly 500 feet over seven huge granite steps at Triberg's **waterfall**, Germany's highest. The pleasant 45-minute walk from the center of town to the top of the spectacular falls is well signposted. You can also take a longer walk that goes by a small pilgrimage church and the old Mesnerhäschen, the sacristan's house. ⊠ *Waterfall €1.50; may be waived in winter.*

Black Forest culture is the focus of Triberg's famous **Schwarzwaldmuseum** (Black Forest Museum), with its impressive collection of cuckoo clocks and other items deriving from the woodworking tradition. ⊠ *Wallfahrtstr. 4* ☎ *07722/4434* ⊕ *www.schwarzwaldmuseum.de* ☞ *€4* ⊙ *Apr.–Nov., daily 10–5.*

You can buy a cuckoo clock, or just about any other souvenir, at the huge **Eble Uhren-Park**, which is also the location of the giant, house-sized cuckoo clock. ⊠ *On Hwy. B–33 between Triberg and Hornberg* ☎ *07722/96220* ⊕ *www.eble-uhren-park.de* ⊙ *Apr.–Oct., Mon.–Sat. 9–6, Sun. 10–6; Nov.–Mar., Mon.–Sat. 9–6.*

The **Haus der 1000 Uhren** (House of 1,000 Clocks) occupies two old houses right at the waterfall. A second store, just off B–33 toward Offenburg, in the suburb of Gremmelsbach, boasts a giant cuckoo clock. ⊠ *Hauptstr. 79–81* ☎ *07722/96300* ⊕ *www.houseof1000clocks.de* ⊙ *Apr.–Oct., Mon.–Sat. 9–5, Sun. 10–4; Nov.–Mar., Mon.–Sat. 10–5, Sun. 10–4.*

Hubert Herr is the only factory that continues to make nearly all their own components for their cuckoo clocks. You can examine the various types and models and, if you wish, buy your own Herbert Herr original. ⊠ *Hauptstr. 8* ☎ *07722/4268* ⊕ *www.hubertherr.de.*

The Horberg–Triberg–St. Georgen segment of the **Schwarzwaldbahn** (Black Forest Railway) is one of Germany's most scenic train rides. The 149-km (93-mi) Schwarzwaldbahn, built from 1866 to 1873, runs from Offenburg to Lake Constance via Freudenstadt and Triberg. It has no fewer than 39 tunnels and at one point climbs 600 meters (656 yards) in just 11 km (6½ mi). It's now part of the German Railway, and you can make inquiries at any station.

Where to Stay & Eat

$$–$$$$ ✕⊞ **Romantik Parkhotel Wehrle.** The steep-eaved, wisteria-covered facade of this large mansion dominates the town center. Rooms are individually furnished in a variety of woods with such pleasant touches as fresh flowers. The main restaurant ($$–$$$$) has international haute cuisine; the Ochsenstube ($–$$) tends toward specialties from Baden, such as trout done a dozen different ways, all delicious. ⊠ *Gartenstr. 24, Triberg im Schwarzwald D–78098* ☎ *07722/86020* 🖷 *07722/860–290* ⊕ *www.parkhotel-wehrle.de* ⌨ *50 rooms, 1 apartment, 1 suite* ♨ *3 restaurants, in-room data ports, cable TV, 2 pools (1 indoors), gym, massage, sauna, parking (fee), some pets allowed (fee), no-smoking rooms; no a/c* ☰ *DC, MC, V* |○| *BP.*

★ $ ✕⊞ **Hotel-Restaurant-Pfaff.** This old post-and-beam restaurant ($–$$), with its blue-tile Kachelofen, attracts people of all types with affordable regional specialties. Try the fresh *Forelle* (trout), either steamed or

Gasthof (in the pan), garnished with mushrooms. The Pfaff family has owned the inn since 1882, and some rooms have balconies overlooking the famous waterfall. ☒ *Hauptstr. 85, D–78098* ☎ *07722/4479* 🖷 *07722/7897* ⊕ *www.hotel-pfaff.com* ⇆ *23 rooms* ⅙ *Restaurant, some in-room data ports, cable TV, some pets allowed (fee), no-smoking rooms; no a/c* ▤ *AE, D, MC, V* ⑩ *BP.*

Rottweil

26 km (16 mi) east of Triberg.

Rottweil has the best of the Black Forest's Fasnet celebrations. Outside the Black Forest, the celebrations are good-natured and sophisticated, but here and in adjacent areas of Switzerland they're pagan and fierce. In the days just before Ash Wednesday, usually in February, witches and devils roam the streets wearing ugly wooden masks and making fantastic gyrations as they crack whips and ring bells. If you can't make it to Rottweil during the Carnival season, you can still catch the spirit of Fasnet. There's an exhibit on it at the **Stadtmuseum**, and tours are organized to the shops where they carve the masks and make the costumes and bells. The name *Rottweil* may be more familiar to you as the name for a breed of dog. The area used to be a center of meat production, and the Rottweiler was bred to herd the cattle.

Furtwangen

⑭ *16 km (10 mi) south of Triberg.*

The somewhat nondescript Furtwangen is on a tourist route dubbed the German Clock Road. You don't have to be a clock enthusiast, however, to drop in on the **Uhren Museum** (Clock Museum), the largest such museum in Germany. In a huge, ingeniously designed space, the museum charts the development of Black Forest clocks and exhibits all types of timepieces, from cuckoo clocks, church clock mechanisms, kinetic wristwatches, and old decorative desktop clocks to punch clocks and digital blinking objects. The oddest piece is the "art clock" by local artisan August Noll, which was built from 1880 to 1885 and features the time in Calcutta, New York, Melbourne, and London, among other places. It emits the sound of a crowing rooster in the morning, and other chimes mark yearly events. It's occasionally demonstrated during tours. You can set your own watch to the sun dial built into the concrete of the square in front of the museum. This remarkable creation nearly ticks off the seconds. ☒ *Robert-Gerwig-Pl. 1* ☎ *07723/920–117* ⊕ *www. deutsches-uhrenmuseum.de* 🎟 *€3* ⊙ *Apr.–Oct., daily 9–6; Nov.–Mar., daily 10–5.*

off the beaten path

NATURPARK SUDSCHWARZWALD – Traveling 7 km (4 mi) northeast of Furtwangen, first along the Katzensteig and then along the Neuweg, gets you into the heart of the Naturpark Sudschwarzwald. There you'll find a little spring with an adjacent mountain guest house called the Kolmenhof. A plaque smugly proclaims this little trickle of water to be the source of one of Europe's longest and mightiest rivers, the Danube. Locals won't admit it, but this fact is disputed. Donaueschingen, a little to the east, also claims this honor for one of its little springs. One thing of which there can be no argument: the Danube isn't "blue," here or anyplace else. Muddy yellow is more like it.

THE SOUTHERN BLACK FOREST

In the south you'll find the most spectacular mountain scenery in the area, culminating in the Feldberg—at 4,899 feet the highest mountain in the Black Forest. The region also has two large lakes, the Titisee and the Schluchsee. Freiburg is a romantic university city that incorporates vineyards, a superb Gothic cathedral, and Schauinsland Mountain.

Titisee

⑮ *37 km (23 mi) south of Furtwangen.*

The Titisee, carved by a glacier in the last ice age, is the most scenic lake in the Black Forest. The landscape is heavily wooded and ideal for long bike tours, which can be organized through the Titisee tourist office. The lake measures 2½ km (1½ mi) long and is invariably crowded in summer. Boats and Windsurfers can be rented at several points along the shore.

Where to Stay & Eat

$ ✕⌷ **Hotel Adler Post.** This solid old building is in the middle of Neustadt, a township to the east of Titisee, about 5 km (3 mi) from the lake. All the rooms are comfortable and traditionally furnished, some with hand-painted furniture and exposed beams. The reception room is full of Biedermeier antiques. The restaurant ($$–$$$$) cooks up excellent local specialties. ⌂ *Hauptstr. 16, Neustadt, D–79822* ☎ *07651/5066* 🖷 *07651/ 3729* ⊕ *www.adler-post-titisee.de* ↪ *28 rooms ⚒ 2 restaurants, cable TV, pool, massage, sauna, some pets allowed (fee), no-smoking rooms; no a/c* ▭ *MC, V* ⫣ *BP.*

Hinterzarten

⑯ *5 km (3 mi) west of Titisee, 32 km (20 mi) east of Freiburg.*

The lovely 800-year-old town of Hinterzarten is the most important resort in the southern Black Forest. Some buildings date from the 12th century, among them St. Oswaldskirche, a church built in 1146. Hinterzarten's oldest inn, the Weisses Rossle, has been in business since 1347. The Park Hotel Adler was established in 1446, although the original building was burned down during the Thirty Years' War. Hinterzarten is known throughout Germany for its summer ski jump, the **Adlerschanze** (⌂ Off Winterhaldenweg, to the south of town), which is used for competitions and for training purposes. Several smaller jumps for "beginners" are currently being built. The town's small **Schwarzwälder Skimuseum** recounts in photographs, paintings, costumes, and equipment the history of Black Forest skiing, which began in the 1890s on the nearby Feldberg. ⌂ *Er-*

lenbruchstr. 35 ☏ *07652/982–192* ⊕ *www.schwarzwaelder-skimuseum. de* ☒ *€3* ⊙ *Mon. and Fri. 2–5, weekends noon–6.*

Where to Stay & Eat

★ **$$$–$$$$** ╳🏨 **Park Hotel Adler.** The proprietress of this 559-year-old hotel was named Germany's "Hotelier of the Year" for 2004. At a gala ceremony in Munich, Katja Trescher was lauded for rescuing the once threatened hotel through such things as a beautiful private park, a very extensive wellness facility, top gastronomy, and superb service. Many of the rooms at the Park Hotel Adler have marble baths and balconies overlooking the park. The rustic Wirtshaus-Stube, with its wood paneling and tile stove, serves Black Forest specialties. ☒ *Adlerpl. 3, D–79856* ☏ *07652/ 1270* 🖷 *07652/127–717* ⊕ *www.parkhoteladler.de* ⤳ *46 rooms, 32 suites* ♿ *2 restaurants, in-room data ports, cable TV, driving range, indoor pool, sauna, Ping-Pong, bar, some pets allowed (fee), no-smoking rooms; no a/c* ▭ *AE, DC, MC, V* ⦿| *BP.*

$–$$ 🏨 **Sassenhof.** Traditional Black Forest style reigns supreme here, from the steep-eaved wood exterior, with window boxes everywhere, to the elegant sitting areas and guest rooms furnished with rustic, brightly painted pieces, many of them decoratively carved. Afternoon tea, like breakfast, is included in the price. ☒ *Adlerweg 17, D–79856* ☏ *07652/1515* 🖷 *07652/484* ⊕ *www.hotel-sassenhof.de* ⤳ *17 rooms, 6 suites* ♿ *Cable TV, pool, massage, sauna, bicycles, some pets allowed (fee); no a/c* ▭ *AE, MC, V* ⊙ *Closed Nov.* ⦿| *BP.*

Sports & the Outdoors

Hinterzarten is at the highest point along the Freiburg–Donaueschingen road; from it a network of far-ranging trails fans out into the forest, making it one of Germany's most popular centers for *Langlauf* (cross-country skiing) in winter and hiking in summer. Cycling is another favorite sport up in these hills and dales. The topology offers something for everyone, gentle excursions or tough mountain-bike expeditions. For more information contact Feldberg's tourist office (☏ 07655/8019).

Schluchsee

❶⑦ *25 km (16 mi) from Hinterzarten; take Hwy. B–317, then pick up B–500.*

The largest of the Black Forest lakes, mountain-enclosed Schluchsee is near Feldberg Mountain. Schluchsee is a diverse resort, where sports enthusiasts swim, windsurf, fish, and, in winter, ski. For details on outfitters contact the tourist office.

Where to Stay

$ 🏨 **Hotel Waldeck.** In summer, geraniums smother the sun-drenched balconies of the Waldeck, and in winter the decorative equivalent is the snow piling up on the slopes outside. Walking trails begin practically at the front door, and the local forest creeps up to the hotel terrace. Some rooms have traditional furnishings; others have a generic, modern look. ☒ *Feldberg Altglashütten, D–79868* ☏ *07655/91030* 🖷 *07655/231* ⊕ *www. hotel-waldeck-feldberg.de* ⤳ *23 rooms* ♿ *Restaurant, cable TV, bar,* *free parking, some pets allowed (fee), no-smoking rooms; no a/c* ⊟ *DC, MC, V* ☉ *Restaurant closed Wed.* ⊙ *BP.*

$ 🏨 **Kur- und Sporthotel Feldberger Hof.** This is the biggest and best-appointed hotel in the area. Set amid the woods and meadows of the Feldberg, and a pleasant walk from the Schluchsee, it has everything for sports lovers—from a large pool to ski lifts, which are right outside the hotel. ⊠ *Dr. Pilet-Spur 1, D–79868* ☎ *07676/180* 🖷 *07676/1220* ⊕ *www. feldberger-hof.de* ⤶ *73 rooms, 26 suites* ⚷ *3 restaurants, café, cable TV, miniature golf, pool (indoor), health club, sauna, steam room, bowling, 2 bars, programs for children 2 and over, some pets allowed (fee); no a/c* ⊟ *AE, DC, MC, V* ⊙ *BP.*

Sports & the Outdoors

HIKING & SKIING The best Alpine skiing in the Black Forest is on the slopes of the Feldberg. The Seebuck, Grafenmatt, and Fahl Alpin area offers 12 lifts and 25 km (15 mi) of slopes (all accessible with a single lift ticket). For more information contact Feldberg's tourist office.

en route To get to Freiburg, the largest city in the southern Black Forest, you have to brave the curves of the winding road through the **Höllental** (Hell Valley). In 1770 Empress Maria Theresa's 15-year-old daughter—the future queen Marie Antoinette—made her way along what was then a coach road on her way from Vienna to Paris. She traveled with an entourage of 250 officials and servants in some 50 horse-drawn carriages. The first stop at the end of the valley is a little village called **Himmelreich,** or Kingdom of Heaven. Railroad engineers are said to have given the village its name in the 19th century, grateful as they were to finally have laid a line through Hell Valley. At the entrance to Höllental is a deep gorge, the **Ravennaschlucht.** It's worth scrambling through to reach the tiny 12th-century chapel of **St. Oswald,** the oldest parish church in the Black Forest (there are parking spots off the road). Look for a bronze statue of a deer high on a roadside cliff, 5 km (3 mi) farther on. It commemorates the legend of a deer that amazed hunters by leaping the deep gorge at this point. Another 16 km (10 mi) will bring you to Freiburg.

Freiburg

⑱ *Via B–31, 23 km (14 mi) from turnoff (317) to Schluchsee.*

Freiburg, or Freiburg im Breisgau (to distinguish it from the Freiberg in Saxony), was founded in the 12th century. After extensive wartime bomb damage, skillful restoration has helped re-create the original and compelling medieval atmosphere of one of the loveliest historic towns in Germany. The 16th-century geographer Martin Waldseemüller was born here; in 1507 he was the first to put the name *America* on a map.

For an intimate view of Freiburg, wander through the streets around the Münster or follow the main shopping artery of Kaiser-Joseph-Strasse. The courageous decision by the municipal government to keep cars off the streets has made the inner city very pleasant for strolling.

After you pass the city gate (Martinstor), follow Gerberau off to the left. You'll come to quaint shops along the bank of one of the city's larger canals, which continues past the former Augustinian cloister to the equally picturesque area around the *Insel* (island). This canal is a larger version of the *Bächle* (brooklets) running through many streets in Freiburg's Old Town. The Bächle, so narrow you can step across them, were created in the 13th century to bring fresh water into the town, but today they serve to cool the air a little on hot summer days. The tourist office sponsors English walking tours mid-April through October, on Monday and Friday at 2:30, Wednesday and Thursday and weekends at 10:30. The two-hour tour costs €6.

The **Münster unserer Lieben Frau** (Cathedral of Our Dear Lady), Freiburg's most famous landmark, towers over the medieval streets. The pioneering 19th-century Swiss art historian Jacob Burckhardt described its delicately perforated 380-foot spire as the finest in Europe. The cathedral took three centuries to build, from around 1200 to 1515. You can easily trace the progress of generations of builders through the changing architectural styles, from the fat columns and solid, rounded arches of the Romanesque period to the lofty Gothic windows and airy interior of the choir. Of particular interest are the luminous 13th-century stained-glass windows. Masterpieces include a 16th-century triptych by Hans Baldung Grien and paintings by Holbein the Younger and Lucas Cranach the Elder. If you can summon the energy, climb the tower. In addition to a magnificent view of the city and the Black Forest beyond, you'll get a closer look at the 16 Minster bells including the 3-ton-plus 1258 "Hosanna," one of Germany's oldest functioning bells. ⊠ *Münsterpl.* ☎ *0761/388–101* ⊠ *Bell tower €1.50* ☉ *Mon.–Sat. 9:30–5, Sun. 1–5.*

The **Münsterplatz**, the square around Freiburg's cathedral, which once served as a cemetery, holds a market (Monday–Saturday) in front of the Renaissance **Kaufhaus** (Market House). You can stock up on local specialties for the road, from wood-oven baked bread to hams, wines, vinegars, fruits, and Kirschwasser. The square is also lined with traditional taverns. The big iron door at No. 12 houses the **Foltermuseum** (Torture Museum), whose explicatory texts do not fail to point out the gruesomeness and often sheer stupidity of jurisprudence in history. ⊠ *Münsterpl. 12* ☎ *0761/292–1900* ⊕ *www.folterkabinett.de* 🖾 *€4.10* ⊙ *Apr.–Oct., Mon.–Sat. 10–6, Sun. 10–7; Nov.–Mar., Mon.–Sat. 10–5, Sun. 10–6.*

Freiburg's famous **Rathaus** is constructed from two 16th-century patrician houses joined together. Among its attractive Renaissance features is an oriel, or bay window, clinging to a corner and bearing a bas-relief of the romantic medieval legend of the Maiden and the Unicorn. ⊠ *Rathauspl. 2–4* ⊙ *Weekdays 8–noon.*

The former house of painter, sculptor, and architect Johann Christian Wentzinger (1710–97), the **Wentzingerhaus,** contains fascinating exhibits on the history of the city, including a 1:50 scale model of the Minster as a construction site, and the poignant remains of a typewriter recovered from a bombed-out bank. The ceiling fresco in the stairway, painted by Wentzinger himself, is the museum's pride and joy. ⊠ *Münsterpl. 30* ☎ *0761/201–2515* ⊕ *www.msg-freiburg.de* 🖾 *€ 3* ⊙ *Tues.–Sun. 10–5.*

A visit to Freiburg's cathedral is not really complete without also exploring the **Augustinermuseum,** at the former Augustinian cloister. Original sculpture from the cathedral is on display, as well as gold and silver reliquaries. The collection of stained-glass windows, dating from the Middle Ages to today, is one of the most important in Germany. ⊠ *Am Augustinerpl.* ☎ *0761/201–2531* ⊕ *www.augustinermuseum.de* 🖾 *€2* ⊙ *Tues.–Sun. 10–5.*

Where to Stay & Eat

$$$$
Fodor'sChoice
★

✕ **Hans Thoma Stube.** It's located in Freiburg's most luxurious hotel, the Colombi. Though the hotel was only built in the 1950s, the restaurant is very traditional. The venerable tables, chairs, and wood paneling of some old establishments have been acquired and installed. Old tile stoves provide a deeply satisfying warmth in winter, and black-tied waiters serve local dishes such as lentil soup and venison. The menu in the Zirbelstube and the Falkenstube pairs innovative sauces with traditional meat and fish dishes. ⊠ *Am Colombi Park/Rotteckring 16, D–79098* ☎ *0761/21060* 🖨 *0761/31410* ⚖ *Reservations essential* ▭ *AE, DC, MC, V.*

★ **$$–$$$$**
✕ **Markgräfler Hof.** The imaginative Baden cuisine in this restaurant ranges from braised tomatoes and artichokes with lukewarm vegetables to fricasseed calf liver with fresh herbs and *brägele* (pan-fried potatoes). It's hard to go wrong with the wide variety of choices. A small but fine wine list complements the menu. ⊠ *Gerberau 22* ☎ *0761/32540* ▭ *AE, D, MC, V.*

$$$
✕ **Weinstube zur Traube.** The fruit of the vine is not the only item on the menu at this cozy old wine tavern; you'll also find a rich and varied selection of classic French and Swabian dishes. Try the saddle of venison wrapped in bacon on a bed of savoy cabbage and pureed celery root. ⊠ *Schusterstr. 17* ☎ *0761/32190* ▭ *AE, MC, V* ⊙ *Closed Tues. and Wed. and 3 wks mid-Aug.*

¢–$$$
✕ **Kühler Krug.** Wild game and goose liver terrine are among the specialties at this restaurant, which has even given its name to a distinctive

saddle-of-venison dish. Those who prefer fish shouldn't despair—there's an imaginative range of freshwater varieties available. ⊠ *Torpl. 1, Günterstal* ☎ *0761/29103* ▤ *MC, V* ⊘ *Closed Wed.*

★ **$$$$** ╳▦ **Colombi.** Freiburg's most luxurious hotel is one of the few still operated on-site by its owners, and one of the few located right downtown. Its tastefully furnished rooms have floor-to-ceiling windows overlooking the romantic old city. Despite its central location, the hotel basks in near-countryside quiet. ⊠ *Am Colombi Park/Rotteckring 16, D–79098* ☎ *0761/21060* ▣ *0761/31410* ⊕ *www.colombi.de* ⟿ *58 rooms, 59 suites* ⚖ *Restaurant, patisserie, room service, in-room data ports, cable TV, indoor pool, gym, sauna, spa, steam room, piano bar, baby-sitting, parking (fee), some pets allowed (fee), no-smoking rooms* ▤ *AE, DC, MC, V.*

★ **$$–$$$** ╳▦ **Zum Roten Bären.** This "Red Bear" hotel claims to be the "oldest in Germany." Two others—the Riesen in Miltenburg on the Main and the Löwen in Seelbach-Schönberg, also in the Black Forest—claim this honor as well, but the Roten Bären's documentation looks best. The inn dates from 1311 and retains its individual character, with very comfortable lodgings and excellent dining in a warren of dining rooms and bars ($–$$$$). Take a tour of the two basement floors, where you'll find cellars dating from the 12th century that are now well stocked with fine wines. ⊠ *Oberlinden 12, D–79098* ☎ *0761/387–870* ▣ *0761/387–8717* ⊕ *www.roter-baeren.de* ⟿ *22 rooms, 3 apartments* ⚖ *Restaurant, in-room data ports, cable TV, sauna, parking (fee), some pets allowed (fee), no-smoking rooms; no a/c* ▤ *AE, DC, MC, V* ⊘ *Restaurant closed Sun.* ▯◎▯ *BP.*

$$ ╳▦ **Oberkirch.** Across from the cathedral, this wine cellar, restaurant, and hotel is a bastion of tradition and Gemütlichkeit (comfort and conviviality). The proprietor personally bags some of the game that ends up on the menu ($$). Fresh trout is another specialty. In summer the dark-oak dining tables spill onto a garden terrace. Approximately 20 Baden wines are served by the glass, many supplied from the restaurant's own vineyards. Twenty-six charming guest rooms are in the Weinstuben and in a neighboring centuries-old house. ⊠ *Münsterpl. 22, D–79098* ☎ *0761/2026868* ⟿ *26 rooms* ⚖ *Restaurant, in-room data ports, cable TV, some pets allowed (fee); no a/c* ▤ *AE, MC, V* ⊘ *Restaurant closed Sun. and for a few wks in Jan.* ▯◎▯ *BP.*

$–$$ ╳▦ **Rappen.** This hotel's brightly painted rooms are on the sunny side of the cobblestoned cathedral square and marketplace. Tables are set out amid the lively chatter in summer. Three rooms are designated as "anti-allergy." The restaurant ($–$$) serves fresh vegetables, game, and fish, and hosts the market people and locals who come in for a glass of wine in the morning (there are about 40 wines available, German and French). ⊠ *Münsterpl. 13, D–79098* ☎ *0761/31353* ▣ *0761/382–252* ⊕ *www.hotelrappen.de* ⟿ *24 rooms* ⚖ *Restaurant, cable TV, some pets allowed (fee); no a/c* ▤ *AE, DC, MC, V* ▯◎▯ *BP.*

$ ╳▦ **Hotel Schwarzwälder Hof.** Part of this hotel occupies a former mint, complete with graceful cast iron railings on the spiral staircase and, unfortunately, paper-thin walls. Despite the low prices it's in the downtown pedestrian zone and is very handy to both a parking garage and public transportation. The Badische Winzerstube (¢–$$) provides all you could want in local atmosphere, wine, and food. ⊠ *Herrenstr. 43, D–79098* ☎ *0761/38030* 🖷 *0761/380–3135* 🖘 *45 rooms* ⚭ *Restaurant, cable TV, bar, some pets allowed (fee); no a/c* ▤ *MC, V* ⍾ *BP.*

¢ ✕⌷ **Gasthaus zur Sonne.** The downside: the bathroom is down the hall, there are no eggs at breakfast, the bedside lamps may or may not work, and it's a long way from the center of town. The upside: the hotel is spotlessly clean, the food in the restaurant (¢–$) sticks to your ribs, a bus at the door gets you downtown with ease, it's just minutes from the Freiburg Nord autobahn exit, and you'll find a piece of chocolate on your bedside table each night. Not a bad choice for travelers on a budget. ⊠ *Hochdorfstr. 1, D–79108* ☎ *07665/2650* 🖷 *07665/1288* 🖘 *15 rooms without bath* ⚭ *Restaurant, cable TV, bar, free parking, some pets allowed; no a/c, no room phones* ▤ *No credit cards* ⍾ *BP.*

$$ ⌷ **Park Hotel Post Meier.** This century-old building, near the train station, has a copper dome and stone balconies overlooking a park. You'll be greeted with a drink upon your arrival, find fruit in your room, and can plug in the phone at the bed, at the desk, or even in the bathroom. ⊠ *Eisenbahnstr. 35, D–79098* ☎ *0761/385–480* 🖷 *0761/31680* 🖘 *43 rooms, 2 apartments* ⚭ *In-room data ports, cable TV, no-smoking rooms; no a/c* ▤ *AE, MC, V* ⍾ *BP.*

$–$$ ⌷ **Victoria.** Owners Astrid and Bertram Späth have received awards for making their elegant 1870s hotel ecofriendly. Black Forest sawdust has replaced oil for heating, solar panels provide some of the electricity and hot water, other electricity comes from a wind farm, windows have thermal panes, bathtubs are ergonomically designed to use less hot water, packaged food and throwaway cans and bottles are avoided, and everything from the stationery to the toilet tissue is of recycled paper. None of this, however, detracts from the hotel's old-world charm. ⊠ *Eisenbahnstr. 54, D–79098* ☎ *0761/207–340* 🖷 *0761/2073–4444* ⊕ *www.hotel-victoria. de* 🖘 *63 rooms* ⚭ *In-room data ports, cable TV, bar, parking (fee), some pets allowed (fee), no-smoking rooms; no a/c* ▤ *AE, DC, MC, V.*

Nightlife & the Arts

Nightlife in Freiburg takes place in the city's *Kneipen* (pubs), wine bars, and wine cellars, which are plentiful on the streets around the cathedral. For student pubs, wander around **Stühlinger,** the neighborhood immediately south of the train station. Plenty of people take their nightcap at the **Cocktailbar Hemingway** (⊠ Eisenbahnstr. 54 ☎ 0761/207–340), which stays open until 2 AM on weekends. **Funpark** (⊠ Hans-Bunte-Str. 16, near the autobahn access road for the Freiburg Nord exit ☎ 0761/ 556–5757), the large-scale, cool nightclub for the young, is in the northern industrial zone of Freiburg. The wild decor includes an airplane. **Jazzhaus** (⊠ Schnewlinstr. 1 ☎ 0761/34973) sometimes has live music and draws big acts and serious up-and-coming artists to its brick cellar. A very mixed crowd meets daily and nightly at **Kagan café bar club lounge** (⊠ Bismarckallee 9 ☎ 0761/767–2766 🖅 on weekends, €6 Sat., €2, including a drink, Sun.) in the skyscraper over the train station. It opens for breakfast at 10 AM, and dancing on weekends goes until 5 AM, with dinner served until 12:30 AM and snacks until somewhat later. The view of the Old Town is incomparable.

Staufen

🔟 *20 km (12 mi) south of Freiburg via B–31.*

Once you've braved Hell Valley to get to Freiburg, a visit to the nearby town of Staufen, where Dr. Faustus is reputed to have made his pact with the devil, should hold no horrors. The Faustus legend is remembered today chiefly because of Goethe's *Faust,* perhaps, the most famous account of a man who sells his soul to the devil in return for eternal youth and knowledge. The original Faustus was a 16th-century alchemist and scientist. His pact was not with the devil but with a local baron who was convinced that Faustus could make his fortune by converting base metal into gold. While attempting to do so, Dr. Faustus caused an explosion that produced such noise and such a sulfurous stink that the townspeople were convinced the devil had carried him off. In fact, he was killed in the accident. You can visit the ancient **Gasthaus zum Löwen** (⊠ Hauptstr. 47), where Faustus lived, allegedly in room number 5, and died. The inn is right on the central square of Staufen, a town with a visible inclination toward modern art in ancient settings.

Where to Stay & Eat

$$–$$$$ ✕▦ **Romantik Hotel Spielweg.** A half-hour's drive from Freiburg, this family-run inn has everything for an indulgent holiday, with pools, tennis courts, Karl-Josef Fuchs's regional cooking ($–$$$$), and its own cheese factory, which you can visit. ⊠ *Hauptstr. 61, D–79244 Obermünstertal, 12 km (7 mi) southeast of Staufen* ☎ *07636/7090* 🖷 *07636/70966* ⊕ *www.spielweg.com* ➟ *43 rooms, 3 suites* ⚘ *2 restaurants, cable TV, 2 pools (1 indoor), massage, sauna, bicycles, some pets allowed (fee), no-smoking rooms; no a/c* ⊟ *AE, DC, MC, V* ⋈ *BP.*

$–$$ ✕▦ **Landgasthaus zur Linde.** Guests have been welcomed here for 350 years, but the comforts inside the inn's old walls are contemporary. The kitchen ($–$$) creates wholesome sustenance out of local ingredients and plays up seasonal specialties, such as asparagus in May and June, and mushrooms from the valley in autumn. The terrace is a favorite for hikers passing through, as are the various snacks. ⊠ *Krumlinden 13, D–79244 Münstertal, 14 km (9 mi) southeast of Staufen* ☎ *07636/7570* 🖷 *07636/447* ⊕ *www.landgasthaus.de* ➟ *10 rooms, 2 suites* ⚘ *Restaurant, cable TV, some pets allowed (fee); no a/c* ⊟ *V* ☺ *Restaurant closed Mon. and Thurs.* ⋈ *BP.*

Kaiserstuhl

🔟 *20 km (12 mi) northwest of Freiburg on B–31.*

One of the incredible sights of the Black Forest is the **Kaiserstuhl** (Emperor's Chair), a volcanic outcrop clothed in vineyards that produce some of Baden's best wines—reds from the Spätburgunder grape and whites that have an uncanny depth. A third of Baden's wines are produced in this single area, which has the warmest climate in Germany. The especially dry and warm microclimate has given rise to tropical vegetation, including sequoias and a wide variety of orchids.

Sample high-quality wines—the Weissherbst, in particular—in one of the taverns of Achkarren or take a short hike along a vineyard path.

The fine little **Weinmuseum** (Wine Museum) is in a renovated barn in the village center. A small vineyard out front displays the various types of grapes used to make wine in the Kaiserstuhl region. ☒ *Schlossstr., D–73235 Vogtsburg-Achkarren* ☎ *07662/81263* ☜ *€1.50* ☺ *Apr.–Oct., Tues.–Fri. 2–5, weekends 11–5.*

Where to Eat & Stay

**$** ✕ Hotel Krone. You could spend an entire afternoon and evening here, either on the terrace or in the dining room, ($–$$$$) trying the wines and enjoying, say, a filet of wild salmon in a horseradish crust, a boar's roast, or some lighter asparagus creation. The house, which also serves as a hotel, has been around since 1561, and the Höfflin-Schüssler family, now in its fourth generation as hoteliers, knows how to make visitors feel welcome. ☒ *Schlossbergstr. 15–17, D–79235 Vogtsburg-Achkarren* ☎ *07662/93130* 🖷 *07662/931-350* ⊕ *www. Hotel-Krone-Achkarren.de* ⇆ *23 rooms* ⚐ *Restaurant, in-room data ports, cable TV, tennis court, some pets allowed (fee); no a/c* ☐ *MC, V* ☺ *Restaurant closed Wed.* ⍾⍨ *BP.*

THE BLACK FOREST A TO Z

To research prices, get advice from other travelers, and book travel arrangements, visit www.fodors.com.

AIRPORTS

The closest international airports in Germany are Stuttgart and Frankfurt. Strasbourg, in neighboring French Alsace, and the Swiss border city of Basel, the latter just 70 km (43 mi) from Freiburg, are also reasonably close.

BUS TRAVEL

The bus system works closely together with the German railways to reach every corner of the Black Forest. Bus stations are usually at or near the train station. For more information, contact the Regionalbusverkehr Südwest (Regional Bus Lines) in Karlsruhe.

🛈 **Regionalbusverkehr Südwest** (Regional Bus Lines) ☎ 0721/84060 in Karlsruhe.

CAR RENTAL

🛈 **Avis** ☒ Maximilianstr. 54, Baden-Baden ☎ 07221/504-190 ☒ St-Georgenerstr. 7, Freiburg ☎ 0761/19719 ☒ Westliche Karl-Friedrich-Str. 141, Pforzheim ☎ 07231/440-828. **Europcar** ☒ Fautenbruchstr. 53, Karlsruhe ☎ 0721/931-550 ☒ Rheinstr. 29, Baden-Baden ☎ 07221/50660 ☒ Lorracherstr. 10, Freiburg ☎ 0761/515-100. **Hertz** ☒ Lörracherstr. 49, Freiburg ☎ 0761/478-090.

CAR TRAVEL

The main autobahns are A–5 (Frankfurt–Karlsruhe–Basel), which runs through the Rhine Valley along the western length of the Black Forest; A–81 (Stuttgart–Bodensee), in the east; and A–8 (Karlsruhe–Stuttgart), in the north. Good two-lane highways crisscross the entire region. B–3 runs parallel to A–5 and follows the Baden Wine Road. Traffic jams on weekends and holidays are not uncommon. Taking the side roads might not save time, but they are a lot more interesting. The Schwarzwald-Hochstrasse is one of the area's most scenic (but also most trafficked) routes, running from Freudenstadt to Baden-Baden. The region's tourist office has mapped out thematic driving routes: the Valley Road, the Spa Road, the Baden Wine Road, the Asparagus Road, and the Clock Road. Most points along these routes can also be reached by train or bus.

Freiburg, the region's major city, is 275 km (170 mi) south of Frankfurt and 410 km (254 mi) west of Munich.

SPORTS & THE OUTDOORS

BIKING Much of the Black Forest is a biker's paradise (provided the rider is stalwart, since there are so many ups and downs). There are many bike rental shops throughout the region, and cycling maps are available at most tourist offices. For information on biking in Germany, contact the National German Cycling Association. To facilitate your bike traveling, you may want to cover certain distances by train. Call the Deutsche Bahn's special line for bicyclists. Deutsche Bahn also rents bikes.

🚲 **Deutsche Bahn** ☎ 01805/151-415 bike hotline. **Baden-Württemberg Regional Cycling Association** ✉ Augustenstr. 99, D-70197 Stuttgart ☎ 0711/628-999.

HIKING & The regional tourist office offers *Wandern ohne Gepäck* (Hike With-
WALKING out Luggage) tours along the old clock carriers' route. The participating hotels are connected by one-day hikes in a circular route, each section ranging from 16 km to 27 km (10 mi to 17 mi). Your bags are transported ahead by car to meet you each evening at that day's destination. Prices are reasonable: three nights with hotel and breakfast start at €185. For reservations and information contact Wandern Ohne Gepäck at the Uhrenträgergemeinschaft in Triberg.

Along the Baden Wine Road spring and summer weekend hikes will take you through vineyard country to five wineries for wine tasting. The package includes two overnights and two meals typical of the region. Information and reservations can be obtained from Mittlere Schwarzwald Tourismus in Offenburg.

🚲 **Wandern Ohne Gepäck** Uhrenträgergemeinschaft ✉ Gartenstr. 24, D-78098 Triberg ☎ 07722/860-2111 🖶 07722/860-290 ⊕ www.uhrentraeger.de.

TOURS Bus tours (some in English) of the Black Forest and parts of neighboring France and Switzerland, as well as walking tours of Freiburg, are available in Freiburg from Freiburg Kultur.

🚲 **Freiburg Kultur** ✉ Rotteckring 14 ☎ 0761/290-7447 🖶 0761/290-7449.

TRAIN TRAVEL

The main rail route through the Black Forest runs north–south, following the Rhine Valley from Karlsruhe to Basel. There are fast and frequent trains to Freiburg and Baden-Baden from most major German cities (you generally have to change at Karlsruhe).

Local lines connect most of the smaller towns. Two east–west routes— the Schwarzwaldbahn (Black Forest Railway) and the Höllental Railway—are among the most spectacular in the country. Details are available from Deutsche Bahn.

VISITOR INFORMATION

For information on the northern Black Forest, contact Touristik Nördlicher Schwarzwald. For the central area, contact Mittlere Schwarzwald Tourismus GmbH. For the southern area, contact Tourismus Südlicher Schwarzwald.

Baden-Baden ✉ Baden-Baden Kur- und Tourismus GmbH, Solmsstrasse 1, D-76530 ☎ 07221/275-2001 ⊕ www.baden-baden.de. **Bad Herrenalb** ✉ Tourismusbüro, Bahnhofplatz 1, D-76332 ☎ 07083/500-555 ⊕ www.badherrenalb.de. **Bad Liebenzell** ✉ Kurverwaltung, Reutlinweg 3, D-75378 ☎ 07052/4080 ⊕ www.bad-liebenzell.de. **Calw** ✉ Stadtinformation Calw, Marktbrücke 1, D-75365 ☎ 07051/968-810 ⊕ www.calw.de. **Feldberg** ✉ Tourist-Information, Kirchgasse 1, D-79868 ☎ 07655/8019 ⊕ www.feldberg-das-hoechste-im-schwarzwald.de. **Freiburg** ✉ Tourist-Information, Rotteckring 14, D-79098 ☎ 0761/388-1880 ⊕ www.freiburg.de. **Freudenstadt** ✉ Kongresse-Touristik-Kur, Marktpl. 64, D-72250 ☎ 07441/8640. **Gengenbach** ✉ Kultur und Tourismus GmbH, Im Winzerhof, D-77723 ☎ 07803/930-143 ⊕ www.gengenbach.info. **Hinterzarten** ✉ Hinterzarten-Breitnau Tourismus GmbH, Freiburgerstr. 1, D-75896 ☎ 07652/12060 ⊕ www.hinterzarten.de. **Karlsruhe** ✉ Tourist-Information, Bahnhofpl. 6, D-76137 ☎ 0721/19433 ⊕ www.karlsruhe.de/tourismus. **Pforzheim** ✉ Tourist-Information, Marktpl. 1, D-75175 ☎ 07231/145-4560 ⊕ www.pforzheim.de. **Schluchsee** ✉ Tourist-Information, Fischbacherstr. 7, D-79859 ☎ 07656/7732 ⊕ www.schluchsee.de. **Mittlere Schwarzwald Tourismus GmbH** ✉ Gerberstr. 8, D-77652 Offenburg ☎ 0781/923-7777 🖷 0781/923-7770 ⊕ www.schwarzwald-tourismus.com. **Titisee-Neustadt** ✉ Tourist-Information, Strandbadstr. 4, D-79822 ☎ 07651/98040 ⊕ www.titisee.de. **Tourismus Südlicher Schwarzwald** ✉ Stadtstr. 2, D-79104 Freiburg ☎ 0761/218-7304 🖷 0761/218-7534 ⊕ www.schwarzwald-sued.de. **Touristik Nördlicher Schwarzwald** ✉ Am Weisenhauspl. 26, D-75172 Pforzheim ☎ 07231/147-380 🖷 07231/147-3820 ⊕ www.noerdlicher-schwarzwald.de. **Triberg** ✉ Tourist-Information, Luisenstr. 10, D-78098 ☎ 07722/953-230 🖷 07722/953-236 ⊕ www.triberg.de.

HEIDELBERG & THE NECKAR VALLEY

8

Updated by
Kerry Brady

THE NECKAR RIVER UNITES BEAUTY and historic resonance as it flows toward the Rhine through the state of Baden-Württemberg, eventually reaching Heidelberg's graceful baroque towers and the majestic ruins of its red sandstone castle. Much of this route follows the west–east course of the Burgenstrasse (Castle Road), which stretches nearly 1,000 km (621 mi) from Mannheim to Prague, taking in some 70 castles and palaces along the way. Every town or bend in the river seems to have its guardian castle, sometimes in ruins but often revived as a museum or hotel. Off the main road, quiet side valleys and little towns slumber in leafy peace.

Exploring Heidelberg & the Neckar Valley

Heidelberg is a destination unto itself, but it can also be seen as the major stop on the Burgenstrasse, which makes its way through the narrower parts of the Neckar Valley. The route in this chapter follows the Neckar River upstream (east, then south) from Heidelberg. The road snakes between the river and the wooded slopes of the Odenwald forest before reaching the rolling, vine-covered countryside around Heilbronn. From there it's a 50-km (31-mi) drive, partly along the Neckar, to Stuttgart. About 40 km (25 mi) farther you rejoin the river at the charming university town of Tübingen.

About the Restaurants

Mittagessen (lunch) in this region is generally served from noon until 2 or 2:30, *Abendessen* (dinner) from 6 until 9:30 or 10. *Durchgehend warme Küche* means that hot meals are also served between lunch and dinner. Slowly but surely, credit cards have gained acceptance, but this is by no means universal, and many restaurants will only accept cash or debit cards issued by a German bank. Casual attire is typically acceptable at restaurants here, and reservations are generally not needed. "Gourmet temples" that require reservations and coat-and-tie are noted as such in this chapter.

About the Hotels

This area is full of castle-hotels and charming country inns that range in comfort from upscale rustic to luxurious. For a riverside view, ask for a *Zimmer* (room) or *Tisch* (table) *mit Neckarblick* (with a view of the Neckar). The Neckar Valley offers idyllic alternatives to the cost and crowds of Heidelberg. Driving time from Eberbach, for example, is a half hour; from Bad Wimpfen, about an hour.

WHAT IT COSTS In Euros				
$$$$	**$$$**	**$$**	**$**	**¢**
RESTAURANTS over €25	€21–€25	€16–€20	€9–€15	under €9
HOTELS over €225	€175–€225	€100–€175	€50–€100	under €50

Restaurant prices are per person for a main course at dinner. Hotel prices are for two people in a standard double room, including tax and service.

Timing

If you plan to visit Heidelberg in summer, make reservations well in advance and expect to pay top rates. To get away from the crowds, con-

8

Numbers in the text correspond to numbers in the margin and on the Neckar Valley and Heidelberg maps.

If you have 3 days

Spend a full day and night exploring the university town of ⬜ **Heidelberg** ①–⑰ ☛. On the second day take a trip up the Neckar to the castles of **Hirschhorn** ⑲ and ⬜ **Burg Hornberg** ㉒ (both have hotels for an overnight stay, with excellent restaurants). On the third day visit the **Staatsgalerie** (State Gallery) in **Stuttgart** ㉖.

If you have 5 days

Spend your first two days and nights in ⬜ **Heidelberg** ①–⑰ ☛. On the third day continue up the Neckar to **Burg Guttenberg** ⑲ (with its aviary of birds of prey) and the castles of **Hirschhorn** ⑲ and ⬜ **Burg Hornberg** ㉒. Stay overnight at one of the many castle hotels in the area. Investigate the remains of the imperial palace and other sights in **Bad Wimpfen** ㉓ on the fourth day, and end the trip in the medieval streets of ⬜ **Tübingen** ㉘.

If you have 7 days

Spend your first two days and nights in ⬜ **Heidelberg** ①–⑰ ☛. On the third day head up the Neckar to **Burg Guttenberg** and the ⬜ **Hirschhorn** ⑲ castle, staying there or in ⬜ **Eberbach** ⑳ for two nights. Continue on to explore **Mosbach** ㉑ and the castle at **Burg Hornberg** ㉒, with time out for a river cruise. Spend the fifth day and night in ⬜ **Bad Wimpfen** ㉓, with a possible side trip to the museum of bicycle and motorcycle technology at **Neckarsulm** ㉔. On the sixth day and night visit the sights and enjoy the nightlife of ⬜ **Stuttgart** ㉖. On Day 7 stop in **Bebenhausen** ㉗ en route to ⬜ **Tübingen** ㉘, where you can spend your final day.

---

sider staying out of town and driving or taking the bus into the city. Hotels and restaurants are much cheaper just a little upriver. A visit in late fall, when the vines turn a faded gold, or early spring, with the first green shoots of the year, can be captivating. In the depths of winter, river mists creep through the narrow streets of Heidelberg's Old Town and awaken the ghosts of a romantic past.

THE NECKAR-RHINE TRIANGLE

The natural beauty of Heidelberg is created by the embrace of mountains, forests, vineyards, and the Neckar River—all crowned by the famous ruined castle. The Neckar and the Rhine meet at nearby Mannheim, a major industrial center and the second-largest river port in Europe. Schwetzingen, known as Germany's asparagus capital, lies in the triangle's center.

Heidelberg

☛ *57 km (35 mi) northeast of Karlsruhe.*

If any city in Germany encapsulates the spirit of the country, it is Heidelberg. Scores of poets and composers—virtually the entire 19th-century German Romantic movement—have sung its praises. Goethe and Mark Twain both fell in love here: the German writer with a beautiful young woman, the American author with the city itself. Sigmund Romberg set his operetta *The Student Prince* in the city; Carl Maria von Weber wrote his lushly Romantic opera *Der Freischütz* here. Composer Robert Schumann was a student at the university. The campaign these artists waged on behalf of the town has been astoundingly successful. Heidelberg's fame is out of all proportion to its size (population 140,000); more than 3½ million visitors crowd its streets every year.

Heidelberg was the political center of the Rhineland Palatinate. At the end of the Thirty Years' War (1618–48), the elector Carl Ludwig married his daughter to the brother of Louis XIV in the hope of bringing peace to the Rhineland. But when the elector's son died without an heir, Louis XIV used the marriage alliance as an excuse to claim Heidelberg, and in 1689 the town was sacked and laid to waste. Four years later he sacked the town again. From its ashes arose what you see today: a baroque town built on Gothic foundations, with narrow, twisting streets and alleyways. Modern Heidelberg changed under the influence of U.S. army barracks and industrial development stretching into the suburbs, but the old heart of the city remains intact, exuding the spirit of romantic Germany.

a good walk

Begin a tour of Heidelberg at the **Königstuhl Bergbahn** (funicular) ❶ ▶, which will take you up to the famous **Schloss** ❷, one of Germany's most memorable sights. It was already in ruins when 19th-century Romantics fell under its spell, drawn by the mystery of its Gothic turrets, Renaissance walls, and abandoned gardens. (You can also choose to hike up the winding Burgweg [castle walk] to the complex.) The fascinating **Deutsches Apotheken–Museum** (German Apothecary Museum) is within the castle walls. The funicular can take you higher from the Schloss to **Molkenkur** ❸, the site of another castle ruin, and **Königstuhl** ❹, a high hill with fine views.

From the Schloss ramparts, take the Burgweg down to the city's Altstadt (Old Town), sandwiched between the Neckar River and the surrounding hills. The steep path from the castle ends abruptly near the **Kornmarkt** (Grain Market). Cross the square north to Hauptstrasse, an elegant pedestrian street that runs straight through the city. Bear right, and you will immediately enter Karlsplatz; on the far side are two traditional pubs, Zum Sepp'l and Zum Roten Ochsen, where fraternity students have engaged in beer-drinking contests for the last 200-some years. As you go left from Kornmarkt, it's only a few steps to the **Marktplatz**, the city's main square. The **Rathaus** (Town Hall) ❺ is a stately baroque building dating from 1701 that fronts the market square. From the center of the square, the late-Gothic **Heiliggeistkirche** ❻ towers over the city. Just as in medieval times, there are shopping stalls between its buttresses. **Hotel zum Ritter** ❼, with an elaborate Renaissance facade of curlicues, columns, and gables, stands opposite Heiliggeistkirche. Walking farther down Hauptstrasse west of Marktplatz, you reach Universitätsplatz and the **Alte Universität** ❽, which was founded in 1386 and rebuilt in the early 18th century. It's one of four separate university complexes in the town. Go behind the Old University and down tiny Au-

8

Festivals Important cultural festivals for music, opera, and theater include the Schlossfestspiele on castle grounds in Schwetzingen (May), Heidelberg (July and August), Zwingenberg (late August), and Ludwigsburg (June to mid-September). Since 1818 thousands have flocked to the Stuttgart suburb of Cannstatt in early October for the annual Volksfest (folk festival), which kicks off with a colorful parade of folk-dance groups and horse-drawn brewery wagons. Two wine festivals of particular note are the Stuttgarter Weindorf, from late August to early September, and the Heilbronner Weindorf in mid-September. Last but not least are the fabulous fireworks and castle illuminations in Heidelberg (with an arts-and-crafts market on the riverbank) on the first Saturday of June and September and the second Saturday of July.

Food & Wine Fish and *Wild* (game) from the streams and woods lining the Neckar Valley, as well as seasonal favorites—*Spargel* (asparagus), *Pilze* (mushrooms), *Morcheln* (morels), *Pfifferlinge* (chanterelles), and *Steinpilze* (cèpes)—are regulars on menus in this area. Pfälzer specialties are also common, but the penchant for potatoes yields to *Knödel* (dumplings) and pasta farther south. The latter includes the Swabian and Baden staples, *Maultaschen* (stuffed "pockets" of pasta) and *spätzle* (roundish egg noodles), as well as *Schupfnudeln* (finger-size noodles of potato dough), also called *Bube-* or *Buwespitzle*. Look for *Linsen* (lentils) and sauerkraut in soups or as sides. *Schwäbischer Rostbraten* (beefsteaks topped with fried onions) and *Schäufele* (pickled and slightly smoked pork shoulder) are popular meat dishes.

Considerable quantities of red wine are produced along the Neckar Valley. Crisp, light Trollinger is often served in the traditional *Viertele*, a round, quarter-liter (8-ounce) glass with a handle. Deeper-color, more substantial reds include Spatburgunder (Pinot Noir) and its mutation Schwarzriesling (Pinot Meunier), Lemberger, and Dornfelder. Riesling, Kerner, and Müller-Thurgau (synonymous with Rivaner), as well as Grauburgunder (Pinot Gris) and Weissburgunder (Pinot Blanc) are the typical white wines. A birch broom or wreath over the doorway of a vintner's home signifies a *Besenwirtschaft* ("broomstick inn"), a rustic pub where you can enjoy wines with snacks and simple fare. Many vintners offer economical bed-and-breakfasts.

gustinerstrasse to find the **Studentenkarzer** 9, or Student Prison. Tradition once dictated that the university rather than the police should deal with unruly students. To the south, the **Neue Universität** 10 is on the southeast corner of Universitätsplatz. Just off Universitätsplatz, on the street called Plöck, stands the **Universitätsbibliothek** 11 (University Library). The Gothic **Peterskirche** 12, the city's oldest parish church, is opposite the library.

Next, return to Hauptstrasse and walk west a couple of blocks to visit the **Kurpfälzisches Museum** 13, Heidelberg's leading museum, housed in

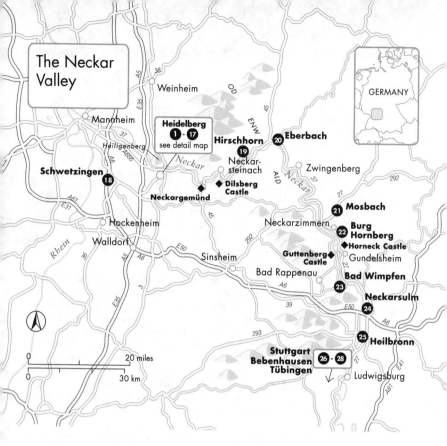

The Neckar Valley

Weinheim

GERMANY

Mannheim

Heiligenberg

Heidelberg
1 - **17**
see detail map

Hirschhorn

19
Neckar-
steinach

20 Eberbach

Zwingenberg

Schwetzingen **18**

Neckar

Neckargemünd

◆ Dilsberg
Castle

Neckarzimmern

21 Mosbach

22 Burg
Hornberg

◆ Horneck Castle

Hockenheim

Walldorf

Sinsheim

Guttenberg ◆
Castle

Gundelsheim

Bad Rappenau

23 Bad Wimpfen

Rhein

24 Neckarsulm

25 Heilbronn

Stuttgart
Bebenhausen
Tübingen

26 - **28**

Ludwigsburg

0   20 miles

0   30 km

a former baroque palace. Six blocks west of the Kurpfälzisches Museum, on the south side of Hauptstrasse, is an alley leading to a courtyard and the entrance to Europe's only museum devoted to the history of industrial packaging, the **Deutsches Verpackungs-Museum** ⑭. Walk back toward Marktplatz and turn left at Dreikönigstrasse; a short block brings you to Untere Strasse, where you go right, then immediately left at the first street, called Pfaffengasse. Halfway down the street on the left-hand side (No. 18) is the **Friedrich-Ebert-Gedenkstätte** ⑮, the birthplace of the president of the ill-fated Weimar Republic. Continue on to the end of the street and turn right along the river to reach the twin turrets of the **Alte Brücke** ⑯. From the bridge you'll have views of the Old Town and the castle above. For the most inspiring view of Heidelberg, climb up the steep, winding **Schlangenweg** ⑰ through the vineyards to the Philosophenweg (Philosophers' Path); then go right and continue through the woods above the river to the Hölderlin Memorial, a grove traditionally frequented by poets and scholars. Try to arrive there as the sun sets and watch the red sandstone castle turn to gold.

TIMING   Allow at least two hours to tour the Schloss—and expect long lines in summer (up to 30 minutes). For the rest of the tour, add another two hours, four if you plan on seeing the collection of the Kurpfälzisches

Museum, the manuscript exhibition at the University Library, and the inside of the Student Prison.

What to See

⑯ Alte Brücke (Old Bridge). Walk onto the bridge from the Old Town under a portcullis spanned by two *Spitzhelm* towers (so called for their resemblance to old German helmets). The twin towers were part of medieval Heidelberg's fortifications. In the west tower are three dank dungeons that once held common criminals. Between the towers, above the gate, are more salubrious lockups, with views of the river and the castle; these were reserved for debtors. Above the portcullis you'll see a memorial plaque that pays warm tribute to the Austrian forces who helped Heidelberg beat back a French attempt to capture the bridge in 1799. The bridge itself is the ninth to be built on this spot; ice floes and floods destroyed its predecessors. The elector Carl Theodor, who built it in 1786–88, must have been confident this one would last: he had a statue of himself erected on it, upon a plinth decorated with river gods and goddesses (symbolic of the Rhine, Danube, Neckar, and Mosel rivers). Just to be safe, he also put up a statue of the saint John Nepomuk. From the center of the bridge you'll have some of the finest views of the Old Town and the castle above.

❽ Alte Universität (Old University). The three-story baroque structure was built between 1712 and 1718 at the behest of the elector Johann Wilhelm on the site of an earlier university building. It houses the impressive Alta Aula (Old Auditorium) and the University Museum, with exhibits that chronicle the history of Germany's oldest university. The present-day Universitätsplatz (University Square) was built over the remains of an Augustinian monastery that was destroyed by the French in 1693. ✉ *Grabeng. 1–3* ☎ *06221/542–152* 🖾 *€2.50* ◷ *Apr.–Sept., Tues.–Sun. 10–4; Oct., Tues.–Sun. 10–4; Nov.–Mar., Tues.–Sat. 10–4.*

⓮ Deutsches Verpackungs-Museum (German Packaging Museum). A former church was innovatively converted to house this fascinating documentation of packaging and package design of brand-name products. Representing the years 1800 to the present, historic logos and slogans are a trip down memory lane. The entrance is not on Hauptstrasse but in the courtyard behind the street, reached via an alley. ✉ *Hauptstr. 22* ☎ *06221/21361* ⊕ *www.verpackungsmuseum.de* 🖾 *€3.50* ◷ *Wed.–Fri. 1–6, weekends 11–6.*

⓯ Friedrich-Ebert-Gedenkstätte (Friedrich Ebert Memorial). The humble rooms of a tiny back-street apartment were the birthplace of Friedrich Ebert, Germany's first democratically elected president (in 1920) and leader of the ill-fated Weimar Republic. Display cases have documents that tell the story of the tailor's son who took charge of a nation accustomed to being ruled by a kaiser. ✉ *Pfaffeng. 18* ☎ *06221/91070* ⊕ *www.ebert-gedenkstaette.de* 🖾 *Free* ◷ *Tues., Wed., and Fri.–Sun. 10–6, Thurs. 10–8.*

❻ Heiliggeistkirche (Church of the Holy Ghost). The foundation stone of the building was laid in 1398, but it was not actually finished until 1544. Unlike that of most other Gothic churches, the facade of the

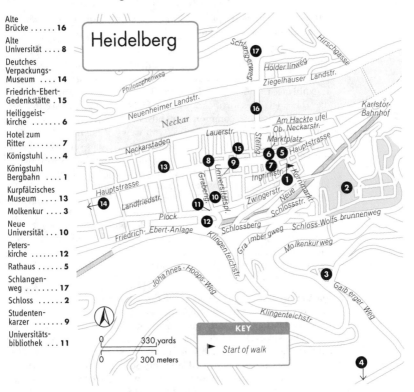

Heiliggeistkirche is uniform—you cannot discern the choir or naves from the outside. The gargoyles looking down on the south side (where Hauptstrasse crosses Marktplatz) are remarkable for their sheer ugliness. The church fell victim to the plundering General Tilly, leader of the Catholic League during the Thirty Years' War. Tilly loaded the church's greatest treasure—the *Bibliotheca Palatina*, at the time the largest library in Germany—onto 500 carts and trundled it off to Rome, where he presented it to the pope. Few volumes found their way back to Heidelberg. At the end of the 17th century, French troops plundered the church again, destroying the family tombs of the Palatinate electors; only the 15th-century tomb of Elector Ruprecht III and his wife, Elisabeth von Hohenzollern, remains today. ✉ *Marktpl.* ☉ *Late Mar.–Oct., Mon.–Sat. 11–5, Sun. 12:30–5; Nov.–late Mar., Fri. and Sat. 11–3, Sun. 12:30–3.*

❼ Hotel zum Ritter. The hotel's name refers to the statue of a Roman knight ("Ritter") atop one of the many gables. Its French builder, Charles Bélier, had the Latin inscription *Persta Invicta Venus* added to the facade in gold letters—"Venus, Remain Unconquerable." It appears this injunction was effective, as this was the city's only Renaissance building to be spared the attentions of the invading French in 1689 and 1693. Between 1695 and 1705 it was used as Heidelberg's town hall; later it became an inn, and it's still a hotel today. ✉ *Hauptstr. 178* ☎ *06221/1350.*

❹ **Königstuhl** (King's Throne). The second-highest hill in the Odenwald range—1,700 feet above Heidelberg—is only a hop, skip, and funicular ride from Heidelberg. On a clear day you can see south as far as the Black Forest and west to the Vosges Mountains of France. The hill is at the center of a close-knit network of hiking trails. Signs and colored arrows from the top lead hikers through the woods of the Odenwald.

▶ ❶ **Königstuhl Bergbahn** (funicular). The funicular hoists visitors in 17 minutes to the summit of Königstuhl. On the way it stops at the ruined Heidelberg Schloss and Molkenkur. The funicular usually leaves every 10 minutes in summer and every 20 minutes in winter. However, renovation work may be under way. During this time buses will run from the funicular station to Königstuhl (weekdays every half hour, weekends every 20 minutes), and Bus 21 from Bismarckplatz to Königstuhl runs the same route (every hour). Both stop at the castle and Molkenkur. ⊠ *Kornmarkt* ▨ *Round-trip to Schloss, Molkenkur, or Königstuhl €3.50.*

Kornmarkt (Grain Market). A baroque statue of the Virgin Mary is in the center of this old Heidelberg square, which has a view of the castle ruins.

❸ **Kurpfälzisches Museum** (Palatinate Museum). The baroque palace that houses the museum was built as a residence for a university professor in 1712. It's a pleasure just to wander around, which is more or less unavoidable, since the museum's layout is so confusing. The collections chart the history of the city and its region. Among the exhibits are two standouts. One is a replica of the jaw of Heidelberg Man, a key link in the evolutionary chain thought to date from a half-million years ago; the original was unearthed near the city in 1907. The larger attraction is the ***Windsheimer Zwölfbotenaltar** (Twelve Apostles Altarpiece),* one of the largest and finest works of early Renaissance sculptor Tilman Riemenschneider. Its exquisite detailing and technical sophistication are evident in the simple faith that radiates from the faces of the Apostles. On the top floor of the museum there's a rich range of 19th-century German paintings and drawings, many depicting Heidelberg. The restaurant in the museum's quiet, shady courtyard is a good place for a break. ⊠ *Hauptstr. 97* ☎ *06221/583–402* ▨ *€2.50* ☉ *Tues.–Sun. 10–6.*

Marktplatz (Market Square). Heidelberg's main square, with the Rathaus on one side and the Heiliggeistkirche on the other, has been its focal point since the Middle Ages. Public courts of justice were held here in earlier centuries, and people accused of witchcraft and heresy were burned at the stake. The baroque fountain in the middle, the Herkulesbrunnen (Hercules Fountain), is the work of 18th-century artist H. Charrasky. Until 1740 a rotating, hanging cage stood next to it. For minor crimes, people were imprisoned in it and exposed to the laughter, insults, and abuse of their fellow citizens. The square is surrounded by narrow side streets that should be explored.

❸ **Molkenkur.** The next stop after the castle on the Königstuhl funicular, Molkenkur was the site of Heidelberg's second castle. Lightning struck it in 1527, and it was never rebuilt. Today it's occupied by a restaurant with magnificent views of the Odenwald and the Rhine plain.

⑩ Neue Universität (New University). The plain building on the south side of Universitätsplatz was erected between 1930 and 1932 through funds raised by the U.S. ambassador to Germany, J. G. Schurman, who had been a student at the university. The only decoration on the building's three wings is a statue of Athena, the Greek goddess of wisdom, above the entrance. The inner courtyard contains a medieval tower from 1380, the **Hexenturm** (Witches Tower). The tower is all that's left of the old city walls and has been incorporated into the newer building. Suspected witches were locked up there in the Middle Ages. It later became a memorial to former students killed in World War I. ⊠ *Grabeng.*

off the beaten path

NEUENHEIM – To escape the crowds of Heidelberg, walk across the Theodor Heuss Bridge to the suburb of Neuenheim. At the turn of the 20th century this old fishing village developed into a residential area full of posh art nouveau villas. North of the Brückenkopf (bridgehead) you'll find antiques and designer shops, boutiques, and cafés on Brückenstrasse, Bergstrasse (one block east), and Ladenburger Strasse (parallel to the river). To savor the neighborhood spirit, visit the charming farmers' market on Wednesday or Saturday morning at the corner of Ladenburger and Luther streets. The beer pubs Vetter's and o'reilly's (once voted best Irish pub in Germany) draw a young crowd; the chic bistros Le Coq and Bar d'Aix cater to a more mature set; and Marktstübel and Dorfschänke serve good food in a casual, cozy atmosphere. All are within a five-minute walk from one another on the streets named above.

⑫ Peterskirche (St. Peter's Church). Many famous Heidelberg citizens' tombstones, some more than 500 years old, line the outer walls of the city's oldest parish church (1485–1500). The church itself is not open for visits. ⊠ *Plöck 62.*

⑤ Rathaus (Town Hall). Work began on the town hall in 1701, a few years after the French destroyed the city. The massive coat of arms above the balcony is the work of sculptor Heinrich Charrasky, who also created the statue of Hercules atop the fountain in the middle of the square. ⊠ *Marktpl.*

⑰ Schlangenweg (Snake Path). This walkway starts just above the Alte Brücke opposite the Old Town and cuts steeply through terraced vineyards until it reaches the woods, where it crosses the Philosophenweg (Philosophers' Path).

② Schloss (Castle). What's most striking is the architectural variety of this

Fodor'sChoice ★ great complex. The oldest parts still standing date from the 15th century, though most of the castle was built in the Renaissance and baroque styles of the 16th and 17th centuries, when the castle was the seat of the Palatinate electors. There's even an "English wing," built in 1612 by the elector Friedrich V for his teenage Scottish bride, Elizabeth Stuart; its plain, square-window facade is positively foreign compared to the more opulent styles of the castle. (The enamored Friedrich also had a charming garden laid out for his young bride; its imposing arched entryway, the Elisabethentor, was put up overnight as a surprise for her 19th birthday.) The architectural highlight remains the Renaissance courtyard—harmonious, graceful, and ornate.

The castle includes the **Deutsches Apotheken–Museum** (German Apothecary Museum; ☎ 06221/25880 ☉ Daily 10–5:30). This museum, on the lower floor of the Ottheinrichsbau (Otto Heinrich Building), is filled with ancient carboys and other flagons and receptacles (each with a carefully painted enamel label), beautifully made scales, little drawers, shelves, a marvelous reconstruction of an 18th-century apothecary shop, dried beetles and toads, and a mummy with a full head of hair.

Even if you have to wait, you should make a point of seeing the **Grosses Fass** (Great Cask), an enormous wine barrel in the cellar, made from 130 oak trees and capable of holding 58,500 gallons. It was used to hold wines paid as taxes by wine growers in the Palatinate. During the rule of the elector Carl Philip, the barrel was guarded by the court jester, a Tyrolean dwarf called Perkeo—when offered wine, he always answered, "*Perche no?*" ("Why not?"), hence his nickname. Legend has it that he could consume frighteningly large quantities of wine and that he died when he drank a glass of water by mistake. A statue of Perkeo stands next to the two-story-high barrel.

The castle may be reached by taking the Königstuhl Bergbahn. Generations of earlier visitors hiked up to it on the Burgweg, a winding road. Of course, it's easier to walk down. In summer there are fireworks displays from the castle terrace (on the first Saturday in June and September and the second Saturday in July). In July and August the castle hosts an open-air theater festival. Performances of *The Student Prince* often figure prominently. ☎ 06221/538–421 castle ⌨ *Courtyard, Great Cask, and Apotheken–Museum €2.50; tours of interior an additional €3.50 ☉ Daily 8–5:30; tours in English daily, when demand is sufficient.*

❾ Studentenkarzer (Student Prison). University officials locked students up here from 1778 to 1914—mostly for minor offenses. They could be held for up to 14 days and were left to subsist on bread and water for the first three days; thereafter, they were allowed to attend lectures, receive guests, and have food brought in from the outside. A stay in the jail became as coveted as a scar inflicted in the university's fencing clubs. There's bravado, even poetic flair, to be deciphered from two centuries of graffiti that cover the walls and ceilings of the narrow cells. ⌨ *Augustinerg.* ☎ 06221/543–554 ⌨ *€2.50 ☉ Apr.–Sept., Tues.–Sun. 10–6; Oct., Tues.–Sun. 10–4; Nov.–Mar., Tues.–Sat. 10–4.*

⓫ Universitätsbibliothek (University Library). Its 2½ million volumes include the 14th-century *Manesse Codex,* a unique collection of medieval songs and poetry once performed in the courts of Germany by the *Minnesänger* (singers). The original is too fragile to be exhibited, so a copy is on display. ⌨ *Plöck 107–109* ☎ 06221/542–380 ⌨ *Free ☉ Mon.–Sat. 10–6.*

Where to Stay & Eat

★ **$$$$** ✕ **Schlossweinstube.** This spacious baroque dining room specializes in *Ente von Heidelberg* (roast duck) and offers refuge from the castle crowds. Bistro Backhaus ($; open daily Apr.–Sept. and Fri.–Sun. in March and Oct.) has rustic furnishings and a nearly 50-foot-high *Backkamin* (baking oven). Light fare as well as coffee and cake are served indoors and on the shady patio until 5 PM. You can sample rare wines (Eiswein, Beerenauslese) by the glass in the Fasskeller, or pick up a bottle with a designer label depicting Heidelberg. Reservations are essential for terrace seating. ⊠ *Schlosshof, on castle grounds* ☎ *06221/ 97970* ⊕ *www.schoenmehl.de* ⊟ *AE, DC, MC, V* ⊘ *Schlossweinstube closed Jan. and Wed. No lunch.*

$$$$ ✕ **schwarz Das Restaurant.** Sleek, contemporary furnishings, soft lighting, stunning panoramic views, and Manfred Schwarz's creative cuisine make for unforgettable dining in this new 12th-floor restaurant, complete with an apéritif bar and cigar lounge. The gourmet and regional menus (three to seven courses) change every month, but Mediterranean accents are a constant, as are dishes flavored with caviar or truffles, such as sautéed goose liver on "truffled" polenta with raspberry vinegar sauce or gratinated scallops with chive sauce and caviar. ⊠ *Print Media Academy, Kurfürsten-Anlage 60, opposite the train station* ☎ *06221/ 757–030* ⊕ *www.schwarzdasrestaurant.com* ⊟ *AE, DC, MC, V* ⊘ *Closed Sun., Mon., and 3 wks in Aug. No lunch.*

★ **$$$** ✕ **Simplicissimus.** Olive oil and herbs of Provence accentuate many of chef Johann Lummer's culinary delights. Saddle of lamb and sautéed liver in honey-pepper sauce are specialties; the *Dessertteller*, a sampler, is a crowning finish to any meal here. The wine list focuses on old-world estates, particularly clarets. The elegant art nouveau interior is done in shades of red with dark-wood accents. In summer dine alfresco in the courtyard. ⊠ *Ingrimstr. 16* ☎ *06221/183–336* ⊕ *www.restaurant-simplicissimus.de* ⊟ *AE, MC, V* ⊘ *Closed Tues., 2 wks in Jan. and Feb., and 2 wks in Aug. and Sept. No lunch.*

★ **$–$$$** ✕ **Zur Herrenmühle.** "Spontaneität" (spontaneity) is the new motto of Ursula and Günter Ueberle's fresh, light cuisine. It's served in a 17th-century grain mill that's been transformed into a romantic, cozy restaurant with an idyllic courtyard. Fish, lamb, homemade pasta, and a delicious Wiener schnitzel are specialties. The prix-fixe menus offer good value. ⊠ *Hauptstr. 239, near Karlstor* ☎ *06221/602–909* ⊕ *www. zur-herrenmuehle.de* ⊟ *AE, DC, MC, V* ⊘ *Closed Sun. and Mon. and 1st half of Jan. No lunch.*

$–$$ ✕ **Schnitzelbank.** A hole-in-the-wall where tourists rarely venture, this former cooper's workshop is now a candlelit pub filled with locals seated at long wooden tables. It's hard not to fall into conversation with the people at your elbow. The menu features wines and specialties from Baden and the Pfalz, such as *Schäufele* (pickled and slightly smoked pork shoulder); or a hearty *Pfälzer Teller*, a platter of bratwurst, *Leberknödel* (liver dumplings), and slices of *Saumagen* (a spicy meat-and-potato mixture encased in a sow's stomach). ⊠ *Bauamtsg. 7* ☎ *06221/21189* ⊟ *MC, V* ⊘ *No lunch weekdays.*

¢–$$ ✕ **Zum Roten Ochsen.** Many of the rough-hewn oak tables here have initials carved into them, a legacy of the thousands who have visited Heidelberg's most famous old tavern. Mark Twain, Marilyn Monroe, and John Wayne may have left their mark—they all ate here. You can wash down simple fare, such as goulash soup and bratwurst, or heartier dishes, such as *Tellerfleisch* (boiled beef) and sauerbraten, with German wines or Heidelberg beer. The "Red Ox" has been run by the Spengel family for 165 years. ✉ *Hauptstr. 217* ☎ *06221/20977* ⊕ *www. roterochsen.de* ⌂ *Reservations essential* ⊟ *No credit cards* ☉ *Closed Sun. and mid-Dec.–mid-Jan. No lunch Nov.–Mar.*

¢–$ ✕ **Café Journal.** Come to this old-world paradise for breakfast, afternoon coffee and cake, and tasty bistro fare. Vegetable lasagne and Florida salad (a combo of chicken, orange, and pineapple) are especially popular. As at its sister cafés in Mannheim and Schwetzingen, newspapers from around the world, hung on hooks, line the walls. It closes after midnight. ✉ *Hauptstr. 162* ☎ *06221/161–712* ⊟ *AE, MC, V.*

¢–$ ✕ **Havana Cocktailbar–Restaurant.** Palm trees and salsa music add Latin zest to the handsome interior of the neoclassical Kongresshaus (convention center) and its broad terrace. It's a perfect backdrop for sipping one of the more than 100 cocktails or the hearty house wine (a Spanish red) with the freshly prepared tapas, *Rollos* (stuffed tortillas), or pasta and vegetarian dishes. There's live piano music some evenings, and on Friday and Saturday 8–10 PM beginners can take a salsa class. ✉ *Neckarstaden 24* ☎ *06221/389–3430* ⊕ *www.heidelberg.havana-restaurants.de* ⊟ *MC, V* ☉ *No lunch.*

¢ ✕ **Café Knösel.** Heidelberg's oldest (1863) coffeehouse has always been a popular meeting place for students and professors. It's still producing café founder Fridolin Knösel's *Heidelberger Studentenkuss* ("student kiss," a chocolate wrapped in paper showing two students touching lips), an acceptable way for 19th-century students to "exchange kisses" in public. ✉ *Haspelg. 20* ☎ *06221/22345* ⊟ *No credit cards* ☉ *Closed Mon.*

★ $$$–$$$$ ✕▦ **Der Europäische Hof–Hotel Europa.** This is the most luxurious of Heidelberg's hotels, centrally located and offering a wide range of facilities. Public rooms are sumptuously furnished, and bedrooms are spacious and tasteful; all suites have whirlpools. In the elegant restaurant, Kurfürstenstube, rich shades of yellow and blue are offset by the original woodwork of 1865. In summer, meals are served on the fountain-lined terrace ($$$–$$$$). There are great views of the castle from the glass-lined fitness and wellness centers. ✉ *Friedrich-Ebert-Anlage 1, D–69117* ☎ *06221/5150* 🖷 *06221/515–506* ⊕ *www.europaeischerhof.com* ⌦ *102 rooms, 13 suites, 3 apartments* ⌂ *Restaurant, cafeteria, in-room data ports, minibars, cable TV, indoor pool, gym, hair salon, sauna, steam room, bar, lobby lounge, babysitting, dry cleaning, laundry service, Internet, business services, some pets allowed, no-smoking rooms; no a/c in some rooms* ⊟ *AE, DC, MC, V* ⍾ *BP.*

$$–$$$$ ✕▦ **Hotel Die Hirschgasse.** A stunning castle view marks this historical
Fodor's Choice inn (1472), located across the river opposite Karlstor (15-minute walk
★ to Old Town). Convivial Ernest Kraft and his British wife, Allison, serve upscale regional specialties (and wines from the vineyard next door) in the Mensurstube ($–$$), once a tavern where university students in-

dulged in fencing duels, as mentioned in Mark Twain's *A Tramp Abroad*. Beamed ceilings, stone walls, and deep red fabrics make for romantic dining in the elegant Le Gourmet ($$$$). ⊠ *Hirschg. 3, D–69120* ☎ *06221/4540* 🖷 *06221/454–111* ⊕ *www.hirschgasse.de* ⤳ *20 suites* ⌂ *2 restaurants, in-room data ports, minibars, cable TV, lobby lounge, babysitting, laundry service, business services, some pets allowed (fee), no-smoking; no a/c* ☰ *AE, DC, MC, V* ☺ *Le Gourmet closed 2 wks in early Jan., 2 wks in early Aug. and Sun. and Mon.; Mensurstube closed Sun. No lunch at either restaurant.*

★ $$–$$$ ✕▥ **Romantik Hotel zum Ritter St. Georg.** If this is your first visit to Germany, try to stay here. It's the only Renaissance building in Heidelberg (1592) and has a top location opposite the market square in the heart of Old Town. The staff is exceptionally helpful and friendly. Some rooms are more modern and spacious than others, but all are comfortable. You can enjoy German and international favorites in the restaurants Belier or Ritterstube ($–$$$). Both are wood paneled and have old-world charm. ⊠ *Hauptstr. 178, D–69117* ☎ *06221/1350* 🖷 *06221/ 135–230* ⊕ *www.ritter-heidelberg.de* ⤳ *39 rooms, 36 with bath; 1 suite* ⌂ *2 restaurants, in-room data ports, minibars, cable TV, babysitting, dry cleaning, laundry service, some pets allowed, no-smoking rooms; no a/c* ☰ *AE, DC, MC, V.*

$$ ✕▥ **KulturBrauerei Heidelberg.** Rooms with warm, sunny colors and modern decor are brilliantly incorporated into this old malt factory in the heart of Old Town. The restaurant ($–$$; no credit cards) is lively until well past midnight. House-brewed Scheffel's beer is the beverage of choice (although there are two wines from the excellent Baden estate Dr. Heger). Try the *Kohlrouladen* (homemade stuffed cabbage rolls) or *Spannferkel* (roast suckling pig). The cellar houses the brewery (tours and tasting possible) and a weekend jazz club; in the courtyard is a huge beer garden. ⊠ *Leyerg. 6, D–69117* ☎ *06221/502–980* 🖷 *06221/502– 9879* ⊕ *www.heidelberger-kulturbrauerei.de* ⤳ *20 rooms, 1 suite* ⌂ *Restaurant, in-room data ports, minibars, cable TV, business services, some pets allowed (fee), no-smoking rooms; no a/c* ☰ *MC, V* ⫿⊙⫿ *BP.*

$$ ✕▥ **Weisser Bock.** Exposed beams and stucco ceilings are part of this hotel's charm. Rooms are individually decorated with warm wood furnishings and offer modern comfort. Art deco fans will be charmed by the restaurant ($–$$$; no credit cards) decor and pretty table settings. Fresh fish is a highlight of the creative cuisine. The homemade smoked salmon and an unusual cream-of-Jerusalem-artichoke soup with crayfish are recommended. The proprietor is a great wine fan, and the extensive wine list reflects it. Smoking is permitted only in the restaurant. ⊠ *Grosse Mantelg. 24, D–69117* ☎ *06221/90000* 🖷 *06221/900–099* ⊕ *www.weisserbock.de* ⤳ *21 rooms, 2 suites* ⌂ *Restaurant, minibars, cable TV, bar, business services; no a/c, no smoking* ☰ *MC, V.*

$–$$ ✕▥ **Gasthaus Backmulde.** This traditional tavern in the heart of Heidelberg has a surprising range of items on its menu ($–$$), from delicately marinated fresh vegetables that accompany the excellent meat dishes to imaginative soups that add modern twists to ancient recipes (a Franconian potato broth, for instance, rich with garden herbs). Guest rooms are small but comfortable. ⊠ *Schiffg. 11, D–69117* ☎ *06221/53660* 🖷 *06221/*

536–660 ⊕ *www.gasthaus-backmulde.de* ⇆ *19 rooms, 12 with bath*
⌂ *Restaurant, cable TV, lobby lounge, Internet, some pets allowed (fee);
no a/c* ⊟ *AE, MC, V* ⊘ *Restaurant closed Sun. No lunch Mon.* ⊖ *BP.*

$ ✕▦ **Schnookeloch.** This lively old tavern ($–$$$) dates from 1703 and
is inextricably linked with Heidelberg's history and university. Young
and old alike crowd around the wooden tables in the wood-panel room,
and piano music adds to the din Thursday through Sunday nights. From
salads and pasta to hearty roasts and steaks, there's a broad selection
of food, including many fish dishes. Upstairs there are modern, pleas-
antly furnished guest rooms. ⊠ *Haspelg. 8, D–69117* ☎ *06221/138–
080* ⊕ *www.schnookeloch.de* 🖷 *06221/138–0813* ⇆ *11 rooms*
⌂ *Restaurant, refrigerators, cable TV, beer garden, some pets allowed;
no a/c* ⊟ *AE, MC, V* ⊖ *BP.*

$–$$ ▦ **Holländer Hof.** The pink-and-white-painted facade of this ornate
19th-century building opposite the Alte Brücke stands out in its row
fronting the Neckar River. Many of its rooms overlook the busy waterway and the forested hillside of the opposite shore. The rooms are
modern and pleasant, and the staff is very friendly. ⊠ *Neckarstaden 66,
D–69117* ☎ *06221/60500* 🖷 *06221/605–060* ⊕ *www.hollaender-hof.
de* ⇆ *38 rooms, 1 suite* ⌂ *In-room data ports, minibars, cable TV, dry
cleaning, laundry service, Internet, business services, some pets allowed
(fee), no-smoking floor; no a/c* ⊟ *AE, DC, MC, V.*

$ ▦ **Hotel Kohler.** It's a little bit of a walk to the city's Old Town but only
a couple of minutes by bus. Rooms are impeccably clean, well lighted,
and equipped with solid hardwood furniture and double-glazed windows.
The staff is very friendly and helpful. ⊠ *Goethestr. 2, D–69115* ☎ *06221/
970–097* 🖷 *06221/970–096* ⊕ *www.hotel-kohler.de* ⇆ *41 rooms*
⌂ *In-room data ports, cable TV, bicycles, no-smoking rooms; no a/c*
⊟ *MC, V* ⊘ *Closed mid-Dec.–mid-Jan.* ⊖ *BP.*

¢ ▦ **Jugendherberge Tiergartenstrasse.** For youth-hostel cardholders (cards
cost €20), these are clean, inexpensive accommodations near miniature
golf, a large pool, stables, and the zoo. Check on the curfew and get a
key if you plan to stay out late. To and from the Hauptbahnhof, take
Bus 33 (10-minute ride)—ask the reception desk for precise times. Reception is open 7:30 AM–9 AM and 1 PM–11:30 PM. ⊠ *Tiergartenstr. 5
D–69120* ☎ *06221/412–066 or 06221/651–190* 🖷 *06221/651–1928*
⊕ *www.djh.de* ⇆ *500 beds* ⌂ *Cafeteria, boccie, Ping-Pong, volleyball,
lounge, recreation room, laundry facilities, no-smoking rooms; no a/c,
no room phones, no room TVs* ⊟ *MC, V* ⊖ *BP.*

Nightlife & the Arts

Information on all upcoming events is given in the monthly *Heidelberg
aktuell,* free and available from the tourist office or on the Internet
(⊕ www.heidelberg-aktuell.de). Theater tickets may be purchased at **hei-
delbergTicket** (⊠ Theaterstr. 4 ☎ 06221/582–000).

THE ARTS Heidelberg has a thriving theater scene. The **Kulturzentrum Karlstor-
bahnhof** (⊠ Am Karlstor 1 ☎ 06221/978–911) is a 19th-century train
station reincarnated as a theater, cinema, and café. The **Theater der Stadt**
(⊠ Theaterstr. 8 ☎ 06221/583–520) is the best-known theater in town.
Avant-garde productions take place at the **Zimmertheater** (⊠ Hauptstr.

118 ☎ 06221/21069). Performances are held at the castle during the annual **Schlossfestspiele** (☎ 06221/582–000).

NIGHTLIFE Heidelberg nightlife is concentrated in the area around the Heiliggeistkirche (Church of the Holy Ghost), in the Old Town. Don't miss a visit to one of the old student taverns that have been in business for ages and have the atmosphere to prove it. Today's students, however, are more likely to hang out in one of the dozen or more bars on **Untere Strasse,** which runs parallel to and between Hauptstrasse and the Neckar River, starting from the market square. Begin at one end of the street and work your way down; you'll find bars that specialize in all sorts of tastes. The fanciest bars and yuppie cafés are along **Hauptstrasse.**

Mark Twain rubbed elbows with students at **Zum Roten Ochsen** (✉ Hauptstr. 217 ☎ 06221/20977). **Zum Sepp'l** (✉ Hauptstr. 213 ☎ 06221/23085) is another traditional, always-packed pub. **Schnookeloch** (✉ Haspelg. 8 ☎ 06221/138–080) has long been patronized by dueling frats.

Billy Blues (im Ziegler) (✉ Bergheimer Str. 1b ☎ 06221/25333) is a restaurant, bar, and disco, with live music Monday and Thursday. The hot sounds of salsa fill the cellar of the **Havana Club** (✉ Neckarstaden 24 ☎ 06221/389–3430) Friday and Saturday after 9 PM, with salsa classes 8–10 PM. The cover charge includes a drink voucher. **Nachtschicht** (Night Shift; ✉ Bergheimer Str. 147 ☎ 06221/438–550), in the Landfried factory, is a popular meeting point for drinks and disco Wednesday through Saturday after 10 PM.

Facing the main train station and futuristic equestrian statue is the chic, modern **print media lounge** (✉ Kurfürsten–Anlage 60 ☎ 06221/653–949), where you can dine inexpensively (breakfast, lunch, dinner, and late-night menu), dance, or simply enjoy delicious cocktails. It's open daily, with DJs Friday and Saturday after 10 PM and soul, funk, and jazz Sunday after 7 PM. Smoky, loud, and always crowded after 10 PM, the old beer hall **Reichsapfel/Lager** (✉ Untere Str. 35 ☎ 06221/485–542) has taken on a sleek, contemporary look after renovations. Seated, or standing around high tables, you can enjoy drinks and light fare, often with live music and/or DJs. Check out the reduced drink prices during the Lounge Hour (nightly, 7–9 PM) or Midnight Express (Friday and Saturday, midnight–1 AM).

The **Schwimmbad Musik Club** (✉ Tiergartenstr. 13, near zoo ☎ 06221/470–201) is a multicultural fixture of Heidelberg nightlife with its ambitious concert program (Nirvana used to play here), DJs, disco, videos, and movies. Theme evenings and parties round out the offerings. It's closed Sunday–Tuesday. For a terrific view of the town and castle, delicious drinks, and relaxing music, head for the glass-lined **Turm Lounge** (✉ Alte Glockengiesserei 9 ☎ 06221/653–949). Choose between trendy sofas and dark-red walls on the seventh floor or an atmosphere shaded in deep blue on the eighth floor. It's worth elbowing your way into **Vetters Alt-Heidelberger Brauhaus** (✉ Steing. 9 ☎ 06221/165–850) for the brewed-on-the-premises beer. There's also a branch in Neuenheim (across the river) with a butcher shop, where the homemade sausage is produced for both pubs.

Shopping

Heidelberg's **Hauptstrasse,** or Main Street, is a pedestrian zone lined with shops, sights, and restaurants that stretches more than 1 km (½ mi) through the heart of town. But don't spend your money before exploring the shops on such side streets as **Plöck, Ingrimstrasse,** and **Untere Strasse,** where there are candy stores, bookstores, and antiques shops on the ground floors of baroque buildings. If your budget allows, the city can be a good place to find reasonably priced German antiques, and the Neckar Valley region produces fine glass and crystal. Heidelberg has open-air **farmers' markets** on Wednesday and Saturday mornings on Marktplatz, and Tuesday and Friday mornings on Friedrich-Ebert-Platz. A *Flohmarkt* (**flea market**) takes place on Messplatz am Kirchheimer Weg several times each month. From the train station take Bus 41 or 42 toward Kirchheim.

In **Aurum & Argentum** (✉ Brückenstr. 22 ☎ 06221/473–453) you'll find a local gold- and silversmith with impeccable craftsmanship; the finely executed pieces start at €150. Its hours are Tuesday–Friday 2:30–6:30 and Saturday 10–2.

The old glass display cases at **Heidelberger Zuckerladen** (✉ Plöck 52 ☎ 06221/24365) are full of lollipops and "penny" candy. If you're looking for an unusual gift, the shop fashions colorful, unique items out of sugary ingredients such as marshmallow and sweetened gum. Drop in weekdays noon–7 and Saturday 11–3.

Buy your cutlery and tableware at **Unholtz** (✉ Hauptstr. 160 ☎ 06221/ 20964) and keep it for life—it's made by famous German manufacturers of some of the world's best knives.

Schwetzingen

⑱ *10 km (6 mi) west of Heidelberg.*

A rare pleasure awaits you if you're in Schwetzingen in April, May, or June: the town is Germany's asparagus center, and nearly every local restaurant has a *Spargelkarte* (a special menu featuring fresh asparagus dishes).

Schwetzingen is famous for its **Schloss,** a formal 18th-century palace constructed as a summer residence by the Palatinate electors. It's a noble, rose-color building, imposing and harmonious; a highlight is the rococo theater in one wing. The extensive park blends formal French and informal English styles, with neatly bordered gravel walks trailing off into the dark woodland. The 18th-century planners of this delightful oasis had fun adding such touches as an exotic mosque, complete with minarets and a shimmering pool (although they got a little confused and gave the building a very baroque portal), and the "classical ruin" that was de rigueur in this period. ☎ *06202/128–828* ⊕ *www.schloesser-und-gaerten.de* ✉ *Palace, including tour and gardens, Apr.–Oct. €6.50, Nov.–Mar. €5; gardens only, Apr.–Oct. €4, Nov.–Mar. €2.50* ☯ *Palace tours, on the hr, Apr.–Oct., Tues.–Fri. 11–4, weekends 11–5; Nov.–Mar., Fri. tour 2 PM, weekends at 11, 2, and 3. Gardens Apr.–Sept., daily 8–8; Nov.–Feb., daily 9–5; Mar. and Oct., daily 9–6.*

The Arts

The annual **Schwetzinger Festspiele,** from late April to early June, features operas and concerts by international artists in the ornate rococo theater of Schwetzingen Palace. The period rooms of the palace are also the venue for the **Mozartfest** (☎ 06202/945–875 tourist office) during the last half of September. The local tourist office has details on both performing-arts festivals.

THE BURGENSTRASSE (CASTLE ROAD)

Upstream from Heidelberg, the Neckar Valley narrows, presenting a landscape of orchards, vineyards, and wooded hills crowned with castles rising above the gently flowing stream. It's one of the most impressive stretches of the Burgenstrasse. The small valleys along the Neckar Valley road (B–37)—the locals call them *Klingen*—that cut north into the Odenwald are off-the-beaten-track territory. One of the most atmospheric is the Wolfsschlucht, which starts below the castle at Zwingenberg. The dank, shadowy little gorge inspired Carl Maria von Weber's opera *Der Freischütz* (The Marksman).

Hirschhorn

⑲ *23 km (14 mi) east of Heidelberg.*

Hirsch (stag) and *Horn* (antlers) make up the name of the Knights of Hirschhorn, the medieval ruling family that gave its name to both its 12th-century castle complex and the village it presided over. The town's coat of arms depicts a leaping stag. Ensconced into the hillside halfway between the castle and the river is a former Carmelite monastery and its beautiful 15th-century Gothic church with remarkable frescoes (open for visits). Hirschhorn's position on a hairpin loop of the Neckar can best be savored from the castle terrace, over a glass of wine, coffee and cake, or a fine meal.

The past comes to life the first weekend of September at the annual, two-day **Ritterfest,** a colorful "Knights' Festival" complete with a medieval arts-and-crafts market.

Where to Stay & Eat

★ **$–$$** ×🔲 **Schlosshotel auf der Burg Hirschhorn.** This very pleasant hotel and restaurant is set in historic Hirschhorn Castle, perched high over the medieval village and the Neckar. The terrace offers splendid views (ask for Table 30 in the corner). The rooms are modern and well furnished. Eight are in the castle and 17 in the old stables. *Wildschwein* (wild boar), *Hirsch* (venison), and fresh fish are the house specialties ($–$$$). The friendly proprietors, the Oberrauners, bake a delicious, warm Apfelstrudel based on a recipe from their home in Vienna. A good selection of wines is available. ✉ D–69434 Hirschhorn/Neckar ☎ 06272/92090 🖷 06272/3267 ⊕ www.castle-hotel.de ⌨ 21 rooms, 4 suites ⟁ Restaurant, café, in-room data ports, minibars, some pets allowed (fee); no a/c ▤ AE, MC, V ⊗ Hotel and restaurant closed Dec. 15–Jan. Restaurant closed Mon. Feb.–Easter and Nov.–mid-Dec. ⏐◎⏐ BP.

Eberbach

⑳ *11 km (7 mi) east of Hirschhorn.*

The Neckar makes a wide bend to the south here. The landscape around romantic Eberbach is punctuated by four square towers from the medieval town fortifications and three castle ruins. The meadows and beechwood forests here provide ideal growing conditions for a regional specialty, *Bärlauch* (wild garlic or ramson). During the "Bärlauch Days" from mid-March to mid-April, restaurants have special Bärlauch menus, and there are guided hikes to gather the greens and learn about their healthful benefits. Historic houses abound, and on **Alter Markt** (old market square) there's a particularly fine graffito facade to admire at the **Hotel Karpfen.** Stop by the **Naturpark-Informationszentrum** (Natural Park Information Center) for details about the extensive hiking trails through the Odenwald forest.

Where to Stay & Eat

$–$$ ✕ **Pleutersbacher Weinstube.** Jürgen and Martina Klier's cozy wine restaurant in Pleutersbach (on the south side of the Neckar, opposite Eberbach proper) is a favorite with locals. Amid exposed beams and rustic furnishings you can enjoy tasty regional fare, such as *Käs'Spätzle* (a cheesegratin version of these wonderful noodles), as well as daily specials and theme menus based on seasonal ingredients, such as matjes herring, kale, or Bärlauch. A good selection of by-the-glass, half bottles, and older-vintage German and international wines is served. ✉ *Eberbacherstr. 5* ☎ *06271/5705* ⊕ *www.pleutersbacher-weinstube.de* ⊟ *No credit cards* ☺ *Closed Mon. No lunch Mon.–Sat.*

$ ✕▥ **Hotel Karpfen.** Behind the beautiful painted facade of this traditional hotel and restaurant a warm welcome from the Rohrlapper and Jung families awaits you. The wooden furnishings and floors lend the rooms warmth and a rustic charm. The restaurant ($–$$$) has wallpapered walls and antique-rose accents, a nice setting for fresh *Forelle* (trout) from the streams of the Odenwald forest, rabbit and game, and regional specialties, including local wines. ✉ *Am Alten Markt 1, D–69412* ☎ *06271/71015* 🖷 *06271/71010* ⊕ *www.hotel-karpfen.com* ⇗ *47 rooms, 2 suites, 1 apartment* ⚕ *Restaurant, some in-room data ports, cable TV, some pets allowed (fee); no a/c* ⊟ *AE, MC, V* ☺ *Restaurant closed Tues. and 4 wks in Jan. and Feb.* ⱺ◎ *BP.*

en route Eight kilometers (5 mi) beyond Eberbach, a castle stands above the village of **Zwingenberg,** its medieval towers thrusting through the dark woodland. Some say it's the most romantic of all the castles along the Neckar (the one at Heidelberg excepted). The annual **Schlossfestspiele** (☎ 06271/71286 ⊕ www.schlossfestspiele-zwingenberg.de), with performances of *Der Freischutz,* takes place within its ancient walls in August. Park at the train station (15-minute walk to the castle, or take the shuttle bus departing from the station 30 minutes before the performance).

Mosbach

㉑ *25 km (16 mi) southeast of Eberbach.*

The little town of Mosbach is one of the most charming towns on the Neckar. Its ancient market square contains one of Germany's most exquisite half-timber buildings—the early 17th-century **Palm'sches Haus** (Palm House), its upper stories laced with intricate timbering. The **Rathaus,** built 50 years earlier, is a modest affair by comparison.

Where to Stay & Eat

★ $–$$$ ✕ **Zum Ochsen.** Chef Achim Münch and his vivacious American wife, Heyley, run this country inn in Nüstenbach, a suburb north of Mosbach. The decor is stylish—one room elegant, the other more rustic. The interesting display of antique silver is for sale. Fresh, seasonal cuisine and fish are always featured, as well as such creative dishes as baked fondue or venison in a pistachio crust. There's a good selection of wines at very fair prices. You can spend the night in the antique-filled cottage next door ($, sleeps four, no smoking). ✉ *Im Weiler 6* ☎ *06261/15428* 🖷 *06261/893–645* ⊕ *www.restaurant-zum-ochsen.de* 🖃 MC ☾ *Closed 2 wks in Feb. or Mar., 2 wks in Aug. or Sept., and Tues. No lunch Mon.–Sat.*

$ ✕🖫 **Zum Lamm.** The half-timber "Lamb" on Mosbach's main street is one of the town's prettiest houses. Its cozy rooms are individually furnished, with flowers filling the window boxes. The restaurant (ce–$$), complete with requisite exposed beams, serves local and international dishes, incorporating meat from the hotel's own butcher shop. ✉ *Hauptstr. 59, D–74821* ☎ *06261/89020* 🖷 *06261/890–291* 🛏 *50 rooms, 1 suite* ⌂ *Restaurant, some minibars, cable TV, lounge, laundry service, some pets allowed, no-smoking rooms; no a/c* 🖃 *AE, MC, V* ¶◎ *BP.*

Neckarzimmern

5 km (3 mi) south of Mosbach.

★ ㉒ The massive, circular bulk of **Burg Hornberg** rises above the woods that drop to the riverbank and the town of Neckarzimmern. The road to the castle leads through vineyards that have been providing dry white wines for centuries. Today the castle is part hotel-restaurant and part museum. In the 16th century it was home to the larger-than-life knight Götz von Berlichingen (1480–1562). When he lost his right arm fighting in a petty dynastic squabble, he had a blacksmith fashion an iron replacement for him. The original designs for this fearsome artificial limb are on view in the castle, as is a suit of armor that belonged to him. Scenes from his life are also represented. For most Germans, the rambunctious knight is best remembered for a remark he delivered to the Palatinate elector that was faithfully reproduced in Goethe's play *Götz von Berlichingen.* Responding to a reprimand, von Berlichingen told the elector, more or less, to "kiss my ass" (the original German is substantially more earthy). To this day the polite version of this insult is known as a *Götz von Berlichingen.* Inquire at the hotel reception for details about visiting the castle ruins. 🖾 €3.

Where to Stay & Eat

★ **$$** ✕⊞ **Burg Hornberg.** Your host is the present baron of the castle. From the heights of the terrace and glassed-in restaurant ($–$$$)—housed in the former *Marstall,* or royal stables—there are stunning views. Fresh fish and game are specialties, as are the estate-bottled wines. There are good Riesling wines and the rarities Traminer and Muskateller—also sold in the wine shops in the courtyard and at the foot of the hill. The hotel's rooms are comfortable and modern in style. ⊠ *D–74865* ☎ *06261/92460* ⊟ *06261/924–644* ⊕ *www.castle-hotel-hornberg.com* 🛏 *22 rooms, 2 suites* ⋔ *Restaurant, some minibars, cable TV, wine shop, some pets allowed (fee), no-smoking rooms; no a/c* ⊟ *MC, V* ⊘ *Closed late Dec.–late Jan.* ⦿⦿ *BP.*

Shopping

The factory **Franz Kaspar** (⊠ Hauptstr. 11, in the courtyard ☎ 06261/ 92400 for tour reservations), known for its fine crystal, gives free tours (weekdays 9–4, Saturday 10–6, Sunday 10:30–6) that demonstrate the manufacturing process. Its outlet shop is open daily.

At the hand of master pastry chef and chocolatier Eberhard Schell of **Café Schell,** an unlikely duo—*essig* (vinegar), made from Spätlese and Auslese wines, and chocolate—is handcrafted into a scrumptious, not-too-sweet delicacy known as *Essig Schleckerle.* The unusual *Pralinen* (chocolates) filled with wine vinegar were the first chocolates to be patented and listed in the *Guinness Book of Records.* Since their debut in 1995, innovative Schell has created a range of exquisite chocolates filled with wine and wine-based products from several of Germany's leading wine estates. ⊠ *Schloss-Str. 31, D–74831 Gundelsheim* ☎ *06269/ 350* ⊕ *www.weinpralinen.de* ⊘ *Closed Mon. afternoon and Tues.*

en route One of the best preserved of the Neckar castles is the 15th-century **Burg Guttenberg.** Within its stout stone walls are a museum and a restaurant (closed January, February, and Monday) with views of the river valley. The castle is also home to Europe's leading center for the study and protection of birds of prey, and some are released on demonstration flights (€8) from the castle walls from April through October, daily at 11 and 3, and in March and November, daily at 3. ⊠ *Neckarmühlbach, 6 km (4 mi) west of Gundelsheim* ☎ *06266/ 388* ⊕ *www.burg-guttenberg.de* ⛫ *Castle €4, castle and flight demonstration €11* ⊘ *Apr.–Oct., daily 10–6.*

Bad Wimpfen

㉓ *8 km (5 mi) south of Neckarzimmern.*

Fodor'sChoice
★ At the confluence of the Neckar and Jagst rivers, Bad Wimpfen is one of the most stunning towns of the Neckar Valley. The Romans built a fortress and a bridge here, on the riverbank site of an ancient Celtic settlement, in the 1st century AD. Wimpfen im Tal (Wimpfen in the Valley), the oldest part of town, is home to the Benedictine monastery Gruessau and its church, **Ritterstiftskirche St. Peter** (⊠ Lindenpl.), which

dates from the 10th and 13th centuries. The cloisters are delightful, an example of German Gothic at its most uncluttered.

On the hilltop, Wimpfen am Berg, the Staufen emperor Barbarossa built his largest **Pfalz** (residence) in 1182. The town not only thrived thereafter but also enjoyed the status of a Free Imperial City from 1300 to 1803. Since then, its fortune has been tied to the local saltworks that enabled it to develop medicinal saline baths and its reputation as a spa—hence the town was renamed Bad Wimpfen in 1930.

A walking tour marked by signs bearing the town arms begins at the Rathaus on the market square, adjacent to the Burgviertel (palace quarter) and the buildings of the former imperial residence. These are nestled along the town wall between the turreted **Blauer Turm** (Blue Tower) and the massive stone **Roter Turm** (Red Tower), the western and eastern strongholds of the palace, respectively. Ascend either for a grand view. The **Steinhaus**, Germany's largest Romanesque living quarters and once the imperial apartments reserved for women, is now a history museum (closed Monday). Next to the Steinhaus are the remains of the northern facade of the palace, an arcade of superbly carved Romanesque pillars that flanked the imperial hall in its heyday. The imperial chapel, next to the Red Tower, holds a collection of ecclesiastical artworks (closed Monday). Other historical houses in the quarter are on Schwibbogengasse (Nos. 5 and 16). ⊠ *Kaiserpl.* ☎ *07063/97200* ☯ *Palace tours daily by advance reservation.*

Among Bad Wimpfen's finest 15- and 16th-century half-timber houses are those on Badgasse (Nos. 8 and 10), Hauptstrasse (Nos. 69 and 83), and Klostergasse (Nos. 4, 6, 8, and 9). The 13th-century stained glass, wall paintings, medieval altars, and the stone pietà in the Gothic **Stadtkirche** (city church) are worth seeing, as are the Crucifixion sculptures (1515) by the Rhenish master Hans Backoffen on Kirchplatz, behind the church.

In late August the Old Town's medieval past comes alive during the **Zunftmarkt,** a historical market dedicated to the *Zünfte* (guilds). "Artisans" in period costumes demonstrate the old trades and open the festivities with a colorful parade on horseback.

☺ In Germany, pigs are a symbol of good luck. At the **Schweine-Museum** (Pig Museum), you'll see them in every form imaginable—depicted on posters and porcelain, modeled into household items, and as toys, including Porky Pig. In all, it's a mixture of historically valuable items and kitsch. ⊠ *Kronengässchen 2* ☎ *07063/6689* ⊕ *www.schweinemuseum. de* ☯ *€2.60* ☯ *Daily 10–5.*

Where to Stay & Eat

$–$$ ✕ **Tafelhaus Perkeo.** The interior and decor of this lovingly restored historical house are warm and inviting. Alfresco dining is also possible. Beate Stiefel oversees service, and Heiko Habelt is in the kitchen, preparing well-made regional dishes, seasonal cuisine (the menu changes frequently), and fresh fish. The ambience, food, and wine offered here set this restaurant well apart from the town's many group-oriented eateries. ⊠ *Hauptstr. 82* ☎ *07063/932–354* ▭ *MC, V* ☯ *Closed Wed.*

★ **$–$$** ✕🏨 **Hotel Schloss Heinsheim.** This baroque castle is in a beautiful park. The rooms are individually furnished—some with antiques, others more rustic in style. You can dine on the terrace or in the country manor–like restaurant ($–$$$$). Start with a Swabian *Hochzeitssuppe* (wedding soup), followed by breast of duck with pink peppercorns or Dover sole in champagne sauce. Most wines on the list are French or German. ✉ *Gundelsheimer Str. 36, D–74906 Bad Rappenau–Heinsheim* 🕿 *07264/ 95030* 🖷 *07264/4208* ⊕ *www.schloss-heinsheim.de* 🛏 *40 rooms, 1 suite* ⟁ *Restaurant, some in-room data ports, minibars, cable TV, 18-hole golf course, pool, bicycles, bar, lobby lounge, babysitting, laundry service, business services, some pets allowed (fee); no a/c* ▤ *AE, DC, MC, V* ⊗ *Closed Jan. Restaurant also closed Mon. and Tues.* ⥁⃝ *BP.*

$ ✕🏨 **Hotel Sonne und Weinstube Feyerabend.** Just before Christmas 2003, the Schachtsiek family's hotel–restaurant in the center of town burned down. Their second house (in a medieval half-timber building) and traditional café–Weinstube Feyerabend (¢; no credit cards) are still in operation and worth a stay or visit. ✉ *Langg. 3, D–74206* 🕿 *07063/245* 🖷 *07063/6591* ⊕ *www.sonne-wimpfen.de* 🛏 *10 rooms* ⟁ *Café, some in-room data ports, cable TV, Weinstube, some pets allowed (fee); no a/c* ▤ *MC, V* ⊗ *Closed late Dec.–mid-Jan. Café and Weinstube closed Mon.* ⥁⃝ *BP.*

$ 🏨 **Hotel Neckarblick.** The Sailer family extends the warmest of welcomes to its guests. There's a peaceful terrace, where you can sit and contemplate the Neckar River. Many rooms have a view and flower boxes in the windows. The furniture is comfortable and modern, like the hotel building. For medieval atmosphere, the heart of Bad Wimpfen is only a few blocks away. Although there is no restaurant, the Sailers serve platters of cold cuts and cheese upon request and offer free shuttle service to and from the train station. ✉ *Erich-Sailer-Str. 48, D–74206* 🕿 *07063/ 961–620* 🖷 *07063/8548* ⊕ *www.neckarblick.de* 🛏 *14 rooms* ⟁ *Minibars, cable TV, bicycles, lounge, dry cleaning, laundry service, some pets allowed (fee), no-smoking rooms; no a/c* ▤ *AE, MC, V* ⥁⃝ *BP.*

Neckarsulm

㉔ *10 km (6 mi) south of Bad Wimpfen.*

Motorbike fans won't want to miss the town of Neckarsulm. It's a busy industrial center, home of the German automobile manufacturer Audi and the **Deutsches Zweirad–Museum** (German Motorcycle Museum). It's close to the factory where motorbikes were first manufactured in Germany. Among its 300 exhibits are the world's first mass-produced motorcycles (the Hildebrand and Wolfmüller); a number of famous racing machines; and a rare Daimler machine, the first made by that legendary name. The museum also has an exhibit of early bicycles, dating from 1816, as well as early automobiles. All are arranged over five floors in a handsome 400-year-old castle that belonged to the Teutonic Knights until 1806. ✉ *Urbanstr. 11* 🕿 *07132/35271* ⊕ *www.zweirad-museum. de* 🎫 *€4* ⊗ *Tues., Wed., and Fri.–Sun. 9–5, Thurs. 9–7.*

SWABIAN CITIES

Heilbronn, Stuttgart, and Tübingen are all part of the ancient province of Swabia, a region strongly influenced by Protestantism and Calvinism. The inhabitants speak the Swabian dialect of German. Heilbronn lies on both sides of the Neckar. Stuttgart, the capital of the state of Baden-Würtemberg and one of Germany's leading industrial cities, is surrounded by hills on three sides, with the fourth side opening up toward its river harbor. The medieval town of Tübingen clings to steep slopes and hilltops above the Neckar.

Heilbronn

㉕ *6 km (4 mi) south of Neckarsulm, 50 km (31 mi) north of Stuttgart.*

Most of the leading sights in Heilbronn are grouped in and around the Marktplatz. The sturdy **Rathaus,** built in the Gothic style in 1417 and remodeled during the Renaissance, dominates the square. Set into the Rathaus's clean-lined facade and beneath the steep red roof is a magnificently ornate 16th-century **clock.** It's divided into four distinct parts. The lowest is an astronomical clock, showing the day of the week, the month, and the year. Above it is the main clock—note how its hour hand is larger than the minute hand, a convention common in the 16th century. Above this there's a smaller dial that shows the phases of the sun and the moon. The final clock is a bell at the topmost level. Suspended from a delicate stone surround, it's struck alternately by the two angels on either side. The entire elaborate mechanism swings into action at noon. As the hour strikes, an angel at the base of the clock sounds a trumpet; another turns an hourglass and counts the hours with a scepter. Simultaneously, the twin golden rams between them charge each other and lock horns while a cockerel spreads its wings and crows. Behind the market square is the **Kilianskirche** (Church of St. Kilian), Heilbronn's most famous church, dedicated to the Irish monk who brought Christianity to the Rhineland in the Dark Ages and who lies buried in Würzburg. Its lofty Gothic tower was capped in the early 16th century with a fussy, lanternlike structure that ranks as the first major Renaissance work north of the Alps. At its summit there's a soldier carrying a banner decorated with the city arms. Walk around the church to the south side (the side opposite the main entrance) to see the well that gave the city its name.

Where to Stay & Eat

$–$$ ✕ **Ratskeller.** Both the handsome table settings in the vaulted cellar and the seats on the spacious terrace in front of the town hall are pleasant settings for the Mosthaf brothers' tasty food, excellent wines, and cheerful service. Try the braised rabbit in mustard sauce or a salmon trout fillet in a whipped lemon sauce. The *Tagessessen* (daily special) is a good value. ✉ *Marktpl. 7* ☎ *07131/84628* ▭ *AE* ☉ *Closed Sun.*

$ ✕ **Vinum.** Whether you want coffee and a croissant, fresh tapas, or a beefsteak with onions, it's all available here from 10 AM 'til midnight, six days of the week. As the name implies, Vinum is also a wine bar—with 140 German and international wines to choose from. ✉ *Marktplatz 1* ☎ *07131/642–7220* ▭ *AE* ☉ *Closed Sun.*

¢–$ ✕ **Restaurant-Café Am Stadtgarten Harmonie.** Eat on the terrace in summer to enjoy the view of the city park. Inside, the decor is traditional with a modern twist, as is the menu. Traditional German dishes and Swabian specialties, such as Rostbraten and *sauere Kutteln* (tripe), are served, and there are two inexpensive specials (€5 and €7) daily. ⊠ *Allee 28* ☎ *07131/87954* ▤ *AE, DC, MC, V* ☺ *Closed Tues. and Aug. No dinner Sun.*

$$ ✕▥ **Hotel und Gutsgaststätte Rappenhof.** This cheerful country inn is on a hill in the midst of the vineyards of Weinsberg (6 km [4 mi] northeast of Heilbronn). You can take in the fresh air and panoramic views from the terrace or on a scenic walk along the signposted Wine Panorama Path. The restaurant ($–$$) features hearty country cooking, such as sauerbraten with *Semmelknödel* (bread dumplings), and regional wines. ⊠ *D–74189 Weinsberg* ☎ *07134/5190* ᐟ *07134/51955* ⊕ *www. rappenhof.de* ➪ *39 rooms* ⚲ *Restaurant, some in-room data ports, minibars, cable TV, bicycles, lobby lounge, some pets allowed (fee), no-smoking rooms; no a/c* ▤ *MC, V* ☺ *Closed mid-Dec.–mid-Jan.* ⅊ *BP.*

$$ ✕▥ **Insel-Hotel.** *Insel* means "island," and that's where the luxurious Insel-Hotel is—on a river island tethered to the city by the busy Friedrich Ebert Bridge. The Mayer family combines a personal touch with polished service and facilities, including 24-hour beverage room service. Enjoy alfresco dining in summer, when chefs fire up the charcoal grill on the Mediterranean-like terrace of the Schwäbisches Restaurant ($$–$$$$). The roof garden affords great views. ⊠ *Friedrich-Ebert-Brücke, D–74072* ☎ *07131/6300* ᐟ *07131/626–060* ⊕ *www.insel-hotel.de* ➪ *122 rooms, 5 suites, 1 apartment* ⚲ *Restaurant, some in-room data ports, cable TV, pool, gym, massage, sauna, bar, business services, free parking, some pets allowed, no-smoking rooms; no a/c* ▤ *AE, DC, MC, V* ⅊ *BP.*

★ $$ ✕▥ **Schlosshotel Liebenstein.** Nestled in the hills above the village of Neckarwestheim, south of Heilbronn, is one of the area's most beautiful castles, Schloss Liebenstein. Within the 3-foot-thick, whitewashed castle walls, the peaceful hush of centuries reigns over a setting of comfort and noble elegance. Guest rooms have views of forests, vineyards, and a golf course. The restaurant Lazuli ($$$$) has gourmet cuisine (three- to seven-course menus only); Kurfürst ($–$$) serves regional fare; and light meals are available in the beer garden. ⊠ *Schloss Liebenstein, D–74382 Neckarwestheim* ☎ *07133/98990* ᐟ *07133/6045* ⊕ *www. liebenstein.com* ➪ *22 rooms, 2 suites* ⚲ *3 restaurants, cable TV, 2 golf courses, bicycles, bar, beer garden, lounge, wine shop, dry cleaning, babysitting, laundry service, business services, some pets allowed, no-smoking rooms; no a/c* ▤ *AE, MC, V* ☺ *Hotel and restaurants closed late Dec.–early Jan. No lunch at Lazuli; no lunch weekdays at Kurfürst.* ⅊ *BP.*

Nightlife & the Arts

The Konzert- und Kongresszentrum Harmonie, Theaterschiff, and Stadttheater are the major (but not the only) venues for theater, dance, opera, musicals, and concerts. The city has two resident orchestras: **Württemberg Chamber Orchestra** and **Heilbronn Symphony Orchestra.** The **Heilbronn tourist office** (☎ 07131/562–270) distributes a bi-monthly *Veranstaltungskalender* (calendar of events) and also sells tickets to cultural events.

Shopping

The city's internationally renowned **Weindorf** wine festival, in mid-September, showcases nearly 300 wines and sparkling wines from the Heilbronn region alone. Most of the year you'll find numerous shops stocking wine along Heilbronn's central pedestrian shopping zone, and you can also sample and purchase directly from private wine estates or a *Weingärtner genossenschaft* (vintners' cooperative winery). One of Württemberg's finest producers, the **Staatsweingut Weinsberg** (State Wine Domain; ⊠ Traubenpl. 5, Weinsberg ☎ 07134/504–167), has an architecturally striking wine shop with 70 wines and 30 other products of the grape on offer. It's open weekdays 9–5.

en route

Ludwigsburg, a scant 15 km (9 mi) north of Stuttgart, merits a stop to visit Germany's largest baroque palace, **Residenzschloss Ludwigsburg.** It celebrated its 300th anniversary in 2004, after 15 years of renovation at a cost of 92 million euros.

The "Versailles of Swabia" is surrounded by the fragrant, colorful 74-acre park **Blühendes Barock** (Blooming Baroque; ☞ €7 ⊕ www.blueba.de ☉ Mid-Mar.–Oct., daily 7:30 AM–8:30 PM; winter hrs shorter), replete with splendid gardens, fountains, aviaries, a Märchengarten (fairy-tale garden), and a "water playground" that delights visitors of all ages. The palace is also home to the **Porzellan-Manufaktur Ludwigsburg** (☉ Store weekdays 9:30–12:30 and 1:30–5:30, Sat. 10–1 ⊕ www.ludwigsburger-porzellan.de), where a film, shown daily, presents the artists who hand-paint the manufactory's exquisite porcelain. A five-minute walk north of the palace (across Marbacher Strasse) brings you to the **Jagdschloss Favorite,** a "small" summer residence and hunting lodge of the dukes of Württemberg.

Additional highlights are the annual **Schlossfestspiele,** with concerts, theater, opera, dance, and exhibitions in the palace and the surrounding park (June–mid-September) and the three new museums that opened in the palace in 2004: the **Barockgalerie,** a collection of German and Italian baroque paintings from the 17th and 18th centuries; the **Keramikmuseum,** a collection of historical treasures from the porcelain manufactories in Meissen, Nymphenburg, Berlin, Vienna, and Ludwigsburg, supplemented by a section devoted to contemporary ceramics; and the **Modemuseum,** showcasing three centuries of fashion, particularly royal clothing of the 18th century. ⊠ *Schloss Str. 30, Ludwigsburg* ☎ *07141/182–004 for information* ⊕ *www.schloesser-und-gaerten.de* ☞ *Residenzschloss €5; Favorite €2.50; museums only €5; Barocke Erlebniskarte (park, 2 palaces, 3 museums) €13* ☉ *Palaces and museums daily 10–5.*

Stuttgart

㉖ *50 km (31 mi) south on B–27 from Heilbronn.*

Stuttgart is a place of fairly extreme contradictions. It has been called, among other things, "Germany's biggest small town" and "the city where work is a pleasure." For centuries Stuttgart, whose name derives from *Stutengarten*, or "stud farm," remained a pastoral backwater along the Neckar. Then the Industrial Revolution propelled the city into the machine age, after which it was leveled in World War II. Since then Stuttgart has regained its position as one of Germany's top industrial centers.

Here, *Schaffen*—"doing, achieving"—is an inherent feature of the modus operandi. This is Germany's can-do city, whose natives have turned out Mercedes-Benz and Porsche cars, Bosch electrical equipment, and a host of other products exported worldwide. Yet Stuttgart is also a city of culture and the arts, with world-class museums, opera, and a ballet company. Moreover, it's the domain of fine local wines; the vineyards actually approach the city center in a rim of green hills. Forests, vineyards, meadows, and orchards compose more than half the city, which is enclosed on three sides by woods.

An ideal introduction to the contrasts of Stuttgart is a guided city bus tour. Included is a visit to the needle-nose TV tower, high on a mountaintop above the city, affording stupendous views. Built in 1956, it was the first of its kind in the world. The tourist office also offers superb walking tours. On your own, the best place to begin exploring Stuttgart is the Hauptbahnhof (main train station, opposite the tourist office); from there walk down the pedestrian street Königstrasse to Schillerplatz, a small, charming square named after the 18th-century poet and playwright Friedrich Schiller, who was born in nearby Marbach. It's surrounded by historic buildings, many of them rebuilt after the war.

Just off Schillerplatz, the **Stiftskirche** (Collegiate Church of the Holy Cross; ⊠ Stiftstr. 12, Mitte) is Stuttgart's most familiar sight, with its two oddly matched towers. Built in the 12th century and then substantially rebuilt in a late-Gothic style (1433–1531), the church became Protestant in 1534. It was reconsecrated in 1958 after being badly damaged in a 1944 bombing raid. The choir has a famous series of Renaissance figures of the counts of Württemberg sculpted by Simon Schlör (1576–1608).

Schlossplatz (Palace Square) is a huge area enclosed by royal palaces, with elegant arcades branching off to other stately plazas. The magnificent baroque **Neues Schloss** (New Castle), now occupied by Baden-Württemberg state government offices, dominates the square. The **Kunstgebäude** (House of Art), the building with a golden stag on its cupola, houses the **Württembergischer Kunstverein** (Württemberg Art Society) and has changing shows of contemporary German artists' works. ⊠ *Schlosspl., Mitte* ☎ *0711/216–2188* ⊡ *Free* ☉ *Tues.–Sun. 11–6, Wed. 11–8* ☞ *At this writing, admission fees and hrs were unavailable; please call ahead for information.*

Kunstmuseum Stuttgart (Stuttgart Art Museum). In autumn 2004 the collection of the former Galerie der Stadt Stuttgart (Stuttgart City Art Gallery) was renamed and moved across the square from the Kunstgebäude to its new home—a sleek structure encased in a glass facade and a work of art in its own right. It features artwork of the 19th and 20th centuries and the world's largest Otto Dix collection (including the *Grossstadt* [*Metropolis*] triptych, which distills the essence of 1920s Germany on canvas). The bistro-café on the rooftop terrace affords great views; the foyer houses a café and the museum shop. ✉ *Kleiner Schlosspl.* ☞ *At this writing, contact details and admission prices were unavailable; please contact tourist office for up-to-date information* ☉ *Tues.–Sun. 10–6; Thurs. 10–9.*

The **Schlossgarten** (Palace Garden) borders the Schlossplatz and extends northeast across Schillerstrasse all the way to Bad Cannstatt on the Neckar River. The park is graced by an exhibition hall, planetarium, lakes, sculptures, and the hot spring–mineral baths Leuze and Berg.

Adjacent to the Schlossgarten is Rosenstein Park, with the city's two natural history museums and the **Wilhelma** zoological and botanical gardens. From here it's but a brief walk along the riverbank to the pier for Neckar-Käpt'n boat trips on the Neckar. ✉ *Neckartalstr., Wilhelma* ☎ *0711/54020* ⊕ *www.wilhelma.de* 🖼 *€9.40; Nov.–Feb. and in summer after 4 PM €6.40* ☉ *May–Aug., daily 8:15–6; Sept.–Apr., daily 8:15–4. Greenhouses and animal halls open 30 min and 45 min longer, respectively, than box office.*

Across the street from the Neues Schloss stands the **Altes Schloss** (Old Castle). This former residence of the counts and dukes of Württemberg was originally built as a moated castle around 1320. Wings were added in the mid-15th century, creating a Renaissance palace. The palace now houses the **Württembergisches Landesmuseum** (Württemberg State Museum), with imaginative exhibits tracing the development of the area from the Stone Age to modern times. The displays of medieval life are especially noteworthy. International design and applied arts during the 20th century are shown in the *Ritterhalle* (knights' hall). ✉ *Schillerpl. 6, Mitte* ☎ *0711/279–3400* 🖼 *€2.60* ☉ *Tues. 10–1, Wed.–Sun. 10–5.*

FodorsChoice ★ The **Staatsgalerie** (State Gallery) possesses one of the finest art collections in Germany. The old part of the complex, dating from 1843, has paintings from the Middle Ages through the 19th century, including works by Cranach, Holbein, Hals, Memling, Rubens, Rembrandt, Cézanne, Courbet, and Manet. Connected to the original building is the **Neue Staatsgalerie** (New State Gallery), designed by British architect James Stirling in 1984 as a melding of classical and modern, sometimes jarring, elements (such as chartreuse window mullions). Considered one of the most successful postmodern buildings, it houses works by such 20th-century artists as Braque, Chagall, de Chirico, Dalí, Kandinsky, Klee, Mondrian, and Picasso. ✉ *Konrad-Adenauer-Str. 30–32, Mitte* ☎ *0711/470–400* ⊕ *www.staatsgalerie.de* 🖼 *€4.50, free Wed.* ☉ *Tues., Wed., and Fri.–Sun. 10–6, Thurs. 10–9, 1st Sat. of month 10 AM–midnight.*

In late 2002, Stuttgart's "cultural mile" was enriched with yet another postmodern architectural masterpiece by James Stirling, the **Haus der Geschichte Baden-Württemberg** (Museum of the History of Baden-Württemberg). It chronicles the state's history during the 19th and 20th centuries. Theme parks and multimedia presentations enable you to interact with the thousands of fascinating objects on display. ✉ *Konrad-Adenauer-Str. 16, Mitte* ☎ *0711/212–3989* ⊕ *www.hdgbw.de* 🖼 *€3* ☉ *Tues., Wed., and Fri.–Sun. 10–6, Thurs. 10–9.*

An extraordinary urban planning project under way is "Stuttgart 21." An area comprising about 250 acres—now covered with train tracks north of the main station—is being converted into a new neighborhood, and the tracks are being moved underground. The **Bahnhofsturm** (train station tower), crowned by the Mercedes star, has an information center with three floors of exhibitions on the project as well as a great viewing platform. ⊠ *Arnulf-Klett-Pl., Mitte* ☎ *0711/2092–2920* 🎟 *Free* ⊙ *Tues.–Sun. 10–6, Thurs. 10–9.*

off the beaten path

GOTTLIEB-DAIMLER-GEDÄCHTNISSTÄTTE (Gottlieb Daimler Memorial Workshop) – The first successful internal combustion engine was perfected here in 1883, and you can see the tools, blueprints, and models of early cars that helped pave the way for the Mercedes line. ⊠ *Taubenheimstr. 13, Stuttgart-Bad Cannstatt* ☎ *0711/569–399* 🎟 *Free* ⊙ *Tues.–Sun. 10–4.*

MERCEDES-BENZ MUSEUM – The oldest car factory in the world shows off a collection of about 100 historic racing and luxury cars. Follow signs to the soccer stadium. New quarters are being built and scheduled to open in spring 2006. ⊠ *Mercedesstr. 137, Stuttgart-Untertürkheim* ☎ *0711/172–2578* 🎟 *Free* ⊙ *Tues.–Sun. 9–5.*

PORSCHE MUSEUM – This Porsche factory in the northern suburb of Zuffenhausen has a small but significant collection of legendary Porsche racing cars. ⊠ *Porschepl. 1, Stuttgart-Zuffenhausen* ☎ *0711/911–5685* 🎟 *Free* ⊙ *Weekdays 9–4, weekends 9–5.*

WEISSENHOFSIEDLUNG – The Weissenhof Colony was a minicity created for a 1927 exhibition of the "New Home." Sixteen leading architects from five countries—among them Mies van der Rohe, Le Corbusier, and Walter Gropius—created residences that offered optimal living conditions at affordable prices. The still-functioning colony is on a hillside overlooking Friedrich-Ebert-Strasse. To get there from the city center, take Bus 43 toward Killesberg/Messe to the Kunstakadamie stop or subway U7 to the Messe. The i-Punkt Weissenhof issues a brochure indicating which architects designed the various homes and is the meeting point for guided tours (Saturday 11 AM). ⊠ *Am Weissenhof 20, Stuttgart-Killesberg* ☎ *0711/854–641 or 0711/257–9187.*

Where to Stay & Eat

★ **$$$$** ✕ **Wielandshöhe.** One of Germany's top chefs, Vincent Klink, and his wife, Elisabeth, are very down-to-earth, cordial hosts. Her floral arrangements add a baroque touch to the otherwise quiet decor, but your vision—and palate—will ultimately focus on the artfully presented cuisine. To the extent possible, all products are sourced locally or are homemade. House specialties, such as saddle of lamb with a potato terrine and ratatouille or the gratinated Breton lobster with basil potato salad, are recommended. The wine list is exemplary. ⊠ *Alte Weinsteige 71, Degerloch* ☎ *0711/640–8848* ⊕ *www.wielandshoehe.com* 🍴 *Reservations essential* ⊟ *AE, DC, MC, V* ⊙ *Closed Sun. and Mon.*

★ **$$$$** ✕🖃 **Am Schlossgarten.** Stuttgart's top accommodation is a modern structure set in spacious gardens, a stone's throw from sights, shops, and the train station. Pretty floral prints and plush chairs add a homey feeling to the elegant rooms. Luxurious baths and business amenities add to the overall comfort. In addition to receiving first-class service, you can wine and dine in the French restaurant Zirbelstube ($$$$); the less-expensive Schlossgarten restaurant ($$–$$$$); the bistro Vinothek ($$); or the café (¢) overlooking the garden. ✉ *Schillerstr. 23, Mitte, D–70173* ☎ *0711/20260* 🖷 *0711/202–6888* ⊕ *www.hotelschlossgarten.com* ⇨ *106 rooms, 10 suites ♨ 3 restaurants, café, in-room data ports, minibars, cable TV, bicycles, bar, lobby lounge, wineshop, babysitting, dry cleaning, laundry service, concierge, business services, some pets allowed (fee), no-smoking rooms* ▤ *AE, DC, MC, V ☺ Zirbelstube closed 4 wks Aug. and Sept., Sun. and Mon. Schlossgarten closed Fri. and Sat. Vinothek closed Sun. and Mon.*

★ **$$–$$$$** ✕🖃 **Der Zauberlehrling.** The "Sorcerer's Apprentice" is aptly named. In addition to their popular restaurant, Z-Bistro ($$$–$$$$; no credit cards)—with magical entertainment on *Tischzauberei* evenings (*Tisch* means "table"; *Zauberei* means "magic")—Karen and Axel Heldmann have conjured up a small luxury hotel. Each room's decor is based on a theme (Asian, Mediterranean, Country Manor), and four have a private whirlpool. Innovative dishes, a three-course menu of organic products, and regional favorites are all part of the culinary lineup, enhanced by a very good wine list. Enjoy the terrace in summer and end the evening with cigars and single malts. ✉ *Rosenstr. 38, Bohnenviertel, D–70182* ☎ *0711/237–7770* 🖷 *0711/237–7775* ⊕ *www.zauberlehrling. de* ⇨ *9 rooms ♨ Restaurant, fans, in-room data ports, minibars, cable TV, lobby lounge, dry cleaning, laundry service, business services, no-smoking rooms; no a/c* ▤ *AE, MC, V ☺ No lunch weekends* ⏐◎⏐ *BP.*

★ **$–$$** ✕🖃 **Alter Fritz.** Katrin Fritsche describes her small country mansion as a "hotel for individualists." With only 10 rooms, she is able to cater to guests with a personal touch. The picturesque house with its steep eaves and shuttered windows, high up on the wooded Killesberg Hill, is ideally located for visitors attending trade fairs and is a 15-minute bus ride from the main railway station. **Der kleine Fritz** serves good food at reasonable prices ($–$$$). House guests can opt to dine in the pretty breakfast room and select from a smaller menu ($). ✉ *Feuerbacher Weg 101, Killesberg, D–70192* ☎ *0711/135–650* 🖷 *0711/135–6565* ⊕ *www. alter-fritz-am-killesberg.de* ⇨ *10 rooms ♨ Restaurant, some in-room data ports, minibars, free parking; no a/c* ▤ *No credit cards ☺ Closed 2 wks in Aug. and 2 wks in Dec. Restaurant closed Mon. No lunch* ⏐◎⏐ *BP.*

$–$$ 🖃 **Hotel Mercure Stuttgart Airport.** This hotel has a light and airy design, with large windows throughout the spacious lobby, restaurant, public rooms, and comfortable bedrooms. Everything is decorated in tasteful, pastel colors. Shuttle service is available to the airport (3 km [2 mi]), and downtown Stuttgart (11 km [7 mi]) can be reached by public transportation or by car in less than a half hour. It's a three-minute drive to the shops, casino, and musical productions at the SI-Erlebnis-Centrum. ✉ *Eichwiesenring 1, Fasanenhof, D–70567* ☎ *0711/72660* 🖷 *0711/ 726–6444* ⊕ *www.mercure.de* ⇨ *148 rooms ♨ 2 restaurants, in-room data ports, minibars, cable TV, fitness room, sauna, bicycles, bar, dry* *cleaning, laundry service, airport shuttle, free parking, some pets allowed (fee), no-smoking rooms* ⊟ *AE, DC, MC, V* ⊺◉⫶ *BP.*

Nightlife & the Arts

The **i-Punkt tourist office** (⊠ Königstr. 1A, Mitte ☏ 0711/222–8243) keeps a current calendar of events and sells tickets via phone weekdays 9–8 and Saturday 9–4; or in the office weekdays 9–8, Saturday 9–6, and Sunday 11–6 (May–October) or 1–6 (November–April). It can also supply information about two cultural highlights in 2005: *Imperum Romanum* (October–Jan. 8, 2006), an exhibition in the State Archaeological Museum about the Roman outposts along the Neckar, Rhine, and Danube rivers, from the 1st to 3rd centuries; and *Theater der Welt* (theater of the world), a high-caliber program with 28 productions (100 performances) from five continents in June and July—primarily in the Staatstheater.

THE ARTS   Stuttgart's internationally renowned ballet company performs in the **Staatstheater** (⊠ Oberer Schlossgarten 6, Mitte ☏ 0711/202–090). The ballet season runs from September through June and alternates with the highly respected State Opera. For program details contact the Stuttgart tourist office. The box office is open weekdays 10–6, Saturday 10–2.

The **SI-Erlebnis-Centrum** is an entire entertainment complex (hotels, bars, restaurants, gambling casino, wellness center, cinemas, shops, theaters) built in 1994 to showcase musicals. *42nd Street* and *Mamma Mia!,* a musical comedy with 22 of ABBA's greatest hits, are playing in 2005. ⊠ *Plieninger Str. 100, Stuttgart-Möhringen* ⊕ *www.si-centrum.de.*

NIGHTLIFE   There's no shortage of rustic beer gardens, wine pubs, or sophisticated cocktail bars in and around Stuttgart. Night owls should head for the **Schwabenzentrum** on Eberhardstrasse; the **Bohnenviertel,** or "Bean Quarter" (Charlotten-, Olga-, and Pfarrstrasse); the "party-mile" along Theodor-Heuss-Strasse; and **Calwer Strasse.**

Sports & the Outdoors

BOAT TRIPS   From the pier opposite the zoo entrance, **Neckar-Käpt'n** (☏ 0711/ 5499–7060 ⊕ www.neckar-kaeptn.de) offers a wide range of boat trips, as far north as scenic Besigheim and Lauffen.

HIKING   Stuttgart has a 53-km (33-mi) network of marked hiking trails in the nearby hills; follow the signs with the city's emblem: a horse set in a yellow ring.

SWIMMING &   Bad Cannstatt's mineral springs are more than 2,000 years old and, with
SPAS   a daily output of about 22 million liters (5.8 million gallons), the second most productive (after Budapest) in Europe. The **MineralBad Cannstatt** (⊠ Sulzerrainstr. 2 ☏ 0711/216–9240) has indoor and outdoor mineral pools, hot tubs, sauna, steam room, and spa facilities. On the banks of the Neckar near the König-Karl bridge is the **Mineralbad Leuze** (⊠ Am Leuzebad 2–6 ☏ 0711/216–4210), with eight pools indoors and out and an open-air mineral-water sauna. **Mineralbad Berg** (⊠ Am Schwanenpl. 9 ☏ 0711/923–6516) has indoor and outdoor pools and sauna and offers therapeutic water treatments.

Shopping

Stuttgart is a shopper's paradise, from the department stores on the Königstrasse, to the boutiques in the Old Town's elegant passages, and the factory outlet stores. Calwer Strasse is home to the glitzy chrome-and-glass arcade **Calwer Passage.** Shops here carry everything from local women's fashion (Beate Mössinger) to furniture. Don't miss the beautiful art nouveau **Markthalle** on Dorotheenstrasse. One of Germany's finest market halls, it's an architectural gem brimming with exotic fruits and spices, meats, and flowers.

Two of Germany's top men's fashion designers—Hugo Boss and Ulli Knecht—are based in Stuttgart. **Holy's** (⊠ Königstr. 54/A, Mitte ☎ 0711/222–9444) is an exclusive boutique that carries clothes (for men and women) by the most sought-after designers.

Günter Krauss (⊠ Kronprinzstr. 21, Mitte ☎ 0711/297–395) specializes in designer jewelry. The shop itself—walls of white Italian marble with gilt fixtures and mirrors—has won many design awards.

Breuninger (⊠ Marktstr. 1–3, Mitte ☎ 0711/2110), a leading regional department-store chain, has glass elevators that rise and fall under the dome of the central arcade.

Bebenhausen

㉗ *6 km (4 mi) north of Tübingen, on west side of B–27/464.*

If you blink, you'll miss the turnoff for the little settlement of Bebenhausen, and that would be a shame, because it's really worth a visit. The **Zisterzienzerkloster** (Cistercian Monastery) is a rare example of an almost perfectly preserved medieval monastery dating from the late 12th century. Owing to the secularization of 1806, the abbot's abode was rebuilt as a hunting castle for King Frederick of Württemberg. Expansion and restoration continued as long as the castle and monastery continued to be a royal residence. Even after the monarchy was dissolved in 1918, the last Württembergs were given lifetime rights here; this came to an end in 1946 with the death of Charlotte, wife of Wilhelm II. For a few years after World War II the state senate convened in the castle; today both castle and monastery are open to the public, although the castle is open for guided tours only. ☎ 07071/602–802 ☜ *Monastery €3, castle €3, both €5.50* ☻ *Monastery Apr.–Oct., Mon. 9–noon and 1–6, Tues.–Sun. 9–6; Nov.–Mar., Tues.–Sun. 9–noon and 1–5. Castle tours on the hr Apr.–Oct., Tues.–Fri. 9–noon and 2–5, weekends 10–noon and 2–5; Nov.–Mar., Tues.–Fri. 9–noon and 2–4, weekends 10–noon and 2–4.*

Where to Eat

$$–$$$$ ✕ **Waldhorn.** Dorothea Schulz-Schilling and her husband, Helmut Schulz, FodorśChoice operate this exceptional restaurant. Old favorites, such as foie gras and ★ fish, the *Vorspeisenvariation* (medley of appetizers), and iced cappuchino are recommended. The wine list features a well-chosen selection of international and top Baden and Württemberg wines. Garden tables have a castle view. A meal here is a perfect start or finale to the concerts held on the monastery-castle grounds in the summer. ⊠ *Schönbuchstr. 49,*

on B–27/464 ☎ *07071/61270* ⊕ *www.waldhorn-bebenhausen.de*
⚲ *Reservations essential* ▭ *No credit cards* ⊙ *Closed Tues. and 10 days in Aug. No lunch Mon.*

Tübingen

㉘ *40 km (25 mi) south of Stuttgart on B–27 on the Neckar River.*

With its half-timber houses, winding alleyways, and hilltop setting overlooking the Neckar, Tübingen provides the quintessential German experience. The medieval flavor is quite authentic, as the town was untouched by wartime bombings. Dating to the 11th century, Tübingen flourished as a trade center; its weights and measures and currency were the standard through much of the area. The town declined in importance after the 14th century, when it was taken over by the counts of Württemberg. Between the 14th and the 19th centuries, its size hardly changed as it became a university and residential town, its castle the only symbol of ruling power.

Yet Tübingen hasn't been sheltered from the world. It resonates with a youthful air. Even more than Heidelberg, Tübingen is virtually synonymous with its university, a leading center of learning since it was founded in 1477. Illustrious students of yesteryear include the astronomer Johannes Kepler and the philosopher G. W. F. Hegel. The latter studied at the Protestant theological seminary, still a cornerstone of the university's international reputation. One of Hegel's roommates was Friedrich Hölderlin, a visionary poet who succumbed to madness in his early thirties. Tübingen's population is around 83,000, of which at least 20,000 are students. During term time it can be hard to find a seat in pubs and cafés; during vacations the town sometimes seems deserted. The best way to see and appreciate Tübingen is simply to stroll around, soaking up its age-old atmosphere of quiet erudition.

a good walk

Tübingen's modest size makes it ideal for a walk. Begin at the Eberhards-Brücke, which crosses an island with a magnificent planting of trees—most of them at least 200 years old—known as the Platanenallee. If time permits, stroll up and down the island. If not, go to the north end of the bridge, take a sharp left down a steep staircase to reach the shore of the Neckar, and follow it to a yellow tower, the **Hölderlinturm**. The poet Friedrich Hölderlin was housed in the tower after he lost his sanity, and it's now a small museum commemorating his life and work. Next, walk away from the river up the steps of Hölderlinsteg and continue left up the Bursagasse to pass by the **Bursa**, a former student dormitory that dates from the Middle Ages. Facing the Bursa, turn left up the street called Klosterberg and then turn left again into the courtyard of the **Evangelisches Stift**. Richer in history than in immediate visual interest, this site was a center of European intellectual thought for centuries. Proceed up Klosterberg to the narrow steps and cobblestones of Burgsteige, one of the oldest thoroughfares in the town and lined with houses dating from the Middle Ages. You might be a little breathless when you finally arrive at the top and enter the portal of the **Schloss Hohentübingen**. The portal is fitted as a Roman-style triumphal arch in true Renaissance spirit.

Cross the Schloss's courtyard and enter the tunnel-like passage directly in front of you; it leads to the other side of the castle. Take a moment to enjoy the view of the river from the ruined ramparts and then descend to your right through tree-shaded Kapitansweg—looking at the remains of the original city walls on your way—to Haaggasse and then left into the narrow Judengasse (Jewish Alley). Jewish citizens lived in this neighborhood until 1477, when they were driven out of the city. Next, stop at the intersection of Judengasse and Ammergasse; all around you are old half-timber buildings. The little stream that runs through Ammergasse was part of the medieval sewage system.

Across the square, Jakobsgasse leads to Jakobuskirche (St. James Church), in medieval times a station on the famous pilgrims' route to Santiago di Compostella in Spain. Go to the other side of the church, make a right into Madergasse, and then turn left at Schmiedtorstrasse, where you will find the Fruchtschranne on the right-hand side—a massive half-timber house built to store fruit and grain in the 15th century. Continue down the street to Bachgasse; turn right, then right again onto the street called Bei der Fruchtschranne and follow it a short distance to a courtyard on the left just before the intersection with Kornhausstrasse. The courtyard leads to the entrance of the 15th-century **Kornhaus,** now a city museum. Continue to Kornstrasse and go left and immediately right into Marktgasse, which takes you uphill to the **Marktplatz,** a sloping, uneven cobblestone parallelogram that dominates the heart of Tübingen's Altstadt (Old City). Its **Neptune Fountain** is graced with a statue of the sea god. The square is bounded on one side by the amazing **Rathaus.**

From the square turn into Wienergasse and then left into Münzgasse; No. 20 is the site of the former **Studentenkarzer.** The large yellow baroque building just beyond is the **Alte Aula,** for many centuries the university's most important building. The well-preserved late-Gothic **Stiftskirche** now rises before you. Climbing the hundred-odd steps up the bell tower will allow you to take a second, faraway look at almost everything you've seen en route.

TIMING   The walk around town takes about 1½ hours. If you go inside the Hölderlinturm, Stadtsmuseum, or Stiftskirche, add a half hour for each.

What to See

Alte Aula (Old Auditorium). Erected in 1547, the half-timber university building was significantly altered in 1777, when it acquired an Italian roof, a symmetrical facade, and a balcony decorated with two crossed scepters, symbolizing the town's center of learning. In earlier times grain was stored under the roof as part of the professors' salaries. The libraries and lecture halls were on the lower floors. ⊠ *Münzg.*

Bursa (Student Dormitory). The word *bursa* meant "purse" in the Middle Ages and later came to refer to student lodgings such as this former student dormitory. Despite its classical facade, which it acquired in the early 19th century, the building actually dates back to 1477. Medieval students had to master a broad curriculum that included the *septem artes liberales* (seven liberal arts) of Grammar, Dialectic, Rhetoric, Arithmetic, Geometry, Astronomy, and Music, in addition to praying several times a day, fasting regularly, and speaking only Latin within the confines of the building. ✉ *Bursag. 4.*

Evangelisches Stift (Protestant Seminary). From the outside you can't tell that this site has served for centuries as a center of European intellectual thought. It was founded in 1534, partly as a political move during the Reformation; the Protestant duke of Württemberg, Ulrich, wanted facilities to train Protestant clerics so that Protestantism could retain its foothold in the region (he would have been disappointed to know a major Catholic seminary arrived near here in 1817). Since that time philosophical rather than political considerations have prevailed within these walls. Hegel, Hölderlin, and the philosopher Schelling all lived and studied here, as have students of Protestant theology ever since. ✉ *Klosterg.*

Hölderlinturm (Hölderlin's Tower). "Mad" Friedrich Hölderlin lived here for 36 years, until his death in 1843, in the care of the master cabinetmaker Zimmer and his daughter. If you don't speak German, the Web site's English version provides good background to help you get the most out of your visit. ✉ *Bursag. 6* ☎ *07071/22040* ⊕ *www.hoelderlin-gesellschaft.de* ✎ *€1.50, with tour €2.50* ☉ *Tues.–Fri. 10–noon and 3–5, weekends 2–5. Tours weekends at 5 PM; English-language tours available by arrangement.*

Kornhaus (Grain House). During the Middle Ages, townspeople stored and sold grain on the first floor of this structure (built in 1453); social events took place on the second floor. Among the Kornhaus's occupants through the centuries were duelists, medieval apprentices, traveling players, 18th-century schoolchildren, an academy for young ladies, the Nazi Women's League, a driving school, and the city's restoration department. It now houses the City Museum. ✉ *Kornhausstr. 10* ☎ *07071/945–460* ⊕ *www.tuebingen.de* ✎ *€2.50* ☉ *Tues.–Fri. 3–6, weekends 11–6.*

off the beaten path

KUNSTHALLE (Art Gallery) – North of the Neckar, the art gallery has become a leading exhibition venue and generates a special kind of "art tourism," making it difficult to find lodging if a popular show is on. ✉ *Philosophenweg 76* ☎ *07071/96910* ⊕ *www.kunsthalle-tuebingen.de* ✎ *€6–€8, depending on exhibit* ☉ *Tues.–Sun. 10–6.*

★ **Marktplatz** (Market Square). Houses of prominent burghers of centuries gone by surround the square. At the open-air market on Monday, Wednesday, and Friday, you can buy flowers, bread, pastries, poultry, sausage, and cheese.

★ **Rathaus** (Town Hall). Begun in 1433, the Rathaus slowly expanded over the next 150 years or so. Its ornate Renaissance facade is bright with colorful murals and a marvelous astronomical clock dating from 1511. The halls and reception rooms are adorned with half-timber and paintings from the late 19th century. ✉ *Marktpl.*

Schloss Hohentübingen. The original castle of the counts of Tübingen (1078) was significantly enlarged and altered by Duke Ulrich during the 16th century. Particularly noteworthy is the elaborate Renaissance portal patterned after a Roman triumphal arch. The coat of arms of the Duchy of Württemberg depicted in the center is framed by the emblems of various orders, including the Order of the Garter. Today the castle houses several university departments, the universityís archaeological and ethnological collections, and reproductions of Greek and Roman sculptures. The castle's main attraction, however, is its magnificent view over the river and town.

★ **Stiftskirche** (Collegiate Church). The late-Gothic church has been well preserved; its original features include the stained-glass windows, the choir stalls, the ornate baptismal font, and the elaborate stone pulpit. The windows are famous for their colors and were much admired by Goethe. The dukes of Württemberg, from the 15th through the 17th centuries, are interred in the choir. ☒ *Holzmarkt.* ☎ *Bell tower €1* ⊙ *Church Feb.–Oct., daily 9–5; Nov.–Jan., daily 9–4; bell tower Fri.–Sun. 11:30–5.*

Studentenkarzer (Student Prison). The oldest surviving university prison in Germany consists of just two small rooms. For more than three centuries (1515–1845) students were locked up here for such offenses as swearing, failing to attend sermons, wearing clothing considered lewd, or playing dice. The figures on the walls are not graffiti but scenes from biblical history that were supposed to contribute to the moral improvement of the incarcerated students. You can enter the prison only on a guided tour organized by the Tübingen Tourist Board. ☒ *Münzg. 20* ☎ *07071/91360 for tour* ☎ *€1* ⊙ *Tour weekends at 2.*

Where to Stay & Eat

$–$$ ✕ **Forelle.** Beautiful ceilings painted with vine motifs, exposed beams, and an old tile oven make for a Gemütlich atmosphere. This small restaurant fills up fast, not least because the Swabian cooking is excellent. All products (and the wines) are sourced locally, including the inn's namesake, trout. Splurge on the saddle of venison in *Wacholdersahnesosse* (juniper-berry cream sauce) with mushroom-filled Maultauschen. ☒*Kronenstr. 8* ☎ *07071/24094* ⊕ *www.weinstube-forelle.de* ☐ *MC, V.*

¢–$ ✕ **Gasthausbrauerei Neckarmüller.** This shady, riverside beer garden and restaurant near the Eberhards-Brücke serves house-brewed beer with snacks, salads, and Swabian specialties (Maultaschen, spätzle, sauerkraut, and beefsteaks in cream sauce). Don't wait to be served. The sign that reads SELBSTABHOLUNG means you fetch it yourself. ☒ *Gartenstr. 4* ☎ *07071/27848* ⊕ *www.neckarmueller.de* ☐ *DC, MC, V.*

¢ ✕ **Neckarbistro.** The café has light and airy 1960s decor and a beautiful view up and down the Neckar. Hölderlin's Tower is just a few houses upriver. The eclectic menu includes vegetarian dishes, pasta, schnitzel, and Swabian fare, or drop in for coffee and delicious pastry. Sunday brunch ($) is a feast (reservations advised). ☒ *Neckarg. 22* ☎ *07071/22122* ⊕ *www.neckarbistro.de* ☐ No credit cards.

★ $–$$ ✕☐ **Hotel Am Schloss.** The climb is steep from the Altstadt to this hotel, next to the castle that towers over the town, but the reward is a lovely view from the windows and terrace. Proprietor Herbert Rösch is an expert on Maultaschen. In his restaurant ($–$$), 28 versions of "Swabian tortellini" are on the menu, together with other regional dishes and wines from Württemberg. The hotel can help you with parking, or with a ride to the airport. ✉ *Burgsteige 18, D–72070* ☎ *07071/92940* 📠 *07071/929–410* 🌐 *www.hotelamschloss.de* *37 rooms* *Restaurant, some minibars, cable TV, bicycles, laundry service, Internet, business services, some pets allowed (fee), no-smoking rooms; no a/c* 💳 *AE, MC, V* *Restaurant closed Tues. Oct.–Mar.* 🍽 *BP.*

$–$$ **Hotel Hospiz.** This modern, family-run hotel provides friendly service, comfort, and a convenient Altstadt location near the castle. Several rooms are small. If you're unhappy about the size of your room, please let the front desk know and they will try to move you into larger quarters. Parking is difficult, so take advantage of the hotel's offer to park the car for you. ✉ *Neckarhalde 2, at Burgsteige, D–72070* ☎ *07071/9240* 📠 *07071/924–200* 🌐 *www.hotel-hospiz.de* *50 rooms, 45 with bath or shower* *In-room data ports, minibars, cable TV, lobby lounge, business services, some pets allowed, no-smoking rooms; no a/c* 💳 *AE, MC, V* 🍽 *BP.*

Nightlife & the Arts

Tübingen has an active small theater scene. Check with the tourist office for a listing of what is going on—the more eclectic offerings are likely to be the better ones. In addition to dozens of Old Town student pubs, there's a lively crowd after 9 at the **Jazzkeller** (✉ Haagg. 15/2 ☎ 07071/550–906). **Die Kelter** (✉ Schmiedtorstr. 17 ☎ 07071/254–675) is good for jazz, music, and light fare, and it has a wine shop. The upstairs cocktail bar at **Café Nass** (✉ Kirchg. 19 ☎ 07071/551–250) opens at 7 PM. From 9 AM until well past midnight there's action at **Tangente-Jour** (✉ Münzg. 17 ☎ 07071/24572), a bistro next to the Stiftskirche. **Zentrum Zoo** (✉ Schleifmühleweg 86 ☎ 07071/94480) has live music, a dance club, and a huge beer garden that is immensely popular with all ages. It's about a 20-minute walk from the town center.

Sports & the Outdoors

The Tübingen tourist office has maps with hiking routes around the town, including historical and geological *Lehrpfade,* or **educational walks.** A classic Tübingen walk goes from the castle down to the little chapel called the **Wurmlinger Kapelle,** taking about two hours. On the way you can stop off at the restaurant Schwärzlocher Hof (closed Monday and Tuesday) for a glass of *Most* (apple wine), bread, and sausages—all are homemade.

off the beaten path

BURG HOHENZOLLERN – The Hohenzollern House of Prussia was the most powerful family in German history. It lost its throne when Kaiser William II abdicated after Germany's defeat in World War I. The Swabian branch of the family owns one-third of the castle, the Prussian branch two-thirds. Today's neo-Gothic structure, perched high on a conical wooded hill, is a successor of a castle dating from the 11th century. Its majestic silhouette is visible from miles away. On the fascinating castle tour you'll see the Prussian royal crown and beautiful period rooms—splendid from floor to ceiling, with playful details, such as door handles carved to resemble peacocks and dogs. The royal tombs, once housed in the Christ Chapel, were returned to Potsdam in 1991 after German reunification. The restaurant on the castle grounds, Burgschänke (closed January and Monday in February and March), is catered by the talented chefs of Hotel

Brielhof (which is at the foot of the hill where the ascent from the B–27 begins). You can enjoy a first-class meal at the Brielhof, then make the one-hour hike up to the castle. From the castle parking lot it's a 20-minute walk to the entrance, or take the shuttle bus (€2.55 round-trip). ⊠ *Hechingen, 25 km (15 mi) south of Tübingen on B–27* 🕾 *07471/2428* ⊕ *www.burg-hohenzollern.com* 🖾 *€5* ☉ *Mid-Mar.–Oct., daily 9–5:30; Nov.–mid-Mar., daily 10–4:30.*

HEIDELBERG & THE NECKAR VALLEY A TO Z

To research prices, get advice from other travelers, and book travel arrangements, visit www.fodors.com.

AIRPORTS

From the Frankfurt and Stuttgart airports, there's fast and easy access, by car and train, to all major centers along the Neckar.

With advance reservations you can get to Heidelberg from the Frankfurt airport via the shuttle service TLS. The trip takes about an hour and costs €29 per person; with four people, €22.25 each. No reservations are needed for the Lufthansa Airport Bus (not restricted to Lufthansa passengers). Service is daily, on the hour, 8–1, 3–7, and 10 or 11 PM. Confirm the schedule by phone or on the Internet. It departs from Frankfurt airport, Terminal One, Hall B, arrivals level. Exit at B4, close to the *Treffpunkt* (Meeting Point) to reach the bus stop. The trip ends at the Crowne Plaza Hotel in Heidelberg and costs €19 per person.

🖪 **TLS** 🕾 06221/770–077 🖷 06221/770–070 ⊕ www.tls-heidelberg.de. **Lufthansa Airport Bus** 🕾 06221/653–256 in Heidelberg ⊕ www.lufthansa-airportbus.com.

BUS TRAVEL

Europabus 189 runs the length of the Burgenstrasse daily from May through September, making stops all along the Neckar. For information, contact Deutsche Touring (⇨ Bus Travel *in* Smart Travel Tips). Local buses run from Mannheim, Heidelberg, Heilbronn, and Stuttgart to most places along the river.

CAR RENTALS

Avis, Europcar, Hertz, and Sixt all have rental offices at the Frankfurt and Stuttgart airports and main train stations.

🖪 **Avis** ⊠ Karlsruherstr. 43, Heidelberg 🕾 06221/22215 ⊠ Salzstr. 112, Heilbronn 🕾 07131/172–077 ⊠ Katharinenstr. 18, Stuttgart 🕾 0711/239–320. **Europcar** ⊠ Bergheimerstr. 159, Heidelberg 🕾 06221/53990 ⊠ Wilhelmstr. 27, Heilbronn 🕾 07131/62110 ⊠ Frankenstr. 3, Stuttgart-Zuffenhausen 🕾 0711/987–9390 ⊠ Eisenbahnstr. 21, Tübingen 🕾 07071/13370. **Hertz** ⊠ Crowne Plaza, Kurfürstenanlage 1, Heidelberg 🕾 06221/23434 ⊠ Weiberstr. 17, Heilbronn 🕾 07131/724–100 ⊠ Hauptbahnhof Arnulf-Klett-Pl. 2, Track 16, Stuttgart 🕾 0711/226–2921. **Sixt** ⊠ Eppelheimer Str. 50C, Heidelberg 🕾 06221/138–990 ⊠ Salzstr. 186, Heilbronn 🕾 07131/580–026 ⊠ Leonhardpl. 17, Stuttgart 🕾 0711/243–925.

CAR TRAVEL

Heidelberg is a 15-minute drive (10 km [6 mi]) on A–656 from Mannheim, a major junction of the autobahn system. Heilbronn is near the east–west

A–6 and the north–south A–81. The route followed in this chapter, the Burgenstrasse (Route B–37), follows the north bank of the Neckar River from Heidelberg to Mosbach, from which it continues south to Heilbronn as B–27, the road parallel to and predating the autobahn (A–81). B–27 still leads to Stuttgart and Tübingen.

TOURS

BOAT TOURS   From Easter through October there are regular boat trips on the Neckar from Heidelberg, Heilbronn, and Stuttgart. If time is short, take a *Rundfahrt* (round-trip excursion). The Tübingen tourist office organizes punting on the Neckar.

CITY TOURS   Medieval Bad Wimpfen offers a town walk year-round, Sunday at 2 (€1.80), departing from the Alter Bahnhof (old train station), and free guided tours in English for visitors who spend at least one night. Upon arrival, ask the hotel to arrange a town tour and ask for the free pass *Bad Wimpfen à la card* for reduced or free admission to historic sights and museums.

From April through October there are daily walking tours of Heidelberg in German (Friday and Saturday in English) at 10:30 AM; from November through March, tours are in German only, Saturday at 10:30; the cost is €6. They depart from the Lion's Fountain on Universitätsplatz. Bilingual bus tours run April–October on Thursday and Friday at 2:30, and on Saturday at 10:30 and 2:30. From November through March bus tours depart Saturday at 2:30. They cost €12 and depart from Universitätsplatz. The *HeidelbergCard* costs €12 (two days) or €20 (four days) and includes free or reduced admission to most tourist attractions as well as free use of all public transportation (including the Bergbahn to the castle) and other extras, such as free guided walking tours, discounts on bus tours, and a city guidebook. It can be purchased at the tourist information office at the main train station, and at many local hotels.

Walking tours (in German) of Heilbronn and Mosbach depart from their respective tourist offices. Heilbronn's year-round tours are Saturday at 11:30, for €2.10. There's also a tour April–September, Tuesday evening at 6:15 (€4.50), that concludes with a Viertele glass of wine in a Heilbronn wine restaurant. Free tours of Mosbach take place May–September, Wednesday at 2:30. In June–September there are free (German) tours of Hirschhorn on Saturday at 10.

The visitor-friendly (three-day) STUTTCARD PLUS (€17) and STUTTCARD (€11.50), with or without access to free public transportation, are available from the Stuttgart tourist office opposite the main train station. This is also the place to book tours and the meeting point for city walking tours in German (year-round, Saturday at 10) for €7.50. There are daily bilingual walks April–October at 11 AM and an extra tour Friday at 5 PM for €6. Bilingual bus tours depart from the bus stop around the corner from the tourist office, in front of Hotel am Schlossgarten (April–October, daily at 1:30; November–March, Friday–Sunday at 1:30) for €17. All tours last from 1½ to 2½ hours. A bilingual Saturday-evening walking tour (7 PM–after midnight) includes a visit to a nightclub (with a show), a pub crawl, and dinner for €60.

The Tübingen tourist office runs guided city tours year-round, weekends at 2:30. From February through October there are also tours on Wednesday at 10 AM and Tuesday, Thursday, and Friday at 2:30 for €3.10. Tours start at the Rathaus on the market square. Overnight guests receive a free *Tourist-Regio-Card* from their hotel (ask for it) for reduced admission fees to museums, concerts, theaters, and sports facilities.

TRAIN TRAVEL

Western Germany's most important rail junction is in nearby Mannheim, with hourly InterCity trains from all major German cities. Heidelberg is equally easy to get to. The super-high-speed InterCity Express service, which reaches 280 kph (174 mph), is Germany's fastest. Travel time between Frankfurt and Stuttgart is less than 1½ hours; between Heidelberg and Stuttgart, 26 minutes. There are express trains to Heilbronn from Heidelberg and Stuttgart and direct trains from Stuttgart to Tübingen. Local services link many of the smaller towns.

VISITOR INFORMATION

For information on the entire Burgenstrasse, contact Die Burgenstrasse. For information on the hilly area south of Stuttgart and Tübingen, contact the Schwäbische Alb Tourismusverband.

🔳 Regional Tourist Offices **Die Burgenstrasse** ✉ Allee 28, D-74072 Heilbronn ☏ 07131/564-028 🖷 07131/564-029 ⊕ www.burgenstrasse.de. **Schwäbische Alb Tourismusverband** ✉ Marktpl. 1, D-72574 Bad Urach ☏ 07125/948-106 🖷 07125/948-108 ⊕ www.schwaebischealb.de.

🔳 Tourist Offices **Bad Wimpfen** ✉ Tourist-Information Bad Wimpfen-Gundelsheim, Carl-Ulrich-Str. 1, D-74206 ☏ 07063/97200 🖷 07063/972-020 ⊕ www.badwimpfen. de. **Heidelberg** ✉ Tourist-Information am Hauptbahnhof, Willy-Brandt-Pl. 1, D-69115 ☏ 06221/19433 🖷 06221/138-8111 ⊕ www.cvb-heidelberg.de. **Heilbronn** ✉ Tourist-Information, Kaiserstr. 17, D-74072 ☏ 07131/562-270 🖷 07131/563-349 ⊕ www. heilbronn-marketing.de. **Hirschhorn** ✉ Tourist-Information, Alleeweg 2, D-69434 ☏ 06272/1742 🖷 06272/912-351 ⊕ www.hirschhorn.de. **Mosbach** ✉ Tourist-Information, Am Marktplatz 4, D-74821 ☏ 06261/91880 🖷 06261/918-815 ⊕ www.mosbach.de. **Schwetzingen** ✉ Stadtinformation, Dreikönigstr. 3, D-68723 ☏ 06202/945-875 🖷 06202/945-877 ⊕ www.schwetzingen.de. **Stuttgart** ✉ Touristik-Information i-Punkt, Königstr. 1A, D-70173 ☏ 0711/222-8246 🖷 0711/222-8253 ⊕ www.stuttgart-tourist.de. **Tübingen** ✉ Verkehrsverein Tübingen, An der Neckarbrücke, D-72072 ☏ 07071/91360 🖷 07071/35070 ⊕ www.tuebingen-info.de.

WINE INFORMATION

The regional wine promotion boards can provide information on the local wines and where to sample them. Ask for details about wine growers who also run economical bed-and-breakfasts. In Baden, which includes Heidelberg, contact Weinwerbezentrale badischer Winzergenossenschaften. The vineyards of Württemberg line the Neckar Valley; contact Werbegemeinschaft Württembergischer Weingärtnergenossenschaften.

🔳 **Weinwerbezentrale badischer Winzergenossenschaften** ✉ Kesslerstr. 5, D-76185 Karlsruhe ☏ 0721/557-028 🖷 0721/557-020 ⊕ www.sonnenmaennchen.de. **Werbegemeinschaft Württembergischer Weingärtnergenossenschaften** ✉ Raiffeisenstr. 6, D-71696 Möglingen ☏ 07141/24460 🖷 07141/244-620 ⊕ www.wwg.de.

FRANKFURT

9

**SEE WHERE EMPERORS
WERE CROWNED**
at the Kaiserdom ➪*p.350*

SAY HI TO EUROPE'S ONLY DINOSAUR
at the Naturkundemuseum Senckenberg
(Natural History Museum) ➪*p.351*

SAVOR THE BEST TAPAS IN TOWN
at La Boveda ➪*p.359*

SIP APFELWEIN WITH THE LOCALS
at Zum Wagner ➪*p.363*

FOLLOW THE FOOTSTEPS OF ROYALTY
with an excursion to Bad Homburg ➪*p.376*

Updated by
Heather Phibbs

STANDING IN THE CENTER of the Römerberg (medieval town square), visitors to Frankfurt at once notice the city's striking contrasts. Re-creations of 15th-, 16th-, 17th-, and 18th-century houses and government buildings line the square while modern skyscrapers tower overhead. Unlike German cities that reclaimed much of their prewar appearance after World War II, Frankfurt looked to the future and focused on erecting skyscrapers to house its many banking institutions (though the city did meticulously restore selected historic buildings in amazing, accurate detail). The city cheekily nicknamed itself Mainhattan, using the name of the Main River that flows through it to suggest that other famous metropolis across the Atlantic. Although modest in size (fifth among German cities, with a population of 652,000), Frankfurt is Germany's financial powerhouse. Not only is the German Central Bank (Bundesbank) here but also the European Central Bank (ECB), which manages the euro. Some 370 credit institutions (more than half of them foreign banks) have offices in Frankfurt, including the headquarters of five of Germany's largest banks.

According to legend, a deer is said to have revealed the ford in the Main River to the Frankish emperor Charlemagne. A stone ridge, now blasted away, made the shallow river a great conduit for trade, and by the early 13th century Frankfurt (*furt* means "ford") had emerged as a major trading center. Frankfurt's first international Autumn Fair was held in 1240; in 1330 it added a Spring Fair. Today these and other trade shows showcase the latest in books, cars, consumer goods, and technology. The city's stock exchange, one of the half dozen most important in the world, was established in 1585, and the Rothschild family opened their first bank here in 1798. The long history of trade might help explain the temperament of many Frankfurters—competitive but open-minded. It's also one of the reasons Frankfurt has become Germany's most international city. Almost 30% of its residents are foreign, including a large number of Turks, Italians, Eastern Europeans, and others who relocated here for business.

So why come to Frankfurt if not on business? Partly for its history, which spans more than 1,200 years. It was one of the joint capitals of Charlemagne's empire; the city where Holy Roman emperors were elected and crowned; the site of Gutenberg's print shop; the birthplace of Goethe (1749–1832), Germany's greatest poet; and the city where the first German parliament met.

Because of its commercialism, Frankfurt has a reputation for being crass, cold, and boring. But people who know the city think this characterization is unfair. The district of Sachsenhausen is as *gemütlich* (fun, friendly, and cozy) as you will find anywhere. The city has world-class ballet, opera, theater, and art exhibitions; an important piece of Germany's publishing industry; a large university (38,000 students); and two of the three most important daily newspapers in Germany. In Frankfurt you find yourself in the heart of a powerful, sophisticated, and cosmopolitan nation. There may not be that much here to remind you of the Old World, but there's a great deal that explains the success story of postwar Germany.

If you have 1 day

Begin at the Goethehaus und Goethemuseum, the home of Germany's greatest poet. The house is within a 5- to 10-minute walk of either the Hauptwache or Willy Brandt Platz subway station. Next, follow Bethmannstrasse as it turns into Braubachstrasse to reach the Museum für Moderne Kunst, one of Frankfurt's modern architectural monuments. Walk a few blocks and several centuries back in time south to the Kaiserdom. The cathedral is next to the heart of the city, the Römerberg. The medieval square holds the Römer, or city hall. After lunch, cross over the Main on the Eiserner Steg to reach the Städelsches Kunstinstitut und Städtische Galerie, with its important collection of old master and impressionist paintings, and the Städtische Galerie Liebieghaus, which contains sculpture from the third millennium BC up to the modern age. In the evening, relax in one of Sachsenhausen's apple-cider taverns.

If you have 2 days

Spend your first morning at the Goethehaus und Goethemuseum and Römerberg Square, with the Römer, Nikolaikirche, Historisches Museum, Paulskirche, and the Kaiserdom all nearby. After viewing the cathedral, continue up Domstrasse to the Museum für Moderne Kunst. Take a midday break before continuing north to Germany's shop-'til-you-drop Zeil district and the Zoologischer Garten, one of Europe's best zoos. End the evening listening to music in the Frankfurter Jazzkeller. The entire second day can be devoted to the Sachsenhausen museums, starting with the Städelsches Kunstinstitut und Städtische Galerie and the Städtische Galerie Liebieghaus. Finally, explore Sachsenhausen's nightlife.

If you have 3 days

Spend your first two days following the itinerary outlined above. On the morning of the third day, see the Naturkundemuseum Senckenberg; it has a famous collection of dinosaurs and giant whales. Afterward visit the nearby Palmengarten und Botanischer Garten, which have climatic zones from tropical to sub-Antarctic and a dazzling range of orchids. Take the U-bahn to Opernplatz, and emerge before the 19th-century splendor of the Alte Oper; lunch on Fressgasse is not far away. In the afternoon, go to the visitors' gallery of the Börse to feel the pulse of Europe's banking capital. Then continue on to the less-worldly Karmeliterkloster. Secularized in 1803, the monastery and buildings house the Museum für Vor- und Frühgeschichte. Just around the corner on the bank of the Main, in the former Rothschild Palais, the Jüdisches Museum tells the 1,000-year story of Frankfurt's Jewish quarter and its end in the Holocaust.

EXPLORING FRANKFURT

The Hauptbahnhof (main train station) area and adjoining Westend district are mostly devoted to business, as evidenced by the banks towering overhead. You'll find the department stores of the Hauptwache and Zeil just a short walk east of the station, but avoid the drug-ridden red-light district southwest of the station. The city's past can be found in the Old Town's restored medieval quarter and in Sachsenhausen, across the river, where pubs and museums greatly outnumber banks.

Numbers in the text correspond to numbers in the margin and on the Frankfurt map.

City Center & Westend

Frankfurt was rebuilt after World War II with little attention paid to the past. Nevertheless, important historical monuments can still be found among the modern architecture. The city is very walkable; its growth hasn't encroached on its parks, gardens, pedestrian arcades, or outdoor cafés.

a good tour

Römerberg ❶ ▶, the historic heart of Frankfurt, has been the center of civic life for centuries. Taking up most of the west side of the square is the city hall, called the **Römer** ❷, a modest-looking building compared with many of Germany's other city halls. In the center of the square stands the fine 16th-century Fountain of Justitia.

On the south side of the Römerberg is the red sandstone **Nikolaikirche** ❸. Beside it stands the **Historisches Museum** ❹, where you can see a perfect scale model of historic Frankfurt. On the east side of the square is a row of painstakingly restored half-timber houses called the Ostzeile, dating from the 15th and 16th centuries.

From the Römerberg, walk up the pedestrian street called Neue Kräme. Looming up on the left is the circular bulk of the **Paulskirche** ❺, a mostly 18th-century church, more interesting for its political than its religious significance. It was here that the short-lived German parliament met for the first time in May 1848. From the Paulskirche keep heading along the Neue Kräme, which becomes Liebfrauenstrasse, and you'll reach the **Liebfrauenkirche** ❻, a late-Gothic church dating from the end of the 14th century.

Liebfrauenstrasse ends at the **Hauptwache** ❼, a square that is the hub of the city's transportation network and is named after the 18th-century building that stands on it. The café in the Hauptwache building can attend to your appetite if you need a break. A vast shopping mall lies below the square. To the south of the Hauptwache is the **Katharinenkirche** ❽, the most important Protestant church in the city. North of the Hauptwache, Schillerstrasse leads to the Börsenplatz and Germany's leading stock exchange, the **Börse** ❾.

To the east of the Hauptwache lies the **Zeil,** Frankfurt's largest pedestrian zone and main shopping street. Its department stores sell every conceivable type of consumer goods and can get very crowded. A 15- to 20-minute walk down the Zeil brings you to Alfred-Brehm-Platz and the entrance to the **Zoologischer Garten** ❿. This is one of Frankfurt's chief attractions, ranking among the best zoos in Europe. If you don't want to walk the Zeil's full length, turn right at the square Konstabler Wache onto Fahrgasse. Follow the signs reading AN DER STAUFENMAUER to the **Staufenmauer** ⓫, which is one of the few surviving stretches of the old city wall.

Continue down Fahrgasse, and turn right onto Battonstrasse. At the corner of Battonstrasse and Domstrasse you'll see the striking wedge-shape outline of the **Museum für Moderne Kunst** ⓬. Walk south down Domstrasse

On the Menu

Many international cuisines are represented in the financial hub of Europe. For vegetarians there's usually at least one meatless dish on a German menu, and substantial salads are popular, too (though often served with bacon). Frankfurt's local cuisine comes from the region's farm tradition. Pork ribs and chops, stewed beef, blood sausage, potato soup, and pancakes with bacon fulfill such proverbs as "Better once full than twice hungry" and "You work the way you eat." The city's most famous contribution to the world's diet is the *Frankfurter Würstchen*— a thin smoked pork sausage—better known to Americans as the hot dog. *Grüne Sosse* is a thin cream sauce of herbs served with potatoes and hard-boiled eggs. The oddly named *Handkäs mit Musik* (hand cheese with music) consists of slices of cheese covered with raw onions, oil, and vinegar, served with bread and butter (an acquired taste for many). All these things are served in *Apfelwein* (apple-wine, or hard cider) taverns in the Sachsenhausen area. Apfelwein is poured from a distinctive gray stoneware pitcher, called a *Bembel,* into an equally distinctive, ribbed tumbler.

Jazz & Techno

Frankfurt was a real pioneer in the German jazz scene and also has done much for the development of techno music. Jazz musicians make the rounds from smoky backstreet cafés all the way to the Old Opera House, and the local broadcaster Hessischer Rundfunk sponsors the German Jazz Festival in the fall. The Frankfurter Jazzkeller has been the most noted venue for German jazz fans for decades.

Museums

Frankfurt is full of museums, and 13 of them were newly built or renovated during the 1980s. Interesting for their architecture as well as for their content, the exhibition halls are Frankfurt's tourist draw. The Sachsenhausen area is home to seven of these museums. They line the side of the Main, on Schaumainkai, known locally as the Museumsufer (Museum Riverbank).

---

a few steps and another silhouette appears, that of the grand Gothic cathedral, **Kaiserdom** ⑬. There is an archaeological site next to the cathedral containing remains of Roman baths; from there walk through the pedestrian zone alongside the modern edifice of the **Schirn Kunsthalle** ⑭, a major venue for art exhibitions.

Continue back to the Römerberg and turn left to get to the Mainkai, the busy street that runs parallel to the tree-lined Main River. On your left you will see the Rententurm, one of the city's medieval gates, with its pinnacled towers at the base of the main spire extending out over the walls. To your right and in front is the **Eiserner Steg** ⑮, an iron footbridge connecting central Frankfurt with the old district of Sachsenhausen. River trips, boat excursions, and the old steam train leave from here.

Past the Eiserner Steg is the **Leonhardskirche** ⑯, which has one of the few 15th-century stained-glass windows to have survived World War II. Continue down the river, just past the Untermainbrücke to the **Jüdisches**

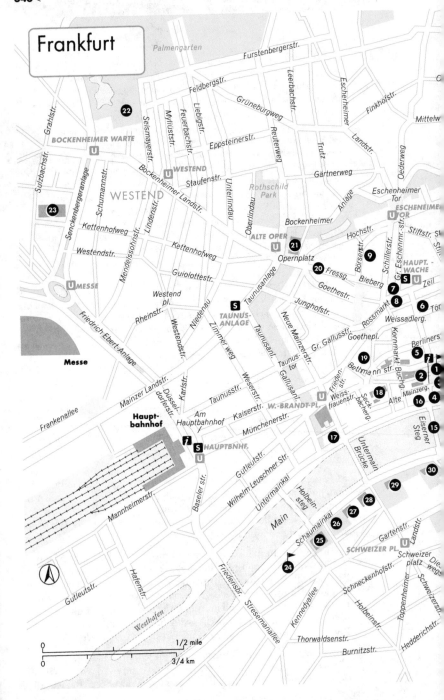

Frankfurt

KEY

🇸 *S-Bahn*

▶ *Start of walk*

🛈 *Tourist information*

🇺 *U-Bahn*

Museum ⑰. At No. 14–15 in the former Rothschild Palais, this museum focuses on the history of Frankfurt's Jewish community.

Backtrack a short way, and turn left into the narrow Karmelitergasse, which will take you to the **Karmeliterkloster** ⑱. The monastery and its buildings house an early history museum and the largest religious fresco north of the Alps. Exit onto Münzgasse, turn left, and go to the junction of Bethmannstrasse and Berlinerstrasse. Use the pedestrian walkway and cross over to the north side of Berlinerstrasse; then turn left again onto Grosser Hirschgraben. At No. 23 there will probably be a small crowd outside the **Goethehaus und Goethemuseum** ⑲, where writer Johann Wolfgang von Goethe was born in 1749.

On leaving the Goethehaus, go to Goetheplatz and continue past the Gutenberg Memorial into the pedestrian zone to Rathenau-Platz. At the end of the square turn left again, this time onto Grosse Bockenheimer Strasse, known locally as **Fressgasse** ⑳ because of its many delicatessens, bakeries, and cafés.

Fressgasse ends at Opernplatz and the **Alte Oper** ㉑, a prime venue for classical concerts as well as conferences and, every now and then, an opera. You can get a good look at Frankfurt's skyline from the opera house steps, or from the street Taunusanlage, opposite. Looking down Taunusanlage, you'll see the twin towers of the Deutsche Bank (the two towers are known as *zoll und haben,* or "debit and credit"). The very tall building to the left, topped by an antenna, is the 849-foot Commerzbank, the tallest building in Europe. Between them is the Maintower, headquarters of the Hessischer Landesbank.

Take the U-bahn two stops from Alte Oper to Bockenheimer Warte, walk down Bockenheimer Landstrasse, and turn left on Palmengartenstrasse to reach the delightful **Palmengarten und Botanischer Garten** ㉒. Also close to the Bockenheimer Warte stop is the **Naturkundemuseum Senckenberg** ㉓, with fun, hands-on exhibits.

TIMING Count on spending a full day on this tour. It's impossible to see all the museums in one trip. You should block out 45 minutes for the Goethehaus und Goethemuseum, an hour and 15 minutes for the Städelsches Kunstinstitut und Städtische Galerie, and an hour for the Städtische Galerie Liebieghaus. For the remaining museums it's a question of time and preference. Pick the one or two that interest you most and allow at least 45 minutes for each. If you intend to visit the Zoologischer Garten, expect to spend 1½ hours there.

What to See

㉑ **Alte Oper** (Old Opera House). Kaiser Wilhelm I traveled from Berlin for the gala opening of the opera house in 1880. Gutted in World War II, the house remained a hollow shell for 40 years while controversy raged over its reconstruction. The exterior and lobby are faithful to the original, though the remainder of the building is more like a modern multipurpose hall. Even if you don't go to a performance, it's worth having a look at the ornate lobby, an example of 19th-century neoclassicism at its most confident. ⊠ *Opernpl., City Center* ☎ *069/134–0400* ⊕ *www.alte-oper-frankfurt.de* Ⓤ *Alte Oper (U-bahn).*

off the beaten path

ALTER JÜDISCHER FRIEDHOF (Old Jewish Cemetery) – The old Jewish quarter is east of Börneplatz, a short walk south of the Konstablerwache, or east of the Römer U-bahn station. Partly vandalized in the Nazi era, the cemetery was in use between the 13th and 19th centuries and is one of the few reminders of prewar Jewish life in Frankfurt. A newer Jewish cemetery is part of the cemetery at Eckenheimer Landstrasse 238 (about 1½ mi north). ⊠ *Kurt-Schumacher-Str. and Battonstr., City Center* ☎ *069/561– 826* ⊠ *Free* ☉ *Daily 8:30–4:30* Ⓤ *Konstablerwache (U-bahn and S-bahn).*

❾ Börse (Stock Exchange). This is the center of Germany's stock and money market. The Börse was founded by Frankfurt merchants in 1585 to establish some order in their often chaotic dealings, but the present building dates from the 1870s. These days computerized networks and international telephone systems have removed some of the drama from the dealers' floor, but it's still an exciting scene to watch from the visitor gallery. ⊠ *Börsepl., City Center* ☎ *069/21010* ⊕ *www.deutsche-boerse.com* ⊠ *Free* ☉ *Visitor gallery weekdays 10:30–6* Ⓤ *Hauptwache (U-bahn and S-bahn).*

⑮ Eiserner Steg (Iron Bridge). A pedestrian walkway and the first suspension bridge in Europe, the Eiserner Steg connects the city center with Sachsenhausen.

Eschenheimer Turm (Eschenheim Tower). Built in the early 15th century, this tower, a block north of the Hauptwache, remains the finest example of the city's original 42 towers. ⊠ *Eschenheimer Tor, City Center* Ⓤ *Eschenheimer Tor (U-bahn).*

⑳ Fressgasse ("Pig-Out Alley"). Grosse Bockenheimer Strasse is the proper name of this pedestrian street, one of the city's liveliest thoroughfares, but Frankfurters have given it this sobriquet because of its amazing choice of delicatessens, wine merchants, cafés, and restaurants. Food shops offer fresh or smoked fish, cheeses, and a wide range of local specialties, including frankfurters. In the summer you can dine alfresco. Ⓤ *Hauptwache (U-bahn and S-bahn), Alte Oper (U-bahn).*

★ ⑲ Goethehaus und Goethemuseum (Goethe's House and Museum). The house where Germany's most famous poet was born in 1749 is furnished with many original pieces that belonged to his family, including manuscripts in his own hand. Though Goethe is associated with Weimar, where he lived most of his life, Frankfurters are proud to claim him as a native son. The original house was destroyed by Allied bombing and has been carefully rebuilt and restored in every detail.

Johann Wolfgang von Goethe studied law and became a member of the bar in Frankfurt. He was quickly drawn to writing, however, and eventually wrote the first version of his masterpiece, *Faust,* here. The adjoining museum contains works of art that inspired Goethe (he was an amateur painter) and works associated with his literary contemporaries. ⊠ *Grosser Hirschgraben 23–25, Altstadt* ☎ *069/138–800* ⊕ *www. goethehaus-frankfurt.de* ⊠ *€5* ☉ *Apr.–Sept., weekdays 9–6, week-*

ends 10–4; Oct.–Mar., weekdays 9–4, weekends 10–4 Ⓤ *Hauptwache (U-bahn and S-bahn).*

❼ Hauptwache. This square is where Grosse Bockenheimer Strasse (Fressgasse) runs into the Zeil, a main shopping street. The attractive baroque building with a steeply sloping roof is the actual Hauptwache (Main Guardhouse), from which the square takes its name. Built in 1729, the building had been tastelessly added to over the years and was demolished to permit excavation for a vast underground shopping mall and subway station, which you'll find beneath the square. The building was then restored to its original appearance. Today it houses a café. Ⓤ *Hauptwache (U-bahn and S-bahn).*

❹ Historisches Museum (Historical Museum). This fascinating museum encompasses all aspects of the city's history over the past eight centuries. It contains a scale model of historic Frankfurt, complete with every street, house, and church. There's also an astonishing display of silver, a children's museum, and a permanent exhibit on Apfelwein. The museum's restaurant, Historix, serves Apfelwein and all the typical food and accoutrements of the hard-cider business. ✉ *Saalg. 19, Altstadt* ☎ *069/ 2123–5599* ⊕ *www.historisches-museum.frankfurt.de* ⌦ *€4, free Wed.* ⊙ *Tues. and Thurs.–Sun. 10–5, Wed. 10–8* Ⓤ *Römer (U-bahn).*

❶❼ Jüdisches Museum (Jewish Museum). The story of Frankfurt's Jewish quarter is told in the former Rothschild Palais. Prior to the Holocaust, the community was the second largest in Germany. The museum contains extensive archives of Jewish history and culture, including a library of 5,000 books, a large photographic collection, and a documentation center. A branch of the museum, **Museum Judengasse** (✉ Kurt-Schumacher-Str. 10, City Center ☎ 069/297–7419 ⌦ €1.50 ⊙ Tues. and Thurs.–Sun. 10–5, Wed. 10–8 Ⓤ Römer [U-bahn]), is built around the foundations of mostly 18th-century buildings, which once made up the ghetto. The branch is also near the Old Jewish Cemetery (Alter Jüdischer Friedhof). ✉ *Untermainkai 14–15, Altstadt* ☎ *069/2123–5000* ⊕ *www.juedischesmuseum. de* ⌦ *€2.60* ⊙ *Tues. and Thurs.–Sun. 10–5, Wed. 10–8.*

❶❸ Kaiserdom. Because the Holy Roman emperors were chosen and crowned here from the 16th to the 18th century, the church is known as the Kaiserdom (Imperial Cathedral), even though it isn't the seat of a bishop. Officially the Church of St. Bartholomew, it was built largely between the 13th and 15th centuries and survived World War II with most of its treasures intact. Its many magnificent, original Gothic carvings include a life-size Crucifixion group and the fine 15th-century *Maria-Schlaf* (Altar of Mary Sleeping). The most impressive exterior feature is the tall, red sandstone tower (almost 300 feet high), which was added between 1415 and 1514. It was the tallest structure in Frankfurt before the skyscrapers, and the view from the top remains an exciting panorama. In 1953 excavations in front of the main entrance revealed the remains of a Roman settlement and the foundations of a Carolingian imperial palace. The **Dommuseum** (Cathedral Museum) occupies the former Gothic cloister. ✉ *Dompl. 1, Altstadt* ☎ *069/1337–6184* ⌦ *Dommuseum €2* ⊙ *Church Apr.–Oct., Mon.–Thurs. and Sat. 9–noon and*

Fodor'sChoice
★

*2:30–6, Fri. and Sun. 2:30–6; Nov.–Mar., Mon.–Thurs. and Sat. 9–noon
and 2:30–5, Fri. and Sun. 2:30–5. Dommuseum Tues.–Fri. 10–5, weekends 11–5* Ⓤ *Römer (U-bahn).*

⑱ Karmeliterkloster (Carmelite Monastery). Secularized in 1803, the church
and adjacent buildings contain the **Museum für Vor- und Frühgeschichte**
(Museum of Prehistory and Early History). The **main cloister** (⊠ Free)
displays the largest religious fresco north of the Alps, a 16th-century representation of Christ's birth and death by Jörg Ratgeb. ⊠ *Karmeliterg.
1, Altstadt* ☎ *069/2123–5896* ⊠ *Museum €4, free Wed.* ☉ *Museum
and cloister Tues. and Thurs.–Sun. 10–5, Wed. 10–8* Ⓤ *Römer (U-bahn).*

❽ Katharinenkirche (St. Catherine's Church). This house of worship, the
first independent Protestant church in Gothic style, was originally built
between 1678 and 1681. The church it replaced, dating from 1343, was
the setting of the first Protestant sermon preached in Frankfurt, in 1522.
Goethe was confirmed here. ⊠ *An der Hauptwache, City Center*
☉ *Weekdays 2–6* Ⓤ *Hauptwache (U-bahn and S-bahn).*

⑯ Leonhardskirche (St. Leonard's Church). Begun in the Romanesque style
and continued in the late-Gothic style, this beautifully preserved Catholic
church contains five naves, two 13th-century Romanesque arches, and
15th-century stained glass. The "pendant," or hanging vaulting, was already a major Frankfurt tourist attraction in the 17th century. Masses
are held in English on Saturday at 5 and Sunday at 10. ⊠ *Am Leon-
hardstor and Untermainkai, Altstadt* ☉ *Tues.–Sun. 10–noon and 3–6*
Ⓤ *Römer (U-bahn).*

❻ Liebfrauenkirche (Church of Our Lady). The peaceful, concealed courtyard of this Catholic church makes it hard to believe you're in the swirl
of the shopping district. Dating from the 14th century, the late-Gothic
church still has a fine tympanum relief over the south door and ornate
rococo wood carvings inside. ⊠ *Liebfrauenberg 3, City Center* ☉ *Daily
7–7, except during services* Ⓤ *Hauptwache (U-bahn and S-bahn).*

Messegelände (Fairgrounds). Also called the congress center, this huge
complex is Europe's busiest trade show center. Important international
trade fairs showcase the latest books, cars, fashion, medical and high
technology, and consumer goods. ⊠ *Ludwig-Erhard-Anlage 1, Messe*
☎ *069/75750* ⊕ *www.messe-frankfurt.de* Ⓤ *Festhalle/Messe (U-bahn).*

⑫ Museum für Moderne Kunst (Museum of Modern Art). Austrian architect
Hans Hollein designed this distinctive triangular building, shaped like a
wedge of cake. The collection features American pop art and works by
such German artists as Gerhard Richter and Joseph Beuys. ⊠ *Domstr.
10, City Center* ☎ *069/2123–0447* ⊕ *www.frankfurt-business.de/mmk*
⊠ *€5* ☉ *Tues. and Thurs.–Sun. 10–5, Wed. 10–8* Ⓤ *Römer (U-bahn).*

❸㉓ Naturkundemuseum Senckenberg (Natural History Museum). An important collection of fossils, animals, plants, and geological exhibits is
upstaged by the famous diplodocus dinosaur, imported from New
York—the only complete specimen of its kind in Europe. Many of the
exhibits of prehistoric animals have been designed with children in
mind, including a series of dioramas featuring stuffed animals. ⊠ *Senck-*

FodorśChoice
★

enberganlage 25, Bockenheim ☎ *069/75420* ⊕ *www.senckenberg.uni-frankfurt.de* 🖾 *€5* ⊙ *Mon., Tues., Thurs., and Fri. 9–5, Wed. 9–8, weekends 9–6* Ⓤ *Bockenheimer Warte (U-bahn).*

❸ **Nikolaikirche** (St. Nicholas Church). This small red sandstone church was built in the late 13th century as the court chapel for emperors of the Holy Roman Empire. Try to time your visit to coincide with the chimes of the carillon, which rings three times a day, at 9, noon, and 5. 🖂 *South side of Römerberg, Altstadt* ⊙ *Oct.–Mar., daily 10–6; Apr.–Sept., daily 10–8* Ⓤ *Römer (U-bahn).*

☾ ㉒ **Palmengarten und Botanischer Garten** (Tropical Garden and Botanical Gardens). A splendid cluster of tropical and semitropical greenhouses contains a wide variety of flora, including cacti, orchids, and palms. The surrounding park, which can be surveyed from a miniature train, has many recreational facilities including a small lake where you can rent rowboats, a play area for children, and a wading pool. Between the Palmengarten and the adjoining Grüneburgpark, the botanical gardens have a wide assortment of wild, ornamental, and rare plants from around the world. Special collections include a 2½-acre rock garden as well as rose and rhododendron gardens. In summer, concerts are held in an outdoor music pavilion. 🖂 *Siesmayerstr. 63, Westend* ☎ *069/2123–3939* ⊕ *www.stadt-frankfurt.de/palmengarten* 🖾 *€3.50* ⊙ *Feb.–Oct., daily 9–6; Nov.–Jan., daily 9–4* Ⓤ *Westend (U-bahn).*

❺ **Paulskirche** (St. Paul's Church). The first all-German parliament was held here in 1848. The parliament lasted only a year, having achieved little more than offering the Prussian king the crown of Germany. Today the church, which has been secularized and not very tastefully restored, remains a symbol of German democracy and is used mainly for ceremonies. The German Book Dealers' annual Peace Prize is awarded in the hall, as is the Goethe Prize. 🖂 *Paulspl., Altstadt* ⊙ *Daily 10–5* Ⓤ *Römer (U-bahn).*

❷ **Römer** (City Hall). Three individual patrician buildings make up the Römer. From left to right, they are the Alt-Limpurg, the Zum Römer (from which the entire structure takes its name), and the Löwenstein. The mercantile-minded Frankfurt burghers used the complex not only for political and ceremonial purposes but also for trade fairs and other commercial ventures. Its gabled Gothic facade with an ornate balcony is widely known as the city's official emblem.

The most important events to take place in the Römer were the festivities celebrating the coronations of the Holy Roman emperors. The first was in 1562 in the glittering **Kaisersaal** (Imperial Hall), which was last used in 1792 to celebrate the election of the emperor Francis II, who would later be forced to abdicate by Napoléon. When no official business is being conducted, you can see the impressive, full-length 19th-century portraits of the 52 emperors of the Holy Roman Empire, which line the walls of the reconstructed banquet hall. 🖂 *West side of Römerberg, Altstadt* ☎ *069/2123–4814* 🖾 *€1.50* ⊙ *Daily 10–1 and 2–5; closed during official functions* Ⓤ *Römer (U-bahn).*

▶ ❶ **Römerberg.** This square north of the Main River, lovingly restored after wartime bomb damage, is the historical focal point of the city. The Römer, the Nikolaikirche, the Historiches Museum, and the half-timber Ostzeile houses are all found here. The 16th-century Fountain of Justitia (Justice) stands in the center of the Römerberg. At the coronation of Emperor Matthias in 1612, wine flowed from the fountain instead of water. This practice has been revived by the city fathers on special occasions. The square is also the site of many public festivals throughout the year, including the Christmas markets in December. ⊠ *Between Braubachstr. and Main River, Altstadt* Ⓤ *Römer (U-bahn).*

❿ **Schirn Kunsthalle** (Schirn Art Gallery). One of Frankfurt's most modern museums is devoted exclusively to changing exhibits of modern art and photography. Past shows have included "Audio-Visual Spaces," "Shopping," Henri Matisse drawings, Mercedes posters, and Polish landscapes of the 19th and 20th centuries. It stands opposite the Kaiserdom. ⊠ *Am Römerberg 6a, Altstadt* ☎ *069/299–8820* ⊕ *www.schirn-kunsthalle.de* ≊ *€5–€7, depending on exhibition* ⊙ *Tues. and Sun. 11–7, Wed.–Sat. 11–10* Ⓤ *Römer (U-bahn).*

⓫ **Staufenmauer** (Staufen Wall). The Staufenmauer is one of the few remaining sections of the old city's fortifications and dates from the 12th century. ⊠ *Fahrg., Altstadt* Ⓤ *Römer (U-bahn).*

Ⓒ **Struwwelpeter-Museum** (Slovenly Peter Museum). This museum contains a collection of letters, sketches, and manuscripts by Dr. Heinrich Hoffmann, a Frankfurt physician and creator of the children's-book hero Struwwelpeter, or Slovenly Peter, the character you see as a puppet or doll in Frankfurt's shops. ⊠ *Benderg. 1, Altstadt* ☎ *069/281–333* ≊ *Free* ⊙ *Tues. and Thurs.–Sun. 11–5, Wed. 11–8* Ⓤ *Römer (U-bahn).*

Zeil. The heart of Frankfurt's shopping district is this bustling pedestrian street, running east from Hauptwache Square. You'll find almost every type of store here, including department stores, boutiques, drugstores, electronics shops, fast-food eateries, restaurants, and more. City officials claim it's the country's busiest shopping street. Ⓤ *Hauptwache, Konstablerwache (U-bahn and S-bahn).*

★ Ⓒ ❿ **Zoologischer Garten** (Zoo). Founded in 1858, this is one of the most important and attractive zoos in Europe. Its remarkable collection includes some 5,000 animals of 600 different species, a bears' castle, an exotarium (aquarium plus reptiles), and an aviary, reputedly the largest in Europe. Nocturnal creatures move about in a special section. The zoo has a restaurant and a café, along with afternoon concerts in summer. ⊠ *Alfred-Brehm Pl. 16, Ostend* ☎ *069/2123–3727* ⊕ *www.zoo-frankfurt.de* ≊ *€5.50* ⊙ *Nov.–Mar., daily 9–5; Apr.–Oct., daily 9–7* Ⓤ *Zoo (U-bahn).*

Sachsenhausen

★ The old quarter of Sachsenhausen, on the south bank of the Main River, has been sensitively preserved, and its cobblestone streets, half-timber houses, and beer gardens make it a very popular area to stroll. Sachsenhausen's two big attractions are the Museumufer (Museum River-bank), which has seven museums almost next door to one another, and the famous *Apfelwein* (apple-wine or cider) taverns around the Ritter-gasse pedestrian area. A green pine wreath above a tavern's entrance tells passersby that a freshly pressed—and alcoholic—apple cider is on tap. You can eat well in these small establishments, too. Formerly a sep-arate village, Sachsenhausen is said to have been established by Charle-magne, who settled the Main's banks with a group of Saxon families in the 8th century. It was an important bridgehead for the crusader Knights of the Teutonic Order and in 1318 officially became part of Frankfurt.

a good walk

The best place to begin is at the charming 17th-century villa housing the **Städtische Galerie Liebieghaus** ㉔ ▶, the westernmost of the museums. It has an internationally famous collection of classical, medieval, and Renaissance sculpture. From it you need only turn to your right and fol-low the riverside road, Schaumainkai, for about 2 km (1 mi), passing all of the museums and winding up around the Rittergasse.

The **Städelsches Kunstinstitut und Städtische Galerie** ㉕ houses one of the most significant art collections in Germany, and the **Museum für Kom-munikation** ㉖ displays postal coaches, ancient telephones that work, and a huge stamp collection. The **Deutsches Architekturmuseum** ㉗ traces man's structures from Stone Age huts to high-rises. Film artifacts and classic film videos are featured at the **Deutsches Filmmuseum** ㉘. After this museum, you could take a break at an Apfelwein tavern on Schweizer Strasse. The next museum, past the Untermain Brucke (Bridge), is the **Museum für Völkerkunde** ㉙, which holds ethnological artifacts from the Pacific, Indonesia, Africa, and America. A stunning collection of Euro-pean and Asian applied art in the **Museum für Angewandte Kunst** ㉚ comes next. Continue down the river road (the name changes from Schaumainkai to Sachsenhäuser Ufer). Just beyond the first bridge carrying car traf-fic, follow Grosse Rittergasse to the right. A bit down this street, on your left, is the **Kuhhirtenturm** ㉛, the only remaining part of Sachsenhausen's original fortifications.

A few steps farther and you will be in the heart of the Apfelwein dis-trict, which is especially lively on summer evenings when it becomes one big outdoor festival. Some of the apple-wine taverns and other water-ing places are also open weekday afternoons. The area has a distinctly medieval air, with narrow back alleys, quaint little inns, and quiet squares that escaped the modern developer, yet it's also full of shops, cafés, and bars thronging with people. This is a great spot to relax and sample some apple-wine at the end of the day.

TIMING   Allow an hour and 15 minutes for the Städelsches Kunstinstitut und Städtische Galerie, and an hour for the Städtische Galerie Liebieghaus. You could spend at least 45 minutes in each of the other museums along the walk.

What to See

㉗ **Deutsches Architekturmuseum** (German Architecture Museum). Created by German architect Oswald Mathias Ungers, this 19th-century villa con-tains an entirely modern interior. There are five floors of drawings, models, and audiovisual displays that chart the progress of architecture through the ages. ⊠ *Schaumainkai 43, Sachsenhausen* ☎ *069/2123–8844* ⊕ *www.dam-online.de* 🖾 *€4* ⊙ *Tues. and Thurs.–Sun. 10–5, Wed. 10–8* Ⓤ *SchweizerPlatz (U-bahn).*

㉘ Deutsches Filmmuseum (German Film Museum). Germany's first museum of cinematography houses an exciting collection of film artifacts. Visitors can view its collection of classic film videos, and a theater in the basement has regular evening screenings of films ranging from avant-garde to Hungarian to silent-era flicks. ⊠ *Schaumainkai 41, Sachsenhausen* ☎ *069/2123–8830* ⊕ *www.deutsches-filmmuseum.de* 🖾 *€2.50* ⊙ *Tues., Thurs.–Fri., and Sun. 10–5, Wed. 10–8, Sat. 2–8* Ⓤ *SchweizerPlatz (U-bahn).*

---

need a break?

Two of Sachsenhausen's liveliest Apfelwein taverns are well removed from the Rittergasse and handy to the Museumufer. You'll find them adjacent to one another if you turn south down Schweizer Strasse, next to the Deutsches Filmmuseum, and walk five minutes. **Zum Gemalten Haus** (⊠ Schweizerstr. 67, Sachsenhausen ☎ 069/614–559) will provide all the hard cider and *gemütlichkeit* you could want. **Zum Wagner** (⊠ Schweizerstr. 71, Sachsenhausen ☎ 069/612–565) reeks so with "old Sachsenhausen" schmaltz that it's downright corny.

㉛ Kuhhirtenturm (Shepherd's Tower). This is the last of nine towers, built in the 15th century, that formed part of Sachsenhausen's fortifications. The composer Paul Hindemith lived in the tower from 1923 to 1927 while working at the Frankfurt Opera. ⊠ *Grosser Ritterg., Sachsenhausen* Ⓤ *SchweizerPlatz (U-bahn).*

㉖ Museum für Kommunikation (Museum for Communication). This is the place for getting in on the electronic age. You can surf the Internet, talk to one another on picture telephones, and learn of glass fiber technology. Exhibitions on historic communication methods include mail coaches, stamps, ancient dial telephones with their clunky switching equipment, and a reconstructed 19th-century post office. ⊠ *Schaumainkai 53, Sachsenhausen* ☎ *069/60600* ⊕ *www.museumsstiftung.de/frankfurt* 🖾 *Free* ⊙ *Tues.–Fri. 9–5, weekends 11–7* Ⓤ *SchweizerPlatz (U-bahn).*

㉚ Museum für Angewandte Kunst (Museum of Applied Arts). More than 30,000 objects representing European and Asian decorative arts are exhibited in this museum designed by American architect Richard Meier. The collection of furniture, glassware, and porcelain has expanded to include Web sites, computers, and graphic design. ⊠ *Schaumainkai 17, Sachsenhausen* ☎ *069/2123–4037* 🖾 *€5, free Wed.* ⊙ *Tues. and Thurs.–Sun. 10–5, Wed. 10–8* Ⓤ *SchweizerPlatz (U-bahn).*

㉙ Museum für Völkerkunde (Ethnological Museum). The lifestyles and customs of aboriginal societies from around the world are examined through items such as masks, ritual objects, and jewelry. ⊠ *Schaumainkai 29, Sachsenhausen* ☎ *069/2123–1510* 🖾 *€3.50; free Wed.* ⊙ *Tues. and Thurs.–Sun. 10–5, Wed. 10–8* Ⓤ *SchweizerPlatz (U-bahn).*

★ ㉕ **Städelsches Kunstinstitut und Städtische Galerie** (Städel Art Institute and Municipal Gallery). You'll find one of Germany's most important art collections at this museum, with paintings by Dürer, Vermeer, Rembrandt, Rubens, Monet, Renoir, and other masters. The section on German expressionism is particularly strong, with representative works by Frankfurt artist Max Beckmann. ⊠ *Schaumainkai 63, Sachsenhausen* ☎ *069/605–0980* ⊕ *www.staedelmuseum.de* ☑ *€5, free Wed.* ⊙ *Tues., Thurs., Fri., and Sun. 10–5, Wed. 10–8, Sat. 2–8* Ⓤ *SchweizerPlatz (U-bahn).*

⬤ ★ ㉔ **Städtische Galerie Liebieghaus** (Liebieg Municipal Museum of Sculpture). The sculpture collection here, from 5,000 years of civilizations and epochs, is considered one of the most important in Europe. From antiquity the collection includes a statue of a Sumarian functionary and a relief from the temple of Egyptian king Sahure (2455–2443 BC). From the Middle Ages there's an 11th-century throned Madonna with child from Trier and from the Renaissance an altar relief by the noted Florentine sculptor Lucca della Robbia (1399–1482). Works such as the *Immaculata,* by Matthias Steinl (1688), represent the baroque era. Some pieces are exhibited in the lovely gardens surrounding the house. ⊠ *Schaumainkai 71, Sachsenhausen* ☎ *069/2123–8617* ☑ *€4* ⊙ *Tues. and Thurs.–Sun. 10–5, Wed. 10–8* Ⓤ *SchweizerPlatz (U-bahn).*

WHERE TO EAT

Business travelers keep the nicer restaurants busy, so be sure to make advance reservations for lunch or dinner whenever possible. Several upscale restaurants serve discounted lunch menus. For example, Erno's Bistro and Gargantua have midday menus for €25. At the apple-wine taverns there's always room for a few more people at the long tables, and patrons are very accommodating when it comes to squeezing together.

WHAT IT COSTS In Euros				
	$$$$	**$$$**	**$$**	**$**	**¢**
AT DINNER	over €25	€21–€25	€16–€20	€9–€15	under €9

Restaurant prices are per person for a main course at dinner.

City Center

$–$$$ ✕ **Central Park.** From Thursday to Saturday, the bar here is just as popular as the restaurant, making this a prime spot for people watching. The menu has a bit of everything: pasta, salads, seafood, vegetarian dishes, and German fare. Located near the Alte Oper (Old Opera), this is an excellent choice for post-concert dining and business entertaining. ⊠ *Kaiserhofstr. 12* ☎ *069/9139–6146* ⊕ *www.central-park.com* ▭ *V, MC* ⊙ *Closed Sun.* Ⓤ *Alte Oper (U-bahn).*

★ **$–$$$** ✕ **Maintower.** Atop the skyscraper that houses Hessischer Landesbank, this popular restaurant-cum-café-cum-bar captures an unbeatable view. Through 25-foot floor-to-ceiling windows, all of "Mainhattan" is at your feet. Prices are surprisingly reasonable, though you will have to pay €4.50 per person just to take the elevator up. The cuisine is part global, part regional. It's hard to get a table for supper, though it's less of a problem for afternoon coffee or an evening at the bar. ⊠ *Neue Mainzerstr. 52–58, City Center* ☎ *069/3650–4770* ⊟ *AE, V* Ⓤ *Alte Oper (U-bahn).*

$–$$ ✕ **Garibaldi.** The fresh pasta and fun atmosphere are equally appealing at this Italian restaurant located between the Alte Oper and Hauptwache. Selections of antipasti, seafood, pizzas, and pasta dishes are extensive, and many entrées are topped with freshly shaved truffles. The waiters are energetic and friendly, as is the chef, who occasionally mingles with diners. Reservations are recommended. ⊠ *Klein Hochstr. 4, City Center* ☎ *069/2199–7644* ⊟ *V* ☽ *Closed Sun.* Ⓤ *Alte Oper (U-bahn).*

$–$$ ✕ **Steinernes Haus.** Diners share long wooden tables beneath prints of old Frankfurt and traditional clothing mounted on the walls. The house specialty is a rump steak brought to the table uncooked with a heated rock tablet on which it is prepared. The beef broth is the perfect antidote to cold weather. The menu has other old German standards along with daily specials. Traditional fare popular with locals includes *Rippchen* (smoked pork) and *Zigeunerhackbraten* (spicy meat loaf). If you don't specify a *Kleines,* or small glass of beer, you'll automatically get a liter mug. ⊠ *Braubachstr. 35, Altstadt* ☎ *069/283–491* ⚄ *Reservations essential* ⊟ *MC, V* Ⓤ *Römer (U-bahn).*

$ ✕ **Café Karin.** An understated café that attracts an interesting cross section of patrons, this is a great place to breakfast (only a few euros), to recover from a shopping spree, or to eat something healthy in preparation for a night out. Sample the goat cheese salad or whole-grain ratatouille crepes. Cakes and baked goods come from a whole-grain bakery. There's a no-smoking section. ⊠ *Grosser Hirschgraben 28, Altstadt* ☎ *069/295–217* ⊟ *No credit cards* Ⓤ *Hauptwache (U-bahn and S-bahn).*

$ ✕ **Metropol.** Brunch is the main attraction at this café near the Römerberg and Dom. The dining room is large, and in the warmer months it's extended to include outdoor seating on a garden patio. In addition to the daily selection of tantalizing cakes and pastries, the menu features eggs, salads, pasta, and a few traditional German dishes. Take a quick break from sightseeing or relax for several hours with a good book. Metropol is open daily until 1 AM. ⊠ *Weckmarkt 13–15, City Center* ☎ *069/288–287* ⊟ *V* Ⓤ *Römer (U-bahn).*

¢ ✕ **Altes Cafe Schneider.** Though it's not striking from the outside, this family-owned establishment has a warm and inviting interior. You can lounge on couches and armchairs while enjoying coffee and a variety of freshly baked treats. The main appeal here is a long list of cakes, pies, and other desserts, but the café also offers light fare such as quiche, soups, and salads. ⊠ *Kaiserstr. 12* ☎ *069/281–447* ⊟ *No credit cards* Ⓤ *Willy-Brandt-Platz (U-bahn).*

¢ ✕ **Nutelleria.** Sweet-tooths will surely want to stop by this eatery just off the Zeil. Everything on the menu, including crepes, waffles, and many other creations, are filled with nutella—the European chocolate-hazelnut treat. This is an occasion to make dessert a meal. ⊠ *Neue Kräme 23* ☎ *069/1388–6938* ⊟ *No credit cards* ☽ *Closed Sun.* Ⓤ *Hauptwache (U-bahn and S-bahn).*

¢ ✕ **Souper.** Germans are among the world's best soup-makers, and one of Frankfurt's best varieties of hearty soups is found here. This small place, a favorite of locals in wintertime, sits on a small street between Hauptwache and the Römer. A selection of six to eight soups is offered daily, including such creations as Thai-coconut chicken and tomato soup with mozzarella. Eat at the counter or take your soup to go. They also serve sandwiches. ☒ *Weissadlerg. 3* ☎ *069/2972–4545* 🖷 *069/2972–4544* ⊕ *www.souper.de* ⊟ *No credit cards* ⊗ *Closed Sun.* Ⓤ *Hauptwache (U-bahn and S-bahn).*

Nordend/Bornheim

$–$$ ✕ **Harvey's.** This restaurant first achieved notoriety as a gay and lesbian hangout, deriving its name from San Francisco's martyred gay supervisor Harvey Milk. But the straight community has been coming here more and more to enjoy the imaginative menu, good music, friendly atmosphere, and chameleonlike changes in design, several times a year. Breakfast is served until 4 PM. ☒ *Bornheimer Landstr. 64, Nordend* ☎ *069/ 497–3032* ⊟ *No credit cards* Ⓤ *Merianplatz (U-bahn).*

¢–$$ ✕ **El Pacifico.** Although Frankfurt lacks a wealth of Mexican cuisine, the best of it is found here. Two blocks from Bergerstrasse, El Pacifico has a festive atmosphere that appeals to patrons of all ages. This warm and cozy restaurant serves a variety of fruit-flavor margaritas, and is well known for its hearty chicken wings appetizer. El Pacifico also offers a full menu of traditional Mexican fare, including burritos, enchiladas, and fajitas. The dimly lit dining room is fairly small; reservations are recommended on weekends. ☒ *Sandweg 79, Bornheim* ☎ *069/446–988* ⊟ *AE* Ⓤ *Bornheim Mitte (U-bahn).*

¢–$$ ✕ **Grossenwahn.** The Nordend is noted for its "scene" establishments, and this corner locale is one of the best. The name translates as "megalomania," which says it all. One whiff of the air tells you that smoking is tolerated without restriction, and the menu is esoteric with German, Greek, Italian, and French elements. ☒ *Lenaustr. 97, Nordend* ☎ *069/ 599–356* ⊟ *AE, MC, V* Ⓤ *Glauburgstr. (U-bahn).*

¢–$ ✕ **Weisse Lilie.** Come to this Bornheim favorite for the fresh garlic aioli and the paella, not to mention the reasonably priced red wines. The dark interior has wooden tables brightened by fresh-cut flowers and candles, making it a good spot for an intimate dinner or a large gathering. A variety of moderately priced tapas is always available. In summer you can dine outside, German style, at long wooden tables. Reservations are recommended on weekends. ☒ *Bergerstr. 275* ☎ *069/453–860* ⊟ *No credit cards* Ⓤ *Bornheim Mitte (U-bahn).*

Westend

★ $$$$ ✕ **Erno's Bistro.** This tiny, unpretentious place in a quiet Westend neighborhood looks like an unlikely candidate for "the best restaurant in Germany." Yet that's what one French critic called it. The bistro's specialty, fish, is often flown in daily from France. It's closed weekends, during the Christmas and Easter seasons, and during much of the summer—in other words, when its clientele, the well-heeled elite of the business community, are unlikely to be in town. ☒ *Liebigstr. 15, Westend* ☎ *069/ 721–997* ⌲ *Reservations essential* ⊟ *AE, DC, MC, V* ⊗ *Closed weekends and July–early Aug.* Ⓤ *Westend (U-bahn).*

$$$ ✕ **Gargantua.** One of Frankfurt's most creative chefs, Klaus Trebes,
Fodor'sChoice who doubles as a food columnist, serves up modern versions of Ger-
★ man classics and French-accented dishes in a laid-back dining room dec-
orated with contemporary art. His menu features dishes such as artichoke
risotto with goose liver, lentil salad with stewed beef, and grilled do-
rado served on pureed white beans and pesto. One corner of the restau-
rant is reserved for those who want only to sample the outstanding wine
list. ⊠ *Liebigstr. 47, Westend* ☎ *069/720–718* ▭ *AE, MC, V* ⊘ *Closed
Sun. No lunch Sat.* Ⓤ *Westend (U-bahn).*

$–$$$ ✕ **La Boveda.** This quaint but expensive restaurant is tucked inside the
dimly lit basement of a Westend residential building. (La Boveda is
Spanish for "wine cellar.") In addition to the smaller plates of tapas,
the menu features a long list of larger dinner entrées. Especially interesting are the creative seafood combinations. And true to its name, La
Boveda offers an extensive wine menu. Patio dining is available May
through September. Reservations are recommended on weekends. ⊠ *Feld-
bergstr 10, Westend* ☎ *069/723–220* ⊕ *www.la-boveda.de* ▭ *AE, MC,
V* ⊘ *Closed Sun.* Ⓤ *Westend (U-bahn).*

$$ ✕ **Omonia.** This cozy cellar locale offers the best Greek cuisine in town.
If you have a good appetite, try the Omonia Platter, with lamb in sev-
eral forms, plus Greek-style pasta and vegetables. The place is popular
and the tables few, so make a reservation. ⊠ *Vogtstr. 43, Westend*
☎ *069/593–314* ⌂ *Reservations essential* ▭ *AE, DC, MC, V* ⊘ *No
lunch weekends* Ⓤ *Holzhausenstr (U-bahn).*

¢–$ ✕ **Café Laumer.** The ambience of an old-time Viennese café is well pre-
served at this popular spot. It owes its literary tradition to Theodor
Adorno, a philosopher and sociologist of the "Frankfurt School," who
drank his daily coffee here. For fear of attracting more patrons than the
often crowded café can handle, it isn't listed in the phone book. The
café is open for breakfast, lunch, and afternoon coffee but closes at 7
PM. ⊠ *Bockenheimer Landstr. 67, Westend* ☎ *069/727–912* ▭ *DC, MC,
V* ⊘ *No dinner* Ⓤ *Westend (U-bahn).*

Sachsenhausen

★ $$$$ ✕ **Maingau Stuben.** Chef Werner Döpfner himself greets you and lights
your candle at this very "in" restaurant. A polished clientele is drawn
by the linen tablecloths, subdued lighting, and such nearly forgotten
practices as carving the meat tableside. The menu includes contem-
porary dishes such as seafood salad with scallops and lobster mousse
and rack of venison in a walnut crust. He also has a cellar full of rare
German wines. ⊠ *Schifferstr. 38–40, Sachsenhausen* ☎ *069/610–752*
▭ *AE, MC, V* ⊘ *Closed Mon. No lunch Sat., no dinner Sun.*
Ⓤ *SchweizerPlatz (U-bahn).*

$$–$$$ ✕ **Holbeins.** Portions are not large here, but everything on the interna-
tional menu is delicious. The elegantly modern dining room was built
in the space between two museums on the Main River. Choose from a
variety of pasta creations, fish, steak, and even a few traditional Ger-
man dishes. Live piano (and sometimes jazz) is performed most evenings.
⊠ *Holbeinstr. 1, Sachsenhausen* ☎ *069/6605–6666* ⌂ *Reservations es-
sential* ▭ *V* ⊘ *Closed Mon.* Ⓤ *SchweizerPlatz (U-bahn).*

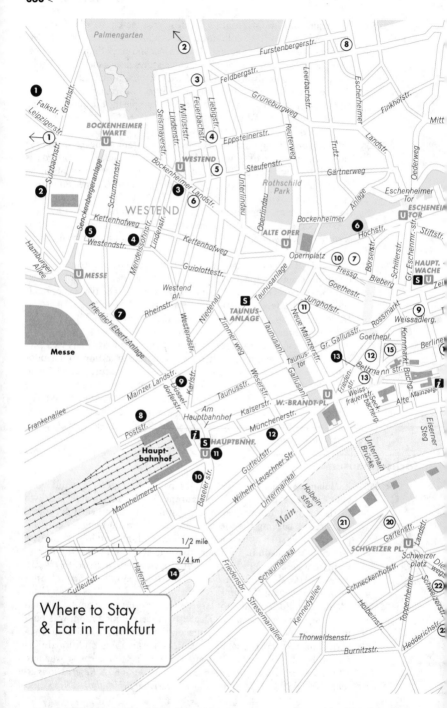

Where to Stay
& Eat in Frankfurt

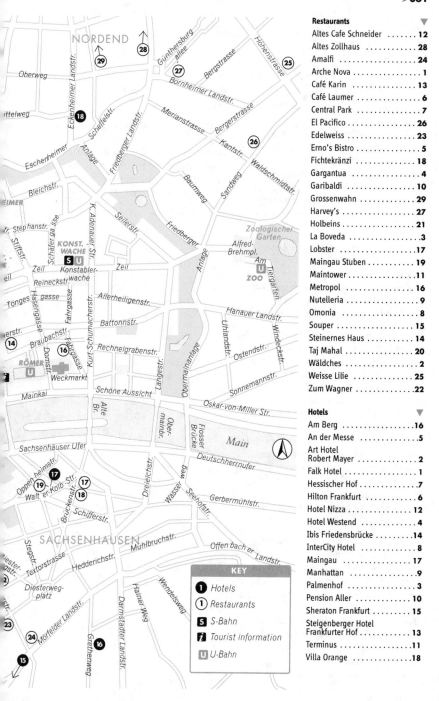

APFELWEIN: SWEET, SOUR, OR STRAIGHT-UP?

DURING A VISIT to one of Frankfurt's traditional German restaurants, you may find that the menu does not include wine. Chances are you are seated in one of the city's better Apfelwein taverns. A restaurant that makes its own Apfelwein, or hard apple cider, will probably not offer any other kind of wine. In fact, some don't even sell beer (aren't we in Germany?).

Apfelwein, sometimes called ebbelwoi by locals, is unique to Frankfurt and the surrounding state of Hessen. The drink was being made here as early as 794, when Charlemagne visited the city. You won't find it anywhere else in the world.

To produce Apfelwein, juice from pressed apples is fermented for approximately eight weeks. Some restaurants make their own; others purchase it from farms outside the city. You may find that Apfelwein tastes like cider, or vinegar. Because it's rather sour, many people choose to mix it with sparkling water (called "sauergespritzt," or sour) or with lemonade (called "süssgespritzt," or sweet). Locals will be impressed, and may even tell you so, if they see you try it straight. Be careful, though: consuming large quantities of Apfelwein will make most stomachs unhappy.

Most Apfelwein bars and restaurants serve the drink in bembels, gray-and-blue clay pitchers, which come in a variety of sizes. The drink is an especially nice accompaniment to the many pork dishes served in restaurants. You will notice that Germans, and especially Frankfurters, use apples heavily in their cooking—not just in Apfelwein. You might want to try some warm apple streudel (usually served with heavy cream or vanilla ice cream) or apple cakes (apfel kuchen) during your visit.

The largest concentration of Frankfurt Apfelwein establishments is found in the old neighborhood of Sachsenhausen. If you want to visit a bar or restaurant that sells its own homemade Apfelwein, look for a pine wreath hanging over the door.

$$–$$$ ✕**Taj Mahal.** Not only is this restaurant often referred to as the best place for Indian food in Frankfurt, but its staff are among the city's most attentive. The menu, a bit pricey, features authentic, delicious tandoori and marsala dishes. ⊠ *Schweizerstr. 28, Sachsenhausen* ☎ *069/620–240* ⊕ *www.tajmahal-restaurant.de* ⚞ *Reservations essential* ⊟ *V* Ⓤ *Schweizer-Platz (U-bahn).*

$–$$ ✕**Lobster.** This small Old Sachsenhausen restaurant is a favorite of locals and visitors alike. The menu, dramatically different from those of neighboring apple-wine taverns, offers mostly seafood. Fish and shellfish are prepared in a variety of international styles, but the strongest influence is French. Contrary to the restaurant's name, lobster does not appear on the regular menu, but it's occasionally offered as a daily special. This cozy restaurant also has a large collection of European wines. Reservations are strongly recommended on weekends. ⊠ *Wallstr. 21, Sachsenhausen* ☎ *069/612–920* ⊟ *V* Ⓤ *SchweizerPlatz (U-bahn).*

$ ✕**Edelweiss.** This is the place for homesick Austrians to enjoy their native cuisine, including the genuine Wiener schnitzel, and Kaiser Franz Josef's favorite, *Tafelspitze,* made of boiled beef with a chive sauce. There's also the roast chicken with a salad made of "earth apples" (potatoes) and the beloved *Kaiserschmarrn* (egg pancakes with raisins, apples, cinnamon, and jam). The interior is rustically wooden, and there's a pleasant terrace. ⊠ *Schweizerstr. 96, Sachsenhausen* ☎ *069/619–696* ⊟ *AE, DC, MC, V* ⊗ *No lunch weekends* Ⓤ *SchweizerPlatz (U-bahn).*

¢–$ ✕**Amalfi.** Many locals say Amalfi turns out the best pizza in town, making it a popular lunch spot. In addition to pizza (both personal and larger sizes), pasta, antipasti, and salads are on the menu. Eat in or take it out. This is a great choice if you're dining on a budget, grabbing a quick meal, or simply craving tasty pizza. ⊠ *Morfelder Landstr. 82, Sachsenhausen* ☎ *069/618–319* ⊟ *No credit cards* Ⓤ *SchweizerPlatz (U-bahn).*

¢–$ ✕**Fichtekränzi.** This is the real thing—a traditional apple-cider tavern in the heart of Sachsenhausen. In summer the courtyard is the place to be; in winter you sit in the noisy tavern at long tables with benches. It's often crowded, so if there isn't room when you arrive, order a glass of apple cider and hang around until someone leaves. Traditional cider-tavern dishes include Rippchen (smoked pork). ⊠ *Wallstr. 5, Sachsenhausen* ☎ *069/612–778* ⊟ *No credit cards* ⊗ *No lunch* Ⓤ *Lokalbahnhof (S-bahn).*

★ **¢–$** ✕**Zum Wagner.** The kitchen produces the same hearty German dishes as other apple-wine taverns, only better. Try the *Tafelspitz mit Frankfurter Grüner Sosse* (stewed beef with a sauce of green herbs), or come on Friday for fresh fish. Beer and wine are served as well as cider. This Sachsenhausen classic, with sepia-tone murals of merrymaking, succeeds in being touristy and traditional all at once. ⊠ *Schweizerstr. 71, Sachsenhausen* ☎ *069/612–565* ⊟ *No credit cards* Ⓤ *SchweizerPlatz (U-bahn).*

Outer Frankfurt

$–$$ ✕**Altes Zollhaus.** Excellent versions of traditional German specialties are served in this beautiful, 200-year-old half-timber house on the edge of town. Try a game dish. In summer you can eat in the beautiful garden. To get here, take Bus 30 from Konstablerwache to Heiligenstock, or drive out on Bundestrasse 521 in the direction of Bad Vilbel. ✉ *Friedberger Landstr. 531, Seckbach* ☎ *069/472–707* ▤ *AE, DC, MC, V* ◷ *Closed Mon. No lunch Mon.–Sat.*

¢–$$ ╳ **Arche Nova.** This sunny establishment is a feature of Frankfurt's Ökohaus, which was built according to environmental principles (solar panels, catching rainwater, etc.). It's more or less vegetarian, with such dishes as a vegetable platter with feta cheese or curry soup with grated coconut and banana. Much of what's served, even some of the beer, is organic. ✉ *Kasselerstr. 1a, Bockenheim* ☎ *069/707–5859* ▤ *No credit cards* Ⓤ *Bockenheimer Warte (U-bahn).*

★ ¢–$ ╳ **Wäldches.** This is Frankfurt's busiest brewpub. Though outside of town, it's a 10-minute walk from the Ginnheim U-bahn station and is a favorite stop for bikers and hikers. By noon on pleasant summer Sundays, the big beer garden is standing room only. The home-brewed light and dark beers go nicely with the largely German cuisine, which is substantial but not stodgy. If you like the beer, you can take some of it with you in an old-fashioned bottle with a wired porcelain stopper. ✉ *Am Ginnheimer Wäldchen 8, Ginnheim* ☎ *069/520–522* ▤ *No credit cards* ◷ *No lunch Oct.–Mar.* Ⓤ *Ginnheim (U-bahn).*

WHERE TO STAY

Businesspeople descend on Frankfurt year-round, so most hotels in the city are expensive (though many offer significant reductions on weekends) and are frequently booked up well in advance. Many hotels add as much as a 50% surcharge during trade fairs (*Messen*), of which there are about 30 a year. You can contact the German National Tourist Office for the trade fair schedule. The majority of the larger hotels are close to the main train station, fairgrounds, and business district (Bankenviertel) and are a 20-minute walk from the Old Town. Lower prices and—for some, anyway—more atmosphere are found at smaller hotels and pensions in the suburbs; the efficient public transportation network makes them easy to reach.

WHAT IT COSTS In Euros				
$$$$	**$$$**	**$$**	**$**	**¢**
FOR 2 PEOPLE over €225	€175–€225	€100–€175	€50–€100	under €50

Hotel prices are for two people in a standard double room, including tax and service.

City Center

★ $$$$ ▦ **Hilton Frankfurt.** This respected chain's downtown Frankfurt location has all the perks the business traveler wants, from fax and modem lines to voice mail and video on command. Its Pacific Colors Restaurant has a large terrace overlooking a park. The Vista Bar & Lounge is just below the hotel's airy and transparent atrium. ✉ *Hochstr. 4, City Center, D–60313* ☎ *069/133–8000* 🖷 *069/1338–1338* ⊕ *www.frankfurt. hilton.com* ⇆ *342 rooms* ⚐ *Restaurant, room service, in-room data ports,* *in-room safes, minibars, cable TV with movies and video games, indoor pool, health club, hair salon, hot tub, massage, sauna, steam room, 2 bars, meeting room, parking (fee), some pets allowed, no-smoking floors* ☰ *AE, DC, MC, V* Ⓤ *Eschenheimer Tor (U-bahn).*

$$$–$$$$ ▦ **Hessischer Hof.** This is the choice of many businesspeople, not just for its proximity to the fairgrounds but also for the air of class that pervades its handsome interior (the exterior is nondescript). Many of the public room furnishings are antiques owned by the family of the Princes of Hessen. Rooms are done in either a British or a Biedermeyer style. The Sèvres Restaurant, so called for the fine display of that porcelain arranged along the walls, features excellent contemporary cuisine. Jimmy's is one of the cult bars in town. ⊠ *Friedrich-Ebert-Anlage 40, Messe, D–60325* ☎ *069/75400* 🖷 *069/7540–2924* ⊕ *www.hessischerhof.de* 🛏 *106 rooms, 11 suites* ⇘ *Restaurant, room service, in-room data ports, minibars, cable TV, bar, meeting rooms, parking (fee), some pets allowed, no-smoking rooms* ☰ *AE, DC, MC, V* Ⓤ *Messe (S-bahn).*

$$–$$$$ ▦ **Steigenberger Hotel Frankfurter Hof.** The neo-Gothic Frankfurter Hof
Fodor'sChoice is one of the city's oldest hotels, but its modern services earn it kudos
★ from business publications around the world. The atmosphere is one of old-fashioned, formal elegance, with burnished woods, fresh flowers, and thick carpet. Kaiser Wilhelm once slept here, and so have modern heads of state. The hotel has rooms and suites, as well as five restaurants. Although it fronts on a courtyard, you must enter it through a modest side entrance. ⊠ *Am Kaiserpl., City Center, D–60311* ☎ *069/ 21502* 🖷 *069/215–900* ⊕ *www.frankfurter-hof.steigenberger.com* 🛏 *286 rooms, 46 suites* ⇘ *5 restaurants, room service, in-room data ports, minibars, cable TV with movies, sauna, bar, concierge, Internet, meeting rooms, parking (fee), some pets allowed (fee)* ☰ *AE, DC, MC, V* Ⓤ *Willy-Brandt-Platz (U-bahn).*

$$–$$$$ ▦ **Villa Orange.** This bright, charming hotel is centrally located, but tucked away from the bustle on a residential street. The moderately priced rooms include country-style furnishings and spacious bathrooms. The high-ceiling lobby and breakfast room are decorated with modern art, and there's a small library with a selection of English books. Hotel staff are friendly and accommodating. ⊠ *Hebelstr. 1, Nordend, D–60318* ☎ *069/405–840* 🖷 *069/4058–4100* ⊕ *www.villa-orange.de* 🛏 *38 rooms* ⇘ *In-room data ports, minibars, cable TV, bar, meeting room, parking (fee), no-smoking rooms* ☰ *AE, MC, V* ⧖ *BP* Ⓤ *Musterschule (U-bahn).*

★ **$–$$** ▦ **Hotel Nizza.** This beautiful Victorian building is furnished with antiques, and the proprietor added a modern touch in some bathrooms with her own artistic murals. There's a pleasant roof garden with lots of potted shrubbery where you can have breakfast with views of rooftops and the skyline. ⊠ *Elbestr. 10, City Center, D–60329* ☎ *069/242– 5380* 🖷 *069/2425–3830* 🛏 *24 rooms, 21 with bath* ⇘ *In-room data ports, cable TV, bar, some pets allowed; no a/c* ☰ *MC, V* ⧖ *CP* Ⓤ *Hauptbahnhof (U-bahn and S-bahn).*

$–$$ ▦ **InterCity Hotel.** InterCity hotels were set up by the Steigenberger chain
Fodor'sChoice with the business traveler in mind, and if there ever was a hotel at the
★ vortex of arrivals and departures, it's this centrally located hostelry in

an elegant old-world building. It's right across the street from the main train station, and guests get a pass good for unlimited travel on local public transportation. The station's underground garage is also at your disposal. ⊠ *Poststr. 8, Bahnhof, D–60329* ☎ *069/273–910* 🖷 *069/ 2739–1999* ⊕ *www.intercityhotel.de* 🛏 *384 rooms, 3 suites* ⚷ *Restaurant, in-room data ports, minibars, cable TV with movies, bar, business services, meeting rooms, some pets allowed (fee), no-smoking floor* ☰ *AE, DC, MC, V* Ⓤ *Hauptbahnhof (U-bahn and S-bahn).*

$–$$ 🏨 **Manhattan.** Get to all parts of town quickly from this modern hotel opposite the Hauptbahnhof. Rooms are fairly spacious, and you can connect to the Internet at one of the terminals in the lobby. There's no restaurant, but the hotel's bar is open around the clock. ⊠ *Düsseldorferstr. 10, City Center, D-60329* ☎ *069/269–5970* 🖷 *069/2695–97777* ⊕ *www. manhattan-hotel.com* 🛏 *60 rooms* ⚷ *Bar, cable TV, meeting room, no-smoking rooms; no a/c* ☰ *AE, MC, V* Ⓤ *Musterschule (U-bahn).*

$ 🏨 **Ibis Friedensbrücke.** The Ibis is a budget hotel offering simple, clean rooms. A short walk from both the main train station and the museums of Sachsenhausen, the hotel sits on a quiet street near the river. Breakfast may be purchased at an additional cost. ⊠ *Speicherstr. 3–5, City Center, D–60327* ☎ *069/273–030* 🖷 *069/237–024* ⊕ *www.accorhotels. com* 🛏 *233 rooms* ⚷ *Bar, cable TV, meeting room, no-smoking rooms, parking (fee)* ☰ *MC, V* Ⓤ *Hauptbahnhof (U-bahn and S-bahn).*

$ 🏨 **Pension Aller.** Quiet, solid comforts for a modest price and a friendly welcome are right near the train station. The third floor of a sociologist's private home offers cozy, well-lighted rooms. Reserve in advance, because it gets a lot of return guests. ⊠ *Gutleutstr. 94, City Center, D–60329* ☎ *069/252–596* 🖷 *069/232–330* 🛏 *10 rooms* ⚷ *Meeting room, some pets allowed; no a/c, no phones in some rooms, no TV in some rooms* ☰ *No credit cards* Ⓤ *Hauptbahnhof (U-bahn and S-bahn).*

$ 🏨 **Terminus.** Across the street from the main train station, this modern, sparkling-clean hotel has its own underground garage. It somehow also manages to keep a quiet summer garden despite its location. The rooms are some of the least expensive in town and include a bath, TV, and phone. ⊠ *Münchenerstr. 59, City Center, D–60329* ☎ *069/242–320* 🖷 *069/ 237–411* 🛏 *107 rooms* ⚷ *Restaurant, in-room data ports, cable TV with movies, bar, meeting rooms, parking (fee), some pets allowed; no a/c* ☰ *AE, DC, MC, V* Ⓤ *Hauptbahnhof (U-bahn and S-bahn).*

Westend

$$–$$$$ 🏨 **An der Messe.** This little place a couple of blocks from the fairgrounds provides a pleasant alternative to the giant hotels of the city. It's stylish, with a pink marble lobby and chicly appointed bedrooms. The staff is courteously efficient. The only drawback is the lack of a restaurant. ⊠ *Westendstr. 104, Messe, D–60325* ☎ *069/747–979* 🖷 *069/748– 349* 🛏 *46 rooms, 2 suites* ⚷ *In-room data ports, cable TV, some pets allowed (fee); no a/c* ☰ *AE, DC, MC, V* Ⓤ *Festhalle/Messe (U-bahn).*

$$–$$$ 🏨 **Hotel Westend.** "*Klein aber fein*" ("small but nice") is what Germans say about a place like this. Everywhere you turn in the stylish, family-run establishment, you'll trip over antiques. The hotel has no restaurant, but the classy neighborhood has plenty—some of which offer delivery service. ✉ *Westendstr. 15, Westend, D–60325* ☎ *069/7898–8180* 📠 *069/745–396* 🛏 *20 rooms, 5 without bath* ⌂ *In-room data ports, cable TV, meeting rooms, some pets allowed; no a/c* ▤ *AE, DC, MC, V* Ⓤ *Westend (U-bahn).*

★ **$$–$$$** 🏨 **Palmenhof.** Near the botanical garden, this luxuriously modern hotel occupies a renovated art nouveau building. The high-ceiling rooms have up-to-date comfort but retain the elegance of the old building. In the basement is a cozy restaurant, L'Artechoc, with a Mediterranean menu. ✉ *Bockenheimer Landstr. 89–91, Westend, D–60325* ☎ *069/753–0060* 📠 *069/7530–0666* 🛏 *46 rooms, 37 apartments, 2 suites* ⌂ *Restaurant, in-room data ports, some microwaves, cable TV with movies, some pets allowed; no a/c* ▤ *AE, DC, MC,* Ⓤ *Westend (U-bahn).*

Sachsenhausen

★ **$–$$** 🏨 **Maingau.** You'll find this pleasant hotel-restaurant in the middle of the lively Sachsenhausen quarter. Rooms are modest but spotless, comfortable, and equipped with TVs; the room rate includes a substantial breakfast buffet. Chef Werner Döpfner has made the restaurant, Maingau-Stuben, one of Frankfurt's best. (Caution: though the hotel is inexpensive, the restaurant is anything but!) ✉ *Schifferstr. 38–40, Sachsenhausen, D–60594* ☎ *069/609–140* 📠 *069/620–790* 🛏 *100 rooms* ⌂ *Restaurant, room service, in-room data ports, minibars, cable TV with video games, meeting rooms, some pets allowed; no a/c* ▤ *AE, MC, V* Ⓤ *SchweizerPlatz (U-bahn).*

¢**–$** 🏨 **Am Berg.** A colorful, romantic inn, the Am Berg is not so much a hotel as a nice guesthouse. Because of its location, hidden away in a residential area near the Sudbahnhof (south train station), many locals aren't even aware it exists. The Mock-Tudor–style hotel was built in the late 1800s and has a quiet backyard garden where guests may relax. Each room has its own unique decor. A stay here is worth much more than the price. ✉ *Grethenweg 23, Sachsenhausen, D–60598* ☎ *069/612–021* 📠 *069/615–109* ⊕ *www.hotel-am-berg-ffm.de* 🛏 *21* ⌂ *No-smoking rooms* ▤ *MC, V* Ⓤ *Sudbahnhof (U-bahn).*

Outer Frankfurt

$$–$$$$ 🏨 **Sheraton Frankfurt.** This huge hotel is immediately accessible to one of Frankfurt Airport's terminals. It, like the airport, is also adjacent to the Frankfurter Kreuz, the major autobahn intersection, with super-highway connections to all of Europe. No need to worry about noise, though—the rooms are all soundproof. In addition to the usual comforts, each room includes an answering machine and a modem. Forty-four of the rooms have ISDN connections that permit fax machines and printers; a few rooms are equipped with fax machines. ✉ *Hugo-Eckener-Ring 15, Flughafen Terminal 1, Airport, D–60549* ☎ *069/69770* 📠 *069/6977–2209* ⊕ *www.sheraton.com/frankfurt* 🛏 *1,006 rooms, 28 suites* ⌂ *2 restaurants, in-room data ports, minibars, cable TV with movies, gym, massage, sauna, steam room, 2 bars, concierge, meeting rooms, parking (fee), some pets allowed, no-smoking rooms* ▤ *AE, DC, MC, V* Ⓤ *Flughafen (S-bahn).*

★ **$$** ☐ **Art Hotel Robert Mayer.** For creative types who shun the sterile decor of hotel chains, this elegant villa dating from 1905 offers an alternative: 11 rooms, each decorated by a different Frankfurt artist, with furniture designs by the likes of Rietveld and Frank Lloyd Wright. The art tradition is stressed in a special weekend arrangement that includes an individual guided tour of an art museum. It has no restaurant, but a large breakfast buffet is included in the price of the room. ⊠ *Robert-Mayer-Str. 44, Bockenheim, D–60486* ☎ *069/970–9100* 🖶 *069/9709–1010* ⊕ *www.art-hotel-robert-mayer.de* ➠ *11 rooms, 1 suite* ⚒ *In-room data ports, cable TV, some pets allowed (fee); no a/c* ⊟ *AE, DC, MC, V* ⑩ *BP* Ⓜ *Bockenheimer Warte (U-bahn).*

$–$$ ☐ **Falk Hotel.** Although it's removed from Frankfurt's city center, this hotel is within walking distance of two U-bahn (subway) stations, and is a relatively inexpensive alternative for those on a budget. The location is especially interesting to younger travelers—two blocks from Leipzigerstrasse, it stands in the heart of the Bockenheim neighborhood, home of Goethe University and numerous ethnic cafés, bars, and shops. Rooms are simple yet comfortable. The staff is friendly and quick to offer help or advice. The room rate includes a full breakfast and discounted rates at a nearby fitness studio. ⊠ *Falkstr. 38 A, Bockenheim, D–60487* ☎ *069/7191–8870* 🖶 *069/7191–88777* ⊕ *www.hotel-falk.de* ➠ *29 rooms* ⚒ *Restaurant, cable TV, meeting room, no-smoking rooms; no a/c* ⊟ *AE, MC, V* ⑩ *CP* Ⓤ *Leipzigerstr. (U-bahn), Bockenheimer Warte (U-bahn).*

NIGHTLIFE & THE ARTS

The Arts

Frankfurt has the largest budget for cultural affairs of any city in the country. The Städtische Bühnen—municipal theaters, including the city's opera company—are the prime venues. Frankfurt has what is probably the most lavish theater in the country, the Alte Oper, a magnificently ornate 19th-century opera house. The building is no longer used for opera but as a multipurpose hall for pop and classical concerts and dances.

Theater tickets can be purchased from the tourist office at Römerberg 27 and from theater box offices. **Best Tickets GmbH** (⊠ Zeil 112–114, City Center ☎ 069/9139–7621) is downtown in the Zeilgalerie. **Frankfurt Ticket GmbH** (⊠ Hauptwache Passage, City Center ☎ 069/134–0400) is one of the best ticket agencies. The **Karstadt department store** (⊠ Zeil 90, City Center ☎ 069/294–848) doubles as a ticket office.

Ballet, Concerts & Opera

Telephone ticket sales for the Alte Oper, Frankfurt Opera, and Frankfurt Ballet are all handled through **Frankfurt Ticket** (☎ 069/134–0400). The most glamorous venue for classical music concerts is the **Alte Oper** (⊠ Opernpl., City Center); tickets to performances can range from €10 to nearly €150. The **Frankfurt Opera** (⊠ Städtische Bühnen, Untermainanlage 11, City Center) has made a name for itself as a company for dramatic artistry. Sharing the same venue as the Frankfurt Opera is the world-renowned **Frankfurt Ballet** (⊠ Städtische Bühnen, Untermainanlage 11, City Center).

The **Festhalle** (⊠ Ludwig-Erhard-Anlage 1, Messe ☎ 069/7575–6404), on the fairgrounds, is the scene of many rock concerts, horse shows, ice shows, sporting events, and other large-scale spectaculars.

The city is also the home of the Radio-Sinfonie-Orchester Frankfurt, part of Hessischer Rundfunk. It performs regularly in the 850-seat **Kammermusiksaal** (⊠ Bertramstr. 8, Dornbusch ☎ 069/550–123), part of that broadcasting operation's campuslike facilities.

Theater

Theatrical productions in Frankfurt are nearly always in German. For English-language productions, try the **English Theater** (⊠ Kaiserstr. 52, City Center ☎ 069/2423–1620), which offers an array of musicals, thrillers, dramas, and comedy with British or American casts. The **Künstlerhaus Mouson Turm** (⊠ Waldschmidtstr. 4, Nordend ☎ 069/4058–9520) is a cultural center that hosts a regular series of concerts of all kinds, as well as plays and exhibits. The municipally owned **Schauspielhaus** (⊠ Willy-Brandt-Pl., City Center ☎ 069/134–0400) has a repertoire including works by Sophocles, Goethe, Shakespeare, Brecht, and Beckett. For a zany theatrical experience, try **Die Schmiere** (⊠ Seckbächerg. 2, City Center ☎ 069/281–066), which offers trenchant satire and also disarmingly calls itself "the worst theater in the world." Renowned for international experimental productions, including dance theater and other forms of nonverbal drama, is **Theater am Turm** (TAT; ⊠ Bockenheimer Warte, Bockenheim ☎ 069/134–0400), in the Bockenheimer Depot, a former trolley barn.

Nightlife

Frankfurt at night is a city of stark contrasts. Old hippies and sharply dressed bankers, Turkish and Greek guest workers, people on pensions, chess players, exhibitionists, and loners all have their piece of the action. People from the banking world seek different amusements than the city's 38,000 students, but their paths cross in such places as the cider taverns in Sachsenhausen and the gay bars of the Nordend. Sachsenhausen (Frankfurt's "Left Bank") is a good place to start for bars, clubs, and Apfelwein taverns. The ever-more-fashionable Nordend has an almost equal number of bars and clubs but fewer tourists. Frankfurt is one of Europe's leading cities for techno, the computer-generated music of ultrafast beats that's the anthem of German youth culture. Please note that most dance and nightclubs charge entrance fees ranging from €5 to €20. In addition, some trendy nightclubs, such as the Living and King Kamehameha, enforce dress codes—usually no jeans, tennis shoes, or khaki pants admitted. Most bars close between 2 AM and 4 AM.

Bars & Live Music Venues

A major trend in the night spots is the "After Work" or "After Hours" happy hour with half-price drinks, lasting usually from 5 or 6 PM to 9 or 10 PM one weekday per week. You can go to Jimmy's every weeknight, EuroDeli on Tuesday, the Studio Bar on Wednesday, and 190 East or King Kamehameha on Thursday.

The tiny, cozy **Balalaika** (⊠ Dreikönigstr. 30, Sachsenhausen ☎ 069/612–226) provides intimacy and live music without charging the high prices you'd expect. The secret is proprietress Anita Honis, a professional American singer from Harlem, who usually gets out her acoustic guitar several times during an evening.

Like much of the Marriott Hotel it's in, the **Champion's Bar** (⊠ Hamburger Allee 2–10, Messe ☎ 069/7955–2540) is designed to make Americans feel at home. The wall is lined with jerseys, and autographed helmets and photographs of American athletes. The TV is tuned to baseball, football, and basketball broadcasts, and the food leans to buffalo wings, potato skins, and hamburgers. Parties take place on American holidays like Halloween, Thanksgiving, and Valentine's Day.

On Tuesday nights, avoid waiting in line by arriving early at **EuroDeli** (⊠ Neue Mainzerstr. 60–66 ☎ 069/2980–1950). Because it's near many of the city's major banks, it's a popular after-work hangout. A mix of popular music is played by a DJ most nights. Order cocktails and food at the bar.

Frankfurt teems with Irish pubs, but **Fox and Hound** (⊠ Niedenau 2, Westend ☎ 069/9720–2009) is the only *English* pub in town. The patrons, mainly British, come to watch constant satellite transmissions of the latest football (soccer to Americans), rugby, and cricket matches. Enjoy the authentic pub grub (try the basket of chips), and participate in the Sunday-night quiz for free drinks and cash prizes. It's a noisy bunch.

★ **Jimmy's Bar** (⊠ Friedrich-Ebert-Anlage 40, Messe ☎ 069/7540–2961) is classy and expensive—like the Hessischer Hof Hotel in which it's located. It's been the meeting place of the business elite since 1951, and what every other bar in town would like to be. The ladies are more chic; the gentlemen more charming; the pianist, who plays from 10 PM onward, more winning. The bar stools and lounge chairs are red leather, the bar of mahogany. There's hot food from the hotel kitchen until 3 AM. You must ring the doorbell to get in, although regulars have a key.

The **Luna Bar** (⊠ Stiftstr. 6, City Center ☎ 069/294–774) is a cocktail lover's paradise, with good drinks at reasonable prices by Frankfurt standards. Dress is smart but casual, and there is live music twice a month.

Though it's also a restaurant, **Coconut Groove** (⊠ Kaiserstr. 53 ☎ 069/2710–7999) is more popular as a drinking destination. A red bar runs half the length of its modern interior. "New world" cuisine, such as Caribbean chicken rolls, pepper-encrusted tuna, and pumpkin soup are served late into the night.

University students and young professionals frequent the **Stereo Bar** (⊠ Abstgässchen 7, Sachsenhausen ☎ 069/617–116), which has cheaper drinks than many other popular bars in town. You'll find it in a former wine cellar beneath a narrow Sachsenhausen alleyway. The carpeted walls are bright red, and there's an aquarium and tiny dance floor. DJs usually spin the music, though there are occasional live acts.

★ The soothing interior attracts many to **Unity** (⊠ Hanauer Landstr. 2, Ostend) lounge in Frankfurt's east end (Ostend). Large couches line the walls of this dimly lit, three-room bar. A mix of rock, funk, and soul is played by a DJ in the center room, where small groups of people sometimes dance.

Caipirinhas and Long Island ice teas are specialties of the house at **Wega** (✉ Schweizerstr. 73, Sachsenhausen ☎ 069/617–564). This bar is especially popular with women who enjoy watching the buff male waiters and bartenders. Many come for dinner—the food is good—then stay late for drinking and mingling. Directly across the street is **Keepers Lounge** (✉ Schweizerstr. 78 ☎ 069/6060–7210), a modern bar that's constantly flooded with young professionals. The cocktail menu looks like a short novel.

Dance & Nightclubs

Beneath the heating pipes of a former brewery, **King Kamehameha** (✉ Hanauer Landstr. 192, Ostend ☎ 069/4800–3701) is designed to suit every type of night owl. You can relax in the quiet cocktail bar, dance to a house band, or see one of the many live concerts, cabarets, comedy acts, or fashion shows that take place on stage. It's closed Monday.

Trendy **Living XXL** (✉ Kaiserstr. 29, City Center ☎ 069/242–9370) is one of the biggest bar-restaurants in Germany and is as hyped as the Eurotower in which it's located, the headquarters of the European Central Bank. On Friday and Saturday it offers a "subdued" disco, geared to the easy-listening preferences of the banking community, but it's not so prudish as to exclude regular gay entertainment. Its spacious, terraced interior has drawn architectural praise.

There's not much that doesn't take place at the **Tigerpalast** (✉ Heiligkreuzg. 16–20, City Center ☎ 069/9200–2250). The best variety shows and circus performances entertain guests, who dine elegantly and get some dancing in themselves. Shows often sell out, so book tickets as far in advance as possible. Closed Monday.

★ Well-known DJs often entertain the crowd at **190 East** (✉ Hanauer Landstr. 190, Ostend ☎ 069/5060–17180). This large, disco-style club is bathed in white and keeps the music playing until 5 AM.

In the fall 2003, a former police headquarters was transformed into **Praesidium** (✉ Friedrich-Ebert-Anlage 11, Ostend ☎ 069/7474–3978), a huge nightclub on Frankfurt's west-side. High ceilings, chandeliers, columns, and a grand staircase fill its stunning interior. Bars and sofas are scattered throughout the club; several DJs will often perform on a single night. Drinks are reasonably priced—compared to those of other Frankfurt dance clubs.

Jazz

The oldest jazz cellar in Germany, **Der Frankfurter Jazzkeller** (✉ Kleine Bockenheimerstr. 18a, City Center ☎ 069/288–537) was founded by legendary trumpeter Carlo Bohländer and has hosted such luminaries as Louis Armstrong. It offers hot, modern jazz, often free (otherwise the cover is around €20). It's closed Monday.

Anything can happen at **Dreikönigskeller** (✉ Färberstr. 71, Sachsenhausen ☎ 069/629–273): you might hear 1940s or '50s jazz, blues, funk, or indie-punk. It's patronized mostly by students, as well as a sprinkling of older hipsters, all smoking as voraciously as the musicians.

Sinkkasten (⊠ Brönnerstr. 5–9, City Center ☎ 069/280–385), a Frankfurt musical institution, is a class act—a great place for jazz, rock, pop, and African music, often by unknown or hardly known groups. It's sometimes hard to get in but worth the effort. There's live music Monday through Wednesday and Saturday.

SPORTS & THE OUTDOORS

Despite the ever-present smog in summer, Frankfurt is full of parks and other green oases where you can breathe easier. South of the city, the huge, 4,000-acre **Stadtwald** makes Frankfurt one of Germany's most forested metropolises. The forest has innumerable paths and trails, bird sanctuaries, impressive sports stadiums, and a number of good restaurants. The Waldlehrpfad trail there leads past a series of rare trees, each identified by a small sign. The Oberschweinstiege stop on streetcar line 14 is right in the middle of the park. Alternately, you can take Bus 36 from Konstablerwache to Hainerweg.

The **Taunus Hills** are also a great getaway for Frankfurters. Take U-bahn 3 to Hohemark. In the Seckbach district, northeast of the city, Frankfurters hike the 590-foot **Lohrberg Hill**. The climb yields a fabulous view of the town and the Taunus, Spessart, and Odenwald hills. Along the way you'll also see the last remaining vineyard within the Frankfurt city limits, the Seckbach Vineyard. Take the U-4 subway to Seckbacher Landstrasse, then Bus 43 to Draisbornstrasse.

Biking

There are numerous biking paths within the city limits. The Stadtwald in the southern part of the city is crisscrossed with well-tended paths that are nice and flat. The city's riverbanks are, for the most part, lined with paths bikers can use. There are not only on both sides of the Main but also on the banks of the little Nidda River, which flows through Heddernheim, Eschersheim, Hausen, and Rödelheim before joining the Main at Höchst. Some bikers also like the Taunus Hills, but note that word *Hills*.

Theo Intra's shop (⊠ Westerbachstr. 273, Sossenheim ☎ 069/342–780) has a large selection of bikes, from tandems to racing models. It's located on the city's northern edge, convenient to the inviting trails of the Taunus. Take the U–6 or U–7 to Bockenheimer Warte, then Bus 50 to Carl-Sonnenschein-Strasse. Also on the edge of the city is **Fahrradverlieh Werkstatt** (⊠ Am Burghof 55, Bonames ☎ 069/9504–1716), reachable by taking the U–2 suburban train from the Hauptwache to Kalbach. Bike rentals will cost you €6–€9 per day.

Fitness Centers

Near the central Hauptwache, the **Fitness Company** (⊠ Zeil 109, City Center ☎ 069/9637–3100) has everything needed to work out. There are more than 60 aerobics and other classes and 150 different fitness machines, from Nautilus to StairMaster. English is spoken. A day's training costs €18. **CityFitness** (⊠ Trakehnerstr. 5, Hausen ☎ 069/703–788) has an extensive program of bodybuilding, aerobics, and stretching, mainly in the evening and on weekends. An hour's course costs €10.

Ice-Skating

Home to the Lions, Frankfurt's ice-hockey team, the **Eissporthalle** (⊠ Bornheimer Hang 4, Ostend ☎ 069/2123–0825, 069/941–4111 Lions schedule and tickets) is open to the public for ice-skating. The indoor and outdoor rinks are open daily 9 AM–10 PM during winter months. Cost is €5.

Jogging

The banks of the Main River are a good place to jog, and to avoid retracing your steps, you can always cross a bridge and return down the opposite side. In the Westend, **Grüneberg Park** is 2 km (1 mi) around, with a *Trimm Dich* (literally, "get fit") exercise facility in the northeast corner. The **Anlagenring,** a park following the line of the old city walls around the city, is also a popular route. For a vigorous forest run, go to the Stadtwald or the Taunus Hills.

Roller-blading

For sports enthusiasts who travel with Rollerblades, the Main riverbanks and Stadtwald are great locations for skating. And Tuesday nights (March through October) give visitors the chance to tour Frankfurt on wheels—join the weekly **In-line Skating Night** at 8 PM in Sachsenhausen. Starting outside the Zwischendurch bar (Dreieichstr. 34), you will cross the river and loop around the city, from west to east. The group returns to Zwischendurch two hours later for post-blading beers. Skates may be rented at **Sport Gräcmann** (⊠ Frankfurterstr. 57, Offenbach ☎ 069/800–3931) for €6–€12 per day.

Swimming

Incredible as it may seem, people used to swim along the banks of the Main. Pictures from the 1930s show happy crowds splashing in a roped-off area. Those days are long gone (you'd probably dissolve), but there are a number of indoor and outdoor pools. The often-crowded **Brentanobad** (⊠ Rödelheimer Parkweg, Rödelheim ☎ 069/2123–9020) is an outdoor pool surrounded by lawns and old trees. The **Stadionbad** (⊠ Morfelder Landstr. 362, Niederrad ☎ 069/678–041) has an outdoor pool, a giant water chute, and exercise lawns. For everything from "adventure pools" and bowling to a sauna and fitness center, head to the **Titus Therme** (⊠ Walter-Möller-Pl. 2, Nordweststadt ☎ 069/958–050) pool complex.

SHOPPING

Shopping Districts

The tree-shaded pedestrian zone of the **Zeil** is said to be the richest shop-'til-you-drop mile in Germany. Other cities ask where Frankfurt gets the figures to prove the boast, but there's no doubt that the Zeil, between Hauptwache and Konstablerwache, is incredible for its variety of department and specialty stores. The area abounds in arcades. The moderately priced **Zeilgallerie** (⊠ Zeil 112–114, City Center ☎ 069/9207–3414) has 56 shops and an IMAX theater. The **Schillerpassage** (⊠ Rahmhofstr. 2, City Center) is strong on men's and women's fashion boutiques.

The Zeil is only the centerpiece of the downtown shopping area. The subway station below the Hauptwache also doubles as a vast underground mall. West of the Hauptwache are two parallel streets highly regarded by shoppers. One is the luxurious **Goethestrasse,** lined with boutiques, art galleries, jewelry stores, and antiques shops. The other is **Grosse Bockenheimer Strasse,** better known as the Fressgasse ("Pig-Out Alley"). Cafés, restaurants, a shopping arcade, and pricey food stores line the street, tempting gourmands with everything from crumbly cheeses and smoked fish to vintage wines and chocolate creams. Heading south toward the cathedral and the river, you'll find an area of art and antiques shops on **Braubachstrasse, Fahrgasse,** and **Weckmarkt.** In addition to these major shopping areas, **Schweizerstrasse** in Sachsenhausen is home to many clothing boutiques, shops, galleries, and cafés. This street runs south through Sachsenhausen, starting from the Main riverbank.

Clothing Stores

Bailly Diehl (⊠ Schweizerstr. 41, Sachsenhausen ☎ 069/9620–0018) is an upscale clothier offering a variety of fashions for both men and women. Most labels in this two-story collection are European.

All of the top women's labels are represented in Inge Winterberg's collection at **Class-X** (⊠ Börsenstr. 7–11, City Center ☎ 069/131–0853). There are bags from Coccinelle, shoes from Free Lance, jewelry from Rio Berlin. Tailors can provide an item in another color or fabric if you like, but the styles can't be altered.

Hype (⊠ Schweizerstr. 65, Sachsenhausen ☎ 069/6199–5117) is on the south side of Schweizer Platz, near Zum Wagner restaurant and Apfelwein tavern. This boutique sells modern women's clothing and accessories in a variety of price ranges and from a selection of European labels, including a number of Italian designers. Items are discounted near the end of each season.

★ **Peek & Cloppenburg** (⊠ Zeil 71–75, City Center ☎ 069/298–950) is a huge, nicely departmentalized clothing store where men and women can find what they need for the office, gym, and nightclub. Clothes range from easily affordable items to pricey labels.

Pfüller Modehaus (⊠ Goethestr. 15–17, City Center ☎ 069/1337–8070) offers a wide range of choices on three floors for women, from classic to trendy, from lingerie to overcoats, from hats to stockings. Gavinci and Hugo Boss are just a few of the many labels sold.

Department Stores

There are two department stores on the Zeil, offering much in the way of clothing, furnishings, electronics, food, and other items. The **Galerie Kaufhof** (⊠ Zeil 116–126, City Center ☎ 060/21910) has an array of up-to-date retailing practices including touch screens that describe products. (One tells you what wines at what temperature go with what food.) The Dinea Restaurant on the top floor has a striking view. The **Karstadt** (⊠ Zeil 90, City Center ☎ 069/929–050) is similar to Galerie Kaufhof in variety, with the best gourmet food department in town.

Flea Markets

Sachsenhausen's weekend flea market takes place on Saturday from 8 to 2 on the riverbank, between **Dürerstrasse** and the **Eiserner Steg.** Purveyors of the cheap have taken over. Get there early for the bargains, as the better-quality stuff gets snapped up quickly. Shopping success or no, the market can be fun for browsing.

Gift Ideas

Cold, hard cash is what springs to mind when in the financial capital of Germany, not souvenirs. Frankfurt does produce fine porcelain, though, and it can be bought at the **Höchster Porzellan Manufaktur,** in the suburb of Höchst.

One thing typical of Frankfurt is the Apfelwein (apple-wine). You can get a bottle of it at any grocery store, but more enduring souvenirs would be Bembel pitchers and glasses that are equally a part of the Apfelwein tradition. The blue-stoneware Bembels have a fat belly, and the glasses, usually with a crest, are ribbed to give them "traction" (in the old days this was good for preventing the glass from slipping from greasy hands). You can get the Bembels and glasses at just about any gift shop, but **Frankfurter Dippemarkt** (⊠ Fahrg. 80, Altstadt ☎ 069/282–559) has a selection that will overwhelm you.

A famous children's book in Germany, *Struwwelpeter* (*Slovenly Peter*), was the work of a Frankfurt doctor, Heinrich Hoffmann. He wrote the poems and drew the rather amateurish pictures in 1844 just to warn his own children of the dire consequences of being naughty. The book has several English translations, one by Mark Twain no less. The **Struwwelpeter-Museum** (⊠ Benderg. 1, Altstadt ☎ 069/281–333) has copies of some of them, including one with the German version on one page and the Mark Twain version facing.

An edible gift you can take home is the Frankfurter sausage. The hot dog, on a long roll, made its first appearance at Chicago's World's Columbian Exhibition in 1893, and this sausage, sent over in cans from Frankfurt, was the basic ingredient. It's still available in cans. Try **Plöger** (⊠ Grosse Bockenheimerstr. 30, City Center ☎ 069/138–7110) on the Fressgasse. One taste of this high-quality smoked sausage will convince you that American imitations resemble the true frankfurter only in size and shape.

Food & Drink

The pastry shop **Konditorei Lochner** (⊠ Kalbächerg. 10, City Center ☎ 069/920–7320) has local delicacies such as *Bethmännchen und Brenten* (marzipan cookies) and *Frankfurter Kranz* (a kind of creamy cake). All types of sweets and pastries are found at the café **Laumer** (⊠ Bockenheimer Landstr. 67, Westend ☎ 069/727–912).

Weinhandlung Dr. Teufel (⊠ Kleiner Hirschgraben 4, City Center ☎ 069/283–236) is as good a place as any for the popular wines, and the best place in town for diversity. There's also a complete line of glasses, carafes, corkscrews and other accessories, and books on all aspects of viticulture.

SIDE TRIPS FROM FRANKFURT

Frankfurt is so centrally located in Germany that the list of possible excursions—day trips and longer treks—is nearly endless. It's the ideal starting point for journeys to the Rhineland, to the west; Heidelberg and the Neckar Valley, to the south; and Würzburg and Franconia, to the southeast.

Destinations reachable by the local transportation system include Höchst, Neu-Isenburg, and the Taunus Hills, which includes Bad Homburg and Kronberg. Just to the northwest and west of Frankfurt, the Taunus Hills are an area of mixed pine and hardwood forest, medieval castles, and photogenic towns that many Frankfurters regard as their own backyard. It's home to Frankfurt's wealthy bankers and businesspeople, and on weekends you can see them enjoying their playground: hiking through the hills, climbing the Grosse Feldberg, taking the waters at Bad Homburg's health-enhancing mineral springs, or just lazing in elegant stretches of parkland.

Bad Homburg

The Taunus Hills area has many royal associations. Emperor Wilhelm II, the infamous "kaiser" of World War I, spent a month each year at Bad Homburg, the area's principal city. And it was the kaiser's mother, the daughter of Britain's Queen Victoria, who built the magnificent palace, now a luxurious hotel, in the Taunus town of Kronberg. Another frequent visitor to Bad Homburg was Britain's Prince of Wales, later King Edward VII, who made the name *Homburg* world famous by attaching it to a hat.

Bad Homburg's greatest attraction has been the **Kurpark** (spa), in the heart of the Old Town, with more than 31 fountains. Romans first used the springs, which were rediscovered and made famous in the 19th century. In the park you'll find not only the popular, highly saline Elisabethenbrunnen Spring but also a Siamese temple and a Russian chapel, mementos left by more royal guests—King Chulalongkorn of Siam and Czar Nicholas II. The Kurpark is a good place to begin a walking tour of the town; Bad Homburg's **tourist office** (⊠ Louisenstr. 58 ☎ 06172/1780) is in the nearby Kurhaus. ⊠ *Between Paul-Ehrlich-Weg and Kaiser-Friedrich-Promenade.*

Adjacent to the Kurpark, the **casino** boasts with some justice that it is the "Mother of Monte Carlo." The first casino in Bad Homburg, and one of the first in the world, was established in 1841 but closed down in 1866 because Prussian law forbade gambling. The proprietor, François Blanc, then moved his operation to the French Riviera, and the Bad Homburg casino wasn't reopened until 1949. A bus runs between the casino and Frankfurt's Hauptbahnhof (south side). It leaves Frankfurt every hour on the hour between 2 PM and 10 PM and then hourly from 10:25 PM to

1:25 AM. Buses back to Frankfurt run every hour on the hour, from 4 PM to the casino's closing. The €6 fare will be refunded after the casino's full entry fee has been deducted. ⊠ *Im Kurpark* 🕾 *06172/17010* 🖾 *Full gaming area €2.50, slot machines only €1* ☺ *Slot machines 2 PM–1:30 AM, remainder 3 PM–3 AM.*

The most historically noteworthy sight in Bad Homburg is the 17th-century **Schloss,** where the kaiser stayed when he was in residence. The 172-foot Weisser Turm (White Tower) is all that remains of the medieval castle that once stood here. The Schloss was built between 1680 and 1685 by Friedrich II of Hesse-Homburg, and a few alterations were made during the 19th century. The state apartments are exquisitely furnished, and the Spiegelkabinett (Hall of Mirrors) is especially worthy of a visit. In the surrounding park look for two venerable cedars from Lebanon, both now about 200 years old. ⊠ *Herrng.* 🕾 *06172/926–2147* 🖾 *€3.50* ☺ *Mar.–Oct., Tues.–Sun. 10–5; Nov.–Feb., Tues.–Sun. 10–4.*

The **Hutmuseum** (Hat Museum), a part of the Museum im Gotisches Haus, is a shrine to headgear. Its collection includes everything from 18th-century three-corner hats to silk toppers, from simple bonnets to the massive, feathered creations of 19th-century milliners. But mainly it's a shrine to the distinguished hat that was developed in Bad Homburg and bears its name. The Homburg hat was made around the turn of the 20th century for Britain's Prince of Wales, later King Edward VII, a frequent visitor. He liked the shape of the Tyrolean hunting hat but found its green color and decorative feather a bit undignified. So, for him, the Homburg hatters removed the feather, turned the felt gray, and established a fashion item once worn by diplomats, state dignitaries, and other distinguished gentlemen worldwide. ⊠ *Tannenwaldweg 102* 🕾 *06172/ 37618* ☺ *Tues. and Thurs.–Sat. 2–5, Wed. 2–7, Sun. noon–6.*

Just a short, convenient bus ride from Bad Homburg is the highest mountain in the Taunus, the 2,850-foot, eminently hikable **Grosse Feldberg.**

Only 6½ km (4 mi) from Bad Homburg, and accessible by direct bus service, is the **Römerkastell-Saalburg** (Saalburg Roman Fort). Built in AD 120, the fort could accommodate a cohort (500 men) and was part of the fortifications along the Limes Wall, which ran from the Danube River to the Rhine River and was meant to protect the Roman Empire from barbarian invasion. On the initiative of Kaiser Wilhelm II, the fort was rebuilt as the Romans originally left it—with wells, armories, parade grounds, and catapults, as well as shops, houses, baths, and temples. All of these are for viewing only. You can't take a bath or buy a souvenir in the shops, though there is a contemporary restaurant on the grounds. There is also a **museum** with Roman exhibits. The Saalburg is north of Bad Homburg on Route 456 in the direction of Usingen. ⊠ *Saalburg-Kastell* 🕾 *06175/93740* 🖾 *€2.50* ☺ *Fort and museum Mar.–Oct., daily 9–6; Nov.–Feb., daily 9–4.*

About a 45-minute walk through the woods along a well-marked path ☾ from the Römerkastell-Saalburg is an open-air museum at **Hessenpark,** near Neu Anspach. The museum presents a clear picture of the world in which 18th- and 19th-century Hessians lived, using 135 acres of rebuilt villages with houses, schools, and farms typical of the time. The park, 15 km (9 mi) outside Bad Homburg in the direction of Usingen, can also be reached by public transportation. Take the Taunusbahn from the Frankfurt main station to Wehrheim; then transfer to Bus 514. ⊠ *Laubweg, Neu-Anspach* ☎ *06081/5880* 🖾 *€4* ⊙ *Mar.–Apr. and Sept.–Oct., daily 9–6; May–Aug., daily 9–8.*

Where to Stay & Eat

Although most of the well-known spas in Bad Homburg have expensive restaurants, there are still enough affordable places to eat.

★ $-$$$ ✕ **Zum Wasserweibchen.** Chef Inge Kuper is a local culinary legend. Although prices are high for some items on the menu, the portions are large. The clientele sometimes includes celebrities, and the service is friendly and unpretentious. You can't go wrong with the potato cakes with salmon mousse, the brisket of beef, or any of the desserts. ⊠ *Am Mühlberg 57* ☎ *06172/29878* 🖃 *AE, MC, V* ⊙ *Closed Sat.*

¢–$ ✕ **Kartoffelküche.** This simple restaurant serves traditional dishes accompanied by potatoes cooked every way imaginable. The potato and broccoli gratin and the potato pizza are excellent, and for dessert try potato strudel with vanilla sauce. ⊠ *Audenstr. 4* ☎ *06172/21500* 🖃 *AE, DC, MC, V.*

$$-$$$ ✕🏨 **Maritim Kurhaus Hotel.** Standing in a quiet location on the edge of the spa park but near the city center, the hotel offers large, richly furnished rooms with king-size beds and deep armchairs. Some rooms have balconies. The cozy Bürgerstube ($$) serves both solid German cuisine and international dishes. For late-night gamblers and those with early planes to catch, the hotel offers "early-bird breakfasts" from 11 PM to 6:30 AM. ⊠ *Ludwigstr. 3, D–61348* ☎ *06172/6600* 🖷 *06172/ 660–100* ⊕ *www.maritim.de* ➳ *148 rooms, 10 suites* ⚭ *Restaurant, café, in-room data ports, cable TV with movies, bar, meeting rooms, some pets allowed (fee), no-smoking rooms; no a/c* 🖃 *AE, DC, MC, V.*

★ $$-$$$ 🏨 **Steigenberger Bad Homburg.** Renowned for catering to Europe's royalty in its pre–World War I heyday, this hotel began as the Ritters Parkhotel in 1883 after Conrad Ritter combined a row of villas opposite Kurpark. Though the Steigenberger group has since dropped the historic and prominent name, it knows how to cater to the still well-heeled clientele. Rooms are furnished in art deco style, and Charley's Bistro evokes the spirit of *gaie Paris* with literary dinners and jazz brunches. The nearby park is ideal for jogging. ⊠ *Kaiser-Friedrich-Promenade 69–75, D–61348* ☎ *06172/1810* 🖷 *06172/181–630* ⊕ *www.bad-homburg.steigenberger.com* ➳ *196 rooms, 17 suites* ⚭ *Restaurant, room service, in-room data ports, in-room safes, minibars, cable TV, gym, sauna, steam room, bar, laundry service, concierge, Internet, meeting rooms, no-smoking floor* 🖃 *AE, DC, MC, V.*

Kronberg

The Taunus town of Kronberg, 15 km (9 mi) northwest of Frankfurt, has a magnificent castle-hotel originally built by the daughter of Queen Victoria, and an open-air zoo. Kronberg's half-timber houses and crooked, winding streets, all on a steep hillside, were so picturesque that a whole 19th-century art movement, the Kronberger Malerkolonie, was inspired by them.

★ ☾ Established by a wealthy heir of the man who created the Opel automobile, the large **Opel Zoo** has more than 1,000 native and exotic animals, plus a petting zoo and an "adventure" playground with more than 100 rides and amusements. There's also a nature path, a geological garden, and a picnic area with grills that can be reserved. Camel and pony rides are offered in summer. ⊠ *Königsteinerstr. 35* ☎ *06173/79749* ⊠ *€6* ☾ *Apr.–Sept., daily 8:30–6; Oct.–Mar., daily 9–5.*

Where to Stay

$$$$ ⊞ **Schlosshotel Kronberg.** This magnificent palace was built for Kaiserin Victoria, daughter of the British queen of the same name and mother of Wilhelm II, the infamous kaiser of World War I. She lived here after she was widowed and until her death in 1901. It's richly endowed with furnishings and works of art and is surrounded by a park with old trees, a grotto, a rose garden, and an 18-hole golf course. It's one of the few hotels left where you can leave your shoes outside your door for cleaning. Jimmy's Bar, with pianist, is a local rendezvous. Hotel guests receive complimentary visits to a nearby fitness center. ⊠ *Hainstr. 25, D–61476 Kronberg im Taunus* ☎ *06173/70101* ⊠ *06173/701–267* ⊕ *www.schlosshotel-kronberg.de* ⊠ *51 rooms, 7 suites* ⚮ *Restaurant, room service, in-room data ports, minibars, cable TV with movies, bar, concierge, meeting rooms, some pets allowed (fee), no-smoking rooms; no a/c* ⊟ *AE, DC, MC, V.*

Bad Homburg & Kronberg A to Z

BUS & TRAIN TRAVEL

Bad Homburg and Kronberg are easily reached by the S-bahn from Hauptwache, the main station, and other points in downtown Frankfurt. S–5 goes to Bad Homburg, S–4 to Kronberg. There's also a Taunusbahn (from the main station only) that stops in Bad Homburg and then continues into the far Taunus, including the Römerkastell-Saalburg and Wehrheim, with bus connections to Hessenpark.

CAR TRAVEL

Bad Homburg is about a 30- to 45-minute drive north of Frankfurt on A–5. You can get to Kronberg in about the same time by taking A–66 (Frankfurt–Wiesbaden) to the Nordwestkreuz interchange and following the signs to Eschborn and Kronberg.

VISITOR INFORMATION

The Bad Homburg tourist office is open until 6:30 PM weekdays, 2 PM Saturday, and is closed on Sunday. Kronberg's office closes at noon on weekdays and is closed the entire weekend.

🚺 **Kur- und Kongress GmbH Bad Homburg** ⊠ Louisenstr. 58, D-61348 Bad Homburg ☎ 06172/1780 ⊕ www.bad-homburg.de. **Verkehrs- und Kulturamt Kronberg** ⊠ Katharinenstr. 7, D-61476 Kronberg ☎ 06173/703-220 ⊕ www.kronberg.de.

Höchst

Take S–1 or S–2 suburban train from Frankfurt's main train station, Hauptwache, or Konstablerwache.

Höchst, a town with a castle and an Altstadt (Old Town) right out of a picture book, was not devastated by wartime bombing, so its castle and the market square, with its half-timber houses, are well preserved. The name *Höchst* is synonymous with chemicals because of the huge firm that has been here for more than a century. The historic part of town is well removed from the industrial area, and, indeed, the company Höchst has made major contributions to the Altstadt's fine state of repair. For a week in July the whole Alstadt is hung with lanterns for the Schlossfest, one of Frankfurt's more popular outdoor festivals.

The **Höchster Schloss,** first built in 1360, houses two **museums,** one about company history and one about Höchst history, the latter with an excellent collection of porcelain. (The castle and a nearby villa were used for decades following the war by the American military broadcaster AFN.) *Museums ☒ Am Burggraben 3 ☎ 069/305–6988 ▣ Free ☉ Daily 10–4.*

Höchst was once a porcelain-manufacturing town to rival Dresden and Vienna. Production ceased in the late 18th century but was revived by an enterprising businessman in 1965. Of special interest in town is the **Höchster Porzellan Manufaktur,** where you can watch the whole porcelain manufacturing process in the attractive "Porzellanhof." The store sells everything from figurines to dinner services, as well as a selection of glassware and silver. *☒ Palleskestr. 32 ☎ 069/300–9020 ▣ €10; €5 off any purchase ☉ Weekdays 9–6, Sat. 9–1.*

Not far from the Höchster Schloss, you can also see a fine exhibit of porcelain at the **Bolongaropalast** (Bolongaro Palace), a magnificent residence facing the river. It was built in the late 18th century by an Italian snuff manufacturer. Its facade—almost the length of a football field—is nothing to sneeze at. *☒ Bolongarostr. at Königsteinerstr. ☎ 069/3106–5520 ▣ Free ☉ Daily 9–4.*

Höchst's most interesting attraction is the **Justiniuskirche** (Justinius Church), Frankfurt's oldest building. Dating from the 7th century, the church is part early Romanesque and part 15th-century Gothic. The view from the top of the hill is well worth the walk. *☒ Justiniuspl. at Bolongarostr.*

Where to Stay

$ ☒ **Hotel-Schiff *Peter Schlott*.** The hotel ship is moored on the Main River, a 15-minute train or tram ride from the city center. Guest cabins are on the small side, but the river views more than compensate, and there's a common room with a television. It's not for you if you're subject to seasickness but ideal if you like to be rocked to sleep. *☒ Bolongarostr. 25, D–65929 ☎ 069/300–4643 ⊞ 069/307–671 ⊕ www.hotel-schiff-schlott.de ⇌ 19 rooms, 10 with bath ⌂ Restaurant, some pets allowed; no a/c, no room phones, no room TVs ⊟ AE, MC, V.*

FRANKFURT A TO Z

To research prices, get advice from other travelers, and book travel arrangements, visit www.fodors.com.

AIRPORTS & TRANSFERS

Flughafen Frankfurt Main is the biggest airport on the Continent, second in Europe only to London's Heathrow. There are direct flights to Frankfurt from many U.S. cities and from all major European cities.

The airport is 10 km (6 mi) southwest of the downtown area by the A–5 autobahn, and has its own railway station for the high-speed InterCity (IC) and InterCity Express (ICE) trains. Getting into Frankfurt from the airport is easy. The S-bahn 8 (suburban train) runs from the airport to downtown. Most travelers get off at the Hauptbahnhof (main train station) or at Hauptwache, in the heart of Frankfurt. Trains run at least every 15 minutes, and the trip takes about 15 minutes. The one-way fare is €3.05. A taxi from the airport into the city center normally takes around 20 minutes; allow double that during rush hours. The fare is around €15. If driving a rental car from the airport, take the main road out of the airport and follow the signs reading STADTMITTE (downtown).
🛈 **Flughafen Frankfurt Main** ☎ 069/6900 ⊕ www.frankfurt-airport.de.

BUS TRAVEL TO & FROM FRANKFURT

Some 100 European cities have bus links with Frankfurt. Buses arrive at and depart from the south side of the Hauptbahnhof.
🛈 **Deutsche Touring** ✉ Am Römerhof 17, Rebstock ☎ 069/79030.

CAR RENTAL

🛈 **Avis** ✉ Schmidtstr. 39, Rebstock ☎ 069/730–111. **Europcar** ✉ Lyonerstr. 68, Niederrad ☎ 069/6772–0291 ✉ Frankfurt Airport Hall A, arrival level ☎ 069/697–970. **Hertz** ✉ Hanauer Landstr. 117, Ostend ☎ 069/449–090 ✉ Cambergerstr. 21, Gallus ☎ 069/2425–2627.

CAR TRAVEL

Frankfurt is the meeting point of a number of major autobahns. The most important are A–3, running south from Köln and then west on to Würzburg and Nürnberg, and A–5, running south from Giessen and then on toward Mannheim and Heidelberg. A complex series of beltways surrounds the city. If you're driving to Frankfurt on A–5 from either north or south, exit at Nordwestkreuz and follow A–66 to the Nordend district, just north of downtown. Driving south on A–3, exit onto A–66 and follow the signs to Frankfurt-Höchst and then the Nordwestkreuz. Driving west on A–3, exit at the Offenbacher Kreuz onto A–661 and follow the signs for Frankfurt-Stadtmitte.

Traffic, accidents, and construction can make driving in Frankfurt irritating. Speeders are caught with hidden cameras, and tow trucks cruise the streets in search of illegal parkers. On the positive side, there are many reasonably priced parking garages around the downtown area and a well-developed "park and ride" system with the suburban train lines.

The transit map shows nearly a hundred outlying stations with a "P" symbol beside them, meaning there is convenient parking there.

CONSULATES
🏢 Australia ⊠ Grüneburgweg 58–62, Westend, D–60322 ☎ 069/905–580
🏢 United Kingdom ⊠ Bockenheimer Landstr. 42, Westend, D–60323 ☎ 069/170–0020
🏢 United States ⊠ Siesmayerstr. 21, Westend, D–60323 ☎ 069/75350

EMERGENCIES
🏢 Ambulance & Fire Services ☎ 112
🏢 Dentists ☎ 069/660–7271
🏢 Doctors ☎ 069/19292
🏢 Police ☎ 110

ENGLISH-LANGUAGE MEDIA
🏢 British Bookshop ⊠ Börsenstr. 17, City Center ☎ 069/280–492.

TELEVISION & RADIO — Though the U.S. military has moved out of Frankfurt, the news, sports, and music of the American Forces Network, the celebrated soldier radio station, is still easy to receive. Its AM broadcast (primarily talk) is at 87.3; the FM signal (primarily music) is at 98.7.

TAXIS
Cabs are not always easy to hail from the sidewalk; some stop, while others will pick up only from the city's numerous taxi stands or outside hotels or the train station. You can always order a cab. Fares start at €2.05 (€2.55 in the evening) and increase by a per-kilometer (½ mi) charge of €1.48 for the first 3, €1.33 thereafter. Count on paying €6.50 for a short city ride.
🏢 Taxi Companies ☎ 069/250–001, 069/230–001, or 069/230–033

TOURS
BOAT TOURS — Day trips on the Main River and Rhine excursions run from March through October and leave from the Frankfurt Mainkai am Eiserner Steg, just south of the Römer complex.
🏢 Frankfurt Personenschiffahrt GmbH ⊠ Mainkai 36, Altstadt ☎ 069/281–884.

BUS TOURS — Two-and-a-half-hour city bus tours with English-speaking guides are offered throughout the year. From April through October tours leave from outside the main tourist information office at Römerberg 27 daily at 10 AM and 2 PM; you can also pick up these tours 15 minutes later from the south side of the train station. The tour includes the price of admission to the Goethehaus and the top of the Maintower. November through March, tours leave daily at 2, stopping at 2:15 at the south side of the train station. The cost is €22.50. Gray Line offers two-hour city tours by bus four times a day for €28.50. They leave from the line's office at Wiesenhüttenplatz 39, or they will pick you up at an inner-city hotel.

APPLEWINE EXPRESS TOUR — Whether your stay in Frankfurt is long or short, you can easily find time for the one-hour Applewine Express (Ebbelwoi Express) tram tour. Offered Friday through Sunday (and holidays), this tour gives you a quick look at the city's neighborhoods, a bit of Frankfurt history, and a chance to sample apple- wine (a bottle, along with pretzels, is included in the €5 fare). You are certain to notice the brightly painted blue-and-red streetcar around town. Departures are from the Heide Strasse tram stop, near the Bornheim Mitte U-bahn station—the route takes you past the zoo, around the city center, across the bridge to Sachsenhausen, and then returns. Timetables change with the season, so it's best to call ahead (☎ 069/2132–2425).

🚩 **Gray Line** ✉ Wiesenhüttenpl. 39, City Center ☎ 069/230–492. **Tourist Office** ✉ Römerberg 27, Altstadt ☎ 069/2123–8708. **Verkehrsgesellschaft Frankfurt am Main** ☎ 069/2132–2425 City Transit Authority.

EXCURSION The Historische Eisenbahn Frankfurt runs a vintage steam train with a
TOURS buffet car along the banks of the Main River on weekends. The train runs from the Eiserner Steg bridge west to Frankfurt-Griesham and east to Frankfurt-Mainkur. The fare is €4.

Deutsche Touring will take you to Rothenburg, Heidelberg, and the Black Forest. Gray Line has trips to the Rhine, the Black Forest, and the Romantic Road.

🚩 **Deutsche Touring** ✉ Am Römerhof 17, Rebstock ☎ 069/79030. **Gray Line** ✉ Wiesenhüttenpl. 39, City Center ☎ 069/230–492. **Historische Eisenbahn Frankfurt** ✉ Eisener Steg, Altstadt ☎ 069/436–093.

WALKING TOURS The tourist office's walking tours cover a variety of topics, including Goethe, Jewish history, literature, transportation, architecture, and business. Tours can also be tailored to your interests. For an English-speaking guide, the cost is €119 for up to two hours, and €59 per hour after that.

🚩 **Tourist office** ✉ Römerberg 27, Altstadt ☎ 069/2123–8800.

TRAIN TRAVEL

EuroCity, InterCity, and InterCity Express trains connect Frankfurt with all German cities and many major European ones. The InterCity Express line links Frankfurt with Berlin, Hamburg, Munich, and a number of other major hubs. All long-distance trains arrive at and depart from the Hauptbahnhof, and many also stop at the long-distance train station at the airport. Be aware that the red-light district is just northeast of the train station.

🚩 **Deutsche Bahn** (German Railways) ☎ 01805/996–633.

TRANSPORTATION AROUND FRANKFURT

Frankfurt's smooth-running, well-integrated public transportation system (called RMV) consists of the U-bahn (subway), S-bahn (suburban railway), Strassenbahn (streetcars), and buses. Fares for the entire system, which includes a very extensive surrounding area, are uniform, though they are based on a complex zone system. Within the time that your ticket is valid (one hour for most inner-city destinations), you can transfer from one part of the system to another.

A basic one-way ticket for a ride in the inner zone costs €1.90 during the peak hours of 6 AM–9 AM and 4 PM–6:30 PM weekdays (€1.60 the rest of the time). There's also a reduced *Kurzstrecke* ("short stretch") fare of €1.50 (€1.05 off-peak). A day ticket for unlimited travel in the inner zones costs €4.35.

DISCOUNT FARES The Frankfurt tourist office offers a one- or two-day ticket—the Frankfurt Card—allowing unlimited travel in the inner zone (and to the airport) and a 50% reduction on admission to 15 museums (€6.15 for one day, €9.75 for two days). If you're attending a conference in Frankfurt, go to the tourist office and ask for a Congress Ticket (€2.60), a one-day ticket valid for unlimited travel in the city and to the airport.

PAYING Tickets may be purchased from automatic vending machines, which are at all U-bahn and S-bahn stations. Each station has a list of short-stretch destinations that can be reached from it, and if you're going to one of them, press the *Kurzstrecke* button on the vending machine. There's a second vertical row of buttons for the lower children's fares. Vending machines also have an extensive list of what might be called "long-stretch" destinations, those beyond the city limits. Each has a number beside it. Press the appropriate buttons for this destination, and then for either the adult or child fare, and the proper fare will appear. If your destination isn't on either list, it's a standard fare. Machines accept coins and notes and make change. If you're caught without a ticket, there's a fine of €30.

Bus drivers also sell tickets, but only if you boarded at a stop that does not have a vending machine. Weekly and monthly tickets are sold at central ticket offices and newsstands.

TRAVEL AGENCIES
🚩 **American Express International** ⊠ Theodor Heuss Allee 112, Bockenheim ☎ 069/97970. **Hapag-Lloyd Reisebüro** ⊠ Kaiserstr. 14, City Center ☎ 069/216-216.

VISITOR INFORMATION
For advance information, write to the Tourismus und Congress GmbH Frankfurt–Main. The main tourist office is at Römerberg 27 in the heart of the Old Town. It's open weekdays 9:30–5:30, weekends 10–4. There are two other information offices. One is in the main hall of the railroad station. The other, at Zeil 94a, is open weekdays 10–6, Saturday 10–4. All three offices can help you find accommodations.

Two airport information offices can also help with accommodations. The airport's Flughafen-Information, on the first floor of Arrivals Hall B, is open daily 6 AM–10 PM. The DER Deutsches Reisebüro, in Terminal 1 Arrivals Hall B, is open weekdays 6 AM–8 PM, weekends 7 AM–1 PM.
🚩 **Tourismus und Congress GmbH Frankfurt/Main** ⊠ Kaiserstr. 56, City Center, D-60329 Frankfurt am Main ☎ 069/2123-8800 ⊕ www.frankfurt.de. **Main tourist office** ⊠ Römerberg 27, Altstadt ☎ 069/2123-8708.

THE PFALZ &
RHINE TERRACE

10

PEEK AT THE CROWN JEWELS
at Burg Trifels ⇨*p.392*

TOUR A CASTLE & VINEYARD
at Schloss Villa Ludwigshöhe ⇨*p.394*

WAVE AT THE GERMAN WINE QUEEN
during the Deutsches Weinlesefest,
in Neustadt ⇨*p.396*

GET YOUR FILL OF POMP AND MAJESTY
at the Kaiserdom
(Imperial Cathedral), in Speyer ⇨*p.400*

RUB ELBOWS WITH THE STARS
at the exclusive Hotel Deidesheimer Hof ⇨*p.403*

Updated by
Kerry Brady

THE ROMANS PLANTED THE FIRST RHINELAND VINEYARDS 2,000 years ago. By the Middle Ages viticulture was flourishing at the hands of the church and the state, and a bustling wine trade had developed. This ancient vineyard area is now the state of Rheinland-Pfalz (Rhineland Palatinate), home to 6 of Germany's 13 wine-growing regions, including the 2 largest, Rheinhessen and the Pfalz. Bordered on the east by the Rhine and stretching from the French border north to Mainz, these two regions were the "wine cellar of the Holy Roman Empire." Thriving viticulture and splendid Romanesque cathedrals are the legacies of the bishops and emperors of Speyer, Worms, and Mainz. Two routes parallel to the Rhine link dozens of wine villages. In the Pfalz follow the Deutsche Weinstrasse (German Wine Road); in the eastern Rheinhessen (Rhine Terrace), the home of the mild wine Liebfraumilch, the Liebfrauenstrasse guides you from Worms to Mainz.

The Pfalz has a mild, sunny climate and an ambience to match. Vines carpet the foothills of the thickly forested Haardt Mountains, an extension of the Alsatian Vosges. The Pfälzerwald (Palatinate Forest) with its pine and chestnut trees is the region's other natural attraction. Hiking and cycling trails lead through the vineyards, the woods, and up to castles on the heights. As the Wine Road winds its way north from the French border, idyllic wine villages beckon with flower-draped facades and courtyards full of palms, oleanders, and fig trees. WEINVERKAUF (wine for sale) or WEINPROBE (wine tasting) signs are posted everywhere, each one an invitation to stop in to sample the wines.

The border between the Pfalz and Rheinhessen is invisible. Yet a few miles into the hinterland, a profile takes shape. Rheinhessen is a region of gentle, rolling hills and expansive farmland, where grapes are but one of many crops; vineyards are often scattered miles apart. The slopes overlooking the Rhine between Worms and Mainz—the so-called Rhine Terrace—are a notable exception. This is a nearly uninterrupted ribbon of vines culminating with the famous vineyards of Oppenheim, Nierstein, and Nackenheim on the outskirts of Mainz.

Exploring the Pfalz & Rhine Terrace

The Pfalz and Rheinhessen wine regions lie west of the Rhine in the central and southern part of the state of Rheinland-Pfalz. The area between Schweigen-Rechtenbach, on the French border, and Neustadt is known as the Südliche Weinstrasse (Southern Wine Road, abbreviated SÜW) and is the most romantic and serpentine part of the Wine Road. The scene farther north is more spacious, and the vineyards fan out onto the vast Rhine Plain. The 45-km (28-mi) stretch between Worms and Mainz along the Rhine takes in Rheinhessen's most prestigious vineyards. From here you are poised to explore the northern portion of the Rhineland.

About the Restaurants

Lunch in this region is generally served from noon until 2 or 2:30, dinner from 6 until 9:30 or 10. Credit cards have gained acceptance, but many restaurants will only accept cash, or debit cards issued by a German bank. Casual attire is typically acceptable at restaurants here and

If time is short, it's best to explore the Pfalz and Rheinhessen by car. There are, however, many scenic paths for hikers and cyclists, and public transportation is excellent.

Numbers in the text correspond to numbers in the margin and on the Pfalz and the Rhine Terrace and Worms maps.

10

If you have 3 days

Start at the French border in **Schweigen-Rechtenbach ❶ ▶**, and then visit two sites west of the Wine Road: enchanting Dörrenbach and the legendary **Burg Trifels,** near **Annweiler ❹**. For a contrast, tour the Pompeian-style palace **Schloss Villa Ludwigshöhe,** overlooking Edenkoben on the Wine Road; then continue uphill via chairlift to the vantage point at the **Rietburg castle.** Stay overnight in ▥ **St. Martin ❺**. The next day travel via **Neustadt ❻** to **Speyer ❼** to see the Romanesque imperial cathedral, the **Kaiserdom,** and the world's oldest bottle of wine, in the **Historisches Museum der Pfalz.** Backtrack to the Wine Road to overnight in either ▥ **Deidesheim ❽** or ▥ **Bad Dürkheim ❾**. Begin your third day with a visit to the magnificent **Limburg Monastery** ruins above Bad Dürkheim. Continue north on the Wine Road, with detours to the romantic medieval towns of **Freinsheim ❿** and Neuleiningen. Your journey and the Wine Road end in **Bockenheim.**

If you have 5 days

From **Schweigen-Rechtenbach ❶ ▶** visit **Dörrenbach** before exploring the cliffs and castles of the **Wasgau** area west of **Bad Bergzabern ❷**. Overnight in ▥**Gleiszellen** or ▥**Herxheim-Hayna.** Devote the second day to the sights between **Klingenmünster** and **Edenkoben,** with an excursion to **Burg Trifels.** After staying in ▥ **St. Martin ❺**, see the **Kalmit,** the region's highest peak, before heading for **Speyer ❼**. Back on the Wine Road, visit ▥ **Deidesheim ❽** en route to ▥ **Bad Dürkheim ❾**, home base for two nights. In the morning visit **Limburg Monastery** or **Hardenburg Fortress;** then relax at the spa, hike or bike through the Palatinate Forest, or tour a wine estate. The final day take in the northern end of the Wine Road via **Freinsheim ❿** and Neuleiningen, before turning east to **Worms ⓫–⓳** for a look at the amazing **Wormser Dom** and the **Judenfriedhof,** Europe's oldest and largest Jewish cemetery.

If you have 7 days

Follow the five-day itinerary above, overnighting in ▥ **Worms ⓫–⓳** the fifth night. Proceed north on B–9 to see Rheinhessen's most famous wine villages. In **Oppenheim ⓴** visit the **Katharinenkirche,** a beautiful Gothic church, and in **Nierstein ㉑** enjoy a Rhine panorama. Spend a peaceful night in ▥ **Nackenheim ㉒** or end the day in ▥ **Mainz ㉓** with a pub crawl. On the seventh day see the **Mainzer Dom** and the **Gutenberg Museum,** devoted to the history of printing. Visit the **Kupferberg Sekt Cellars** for a sparkling finale to your trip.

reservations are generally not needed. "Gourmet temples" that require reservations and jacket and tie are noted as such in this chapter.

About the Hotels

Accommodations in all price categories are plentiful, but book in advance if your visit coincides with a large festival. Bed-and-breakfasts abound. Look for signs reading FREMDENZIMMER or ZIMMER FREI (rooms available). A *Ferienwohnung* (holiday apartment), abbreviated FeWo in tourist brochures, is an economical alternative if you plan to stay in one location for several nights.

WHAT IT COSTS In Euros				
	$$$$	**$$$**	**$$**	**$**	**¢**
RESTAURANTS	over €25	€21–€25	€16–€20	€9–€15	under €9
HOTELS	over €225	€175–€225	€100–€175	€50–€100	under €50

Restaurant prices are per person for a main course at dinner. Hotel prices are for two people in a standard double room, including tax and service.

Timing

The wine-festival season begins in March with the *Mandelblüten* (blossoming of the almond trees) along the Wine Road and continues through October. By May the vines' tender shoots and leaves appear. As the wine harvest progresses in September and October, foliage takes on reddish-golden hues.

THE GERMAN WINE ROAD

The Wine Road spans the length of the Pfalz wine region. You can travel from north to south or vice versa. Given its central location, the Pfalz is convenient to visit before or after a trip to the Black Forest, Heidelberg, or the northern Rhineland.

Schweigen-Rechtenbach

▶ ❶ *21 km (13 mi) southwest of Landau on B–38.*

The southernmost wine village of the Pfalz lies on the French border. During the economically depressed 1930s, local vintners established a route through the vineyards to promote tourism. The German Wine Road was inaugurated in 1935; a year later the massive stone **Deutsches Weintor** (German Wine Gate) was erected to add visual impact to the marketing concept. Halfway up the gateway is a platform that offers a fine view of the vineyards—to the south, French; to the north, German. Schweigen's 1-km (½-mi) **Weinlehrpfad** (educational wine path) wanders through the vineyards and, with signs and exhibits, explains the history of viticulture from Roman times to the present.

en route | Drive north on B–38 toward Bad Bergzabern. Two kilometers (1 mi) before you reach the town, turn left to see the enchanting village of **Dörrenbach.** It has an uncommon Gothic *Wehrkirche* (fortified

Biking, Hiking & Walking

Country roads and traffic-free vineyard paths are a cyclist's paradise. There are also well-marked cycling trails, such as the *Radwanderweg Deutsche Weinstrasse,* which runs parallel to its namesake from the French border to Bockenheim, and the *Radweg* (cycling trail) along the Rhine between Worms and Mainz. The Palatinate Forest, Germany's largest single tract of woods, has more than 10,000 km (6,200 mi) of paths.

The Wanderweg Deutsche Weinstrasse, a walking route that traverses vineyards, woods, and wine villages, covers the length of the Pfalz. It connects with many trails in the Palatinate Forest that lead to Celtic and Roman landmarks and dozens of castles dating primarily from the 11th to 13th centuries. In Rheinhessen you can hike along two marked trails parallel to the Rhine: the Rheinterrassenwanderweg and the Rheinhöhenweg along the heights.

Festivals

Wine and *Sekt* (sparkling wine) flow freely from March through October at festivals that include parades, fireworks, and rides. The Pfalz is home to the world's largest wine festival in mid-September, the Dürkheimer Wurstmarkt ("sausage market," so named because of the 400,000 pounds of sausage consumed during eight days of merrymaking). In Neustadt, the German Wine Queen is crowned during the 10-day Deutsches Weinlesefest (German wine harvest festival) in October. The Mainzer Johannisnacht (in honor of Johannes Gutenberg) in late June, the Wormser Backfischfest (fried-fish festival) in late August, and the Brezelfest (pretzel festival) in Speyer on the second weekend in July are the major wine and folk festivals along this part of the Rhine.

On the Menu

The best introduction to regional country cooking is the *Pfälzer Teller,* a platter of bratwurst (grilled sausage), *Leberknödel* (liver dumplings), and slices of *Saumagen* (a spicy meat-and-potato mixture encased in a sow's stomach), with *Weinkraut* (sauerkraut braised in wine) and *Kartoffelpüree* (mashed potatoes) on the side. Rheinhessen is known for the hearty casseroles *Dippe-Has* (hare and pork baked in red wine) and *Backes Grumbeere* (scalloped potatoes cooked with bacon, sour cream, white wine, and a layer of pork). *Spargel* (asparagus); *Wild* (game); chestnuts; and mushrooms, particularly *Pfifferlinge* (chanterelles), are seasonal favorites. During the grape harvest, from September through November, try *Federweisser* (fermenting grape juice) and *Zwiebelkuchen* (onion quiche)—specialties unique to the wine country.

Local Wine

Savor the local wines. Those from Rheinhessen are often sleeker and less voluminous than their Pfälzer counterparts. Many are sold as *offene Weine* (wines by the glass) and are *trocken* (dry) or *halbtrocken* (semidry). The classic white varieties are Riesling, Silvaner, Müller-Thurgau (also called Rivaner), Grauburgunder (Pinot Gris), and Weissburgunder (Pinot Blanc); Spätburgunder (Pinot Noir), Dornfelder, and Portugieser are the most popular red wines. The word *Weissherbst,* after the grape variety, signals a rosé wine.

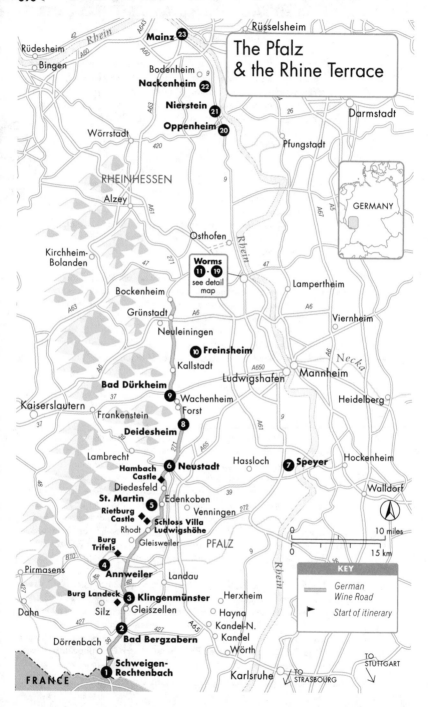

church) that overlooks the Renaissance town hall, considered the most beautiful half-timber building in the Pfalz.

Bad Bergzabern

② *10 km (6 mi) north of Schweigen-Rechtenbach on B–38.*

The landmark of this little spa town is the baroque **Schloss** (palace) of the dukes of Zweibrücken. Walk into the courtyard to see the elaborate portals of earlier residences on the site. The town's other gem is an impressive stone building with scrolled gables and decorative oriels. Built about 1600, it houses the wine restaurant **Zum Engel.** There are many historic facades to admire along Marktstrasse. Stop at No. 48, **Café Herzog,** to sample *Weinperlen* (wine pearls), unusual wine-filled chocolates, or the ice cream version, *Weinperleneis.* "Adam and Eve," sweet and peppery chocolates, and ice cream flavored with almond blossoms debuted in 2004. The café is closed Monday.

Where to Stay & Eat

¢–$$ ✕ **Zum Engel.** Enjoy Palatinate specialties or *Käs'Spätzle mit Rostzwiebeln* (a cheese-gratin pasta dish topped with fried onions) in the prettiest Renaissance house of the Pfalz. The wines are from local producers and very reasonably priced. ✉ *Königstr. 45, Bad Bergzabern* ☎ *06343/989–300* ▤ *MC, V* ☉ *Closed Mon., 2 wks in Feb., and 2 wks in July and Aug.*

$$ ✕▣ **Hotel–Restaurant Zur Krone.** The simple facade belies this upscale inn
Fodor'sChoice that offers modern facilities, tasteful decor, and above all, a warm wel-
★ come from the Kuntz family. Reservations are essential at the main restaurant ($$$$). Start with chef Karl-Emil Kuntz's *Gruss aus der Küche* ("greetings from the kitchen"), a medley of appetizers. Terrines and parfaits are specialties, as is the homemade goat cheese. The same kitchen team cooks for the Pfälzer Stube ($$–$$$; no lunch Tuesday). The wine list is excellent. Hayna, an idyllic suburb of Herxheim, lies between the Rhine and the Wine Road, 20 km (12 mi) east of Bad Bergzabern via B–427. ✉ *Hauptstr. 62–64, D–76863 Herxheim-Hayna* ☎ *07276/5080* 🖷 *07276/50814* ⊕ *www.hotelkrone.de* ⇥ *50 rooms, 3 suites* ⚐ *2 restaurants, in-room data ports, minibars, cable TV, 2 tennis courts, indoor pool, massage, sauna, steam room, bicycles, bar, lobby lounge, pub, babysitting, laundry service, Internet, some pets allowed (fee), no-smoking rooms; no a/c* ▤ *AE, MC, V* ☉ *Restaurant Zur Krone closed Mon. and Tues., 1st 2 wks in Jan., and 2 wks July and Aug. No lunch* ⦿ *BP.*

$ ✕▣ **Gasthof Zum Lam.** Flowers cascade from the windowsills of this half-timber inn in the heart of Gleiszellen (to the north of Bad Bergzabern). Exposed beams add rustic charm to the airy rooms; the bathrooms are bright and very modern. The restaurant ($–$$) is no less inviting with its dome-shape tile stove and natural stone walls. In summer you can dine on the vine-shaded terrace. ✉ *Winzerg. 37, D–76889 Gleiszellen* ☎ *06343/939–212* 🖷 *06343/939–213* ⊕ *www.zum-lam.de* ⇥ *11 rooms, 1 suite* ⚐ *Restaurant, cable TV, beer garden, some pets allowed (fee); no a/c, no smoking* ▤ *No credit cards* ☉ *Restaurant closed Wed. No lunch Nov.–Apr.* ⦿ *BP.*

en route   Continue north on the Wine Road—now B–48 (B–38 leads to Landau)—toward Klingenmünster. Four kilometers (2½ mi) north of Bad Bergzabern turn left and drive to **Gleiszellen** to see the Winzergasse (Vintners' Lane). This little vine-canopied street is lined with a beautiful ensemble of half-timber houses. Try a glass of the town's specialty: spicy, aromatic Muskateller wine, a rarity seldom found elsewhere in Germany.

Klingenmünster

❸ *8 km (5 mi) north of Bad Bergzabern on B–48.*

The village grew out of the **Benedictine monastery** founded here by the Merovingian king Dagobert in the 7th century. The monastery church is still in use. Despite its baroque appearance, parts of it date from the 12th century, as do the remains of the cloister. On the hillside are ruins of **Burg Landeck,** built around 1200 to protect the monastery. The keep and inner walls are accessible via a drawbridge that spans a 33-foot-deep moat. A walk through the chestnut forest from the monastery to the castle takes a half hour. Your reward will be a magnificent view over the Rhine Valley and south as far as the Black Forest.

Annweiler

❹ *11 km (7 mi) northwest of Klingenmünster at junction of B–48 and B–10.*

In 1219 Annweiler was declared a Free Imperial City by Emperor Friedrich II. Stroll along Wassergasse, Gerbergasse (Tanners' Lane), and Quodgasse to see the half-timber houses and the waterwheels on the Queich River, which is more like a creek. Annweiler is a gateway to the **Wasgau,** the romantic southern portion of the Palatinate Forest, marked by sandstone cliffs and ancient castles. Festivities at the Triftfest in late June focus on the history of the once-important timber industry and the work of lumberjacks a century ago. The fruits of the forest are celebrated in early October, when local chefs present chestnut-theme menus during the *Käschdefescht* (chestnut festival).

★ **Burg Trifels,** one of Germany's most imposing castles, is perched on the highest of three sandstone bluffs overlooking Annweiler. Celts, Romans, and Salians all had settlements on this site, but it was under the Hohenstaufen emperors (12th and 13th centuries) that Trifels was built on a grand scale. It housed the crown jewels from 1125 to 1274 (replicas are on display today). It was also an imperial prison, perhaps where Richard the Lion-Hearted was held captive in 1193–94.

Although it was never conquered, the fortress was severely damaged by lightning in 1602. Reconstruction began in 1938, shaped by visions of grandeur to create a national shrine of the imperial past. Accordingly, the monumental proportions of some parts of today's castle bear no resemblance to those of the original Romanesque structure. The imperial hall is a grand setting for the *Serenaden* (concerts) held in summer. ☎06346/8470 ⊕*www.burgen-rlp.de* ⊠*€2.60* ☉*Apr.–Sept., daily 10–6; Oct., Nov., and, Jan.–Mar., daily 10–5.*

🐾 **Museum unterm Trifels.** A historic mill, tanners' houses, and a tannery "beneath Trifels" showcase diverse artifacts and models that chronicle the development of Burg Trifels, Annweiler, and the natural surroundings. The museum ticket entitles reduced admission at Burg Trifels and the Shoe Factory Museum in Hauenstein. ⊠ *Am Schipkapass 4* ☎ *06346/ 1682* ⊠ *€2.60* ☾ *Mid-Mar.–Oct., Tues.–Sun. 10–5; Nov.–mid-Mar., weekends 1–5.*

off the beaten path

MUSEUM "DIE SCHUHFABRIK" (Shoe Factory Museum) – In this former shoe factory in Hauenstein, 12 km (7½ mi) west of Annweiler on B–10, you can learn about the history of shoemaking, once an important industry in this part of Germany. Demonstrations on historical machinery and 14 factory outlet stores nearby make this a worthwhile excursion. ⊠ *Turnstr. 5* ☎ *06392/915–165* ⊕ *www. deutsches-schuhmuseum.de* ⊠ *€3.20* ☾ *Dec.–Feb., weekdays 1–4, weekends 10–4; Mar.–Nov., daily 10–5.*

DIE GLÄSERNE SCHUHFABRIK – You can watch workers produce handmade footwear during working hours and on tours at the Seibel family's glass-lined shoe factory—home of The European Comfort Shoe™. ⊠ *Waldenburgerstr. 1* ☎ *06392/922–1371* ⊕ *www. glaeserne-schuhfabrik.de* ⊠ *Free* ☾ *Apr.–Oct., weekdays 10–5, weekends 1–5; Nov.–Mar., weekdays 10–noon and 12:45–4. Year-round, weekday tours 10:30 and 2:30; Apr.–Oct., weekends 2:30.*

Where to Stay & Eat

$–$$ ✕ **Restaurant s'Reiwerle.** Enjoy Pfälzer cuisine and chestnut-based dishes, such as *Keschtebrieh* (chestnut soup), in Annette Neumann's 300-year-old half-timber house. *Reiwerle* (RYE vair leh) is dialect for a spigot to tap wine from a cask. At this writing she plans to extend the opening hours. ⊠*Flitschberg 7* ☎*06346/929–362* ⊟*No credit cards* ☾*Closed Nov.–Aug.*

★ **¢–$** ✕ **Zur alten Gerberei.** An open fireplace, exposed beams, and sandstone walls give this old *Gerberei* (tannery) a cozy feel. The Queich flows right past the outdoor seats. In addition to Pfälzer specialties and vegetarian dishes, you can try Alsatian *Flammkuchen,* similar to pizza but baked on a wafer-thin crust. There are 15 Pfälzer wines available by the glass. ⊠ *Am Prangertshof 11, at Gerberg.* ☎ *06346/3566* ⊕ *www.gerberei. de* ⊟ *No credit cards* ☾ *Closed Mon. and 4 wks Jan. and Feb. No lunch Tues.–Sat.*

$ ✕🏨 **Landhaus Herrenberg.** A flower-filled courtyard welcomes guests to this country inn. The rooms are modern and spacious (there's a whirlpool in the suite), with blond-wood furnishings. The Lergenmüllers are vintners known for excellent red wines. In the restaurant ($–$$), Clemens Sulzmann showcases their wines with fine regional cuisine using local fish and game, and adds contemporary flavors to traditional dishes, such as breast of duck in balsamic sauce. ⊠ *Lindenbergstr. 72, D–76829 Landau-Nussdorf* ☎ *06341/60205* 🖷 *06341/60709* ⊕ *www.landhaus-herrenberg.de* ⇆ *8 rooms, 1 suite* ♿ *Restaurant, minibars, cable TV, Weinstube, wine shop, some pets allowed (fee), no-smoking rooms; no a/c* ⊟ *AE, MC, V* ☾ *Hotel closed 3 wks in Jan. Restaurant closed Thurs. No lunch Mon.–Sat.* ⏀ *BP.*

Sports & the Outdoors

BIKING, Dozens of marked trails guide you to the Wasgau's striking geological
CLIMBING & formations and castles carved into the sandstone cliffs. From Annweiler
HIKING you can access many of these trails via a circular tour by car (55½ km
[35 mi]). Proceed west on B–10 to Hinterweidenthal (16½ km [10 mi]),
then south on B–427 to Dahn (7 km [4 mi]), and continue southeast to
Erlenbach (9 km [5½ mi]). Return to Annweiler via Vorderweidenthal
(1 km [½ mi]) and Silz (7 km [4 mi]). Each town is a good starting point
for a scenic ride, climb, or hike.

Shopping

The **süw Shop** (⊠ An der Kreuzmühle 2 ☎ 06341/940–407), in Landau's
Südliche Weinstrasse regional tourist office, sells gift items, grape products, wine-related accessories, and detailed maps of cycling and hiking
trails. The shop is closed Friday afternoon and weekends.

Schloss Villa Ludwigshöhe

★ *8 km (5 mi) north of Gleisweiler, slightly west of Edenkoben on the
Wine Road.*

Bavaria's King Ludwig I built a summer residence on the slopes overlooking Edenkoben, in what he called "the most beautiful square mile
of my realm." You can reach the neoclassical Schloss Villa Ludwigshöhe
by car or bus from Edenkoben or take a scenic 45-minute walk through
the vineyards along the Weinlehrpfad. Historical wine presses and vintners' tools are displayed at intervals along the path. It starts at the corner of Landauer Strasse and Villa Strasse in Edenkoben.

The layout and decor—Pompeian-style murals, splendid parquet floors,
and Biedermeier and Empire furnishings—of the palace provide quite
a contrast to medieval castles elsewhere in the Pfalz. An extensive collection of paintings and prints by the leading German impressionist Max
Slevogt (1868–1932) is on display. ☎ *06323/93016* ⊕ *www.burgen-rlp.
de* ⊠ *€2.60* ☉ *Apr.–Sept., Tues.–Sun. 10–6; Oct., Nov., and Jan.–Mar.,
Tues.–Sun. 10–5.*

From Schloss Villa Ludwigshöhe you can hike (30 minutes) or ride the
☺ Rietburgbahn chairlift (10 minutes) up to the **Rietburg** castle ruins for
a sweeping view of the Pfalz. A restaurant, game park, and playground
are on the grounds. ⊠ *Chairlift €4.50 round-trip, €3.50 one-way*
☉ *Mar., Sun. 9–5; Apr.–Oct., weekdays 9–5, weekends 9–6.*

Where to Stay & Eat

$$ ▦ **Alte Rebschule.** In 2004 Sonja Hafen converted the old *Rebschule* (vine
nursery), nestled between the forest and vineyards, into a pleasant,
modern hotel. All rooms have country-style furniture and balconies
overlooking the vineyards and Rhine Plain. She plans to add a small spa
and offer themed excursions (wine, culture, nature). In the evenings, house
guests can opt for a prix-fixe menu ($–$$). ⊠ *3 km (2 mi) west of Schloss
Villa Ludwigshöhe, Theresienstr. 200 D–76835 Rhodt u. Rietburg*
☎ *06323/987–113* ⊕ *www.alte-rebschule.de* ↩ *29 rooms, 1 suite*
↻ *Dining room, in-room data ports, minibars, cable TV, sauna, bar, lobby*

lounge, babysitting, laundry service, some pets allowed (fee), no smoking; no a/c ▭ *MC, V* ¶◎¶ *BP.*

St. Martin

❺ *10 km (6 mi) north of Gleisweiler, slightly west of the Wine Rd. Turn left at the northern edge of Edenkoben.*

★ This is one of the most charming wine villages of the Pfalz. The entire **Altstadt** (Old Town) is under historical preservation protection. For 350 years the Knights of Dalberg lived in the castle **Kropsburg,** the romantic ruins of which overlook the town. The Renaissance tombstones are among the many artworks in the late-Gothic Church of **St. Martin.** The town's namesake is honored with a parade and wine festival on November 11.

Where to Stay & Eat

$ ✕▦ **Landhaus Christmann.** This bright, modern house in the midst of the vineyards has stylish rooms decorated with both antiques and modern furnishings. Some rooms have balconies with a view of the Hambacher Schloss. Vintners and distillers, the Christmanns offer 20 wines by the glass in their restaurant, Gutsausschank Kabinett (¢–$), as well as culinary wine tastings. In addition to their wines and spirits, they sell antiques. ✉ *Riedweg 1, D–67487* ☎ *06323/94270* 🖷 *06323/942–727* ⊕ *www.landhaus-christmann.de* ⇆ *6 rooms, 3 apartments* ⚭ *Restaurant, cable TV, Internet, some pets allowed (fee); no a/c, no room phones, no smoking* ▭ *MC, V* ⊗ *Hotel and restaurant closed 2 wks Jan. and Feb. and 2 wks July and Aug. Restaurant closed Mon.–Wed. No lunch* ¶◎¶ *BP.*

★ $ ✕▦ **St. Martiner Castell.** The Mücke family transformed a simple vintner's house into a fine hotel and restaurant, retaining many of the original features, such as exposed beams and an old wine press. Though it's in the heart of town, the hotel is an oasis of peace, particularly the rooms with balconies overlooking the garden. A native of the Loire Valley, Frau Mücke adds French flair to the menu ($–$$$), including a six-course *Schlemmer-Menü* (gourmet menu). The wine list offers a good selection of bottles from a neighboring wine estate. ✉ *Maikammerer Str. 2, D–67487* ☎ *06323/9510* 🖷 *06323/951–200* ⊕ *www.hotelcastell.de* ⇆ *26 rooms* ⚭ *Restaurant, in-room data ports, cable TV, sauna, babysitting, laundry service, some pets allowed (fee), no-smoking rooms; no a/c* ▭ *MC, V* ⊗ *Hotel and restaurant closed Feb. Restaurant closed Tues.* ¶◎¶ *BP.*

The Arts

Schloss Villa Ludwigshöhe, Kloster Heilsbruck (a former Cistercian convent near Edenkoben), and **Schloss Edesheim** are backdrops for concerts and theater in summer. For a calendar of events contact the Südliche Weinstrasse regional tourist office in Landau.

Shopping

Artist Georg Wiedemann is responsible for both content and design of the exquisite products of Germany's premier wine-vinegar estate, **Doktorenhof** (✉ Raiffeisenstr. 5 ☎ 06323/5505 ⊕ www.doktorenhof.de)

in Venningen, 2 km (1 mi) east of Edenkoben. Make an appointment for a unique vinegar tasting and tour of the cellars or pick up a gift at his shop. He's open weekdays 8–4, Wednesday until 6, and Saturday 9–2 (no credit cards).

en route Depart St. Martin via the Totenkopf-Höhenstrasse, a scenic road through the forest. Turn right at the intersection with Kalmitstrasse and proceed to the vantage point atop the **Kalmit,** the region's highest peak (2,200 feet). The view is second to none. Return to the Kalmitstrasse, drive toward Maikammer, and stop at **Mariä-Schmerzen-Kapelle** (Our Lady of Sorrows Chapel) in Alsterweiler. It houses the work of an unknown master, a remarkable Gothic triptych depicting the Crucifixion. Maikammer has half-timber houses, patrician manors, and a baroque church and is the last (or first) wine village in the Südliche Weinstrasse district.

Back on the Wine Road it's a brief drive to the Neustadt suburb of Hambach. The sturdy block of **Hambacher Schloss** is considered the "cradle of German democracy." It was here, on May 27, 1832, that 30,000 patriots demonstrated for German unity, raising the German colors for the first time. Inside there are exhibits about the uprising and the history of the castle. The French destroyed the 11th-century imperial fortress in 1688. Reconstruction finally began after the Second World War, in neo-Gothic style, and the castle is now an impressive setting for theater and concerts. On a clear day you can see the spire of Strasbourg Cathedral and the northern fringe of the Black Forest from the terrace restaurant. ⊠ *Hambach* ☎ *06321/30881* ⊕ *www.hambacher-schloss.de* 🖾 *€4.50* ☉ *Mar.–Nov., daily 10–6.*

Neustadt

❻ *8 km (5 mi) north of St. Martin, 5 km (3 mi) north of Hambach on the Wine Rd.*

Neustadt and its nine wine suburbs are at the midpoint of the Wine Road and the edge of the district known as Deutsche Weinstrasse–Mittelhaardt. With around 5,000 acres of vines, they jointly compose Germany's largest wine-growing community. The **Deutsches Weinlesefest** (German Wine Harvest Festival) culminates every October with the coronation of the German Wine Queen and a parade with more than 100 floats. You can sample some 30 of the 100 Neustadt wines sold at the **Haus des Weines** (House of Wine), which is opposite the town hall. The Gothic house from 1276 is bordered by a splendid Renaissance courtyard, the Kuby'scher Hof. ⊠ *Rathausstr. 6* ☎ *06321/355–871* ☉ *Closed Sun. and Mon.*

The **Marktplatz** (market square) is the focal point of the Old Town and a beehive of activity on Tuesday, Thursday, and Saturday, when farmers come to sell their wares. The square itself is ringed by baroque and Renaissance buildings (Nos. 1, 4, 8, and 11) and the Gothic **Stiftskirche**

(Collegiate Church), built as a burial church for the Palatinate counts. In summer, concerts take place in the church (Saturday 11:30–noon). Afterward, you can ascend the southern tower (187 feet) for a bird's-eye view of the town (the tower is only open after concerts). The world's largest cast-iron bell—weighing more than 17 tons—hangs in the northern tower. Indoors, see the elaborate tombstones near the choir and the fanciful grotesque figures carved into the baldachins and corbels.

The Pfalz is home to the legendary, elusive *Elwetritschen,* part bird and part human, said to roam the forest and vineyards at night. "Hunting Elwetritschen" is both a sport and an alibi. Local sculptor Gernot Rumpf has immortalized these creatures by depicting them in a **fountain** on Marstallplatz. No two are alike. Near the market square, hunt for the one that "escaped" from its misty home. End a walking tour of the Old Town on the medieval lanes Metzgergasse, Mittelgasse, and Hintergasse to see beautifully restored half-timber houses, many of which are now pubs, cafés, and boutiques.

Otto Dill Museum. The late Impressionist painter Otto Dill (1884–1957), a native of Neustadt, is known for powerful animal portraits (especially lions, tigers, horses) and vivid landscapes. Some 100 oil paintings and 50 drawings and watercolors of the Manfred Vetter collection are on display. ⊠ *Rathausstr. 12, at Bachgängel 8* ☎ *06321/398–321* ⊕ *www.otto-dill-museum.de* 🎫 *€2.50* 🕙 *Wed. and Fri. 5–7, Sat. 2–6, and Sun. 11–6.*

Thirty historical train engines and railway cars are on display at the **Eisenbahn Museum,** behind the main train station. Take a ride through the Palatinate Forest on one of the museum's historical steam trains, the *Kuckucksbähnel* (€12), which departs from track 5 around 10:30 AM every other Sunday between Easter and mid-October. It takes 1½ hours to cover the 13-km (8-mi) stretch from Neustadt to Elmstein. ⊠ *Neustadt train station, Schillerstr. entrance* ☎ *06325/8626* ⊕ *www.eisenbahnmuseum-neustadt.de* 🎫 *€3* 🕙 *Tues.–Fri. 10–1, weekends 10–4.*

Where to Stay & Eat

$$–$$$ ✕ **Brezel.** The gilded *Brezel* (pretzel) hanging in front of the 17th-century half-timber house (once a bakery) is the namesake of Helga and Stefan Braun's classy yet comfortable wine restaurant. White walls, softened by light wooden floors and beams, are hung with paintings by the late Impressionist Otto Dill. In the back, dine beneath the vaulted ceiling of a former wine cellar. Fish is the specialty, but the entire menu is based on fresh, seasonal ingredients. The luncheon special is a good value, and the excellent wines are reasonably priced. ⊠ *Rathausstr. 32, between Ludwigstr. and Sauter Str.* ☎ *06321/481–971* ⊕ *www.brezel-restaurant.de* 🖃 *MC, V* 🕙 *Closed 1 wk in Jan., 2 wks in late July, and Tues. and Wed.*

$–$$$ ✕ **Altstadtkeller bei Jürgen.** Tucked behind a wooden portal, this vaulted sandstone "cellar" (it's actually on the ground floor) is a cozy setting for very tasty food. Equally inviting is the terrace, with its citrus, olive, palm, and fig trees. The regular menu includes a number of salads and a good selection of fish and steaks, and the daily specials are geared to what's in season. Owner Jürgen Reis is a wine enthusiast, and his well-chosen list shows it. ✉ *Kunigundenstr. 2* ☎ *06321/32320* ⊕ *www.altstadtkeller-neustadt.de* ▤ *DC, MC, V* ☉ *Closed 10 days in early Aug., 2 wks in Feb., and Mon. No dinner Sun.*

¢–$ ✕ **Weinstube Eselsburg.** The *Esel* (donkey) lends its name to Mussbach's best-known vineyard, Eselshaut (donkey's hide); this wine pub; and one of its specialties, *Eselssuppe,* a hearty soup of pork, beef, and vegetables. Always packed with regulars, the Eselsburg is decorated with original artwork by the owner, Peter Wiedemann, and his late father, Fritz, the pub's founder. Enjoy top Pfälzer wines in the flower-filled courtyard in summer or in the warmth of an open hearth in winter. From October to May, try the *Schlachtfest* (meat and sausages from freshly slaughtered pigs) the first Tuesday of the month. ✉ *Kurpfalzstr. 62, Neustadt-Mussbach* ☎ *06321/66984* ⊕ *www.eselsburg.de* ▤ *MC, V* ☉ *Closed Sun.–Tues. and mid-Dec.–mid-Jan. No lunch.*

$$ ✕▥ **Steinhäuser Hof.** The 14th-century Kuby'scher Hof is an architectural gem in the heart of the Old Town. The former stables have been converted into modern rooms with light wood furnishings and a cozy restaurant (**¢–$$$**) run by cheerful Ilona Jochim. She serves regional, seasonal, and vegetarian specialties beneath a 16th-century vaulted brick ceiling and in the beautiful courtyard. There's fresh fish on Friday and *Pfälzer Dampfnudeln* (tasty yeast dumplings with wine or vanilla sauce) on Tuesday. ✉ *Turmsstr. 11, D–67433 Neustadt* ☎ *06321/480–706* ▤ *06321/480–712* ⤳ *6 rooms* ⌂ *Restaurant, cable TV, some pets allowed (fee), no-smoking rooms; no a/c, no room phones* ▤ *No credit cards* ☉ *Closed 4 wks in Jan. and Feb. Restaurant closed Wed. No dinner Sun.* ¶◯⟨ *BP.*

★ $ ✕▥ **Mithras-Stuben/Weinstube Kommerzienrat.** Convivial proprietor and wine devotee Bernd Hagedorn named his four spacious apartments after Mithras, the ancient Persian god of light and deity of a religious cult embraced by Roman legionnaires. The contemporary furnishings, Oriental rugs, and modern baths are a far cry from what the Romans had in the Pfalz 2,000 years ago. Upon request, cell phones are available for the two apartments with no in-room phones. In the restaurant ($), an incredible 300 Pfälzer wines can be sampled by the glass (and 250 imported wines by the bottle). *Rumpsteak* (beef steak), served with tasty *Bratkartoffeln* (home-fried potatoes) or *Rösti* (potato pancakes), and Pfälzer Gyros (a unique meat-and-cheese dish) are favorites. ✉ *Kurpfalzstr. 161/Loblocherstr. 34, D–67435 Neustadt-Gimmeldingen* ☎ *06321/679–0335 or 06321/68200* ▤ *06321/679–0331* ⊕ *www.weinstube-kommerzienrat.de* ⤳ *4 apartments* ⌂ *Restaurant, some in-room data ports, cable TV, kitchenettes, wine shop, some pets allowed (fee), no-smoking rooms; no a/c, no phones in some rooms* ▤ *MC, V* ☉ *Restaurant closed Thurs. No lunch.*

$ ✕▥ **Rebstöckel/Weinstube Schönhof.** Enjoy vintner's hospitality in Hannelore and Stephan Hafen's 17th-century stone guesthouse at the Weingut Schönhof estate. All rooms have blond-wood furnishings; some have kitchenettes. A common refrigerator is stocked with the estate's wines (and other drinks), or try them in the Weinstube with a hearty *Schönhof Pfännchen* (ham gratin in a brandy cream sauce). Wine tastings and vineyard hikes can be arranged and cycling fans can rent bikes at a shop around the corner. Neustadt proper is 5 km (3 mi) north. ⊠ *Weinstr. 600, D–67434 Neustadt-Diedesfeld* ☎ *06321/86198* 🖷 *06321/86823* ⊕ *www.weingut-schoenhof.de* ⟋ *1 room, 4 apartments* ⚶ *Restaurant, refrigerators, wine shop; no a/c, no smoking* ▤ *No credit cards* ⊙ *Restaurant closed Dec.–mid-Mar. and Mon.–Thurs. No lunch* ⑂ *BP.*

Nightlife & the Arts

The **Saalbau** (⊠ Bahnhofstr. 1 ☎ 06321/926–892), opposite the train station, is Neustadt's convention center and main venue for concerts, theater, and events. In summer there's open-air theater at **Villa Böhm** (⊠ Maximilianstr. 25), which also houses the city's history museum. Concerts, art exhibits, and wine festivals are held at the **Herrenhof** (⊠ An der Eselshaut 18) in the suburb of Mussbach. Owned by the Johanniter-Orden (Order of the Knights of St. John) from the 13th to 18th century, it's the oldest wine estate of the Pfalz. Contact the Neustadt tourist office for program details and tickets.

Shopping

After seeing the water-spewing Elwetritschen in action, you might want to take one home. The pottery store, **Keramik-Atelier Ingrid Zinkgraf** (⊠ Badstubeng. 5, Am Klemmhof ☎ 06321/30162), has amusing ceramic renditions of the mythical birds, as well as modern and traditional pottery and sculptures.

Sports & the Outdoors

The Neustadt tourist office has brochures and maps that outline circular biking and hiking routes, including the educational wine paths in Gimmeldingen and Haardt.

en route The **Holiday Park,** in Hassloch, 10 km (6 mi) east of Neustadt, is one of Europe's largest amusement parks. The admission fee (free on your birthday) covers all attractions, from shows to giant-screen cinema, and special activities for children. The free-fall tower, hell barrels, and Thunder River rafting are standing favorites, and *Expedition GeForce,* has the steepest drop (82 degrees) of any roller coaster in Europe. ☎ *06324/599–3318* ⊕ *www.holidaypark.de* 🖼 *€22.50* ⊙ *Early Apr.–Oct., daily 10–6.*

Speyer

❼ *25 km (15 mi) east of Neustadt via B–39, 22 km (14) mi south of Mannheim via B–9 and B–44.*

Speyer was one of the great cities of the Holy Roman Empire, founded in pre-Celtic times, taken over by the Romans, and expanded in the 11th century by the Salian emperors. Between 1294, when it was declared a Free Imperial City, and 1570, no fewer than 50 imperial diets were convened here. The term "Protestant" derives from the diet of 1529, referring to those who protested when the religious freedom granted to evangelicals at the diet of 1526 was revoked and a return to Catholicism was decreed. The neo-Gothic **Gedächtniskirche** on Bartolomäus-

Weltz-Platz commemorates those 16th-century Protestants. Ascend the **Altpörtel**, the impressive town gate, for a grand view of Maximilianstrasse, the street that led kings and emperors straight to the cathedral. 🎫 €1 🕙 *Apr.–Oct., weekdays 10–noon and 2–4, weekends 10–5.*

Fodor'sChoice ★ The **Kaiserdom** (Imperial Cathedral), one of the finest Romanesque cathedrals in the world and a UNESCO World Heritage site, conveys the pomp and majesty of the early Holy Roman Emperors. It was built between 1030 and 1061, by the emperors Konrad II, Henry III, and Henry IV. The last replaced the flat ceiling with groined vaults in the late 11th century, an innovative feat in its day. A restoration program in the 1950s returned the building to almost exactly its original condition.

See the exterior before venturing inside. You can walk most of the way around it, and there's a fine view of the east end from the park by the Rhine. Much of the architectural detail, including the dwarf galleries and ornamental capitals, was inspired and executed by stone masons from Lombardy, which belonged to the German Empire at the time. The four towers symbolize the four seasons and the idea that the power of the empire extends in all four directions. Look up as you enter the nearly 100-foot-high portal. It's richly carved with mythical creatures. In contrast to Gothic cathedrals, whose walls are supported externally by flying buttresses, allowing for a minimum of masonry and a maximum of light, at Speyer the columns supporting the roof are massive. The **Krypta** (crypt) lies beneath the chancel. It's the largest crypt in Germany and is strikingly beautiful in its simplicity. Four emperors, four kings, and three empresses are buried here. ⊠ *Dompl.* 🎫 *Donation requested* 🕙 *Apr.–Oct., daily 9–7; Nov.–Mar., daily 9–5; closed during services.*

★ Opposite the cathedral, the **Historisches Museum der Pfalz** (Palatinate Historical Museum) houses the **Domschatz** (Cathedral Treasury). Other collections chronicle the art and cultural history of Speyer and the Pfalz from the Stone Age to modern times. Don't miss the precious "Golden Hat of Schifferstadt," a golden, cone-shape object used for religious purposes during the Bronze Age. The **Wine Museum** exhibits artifacts from Roman times to the present, including the world's oldest bottle of wine, from circa AD 300. A major exhibition, "The Jews of Europe in the Middle Ages," runs from mid-November 2004 to mid-March 2005. ⊠ *Dompl. 4* 🕾 *06232/132–528* 🖷 *06232/132–540* ⊕ *www.museum.speyer.de* 🎫 *€7, combination ticket with Sea Life €14* 🕙 *Tues.–Sun. 10–6.*

Speyer was an important medieval Jewish cultural center. In the **Jewish quarter,** behind the Palatinate Historical Museum, you can see synagogue remains from 1104 and Germany's oldest (pre-1128) ritual baths, the 33-foot-deep *Mikwe.* ⊠ *Judeng.* 🕾 *06232/291–971* 🎫 *€1* 🕙 *Apr.–Oct., daily 10–5.*

☾ A turn-of-the-20th-century factory hall houses the **Technik-Museum** (Technology Museum), a large collection of locomotives, aircraft, old automobiles, and fire engines. Automatic musical instruments, historical dolls and toys, and 19th-century fashion are displayed in the Wilhelmsbau. Highlights of the complex are the 420-ton U-boat (you can go inside) and the massive 3-D IMAX cinemas. ⊠ *Am Technik Museum 1* ☎ *06232/ 67080* ⊕ *www.technik-museum.de* 🖼 *Museum €11, IMAX €7.50, combined ticket €15.50* ⊘ *Daily 9–6.*

Sea Life, in the old harbor of Speyer, enables you to travel the length of the Rhine from the Alps to the North Sea via a walk through a 33-foot-long tunnel. All types of marine life native to this region glide through 105,600 gallons of water. ⊠ *Hafenstr. 2/Im Hafenbecken, 15-min walk from large parking lot on Festpl.* ☎ *06232/686–798* ⊕ *www.sealife.de* 🖼 *€10, combination ticket with historical museum €14* ⊘ *Daily 10–5.*

Where to Stay & Eat

★ **$$–$$$$** ✕ **Backmulde.** Bread is still baked daily in this historic bakery, now a friendly, comfortable, and upscale wine restaurant. Homemade bread, homegrown fruits and vegetables, and local products are all part of chef and proprietor Gunter Schmidt's requirement for freshness. The aromas and flavors of his fare often have a Mediterranean accent, and the menu changes according to season. The wine list features an array of champagnes, and more than 850 wines—half from the Pfalz and a well-chosen selection from abroad—spanning decades of vintages. Schmidt's own wines are from the Heiligenstein vineyard on the outskirts of Speyer. ⊠ *Karmeliterstr. 11–13* ☎ *06232/71577* ⊕ *www. backmulde.de* ⊟ *AE, DC, MC, V* ⊘ *Closed Sun. and Mon. and mid-Aug.–early Sept.*

$–$$ ✕ **Wirtschaft Zum Alten Engel.** This 200-year-old vaulted brick cellar, with its rustic wood furnishings and cozy niches, is an intimate setting for a hearty meal. Seasonal dishes supplement the large selection of Pfälzer and Alsatian specialties, such as *Ochsenfetzen* (slices of beef), coq au vin, or *Choucroute* (similar to a Pfälzer Teller). The wine list features about 180 Pfälzer, European, and New World wines. ⊠ *Mühlturmstr. 7* ☎ *06232/70914* ⊕ *www.zumaltenengel.de* ⊟ *V* ⊘ *Closed Sun. June–Aug. and 2 wks in Aug. No lunch.*

$ ✕ **Ratskeller.** Friendly service and Gunter Braun's fresh seasonal dishes make for an enjoyable dining experience in the town hall's vaulted cellar (1578). The menu changes frequently and offers more than standard fare: creative soups (pretzel soup, Tuscan bread soup) and entrées, such as *Kalbsnieren* (veal kidneys), or *Bachsaibling* (brook char on a red-wine-butter sauce). Wines from the Pfalz predominate, with 18 available by the glass. Small fare and drinks are served in the idyllic courtyard. ⊠ *Maximilianstr. 12* ☎ *06232/78612* ⊟ *AE, MC, V* ⊘ *Closed 2 wks in late Feb., 1 wk in late Oct., and Mon. No dinner Sun.*

$ ✕🖼 **Kutscherhaus.** Charming rustic decor and a profusion of flowers have replaced the *Kutschen* (coaches) in this turn-of-the-20th-century coachman's house. The menu (¢–$$) offers regional cuisine as well as creative vegetarian and pasta dishes. In summer you can sit beneath the old plane trees in the beer garden and select from a sumptuous buffet. Three modern, comfortable suites can sleep up to four persons each. ⊠ *Fischmarkt 5a, D–67346* ☎ *06232/70592* 🖨 *06232/620–922* ⊕ *www. kutscherhaus-speyer.de* ⮞ *3 suites* ⚒ *Restaurant, minibars, cable TV, bicycles, beer garden, some pets allowed; no a/c* ⊟ *MC, V* ⊘ *Restaurant closed Wed.* ¶⊘ *BP.*

$ 🏨 **Hotel Goldener Engel.** A scant two blocks west of the Altpörtel is the "Golden Angel," a friendly, family-run hotel furnished with antiques and innovative metal-and-wood designer furniture. Paintings by contemporary artists and striking photos of Namibia and the Yukon line the walls—the photos are a tribute to proprietor Paul Schaefer's wanderlust. The restaurant Wirtschaft Zum Alten Engel is in the cellar. ✉ *Mühlturmstr. 5–7, D–67346* ☎ *06232/13260* 🖷 *06232/132–695* 🌐 *www.goldener-engel-speyer.de* 🖙 *44 rooms, 2 suites* ⚒ *Restaurant, in-room data ports, cable TV, bicycles, some pets allowed (fee); no a/c in some rooms* ▱ *MC, V* ☺ *Closed 2 wks late Dec.–early Jan.* ¶ *BP.*

Nightlife & the Arts

Highlights for music lovers are **Orgelfrühling,** the organ concerts in the Gedächtniskirche (Memorial Church) in spring, and the concerts in the cathedral during September's **Internationale Musiktage.** Call the Speyer tourist office for program details and tickets. Walk into the town-hall courtyard to enter the **Kulturhof Flachsgasse,** home of the city's art collection and special exhibitions. ✉ *Flachsg.* ☎ *06232/142–399* 🖷 *Free* ☺ *Tues.–Sun. 11–6.*

The music, dancing, acrobatics, magic, and comedy of the 3½-hour shows at **Varieté-Palast Speyer** make for lively entertainment. A five-course dinner is served during evening performances. Showtime is Monday–Saturday 7 PM and Sunday 3 PM. ✉ *Untere Langg. 6* ☎ *06232/676–767* 🖷 *06232/676–768* 🌐 *www.varietepalast.cqr.de* 🖾 *Mon.–Thurs. €89, Fri. and Sat. €98, Sun. €39.*

Deidesheim

❽ *8 km (5 mi) north of Neustadt via the Wine Road, now B–271.*

Deidesheim is the first of a trio of villages on the Wine Road renowned for their vineyards and the wine estates known as the Three Bs of the Pfalz—Bassermann, Buhl, and Bürklin.

The half-timber houses and historical facades framing Deidesheim's **Marktplatz** form a picturesque group, including the Church of St. Ulrich, a Gothic gem inside and out, and the old **Rathaus** (Town Hall), whose doorway is crowned by a baldachin and baroque dome. The attractive open staircase leading up to the entrance is the site of the festive *Geissbock-Versteigerung* (billy-goat auction) every Pentecost Tuesday, followed by a parade and folk dancing. The goat is the tribute neighboring Lambrecht has paid Deidesheim since 1404 for grazing rights. Inside see the richly appointed **Ratssaal** (council chamber) and the museum of wine culture. ✉ *Marktpl.* 🖾 *€2* ☺ *Mar.–Dec., Wed.–Sun. 4–6.*

Vines, flowers, and *Feigen* (fig trees) cloak the houses behind St. Ulrich on Heumarktstrasse and its extension, Deichelgasse (nicknamed Feigengasse). To see the workshops and ateliers of about a dozen local artists, follow the *Künstler-Rundweg,* a signposted trail (black "K" on yellow signs). The tourist office has a list of their opening hours. Cross the Wine Road to reach the grounds of **Schloss Deidesheim,** now a wine estate and pub (closed Wednesday and Thursday; lunch on Sunday only). The bishops of Speyer built a moated castle on the site in the 13th century. Twice destroyed and rebuilt, the present castle dates from 1817 and the moats have been converted into gardens.

Where to Stay & Eat

$$ ✕ **Weinschmecker.** The restaurant and Vinothek of Herbert Nikola, an expert on Pfälzer wines and festivals, is on the eastern edge of town. Italian tiles and whitewashed walls give it a light, airy Mediterranean look—the menu reflects the same. The focus, however, is on top-quality Pfälzer wines, 200 of which (from about 40 estates) are featured; 120 are available by the glass. ⊠ *Steing. 2* ☎ *06326/980–460* 🖃 *No credit cards* ☽ *Closed Sun. and Mon. No lunch.*

$–$$ ✕ **Gallino.** The Hotel Deidesheimer Hof's outdoor restaurant sits in a quiet little courtyard and embodies the Pfalz's nickname, the "Tuscany of Germany." Lots of fresh herbs and tomatoes are featured in pasta dishes such as porcini-filled ravioli with a salad dressed in tomato vinaigrette, or basil-spiced spaghetti salad with shrimp kebabs. Open only if weather permits. ⊠ *Am Marktpl. 1* ☎ *06326/96870* 🖃 *AE, DC, MC, V* ☽ *May–Aug., Wed.–Sun. No lunch.*

$–$$ ✕ **Weinstube St. Urban.** Named after St. Urban, the vintners' patron saint, this is not a "typical" Weinstube but rather an upscale wine restaurant offering excellent regional cuisine and wines in beautiful rooms. Try the homemade *Entenbratwurst* (duck sausage) with potato salad. The restaurant is in (and on the front patio of) the Hotel Deidesheimer Hof. ⊠ *Am Marktpl. 1* ☎ *06326/96870* 🖃 *AE, DC, MC, V.*

$$–$$$ ✕🖼 **Hotel Deidesheimer Hof.** If your timing's right, you could rub elbows
FodorśChoice with the heads of state, entertainers, or sports stars who frequent this
★ house. Despite the aura of the guest book, the hotel retains its country charm and friendly service. Rooms are luxurious, and several have baths with round tubs or whirlpools. The restaurant Schwarzer Hahn ($$–$$$$) is for serious wining and dining. Chef Stefan Neugebauer's set menus are an excellent choice. À la carte you can sample Pfälzer specialties, including sophisticated renditions of the region's famous dish, Saumagen, with foie gras and truffles. More than 600 wines grace the wine list. ⊠ *Am Marktpl. 1, D–67146* ☎ *06326/96870* 🖨 *06326/ 7685* ⊕ *www.deidesheimerhof.de* ⇆ *24 rooms, 4 suites* ⚫ *3 restaurants, some in-room data ports, minibars, cable TV, bicycles, bar, lobby lounge, lounge, Weinstube, wineshop, library, babysitting, dry cleaning, laundry service, business services, some pets allowed (fee), no-smoking rooms; no a/c in some rooms* 🖃 *AE, DC, MC, V* ☽ *Restaurant closed Sun. and Mon., Jan., and 7 wks July and Aug. No lunch.*

$$ ✕🖼 **Hatterer's Hotel-Restaurant Le Jardin d'Hiver.** Clément Hatterer, the hospitable Alsatian owner and chef, has anticipated all the comforts you could ask for in his stylish hotel. Whether you dine in the winter garden, decorated in soothing shades of lilac, or in the sunny courtyard garden filled with exotic plants, the food and wine are exceptional. Like the menu ($$–$$$), the wine list features Pfälzer and Alsatian specialties. First-floor guest rooms have a contemporary look; those on the second floor are more spacious and are outfitted in a country style with wood furniture. ⊠ *Weinstr. 12, D–67146* ☎ *06326/6011* 🖨 *06326/7539* ⊕ *www.hotel-hatterer.com* ⇆ *57 rooms* ⚫ *Restaurant, minibars, cable*

TV, bicycles, bar, lobby lounge, dry cleaning, laundry service, Internet, business services, some pets allowed (fee), no-smoking rooms; no a/c ▤ *AE, DC, MC, V* ⊗ *Hotel and restaurant closed 2 wks early Jan. Restaurant closed Jan.–Mar. No dinner Sun. or Mon.* ⊠ *BP.*

$ ▥ **Landhotel Lucashof.** Klaus and Christine Lucas are well known for their wines and hospitality. Their beautifully decorated, modern guest rooms are named after famous vineyards in Forst, and four have balconies—the room called Pechstein is particularly nice. You can enjoy their excellent wines in the tasting room, beneath a shady pergola in the courtyard, or in the privacy of your room (the refrigerator in the breakfast room is stocked for guests). Delicious food and wine at pubs in Forst's Old Town are a three-minute walk away. ⊠ *Wiesenweg 1a, D–67147 Forst* ☎ *06326/336* ⊟ *06326/5794* ⊕ *www.lucashof.de* ⇨ *7 rooms* ⌂ *Cable TV, wineshop, some pets allowed (fee), no-smoking rooms; no a/c* ▤ *No credit cards* ⊗ *Closed mid-Dec.–Jan.*

Shopping

The Biffar family not only runs a first-class **wine estate** but also manufactures very exclusive candied fruits and ginger (delicious souvenirs). ⊠ *Niederkircher Str. 13* ☎ *06326/96760* ⊕ *www.biffar.com* ▤ *No credit cards* ⊗ *Weekdays 9–noon and 1–5:30, Sat. 10–noon and 1:30–4.*

> **en route**
>
> **Forst** and **Wachenheim**, both a few minutes' drive north of Deidesheim, complete the trio of famous wine villages. As you approach Forst, depart briefly from B–271 (take the left fork in the road) to see the Old Town with its vine- and ivy-clad sandstone and half-timber vintners' mansions. Peek through the large portals to see the lush courtyards. Many estates on this lane have pubs, as does the town's *Winzerverein* (cooperative winery). Wachenheim is another 2 km (1 mi) down the road. Its cooperative, Wachtenburg Winzer (with a good restaurant), is on the left at the entrance to town. Head for the Wachtenburg (castle) ruins up on the hill for a glass of wine. The Burgschänke (castle pub) is open if the flag is flying.

Bad Dürkheim

❾ *6 km (4 mi) north of Deidesheim on B–271.*

This pretty spa is nestled into the hills at the edge of the Palatinate Forest and ringed by vineyards. The saline springs discovered here in 1338 are the source of today's drinking and bathing cures, and at harvesttime there's also a detoxifying *Traubenkur* (grape-juice cure). A trip to the neoclassical **Kurhaus** and its beautiful gardens might be just the ticket if you've overindulged at the Dürkheimer Wurstmarkt, the world's largest wine festival, held in mid-September. Legendary quantities of *Weck, Worscht, un Woi* (dialect for rolls, sausage, and wine) are consumed at the fair, including half a million *Schoppen*, the region's traditional pint-size glasses of wine. The festival grounds are also the site of the world's largest wine cask, the **Dürkheimer Riesenfass**, with a capacity of 1.7 million liters (450,000 gallons). Built in 1934 by an ambitious cooper, the cask is now a restaurant that can seat well over 450 people.

Northwest of town is the **Heidenmauer** (heathen wall), the remains of an ancient Celtic ring wall more than 2 km (1 mi) in circumference and up to 20 feet thick in parts, and nearby are the rock drawings at **Kriemhildenstuhl,** an old Roman quarry where the legionnaires of Mainz excavated sandstone.

Overlooking the suburb of Grethen are the ruins of **Kloster Limburg** (Limburg Monastery). Emperor Konrad II laid the cornerstone in 1030, supposedly on the same day that he laid the cornerstone of the Kaiserdom in Speyer. The monastery was never completely rebuilt after a fire in 1504, but it's a majestic backdrop for open-air performances in summer. From the tree-shaded terrace of the Klosterschänke restaurant, adjacent to the ruins, you can combine good food and wine with a great view of the ruins (open daily).

The massive ruins of 13th-century **Burgruine Hardenburg** (Hardenburg Fortress) lie 3 km (2 mi) west (via B–37) of the Kloster Limburg. In its heyday it was inhabited by more than 200 people. It succumbed to fire in 1794. ⊠ *B–37* ☐ *€2.10* ☉ *Apr.–Sept., Tues.–Sun. 10–6; Jan.–Mar., Oct., and Nov., Tues.–Sun. 10–5.*

Where to Stay & Eat

★ **$-$$$** ✕ **Weinstube Bach-Mayer.** From the warmth of the tile stove to the polished wooden tables and benches, this small wine pub pleases customers with its down-home atmosphere, tasty country cooking (including favorites, such as rack of lamb and, in late autumn, roast goose), and hearty Pfälzer wines. You can dine in the garden from May until autumn. It's a local favorite. ⊠ *Gerberstr. 13* ☎ *06322/92120* ☐ *MC, V* ☉ *Closed Sun., 2 wks mid-Jan., and during Wurstmarkt. No lunch.*

$-$$ ✕ **Dürkheimer Riesenfass.** The two-story "giant cask" is divided into various rooms and niches with rustic wood furnishings. Ask to see the impressive *Festsaal mit Empore* (banquet hall with gallery) upstairs. Regional wines, Pfälzer specialties, and international dishes are served year-round. ⊠ *St. Michael Allee 1* ☎ *06322/2143* ⊕ *www.duerkheimerfass.de* ☐ *AE, MC, V.*

★ **$$** ✕▥ **Kurparkhotel.** Part of the Kurhaus complex, the Kurparkhotel is the place to be pampered from head to toe. Haus A has the most elegant rooms, several with balconies. Haus B, also modern and comfortable, is less exclusive. This is a typical, elegant spa hotel, with extensive health and beauty facilities, thermal baths, a casino, and concerts in the garden. The flower-lined terrace at the restaurant Graf zu Leiningen ($–$$$) is a beautiful setting for coffee or tea with delicious homemade pastries in the afternoon or an elegant *Feinschmecker-Menü* (five-course gourmet menu) in the evening. ⊠ *Schlosspl. 1–4, D–67098* ☎ *06322/ 7970* 📠 *06322/797–158* ⊕ *www.kurpark-hotel.de* ⏣ *113 rooms* ⚅ *Restaurant, in-room data ports, minibars, cable TV, pool, sauna, spa, steam room, Turkish baths, bicycles, bowling, bar, lobby lounge, casino, laundry service, Internet, business services, some pets allowed (fee), nosmoking floors; no a/c* ☐ *AE, DC, MC, V* ▥| *BP.*

$ ✕▥ **Weingut und Gästehaus Ernst Karst und Sohn.** This cheerful guesthouse is adjacent to the Karst family's wine estate, in the midst of the vineyards. Rooms are light and airy, furnished mostly in pine; all of them have splendid views of the countryside—which you are invited to explore on the bikes the Karsts loan. Tastings and cellar tours are possible, or sample the wines with regional dishes at the nearby restaurant, Weinrefugium ($–$$), located at Schlachthausstrasse 1a. (Restaurant days and hours vary; call ahead.) ⊠ *In den Almen 15, D–67098* ☎ *06322/ 2862 for guesthouse, 06322/791–0980 for restaurant* 🖷 *06322/65965* ⊕ *www.weingut-karst.de or www.weinrefugium-klotz.de* ➪ *3 rooms, 6 apartments* ♤ *Restaurant, minibars, bicycles, wineshop, no-smoking rooms; no a/c* ▭ *No credit cards (hotel); MC, V (restaurant)* ☉ *Closed Nov.–Jan.* ⍾ *BP.*

★ $$ 🖭 **Weingut Fitz-Ritter.** Konrad Fitz and his American wife, Alice, have a centuries-old stone cottage that sleeps up to four people on the parklike grounds of their 220-year-old wine estate. You'll have a pool all to yourself, and there are concerts and festivals in the garden, courtyard, and vaulted cellars (request a calendar of events). Tastings and tours of the cellars, vineyards, and garden are possible. The minimum stay is seven nights. ⊠ *Weinstr. Nord 51, D–67098* ☎ *06322/5389* 🖷 *06322/66005* ⊕ *www.fitz-ritter.de* ➪ *1 cottage* ♤ *Kitchen, cable TV, pool, wine shop, some pets allowed; no a/c, no smoking* ▭ *MC, V.*

Nightlife & the Arts

The **Spielbank** (Casino) (🖅 €2.50), in the Kurparkhotel, is a daily diversion after 2 PM; jacket and tie are required. Concerts and theater take place at the **Limburg Monastery.** Contact the local tourist office for program details.

> **en route**   When the vineyards of Ungstein, a suburb north of Bad Dürkheim, were modernized in 1981, a **Roman wine estate** was discovered. Among the finds was an ancient *Kelterhaus* (pressing house). A romantic wine festival is held on this historic site every year, in late June. Watch for signs to Villa Weilberg, to the left of the Wine Road (B–271).

Around Freinsheim

❿ *7 km (4½ mi) northeast of Bad Dürkheim, via Kallstadt, right turn to Freinsheim is signposted midway through Kallstadt.*

The next village on the Wine Road north of Bad Dürkheim is **Kallstadt,** where you can enjoy Saumagen in your glass and on your plate—for this is the home of the excellent **Saumagen Vineyard.** Both its wine and the specialty dish are served with pride everywhere in town, not just at the *Saumagenkerwe* (wine festival) the first weekend in September.

Off the Wine Road to the east, **Freinsheim's** *Stadtmauer* (town wall), probably built between 1400 and 1540, is one of the best-preserved fortifications in the Pfalz. Walk along it to see the massive town gates (Eisentor and Haintor) and the numerous towers, two of which can be rented as holiday apartments. Many of the town's historical houses are baroque, including the **Rathaus** (1737), with its covered stairway and sandstone balustrade. Next to it is a **Protestant church,** a Gothic structure to which Renaissance and baroque elements were added over the years.

No fewer than five large festivals are celebrated here between April and September—quite a showing for a town this small.

Drive 5 km (3 mi) west to Weisenheim am Berg (you'll cross over the Wine Road at Herxheim) and watch for signs toward Bobenheim and Kleinkarlbach. This road, which runs parallel to the Wine Road and along the vineyard heights, affords a wonderful panorama of the expansive vineyards stretching onto the Rhine Plain. Follow the signs to **Neuleiningen,** and then wind your way uphill to reach the romantic Old Town, ringed by a medieval wall. The ruins of the 13th-century castle are a good start for a town walk.

Where to Stay & Eat

★ **$–$$** ✕ **Alt Freinsheim.** Cordial chef Axel Steffl's domain is tucked away on a narrow lane between Hauptstrasse and Freinsheim's town wall (northern edge). Old stone walls, exposed beams, and the tiny size of the restaurant make for a cozy dining experience. Whether you opt for his country cooking, or a refined entrée with one of his creative sauces (lamb filet in red wine-thyme sauce or crayfish tails in Pernod cream sauce), everything is homemade. The good selection of local wines is as reasonably priced as the food. ✉ *Korngasse 5, Freinsheim* ☎ *06353/2582* ⊕ *www.restaurant-alt-freinsheim.de* 🖃 *No credit cards* ☉ *Closed Wed. and 3 wks in July and Aug. No lunch.*

$–$$ ✕ **Weinhaus Henninger.** Walter Henninger numbers among the elite of Pfälzer vintners, but there's nothing pretentious about the atmosphere or cooking at his wood-panel wine pub. It's a jovial place, frequented by locals who come for the delicious, hearty fare and excellent wines. The soups and *Eintopf* dishes (stews), rumpsteak with sautéed onions, and daily specials are recommended. ✉ *Weinstr. 93, Kallstadt* ☎ *06322/2277* ⊕ *www.weinhaus-henninger.de* 🖃 *No credit cards* ☉ *No lunch Mon.*

★ **$–$$** ✕🖃 **Hotel–Restaurant Alte Pfarrey.** Once a rectory, this hotel-restaurant is on the hilltop above the Old Town of Neuleiningen. The comfortable inn with modern facilities is made up of several Gothic houses. Rooms are distinctive for their antique furnishings. Susanne and Utz Ueberschaer tend to the personal service and first-rate culinary delights ($$–$$$$). The menu focuses on light international favorites prepared with fresh, local ingredients. The wine list is very good, with offerings from the New and Old World. Jewelry fans: don't miss the vitrine showcasing son Tobias's designer jewelry. ✉ *Unterg. 54, D–67271 Neuleiningen* ☎ *06359/86066* 🖷 *06359/86060* ⊕ *www.altepfarrey.de* 🛏 *9 rooms* ♿ *Restaurant, some pets allowed (fee); no a/c, no room TVs* 🖃 *DC, MC, V* ☉ *Restaurant closed Mon. and Tues.* ❢⦿❢ *BP.*

$–$$ ✕🖃 **Hotel–Restaurant Luther.** This elegant country inn is set in a baroque manor next to Freinsheim's town wall. The rooms provide modern comfort amid refined decor, with fresh flowers throughout the house. Gisela Luther's handsome table settings and Dieter Luther's artistic food presentations make dining here ($$$–$$$$) a joy for all the senses. One of Germany's leading chefs, Dieter is known for his imaginative combinations, such as lobster with fennel or venison with kumquats. Save room for a chocolate creation or the crème brûlée quintet. Spanish, Bordeaux, and top Pfälzer wines are focal points of the wine list. ✉ *Hauptstr. 29,*

Fodor'sChoice
★

D–67251 Freinsheim ☎ 06353/93480 🖷 06353/934–845 ⊕ *www. luther-freinsheim.de* ⇨ 23 rooms ⚘ *Restaurant, in-room data ports, minibars, cable TV, no-smoking rooms; no a/c* ⊟ *AE, MC, V* ⊘ *Hotel closed Feb. Restaurant closed Sun. and Feb. No lunch* ⵏⵧ *BP.*

★ **$–$$** ✕⊞ **Hotel–Restaurant Weinkastell Zum Weissen Ross.** Behind the cheerful facade of this half-timber house, with its wrought-iron sign depicting a *weisser Ross* (white stallion), you can experience Pfälzer hospitality at its best. Rooms have warm colors, solid oak furnishings, and modern baths, and several have romantic alcoves or four-poster beds. Jutta and Norbert Kohnke offer service and cuisine ($$$–$$$$) that are top-notch. Most of the superb wines come from her brother's wine estate next door, Weingut Koehler-Ruprecht (tours and tastings are possible), as well as red wines from his affiliated estates in Portugal and South Africa. This is the best place in the Pfalz to sample "Saumagen twice." ⊠ *Weinstr. 80–82, D–67169 Kallstadt* ☎ 06322/5033 🖷 06322/66091 ⊕ *www.diepfalz.de* ⇨ 13 rooms, 1 apartment ⚘ *Restaurant, in-room data ports, room TVs, bicycles, business services, some pets allowed; no a/c* ⊟ *AE, MC, V* ⊘ *Hotel closed Jan.–mid-Feb. Restaurant closed Mon. and Tues., Jan.–mid-Feb., and 1 wk late July–early Aug.* ⵏⵧ *BP.*

$ ⊞ **Town Wall Tower.** For a room with a view in a highly original setting, stay overnight in a medieval *Turm* (tower). The Hahnenturm sleeps two; the Herzogturm can accommodate a family. Contact the Freinsheim tourist office for reservations. ⊠ *Hauptstr. 2, D–67251 Freinsheim* ☎ 06353/ 989–294 🖷 06353/989–904 ⊕ *www.stadt.freinsheim.de* ⇨ 2 rooms ⚘ *Kitchenettes; no a/c, no room phones, no room TVs* ⊟ *No credit cards.*

> **en route** Neuleiningen is 4 km (2½ mi) west of the Wine Road town Kirchheim. **Bockenheim,** 10 km (6 mi) north, is dominated by an imposing gateway. There's a panoramic view of the Pfalz's "sea of vineyards" from the viewing platform. Like its counterpart in Schweigen-Rechtenbach, the **Haus der Deutschen Weinstrasse** marks the end (or start) of its namesake, the German Wine Road.

THE RHINE TERRACE

Like Speyer, the cities of Worms and Mainz were Free Imperial Cities and major centers of Christian and Jewish culture in the Middle Ages. Germany's first synagogue and Europe's oldest surviving Jewish cemetery, both from the 11th century, are in Worms. The imperial diets of Worms and Speyer in 1521 and 1529 stormed around Martin Luther (1483–1546) and the rise of Protestantism. In 1455 Johannes Gutenberg (1400–68), the inventor of movable type, printed the Gutenberg Bible in Mainz.

Worms

15 km (9 mi) east of Bockenheim via B–47 from Monsheim, 45 km (28 mi) south of Mainz on B–9.

Although devastated in World War II, Worms (pronounced *vawrms*) is among the most ancient cities of Germany, with a history going back some 6,000 years. Once settled by the Romans, Worms later became one of the imperial cities of the Holy Roman Empire. More than 100 imperial diets were held here, including the 1521 meeting where Martin Luther pleaded his cause. In addition to having a great Romanesque cathedral, Worms is a center of the wine trade.

Worms developed into an important garrison town under the Romans, but it's better known for its greatest legend, the *Nibelungenlied,* derived from the short-lived kingdom established by Gunther and his Burgundian tribe in the early 5th century. The complex and sprawling story was given its final shape in the 12th century and tells of love, betrayal, greed, war, and death. It ends when Attila the Hun defeats the Nibelungen (Burgundians), who find their court destroyed, their treasure lost, and their heroes dead. One of the most famous incidents tells how Hagen, treacherous and scheming, hurls the court riches into the Rhine. Near the Nibelungen Bridge there's a bronze statue of him caught in the act. The *Nibelungenlied* may be legend, but the story is based on fact. A Queen Brunhilda, for example, is said to have lived here. It's also known that a Burgundian tribe was defeated in 436 by Attila the Hun in what is present-day Hungary.

Not until Charlemagne resettled Worms almost 400 years later, making it one of the major cities of his empire, did the city prosper again. Worms was more than an administrative and commercial center; it was a great ecclesiastical city as well. The first expression of this religious importance was the original cathedral, consecrated in 1018. Between 1130 and 1181 it was rebuilt in three phases into the church you see today.

★ ⓫ The *Nibelungenlied* comes to life in the **Nibelungen Museum,** a stunning sight-and-sound exhibition cleverly installed in two medieval towers and the portion of the Old Town wall between them. The structure itself is architecturally fascinating inside and out, and the rampart affords a wonderful view of the town. Language is no problem: the tour script (via headphones and printed matter) is offered in English. Allow 1½ hours for a thorough visit. ⊠ *Fischerpförtchen 10* ☎ *06241/202–120* ⊕ *www.nibelungen-museum.de* 🎫 *€5.50* ☉ *Tues.–Thurs. and weekends 10–5, Fri. 10 AM–10 PM.*

★ ⓬ If you've seen Speyer Cathedral, you'll quickly realize that the **Wormser Dom St. Peter** (Cathedral of St. Peter), by contrast, contains many Gothic elements. In part this is simply a matter of chronology. Speyer Cathedral was completed nearly 70 years before the one in Worms was even begun, long before the lighter, more vertical lines of the Gothic style evolved. Furthermore, once built, Speyer Cathedral was left largely untouched in later periods; the Worms Cathedral was remodeled frequently as new architectural styles and new values developed. The Gothic influence can be seen both inside and out, from the elaborate tympanum with biblical scenes over the southern portal (today's entrance) to the great rose window in the west choir to the five sculptures in the north aisle recounting the life of Christ. The cathedral was completely gutted by fire in 1689 in the War of the Palatinate Succession. For this reason many of the furnishings are baroque, including the magnificent

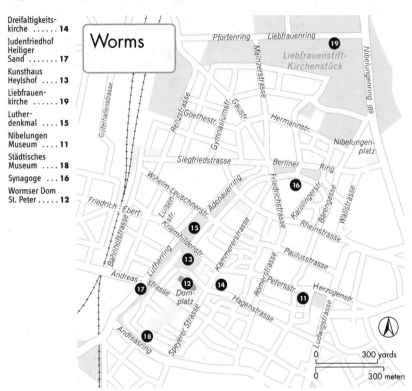

gilt high altar from 1742, designed by the master architect Balthasar Neumann (1687–1753). The choir stalls are no less decorative. They were built between 1755 and 1759 in rococo style. Walk around the building to see the artistic detail of the exterior. ⊠ *Dompl.* ☎ *06241/6115* 🖾 *Donation requested* ☉ *Apr.–Oct., daily 9–6; Nov.–Mar., daily 9–5; closed during services.*

An imperial palace once stood in what is now the **Heylshofgarten,** a park just north of the cathedral. This was the site of the fateful meeting between Luther and Emperor Charles V in April 1521 that ultimately led to the Reformation. Luther refused to recant his theses demanding Church reforms and went into exile in Eisenach, where he translated the New Testament in 1521 and 1522.

★ ⑬ The **Kunsthaus Heylshof** (Heylshof Art Gallery) in the Heylshofgarten is one of the leading art museums of the region. It has an exquisite collection of German, Dutch, and French paintings as well as stained glass, glassware, porcelain, and ceramics from the 15th to the 19th centuries. ⊠ *Stephansg. 9* ☎ *06241/22000* ⊕ *www.museum-heylshof.de* 🖾 *€2.50* ☉ *May–Sept., Tues.–Sun. 11–5; Oct.–Dec. and mid-Feb.–Apr., Tues.–Sat. 2–5, Sun. 11–5.*

⑭ The Lutheran **Dreifaltigkeitskirche** (Church of the Holy Trinity) is just across the square from the Heylshofgarten. Remodeling during the 19th and 20th centuries produced today's austere interior, although the facade and tower are still joyfully baroque. ✉ *Marktpl.* ⊙ *Apr.–Sept., daily 9–5; Oct.–Mar., daily 9–4.*

⑮ The **Lutherdenkmal** (Luther Monument) commemorates Luther's appearance at the Diet of Worms. He ended his speech with the words: "Here I stand. I have no choice. God help me. Amen." The 19th-century monument includes a large statue of Luther ringed by other figures from the Reformation. It's set in a small park on the street named Lutherring.

The Jewish quarter is along the town wall between Martinspforte and Friesenspitze and between Judengasse and Hintere Judengasse. The first **★ ⑯ Synagoge** (synagogue) was built in 1034, rebuilt in 1175, and expanded in 1212 with a building for women. Destroyed in 1938, it was rebuilt in 1961 using as much of the original masonry as had survived. ✉ *Hintere Judeng.* ⊙ *Apr.–Oct., daily 10–12:30 and 1:30–5; Nov.–Mar., daily 10–noon and 2–4; closed during services.*

The **Raschi-Haus,** the former study hall, dance hall, and Jewish home for the elderly, is next door to the synagogue. It houses the city archives and the **Jewish Museum.** The well-written, illustrated booklet *Jewish Worms* chronicles a millennium of Jewish history in Worms. A bilingual exhibition about the life and work of Rashi (Rabbi Solomon ben Isaac of Troyes [1040-1105]), who studied at the Worms Talmud academy in circa 1060, will run from April to October 2005. Bilingual walking tours of Jewish Worms and concerts are also planned. For more details contact: ✍ gerold.boennen@worms.de. ✉ *Hintere Judeng. 6* ☎ *06241/853–4701* 🖃 *€1.50* ⊙ *Apr.–Oct., Tues.–Sun. 10–12:30 and 1:30–5; Nov.–Mar., Tues.–Sun. 10–12:30 and 1:30–4:30.*

⑰ The **Judenfriedhof Heiliger Sand** (Holy Sand Jewish Cemetery) is the oldest Jewish cemetery in Europe. The oldest of some 2,000 tombstones date from 1076. ✉ *Andreasstr. and Willy-Brandt-Ring* ⊙ *Daily.*

⑱ To bone up on the history of Worms, visit the **Städtisches Museum** (Municipal Museum), housed in the cloisters of a Romanesque church in the Andreasstift. ✉ *Weckerlingpl. 7* ☎ *06241/946–3911* 🖃 *€2* ⊙ *Tues.–Sun. 10–5.*

⑲ On the northern outskirts of Worms, the twin-tower Gothic **Liebfrauenkirche** (Church of Our Lady) is set amid vineyards. The church is the namesake of the mild white wine named Liebfraumilch, literally, the "Milk of Our Lady." Today this popular wine can be made from grapes grown throughout Rheinhessen, the Pfalz, the Nahe, and the Rheingau wine regions, since the original, small vineyard surrounding the church could not possibly meet demand.

Where to Stay & Eat

★ $$$ ✕ **Rôtisserie Dubs.** A pioneer of the Rheinhessen restaurant scene, Wolfgang Dubs focused on creative regional cuisine and seasonal specialties long before it was in vogue. Fish, fowl, meat, and game are all expertly prepared and garnished. For a more casual meal, try his cozy Gasthaus

Zum Schiff (¢–$), next door. The daily specials are a very good value. A wine enthusiast, Dubs offers his own wines, top German and French estates, and a few New World wines, such as Opus One. Rheindürkheim is 9 km (5½ mi) north of Worms via B–9. The restaurant is near the *Kirche* (church), not far from the riverbank. ⊠ *Kirchstr. 6 Worms-Rheindürkheim* ☎ *06242/2023* ⊕ *www.dubs.de* ⊟ *MC, V* ⊙ *Closed Tues. and 2–3 wks in Jan. No lunch Sat.*

$–$$ ✕⊞ **Dom-Hotel.** The appeal of this hotel with modern, comfortable rooms lies in its friendly staff and its terrific location in the heart of the pedestrian zone (a parking garage is available). At the hotel's upscale restaurant ($–$$$) you can watch the happenings on the square below. The focus is on international and regional cuisine and wines. ⊠ *Obermarkt 10, D–67547* ☎ *06241/9070* ⊟ *06241/23515* ⊕ *www.dom-hotel.de* ➳ *60 rooms, 2 apartments* ⚐ *Restaurant, in-room data ports, minibars, cable TV, bicycles, babysitting, dry cleaning, laundry service, business services, some pets allowed (fee), no-smoking rooms; no a/c* ⊟ *AE, DC, MC, V* ⊙ *Restaurant closed Sun. and 2 wks in July. No lunch Sat.* ⅢⅠ *BP.*

$–$$ ✕⊞ **Landhotel Zum Schwanen.** Bärbel Berkes runs this lovingly restored country inn in Osthofen (10 km [6 mi] northwest of Worms). You can linger over a meal or a glass of wine in its pretty courtyard, the hub of the 18th-century estate. Like the rooms, the restaurant ($$) is light, airy, and furnished with sleek, contemporary furniture. Regional favorites are served as well as dishes with a Mediterranean touch. The lineup of fine, local wines is exemplary. The beer garden is also inviting. ⊠ *Friedrich-Ebert-Str. 40, D–67574 Osthofen, West of B–9* ☎ *06242/9140* ⊟ *06242/ 914–299* ⊕ *www.zum-schwanen-osthofen.de* ➳ *30 rooms* ⚐ *Restaurant, some in-room data ports, minibars, cable TV, bicycles, beer garden, some pets allowed (fee), no-smoking rooms; no a/c* ⊟ *AE, MC, V* ⊙ *No lunch Sat. or Mon.* ⅢⅠ *BP.*

$ ✕⊞ **Hotel and Weinstube Römischer Kaiser.** Housed in an 18th-century baroque patrician manor, the Lehr family's "Roman Emperor" is a down-to-earth, friendly little hotel and wine pub (¢) that quickly fills up with regulars in the evening. The nearly two dozen wines-by-the-glass are as moderately priced as the simple, hearty fare, such as Flammkuchen, Saumagen, or the daily specials. ⊠ *Römerstr. 72* ☎ *06241/93370* ⊟ *06241/413–126* ⊕ *www.roemischer-kaiser-worms.de* ➳ *11 rooms* ⚐ *Restaurant, cable TV; no a/c* ⊟ *AE, MC, V* ⊙ *Closed 1 wk in Jan., 1 wk July and Aug. No lunch* ⅢⅠ *BP.*

¢–$ ✕⊞ **Land- und Winzerhotel Bechtel.** The friendly Bechtel family, winegrowers and proud parents of a former German Wine Queen, offer very pleasant accommodations on the grounds of their wine estate in the suburb of Heppenheim, about 10 km (6 mi) west of Worms (depart Worms on Speyerer Strasse, an extension of Valckenbergstrasse, which runs parallel to the east side of the Dom). The rooms are modern, and all have balconies. You can enjoy country cooking (daily specials) as well as more refined fare in the restaurant ($) or on its terrace with the estate's own wine. Wine tastings in the vaulted cellars are also possible. ⊠ *Pfälzer Waldstr. 100, D–67551 Worms-Heppenheim* ☎ *06241/36536* ⊟ *06241/ 34745* ⊕ *www.landhotel-bechtel.de* ➳ *15 rooms, 1 apartment* ⚐ *Restau-*

rant, in-room data ports, minibars, cable TV, gym, sauna, bicycles, lounge, wineshop, some pets allowed (fee), no-smoking rooms; no a/c ☰ *AE, MC, V* ❍ *BP.*

$ ☷ **Haus Kalisch am Dom.** For more than 30 years the Kalisch family has welcomed guests to its little inn opposite the cathedral. There are no frills, but the rooms are comfortable and have private baths and TVs. ⊠ *Neumarkt 9, D–67547* ☎ *06241/27666* 🖷 *06241/25073* ❧ *13 rooms* ⚬ *Cable TV, some pets allowed; no a/c, no room phones* ☰ *No credit cards* ❍ *Closed 3 wks Dec. and Jan.* ❍ *BP.*

Nightlife & the Arts

Worms's nine-day wine and folk festival, the **Backfischfest** (Fried-Fish Festival), begins the last weekend of August. It evolved from the thanksgiving celebrations held by the once-powerful fishers' guild. There are rides, entertainment, a parade, fireworks, and *Fischerstechen* (jousting) in the harbor.

The **Städtisches Spiel- und Festhaus** (⊠ Rathenaustr. ☎ 06241/22525) is the cultural hub of Worms, presenting theater, concerts, ballet, and special events. Concerts are also held in the Municipal Museum, in the Andreasstift, and at the 19th-century palace Schloss Herrnsheim, in the northern suburb of Herrnsheim. The annual **jazz festival** (mid-July) is staged primarily around Weckerlingplatz and the cathedral. Contact the tourist office for program details.

Shopping

For tasteful wine accessories and excellent wines, drop by P. J. Valckenberg's wine shop, **Der Weinladen** (⊠ Weckerlingpl. 1 ☎ 06241/911-180), near the Municipal Museum. The winery owns nearly all of the Liebfrauenstift-Kirchenstuck vineyard surrounding the Liebfrauenkirche. The store is closed Sunday and Monday and does not accept credit cards.

Oppenheim

⑳ *26 km (16 mi) north of Worms, 23 km (16 mi) south of Mainz on B–9.*

En route to Oppenheim, the vine-covered hills parallel to the Rhine gradually steepen. Then, unexpectedly, the spires of Oppenheim's Gothic ★ **Katharinenkirche** (St. Katharine's Church) come into view. The contrast of its pink sandstone facade against a bright blue sky is striking. Built between 1220 and 1439, it's the most important Gothic church between Strasbourg and Köln. The interior affords a rare opportunity to admire original 14th-century stained-glass windows and two magnificent rose windows, the Lily Window and the Rose of Oppenheim. The church houses masterfully carved tombstones, while the chapel behind it has a *Beinhaus* (charnel house) that contains the bones of 20,000 citizens and soldiers from the 15th to 18th century. ⊠ *Katharinenstr. at Merianstr., just north of market square* ❍ *Apr.–Oct., daily 8–6; Nov.–Mar., daily 9–5.*

Oppenheim and its neighbors to the north, Nierstein and Nackenheim, are home to Rheinhessen's finest vineyards. The **Deutsches Weinbaumuseum** (German Viticultural Museum) has wine-related artifacts that chronicle the region's 2,000-year-old wine-making tradition and the world's largest collection of mousetraps. ⊠ *Wormser Str. 49* ☎ *06133/ 2544* ▣ *€3.50* ☉ *Apr.–Oct., Tues.–Fri. 2–5, weekends 10–noon and 2–5.*

Nightlife & the Arts

Concerts are held in St. Katharine's, and open-air theater takes place in the **Burgruine Landskrone,** the 12th-century imperial fortress ruins a few minutes' walk northwest of the church. From here there's a wonderful view of the town and the vineyards, extending all the way to Worms on a clear day. For more jovial entertainment, accompanied by *Blasmusik* (brass-band oompah music), attend the **wine festival** in mid-August on the market square, which is ringed by half-timber houses and the 16th-century Rathaus.

Nierstein

㉑ *3 km (2 mi) north of Oppenheim on B–9.*

Surrounded by 2,700 acres of vines, Nierstein is the largest wine-growing community on the Rhine and boasts Germany's oldest documented **vineyard** (AD 742), the Glöck, surrounding St. Kilian's Church. You can sample wines at the **Winzergenossenschaft** (Cooperative winery; ⊠ Karolingerstr. 6), which is the starting point of an easy hike or drive to the vineyard heights and the vantage point at the *Wartturm* (watch tower). Tasting stands are set up along the route, providing delightful wine presentations in the vineyards *am roten Hang* (referring to the steep sites of red soils of slate, clay, and sand) in mid-June. Early August brings the wine festival, with stands throughout the town and a festive parade in medieval costumes.

Where to Stay & Eat

★ **$$** ✕▦ **Best Western Wein & Parkhotel.** Quiet elegance and Mediterranean flair mark this country inn. Spacious, light rooms decorated in warm shades of ocher, chic bathrooms, and an inviting lounge and terrace make for comfortable, relaxing quarters. Cuisine at the restaurant Am Heyl'schen Garten ($–$$$) ranges from barbecue on the terrace to Sunday brunch to well-prepared regional specialties and dishes with an Asian touch; the Irish pub serves light fare. The staff is exceptionally cheerful and competent. ⊠ *An der Kaiserlinde 1, D–55283* ☎ *06133/5080* ▤ *06133/508–333* ⊕ *www.weinhotel.bestwestern.de* ⇗ *47 rooms, 8 suites* ⚭ *Restaurant, in-room data ports, cable TV, minibars, indoor pool, gym, hot tub, sauna, bicycles, bar, lobby lounge, pub, babysitting, Internet, business services, some pets allowed (fee), no-smoking rooms* ▭ *AE, MC, V* ⦿ *BP.*

Nackenheim

㉒ *5 km (3 mi) north of Nierstein on B–9.*

This wine village lies slightly to the west of B–9; from the south, turn left and cross the railroad tracks (opposite the tip of the island in the Rhine) to reach the town center, 2 km (1 mi) down the country road. The writer Carl Zuckmayer (1896–1977) was born here and immortalized the town in his farce *Der fröhliche Weinberg* (*The Merry Vineyard*) in 1925. He described Rheinhessen wine as "the wine of laughter . . . charming and appealing." You can put his words to the test the last weekend of July, when wine-festival booths are set up between the half-timber town hall on Carl-Zuckmayer-Platz and the baroque **Church of St. Gereon.** The church's scrolled gables, belfry, and elaborate altars are worth seeing.

Where to Stay & Eat

$–$$ ✕ **Zum alten Zollhaus.** Walk through the arched gateway to reach the beautiful garden and entrance to this historical house. Cozy niches, fresh flowers, and handsome antiques provide a pleasant setting for good food and wine. Ilse Hees, the friendly proprietor, offers daily specials as well as standards such as roast breast of duck. The *Trilogie vom Lachs* (cold salmon) served with a mustard sauce is excellent. The wine list focuses on Rheinhessen wines, and a good number are available by the glass. ✉ *Wormser Str. 7, at Carl-Gunderloch-Pl.* ☎ *06135/8726* ⊕ *www. zum-alten-zollhaus.de* ⊟ *No credit cards* ⊙ *Closed Sun. and Mon., 2 wks in late Feb., and 2 wks in late Sept. No lunch.*

★ **$** ✕⊞ **Jordan's Landhotel und Restaurant St. Gereon.** The Jordan family's charming half-timber country inn has modern rooms that feature blond-wood floors and light-color furnishings. Stone walls and light pine furniture on terra-cotta tiles give the restaurant ($$) a warm, rustic look, too. Ask if the hearty regional specialties *Dippe-Has* or *Backes Grumbeere* are available, or try the unique *Handkäs'carpaccio* in Zuckmeyer's Weingewölbe in the cellar (open daily, evenings). All 20 wines served come from Rheinhessen. ✉ *Carl-Zuckmayer-Pl. 3, D–55299* ☎ *06135/ 92990* ⊞ *06135/929–992* ⊕ *www.landhotel-st-gereon.de* ⇆ *15 rooms* ⚫ *Restaurant, in-room data ports, cable TV, bicycles, Weinstube, laundry service, some pets allowed (fee), no-smoking rooms; no a/c* ⊟ *DC, MC, V* ⊙ *Restaurant closed Tues. and Wed.* ⦿ *BP.*

¢–$ ⊞ **Jordan's Gästehaus im Karthäserhof.** The Jordan family in Nackenheim has opened a *dépendance* in the wine village of Bodenheim, 9 km (5½ mi) south of Mainz. The historic house has rooms with modern amenities. Its location within walking distance of many local vintners' pubs and the personal service offered make it an attractive overnight possibility. ✉ *Gaustr. 21, D–55294 Bodenheim* ☎ *06135/702–880* ⊞ *06135/ 7028–8288* ⊕ *www.landhotel-st-gereon.de* ⇆ *11 rooms* ⚫ *In-room data ports, cable TV, bicycles, laundry service, some pets allowed (fee), no-smoking rooms; no a/c* ⊟ *DC, MC, V* ⦿ *BP.*

Sports & the Outdoors

BIKING The old towpath along the riverbank is an ideal cycling trail to Mainz or Worms, and the vineyard paths are well suited for exploring the countryside.

HIKING Enjoy the views from the vineyard heights on the **Rheinhöhenweg** trail. Allow three hours to hike the 10-km (6-mi) stretch between Nackenheim, Nierstein, and Oppenheim. Start at the corner of Weinbergstrasse and Johann-Winkler-Strasse. The educational wine path through the St. Alban vineyard is a pleasant walk in Bodenheim (4 km [2½ mi] northwest of Nackenheim).

Mainz

❷❸ *14 km (9 mi) north of Nackenheim, 45 km (28 mi) north of Worms on B–9, and 42 km (26 mi) west of Frankfurt on A–3.*

Mainz is the capital of the state of Rheinland-Pfalz. Today's city was built on the site of a Roman citadel from 38 BC, though some of the local artifacts in its Landesmuseum date from 300,000 BC. Given its central location at the confluence of the Main and Rhine rivers, it's not surprising that Mainz has always been an important trading center, rebuilt time and time again in the wake of wars. The city's fine museums and historical buildings bear witness to a splendid past.

To see the sights, head for the Touristik Centrale (tourist office) to pick up a *Mainz Card,* a terrific one-day pass for €6 that includes a basic walking tour, unlimited use of public transportation, and free entry to museums and the casino, as well as a reduction in price on some hotel rooms, KD cruises, and theater tickets.

The **Marktplatz** and *Höfchen* (little courtyard) around the cathedral, the focal points of the town, are especially colorful on Tuesday, Friday, and Saturday, when farmers set up their stands to sell produce and flowers. This is also the site of the *Sektfest* (sparkling wine festival) in late May or early June and *Johannisnacht,* a huge wine festival with fireworks, a few weeks later.

★ The entrance to the **Dom** (Cathedral of St. Martin and St. Stephan) is on the south side of the market square, midway between the eastern and western chancels, which symbolize the worldly empire and the priestly realm, respectively. Emperor Otto II began building the oldest of the Rhineland's trio of grand Romanesque cathedrals in 975, the year in which he named Willigis archbishop and chancellor of the empire. Henry II, the last Saxon emperor of the Holy Roman Empire, was crowned here in 1002, as was his successor, Konrad II, the first Salian emperor, in 1024. In 1009, on the very day of its consecration, the cathedral burned to the ground. It was the first of seven fires the Dom has endured in the course of its millennium. Today's cathedral dates mostly from the 11th to 13th century. During the Gothic period, remodeling diluted the Romanesque identity of the original; an imposing baroque spire was added in the 18th century. Nevertheless, the building remains essentially Romanesque, and its floor plan demonstrates a clear link to the cathedrals in Speyer and Worms. The interior is a virtual sculpture gallery of elaborate monuments and tombstones of archbishops, bishops, and canons, many of which are significant artworks from the 13th to 19th century. ⊠ *Domstr. 3 (Markt)* ☎ *06131/253–412* 🖅 *Donations requested* 🕓 *Mar.–Oct., weekdays 9–6:30, Sat. 9–4, Sun. 12:45–3 and 4–6:30; Nov.–Feb., weekdays 9–5, Sat. 9–4, Sun. 12:45–3 and 4–5; closed during services.*

From the Middle Ages until secularization in the early 19th century, the archbishops of Mainz, who numbered among the imperial electors, were extremely influential politicians and property owners. The wealth of religious art treasures they left behind can be viewed in the **Dom und**

THE FATHER OF MODERN PRINTING

His invention—printing with movable type—transformed the art of communication, yet much about the life and work of Johannes Gutenberg is undocumented, starting with his year of birth. It's estimated that he was born in Mainz circa 1400 into a patrician family that supplied the city mint with metal to be coined. Gutenberg's later accomplishments attest to his own skill in working with metals. Details about his education are unclear, but he probably helped finance his studies by copying manuscripts in a monastic scriptorium. He moved to Strasbourg circa 1434, where he was a goldsmith by day and an inventor by night. It was here that he worked—in great secrecy—to create movable type and develop a press suitable for printing by adapting the conventional screw press used for winemaking. By 1448 Gutenberg had returned to Mainz. Loans from a wealthy businessman enabled him to set up a printer's workshop and print the famous 42-line Bible. The lines of text are in black ink, yet each of the original 180 Bibles printed from 1452 to 1455 is unique, thanks to the artistry of the handpainted illuminated letters.

Despite its significance, Gutenberg's invention was not a financial success. His quest for perfection rather than profit led to a legal battle during which his creditor was awarded the workshop and the Bible type. Gutenberg's attempts to set up another print shop in Mainz failed, but from 1465 until his death in 1468, he received an allowance for service to the archbishop of Mainz, which spared the "father of modern printing" from dying in poverty.

Diözesanmuseum, in the cathedral cloisters. ✉ *Domstr. 3* ☎ *06131/ 253–344* ⊕ *www.bistum-mainz.de* ✉ *Free, Schatzkammer (treasure chamber)* €3 ♥ *Tues.–Sun. 10–5.*

★ Opposite the east end of the cathedral (closest to the Rhine) is the **Gutenberg Museum,** devoted to the history of writing and printing from Babylonian and Egyptian times to the present. Exhibits include historical printing presses, incunabula, and medieval manuscripts with illuminated letters, as well as two precious 42-line Gutenberg Bibles printed circa 1455. A replica workshop demonstrates how Gutenberg implemented his invention of movable type. ✉ *Liebfrauenpl. 5* ☎ *06131/122– 640* ⊕ *www.gutenberg-museum.de* ✉ €3 ♥ *Tues.–Sat. 9–5, Sun. 11–3.*

★ The Kurfürstliches Schloss (Electoral Palace) houses the **Römisch-Germanisches Zentralmuseum,** a wonderful collection of original artifacts and copies of items that chronicle cultural developments in the area up to the early Middle Ages. ✉ *Ernst-Ludwig-Pl. on Grosse Bleiche* ☎ *06131/ 91240* ✉ *Free* ♥ *Tues.–Sun. 10–6.*

The remains of five 4th-century wooden Roman warships and two full-size replicas are on display at the **Museum für Antike Schiffahrt** (Museum of Ancient Navigation). These were unearthed in 1981 when the foundation for the Hilton's wing was dug. For more than a decade the wood was injected with a water-and-paraffin mixture to restore hardness. ⊠ *Neutorstr. 2b* ☎ *06131/286–630* ✆ *Free* ☉ *Tues.–Sun. 10–6.*

The various collections of the **Landesmuseum** (Museum of the State of Rheinland-Pfalz) are in the former electors' stables, easily recognized by the statue of a golden stallion over the entrance. Exhibits range from the Stone Age to the 20th century. Among the highlights are a tiny Celtic glass dog from the 1st or 2nd century BC, Roman masonry, paintings by Dutch masters, artworks from the baroque to art nouveau period, and collections of porcelain and faience. ⊠ *Grosse Bleiche 49–51* ☎ *06131/28570* ⊕ *www.landesmuseum-mainz.de* ✆ *€2, free Sat.* ☉ *Tues. 10–8, Wed.–Sun. 10–5.*

☺ The animals in Mainz's **Naturhistorisches Museum** (Natural History Museum) may all be stuffed and mounted, but these lifelike groups can demonstrate the relationships among various families of fauna better than any zoo. Fossils and geological exhibits show the evolution of the region's plants, animals, and soils. ⊠ *Reichklarastr. 1* ☎ *06131/122–646* ✆ *€1.50, free Sun.* ☉ *Tues. 10–8, Wed. 10–2, Thurs.–Sun. 10–5.*

Schillerplatz, ringed by beautiful baroque palaces, is the site of the ebullient **Fastnachtsbrunnen** (Carnival Fountain), with 200 figures related to Mainz's "fifth season" of the year.

★ From Shillerplatz it's but a short walk up Gaustrasse to **St. Stephanskirche** (St. Stephen's Church), which affords a hilltop view of the city. In 990 Willigis built a basilica on the site; today's Gothic church dates from the late 13th and early 14th centuries. Postwar restoration included the installation of six vividly blue stained-glass windows depicting scenes from the Bible, designed in the 1970s by the Russian-born painter Marc Chagall. ⊠ *Kleine Weissg. 12, via Gaustr.* ☎ *06131/231–640* ☉ *Feb.–Nov., Mon.–Sat. 10–noon and 2–5, Sun. afternoon only; Dec. and Jan., Mon.–Sat. 10–noon and 2–4:30, Sun. afternoon only.*

The hillside **Kupferberg Sektkellerei** (sparkling wine cellars) were built in 1850 on a site where the Romans cultivated vines and built cellars. The Kupferberg family expanded the cellars into 60 seven-story-deep vaulted cellars—the deepest in the world. The winery has a splendid collection of glassware; posters from the Belle Epoque period (1898–1914); richly carved casks from the 18th and 19th centuries; and the **Traubensaal** (Grape Hall), a tremendous example of the art nouveau style. Two-hour tours include a tasting of five sparkling wines; 1½-hour tours include three sparkling wines; one-hour tours include one glass of Sekt. Reservations are required. ⊠ *Kupferbergterrasse 17–19* ☎ *06131/9230* ⊕ *www.kupferberg.de* ✆ *2-hr tours €12, 1½-hr tours € 9.50, 1-hr tours €6.50* ☉ *Shop weekdays 10–6* ▭ *MC, V.*

Where to Stay & Eat

★ **$–$$$** ✕ **Gebert's Weinstuben.** Gebert's traditional wine restaurant serves refined versions of regional favorites in a very personal atmosphere. Try the *Handkäs-Suppe* (cheese soup) or Saumagen made not of pork but *Wildschwein* (wild boar). *Gans mit Schmoräpfel und Klöse* (goose with braised apples and dumplings) is served from November 11 until Christmas. The seasonal specialties, homemade noodles and handmade chocolate pralines, are always delicious. German wines (especially Rheinhessen) dominate the excellent wine list. Summer dining alfresco is possible in the smartly renovated courtyard. ☒ *Frauenlobstr. 94, near Rhine* ☏ *06131/611–619* ⊕ *www.geberts-weinstuben.de* ☐ *AE, DC, MC, V* ☉ *Closed Sat. and 3 wks in July or Aug. No lunch Sun.*

★ **$-$$** ✕ **Haus des Weines.** In addition to the pleasant ambience, tasty food, and a great selection of wines, the late hours are customer-friendly. The luncheon specials (€5.20) and huge salads are a very good value, and the menu covers a broad range, from snacks to full-course meals. Game is a specialty and available year-round. Enjoy a glass of wine with the Mainz specialties *Spundekäs* (cheese whipped with cream and onions) or *Handkäse mit Musik* (pungent, semihard cheese served with diced onions in vinaigrette). ☒ *Gutenbergpl. 3* ☏ *06131/221–300* ⊕ *www.hdw-mainz. de* ☐ *AE, MC, V.*

$-$$ ✕ **Mollers im Staatstheater.** For a fabulous view of Mainz, head for the terrace (5th floor) or glass-lined restaurant atop the state theater (6th floor). Walk through the bistro (open daily 9–9) to reach the elevator. Sumptuous buffets, traditional favorites, and creative dishes, such as monkfish wrapped in ham with coconut risotto or couscous-coated rabbit, offer something for every taste. Brunch is served (11–2:30) Sunday. ☒ *Gutenbergplatz 7* ☏ *06131/627–9211* ⊕ *www.mollers.de* ☐ *MC, V* ☉ *Closed Wed.*

¢-$$ ✕ **Fischrestaurant Jackob.** Gernot Grundmann's fish shop supplies his restaurant with an array of absolutely fresh fish and, when in season, *Muscheln* (mussels). Half portions and the daily special are especially good values. At this writing, a move to new quarters (near the fish shop) is planned. Check with the shop for details. ☒ *Fish shop: Fischtor 5* ☏ *06131/231–729* ⊕ *www.fischjackob.de* ☐ *V* ☉ *Closed Sun. No dinner except Fri., Oct.–May.*

¢-$$ ✕ **Heiliggeist.** Meals are served until after midnight at this lively cafébistro-bar. Modern, minimal decor provides an interesting contrast to the historic vaulted ceilings, and in summer the beer garden is always packed. The compact menu includes elaborate salad platters as well as creatively spiced and sauced fish and meat dishes. One house specialty worth trying is the *Croustarte,* an upscale version of pizza. There's an extensive drink list. ☒ *Mailandsg. 11* ☏ *06131/225–757* ⊕ *www. heiliggeist-online.de* ☐ *No credit cards* ☉ *No lunch Mon.–Thurs.*

¢-$ ✕ **Eisgrub-Bräu.** It's loud, it's lively, and the beer is brewed in the vaulted cellars on-site. An Eisgrub brew is just the ticket to wash down a hearty plate of *Haxen* (pork hocks) or *Meterwurst* (yard-long, rolled bratwurst), *Bratkartoffeln* (home fries), and sauerkraut. Breakfast (daily) and a buffet lunch (weekdays) are also served. Brewery tours are free, but make a reservation in advance. It's open daily 9 AM–1 AM. ☒ *Weisslilieng. 1a* ☏ *06131/221–104* ⊕ *www.eisgrub.de* ☐ *MC, V.*

$$$-$$$$ ▥ **Hyatt Regency Mainz.** The blend of contemporary art and architecture with the old stone walls of historical Fort Malakoff on the Rhine is a visually stunning success. From the spacious atrium lobby to the luxurious rooms, everything is sleek, modern, and designed for comfort. The M-Lounge & Bar in the lobby serves light fare from 10 to midnight (drinks until 1:30 AM), and tables in the garden courtyard are always at a premium in the summer. The boutiques and pubs of the Old Town are only a 5- to 10-minute walk away. ⊠ *Malakoff-Terrasse 1, D–55116* ☎ *06131/731–234* 📠 *06131/731–235* ⊕ *www.mainz.regency. hyatt.com* 🛏 *265 rooms, 3 suites* ⚭ *Restaurant, room service, in-room data ports, cable TV, minibars, indoor pool, gym, massage, sauna, steam room, bicycles, bar, lobby lounge, laundry service, concierge, Internet, business services, some pets allowed (fee), no-smoking rooms* 🖃 *AE, DC, MC, V.*

$ 🏨 **Hotel Ibis.** Modern, functional rooms and a great location on the edge of the Old Town are what the Ibis offers. Ask about the various discount rates that are available (except during trade fairs and major events). ⊠ *Holzhofstr. 2, at Rheinstr., D–55116* ☎ *06131/2470* 📠 *06131/ 234–126* ⊕ *www.ibishotel.com* 🛏 *144 rooms* ⚭ *In-room data ports, cable TV, bar, laundry service, some pets allowed (fee), no-smoking rooms* 🖃 *AE, DC, MC, V.*

$ 🏨 **Hotel Weinhaus Rebstock.** This 15th-century house is tucked away in the Old Town's pedestrian zone. A family-run operation, it offers friendly service and comfortable rooms, seven with a view of the cathedral. Park at the garage of the Karstadt department store (entrance on Weissliliengasse), a minute's walk away. ⊠ *Heiliggrabg. 6, near Bischofspl., D–55116* ☎ *06131/230–317* 📠 *06131/230–318* 🛏 *11 rooms, 5 with bath* ⚭ *Some pets allowed; no a/c, no room phones* 🖃 *MC, V* ⊘ *Closed mid-Dec.–mid-Jan.* 🍴 *BP.*

Nightlife & the Arts

Mainz supports a broad spectrum of cultural events—music (from classical to avant-garde), dance, opera, and theater performances—at many venues throughout the city. Music lovers can attend concerts in venues ranging from the cathedral, the Kurfürstliches Schloss, and the Kupferberg sparkling wine cellars to the Rathaus, market square, and historic churches. The home stage of the Staatstheater Mainz is the **Grosses Haus** (⊠ Gutenbergpl. ☎ 06131/28510 or 06131/285–1222). A smaller stage, the Kleines Haus, is also on the premises. **TiC** (⊠ Spritzeng. 2 ☎ 06131/28510) is a sister stage of the Grosses Haus that features works of contemporary artists. **Mainzer Kammerspiele** (⊠ Rheinstr. 4, Fort Malakoff Park ☎ 06131/225–002) is a multi-arts venue. The Mainzer Forum-Theater (cabaret) performs in the **Unterhaus** (⊠ Münsterstr. 7 ☎ 06131/232–121).

Musicals and large-scale concerts are held in the high-tech **Phönix Halle** (⊠ Hauptstr. 17–19 ☎ 06131/962–830) in the suburb of Mombach. **KUZ** (⊠ Dagobertstr. 20b ☎ 06131/286–860) and its beer garden attract young and old for international rock, jazz, and pop concerts. The **Frankfurter Hof** (⊠ Augustinerstr. 55) hosts many (often contemporary) musical events and lively dance parties. A traditional setting for concerts is the **Villa Musica** (⊠ Auf der Bastei 3), with a repertoire ranging from classical to modern.

Nightlife is centered in the numerous wine pubs. Rustic and cozy, they're packed with locals who come to enjoy a meal or snack with a glass (or more) of local wine. Most are on the Old Town's main street, **Augustinerstrasse,** and its side streets (Grebenstrasse, Kirschgarten, Kartäuserstrasse, Jakobsbergstrasse) and around the Gutenberg Museum, on Liebfrauenplatz. The wood-panel pub **Wilhelmi** (⊠ Rheinstr. 51 ☎ 06131/ 224–949) is a favorite with the post-student crowd. **Schreiner** (⊠ Rheinstr. 38 ☎ 06131/225–720) attracts a mature clientele and is an old, traditional Mainz favorite.

Carnival season runs from November 11 at 11:11 AM to Ash Wednesday. There are dozens of costume balls, parties, and political cabaret sessions that culminate in a huge parade of colorful floats and marching bands through downtown on the Monday before Lent.

Shopping

The Old Town is full of boutiques, and the major department stores (Karstadt and Kaufhof-Galeria) sell everything imaginable, including gourmet foods in their lower levels. The shopping district lies basically between the Grosse Bleiche and the Old Town and includes the **Am Brand** Zentrum, an ancient marketplace that is now a pedestrian zone brimming with shops. At the shopping mall **Römerpassage** (Lotharstrasse, near Grosse Bleiche), head for the cellar to see the remains of a Roman temple (AD 1) dedicated to the goddesses Isis and Mater Magna. The discovery was made in 1999 during construction of the mall.

The **Gutenberg-Shop** (⊠ Markt 17 ⊕ www.gutenberg-shop.de ⊙ Closed Sun.) on the first floor of the *AZ* (local newspaper) customer center has a better selection of splendid souvenirs and gifts—including pages from the Bible, books, posters, stationery, pens, and games—than the shop in the Gutenberg Museum. The excellent **Weincabinet** (⊠ Leichhofstr. 10, behind cathedral ☎ 06131/228–858) sells an array of the region's best wines and accessories. The flea market **Krempelmarkt** is on the banks of the Rhine between the Hilton hotel and Kaiserstrasse. It takes place from 7 to 1 the first and third Saturday of the month from April to October and the first Saturday from November to March.

THE PFALZ & RHINE TERRACE A TO Z

To research prices, get advice from other travelers, and book travel arrangements, visit www.fodors.com.

AIRPORTS

Frankfurt is the closest major international airport for the entire Rhineland. International airports in Stuttgart and France's Strasbourg are closer to the southern end of the German Wine Road.

BIKE TRAVEL

There's no charge for transporting bicycles on local trains throughout Rheinland-Pfalz weekdays after 9 AM and anytime weekends and holidays. The train stations in the towns of this chapter, however, do not rent bicycles. For maps, suggested routes, bike-rental locations, and details on *Pauschal-Angebote* (package deals) or *Gepäcktransport* (luggage-forwarding service), contact Pfalz-Touristik or Rheinhessen-Information.

CAR RENTAL

Avis, Europcar, Hertz, and Sixt have rental offices at Frankfurt's airport and main train station.

◫ **Avis** ✉ Hattenbergstr. 30, Mainz ☎ 06131/625–523 ✉ Wormser Landstr. 22, Speyer ☎ 06232/31680 ✉ Alzeyerstr. 44, Worms ☎ 06241/30280. **Europcar** ✉ Am Mombacher Kreisel 1, Mainz ☎ 06131/913–500 ✉ Gutleutstr. 8, Worms ☎ 06241/45767. **Hertz** ✉ Alte Mainzer Str. 127, Mainz ☎ 06131/985–644 ✉ Klosterstr. 45, Worms ☎ 06241/411–462. **Sixt** ✉ Bingerstr. 19, Mainz ☎ 06131/270–710.

CAR TRAVEL

It's 162 km (100 mi) between Schweigen-Rechtenbach and Mainz, the southernmost and northernmost points of this itinerary. The main route is the Deutsche Weinstrasse, which is a *Bundesstrasse* (two-lane highway), abbreviated "B," as in B–38, B–48, and B–271. The route from Worms to Mainz is B–9. The autobahn, abbreviated "A," parallel to the Wine Road in the Pfalz is A–65 from Kandel to Kreuz Mutterstadt (the junction with A–61, south of Ludwigshafen), and in Rheinhessen, A–61 to Alzey, and, finally, A–63 to Mainz. The A–6 runs west to east through the Pfalz from Kaiserslautern to Kreuz Frankenthal (the junction with A–61, north of Ludwigshafen).

Autobahn access to Mainz, the northernmost point of the itinerary, is fast and easy. A–63, A–61, and A–65 run through the area roughly north–south, and A–8 approaches the southern part of the German Wine Road via Karlsruhe.

TOURS

Town walking tours usually begin at the tourist-information office. Annweiler tours are at 10 AM on Wednesday from May to October, free of charge. Bad Dürkheim has free tours March to mid-November, departing Monday at 10:30 from the fountain in front of the train station. Deidesheim conducts tours from May to October on Saturday at 10 (€3). Mainz has year-round tours departing Saturday at 2 (€5) from the Touristik Centrale. The office is one story above street level on the footbridge over Rheinstrasse. There are additional tours from May to October, Wednesday and Friday at 2.

Neustadt tours cost €3 and take place April through mid-November, Wednesday and Saturday at 10:30. Speyer tours are at 11 on weekends between April and November; the cost is €3.50. Wachenheim tours start at the market square in September and October, Thursday at 4, and cost €1. Worms begins its tours at the southern portal (main entrance) of the cathedral on Saturday at 10:30 and Sunday at 2, between March and October. The cost is €4.

The Köln-Düsseldorfer Deutsche Rheinschiffahrt (KD Rhine Line; ⇨ Cruise Travel *in* Smart Travel Tips) travels down the Rhine from Mainz to Köln.

TRAIN TRAVEL

Mainz and Mannheim are hubs for IC (InterCity) and ICE (InterCity Express) trains.

TRANSPORTATION AROUND THE PFALZ & RHINE TERRACE

An excellent network of public transportation called *Rheinland-Pfalz-Takt* operates throughout the region with well-coordinated *RegioLinie* (buses) and *Nahverkehrszüge* (local trains). The travel service of the Deutsche Bahn (German Railway) provides schedules, connections, prices, and so on, 24 hours daily from anywhere in Germany.

VISITOR INFORMATION

The *KulturCard* (€5) entitles you to a 50% discount at many cultural events, museums, and sights in Rheinland-Pfalz. The card is sold by mail through the regional broadcaster SWR and at the newspaper *RZ* (RheinZeitung) shops. For discounts in Mainz, buy the *MainzCard* (€6) at the tourist office or at a hotel.

The regional and local tourist and wine information offices in the southern Pfalz, the northern Pfalz, and Rheinhessen can help make the most of your visit. The German Wine Information Bureau (⇨ Wine, Beer & Spirits *in* Smart Travel Tips) promotes the wines of all the regions.

KulturCard SWR Stichwort KulturCard, D-55114 Mainz or at the *RZ* shop ⊠ Grosse Bleiche 17-23, Mainz.

Pfalz Region Pfalz.Touristik ⊠ Landauer Str. 66, D-67434 Neustadt a.d. Weinstrasse ☎ 06321/39160 🖷 06321/391-619 ⊕ www.pfalz-touristik.de. **Pfalzwein** ⊠ Martin-Luther-Str. 69, D-67433 Neustadt a.d. Weinstrasse ☎ 06321/912-328 🖷 06321/12881 ⊕ www.zum-wohl-die-pfalz.de.

Northern Pfalz Deutsche Weinstrasse ⊠ Martin-Luther-Str. 69, D-67433 Neustadt a.d. Weinstrasse ☎ 06321/912-333 🖷 06321/912-330 ⊕ www.deutsche-weinstrasse.de.

Southern Pfalz Südliche Weinstrasse ⊠ An der Kreuzmühle 2, D-76829 Landau ☎ 06341/940-407 🖷 06341/940-502 ⊕ www.suedlicheweinstrasse.de.

Rheinhessen Area Rheinhessen-Information ⊠ Wilhelm-Leuschner-Str. 44, D-55218 Ingelheim ☎ 06132/44170 🖷 06132/441-744 ⊕ www.rheinhessen-info.de. **Rheinhessenwein** ⊠ Otto-Lilienthal-Str. 4, D-55232 Alzey ☎ 06731/951-0740 🖷 06731/9510-7499 ⊕ www.rheinhessenwein.de.

Annweiler ⊠ Büro für Tourismus, Hauptstr. 20, D-76855 ☎ 06346/2200 🖷 06346/7917 ⊕ www.trifelsland.de. **Bad Dürkheim** ⊠ Tourist-Information, Kurbrunnenstr. 14, D-67098 ☎ 06322/956-6250 🖷 06322/956-6259 ⊕ www.bad-duerkheim.de. **Deidesheim** ⊠ Tourist Service, Bahnhofstr. 5, D-67146 ☎ 06326/96770 🖷 06326/967-718 ⊕ www.deidesheim.de. **Landau** ⊠ Büro für Tourismus, Marktstr. 50, D-76829 ☎ 06341/13182 🖷 06341/13195 ⊕ www.landau.de. **Mainz** ⊠ Touristik Centrale, Brückenturm am Rathaus, D-55116 ☎ 06131/286-210 🖷 06131/286-2155 ⊕ www.info-mainz.de. **Neustadt-an-der-Weinstrasse** ⊠ Tourist-Information, Hetzelpl. 1, D-67433 ☎ 06321/926-892 🖷 06321/926-891 ⊕ www.neustadt.pfalz.com. **Speyer** ⊠ Tourist-Information, Maximilianstr. 13, D-67346 ☎ 06232/142-392 🖷 06232/142-332 ⊕ www.speyer.de. **Wachenheim** ⊠ Tourist-Information, Weinstr. 15, D-67157 ☎ 06322/958-032 🖷 06322/958-01159 ⊕ www.wachenheim.de. **Worms** ⊠ Tourist-Information, Neumarkt 14, D-67547 ☎ 06241/25045 🖷 06241/26328 ⊕ www.worms.de/tourismus.

THE RHINELAND

11

Updated by
Kerry Brady

VATER RHEIN, OR "FATHER RHINE," is Germany's historic lifeline, and the region from Mainz to Koblenz is its heart. Its banks are crowned by magnificent castle after castle and by breathtaking, vine-terraced hills that provide the livelihood for many of the villages hugging the shores. In the words of French poet Victor Hugo, "The Rhine combines everything. The Rhine is swift as the Rhône, wide as the Loire, winding as the Seine . . . royal as the Danube and covered with fables and phantoms like a river in Asia. . . ."

The importance of the Rhine can hardly be overestimated. Although not the longest river in Europe (the Danube is more than twice its length), the Rhine has been the main river-trade artery between the heart of the Continent and the North Sea (and Atlantic Ocean) throughout recorded history. The Rhine runs 1,320 km (820 mi) from the Bodensee (Lake Constance) west to Basel, then north through Germany, and, finally, west through the Netherlands to Rotterdam.

Vineyards, a legacy of the Romans, are an inherent part of the Rhine landscape from Wiesbaden to Bonn. The Rhine tempers the climate sufficiently for grapes to ripen this far north. Indeed, the wine regions along the Rhine, such as the Rheingau, and its most important tributary, the Mosel, are synonymous with the world's finest Riesling wines. Thanks to the river, these wines were shipped far beyond the borders of Germany, which in turn gave rise to the wine trade that shaped the fortune of many riverside towns. Rüdesheim, Bingen, Koblenz, and Köln (Cologne) remain important commercial wine centers to this day.

The Rhine became Germany's top tourist site more than 200 years ago. Around 1790 a spearhead of adventurous travelers from throughout Europe arrived by horse-drawn carriages to explore the stretch of the river between Bingen and Koblenz, now known as the Rhine gorge, or Mittelrhein (Middle Rhine)—and declared a UNESCO World Heritage site in June 2002. The Prussian-Rhine Steamship Co. (forerunner of the Köln-Düsseldorfer) started passenger service between Mainz and Köln in 1827. Shortly thereafter, the railroad opened the region to an early form of mass tourism.

The river is steeped in legend and myth. The Loreley, a jutting sheer slate cliff, was once believed to be the home of a beautiful and bewitching maiden who lured boatmen to a watery end in the swift currents. Heinrich Heine's poem *Song of Loreley* (1827), inspired by Clemens Brentano's *Legend of Loreley* (1812) and set to music in 1837 by Friedrich Silcher, has been the theme song of the landmark ever since. The Nibelungen, a Burgundian race said to have lived on the banks of the Rhine, serve as subjects for Wagner's epic opera cycle *Der Ring des Nibelungen* (1852–72).

William Turner captured misty Rhine sunsets on canvas. Famous literary works, such as Goethe's *Sanct Rochus-Fest zu Bingen* (The Feast of St. Roch; 1814), Lord Byron's *Childe Harold's Pilgrimage* (1816), and Mark Twain's *A Tramp Abroad* (1880), captured the spirit of Rhine Romanticism on paper, encouraging others to follow in their footsteps.

No less romantic is the dreamy landscape of the Mosel Valley. Vines and forests still carpet the steep slate slopes lining the river from Trier, the former capital of the western Roman Empire, to its confluence with the Rhine at Koblenz. En route there's a wealth of Roman artifacts, medieval churches, and castle ruins to admire.

About the Restaurants

Although Düsseldorf, Köln, and Wiesbaden are home to many talented chefs, some of Germany's most creative classic and contemporary cooking is found in smaller towns or country inns.

About the Hotels

The most romantic places to lay your head are the old riverside inns and castle hotels. Ask for a *Rheinblick* (Rhine view) room. Hotels are often booked well in advance, especially for festivals and when there are trade fairs in Köln, Düsseldorf, or Frankfurt, making rooms in Wiesbaden and the Rheingau scarce and expensive. Many hotels close for the winter.

WHAT IT COSTS In Euros					
	$$$$	**$$$**	**$$**	**$**	**¢**
RESTAURANTS	over €25	€21–€25	€16–€20	€9–€15	under €9
HOTELS	over €225	€175–€225	€100–€175	€50–€100	under €50

Restaurant prices are per person for a main course at dinner. Hotel prices are for two people in a standard double room, including tax and service.

Timing

The peak season for cultural, food, and wine festivals is March–mid-November, followed by colorful Christmas markets in December. The season for many hotels, restaurants, riverboats, cable cars, and sights is from Easter through October, particularly in smaller towns. Opening hours at castles, churches, and small museums are shorter during winter. Orchards blossom in March, and the vineyards are verdant from May until mid-September, when the vines turn a shimmering gold.

THE RHEINGAU

Updated by
Kerry Brady

The heart of the region begins in Wiesbaden, where the Rhine makes a sharp bend and flows east to west for some 30 km (19 mi) before resuming its south–north course at Rüdesheim. Wiesbaden is a good starting point to follow any of the well-marked cycling, hiking, and driving routes through the Rheingau's villages and vineyards. The cycling and hiking trails extend to Kaub in the Mittelrhein. Nearly every Rheingau village has an outdoor *Weinprobierstand* (wine-tasting stand), usually near the riverbank. They are staffed and stocked by a different wine estate every weekend in summer.

11

Driving is the ideal way to travel—up one side of the Rhine and down the other—with time out for a cruise. But even the train route between Wiesbaden and Koblenz offers thrilling views.

If you have 3 days

Travel down the Rhine toward Rüdesheim, stopping near **Eltville ②** ⌐ to visit the historical monastery **Kloster Eberbach,** the cultural wine center of the Rheingau. Take in the beauty of the Rhine Gorge, with its steep vineyards, legendary castles, and the **Loreley** rock, on a Rhine steamer cruise from ⬚ **Rüdesheim ④** to **St. Goarshausen ⑩**. Return by train and stay overnight in a Rheingau wine village between Eltville and Rüdesheim. The second day, ferry from Rüdesheim to **Bingen ⑤** for a closer look at the romantic Mittelrhein. The period rooms in Rheinstein, Reichenstein, and Sooneck castles evoke the region's medieval past, as do the town walls, towers, and historic buildings in the wine villages of **Bacharach ⑥, Oberwesel ⑧, St. Goar ⑨,** and **Boppard ⑪**. The last also has significant relics from Roman times. From there drive about 20 km (12 mi) to the Mosel Valley (toward Brodenbach) to spend the night in a wine village such as ⬚ Dieblich, ⬚ **Alken ㉓,** or ⬚ **Treis-Karden ㉔**. Start the third day with a visit to the fairy-tale castle **Burg Eltz.** Follow the Mosel downstream to its confluence with the Rhine at ⬚ **Koblenz ⑫–㉑,** spending the rest of the day exploring the sights of the city or the nearby castles **Stolzenfels, Marksburg,** and **Ehrenbreitstein.**

If you have 5 days

Spend an afternoon and night in ⬚ **Wiesbaden ①** ⌐ to enjoy the thermal springs, elegant shops, and nightlife. The next morning visit **Kloster Eberbach** and a wine estate, or proceed to ⬚ **Rüdesheim ④** for a Rhine steamer cruise to **St. Goarshausen ⑩**. Return by train and take the cable car to the Niederwald-Denkmal (monument) overlooking Rüdesheim for an outstanding panoramic view of the Rhine Valley. The third morning continue downstream to **Kaub ⑦** to visit the **Pfalz,** a medieval fortress. Ferry across the Rhine to **Bacharach ⑥**. See the medieval towns of **Oberwesel ⑧, St. Goar ⑨,** and **Boppard ⑪**. Overnight in ⬚ **Koblenz ⑫–㉑**. The fourth day travel along the Mosel River to **Burg Eltz,** followed by stops in ⬚ **Cochem ㉕** and a few of the charming wine villages upstream. Stay overnight in or near ⬚ **Bernkastel-Kues ㉘,** with its picturesque market square, wine museum, and wine-tasting centers. On Day 5 enjoy the natural beauty of the Mosel during an hour-long boat excursion from Bernkastel before following the river upstream to ⬚ **Trier ㉙–㊷,** the former capital of the western Roman Empire.

If you have 7 days

Follow the five-day itinerary above. Travel from ⬚ **Trier ㉙–㊷** to ⬚ **Köln ㉝–㊿** via the autobahn. Spend the sixth day and night in Köln, visiting the Dom, a masterpiece of Gothic architecture, and one or more of the Romanesque churches and excellent museums. Devote the last day to **Aachen,** an elegant spa and the single-greatest storehouse of Carolingian architecture in Europe.

Wiesbaden

► ❶ *40 km (25 mi) west of Frankfurt via A–66.*

Wiesbaden, the capital of the state of Hesse, is a small city of tree-lined avenues with elegant shops and handsome facades. Its hot mineral springs have been a drawing card since the days when it was known as Aquis Mattiacis ("the waters of the Mattiaci")—the words boldly inscribed on the portal of the Kurhaus—and Wisibada ("the bath in the meadow"). In the first century AD the Romans built thermal baths here, a site then inhabited by a Germanic tribe, the Mattiaci. Modern Wiesbaden dates from the 19th century, when the dukes of Nassau and, later, the Prussian aristocracy commissioned the grand public buildings and parks that shape the city's profile today. Wiesbaden developed into a fashionable spa that attracted the rich and the famous. Their ornate villas on the Neroberg and turn-of-the-20th-century town houses are part of the city's flair.

★ Built in 1907, the neoclassical **Kurhaus** (✉ Kurhauspl.) is the social-cultural center of town. It houses the casino and the Thiersch-Saal, a splendid setting for concerts. The Staatstheater (1894), opulently appointed in baroque and rococo revival styles, and two beautifully landscaped parks flank the Kurhaus. Today you can "take the waters" in an ambience reminiscent of Roman times in the **Irisch-Römisches Bad** (Irish-Roman Bath; ✉ Langg. 38–40) at the Kaiser-Friedrich-Therme, a superb art nouveau bathhouse from 1913. On Kranzplatz, 15 of Wiesbaden's 26 springs converge at the steaming **Kochbrunnen Fountain,** where the healthful waters are there for the tasting.

Historical buildings ring the Schlossplatz (Palace Square) and the adjoining **Marktplatz** (Market Square), site of the farmers' market (Wednesday and Saturday). Behind the neo-Gothic brick Marktkirche (Market Church), food and wine vendors ply their wares in the vaulted cellars of the Marktkeller. The **Altstadt** (Old Town) is just behind the Schloss (now the seat of parliament, the Hessischer Landtag) on Grabenstrasse, Wagemannstrasse, and Goldgasse. The **Museum Wiesbaden** is known for its collection of expressionist paintings, particularly the works of Russian artist Alexej Jawlensky. A major retrospective of his works runs from October 31, 2004, to March 13, 2005. During renovations, the entrance is on the back side of the building (August-Viktoria-Str.). ✉ *Friedrich-Ebert-Allee 2* ☏ *0611/335–2250* ⊕ *www.museum-wiesbaden.de* ⌨ *€2.50, free Tues. 4–8* ☉ *Tues. 10–8, Wed.–Sun. 10–5.*

Where to Stay & Eat

$–$$$$ ✕ **Käfer's.** This popular Kurhaus bistro with striking art nouveau decor, a grand piano (live music nightly), and a good-size bar attracts an upscale clientele. Ambience is the main attraction here. Book a table for two in one of the window alcoves (Nos. 7, 12, 25, and 29) for some privacy among the otherwise close-set tables. *Lachstatar* (salmon tartare on a potato pancake, garnished with lime crème fraîche) and *Bauernente* (farmer's duck with pretzel-dough dumplings) are standard favorites. There's a good international selection of wines, and a bottle of Veuve

11

Festivals

The Rhineland is a stronghold of Germany's Fastnacht (Carnival festivities), which takes place from 11:11 AM on November 11 to Ash Wednesday, culminating with huge parades in Düsseldorf, Köln, and Mainz on the Monday before Lent. Some attractions close for the five days leading up to Ash Wednesday.

Festivals lasting well over a week at venues throughout the Rheingau are the Gourmet Festival (mid-March) and Glorreiche Tage (mid-November); the Rheingau Musik Festival (mid-June through August), with more than 100 concerts, often held at Kloster Eberbach, Schloss Johannisberg, or Wiesbaden's Kurhaus; and theater and concerts during the Burghof Spiele in and near Eltville (late June to late August). Wiesbaden hosts the region's largest wine festival, the Rheingauer Weinwoche (mid-August), and the Internationale Maifestspiele (throughout May), featuring performances by world-renowned artists. Bonn is home to the International Beethoven Festival (mid-September).

The spectacular fireworks display Rhein in Flammen (Rhine in Flames) takes place the first Saturday evening in May (Linz–Bonn), July (Bingen–Rüdesheim), and August (Andernach); the second Saturday evening in August (Koblenz) and September (Oberwesel); and the third Saturday evening in September (St. Goar).

Throughout the Mosel, Saar, and Ruwer valleys top chefs and winemakers present fine wine and food at 135 events, often with musical entertainment, during the International Wein & Gourmet Festival (mid-April to mid-May).

On the Menu

Regional cuisine features fresh fish and *Wild* (game), as well as sauces and soups based on the local Riesling and Spätburgunder (Pinot noir) wines. *Tafelspitz* (boiled beef) and *Rheinischer Sauerbraten* (Rhenish marinated pot roast in a sweet-and-sour raisin gravy) are traditional favorites. The *Kartoffel* (potato) is prominent in soups, *Reibekuchen* and *Rösti* (potato pancakes), and *Dibbe-* or *Dippekuchen* (dialect: *Döppekoche*), a casserole baked in a cast-iron pot and served with apple compote. *Himmel und Erde,* literally "heaven and earth," is a mixture of mashed potatoes and chunky applesauce, topped with pan-fried slices of blood sausage and onions.

Classical Music

Few regions in Europe rival the quality of classical music performances and venues on the Rhine. Beethoven was born in Bonn, and the city hosts a Beethoven festival every year in mid- to late September. Düsseldorf, once home to Mendelssohn, Schumann, and Brahms, has the finest concert hall in Germany after Berlin's Philharmonie: the Tonhalle, in a former planetarium. Köln also has one of Germany's best concert halls, and its opera company is known for exciting classical and contemporary productions. The cathedrals of Aachen, Köln, and Trier are magnificent settings for concerts and organ recitals.

Wine Regions Riesling is the predominant white grape, and Spätburgunder (Pinot noir) the most important red variety in the Rheingau, Mittelrhein, and Mosel wine regions covered in this chapter. Three abutting wine regions—Rheinhessen and the Nahe, near Bingen, and the Ahr, southwest of Bonn—add to the variety of wines available along the route.

Clicquot Brut Champagne at €45.60 is an excellent value. Käfer's also caters the beer garden behind the Kurhaus. ✉ *Kurhauspl. 1* ☎ *0611/536–200* 🌐 *www.kurhaus-gastronomie.de* 💳 *AE, MC, V.*

¢–$ ✕ **Sherry & Port.** Gerd Royko's friendly neighborhood bistro-pub hosts live music on Fridays from October through March. During warm months, dine at outdoor tables surrounding a huge fountain on tree-lined Adolfsallee. In addition to the fantastic number of sherries (30), ports (17), and malt whiskeys (18) by the glass, there's a good selection of beers (Guinness on tap) and wines to accompany everything from tapas and salads to steaks and popularly priced daily specials (€5.55). ✉ *Adolfsallee 11* ☎ *0611/373–632* 🌐 *www.sherry-und-port.de* 💳 *No credit cards* ⏲ *Closed weekends Oct.–Mar.*

$$$$ Fodor's Choice ★ ✕🏨 **Nassauer Hof.** Wiesbaden's premier address for well over a century, this elegant hotel opposite the Kurhaus lies on the site of a Roman fortress that was converted into a spa and, ultimately, a guesthouse. It's internationally renowned for its luxuriously appointed rooms, topflight service, and restaurants—Ente ($$$$, closed one week in January and Sunday) and Orangerie ($–$$$)—both open for lunch and dinner. ✉ *Kaiser-Friedrich-Pl. 3–4, D–65183* ☎ *0611/1330* 📠 *0611/133–632* 🌐 *www.nassauer-hof.de* *139 rooms, 30 suites* *2 restaurants, in-room data ports, minibars, cable TV, indoor pool, gym, sauna, spa, bicycles, lobby lounge, piano bar, wineshop, babysitting, dry cleaning, laundry service, concierge, Internet, business services, no-smoking rooms* 💳 *AE, DC, MC, V.*

★ $$–$$$ ✕🏨 **Trüffel.** For years truffle lovers have indulged in the "diamonds of the kitchen"—or the sumptuous chocolate versions—at Cristina and Dr. Manuel Stirn's first-rate delicatessen and bistro. A classy hotel and restaurant round out operations. Personal service, stylish decor, and luxury baths make for a very pleasant stay. Trüffel (truffles) are still on the menu at the bistro ($) and at the restaurant Trüffel First Floor ($$–$$$). The chocolates (and superb foods and beverages) merit a detour to the delicatessen. ✉ *Weberg. 6–8, D–65183* ☎ *0611/990–550* 📠 *0611/990–5511* 🌐 *www.trueffel.net* *24 rooms, 4 suites* *2 restaurants, café, patisserie, in-room data ports, minibars, cable TV, 2 bars, shop, babysitting, dry cleaning, laundry service, some pets allowed (fee); no smoking* 💳 *AE, DC, MC, V* ⏲ *Restaurant closed Sun.* *BP.*

$$ 🏨 **Best Western Hotel Hansa.** This very comfortable, modern hotel in an art nouveau house is centrally located and but a brief walk to the main train station, the Kurhaus, and the Old Town. Enjoy the hearty breakfast buffet on the ground floor, or head for one of the many cafés nearby. ✉ *Bahnhofstr. 23, D–65185* ☎ *0611/901–240* 📠 *0611/9012–4666* 🌐 *www.bestwestern.de* *80 rooms, 1 suite* *In-room*

data ports, cable TV, laundry service, some pets allowed (fee), no-smoking rooms; no a/c ☰ *AE, DC, MC, V.*

$ ▨ **Ibis.** This modern hotel opposite the Kochbrunnen on Kranzplatz offers excellent value and a location within walking distance of the shop-filled pedestrian zone, the Old Town, and all sights. ✉ *Georg-August-Zinn-Str. 2, D–65183* ☎ *0611/36140* 📠 *0611/361–4499* ⊕ *www.ibishotel.com* ☞ *131 rooms* ⚴ *In-room data ports, cable TV, bar, lobby lounge, some pets allowed (fee), no-smoking rooms; no a/c* ☰ *AE, DC, MC, V.*

Nightlife & the Arts

In addition to the casino, restaurants, bars, and beer garden at the Kurhaus, nightlife is centered in the many bistros and pubs on Taunusstrasse and in the Old Town. The tourist office provides schedules and sells tickets for most venues listed below.

The **Hessisches Staatstheater** (✉ Chr.-Zais-Str. 3 ☎ 0611/132–325) presents classical and contemporary opera, theater, ballet, and musicals on three stages: Grosses Haus, Kleines Haus, and Studio. Great classics and avant-garde films, as well as dance and small theatrical productions, are specialties of the **Caligari Filmbühne** (✉ Marktpl. 9, behind Marktkirche ☎ 0611/313–779). Smaller dramatic productions and cabaret are performed at the intimate **Pariser Hoftheater** (✉ Spiegelg. 9 ☎ 0611/300–607). **Thalhaus** (✉ Nerotal 18 ☎ 0611/185–1267) is a lively, multiarts venue. Live concerts (jazz, blues, rock, and pop), often accompanied by readings or theater, are held at the **Walhalla Studio Theater** (✉ Mauritiusstr. 1a [use entrance of movie theater Bambi Kino] ☎ 0611/910–3743 ⊕ www.walhalla-studio.de).

The Hessian State Orchestra performs in the **Kurhaus** (✉ Kurhauspl. 1 ☎ 0611/17290). Concerts and musicals are staged at the **Rhein-Main-Hallen** (✉ Rheinstr. 20 ☎ 0611/1440). The **Villa Clementine** (✉ Frankfurter Str. 1 ☎ 0611/313–642) is a regular concert venue. The sparkling wine cellars of **Henkell & Söhnlein** (✉ Biebricher Allee 142 ☎ 0611/630) host a series of concerts in their splendid foyer. Many churches offer concerts, including the free organ concerts Saturday at 11:30 in the **Marktkirche.**

At the **Spielbank** (casino), the Grosses Spiel (roulette, blackjack) in the Kurhaus is lively from 3 PM to 3 AM, while the Kleines Spiel (slots) in the neighboring Kolonnade, is hopping from 1 PM to 4 AM. The former is one of Europe's grand casinos, where jacket and tie are required. Minimum age is 18 (bring your passport). ✉ *Kurhauspl. 1* ☎ *0611/536–100* ⊕ *www. spielbank-wiesbaden.de* 💶 *Grosses Spiel €2.50, Kleines Spiel €1.*

Thermal Springs, Spas & Pools

Pamper yourself with the **Kaiser-Friedrich-Therme**'s thermal spring and cold-water pools, various steam baths and saunas, two solaria, and a score of health and wellness treatments in elegant art nouveau surroundings. Towels and robes can be rented on-site, but come prepared for "textile-free" bathing. Children under 16 are not admitted. ✉ *Langg. 38–40, entrance faces Weberg.* ☎ *0611/172–9660* 💶 *4 hrs in pools, steam baths, and saunas €17.50* ⊙ *Sat.–Thurs. 10–10, Fri. 10 AM–midnight; Tues. women only; massage and treatments by appointment.*

The Rhineland

TO DÜSSELDORF

Bonn 43 - 52 see detail map

Köl 53 - see de ma

Mayen

Kobe Gonc

Lissingen

Daun

Burg Eltz

Mose

24 **Treis-Karden**

Mosel

25 **Cochem**

26 **Ediger-Eller**

Beilstein

TO AACHEN

Zell

Kappel

Wittlich

Zeltingen

Wehlen

27 **Traben-Trarbach**

Klausen

28 **Bernkastel-Kues**

Mülheim

Bitburg

Piesport

Mosel

Neumagen-Dhron

Trittenheim

Morbach

Schweich

LUXEMBOURG

Büdlicherbrück

Thalfang

Ruwer

Trier 29 - 42 see detail map

Zewen

Konz

Hermeskeil

0   10 miles

0   15 km

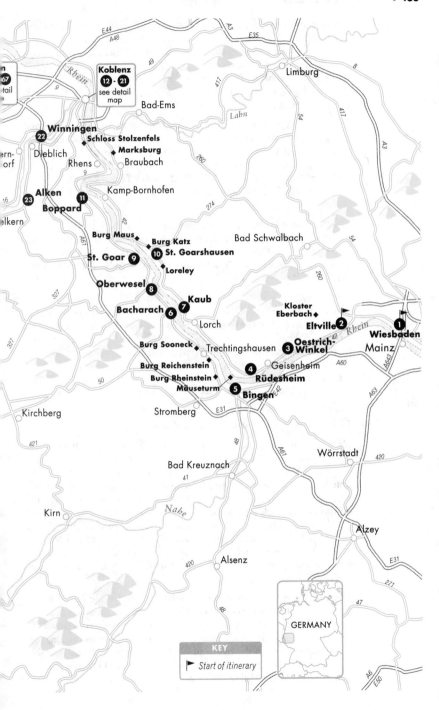

Another art nouveau spa with its own thermal spring is the **Badhaus** in the Radisson SAS Schwarzer Bock Hotel opposite the Kochbrunnen. The very professional, personalized service for massage and individual therapeutic and beauty baths is excellent. ⊠ *Kranzplatz 12* ☎ *0611/1550 or 0611/155–630* ☜ *Pool, sauna, fitness room, no time limit €13* ⊙ *Weekdays 7 AM–9 PM, weekends 9 AM–6 PM; massage and treatments by appointment.*

There's year-round swimming indoors and out thanks to the thermal springs (32°C [90°F]) that feed the pools at the **Thermalbad Aukammtal.** The facility includes eight saunas, a whirlpool, massage, and balneological treatments. ⊠ *Leibnizstr. 7, bus No. 18 from Wilhelmstr. to Aukamm Valley* ☎ *0611/172–9880* ☜ *Pools €15; saunas €8.50; combination €20. Ticket valid for one day* ⊙ *Sun.–Thurs. 8 AM–10 PM, Fri. and Sat. 8 AM–midnight.*

The **Opelbad,** a large, outdoor swimming pool on the Neroberg, is idyllically set on the edge of the city forest, overlooking Wiesbaden and the Rheingau. To get there, you can drive, walk, or take the **Nerobergbahn,** a historical railway dating from 1888. ⊠ *Neroberg* ☎ *0611/172–9885* ☜ *€6* ⊙ *May–Sept., daily 7 AM–8 PM.*

Shopping

Broad, tree-lined Wilhelmstrasse, with designer boutiques housed in its fin-de-siècle buildings, is one of Germany's most elegant shopping streets. Wiesbaden is also known as one of the best places in the country to find antiques; Taunusstrasse has excellent antiques shops. The Altstadt is full of upscale boutiques; Kirchgasse and its extension, Langgasse, are the heart of the shop-filled pedestrian zone.

Eltville

▶ ❷ *14 km (9 mi) west of Wiesbaden via A–66 and B–42.*

Eltville, Alta Villa in Roman times, was first in the Rheingau to receive town rights (1332). Eltville flourished as a favorite residence of the archbishops of Mainz in the 14th and 15th centuries, and it was during this time that the **Kurfürstliche Burg** (Electors' Castle) was built. The castle has an exhibition commemorating Johannes Gutenberg (1400–68), the inventor of movable type. He lived in Eltville on and off, and it was here that he was named a courtier by elector Adolf II of Nassau in 1465. ⊠ *Burgstr. 1* ☎ *06123/90980* ☜ *Tower €1.50, rose garden free* ⊙ *Tower open Apr.–mid-Oct., Fri. 2–6 and weekends 11–6; exhibition Sun. 3–5; rose garden Easter–mid-Oct., daily 9:30–7 and mid-Oct.–Easter, daily 10:30–5.*

The parish church of **Sts. Peter und Paul** has late-Gothic frescoes, Renaissance tombstones, and a carved baptismal by the Rhenish sculptor Hans Backoffen (or his studio). Worth seeing are Burg Crass (Crass Castle) on the riverbank and the half-timber houses and aristocratic **manors** on the lanes between the river and Rheingauer Strasse (B–42), notably the Bechtermünzer Hof (Kirchgasse 6), Stockheimer Hof (Ellenbogengasse 6), and Eltzer Hof (at the Martinstor gateway).

Sekt (sparkling wine) production in the Rheingau is concentrated in Eltville, Wiesbaden, and Rüdesheim. The tree-lined Rhine promenade here hosts the annual Sekt festival during the first weekend of July. The administrative headquarters and main cellars of the **Hessian State Wine Domains,** Germany's largest wine estate, are in town. The estate owns nearly 500 acres of vineyards throughout the Rheingau and in the Hessische Bergstrasse wine region south of Frankfurt. Its shops—in the art nouveau press house built in 1911 and at nearby Kloster Eberbach—offer a comprehensive regional selection. ⊠ *Schwalbacher Str. 56–62* ☎ *06123/92300* ⊕ *www.weingut-kloster-eberbach.de* ⊟ *AE, MC, V* ⊙ *Weekdays 10–6, Sat. 10–4.*

For a good look at the central Rheingau, make a brief circular tour from Eltville. Drive 3 km (2 mi) north via the Kiedricher Strasse to the Gothic village of **Kiedrich.** In the distance you can see the tower of Scharfenstein castle (1215) and the spires of **St. Valentine's Church** and St. Michael's Chapel, both from the 15th century. If you attend the church's 9:30 AM mass on Sunday, you can admire the splendid Gothic furnishings and star vaulting amid the sounds of Gregorian chants and one of Germany's oldest organs. The chapel next door, once a charnel house, has a unique chandelier sculpted around a nearly life-size, two-sided Madonna.

These Gothic gems have survived intact thanks to 19th-century restorations patronized by the English baronet John Sutton. Today Sutton's beautiful villa south of the church is home to one of Germany's leading wine estates, **Weingut Robert Weil.** Its famed Kiedricher Gräfenberg Riesling wines can be sampled in the ultramodern wein*galerie* (tasting room and wine shop). ⊠ *Mühlberg 5* ☎ *06123/2308* ⊕ *www.weingut-robert-weil.com* ⊙ *Weekdays 8–5:30, Sat. 10–4, Sun. 11–5.*

Fodor'sChoice ★ The former Cistercian monastery **Kloster Eberbach** is idyllically set in a secluded forest clearing 3 km (2 mi) west of Kiedrich. Its Romanesque and Gothic buildings (12th–14th centuries) look untouched by time—one reason why the film of Umberto Eco's medieval murder mystery *The Name of the Rose,* starring Sean Connery, was partially filmed here. The monastery's impressive collection of old wine presses and the historic Cabinet Cellar, once reserved for the best barrels, bear witness to a viticultural tradition that spans nearly nine centuries. The wines can be sampled year-round in the **wine shop** or restaurants on the grounds. The church, with its excellent acoustics, and the large medieval dormitories are the settings for concerts, wine auctions, and festive wine events. *Stiftung Kloster Eberbach* ⊠ *Postfach 1453, D–65334 Eltville* ☎ *06723/91780* ⊕ *www.klostereberbach.de* ⊠ *€3* ⊙ *Easter–Oct., daily 10–6; Nov.–Easter, daily 11–4.*

From Eberbach take the road toward Hattenheim, stopping at the first right-hand turnoff to admire the monastery's premier vineyard, **Steinberg.** It's encircled by a 3-km-long (2-mi-long) stone wall (13th–18th centuries). The vineyard has an **outdoor pub,** Brot und Wein ("bread and wine"). ⊙ *May–Sept., weekends 11–7.*

The *Brunnen* (springs) beneath the vineyards of Hattenheim and Erbach, both on the Rhine, lend their name to three excellent **vineyards:** Nussbrunnen, Wisselbrunnen, and Marcobrunnen—on the boundary between the two towns. As you return to Eltville (2 km [1 mi] east of Erbach on B–42), you will pass the elegant 19th-century palace Schloss Reinhartshausen (now a hotel and wine estate).

Where to Stay & Eat

$ ✕ **Gutsausschank im Baiken.** Andrea and Stefan Seyffardt's cozy wine restaurant is set on a hilltop amid the famed Rauenthaler Baiken vineyard. The magnificent panorama from the vine-canopied terrace, the fresh country cooking, and superb wines—from the Hessian State Wine Domains—make for a "Rheingau Riesling" experience par excellence. The Domaine Pfännchen (pork medallions in a creamy mushroom sauce) is a house specialty. ⊠ *Wiesweg 86, via Eltville* ☎ *06123/900–345* ⊟ *MC, V* ☯ *Closed Mon. and Nov.–mid-Apr. No lunch.*

$$$$ ✕⌂ **Schloss Reinhartshausen.** A palace in every sense of the word, this
FodorśChoice hotel and wine estate majestically overlooks the Rhine and beautifully
★ landscaped gardens. Antiques and artworks fill the house, and some rooms have fireplaces and whirlpools. From morning until night you can dine in the airy, glass-lined Wintergarten ($$$$) or on its terrace facing the parklike garden. Homemade pastries are served afternoons, including the house specialty *Rieslingtorte* (cake prepared with Riesling wine). Upscale regional cuisine and dishes with a Mediterranean accent are served in a vaulted stone cellar at Balzer's Schlosskeller ($$–$$$; MC, V; no lunch). The casual Schloss Schänke (¢; no credit cards; no lunch weekdays) in the old press house offers light fare and hearty snacks. The estate's wines are also sold in the Vinothek. ⊠ *Hauptstr. 43, D–65346 Eltville-Erbach* ☎ *06123/6760* ⊟ *06123/676–400* ⊕ *www.schloss-hotel.de* ⊃ *39 rooms, 15 suites, 1 apartment* ⌂ *3 restaurants, in-room data ports, minibars, cable TV, indoor pool, sauna, bicycles, bar, lobby lounge, Weinstube, shop, babysitting, dry cleaning, laundry service, business services, some pets allowed (fee), no-smoking rooms; no a/c* ⊟ *AE, DC, MC, V.*

$$ ✕⌂ **Klosterschänke und Gästehaus Kloster Eberbach.** The monks never had it this good: the Marschollek family's modern and comfortable rooms are a far cry from the unheated stone dormitories of the past. Beneath the vaulted ceiling of the Klosterschänke ($–$$) you can sample the wines of the Hessian State Wine Domains with regional cuisine. Try the *Weinfleisch* (pork goulash in Riesling sauce) or *Zisterzienser Brot,* which translates to "Cistercian bread" (minced meat in a plum-and-bacon dressing with boiled potatoes). ⊠ *Kloster Eberbach, D–65346 Eltville, Via Kiedrich or Hattenheim* ☎ *06723/9930* ⊟ *06723/993–100* ⊕ *www. klostereberbach.com* ⊃ *28 rooms* ⌂ *Restaurant, in-room data ports, cable TV, sauna, shop, some pets allowed, no-smoking rooms; no a/c* ⊟ *AE, MC, V* ⊠ *BP.*

$$ ✕⌂ **Kronenschlösschen.** The atmosphere of this stylish art nouveau
FodorśChoice house (1894) is intimate, and the individually designed rooms have an-
★ tique furnishings and marble baths. Chef Patrik Kimpel oversees both the gourmet restaurant Kronenschlösschen ($$$$) and the more casual Bistro ($–$$). Fish, poultry, beef, and lamb are always beautifully presented with very flavorful sauces. You can also dine in the parklike garden. The wine list focuses on the finest Rheingau estates for whites and Old and New World estates for reds. ⊠ *Rheinallee, D–65347 Eltville-*

Hattenheim ☎ 06723/640 🖷 06723/7663 ⊕ *www.kronenschloesschen. de* ⌕ *8 rooms, 10 suites* ⚭ *2 restaurants, in-room data ports, minibars, cable TV, bar, babysitting, laundry service, some pets allowed, no-smoking rooms; no a/c* ▤ *AE, DC, MC, V.*

★ **$$** ✕▦ **Zum Krug.** Winegrower Josef Laufer more than lives up to the hospitality promised by the wreath and *Krug* (earthenware pitcher) hanging above the front door. The rooms have modern baths and dark-wood furnishings. Equally cozy is the wood-panel restaurant ($$–$$$), with its old tiled oven. The German fare includes wild duck, goose, game, or sauerbraten served in rich, flavorful gravies. The wine list is legendary for its scope (600 Rheingau wines) and large selection of older vintages. ✉ *Hauptstr. 34, D–65347 Eltville-Hattenheim* ☎ 06723/99680 🖷 06723/ 996–825 ⊕ *www.hotel-zum-krug.de* ⌕ *8 rooms* ⚭ *Restaurant, minibars, cable TV, Weinstube, shop, laundry service, business services, some pets allowed; no smoking, no a/c* ▤ *DC, MC, V* ⊙ *Closed 1st half of Jan. and 2nd half of July. Restaurant also closed Mon. No dinner Sun., no lunch Tues.* ¶◎¶ *BP.*

$ ✕▦ **Maximilianshof.** For generations the von Oetinger family has shared its home, its wines, and its simple, hearty cooking (¢–$) with guests from near and far. In winter the warm art nouveau parlor beckons with its plush sofas; in summer, tables are set out on the pretty terrace. Across the courtyard, there's a cheerful, modern guesthouse with nine rooms, each named after a local vineyard. Honigberg has a private sauna; Hohenrain has a nifty little kitchen and can be booked as a holiday flat for up to five people. ✉ *Rheinallee 2, D–65346 Eltville-Erbach* ☎ 06123/ 92240 🖷 06123/922–425 ⊕ *www.maximilianshof.de* ⌕ *9 rooms* ⚭ *Restaurant, in-room data ports, cable TV, laundry service, Internet, business services, some pets allowed; no a/c* ▤ *AE, DC, MC, V (hotel); V (restaurant)* ⊙ *Restaurant closed Mon. and mid-Jan.–mid-Feb. No lunch weekdays Apr.–Oct. or Mon.–Sat. Nov.–Mar.* ¶◎¶ *BP.*

Oestrich-Winkel

❸ *21 km (13 mi) west of Wiesbaden, 7 km (4½ mi) west of Eltville on B–42.*

Oestrich's vineyard area is the largest in the Rheingau. Lenchen and Doosberg are the most important vineyards. You can sample the wines at the outdoor wine-tasting stand, opposite the 18th-century crane.

The village of Winkel (pronounced *vin*-kle) lies west of Oestrich. A Winkeler Hasensprung wine from the fabulous 1811 vintage was Goethe's wine of choice during his stay here with the Brentano family in 1814. The Brentanos' descendants still welcome visitors to the restaurant at their home. The oldest (1211) of Germany's great private wine

★ estates, **Schloss Vollrads,** lies 3 km (2 mi) north of town. The moated tower (1330) was the Greiffenclau residence for 350 years until the present palace was built in the 17th century. The period rooms are open during concerts, festivals, and wine tastings. ✉ *North on Schillerstr., turn right on Greiffenclaustr.* ☎ 06723/660 ⊕ *www.schlossvollrads.com* ▤ *MC, V* ⊙ *Vinothek Easter–Oct., weekdays 9–6, weekends 11–7; Nov.–Easter, weekdays 9–5, weekends noon–5. Outdoor tasting stand Easter–late Oct., weekends 11–7.*

★ The origins of the grand wine estate, **Schloss Johannisberg,** date from 1100, when Benedictine monks built a monastery and planted vines on the slopes below. The palace and remarkable cellars (visits by appointment only) were built in the early 18th century by the prince-abbots of Fulda. Every autumn a courier was sent from Johannisberg to Fulda to obtain permission to harvest the grapes. In 1775 the courier returned after considerable delay. The harvest was late and the grapes were far riper than usual; the resulting wines were exceptionally rich and fruity. *Spätlese* (literally, "late harvest," pronounced *shpate*-lay-zeh) wines have been highly esteemed ever since. A statue in the courtyard commemorates the "late rider." There are tastings at the Vinothek and the Gutsauschank (estate's restaurant). To get here from Winkel's main street, drive north on Schillerstrasse and proceed all the way uphill (there's a fine view at the top). After the road curves to the left, watch for the left turn to the castle. ⊠ *Weinbaudomäne Schloss Johannisberg, Geisenheim-Johannisberg* ☎ *06722/70090 or 06722/700–935* ⊕ *www.schloss-johannisberg. de* ☽ *Vinothek Mar.–Oct., weekdays 10–1 and 2–6, weekends 11–6; Nov.–Feb., weekdays 10–1 and 2–6, weekends 11–5.*

Where to Stay & Eat

$–$$ ✕ **Gutsausschank Brentano Haus.** Part of the Brentano family's home, once a favorite meeting place of the Rhine Romanticists, has been converted into a cozy wine pub that serves regional cuisine—try the *Woihinkel* (chicken in Riesling sauce) or a Goethe Menü. In summer there are BBQs on the terrace Tuesday night. The Goethe Zimmer (Goethe Room), with mementos and furnishings from Goethe's time, may be visited by appointment only. ⊠ *Am Lindenpl. 2, Winkel* ☎ *06723/7426 pub, 06723/2068 estate* ⊕ *www.brentanohaus.de* ▭ *No credit cards* ☽ *Closed Thurs. Apr.–Sept.; Wed. and Thurs. Oct.–Dec. and Feb. and Mar; all of Jan. No lunch weekdays Oct.–Mar.*

$–$$ ✕ **Gutsausschank Schloss Johannisberg.** The glassed-in terrace affords a spectacular view of the Rhine and the vineyards from which the wine in your glass originated. Rheingau Riesling soup and *Bauernente* (farmer's duck) are house specialties. ⊠ *Schloss Johannisberg* ☎ *06722/96090* ▭ *AE, MC, V.*

$–$$ ✕ **Gutsrestaurant Schloss Vollrads.** Chef Matthias Böhler's "farmers' specialties" and creative seasonal menus are served with the estate's wines in the cavalier house (1650) or on the flower-lined terrace facing the garden. Check the Schloss Vollrads Web site (www.schlossvollrads.com) for a calendar of the many food-and-wine events throughout the year. ⊠ *Schloss Vollrads, north of Winkel* ☎ *06723/5270* ▭ *MC, V* ☽ *Closed Wed. Apr.–Oct.; Tues.–Thurs. Nov.–Mar.; all of Jan. and 2 wks in Nov.*

$$ ▨ **Hotel Schwan.** This green-and-white half-timber inn has been in the Wenckstern family since it was built in 1628. All rooms offer modern comfort; the decor in the guesthouse is simpler than in the historic main building. Many rooms afford a Rhine view, as does the beautiful terrace. The staff is friendly and helpful, and you can sample the family's wines in the historic wine cellar and purchase them on site. ⊠ *Rheinallee 5, in Oestrich, D–65375 Oestrich-Winkel* ☎ *06723/8090* 🖷 *06723/7820* ⊕ *www.hotel-schwan.de* ⇔ *56 rooms* ♿ *Restaurant, in-room data ports, minibars, cable TV, bar, lobby lounge, babysitting, laundry ser-*

vice, business services, some pets allowed, no-smoking rooms; no a/c
🖃 *AE, DC, MC, V* 🍴 *BP.*

Rüdesheim

❹ *30 km (19 mi) west of Wiesbaden, 9 km (5½ mi) west of Oestrich-Winkel on B–42.*

Tourism and wine are the heart and soul of Rüdesheim and best epitomized by the **Drosselgasse** (Thrush Alley). Less than 500 feet long, this narrow, pub-lined lane is abuzz with music and merrymaking from noon until well past midnight every day from Easter through October.

The **Asbach Weinbrennerei** (wine distillery) has produced Asbach, one of Germany's most popular brands of *Weinbrand* (wine brandy, the equivalent of cognac) here since 1892. It's a key ingredient in its brandy-filled *Pralinen* (chocolates) and in the local version of Irish coffee, Rüdesheimer Kaffee. A tour of the distillery operations concludes with a tasting. ⊠ *Asbach Besucher Center, Ingelheimer Str. 4, on eastern edge of town* 🕿 *06722/497–345* ⊕ *www.asbach.de* 🎫 *€5* 🕙 *Jan.–Mar. and Nov., Mon.–Thurs. 9–6, Fri. 9–1; Apr.–Oct. and Dec., Mon.–Thurs. 9–6, Fri. 9–1, Sat. 9–6; Sun. on request.*

The **Weinmuseum Brömserburg** (Brömserburg Wine Museum), housed in one of the oldest castles on the Rhine (circa AD 1000), displays wine-related artifacts and drinking vessels dating from Roman times. There are great views from the roof and the terrace, where you can sample local wines on weekends from mid-March to October. ⊠ *Rheinstr. 2* 🕿 *06722/2348* ⊕ *www.rheingauer-weinmuseum.de* 🎫 *€3* 🕙 *Mid-Mar.–Oct., daily 9–6.*

☾ The 15th-century **Brömserhof** (Brömser Manor) holds Germany's largest collection of mechanical music instruments. Tours are educational and entertaining. ⊠ *Siegfried's Mechanisches Musikkabinett, Oberstr. 29* 🕿 *06722/49217* 🎫 *€5.50* 🕙 *Mar.–Dec., daily 10–6.*

High above Rüdesheim and visible for miles stands *Germania,* a colossal female statue crowning the **Niederwald-Denkmal** (Niederwald Monument). It was built between 1877 and 1883 to commemorate the rebirth of the German Empire after the Franco-Prussian War (1870–71). There are splendid panoramic views from the monument and from other vantage points on the edge of the forested plateau. You can reach the monument on foot, by car (via Grabenstrasse), or over the vineyards in the *Seilbahn* (cable car). There's also a *Sessellift* (chairlift) to and from Assmannshausen, a red-wine enclave, on the west side of the hill. ⊠ *Oberstr. 37* 🕿 *06722/2402* ⊕ *www.seilbahn-ruedesheim.de* 🎫 *One-way €4, round-trip or combined ticket for cable car and chairlift €6. Ring-Ticket €10 for cable car, chairlift, and Rhine cruise* 🕙 *Mid-Mar.–May and Oct., daily 9:30–4; June–Sept., daily 9:30–6:30.*

With the wings of a glider you can silently soar over the Rhine Valley. At the **Luftsport-Club Rheingau** you can catch a 30- to 60-minute *Segelflug* (glider flight) on a glider plane between Rüdesheim and the Loreley; allow 1½ hours for pre- and postflight preparations. ⊠ *3 km (2 mi) north of*

Niederwald-Denkmal and Landgut Ebenthal ☎ 06722/2979 ⊕ *www. lcr.rheingau-media.com* ✉ *1st 5 min €12, each additional min €0.50; €1.50 per min in glider with motor* ⊗ *Apr.–Oct., weekends 10–7.*

Where to Stay & Eat

¢–$$ ✕ **Rüdesheimer Schloss.** In a tithe house built in 1729, this wine tavern specializes in Hessian cuisine and Rheingauer Riesling and Spätburgunder wines from the Breuer family's own estate and those of its illustrious neighbors. The selection of older vintages is remarkable. Start with the delectable *Sauerkrautsuppe* (sauerkraut soup). Benedictine-style *Schloss Ente* (duck with dates and figs), *Ochsenbrust* (boiled breast of beef), and Woihinkel are all excellent. Typical Drosselgasse music and dancing are an entertaining backdrop indoors and in the tree-shaded courtyard. ⊠ *Drosselg.* ☎ *06722/ 90500* ⊟ *AE, DC, MC, V* ⊗ *Closed Jan. and Feb., except on request.*

$$–$$$ ✕▣ **Hotel Krone Assmannshausen.** This elegant, antiques-filled hotel and
Fodor'sChoice restaurant ($$$–$$$$) offers first-class service and fine wining and din-
★ ing. Classic cuisine prepared by chef Willi Mittler and a superb collection of wines, including the famed Spätburgunder red wines of Assmannshausen, make for very memorable meals indoors or on the terrace overlooking the Rhine. Two of the suites have their own sauna. ⊠ *Rheinuferstr. 10, D–65385 Rüdesheim-Assmannshausen* ☎ *06722/ 4030* 🖷 *06722/3049* ⊕ *www.hotel-krone.com* ⊅ *52 rooms, 13 suites, 1 apartment* ⟺ *Restaurant, in-room data ports, minibars, cable TV, pool, bar, shop, babysitting, dry cleaning, laundry service, Internet, some pets allowed (fee), no-smoking rooms; no a/c* ⊟ *AE, DC, MC, V.*

★ $$ ▣ **Breuer's Rüdesheimer Schloss.** Gracious hosts Susanne and Heinrich Breuer have beautifully integrated modern designer decor into the historic walls of this stylish hotel. The Constantinescu Suite (No. 20) and the Rhine Suite (No. 14), with its large terrace, are popular; most rooms offer a vineyard view. Cellar or vineyard tours and wine tastings can be arranged. Wines from the family's Rheingau estate, Weingut Georg Breuer, and tasteful wine accessories are available at the Vinothek (on Grabenstr. 8). ⊠ *Steing. 10, D–65385 Rüdesheim* ☎ *06722/90500* 🖷 *06722/905–050* ⊕ *www.ruedesheimer-schloss.com* ⊅ *23 rooms, 3 suites* ⟺ *Restaurant, in-room data ports, minibars, cable TV, bicycles, Ping-Pong, bar, lobby lounge, shop, babysitting, dry cleaning, laundry service, some pets allowed (fee), no-smoking rooms; no a/c* ⊟ *AE, DC, MC, V* ⊗ *Closed Christmas–early Jan.* ⏴⏵ *BP.*

THE MITTELRHEIN

Updated by
Kerry Brady

Bingen, like Rüdesheim, is a gateway to the Mittelrhein. From here to Koblenz lies the greatest concentration of Rhine castles. Most date from the 12th and 13th centuries but were destroyed in 1689 when French troops systematically blew them up and burned them down during the war of Palatinate succession. It's primarily thanks to the Prussian royal family and its penchant for historical preservation that numerous Rhine castles were rebuilt or restored in the 19th and early 20th centuries.

Two roads run parallel to the Rhine: B–42 (east side) and B–9 (west side). The spectacular views from the heights can best be enjoyed via the routes known as the Loreley-Burgenstrasse (east side), from Kaub to the Loreley to Kamp-Bornhofen; or the Rheingoldstrasse (west side), from Rheindiebach to Rhens. The Rheinhöhenweg (Rhine Heights Path) affords hikers the same splendid views, including descents into the villages en route. These marked trails run between Oppenheim on the Rhine Terrace and Bonn for 240 km (149 mi) and between Wiesbaden and Bonn-Beuel for 272 km (169 mi). The traffic-free paths through the vineyards and along the riverbanks are wonderful routes for hikers and cyclists alike.

Bingen

⑤ *35 km (22 mi) west of Wiesbaden via Mainz and A–60; ferry from wharf opposite Rüdesheim's train station.*

Bingen overlooks the Nahe-Rhine conflux near a treacherous stretch of shallows and rapids known as the Binger Loch (Bingen Hole). Early on, Bingen developed into an important commercial center, for it was here—as in Rüdesheim on the opposite shore—that goods were moved from ship to shore to circumvent the unnavigable waters. Bingen was also the crossroad of Roman trade routes between Mainz, Koblenz, and Trier. Thanks to this central location, it grew into a major center of the wine trade and remains so today. Wine is celebrated during 11 days of merrymaking in early September at the annual **Winzerfest**.

Bingen was destroyed repeatedly by wars and fires; thus there are many ancient foundations but few visible architectural remains of the past. Since Celtic times the Kloppberg (Klopp Hill), in the center of town, has been the site of a succession of citadels, all named **Burg Klopp** since 1282. The existing terrace has good views of the Rhine, the Nahe, and the surrounding hills.

Not far from the thousand-year-old Drususbrücke, a stone bridge over the Nahe, is the late Gothic **Basilika St. Martin**. It was originally built in 793 on the site of a Roman temple. The 11th-century crypt and Gothic and baroque furnishings merit a visit.

★ The **Historisches Museum am Strom** (History Museum) is housed in a former power station (1898) on the riverbank. Here you can see an intact set of Roman surgical tools (2nd century), period rooms from the Rhine Romantic era, and displays about the Abbess St. Hildegard von Bingen (1098–1179), one of the most remarkable women of the Middle Ages. An outspoken critic of papal and imperial machinations, she was a highly respected scholar, naturopath, and artist whose mystic writings and music are much in vogue today. An excellent illustrated booklet in English on Rhine Romanticism, *The Romantic Rhine,* is sold at the museum shop. ✉ *Museumsstr. 3* ☎ *06721/990–654* ⊕ *www.bingen.de* 💶 *€3* ⊙ *Tues.–Sun. 10–5.*

The forested plateau of the Rochusberg (St. Roch Hill) is the pretty setting of the **Rochuskapelle** (St. Roch Chapel). Originally built in 1666 to celebrate the end of the plague, it has been rebuilt twice. On August 16, 1814, Goethe attended the consecration festivities, the forerunner of today's Rochusfest, a weeklong folk festival in mid-August. The chapel (open during Sunday services at 8 and 10) contains an altar dedicated to St. Hildegard and relics and furnishings from the convents she founded on the Ruppertsberg (in the suburb of Bingerbrück) and in Eibingen (east of Rüdesheim). The **Hildegard Forum** (☎ 06721/181–000 ⊕ www. hildegard-forum.de ⊙ Tues.–Sun. 11–6), near the chapel, has exhibits related to St. Hildegard, a medieval herb garden, and a restaurant serving tasty, wholesome foods (*Dinkel,* or spelt, is a main ingredient) based on Hildegard's nutritional teachings.

Where to Stay & Eat

$–$$ ✕ **Schlösschen am Mäuseturm.** Dining on the terrace of this Schlösschen (little castle) with its view of the Mäuseturm and the Rhine makes for a very pleasant evening. The Steiningers serve fresh, seasonal cuisine as well as Pfälzer specialties. The wine list offers 24 wines by the glass, including *Trockenbeerenauslese,* a rare, liqueurlike wine. ⊠ *Stromberger Str. 28A, in suburb of Bingerbrück* ☎ *06721/36699* ▤ *MC* ⊙ *Closed Sun. No lunch.*

★ **$** ✕ **Weinstube Kruger-Rumpf.** It's well worth the 10-minute drive from Bingen (just across the Nahe River) to enjoy Cornelia Rumpf's refined country cooking with Stefan Rumpf's exquisite Nahe wines (Riesling, Weissburgunder [Pinot Blanc], and Silvaner are especially fine). House specialties are *geschmorte Schweinebacken* (braised pork jowls) with kohlrabi, boiled beef with green herb sauce, and *Winzerschmaus* (casserole of potatoes, sauerkraut, bacon, cheese, and herbs). The house dates from 1790; the wisteria-draped garden beckons in summer. ⊠ *Rheinstr. 47, Münster-Sarmsheim, 4 km (2½ mi) southwest of Bingen* ☎ *06721/ 43859* ⚑ *Reservations essential* ▤ *MC* ⊙ *Closed Mon. and 3 wks late Dec.–early Jan. No lunch.*

$$–$$$$ ✕▥ **Johann Lafer's Stromburg.** It's a pretty 15-minute drive through the
Fodor'sChoice Binger Wald (Bingen Forest) to this luxurious castle hotel and restau-
★ rant overlooking Stromberg. Johann Lafer is a prolific chef who pioneered cooking shows in Germany. In the elegant Le Val d'Or ($$$$, reservations essential), the *Variationen* (medley) of foie gras and the *Dessert–Impressionen* are classics. The less formal Turmstube ($$–$$$) offers tasty regional dishes. The wine list features 200 top Nahe wines and several hundred old- and new-world wines, with a particularly fine collection from Bordeaux and Burgundy. ⊠ *Am Schlossberg 1, D–55442 Stromberg, 12 km (7½ mi) west of Bingerbrück via Weiler and Waldalgesheim* ☎ *06724/93100* 🖷 *06724/931–090* ⊕ *www.johannlafer.de* ⊷ *13 rooms, 1 suite* ⚐ *2 restaurants, in-room data ports, minibars, cable TV, bar, lobby lounge, shop, babysitting, dry cleaning, laundry service, some pets allowed (fee); no a/c* ▤ *AE, DC, MC, V* ⊙ *Le Val d'Or closed Mon. No lunch weekdays.*

en route On the 5-km (3-mi) drive on B–9 to Trechtingshausen, you will pass by Bingen's landmark, the **Mäuseturm** (Mice Tower), perched on a rocky island near the Binger Loch. The name derives from a gruesome legend. One version tells that during a famine in 969, the miserly Archbishop Hatto hoarded grain and sought refuge in the tower to escape the peasants' pleas for food. The stockpile attracted scads of mice to the tower, where they devoured everything in sight, including Hatto. In fact, the tower was built by the archbishops of

Mainz in the 13th and 14th centuries as a *Mautturm* (watch tower and toll station) for their fortress, Ehrenfels, on the opposite shore (now a ruin). It was restored in neo-Gothic style by the king of Prussia in 1855, who also rebuilt Burg Sooneck.

The three castles open for visits near Trechtingshausen (turnoffs are signposted on B–9) will fascinate lovers of history and art. As you enter each castle's gateway, consider what a feat of engineering it was to have built such a massive *Burg* (fortress or castle) on the stony cliffs overlooking the Rhine. They have all lain in ruin once or more during their turbulent histories. Their outer walls and period rooms still evoke memories of Germany's medieval past as well as the 19th-century era of Rhine Romanticism. You can enjoy superb Rhine vistas from the castles' terraces, where coffee, cake, and local wines are served (except Monday). Reichenstein also serves meals.

Burg Rheinstein was the home of Rudolf von Habsburg from 1282 to 1286. To establish law and order on the Rhine, he destroyed the neighboring castles of Burg Reichenstein and Burg Sooneck and hanged their notorious robber barons from the oak trees around the Clemens Church, a late-Romanesque basilica near Trechtingshausen. The Gobelin tapestries, 15th-century stained glass, wall and ceiling frescoes, and antique furniture—including a rare "giraffe spinet" upon which Kaiser Wilhelm I is said to have tickled the ivories—are well worth seeing. In 2004 a new floor of royal apartments, featuring additional period rooms, was opened. Rheinstein was the first of many a Rhine ruin to be rebuilt by a royal Prussian family in the 19th century. ☎ 06721/6348 ⊕ *www.burg-rheinstein.de* 🎫 €4 🕐 *Mid-Mar.–mid-Nov., daily 9:30–5:30; mid-Nov.–mid-Mar., Mon.–Thurs. 2–5, Sun. 10–5* 🕐 *Terrace café closed Mon.*

Burg Reichenstein has collections of decorative cast-iron slabs (from ovens and historical room-heating devices), hunting weapons and armor, period rooms, and paintings. ☎ 06721/6117 🎫 €3.40 🕐 *Mar.–mid-Nov., Tues.–Sun. 10–6.*

Burg Sooneck, on the edge of the Soon (pronounced *zone*) Forest, houses a valuable collection of Empire, Biedermeier, and neo-Gothic furnishings, medieval weapons, and paintings from the Rhine Romantic era. ✉ *Niederheimbach* ☎ 06743/6064 ⊕ *www.burgen-rlp.de* 🎫 €2.60 🕐 *Apr.–Sept., Tues.–Sun. 10–6; Oct., Nov., and Jan.–Mar., Tues.–Sun. 10–5.*

Bacharach

❻ *16 km (10 mi) north of Bingen; ferry 3 km (2 mi) north of town, to Kaub.*

Bacharach, a derivative of the Latin *Bacchi ara* (altar of Bacchus), has long been associated with wine. Like Rüdesheim, Bingen, and Kaub, it was a shipping station where barrels would interrupt their Rhine journey for land transport. Wine from the town's most famous vineyard, the Bacharacher Hahn, is served on the KD Rhine steamers. In late June you can sample wines at the Weinblütenfest (vine blossom festival) in the side valley suburb of Steeg and, in early October, at the Winzerfest (wine festival) in Bacharach proper.

Park on the riverbank and enter the town through one of its medieval gateways. You can ascend the 14th-century town wall for a walk along the ramparts facing the Rhine, then stroll along the main street (one street, but three names: Koblenzer Strasse, Oberstrasse, and Mainzer Strasse) for a look at patrician manors, typically built around a *Hof* (courtyard), and half-timber houses. Haus Sickingen, Posthof, Zollhof, Rathaus (Town Hall), and Altes Haus are fine examples. The massive tower in the center of town belongs to the parish church of **St. Peter.** A good example of the transition from Romanesque to Gothic styles, it has an impressive four-story nave. From the parish church a set of stone steps (signposted) leads to Bacharach's landmark, the sandstone ruins of the Gothic **Werner Kapelle,** highly admired for its filigree tracery. The chapel's roof succumbed to falling rocks in 1689, when the French blew up Burg Stahleck. Originally a Staufen fortress (11th century), the castle lay dormant until 1925, when a youth hostel was built on the foundations. The sweeping views it affords are worth the 10-minute walk.

Where to Stay & Eat

★ **$–$$$** ✕ **Weinhaus Altes Haus.** Charming inside and out, this medieval half-timber house is a favorite setting for films and photos. The cheerful proprietor, Reni Weber, uses the freshest ingredients possible and buys her meat and game from local butchers and hunters. *Rieslingrahmsuppe* (Riesling cream soup), *Reibekuchen* (potato pancakes), and the hearty *Hunsrücker Tellerfleisch* (boiled beef with horseradish sauce) are favorites, in addition to the seasonal specialties. She offers a good selection of wines from the family's vineyards. ⊠ *Oberstr. 61* ☎ *06743/1209* ☐ *AE, MC, V* ☉ *Closed Wed. and Dec.–Easter.*

¢ ✕ **Gutsausschank Zum Grünen Baum.** Winegrower Fritz Bastian runs this cozy tavern in a half-timber house (1579). He is the sole owner of the vineyard Insel Heyles'en Werth, on the island opposite Bacharach. The "wine carousel" is a great way to sample a full range of flavors and styles (15 wines) under the tutelage of the congenial host. Snacks are served (from 1 PM), including delicious homemade, air-dried *Schinken* (ham); sausages; and cheese. ⊠ *Oberstr. 63* ☎ *06743/1208* ☐ *No credit cards* ☉ *Closed Thurs. and Feb.*

$ ✕▦ **RheinHotel Andreas Stüber.** This friendly, family operation offers modern rooms (each named after a vineyard) with Rhine or castle views. The restaurant ($–$$) has an excellent selection of Bacharacher wines to help wash down hearty regional specialties, such as *Hinkelsdreck* (chicken liver pâté), *Rieslingbraten* (beef marinated in wine), or *Wildschwein Sauerbraten* (wild boar sauerbraten). ⊠ *Langstr. 50, on town wall, D–55422* ☎ *06743/1243* 🖷 *06743/1413* ⊕ *www.rhein-hotel-bacharach.de* ➴ *14 rooms, 1 apartment* ⟳ *Restaurant, fans, minibars, cable TV, bicycles, lounge, Weinstube, shop, laundry service, business services, some pets allowed (fee); no smoking* ☐ *MC, V* ☉ *Closed Nov.–mid-Mar. Restaurant closed Tues.* ⚞⚟ *BP.*

$–$$ ⊡ **Altkölnischer Hof.** Flowers line the windows of the Scherschlicht family's pretty, half-timber hotel near market square. The rooms are simply but attractively furnished in country style, and some have balconies. ⊠ *Blücherstr. 2, D–55422* ☎ *06743/1339* 🖷 *06743/2793* ⊕ *www. hotel-bacharach-rhein.de* ⟿ *20 rooms, 2 suites* ⌂ *Restaurant, some minibars, cable TV, bicycles, Weinstube, Internet, business services, some pets allowed (fee), no-smoking rooms; no a/c* ⊟ *MC, V* ⊙ *Closed Nov.–Mar.* ⟦⊙⟧ *BP.*

Kaub

❼ *19 km (12 mi) north of Rüdesheim; ferry from Bacharach.*

The village of Kaub (pronounced *cowp*), once a major customs post, has profited from its slate quarries and wine for centuries. On New Year's Eve 1813–14, General Blücher led his troops from here across the Rhine on a pontoon bridge of barges to expel Napoleon's troops from the Rhineland. The small **Blüchermuseum** with furnishings and militaria from that time is housed in his former headquarters. ⊠ *Metzgerg. 6* ☎ *06774/400* 🖾 *€2* ⊙ *Apr.–Oct., Tues.–Sun. 11–4; Nov.–Mar., Tues.–Sun. 2–5.*

★ ℃ Pfalzgrafenstein castle—known locally as the Pfalz—is built on a rock in the middle of the Rhine. Originally a five-sided tower, it was later enclosed by a six-sided defense wall that makes it look like a stone ship anchored in the Rhine. It was never destroyed. Unlike the elaborate period rooms of many Rhine castles, the Pfalz provides a good look at sparse medieval living quarters and has an interesting collection of ordinary household goods. ☎ *0172/262–2800* ⊕ *www.burgen-rlp.de* 🖾 *€4.10, including boat ride to and from Kaub* ⊙ *Apr.–Sept., Tues.–Sun. 10–1 and 2–6; Oct., Nov., and Jan.–Mar., Tues.–Sun. 10–1 and 2–5.*

Where to Stay & Eat

$ ✕⊡ **Zum Turm.** Set next to a medieval *Turm* (tower) near the Rhine, this little inn offers spacious, comfortable guest rooms on the floors above its cozy restaurant ($–$$$$) and terrace. Any fish, game, and produce chef Harald Kutsche can't find at local farms are imported from the market stalls of Paris. For a starter try the home-smoked salmon or splurge on anglerfish on lobster ragout. The daily set menus are excellent options. The Mittelrhein and Rheingau are the focus of the wine list. ⊠ *Zollstr. 50, D–56349* ☎ *06774/92200* 🖷 *06774/922–011* ⊕ *www. rhein-hotel-turm.com* ⟿ *6 rooms* ⌂ *Restaurant, in-room data ports, minibars, cable TV, bicycles, laundry service, Internet, business services, some pets allowed (fee), no-smoking rooms* ⊟ *AE, DC, MC, V* ⊙ *Hotel and restaurant closed 1 wk in Jan., 1 wk in Aug., and 1st half Nov. Restaurant closed Tues.; lunch weekdays on request only Nov.–Mar.* ⟦⊙⟧ *BP.*

Oberwesel

❽ *8 km (5 mi) north of Bacharach.*

Oberwesel retains its medieval silhouette. Sixteen of the original 21 towers and much of the town wall still stand in the shadow of Schönburg

Castle. The "town of towers" is also renowned for its Riesling wines, celebrated at a lively wine festival, the Weinmarkt, during the first half of September. Both Gothic churches on opposite ends of town are worth visiting. The **Liebfrauenkirche** (Church of Our Lady), popularly known as the "red church" because of its brightly colored exterior, has a superb rood screen, masterful sculptures, tombstones and paintings, and one of Germany's oldest altars (1331). Set on a hill, **St. Martin**—the so-called white church—with a fortresslike tower, has beautifully painted vaulting and a magnificent baroque altar.

Where to Stay & Eat

$–$$ ✕ **Historische Weinwirtschaft.** Tables in the flower-laden garden in front of this lovingly restored stone house are at a premium in summer, yet seats in the nooks and crannies indoors are just as inviting. Dark beams, exposed stone walls, and antique furniture set the mood on the ground and first floors, and the vaulted cellar houses contemporary art exhibitions. Ask Iris Marx, the ebullient proprietor, to translate the menu (it's in local dialect) of regional dishes. She offers country cooking at its best. The wine list is excellent and features 32 wines by the glass. ⊠ *Liebfrauenstr. 17* ☎ *06744/8186* ⊕ *www.historische-weinwirtschaft.de* ▤ *AE, MC, V* ⊗ *Closed Tues. and Jan. No lunch except Sun. May–Sept.*

$$–$$$ ✕▥ **Burghotel Auf Schönburg.** Part of the Schönburg Castle complex (12th
FodorśChoice century) has been lovingly restored as a romantic hotel and restaurant
★ ($$–$$$$; closed Monday except for hotel guests, who can opt for a prix-fixe dinner), with terraces in the courtyard and overlooking the Rhine. Antique furnishings and historical rooms (library, chapel, prison tower) make for an unforgettable stay, enhanced by the extraordinarily friendly, personal service of your hosts, the Hüttls, and staff. If you have only a night or two in the area, go for this hotel's first-rate lodging, food, and wine. Luggage transfer from the parking lot below the entrance is easily arranged at the front desk. The winding, uphill route to the hotel is signposted ⊠ *D–55430* ☎ *06744/93930* 🖷 *06744/1613* ⊕ *www.hotelschoenburg.com* ▱ *20 rooms, 2 suites* ⟲ *Restaurant, some in-room data ports, minibars, cable TV, lounge, library, some pets allowed (fee), nosmoking rooms; no a/c* ▤ *MC, V* ⊗ *Hotel and restaurant closed Jan.–Mar.* ❯◎❮ *BP.*

$–$$ ✕▥ **Römerkrug.** Rooms with exposed beams, pretty floral prints, and historic furnishings are tucked within the half-timber facade (1458) of Elke Matzner's small inn on the market square. Fish and game are house specialties ($–$$$), but there's also light cuisine with Asian accents as well as Rhine specialties, such as Himmel und Erde. There's a well-chosen selection of Mittelrhein wines. ⊠ *Marktpl. 1, D–55430* ☎ *06744/7091* 🖷 *06744/1677* ⊕ *www.roemerkrug.de* ▱ *6 rooms, 1 apartment* ⟲ *Restaurant, cable TV, some pets allowed; no a/c* ▤ *MC, V* ⊗ *Hotel closed Jan. Restaurant closed Wed. and Jan.* ❯◎❮ *BP.*

St. Goar

❾ *7 km (4½ mi) north of Oberwesel; ferry to St. Goarshausen.*

St. Goar and its counterpoint on the opposite shore, St. Goarshausen, are named after a Celtic missionary who settled here in the 6th century.

He became the patron saint of innkeepers—an auspicious sign for both towns, which now live off tourism and wine. September is especially busy, with Weinforum Mittelrhein (a major wine-and-food presentation in Burg Rheinfels) on the first weekend, and wine festivals and the splendid fireworks display "Rhine in Flames" on the third weekend.

St. Goar's tomb once rested in the 15th-century collegiate church, the **Stiftskirche,** built over a Romanesque crypt reminiscent of those of churches in Speyer and Köln. ⊠ *Kirchpl.* ⊙ *Apr.–Oct., daily 11–5.*

The castle ruins of **Burg Rheinfels,** overlooking the town, bear witness to the fact that St. Goar was once the best-fortified town in the Mittelrhein. From its beginnings in 1245, it was repeatedly enlarged by the counts of Katzenelnbogen, a powerful local dynasty, and their successors, the landgraves of Hesse. Although it repelled Louis IV's troops in 1689, Rheinfels was blasted by the French in 1797. Take time for a walk through the impressive ruins and the museum, which has an exquisite model of how the fortress looked in its heyday. To avoid the steep ascent on foot, buy a round-trip ticket (€3) for the *Burgexpress,* which departs from the bus stop on Heerstrasse, opposite the riverside parking lot for tour buses. ⊠ *Off Schlossberg Str.* ☎ *06741/383* ⊕ *www. burg-rheinfels.com* ⊠ *€4* ⊙ *Mid-Mar.–Oct., daily 9–6; Nov.–mid-Mar., weekends, weather permitting, 10–4.*

Where to Stay & Eat

★ **$$** ✕⊞ **Schloss-Hotel & Villa Rheinfels.** Directly opposite Burg Rheinfels, this hotel offers modern comfort and expansive views from the terrace of its restaurant, Auf Scharfeneck ($$–$$$; try to book a window alcove—Nos. 51, 52, 61, or 62). Game from the Hunsrück Hills or the *Wispertal Forelle* (trout from the Wisper Valley) are recommended, as are the seasonal specialties. In 2004 spa facilities and a second terrace overlooking the Rhine were added. ⊠ *Schlossberg 47, D–56329* ☎ *06741/8020* 🖷 *06741/802–802* ⊕ *www.schlosshotel-rheinfels.de* ⮡ *60 rooms, 4 suites* ⋄ *2 restaurants, snack bar, some in-room data ports, minibars, cable TV, indoor pool, sauna, spa, steam room, Turkish bath, (2) tennis courts, bicycles, bar, lobby lounge, shop, Internet, business services, babysitting, dry cleaning, laundry service, some pets allowed (fee); no a/c* ⊟ *AE, DC, MC, V* ⦿⦿ *BP.*

$–$$ ✕⊞ **Hotel Landsknecht.** The Nickenig family makes everyone feel at home in its riverside restaurant ($–$$) and hotel north of St. Goar. Daughter Martina, a former wine queen, and her wine-maker husband, Joachim Lorenz, operate the Vinothek, where you can sample his delicious Bopparder Hamm wines. These go well with the restaurant's hearty local dishes, such as Rhine-style sauerbraten or seasonal specialties (asparagus, game). Rooms are individually furnished and quite comfortable; some offer a Rhine view (Nos. 4, 5, and 8 are especially nice). ⊠ *Rheinuferstr. (B–9), D–56329 St. Goar–Fellen* ☎ *06741/2011* 🖷 *06741/ 7499* ⊕ *www.hotel-landsknecht.de* ⮡ *14 rooms, 1 suite, 2 apartments* ⋄ *Restaurant, in-room data ports, minibars, cable TV, bicycles, shop, laundry service, some pets allowed (fee), no-smoking rooms; no a/c* ⊟ *AE, DC, MC, V* ⊙ *Hotel and restaurant closed Jan. and Feb.* ⦿⦿ *BP.*

Shopping

The two **Montag shops** (⊠ Heerstr. 128 ☎ 06741/2488 ⊠ Schlossberg 2 ☎ 06741/93093) sell highly esteemed "made in Germany" collectibles: 12 dozen different beer steins; elaborate pewter drinking vessels; superb German cutlery; and a zoo of Steiff stuffed animals and teddy bears (in the Schlossberg location). Videos, CDs, and cassettes highlighting the region's landscape and folk music are also for sale. They issue tax-free documents and ship worldwide.

St. Goarshausen

❿ *29 km (18 mi) north of Rüdesheim, ferry from St. Goar.*

St. Goarshausen lies at the foot of two 14th-century castles whose names, Katz (cat) and Maus (mouse), reflect but one of the many power plays on the Rhine in the Middle Ages. Territorial supremacy and the concomitant privilege of collecting tolls fueled the fires of rivalry. In response to the construction of Burg Rheinfels, the archbishop of Trier erected a small castle north of St. Goarshausen to protect his interests. In turn the masters of Rheinfels, the counts of Katzenelnbogen, built a bigger castle directly above the town. Its name was shortened to Katz, and its smaller neighbor was scornfully referred to as Maus. Katz is not open to the public. **Maus** has a terrace café (great views) and demonstrations featuring eagles and falcons in flight. ☎ 06771/7669 ⊕ *www.burg-maus.de* ⊠ *€6.50* ⊗ *Mid-Mar.–mid-Oct., Mon.–Sat. at 11 and 2:30, Sun. at 11, 2:30, and 4:30.*

Some 10 km (6 mi) north of the Maus castle, near Kamp-Bornhofen, is a castle duo separated by a "quarrel wall": **Liebenstein and Sterrenberg,** known as the *Feindliche Brüder* (rival brothers). Both impressive ruins have terrace cafés that afford good views.

One of the Rhineland's main attractions lies 4 km (2½ mi) south of St. Goarshausen: the steep (430-foot-high) slate cliff named after the beautiful blond nymph **Loreley.** Here she sat, singing songs so lovely that sailors and fishermen were lured to the treacherous rapids—and their demise. The legend stems from a tale by Clemens Brentano, retold as a ballad by Heinrich Heine and set to music by Friedrich Silcher at the height of Rhine Romanticism in the 19th century. The summit is a great vantage point.

off the beaten path

BESUCHERZENTRUM LORELEY – The 10-minute film and hands-on exhibits at this visitor center are entertaining ways to learn about the region's flora and fauna, geology, wine, shipping, and, above all, the myth of the Loreley. You can stock up on souvenirs in the shop and have a snack at the bistro before heading for the nearby vantage point at the cliff's summit. Hiking trails are signposted in the landscaped park. ⊠ *Auf der Loreley* ☎ 06771/599–093 ⊕ *www.besucherzentrum-loreley.de* ⊠ *€2.50* ⊗ *Apr.–Oct., Tues.–Sun. 10–5.*

Boppard

🔟 *17 km (11 mi) north of St. Goar; ferry to Filsen.*

Boppard is a pleasant little resort that evolved from a Celtic settlement into a Roman fortress, Frankish royal court, and Free Imperial City. The Roman garrison Bodobrica, established here in the 4th century, was enclosed by a 26-foot-high rectangular wall (1,010 by 505 feet) with 28 defense towers. You can see portions of these in the fascinating open-air **archaeological park** (⊠ Angertstr. near B–9 and the railroad tracks). The **Stadtmuseum** (town museum), housed in the 14th-century Kurfürstliche Burg (elector's castle) built by the archbishop of Trier, has exhibits on Boppard's Roman and medieval past, as well as an extensive collection of bentwood furniture designed by the town's favorite son, Michael Thonet (1796–1871). The cane-bottom *Stuhl Nr. 14* (Chair No. 14) is the famous classic found in coffeehouses around the world since 1859. ⊠ *Burgstr.near ferry dock* ☎ *06742/10369* 🎟 *Free* ☉ *Apr.–Oct., Tues.–Sun. 10–12:30 and 1:30–5.*

Excavations in the 1960s revealed ancient Roman baths beneath the twin-tower, Romanesque **Severuskirche** (Church of St. Severus; 1236) on the market square. The large triumphal crucifix over the main altar and a lovely statue of a smiling Madonna date from the 13th century. Two baroque altars dominate the interior of the Gothic **Karmeliterkirche** (Carmelite Church) on Karmeliterstrasse, near the Rhine. It houses intricately carved choir stalls and tombstones and several beautiful Madonnas. Winegrowers still observe the old custom of laying the first-picked *Trauben* (grapes) at the foot of the Traubenmadonna (1330) to ensure a good harvest. The annual wine festival takes place in late September, just before the Riesling harvest.

On the northern edge of Boppard, the Rhine makes its largest loop, skirting the majestic hillside vineyard known as the **Bopparder Hamm.** From the Mühltal station, let the *Sessellift* (chairlift) whisk you 1,300 feet uphill to the **Vierseenblick** (four-lake vista), a vantage point from which the Rhine looks like a chain of lakes. 🎟 *Round trip €6.20, one way €4.20* ☉ *Apr.–Oct., daily 10–5.*

Where to Stay & Eat

$$ ✕🏨 **Best Western Hotel Bellevue.** You can enjoy a Rhine view from many of the rooms in this traditional hotel or from the terrace next to the pretty Rhine promenade. Afternoon tea, dinner, and Sunday lunch are served in the main restaurant ($$$), Le Chopin. Le Bristol ($$) has fabulous luncheon buffets. Both restaurants serve specialties using local products, such as Hunsrück beef, or lamb from the meadows of Bacharach. ⊠ *Rheinallee 41, D–56154* ☎ *06742/1020* 🖨 *06742/102–602* ⊕ *www. bellevue-boppard.de* ⇥ *92 rooms, 1 suite* ⚹ *2 restaurants, some in-room data ports, minibars, indoor pool, gym, spa, steam room, sauna, bar, recreation room, shop, babysitting, laundry service, Internet, business services, some pets allowed (fee), no-smoking rooms; no a/c in some rooms* ⊟ *AE, DC, MC, V* ☉ *Le Chopin closed Mon. No lunch Mon.–Sat.*

¢–$ ╳▦ **Weinhaus Heilig Grab.** This wine estate's tavern (¢), Boppard's oldest, is full of smiling faces: the wines are excellent, the fare is simple but hearty, and the welcome is warm. Old chestnut trees shade tables in the courtyard. Rooms are furnished with rustic pine furniture. If you'd like to visit the cellars or vineyards, ask your friendly hosts, Rudolf and Susanne Schoeneberger. They also arrange wine tastings. ⊠ *Zelkesg. 12, D–56154* ☎ *06742/2371* 🖷 *06742/81220* ⊕ *www.heiliggrab.de* 🖙 *5 rooms* ♿ *Restaurant, cable TV, shop, no-smoking rooms; no a/c, no room phones* ▤ *MC, V* ⊘ *Hotel closed Nov.–Easter. Restaurant closed Tues. No lunch* ◯| *BP.*

Sports & the Outdoors

HIKING   The 10-km (6-mi) **Weinwanderweg** (Wine Hiking Trail) through the Bopparder Hamm, from Boppard to Spay, begins north of town on Peternacher Weg. Many other marked trails in the vicinity are outlined on maps and in brochures available from the tourist office.

en route   On the outskirts of Koblenz, the neo-Gothic towers of **Schloss Stolzenfels** come into view. The castle's origins date from the mid-13th century, when the archbishop of Trier sought to counter the influence (and toll rights) of the archbishop of Mainz, who had just built Burg Lahneck, a castle at the confluence of the Lahn and Rhine rivers. Its superbly furnished period rooms and beautiful gardens are well worth a visit. It's a wonderful setting for concerts. From B–9 (curbside parking) it's about a 15-minute walk to the castle entrance. ☎ *0261/51656* ⊕ *www.burgen-rlp.de* 🖾 *€2.60* ⊘ *Apr.–Sept., Tues.–Sun. 10–6; Oct., Nov., and Jan.–Mar., Tues.–Sun. 10–5.*

On the eastern shore overlooking the town of Braubach is the **Marksburg.** Built in the 12th century to protect the silver and lead mines in the area, it's the only land-based castle on the Rhine to have survived the centuries intact. Within its massive walls are a collection of weapons and manuscripts, a medieval botanical garden, and a snack bar. ☎ *02627/206* ⊕ *www.deutsche-burgen.org* 🖾 *€4.50* ⊘ *Easter–Oct., daily 10–5; Nov.–late Dec. and Jan.–Easter, daily 11–4; snack bar open daily.*

Koblenz

20 km (12 mi) north of Boppard.

The ancient city of Koblenz is at a geographic nexus known as the **Deutsches Eck** (German Corner) in the heart of the Mittelrhein region. Rivers and mountains converge here: the Mosel flows into the Rhine on one side; the Lahn flows in on the other a few miles south; and three mountain ridges intersect. Koblenz is one of the Rhineland-Palatinate's cultural, administrative, and business centers.

Founded by the Romans in AD 9, the city was first called Castrum ad Confluentes (Fort at the Confluence). It became a powerful city in the Middle Ages, when it controlled trade on both the Rhine and the Mosel. Air raids during World War II destroyed 85% of the city, but extensive restoration has done much to re-create its former atmosphere. English-speaking walking tours of the Old Town can be arranged by the tourist office on request.

⑫ Koblenz is centered on the west bank of the Rhine. On the east bank stands Europe's largest fortress, **Festung Ehrenbreitstein**, offering a commanding view from 400 feet above the river. The earliest buildings date from about 1100, but the bulk of the fortress was constructed in the 16th century. In 1801 it was partially destroyed by Napoléon, and the French occupied Koblenz for the next 18 years. As for the fortress's 16th-century Vogel Greif cannon, the French absconded with it in 1794, the Germans took it back in 1940, and the French commandeered it again in 1945. The 15-ton cannon was peaceably returned by French president François Mitterrand in 1984 and is now part of the exhibit on the history of local technologies, from wine growing to industry, in the fortress's **Landesmuseum** (State Museum; ☎ 0261/97030 🖃 €3.10, including fortress grounds ⊗ mid-Mar.–mid-Nov., daily 9:30–5).

To reach the fortress on the east bank of the Rhine, take Bus No. 9 from the train station or the **ferry** (☎ 0261/72783 🖃 €2.40 round-trip ⊗ Mar.–Apr., Oct., and Nov., daily 8–5; May–Sept., daily 8–7) from the Pegelhaus on the Koblenz riverbank (near Rheinstrasse). Take the **Sesselbahn** (Cable car; 🖃 €6.90 round-trip, including fortress grounds ⊗ Apr., May, and Oct., daily 10–4:50; June–Aug., daily 9–5:50; Sept., daily 10–5:50) to ascend to the fortress. For the best value, purchase the combination ticket that includes the grounds, museum, and a 45-minute tour. ☎ 0261/974–2440 🖃 *Grounds €1.10, combined ticket and tour €4.20* ⊗ *Mid-Mar.–mid-Nov., daily 9–5.*

⑬ The **Pfaffendorfer Brücke** (Pfaffendorf Bridge) marks the beginning of the Old Town. Just off the Pfaffendorf Bridge, between the modern blocks **⑭** of the Rhein-Mosel-Halle and the Hotel Mercure, is the **Weindorf** (⊕ www.weindorf-koblenz.de), a wine "village" constructed for a mammoth exhibition of German wines in 1925, which is now a restaurant.

⑮ The **Rheinanlagen** (Rhine Gardens), a 10-km (6-mi) promenade, runs along the riverbank past the Weindorf. Strolling along the promenade toward **⑯** town, you'll pass the gracious **Kurfürstliches Schloss**, the prince-elector's palace. It was built in 1786 by Prince-Elector Clemens Wenzeslaus as an elegant escape from the grim Ehrenbreitstein fortress. He lived here for only three years, however; in 1791 he was forced to flee to Augsburg when the French stormed the city. The palace is used for city offices and is closed to visitors. It's open to the public the first Sunday in May for *Wein im Schloss,* a large presentation of Lower Mosel, Nahe, Mittelrhein, and Ahr wines. In the garden behind the palace, don't miss the handsome statue of "Father Rhine & Mother Mosel."

⑰ The squat form of the **Rheinkran** (Rhine Crane), built in 1611, is one of Koblenz's landmarks. Marks on the side of the building indicate the heights reached by floodwaters of bygone years. In the mid-19th century a pontoon bridge consisting of a row of barges spanned the Rhine here; when ships approached, two or three barges were simply towed out of the way to let them through.

18 The **Deutsches Eck** (German Corner) is at the sharp intersection of the Rhine and Mosel, a pointed bit of land jutting into the river like the prow of some early ironclad warship. One of the more effusive manifestations of German nationalism—an 1897 statue of Kaiser Wilhelm I, first emperor of the newly united Germany—was erected here. It was destroyed at the end of World War II and replaced in 1953 with a ponderous, altarlike monument to Germany's unity. After German reunification a new statue of Wilhelm was placed atop this monument in 1993. Pieces of the Berlin Wall stand on the Mosel side—a memorial to those who died as a result of the partitioning of the country.

From the Deutsches Eck, the Moselanlagen (Mosel Promenade) leads to Koblenz's oldest restaurant, the Deutscher Kaiser, which marks the start of the Old Town.

19 The **Ludwig Museum** stands just behind the Deutsches Eck, housed in the spick-and-span Deutschherrenhaus, a restored 13th-century building. Industrialist Peter Ludwig, one of Germany's leading contemporary art collectors, has filled this museum with part of his huge collection. ✉ *Danziger Freiheit 1* ☎ *0261/304–040* ⊕ *www.ludwigmuseum.de* 💶 *€2.50, combined ticket with Mittelrhein Museum €3.50* 🕐 *Tues.–Sat. 10:30–5, Sun. 11–6.*

★ ❷⓿ The **St. Kastor Kirche** (St. Castor Church) is a sturdy Romanesque basilica consecrated in 836. It was here in 842 that plans were drawn for the Treaty of Verdun, formalizing the division of Charlemagne's great empire and leading to the creation of Germany and France as separate states. Inside, compare the squat Romanesque columns in the nave with the intricate fan vaulting of the Gothic sections. The **St. Kastor Fountain** outside the church is an intriguing piece of historical one-upmanship. It was built by the occupying French to mark the beginning of Napoléon's ultimately disastrous Russian campaign of 1812. ⊠ *Kastorhof* ☉ *Daily 9–6 except during services.*

The **Mittelrhein Museum** houses the city's art collection in a lovely 16th-century building near the Old Town's central square, Am Plan. ⊠ *Florinsmarkt 15* ☎ *0261/129–2520* ⊕ *www.mittelrhein-museum.de* 🖪 *€2.50, combined ticket with Ludwig Museum €3.50* ☉ *Tues.–Sat. 10:30–5, Sun. 11–6.*

❷⓵ War damage is evidenced by the blend of old buildings and modern store blocks on and around Am Plan. The **Liebfrauenkirche** (Church of Our Lady) stands on Roman foundations at the Old Town's highest point. The bulk of the church is of Romanesque design, but its choir is one of the Rhineland's finest examples of 15th-century Gothic architecture, and the west front is graced with two 17th-century baroque towers. ⊠ *Am Plan* ☉ *Mon.–Sat. 8–6, Sun. 9–8 except during services.*

Where to Stay & Eat

$–$$ ✕ **Café Einstein.** Portraits of Einstein line the walls of this lively café-restaurant-bar just off Görresplatz. The friendly Tayhus family serves tasty fare daily, from a hearty breakfast buffet (brunch on Sunday—reservations recommended) to late-night finger food. Fish is a specialty in summer. This place fills up quickly on nights with live music—jazz on Wednesday and Thursday, contemporary music on Friday and Saturday. ⊠ *Firmungstr. 30* ☎ *0261/914–4999* ▤ *DC, MC, V.*

¢–$$ ✕ **Grand Café.** The multistory atrium of a historic house (once a furniture store) has been turned into a very classy yet comfortable meeting point. From early morning until late at night, food and drinks are served amid fabulous art nouveau decor, complete with huge palm trees. Thursday through Saturday, the lower level is a disco. Thursday evening (5–9) there's a cigar club on the upper level. The huge terrace on Görres Square is a perfect spot for people-watching and soaking up the sun. ⊠ *Firmungstr. 2, Am Görrespl.* ☎ *0261/100–5833* ▤ *AE, MC, V.*

¢–$$ ✕ **Weindorf–Koblenz.** The Bastian family has upgraded the food and wine selection at this reconstructed "wine village" of half-timber houses grouped around a tree-shaded courtyard. Fresh renditions of traditional Rhine and Mosel specialties, a good selection of local wines, and a fabulous Sunday brunch—wine, beer and nonalcoholic beverages are included in the price (€20)—make this a popular spot. ⊠ *Julius-Wegeler-Str. 2-4* ☎ *0261/133–7190* ▤ *AE, MC, V* ☉ *Closed Mon. Nov.–Mar.*

$ ✕ **Weinhaus Hubertus.** Hunting scenes and trophies line the wood-panel walls of this cozy wine restaurant named after the patron saint of hunters. Karin and Dieter Spahl serve hearty portions of traditional fare, such as Himmel und Erde, and local wines. Try their dessert specials,

Feigenmus (fig puree) and *Tête de Moine* cheese, served with a glass of the rare dessert wine Beerenauslese. ⊠ *Florinsmarkt 6* ☎ *0261/31177* ⊟ *AE, DC, MC, V* ⊘ *Closed Tues. No lunch.*

¢–$ ✕ **Circus Maximus.** Here's a laid-back setting for breakfast, lunch, dinner, or drinks with live music and theme parties from Thursday to Saturday evening. Weekdays, the *Mittagstisch* (luncheon special) at €4.80 is an excellent value. The menu offers everything from sandwiches, salads, and baked potatoes to potato gratins, steaks, and pizza. New items include couscous with chicken and hummus. ⊠ *Stegemannstr. 30, at Viktoriastr.* ☎ *0261/300–2357* ⊟ *No credit cards* ⊘ *No lunch weekends.*

★ $ ✕🏠 **Zum weissen Schwanen.** Guests have found a warm welcome in this half-timber inn and mill since 1693, a tradition carried on by the Kunz family. Located next to a 13th-century town gateway, this is a charming place to overnight or enjoy well-prepared, contemporary German cuisine ($–$$$) and excellent local wines. Brasserie Brentano ($) serves lighter fare and Sunday brunch. Rooms are individually decorated with period furniture ranging from Biedermeier to Belle Epoque. ⊠ *Brunnenstr. 4, D–56338 Braubach, 12 km (7½ mi) south of Koblenz via B–42* ☎ *02627/9820* 🖨 *02627/8802* ⊕ *www.zum-weissen-schwanen.de* 🛏 *19 rooms, 1 suite* ⟐ *2 restaurants, some in-room data ports, some minibars, cable TV, bicycles, bar, lounge, babysitting, dry cleaning, laundry service, some pets allowed, no-smoking rooms; no a/c* ⊟ *AE, DC, MC, V* ⊘ *Restaurant closed Wed. and Jan. No lunch Mon.–Sat. Brasserie closed Sat. No dinner Sun.* ⏉⏉ *BP.*

$$–$$$ 🏠 **Hotel Mercure.** This modern high-rise on the Rhine is next to the city's conference and events center, the Rhein-Mosel-Halle, and within a short walk of all major sights. Rooms are modern and well appointed; rooms on the fifth floor and above have fabulous Rhine views. ⊠ *Julius-Wegeler-Str. 6, D–56068* ☎ *0261/1360* 🖨 *0261/136–1199* ⊕ *www.mercure.com* 🛏 *167 rooms, 1 suite* ⟐ *2 restaurants, minibars, cable TV, gym, hot tub, sauna, bicycles, bar, dry cleaning, laundry service, Internet, business services, some pets allowed (fee), no-smoking rooms* ⊟ *AE, DC, MC, V* ⏉⏉*BP.*

Nightlife & the Arts

The **Staatsorchester Rheinische Philharmonie** (Rhenish Philharmonic Orchestra; ⊠ Julius-Wegeler-Str. ☎ 0261/301–2272) plays regularly in the Rhein-Mosel-Halle. The gracious neoclassic **Theater der Stadt Koblenz** (⊠ Clemensstr. 1–5 ☎ 0261/129–2840), built in 1787, is still in regular use.

Night owls frequent the bar and Abaco Club (a disco Thursday–Saturday) at **Grand Café** (⊠ Firmungstr. 2, Am Görrespl. ☎ 0261/100–5833). **Café Einstein** (⊠ Firmungstr. 30, near Görresplatz ☎ 0261/914–4999) usually has live music Wednesday to Saturday nights. **Circus Maximus** (⊠ Stegemannstr. 30, at Viktoriastr. ☎ 0261/300–2357) offers disco sounds, live music, and theme parties from Thursday to Saturday. For Latin American music and good cocktails, head for **Enchilada** (⊠ Gerichtsstr. 2 ☎ 0261/100–4666). There are also many pubs and bars on or near Florinsmarkt. **Café Hahn** (⊠ Neustr. 15 ☎ 0261/42302), in the suburb of Güls, features everything from cabaret and stand-up comedians to popular musicians and bands.

Shopping

Koblenz's most pleasant shopping is in the Old City streets around the market square Am Plan. **Löhr Center** (⌧ Hohenfelder Str., at Am Wöllershof), a modern, American-style, windowless mall, has some 130 shops and restaurants and will give you an authentic German shopping experience.

---

en route Take a fascinating walk through the **Garten der Schmetterlinge Schloss Sayn** (Garden of Butterflies), where butterflies from South America, Asia, and Africa flit back and forth over your head between the branches of banana trees and palms. The palace proper houses a small local history museum, a restaurant, and a café. It's 15 km (9 mi) north of Koblenz (Bendorf exit off B–42). ⌧ *Im Fürstlichen Schlosspark, D–56170 Bendorf-Sayn* ☎ *02622/15478* ⊕ *www.sayn. de* ☞ *Butterfly garden and museum €6* ☼ *Mar.–Sept., daily 9–6; Oct., daily 10–5; Nov., daily 10–4.*

THE MOSEL VALLEY

Updated by
Kerry Brady

The Mosel is one of the most hauntingly beautiful river valleys on Earth. Here, as in the Rhine Valley, forests and vines carpet steep hillsides; castles and church spires dot the landscape; and medieval wine villages line the riverbanks. The Mosel landscape is no less majestic, but it's less narrow and more peaceful than that of the Rhine Gorge; the river's countless bends and loops slow its pace and lend the region a special charm.

From Koblenz to Treis-Karden, two roads run parallel to the Mosel: B–416 (west side) and B–49 (east side). Thereafter, only one road continues upstream, occasionally traversing the river as it winds toward Trier: until Alf, it's B–49; afterward, B–53.

The signposted routes between Koblenz and Trier include the Mosel Weinstrasse (Mosel Wine Road) along the riverbank and, on the heights, the hiking trails on both sides of the river known as the Moselhöhenweg. The latter extends 224 km (140 mi) on the Hunsrück (eastern) side and 164 km (102 mi) on the Eifel (western) side of the river. Driving time for the river route is at least three hours. On the autobahn (A–1) the distance between Koblenz and Trier can be covered in about an hour.

Winningen

㉒ *11 km (7 mi) southwest of Koblenz on B–416.*

Winningen is a gateway to the Terrassenmosel (Terraced Mosel), the portion of the river characterized by steep, terraced vineyards. Monorails and winches help winegrowers and their tools make the ascent, but tending and harvesting the vines are all done by hand. For a bird's-eye view of the valley, drive up Fährstrasse to Am Rosenhang, the start of a pleasant walk along the Weinlehrpfad (Educational Wine Path).

As you head upstream toward Kobern-Gondorf, you'll pass the renowned vineyard site Uhlen. In Kobern the Oberburg (upper castle) and the St.

Matthias Kapelle, a 12th-century chapel, are good vantage points. Near the market square in the village below, you can see an old half-timber house (1321), now quarters for Kobern's tourist office.

Where to Stay & Eat

★ $$ ✕▦ **Höreth im Wald/Alte Mühle.** At Thomas and Gudrun Höreth's country inn and restaurant ($$–$$$$), a labyrinth of little rooms and cellars is grouped around romantic oleander-lined courtyards. The menu offers something for every taste, but the absolute hits are the homemade cheeses, terrines, pâtés, and *Entensülze* (goose in aspic), served with the Höreths' own wines as well as mature Bordeaux selections. ⊠ *Mühlental 17, via B–416, D–56330 Kobern* ☎ *02607/6474* 🖷 *0261/6848* ⊕ *www. thomas-hoereth.de* ⇌ *10 rooms, 2 apartments nearby* ⚿ *Restaurant, cable TV, bicycles, shop, babysitting, dry cleaning, laundry service, business services, some pets allowed (fee), no-smoking rooms; no a/c* ⊟ *MC, V* ☺ *No lunch weekdays* ❡❙ *BP.*

$ ✕▦ **Halferschenke.** This *Schenke* (inn) was once an overnight stop for *Halfer*, who, with their horses, towed cargo-laden boats upstream. Today the stone-house inn (1832) is run by a friendly young couple, Thomas and Eva Balmes. Light walls, dark wood, and lots of candles and flowers are a lovely setting for his artfully prepared food ($$–$$$). An excellent selection of Terrassenmosel wines is available. The rooms, each named after an artist, are modern, airy, and bright. ⊠ *Hauptstr. 63, D–56332 Dieblich, Via B–49, opposite Kobern* ☎ *02607/1008* 🖷 *02607/960–294* ⊕ *www.halferschenke.de* ⇌ *4 rooms* ⚿ *Restaurant, some pets allowed; no a/c, no room phones, no TV in some rooms* ⊟ *AE, MC, V* ☺ *Restaurant closed Mon. No lunch Tues.–Sat.* ❡❙ *BP.*

Alken

㉓ *22 km (13½ mi) southwest of Koblenz.*

The 12th-century castle **Burg Thurant** towers over the village and the Burgberg (castle hill) vineyard. Wine and snacks are served in the courtyard; castle tours take in the chapel, cellar, tower, and a weapons display. Allow a good half hour for the climb from the riverbank. ☎ *02605/2004* ⊕ *www.thurant.de* ▣ *€3* ☺ *Mar.–Nov., daily 10–5; Dec.–Feb., weekends 10–4.*

Where to Stay & Eat

$–$$ ✕▦ **Burg Thurant.** The Kopowskis' stylish restaurant ($–$$) and guesthouse lie at the foot of the castle, next to a venerable stone tower on the riverbank (B–49). They serve tasty renditions of *Mosel Aal* (Mosel eel), *Bachforelle* (fresh stream trout) in almond butter, and *Entenbrust an Brombeerjus* (breast of duck in blackberry sauce), accompanied by wines from the region's finest producers. The guest rooms are outfitted with a mixture of antiques and country-style furnishings. ⊠ *Moselstr. 16, D–56332* ☎ *02605/3581* 🖷 *02605/2152* ⊕ *www.terrassenmosel. de* ⇌ *3 rooms* ⚿ *Restaurant, bicycles, Weinstube, laundry service, some pets allowed (fee), no-smoking rooms; no a/c, no room TVs* ⊟ *MC* ☺ *Hotel and restaurant closed Mon. and Feb. No lunch Mon.–Sat. Nov.–late May* ❡❙ *BP.*

en route

Burg Eltz (Eltz Castle) is one of Germany's most picturesque, genuinely medieval castles (12th–16th centuries) and merits as much attention as King Ludwig's trio of castles in Bavaria. The 40-minute tour, with excellent commentary on the castle's history and furnishings, guides you through the period rooms and massive kitchen but does not include the treasure chamber, a collection of fascinating artworks displayed in five historical rooms. In summer the lines are long, so bring some water, particularly if you're traveling with children. To get here, exit B–416 at Hatzenport (opposite and southwest of Alken), proceed to Münstermaifeld, and follow signs to the parking lot near the Antoniuskapelle. From here it's a 15-minute walk, or take the shuttle bus (€1.50). Hikers can reach the castle from Moselkern in 40 minutes. ✉ *Burg Eltz/Münstermaifeld* ☎ *02672/950–500* 🌐 *www.burg-eltz.de* 🎫 *Castle tour €6, treasure chamber €2.50* ⏲ *Apr.–Oct., daily 9:30–5:30.*

11

Treis-Karden

24 *39 km (24 mi) southwest of Koblenz; Karden is on B–416; Treis is on B–49.*

Treis-Karden consists of two towns joined for administrative purposes. You can visit the richly furnished Romanesque and Gothic **Stiftskirche St. Castor** (Church of St. Castor), named after the saint who introduced Christianity to the area in the middle of the 4th century, as well as is the **Stiftsmuseum** (Foundation Museum) in the historical tithe house (1238) behind the church. Exhibits illustrate Karden's history as a religious center, starting with the Celtic and Roman eras. The two stars on the weather vane symbolize the star of Bethlehem and allude to the church's precious "altar of the three kings," Europe's only remaining terra-cotta altar shrine (1420). Attend Sunday service to hear the magnificent baroque organ (1728) built by Johann Michael Stumm, founder of one of the world's greatest organ-building dynasties. ✉ *St.-Castor-Str. 1, Karden* ☎ *02672/6137* 🎫 *Museum €3* ⏲ *Easter and May–Oct., Wed.–Fri. 2–5, weekends 10–noon and 2–5.*

Where to Stay & Eat

$–$$ ✕🏨 **Schloss-Hotel Petry.** From a simple guesthouse a century ago, this family-run hotel has developed into a complex of buildings with very attractive, comfortably furnished rooms and modern facilities. House specialties at the two restaurants (Schloss Stube $$$, Weinstube $–$$) are *Mosel Aal,* eel cooked and served cold with a green herb sauce, and rib roast of lamb. The wine list has a good selection of Mosel wines. ✉ *St.-Castor-Str. 80 (B–416), D–56253* ☎ *02672/9340* 📠 *02672/934–440* 🌐 *www.schloss-hotel-petry.de* *55 rooms, 19 suites* *2 restaurants, in-room data ports, some minibars, cable TV, gym, hot tub, sauna, billiards, bowling, Ping-Pong, bar, lounge, shop, babysitting, dry cleaning, laundry service, business services, some pets allowed (fee), no-smoking rooms; no a/c* 💳 *AE, DC, MC, V restaurant only* ⏲ *Schloss Stube closed Tues. and Wed.* 🍽 *BP.*

Cochem

㉕ *51 km (31½ mi) southwest of Koblenz on B–49, approximately 93 km (58 mi) from Trier.*

Cochem is one of the most attractive towns of the Mosel Valley, with a riverside promenade to rival any along the Rhine. It's especially lively during the wine festivals in June and late August. If time permits, savor the landscape from the deck of a boat—many excursions are available, lasting from one hour to an entire day. The tourist office on Endertplatz has an excellent English-language outline for a walking tour of the town. From the **Enderttor** (Endert Town Gate) you can see the entrance to Germany's longest railway tunnel, the Kaiser-Wilhelm, an astonishing example of 19th-century engineering. The 4-km-long (2½-mi-long) tunnel saves travelers a 21-km (13-mi) detour along one of the Mosel's great loops.

The 15-minute walk to the **Reichsburg** (Imperial Fortress), the 1,000-year-old castle overlooking the town, will reward you with great views of the area. Flight demonstrations (eagles and falcons) take place Tuesday through Sunday at 11, 1, 2:30, and 4. With advance reservations, you can get a taste of the Middle Ages at a medieval banquet, complete with costumes, music, and entertainment. Banquets take place on Friday (7 PM) and Saturday (6 PM), and last four hours; the price (€39) includes a castle tour. ☎ 02671/255 ⊕ *www.reichsburg-cochem.de* ✉ €4, *including 40-min tour; flight demonstration €3* ⊙ *Mid-Mar.–mid-Nov., daily 9–5.*

Historische Senfmühle. On tours of his 200-year-old mustard mill (daily at 11, 2, 3, and 4), Wolfgang Steffens shows how he produces his gourmet mustard. Garlic, cayenne, honey, curry, and even Riesling wine are among the types you can sample and purchase in the shop. From the Old Town, walk across the bridge toward Cond. The mill is to the left of the bridgehead. ⊠ *Stadionstr. 1* ☎ *02671/607–665* ⊕ *www. senfmuehle.net* ✉ *Tours €2* ⊙ *Daily 10–6.*

A ride on the **cable car** to the Pinner Kreuz provides great vistas. ⊠ *Endertstr.* ☎ *02671/989–063* ✉ *Round-trip €5.50* ⊙ *Late Mar.–mid-Nov., daily 10–6.*

Where to Stay & Eat

$–$$ ✕▥ **Alte Thorschenke.** Next to the Enderttor, near the river, this inn dates from 1332. Winding staircases, ancient wooden beams, and historic decor set the mood. Many of the rooms have period furniture (some with four-poster beds). Hunting trophies and portraits of prince electors adorn the wood-panel walls of the restaurant ($$–$$$). There's also a cozy Weinstube and a patio for alfresco dining. Highly recommended are the fresh trout and the *Wildplatte* (game platter). The parent firm, Weingut Freiherr von Landenberg, supplies the excellent Mosel wine and welcomes visitors to tour the estate. ⊠ *Brückenstr. 3, D–56812* ☎ *02671/ 7059* 🖶 *02671/4202* ⊕ *www.castle-thorschenke.com* ⇱ *31 rooms, 3 suites, 1 apartment* ♨ *Restaurant, minibars, cable TV, bicycles, Weinstube, shop, laundry service, some pets allowed (fee), no-smoking rooms; no a/c* ▭ *AE, DC, MC, V* ⦿I *BP.*

$–$$ ✕🏠 **Weissmühle.** This lovely inn is set amid the forested hills of the En-
derttal (Endert Valley) on the site of a historic mill dating from ca. 1820.
The fire department's efforts to put out a small fire in 1976 caused considerable water damage to the original half-timber construction, but the
present inn is lined with photos and memorabilia from the original
mill. It's an oasis from traffic and crowds yet only 2½ km (1½ mi) from
Cochem. The rooms are individually decorated—some in an elegant coun-
try-manor style, others with rustic farmhouse furnishings. Beneath the
exposed beams and painted ceiling of the restaurant ($$–$$$), food from
the hotel's own bakery, butcher shop, and trout farm will grace your
table. German and French wines are served. ⊠ *Im Enderttal, via Endertstr., toward Greimersburg; from A–48 exit Kaisersesch, D–56812*
☎ *02671/8955* 🖷 *02671/8207* ⊕ *www.weissmuehle.de* 🛏 *36 rooms*
⌂ *Restaurant, some in-room data ports, minibars, cable TV, sauna, spa,
steam room, bowling, bar, lounge, some pets allowed (fee); no a/c*
▤ *DC, MC, V* ⟟⟨ *BP.*

$ ✕🏠 **Lohspeicher–l'Auberge du Vin.** In times past, oak bark for leather tan-
ners was dried and stored in this house (1834) near the market square.
Today it's a charming inn with a pretty terrace, run by a vivacious young
couple, Ingo and Birgit Beth. His delicacies ($$–$$$) are a pleasure for
the palate and the eye. At least one saltwater and one freshwater fish
are featured daily. Some 20 French and Italian wines supplement the family's own estate-bottled wines. The rooms are pleasant and modern.
⊠ *Oberg. 1, at Marktpl., D–56812* ☎ *02671/3976* 🖷 *02671/1772*
🛏 *9 rooms* ⌂ *Restaurant, cable TV, shop, some pets allowed (fee), no-
smoking rooms; no a/c* ▤ *MC, V* ⊘ *Restaurant closed Wed.* ⟟⟨ *BP.*

⌜ **en route** ⌏ Ten kilometers (6 mi) south of Cochem, on the opposite shore, the
ruins of Metternich Castle crown the Schlossberg (Castle Hill)
vineyard next to the romantic village of **Beilstein.** Take in the
stunning Mosel loop panorama from the castle's terrace café before
heading for the market square below. Then ascend the *Klostertreppe*
(monastery steps) leading to the baroque monastery church for views
of the winding streets lined with half-timber houses.

Ediger-Eller

㉖ *61 km (38 mi) southwest of Koblenz on B–49.*

Ediger is another photogenic wine village with well-preserved houses
and remnants of a medieval town wall. The **Martinskirche** (St. Martin's
Church; ⊠ Kirchstr.) is a remarkable amalgamation of art and architectural styles, inside and out. Take a moment to admire the 117 carved
bosses in the star-vaulted ceiling of the nave. Among the many fine sculptures throughout the church and the chapel is the town's treasure: a Renaissance stone relief, *Christ in the Wine Press.*

Where to Stay & Eat

$ ✕🏠 **Zum Löwen.** This hotel and wine estate, run by the Saffenreuther
family, boasts friendly service and excellent wine and cuisine ($–$$$$).
The house specialties are game (from their own preserve) and fine,

fruity Rieslings (a mature Riesling with a balance of acidity and naturally ripe sweetness is superb with venison and boar). The rooms have simple decor; some have a balcony facing the Mosel. In addition to wine tastings and hikes in Calmont, Europe's steepest vineyard site, fishing or hunting trips can be arranged. ⊠ *Moselweinstr. 23, D–56814 Ediger-Eller* ☎ *02675/208* 🖷 *02675/214* ⊕ *www.mosel-hotel-loewen.de* 🛏 *21 rooms* ⚭ *Restaurant, cable TV, bicycles, Weinstube, shop, some pets allowed (fee); no a/c, no room phones* ⊟ *AE, MC, V* ⊘ *Hotel and restaurant closed Jan.–mid-Mar. Restaurant closed Tues. and Wed. mid-Mar.–Apr.* ❏⊘ *BP.*

en route | As you continue along the winding course of the Mosel, you'll pass Europe's steepest vineyard site, **Calmont**, opposite the romantic ruins of a 12th-century Augustinian convent and before the loop at Bremm. **Zell** is a popular village full of pubs and wineshops plying the crowds with Zeller Schwarze Katz, "Black Cat" wine, a commercially successful product and the focal point of a large wine festival in late June. Some 6 million vines hug the slopes around Zell, making it one of Germany's largest wine-growing communities. The area between Zell and Schweich (near Trier), known as the Middle Mosel, is home to some of the world's finest Riesling wines.

Traben-Trarbach

❷ *30 km (19 mi) south of Cochem.*

The Mosel divides Traben-Trarbach, which has pleasant promenades on both sides of the river. Its wine festivals are held the second and last weekends in July. Traben's art nouveau buildings are worth seeing (Hotel Bellevue, the gateway on the Mosel bridge, the post office, the train station, and town hall). For a look at fine period rooms and exhibits on the historical development of the area, visit the **Mittelmosel Museum**, in the Haus Böcking (1750). ⊠ *Casino Str. 2* ☎ *06541/9480* ⊕ *www.mittelmosel-museum.de* 🎫 *€2.50* ⊘ *Mid-Apr.–Oct., Tues.–Fri. 9:30–noon and 1:30–5, weekends 10–1.*

en route | During the next 24 km (15 mi) you'll pass by world-famous vineyards, such as Erdener Treppchen, Ürziger Würzgarten, the *Sonnenuhr* (sundial) sites of Zeltingen and Wehlen, and Graacher Himmelreich, before reaching Bernkastel-Kues.

Bernkastel-Kues

❸ *22 km (14 mi) southwest of Traben-Trarbach, 100 km (62 mi) southwest of Koblenz on B–53.*

Bernkastel and Kues straddle the Mosel, on the east and west banks, respectively. Elaborately carved half-timber houses (16th–17th centuries) and a Renaissance town hall (1608) frame St. Michael's Fountain (1606), on Bernkastel's photogenic **market square.** In early September the square and riverbank are lined with wine stands for one of the region's largest wine festivals, the Weinfest der Mittelmosel. From the hilltop ruins of the 13th-century castle, **Burg Landshut,** there are splendid views. It was here that Trier's Archbishop Boemund II is said to have recovered from an illness after drinking the local wine. This legendary vineyard, still known as the "Doctor," soars up from Hinterm Graben street near the town gate, Graacher Tor. You can purchase these exquisite wines from Weingut J. Lauerburg (one of the three original owners of the tiny site) at the estate's tasteful wineshop. ⊠ *Am Markt 27* ☎ *06531/ 2481* ⊘ *Apr.–Oct., weekdays 10–5, Sat. 11–5.*

The philosopher and theologian Nikolaus Cusanus (1401–64) was born in Kues. The **St.-Nikolaus-Hospital** is a charitable *Stiftung* (foundation) he established in 1458, and it still operates a home for the elderly and a wine estate. Within it is the **Mosel-Weinmuseum** (Wine museum; ⊠ €2 ⊘ Mid-Apr.–Oct., daily 10–5; Nov.–mid-Apr., daily 2–5), as well as a bistro and a wineshop. You can sample more than 100 wines from the entire Mosel-Saar-Ruwer region in the **Vinothek** (⊠ €9 ⊘ Mid-Apr.–Oct., daily 10–5; Nov.–mid-Apr., daily 2–5) in the vaulted cellar. The hospital's famous library, with precious manuscripts, cloister, and Gothic chapel, may be visited only on tours. ⊠ *Cusanus-Str. 2* ☎ *06531/ 4141* ⊠ *Historic room tours €4* ⊘ *Mid-Apr.–Oct., Tues. at 10:30, Fri. at 3, or by appointment.*

Some 3,100 winegrowers throughout the region deliver their grapes to the **Moselland Winzergenossenschaft** (Cooperative Winery), where wines are produced, bottled, and marketed. It's an impressive operation, and the large wine shop is excellent. ⊠ *Bornwiese 6, in industrial park* ☎ *06531/570* ⊠ *Tours with wine tasting €3.50* ⊘ *Tours with wine tasting Tues. and Thurs. at 2 or by appointment. Wine shop Jan.–Mar., weekdays 9–noon and 1–5, Sat. 9–12:30; Apr.–Dec., weekdays 9–noon and 1–6, Sat. 9–12:30.*

Where to Stay & Eat

$$–$$$$
Fodor'sChoice
★

✕▥ **Waldhotel Sonnora.** Helmut and Ulrike Thieltges offer guests one of Germany's absolute finest dining ($$$$, reservations essential) and wining experiences in their elegant country inn set within the forested Eifel Hills. Mr. Thieltges is an extraordinary chef, renowned for transforming exclusive ingredients (foie gras, truffles, Persian caviar) into culinary masterpieces. The wine list is equally superb. The dining room, with gilded and white-wood furnishings and plush red carpets, has a Parisian look. Attractive guest rooms and pretty gardens add to a memorable visit. ⊠ *Auf dem Eichelfeld, D–54518 Dreis, 8 km (5 mi) southwest of Wittlich, which is 18 km (11 mi) west of Kues via B–50; from A–1, exit Salmtal* ☎ *06578/98220* 🖷 *06578/1402* ⊕ *www.hotel-sonnora.de* 🗗 *20 rooms* 🖏 *Restaurant, minibars, babysitting; no a/c* 🗖 *AE, MC, V* ⊘ *Restaurant closed Mon. and Tues. Hotel and restaurant closed Jan. and 1st 2 wks in July* ⍾ *BP.*

$$

✕▥ **Weinromantikhotel Richtershof.** Very comfortable, individually furnished rooms and first-class friendly service make for a pleasant stay in this 17th-century manor house set in a shady park. Relax over breakfast or a glass of wine on the garden terrace, or take advantage of the 24-hour room service. Culinarium R ($$–$$$) serves innovative regional cuisine, including a local version of Riesling soup, in handsome surroundings. The Richtershof wine estate is open for cellar and vineyard tours as well as tastings. ⊠ *Hauptstr. 81–83, D–54486 Mülheim, 6 km (4 mi) south of Bernkastel via B–53* ☎ *06534/9480* 📠 *06534/ 948–100* ⊕ *www.weinromantikhotel.de* ⤳ *40 rooms, 4 suites* ♻ *Restaurant, in-room data ports, cable TV, gym, sauna, spa, steam room, bicycles, bar, lobby lounge, babysitting, laundry service, Internet, business services, some pets allowed (fee), no-smoking rooms; no a/c* ⊟ *MC, V* ⊘ *No lunch Mon.–Sat.* ⏀ *BP.*

$ ⨯🏠 **Zur Post.** The Rössling family will make you feel welcome in their house (1827) with its comfortable guest rooms and cozy restaurant, Poststube ($–$$$), and Weinstube. It's near the riverbank, and the market square is just around the corner. Try the Mosel trout *nach Müllerin Art* (dredged in flour and fried). The wine list is devoted exclusively to Mosel Rieslings. ⊠ *Gestade 17, D–54470 Bernkastel-Kues* ☎ *06531/ 96700* 📠 *06531/967–050* ⊕ *www.hotel-zur-post-bernkastel.de* ⤳ *42 rooms, 1 suite* ♻ *Restaurant, minibars, cable TV, sauna, Weinstube, some pets allowed (fee), no-smoking rooms; no a/c* ⊟ *DC, MC, V* ⊘ *Closed Jan.* ⏀ *BP.*

$ 🏠 **Gästehaus Erika Prüm.** The traditional wine estate S. A. Prüm has state-of-the-art cellars, a tastefully designed Vinothek, and a beautiful guesthouse with an idyllic patio facing the Mosel. The spacious rooms and baths are individually decorated in a winning mixture of contemporary and antique furnishings. Erika Prüm is a charming hostess, and her husband, Raimund (the redhead), is an excellent winemaker who offers tastings and cellar tours. ⊠ *Uferallee 25, D–54470 Bernkastel-Wehlen, North of Kues* ☎ *06531/3110* 📠 *06531/8555* ⊕ *www.sapruem.com* ⤳ *8 rooms* ♻ *In-room data ports, cable TV, lounge, shop, business services, some pets allowed (fee); no a/c* ⊟ *AE, MC, V* ⊘ *Closed Dec.–mid-Feb.* ⏀ *BP.*

---

en route

The 55-km (34-mi) drive from Bernkastel to Trier takes in another series of outstanding hillside vineyards, including those 10 km (6 mi) upstream at **Brauneberg** (⊠ Paulinsstr. 14, Kesten ☎ 06535/544 ⊕ www.paulinshof.de ⊘ Weekdays 8–6, Sat. 9–6), where Thomas Jefferson was enchanted by a 1783 Brauneberger Kammer Auslese during his visit here in 1788. Today, the vineyard is solely owned by Weingut Paulinshof. You can sample contemporary vintages of this wine in the beautiful chapel on the estate grounds. On a magnificent loop 12 km (7½ mi) southwest of Brauneberg is the famous village of **Piesport,** whose steep, slate cliff is known as the "Loreley of the Mosel." The village puts on the Mosel in Flammen (Mosel in Flames) fireworks display and festival the first weekend in July. Wines from its 35 vineyards are collectively known as Piesporter Michelsberg; however, the finest individual vineyard site, and one of Germany's very best, is the Goldtröpfchen ("little droplets of gold"). On the western edge of the town, the largest Roman press house (4th century) north of the Alps is on display.

Dhrontal

If the heat of the Mosel's slate slopes becomes oppressive in summer, revitalize body and soul with a scenic drive through the cool, fragrant forest of the Dhrontal (Dhron Valley), south of Trittenheim, and make a stop at this oasis for food-and-wine lovers.

Where to Stay & Eat

★ $–$$ ✕⊡ **Landhaus St. Urban.** Talented chef Harald Rüssel, his charming wife, Ruth, and their friendly staff see to it that guests enjoy excellent food, wine, and service in comfortable surroundings. Aromatic, visually stunning food presentations are served with wines from Germany's leading producers, including the family's Weingut St. Urbans-Hof in Leiwen, where visitors are welcome for tours and tastings. The house decor is stylish, and like the food, it reflects Mediterranean flair. ✉ *Büdlicherbrück 1, D–54426 Naurath/Wald, 8 km (5 mi) south of Trittenheim, toward Hermeskeil; from A–1, exit Mehring* ☎ *06509/91400* 🖷 *06509/914–040* ⊕ *www.landhaus-st-urban.de* 🛏 *14 rooms, 2 suites* ♧ *Restaurant, some in-room data ports, minibars, cable TV, shop, laundry service, some pets allowed (fee); no a/c* ☰ *AE, MC, V* ☾ *Hotel and restaurant closed 2 wks in Jan. Restaurant also closed Tues. and Wed.* ⊠ *BP.*

Trier

55 km (34 mi) southwest of Bernkastel-Kues via B–53, 150 km (93 mi) southwest of Koblenz; 30 min by car to Luxemburg airport.

By 400 BC a Celtic tribe, the Treveri, had settled the Trier Valley. Eventually Julius Caesar's legions arrived at this strategic point on the river, and Augusta Treverorum (the town of Emperor Augustus in the land of the Treveri) was founded in 16 BC. It was described as a most opulent city, as beautiful as any outside Rome.

Around AD 275 an Alemannic tribe stormed Augusta Treverorum and reduced it to rubble. But it was rebuilt in even grander style and renamed Treveris. Eventually it evolved into one of the leading cities of the empire and was promoted to "Roma secunda" (a second Rome) north of the Alps. As a powerful administrative capital it was adorned with all the noble civic buildings of a major Roman settlement, as well as public baths, palaces, barracks, an amphitheater, and temples. The Roman emperors Diocletian (who made it one of the four joint capitals of the empire) and Constantine both lived in Trier for years at a time.

Trier survived the collapse of Rome and became an important center of Christianity and, ultimately, one of the most powerful archbishoprics in the Holy Roman Empire. The city thrived throughout the Renaissance and baroque periods, taking full advantage of its location at the meeting point of major east–west and north–south trade routes and growing fat on the commerce that passed through. It also became one of Germany's most important wine-exporting centers. A later claim to fame is the city's status as the birthplace of Karl Marx. Trier is a city of wine as well as history, and beneath its streets are cellars capable of storing nearly 8 million gallons. To do justice to Trier, consider staying for at least two full days. The **Trier Card** entitles the holder to free public transportation and discounts on tours and admission fees to Roman sights, museums, and sports and cultural venues. It costs €9 and is valid for three days. There's also a ticket good for all the Roman sights for €6.20.

a good walk

Nearly all of Trier's main sights are close together. Begin your walk where Simeonstrasse passes around the city gate of the Roman city—the **Porta Nigra** ㉙ —one of the grandest Roman buildings still standing. Climb up inside for a good view of Trier from the tower gallery. **Tourist-Information Trier** ㉚, next to the Porta Nigra, sells various tours, the discount *Trier Card*, wines, and souvenirs. In a courtyard off the Porta Nigra, the **Städtisches Museum Simeonstift** ㉛ holds remains of the Romanesque church honoring the early medieval hermit Simeon. From here follow Simeonstrasse to the **Hauptmarkt** ㉜, in the center of the Old Town. You'll find yourself surrounded by old gabled houses, with facades from several ages—medieval, baroque, and 19th century. Turn left onto Domstrasse and come almost immediately face-to-face with Trier's **Dom** ㉝, the oldest Christian church north of the Alps. The 13-century Gothic **Liebfrauenkirche** ㉞ stands next door. Just behind the Dom, the **Bischöfliches Museum** ㉟ houses many antiquities unearthed in excavations around the cathedral.

Next, walk south of the cathedral on Liebfrauenstrasse, curving left through a short street (An-der-Meer-Katz) to Konstantinplatz for a look at the **Römische Palastaula** ㊱, the largest surviving single-hall structure of the ancient world. The **Rheinisches Landesmuseum** ㊲, with an extensive collection of Roman antiquities, stands south of the Palastaula, facing the grounds of the prince-elector's palace. The ruins of the **Kaiserthermen** ㊳, or Imperial Baths, are just 200 yards from the museum. The smaller **Barbarathermen** ㊴ lies west of the Kaiserthermen on Südallee, while the remains of the **Amphitheater** ㊵ are just east of the Kaiserthermen. Continue from the Barbarathermen toward the town center along Lorenz-Kellner-Strasse to Brückenstrasse to visit the **Karl-Marx-Haus** ㊶. Then proceed to Viehmarkt, east of St. Antonius Church, to visit the **Viehmarktthermen** ㊷, and an excavated Roman bath. From here Brotstrasse will lead you back to the main market square.

TIMING The walk will take a good two hours. It takes extra time to climb the tower of the Porta Nigra, walk through the vast interior of the Dom and its treasury, visit the underground passageways of the Kaiserthermen, and examine the cellars of the Amphitheater. Allow at least another half hour each for the Städtisches Museum Simeonstift, the Bischöfliches Museum, and Viehmarktthermen, as well as an additional hour for the Rheinisches Landesmuseum.

What to See

★ ㊵ **Amphitheater.** The sheer size of Trier's oldest Roman structure (circa AD 100) is impressive. In its heyday it seated 20,000 spectators; today it's a stage for the Antiquity Festival. You can climb down to the cellars beneath the arena—animals were kept in cells here before being unleashed to do battle with gladiators. There's a highly original tour through the cellars during which the slave Valerius, played by an actor of the state theater, explains how he trained to become a gladiator to win his freedom. If you don't speak German, speak up! The tour guide and/or someone in the group probably speaks some English and will translate the basic points. Reservations are essential. ⊠ *Olewiger Str. 25* ☎ *0651/ 9778–080 for tour reservations* 🖳 *0651/44759* ⊕ *www.valerius-trier. de* 🎫 *€2.10, tour with Valerius €8.50* ⊙ *Apr.–Sept., daily 10–6; Oct.–Mar., daily 10–5; tours Apr.–Sept., Fri. and Sat., 6 and 7:30* PM, *Sun. at 6* PM.

㊴ Barbarathermen (Barbara Baths). These Roman baths are much smaller and two centuries older than the Kaiserthermen. ⊠ *Südallee 48, near Friedrich-Wilhelm-Str. and river* 🎫 *€2.10* ⊙ *Apr.–Sept., daily 10–6; Oct.–Mar., daily 10–5. At this writing, closed for renovation.*

㉟ Bischöfliches Museum (Episcopal Museum). The collection here focuses on medieval sacred art, but there are also fascinating models of the cathedral as it existed in Roman times and 15 Roman frescoes (AD 326), discovered in 1946, that may have adorned the emperor Constantine's palace. ⊠ *Windstr. 6* ☎ *0651/710–5255* 🎫 *€2; combination ticket with Domschatzkammer €3* ⊙ *Apr.–Oct., Mon.–Sat. 9–5, Sun. 1–5; Nov.–Mar., Tues.–Sat. 9–5, Sun. 1–5.*

★ ㉝ Dom (Cathedral). Practically every period of Trier's past is represented here. The Dom stands on the site of the Palace of Helen, named for the mother of the emperor Constantine, who tore the palace down in AD 330 and put up a large church in its place. The church burned down in 336, and a second, even larger one was built. Parts of the foundations of this third building can be seen in the east end of the present structure (begun in about 1035). The cathedral you see today is a weighty and sturdy edifice with small round-head windows, rough stonework, and asymmetrical towers, as much a fortress as a church. Inside, Gothic styles predominate—the result of remodeling in the 13th century—although there are also many baroque tombs, altars, and confessionals. ⊠ *Domfreihof* ☎ *0651/979–0790* ⊕ *www.dominformation.de* 🎫 *Tours €3* ⊙ *Apr.–Oct., daily 6:30–6; Nov.–Mar., daily 6:30–5:30; tours Apr.–Oct., daily at 2* PM.

The **Domschatzkammer** (Cathedral Treasure Chamber; 🎫 €1.50; combination ticket with Bischöfliches Museum €3 ⊙ Apr.–Oct., Mon.–Sat. 10–5, Sun. 2–5; Nov.–Mar., Mon.–Sat. 11–4, Sun. 2–4) houses many extraordinary objects. The highlight is the 10th-century Andreas Tragaltar (St. Andrew's Portable Altar), constructed of oak and covered with gold leaf, enamel, and ivory by local craftsmen. It's a reliquary for the soles of St. Andrew's sandals, symbolized by the gilded, life-size foot on the top of the altar.

㉜ Hauptmarkt. The main market square of Old Trier is easily reached via Simeonstrasse. The market cross (958) and richly ornate St. Peter's Fountain (1595), dedicated to the town's patron saint, stand in the square. The farmers' market is open weekdays 7–6 and Saturday 7–1.

㊳ Kaiserthermen (Imperial Baths). This enormous 4th-century bathing palace once housed cold- and hot-water baths and a sports field. Although

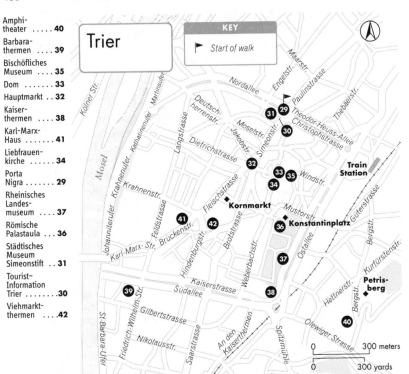

only the masonry of the **Calderium** (hot baths) and the vast basements remain, they are enough to give a fair idea of the original splendor and size of the complex—it covered an area 270 yards long and 164 yards wide. Originally 98 feet high, the walls you see today are 62 feet high. ⊠ *At Weimarer-Allee and Kaiserstr.* 🎟 *€2.10* ⊙ *Apr.–Sept., daily 10–6; Oct.–Mar., daily 10–5.*

㊶ Karl-Marx-Haus. Marx was born in this bourgeois house in 1818. Visitors with a serious interest in social history will be fascinated by its small museum. A signed first edition of *Das Kapital*, the study in which Marx sought to prove the inevitable decline of capitalism, has a place of honor. ⊠ *Brückenstr. 10* 🕾 *0651/970–680* 🎟 *€2* ⊙ *Apr.–Oct., Mon. 1–6, Tues.–Sun. 10–6; Nov.–Mar., Mon. 2–5, Tues.–Sun. 10–1 and 2–5.*

㉞ Liebfrauenkirche (Church of Our Lady). This is the first Gothic church in Germany, built in the 13th century on the site of a Roman basilica. The original statues from the portal (those that have survived) are in the **Bischöfliches Museum.** Inside, the decoration is austere except for Karl von Metternich's 17th-century tomb. ⊠ *Liebfrauenstr.* ⊙ *Apr.–Oct., daily 7:30–6; Nov.–Mar., daily 7:30–5:30.*

★ ▶ **㉙ Porta Nigra** (Black Gate). The best-preserved Roman structure in Trier was originally a city gate, built in the 2nd century (look for holes left by the iron clamps that held the structure together). Its name is misleading, however; the sandstone gate is not black but dark gray. The gate also served as part of Trier's defenses and was proof of the sophistication of Roman military might and its ruthlessness. Attackers were often lured into the two innocent-looking arches of the Porta Nigra, only to find themselves enclosed in a courtyard. In the 11th century the upper stories were converted into two churches, in use until the 18th century. The tourist office is next door. ⊠ *Porta-Nigra-Pl.* 📧 €2.10 🕓 *Apr.–Sept., daily 10–6; Oct.–Mar., daily 10–5.*

★ **37** **Rheinisches Landesmuseum** (Rhenish State Museum). The largest collection of Roman antiquities in Germany is housed here. The highlight is the 4th-century stone relief of a Roman ship transporting barrels of wine up the river. This tombstone of a Roman wine merchant was discovered in 1874 when Constantine's citadel in Neumagen was excavated. Have a look at the 108-square-foot model of the city as it looked in the 4th century—it provides a sense of perspective to many of the sights you can still visit today. ⊠ *Weimarer-Allee 1* 📞 *0651/97740* ⊕ *www. landesmuseum-trier.de* 📧 *€5.50* 🕓 *May–Oct., weekdays 9:30–5, weekends 10:30–5; Nov.–Apr., Tues.–Fri. 9:30–5, weekends 10:30–5.*

★ **36** **Römische Palastaula** (Roman Basilica). An impressive reminder of Trier's Roman past, this edifice is now Trier's major Protestant church. When first built by the emperor Constantine around AD 310, it was the imperial throne room of the palace. At 239 feet long, 93 feet wide, and 108 feet high, it demonstrates the astounding ambition of its Roman builders and the sophistication of their building techniques. The basilica is one of the two largest Roman interiors in existence (the other is the Pantheon in Rome). Look up at the deeply coffered ceiling; more than any other part of the building, it conveys the opulence of the original structure. ⊠ *Konstantinpl.* 📞 *0651/72468 or 0651/42570* 🕓 *Apr.–Oct., Mon.–Sat. 9–6, Sun. noon–6; Nov.–Mar., Tues.–Sat. 11–noon and 3–4, Sun. noon–1.*

31 **Städtisches Museum Simeonstift** (Simeon Foundation City Museum). Built around the remains of the Romanesque Simeonskirche, this church is now a museum. It was constructed in the 11th century by Archbishop Poppo in honor of the early medieval hermit Simeon, who for seven years shut himself up in the east tower of the Porta Nigra. Collections include art and artifacts produced in Trier from the Middle Ages to the 19th century. ⊠ *An der Porta Nigra* 📞 *0651/718–1454* 📧 *€2.60* 🕓 *Apr.–Oct., daily 9–5; Nov.–Mar., Tues.–Fri. 9–5, weekends 9–3.*

30 **Tourist-Information Trier.** In addition to dispensing city information, this tourist office sells regional wines and souvenirs. ⊠ *An der Porta Nigra* 📞 *0651/978–080* 🕓 *Apr.–Oct., Mon.–Sat. 9–6, Sun. 10–3; Mar., Nov., and Dec., Mon.–Sat. 9–6, Sun. 10–1; Jan. and Feb., Mon.–Sat. 10–5.*

42 **Viehmarktthermen.** Trier's third Roman bath (early 1st century) was discovered beneath Viehmarktplatz when ground was broken for a parking garage. Finds of the excavations from 1987 to 1994 are now beneath a protective glass structure. You can visit the baths and see the cellar of a baroque Capuchin monastery. ⊠ *Viehmarktpl.* 📞 *0651/994–1057* 📧 *€2.10* 🕓 *Tues.–Sun. 10–5.*

off the
beaten
path

ROSCHEIDER HOF – For a look at 19th- and 20th-century rural life in the Mosel-Saar area, visit the hilltop open-air Freilichtmuseum near Konz–Saar (10 km [6 mi]:southwest of Trier via B–51). Numerous farmhouses and typical village buildings in the region were saved from the wrecking ball by being dismantled and brought to the Roscheider Hof, where they were rebuilt and refurnished as they were decades ago. Old school rooms, a barber shop and beauty salon, a tavern, a shoemakerís workshop, a pharmacy, a grocery, and a dentistís joffice have been set up in the rooms of the museum proper, along with period rooms and exhibitions on local trades and household work, such as the history of laundry. A Beidermeier rose garden, museum shop, and restaurant are also on the grounds. ✉ *Konz* ☎ *06501/92710* ⊕ *www.roscheiderhof.de* 🎟 *€3* ☉ *Tues.–Fri. 9–6, weekends 10–6.*

Where to Stay & Eat

$$$ ✕ **Pfeffermühle.** For nearly three decades chef Siegbert Walde has offered guests classic cuisine in elegant surroundings. The 18th-century house on the northern edge of town has two stories of cozy niches, with beautiful table settings in shades of pink; the terrace directly overlooks the Mosel. Foie gras is a favorite ingredient, served in a terrine or sautéed and served in *Ahorn-jus* (maple-flavor juices). White wines from the Mosel's finest producers and top red Bordeaux wines make up a good part of the excellent wine list. ✉ *Zurlaubener Ufer 76* ☎ *0651/26133* ♨ *Reservations essential* 🟰 *MC, V* ☉ *Closed Sun. No lunch Mon.*

$$–$$$ ✕ **Palais Kesselstatt.** This baroque palace opposite the Liebfrauenkirche is a wonderful setting for fine dining—elegant but not pretentious. There's also seating in the beautiful courtyard in the summer. Katja Weiler is responsible for the efficient, friendly service; Burkhard Weiler reigns in the kitchen. Specialties include rack of lamb or lamb medallions as well as daily fish menus. Wines from the Reichsgraf von Kesselstatt estate dominate the wine list, supplemented by old- and new-world reds. ✉ *Liebfrauenstr. 10* ☎ *0651/40204* ⊕ *www.restaurant-kesselstatt.de* 🟰 *AE, DC, MC, V* ☉ *Closed Sun. and Mon. and Jan.*

★ $–$$$ ✕ **Schlemmereule.** The name literally means "gourmet owl," and, indeed, chef Peter Schmalen caters to gourmets within the 19th-century Palais Walderdorff complex opposite the cathedral. Lots of windows lend a light, airy look, and there's courtyard seating in summer. The fish is always excellent, or try the *Gänsestopfleber* (foie gras) with port wine aspic. The daily specials at lunch ($) include a glass of wine. The wine list features 10 wines by the glass and 180 by the bottle, with an emphasis on Mosel wines. ✉ *Palais Walderdorff, Domfreihof 1B* ☎ *0651/73616* ⊕ *www.schlemmereule.de* ♨ *Reservations essential* 🟰 *AE, DC, MC, V* ☉ *Closed Tues.*

★ $–$$ ✕ **Zum Domstein.** Whether you dine inside or out, don't miss the collection of Roman artifacts displayed in the cellar. You can order prix-fixe menus based on the recipes of Roman gourmet Marcus Gavius Apicius in the evening. Proprietor Rose-Marie Gracher is an expert on the subject. It's a unique experience and highly recommended. ✉ *Am Hauptmarkt 5* ☎ *0651/74490* ⊕ *www.domstein.de* 🟰 *MC, V.*

¢–$ ✕ **Walderdorff's Vinothek-Café-Club.** This trio has added a lively note to the 19th-century palace opposite Trier cathedral. The café-bistro offers breakfast, sandwiches, salads, pasta, and light fare—prepared by the Schlemmereule team. Some 250 local and old- and new-world wines are sold in the Vinothek, where tastings are offered. The club offers music and dancing in the baroque cellars. ✉ *Palais Walderdorff, Domfreihof 1* ☎ *0651/9946–9210* ⊕ *www.walderdorffs.de* ⊟ *DC, MC, V.*

¢–$ ✕ **Weinstube Palais Kesselstatt.** The Hilgers family runs this casual off-shoot of Palais Kesselstatt. The interior has exposed beams and polished wood tables; the shady terrace is popular in summer. Two soups daily, light fare, and fresh, regional cuisine are served with wines from the Reichsgraf von Kesselstatt estate. With the sampler "Das Beste aus der Region" you can taste several local specialties. ✉ *Liebfrauenstr. 10* ☎ *0651/41178* ⊕ *www.weinstube-kesselstatt.de* ⊟ *MC, V* ☉ *Closed Jan.*

$ ✕▥ **Ambiente.** Modern flair marks the style and decor that Markus and Monika Stemper—a passionate cook and a gracious hostess—offer in their country inn. Their legendary garden (with palms, ponds, and flowers galore), comfortable rooms, and personal service are remarkable. Both Restaurant Jardin ($$–$$$) and Stempers Brasserie ($–$$) serve dishes with Mediterranean accents, enhanced by an extensive wine list. ✉ *In der Acht 1–2, D–54294 Trier-Zewen, 7 km (4½ mi) southwest of Trier via B–49* ☎ *0651/827–280* 📠 *0651/827–2844* ⊕ *www.ambiente-hotel. com* ☞ *11 rooms* ⚲ *2 restaurants, in-room data ports, some minibars, cable TV, bicycles, bar, babysitting, dry cleaning, laundry service, no-smoking rooms; no a/c* ⊟ *AE, DC, MC, V* ☉ *Restaurants closed Thurs.* ▦ *BP.*

★ $ ✕▥ **Weinhaus Becker.** This family-run hotel, gourmet restaurant ($$$$), and wine estate is in the peaceful suburb of Olewig, near the amphitheater. The rooms are individually decorated with light-wood furnishings; some have balconies. You can dine in the restaurant's romantic, candlelighted niches or on the terrace. The three-course menu for hotel guests ($$$) offers very good value. Bordeaux and Burgundy wines are available in addition to the estate's own wines—and wine tastings, cellar visits, and guided tours on the wine path can be arranged. ✉ *Olewiger Str. 206, D–54295 Trier-Olewig* ☎ *0651/938–080* 📠 *0651/938–0888* ⊕ *www.weinhaus-becker.de* ☞ *19 rooms* ⚲ *Restaurant, cable TV, bicycles, shop, babysitting, Internet, business services, some pets allowed (fee); no a/c* ⊟ *AE, MC, V* ☉ *Restaurant closed Mon., 3 wks Jan. and Feb., and 1 wk late July. No lunch Tues., no dinner Sun.* ▦ *BP.*

$–$$ ▥ **Römischer Kaiser.** Centrally located near the Porta Nigra, this handsome patrician manor from 1895 offers well-appointed, attractive, modern rooms. The staff is friendly and helpful, and while some of Trier's other restaurants offer more flair, the food here is tasty, as is the hearty breakfast buffet. ✉ *Am Porta-Nigra-Pl. 6, D–54292* ☎ *0651/97700* 📠 *0651/977–099* ⊕ *www.hotels-trier.de* ☞ *43 rooms* ⚲ *Restaurant, some in-room data ports, minibars, cable TV, bar, laundry service, some pets allowed (fee); no a/c* ⊟ *AE, DC, MC, V* ▦ *BP.*

$ ▥ **Hotel Petrisberg.** The Pantenburgs' friendly, family-run hotel is high on Petrisberg hill overlooking Trier, not far from the amphitheater. You can walk to the Old Town in 20 minutes. The individually decorated rooms have solid pine furnishings; all have balconies—some with a fabulous view of the city. All rooms are no-smoking. In the evenings, you can enjoy snacks and good local wines in the wine pub. ⊠ *Sickingenstr. 11–13, D–54296* ☎ *0651/4640* ⊟ *0651/46450* ⊕ *www. hotelpetrisberg.de* ⤳ *26 rooms, 4 apartments* ⚲ *Some in-room data port, cable TV, bicycles, Weinstube; no a/c, no smoking* ⊟ *MC, V* ⦿ *BP.*

Festivals

The **Europa-Volksfest** (European Folk Festival), in May or early June, features wine and food specialties from several European countries, in addition to rides and entertainment. In late June the entire Old Town is the scene of the **Altstadtfest.** The amphitheater is an impressive setting for the theatrical performances of the **Antikenfestspiele** (Antiquity Festival) from late June to mid-July. The **Moselfest,** with wine, sparkling wine, beer, and fireworks, takes place in July along the riverbank in Zurlauben, followed by a large **Weinfest** (Wine Festival) in Olewig in early August, the **Elblingfest** (festival with still and sparkling wines from the grape variety Elbling) in mid-August, and the **Sektgala** (sparkling wine gala) in front of the Porta Nigra in late August. From late November until December 22, the annual **Weihnachtsmarkt** (Christmas market) takes place on the market square and in front of the cathedral.

Nightlife & the Arts

For absolutely up-to-the-minute information on performances, concerts, and events all over town, visit the Web site **www.trier-today.de.** Pop-up maps show exactly where everything is located.

Theater Trier (⊠ Am Augustinerhof ☎ 0651/718–1818 for box office) offers opera, theater, ballet, and concerts.

Concerts, theater, and cultural events are staged at **TUFA–Tuchfabrik** (⊠ Wechselstr. 4, at Weberstr. ☎ 0651/718–2412).

Pubs and cafés are centered on Viehmarktplatz and Stockplatz in the Old Town. **Walderdorff's** (⊠ Domfreihof 1 ☎ 0651/9946–9210) in the Palais Walderdorff has trendy DJ nights, early after-work parties, and occasional live bands.

The restaurant-lounge-café **FORUM** (⊠Hindenburgstr. 4 ☎0651/170–4363) features international DJs, theme parties, and live music. There's music and dancing at **Riverside** (⊠Zurmaiener Str. 173, near traffic circle on northern edge of town ☎ 0651/21006), a large entertainment center.

BONN & THE COLOGNE LOWLANDS

Updated by Jürgen Scheunemann

Bonn, the former capital of Germany, is the next major stop after Koblenz on the Rhine. It's close to the legendary Siebengebirge (Seven Hills), a national park and site of Germany's northernmost vineyards. According to German mythology, Siegfried (hero of the Nibelungen saga) killed a dragon here and bathed in its blood to make himself invincible. The lowland, a region of gently rolling hills north of Bonn, lacks the drama of the Rhine gorge upstream but offers the urban pleasures of Köln (Cologne), an ancient cathedral town, and Düsseldorf, an elegant city of art and fashion. Although not geographically in the Rhineland proper, Aachen is an important side trip for anyone visiting the region. Its stunning cathedral and treasury are the greatest storehouses of Carolingian art and architecture in Europe.

Bonn

44 km (27 mi) north of Koblenz, 28 km (17 mi) south of Köln.

Bonn was the postwar seat of the federal government and parliament until the capital returned to Berlin in 1999. Aptly described by the title of John le Carré's spy novel *A Small Town in Germany,* the quiet university town was chosen as a stopgap measure to prevent such weightier contenders as Frankfurt from becoming the capital, a move that would have lessened Berlin's chances of regaining its former status. With the exodus of the government from Bonn, the city has lost some of its international flair. Still, other organizations and industries have moved to Bonn to fill the gap, and its status as a U.N. city has been strengthened. The fine museums and other cultural institutions that once served the diplomatic elite are still here to be enjoyed.

Although Bonn seems to have sprung into existence only after the war, the Romans settled this part of the Rhineland 2,000 years ago, calling it Castra Bonnensia. Life in Bonn's streets, old markets, pedestrian malls, and handsome Sudstadt residential area is unhurried. The town center is a car-free zone; an inner ring road circles it with parking garages on the perimeter. A convenient parking lot is just across from the railway station and within 50 yards of the tourist office. Check with the tourism office for *RegioBonnCard* packages, which offer free or reduced entry into museums, low-cost transportation, and more.

a good tour

After picking up what you need at the tourist office at Windeckstrasse 2, continue to the cathedral **Münster** ㊸ ►, the site where two Roman soldiers were executed in AD 253 for holding Christian beliefs. Across from the cathedral are the **Kurfürstliches Residenz** ㊹, now the main Friedrich-Wilhelm University building, and its gardens (Hofgarten). Walk away from the river and down chestnut-tree-lined Poppelsdorfer Allee to the **Poppelsdorfer Schloss** ㊺, which has a tropical garden. Return toward the Kurfürstliches Residenz along Am Hof, and turn left onto the Marktplatz to arrive at the lavish, rococo **Rathaus** ㊻. Off the square, Bonngasse leads to the modest **Beethoven-Haus** ㊼, the residence of the great composer until he was 22. Backtrack to the Markt, and take Stockenstrasse past the palace gardens to Adenauerallee. Walk south along Adenauerallee and turn right onto Am Hofgarten. At the corner of Lennéstrasse is the glassed-in building of the offbeat **Arithmeum** ㊽. Return via Am Hofgarten to Adenauerallee. About 1½ km (1 mi) southeast along the Rhine is the Museum Mile. There you'll find the **Haus der Geschichte** ㊾, the **Kunst- und Ausstellungshalle der Bundesrepublik Deutschland** ㊿, and the **Kunstmuseum Bonn** ⓷, among others. To save yourself the walk, catch Bus No. 610 or take U-bahn 16 at the Juridicum subway on Adenauerallee, between Am Hofgarten and Weberstrasse. Get off at the Heussallee–Museumsmeile stop. Finally, take a casual walk

Bonn

KEY

▶ *Start of walk*

🛈 *Tourist information*

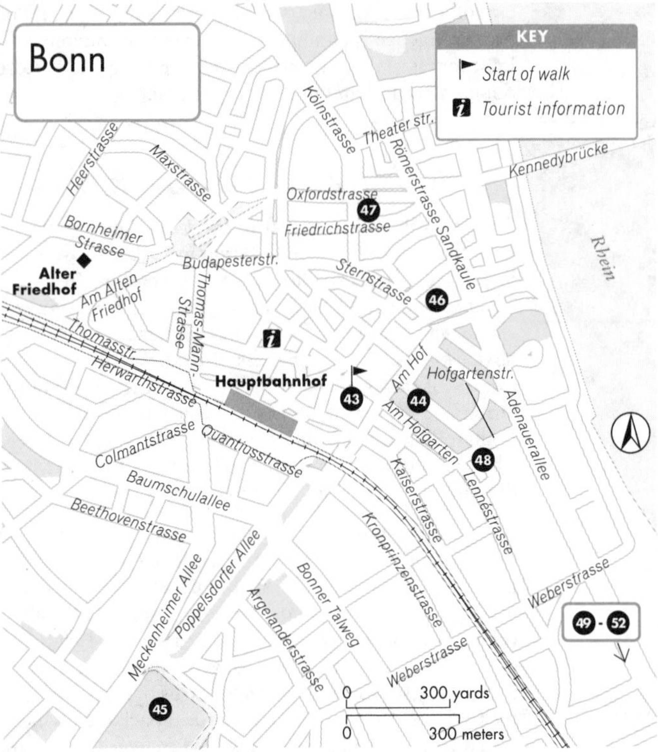

through the **Bundesviertel** 52, West Germany's government district for half a century. Most of the sights can be toured by walking down Adenauerallee to Willy-Brandt-Allee (you can also take the U-bahn to the Museum Koenig station).

If you'd like to spend more time inside Bonn's museums, follow the above route, but skip the long walk to the Poppelsdorfer Schloss.

TIMING Allow a little more than 2 hours for the first walk and 1½ for the shorter version, not including time spent in museums or shopping.

What to See

48 **Arithmeum.** Technophiles and technophobes alike enjoy this university-run museum, where even the abstract theme of discrete mathematics is made comprehensible. Its stated aim is to show "the interface of art and technology," and the core of the exhibit is a 1,200-piece collection of historical mechanical calculating machines, which became obsolete with the advent of computers. The art comes in the form of a collection of constructivist paintings that resemble enlarged, colorful computer-chip designs. ⊠ *Lennéstr. 2* ☎ *0228/738–790* ⊕ *www.arithmeum.uni-bonn. de* ☞ *€3* ☉ *Tues.–Sun. 11–6.*

off the
beaten
path

ALTER FRIEDHOF (Old Cemetery) – This ornate, leafy cemetery is the resting place of many of the country's most celebrated sons and daughters. Look for the tomb of composer Robert Schumann (1810–56) and his wife, Clara, also a composer and accomplished pianist. To reach the cemetery from the main train station, follow Quantiusstrasse north until it becomes Herwarthstrasse; before the street curves, turning into Endenlicherstrasse, take the underpass below the railroad line. You'll then be on Thomastrasse, which borders the cemetery. ⊠ *Am Alten Friedhof* ☉ *Jan., daily 9–5; Feb., daily 8–6; Mar.–Aug., daily 7:15 AM–8 PM; Sept., daily 8–8; Oct., daily 8–7; Nov. and Dec., daily 8–5.*

㊼ Beethoven-Haus (Beethoven House). Beethoven was born in Bonn in 1770 and, except for a short stay in Vienna, lived there until the age of 22. The house where he grew up is a museum celebrating his career. You'll find scores, paintings, a grand piano (his last, in fact), and an ear trumpet or two. Perhaps most impressive is the room in which Beethoven was born—empty save for a bust of the composer. The attached museum shop carries everything from kitsch to elegant Beethoven memorabilia. ⊠ *Bonngasse 20* ☎ *0228/981–7525* ⊕ *www.beethoven-haus-bonn.de* ▤ *€4* ☉ *Apr.–Sept., Mon.–Sat. 10–6, Sun. 11–4; Oct.–Mar., Mon.–Sat. 10–5, Sun. 11–4.*

㊽ Bundesviertel (Federal Government District). Walking through the amiable, former government district is like taking a trip back in time to an era when Bonn was still the sleepy capital of West Germany. Bordered by Adenauerallee, Willy-Brandt-Allee, Friedrich-Ebert-Allee, and the Rhine, the quarter boasts sights such as the **Bundeshaus** with the Plenarsaal. This building, designed to serve as the new Federal Parliament, was completed only six years before the capital was relocated to Berlin in 1999. A few steps away, you'll find the historic **Villa Hammerschmidt,** the German equivalent of the White House. This stylish classicist mansion began serving as the Federal president's permanent residence in 1950 and is still his home when he stays in Bonn. Equally impressive is the **Palais Schaumburg,** another fine example of the Rhein Riveria estates that once housed the Federal Chancellery (1949–76). It became the center of Cold War politics during the Adenauer administration. Tours of the quarter, including a visit to the Villa Hammerschmidt, are offered by the Bonn Tourist Office. ⊠ *Adenauerallee.*

★ ㊾ Haus der Geschichte (House of History). German history since World War II is the subject of this museum, which begins with "hour zero," as the Germans call the unconditional surrender of 1945. The museum displays an overwhelming amount of documentary material organized on five levels and engages various types of media. It's not all heavy either—temporary exhibits have featured political cartoonists, "Miss Germany" pageants, and an in-depth examination of the song *Lili Marleen,* sung by troops of every nation during World War II. Take a look at the historical reconstructions of typical German backyards, behind the museum. ⊠ *Adenauerallee 250* ☎ *0228/91650* ⊕ *www.hdg.de* ▤ *Free* ☉ *Tues.–Sun. 9–7.*

★ ⑤ **Kunst- und Ausstellungshalle der Bundesrepublik Deutschland** (Art and Exhibition Hall of the German Federal Republic). This is one of the Rhineland's most important venues for major exhibitions about culture and science. Recent exhibits included treasures from Venetian palaces, mythical representations and reality of Troy, and art from the Iranian national museum. Its modern design, by Viennese architect Gustave Peichl, is as interesting as anything on exhibit in the museum. It employs three enormous blue cones situated on a lawnlike rooftop garden. ⊠ *Friedrich-Ebert-Allee 4* ☎ *0228/917–1200* ⊕ *www.bundeskunsthalle. de* ◻ *€7* ۞ *Tues. and Wed. 10–9, Thurs.–Sun. 10–7.*

⑤ **Kunstmuseum Bonn** (Art Museum). Devoted to contemporary art, this large museum is renowned for the high standard of its collection. The two main focuses are on Rheinish Expressionists and German art since 1945 (Beuys, Baselitz, and Kiefer, for example). Changing exhibits are generally excellent and help maintain a link to the international art scene. The museum's airy and inexpensive café is preferable to the stuffier version across the plaza at the Kunst- und Ausstellungshalle. ⊠ *Friedrich-Ebert-Allee 2* ☎ *0228/776–260* ⊕ *www.bonn.de/kunstmuseum* ◻ *€5* ۞ *Tues. and Thurs.–Sun. 10–6, Wed. 10–9.*

④ **Kurfürstliche Residenz** (Prince-Electors' Residence). Built in the 18th century by the prince-electors of Köln, this grand palace now houses a university. If the weather is good, stroll through the Hofgarten (Palace Gardens). ⊠ *Am Hofgarten.*

▶ ④ **Münster** (Cathedral). The 900-year-old cathedral is vintage late Romanesque, with a massive octagonal main tower and a soaring spire. It saw the coronations of two Holy Roman Emperors (in 1314 and 1346) and was one of the Rhineland's most important ecclesiastical centers in the Middle Ages. The 17th-century bronze figure of St. Helen and the ornate rococo pulpit are highlights of the interior. ⊠ *Münsterpl.* ☎ *0228/985–880* ◻ *Free* ۞ *Daily 9–7.*

④ **Poppelsdorfer Schloss** (Poppelsdorf Palace). This former electors' palace was built in the baroque style between 1715 and 1753 and now houses the university's mineralogical collection. Its botanical gardens are open to the public and have an impressive display of tropical plants. The best exhibit is the mammoth Amazon water lilies, which can support up to 175 pounds. ⊠ *Meckenheimer Allee 171* ☎ *0228/732–764* ◻ *Free* ۞ *Apr.–Sept., weekdays 9–6, weekends 9–1; Oct.–Mar., weekdays 9–4.*

④ **Rathaus** (Town Hall). Not very austere, this 18th-century town hall looks somewhat like a pink dollhouse. Its elegant steps and perron have seen a great many historic figures, including French president Charles de Gaulle and U.S. president John F. Kennedy. ⊠ *Am Markt* ☎ *0228/750* ◻ *Free* ۞ *By tour only; May–Oct., 1st Sat. of month.*

Where to Stay & Eat

$–$$$ ✕ **Sassella.** When the Bundestag was still in town, this Bonn institution used to be cited in the press as frequently for its back-room political dealings as for its Lombardi-influenced food. But locals, prominent and otherwise, still flock to the restaurant, in an 18th-century house outside the town center. The style is pure Italian farmhouse, with stone walls and exposed beams, but the handmade pastas often stray from the typical—note the salmon-filled black-and-white pasta pockets in shrimp sauce. ⊠ *Karthäuserpl. 21* ☎ *0228/5308–1512* ▤ *AE, DC, MC, V* ⊘ *Closed Mon.*

$–$$ ✗ **Amadeo.** The popularity of this neighborhood restaurant is due in part to the German affinity for all things Spanish but also because its food—40 different tapas (€2–€6), inventive salads, and main dishes—rarely misses the mark. The seafood kebabs with Spanish potatoes and spicy tomato sauce are recommended, and the mixed-tapas plate is excellent. ⊠ *Mozartstr. 1* ☎ *0228/635–534* ▤ *No credit cards* ⊘ *No lunch.*

$–$$ ✗ **Pirandello.** This trattoria with its frescoed brick walls is so cozy that it borders on kitsch. But the decor is redeemed by the quality of chef-owner Fausto Langui's Italian regional dishes and the wines he recommends to go with them. The seasonally changing menu features pizzas, pastas, fish, and meats—all, as a rule, excellently prepared. ⊠ *Brüderg. 22* ☎ *0228/656–606* ▤ *No credit cards* ⊘ *Closed Sun.*

¢–$ ✗ **Em Höttche.** Travelers and Bonn residents (Beethoven was a regular) have taken sustenance at this tavern since the late 14th century, and today it offers one of the best-value lunches in town. The interior is rustic; the food stout and hearty. ⊠ *Markt 4* ☎ *0228/690–009* ▤ *No credit cards.*

$$$ ▦ **Best Western Domicil.** A group of buildings around a quiet, central courtyard has been converted into a charming and comfortable hotel. The rooms are individually furnished and decorated—in styles ranging from fin-de-siècle romantic to Italian modern. Huge windows give the public rooms a spacious airiness. ⊠ *Thomas-Mann-Str. 24–26, D–53111* ☎ *0228/729–090* 🖷 *0228/691–207* ⊕ *www.bestwestern.de* ➳ *43 rooms, 1 apartment* ♿ *Restaurant, room service, in-room data ports, cable TV, sauna, Internet, some free parking, some pets allowed (fee), no-smoking rooms; no a/c* ▤ *AE, DC, MC, V* ¶◎¶ *BP.*

$$ ▦ **Sternhotel.** For solid comfort and a central location in the Old Town, the Stern is tops. About 80% of the rooms have been renovated in a Danish modern style; the rest are more old-fashioned. Weekend rates are a particular bargain. ⊠ *Markt 8, D–53111* ☎ *0228/72670* 🖷 *0228/726–7125* ⊕ *www.sternhotel-bonn.de* ➳ *80 rooms* ♿ *In-room data ports, cable TV, some pets allowed (fee), no-smoking rooms; no a/c* ▤ *DC, MC, V* ¶◎¶ *CP.*

$ ▦ **Mozart.** Elegant on the outside and simple on the inside, this small, attractive hotel is often recommended to friends by Bonn residents. Part of its appeal is its location amid traditional town houses in the romantic, residential "musician's quarter," just a four-minute walk from the main train station and the city center. ⊠ *Mozartstr. 1, D–53115* ☎ *0228/659–071* 🖷 *0228/659–075* ⊕ *www.hotel-mozart-bonn.de* ➳ *39 rooms* ♿ *Cable TV, parking (fee); no a/c* ▤ *AE, DC, MC, V* ¶◎¶ *CP.*

The Arts

MUSIC The Bonn Symphony Orchestra opens its season in grand style every September with a concert on the market square, in front of city hall. Otherwise, concerts are held in the **Beethovenhalle** (⊠ Wachsbleiche 16 ☎ 0228/72220). Indoor and outdoor concerts are held at numerous venues during September's **Beethoven-Festival** (☎ 0228/201–0345

⊕ www.beethovenfest-bonn.de). In the **Beethoven-Haus** (⊠ Bonngasse 20 ☎ 0228/981–750), intimate recitals are sometimes given on an 18th-century grand piano.

Operas are staged regularly at the **Oper der Stadt Bonn** (⊠ Am Boese-lagerhof 1 ☎ 0228/778–000 ⊕ www.oper.bonn.de), popularly known as La Scala of the Rhineland. The **Pantheontheater** (⊠ Bundeskanzlerpl. ☎ 0228/212–521) is a prime venue for all manner of pop concerts and cabaret. Chamber-music concerts are given regularly at the **Schuman** (⊠ Sebastianstr. 182 ☎ 0228/773–656).

THEATER &   Musicals and ballet are performed at the **Oper der Stadt Bonn.** From May
DANCE   through October, the **Bonner Sommer** (⊠ Tourist office, Windeckstr. 1 ☎ 0228/775–000) festival offers folklore, music, and street theater, much of it outdoors and most of it free. Information is available at the tourist office.

Shopping

There are plenty of department stores and boutiques in the pedestrian shopping zone around the Markt and the Münster. Bonn's **Wochen-markt** (Weekly Market) is open daily except Sunday, filling the Markt with vendors of produce and various edibles. Bargain hunters search for secondhand goods and knickknacks at the city's renowned—and huge—**Flohmarkt** (Flea Market; ⊠ Ludwig-Erhard-Allee), held in Rheinaue park under the Konrad-Adenauer-Brücke on the third Saturday of each month from April through October. **Pützchens Markt,** a huge country fair, takes place in the Bonn area the second weekend of September.

Königswinter

12 km (7 mi) southeast of Bonn.

The town of Königswinter has one of the most visited castles on the Rhine, the **Drachenfels.** Its ruins crown one of the highest hills in the Siebengebirge, Germany's oldest nature reserve, with a spectacular view of the Rhine. The reserve has more than 100 km (62 mi) of hiking trails. The castle was built in the 12th century by the archbishop of Köln. Its name commemorates a dragon said to have lived in a nearby cave. As legend has it, the dragon was slain by Siegfried, hero of the epic *Nibelungenlied.* You can reach the castle ruins by taking the **Drachenfelsbahn** (⊠ Drachenfelsstr. 53 ☎ 02223/92090 ⊕ www.drachenfelsbahn-koenigswinter.de ☉ Mar. and Oct., daily 10–6; Apr., daily 10–7; May–Sept., daily 9–7; Nov.–Feb., weekdays noon–5, weekends 11–6), a steep, narrow-gauge train that makes trips to the summit every hour or occasionally every half hour. The trip costs €6.50 one way, €8 round trip.

Where to Eat

$–$$$ ✕ **Gasthaus Sutorius.** Across from the church of St. Margaretha, this wine tavern serves refined variations on German cuisine with a nice selection of local wines. In summer, food is served outdoors beneath the linden trees. ⊠ *Oelinghovener Str. 7* ☎ *02244/912–240* ▭ *MC* ☉ *No dinner Sun. and Mon. No lunch Tues.–Sat.*

Brühl

20 km (12 mi) southwest of Bonn.

In the heart of Brühl you'll discover the Rhineland's most important baroque palace. **Schloss Augustusburg** and the magnificent pleasure park that surrounds it were created in the time of Prince Clemens August, between 1725 and 1768. The palace contains one of the most famous achievements of rococo architecture, a staircase by Balthasar Neumann. The castle can be visited only on guided tours, which leave the reception area every hour or so. An English cassette guide is available. Concerts (☎ 02232/792–640) are held here in summer. ⊠ *Schlossstr. 6* ☎ *02232/44000* ⊕ *www.schlossbruehl.de* 🎫 *€4* ☉ *Feb.–Nov., Tues.–Fri. 9–noon and 1:30–4, weekends 10–5.*

The smaller **Jagdschloss Falkenlust,** at the end of an avenue leading straight through Schloss Augustusburg's grounds, was built as a getaway where the prince could indulge his passion for falconry. ⊠ *Schlossstr. 6* ☎ *02232/12111* 🎫 *€3* ☉ *Feb.–Nov., Tues.–Sun. 9–noon and 2–4:30.*

Köln

28 km (17 mi) north of Bonn, 47 km (29 mi) south of Düsseldorf, 70 km (43 mi) southeast of Aachen.

Köln is the largest city on the Rhine (the fourth largest in Germany) and one of the most interesting. Although not as old as Trier, it has been a dominant power in the Rhineland since Roman times. Known throughout the world for its "scented water," eau de cologne (first produced here in 1705 from an Italian formula), Köln is today a major commercial, intellectual, and ecclesiastical center. The city is vibrant and bustling, with a light and jolly flair that is typical of the Rhineland. At its heart is tradition, manifested in the abundance of bars and brew houses serving the local Kölsch beer and old Rhine cuisine. These meeting places are a good place to start a night on the town. Köln also puts on Germany's most exciting carnival every February, when the whole city follows the famous motto of *Kölle alaaf!* ("Cologne is alive") in an orgiastic revelry with bands, parades, and parties that last all night. Tradition, however, is mixed with the contemporary, found in a host of elegant shops, sophisticated restaurants, modern bars and dance clubs, and an important modern-art scene.

Köln was first settled by the Romans in 38 BC. For nearly a century it grew slowly, in the shadow of imperial Trier, until a locally born noblewoman, Julia Agrippina, daughter of the Roman general Germanicus, married the Roman emperor Claudius. Her hometown was elevated to the rank of a Roman city and given the name Colonia Claudia Ara Agrippinensium. For the next 300 years Colonia (hence Cologne, or Köln) flourished. Evidence of the Roman city's wealth resides in the Römisch-Germanisches Museum. In the 9th century, Charlemagne, the towering figure who united the sprawling German lands (and ruled much of present-day France) as the first Holy Roman Emperor, restored Köln's fortunes and elevated it to its preeminent role in the Rhineland. Charlemagne also appointed the first archbishop of Köln. The city's ecclesiastical heritage is one of its most striking features; it has a full dozen Romanesque churches and one of the world's largest and finest Gothic cathedrals. In the Middle Ages it was a member of the powerful Hanseatic League, occupying a position of greater importance in European commerce than either London or Paris.

Köln was a thriving modern city until World War II, when bombings destroyed 90% of it. Only the cathedral remained relatively unscathed. But like many German cities that rebounded during the "Economic Miracle" of the 1950s, Köln is a mishmash of old and new, sometimes awkwardly juxtaposed. A good part of the former Old Town along the Hohe Strasse (old Roman High Road) was turned into a remarkably charmless pedestrian shopping mall. The ensemble is framed by six-lane expressways winding along the rim of the city center—barely yards from the cathedral—perfectly illustrating the problems of postwar reconstruction. However, much of the Altstadt (Old Town), ringed by streets that follow the line of the medieval city walls, is closed to traffic. Most major sights are within this area and are easily reached on foot. Here, too, you'll find the best shops.

Modern Cologne is proud to be one of Europe's media capitals, with RTL and WDR, two of the Continent's biggest private and public TV companies, based here. The arrival of a new business elite has also ended decades of the infamous rule of *Klüngel* in the city, a legendary system of old boys' political and economic networks, which has been uprooted after a series of cover-ups and political scandals.

At the tourist office, ask about the KölnTourismus card, which offers free or reduced entry into museums and other attractions, combined with free transit in and around the city.

a good walk

Any tour of the city should start beneath the towers of the extraordinary Gothic cathedral, the **Dom** ㊾ ⬆, comparable to the great French cathedrals and a highlight of a trip to Germany. Spend some time admiring the outside of the building (you can walk almost all the way around it). Notice how there are practically no major horizontal lines—all the accents of the building are vertical. The cathedral's treasures are kept in the **Domschatzkammer,** the cathedral treasury. Behind the Dom toward the river is the **Museum Ludwig** ㊿, which holds artworks from the early 20th century onward. Sharing the Roncalliplatz plaza with the Museum Ludwig is the **Römisch-Germanisches Museum** ㊿, which has a large, well-preserved floor mosaic dating from Roman times. From the museum, walk away from the cathedral across Roncalliplatz, go down the steps, and turn left on Am Hof Strasse. Walk one block and turn right onto Unter Taschenmacher, which, after crossing Kleine Budengasse, becomes Burgerstrasse. Continue down Burgerstrasse to the **Altes Rathaus** ㊿. To your right as you face the Rathaus, on the other side of Obenmarspforten, is the basalt-and-glass building housing the **Wallraf-Richartz-Museum** ㊿ and its fine and massive collection of 13th- to 19th-century art. Just south of the museum on Martinstrasse is the 15th-century hall, **Gürzenich** ㊿. Crossing back to the Rathaus, enter the small alley beneath the Rathaus tower (to the left as you face it) and walk down a flight of steps to the **Alter Markt** ⓢ. Cross the square and enter Lintgasse; after taking a few steps, you will be in the shadow of the outstanding **Gross St. Martin** ⓪, one of Köln's 12 Romanesque churches. You are also near the bank of the Rhine. Turn left and walk north through the Rhein Garten park for a view of the river. Soon you'll reach Heinrich-Böll-Platz, named after the native son who was Germany's greatest postwar novelist. (Five blocks north, along the Rhine, stands **St. Kunibert** ⓵, the last of Köln's famous Romanesque churches to be built.) Continuing from Heinrich-Böll-Platz, go up the steps and walk past the cathedral again, continuing beyond the Dom Hotel and across Hohe Strasse, an ugly pedestrian shopping street, into Burgmauer Strasse. Follow the waist-high, block-long remnant of the old city walls to Mohrenstrasse. Go right two blocks, then left to a square. On the other side of the square stands **St. Gereon** ⓶, the jewel of the city's Romanesque churches.

From the church, just walk back on Zeughausstrasse toward the cathedral, and you'll pass the **Kölnisches Stadtmuseum** ⓷, the city's history museum, on your right. Sights to the south can easily be reached on foot. Head down Mohrenstrasse, which becomes Auf dem Berlich and then Richmodstrasse. Here, on the top floor of a shopping center, is the **Käthe Kollwitz Museum** ⓸, one of two collections in the country. Cut diagonally across the Neumarkt to Cäcilienstrasse, and continue walking east to the **Museum Schnütgen** ⓹, which holds a fine collection of medieval art. Farther east on Cäcilienstrasse is the somber 11th-century **St. Maria im Kapitol** ⓺. Need a sugar boost? On the Rhine, about four blocks south of the Deutzer Bridge, is the impressive building—part postmodern ship, part medieval castle—housing the **Imhoff-Stollwerck-Museum** ⓻—free samples available.

TIMING Allow two hours just for the walk. To see the interior of the cathedral and the cathedral treasury and to climb the cathedral tower will add almost an hour. The museum collections could take several hours depending on your interests. Visits to the Wallraf-Richartz Museum and the Römisch-Germanisches Museum require at least 45 minutes each.

What to See

ⓢ **Alter Markt** (Old Market). The square has an eclectic assembly of buildings, most of them postwar; two 16th-century houses survived the war intact—Nos. 20 and 22. The oldest structure dates from 1135. ✉ *Altstadt*.

⓺ **Altes Rathaus** (Old Town Hall). After a lengthy renovation, the Rathaus is open to visitors (call for tour information as hours vary). It's worth a look even from the outside, for it's the oldest town hall in Germany, even if it was entirely rebuilt after the war (it was originally erected in the 14th century). The famous bell tower rings its bells daily at noon and 5 PM. Standing on pedestals at one end of the town hall are figures of prophets, made in the early 15th century. Ranging along the south wall are nine additional statues, the so-called *Nine Good Heroes*, carved in 1360. Charlemagne and King Arthur are among them. Beneath a small glass pyramid near the south corner of the Rathaus is the **Mikwe**, a 12th-

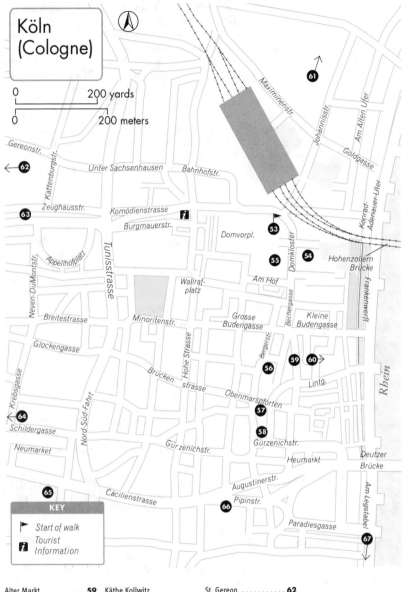

Köln (Cologne)

0 — 200 yards
0 — 200 meters

KEY

⚑ Start of walk
ℹ Tourist Information

century ritual bath from the medieval Jewish quarter. When the Rathaus is open, you can request a key from the guard and descend to the Mikwe's interior. Directly below the Rathaus are the remains of the Roman city governor's headquarters, the Praetorium. ⊠ *Rathauspl., Altstadt* ☎ *0221/30400* ⊙ *Mon.–Thurs. 7:30–4:45, Fri. 7:30–2.*

► ⑬ **Dom** (Cathedral). Köln's landmark embodies one of the purest expres-
Fodor'sChoice sions of the Gothic spirit in Europe. The cathedral, meant to be a tan-
★ gible expression of God's kingdom on earth, was conceived with such immense dimensions that construction, begun in 1248, was not completed until 1880, though builders adhered to the original plans. At 515 feet high, the two west towers of the cathedral were by far the tallest structures in the world when they were finished. The cathedral was built to house what were believed to be the relics of the Magi, the three kings who paid homage to the infant Jesus (the trade in holy mementos was big business in the Middle Ages—and not always scrupulous). The size of the building was not simply an example of self-aggrandizement on the part of the people of Köln, however; it was a response to the vast numbers of pilgrims who arrived to see the relics. The ambulatory, the passage that curves around the back of the altar, is unusually large, allowing cathedral authorities to funnel large numbers of visitors up to the crossing (where the nave and transepts meet and where the relics were originally displayed), around the back of the altar, and out again.

Today the relics are kept just behind the altar, in the original enormous gold-and-silver **reliquary.** The other great treasure of the cathedral, in the last chapel on the left as you face the altar, is the **Gero Cross,** a monumental oak crucifix dating from 971. The *Adoration of the Kings* (1440), a triptych by Stephan Lochner, Köln's most famous medieval painter, is to the right. The **Domschatzkammer** (Cathedral Treasury; 🖼 €4 ⊙ Daily 10–6) includes the silver shrine of Archbishop Engelbert, who was stabbed to death in 1225. Other highlights are the stained-glass windows, some dating from the 13th century; the 15th-century altarpiece; and the early 14th-century high altar with its glistening white figures and intricate choir screens. Climb to the top of the bell tower to get the complete vertical experience. ⊠ *Dompl., Altstadt* ☎ *0221/9258–4730* ⊕ *www.koelner-dom.de* 🖼 *Tower € 2; tour of tower and cathedral treasury €5* ⊙ *Daily 6 AM–7 PM; tower and stairwell Nov.–Feb., daily 9–4; Mar. and Apr., daily 9–5; May–Sept., daily 9–6; Oct., daily 9–5; guided tours in English Mon.–Sat. at 10:30 and 2:30, Sun. at 2:30.*

⑳ **Gross St. Martin** (Big St. Martin). This remarkable Romanesque parish church was rebuilt after being flattened in World War II. Its massive 13th-century tower, with distinctive corner turrets and an imposing central spire, is another landmark of Köln. The church was built on the site of a Roman granary. ⊠ *An Gross St. Martin 9, Altstadt* ☎ *0221/257–7924* ⊙ *Mon.–Sat. 10–6, Sun. 2–4.*

⑱ **Gürzenich.** This Gothic structure, located at the south end of Martinsviertel, was all but demolished in World War II but carefully reconstructed afterward. It's named after a medieval knight from whom the city acquired valuable real estate in 1437. The official reception and festival hall here has played a central role in civic life through the centuries. At one end of the complex are the remains of the 10th-century Gothic church of **St. Alban,** which were left ruined after the war as a memorial. On what's left of the church floor, you can see a sculpture of a couple kneeling in prayer, *Mourning Parents,* by Käthe Kollwitz, a fitting memorial to the ravages of war. ⊠ *Gürzenichstr., Altstadt.*

Imhoff-Stollwerck-Museum. This riverside museum recounts 3,000 years of civilization's production and delectation of chocolate, from the Central American Maya to the colonizing and industrializing Europeans. It's also a real factory with lava flows of chocolate and a conveyer belt jostling thousands of truffles. Visitors get a free tasting. The museum shop, with candy bars stacked to the ceiling, is a great place to pick up interestingly packaged edible gifts. ⊠ *Rheinauhafen 1a, Rheinufer* ☎ *0221/931–8880* ⊕ *www.schokoladenmuseum.de* ⊠ *€6* ⊙ *Tues.–Fri. 10–6, weekends 11–7; closed 1 wk mid-Feb.*

Käthe Kollwitz Museum. The works of Käthe Kollwitz (1867–1945), the most important German female artist of the 20th century, focus on social themes like the plight of the poor and the atrocities of war. This is the larger of the country's two Kollwitz collections and comprises all of her woodcuts, as well as paintings, etchings, lithographs, and sculptures. There are also changing exhibits of other modern artists. ⊠ *Neumarkt 18–24, in Neumarkt Galerie, Innenstadt* ☎ *0221/227–2363* ⊕ *www.kollwitz.de* ⊠ *€3* ⊙ *Tues.–Fri. 10–6, weekends 11–6.*

Kölnisches Stadtmuseum (Cologne City History Museum). The triumphs and tragedies of Cologne's rich past are packed into this museum at the historic *Zeughaus,* the city's former arsenal. Here, you'll find an in-depth chronicle of Cologne's history—including information about the lives of ordinary people and high-profile politicians, the industrial revolution (car manufacturer Henry Ford's influence on the city is also retraced), and the destruction incurred during World War II. For those who've always wanted to be privy to the inside stories surrounding local words such as *Klüngel, Kölsch,* and *Karneval,* the answers are waiting to be discovered within the museum's walls. ⊠ *Zeughausstr. 1–3, Altstadt* ☎ *0221/2212–5790* ⊕ *www.museenkoeln.de* ⊠ *€4.20* ⊙ *Mon.–Sun. 10–5, Tues. 10–8; closed 1 wk mid-Feb.*

Museum Ludwig. This museum is dedicated to art from the beginning of the 20th century to the present day. Its American pop art collection (including Andy Warhol, Jasper Johns, Robert Rauschenberg, Claes Oldenburg, and Roy Lichtenstein) rivals that of New York's Guggenheim Museum. Within the building and at no extra cost is the **Agfa Foto-Historama** (Agfa Photography Museum), which has one of the world's largest collections of historic photographs and cameras. ⊠ *Bischofsgartenstr. 1, Innenstadt* ☎ *0221/2212–6165* ⊕ *www.museum-ludwig.de* ⊠ *€5.80* ⊙ *Tues., Thurs., weekends 10–6, Fri. 11–6; closed 1 wk mid-Feb.*

Museum Schnütgen. A treasure house of medieval art from the Rhine region, the museum has an ideal setting in a 12th-century basilica. Don't miss the crucifix from the St. Georg Kirche or the original stained-glass windows and carved figures from the Dom. Many of the exhibits—intricately carved ivory book covers, rock crystal reliquaries, illuminated manuscripts—require intense concentration to be fully appreciated. ⊠ *Cäcilienstr. 29, Innenstadt* ☎ *0221/2212–3620* ⊕ *www.museenkoeln. de* ⊠ *€3.20* ☉ *Tues.–Fri. 10–5, every 1st Wed. until 8, weekends 11–5; closed Feb. 19–24; Dec. 24, 25, and 31, and Jan. 1.*

> **need a break?** Cologne's main pedestrian shopping street is practical but utterly uninspiring—some even say ugly. An airy, artsy oasis is **Café Stanton, The Fine Art of Leisure** (⊠ Schilderg. 57, behind Antoniterkirche ☎ 0221/271–0710), with outdoor terrace seating and a view of the Antoniter church's late-Gothic walls. The food is international with an emphasis on the Mediterranean; the selection of cakes is divinely German. Three enormous, surprisingly delicate chandeliers, made entirely of plastic waste, provide lighting.

★ ⑤ **Römisch-Germanisches Museum** (Roman-Germanic Museum). This cultural landmark was built in the early 1970s around the famous Dionysius mosaic discovered there during the construction of an air-raid shelter in 1941. The huge mosaic, more than 100 yards square, once formed the dining-room floor of a wealthy Roman trader's villa. Its millions of tiny earthenware and glass tiles depict some of the adventures of Dionysius, the Greek god of wine and, to the Romans, the object of a widespread and sinister religious cult. The pillared 1st-century tomb of Lucius Publicius (a prominent Roman officer), some stone Roman coffins, and everyday objects of Roman life are among the museum's other exhibits. Bordering the museum on the south is a restored 90-yard stretch of the old Roman harbor road. ⊠ *Roncallipl. 4, Altstadt* ☎ *0221/ 2212–4438* ⊕ *www.museenkoeln.de* ⊠ *€4.70* ☉ *Tues.–Sun. 10–5* ☉ *Closed Feb. 19–24, Dec. 24, 25, and 31, and Jan. 1.*

⑫ **St. Gereon.** Experts regard St. Gereon as one of the most noteworthy medieval structures in existence. This exquisite Romanesque church stands on the site of an old Roman burial ground six blocks west of the train station. An enormous dome rests on walls that were once clad in gold mosaics. Roman masonry forms part of the structure, which is believed to have been built over the grave of its namesake, the 4th-century martyr and patron saint of Köln. ⊠ *Gereonsdriesch 2–4, Ringe* ☎ *0221/ 134–922* ⊠ *Free* ☉ *Mon.–Sat. 9–12:30 and 1:30–6, Sun. 1:30–6.*

⑪ **St. Kunibert.** The most lavish of the churches from the late Romanesque period is by the Rhine, three blocks north of the train station. Its precious stained-glass windows have filtered light for more than 750 years. Consecrated in 1247, the church contains an unusual room, concealed under the altar, which gives access to a pre-Christian well once believed to promote fertility in women. ⊠ *Kunibertsklosterg. 2, Altstadt-Nord* ☎ *0221/121–214* ⊠ *Free* ☉ *Daily 9–noon and 2:30–6:30.*

⑯ **St. Maria im Kapitol.** Built in the 11th and 12th centuries on the site of a Roman temple, St. Maria is best known for its two beautifully carved 16-foot-high doors and its enormous crypt, the second largest in Germany after the one in Speyer's cathedral. ⊠ *Marienpl. 19, Altstadt* ☎ *0221/214–615* ⊠ *Free* ☉ *Daily 9:30–6.*

㊼ Wallraf-Richartz-Museum. The Wallraf-Richartz-Museum contains paintings spanning the years 1300 to 1900. The Dutch and Flemish schools are particularly well represented, as is the 15th- to 16th-century Cologne school of German painting. Its two most famous artists are the Master of the St. Veronica (whose actual name is unknown) and Stefan Lochner, represented by two luminous works, *The Last Judgment* and *The Madonna in the Rose Bower.* Large canvases by Rubens, who spent his youth in Köln, hang prominently on the second floor. There are also outstanding works by Rembrandt, Van Dyck, and Frans Hals. Among the other old masters are Tiepolo, Canaletto, and Boucher. ⊠ *Martinstr. 39, Altstadt* ☎ *0221/2212–2393* ⊕ *www.museenkoeln.de* ☜ *€5.80* ⊗ *Tues. 10–8, Wed.–Fri. 10–6, weekends 11–6* ⊗ *Closed Feb. 19–24, Dec. 24, 25, and 31, and Jan. 1.*

Where to Stay & Eat

The tourist office, across from the cathedral, can make hotel bookings for you for the same night, at a cost of €10 per room. If you plan to be in town for the Karneval, be sure to reserve a room well in advance.

$$$$ ✕ **Capricorn i Aries.** This hip, fine-dining establishment houses but four

Fodor'sChoice tables, each covered with crisp, white linens and enhanced by sur-

★ rounding dark wood and sophisticated lighting. You'll be personally waited on by the owners, Judith Werner (Capricorn) and Klaus Jaquemod (Aries), as you indulge in truly heavenly French cuisine with a Rhineland twist. Just opposite this intimate little restaurant, a new and somewhat larger Brasserie serves the staples in French rural cuisine. ⊠ *Alteburger Str. 34, Neustadt* ☎ *0221/323–182* ⌂ *Reservations essential* ▭ *No credit cards* ⊗ *Closed Mon. and Tues. No lunch.*

$$$–$$$$ ✕ **Le Moissonnier.** Part of the charm of this restaurant—arguably the best in the city—is its lack of pretension. The turn-of-the-20th-century bistro decor radiates warmth from its mirrors, Tiffany lamps, and painted flowers. Owners Vincent and Liliane Moissonnier greet their guests in person, seating them at one of 20 tables. The cuisine is French at its base but intertwines an array of global influences. ⊠ *Krefelder Str. 25, Neustadt-Nord* ☎ *0221/729–479* ⌂ *Reservations essential* ▭ *No credit cards* ⊗ *Closed Sun. and Mon.*

$$$ ✕ **Bizim.** The extraordinary chef Enis Akisik has made his Bizim one of the best Turkish restaurants in Germany. Forget shish kebab and prepare yourself for a leisurely gourmet experience that might include scampi with tarragon sauce, eggplant-coated lamb fillets with a garlic yogurt sauce, or quail grilled on a rosemary spit and served in its own juices. There are four-course tasting menus for lunch (€28) and dinner (€50). ⊠ *Weideng. 47–49, Nordstadt* ☎ *0221/131–581* ⌂ *Reservations essential* ▭ *AE, D, MC, V* ⊗ *Closed Sun. and Mon. No lunch Sat.*

$$–$$$ ✕ **Casa di Biase.** This romantic eatery serves sophisticated Italian cuisine in a warm, elegant setting. The seasonally changing menu focuses on fish and game, and the wine list is interesting and extensive—although sometimes pricey. Just next door is the Casa's smaller and more casual sister, the Teca di Biasi. This cozy, wood-panel wine bar serves antipasti, salads, and main dishes for up to €13. ⊠ *Eifelpl. 4, Sudstadt* ☎ *0221/ 322–433* ▭ *AE, MC, V* ⊗ *Closed Sun. No lunch Sat.*

$–$$$ ✕ **Fischers Weingenuss und Tafelfreuden.** If someone were to create a shrine to wine, it would look a lot like this restaurant. Run by one of Germany's star sommeliers (who happens to be a woman), the restaurant offers 800 wines, 40 of which can be bought by the glass. The kitchen experiments with regional cuisine, with influences from France, the Mediterranean, and even Southeast Asia. The dining experience is always elegant, and an expert staff will help you pick the perfect wine for each dish. ✉ *Hohenstaufenring 53, Ringe* ☎ *0221/310–8470* ▭ *DC, MC, V* ☽ *Closed Sun. No lunch Sat.*

¢–$$$ ✕ **Früh am Dom.** For real down-home Cologne food, there are few places that compare with this time-honored former brewery. Bold frescoes on the vaulted ceilings establish the mood, and the authentically Teutonic experience is completed by such dishes as *Hämmchen* (pork knuckle). The beer garden is delightful for summer dining. ✉ *Am Hof 12–14, Altstadt* ☎ *0221/26130* ▭ *No credit cards.*

$–$$ ✕ **Paeffgen.** There's no better *Brauhaus* in Köln in which to imbibe Kölsch,
Fodor's Choice   the city's home brew. You won't sit long in front of an empty glass be-
★   fore a blue-aproned waiter sweeps by and places a full one before you. With its worn wooden decor, colorful clientele, and typical German fare (sauerbraten, Hämmchen, and Reibekuchen), Paeffgen sums up tradition—especially when compared to the trendy nightspots that surround it. ✉ *Friesenstr. 64–66, Friesenviertel* ☎ *0221/135–461* ▭ *No credit cards.*

$$$$ ✕▥ **Excelsior Hotel Ernst.** The Empire-style lobby in this 1863 hotel is striking in sumptuous royal blue, bright yellow, and gold. Old-master paintings (including a Van Dyck) grace the lobby walls; Gobelins tapestries hang in the ballroom of the same name. Breakfast is served either in the "petit palais" ballroom or in the two-story atrium. The Hanse-stube restaurant ($$–$$$$) attracts a business crowd with its lunch specials and has a more hushed ambience in the evening, when it serves French haute cuisine. A sleek, hip restaurant, Taku ($$–$$$$), serves pan-Asian cuisine at slightly less-elevated prices. ✉ *Trankg. 1, Altstadt, D–50667* ☎ *0221/2701* ⊟ *0221/135–150* ⊕ *www.excelsiorhotelernst. de* ➲ *140 rooms, 20 suites* ♻ *2 restaurants, room service, minibars, cable TV with movies, gym, massage, sauna, bar, babysitting, dry cleaning, laundry service, concierge, Internet, business services, meeting rooms, parking (fee), some pets allowed (fee), no-smoking rooms; no a/c in some rooms* ▭ *AE, DC, MC, V* ⊠ *BP.*

★ **$$$–$$$$** ✕▥ **Hotel im Wasserturm.** What used to be Europe's tallest water tower is now an 11-story luxury hotel-in-the-round. The neoclassic look of the brick exterior remains, and few modern architects could create a more unusual setting. The ultramodern interior was the work of the French designer Andrée Putman, known for her minimalist work on Morgans, a stylish hotel in New York City. The 11th-floor restaurant-in-the-round ($$$$) has a stunning view of the city. The menu, which changes daily, offers Continental haute cuisine. ✉ *Kayg. 2, Altstadt, D–50676* ☎ *0221/20080* ⊟ *0221/200–8888* ⊕ *www.hotel-im-wasserturm.de* ➲ *48 rooms, 40 suites* ♻ *Restaurant, room service, in-room data ports, in-room safes, minibars, cable TV, gym, sauna, bar, dry cleaning, laundry service, concierge, business services, meeting rooms, parking (fee), some pets allowed* ▭ *AE, DC, MC, V* ⊠ *BP.*

$$$–$$$$ ╳▣ **Hyatt Regency Köln.** This sleek glass-and-steel building, sitting like a huge futuristic cube on the right bank of the Rhine, relies on high-tech, luxurious comfort and excellent service to compensate for what it lacks in atmosphere. It's favored by business travelers for its quiet and spacious rooms (even standard rooms come with fully equipped computer data ports and interactive TV screens), but all will relish the hotel's spectacular views of Cologne's skyline, particularly at night. All this, along with a world-class spa and pool, and two superb restaurants (the Glashaus restaurant offers the better view) may indeed make the Hyatt the region's finest hotel. ⊠ *Kennedy-Ufer 2a, Deutz, D–50679* ☎ *0221/828–1234* 🖷 *0221/828–1370* ⊕ *www.cologne.hyatt.com* ⤶ *289 rooms, 16 suites* ⚫ *2 restaurants, room service, in-room data ports, minibars, cable TV with movies, indoor pool, health club, hair salon, massage, sauna, bar, babysitting, dry cleaning, laundry service, concierge, business services, meeting rooms, parking (fee), some pets allowed (fee), no-smoking rooms* ▤ *AE, DC, MC, V* ▮◉▮ *CP.*

$$ ╳▣ **Hopper Hotel et cetera.** The rooms in this chicly renovated monastery are spare but not spartan, although a startlingly realistic sculpture of a bishop, sitting in the reception area, serves as a constant reminder of the building's ecclesiastic origins. The rooms are decorated with modern works by Cologne artists. The courtyard Hopper Restaurant et cetera ($–$$) serves upscale Mediterranean cuisine and has delightful garden seating. ⊠ *Brüsselerstr. 26, Belgisches Viertel, D–50674* ☎ *0221/924–400* 🖷 *0221/924–406* ⊕ *www.hopper.de* ⤶ *48 rooms, 1 suite* ⚫ *Restaurant, café, in-room data ports, cable TV, gym, sauna, Internet, business services, parking (fee), some pets allowed (fee), no-smoking rooms; no a/c* ▤ *AE, DC, MC, V* ▮◉▮ *BP.*

$–$$ ╳▣ **Chelsea.** This designer hotel has a very strong following among artists and art dealers, as well as the musicians who come to play in the nearby Stadtgarten jazz club. Breakfast is served until noon for these late-risers. The best features of the rooms are the luxuriously large bathrooms and bathtubs. The restaurant-café ($–$$) is great for informal gatherings and for people-watching. It's 20 minutes to the city center on foot, 10 by subway or tram. ⊠ *Jülicherstr. 1, Belgisches Viertel, D–50674* ☎ *0221/207–150* 🖷 *0221/239–137* ⊕ *www.hotel-chelsea.de* ⤶ *36 rooms, 2 suites, 1 apartment* ⚫ *Restaurant, cable TV, parking (fee), some pets allowed; no a/c* ▤ *AE, DC, MC, V* ▮◉▮ *EP.*

$ ╳▣ **Das Kleine Stapelhäuschen.** One of the few houses along the riverbank that survived World War II bombings, this is among the oldest buildings in Köln. You can't beat the location, overlooking the river and right by Gross St. Martin; yet the rooms are reasonably priced, making up in age and quaintness for what they lack in luxury. The restaurant ($$–$$$$) is in a slightly higher price bracket and does a respectable enough job with spruced-up versions of German specialties. ⊠ *Fischmarkt 1–3, Altstadt, D–50667* ☎ *0221/257–7862* 🖷 *0221/257–4232* ⊕ *www.koeln-altstadt.de/stapelhaeuschen* ⤶ *31 rooms* ⚫ *Restaurant, in-room data ports, cable TV, parking (fee), some pets allowed; no a/c, no-smoking rooms* ▤ *AE, MC, V* ▮◉▮ *BP.*

$ ▣ **Hotel Good Sleep.** What it lacks in personality this hotel makes up for in price and location. A favorite with students and backpackers, Hotel

Good Sleep is just steps from the Dom. The small rooms are bland but bright and clean. Cheaper rooms, with a shower in the hallway, are also available. ⊠ *Komödienstr. 19–21, Altstadt, D–50667* ☎ *0221/257–2257* 🖷 *0221/257–2259* ⊕ *www.goodsleep.de* ⮔ *33 rooms* ♻ *Cable TV, some pets allowed; no a/c* ☰ *AE, D, MC, V* ⏏ *CP.*

¢–$ 🖫 **Hotel Im Kupferkessel.** The best things about this small, unassuming hotel are its location (in the shadow of St. Gereon church and a 15-minute walk from the Dom) and the price (single rooms with shared bath can be had for as low as €30). The slightly shabby lobby and breakfast room look like they might have been decorated by someone's grandmother, circa 1950, but the rooms are clean and functional. Be prepared to deal with stairs here, as most of the rooms are on the third and fourth floors. ⊠ *Probsteig. 6, Ringe, D–50670* ☎ *0221/270–7960* ⊕ *www.im-kupferkessel.de* 🖷 *0221/2707–9629* ⮔ *13 rooms* ♻ *Cable TV, parking (fee); no a/c* ☰ *AE, D, MC, V* ⏏ *CP.*

Nightlife & the Arts

THE ARTS Köln's Westdeutsche Rundfunk Orchestra performs regularly in the city's excellent concert hall, the **Philharmonie** (⊠ Bischofsgartenstr. 1, Altstadt ☎ 0221/280–280 ⊕ www.koelnticket.de). The Gürzenich Orchestra gives regular concerts in the Philharmonie, but the primary setting for its music is the restored **Gürzenich** (⊠ Martinstr. 29/37, Altstadt ☎ 0221/925–8990), medieval Köln's official reception mansion. Köln's opera company, the **Oper der Stadt Köln** (⊠ Offenbachpl. 1, Innenstadt ☎ 0221/2212–8400), is known for exciting classical and contemporary productions. Year-round organ recitals in Köln's cathedral are supplemented from June through August with a summer season of organ music. Organ recitals and chamber concerts are also presented in many of the Romanesque churches and in **Antoniterkirche** (⊠ Schilderg. 57, Innenstadt ☎ 0221/257–8674).

Köln's principal theater is the **Schauspielhaus** (⊠ Offenbachpl. 1, Innenstadt ☎ 0221/2212–8252), home to the 20 or so private theater companies in the city.

NIGHTLIFE Köln's nightlife is centered in three distinct areas: between the Alter Markt and Neumarkt in the Old Town; on Zulpicherstrasse; and around the Friesenplatz S-bahn station. Many streets off the Hohenzollernring and Hohenstaufenring, particularly Roonstrasse, also provide a broad range of nightlife.

In summer head straight for the **Stadtgarten** (⊠ Venloerstr. 40, Friesenviertel ☎ 0221/9529–9410) and sit in the Bier Garten for some good outdoor Gemütlichkeit. At other times of the year it's still worth a visit for its excellent jazz club. In summer, the Martinsviertel, a part of the Altstadt around the Gross St. Martin church, which is full of restaurants, brew houses, and *Kneipen* (pubs), is a good place to go around sunset. One particular spot to check out there is **Papa Joe's Biersalon** (⊠ Alter Markt 50–52, Altstadt ☎ 0221/258–2132), which is kind of kitschy but often has classic and Dixieland jazz.

Das Ding (⊠ Hohenstaufenring 30–34, Ringe ☎ 0221/246–348), literally "The Thing," is a student club that is never empty, even on weeknights.

For a true disco experience, make for the **Alter Wartesaal** (✉ Am Haupt-bahnhof, Johannisstr. 11, Altstadt ☎0221/912–8850) in the Hauptbahnhof on Friday or Saturday night. The old train-station waiting room has been turned into a concert hall and disco, where dancers swivel on ancient polished parquet and check their style in original mahogany-frame mirrors. In the cellar of the street café **Petit Prince** (✉ Hohenzollernring 90, Ringe ☎ 0221/124–499), salsa and other Latin music plays five nights a week. Free dance classes are also frequently given.

Shopping

A good shopping loop begins at the **Neumarkt Galerie** (✉ Richmodstr. 8, Innenstadt), a bright, modern indoor shopping arcade with a web of shops and cafés surrounding an airy atrium. From there, head down the charmless but practical pedestrian shopping zone of the Schildergasse. The big department store **Kaufhof** (✉ Hohestr. 41–53, Innenstadt ☎0221/2230) is off the mall and central to city life. Its offerings are rich in quantity and quality.

From Schildergasse, go north on Herzogstrasse to arrive at **Glockengasse** (✉ No. 4711, Innenstadt ☎ 0221/925–0450), where Köln's most celebrated product, eau de cologne No. 4711, was first concocted by the 18th-century Italian chemist Giovanni-Maria Farina. The shop has extended its selection to include other scents, but the original product remains the centerpiece, available in all sizes from a purse-size bottle to a container that holds a quart or so.

On Breite Strasse, another pedestrian shopping street, **Heubel** (✉ Breite Str. 118, Innenstadt ☎ 0221/257–6013) carries unusual, beautiful, and often inexpensive imported antiques, housewares, and jewelry. At the end of Breite Strasse is Eherenstrasse, where the young and young-at-heart can shop for hip fashions and trendy housewares. After a poke around here, explore the small boutiques on Benesisstrasse, which will lead you to Mittelstrasse, best known for high-tone German fashions and luxury goods. Follow Mittelstrasse to the end to return to the Neumarkt.

Because train stations are exempt from restrictive German laws on store-opening hours, the shopping arcade in the **Hauptbahnhof** (main train station) offers the rare opportunity to shop in Germany on Sunday, and on weekdays until as late as 10 PM.

Aachen

70 km (43 mi) west of Köln.

At the center of Aachen, the characteristic *drei-Fenster* facades, three windows wide, give way to buildings dating from the days when Charlemagne made Aix-la-Chapelle (as it was then called) the great center of the Holy Roman Empire. Thirty-two German emperors were crowned here, gracing Aachen with the proud nickname Kaiserstadt (Emperors' City). Roman legions had been drawn here for the healing properties of the sulfur springs emanating from the nearby Eifel Mountains. Charlemagne's father, Pepin the Short, also settled here to enjoy the waters that gave Bad Aachen—as the town is also known—its name; the waters continue to attract visitors today. But it was certainly Charlemagne who was responsible for the town's architectural wealth. After his coronation in Rome in 800, he spent more and more time in Aachen, building his spectacular palace and ruling his vast empire from within its walls. Aachen is now home to almost 30,000 students, keeping this beautiful old town a bustling center of activity. One-and-a-half-hour walking tours depart from the tourist information office weekends at 11, year-round, and weekdays at 2, from April through October. **English-language tours** can be set up by prior arrangement. ☎ *0241/180–2960.*

★ The stunning **Dom** (Cathedral) in Aachen, the "Chapelle" of the town's earlier name, remains the single greatest storehouse of Carolingian architecture in Europe. Though it was built over the course of 1,000 years and reflects architectural styles from the Middle Ages to the 19th century, its commanding image is the magnificent octagonal royal chapel, rising up two arched stories to end in the cap of the dome. It was this section, the heart of the church, that Charlemagne saw completed in AD 800. His bones now lie in the Gothic choir, in a golden shrine surrounded by wonderful carvings of saints. Another treasure is his marble throne. Charlemagne had to journey all the way to Rome for his coronation, but the next 32 Holy Roman emperors were crowned here in Aachen, and each marked the occasion by presenting a lavish gift to the cathedral. In the 12th century Barbarossa donated the great chandelier now hanging in the center of the imperial chapel; his grandson, Friedrich II, donated Charlemagne's shrine. Emperor Karl IV journeyed from Prague in the late 14th century for the sole purpose of commissioning a bust of Charlemagne for the cathedral; now on view in the treasury, the bust incorporates a piece of Charlemagne's skull. ⊠ *Münsterpl.* ☎ *0241/477– 090* 🎫 *Free* ⊕ *www.aachendom.de* ⊗ *Daily 7–7.*

The **Domschatzkammer** (Cathedral Treasury) houses sacred art from late antiquity and the Carolingian, Ottonian, and Hohenstaufen eras; highlights include the Cross of Lothair, the Bust of Charlemagne, and the Persephone Sarcophagus. ⊠ *Am Domhof, entrance via Klosterg.* ☎ *0241/ 4770–9127* 🎫 *€2.50* ⊗ *Mon. 10–1, Tues., Wed., and Fri.–Sun. 10–6, Thurs. 10–9.*

The back of the **Rathaus** (Town Hall) is opposite the Dom, across Katschhof Square. It was built in the early 14th century on the site of the *Aula,* or "great hall," of Charlemagne's palace. Its first major official function was the coronation banquet of Emperor Karl IV in 1349, held in the great Gothic hall you can still see today (though this was largely rebuilt after the war). On the north wall of the building are statues of 50 emperors of the Holy Roman Empire. The greatest of them all, Charlemagne, stands in bronze atop the Kaiserbrunnen (Imperial Fountain) in the center of the market square. ⊠ *Marktpl.* ☎ *0241/432– 7310* 🎫 *€2* ⊗ *Daily 10–1 and 2–5.*

An old Aachen tradition that continues today is "taking the waters." The arcaded, neoclassical **Elisenbrunnen** (Elisa Fountain), built in 1822, is south of the cathedral and contains two fountains with thermal drinking water. Experts agree that the spa waters here—the hottest north of the Alps—are effective in helping to cure a wide range of ailments. Drinking the sulfurous water in the approved manner can be unpleasant, but as you hold your nose and gulp away, you're emulating the likes of Dürer, Frederick the Great, and Charlemagne.

You can try sitting in the spa waters at **Carolus-Thermen Bad Aachen**, a high-tech sauna-spa facility. In Dürer's time there were regular crackdowns on the orgiastic goings-on at the baths. Today taking the waters is done with a bathing suit on, but beware—the casual German attitude toward nudity takes over in the sauna area, which is declared a "textile-free zone." ⊠ *Passstr. 79* ☎ *0241/182–740* ⊕ *www.carolus-thermen. de* 🖾 *€9–€26* ☉ *Daily 9 AM–11 PM.*

Like many other German spa towns, Aachen has its **Spielbank** (casino). It's housed in the porticoed former Kurhaus, on the parklike grounds fronting Monheimsallee and facing the Kurbad Quellenhof. Jacket and tie are required. Bring your passport for identification. ⊠ *Monheimsallee 44* ☎ *0241/18080* 🖾 *€5* ☉ *Sun.–Fri. 3 PM–3 AM, Sat. 3 PM–4 AM.*

Aachen has its modern side as well—one of the world's most important art collectors, Peter Ludwig, has endowed two museums in his hometown. The **Ludwig Forum für Internationale Kunst** holds a portion of Ludwig's truly enormous collection of contemporary art and hosts traveling exhibits. ⊠ *Jülicher Str. 97–109* ☎ *0241/180–7103 or 0241/180–7104* ⊕ *www.heimat.de/ludwigsforum* 🖾 *€3* ☉ *Tues.–Sun. noon–6.*

The **Suermont-Ludwig Museum** is devoted to classical painting up to the beginning of the 20th century. ⊠ *Wilhelmstr. 18* ☎ *0241/479–800* 🖾 *€3* ☉ *Tues. and Thurs.–Sun. noon–6, Wed. noon–9.*

Where to Stay & Eat

$$$–$$$$ ✕ **La Becasse.** Sophisticated French nouvelle cuisine is offered in this modern restaurant just outside the Old Town by the Westpark. Try the distinctively light calves' liver. ⊠ *Hanbrucherstr. 1* ☎ *0241/74444* 🍴 *Reservations essential* 🝔 *MC, V* ☉ *Closed Sun. No lunch Sat. and Mon.*

$–$$ ✕ **Der Postwagen.** This annex of the more upscale Ratskeller is worth a stop for the building alone, a half-timber medieval edifice at one corner of the old Rathaus. Sitting at one of the low wooden tables, surveying the marketplace through the wavy old glass, you can dine very respectably on solid German fare. If you really want to go local, try *Himmel und Erde* ("Heaven and Earth"), a hearty Westphalian specialty made of potatoes, apples, and blood sausage. ⊠ *Am Markt* ☎ *0241/35001* 🝔 *AE, DC, MC, V.*

¢–$$ ✕ **Am Knipp.** At this historic old Aachen Bierstube, guests dig into their German dishes at low wooden tables next to the tile stove. Pewter pots and beer mugs hang from the rafters. ⊠ *Bergdriesch 3* ☎ *0241/33168* 🝔 *No credit cards* ☉ *Closed Tues., Dec. 24–Jan. 2, and 2 wks in Oct.*

$ ✕ **Magellan.** Nestling against part of Aachen's ancient 13th-century city wall, this historic and upscale establishment, true to the city's international heritage and the restaurant's namesake, serves up a varied selection of Mediterranean cuisine under an imposing Greek-Orthodox chandelier. Despite the elegant background, the atmosphere is very lively and relaxed. ⊠ *Pontstr. 78* ☎ *0241/401–6440* 🝔 *DC, MC, V.*

$$–$$$$ ╳⊞ **Dorint Quellenhof Aachen.** Built during World War I as a country home for the kaiser, this is one of Europe's grande dames: spacious, elegant, and formal. Rooms have high ceilings, a mix of conservative-style furniture, a walk-in closet, and huge, modern bathrooms. Flowers fill the bistro La Brasserie, and the restaurant Lakmé ($$$$) is an oasis of Asian-accented cuisine where diners can create their own three- to five-course menus. ⊠ *Monheimsallee 52, D–52062* ☎ *0241/91320* ᐟ *0241/91100* ⊕ *www.dorint.de* ⇆ *185 rooms, 2 suites* ᐣ *2 restaurants, room service, in-room data ports, minibars, cable TV with movies, health club, hair salon, massage, sauna, bar, babysitting, dry cleaning, laundry service, concierge, business services, meeting rooms, parking (fee), some pets allowed (fee), no-smoking rooms* ⊟ *AE, DC, MC, V* ⦿*⦆ BP.*

$ ⊞ **Hotel Brülls am Dom.** In the historic heart of the city, this family-run hotel offers tradition, convenience, and considerable comfort. It's a short walk to nearly all the major attractions. ⊠ *Hühnermarkt 2–3, D–52062* ☎ *0241/31704* ᐟ *0241/404–326* ⇆ *10 rooms* ᐣ *Cable TV, parking (fee); no a/c* ⊟ *No credit cards* ⦿*⦆ CP.*

$ ⊞ **Hotel Dura.** This small, family-run hotel, one block from the train station, on a noisy street, is one of the few low-budget options in the city. There's no restaurant, but you can buy snacks in the kiosk downstairs. ⊠ *Lagerhausstr. 5, D–52064* ☎ *0241/403–135* ᐟ *0241/401–8450* ⇆ *8 rooms, 1 apartment* ᐣ *Cable TV, bar; no a/c* ⊟ *DC, MC, V* ⦿*⦆ CP.*

Nightlife & the Arts

Most activity in town is concentrated around the market square and Pontstrasse, a pedestrian street that radiates off the square. Start out at Aachen's most popular bar, the **Dom Keller** (⊠ Hof 1 ☎ 0241/34265), to mingle with locals of all ages at old wooden tables. The Irish pub **Wild Rover** (⊠ Hirschgraben 13 ☎ 0241/35453) serves Guinness on tap to live music every night starting at 9:30. The municipal orchestra gives regular concerts in the **Kongresszentrum Eurogress** (⊠ Monheimsallee 48 ☎ 0241/91310).

Shopping

Don't leave Aachen without stocking up on the traditional local gingerbread, *Aachener Printen.* Most bakeries in town offer assortments. Some of the best are at the **Alte Aachener Kaffeestuben** (⊠ Büchel 18 ☎ 0241/35724), also known as the *Konditorei van den Daele.* The store-café is worth a visit for its atmosphere and tempting aromas, whether or not you intend to buy anything. It also ships goods.

Düsseldorf

47 km (29 mi) north of Köln.

Düsseldorf may suffer by comparison to Köln's remarkable skyline, but the elegant city has more than enough charm—and money—to boost its confidence. It has a reputation for being one of the richest cities in Germany, with an extravagant lifestyle that epitomizes the economic success of postwar Germany. Since 80% of Düsseldorf was destroyed in World War II, the city has since been more or less rebuilt from the ground up—in part re-creating landmarks of long ago and restoring a medieval riverside quarter.

At the confluence of the Rivers Rhine and Düssel, this dynamic city started as a small fishing town. The name means "village on the Düssel," but obviously this Dorf is a village no more. Raised expressways speed traffic past towering glass-and-steel structures; within them, glass-enclosed shopping malls showcase the finest clothes, furs, jewelry, and other goods that money can buy.

The **Königsallee,** the main shopping avenue, is the epitome of Düsseldorf affluence; it's lined with the crème de la crème of designer boutiques and stores. Known as the Kö, this wide, double boulevard is divided by an ornamental waterway that is actually a part of the River Düssel. Rows of chestnut trees line the Kö, shading a string of sidewalk cafés. Beyond the Triton Fountain, at the street's north end, begins a series of parks and gardens. In these patches of green you can sense a joie de vivre hardly expected in a city devoted to big business.

The lovely **Hofgarten Park,** once the garden of the elector's palace, is reached by heading north to Corneliusplatz. Laid out in 1770 and completed 30 years later, the Hofgarten is an oasis of greenery at the heart of downtown and a focal point for Düsseldorf culture.

The baroque **Schloss Jägerhof,** at the far-east edge of the Hofgarten, is more a combination town house and country lodge than a castle. It houses the **Goethe Museum,** featuring original manuscripts, first editions, personal correspondence, and other memorabilia of Germany's greatest writer. There's also a museum housing a collection of **Meissner porcelain.** ✉ *Jacobistr. 2* ☎ *0211/899–6262* ⊕ *www.goethe-museum.com* 🖼 *€2* ☽ *Tues.–Fri. and Sun. 11–5, Sat. 1–5.*

The **museum kunst palast** (art museum foundation) lies at the northern extremity of the Hofgarten, close to the Rhine. The collection of paintings runs the gamut from Rubens, Goya, Tintoretto, and Cranach the Elder to the romantic Düsseldorf school and such modern German expressionists as Beckmann, Kirchner, Nolde, Macke, and Kandinsky. The collection also includes works from Asia and Africa. ✉ *Ehrenhof 4–5* ☎ *0211/899–2460* ⊕ *www.museum-kunst-palast.de* 🖼 *€8* ☽ *Tues.–Sun. 11–8.*

The **Kunstsammlung Nordrhein-Westfalen** (Art Collection of North Rhine–Westphalia) displays a dazzling array of 20th-century classic modern paintings, including works by Bonnard, Braque, Matisse, Léger, Johns, and Pollock; there are also many by Paul Klee, the Swiss painter who lived in Düsseldorf for a time and taught at the National Academy of Art. The collection is across the street from the city opera house. ✉ *Grabbepl. 5* ☎ *0211/83810* ⊕ *www.kunstsammlung.de* 🖼 *€6.50* ☽ *Tues.–Fri. 10–6, weekends 11–6, 1st. Wed. of each month 10–10.*

The restored **Altstadt** (Old Town) faces the Rhine. Narrow alleys thread their way to some 200 restaurants and taverns offering a wide range of cuisines, all crowded into the 1-square-km (½-square-mi) area between the Rhine and Heine Allee. Traffic is routed away from the river and underneath the **Rhine Promenade,** which is lined by chic shopping arcades and cafés. Joggers, rollerbladers, and folks out for a stroll make much use of the promenade as well. Occasionally you can still see the *Radschläger,* young boys who demonstrate their cartwheeling abilities, a Düsseldorf tradition, for the admiration (and tips) of visitors.

A plaque at **Bolkerstrasse 53** indicates where poet Heinrich Heine was born in 1797. The **Heinrich Heine Institute** has a museum and an archive of significant manuscripts. Part of the complex was once the residence of the composer Robert Schumann. ⊠ *Bilkerstr. 12–14* ☎ *0211/899– 2902* ⊕ *www.duesseldorf.de/kultur/heineinstitut* ⊠ € 2 ⊙ *Tues.–Fri. and Sun. 11–5, Sat. 1–5.*

The stylish **MedienHafen** is an eclectic mixture of late-19th-century warehouses and ultramodern new businesses, shopping, and entertainment amenities. The now fashionable and hip neighborhood is one of Europe's masterpieces in urban redevelopment. Surrounding the historic, commercial harbor, now occupied by yachts and leisure boats, at the foot of the Rhine Tower, many media companies have made this area their new home. International star architects including David Chipperfield, Fumihiko Maki, Claude Vasconi, and Frank O. Gehry have left their mark. On the riverbank, you'll find Gehry's **Neuer Zollhof,** a particularly striking ensemble of three organic-looking high-rises. The best way to tackle the buzzing architecture is to take a stroll down the promenade Am Handelshafen from the Rhine Tower toward Franziusstrasse, and then back along the opposite side on Speditionsstrasse.

The traffic-free cobblestone streets of the Old Town lead to **Burgplatz** (Castle Square). The 13th-century **Schlossturm** (Castle Tower) is all that remains of the castle built by the de Berg family, which founded Düsseldorf. The tower also houses the **Schifffahrtsmuseum,** which charts 2,000 years of Rhine boatbuilding and navigation. ⊠ *Burgpl. 30* ☎ *0211/899– 4195* ⊠ *€3* ⊙ *Tues.–Sun. 11–6.*

The Gothic **St. Lambertus** (St. Lambertus Church; ⊠ Stiftspl.) is near the castle tower on Burgplatz. Its spire became distorted because unseasoned wood was used in its construction. The Vatican elevated the 14th-century brick church to a basilica minor (small cathedral) in 1974 in recognition of its role in church history. Built in the 13th century, with additions from 1394, St. Lambertus contains the tomb of William the Rich and a graceful late-Gothic tabernacle.

Where to Stay & Eat

$$$$ ✕ **Im Schiffchen.** Although it's a bit out of the way, dining in one of Germany's best restaurants makes it worth a trip. This is grande luxe, with cooking that's a fine art. A typical dish might be fried saddle of French milk calf in vervain sauce. The restaurant Aalschokker, on the ground floor, features local specialties created by the same chef but at lower prices. There are 900 wines on the menu. ⊠ *Kaiserwerther Markt 9* ☎ *0211/ 401–050* ⌂ *Reservations essential* ⌂ *Jacket and tie* ▭ *AE, DC, MC, V* ⊙ *Closed Sun. and Mon. No lunch.*

$$–$$$ ✕ **Weinhaus Tante Anna.** This charming restaurant is furnished with antiques. The cuisine presents modern versions of German classics, demonstrating that there's a lot more to the country's cooking than wurst and

sauerkraut—a specialty is the hearty roast beef with mustard. ⊠ *Andreasstr. 2* ☎ *0211/131–163* ▭ *AE, DC, MC, V* ⊘ *Closed Sun. No lunch.*

$–$$$ ✕ **Malkasten.** If artists seem to live in restaurants and pubs, then the Malkasten ("paint box") shines as a most favored haven. The stylish bar and restaurant is a designer's dream come true. Chef Aldo Villani serves a wild mix of German-Italian and French cooking as colorful as his restaurant's name suggests. ⊠ *Jacobistr. 6* ☎ *0211/173–040* ▭ *AE, MC, V* ⊘ *No lunch Sat.*

$–$$$ ✕ **PianPolvere.** Members of Düsseldorf's high-society crowd congregate
FodorśChoice for their nightly see-and-be-seen ballet at this ultrastylish Italian restau-
★ rant. Good taste is available here at a price. The ambience is dictated by four huge 16th-century chandeliers suspended over minimalist tables made of varying fine, dark woods, set off by high-back leather seats and an 82-foot-long tin-covered bar. The food is delicious, hearty country fare featuring dishes such as lamb chops with almonds and duck liver. The adjoining cigar lounge beckons you to puff the night away. ⊠ *Grünstr. 15, at Stilwerk department store* ☎ *0211/8622–8880* ▭ *AE, DC, MC, V.*

¢–$ ✕ **Brauerei Zur Uel.** A nontraditional brew house, the Uel is the popular hangout for Düsseldorf's students. The basic menu consists of soups, salads, and pastas; the ingredients are fresh and the portions are generous. Every cultural and political event in the city is advertised in the entry hall. ⊠ *Ratingerstr. 16* ☎ *0211/325–369* ▭ *MC, V.*

¢–$ ✕ **Zum Uerige.** Among beer buffs, Düsseldorf is famous for its *Altbier,* so called because of the old-fashioned brewing method. The mellow and malty copper-color brew is produced by eight breweries in town. This tavern provides the perfect atmosphere for drinking it. The beer is poured straight out of polished oak barrels and served with hearty local food by busy waiters in long blue aprons. ⊠ *Bergerstr. 1* ☎ *0211/866–990* ▭ *No credit cards.*

$$$$ 🖼 **Steigenberger Parkhotel.** Miraculously quiet despite its central location on the edge of the Hofgarten and at the beginning of the Königsallee, this old hotel is anything but stodgy. The soaring ceilings add to the spaciousness of the guest rooms, each individually decorated in a restrained, elegant style. The pampering continues at the breakfast buffet, served in the Menuette restaurant, where champagne and smoked salmon are appropriate starters for a shopping expedition on the Kö. ⊠ *Corneliuspl. 1, D–40213* ☎ *0211/13810* 🖷 *0211/138–1592* ⊕ *www. steigenberger.de* 🛏 *122 rooms, 11 suites* ⌂ *Restaurant, café, some in-room data ports, in-room safes, minibars, cable TV, 2 bars, dry cleaning, laundry service, concierge, business services, meeting rooms, free parking, some pets allowed (fee), no-smoking rooms; no a/c in some rooms* ▭ *AE, DC, MC, V* ⦾ *BP.*

$$–$$$$ 🖼 **Günnewig Hotel Esplanade.** This small, modern hotel has an exceptionally quiet, leafy location still close to the action. From the inviting lobby to the attractive rooms, the ambience here is one of intimacy. Room rates vary depending on the view. ⊠ *Fürstenpl. 17, D–40215* ☎ *0211/386–850* 🖷 *0211/3868–5555* ⊕ *www.guennewig.de* 🛏 *80 rooms, 2 suites* ⌂ *In-room data ports, cable TV, pool, sauna, bar, business services, parking (fee), some pets allowed (fee), no-smoking floors; no a/c* ▭ *AE, DC, MC, V* ⦾ *BP.*

$$ ☷ **Carathotel.** Besides bright, well-sized rooms, the true strength of this modern hotel is its location, at the southern edge of the Altstadt. After a generous buffet breakfast you can quickly reach either the Rhine or the Kö with a three-block walk. ⊠ *Benratherstr. 7a, D–40213* ☎ *0211/ 13050* 📠 *0211/322–214* ⊕ *www.horega.de* 🛏 *72 rooms, 1 suite* � *Some in-room data ports, cable TV, sauna, Internet, business services, meeting room, parking (fee), some pets allowed (fee), no-smoking floors; no a/c in some rooms* ▭ *AE, DC, MC, V* ⍟❘ *BP.*

$ ☷ **Diana.** If a trade fair hasn't filled this place, it's one of the best bets for a low-price stay in this high-price town. The small rooms with adjoining bathrooms are comfortable, if somberly furnished. The Altstadt is a 15-minute walk away. ⊠ *Jahnstr. 31, D–40215* ☎ *0211/375–071* 📠 *0211/385–0070* 🛏 *20 rooms* � *Cable TV, some pets allowed (fee); no a/c* ▭ *AE, DC, MC, V* ⍟❘ *BP.*

Nightlife & the Arts

The **Altstadt** is a landscape of pubs, dance clubs, ancient brewery houses, and jazz clubs in the vicinity of the Marktplatz and along cobblestone streets named Bolker, Kurze, Flinger, and Mühlen. These places may be crowded, but some are very atmospheric. The local favorite for nightlife is the **Hafen** neighborhood. Its restaurants and bars cater to the hip thirtysomething crowd that works and parties there. **Front Page** (⊠ Mannesman Ufer 9 ☎ 0211/323–264) is a slick watering hole. The most popular dance club is **Sam's West** (⊠ Königsallee 52 ☎ 0211/328–171).

Düsseldorf, once home to Mendelssohn, Schumann, and Brahms, has the finest concert hall in Germany after Berlin's Philharmonie, the **Tonhalle** (⊠ Ehrenhof 1 ☎ 0211/899–6123), a former planetarium on the edge of the Hofgarten. It's the home of the Düsseldorfer Symphoniker, which plays from September to mid-June. **Deutsche Oper am Rhein** (⊠ Heinrich Heine Allee 16a ☎ 0211/890–8211) showcases the city's highly regarded opera company and ballet troupe. The **Robert Schumann Saal** (⊠ Ehrenhof 4 ☎ 0211/899–6211 ⊕ www.museum-kunst-palast. de) has classic and pop concerts, symposia, film, and international theater. One of Germany's finest variety and artistic shows is presented nightly at the **Roncalli's Apollo Varieté** (⊠ Apollopl./Haroldstr. 1 ☎ 0211/828–9090 ⊕ www.apollo-variete.com).

A 30-minute ride outside Düsseldorf by car, train, or S-bahn (from the Hauptbahnhof) will get you to the industrial city of Wuppertal, whose main claim to fame is its transit system of suspended trains, the *Schwebebahn*. It is also home to the **Tanztheater Wuppertal** (⊠ Spinnstr. 4 ☎ 0202/569–4444 ⊕ www.pina-bausch.de), the dance-theater company of world-famous choreographer Pina Bausch.

Shopping

For antiques, go to the area around Hohe Strasse. The east side of the **Königsallee** is lined with some of Germany's trendiest boutiques, grandest jewelers, and most extravagant furriers. The shopping arcade **Kö Center** (⊠ Königsallee 30) features the most famous names in fashion, from Chanel to Louis Vuitton. **Kö Galerie** (⊠ Königsallee 60) has trendy boutiques and includes a Mövenpick restaurant on its luxurious two-story premises. **Schadow Arcade** (⊠ Off Schadowpl., at end of Kö Galerie) caters to normal budgets, with such stores as Hennes & Mauritz (H&M) and Habitat.

THE RHINELAND A TO Z

To research prices, get advice from other travelers, and book travel arrangements, visit www.fodors.com.

AIRPORTS

The Rhineland is served by three international airports: Frankfurt, Düsseldorf, and Köln-Bonn. Bus and rail lines connect each airport with its respective downtown area and provide rapid access to the rest of the region. No-frills carriers that fly within Europe are based at Frankfurt-Hahn Airport in Lautzenhausen, between the Rhine and Mosel valleys (a 45-minute drive from Wiesbaden; a 1½-hour bus ride from Frankfurt Airport). The Luxembourg Findel International Airport (a 30-minute drive from Trier) is close to the upper Mosel River Valley.

▪ **Flughafen Düsseldorf** ☎ 0211/421-2223. **Flughafen Köln/Bonn** ⊠ Waldstr. 247, Köln ☎ 02203/404-001.

BIKE TRAVEL

The Mosel Valley, with its small hamlets lining the riverbanks, is an excellent area for biking. The train station in Trier rents bikes; call the Deutsche Bahn bicycle hotline to reserve. Cyclists can follow the marked route of the *Radroute Nahe-Hunsrück-Mosel* from Trier to Bingen, which partially overlaps with the *Moselradwanderweg* from Koblenz to Trier. Both Bonn and Köln have extensive bike paths downtown; these are designated, red-painted or red-brick paths on the edges of roads or sidewalks. (Pedestrians, beware: anyone walking on a bike path risks getting mowed down.) Bicyclists are expected to follow the same traffic rules as cars. In Bonn, the Radstation, at the main train station, not only will rent you a bike and provide maps, but will fill your water bottle and check the pressure in your tires for free. In Köln, Rent-a-Bike offers bike rental by the day from April through October as well as a daily three-hour bike tour of the city.

▪ **Deutsche Bahn bicycle hotline** ☎ 01805/151-415. **Radstation** ⊠ Quantiusstr. 26, Bonn ☎ 0228/981-4636. **Rent-a-Bike** ⊠ Markmannsg. under Deutzer Brücke, Köln ☎ 0171/629-8796.

CAR RENTAL

Each of the companies below has a rental office at the Frankfurt Airport. Avis, Europcar, and Hertz have offices at the Luxembourg Airport as well. Sixt has an office at Wiesbaden's main train station.

▪ **Avis** ⊠ Römerstr. 4, Bonn ☎ 0228/631-433 ⊠ Berliner Allee 32, Düsseldorf ☎ 0211/865-6220 ⊠ Andernacher Str. 190-192, Koblenz ☎ 0261/800-366 ⊠ Köln-Bonn Airport, Köln ☎ 02203/402-343 ⊠ Herzogenbuscher Str. 35, Trier ☎ 0651/270-770 ⊠ Dotzheimer Str. 93-95, Wiesbaden ☎ 0611/449-030. **Europcar** ⊠ Potsdammer Pl. 7, Bonn ☎ 0228/604-340 ⊠ Burgunderstr. 53, Düsseldorf ☎ 0211/950-980 ⊠ Andernacher Str. 199, Koblenz ☎ 0261/889-180 ⊠ Köln-Bonn Airport, Köln ☎ 02203/955-880 ⊠ Wasserweg 16, Trier ☎ 0651/146-540 ⊠ Kasteler Str. 42, Wiesbaden

☎ 0611/186−330. **Hertz** ✉ Juelicherstr. 250, Aachen ☎ 0241/162−686 ✉ Adenauer-allee 216, Bonn ☎ 0228/201−530 ✉ Immermannstr. 65, Düsseldorf ☎ 0211/357−025 ✉ Bismarckstr. 19−21, Köln ☎ 0221/515−084 ✉ Loeb Str. 4, Trier ☎ 0651/23137 ✉ Schwalbacher Str. 38, Wiesbaden ☎ 0611/945−0845. **Sixt** ✉ Tilde-Klose-Weg 6, Düsseldorf ☎ 0211/471−310 ✉ Friedrich-Mohr-Str. 10A, Koblenz ☎ 0261/86095 ✉ Aachenerstr. 226−232, Köln ☎ 0221/954−2300 ✉ Bahnhof, Wiesbaden ☎ 0611/840−300.

CAR TRAVEL

The autobahns and other highways of the Rhineland are busy, so allow plenty of time for driving. Frankfurt is 126 km (78 mi) from Koblenz, 175 km (109 mi) from Bonn, 190 km (118 mi) from Köln, and 230 km (143 mi) from Düsseldorf (the A−3 links Frankfurt with Köln and Düsseldorf and passes near Koblenz and Bonn). The most spectacular stretch of the Rhineland is along the Middle Rhine, between Mainz and Koblenz, which takes in the awesome castles and vineyards of the Rhine gorge. Highways hug the river on each bank (B−42 on the north and eastern sides, and B−9 on the south and western sides), and car ferries crisscross the Rhine at many points.

CONSULATES

🇨🇦 Canada **Canadian Consulate** ✉ Benratherstr. 8, D−40213 Düsseldorf ☎ 0211/172−170.

🇬🇧 United Kingdom **British General Consulate** ✉ Yorckstr. 19, D−40476 Düsseldorf ☎ 0211/94480.

🇺🇸 United States **US Consulate General** ✉ Willi-Becker-Allee 10, D−40227 Düsseldorf ☎ 0211/788−8927.

TOURS

BOAT TOURS   No visit to the Rhineland is complete without at least one river cruise, and there are many options from which to choose. Even rowboats and canoes can be rented at most Rhine and Mosel river resorts.

Trips along the Rhine and Mosel range in length from a few hours to days or even a week or more (⇨ see Cruise Travel *in* Smart Travel Tips). Viking River Cruises offers various multiday cruises on cabin ships. A major day-trip line is Köln-Düsseldorfer Deutsche Rheinschiffahrt (KD Rhine Line). Its fleet travels the Rhine between Köln and Mainz, daily from Easter to late October, and the Mosel from Koblenz to Cochem, daily from June to September (and reduced service during the spring and fall). There are many special offers, such as free travel on your birthday (bring your passport as proof); half-price for senior citizens on Monday and Friday; two cyclists for the price of one on Tuesday, with no charge for the bikes; family day on Wednesday (three children travel free per paying adult); and economical fares for time-saving round-trip travel—one way by train, return by boat.

Many smaller, family-operated boat companies offer daytime trips and, often, nighttime dinner-dance cruises. The Koblenz operator Rhein-und Moselschiffahrt Hölzenbein travels between Koblenz and Winningen on the Mosel and between Bonn and Rüdesheim on the Rhine. From Koblenz, Personenschiffahrt Merkelbach makes round-trip "castle cruises" to Schloss Stolzenfels (one hour) or the Marksburg (two hours), passing by six castles en route. The Hebel-Line has Loreley Valley trips from Boppard. Another important Mittelrhein specialist traveling to the Loreley is the Bingen-Rüdesheimer Fahrgastschiffahrt. The Frankfurt-based Primus-Linie cruises between Frankfurt and the Loreley via Wiesbaden and between Wiesbaden and Heidelberg. The spacious, luxurious boat *Princesse Marie-Astrid,* headquartered in Grevenmacher, Luxembourg, offers gourmet dining, and occasionally evening shows or live music, during Mosel cruises along the German-Luxembourgian border from Trier or Grevenmacher to Schengen. Costs range from €14 to €19, excluding food; entertainment cruises vary in price. Cruises depart from Trier from July through mid-September; and from Grevenmacher from Easter through mid-November.

Three shipping companies in Köln leave from the Rhine landing stages near the Hohenzollern Brücke, a short walk from the cathedral.

🚢 For Rhine Trips **Bingen-Rüdesheimer Fahrgastschiffahrt** ✉ Bingen ☎ 06721/14140 🖷 06721/17398. **Dampfschiffahrt Colonia** ✉ Köln ☎ 0221/257-4225. **Hebel-Line** ✉ Boppard ☎ 06742/2420 🖷 06742/4727. **KD Rhine Line** ✉ Köln ☎ 0221/208-8318, 800/346-6525 in U.S. ⊕ www.k-d.com. **Kölntourist Personenschiffahrt am Dom** ✉ Köln ☎ 0221/121-714. **Personenschiffahrt Merkelbach** ✉ Koblenz ☎ 0261/76810 🖷 0261/973-3264. **Primus-Linie** ✉ Frankfurt ☎ 069/133-8370 ⊕ www.primus-linie.de. **Rhein-und Moselschiffahrt Hölzenbein** ✉ Koblenz ☎ 0261/37744 🖷 0261/16640. **Viking River Cruises** ✉ Köln ☎ 0221/25860, 877/668-4546 in U.S. ⊕ www.vikingkd.com.

🚢 For Mosel Trips **Personenschiffahrt Hans Michels** ✉ Bernkastel-Kues ☎ 06531/8222 🖷 06531/7603. **Personenschiffahrt Kolb** ☎ 02673/1515 🖷 02673/1510. **Princesse Marie-Astrid** ✉ Grevenmacher Luxembourg ☎ (country code for Luxembourg is 352) 758-275 ⊕ www.moselle-tourist.lu. **Rhein- und Moselschiffahrt Hölzenbein** ☎ 0261/37744 🖷 0261/16640.

BUS TOURS Limousine Travel Service has a daily bus trip from Frankfurt to Rhine wine country. From Rüdesheim, travel continues by boat to St. Goarhausen; return to Frankfurt is by bus. The €69 fee includes lunch and a wine tasting.

Bus trips into the Köln countryside (to the Eifel Hills, the Ahr Valley, and the Westerwald) are organized by several city travel agencies. Reisebüro Knipper sells tours to individuals looking for trips outside the city. 🚌 **Limousine Travel Service** ✉ Wiesenhüttenpl. 39, Frankfurt/Main ☎ 069/230-492 ⊕ www.ets-frankfurt.de. **Reisebüro Knipper** ✉ Hahnenstr. 41, near Neumarkt ☎ 0221/205-0820.

CITY TOURS Tours of Bonn start from the tourist office and are conducted April–October, Tuesday–Sunday, and November–March, Saturday only. Call ahead to check times for tours in English.

Bus tours of Düsseldorf leave year-round at 11 daily and also at 2:30 on Saturday, from the corner of Steinstrasse and Königsallee. From April to October, the 2:30 tour is daily as well. Tickets (€17.50 in summer, and €15 in winter) can be purchased on the bus, at the information center, or through Adorf Reisebüro.

The Koblenz tourist office has guided tours on Saturday at 2:30, in April, and on Friday, Saturday, and Sunday at 2:30, May through October, departing from the Historisches Rathaus on Jesuitenplatz (€2.50). English-language tours are available upon request.

Bus tours of Köln leave from outside the tourist office, opposite the main entrance to the cathedral, at the Köln Tourismus Office, hourly 10–3, April–October (more frequently on weekends), and at 11 and 2, November–March. The tour lasts two hours and costs €10; it's conducted in English and German. A two-hour Köln walking tour is available by prior arrangement with the tourist office.

In Trier you can circumnavigate the town with the narrated tours of the Römer-Express trolley, the CityTour double-decker bus, or a tourist office bus; all cost €6 and depart from Porta Nigra, near the tourist office. You can board the hop-on, hop-off bus TrierTour (€5.60; no narration) at any of its 16 stops in town. The tourist office sells tickets for all tours and also leads various walks. A tour in English (€6) departs Saturday, May through October, at 1:30.

Bilingual walking (€6) and bus (€10) tours of Wiesbaden depart from the bus stop in front of the Staatstheater on Kurhausplatz. The walking tour is conducted April–October, Saturday at 10 (November–March, the first and third Saturday). The bus tour is offered year-round, Saturday at 2.

🚩 **Adorf Reisebüro** ✉ Bismarkstr. 45, Düsseldorf ☎ 0211/418-970.

TRAIN TRAVEL

InterCity and EuroCity expresses connect all the cities and towns of the area. Hourly InterCity routes run between Düsseldorf, Köln, Bonn, and Mainz, with most services extending as far south as Munich and as far north as Hamburg. The Mainz–Bonn route runs beside the Rhine, providing spectacular views all the way. The city transportation networks of Bonn, Köln, and Düsseldorf are linked by S-bahn (for information contact the KVB).

🚩**Deutsche Bahn** ☎0180/599-6633. **Kölner Verkehrs-Betriebe** (KVB) ☎0221/547-3333.

TRAVEL AGENCIES

🚩 **American Express** ✉ Immamannstr. 65b, D-40215 Düsseldorf ☎ 0211/385-0069 ✉ Burgmauer 14, D-50667 Köln ☎ 0221/257-5186.

VISITOR INFORMATION

The Rhineland regional tourist office, Rheinland-Pfalz Tourismus, provides general information on the entire region. The events calendar *Veranstaltungskalender Rheinland-Pfalz* gives a comprehensive overview of the wine, regional, and folk festivals, as well as concerts, theater, and art exhibitions taking place in many parts of this area.

Many cultural events and museums in the state of Rhineland-Pfalz accept the *KulturCard* (€5), which grants up to 50% discounts. The card is sold by mail through the regional broadcaster SWR and in person at the newspaper *RZ* (RheinZeitung) shops. The *Mittelrhein Burgen-Ticket*, sold at 10 participating castles in the Mittelrhein area between Rüdesheim and Koblenz, offers a tremendous savings on admission fees to 10 castles. The cost is €14 for adults and allows free admission to the castles.

Bonn's tourism office sells the *RegioBonnCard* package, which offers an array of reductions, plus free entry into most museums, in combination with low- or no-cost transportation for €12.25 per day or €23.50 for two days.

In Köln, most central hotels sell the *KölnTourismus Card* (€15.50), which entitles you to a sightseeing tour, admission to all the city's museums, free city bus and tram travel, and other reductions.

🚩 Discount Tickets **KulturCard** ☏ SWR, Stichwort KulturCard, D-55114 Mainz. **Mittelrhein Burgen-Ticket** ⊕ www.burgen-am-rhein.de.

🚩 Tourist-Information **Aachen** ✉ Aachen Tourist Service, Friedrich-Wilhelm-Pl., Postfach 2007, D-52022 ☎ 0241/180-2960 ⊕ www.aachen-tourist.de. **Bacharach** ✉ Tourist-Information, Oberstr. 45, D-55422 ☎ 06743/919-303 🖶 06743/919-304 ⊕ www.rhein-nahe-touristik.de. **Bernkastel-Kues** ✉ Tourist-Information, Gestade 6, D-54470 ☎ 06531/402-3 🖶 06531/7953 ⊕ www.bernkastel.de. **Bingen** ✉ Tourist-Information; Rheinkai 21, D-55411 ☎ 06721/184-205 🖶 06721/184-214 ⊕ www.bingen.de. **Bonn** ✉ Bonn Information, Windeckstr. 2 am Münsterpl., D-53111 ☎ 0228/775-000 ⊕ www.bonn.de. **Boppard** ✉ Tourist-Information, Marktpl., D-56154 ☎ 06742/3888 🖶 06742/81402 ⊕ www.boppard.de. **Cochem** ✉ Tourist-Information, Endertpl. 1, D-56812 ☎ 02671/60040 🖶 02671/600-444 ⊕ www.cochem.de. **Düsseldorf** ✉ Verkehrsverein, Konrad Adenauer Pl. 12, D-40210 ☎ 0211/172-020 ⊕ www.duesseldorf.de. **Koblenz** ✉ Tourist-Information, Jesuitenplatz 2-4, D-56068 ☎ 0261/129-1610 🖶 0261/130-9211 ⊕ www.koblenz.de. **Köln** ✉ Köln Tourismus Office, Unter Fettenhenen 19, D-50667 ☎ 0221/2213-0400 ⊕ www.koeln.de. **Rheingau-Taunus Kultur & Tourismus** ✉ An der Basilika 11a, D-65375 Oestrich-Winkel ☎ 06723/99550 🖶 06723/995-555 ⊕ www.rheingau-taunus-info.de. **Rheinland-PfalzTourismus** ✉ Löhrstr. 103-105, D-56068 Koblenz ☎ 0261/915-200 🖶 0261/915-2040 ⊕ www.rlp-info.de. **Rüdesheim** ✉ Tourist-Information, Geisenheimer Str. 22, D-65385 ☎ 06722/19433 🖶 06722/3485 ⊕ www.ruedesheim.de. **Trier** ✉ Tourist-Information, An der Porta Nigra, D-54290 ☎ 0651/978-080 🖶 0651/44759 ⊕ www.trier.de/tourismus. **Wiesbaden** ✉ Tourist-Information, Marktstr. 6, D-65183 ☎ 0611/17290 🖶 0611/172-9798 ⊕ www.wiesbaden.de.

WINE
INFORMATION

The German Wine Information Bureau provides background information and brochures about all German wine-growing regions. Tips on wine-related events and package offers are available from regional wine information offices.

The tiny red-wine region near Bonn is called the Ahr. Mosel-Saar-Ruwer Wein supplies wine information about the Mosel, Saar, and Ruwer River valleys. Between the Mosel and Rhine valleys lies the Nahe region.

🚩 **German Wine Information Bureau** ✉ 245 Park Ave., 39th fl., New York, NY 10167 ☎ 212/792-4134 🖶 212/792-4001 ⊕ www.germanwineusa.org. **Gesellschaft für Rheingauer Weinkultur** ✉ Adam-von-Itzstein-Str. 20, D-65375 Oestrich-Winkel ☎ 06723/91757 🖶 06723/917-591 ⊕ www.rheingau.de. **Mittelrhein-Wein** ✉ Am Hafen 2, D-56329 St. Goar ☎ 06741/7712 🖶 06741/7723 ⊕ www.mittelrhein-wein.com. **Mosel-Saar-Ruwer Wein** ✉ Gartenfeldstr. 12a, D-54295 Trier ☎ 0651/710-280 🖶 0651/45443 ⊕ www.msr-wein.de. **Tourisismus & Service Ahr Rhein Eifel** ✉ Felix-Rütten-Str. 2, D-53474 Bad Neuenahr-Ahrweiler ☎ 02641/97730 🖶 02641/977-373 ⊕ www.wohlsein365.de. **Weinland Nahe** ✉ Dessauer Str. 6, D-55545 Bad Kreuznach ☎ 0671/834-050 🖶 0671/834-0525 ⊕ www.weinland-nahe.de.

THE FAIRY-TALE ROAD

12

Updated by
Ted Shoemaker

IF YOU'RE IN SEARCH OF SLEEPING BEAUTY, the Pied Piper, or Rumpelstiltskin, the Fairy-Tale Road, or Märchenstrasse, is the place to look. One of Germany's special tour routes, it leads deep into the heart of the country, as well as the German character, through the landscapes that inspired the Brothers Grimm. It begins 20 minutes east of Frankfurt in the city of Hanau and from there wends its way north 600 km (about 370 mi), mainly through the states of Hesse and Lower Saxony, following the Fulda and Weser rivers and traversing a countryside as beguiling as any other in Europe.

This designated tour route doesn't have the glamour of the Romantic Road, but it also doesn't have the crowds and commercialism. It's a route perhaps even more in tune with romantics. Fairy tales come to life in forgotten villages, ancient castles, and misty valleys where the silence of centuries is broken only by the splash of a ferryman's oar. The meandering, progressive path seems to travel back in time, into the reaches of childhood, imagination, and the German folk consciousness. These old-world settings are steeped in legend and fantasy.

This part of Germany shaped the lives and imaginations of the two most famous chroniclers of German folk history and tradition, the Brothers Grimm. They sought out the region's best storytellers to bring us such unforgettable characters as Cinderella, Hansel and Gretel, Little Red Riding Hood, Rapunzel, Rumpelstiltskin, Sleeping Beauty, and Snow White.

The zigzag course detailed in this chapter follows the spine of the Fairy-Tale Road and includes a number of side trips and detours. The route is best explored by car, though train service is available to the larger cities.

Exploring the Fairy-Tale Road

This isn't a route for travelers in a hurry. The road extends about half the length of Germany, from the banks of the Main River, which marks the border between northern and southern Germany, to the North Sea ports of Bremen and Bremerhaven. The diverse regions have been linked together to highlight the region's connection with the Grimm brothers and their stories, and to create a meandering tour route for travelers seeking a quieter, more intimate view of Gernmany's many charms. Some towns on the journey—Bremerhaven and Hanau, for example—are modern, while others, such as Steinau an der Strasse, Hannoversch-Münden, and Hameln, might have stepped right out of a Grimm story.

About the Restaurants

Old restaurant habits persist to some extent on the Fairy-Tale Road. In urban areas you can find restaurants that serve hot meals around the clock, even at breakfast time. But don't count on that in this largely rural area. Many restaurants serve hot meals only between 11:30 AM and 2 PM, and 6 PM and 9 PM. You rarely need a reservation here and casual clothing is generally acceptable.

About the Hotels

Make advance reservations if you plan to visit in summer. Though it's one of the less-traveled tourist routes in Germany, the main points of the Fairy-Tale Road are popular. Hannover is particularly busy during trade fair times.

The itineraries below assume you'll be starting off from Frankfurt, Germany's transportation hub. You could also approach the Fairy-Tale Road from Hamburg in the north.

Numbers in the text correspond to numbers in the margin and on the Fairy-Tale Road map.

If you have
3 days

12

You won't get much farther than the first stretch of the route, but that's enough for an introduction to the influence of the region on the Grimm brothers. Skip downtown **Hanau** ① altogether and begin with **Schloss Philippsruhe** ▶, the oldest French-style baroque palace east of the Rhine, and the spa district of **Wilhelmsbad,** where European royalty and aristocrats once took the waters. Make 🏨 **Gelnhausen** ② your next stop, for a visit to the remains of Barbarossa's greatest castle. Plan an overnight stay at the **Romantisches Hotel Burg Mühle** or at least dine in its restaurant. Devote your second day to exploring **Steinau an der Strasse** ③, where the Grimm brothers spent much of their childhood, and then continue on to 🏨 **Fulda** ④, which has an impressive palace and cathedral. On your third day proceed north of Fulda, calling at the medieval towns of **Lauterbach, Alsfeld,** and **Marburg** ⑤, all of which are perfect settings for Grimm tales.

5 days

Follow the itinerary described above but include a short stop in **Hanau** ① ▶. From Marburg, continue on to 🏨 **Kassel** ⑥ for the night, and try to catch the sunset from the heights of the Wilhelmshöhe. On the fourth day, traverse the valley of the Fulda River to where it meets the Werra to form the Weser at **Hannoversch-Münden** ⑦, which claimed a place on geographer Alexander von Humboldt's list of the world's most beautiful towns. Follow the lazily winding Weser northward now, making a short detour to **Göttingen** ⑧ for lunch in one of the student taverns in this busy university city. Try to fit in an overnight stay at Sleeping Beauty's Castle in 🏨 **Sababurg** ⑨, half hidden in the depths of the densely wooded Reinhardswald. On the fifth day return to the Weser River valley road and take time for stops at **Bad Karlshafen** ⑩, **Höxter** ⑪, and **Bodenwerder** ⑫ to explore their streets of half-timber houses, examples of the Weser Renaissance style of building. End your trip at 🏨 **Hameln** ⑬, the Pied Piper's town.

If you have
7 days

After the five-day itinerary described above, leave the Fairy-Tale Road at Hameln for a detour to 🏨 **Hannover** ⑭–⑲, which has a magnificent royal park. An overnight stay in Hannover will give you the opportunity to enjoy some nightlife after the tranquillity of the Weser Valley route. Or you can postpone that amusement until 🏨 **Bremen** ㉒, 110 km (68 mi) northwest. Bremen is the northernmost frontier of the Grimm brothers' influence, represented by several statues of the donkey, dog, cat, and rooster of the Bremen Town Musicians fable. It would be a shame to travel all this way without venturing the final 66 km (40 mi) to the seaport of **Bremerhaven,** which has Germany's largest maritime museum.

	WHAT IT COSTS In Euros				
	$$$$	**$$$**	**$$**	**$**	**¢**
RESTAURANTS	over €25	€21–€25	€16–€20	€9–€15	under €9
HOTELS	over €225	€175–€225	€100–€175	€50–€100	under €50

Restaurant prices are per person for a main course at dinner. Hotel prices are for two people in a standard double room, including tax and service.

Timing

Summer is the ideal time to travel through this varied landscape, although in spring you'll find the river valleys carpeted in the season's first flowers and in fall the sleepy current of the Weser is often blanketed in mist. Keep in mind that retail stores and shops in the smaller towns in this area often close for two to three hours at lunchtime.

HESSE

The first portion of the Fairy-Tale Road, from Hanau to Kassel, lies within the state of Hesse. Frankfurt, the gateway to the state, is less than a half hour west of the road's starting point in Hanau.

Hanau

➤ ❶ *16 km (10 mi) east of Frankfurt.*

The Fairy-Tale Road begins in once-upon-a-time fashion at Hanau, the town where the Brothers Grimm were born. Although Grimm fans will want to start their pilgrimage here, Hanau is now a traffic-congested suburb of Frankfurt, with post–World War II buildings that are not particularly attractive. Hanau was almost completely obliterated by wartime bombing raids, and there's little of the Altstadt (Old Town) that the Grimm brothers would recognize now.

Hanau's main attraction can be reached only on foot—the **Nationaldenkmal Brüder Grimm** (Brothers Grimm Memorial) in the Marktplatz. The bronze memorial, erected in 1898, is a larger-than-life-size statue of the brothers, one seated, the other leaning on his chair, the two of them pondering an open book—a fitting pose for these scholars who unearthed so many medieval myths and legends, earning their reputation as the fathers of the fairy tale.

The solid bulk of Hanau's 18th-century **Rathaus** (Town Hall) stands behind the Grimm brothers statue. Every day at noon, 4, and 6 its bells play tribute to another of the city's famous sons, the composer Paul Hindemith (1895–1963), by chiming out one of his canons. On Wednesday and Saturday mornings the Rathaus is the backdrop for the largest street market in the state of Hesse. ✉ *Marktpl. 14.*

The **Altes Rathaus** (Old Town Hall), behind the Rathaus, dominates a corner that has been faithfully reconstructed. This handsome 16th-century Renaissance building has two half-timber upper stories weighted down by a steep slate roof. Today it's a museum. Known as the **Deutsches**

On the Menu

A specialty of northern Hesse is sausages with *Beulches,* made from potato balls, leeks, and black pudding. *Lauterbacher Strolch* is a special Camembert named after the little fellow who lost his sock in that town. *Weck,* which is local dialect for "heavily spiced pork," appears either as *Musterweck,* served on a roll, or as *Weckewerk,* a frying-pan concoction with white bread. Heading north into Lower Saxony, you'll encounter the ever-popular *Speckkuchen,* a heavy and filling onion tart. Another favorite main course is *Pfefferpothast,* a sort of heavily browned goulash with lots of pepper. Trout and eels are common in the rivers and streams around Hameln, and by the time you reach Bremen, north German cuisine has taken over the menu. *Aalsuppe grün,* eel soup seasoned with dozens of herbs, is a must in summer, and the hearty *Grünkohl mit Pinkel,* a cabbage dish with sausage, bacon, and cured pork, appears in winter. Be sure to try the coffee. Fifty percent of the coffee served in Germany comes from beans roasted in Bremen. The city has been producing the stuff since 1673 and knows just how to serve it in pleasantly cozy or, as locals say, *gemütlich* surroundings.

Golf Courses

There are golf courses at Bad Orb, Bad Pyrmont, Bremen, Göttingen, Hanau, Kassel, Hameln, Hannover, and Celle; visiting golfers are welcome, preferably Monday to Thursday, at most locations (provided they can produce a handicap from their local clubs). The courses at Hanau (on the former hunting grounds at Wilhelmsbad) and Kassel (high above the city on the edge of Wilhelmshöhe Park) are particularly attractive. At Schloss Schwöbber, near Hameln, golfers tee off on the extensive castle grounds.

Hiking & Walking

Two protected nature parks—the Weserergland and the Lüneburg Heath—are in or near the Fairy-Tale Road. You can hike the banks of the Weser, stopping at ancient waterside inns, from Hannoversch-Münden, in the south, to Porta-Westfalica, where the Weser River breaks through the last range of north German hills and into the plain of Lower Saxony. The Lüneburg Heath is flat, and hiking is particularly pleasant in late summer, when the heather is in bloom. The tourist offices in the area can give you good tips on where to find nearby trails. A book entitled *Weserbergland: Rother Wanderführer,* by Ulrich Tubbesing, describes 50 selected walks in the area, several of them lasting two or more days. It's available at area bookstores in German only, but the many maps may be useful to non–German speakers as well.

Goldschmiedehaus (German Goldsmiths' House), it has exhibitions about the craft, contemporary and historical, of the goldsmith and silversmith. ⊠ *Altstädter Markt 6* ☎ *06181/4288–888* ⊡ *€2* ⊙ *Tues.–Sun. 10–noon and 2–5.*

The baroque **Schloss Philippsruhe** (Palace of Philipp's Rest), on the bank of the Main River in the suburb of Kesselstadt (Bus 1 will take you there

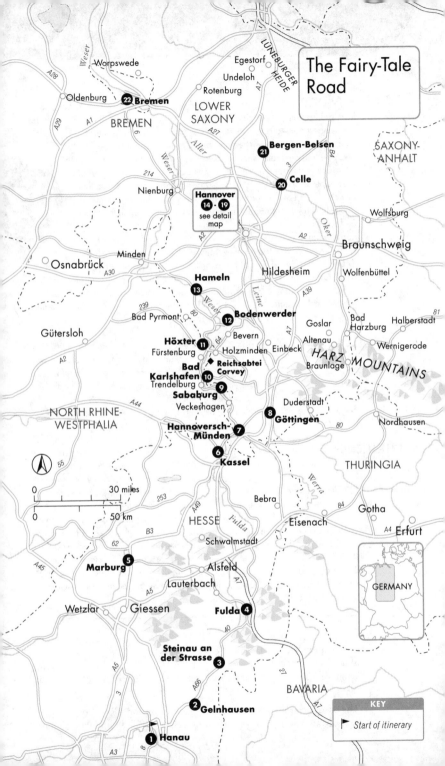

in 10 minutes), has much more than Grimm exhibits. Count Philipp Reinhard von Hanau laid the cornerstone in 1701. Historical Hanau treasures, including a priceless collection of faience, are on display in the palace museum, as are exhibits of 17th-century Dutch paintings, silver and cast-iron crafts, and cardboard toy theaters popular in the 19th century. A café with a terrace overlooks the Main.

In the early 19th century, following the withdrawal of the French from Hanau, the original formal gardens were replanned as an informal, English-style park. The contrast between the formal palace and informal wooded grounds is striking. Pause to study the entrance gate—its gilding was the work of Parisian masters. ⊠ *Phillipsruher Allee 45* ☏ *06181/20209* ⊕ *www.museen-hanau.de* ✍ *€2.50* ⊙ *Tues.–Sun. 11–6.*

A short bus ride west from the center of Hanau is its spa district, **Wilhelmsbad,** once a magnet for Europe's wealthy and titled. It was built at the end of the 18th century by Crown Prince Wilhelm von Hessen-Kassel at the site where two peasant women, out gathering herbs, discovered mineral springs. Today you'll find baroque buildings and bathhouses; informal, English-style parkland; riding stables; three restaurants; and one of Germany's loveliest golf courses laid out where the leisure classes once hunted pheasants.

The spa's Arkadenbau (arcade) contains the **Hessisches Puppenmuseum** (Hesse Doll Museum), one of Germany's largest doll museums, with examples dating back to 1750. They also have a room full of antique toys, a few of which date back more than 2,000 years. ⊠ *Parkpromenade 4* ☏ *06181/86212* ✍ *€2.50* ⊙ *Tues.–Sun. 10–noon and 2–5.*

Where to Stay & Eat

$ ✕⌂ **Golfhotel.** An occasional "fore" heard from the neighboring golf course and birdsong coming from the backyard are the only sounds likely to disturb you at this rural retreat on the edge of the Wilhelmsbad park. Nonsporting types relax at the friendly bar or, in warm weather, on the outside terrace (overlooking the golf links, of course). The hotel's da Enzo restaurant ($$–$$$) serves excellent Italian cuisine. There are only seven rooms, so it's essential to book in advance. ⊠ *Wilhelmsbader Allee 32, D–63454* ☏ *06181/99550* ᵬ *06181/87722* ⊕ *www.golfclub-hanau.de* ⊅ *7 rooms* ⌂ *Restaurant, cable TV, bar, meeting rooms, some pets allowed; no a/c* ⊟ *AE, DC, MC, V* ⦿ *BP.*

Gelnhausen

❷ *20 km (12 mi) northeast of Hanau, 35 km (21 mi) northeast of Frankfurt.*

If you're flying into Frankfurt, Gelnhausen is an ideal spot for your first night on the Fairy-Tale Road. It's smaller and more charming than Hanau and is still less than an hour's drive from Frankurt's main airport. The town's picturesque *Altstadt* (old town) will give you a first taste of the half-timber architecture and cobblestone streets that await you in abundance further north.

On an island in the sleepy little Kinzig River you'll find the remains of **Burg Barbarossa,** a castle that may well have stimulated the imagination of the Grimm brothers. Emperor Friedrich I—known as Barbarossa, or Red Beard—built the castle in this idyllic spot in the 12th century; in 1180 it was the scene of the first all-German Imperial Diet, a gathering of princes and ecclesiastical leaders. Today only parts of the russet walls and colonnaded entrance remain. Still, stroll beneath the castle's ruined ramparts on its water site, and you'll get a tangible impression of the medieval importance of the court of Barbarossa. ⊠ *Burgstr. 14* ☎ *06051/ 3805* 🖾 *€1.80* 🕙 *Mar.–Oct., Sun., Tues.–Fri. 10–5, Sat. 3–5; Nov.–Dec., Sun., Tues.–Fri. 10–4, Sat. 3–4.*

The **Hexenturm** (Witches Tower), a grim prison, remains from the time when Gelnhausen was the center of a paranoiac witch hunt in the late 16th century; dozens of women were burned at the stake or thrown— bound hand and foot—into the Kinzig River. Suspects were held in the Hexenturm of the town battlements. Today it houses a bloodcurdling collection of medieval torture instruments. A visit to the tower is possible only as part of a weekly summer-season tour of the town, beginning at the Rathaus. The tour, which costs €5, also includes a tour of Burg Barbarossa. ⊠ *Am Fretzenstein* ☎ *06051/380–300* 🕙 *May–Oct., tour Sun., except 1st Sun. of month, at 2:30.*

Where to Stay & Eat

$ ✕🖾 **Romantisches Hotel Burg Mühle.** *Mühle* means "mill," and this hotel was once the mill of the neighboring castle, delivering flour to the community until 1958. In the restaurant ($$) the mill wheel churns away as you eat. The furniture and carpeting in the hotel is showing a little wear, but the rooms are large (many with small balconies), and spotlessly clean. There is no elevator; reserve a room on the ground floor if this is a problem. ⊠ *Burgstr. 2, D–63571* ☎ *06051/82050* 🖷 *06051/820–554* ⊕ *www.burgmuehle.de* 🛏 *42 rooms* 🛁 *Restaurant, minibars, cable TV, gym, massage, sauna, bar, no-smoking rooms; no a/c* ▭ *DC, MC, V* 🍴*BP.*

Steinau an der Strasse

❸ *30 km (18 mi) northeast of Gelnhausen, 65 km (40 mi) northeast of Frankfurt.*

For clear evidence of its formative influence on the Brothers Grimm, you need only travel to the little town of Steinau—full name Steinau an der Strasse (Steinau "on the road," referring to an old trade route between Frankfurt and Leipzig). They were preschoolers on arrival and under 12 when they left after their father's untimely death.

Steinau dates from the 13th century and is typical of villages in the region. Marvelously preserved half-timber houses are set along cobblestone streets; an imposing castle bristles with towers and turrets. In its woodsy surroundings you can well imagine encountering Little Red Riding Hood, Snow White, or Hansel and Gretel. A major street is named after the brothers; the building where they lived is now known as the Brothers Grimm House.

★ **Schloss Steinau** (Steinau Castle), straight out of a Grimm fairy tale, stands at the top of the town. Originally an early medieval fortress, it was rebuilt in Renaissance style between 1525 and 1558 and first used by the

THE BROTHERS GRIMM

THE TWO ESSENTIAL FEATURES of a Grimm's fairy tale are generally deep, gloomy forests (Hansel and Gretel, Snow White) and castles (Cinderella, The Sleeping Beauty). It would seem logical that the region where the stories originated would be abundantly endowed with both. And, as you will see if you explore the Fairy-Tale Road, it is indeed.

This area, mainly in the state of Hesse, was the home region of the brothers Jacob (1785–1863) and Wilhelm (1786–1859) Grimm. They didn't originate the stories for which they are famous. Their feat was to mine the great folklore tradition that was already deeply engrained in local culture.

For generations eager children had been gathering at dusk around the village storyteller to hear wondrous tales of fairies, witches, and gnomes; tales passed down from storytellers who had gone before. The Grimms sought out these storytellers and recorded their tales.

The result was the two volumes of their work **Kinder und Hausmärchen** (Children and Household Tales), published in 1812 and 1814, and revised and expanded six times during their lifetimes. The last edition, published in 1857, is the basis for the stories we know today. Earlier versions contained more violence and cruelty than deemed suitable for children.

That is how the world got the stories of Cinderella, Sleeping Beauty, Hansel and Gretel, Little Red Riding Hood, Snow White and the Seven Dwarfs, Rumpelstiltskin, Puss-in-Boots, Mother Holle, Rapunzel, and some 200 others, most perhaps unfamiliar.

Both Jacob and Wilhelm Grimm had distinguished careers as librarians and scholars, and probably would be unhappy to know that they are best remembered for the fairy tales. Among other things they compiled the first dictionary of the German language and an analysis of German grammar.

The brothers were born in Hanau, near Frankfurt, which has a statue memorializing them and a Grimm exhibit at Schloss Phillipsruhe. They spent their childhood in Steinau, 30 km (18 mi) to the north, where their father was magistrate. There are two Grimm museums there, one in their home. On their father's untimely death they moved to their mother's home city of Kassel, which also has an important Grimm museum. They attended the university at Marburg from 1802 to 1805, then worked as librarians in Kassel. It was in the Kassel area that they found the best of their stories. They later worked as librarians and professors in the university town of Göttingen and spent their last years as academics in Berlin.

counts of Hanau as their summer residence. Later, it was used to guard the increasingly important trade route between Frankfurt and Leipzig. It's not difficult to imagine the young Grimm boys playing in the shadow of its great gray walls or venturing into the encircling dry moat.

The castle houses a **Grimm Museum**, one of two in Steinau, as well as an **exhibition of marionettes** from the marionette theater. The Grimm Museum exhibits the family's personal effects, including portraits of the Grimm relatives, the family Bible, an original copy of the Grimms' dictionary (the first in the German language), and all sorts of mundane things such as spoons and drinking glasses. Climb the tower for a breathtaking view of Steinau and the countryside. ☎ 06663/6843 ✉ *Museum €2, tower €1, tour of castle and museum €3.20* ⊘ *Mar.–Sept., Tues.–Thurs. and weekends 10–5; Oct.–mid-Dec., Tues.–Thurs. and weekends 10–4.*

♻ The **Steinauer Marionettentheater** (Steinau Marionette Theater) is in the castle's former stables and portrays Grimm fairy tales and other children's classics. Performances are held most weekends at 3. ✉ *Am Kumpen 4* ☎ *06663/245* ✉ *€6.50.*

★ The carefully restored **Brüder-Grimm-Haus,** where the brothers lived as children and where their father had his office, is the only Grimm residence that's still extant. Other Grimm houses, in Hanau and Kassel, were destroyed during World War II. The house is a few hundred yards from the castle and contains a museum devoted to the Grimms. Among the exhibits are books and pictures, some dating from their time, plus reminders of the Grimms' work as lexicographers. ✉ *Brüder-Grimm-Str. 80* ☎ *06663/ 7605* ✉ *€2* ⊘ *Mar.–Dec., daily 2–5; Jan. and Feb., weekends 2–5.*

Where to Stay & Eat

$ ✕▥ **Brathähnchenfarm.** All meat here is charcoal-grilled, something your nose will tell you the minute you step into the cheery hotel-restaurant ($$–$$$). The name *Roast Chicken Farm* tells you right away what the specialty is, but lamb or pork kebabs, spare ribs, and other grilled delicacies can also be had. Many of the rooms face the surrounding forest. ✉ *Im Ohl, D–36396* ☎ *06663/961–228* ☖ *06663/1579* ⊕ *www. brathaehnchenfarm.de* ⇆ *14 rooms* ⚒ *Restaurant, cable TV, bowling, bar, meeting rooms, some pets allowed; no a/c* ▭ *AE, DC, MC, V.*

$ ▥ **Weisses Ross.** It may be a simple inn, but you can sleep within its gnarled walls in the knowledge that the Grimm brothers dined and imbibed in its tavern almost 200 years ago. Rooms facing the street have views of ancient buildings but suffer from traffic noise. ✉ *Brüder-Grimm-Str. 48, D–36396* ☎ *06663/5804* ⇆ *7 rooms, 5 with shower* ⚒ *Meeting room; no a/c, no room phones, no room TVs* ▭ *No credit cards* ¶⊙ *BP.*

Fulda

④ *32 km (20 mi) northeast of Steinau an der Strasse, 100 km (62 mi) northeast of Frankfurt.*

The episcopal city of Fulda is well worth a detour off the Fairy-Tale Road. There are two distinct parts to its downtown area. One is a stunning display of baroque architecture, replete with cathedral, Orangerie, and formal garden, that grew up around the palace. The other is the Old Town, where the incredibly narrow and twisty streets are lined with boutiques, bistros, and a medieval tower.

The city's grandest example of baroque design is the immense **Stadtschloss** (City Palace), formerly the residence of the prince bishops. Much of the palace is used as municipal offices, but there are a few public areas. The **Fürstensaal** (Princes' Hall), on the second floor, provides a breathtaking display of baroque decorative artistry, with ceiling paintings by the 18th-century Bavarian artist Melchior Steidl, and fabric-clad walls. The palace also has permanent displays of the faience for which Fulda was once famous, as well as some fine Fulda porcelain.

Also worth seeing is the **Spiegelsaal,** with its many tastefully arranged mirrors. Pause at the windows of the Grünes Zimmer (Green Chamber) to take in the view across the palace park to the **Orangerie,** a large garden with summer-flowering shrubs and plants. If you have time after your palace tour, stroll over for a visit. ⊠ *Schlossstr. 1* ☎ *0661/102–1813* 🖼 *€2* ⊗ *Sat.–Thurs. 10–6, Fri. 2–6.*

The **Dom** (cathedral), Fulda's 18th-century cathedral with tall twin spires, stands on the other side of the broad boulevard that borders the palace park. The basilica accommodated the ever-growing number of pilgrims who converged on Fulda to pray at the grave of the martyred St. Boniface, the "Apostle of the Germans." A black alabaster bas-relief depicting his death marks the martyr's grave in the crypt. The **Cathedral Museum** (☎ *0661/0661–87207* 🖼 *€2.10* ⊗ Apr.–Oct., Tues.–Sat. 10–5:30, Sun. 12:30–5:30; Nov.–Mar., Tues.–Sat. 10–12:30 and 1:30–4, Sun. 12:30–4) contains a document bearing St. Boniface's writing, along with several other treasures, including Lucas Cranach the Elder's fine 16th-century painting of Christ and the Adulteress. ⊠ *Dompl.* ⊗ *Apr.–Oct., weekdays 10–6, Sat. 10–3, Sun. 1–6; Nov.–Mar., weekdays 10–5, Sat. 10–3, Sun. 1–6.*

Directly across from the Dom is the two-towered **Michaelskirche** (Church of St. Michael), one of Germany's oldest churches. Built in the 9th century, its Carolingian and Romanesque architecture contrasts strikingly with the neighboring Baroque cathedral. A brochure is available in English for a small fee. ⊠ *Michaelsberg. 1* ⊗ *Apr.–early Oct., daily 10–6; mid-Oct.–March, daily 2–4.*

The **Vonderau Museum** is housed in a former Jesuit seminary. Its exhibits chart the cultural and natural history of Fulda and eastern Hesse. A popular section of the museum is its **planetarium,** with a variety of shows, including one for children. Since it has only 35 seats, an early reservation is advisable. You get a unique impression of wandering alone through the stars to the sound of music. Shows take place Thursday at 7, Friday at 5 and 8, Saturday at 3 and 8, and Sunday at 10:30 and 3. ⊠ *Jesuitenpl. 2* ☎ *0661/928–3510* 🖼 *Museum €2, planetarium €2.50* ⊗ *Tues.–Sun. 10–6.*

The **Rathaus** (Town Hall) is possibly the finest in this part of the country. The particularly delicate half-timber separates the arcaded first floor from the steep roof and its incongruous but charming battery of small steeples. It can be viewed only from the outside. ⊠ *Schlossstr. 1.*

If you need a break from cultural pursuits, head to the **Gokart Bahn** (Go-Cart Track) on the southern outskirts of Fulda. Hop into one of the 5.5 HP Honda machines and navigate the 11 curves of a 1,320-foot-long indoor track. A special "top grip" surface keeps you safely on the piste. It's expensive fun, but where else can you play at being a top Formula One driver? ⊠ *Frankfurter Str. 142* ☎ *0661/402–053* ✉ *€9.50 per ride* ☉ *Mon.–Thurs. 3–11, Fri. 3 PM–midnight, Sat. 1 PM–midnight, Sun. 10 AM–11 PM.*

Where to Stay & Eat

¢–$$ ✕ **Zum Stiftskämmerer.** This former episcopal treasurer's home is now a charming tavern-restaurant, its menu packed with local fare prepared with imagination. A four-course menu priced around €30 is an excellent value, although à la carte dishes can be ordered for as little as €5. Try the *Schlemmertöpfchen,* a delicious (and very filling) combination of pork, chicken breast, and venison steak. ⊠ *Kämmerzeller Str. 10* ☎ *0661/52369* ▭ *DC, MC, V* ☉ *Closed Tues.*

★ $$–$$$$ 🏨 **Romantik Hotel Goldener Karpfen.** Fulda is famous for its baroque buildings, and this hotel is a short walk from the finest of them. The hotel, too, dates from the baroque era (circa. 1750), though the facade was redone around 1900. Inside it's been renovated to a high standard of comfort. Afternoon coffee in the tapestry-upholstered chairs of the hotel's lounge is one of Fulda's delights, while dining in the elegant restaurant, with linen tablecloths, Persian rugs, and subdued lighting, is another. ⊠ *Simpliciusbrunnen 1, D–36037* ☎*0661/86800* 🖷*0661/868–0100* ⊕*www.hotel-goldener-karpfen.com* ✒ *50 rooms* ⅗ *Restaurant, in-room data ports, cable TV, sauna, Weinstube, meeting rooms, some pets allowed (fee), no-smoking rooms; no a/c in some rooms* ▭ *AE, DC, MC, V* ⋓⃒ *BP.*

$$–$$$ 🏨 **Maritim Hotel am Schlossgarten.** This is the luxurious showpiece of the Maritim chain. The large breakfast room and conference rooms are housed in a stunning 18th-century orangerie overlooking Fulda Palace Park. Guest rooms are in a modern wing with a large central atrium. The historic atmosphere of the grand old building extends to the basement foundations, where you can dine beneath centuries-old vaulted arches in the Dianakeller restaurant ($–$$$). The rooms are large and comfortable; many have balconies with views over the park. ⊠ *Pauluspromenade 2, D–36037* ☎ *0661/2820* 🖷 *0661/282–499* ⊕ *www.maritim.de* ✒ *111 rooms, 1 suite* ⅗ *Restaurant, café, cable TV, indoor pool, sauna, bar, beer garden, some pets allowed (fee); no a/c* ▭ *AE, DC, MC, V* ⋓⃒ *BP.*

¢–$ 🏨 **Zum Kronhof.** This homey hotel vies for "funkiest decor" around. There's an array of clashing colors in every room, but it's clean and friendly. You're right behind the Dom, so you won't need an alarm clock. A room is usually available, but call ahead just to be safe. ⊠ *Am Kronhof 2, D–36037* ☎*0661/74147* 🖷*0661/74147* ✒*22 rooms* ⅗*Restaurant, café, cable TV, meeting rooms, free parking, some pets allowed, no-smoking rooms; no a/c, no room phones* ▭ *No credit cards* ⋓⃒ *BP.*

The Arts

One wing of the bishop's palace is now the city's main theater. Organ recitals are given regularly in Fulda's Dom. Call 0661/102–1814 for details on all of Fulda's **cultural events.**

en route

Marburg is the next major stop on the road. Take B–254 to Alsfeld, making a short stop in Lauterbach along the way. From Alsfeld, take B–62 into Marburg.

The resort town of **Lauterbach** has many medieval half-timber houses and is the setting of a well-known folk song in which a little fellow complains of having lost his sock. (The lyrics never crossed the Atlantic, but the tune did, as "Oh Where, Oh Where Has My Little Dog Gone?") There's a statue of the little fellow in town.

Lauterbach's garden gnomes are renowned as a beloved, folklorish German export. These gnomes, made in all shapes and sizes by the firm of **Heissner AG,** stand out on lawns at night with lighted lanterns, direct choruses of birds with batons, or fish in goldfish ponds. You can examine them, and perhaps buy one, at the factory. (⊠ Schlitzerstr. 24, D–36341 ☎ 06641/860)

The Fairy-Tale Road continues north to **Alsfeld** (34 km [21 mi] northwest of Fulda), notable for its beautifully preserved half-timber houses on narrow, winding cobbled streets. The numerous cafes and restaurants make this an ideal place to stop for lunch. The jewel of Alsfeld—and one of Germany's showpieces—is the **Altes Rathaus** (Old Town Hall), built in 1512. Its facade—combining a ground floor of stone arcades; half-timber upper reaches; and a dizzyingly steep, top-heavy slate roof punctuated by two pointed towers shaped like witches' hats—would look right at home in Walt Disney World. To get an unobstructed snapshot of this remarkable building (which is closed to the public), avoid the Marktplatz on Tuesday and Friday, when market stalls clutter the square. Information and a self-guided walking tour of the town are available in English at the tourist office, located across from the Altes Rathaus.

Marburg

5 *60 km (35 mi) northwest of Fulda.*

"I think there are more steps in the streets than in the houses." That is how Jacob Grimm described the half-timber hillside town of Marburg. He and his brother Wilhelm studied at the town's famous university from 1802 to 1805.

Marburg rises steeply from the Lahn River to the spectacular castle that crowns the hill, 335 feet up. Many of the winding, crooked "streets" are indeed stone staircases; a free elevator near the tourist information office on Pilgrimstein can transport you from the level of the river to the marketplace. Several of the hillside houses have a back door five stories above the front door.

A great deal of money went into restoring the buildings to their original appearance (half-timbering went out of fashion after the 1600s, and the building facades had been stuccoed over). Much of the old city is closed to automobile traffic, which is just as well, because the cobblestone streets are slippery when wet, especially on a steep hillside. One of the main streets of the old city is named Barfüsserstrasse (Barefoot Street) because it led to a Franciscan monastery, the residents of which were sworn to humility and poverty.

The university and its students are the main influence on the town's social life, which pulses through the many street cafés, restaurants, and student hangouts around the marketplace. Because so many of the streets are traffic-free, the whole area is filled with outdoor tables when the weather cooperates.

Marburg's most important building is the **Elisabethkirche** (St. Elizabeth Church; ⊠ Elisabethstr. 3), which marks the burial site of St. Elizabeth (1207–31), the town's favorite daughter. She was a Hungarian princess, betrothed at 4 and married at 12 to a member of the nobility, Ludwig IV of Thuringia. She was widowed in 1228 when her husband fell in one of the Crusades and thereafter gave up all worldly pursuits. She moved to Marburg, founded a hospital, gave her wealth to the poor, and spent the rest of her very short life in poverty, caring for the sick and the aged. She is largely responsible for what Marburg became. Because of her selflessness she was made a saint only four years after her death at only 24. The Teutonic Knights built the Elisabethkirche, which quickly became the goal of pilgrimages, enabling the city to prosper. You can visit the shrine in the sacristy that once contained her bones, a masterpiece of the goldsmith's art. The church is a veritable museum of religious art, full of statues and frescoes.

Where to Stay & Eat

¢ ✕ **Cafe Vetter.** This has unquestionably the most spectacular view in a town famous for its panoramas. The outdoor terrace is pleasant in good weather, but there's also a glassed-in terrace and two floors of dining rooms with plush chairs and windows facing the valley. It bakes its own cakes and is known for its literary Sundays and Friday-evening cabarets. ⊠ *Reitg. 4* ☎ *06421/25888* ▭ *No credit cards* ◷ *No dinner.*

$$ ✕▦ **Sorat Hotel Marburg.** This rather unconventional luxury hotel is at the river level, just across the street from the elevator to the marketplace. The color scheme is orange, apricot, and yellow, contrasted with fiery-red tables and upholstered furniture. Its Tartagua Restaurant ($–$$), with bar, terrace, and beer cellar, has become a hip meeting place for those who can afford it. In addition to the usual rolls, eggs, and sausages, the breakfast buffet includes smoked salmon and champagne. ⊠ *Pilgrimstein 29, D–35037* ☎ *06421/9180* 🖶 *06421/918–444* ⊕ *www.sorat-hotels.com/marburg* 🛏 *143 rooms, 3 suites* ☝ *Restaurant, in-room data ports, minibars, cable TV, gym, sauna, bar, meeting room, parking (fee), some pets allowed (fee), no-smoking rooms* ▭ *AE, DC, MC, V* ⦿| *BP.*

en route | The next major stop is Kassel. Travel via Stadtallendorf (B-62 to B-454) to a region so inextricably linked with the Grimm fairy tales that it's known as Rotkäppchenland (Little Red Riding Hood Country). **Schwalmstadt** is the capital of the area, and during the town's many festival days, local people deck themselves out in traditional folk costumes. You'll notice that the women's costume includes a little red cap (*Rotkäppchen*) covering a topknot. This is what gave Little Red Riding Hood her name. You'll meet B–254 again at Schwalmstadt and can follow it into Kassel.

Kassel

❻ *100 km (62 mi) northeast of Marburg.*

The Brothers Grimm lived in Kassel, their mother's home town, as teenagers, and also worked there as librarians at the court of the king of Westphalia, Jerome Bonaparte (Napoléon's youngest brother), and for the elector of Kassel. In researching stories and legends, their best source was not books but storyteller Dorothea Viehmann, who was born in the Knallhütte tavern, which is still in business in nearby Baunatal.

Much of Kassel was detroyed in World War II and the city was rebuilt with little regard for its architectural history. The city's museums and the beautiful Schloss Wilhelmshöhe and Schlosspark, however, are well worth a day or two of exploration. When you arrive, you may want to purchase a ServiceCard. This entitles you to a city bus tour, free travel on the local transportation system, and reduced admission to the museums and the casino. It's available at the **tourist office** (⌧ Tourist GmbH, Obere Königstr. 15 ☎ 0561/707–707) for €7 per day.

The **Brüder Grimm Museum,** in the center of Kassel, occupies five rooms of the Palais Bellevue, where the brothers once lived and worked. Exhibits include furniture, memorabilia, letters, manuscripts, and editions of their books, as well as paintings, watercolors, etchings, and drawings by Ludwig Emil Grimm, a third brother and a graphic artist of note. ⌧ *Palais Bellevue, Schöne Aussicht 2* ☎ *0561/770–550* ⌧ *€1.50* ☉ *Daily 10–4:30.*

The **Deutsches Tapeten Museum** (German Wallpaper Museum), the world's most comprehensive museum of wallpaper, has more than 600 exhibits tracing the art through the centuries. ⌧*Brüder-Grimm-Pl. 5* ☎*0561/78460* ⊕ *www.museum-kassel.de* ⌧ *€3.50, free Fri.* ☉ *Tues.–Sun. 10–5.*

The magnificent grounds of the 18th-century **Schloss und Schlosspark Wilhelmshöhe** (Wilhelmshöhe Palace and Palace Park), at the western edge of Kassel, are said to be Europe's largest hill park. If you have time, plan to spend an entire day here exploring the various gardens, museums, and wooded pathways. Wear good walking shoes and bring some water if you want to hike all the way up to the giant statue of Hercules that crowns the hilltop. Tramline 1 runs from the city to the bottom of the palace grounds. Bus 43 runs from the city to the base of the Hercules statue.

The Wilhelmshöher Park was laid out as a baroque park in the early 18th century, its elegant lawns separating the city from the thick woods of the Habichtswald (Hawk Forest). Schloss Wilhelmshöhe was added between 1786 and 1798. It served as a royal residence from 1807 to 1813, when Jerome was king of Westphalia. Later it became the summer residence of the German emperor Wilhelm II. The great palace stands at the end of the 5-km-long (3-mi-long) Wilhelmshöher Allee, an avenue that runs straight as an arrow from one side of the city to the other.

Kassel's leading art gallery and the state art collection lie within Schloss Wilhelmshöhe as part of the **Staatliche Museen.** Its esteemed collection includes 11 Rembrandts as well as outstanding works by Rubens, Hals, Jordaens, Van Dyck, Dürer, Altdorfer, Cranach, and Baldung Grien. ⊠ *Schloss Wilhelmshöhe* ☎ *0561/93777* ⊕ *www.museum-kassel.de* ⌼ *€3.50, free Fri.* ☉ *Tues.–Sun. 10–5.*

Amidst the thick trees of the Wilhelmshöher Park, it comes as something of a surprise to see the turrets of a romantic medieval castle, the **Löwenburg** (Lion Fortress), breaking the harmony. There are more surprises, for this is no true medieval castle but a fanciful, stylized copy of a Scottish castle, built 70 years after the Hercules statue that towers above it. The architect was a Kassel ruler who displayed an early touch of the mania later seen in the castle-building excesses of Bavaria's eccentric Ludwig II. The Löwenburg contains a collection of medieval armor and weapons, tapestries, and furniture. ⊠ *Schloss Wilhelmshöhe* ☎ *0561/ 3168–0224* ⌼ *€3.50 including tour* ☉ *Mar.–Oct., Tues.–Sun. 10–5; Nov.–Feb., Tues.–Sun. 10–4.*

The giant 18th-century **statue of Hercules** that crowns the Wilhelmshöhe Heights is an astonishing sight, standing on a massive stone octagon that resembles an open-air castle of sorts. At 2:30 PM on Sunday and Wednesday from mid-May through September, water gushes from a fountain beneath the statue, rushes down a series of cascades to the foot of the hill, and ends its precipitous journey in a 175-foot-high jet of water. An open-air concert follows this *wasserspiel* at 4:30. It takes so long to accumulate enough water that the sight can be experienced only on those two days, on holidays, and on the first Saturday evening of June, July, August, and September. On these evenings the cascade is also floodlighted. You can climb the castlelike octagon and the statue from within for a rewarding look over the entire city, spread out over the plain and bisected by the straight line of the Wilhelmshöher Allee. A café lies a short walk from the statue. ⊠ *Schlosspark 3* ☎ *0561/93570* ⌼ *€2* ☉ *Mar.–Oct., Tues.–Sun. 10–4; Nov.–Feb., Tues.–Sun. 10–3.*

Where to Stay & Eat

¢–$$ ✕ **Autobahnrastätte Knallhütte.** This brewery-cum-inn, established in 1752, was the home of village storyteller Dorothea Viehmann. The Grimms got the best of their stories from her, including *Little Red Riding Hood, Hansel and Gretel,* and *Rumpelstiltskin.* Numerous reminders of the tavern's history begin with its name: the crack of a whip (*knall*) sounded the arrival of horse-drawn carriages struggling up the hill. You can dine at the restaurant at any time. With prior notice, you can tour the brewery and sample the beer and food for €12.80. ⊠ *a few miles southwest of Kassel in Baunatal* ☎ *0561/492–076* ▤ *MC, V.*

¢–$ ✕ **Ratskeller.** Rustic German cuisine is served here within the embracing cellar vaults. The kitchen's North Hessian duck, fresh daily from the oven, is much beloved, as is its *Riesenbratwurst,* a 1½-foot coiled roast sausage, served with sauerkraut. ⊠ *Obere Konigstr. 8* ☎ *0561/ 15928* ▤ *AE, DC, MC, V.*

$$ ✕⊡ **Hotel Gude.** This modern hotel is 10 minutes by public transportation from the city center. Rooms are spacious and come with marble bathrooms. The Pfeffermühle ($–$$$) is one of the region's finest restaurants, with an inventive international menu that includes German fare. The hotel is ideal for conferences and has its own underground garage. ⊠ *Frankfurter Str. 299, D–34134* ☎ *0561/48050* 🖷 *0561/ 480–5101* ⊕ *www.hotel-gude.de* 🛏 *85 rooms* ♨ *Restaurant, in-room data ports, in-room safes, minibars, cable TV, indoor pool, gym, massage, sauna, bicycles, bar, meeting room, parking (fee), some pets allowed, no-smoking rooms; no a/c in some rooms* ☰ *AE, DC, MC, V* ⎪⊙⎪ *BP.*

$–$$ ⊡ **Mövenpick Hotel Kassel.** Located in the heart of the city, this modern hotel is all about convenience. The rooms may lack charm, but they are large and comfortable and include amenities such as a kettle with teabags and coffee (a rarity in this region). The hotel is attached to a shopping mall, which has a large food court in the lower level. A 32,000-square-foot fitness center and spa opened in the hotel in 2004 and is accessible to hotel guests for €5 per day. Discounted room rates are available on weekends. ⊠ *in der Kurfürsten Galerie Spohrstr. 4, 34117* ☎ *0561/72850* 🖷 *0561/728–5118* ⊕ *www.movenpick-kassel.com* 🛏 *110 rooms, 18 suites* ♨ *Restaurant, room service, in-room data ports, in-room safes, minibars, cable TV, bar, dry cleaning, laundry service, meeting rooms, parking (fee), some pets allowed* ☰ *AE, DC, V.*

$–$$ ⊡ **Schlosshotel Wilhelmshöhe.** Set in the beautiful baroque Wilhelmshöhe Park, 5 km (3 mi) from town, this is no ancient palace but a contemporary hotel with a sleek gambling casino. Secure a window table in the elegant restaurant for a view of the park grounds. Sports facilities in the immediate vicinity include an 18-hole golf course, tennis courts, pool, and horse stables. The park's palace is a two-minute walk away. ⊠ *Am Schlosspark 8, D–34131* ☎ *0561/30880* 🖷 *0561/308–8428* ⊕ *www. schlosshotel.com* 🛏 *94 rooms, 7 suites* ♨ *Restaurant, café, in-room data ports, cable TV, bar, casino, meeting rooms, some pets allowed (fee), no-smoking rooms; no a/c* ☰ *AE, DC, MC, V* ⎪⊙⎪ *BP.*

$ ⊡ **Hotel Lenz.** All rooms have a bath or shower in this clean and quiet hotel, which is somewhat out of the way. To get here take Tram 5 or 9 to Bahnhof Niederzwehren, and then walk down Frankfurter Strasse. ⊠ *Frankfurter Str. 176, D–34134* ☎ *0561/43373* 🖷 *0561/41188* ⊕ *www.hotel-lenz-kassel.de* 🛏 *13 rooms* ♨ *Restaurant, cable TV, bar, free parking, some pets allowed; no a/c, no phones in some rooms* ☰ *AE, DC, MC, V* ⎪⊙⎪ *BP.*

Nightlife & the Arts

THE ARTS The Kasseler Musiktage (Kassel Music Days) at the end of October has the motto "New forms of the concert, with music of the classic and the modern." The municipal orchestra gives classical concerts in the **Stadttheater** (⊠ Friedrichspl. 15). Kassel has no fewer than 35 theater companies. The principal venues are the Schauspielhaus, the Stadthalle, and the Stadttheater. Call ☎ 0561/109–4222 for program details and tickets for all.

NIGHTLIFE Kassel's pulsating nightlife is concentrated in the bars and discos of Friedrich-Ebert-Strasse. The **casino** (⊠ Schlosspark 8 ☎ 0561/930–850) in the Schlosshotel Wilhelmshöhe provides a note of elegance with its gray-blue-silver decor and windows that afford a spectacular view of the city below. It's open daily 3 PM–3 AM. Admission is €1 for roulette, card games, and slot machines.

Shopping

Königstrasse, Kassel's pedestrian-only shopping street, offers numerous department stores, shops, and cafes. The **Königsgalerie** (⊠ Obere Königstr. 39), is a chic, glass-roof atrium that's packed with boutiques, restaurants, and bars.

In the village of Immenhausen, just north of Kassel, a local glass museum, **Glasmuseum Immenhausen,** exhibits work by German glassblowers; many of the pieces are for sale. The museum has an extensive collection of modern glass, but its centerpiece is work by the celebrated but now-closed Immenhausen glass foundry, the Glashütte Süssmuth. ⊠ *Am Bahnhof 3* ☎ *05673/2060* ✉ *€2.50* ⊙ *May–Oct., Tues.–Fri. 10–5, Sat. 1–5, Sun. 10–5; Nov.–Apr., Tues.–Fri. 1–5.*

LOWER SAXONY

Lower Saxony (Niedersachsen), Germany's second-largest state after Bavaria, was formed from an amalgamation of smaller states in 1946. Its landscape is quite diverse, but the focus here is on the Weser River's course from Hannoversch-Münden, in the south, to its end in the North Sea at Bremenhaven. Between Hannoversch-Münden and Hameln is one of Germany's most haunting river roads (B–80 to Bad Karlshafen, B–83 the rest of the way), where the fast-flowing Weser snakes between green banks that hardly show where land ends and water begins. Standing sentinel along the banks are superb little towns, whose half-timber architecture has given rise to the expression "Weser Renaissance."

The states of Lower Saxony and Saxony-Anhalt share the Harz Mountains; *see* Saxony-Anhalt *in* Chapter 16 for more coverage of the region.

Hannoversch-Münden

★ ❼ *24 km (15 mi) north of Kassel, 150 km (93 mi) south of Hannover.*

This delightful town, known as Hann.Münden and seemingly untouched by the modern age, shouldn't be missed. You'll have to travel a long way through Germany to find a grouping of half-timber houses (700 of them) as harmonious as these. The town is surrounded by forests and the Fulda and Werra rivers, which join and flow northward as the Weser River.

Much is made of the fact that the quack doctor to end all quacks died here. Dr. Johann Andreas Eisenbart (1663–1727) would be forgotten today if a ribald 19th-century drinking song (*"Ich bin der Doktor Eisenbart, widda, widda, wit, boom! boom!"*) hadn't had him shooting out aching teeth with a pistol, anesthetizing with a sledgehammer, and removing boulders from the kidneys. He was, as the song has it, a man who could make "the blind walk and the lame see." This is terribly exaggerated, of course, but the town takes advantage of it. It stages Eisenbart plays at 11:15 AM on summer Sundays, the doctor has "office hours" at 1:30 on Saturday from mid-May through September, and a glockenspiel on the city hall depicts his feats. There's a statue of the doctor in front of his home at Langestrasse 79, and his grave is outside the St. Ägidien Church. For information on the Dr. Eisenbart plays, contact the **Touristik Naturpark Münden** (⊠ Lotzestr. 2 ☎ 05541/75313 🖷 05541/75404 ⊕ www.hann.muenden.de).

Göttingen

❽ *30 km (19 mi) northeast of Hannoversch-Münden, 110 km (68 mi) south of Hannover.*

Although Göttingen is not strictly on the Fairy-Tale Road, it's closely associated with the Brothers Grimm, for they served as professors and librarians at the city's university from 1830 to 1837.

The university dominates life in Göttingen, and most houses more than a century old bear plaques that link them to a famous student or professor. In a house now known as the **Bismarckhäuschen,** beyond the city's old defense wall, Otto von Bismarck, the Iron Chancellor and founder of the 19th-century German Empire, pored over his books as a 17-year-old law student. Bismarck was a reluctant tenant—he was banned from living within the city center because of his "riotous behavior" and fondness for wine. ⊠ *Auf dem Wall* ☎ *0551/499–800 tourist office* 🖾 *Free* ☉ *Tues. 10–1, Wed., Thurs., and Sat. 3–5.*

Among the delights of Göttingen are the **ancient taverns** where generations of students have lifted their steins. Among the best known are **Mutter Jütte** (⊠ Heiligstädterstr. 4 in the Bremke district) and the **Kleine Ratskeller** (⊠ Judenstr. 30). Don't be shy about stepping into either of these taverns or any of the others that catch your eye; the food and drink are inexpensive, and the welcome is invariably warm and friendly.

The statue of **Gänseliesel,** the little Goose Girl of German folklore, stands in the central market square, symbolizing the strong link between the students and their university city. The girl, according to the story, was a princess who was forced to trade places with a peasant, and the statue shows her carrying her geese and smiling shyly into the waters of a fountain. Above her pretty head is a charming wrought-iron art nouveau bower of entwined vines. The students of Göttingen contributed money toward the bronze statue and fountain in 1901 and gave it a ceremonial role: traditionally, graduates who earn a doctorate bestow a kiss of thanks upon Gänseliesel. Göttingen's citizens say she's the most-kissed girl in the world.

Behind the Gänseliesel statue is the **Altes Rathaus** (Old Town Hall), begun in the 13th century but basically a part-medieval, part-Renaissance building. The bronze lion's-head knocker on the main door dates from the early 13th century. Inside, the lobby's striking murals tell the city's story. Beneath the heavily beamed ceiling of the medieval council chamber, the council met, courts sat in judgment, visiting dignitaries were officially received, receptions and festivities were held, and traveling theater groups performed. The Tourist-Information office is located on the first floor. ⊠ *Markt 9* ☎ *0551/499–800* 💷 *Free* ⊗ *Apr.–Oct., weekdays 9:30–6, weekends 10–4; Nov.–Mar., weekdays 9:30–6, Sat. 10–1.*

In the streets around the Rathaus you'll find magnificent examples of Renaissance architecture. Many of these half-timber, low-gable buildings house businesses that have been here for centuries. The **Ratsapotheke** (pharmacy) across from the Rathaus is one of the town's oldest buildings; medicines have been doled out here since 1322. ⊠ *Weenderstr. 30* ☎ *0551/57128.*

The 16th-century **Schrödersches Haus** (Schröder House), a short stroll from the Altes Rathaus up Weenderstrasse, is possibly the most appealing storefront—with an ornate, half-timber front—in all Germany. A clothing store, the Camel Shop, is inside. ⊠ *Weenderstr. 62.*

The **Städtisches Museum** (City Museum) is in Göttingen's only noble home, a 16th-century palace. It charts the history of Göttingen and its university with exhibits of church art, glass objects, and Judaica and has a valuable collection of antique toys and a reconstructed apothecary's shop. ⊠ *Ritterplan 7–8* ☎ *0551/400–2843* 💷 *€1.50* ⊗ *Tues.–Fri. 10–5, weekends 11–5.*

Just to the east of Göttingen is the **Wilhelm Busch Mühle,** a rustic mill and museum honoring a man who could justifiably be called "the godfather of the comic strip." The mill, with a wheel that still turns, belonged to Busch's uncle, and Busch lived there for five years. The admission price includes a tour of the mill, in English if desired. There is a more extensive Busch Museum in Hannover. ⊠ *Mühleng. 8, Ebergötzen* ☎ *05507/7181* 💷 *€3.50* ⊗ *March–Dec., Tues.–Sat. 9–1 and 2–5, Sun. 10–1 and 2–5.*

Where to Stay & Eat

¢–$ ✕ **Historischer Rathskeller.** Dine in the vaulted underground chambers of Göttingen's Altes Rathaus and choose from a traditional menu. If you're tired of cream sauces, try the *Altdeutscher Bauernschmaus,* which includes a small portion of grilled chicken, pork, and sausage—with no cream sauce—as well as fried potatoes and a side salad. ⊠ *Altes Rathaus, Markt 9* ☎ *0551/56433* ▤ *AE, DC, MC, V.*

★ ¢–$ ✕ **Zum Schwarzen Bären.** The Black Bear is one of Göttingen's oldest tavern-restaurants, a 16th-century half-timber house that breathes history and hospitality. Its specialties are *Bärenpfanne,* a generous mixture of beef, pork, and lamb (but no bear meat), and its wide selection of fried potato dishes. ⊠ *Kurzestr. 12* ☎ *0551/58284* ▤ *AE, DC, MC, V* ⊗ *Closed Mon. No dinner Sun.*

$$ 🏨 **Romantik Hotel Gebhards.** Though just across a busy road from the train station, this family-run hotel stands aloof and unflurried on its own grounds, a modernized 18th-century building that's something of a local landmark. Rooms are furnished in dark woods and floral prints highlighted by bowls of fresh flowers. The suites are particularly spacious, with completely separate bedrooms. ⊠ *Goethe-Allee 22–23, D–37073* ☎ *0551/49680* 🖷 *0551/496–8110* ⊕ *www.hotel-gebhards.de* 🛏 *53 rooms, 7 suites* ⌂ *Restaurant, some in-room data ports, in-room safes,*

minibars, cable TV, sauna, meeting rooms, parking (fee), some pets allowed (fee), no-smoking rooms; no a/c ⊟ AE, DC, MC, V ⎜○⎜ BP.

$–$$ ⊡ **Hotel Stadt Hannover.** The Netke family has run this charming hotel, an 18th-century town house in the historic Altstadt, for four generations. The somewhat spacious rooms are simply outfitted with wooden furnishings, brass fixtures, and light blue curtains. The location, two minutes from the train station and just down the street from the pedestrian zone, is ideal. ⊠ Goethe-Allee 21, 37073 ☎ 0551/547–960 🖷 0551/45470 ⊕ www.hotelstadthannover.de ⌂ In-room safe, cable TV, laundry service, Internet, meeting room, parking (fee); no a/c ⊟ AE, D, MC, V ⎜○⎜ BP.

¢–$ ⊡ **Landgasthaus Lockemann.** If you like to walk and hike, consider this half-timber lodge at the edge of the Stadtwald (city forest). Locals descend on the friendly, country-style restaurant for hearty German cooking. Take Bus 10 from the Busbahnhof, direction Herbershausen, to the last stop then walk left on Im Beeke. The trip will take 20 minutes. ⊠ Im Beeke 1, D–37075 ☎ 0551/209–020 🖷 0551/209–0250 ⇥ 18 rooms, 8 with bath ⌂ Restaurant, cable TV, beer garden, some pets allowed; no a/c, no phones in some rooms ⊟ No credit cards ⎜○⎜ BP.

Nightlife & the Arts

Göttingen's symphony orchestra presents about 20 concerts a year. In addition, the city has a nationally known boys' choir and an annual Handel music festival in May and June. Call the tourist office for program details and tickets for all three.

Göttingen's elegant **Deutsches Theater** (⊠ Theaterpl. 11 ☎ 0551/496–911), built in 1890, is known throughout Germany. It has four performing areas, including the large Grösse Bühne, with its two tiers of horseshoe-shape balconies, where much experimental theater is performed, and the intimate Keller, with its cabaretlike performances.

en route | To pick up the Fairy-Tale Road where it joins the scenic Weser Valley Road, return to Hannoversch-Münden and head north on B–80. In the village of Veckerhagen take a left turn to the signposted Sababurg.

Sababurg

★ ➒ 60 km (36 mi) west of Göttingen, 100 km (62 mi) south of Hannover.

Sababurg is home to the **Dornröschenschloss** (Sleeping Beauty's Castle). It stands just as the Grimm fairy tale tells us it did, in the depths of the densely wooded Reinhardswald, still inhabited by deer and wild boar. Today it's a fairly fancy hotel. Even if you don't stay the night, a drive to the castle is scenic. There's a nominal fee to tour the grounds, which include a rose garden and ruins.

☼ The **Tierpark Sababurg** is one of Europe's oldest wildlife refuges. Bison, red deer, wild horses, and all sorts of waterfowl populate the park. There's also a petting zoo for children. ⊠ Kasinoweg 22 ☎ 05671/800–1251 🎟 Apr.–Nov. €4, Dec.–Mar. €3.50 ⊙ Apr.–Sept., daily 8–7; Oct. and Mar., daily 9–5; Nov.–Feb., daily 10–4.

Where to Stay & Eat

★ **$$–$$$** ✕▦ **Dornröschenschloss Sababurg.** The medieval fortress thought to have inspired *The Sleeping Beauty* is now a small luxury hotel surrounded by a forest of oaks. It's a popular place for weddings, and on request, a "prince" and "princess" will present a version of the Sleeping Beauty story. The restaurant ($$–$$$) serves fine venison in the autumn, and the fresh trout with a Riesling-based sauce in the spring is equally satisfying. ✉ *Im Reinhardswald, D–34369 Hofgeismar* ☎ *05671/8080* 🖷 *05671/808–200* ⊕ *www.sababurg.de/dornroeschenschloss* ⇨ *18 rooms* ⌂ *Restaurant, bicycles, meeting rooms, some pets allowed (fee); no a/c* ▭ *AE, DC, MC, V* ¶⊙| *BP.*

en route   A short distance over back roads is another hilltop castle hotel, **Trendelburg.** Legend has it that its tower is the one in which a wicked witch imprisoned Rapunzel. Since it had neither a door nor stairs, the witch, and eventually a handsome prince, could get to Rapunzel only by climbing her long, golden tresses. From Trendelburg follow more back roads to the Weser Valley riverside village of Oberweser.

Though it has no historic connection with the stories, Oberweser is using its position on the Fairy-Tale Road to celebrate two more stories—*Puss-in-Boots* and *Snow White*—with festivals and other events. Turn left and take B–80 north to Bad Karlshafen.

Bad Karlshafen

❿   *42 km (26 mi) north of Hannoversch-Münden, 55 km (34 mi) northwest of Göttingen, 125 km (77 mi) south of Hannover.*

From the inland harbor of the pretty little spa of Bad Karlshafen, German troops of the state of Waldeck embarked to join the English forces in the American War of Independence. Flat barges took the troops down the Weser to Bremen, where they were shipped across the North Sea for the long voyage west. Many American families can trace their heritage to this small spa and the surrounding countryside.

Viewed from one of the benches overlooking the harbor, there's scarcely a building that's not in the imposing baroque style—grand and starkly white. The **Rathaus** (✉ Hafenpl. 8) behind you is the best example. Bad Karlshafen stands in surprising contrast to the abundance of half-timber architecture of other riverside towns.

Where to Stay & Eat

$$ ✕▦ **Hotel Menzhausen.** The half-timber exterior of this 16th-century establishment in the small town of Uslar, 12 km (7 mi) east of the Weser River, is matched by the elegant interior of its comfortable restaurant ($–$$). Ask for a guest room in the Mauerschlösschen, a luxurious extension that incorporates traditional Weser Renaissance design, such as half-timber and carved beams. ✉ *Langestr. 12, D–37170 Uslar* ☎ *05571/ 92230* 🖷 *05571/922–330* ⇨ *40 rooms* ⌂ *Restaurant, in-room data ports,* *cable TV, indoor pool, sauna, meeting room, some pets allowed (fee); no a/c* ⊟ *V* ⏀ *BP.*

$ ✕⊡ **Gaststätte-Hotel Weserdampfschiff.** You can step right from the deck of a Weser pleasure boat into the welcoming garden of this popular hotel-tavern. Fish from the river land straight into the tavern's frying pan. The rooms are snug; ask for one with a river view. The restaurant ($–$$) is closed Monday. ⊠ *Weserstr. 25, D–34385* ☎ *05672/2425* 🖷 *05672/ 8119* ⇩ *14 rooms* ⚲ *Restaurant, some pets allowed (fee); no a/c* ⊟ *No credit cards* ⏀ *BP.*

$ ✕⊡ **Hessischer Hof.** In the heart of town, this inn started as a tavern for the locals and now includes several comfortably furnished bedrooms, plus an apartment suitable for larger families and the numerous cycling groups that visit. The restaurant ($–$$) serves good, hearty fare. Breakfast is included in the room price, or you may request half-pension. ⊠ *Carlstr. 13–15, D–34385* ☎ *05672/1059* 🖷 *05672/2515* ⊕ *www.hess-hof. de* ⇩ *17 rooms* ⚲ *Restaurant, in-room safes, cable TV, bar, meeting rooms, some pets allowed; no a/c* ⊟ *AE, DC, MC, V.*

<table>
<tr><td>en route</td><td>Germany's oldest porcelain factory is at Fürstenberg, 8 km (5 mi) south of Höxter, in a baroque castle high above the Weser River. The crowned Gothic letter F, which serves as its trademark, is world</td></tr>
</table>

famous. You'll find Fürstenberg porcelain in Bad Karlshafen and Höxter, but it's more fun to journey to the 18th-century castle, where production first began in 1747, and buy directly from the manufacturer. Fürstenberg and most dealers will take care of shipping arrangements and any tax refunds. Tours of the factory in English are possible with advance notice. There's also a sales outlet, museum, and café. ⊠ *Schloss Fürstenberg* ☎ *05271/401–161* 🖾 *Museum* €*3.50* ⊙ *Museum Apr.–Oct., Tues.–Sun. 10–5; Nov.–Mar., weekends 10–5. Shop Apr.–Oct., Tues.–Sun. 10–6; Nov.–Mar., Tues.–Sat. 10–6.*

Höxter

⓫ *24 km (14 mi) north of Bad Karlshafen, 100 km (62 mi) south of Hannover.*

Stop at Höxter to admire its **Rathaus,** a perfect example of the Weser Renaissance style, combining three half-timber stories with a romantically crooked tower. Though it has no better claim than any other town to the story of Hansel and Gretel, Höxter presents a free performance of the story on the first Saturday of each month, from May to September.

The **Reichsabtei Corvey** (Imperial Abbey of Corvey) is idyllically set between the wooded heights of the Solling region and the Weser River. During its 1,200-year history it has provided lodging for several Holy Roman emperors. Heinrich Hoffmann von Fallersleben (1798–1874), author of the poem "Deutschland, Deutschland über Alles," worked as librarian here in the 1820s. The poem, set to music by Joseph Haydn, became the German national anthem in 1922. A music festival is held in the church and great hall, the Kaisersaal, in May and June. Corvey, also the name of the village, is reached on an unnumbered road heading east from Höxter (3 km [2 mi]) toward the Weser. There are signposts to the abbey. ☎ *05271/694–010* 🗺 *€4.20, abbey church €0.60* ⊙ *Apr.–Oct., daily 9–6.*

off the beaten path

EINBECK – Bock beer originated in this storybook town 20 km (12 mi) east of Höxter. Starting in 1341 the good burghers brewed it in their houses, and the name *Bockbier* is a corruption of the original Einbecker Bier. The **Einbecker Brauhaus** (Brewery; ⊠ Papenstr. 4–7, D-37574 Einbeck ☎ 05561/7970 🖨 05561/797223) still makes the strong brew, and groups can visit it with an advance request by telephone, fax or letter.

Where to Stay & Eat

★ **¢–$$** ✕ **Schlossrestaurant Corvey.** In summer you can dine under centuries-old trees at the Reichsabtei Corvey's excellent restaurant. With advance notice, a *Fürstenbankett*, or "princely banquet," can be arranged for groups in the vaulted cellars. ⊠ *Reichsabtei Corvey* ☎ *05271/8323* 🚇 *MC, V* ⊙ *Closed Jan.–Mar. No dinner Apr.–Oct. No lunch Nov. and Dec.*

$–$$ ✕🏨 **Niedersachsen Ringhotel.** Behind the three-story half-timber facade of this fine old Höxter house is a hotel with modern comfort and amenities, a member of the respected Ring group. Rooms are spacious, and equipped with everything you'd expect in a luxury hotel,including voice mail and turn-down service. The restaurant ($–$$) has a shady garden terrace and features fresh river fish. ⊠ *Grubestr. 3–7, D-37671* ☎ *05271/ 6880* 🖨 *05271/688–444* 🛏 *80 rooms* ⚘ *2 restaurants, in-room data ports, cable TV with movies, indoor pool, sauna, bar, some pets allowed (fee); no a/c* 🚇 *AE, DC, MC, V* ⊙ *BP.*

Sports & the Outdoors

Busch Freizeitservice (⊠ Postweg Nord 7 ☎ 05271/921–363) organizes canoe trips on the Fulda, Weser, and Werra rivers, as well as bicycle tours in the surrounding countryside.

Bodenwerder

⑫ *34 km (21 mi) north of Höxter, 70 km (43 mi) south of Hannover.*

The charming Weser town of Bodenwerder plays a central role in German popular literature. It's the home of the Lügenbaron (Lying Baron) von Münchhausen (1720–97), who was known as a teller of whoppers. His reputation was not without foundation, but it was mainly created by a book based in part on the baron's stories and published anonymously by an acquaintance. According to one tale, the baron rode a cannonball toward an enemy fortress but then, having second thoughts, returned to where he started by leaping onto a cannonball heading the other way.

The **Münchhausen-Erinnerungszimmer** (Münchhausen Memorial Room), in the imposing family home in which Baron von Münchhausen grew up (now the Rathaus), is crammed with mementos of his adventurous life, including his cannonball. A fountain in front of the house represents another story. The baron, it seems, was puzzled when his horse kept drinking insatiably at a trough. Investigating, he discovered that the horse had been cut in two by a closing castle gate and that the water ran out as fast as the horse drank. The water in the fountain, of course, flows from the rear of a half-horse. Other statues in the town show the other half of the horse and the baron mounted on his cannonball. On the first Sunday of the month from May through October, townspeople retell von Münchhausen's life story with performances in front of the Rathaus. ⊠ *Münchhausenpl. 1* ☎ *05533/409–147* 🖼 *Museum €2* 🕙 *Apr.–Oct., daily 10–noon and 2–5.*

Where to Stay & Eat

$ ✕🏠 **Hotel Goldener Anker.** The Weser boats tie up outside this half-timber tavern and hotel, and the sleepy river flows right past your bedroom window. The restaurant ($–$$) prepares hearty German fare and sometimes fresh Weser fish; in summer a beer garden right on the river beckons. ⊠ *Brückenstr. 5, D–37619* ☎ *05533/400–730* 🖶 *05533/400–733* ⊕ *www.goldeneranker.com* 🛏 *11 rooms* ⚒ *Restaurant, in-room data ports, cable TV, bicycles, meeting room, some pets allowed, no-smoking rooms; no a/c* ▭ *MC, V* ¶◎¶ *BP.*

$ ✕🏠 **Parkhotel Deutsches Haus.** The fine half-timber facade of this comfortable country hotel vies for attention with the nearby home of Baron von Münchhausen, now Bodenwerder's town hall. Original wood beams and oak paneling add to the rural feel inside. The hotel's own extensive grounds adjoin the town park, and the Weser River is a short walk away. The restaurant's ($) terrace adjoins the Münchhausen house. A specialty is *Münchhausen Kugeln* (Cannonballs), a dish with turkey, pork, vegetables, and croquettes. ⊠ *Münchhausenpl. 4, D–37619* ☎ *05533/3925* 🖶 *05533/4113* ⊕ *www.hotel-deutsches-haus-bodenwerder.de* 🛏 *42 rooms* ⚒ *2 restaurants, in-room data ports, cable TV, bowling, beer garden, some pets allowed (fee), no-smoking rooms; no a/c* ▭ *AE, MC, V.*

Hameln

★ ⑬ *24 km (15 mi) north of Bodenwerder, 47 km (29 mi) southwest of Hannover.*

Hameln (or Hamelin, in English) is home to the story of the gaudily attired Pied Piper, who rid the town of rats by playing seductive melodies on his flute. The rodents followed him willingly, waltzing their way right into the Weser. When the town defaulted on its contract and refused to pay the piper, he settled the score by playing his merry tune to lead Hameln's children on the same route. As the children reached the river, the Grimms wrote, "they disappeared forever." The tale is included in the Grimms' book *German Legends.* The origin of the story is lost in the mists of time, but the best guess is that it is associated with the forced resettlement of young people to the sparsely populated eastern territories. Also, during the 13th century, an inordinate number of Hameln's young men were conscripted to fight in an unpopular war in Bohemia and Moravia.

The Pied Piper tale is immortalized in an ultramodern sculpture set above a reflecting pool in the town's pedestrian zone. And there are rat-shape pastries in the windows of Hameln's bakeries. On central Osterstrasse you'll see several beautiful half-timber houses, including the Ratten-fängerhaus (Rat-Catcher's House) and the **Hochzeitshaus** (Wedding House), a 17th-century Weser Renaissance building now containing city offices. Between mid-May and mid-September the Hochzeithaus terrace is the scene of two free open-air events commemorating the legend. Local actors and children present a half-hour reenactment each Sunday at noon, and there is now also a 40-minute musical, *Rats,* each Wednesday at 4:30. Get there early to ensure a good seat. The carillon of the Hochzeitshaus plays tunes every day at 9:35 and 11:35, and mechanical figures enact the piper story on the west gable of the building at 1:05, 3:35, and 5:35.

Where to Stay & Eat

★ ¢–$$ ✕ **Rattenfängerhaus.** This brilliant example of Weser Renaissance architecture is Hameln's most famous building, reputedly where the Pied Piper stayed during his rat-extermination assignment (actually, it wasn't built until centuries after his supposed exploits). A plaque in front of it fixes the date of the incident at June 26, 1284. Rats are all over the menu, from the "rat-killer cocktail" to a "rat-tail flambé." But don't be put off: the traditional dishes are excellent, and the restaurant is guaranteed rodent free. ✉ *Osterstr. 28* ☎ *05151/3888* ▭ *AE, DC, MC, V.*

$ ▦ **Hotel zur Börse.** This upscale hotel is in the pedestrian zone in the heart of the old city. It offers comfortable accommodations and friendly service, and its Börsenbistro serves Mediterranean food. ✉ *Osterstr. 41a, entrance on Kopmanshof, D–31785* ☎ *05151/7080* 📠 *05151/25485* 🛏 *31 rooms* ⚒ *Restaurant, in-room data ports, minibars, cable TV with movies, bar, meeting rooms, some pets allowed (fee); no a/c* ▭ *AE, DC, MC, V* ⦿ *BP.*

★ $ ▦ **Hotel zur Krone.** If you fancy a splurge, ask for one of the hotel's elegant suites, with prices starting at €128 a night. It's an expensive but delightful comfort. The building dates from 1645 and is a half-timber marvel. Avoid the modern annex, however; it lacks all charm. ✉ *Osterstr. 30, D–31785* ☎ *05151/9070* 📠 *05151/907–217* ⊕ *www. hotelzurkrone.de* 🛏 *27 rooms, 5 suites* ⚒ *Restaurant, in-room data ports, minibars, cable TV, meeting rooms, some pets allowed (fee), no-smoking rooms; no a/c* ▭ *AE, MC, V* ⦿ *BP.*

$ ▦ **Pension Ragazzi.** Don't be fooled by the inappropriate Italian name, which derives from a pizzeria on the ground floor. This very reasonable little hostelry, with simple but modern rooms, is pure Fairy-Tale Road, situated in the pedestrian zone in the old part of the town. A continental breakfast is included in the rate. ✉ *Fischpfortenstr. 25, D–31785* ☎ *05151/21513* 📠 *05151/923–667* 🛏 *8 rooms* ⚒ *Pizzeria, cable TV, some pets allowed; no a/c* ▭ *No credit cards* ⦿ *BP.*

Hannover

47 km (29 mi) northeast of Hameln.

Hannover is somewhat off the Fairy-Tale Road, yet its culture and commerce influence the quieter surrounding towns. As a trade-fair center, Hannover competes with such cities as Munich and Leipzig. It's also an

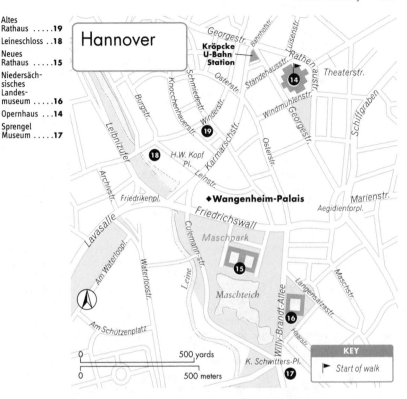

exemplary arts center, with leading museums, an opera house of international repute, and the finest baroque park in the country. Its patronage of the arts is evident in unexpected places: in an international
competition, architects and designers created nine unique bus stops for
the city. A Hannover Card entitles you to free travel on local transportation, reduced admission to five museums, and discounts on certain sightseeing events and performances. It's available through the
tourist office (✉ Hannover Tourismus Service, Ernst-August-Pl. 2,
D–30159 ☎0511/1684–9700 ⊕ www.hannover.de), for €8 per day (€12
for three days).

The major sights of Hannover are strung together on an easy-to-follow
tourist trail known as the "Red Thread." The trail begins at the tourism
office next to the main train station. Just follow the red line that is literally painted on the sidewalks and streets to 35 points of interest. A
map and information booklet explaining the various sites is available
at the tourism office for a nominal fee. The route takes about two hours
and follows a loop that brings you back to where you started.

What to See

19 Altes Rathaus. It took nearly 100 years, starting in 1410, to build this
gabled brick edifice, which once contained a merchants hall and an apothe-

cary. In 1844 it was restored to the style of about 1500. The facade's fired-clay frieze depicts coats of arms and representations of princes, and a medieval game somewhat comparable to arm wrestling. Inside is a modern interior with boutiques and a restaurant. ☒ *Köbelingerstr. 2.*

Herrenhausen. The gardens of the former Hannoverian royal summer residence are the city's showpiece (the 17th-century palace was never rebuilt after wartime bombing). The baroque park is unmatched in Germany for its formal precision, with patterned walks, gardens, hedges, and chestnut trees framed by a placid moat. There is a "fig garden" with a collapsible shelter to protect it in the winter and a gastronomy pavilion behind a grotto. From Easter until October, fountains play for a few hours daily (weekdays 11–noon and 3–5, weekends 11–noon and 2–5). Herrenhausen is outside the city, a short ride on Tramline 4 or 5. ☒ *Herrenhauserstr.* ☎ *0511/1684–7576* ⌨ *€4* ⊙ *Mar. and Oct., daily 9–6; Apr. and Sept., daily 9–7; May–Aug., daily 9–8; Nov.–Jan., daily 9–4:30; Feb., daily 9–3:30.*

An 18th-century residence at the edge of the park is now a museum, the **Fürstenhaus Herrenhausen-Museum,** affording fascinating insight into Hannoverian court life and its links with England. ☒ *Alte Herrenhauser Str. 14* ☎ *0511/750–947* ⌨ *€3.30* ⊙ *Apr.–Sept., Tues.–Sun. 10–6; Oct.–Mar., Tues.–Sun. 10–5.*

🔞 **Leineschloss.** The former Hannoverian royal palace stands above the River Leine and is now the seat of the Lower Saxony State Parliament. From 1714 until 1837, rulers of the house of Hannover sat on the British throne as Kings George I–IV. The first of them, George I, spoke no English. George III presided over the loss of the American colonies in the Revolutionary War but sent no Hannoverian troops to help fight, even though he hired troops from other German states for this purpose. The period of joint rule came to an end when Queen Victoria ascended the throne (Hannover didn't allow female monarchs). Tours are conducted weekdays. Brochures in English are available. ☒ *Heinrich-Wilhelm-Kopf-Pl. 1* ☎ *0511/3030–2042* ⌨ *Free* ⊙ *Tours Mon.–Thurs. at 10:30 and 1:30, Fri. at 10:30.*

🔞 **Neues Rathaus.** The new town hall was built at the start of the 20th century in Wilhelmine style (for Kaiser Wilhelm), at a time when pomp and circumstance were important ingredients of heavy German bureaucracy. Four scale models on the ground floor depict Hannover in various stages of development and destruction: as a medieval walled city, in the years before World War II, immediately following World War II, and in its present-day form. An elevator rises diagonally to the dome for a splendid view. ☒ *Trammpl. 2* ☎ *0511/1684–5333* ⌨ *Dome €2* ⊙ *Apr.–Oct., daily 9:30–6.*

🔞 **Niedersächsisches Landesmuseum** (Lower Saxony State Museum). The priceless art collection of this prestigious museum includes works by Tilman Riemenschneider, Veit Stoss, Hans Holbein the Younger, and Lucas Cranach. There are also historical and natural history sections. ☒ *Willy-Brandt-Allee 5* ☎ *0511/98075* ⌨ *€4* ⊙ *Tues., Wed., and Fri.–Sun. 10–5, Thurs. 10–7.*

▶ ⑭ **Opernhaus.** Hannover's late classical opera house, completed in 1852, has two large wings and a covered, colonnaded portico adorned with statues of great composers and poets. This enabled the finely attired oper-agoers to disembark from their coaches with dry feet, a function now taken over by an underground garage. The building originally served as the court theater but now is used almost exclusively for opera. It was gutted by fire in a 1943 air raid and restored in 1948. Unless you have tickets to a performance, the only part of the interior you can visit is the foyer with ticket windows. ⊠ *Opernpl. 1* ☎ *0511/9999–1298.*

⑰ **Sprengel Museum.** An important museum of modern art, the Sprengel holds major works by Max Beckmann, Max Ernst, Paul Klee, Emil Nolde, and Pablo Picasso. The street where it's located is named after Kurt Schwitters, a native son and prominent dadaist, whose works are also exhibited. ⊠ *Kurt-Schwitters-Pl. 1* ☎ *0511/1684–3875* 🖾 *€3.50* ☉ *Tues. 10–8, Wed.–Sun. 10–6.*

off the beaten path

WILHELM BUSCH MUSEUM – This section of the Georgenpalais, near Herrenhausen, is devoted to the works of cartoonists and caricaturists through the centuries. Emphasis is on Wilhelm Busch, the "godfather of the comic strip," whose original drawings and effects are on display. More than a century ago, Busch (1832–1908) wrote and illustrated a very popular children's book, still in print, called *Max und Moritz.* The story tells of two boys who mixed gunpowder in the village tailor's pipe tobacco and, with fishing lines down the chimney, filched roasting chickens off the fire. The first American comic strip, *The Katzenjammer Kids* (1897), drew not only on Busch's naughty boys (they even spoke with a German accent) but also on his loose cartoon style. ⊠ *Georgengarten 1* ☎ *0511/ 1699–9911* 🖾 *€4.50* ☉ *Apr.–Sept., Tues.–Sat. 11–5, weekends 11–6; Oct.–Mar., Tues.–Fri. 11–4, weekends 11–6.*

Where to Stay & Eat

\$\$–\$\$\$ ✕ **Basil.** Constructed in 1867 as a riding hall for the Royal Prussian military, this hip restaurant's home is as striking as the menu. Cast-iron pillars support the vaulted brick ceiling, and two-story drapes hang in the huge windows. The menu changes every three weeks and includes eclectic dishes from the Mediterranean to Asia. Game and white *Spargel* (asparagus) are served in season. ⊠ *Dragonerstr. 30* ☎ *0511/622–636* ▭ *AE, MC, V* ☉ *Closed Sun.*

¢–\$\$ ✕ **Brauhaus Ernst August.** This brewery has so much artificial greenery that you could imagine yourself in a beer garden. Hannoverian pilsner is brewed on the premises, and regional specialties are the menu's focus. There's a souvenir shop where, besides beer paraphernalia such as mugs and coasters, you can purchase, empty or full, a huge old-fashioned beer bottle with a wired porcelain stopper. The pub's own potent schnapps is also sold in a miniature version of this bottle. There's live music at least five evenings a week. ⊠ *Schmiedstr. 13* ☎ *0511/365–950* ▭ *AE, MC, V.*

¢–\$ ✕ **Grapenkieker.** An ancient pot steams in the aromatic, farmhouse-style kitchen, and simple, hearty fare prevails. Proprietors Gabriele and Karl-Heinz Wolf are locally famous for their culinary prowess and the warm welcome they give their guests. The half-timber restaurant is 5 km (3 mi) from the city center, in the Isernhagen District, but it's well worth seeking out. ⊠ *Hauptstr. 56, Isernhagen* ☎ *05139/88068* 🖃 *AE, DC, MC, V* ☺ *Closed Sun. and Mon.*

\$\$ ✕🖼 **Kastens Hotel Luisenhof.** This very traditional hotel, both in appearance and service, is a few steps from the main train station. Antiques are everywhere: tapestries on the lobby walls, oil paintings in the foyer, copper engravings in the bar, and an elegant wardrobe on every floor. In-room facilities don't include pay-per-view movies, as most mass-market films wouldn't appeal to the taste of the clientele here. The restaurant (\$\$\$–\$\$\$\$) is international with French touches. ⊠ *Luisenstr. 1–3, D–30159* ☎ *0511/30440* 🖷 *0511/304–4807* ⊕ *www.kastens-luisenhof. de* ↪ *124 rooms, 7 suites* ⚐ *Restaurant, in-room data ports, in-room safes, minibars, cable TV, bar, meeting rooms, some pets allowed (fee), no-smoking rooms; no a/c in some rooms* 🖃 *AE, DC, MC, V* ◎ *BP.*

\$\$ 🖼 **Hotel Körner.** The modern Körner has an old-fashioned feel, probably created by the friendly and personal service. Rooms are comfortably furnished in light veneers and pastel shades. The small courtyard terrace has a fountain; breakfast is served here in summer. ⊠ *Körnerstr. 24–25, D–30159* ☎ *0511/16360* 🖷 *0511/18048* ⊕ *www. hotelkoerner.de* ↪ *77 rooms* ⚐ *In-room data ports, minibars, cable TV, indoor pool, gym; no a/c* 🖃 *AE, DC, MC, V* ◎ *BP.*

Nightlife & the Arts

Hannover's nightlife is centered on the Bahnhof and the Steintor red light district. The **opera company** of Hannover is internationally known, with productions staged in one of Germany's finest 19th-century classical opera houses. Call 0511/9999–1298 for program details and tickets. Hannover's elegant **casino** (⊠ Osterstr. 40 ☎ 0511/980–660) is open from 3 PM to 3 AM.

Shopping

Hannover is one of northern Germany's most fashionable cities, and its central pedestrian zone has international shops and boutiques, as well as the very best of German-made articles, from stylish clothes to handmade jewelry. In the glassed-over **Galerie Luise** (⊠ Luisenstr. 5) you can spend a couple of hours browsing, with a leisurely lunch or afternoon tea at one of the several restaurants and cafés.

Hannover has what it claims is Germany's oldest **Flohmarkt** (flea market; ⊠ Am Hohen Ufer)—certainly one of the largest and most interesting. It's held every Saturday on the bank of the River Leine from 7 to 4.

en route   The Fairy-Tale Road continues north of Hannover as far as Bremen, though any connection to the Grimm brothers is faint here. You can reach Bremen in less than an hour by taking autobahn A–7 to the Walsrode interchange and then continuing on autobahn A–27. An alternative is to return to Hameln and follow the Weser as it breaks free of the Wesergebirge uplands at Porta Westfalica. The meandering route runs through the German plains to the sea and Bremen. Another alternative is a quick side trip to the northeast, to Celle and the Lüneburg Heath.

Celle

② *60 km (35 mi) northeast of Hannover.*

The main street of Celle's Old Town is quite different from the narrow, twisting streets you'd expect to find in a half-timber town. The **Stechbahn** is very broad and was once used for jousting tournaments. A horseshoe sunk in the pavement in front of the Löwenapotheke supposedly marks where the man who established Celle's present location, Duke Otto the Severe, died in such a tournament.

This charming city, with more than 500 half-timber buildings, is also the southern gateway to the Lüneburg Heath, one of Germany's most pleasant pastoral areas. It's a landscape of bizarrely shaped juniper bushes, of heather that flowers in pinkish purple in the late summer, and of grazing flocks of the heath's own breed of sheep, the cuddly Heidschnucken.

Thanks to a bend in the Aller River and a small tributary, Celle was protected on three sides by streams. To guard the fourth side from invasion by robber barons, Duke Otto built a fortified castle. This became the city's present palace, set in a lush park with the oldest baroque theater in Germany still used for performances. The castle chapel is an important example of north German Renaissance. The town hall (Rathaus) also traces its origins back to Duke Otto's time. It was extended and elaborately decorated in the 14th and 16th centuries.

The **Bomann Museum,** which concentrates on the local history and culture, is a must for anyone charmed by old furnishings. Its aim is to depict the folk culture of the area along with the history of Celle and of the Kingdom of Hannover. You can see a completely furnished reconstruction of a farmhouse and numerous reconstructed interiors, including a wagon maker's shop and a smithy. ⊠ *Schlosspl. 7* ☎ *05141/ 12544* ⊠ €3 ☉ *Tues.–Sun. 10–5.*

Where to Stay & Eat

$$$$ ✕ **Endtenfang.** Chef Hans Sobotka, a master of French cuisine, has
Fodor'sChoice turned this elegant restaurant, part of the Hotel Fürstenhof, into one of
★ the culinary magnets of northern Germany. With his *le canard du duc,* the duck breast is served with a pepper sauce and potatoes au gratin, and the legs, after a sorbet to clear the palate, with a port wine sauce and mushrooms. The menu otherwise leans toward seafood, and there's an imaginative dessert menu that could include crepes flambée and cheese from the cart. ⊠ *Hannoverische Str. 55* ☎ *05141/2010* ▭ *AE, DC, MC, V* ☉ *Closed Mon.*

$$ ✕ **Ratskeller Celle.** This subterranean establishment with a vaulted stone ceiling lays claim to being the oldest restaurant in Lower Saxony. If you can stand slow service, it's a good place to try the regional specialties, notably dishes from the Heidschnucken lamb. Boar is also a regional specialty, as are seasonal tender white asparagus and chanterelle mushrooms, served with an endless variety of accompaniments. ⊠ *Markt 14* ☎ *05141/29099* ▭ *AE, V.*

$$–$$$ ✕▥ **Hotel Fürstenhof.** This baroque hunting château, surrounded by huge chestnut trees in the center of town, proudly displays its patrician past. The grand salon, with its groupings of overstuffed chairs, has a mirror ceiling supported by Grecian columns, the oak-panel library has a fireplace, and conferences can be held in an ornate room hung with tapestries. Its restaurant, the Endtenfang ($$$$), is famous throughout the region. Try to book one of the four rooms with antique furnishings in the original lodge. The other rooms are in a modern wing with less character. ✉ *Hannoverische Str. 55, D–29221* ☎ *05141/201–140* 🖷 *05141/201–120* 🌐 *www.fuerstenhof.de* *69 rooms* *3 restaurants, in-room data ports, minibars, cable TV, indoor pool, gym, sauna, bar, meeting rooms, some pets allowed (fee); no a/c* 💳 *AE, DC, MC, V* 🍽 *BP.*

$ **Best Western Celler Hof.** This moderately priced hotel is right in the heart of the half-timber old city, just steps from the Rathaus, palace, and Bomann Museum. Guests are welcome to use the indoor pool and solarium at the nearby Fürstenhof. ✉ *Stechbahn 11, D–29221* ☎ *05141/911–960* 🖷 *05141/911–9644* *47 rooms* *Minibars, cable TV, gym, sauna, bar, some pets allowed (fee); no a/c* 💳 *AE, DC, MC, V* 🍽 *BP.*

Bergen-Belsen

21 *25 km (15 mi) north of Celle.*

Just outside Celle is a sobering contrast to the charm of half-timber and heather. At the site of the infamous concentration camp on the Lüneburg Heath, the **Gedenkstätte Bergen-Belsen** (Bergen-Belsen Memorial) pays tribute to the victims of the Holocaust. Diarist Anne Frank was among the more than 80,000 persons who died here.

Only the gruesome photographs on display will tell what the camp looked like. There's nothing left of it. The British liberators found thousands and thousands of unburied corpses all over the camp, so as a precaution against disease, all structures were burned to the ground. Volunteer youth groups have unearthed the foundations of the barracks.

Those who venture onto the site of the camp may be surprised at its pleasant, parklike appearance. Reminders of the horrors that once happened here include numerous burial mounds, mostly overgrown with heather and with stones with such inscriptions as HERE LIE 1,000 DEAD. Anne Frank probably lies in one of them. The SS officers had hoped to have the dead buried and out of sight before the British forces arrived, but the starving prisoners were too weak for the job. Under the direction of the British, the graves you see were dug and filled by the SS officers themselves. The British tried and executed the camp's SS commandant, Josef Kramer, the "Beast of Belsen."

Monuments and shrines include a Jewish memorial dating to 1946, with a commemorative stone dedicated by the Israeli president in 1987; an obelisk and memorial wall erected by the British; a wooden cross dating to only weeks after the liberation; and a commemorative stone from the German government. The main feature of the memorial is a permanent exhibition on the history of the camp and the Nazi persecution system. Though all signs are in German, there are supplementary guides (€2.50) in English and eight other languages. There are also regular showings of a movie on the camp in English, German, and French. Children under

12 are not admitted to the showings, and it's said that one of the British photographers who made the footage couldn't bear to look at his work in later years. ✉ *Just off the unnumbered hwy. connecting Bergen and Winsen* ☎ *05051/6011* ⊕ *www.bergenbelsen.de* ⊡ *Free* ☉ *Daily 9–6.*

Where to Stay

✆ **$** ▦ **Hof Averbeck.** This typical heath farm doubling as a bed-and-breakfast proves the Lüneburg Heath is an ideal place for a farm vacation. Well off the main highway, it's great for children, with ponies to ride, animals to feed, and a playground. The farm, which is close to the Bergen-Belsen Memorial and central for day trips to Hamburg and Hannover, also has cattle, with boar and deer in the surrounding forest and meadows. ✉ *Hassel 3, D–29303 Bergen* ☎ *05054/249* 📠 *05054/269* ⊕ *www. hofaverbeck.de* ➳ *14 rooms, 2 apartments* ♿ *Cable TV, some pets allowed (fee); no a/c, no room phones* ▭ *MC, V* ⧖ *BP.*

Bremen

㉒ *110 km (68 mi) northwest of Hannover.*

Germany's smallest city-state, Bremen, is also Germany's oldest port, and second in size to Hamburg. Together with Hamburg and Lübeck, Bremen was an early member of the merchant-run Hanseatic League, and its rivalry with the larger port on the Elbe River is still tangible. Though Hamburg may still claim its title as Germany's "door to the world," Bremen likes to boast: "But we have the key." Bremen's symbol is, in fact, a golden key, which you will see displayed on flags and signs throughout the city.

Bremen is also central to the fable of the Bremer Stadtmusikanten, or Bremen Town Musicians—a rooster, cat, dog, and donkey quartet that came to Bremen to seek its fortune. (Their music and singing were so awful that they caused a band of robbers to flee in terror.) You'll find statues of this group in various parts of the city.

There are numerous sights to see in Bremen's charming Altstadt. The **Marktplatz** is one of Europe's most impressive market squares. It's bordered by the St. Petri Dom, an imposing 900-year-old Gothic cathedral; an ancient Rathaus; a 16th-century guildhall; and a modern glass-and-steel state parliament building, with gabled town houses finishing the panorama. Alongside the northwest corner of the Rathaus is the famous bronze statue of the four **Bremen Town Musicians,** one atop the other in a sort of pyramid. Their feats are reenacted in a free, open-air play in the courtyard of the Liebfrauenkirche, near the Marktplatz, at noon and 1:30 each Sunday, from May to October. Another well-known figure on the square is the stone statue of the knight in service to Charlemagne, **Roland,** erected in 1404. Three times larger than life, the statue serves as Bremen's good-luck piece and a symbol of freedom and independence. It is said that as long as Roland stands, Bremen will remain a free and independent state.

Construction of the **St. Petri Dom** (St. Peter's Cathedral) began in the mid-11th century. Its two prominent towers are Gothic, but in the late 1800s the cathedral was restored in the Romanesque style. It served as the seat of an archbishop until the Reformation turned the cathedral Protestant. ⊠ *Marktpl.* 🎫 *Free* ☉ *Weekdays 10–5, Sat. 10–2, Sun. 2–5.*

Charlemagne had established a diocese here in the 9th century, and a 15th-century statue of him, together with seven princes, adorns the Gothic **Rathaus,** which acquired a Weser Renaissance facade during the early 17th century. Tours are given in German. ⊠ *Marktpl.* 🎫 *Tour €4* ☉ *Tours Mon.–Sat. at 11, noon, 3, and 4; Sun. at 11 and noon, unless an official function is in progress.*

Don't leave Bremen's Altstadt without strolling down **Böttcherstrasse** (Barrel Maker's Street), at one time inhabited by coopers. Between 1924 and 1931 their houses were torn down and reconstructed, in a style at once historically sensitive and modern, by Bremen coffee millionaire Ludwig Roselius. (He was the inventor of decaffeinated coffee and held the patent for many years; Sanka was its brand name in the United States.) Many of the restored houses are used as galleries for local artists.

At one end of Böttcherstrasse is the **Roselius-Haus,** a 14th-century building that is now a museum, established on the initiative of the coffee baron. It showcases German and Dutch paintings, as well as wood carvings, furniture, textiles, and decorative arts from the 12th through the 18th centuries. Notice also the arch of Meissen bells at the rooftop. Except when freezing weather makes them dangerously brittle, these chime daily on the hour from noon to 6 (only at noon, 3, and 6, January–April). ⊠ *Böttcherstr. 6–10* 📞 *0421/336–5077* 🎫 *€5* ☉ *Tues.–Sun. 11–6.*

★ Also take a walk through the nearby narrow streets of the idyllic **Schnoorviertel** (Schnoor District), a jumble of houses, taverns, and shops once occupied or frequented by fishermen and tradespeople. This is Bremen's oldest district, dating back to the 15th and 16th centuries. The neighborhood is fashionable among artists and craftspeople, who have restored the tiny cottages to serve as galleries and workshops. Other buildings have been converted into popular antiques shops, small cafés, and pubs.

At the **Universum Science Center,** you can study the earth and cosmos through interactive exhibits, videos, and simulations. ⊠ *Wiener Str. 2* 📞 *0421/334–6333* 🎫 *€10* ☉ *Mon., Tues., Thurs., and Fri. 9–6, Wed. 9–9, weekends 10–7.*

The **Übersee Museum** (Overseas Museum) has unusual displays on the histories and cultures of the many peoples with whom Bremen traders came into contact. One section is devoted to North America. ⊠ *Bahnhofspl. 13* 📞 *0421/1603–8101* 🎫 *€6* ☉ *Tues.–Fri. 9–6, weekends 10–6.*

off the beaten path

BREMERHAVEN – This busy port city belongs to Bremen and is 66 km (41 mi) upriver, where the Weser empties into the North Sea. You can take in the enormity of the port from a promenade or from a platform in the North Harbor. The country's largest and most fascinating maritime museum, the **Deutsches Schifffahrtsmuseum** (German Maritime Museum), is a fun place to explore. Part of the museum consists of a harbor, open from April through October, with seven old trading ships. A train to Bremerhaven from Bremen takes about one hour. ☒ *Hans-Scharoun-Pl. 1, from Bremen take A–27 to exit for Bremerhaven-Mitte* ☎ *0471/482–070* ☜ *€5* ☉ *Tues.–Sun. 10–6.*

Where to Stay & Eat

★ **$$$–$$$$** ✕ **Grashoffs Bistro.** Chef Jürgen Schmidt, a culinary TV personality and honorary citizen of Cognac, France, draws an enthusiastic lunchtime crowd that's willing to put up with incredibly cramped conditions to dine his way. The room is so small that there's no room between the square tables; a table has to be pulled out for anyone who has a seat next to the wall. The menu has a French touch, with an emphasis on fresh fish from the Bremerhaven market. The place is also a deli in the Chef Schmidt tradition. There's a whole wall of teas, another of cheeses, and a huge assortment of wines. ☒ *Contrescarpe 80* ☎ *0421/14740* ▭ *DC, MC, V* ☉ *Closed Sun. No dinner.*

★ **$$–$$$$** ✕ **Park Restaurant.** Thanks to chef Henri Precht, the Park, within the Park Hotel Bremen, is one of the finest dining establishments in Germany. The stunning dining room is decorated in yellow and cream, with shimmering crystal chandeliers, classical moldings, marble urns, Louis XVI chairs, floor-to-ceiling windows, and a lacquered ceiling. Chef Precht includes a dash of fantasy in his classic French and German dishes. Fish is filleted at the table and specialties include a three-soup starter and a four-course dessert meal. The latter sounds caloric but actually includes kumquats, almonds, passion fruit, buttermilk, a Granny Smith apple sorbet, and other healthy-sounding things in addition to the chocolate and pudding. ☒ *Im Bürgerpark* ☎ *0421/340–8633* ▭ *AE, DC, MC, V.*

★ **¢–$** ✕ **Ratskeller.** This cavernous cellar, with a three-story-high vaulted ceiling, is said to be Germany's oldest and most renowned town-hall restaurant—it's been here for 600 years. The waiters and waitresses wear medieval costumes and serve solid, typical northern German fare, including creatively prepared poultry and fresh seafood. The walls are lined with wine casks, and despite the vastness, there are intimate alcoves with closable doors, once used by merchants as they closed their deals. The Ratskeller's wine cellar has the largest variety of German wines in the country. Some 655 of them are offered; every one German. ☒ *Am Markt* ☎ *0421/321–676* ▭ *AE, DC, MC, V.*

$$$$ ▦ **Park Hotel Bremen.** This palatial hotel, with a lake on one side and an extensive area of park and forest on the other sides, is nevertheless only minutes from the central station. In winter, guests can swim in a heated outdoor pool or sit cozily beside a fireplace in the lobby. In summer they can dine on a lakeside terrace. Waiters wear white ties and bellhops wear flat caps and brass buttons right out of the old days. Each room is decorated in a different style, from opulently Moorish to minimalist Japanese, and the bathrooms are exquisite marble affairs. The Park Restaurant is the best fine dining around. ☒ *Im Bürgerpark, D–28209* ☎ *0421/34080* ▤ *0421/340–8602* ⊕ *www.parkhotel-bremen. de* ☞ *150 rooms, 12 suites* ☖ *2 restaurants, café, in-room data ports,*

FodorśChoice
★

some cable TV with movies and video games, hair salon, massage, bicycles, bar, meeting rooms, some pets allowed (fee), no-smoking rooms; no a/c in some rooms ⊟ *AE, DC, MC, V* ⊚ *BP.*

★ $ ⊞ **Hotel Landhaus Louisenthal.** This charming complex of buildings, all under the hotel's management, consists of two half-timber restaurants and a 150-year-old hotel. Across the street is a windmill right out of a Dutch landscape. It's all about as far from downtown as you can get and still be in Bremen, but the price is right, the service and food are fine, a streetcar at the door takes you downtown in minutes, it's near the Hohe-Lehe Autobahn exit, and there's plenty of parking. ⊠ *Leher Heerstr. 105, D–28359* ☎ *0421/232–076* ⊟ *0421/236–716* ⊕ *www. landhaus-louisenthal.de* ⇆ *61 rooms* ♨ *2 restaurants, cable TV, sauna, meeting rooms, some pets allowed (fee), no-smoking rooms; no a/c* ⊟ *AE, DC, MC, V* ⊚ *BP.*

Nightlife & the Arts

Bremen may be Germany's oldest seaport, but it can't match Hamburg for racy nightlife. Nevertheless, the streets around the central Marktplatz and in the historic Schnoor District are filled with all sorts of taverns and bars.

Try your luck at American or French roulette and blackjack at the **Bremen casino** (⊠ Böttcherstr. 3–5 ☎ 0421/329–000), open daily 5 PM–3 AM. The **Bremerhaven casino** (⊠ Theodor-Heuss-Pl. 3 ☎ 0471/413–641), open daily 11 AM until midnight, is strictly for one-arm bandits and machine players.

Music and theater lovers have much to choose from. The **Theater am Goetheplatz** (⊠ Goethepl. 1–3) presents operas, operettas, music, and dance programs. The **Concordia** (⊠ Schwachhäuser Heerstr. 1) is a multipurpose theater whose stage and audience area can be adjusted to suit the needs of the mostly experimental programs it presents. The **Schauspielhaus** (⊠ Goethepl. 1–3) presents theater, everything from Goethe to Brecht to Woody Allen, but nearly always in German. Program and ticket information for the Theater am Goetheplatz, Concordia, and Schauspielhaus is available through a single **box office** (☎ 0421/365–300). The **philharmonic orchestra,** which plays regularly at the city's concert hall, **Die Glocke** (⊠ Domsheide 4–5 ☎ 0421/336–699), is of national stature. Bremen's **Shakespeare Company** (⊠ Schulstr. 26 ☎ 0421/500–333) presents the works of the Bard and other plays in German.

Shopping

Bremen's **Schnoorviertel** is the place to go for souvenirs. Its stores are incredibly specialized, selling porcelain dolls, teddy bears, African jewelry, and smoking pipes among many other things. One of the most whimsical shops in town is **Atelier GAG** (⊠ Auf den Häfen 12-15 ☎ 0421/701-137). The tiny shop is overflowing with paper models of lighthouses, famous buildings, spaceships, and other fun creations. All of the models are for sale as flat sheets of paper, ready to be cut and pasted into their various forms.

THE FAIRY-TALE ROAD A TO Z

To research prices, get advice from other travelers, and book travel arrangements, visit www.fodors.com.

AIRPORTS

Frankfurt, Hannover, and Hamburg have the closest international airports to the area. Frankfurt is less than a half hour from Hanau, and Hamburg is less than an hour from Bremen.

🚩 **Langenhagen Airport** ⊠ Petzelstr. 84, Hannover ☎ 0511/9770.

BIKE & MOPED TRAVEL

The Fulda and Werra rivers have 190 km (118 mi) of cycle paths, and you can cycle the whole length of the Weser River from Hannoversch-Münden to the outskirts of Bremen without making too many detours from the river valley. Five- and seven-day cycle tours of the Fulda and Werra river valleys are possible, including bike rentals, overnight accommodations, and luggage transport between stops.

🚩 **Boots- und Fahrrad Verleih Ilona Cleff** ⊠ Rathaus, Gerstembrunnenhöhe 9, D–37124 Rosdorf ☎ 05545/950–810. **SRJ Gasteservice** ⊠ Gneisenaustr. 4, D–32423 Minden ☎ 0571/889–1900.

BOAT & FERRY TRAVEL

Rehbein-Linie Kassel operates a boat service between Kassel, Hannoversch-Münden, and Bad Karlshafen.

🚩 **Rehbein-Linie Kassel** ⊠ Weserstr. 5, D–34125 Kassel ☎ 0561/18505 🖷 0561/102–839.

BUS TRAVEL

Bremen, Kassel, Göttingen, Fulda, and Hanau all are reachable via Europabus (⇨ Deutsche Touring in Bus Travel *in* Smart Travel Tips). Frankfurt, Kassel, Göttingen, and Bremen all have city bus services that extend into the countryside along the Fairy-Tale Road. A local bus serves the scenic Weser Valley Road stretch.

CAR RENTAL

🚩 **Avis** ⊠ Kirchbachstr. 200, Bremen ☎ 0421/201–060 🖾 Am Klagesmarkt 22, Hannover ☎ 0511/121–740. **Hertz** ⊠ Flughafenallee 22, Bremen ☎ 0421/555–350 🖾 Langenhagen Airport, Hannover ☎ 0511/779–041. **Sixt** ⊠ Flughafenallee 22, Bremen ☎ 0421/552–081 🖾 Schulenburger Landstr. 66, Hannover ☎ 0511/352–1213 🖾 Weserstr. 6, Kassel ☎ 0561/500–880.

CAR TRAVEL

The Fairy-Tale Road incorporates one of Germany's loveliest scenic drives, the Wesertalstrasse, or Weser Valley Road (B–80 and B–83), between Hannoversch-Münden and Hameln; total mileage is approximately 103 km (64 mi). The autobahn network penetrates deep into the area, serving Hanau, Fulda, Kassel, Göttingen, and Bremen directly. Bremen is 60 km (35 mi) northwest of Hannover and 100 km (60 mi) northwest of Celle.

TOURS

BOAT TOURS Reederei Warrings has two excursions from Bremerhaven: a one-hour trip around the harbor for €7 and an all-day round-trip to the fortress

North Sea island of Helgoland for €31.50. Book through the Bremerhaven tourist office or through Reederei Warrings. (If you're in a hurry to see the stark, red-cliff island Helgoland, there's a daily round-trip flight for €145 per person with OLT Airlines.)

The six boats of Flotte Weser operate short summer excursions along a considerable stretch of the Weser River between Bremen and Bad Karlshafen. The trip Hameln–Bad Karlshafen–Hameln, for example, takes slightly under three hours and costs €13.50.

Rehbein-Linie Kassel (⇨ Boat & Ferry Travel) operates a service from Kassel to Bad Karlshafen. It also prides itself on the only "three-river tour" in the area. In a single trip you travel a little on the Fulda and Werra rivers and also on the river formed when these two meet at the tour's starting point of Hannoversch-Münden, the Weser. One of its three boats, the *Deutschland,* has a bowling alley aboard. For schedule information and bookings, contact the company at its Kassel headquarters. Another Kassel company, Personenschifffahrt K. & K. Söllner, has two excursion boats plying between Kassel and Hannoversch-Münden.
🚢 **OLT Airlines** ⊠ Flughafen, Am Luneort 15, D-27572 Bremerhaven ☎ 0471/77-188. **Flotte Weser** (⇨ Boat & Ferry Travel). **Personenschifffahrt K. & K. Söllner** ⊠ Die Schlagd, D-34125 Kassel ☎ 0561/774-670. **Reederei Warrings** ⊠ Neuestr. 9, D-26409 Wittmund/Carolinensiel ☎ 04464/94950.

BUS TOURS   Year-round tours of the region are offered by Herter-Reisen. Guided bus tours of Kassel set off from the Stadttheater on Saturday at 2 PM from Easter through October, and at 11 AM in November and December. Tours are free if you buy a ServiceCard at the tourist office. Some local authorities—those in Bad Karlshafen, for example—also organize bus tours. Contact individual tourist offices for details.
🚌 **Herter-Reisen** ⊠ Am Klei 26, D-31863 Coppenbrügge ☎ 05159/969-244.

WALKING TOURS   Bremen's tours depart daily at 10:30 from the central bus station on Breiteweg. Fulda has tours of the Old Town, starting at the tourist office on Bonifatiusplatz, April–October, daily at 11:30 and 3; November–March, weekends and holidays at 11:30. Göttingen shows visitors around April–October, Friday, Saturday, and Sunday at 11:30 (starting from the Old Town Hall).

Hameln offers tours April–October, Monday–Saturday at 2:30 and Sunday at 10:15 and 2:30, leaving from the tourist office. The tourist office of Steinau an der Strasse conducts tours at 11:15 on the first Sunday of each month, April–October, departing from the Märchenbrunnen.
🚶 Contact the respective tourist offices for details.

TRAIN TRAVEL
Hanau, Fulda, Kassel, and Göttingen all are on both the InterCity Express Frankfurt–Hamburg line and the Frankfurt–Berlin line (not all of these trains stop at Hanau). The Frankfurt-Hamburg line also stops in Hannover, and there's additional ICE service to Hannover and to Bremen from Frankfurt and other major cities.

Four cities, though too small for ICE service, are big enough for rail service. They are Hannoversch-Münden, Marburg, Hameln, and Celle.

VISITOR INFORMATION

Information on the entire Fairy-Tale Road can be obtained from the Deutsche Märchenstrasse.

Alsfeld ⊠ Verkehrsbüro Touristcenter, Am Markt 13, D–36304 ☎ 06631/182–165 ⊕ www.tca-alsfeld.de. **Bad Karlshafen** ⊠ Kurverwaltung, Hafenplatz 8, D–34385 ☎ 05672/9999–22 ⊕ www.hessennet.de/badkarlshafen. **Bad Pyrmont** ⊠ Touristik Information, Europapl. 1, D–31812 ☎ 05281/940–511 ⊕ www.badpyrmont.de. **Bodenwerder** ⊠ Städtische Verkehrsamt, Münchausenplatz 3, D–37619 ☎ 05533/40542 ⊕ www.bodenwerder.de. **Bremen** ⊠ Touristik-Zentrale, Findorffstr. 105, D–28215 ☎ 01805/101–030 ⊕ www.bremen-tourism.de. **Bremerhaven** ⊠ Bremerhaven Touristik, H.-H.-Meierstr. 6, D–27568 ☎ 0471/946–4610 ⊕ www.seestadt-bremerhaven.de. **Celle** ⊠ Tourismus Region Celle, Markt 14–16, D–29221 ☎ 05141/1212 ⊕ www.region-celle.de. **Deutsche Märchenstrasse** ⊠ Obere Königstr. 15, D–34117 Kassel ☎ 0561/707–7120 ⊕ www.deutsche-maerchenstrasse.de. **Fulda** ⊠ Tourismus- und Kongressmanagement, Bonifatiuspl. 1, D–36037 ☎ 0661/102–1813 ⊕ www.fulda.de. **Gelnhausen** ⊠ Verkehrsbüro, Obermarkt 7, D–63571 ☎ 06051/830–300 ⊕ www.gelnhausen.de. **Göttingen** ⊠ Tourist-Information, Altes Rathaus, Markt 9, D–37073 ☎ 0551/499–800 ⊕ www.goettingen.de. **Hameln** ⊠ Hameln Marketing und Tourismus, Deisterallee 1, D–31785 ☎ 05151/202–617 ⊕ www.hameln.de. **Hanau** ⊠ Tourist-Information Hanau, Am Markt 14–18, D–63450 ☎ 06181/295–950 ⊕ www.hanau.de. **Hannover** ⊠ Hannover Tourismus Service, Ernst-August-Pl. 2, D–30159 ☎ 0511/1684–9700 ⊕ www.hannover.de. **Hannoversch-Münden** ⊠ Touristik Naturpark Münden, Lotzstr. 2, D–34346 ☎ 05541/75313 ⊕ www.hann.muenden.de. **Höxter** ⊠ Touristik- und Kulturinformation, Historisches Rathaus, Weserstr. 11, D–37671 ☎ 05271/963–431 ⊕ www.hoexter.de. **Kassel** ⊠ Tourist GmbH, Obere Königstr. 15, D–34117 ☎ 0561/707–707 ⊕ www.kassel.de. **Lauterbach** ⊠ Verkehrsamt, Marktplatz 14, D–36341 ☎ 06641/1840 ⊕ www.lauterbach-hessen.de. **Marburg** ⊠ Tourismus und Marketing, Pilgrimstein 26, D–35037 ☎ 06421/99120 ⊕ www.marburg.de. **Steinau an der Strasse** ⊠ Verkehrsbüro, Bruder-Grimm-Str. 70, D–36396 ☎ 06663/96310 ⊕ www.steinau.de.

HAMBURG

13

Updated by
Jürgen
Scheunemann

WATER—IN THE FORM OF THE ALSTER LAKES AND THE ELBE RIVER—is Hamburg's defining feature and the key to the city's success. A harbor city with an international past, Hamburg is the most tolerant and open-minded of German cities. The media have made Hamburg their capital by planting some of the leading newspapers, magazines, and television stations here. Add to that the slick world of advertising, show business, and model agencies, and you have a populace of worldly and fashionable professionals. Not surprisingly, the city of movers and shakers is also the city with most of Germany's millionaires.

But for most Europeans, the port city invariably triggers thoughts of the gaudy Reeperbahn underworld, that sleazy strip of clip joints, sex shows, and wholesale prostitution that helped earn Hamburg its reputation as "Sin City." Today the infamous red-light district is just as much a hip meeting place for young Hamburgers and tourist crowds, who flirt with the bright lights and chic haunts of the not-so-sinful Reeperbahn, especially on warm summer nights.

Hamburg, or "Hammaburg," was founded in 810 by Charlemagne. For centuries it was a walled city, its gigantic outer fortifications providing a tight little world relatively impervious to outside influences. The city is at the mouth of the Elbe, one of Europe's great rivers and the 97-km (60-mi) umbilical cord that ties the harbor to the North Sea. Its role as a port gained it world renown. It was a powerful member of the Hanseatic League, the medieval union of northern German merchant cities that dominated shipping in the Baltic and North seas.

The Thirty Years' War left Hamburg unscathed, and Napoléon's domination of much of the Continent in the early 19th century also failed to affect it. Indeed, it was during the 19th century that Hamburg reached the crest of its power, when the largest shipping fleets on the seas with some of the fastest ships afloat were based here. Its merchants traded with the far corners of the globe. During the four decades leading up to World War I, Hamburg became one of the world's richest cities. Its aura of wealth and power continued right up to the outbreak of World War II. These days, about 15,000 ships sail up the lower Elbe each year, carrying more than 50 million tons of cargo—from petroleum and locomotives to grain and bananas.

What you see today is the "new" Hamburg. The Great Fire of 1842 all but obliterated the original city; a century later World War II bombing raids destroyed port facilities and leveled more than half of the city proper. In spite of the 1940–44 raids, Hamburg now stands as a remarkably faithful replica of that glittering prewar city—a place of enormous style, verve, and elegance, with considerable architectural diversity, including turn-of-the-20th-century art nouveau buildings.

The comparison that Germans like to draw between Hamburg and Venice is somewhat exaggerated. But the city *is* threaded with countless canals and waterways spanned by about 1,000 bridges, even more than you'll find in Venice. Swans glide on the canals. Arcaded passageways run along the waterways. In front of the Renaissance-style Rathaus (Town Hall) is a square that resembles the Piazza San Marco.

The distinguishing feature of downtown Hamburg is the Alster (Alster Lakes). Once an insignificant waterway, it was dammed in the 18th century to form an artificial lake. Divided at its south end, it's known as the Binnenalster (Inner Alster) and the Aussenalster (Outer Alster)—the two separated by a pair of graceful bridges, the Lombard Brücke and the John F. Kennedy Brücke. The Inner Alster is lined with stately hotels, department stores, fine shops, and cafés; the Outer Alster is framed by parks and gardens against a backdrop of private mansions. From late spring into fall, sailboats and windsurfers skim across the surface of the Outer Alster and white excursion steamers ferry back and forth. The view from these vessels (or from the shore of the Outer Alster) is of the stunning skyline of six spiny spires (five churches and the Rathaus) that is Hamburg's identifying feature. It all creates one of the most distinctive downtown areas of any European city.

EXPLORING HAMBURG

Hamburg's most important attractions stretch between the Alster Lakes to the north, and the harbor and Elbe River to the south. This area consists of four distinct quarters. St. Georg is the business district around the Hauptbahnhof (main train station). The historic Altstadt (Old City) clusters near the harbor and surrounds the Rathaus (Town Hall). West of Altstadt is Neustadt (New City). The shabby but thrilling district of St. Pauli includes the Reeperbahn, a strip of sex clubs and bars.

Downtown Hamburg

The city's heart (and shops) is centered on two long boulevards, the Jungfernstieg and the Mönckebergstrasse. The area was heavily bombarded during World War II, so most of the buildings here were constructed after the war; they now house banks, insurance companies, and other big businesses. Downtown may not be the most beautiful part of town, but its atmosphere is invigorating.

Numbers in the text correspond to numbers in the margin and on the Hamburg map.

a good walk

Begin at **Dammtorbahnhof** ❶ ▶, a fine example of Hamburg's art nouveau architecture. Departing from the south exit, you can easily take a detour to Hamburg's zoo, **Hagenbecks Tierpark** ❷, one of Germany's oldest and most popular urban animal habitats. It has its own subway stop on the U–2 line. After visiting the zoo, return to the south exit of the Dammtor station; on your right you'll see the SAS Plaza Hotel and the Congress Centrum Hamburg (CCH), a vast, modern conference-and-entertainment complex. Continue past the Congress Centrum and bear left in a sweeping arc through the ornamental park **Planten un Blomen** ❸. Leave the park at Marseillerstrasse and cross over into the less formal **Alter Botanischer Garten** ❹. Both the park and the gardens are in the larger Wallringpark, which encompasses four parks in all. At the garden's southeast exit at Stephansplatz, cross over the Esplanade and walk down Colonnaden to reach the **Alster Lakes** ❺ and the **Jungfernstieg** ❻, the most elegant boulevard in downtown Hamburg.

If you have 2 days

Start at the Alster Lakes and head toward the main shopping boulevards of Jungfernstieg and Mönckebergstrasse. A short walk south of Mönckebergstrasse takes you to the majestic Rathaus Square, while a brief walk north on the same street leads to the equally impressive Hauptbahnhof. To the southeast, the Kontorhausviertel is one of the nicest parts of town, a collection of old brick warehouses dating back to the 1920s. On your second day, take a quick tour of the Freihafen Hamburg, Hamburg's port. Compare the port's modern warehouses with their antique counterparts on photogenic Deichstrasse in the Altstadt (Old City). You may want to inspect at least one of the city's great churches; a good choice is the city's premier baroque landmark, St. Michaeliskirche. Finally, head over to the Landungsbrücken, the starting point for boat rides in the harbor and along the Elbe River. And don't leave Hamburg without a jaunt down St. Pauli's Reeperbahn.

If you have 3 days

Begin watching wild animals roam free at Hagenbecks Tierpark. Equally green are the two parks, Planten un Blomen and the Alter Botanischer Garten, in the business district. After exploring the downtown's other attractions, from the Alster to the Hauptbahnhof, detour to the Kunsthalle and the Museum für Kunst und Gewerbe, both showcasing some of the best art in Germany. Devote your second day to historic Hamburg and the harbor. Take in the docks and don't miss the Speicherstadt's 19th-century warehouses. After a walk among the charming houses on Deichstrasse, continue on to the meticulously restored Krameramtswohnungen, the late-medieval Shopkeepers' Guild Houses. Next, visit the Museum für Hamburgische Geschichte for an excellent overview of the city's dramatic past. Save your third day for St. Pauli. Board one of the boats at the Landungsbrücken for a sightseeing tour through the harbor. One evening should be spent along the Reeperbahn, perhaps including the Erotic Art Museum, one of the few tasteful displays of eroticism on the strip.

If you have 4 days

To get a glimpse of Hamburg's playful art nouveau architecture, start the first day west of the lakes at the Dammtorbahnhof and make quick trips to Hagenbecks Tierpark and the Planten un Blomen and Alter Botanischer Garten parks. The inner-city district has many highlights, from the Alster to the Kontorhausviertel, including the Chilehaus and St. Jacobikirche, a medieval church with Gothic altars. On the second day, explore Hamburg's past at the harbor and in other old parts of town. Begin with the St. Katharinenkirche, the city's perfectly restored baroque church. Then spend the afternoon at Hamburg's harbor and its historic attractions, from the Freihafen Hamburg to Krameramtswohnungen, including the Alte St. Nikolaikirche, a church ruin now preserved as a memorial. End the day by viewing the city from the giant Bismarck-Denkmal. Spend a third day in St. Pauli. On the fourth day, return to the Landungsbrücken and embark on a boat ride to the village of Blankenese and the historic ships at the Museumshafen Övelgönne.

13

Turn right off the Jungfernstieg onto Reesendamm and make your way to the **Rathaus** ❼ and its square. Leave by its east side, perhaps pausing to join those relaxing on the steps of the memorial to the poet Heinrich Heine, a great fan of the city.

Beyond the memorial lies **Mönckebergstrasse** ❽, Hamburg's not-so-elegant but always-bustling shopping boulevard. At its end you'll meet the busy main road of Steintorwall, which was the easternmost link of the defense wall encircling the Old Town in the 17th century. Take the pedestrian underpass to the **Hauptbahnhof** ❾, Hamburg's impressive central train station. Leave the Hauptbahnhof the way you entered and turn right on Steintorwall, which continues as Glockengiesserwall, until you come to the major art museum, **Kunsthalle** ❿, on the corner of Ernst-Merck-Strasse.

A quite different but equally fascinating perspective on art is offered at the nearby **Museum für Kunst und Gewerbe** ⓫. To reach it, head in the direction from which you came and turn left on Steintordamm, crossing over the railroad tracks. The large, yellow museum is across the street, its entrance on Brockestrasse.

Turn right when leaving the museum, then right again onto Kurt-Schumacher-Allee. Cross over Steintorwall near the subway and continue west along Steinstrasse to the **St. Jacobikirche** ⓬—you'll recognize it by its needle spire. Cross over Steinstrasse when leaving the church and head down Burchardstrasse, which will bring you to Burchardplatz. This area between Steinstrasse and Messberg is known as the Kontorhausviertel, a restored quarter with redbrick commercial buildings dating to the 1920s. The most famous building is at the south end of Burchardplatz—the **Chilehaus** ⓭ resembles a huge ship.

TIMING You need half a day just to walk the proposed tour, depending on how much time you devote to the parks, the zoo (both are crowded but most enjoyable on summer weekends), and to shopping (which isn't advisable on Saturday morning because of the crowds). If you add two hours for visits to the museums and the Rathaus and two more hours for the delightful boat tour on the Alster Lakes, you'll end up spending more than a full day downtown.

What to See

❺ **Alster** (Alster Lakes). These twin lakes provide downtown Hamburg with one of its most memorable vistas. The two lakes meet at the Lombard and Kennedy bridges. In summer the boat landing at the Jungfernstieg, below the Alsterpavillion, is the starting point for the *Alsterdampfer,* the flat-bottom passenger boats that traverse the lakes. Small sailboats and rowboats, hired from yards on the shores of the Alster, are very much a part of the summer scene.

Every Hamburger dreams of living within sight of the Alster, but only the wealthiest can afford it. Some lucky millionaires own the magnificent garden properties around the Alster's perimeter, known as the Millionaire's Coast. But you don't have to be a guest on one of these estates to enjoy the waterfront—the Alster shoreline has 6 km (4 mi) of tree-

13

On the Menu
Hamburg is undoubtedly one of the best places in the country to enjoy fresh seafood. The flotilla of fishing boats brings a wide variety of fish to the city—to sophisticated upscale restaurants as well as simple harborside taverns. One of the most celebrated dishes among the robust local specialties is *Aalsuppe* (eel soup), a tangy concoction not entirely unlike Marseilles's famous bouillabaisse. A must in summer is *Aalsuppe grün* (eel soup seasoned with dozens of herbs); *Räucheraal* (smoked eel) is equally good. In the fall, try *Bunte oder Gepflückte Finten,* a dish of green and white beans, carrots, and apples. Available any time of year is *Küken* ragout, a concoction of sweetbreads, spring chicken, tiny veal meatballs, asparagus, clams, and fresh peas cooked in a white sauce. Other northern German specialties include *Stubenküken* (young, male oven-fried chicken); *Vierländer Mastente* (duck stuffed with apples, onions, and raisins); *Birnen, Bohnen, und Speck* (pears, beans, and bacon); and the sailors' favorite, *Labskaus*—a stew made from pickled meat, potatoes, and (sometimes) herring, garnished with a fried egg, sour pickles, and lots of beets.

The Harbor
A cruise of Germany's gateway to the world is a must. The energy from the continuous ebb and flow of huge cargo vessels and container ships, the harbor's prosperity, and its international flavor best symbolize the city's spirit. The surrounding older parts of town, with their narrow cobblestone streets and late-medieval warehouses, testify to Hamburg's powerful Hanseatic past. Bars and nightclubs have transformed some of the harbor area into a hot spot for eyebrow-raising entertainment.

Shopping
Although not as rich or sumptuous on first sight as Düsseldorf or Munich, Hamburg is nevertheless expensive and ranks first among Germany's shopping experiences. Chic boutiques sell primarily distinguished and somewhat conservative fashion; understatement is the style here. Some of the country's premier designers, such as Karl Lagerfeld, Jil Sander, and Wolfgang Joop, are native Hamburgers or at least worked here for quite some time. Hamburg has the greatest number of shopping malls in the country, mostly small but elegant downtown arcades offering entertainment, fashion, and fine food.

---

lined public pathways. Popular among joggers, these trails are a lovely place for a stroll. Ⓤ *Jungfernstieg (U-bahn).*

❹ **Alter Botanischer Garten** (Old Botanical Gardens). This green and open park within Wallringpark cultivates rare and exotic plants. Tropical and subtropical species grow under glass in five hothouses, including the large Schaugewächshaus (Show Greenhouse). Specialty gardens, including herbal and medicinal plantings, are clustered around the moat. ✉ *Stephanspl., Neustadt* ☎ *040/4283–82327* 🎫 *Free* ☉ *Schaugewächshaus Mar.–Oct., daily 9–4:15; Nov.–Feb., weekdays 9–3:15, weekends 10–3:15* Ⓤ *Stefanspl. (U-bahn).*

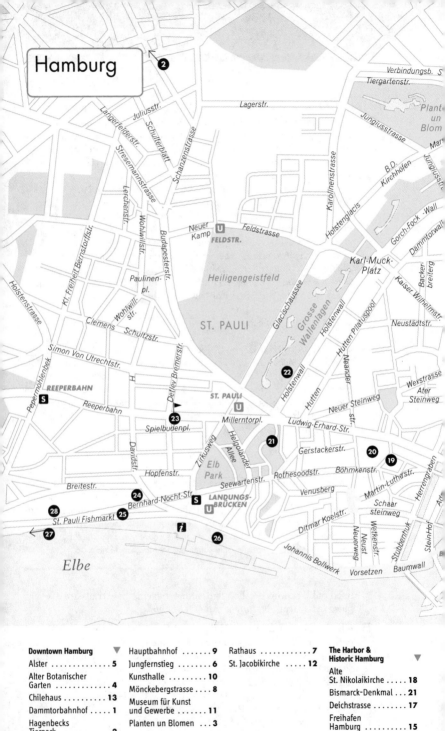

Hamburg

2

Verbindungsb. S
Tiergartenstr.

Langerfelderstr.
Juliusstr.
Schulterblatt
Schanzenstrasse
Lagerstr.
Plant
un
Blom
Jungiusstrasse
Mark
Stresemannstrasse
Lerchenstr.
Wohlwillstr.
Budapesterstr.
Karolinenstrasse
B.D.
Kirchhöfen
Gorch-Fock-Wall
Dammtorwall

Neuer
Kamp
U
FELDSTR.
Feldstrasse
Holstenglacis
Karl-Muck-
Platz
Kaiser Wilhelmstr.

Holstenstrasse
Kl. Freiheit Bernstorfstr.
Paulinen-
pl.
Wohlwill-
str.
Heiligengeistfeld
Glacischaussee
Grosse
Wallanlagen
Holstenwall
Backer
breiter.
Neustädtstr.

Clemens Schultzstr.
ST. PAULI
Hütten Plätuspool
Neander

Simon Von Utrechtstr.
Holstenwall
22
Wexstrasse
Ater
Steinweg

REEPERBAHN
S
Pepermöhlenbek
Detlev Bremerstr.
ST. PAULI
U
Millerntorpl.
Hütten
Neuer Steinweg
str.

Reeperbahn
23
Spielbudenpl.
Ludwig-Erhard-Str.

Davidstr.
Zirkusweg
Helgoländer
Allee
21
Gerstackerstr.
20
19
Martin-Luthstr.
Herrengraben
Acd

Hopfenstr.
Elb
Park
Rothesoodstr.
Böhmkenstr.
Schaar
steinweg
Steinhof

Breitestr.
Seewartenstr.
Venusberg
Wetkenstr.
Stubbenhuk
Steinhof

24
Bernhard-Nocht-Str.
S
LANDUNGS-
BRÜCKEN
U
Ditmar Koelstr.
Neuerweg
Neust.
Baumwall

28
St. Pauli Fishmarkt
25
26
Johannis Bollwerk
Vorsetzen

27
Elbe

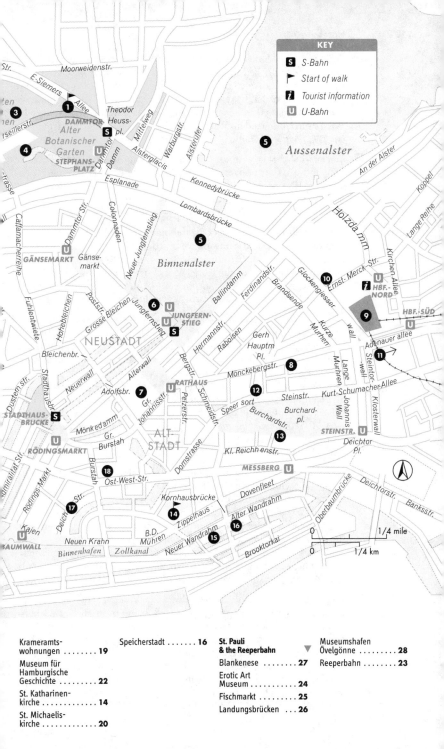

KEY

S S-Bahn

▶ Start of walk

ℹ Tourist information

U U-Bahn

⑬ Chilehaus (Chile House). This fantastical 10-story structure, which looks like a vast landlocked ship, is the standout of the **Kontorhausviertel**, a series of imaginative clinker-brick buildings designed in the New Objectivity style of 1920s civic architect Fritz Schumacher. The building was commissioned by businessman Henry Sloman, who traded in saltpeter from Chile, and now houses modern offices. ⊠ *Buchardspl., Altstadt* ⊕ *www.chilehaus.de* Ⓤ *Messberg (U-bahn).*

➤ ① Dammtorbahnhof (Dammtor Train Station). Built in 1903, this elevated steel-and-glass art nouveau structure is among Hamburg's finest train stations. It's one of many art nouveau buildings you'll see in the city. You can buy a city map at the newsstand in the station. ⊠ *Ernst-Siemers-Allee, Altstadt* Ⓤ *Dammtor (U-bahn).*

Deichtorhallen. This complex of warehouses built in 1911–12 is near the Kontorhausviertel and is now one of the country's largest exhibition halls for modern art. Its interior resembles an oversize loft, and its changing exhibits have presented the works of such artists as Andy Warhol, Roy Lichtenstein, and Miró. ⊠ *Deichtorstr. 1–2, Altstadt* ☎ *040/321–0307* ⊕ *www.deichtorhallen.de* ⊠ *Varies depending on exhibit* ☉ *Tues.–Sun. 11–6* Ⓤ *Steinstrasse (U-bahn).*

☾ ② Hagenbecks Tierpark (Hagenbecks Zoo). One of the country's oldest and most popular zoos is family-owned. Founded in 1848, it was the world's first city park to let wild animals such as lions, elephants, chimpanzees, and others roam freely in vast, open-air corrals. Weather permitting, you can ride one of the elephants. In the Troparium, an artificial habitat creates a rain forest, an African desert, and a tropical sea. ⊠ *Lokstedter Str. at Hamburg-Stellingen, Niendorf* ☎ *040/540–0010* ⊕ *www.hagenbeck.de* ⊠ *€14.50* ☉ *Mar.–Oct., daily 9–6; Nov.–Feb., daily 9–4:30; last admission at 3:30* Ⓤ *Hagenbecks Tierpark (U-bahn).*

⑨ Hauptbahnhof (Main Train Station). This central train station's cast-iron-and-glass architecture evokes the grandiose self-confidence of imperial Germany. The chief feature of the enormous 394-foot-long structure is its 460-foot-wide glazed roof supported only by pillars at each end. The largest structure of its kind in Europe, it's remarkably spacious and light inside. Though built in 1906 and having gone through many modernizations, it continues to have tremendous architectural impact. Today it sees a heavy volume of international, national, and suburban rail traffic. ⊠ *Steintorpl., St. Georg* Ⓤ *Hauptbahnhof (U-bahn).*

⑥ Jungfernstieg. This wide promenade looking out over the Alster Lakes is the city's premier shopping boulevard. Laid out in 1665, it used to be part of a muddy millrace that channeled water into the Elbe. Hidden from view behind the sedate facade of Jungfernstieg is a network of nine covered arcades that together account for almost a mile of shops selling everything from souvenirs to haute couture. Many of these air-conditioned passages have sprung up in the past two decades, but some have been here since the 19th century; the first glass-covered arcade, called Sillem's Bazaar, was built in 1845. ⊠ *Neustadt* Ⓤ *Jungfernstieg (U-bahn).*

need a break? Hamburg's best-known and oldest café, the **Alex im Alsterpavillon** (⊠ Jungfernstieg 54, Neustadt ☎ 040/350–1870) is a sleek 1950s retro café with an ideal vantage point from which to observe the constant activity on the Binnenalster.

★ ⓾ **Kunsthalle** (Art Gallery). One of the most important art museums in Germany, the Kunsthalle has 3,000 paintings, 400 sculptures, and a coin and medal collection that dates from the 14th century. In the postmodern, cube-shape building designed by Berlin architect O. M. Ungers, the **Galerie der Gegenwart** has housed a collection of international modern art since 1960, including works by Andy Warhol, Joseph Beuys, Georg Baselitz, and David Hockney. Graphic art is well represented, with a special collection of works by Pablo Picasso and the late Hamburg artist Horst Janssen, famous for his satirical worldview. In the old wing, you can view works by local artists dating from the 16th century. The outstanding collection of German Romantic paintings includes works by Runge, Friedrich, and Spitzweg. Paintings by Holbein, Rembrandt, Van Dyck, Tiepolo, and Canaletto are also on view, while late-19th-century impressionism is represented by works by Leibl, Liebermann, Manet, Monet, and Renoir. ⊠ *Glockengiesserwall, Altstadt* ☎ *040/4285–45765* ⊕ *www.hamburger-kunsthalle.de* 🖃 *€7.50* ⊙ *Tues., Wed., and Fri.–Sun. 10–6, Thurs. 10–9* Ⓤ *Hauptbahnhof (U-bahn).*

⓼ **Mönckebergstrasse.** This broad, bustling street of shops—Hamburg's major thoroughfare—cuts through both the historic and the new downtown areas. It was laid out in 1908 when this part of the Old Town was redeveloped. The shops here are not as exclusive as those on Jungfernstieg; the stores and shopping precincts on both sides of the street provide a wide selection of goods at more affordable prices. ⊠ *Altstadt* Ⓤ *Jungfernstieg (U-bahn).*

⓫ **Museum für Kunst und Gewerbe** (Arts and Crafts Museum). The museum houses a wide range of exhibits, from 15th- to 18th-century scientific instruments to an art nouveau interior complete with ornaments and furnishings. It was built in 1876 as a combination museum and school. Its founder, Justus Brinckmann, intended it to be a bastion of the applied arts that would counter what he saw as a decline in taste owing to industrial mass production. A keen collector, Brinckmann amassed a wealth of unusual objects, including a collection of ceramics from around the world. ⊠ *Steintorpl. 1, Altstadt* ☎ *040/4285–42630* ⊕ *www.mkg-hamburg.de* 🖃 *€7.20 or €8.20 depending on exhibit, Thurs. after 5 €4.10* ⊙ *Tues., Wed., and Fri.–Sun. 10–6, Thurs. 10–9* Ⓤ *Hauptbahnhof (U-bahn).*

☝ ⓷ **Planten un Blomen** (Plants and Flowers Park). Opened in 1935, this huge, tranquil park is renowned in Germany for its well-kept gardens. The park lies within the remains of the 17th-century fortified wall that guarded the city during the Thirty Years' War. If you visit on a summer evening, you'll see the Wasserballet, the play of an illuminated fountain set to organ music. Make sure you get to the lake in good time for the show—it begins at 10 PM each evening during the summer (at 9 PM in September). Also in summer, traditional tea ceremonies are presented in the Japanese Garden, the largest of its kind in Europe. *Planten un Blomen* ⊠ *Stephanspl., Neustadt* ☎ *040/4285–44723* 🖼 *Free* 🕙 *Mar.–Oct., daily 6 AM–10 PM; Nov.–Feb., daily 7 AM–8 PM* Ⓤ *Stephansplatz (U-bahn).*

❼ **Rathaus** (Town Hall). To most Hamburgers this large building is the symbolic heart of the city. As a city-state—an independent city and simultaneously one of the 16 federal states of Germany—Hamburg has a city council and a state government, both of which have their administrative headquarters in the Rathaus. A pompous neo-Renaissance affair, the building dictates political decorum in the city. To this day, the mayor of Hamburg never welcomes VIPs at the foot of its staircase but always awaits them at the very top—whether it's a president or the queen of England.

FodorsChoice
★

Both the Rathaus and the **Rathausmarkt** (Town Hall Market) lie on marshy land, a fact vividly brought to mind in 1962, when the entire area was severely flooded. The large square, with its surrounding arcades, was laid out after Hamburg's Great Fire of 1842. The architects set out to create a square with the grandeur of Venice's Piazza San Marco. The Rathaus was begun in 1866, when 4,000 piles were sunk into the moist soil to support the structure. It was completed in 1892, the year a cholera epidemic claimed the lives of 8,605 people in 71 days. A fountain and monument to that unhappy chapter in Hamburg's history are in a rear courtyard of the Rathaus.

The immense building, with its 647 rooms (6 more than Buckingham Palace) and imposing central clock tower, is not the most graceful structure in the city, but the sheer opulence of its interior is astonishing. A 45-minute tour begins in the ground-floor Rathausdiele, a vast pillared hall. Although you can only view the state rooms, their tapestries, huge staircases, glittering chandeliers, coffered ceilings, and grand portraits give you a sense of the city's great wealth in the 19th century and its understandable civic pride. ⊠ *Rathausmarkt, Altstadt* ☎ *040/428–310* ⊕ *www.hamburg.de* 🖼 *English-language tour €1.50* 🕙 *Tours Mon.–Thurs., hourly 10:15–3:15, Fri.–Sun., hourly 10:15–1:15* Ⓤ *Mönckebergstr. (U-bahn).*

⓬ **St. Jacobikirche** (St. James's Church). This 13th-century church was almost completely destroyed during World War II. Only the furnishings survived, and reconstruction was completed in 1962. The interior is not to be missed—it houses such treasures as the vast baroque organ on which Bach played in 1720 and three Gothic altars from the 15th and 16th centuries. ⊠ *Jacobikirchhof 22, at Steinstr., Altstadt* ☎ *040/303–7370* 🕙 *Mon.–Sat. 10–5, Sun. 10–noon* Ⓤ *Mönckebergstr. (U-bahn).*

The Harbor & Historic Hamburg

Hamburg's historic sections are a fascinating patchwork of time periods where buildings restored to their medieval splendor hold ground next to sleek high-rises. Along the waterfront, late-medieval and 19th-century warehouses contrast with the high-tech harbor installations nearby. Narrow cobblestone streets with richly decorated mansions lead to churches of various faiths, reflecting the diverse origins of the sailors and merchants drawn to the city. Small museums and old restaurants occupy buildings that once served as sailor taverns.

a good
walk

This tour takes you south to the picturesque quarters around the harbor area (bring your passport, as there's a customs point on the walk). Start with a visit to the restored **St. Katharinenkirche** ⑭ ▶. To get there from the Messberg U-bahn station, cross the busy Ost-West-Strasse and continue down Dovenfleet, which runs alongside the Zollkanal (Customs Canal). On your way, you will pass the Kornhausbrücke, a bridge with a sign on it announcing your entrance to the **Freihafen Hamburg** ⑮ (Free Port) and the **Speicherstadt** ⑯, a complex of 19th-century warehouses. Continue until Dovenfleet turns into Bei den Mühren, and you'll see the church's distinctive green-copper spire.

As you leave the Free Port over the Brooksbrücke (two bridges down from the Kornhausbrücke), you'll pass through a customs control point, at which you may be required to make a customs declaration. Turn left after the bridge, where Bei den Mühren becomes Bei dem Neuen Krahn. Take your second right onto **Deichstrasse** ⑰, the city's 18th-century business district, which runs alongside Nikolaifleet, a former channel of the Alster and one of Hamburg's oldest canals. After exploring this lovely area, take the Cremon Bridge, at the north end of Deichstrasse. This angled pedestrian bridge spans Ost-West-Strasse. You may wish to make a small detour down one of the narrow alleys (Fleetgänge) between the houses to see the fronts of the houses facing the Nikolaifleet.

The Cremon Bridge will take you to Hopfenmarkt Square, just a stone's throw from the ruins of the **Alte St. Nikolaikirche** ⑱. From here head west on Ost-West-Strasse and cross to the other side at the Rödingsmarkt U-bahn station. Continue along Ost-West-Strasse, which turns into Ludwig-Erhard-Strasse, until you reach Krayenkamp, a side street to your left that will take you to the historic **Krameramtswohnungen** ⑲ (Shopkeepers' Guild Houses). The distance from the Nikolaikirche to Krayenkamp is about 1 km (½ mi). Hamburg's best-loved and most famous landmark, the **St. Michaeliskirche** ⑳, is on the other side of the alley Krayenkamp.

From St. Michaeliskirche, walk west on Bömkenstrasse until you reach a park and the enormous **Bismarck-Denkmal** ㉑, rising high above the greenery. From the monument's northeast exit cross Ludwig-Erhard-Strasse and continue on Holstenwall to the **Museum für Hamburgische Geschichte** ㉒, with exhibits depicting the city's past.

TIMING This can be a rather short walk, manageable in a half day if you stroll only through the historic harbor quarters. You may wish to spend another 1½ hours at the Museum of Hamburg History and still another hour taking a closer look inside the churches.

What to See

⑱ **Alte St. Nikolaikirche** (Old St. Nicholas's Church). The tower and outside walls of this 19th-century neo-Gothic church are all that survived World War II. Today these ruins serve as a monument to those killed and persecuted during the war. Next to the tower is a center documenting the church. It's run by a citizens' organization that is also spearheading private efforts to partially rebuild the church and redesign the surrounding area. A cellar wine store is open for browsing and wine tasting. ⊠ *Ost-West-Str. at Hopfenmarkt, Altstadt* ☎ *040/441–1340* ⊙ *Apr.–Sept., weekdays 10–5, weekends 11–4; Oct.–Mar., Thurs. and Fri. 10–5, weekends 11–4* Ⓤ *Rödingsmarkt (U-bahn).*

㉑ **Bismarck-Denkmal** (Bismarck Memorial). The colossal 111-foot granite monument, erected between 1903 and 1906, is an equestrian statue of Otto von Bismarck, Prussia's Iron Chancellor, who was the force behind the unification of Germany. The plinth features bas-reliefs of various German tribes. Created by sculptor Hugo Lederer, the statue calls to mind Roland, the famous warrior from the Middle Ages, and symbolizes the German Reich's protection of Hamburg's international trade. ⊠ *St. Pauli* Ⓤ *St. Pauli (U-bahn).*

★ ⑰ **Deichstrasse.** The oldest residential area in the Old Town of Hamburg, which dates from the 14th century, now consists of lavishly restored houses from the 17th through the 19th centuries. Many of the original houses on Deichstrasse were destroyed in the Great Fire of 1842, which broke out in No. 42 and left approximately 20,000 people homeless; only a few of the early dwellings escaped its ravages. Today Deichstrasse and neighboring **Peterstrasse** (just south of Ost-West-Strasse) are of great historical interest. At No. 39 Peterstrasse, for example, is the baroque facade of the Beylingstift complex, built in 1700. Farther along, No. 27, constructed as a warehouse in 1780, is the oldest of its kind in Hamburg. All the buildings in the area have been painstakingly restored, thanks largely to the efforts of individuals. ⊠ *Altstadt* Ⓤ *Rödingsmarkt (U-bahn).*

need a break? There are two good basement restaurants in this area. The **Alt-Hamburger Aalspeicher** (⊠ Deichstr. 43, Altstadt ☎ 040/362–990) serves fresh fish dishes, including Hamburg's famous eel soup with dried fruits. **Das Kontor** (⊠ Deichstr. 32, Altstadt ☎ 040/371–471), an upscale historic Hamburg tavern, offers some of the city's best fried potatoes and delicious, traditional desserts.

★ ☾ ⑮ **Freihafen Hamburg.** Hamburg's Free Port, the city's major attraction, dates to the 12th century, when the city was granted special privileges by Holy Roman Emperor Frederick I (Barbarossa). One of these was freedom from paying duties on goods transported on the Elbe River. The original Free Port was where the Alster meets the Elbe, near Deichstrasse, but it was moved farther south as Hamburg's trade expanded. When Hamburg joined the German Empire's Customs Union in the late 1800s, the Free Port underwent major restructuring to make way for additional storage facilities. An entire residential area was torn down (including many Renaissance and baroque buildings), and the **Speicherstadt** warehouses, the world's largest block of continuous storage space, came into being between 1885 and 1927. Ⓤ *St. Pauli Landungsbrücken (U-bahn).*

⑲ **Krameramtswohnungen** (Shopkeepers' Guild Houses). The shopkeepers' guild built this tightly packed group of courtyard houses between 1620 and 1626 for members' widows. The houses became homes for the elderly after 1866. The half-timber, two-story dwellings, with unusual twisted chimneys and decorative brick facades, were restored in the 1970s and are now protected. The house marked "C" is open to the public. A visit inside gives you a sense of what life was like in these 17th-century dwellings. ⊠ *Historic House "C," Krayenkamp 10, Speicherstadt* ☎ *040/3750–1988* 🎟 *€1, Fri. €.50* ☉ *Tues.–Sun. 10–5* Ⓤ *Rödingsmarkt (U-bahn).*

need a break? Krameramtsstuben (⊠ Krayenkamp 10, Speicherstadt ☎ 040/365-800) is a rustic bar-cum-restaurant, in the heart of the historic harbor, where you can sample hearty local dishes, mostly made with fish. It's open daily 10 AM–midnight.

☾ ㉒ **Museum für Hamburgische Geschichte** (Museum of Hamburg History). The museum's vast and comprehensive collection of artifacts gives you an excellent overview of Hamburg's development, from its origins in the 9th century to the present. Pictures and models portray the history of the port and shipping between 1650 and 1860. One exhibit chronicles pirates in the North Sea during the late Middle Ages. ⊠ *Holstenwall 24, Neustadt* ☎ *040/4284–12380* ⊕ *www.hamburgmuseum.de* 🎟 *€7.50* ☉ *Tues.–Sat. 10–5, Sun. 10–6* Ⓤ *St. Pauli (U-bahn).*

▶ ⓮ **St. Katharinenkirche** (St. Catherine's Church). Completed in 1660, this house of worship was severely damaged during World War II but has since been carefully reconstructed. Only two 17th-century epitaphs (to Moller and to von der Feehte) remain from the original interior. ⊠ *Katharinenkirchhof 1, near Speicherstadt, Altstadt* ☎ *040/3037–4730* ☉ *Apr.–Sept., Mon.–Sat. 9–5, Sun. noon–5; Oct.–Mar., Sat. 9–4, Sun. noon–4* Ⓤ *Messberg (U-bahn).*

⓴ **St. Michaeliskirche** (St. Michael's Church). The Michel, as it's called locally, is Hamburg's principal church and northern Germany's finest baroque-style ecclesiastical building. Constructed between 1649 and 1661 (the tower followed in 1669), it was razed after lightning struck almost a century later. It was rebuilt between 1750 and 1786 in the decorative Nordic baroque style but was gutted by a terrible fire in 1906. The replica, completed in 1912, was demolished during the Second World War. The present church is a reconstruction.

FodorśChoice ★

The distinctive 433-foot brick-and-iron tower bears the largest tower clock in Germany, 26 feet in diameter. Just above the clock is a viewing platform (accessible by elevator or stairs) that affords a magnificent panorama of the city, the Elbe River, and the Alster Lakes. Twice a day, at 10 AM and 9 PM (Sunday at noon), a watchman plays a trumpet solo from the tower platform, and during festivals an entire wind ensemble crowds onto the platform to perform. The **Multivisionsshow** (slide and audio show), located one floor beneath the viewing platform, recounts Hamburg's history on a 16.4-foot screen and a refined audio system. ⊠ *St. Michaeliskirche, Altstadt* ☎ *040/376–780* ⊕ *www.st-michaelis. de* 🎟 *Tower €2.50; crypt €1.25; tower and show €4; crypt and show €2.75; show, tower, and crypt €4.50* ☉ *Apr.–Sept., Mon.–Sat. 9–6, Sun. 12:30–6; Oct.–Mar., Mon.–Sat. 10–5, Sun. 11–5; multimedia screening*

Thurs. and weekends on the half hr, 12:30–3:30 Ⓤ *Landungsbrücken, Rödingsmarkt (U-bahn).*

need a break? Just opposite St. Michaeliskirche is one of Hamburg's most traditional restaurants, the **Old Commercial Room** (✉ Englische Planke 10, Speicherstadt ☎ 040/366–319). Try one of the local specialties, such as Labskaus or Aalsuppe. If you don't make it to the restaurant, you can buy its dishes (precooked and canned) in department stores in both Hamburg and Berlin.

⓰ Speicherstadt (Warehouse District). These imposing warehouses in the Freihafen Hamburg reveal yet another aspect of Hamburg's extraordinary architectural diversity. A Gothic influence is apparent here, with a rich overlay of gables, turrets, and decorative outlines. These massive rust-brown buildings are still used to store and process every conceivable commodity, from coffee and spices to raw silks and handwoven Oriental carpets.

Hamburg's proud past as Europe's gateway to the world comes to life at the tiny but fascinating **Spicy's Gewürzmuseum,** where you can smell, touch, and feel close to 50 spices. More than 700 objects chronicle five centuries of the once-prosperous spice trade in Hamburg. ✉ *Am Sandtorkai 32, Speicherstadt* ☎ *040/367–989* ⊕ *www.spicys.de* ✉ *€3* ☉ *Tues.–Sun. 10–5* Ⓤ *Messberg (U-bahn).*

Although you won't be able to enter the buildings, the nonstop comings and goings will give you a good sense of a port at work. If you want to learn about the history and architecture of the old warehouses, detour to the **Speicherstadtmuseum.** ✉ *St. Annenufer 2, Block R, Speicherstadt* ☎ *040/321–191* ⊕ *www.speicherstadtmuseum.de* ✉ *€2.80* ☉ *Tues.–Sun. 10–5* Ⓤ *Messberg (U-bahn).*

Opposite the historic Speicherstadt, one of Germany's largest urban-development projects, the **HafenCity,** is currently under construction. This new city district with business and living areas encompasses 387 acres. You can see a model of the project, slated for final completion in 2025, in the Speicherstadt's old power plant, along with an exhibition of the architectural and economic aspects of the new harbor district. ✉ *Am Sandtorkai 30, Speicherstadt* ☎ *040/3690–1799* ⊕ *www.hafencity.info* ✉ *Free* ☉ *Tues.–Sun. 10–6* Ⓤ *Messberg (U-bahn).*

St. Pauli & the Reeperbahn

The run-down maritime district of St. Pauli is sometimes described as a "Babel of sin," but that's not entirely fair. The Reeperbahn, its major thoroughfare as well as a neighborhood moniker, offers a broad menu of entertainment in addition to the striptease and sex shows. Beyond this strip of pleasure, St. Pauli and Altona are defined by their Elbe waterfront.

a good walk At the St. Pauli U-bahn station, you'll find yourself at the beginning of a long, neon-lit street stretching nearly 1 km (½ mi). This is the red-light **Reeperbahn** ㉓ ▶, full of nightlife entertainment and sex clubs. The best areas to check out are the Grosse Freiheit, Hans-Albers-Platz, and Davidstrasse. Walk down Davidstrasse to reach the not-to-be-missed **Erotic**

Art Museum ㉔, exhibiting all aspects of human sexuality. From the museum, walk west on Hafenstrasse until you see the first market booths of the **Fischmarkt** ㉕, a shopper's paradise stocked with fresh fish, meat, and produce (open Sunday only).

From the market you can head back on Hafenstrasse to the nearby piers at **Landungsbrücken** ㉖, where ferries depart for short round-trips. Walk through the long limestone building with two towers to reach the ticket booths.

Try to make the trip to the riverside village of **Blankenese** ㉗, 14½ km (9 mi) west of Hamburg. You can get there by ferry, S-bahn, or on foot. The celebrated Elbe River walk is long, but it's one of Hamburg's prettiest. On the way to Blankenese (or on the return trip), stop by **Museumshafen Övelgönne** ㉘, a quaint little fishing town and harbor filled with historic vessels.

TIMING   This tour can last a full day and a long night, including a very enjoyable boat trip through the harbor, and a few hours in the theaters and bars along the Reeperbahn. However, you can walk down the red-light strip and check out the Erotic Art Museum and the Landungsbrücken in less than three hours. You have to be either a night owl or an early riser to catch the Fischmarkt on Sunday.

What to See

㉗ **Blankenese.** Blankenese is one of Hamburg's surprises—a suburb west of the city with the character of a quaint 19th-century fishing village. Some Germans like to compare it to the French and Italian rivieras; many consider it the most beautiful part of Hamburg. The most picturesque part of town is the steeply graded hillside, where paths and stairs barely separate closely placed homes. The town has a lively fruit and vegetable market, open Tuesday 8–2, Friday 8–6, and Saturday 8–1. Weekday ferries to Blankenese leave from Pier 3 every 10 to 15 minutes and involve two transfers. ۞ *Nonstop HADAG ferries depart from Pier 2 for Blankenese late Mar.–Oct., weekends at 10:30 and 2:30* Ⓤ *Blankenese (S-bahn).*

need a break?   A fine view and well-prepared fish await you at one of Hamburg's most traditional fish restaurants, the **Sagebiel's Fährhaus** (✉ Blankeneser Hauptstr. 107, Blankenese ☎ 040/861–514), a former farmhouse where Kaiser Wilhelm once celebrated his birthday.

㉔ **Erotic Art Museum.** Sexually provocative art from 1520 to the present— 1,800 original works (mostly photographs) in all—is showcased here. The collection is presented with such great taste and decorum that it has won the respect of many who doubted the museum's seriousness. Special exhibits of modern erotic photography and events are staged in a building on Bernhard-Nocht-Strasse. ✉ *Bernhard-Nocht-Str. 69, St. Pauli* ☎ *040/3178–4126* ⊕ *www.eroticartmuseum.de* ☞ *Minimum age 16* 💶 *€8* ۞ *Sun.–Thurs. 10 AM–midnight, Fri. and Sat. 10 AM–2 AM* Ⓤ *St. Pauli (U-bahn).*

🕒 **㉕ Fischmarkt** (Fish Market). The open-air Altona Fischmarkt is worth getting out of bed early for (or staying up all night). The pitch of fervent deal making is unmatched in Germany. Offering real bargains, the market's barkers are famous for their sometimes rude but usually successful bids to shoppers. Sunday fish markets became a tradition in the 18th century, when fishermen sold their catch before church services. Today, freshly caught fish are only a part of the scene. You can find almost anything here—from live parrots and palm trees to armloads of flowers and bananas, valuable antiques, and fourth-hand junk. ⊠ *Between Grosse Elbestr. and St. Pauli Landungsbrücken, St. Pauli* 🕙 *Sun. 5:30 AM–10:30 AM* Ⓤ *Landungsbrücken (U-bahn).*

🕒 **㉖ Landungsbrücken** (Piers). A visit to the port is not complete without a tour of one of the most modern and efficient harbors in the world. Hamburg is Germany's largest seaport, with 33 individual docks and 500 berths lying within its 78 square km (30 square mi). Barge tours of the harbor leave from the main passenger terminal, along with a whole range of ferries and barges heading to other destinations in the North Sea. There's usually a breeze, so dress warmly. ***Rickmer Rickmers***, an 1896 sailing ship that once traveled as far as the West Indies, is open to visitors and is docked at Pier 1. ⊠ *St. Pauli Landungsbrücken 1, St. Pauli* ☎ *040/319–5959* ⊕ *www.rickmer-rickmers.de* ⊠ *Rickmer Rickmers €3* 🕙 *Daily 10–6* Ⓤ *Landungsbrücken (U-bahn).*

🕒 **㉘ Museumshafen Övelgönne** (Museum Harbor Övelgönne). The glorious days of *Windjammern*, Hamburg's commercial fleet, come alive in this small harbor museum on the Elbe River. Eighteen antique steam and sailing vessels from the late 19th century can be inspected from the pier, or boarded on weekends if a crew is around. Behind the harbor, along the quay, are charming little cottages with tidy gardens. ⊠ *Anleger Neumühlen, Ottensen* ☎ *040/397–383* ⊕ *www.museumshafen-oevelgoenne.de* ⊠ *Free* 🕙 *Daily.*

need a break? No Hanseatic Sunday would be complete without a visit to the **Strandperle** (⊠ Am Schulberg, Ottensen ☎ 040/880–1112), a small but stylish kiosk on the riverbanks near Övelgönne. Join the Hamburg locals and watch the cargo ships pass while downing your beer with lemonade (an *Alsterwasser*) and munching on a bratwurst.

▶ **㉓ Reeperbahn.** The hottest spots in town are concentrated in the St. Pauli Harbor area on the Reeperbahn thoroughfare and on a little side street known as the Grosse Freiheit (Great Liberty—and that's putting it mildly). In the early '60s, a then obscure band called The Beatles had their first live acts at the now demolished Star Club. The striptease shows are expensive and explicit, but a walk through this area is an experience in itself and costs nothing. Saturday night finds St. Pauli pulsating with people determined to have a good time. It's *not* advisable, however, to travel through this part of the city alone in the wee hours of the morning.

Although some of the sex clubs may be relatively tame, a good many others are pornographic in the extreme. They all get going around 10 PM and will accommodate you until the early hours. Order your own drinks rather than letting the hostess do it, and pay for them as soon as they arrive, double-checking the price list again before handing over the money.

Among the attractions in the St. Pauli area are theaters, clubs, music pubs, discos, and a bowling alley. Ⓤ *St. Pauli (U-bahn).*

WHERE TO EAT

Hamburg has plenty of chic restaurants to satisfy the fashion-conscious local professionals, as well as the authentic salty taverns typical of a harbor town.

WHAT IT COSTS In Euros				
	$$$$	**$$$**	**$$**	**$**	**¢**
AT DINNER	over €25	€21–€25	€16–€20	€9–€15	under €9

Restaurant prices are per person for a main course at dinner.

Downtown & Historic Hamburg

$–$$$$ ✕ **Ratsweinkeller.** For atmosphere and robust local specialties, there are few more-compelling restaurants than this cavernous, late-19th-century haunt under the city hall. The simple tables are wooden, and ship models hang from the high stone-and-brick arches. You can order surprisingly fancy or no-nonsense meals. Fish specialties predominate, but there's a wide range of choices. ⊠ *Grosse Johannisstr. 2, Altstadt* ☎ *040/ 364–153* ▭ *AE, DC, MC, V* ⊗ *No dinner Sun.* Ⓤ *Rathaus (U-Bahn).*

$$–$$$ ✕ **Deichgraf.** This small and elegant fish restaurant in the heart of the old harbor warehouse district is a Hamburg classic. It's one of the best places to get traditional dishes such as *Hamburger Pannfisch* (fried pieces of the day's catch prepared in a wine and mustard sauce) at a very reasonable price of €17.40. The restaurant is in an old merchant house, and historic oil paintings in the dining room depict the hardships of the fisherman of the late 19th century. Reservations are essential on weekends. ⊠ *Deichstr. 23, Altstadt* ☎ *040/364–208* ▭ *MC, V* ⊗ *Closed Sun. No lunch Sat.* Ⓤ *Rödingsmarkt (U-bahn).*

$–$$$ ✕ **Das Feuerschiff.** This bright-red lightship served in the English Channel before it retired to the city harbor in 1989 and became a landmark restaurant and pub. Fresh and tasty fish dishes are on the menu, as well as traditional seafood entrées from Scandinavia, Poland, and other seafaring nations. On Monday, local bands jam, and once a month a cabaret show is staged. ⊠ *Vorsetzen, Hamburg City Sporthafen, Speicherstadt* ☎ *040/362–553* ▭ *AE, DC, MC, V* Ⓤ *Baumwall (U-bahn).*

St. Pauli & Altona

$$–$$$$ ✕ **Fischereihafen-Restaurant Hamburg.** For the best fish in Hamburg, book a table at this big, upscale restaurant in Altona, just west of the downtown area, along the Elbe. The menu changes daily according to

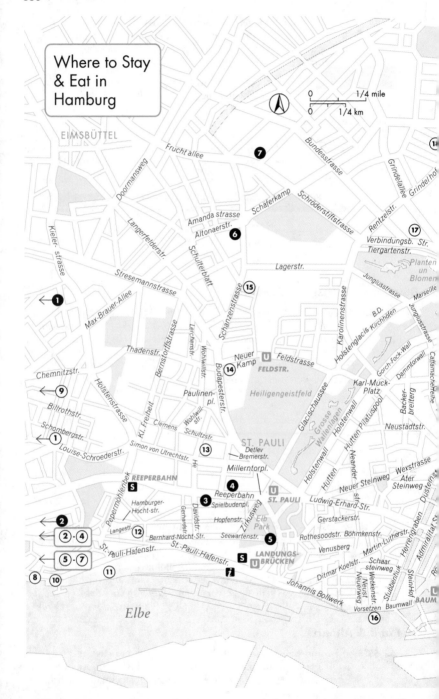

Where to Stay
& Eat in
Hamburg

0   1/4 mile
0   1/4 km

EIMSBÜTTEL

Frucht allee

Bundesstrasse

Kieler- strasse

Doormansweg

Langerfelderstr.

Amanda strasse
Altonaerstr.

Schäferkamp

Schröderstiftstrasse

Grindelallee

Grindelhof

Rentzelstr.

⑰

Verbindungsb. Str.
Tiergartenstr.

Schulterblatt

Lagerstr.

Planten
un
Blomen

Stresemannstrasse

Max-Brauer-Allee

Karolinenstrasse

Junglusstrasse

Marseille

Thadenstr.

Schanzenstrasse

⑮

B.D.

Holstenglacis Kirchhöfen

Chemnitzstr.

Bernstorffstrasse

Neuer
Kamp

⑭

Ⓤ Feldstrasse
FELDSTR.

Gorch-Fock-Wall

Dammtorwall

Caffamachereihe

⑨

Lerchenstr.

Wohlwillstr.

Budapesterstr.

Holstenwall

Karl-Muck-
Platz

Bäcker-
breiteng

Biltrothstr.

Holstenstrasse

Paulinen-
pl.

Heiligengeistfeld

Glacischaussee

Grosse
Wallanlagen

Hütten Pilatuspool

Neustädtstr.

Schombergstr.

Kl. Freiheit

Clemens

Wohlwill-
str.

Schultzstr.

⑬

ST. PAULI
Detlev
Bremerstr.

Holstenwall

Neander

Wexstrasse

①

Louise-Schroederstr.

Simon von Utrechtstr.

He

Millerntorpl.

Neuer Steinweg

Ater
Steinweg

Dusterns

REEPERBAHN

Ⓢ

④

Reeperbahn

Ⓤ
ST. PAULI

Hütten

Ludwig-Erhard-Str.

②

Hamburger-
Hocht-str.

③ Spielbudenpl.

Gerstackerstr.

② · ④

Langestr.

⑫

Bernhard-Nocht-Str.

Hopfenstr.

Davidstr.

Zirkusweg

Elb
Park

Rothesoodstr. Böhmkenstr.

Martin-Lutherstr.

Herrengraben

Admiralitäts St

⑤ · ⑦

St.-Pauli-Hafenstr.

Seewartenstr.

⑤

Venusberg

⑧   ⑩

⑪

St.-Pauli-Hafenstr.

Ⓢ

LANDUNGS-
BRÜCKEN
Ⓤ

Ⓘ

Ditmar Koelstr.

Schaar
steinweg

Neust
Neuerweg

Stubbenhuk

Steinhö

BAUM

Johannis Bollwerk

Wettkenstr.

Baumwall

Stubbenhuk

Elbe

Vorsetzen

Vorsetzen

⑯

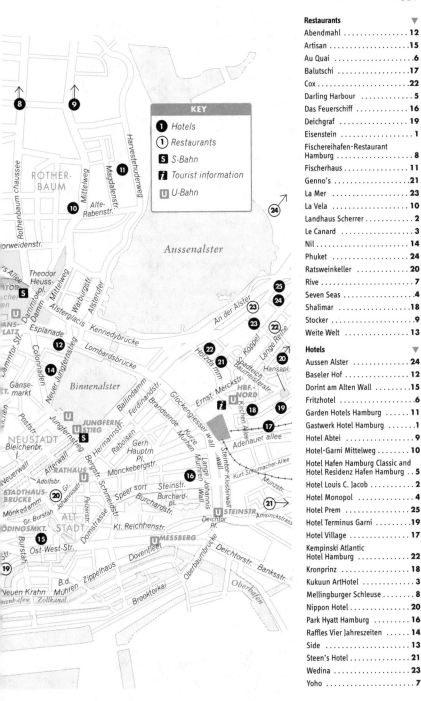

what's available in the fish market that morning. The restaurant and its oyster bar are a favorite with the city's beau monde. In summer, try to get a table on the sun terrace for a great view of the Elbe. ⊠ *Grosse Elbstr. 143, Altona* ☎ *040/381–816* ⌂ *Reservations essential* ▤ *AE, DC, MC, V* Ⓤ *Altona (S-bahn).*

★ **$–$$$$** ✕ **Au Quai.** The Au Quai is the hippest addition to a row of upscale, romantic restaurants nestled on the harbor's waterfront. The terrace, situated directly over the water, makes the elegant yet stylishly modern Au Quai a summer must. Indulge in French-Asian fusion cuisine, while taking in chugging tugboats, container ships, and sightseeing boats. The staff, dressed in blue-and-white-stripe scoop-neck sailor sweaters, enriches the maritime flair, and the menu offers a tasty selection of fish. ⊠ *Grosse Elbstr. 145, Altona* ☎ *040/3803–7730* ▤ *AE, DC, MC, V* ☾ *No lunch Sat., no dinner Sun.* Ⓤ *Königstrasse (S-bahn).*

$–$$$$ ✕ **Rive.** This harborside oyster bar is a Hamburg establishment, known for both its German nouvelle cuisine and its classic local dishes. Choose between dishes such as hearty *Matjes mit drei Saucen* (herring with three sauces), or *Dorade in der Salzkruste* (dorado fried in salt crust). Media types come to this shiplike building for the fresh oysters, clams, and the spectacular view. ⊠ *Van der Smissen Str. 1, Kreuzfahrt-Center, Altona* ☎ *040/380–5919* ⌂ *Reservations essential* ▤ *AE* Ⓤ *Königstrasse (S-bahn).*

$$–$$$ ✕ **Stocker.** *Nordlichter,* as northern Germans are affectionately called, love Austrian cuisine, and for delicacies including Viennese classics such as schnitzel or boiled beef brisket, they come to Stocker, the city's expert. The restaurant is casual and full of charm. A good choice is the *Schmankerlteller,* a hearty sampler with Austrian favorites, or the three-course lunch menu for just €18. In summer request a table in the quaint garden. ⊠ *Max-Brauer-Allee 80, Altona* ☎ *040/3861–5056* ▤ *AE, DC, MC, V* ☾ *Closed Mon.* Ⓤ *Altona (U-Bahn).*

$–$$$ ✕ **Darling Harbour.** True to its name, the Darling Harbour, named after the world-famous Sydney attraction, has become everybody's darling—at least that of Hamburg's bold and beautiful. Familiar faces from the media world come to this fine yet understated restaurant to see and be seen. Though some may find the menu lacking, the chef pulls out every stop to create an innovative and daring cuisine. The stunning view from the bay windows is worth a visit in itself. ⊠ *Neumühlen 17, Altona* ☎ *040/ 380–8900* ▤ *AE, DC, MC, V* ☾ *No lunch Sat.* Ⓤ *Altona (U-bahn).*

★ **$–$$$** ✕ **Fischerhaus.** The family-owned fish restaurant may look mediocre, but the food, prepared from family recipes, is outstanding. Most dishes focus on North Sea fish and Hamburg classics such as Labskaus or a plaice (a kind of flounder) dish. A favorite is the *Scholle Finkenwerder Art* (pan-fried plaice with smoked ham and potato salad). When making a reservation, ask for a table upstairs to get a harbor view. ⊠ *Fischmarkt 14, St. Pauli* ☎ *040/314–053* ▤ *MC, V* Ⓤ *Landungsbrücken (U-Bahn).*

¢–$$$ ✕ **Weite Welt.** Weite Welt is an absolute must if you are visiting St. Pauli. The restaurant's name recalls the longing of Hamburg's seafaring folk to see the "great wide world." In an old fish smokehouse on the Reeperbahn's notorious Grosse Freiheit (the live sex shows are just a few steps away), regulars feel right at home thanks to owner Nikolaus Bornhofen's hospitality. The fish dishes cross the continents of Europe and Asia and the theme dishes (such as the "Last Supper of the *Titanic*") are a good value. Reservations are essential on weekends. ⊠ *Grosse Freiheit 70, St. Pauli* ☎ *040/319–1214* ▤ *No credit cards* ⊗ *No lunch* Ⓤ *Reeperbahn (U-bahn).*

★ **$–$$** ✕ **Artisan.** Don't be surprised to see the words *I hate people who are not serious about their meals* scribbled on the slate, where one would normally find the specials. Artisan chef Thorsten Gillert has adopted this Oscar Wilde quote as his personal credo. This subdued, minimalist restaurant—Hamburg's newcomer of recent years—is the perfect place to acquaint yourself with the revolutionary fusion cuisine of international and local culinary favorites. The ever-changing selection of the three- and seven-course prix fixe meals go for €28 and €55, respectively. ⊠ *Kampstr. 27, Altona* ☎ *040/4210–2915* ▤ *No credit cards* ⊗ *Closed Mon.* Ⓤ *Sternschanze (U-bahn).*

$–$$ ✕ **La Vela.** Waiting at the gate of Hamburg's harbor next to the historic fish auction hall, this sophisticated Italian eatery serves up the market's freshest catches. If it's available, try the grilled *Dorade Royal* topped with a caramelized lemon and herb vinaigrette. A dark oak parquet floor and cozy cherrywood furniture complement the bare redbrick walls of the (former) harbor mill, providing the interior with a subtle spin on traditional Tuscan style. Try not to be swept away, as *La Vela* is Italian for "sail." ⊠ *Grosse Elbstr. 27, St. Pauli* ☎ *040/3869–9393* ▤ *AE, MC, V* Ⓤ *Landungsbrücken (U-bahn).*

$–$$ ✕ **Nil.** Media types—the intellectual and cultural elite of Hamburg—gather at this trendy venue for business lunches and prepartying on weekends. The Nil is worth a visit for its interior alone: it's in an old 1950s-style, three-floor shoe shop. The kitchen serves seafood and modern German cuisine, including four different three- to six-course menus, offering fare such as *Entenkeule Hamburger Art* (roasted duck joint in spicy sauce) in winter or lighter Italian-oriented fare in summer. Reservations are essential for dinner. ⊠ *Neuer Pferdemarkt 5, St. Pauli* ☎ *040/439–7823* ▤ *No credit cards* ⊗ *Closed Tues.* Ⓤ *Feldstrasse (U-bahn).*

$ ✕ **Abendmahl.** Off the Reeperbahn, the small Abendmahl is a launching point for crowds getting ready for bars and clubs. The fresh dishes on the small menu change daily and focus on French and Italian recipes. But the food plays second fiddle to the inexpensive and inventive drinks and the flirtatious atmosphere. The three-course dinner meal for just €24 is a great deal. ⊠ *Hein-Köllisch-Pl. 6, St. Pauli* ☎ *040/312–758* ▤ *No credit cards* Ⓤ *St. Pauli (U-bahn).*

St. Georg

$$–$$$ ✕ **La Mer.** The old-fashioned dining room of the Hotel Prem is perhaps the best hotel restaurant in the city, beautifully set on the Aussenalster, a 10-minute ride from downtown. A host of specialties changes daily, including *Zanderfilet auf Pfefferkraut mit gefüllten Waffelkartoffeln* (pike-perch fillet on pepper sauerkraut with stuffed waffle potatoes) or *Brust und Keule vom Perlhuhn auf Schwarzwurzeln mit Kartoffelgratin* (breast and leg of guinea fowl on black salsify with potato gratin). ⊠ *An der Alster 9, St. Georg* ☎ *040/2483–4040* ⋔ *Jacket and tie*

⊟ *AE, DC, MC, V* ⊘ *Closed Sun. No lunch Mon.* Ⓤ *Hauptbahnhof (U-or S-bahn).*

★ **$$** ✕ **Cox.** The Cox has been a reliably stylish restaurant for several years. It remains one of the hippest places around, with waitstaff (and patrons, for that matter) who won't give you any attitude. The dishes, mostly German nouvelle cuisine, are known for the careful use of fresh produce and spices from around the globe. The simple and cool interior with red leather banquettes is reminiscent of a French brasserie. ⊠ *Lange Reihe 68, at Greifswalder Str. 43, St. Georg* ☎ *040/249–422* ⊟ *AE* ⊘ *No lunch weekends* Ⓤ *Hauptbahnhof (U-bahn and S-Bahn).*

Rotherbaum

¢–$ ✕ **Balutschi.** A favorite among neighborhood students, Balutschi serves affordable and tasty Pakistani food, prepared with organic products. The richly decorated restaurant always seems to be crowded, and the smell of fresh spices and meat dishes, mostly lamb, hangs thick in the air. On weekend nights, a reservation is a must. ⊠ *Grindelallee 33, Rotherbaum* ☎ *040/452–479* ⊟ *AE, MC, V* Ⓤ *Dammtor (S-bahn).*

Ottensen, Uhlenhorst & Elsewhere

$$$$ ✕ **Seven Seas.** Süllberg, a small hill in the countryside along the River
Fodor'sChoice Elbe, boasts one of northern Germany's most traditional "getaway
★ restaurants." The Seven Seas is run by one of Europe's premier chefs, Karlheinz Hauser, and features international and French fish specialties in four- to six-course dinners only. If you don't want all the frills, try the Bistro dining room or come on a Sunday, when you can enjoy a bountiful Sunday brunch (€45 per person). ⊠ *Süllbergsterrasse 12, Blankenese* ☎ *040/866–2520* ⊟ *AE, DC, MC, V* ⊘ *Seven Seas closed Mon. and Tues. No lunch at Seven Seas* Ⓤ *Blankenese (S-bahn).*

$$$–$$$$ ✕ **Landhaus Scherrer.** Though this establishment is a 10-minute drive from downtown, its parklike setting seems worlds away from the high-rise bustle of the city. Wood-panel walls and soft lighting create a low-key mood in the building, which was originally a brewery. The food fuses sophisticated specialties with more down-to-earth local dishes. The wine list is exceptional. ⊠ *Elbchaussee 130, Ottensen* ☎ *040/880–1325* ⊟ *AE, MC, V* ⊘ *Closed Sun.* Ⓤ *Altona (S-bahn).*

★ **$$$–$$$$** ✕ **Le Canard.** One of Hamburg's top restaurants, Le Canard enjoys a much-coveted location overlooking the harbor and historic vessels at Övelgönne, with enviably elegant decor and cuisine to match. Chef Josef Viehhauser's skills and creativity keep the restaurant's standards high. Fish dishes such as pan-fried turbot predominate, but the roasted duck with red cabbage, traditionally served during the pre-Christmas season, is worth sampling. ⊠ *Elbchaussee 139, Ottensen* ☎ *040/880–5057* ⌕ *Reservations essential* ⊟ *AE, DC, MC, V* ⊘ *Closed Sun.* Ⓤ *Altona (S-bahn).*

$$–$$$ ✕ **Eisenstein.** The food is fantastic considering the low prices, and the crowd bubbly and mostly stylish. A sure bet are the daily menus or the Italian-Mediterranean dishes, including pastas and some excellent pizzas. The Pizza Helsinki (made with sour cream, onions, and fresh gravlax) is truly delicious. The setting, a 19th-century industrial complex with high ceilings and dark redbrick walls, is very rustic. Reservations are essential for dinner. ✉ *Friedensallee 9, Ottensen* ☎ *040/390–4606* ▤ *No credit cards* Ⓤ *Altona (S-bahn).*

★ **$$** ✕ **Shalimar.** The spices and exotic fare the locals have come to know at Freihafen Hamburg are commonplace at Shalimar, *the* Indian restaurant that has been dazzling Hamburg for 22 years strong. Its refined atmosphere, compliments of the gentle sitar sounds and swift, silent waiters, beguiles its guests as much as its prices. Neither, however, can hold a candle to the food itself. A mixed crowd of students, hipsters, bankers, and Indian businessmen make for an exciting evening. And be sure to try the mango ice cream—no meal is complete without it. ✉ *Dillstr. 16, Harvestehude* ☎ *040/442–484* ▤ *AE, DC, MC, V* ⊘ *No lunch* Ⓤ *Hallerstrasse (U-bahn).*

★ **$–$$** ✕ **Phuket.** Though it has an unimaginative name and dull facade, Phuket is by far the best Thai, or Asian for that matter, restaurant in town. The place is often jammed with Hamburgers from all districts who come to sample the truly hot fish dishes or the famous chicken in red wine sauce. ✉ *Adolph-Schönfelder-Str. 33–35, Uhlenhorst* ☎ *040/2982–3380* ▤ *AE, V* Ⓤ *Hamburger Strasse (U-bahn).*

★ **$** ✕ **Genno's.** Genno's is far from the downtown district, in Hamburg-Ham—a run-down residential area where you would hardly expect to find such a gem of high-quality dining. Owner Eugen Albrecht makes you feel at home with warm service and equally tasty dishes. The cuisine is a mixture of his personal preferences, including dishes such as *Lammfilet mit Senfsauce* (fillet of lamb with mustard sauce). ✉ *Hammer Steindamm 123, Hamm* ☎ *040/202–567* ▤ *No credit cards* ⊘ *Closed Sun. No lunch* Ⓤ *Hasselbrook (S-bahn).*

WHERE TO STAY

Hamburg has a full range of hotels, from five-star, grande-dame luxury enterprises to simple pensions. Nearly year-round conference and convention business keeps most rooms booked well in advance, and the rates are high. But many of the more expensive hotels lower their rates on weekends, when businesspeople have gone home. The tourist office can help with reservations if you arrive with nowhere to stay; ask about the many Happy Hamburg special-accommodation packages.

WHAT IT COSTS In Euros				
	$$$$	**$$$**	**$$**	**$**	**¢**
FOR 2 PEOPLE	over €225	€175–€225	€100–€175	€50–€100	under €50

Hotel prices are for two people in a standard double room, including tax and service.

Downtown & Historic Hamburg

$$$$ 🏨 **Raffles Vier Jahreszeiten.** Some claim that this 19th-century town house on the edge of the Binnenalster is the best hotel in Germany. Antiques—the hotel has a set of near-priceless Gobelin tapestries—fill the public rooms and accentuate the stylish bedrooms; fresh flowers overflow from massive vases; rare oil paintings adorn the walls; and all rooms are individually decorated with superb taste. One of the three restaurants, the Jahreszeiten-Grill, has been restored to its 1920s art deco look with dark woods, making it worth a visit. ⊠ *Neuer Jungfernstieg 9–14, Neustadt, D–20354* ☎ *040/34940* 🖷 *040/3494–2600* ⊕ *www.hvj.de* 🖘 *156 rooms, 23 suites* ♨ *3 restaurants, room service, in-room data ports, in-room safes, minibars, cable TV with movies, health club, hair salon, massage, sauna, bar, wine shop, babysitting, dry cleaning, laundry service, concierge, business services, meeting room, parking (fee), some pets allowed (fee), no-smoking rooms* ⊟ *AE, DC, MC, V* ℐℴℐ *EP* Ⓤ *Jungfernstieg (U-bahn).*

$$$–$$$$ 🏨 **Dorint am Alten Wall.** The flagship hotel of the German hotel chain, the Dorint is one of the city's finest. Behind the facade of Hamburg's 19th-century Postsparkassenamt, the German mail service's customer bank, is a sleek decor dominated by gray, white, and dark brown hues. All rooms are furnished with timelessly stylish furniture, huge beds (by German standards), and even bigger marble bathrooms. ⊠ *Alter Wall 38–46, Altstadt, D–20457* ☎ *040/369–500* 🖷 *040/3695–01000* ⊕ *www.dorint.de* 🖘 *224 rooms, 18 suites* ♨ *Restaurant, room service, in-room safes, minibars, cable TV with movies, pool, health club, massage, sauna, bar, babysitting, dry cleaning, laundry service, business services, meeting rooms, parking (fee), some pets allowed (fee), no-smoking rooms* ⊟ *AE, DC, MC, V* ℐℴℐ *BP* Ⓤ *Rödingsmarkt (U-bahn).*

★ $$$–$$$$ 🏨 **Park Hyatt Hamburg.** This ultramodern hotel is built within the historic walls of the Levantehaus, an old warehouse, not far from the train station. Guest rooms have bright and modern furnishings, somewhat minimalist and Asian in style. Original artwork by local painters adorns the suites. The Club Olympus pool and fitness area is breathtaking, both for its streamlined design and the variety of activities. ⊠ *Bugenhagenstr. 8, Neustadt, D–20095* ☎ *040/3332–1234* 🖷 *040/3332–1235* ⊕ *www.hamburg.hyatt.com* 🖘 *252 rooms, 30 apartments* ♨ *2 restaurants, room service, in-room data ports, minibars, cable TV with movies, indoor pool, health club, hair salon, massage, sauna, bar, babysitting, dry cleaning, laundry service, concierge, business services, meeting room, parking (fee), some pets allowed (fee), no-smoking room* ⊟ *AE, DC, MC, V* ℐℴℐ *BP* Ⓤ *Steinstrasse (U-bahn).*

★ $$$ 🏨 **Side.** Deeming itself to be "the luxury hotel of the 21st century," this ambitious newcomer is one of Germany's most architecturally sophisticated hotels. Premier Milanese designer Matteo Thun served as the driving force behind the five-star resort in the heart of the city. His vision provided for the stunning lighting arrangement as well as the interior design. Whether soothed by the eggshell-white accents in your room or wowed by the lobby's soaring and stark atrium, you won't ever want to leave. ⊠ *Drehbahn 49, Altstadt, D–20304* ☎ *040/309–990* 🖷 *040/3099–9399* ⊕ *www.side-hamburg.de* 🖘 *158 rooms, 10 suites* ♨ *Restaurant, room service, in-room safes, minibars, cable TV with movies, health club, sauna, spa, bar, dry cleaning, laundry service, meeting rooms, parking (fee), some pets allowed (fee), no-smoking rooms* ⊟ *AE, DC, MC, V* ℐℴℐ *EP* Ⓤ *Gänsemarkt (U-bahn).*

$$ 🏨 **Baseler Hof.** It's hard to find a fault in this central hotel near the Binnenalster and the opera house. Service is friendly and efficient, all rooms are neatly furnished, and prices are quite reasonable for this expensive city. The hotel caters to both individuals and convention groups, so the lounge area can be crowded at times. ⊠ *Esplanade 11, Neustadt, D–20354* ☎ *040/359–060* 🖷 *040/3590–6918* ⊕ *www.baselerhof.de* ➷ *151 rooms, 2 suites* ⋄ *Restaurant, room service, in-room data ports, bar, babysitting, dry cleaning, laundry service, concierge, meeting room, parking (fee), some pets allowed (fee), no-smoking rooms; no a/c* ⊟ *AE, DC, MC, V* ⍟ *CP* Ⓤ *Stephansplatz (U-bahn).*

$ 🏨 **Hotel Terminus Garni.** Unlike its famous namesake in Paris, the Hamburg Hotel Terminus is a simple and inexpensive hotel near the central train station. It's popular among British and American budget travelers who appreciate its relaxed atmosphere and reliable service (the hotel is part of the Garni hotel chain). Double rooms share either a bath or a shower. ⊠ *Steindamm 5, Altstadt, D–20999* ☎ *040/280–3144* 🖷 *040/241–518* ⊕ *www.hotel-terminus-hamburg.de* ➷ *20 rooms, 4 with shared bath; 1 apartment* ⋄ *Cable TV; no a/c, no room phones* ⊟ *AE, DC, MC, V* ⍟ *CP* Ⓤ *Hauptbahnhof-Süd (U-bahn, S-bahn).*

★ $ 🏨 **Hotel Village.** The small and charming Hotel Village was once a thriving brothel near the central train station. Red-and-black carpets and glossy wallpaper in the rooms are a nod to the hotel's past. Some rooms even have their old large beds, replete with canopy and a revolving mirror. The service (including a 24-hour coffee bar) is extremely friendly and casual. ⊠ *Steindamm 4, Altstadt, D–20099* ☎ *040/246–137* 🖷 *040/486–4949* ⊕ *www.hotel-village.de* ➷ *20 rooms* ⋄ *Cable TV, parking (fee), some pets allowed (fee); no a/c* ⊟ *AE, MC, V* ⍟ *CP* Ⓤ *Hauptbahnhof (U-bahn and S-bahn).*

$ 🏨 **Kronprinz.** For its humble position (on a busy street opposite the railway station) and its moderate price, the Kronprinz is a surprisingly attractive hotel, with a whiff of four-star flair. Rooms are individually styled, modern but homey. ⊠ *Kirchenallee 46, Altstadt, D–20099* ☎ *040/243–258* 🖷 *040/280–1097* ➷ *73 rooms* ⋄ *Restaurant, minibars, cable TV, babysitting, parking (fee), some pets allowed (fee), no-smoking rooms; no a/c* ⊟ *AE, DC, MC, V* ⍟ *CP* Ⓤ *Hauptbahnhof (U-bahn and S-bahn).*

St. Pauli & Altona

★ $$–$$$ 🏨 **Gastwerk Hotel Hamburg.** Proudly dubbing itself Hamburg's first design hotel, the Gastwerk, in a century-old, redbrick gas plant, certainly is the most stylish accommodation in town. The simple but incredibly chic furnishings reflect the building's industrial design but are warmed by the use of natural materials, various woods, and thick carpets. The loft rooms with large windows, bare walls, and a lot of space are probably the most exciting hotel rooms in Hamburg. ⊠ *Beim alten Gaswerk 3, at Daimlerstr. 67, Altona, D–22761* ☎ *040/890–620* 🖷 *040/890–6220* ⊕ *www.gastwerk-hotel.de* ➷ *122 rooms, 13 suites* ⋄ *Restaurant, room service, in-room safes, minibars, cable TV, health club, massage, sauna, bar, dry cleaning, laundry service, meeting rooms, free parking,* *some pets allowed (fee), no-smoking rooms* ⊙ *EP* ▭ *AE, DC, MC, V* Ⓤ *Bahrenfeld (S-bahn).*

$$ 🏨 **Hotel Hafen Hamburg Classic and Hotel Residenz Hafen Hamburg.** Located in one building complex just across from the famous St. Pauli Landungsbrücken, both hotels are good value considering their three- and four-star status, respectively. The older Hotel Hafen Hamburg, with its small but nicely renovated rooms, offers a great view of the harbor, while the larger, ultramodern and upscale Hotel Residenz Hafen annex has less flair but more comfort. The location makes this hotel a perfect starting point for exploring St. Pauli and the Reeperbahn. ⊠ *Seewartenstr. 7–9, St. Pauli, D–20459* ☎ *040/3111–3600* 📠 *040/3111–3751* ⊕ *www. hotel-hamburg.de* ⇄ *Hotel Hafen: 230 rooms; Hotel Residenz: 125 rooms* △ *Restaurant, in-room safes, minibars, cable TV with movies, sauna, 3 bars, babysitting, dry cleaning, laundry service, meeting room, parking (fee), some pets allowed (fee), no-smoking floor; no a/c in some rooms* ▭ *AE, DC, MC, V* ⊙ *EP* Ⓤ *Landungsbrücken (U-bahn).*

$ 🏨 **Fritzhotel.** This intimate yet stylish hotel, squeezed into an old city apartment complex, has small but bright designer rooms complete with amenities such as TV and Internet access. The hotel does not offer breakfast but it shares the relatively quiet street with many bistros and breakfast cafés. ⊠ *Schanzenstr. 101, St. Pauli, D–20357* ☎ *040/ 8222–2830* 📠 *040/8222–28322* ⊕ *www.fritzhotel.com* ⇄ *17 rooms* △ *Cable TV; no a/c* ▭ *No credit cards* Ⓤ *Sternschanze (U-bahn).*

$ 🏨 **Kukuun ArtHotel.** This enchanting, offbeat hotel in the heart of St. Pauli is a treat for the budget traveler. Each room, as well as its appliances and gadgets, was exclusively designed in painstaking detail by a different artist. Not all of its quarters are intended for the same audience. For instance, in the room entitled Camera Obscura, street imagery from the red-light Reeperbahn is projected right before your eyes. The two new, modern apartments on the second floor are quiet and secluded alternatives and a fairly good deal. ⊠ *Spielbudenpl. 22, St. Pauli, D–20359* ☎ *040/314–393* 📠 *040/3023–7947* ⇄ *13 rooms without bath; 2 apartments with bath* △ *2 bars, some pets allowed; no a/c, no room phones* ▭ *No credit cards* ⊙ *EP* Ⓤ *St. Pauli (U-bahn).*

$ 🏨 **Hotel Monopol.** There's no other hotel in the Reeperbahn neighborhood where budget travelers can enjoy a safe and clean stay in the heart of Europe's most bizarre red-light district. Despite a makeover in 2002, the small rooms are mostly old-fashioned, and some look like an odd mixture of 1950s and '80s designs, but the service is warm and has a touch of Hamburger Kiez. You might run into an artist performing in a Hamburg musical—or in the live sex shows on Reeperbahn. ⊠ *Reeperbahn 48, St. Pauli, D–20359* ☎ *040/311–770* 📠 *040/3117–7151* ⊕ *www. monopol-hamburg.de* ⇄ *82 rooms* △ *Restaurant, room service, cable TV, bar, dry cleaning, laundry service, meeting room, free parking, some pets allowed (fee); no a/c* ▭ *AE, DC, MC, V* ⊙ *BP* Ⓤ *St. Pauli (U-bahn).*

St. Georg

$$$$ 🏨 **Kempinski Atlantic Hotel Hamburg.** There are few hotels in Germany more sumptuous than this gracious Edwardian palace facing the Aussenalster. The stylish mood is achieved with thick carpet, marble-inlaid

FodorsChoice
★

floors and walls, sophisticated lighting, and a newly refurbished lobby that is positively baronial. Some rooms are traditionally furnished while others are more modern, but all are typical of Hamburg in their understated luxury. Each room has a spacious sitting area and large bathroom. Guests can lounge in the formal outdoor courtyard, where only the gurgling fountain disturbs the peace. ⊠ *An der Alster 72–79, St. Georg, D–20099* ☎ *040/28880* 🖷 *040/247–129* ⊕ *www.kempinski.atlantic. de* 🖙 *241 rooms, 13 suites* ♻ *2 restaurants, café, room service, in-room data ports, in-room safes, minibars, cable TV with movies, pool, health club, massage, sauna, boating, bicycles, bar, shops, babysitting, dry cleaning, laundry service, concierge, business services, meeting room, parking (fee), some pets allowed (fee), no-smoking rooms* 🖃 *AE, DC, MC, V* 🍴 *EP* Ⓤ *Hauptbahnhof (U-bahn, S-bahn).*

$$–$$$ 🏨 **Hotel Prem.** Facing the Aussenalster, this extremely personable, quiet hotel is Hamburg's gem. Most guests are regulars and have favorite rooms; no two rooms are the same. The Adenauer Suite (named after the chancellor, who stayed here) is traditionally furnished, including an antique chaise longue and a period writing desk in an alcove with a lake view. Room 102, across the hall, has contemporary furnishings and a platform bed. Suite 2 has two rooms with modern furnishings and a terrace overlooking the lake. The bar is intimate, and the dining at La Mer is superb. ⊠ *An der Alster 9, St. Georg, D–20099* ☎ *040/2483–4040* 🖷 *040/280–3851* ⊕ *www.hotel-prem.de* 🖙 *51 rooms, 3 suites* ♻ *Restaurant, room service, in-room data ports, in-room safes, minibars, cable TV, sauna, bar, babysitting, dry cleaning, laundry service, concierge, business services, meeting room, free parking, some pets allowed (fee); no a/c* 🖃 *AE, DC, MC, V* 🍴 *BP* Ⓤ *Hauptbahnhof (U-bahn and S-bahn).*

$$ 🏨 **Aussen Alster.** Crisp and contemporary in design, this boutique hotel prides itself on the personal attention it gives its guests. Rooms are compact; most have a full bathroom, but three have a shower only, no bathtub. Stark white walls, white bedspreads, and light-hue carpets create a bright, fresh ambience. A small bar is open in the evening, and there's a tiny garden for summer cocktails. The restaurant serves Italian fare for lunch and dinner. The Aussenalster, where the hotel keeps a sailboat for guests to use, is at the end of the street. ⊠ *Schmilinskystr. 11, St. Georg, D–20099* ☎ *040/241–557* 🖷 *040/280–3231* ⊕ *www.aussen-alster.de* 🖙 *27 rooms* ♻ *Restaurant, room service, in-room safes, cable TV, sauna, boating, bicycles, bar, babysitting, dry cleaning, laundry service, meeting room, parking (fee), some pets allowed (fee); no a/c* 🖃 *AE, DC, MC, V* 🍴 *BP* Ⓤ *Hauptbahnhof (U-bahn and S-bahn).*

$$ 🏨 **Wedina.** Rooms at this small hotel are neat and compact. When you make a reservation, either ask for a room in the Italian-style Yellow House, with its elegant parquet floor, or check out the rooms in the new, minimalist-style Green House. In the main building, the bar and breakfast area face the veranda and a small garden and pool that bring Tuscany to mind. All lodgings are a half block from the Aussenalster and a brisk 10-minute walk from the train station. ⊠ *Gurlittstr. 23, St. Georg, D–20099* ☎ *040/280–8900* 🖷 *040/280–3894* ⊕ *www.wedina.de* 🖙 *48 rooms, 11 apartments* ♻ *In-room safes, cable TV, bicycles, bar, concierge, business services, parking (fee), some pets allowed (fee), no-smoking* *rooms; no a/c* ▭ *AE, DC, MC, V* 🍽 *CP* Ⓤ *Hauptbahnhof (U-bahn and S-bahn).*

$ **Steen's Hotel.** This small, family-run hotel in a narrow, four-story town house near the central train station provides modest but congenial service. The rooms are spacious and clean but lack atmosphere. Bathrooms are tiny. A great plus are the comfortable beds with reclining head and foot rests. The breakfasts amply make up for the uninspired rooms, and the hotel's garage is a blessing, since there's never a parking space in this neighborhood. ✉ *Holzdamm 43, St. Georg, D–20099* ☎ *040/244–642* 🖷 *040/280–3593* 🌐 *www.steens-hotel.com* *11 rooms* *Minibars, cable TV, parking (fee); no a/c* ▭ *AE, DC, MC, V* 🍽 *CP* Ⓤ *Hauptbahnhof (U-bahn and S-bahn).*

Elsewhere

★ $$$$ **Hotel Louis C. Jacob.** Would-be Hanseats frequent this small yet luxurious hotel nestled amid the older wharf dwellings along the banks of the Elbe. Far from the hustle-bustle of the city, the intimate Louis C. Jacob, named after the French landscape gardener who founded it in 1791, makes a point of meticulously pampering its guests. Artist Max Liebermann stayed here and painted the terrace with its linden trees. One of the classically furnished suites even bears his name. From a river-view room, you'll be able to watch passing ships and listen as their foghorns bid Hamburg farewell. ✉ *Elbchaussee 401–403, Blankenese, D–22609* ☎ *040/822–550* 🖷 *040/8225–5555* 🌐 *www.hotel-jacob.de* *66 rooms, 19 suites* *2 restaurants, room service, in-room safes, minibars, cable TV with movies, hot tub, massage, sauna, bar, dry cleaning, laundry service, meeting rooms, parking (fee), some pets allowed (fee), no-smoking rooms* ▭ *AE, DC, MC, V* 🍽 *EP* Ⓤ *Hochkamp (S-bahn).*

$$$–$$$$ **Hotel Abtei.** On a quiet, tree-lined street about 2 km (1 mi) north of the downtown area, in Harvestehude, this elegant period hotel offers understated luxury and friendly, personal service. If you want a room with a four-poster bed, ask when making a reservation. One of the nicest rooms in the small hotel is No. 7 with its antique 19th-century washing tables. All guest rooms have English antique cherrywood and mahogany furniture. ✉ *Abteistr. 14, Harvestehude, D–20149* ☎ *040/442–905* 🖷 *040/449–820* 🌐 *www.abtei-hotel.de* *8 rooms, 3 suites* *Restaurant, room service, in-room safes, minibars, cable TV, dry cleaning, laundry service, free parking, some pets allowed (fee); no a/c* ▭ *AE, MC, V* 🍽 *BP* Ⓤ *Klosterstern (U-bahn).*

$$–$$$ **Garden Hotels Hamburg.** The location in chic Pöseldorf, 2 km (1 mi) from the downtown area, may discourage those who want to be in the thick of things, but this is one of the most appealing hotels in Hamburg, offering outstanding personal service and classy accommodations in three attractive mansions. ✉ *Magdalenenstr. 60, Pöseldorf, D–20148* ☎ *040/414–040* 🖷 *040/414–0420* 🌐 *www.garden-hotels.de* *57 rooms, 3 suites* *Room service, in-room data ports, minibars, cable TV, bicycles, bar, babysitting, dry cleaning, laundry service, concierge, business services, meeting room, free parking, some pets allowed (fee), no-smoking rooms; no a/c* ▭ *AE, MC, V* 🍽 *EP* Ⓤ *Hallerstrasse (U-bahn).*

$$ 🏨 **Hotel-Garni Mittelweg.** With chintz curtains, flowered wallpaper, old-fashioned dressing tables, and a country-house-style breakfast room, this hotel exudes small-town charm in big-business Hamburg. The converted mansion is in upmarket Pöseldorf, a short walk from the Aussenalster and a quick bus ride from the city center. ✉ *Mittelweg 59, Pöseldorf, D–20149* ☎ *040/414–1010* 🖷 *040/4141–0120* ⊕ *www. hotel-mittelweg.de* ⤶ *30 rooms, 1 apartment* ♿ *Room service, in-room safes, minibars, cable TV, babysitting, parking (fee), some pets allowed (fee), no-smoking rooms; no a/c* ▭ *AE, DC, MC, V* ⊚ *CP* Ⓤ *Klosterstern (U-bahn).*

$$ 🏨 **Nippon Hotel.** You'll be asked to remove your shoes before entering your room at the Nippon. Tatami mats line the floor, futon mattresses are on the beds, and an attentive Japanese staff is at your service. The authenticity might make things a bit *too* spartan and efficient for some, but by cutting some Western-style comforts, the hotel offers a good value in the attractive Uhlenhorst District. The Nippon has a Japanese restaurant and sushi bar. ✉ *Hofweg 75, Uhlenhorst, D–22085* ☎ *040/227–1140* 🖷 *040/2271–1490* ⊕ *www.nippon-hotel-hh.de* ⤶ *41 rooms, 1 suite* ♿ *Restaurant, in-room safes, minibars, cable TV, bicycles, dry cleaning, laundry service, concierge, business services, meeting room, parking (fee), no-smoking rooms; no a/c* ▭ *AE, DC, MC, V* ⊚ *BP* Ⓤ *Mundsburg (U-bahn).*

$–$$ 🏨 **Mellingburger Schleuse.** If you prefer off-the-beaten-track lodgings, this member of the Ringhotel-Association is a 20-minute drive from the downtown area, idyllically set in a forest. The Alsterwanderweg hiking trail passes right by the doorstep. The hotel is more than 200 years old, with a thatch roof, peasant-style furnishings, and a restaurant that serves traditional northern German dishes. ✉ *Mellingburgredder 1, Sasel, D–22395* ☎ *040/6024–00103* 🖷 *040/602–7912* ⤶ *40 rooms* ♿ *2 restaurants, cable TV, pool, billiards, bowling, bar, concierge, meeting room, free parking, some pets allowed (fee), no-smoking rooms; no a/c* ▭ *AE, DC, MC, V* ⊚ *BP* Ⓤ *Poppenbüttel (U-bahn).*

★ $ 🏨 **Yoho.** Centrally located between the hip Schanzenviertel and the downtown area, the new Yoho is the budget youth hostel of the 21st century. Housed in an historic, imposing villa with contemporary interior design, it offers simple yet elegant rooms with modern amenities otherwise not found in a hostel. Guests under 26 receive a special rate of €57 for a single or €67 for a double room. This is the perfect place for international backpackers with an edge. ✉ *Moorkamp 5, Eimsbüttel, D–20357* ☎ *040/284–1910* 🖷 *040/2841–9141* ⊕ *www.yoho-hamburg. de* ⤶ *30 rooms* ♿ *Restaurant, cable TV, free parking, some pets allowed; no a/c* ▭ *AE, MC, V* ⊚ *CP* Ⓤ *Schlump (U-bahn).*

NIGHTLIFE & THE ARTS

The Arts

The arts flourish in this cosmopolitan metropolis. The city's ballet company is one of the finest in Europe, and the Ballet Festival in July is a cultural high point. Information on events is available in the magazines

Hamburger Vorschau—pick it up for free in tourist offices and most hotels—and *Szene Hamburg,* sold at newsstands for €2.50.

The best way to order tickets for all major Hamburg theaters, musicals, and most cultural events is the central phone **Hamburg-Hotline** (☎ 040/3005–1300). A number of travel agencies also sell tickets for plays, concerts, and the ballet. The tourist office at the **Landungsbrücken** (⊠ Between Piers 4 and 5, St. Pauli ☎ 040/3005–1200 or 040/3005–1203) has a ticket office. One of the large downtown ticket agencies is the **Theaterkasse im Alsterhaus** (⊠ Jungfernstieg 16, Neustadt ☎ 040/353–555). The downtown **Theaterkasse Central** (⊠ Gerhart-Hauptmann-Pl. 48, Neustadt ☎ 040/337–124) is at the Landesbank-Galerie.

Ballet & Opera

One of the most beautiful theaters in the country, **Hamburgische Staatsoper** (⊠ Grosse Theaterstr. 35, Altstadt ☎ 040/356–868) is the leading northern German venue for opera and ballet. The Hamburg Ballet is directed by American John Neumeier.

The **Operettenhaus Hamburg** (⊠ Spielbudenpl. 1, St. Pauli ☎ 01805/114–113) is currently running *Mamma Mia,* a fun and popular musical about the pop band Abba.

Concerts

Both the Hamburg Philharmonic and the Hamburg Symphony Orchestra appear regularly at the **Musikhalle** (⊠ Johannes-Brahms-Pl., Neustadt ☎ 040/346–920). Visiting orchestras from overseas are also presented.

Film

Independent and mainstream English-language movies are shown at the **Metropolis** (⊠ Dammtorstr. 30, Neustadt ☎ 040/342–353) and are often subtitled in German. Students often show up at the **Grindel Kino** (⊠ Grindelberg 7a, Harvestehude ☎ 040/449–333) for blockbuster English-language movies.

Theater

Deutsches Schauspielhaus (⊠ Kirchenallee 39, St. Georg ☎ 040/248–713), one of Germany's leading drama stages, is lavishly restored to its full 19th-century opulence and is the most important Hamburg venue for classical and modern theater.

English Theater (⊠ Lerchenfeld 14, Uhlenhorst ☎ 040/227–7089) is the city's only theater presenting English-language drama.

Theater im Hamburger Hafen (⊠ Norderelbstr. 6, at Hamburger Hafen, follow signs to Schuppen 70, St. Pauli ☎ 040/3005–1150) is currently staging a German version of the Broadway musical hit *The Lion King.*

Hamburg is by far Germany's capital for musicals, and the **Neue Flora Theater** (⊠ Stresemannstr. 159a, at Alsenstr., Altona ☎ 01805–4444 or 040/4316–5490) offers the best deal. At this writing, the theater was presenting the musical *Dance with Vampires.*

Nightlife

The Reeperbahn

Whether you think it sordid or sexy, the Reeperbahn, in the St. Pauli District, is as central to the Hamburg scene as the classy shops along Jungfernstieg. A walk down **Herbertstrasse** (men only, no women or children permitted), just two blocks south of the Reeperbahn, can be quite an eye-opener. Here, prostitutes sit displayed in windows as they await customers. On nearby **Grosse Freiheit**, you'll find a number of the better-known sex-show or table-dance clubs: **Colibri**, at No. 30; **Safari**, at No. 24; and **Dollhouse**, at No. 11. They cater to the package-tour trade as well as those on the prowl by themselves. Prices are high. If you order a drink, ask for the price list, which must be displayed by law, and pay as soon as you're served. Not much happens here before 10 PM.

Schmidts Tivoli (✉ Spielbudenpl. 27–28, St. Pauli ☎ 040/3177–8899 or 040/3005–1400) has become Germany's most popular variety theater, presenting a classy repertoire of live music, vaudeville, chansons, and cabaret.

Bars

The Hansestadt has a buzzing and upscale bar scene, with many spots that feature live music or DJs and dancing. A nightlife institution still going strong is the fashionable but cozy **Bar Hamburg** (✉ Rautenbergstr. 6–8, St. Georg ☎ 040/2805–4880). The **Bereuther** (✉ Klosterallee 100, Hoheluft ☎ 040/4140–6789) is a sleek bar and bistro for thirtysomethings. **Christiansen's** (✉ Pinnasberg 60, St. Pauli ☎ 040/317–2863), near the Fischmarkt, is said to mix the best cocktails in town.

Dance Clubs

One of the hottest clubs in Hamburg, **Gum** (✉ Hamburger Berg 12–13, St. Pauli ☎ No phone) is packed with young, trendy, and very flirtatious Hamburgers dancing to house or electropop music. The new **China Lounge** (✉ Nobistor 10, St. Pauli ☎ 040/3197–6622), in a former Chinese restaurant, is Hamburg's coolest lounge and bar, mostly attracting hip and beautiful twentysomethings. The stylish **Funky Pussy Club** (✉ Grosse Freiheit 34, St. Pauli ☎ 040/314–236) is a small dance club with '70s retro design, where a young crowd dances to techno, hip-hop, and Latin music. The more mature business crowd meets at Hamburg's smallest dance club, **Top of Town** (✉ Marseillerstr. 2, Rotherbaum ☎ 040/3502–3432), on the 26th floor of the SAS Radisson Hotel. It's both elegant and expensive, as most Hamburg clubs are.

Jazz & Live Music Clubs

Birdland (✉ Gärtnerstr. 122, Hoheluft ☎ 040/405–277) is one of the leading clubs among Hamburg's more than 100 venues, offering everything from traditional New Orleans sounds to avant-garde electronic noise. The **Cotton Club** (✉ Alter Steinweg 10, Neustadt ☎ 040/343–878), Hamburg's oldest jazz club, books classic New Orleans jazz as well as swing. **Docks** (✉ Spielbudenplatz 19, St. Pauli ☎ 040/317–8830) has a stylish bar and is Hamburg's largest venue for live music. It also puts on disco nights.

SPORTS & THE OUTDOORS

Biking

Most major streets in Hamburg have bicycle lanes. Some of the major hotels will lend their guests bikes. The most central location for renting bikes is at the **Hauptbahnhof** (⊠ Entrance on Kirchenallee, St. Georg ☎ 040/3918–50475). Bikes rent for €8 a day (7 AM–9:30 PM). A wide selection of bikes, including racing, mountain, and children's bikes, are rented at Mr. Petersen's **Hamburg anders erfahren** (⊠ Insterburger Str. 15, Bramfeld ☎ 040/640–1800). The bikes cost between €7.50 and €20 a day. There's a discount on multiday rentals. A complete list of bike rentals in Hamburg and the surrounding countryside can be obtained from the **ADFC Hamburg** (⊠ Markstr. 18, D–22041 ☎ 040/393–933 or 040/390–7050).

Jogging

The best places for jogging are the Planten un Blomen and Alter Botanischer Garten parks and along the leafy promenade around the Alster. The latter route is about 6 km (4 mi) long.

Sailing

You can rent rowboats and sailboats on the Alster in summer between 10 AM and 9 PM. Rowboats cost around €12 an hour, sailboats around €16 an hour. The largest selection of boats is at the Gurlittinsel pier off An der Alster (on the east bank of the Aussenalster). Another rental outlet is at the very tip of the Alster, at the street Fernsicht.

SHOPPING

Shopping Districts

Hamburg's shopping districts are among the most elegant on the Continent, and the city has Europe's largest expanse of covered shopping arcades, most of them packed with small, exclusive boutiques. The streets **Grosse Bleichen** and **Neuer Wall,** which lead off Jungfernstieg, are a high-price-tag zone. The Grosse Bleichen leads to six of the city's most important covered (or indoor) malls, many of which are connected. The marble-clad **Galleria** is modeled after London's Burlington Arcade. Daylight streams through the immense glass ceilings of the **Hanse-Viertel,** an otherwise ordinary reddish-brown brick building. The **Kaufmannshaus,** also known as the Commercie, and the upscale (and former first-class hotel) **Hamburger Hof** are two of the oldest and most fashionable indoor malls. There are also the **Alte Post** and the **Bleichenhof.**

Hamburg's premier shopping street, **Jungfernstieg,** is just about the most expensive in the country. It's lined with jewelers' shops—Wempe, Brahmfeld & Guttruf, and Hintze are the top names—and chic clothing boutiques such as Linette, Ursula Aust, Selbach, Windmöller, and Jäger & Koch.

In the fashionable **Pöseldorf** district north of downtown, take a look at Milchstrasse and Mittelweg. Both are filled with small boutiques, restaurants, and cafés.

Running from the main train station to Gerhard-Hauptmann-Platz, the boulevard **Spitalerstrasse** is a pedestrians-only street lined with stores. Prices here are noticeably lower than those on Jungfernstieg.

Antiques

Take a look at the shops in the **St. Georg** district behind the train station, especially those between Lange Reihe and Koppel. You'll find a mixture of genuine antiques (*Antiquitäten*) and junk (*Trödel*). You won't find many bargains, however. ABC-Strasse is another happy hunting ground for antiques lovers.

The **Antik-Center** (⊠ Klosterwall 9–21, Altstadt ☎ 040/326–285) is an assortment of 39 shops in the old market hall, close to the main train station. It features a wide variety of antiques from all periods.

Department Stores

Alsterhaus (⊠ Jungfernstieg 16–20, Neustadt ☎ 040/359–010) is Hamburg's most famous department store. It's large and elegant, and a favorite with locals.

GaleriaKaufhof (⊠ Mönckebergstr. 3, Altstadt ☎ 040/333–070) offers far more bargains than most other department stores.

Karstadt (⊠ Mönckebergstr. 16, Altstadt ☎ 040/30940) is Germany's leading department-store chain and offers the same goods as the Alsterhaus at similar prices. Hamburg's downtown Karstadt is the city's best place to shop for sports clothing.

Stilwerk (⊠ Grosse Elbstr. 68, Altona ☎ 040/306–210), Hamburg's most fashionable shopping mall, resembles a department store and primarily houses furniture and home-accessory shops.

Flea & Food Markets

A lively fruit-and-vegetable market in the heart of **Blankenese** manages to preserve the charm of a small village. ⊠ Bahnhofstr., Blankenese ☉ *Tues. 8–2, Fri. 8–6, Sat. 8–1* Ⓤ *Blankenese (S-bahn).*

Fischmarkt (⇨ St. Pauli and the Reeperbahn *in* Exploring Hamburg).

Gift Ideas

Binikowski (⊠ Lokstedter Weg 68, Eppendorf ☎ 040/462–852) sells the most famous must-buy *Buddelschiffe* (ships in bottles). There are few better places to shop for one, or for a blue-and-white-stripe sailor's shirt, a sea captain's hat, ship models, or even ships' charts.

Captain's Cabin (⊠ St. Pauli Landungsbrücken, St. Pauli ☎ 040/316–373), a Hamburg institution, is an experience not to be missed. It's the best place for all of the city's specialty maritime goods.

Harry's Hafenbasar (⊠ Balduinstr. 18, St. Pauli ☎ 040/312–482) is full of dusty goods traders and seamen have brought back from the corners of the globe. This eerie, bazaarlike store is jam-packed and is a bargain-hunter's paradise for anything maritime.

Seifarth and Company (⊠ Robert-Koch-Str. 19, Norderstedt ☎ 040/524–0027) is one of the best places to buy tea in Hamburg, and Hamburg is one of the best places to buy tea in Europe. Smoked salmon and caviar are terrific buys here as well.

Jewelry

Wempe (⊠ Jungfernstieg 8, Neustadt ☎ 040/3344–8824) is Germany's largest and most exclusive jeweler. This is its flagship store (one of three Hamburg locations); the selection of watches here is particularly outstanding.

Men's Clothing

The stylish store **Doubleeight. Another Level** (⊠ Jungfernstieg 52, Neustadt ☎ 040/3571–5510) carries both designer and less-expensive everyday fashions. A Hamburg classic and a must for the fashion-conscious traveler, **Thomas I-Punkt** (⊠ Mönckebergstr. 21, Altstadt ☎ 040/327–172) sells hip designer clothes and suits of its own label.

Women's Clothing

High-price fashion, designed by one of Hamburg's newcomers, Petra Rodeck, is found at **balcony** (⊠ Fehlandstr. 41, Neustadt ☎ 040/343–606). The clothing here is daring, cool, and definitely not mainstream. The upscale shopping complex **Kaufrausch** (⊠ Isestr. 74, Eppendorf ☎ 040/480–8313) has mostly clothing and accessories stores for women. **Kleidermacher** (⊠ Michaelisbrücke 1–3, Neustadt ☎ 040/3751–8787) carries several young local designers' labels. A small but elegant and very personal store, **Linette** (⊠ Eppendorfer Baum 19, Eppendorf ☎ 040/460–4963), stocks only top names.

SIDE TRIPS FROM HAMBURG

Hamburg is surrounded by the fertile green marshlands of the neighboring states of Schleswig-Holstein and Lower Saxony (Niedersachsen). Two popular side trips are described here.

Altes Land

23 km (14 mi) west of downtown Hamburg (on Finkenwerder Str. and Cranzer Hauptdeich).

The marshy Altes Land extends 30 km (19 mi) west from Hamburg along the south bank of the Elbe River to the town of Stade. This fruit-growing region is dotted with huge half-timber farmhouses and crisscrossed by canals. Hikers come out for walks, especially in spring, when the apple and cherry trees are in blossom. Some of the prettiest trails take you along the dikes running next to the Este and Lühe rivers. Much of the territory is best covered on foot, so wear walking shoes. You may want to bring a picnic lunch as well and spend a long (summer) day here.

From the dock at Cranz, walk south into the suburb of **Neuenfelde**. Visit the **St. Pancratius Kirche** (Church of St. Pancratius), a baroque church with an unusual painted barrel roof, worth a visit for its northern German Baroque-style altar. It was built in 1688, and the organ, dating from the same period, was designed by Arp Schnitger, an organ builder and local farmer. ⊠ *Am Organistenweg, Altes Land* ☎ *040/745–9296* ⊙ *Daily 9–5.*

The 18th-century church and decorative farmhouses of the village of **Jork** lie some 9 km (5½ mi) on foot to the west of Neuenfelde, just beyond the confluence of the Este and Elbe rivers (Bus No. 257 travels to and from Neuenfelde as well). The windmill in **Borstel,** a 10-minute walk from Jork, is worth a short detour.

Stade

60 km (37 mi) west of Hamburg on B–73.

The medieval town of Stade is skirted by marshland, rivers, and small lakes on the western edge of the Altes Land. Founded sometime before AD 994, and once a thriving member of the Hanseatic League, Stade was later conquered by the Swedes, who controlled the city for 70 years: and their heritage is still visible.

Close to the **Alter Hafen** (Old Harbor), which looks rather like a narrow canal, is Stade's most beautiful (and lively) square, the tiny Fischmarkt. Nearby streets, particularly **Wasser West,** have many cafés and restaurants as well as some of the best-preserved Renaissance and baroque merchants' mansions. The **Schwedenspeicher-Museum** (Swedish Warehouse Museum) once stored food for the Swedish garrison and now traces the city's history from the Stone Age to the present. ⊠ *Wasser West 39, Stade* ☎ *04141/3222* ✉ *€1* ۞ *Tues.–Fri. 10–5, weekends 10–6.*

A walk through the **Altstadt** (Old Town), which is set on a little island in the River Elbe, gives you a vivid impression of what a northern German city looked like 300 years ago. Many of the buildings are built in the half-timber or redbrick style typical of the region. The heart of the Old City is the **Altes Rathaus** (Old Town Hall), built in 1667, a redbrick blend of Dutch Renaissance and early baroque recalling the city's proud mercantile days. Exhibitions are sometimes held in the historic main hall. ⊠ *Hökerstr. 22, Stade* ☎ *04141/4010* ۞ *Weekdays 8:30–5.*

HAMBURG A TO Z

To research prices, get advice from other travelers, and book travel arrangements, visit www.fodors.com.

AIR TRAVEL

Hamburg's international airport, Fuhlsbüttel, is 11 km (7 mi) northwest of the city. The Airport-City-Bus (the private Jasper Airport-Shuttle) runs nonstop between the airport and Hamburg's main train station daily at 30-minute intervals between 5 AM and 10:30 PM. Tickets are €4.60. The (public) Airport-Express (Bus 110) runs every 10 minutes between the airport and the Ohlsdorf U- and S-bahn stations, a 15-minute ride from the main train station. The fare is €1.45. A taxi to the downtown area will cost about €16. If you're driving a rental car from the airport, follow the signs to STADTZENTRUM (downtown).

🚩 **Fuhlsbüttel** ☎ 040/50750 ⊕ www.ham.airport.de.

BOAT & FERRY TRAVEL

HADAG ferries to Altes Land and Lühe depart from the Landungsbrücken (⇨ Tours) twice daily during the week and four times daily on the weekends from mid-April through August and on weekends only in September. Get off at the stop in Lünhe. To reach Neunfelde, take the ferry from Blankenese.

A more exciting way to reach Altes Land or Stade is via a 45-minute ride on a high-speed boat. Elbe-city-jets depart four times a day for Stade from the St. Pauli Landungsbrücken, between 9 AM and 6 PM, and cost €17 (round-trip). You can also reach the Cranz dock in Altes Land by Elbe-city-jet.

HADAG ☎ 040/311-7070. **SAL Schiffahrtskontor** ☎ 04142/81170, 040/317-7170 Elbe-city-jet ⊕ www.elbe-city-jet.de.

BUS TRAVEL

Hamburg's bus station, the Zentral-Omnibus-Bahnhof, is directly behind the main train station.

Zentral-Omnibus-Bahnhof (ZOB) ✉ Adenauerallee 78, St. Georg ☎ 040/247-575.

CAR TRAVEL

Hamburg is easier to handle by car than many other German cities, and traffic is relatively uncongested. During rush hour, however, there can be gridlock. Several autobahns (A–1, A–7, A–23, A–24, and A–250) connect with Hamburg's three beltways, which then easily take you to the downtown area. Follow the STADTZENTRUM signs. To reach Altes Land and Stade from Hamburg, take B–73 west.

Avis ✉ Airport, Fuhlsbüttel ☎ 040/5075-2314 ✉ Drehbahn 15-25, Neustadt ☎ 040/341-651. **Hertz** ✉ Airport, Fuhlsbüttel ☎ 040/5935-1367 ✉ Kirchenallee 34-36, opposite Hauptbahnhof, Altstadt ☎ 040/280-1201. **Sixt** ✉ Airport, Fuhlsbüttel ☎ 040/593-9480 ✉ Hauptbahnhof-Wandelhalle, St. Georg ☎ 040/322-419.

CONSULATES

Ireland ✉ Feldbrunnenstr. 43, Winterhude ☎ 040/4418-6213. **New Zealand** ✉ Domstr. 19, Neustadt ☎ 040/442-5550. **U.K** ✉ Harvestehuder Weg 8a, Harvestehude ☎ 040/448-0320. **U.S** ✉ Alsterufer 27, Neustadt ☎ 040/4117-1100.

EMERGENCIES

For medical emergencies: 112 is a direct line to the ambulance service operated by the fire department; 110 is the general ambulance service; 040/228–022 is a special city ambulance service providing doctors in an ambulance. The kind of service provided does not differ, only the institution behind it.

Pharmacies offer late-night service on a rotating basis. Every pharmacy displays a notice indicating the schedule. For emergency pharmaceutical assistance, inquire at the nearest police station or call 112.

Ambulance & Police ☎ 110. **Central Poison Center** ☎ 0551/19240 or 030/19240. **Dentist** ☎ 040/11500. **Emergency medical aid and Fire** ☎ 112. **Medical emergencies** ☎ 040/228-022. **Pharmacies** ☎ 112.

ENGLISH-LANGUAGE BOOKSTORE

Frensche International ✉ Spitalerstr. 26c, Altstadt ☎ 040/327-585.

TOURS

BOAT TOURS There are few better ways to get to know the city than by taking a trip around the massive harbor. The HADAG line and other companies organize round-trips in the port, lasting about one hour (€8.50–€9). Between April and late September, excursion boats and barges leave every half hour from the Landungsbrücken—Piers 1, 2, 3, and 7—between 10 AM and 6:30 PM. From early October through March, departures are every hour. From March through November, an English-language tour leaves at noon daily from Pier 1.

From April through October, Alster Touristik operates boat trips around the Alster Lakes and through the canals. There are two tour options; both leave from the Jungfernstieg promenade in the city center. The Aussenalster 50-minute lake tour ("Alster-Rundfahrt") costs €9 and leaves every half hour, April–October 3, daily 10–6. A two-hour-long *Fleet-Fahrt* costs €14 and explores the canals of the historic Speicherstadt (late March–November, daily at 10:45, 1:45, and 4:45). From May through September there's also the romantic twilight tour, called Dämmertour, every evening (Wednesday–Saturday in September) at 8 (€14).

🚢 **Alster Touristik** ☎ 040/357-4240. **Bordparty-Service** ⊠ Landungsbrücken, Pier 9, St. Pauli ☎ 040/313-687. **HADAG** ☎ 040/311-7070, 040/313-130, 040/313-959, 040/3178-2231 for English-language tour.

ORIENTATION TOURS Sightseeing bus tours of the city, all with guides who rapidly narrate in both English and German, leave from Kirchenallee by the main train station. A bus tour lasting 1¾ hours sets off at varying times daily and costs €13. For €20, one of the bus tours can be combined with two one-hour boat trips on the Alster Lake and the Elbe River. Departure times for tours vary, according to season. City tours aboard the nostalgic *Hummelbahn* (a converted railroad wagon pulled by a tractor) start from the Kirchenallee stop. They run daily April–October. The fare is €13 for 1¾ hours.

🚢 *Hummelbahn* ☎ 040/792-8979.

WALKING TOURS Tours of downtown, the harbor district, and St. Pauli are offered from April through November, weekdays at 2:30 by the Hamburg Tourismus GmbH. All guided walking tours (€6) are conducted in German and start at different locations. Downtown tours by Stattreisen Hamburg are held on Saturday (February–November) and are conducted in German only. Tours of the historic Speicherstadt district are conducted by the Speicherstadtmuseum (Sunday at 11, €6).

🚢 **Speicherstadtmuseum** ⊠ St. Annenufer 2, Block R, Speicherstadt ☎ 040/321-191 ⊕ www.speicherstadtmuseum. **Stattreisen Hamburg** ☎ 040/430-3481. **Hamburg Tourismus GmbH** ⊠ Steinstr. 7, Altstadt, D-20015 ☎ 040/3005-1144.

TAXIS

Taxi meters start at €2, and the fare is €1.30–€1.50 per km or ½ mi. You can hail taxis on the street or at stands, or order one by phone.

🚕 Taxi Information ☎ 040/441-011, 040/686-868, or 040/666-666.

TRAIN TRAVEL

There are two principal stations: the central Hauptbahnhof (main train station) and Hamburg-Altona, west of the downtown area. EuroCity and InterCity trains connect Hamburg with all German cities and many major European ones. Two InterCity Express "supertrain" lines link Hamburg with Berlin, Frankfurt, and Munich, and with Würzburg and Munich. Trains to Stade depart from the Hauptbahnhof.

🚉 **Hauptbahnhof** ✉ Steintorpl., Altstadt ☎ 0180/599-6633.

TRANSPORTATION AROUND HAMBURG

The HVV, Hamburg's public transportation system, includes the U-bahn (subway), the S-bahn (suburban train), and buses. A one-way fare starts at €1.35; €1.85 covers one unlimited ride in the Hamburg city area. Tickets are available on all buses and at automatic machines in all stations and at most bus stops. A *Ganztageskarte* (all-day ticket), valid until 1 AM on the day of purchase, costs €5.25. A *9 Uhr-Tageskarte* for just €4.45 is valid between 9 AM and 1 AM on the day of purchase. If you're traveling with family or friends, a *Gruppen-* or *Familienkarte* (group or family ticket) is a good value—a group of up to five can travel for the entire day for only €7.40–€17.70 (depending on the number of fare zones the ticket covers).

Available from all Hamburg tourist offices, the Hamburg CARD allows unlimited travel on all public transportation within the city and admission to state museums. The Hamburg CARD is valid for 24 hours (beginning at 6 PM through 6 PM the following day) and costs €7 for one adult and up to three children under the age of 12. The Hamburg CARD for three days (valid starting at noon the first day) costs €14.50. The Hamburg CARD *Gruppenkarte* costs €23 for any group of five and is valid for three days; a *Gruppenkarte* for just one day is available for €13.

You must validate your ticket at a machine at the start of your journey. If you are found without a validated ticket, the fine is €32.

In the north of Hamburg, the HVV system connects with the A-bahn (Alsternordbahn), a suburban train system that extends into Schleswig-Holstein. Night buses (Nos. 600–640) serve the downtown area all night, leaving the Rathausmarkt and Hauptbahnhof every hour.

🚉 **Hamburg Passenger Transport Board** (Hamburger Verkehrsverbund) ✉ Steinstr. 7, Altstadt ☎ 040/19449 ⊕ www.hvv.de is open daily around the clock.

TRAVEL AGENCIES

🚉 **Agencies Reiseland American Express** ✉ Ballindamm 39, Neustadt ☎ 040/309-080. **Hapag-Lloyd** ✉ Verkehrspavillon Jungfernstieg, Neustadt ☎ 040/325-8560.

VISITOR INFORMATION

Hamburg has tourist offices around the city. The main office is in the Hauptbahnhof (main train station) and is open daily 7 AM–11 PM. At the harbor there's an office at the St. Pauli Landungsbrücken, between Piers 4 and 5, open November–February, daily 10–7, and March–October, daily 10–5:30.

In addition to its comprehensive hotel guide, the tourist office also co-publishes *Hamburger Vorschau*, a free monthly program of events in the city. The free magazine *Hamburg Tips* is issued quarterly and details major seasonal events.

All tourist offices can help with accommodations, and there's a central call-in booking office for hotel and ticket reservations and general information, the Hamburg-Hotline. A €4 fee is charged for every room reserved.

Hamburg-Hotline ☎ 040/3005-1300 ⊕ www.hamburg-tourism.de. **Hamburg Tourismus GmbH** ✉ Hauptbahnhof, Altstadt ☎ 040/3005-1200 ✉ St. Pauli Landungsbrücken, St. Pauli ☎ 040/3005-1200 or 040/3005-1203 ✉ Steinstr. 7, Altstadt D-20015 ☎ 040/3005-1144. **Stade Tourismus GmbH** ✉ Schiffertorstr. 6, D-21682 Stade Stade ☎ 04141/4091-7074 🖷 04141/409-110 ⊕ www.stade.de.

SCHLESWIG-HOLSTEIN & THE BALTIC COAST

14

By Jürgen Scheunemann

GERMANY'S TRUE NORTH IS A QUIET AND PEACEFUL REGION that belies its past status as one of the most powerful trading centers in Europe. The salty air and lush, green landscape of marshlands, endless beaches, fishing villages, and lakes are the main pleasures here, not sightseeing. On foggy November evenings, or during the hard winter storms that sometimes strand islanders from the mainland, you can well imagine the fairy tales spun by the Vikings who lived here.

The Danish-German heritage in Schleswig-Holstein, Germany's northernmost state, is the result of centuries of land disputes between the two nations—you could call this area southern Scandinavia. Since the early 20th century, its shores and islands have become popular weekend and summer retreats for the well-to-do from Hamburg and Berlin. The island of Sylt, in particular, is known throughout Germany for its rich and beautiful sunbathers.

The rest of Schleswig-Holstein, though equally appealing in its green and mostly serene landscape, is far from rich and worldly. Most people farm or fish and often speak Plattdütsch, or low German, which is difficult for outsiders to understand. Cities such as Flensburg, Husum, Schleswig, Kiel (the state capital), and even Lübeck all exude a laid-back, small-town charm.

The neighboring state of Mecklenburg-Vorpommern includes the Baltic Coast and is even more rural. On the resort islands of Hiddensee and Usedom, the clock appears to have stopped before World War II; the architecture, the pace of life, even the old-fashioned trains seem like products of a magical time warp. Though it has long been a popular summer destination for families, few foreign tourists venture here.

This area was not always a restful retreat. Between the 12th and 16th centuries the sea was crucial to the rise of the Hanseatic League, a consortium of merchants who monopolized trade across the Baltic. You'll see their wealth invested in some of the finest examples of northern German Gothic and Renaissance redbrick architecture, with buildings topped by tall, stepped gables. The shipbuilding industry in Schleswig-Holstein closed down more than 20 years ago, however, and the mid-1990s bankruptcy of the industry in Rostock and Stralsund further depressed the economy. The unemployment rate in Mecklenburg-Vorpommern is among the highest in Germany, and a dramatic, westward migration is further depleting this sparsely populated region.

Exploring Schleswig-Holstein & the Baltic Coast

This chapter follows a route through five main ports of the medieval Hanseatic League—Flensburg, Lübeck, Wismar, Rostock, and Stralsund. Except for these main cities, both states are essentially rural, with a countryside of lakes, meadows, fertile fields, and tree-lined roads. The three major areas of interest are the western coastline of Schleswig-Holstein—primarily Sylt island, eastern Mecklenburg, and Vorpommern's secluded, tundralike landscape of sandy heath and dunes. In Mecklenburg-Vorpommern any interesting roads that head off to the north are likely to lead to the coast. Vorpommern ends at the Polish border. Barring summer traffic jams, you could easily drive through the whole region from west to east in less than two days, but that would be the surest way to miss all the hidden treasures in the villages and medieval cities along the way. Instead, try to do it like the locals—at a slow pace.

About the Restaurants & Hotels

In urban areas you can find restaurants that serve hot meals around the clock, even at breakfast time. But don't count on that in this largely rural area. Many restaurants serve hot meals only between 11:30 AM and 2 PM, and 6 PM and 9 PM. You rarely need a reservation here and casual clothing is generally acceptable.

In northern Germany you'll find both small *Hotelpensionen* and fully equipped large hotels; along the eastern Baltic Coast, some hotels are renovated high-rises dating from GDR (German Democratic Republic) times. Many of the small hotels and pensions in towns such as Kühlungsborn, Binz, and Albeck have been restored to their romantic, quaint splendor of German *Bäderarchitektur* (spa architecture) from the early 20th century. In high season all accommodations, especially on the islands, are in great demand. If you can't book well in advance, inquire at the local tourist office, which will also have information on the 150 campsites along the Baltic coast and on the islands.

WHAT IT COSTS In Euros				
$$$$	**$$$**	**$$**	**$**	**¢**
RESTAURANTS over €25	€21–€25	€16–€20	€9–€15	under €9
HOTELS over €225	€175–€225	€100–€175	€50–€100	under €50

Restaurant prices are per person for a main course at dinner. Hotel prices are for two people in a standard double room, including tax and service.

Timing

The region's climate is at its best when the two states are most crowded with vacationers—in July and August. Winter is extremely harsh in this area, and even spring and fall are rather windy, chilly, and rainy. To avoid the crowds, schedule your trip for June or September. But don't expect tolerable water temperatures or hot days on the beach.

SCHLESWIG-HOLSTEIN

This region once thrived, thanks to the Hanseatic League and the Salzstrasse (Salt Route), a merchant route connecting northern Germany's cities. The kings of Denmark warred with the dukes of Schleswig and, later, the German Empire over the prized northern territory of Schleswig-Holstein. The northernmost strip of land surrounding Flensburg became German in 1864. The quiet, contemplative spirit of the region's people, the marshland's special light, and the ever-changing face of the sea are inspiring. Today the world-famous Schleswig-Holstein-Musikfestival ushers in classical concerts to farmhouses, palaces, and churches.

Numbers in the text correspond to numbers in the margin and on the Schleswig-Holstein and Baltic Coast maps.

If you have
3 days

Start your trip in **Flensburg** ❶ ☞, less than two hours from Hamburg, and make **Schleswig** ❹ a stop as you head toward 🖼 **Lübeck** ❼, western Germany's only Hanseatic town. On the following day visit **Wismar's** ❽ delightful market square and grand churches and make a side trip south to **Schwerin** ❾, known for its lakes and magnificent castle. Next, head to 🖼 **Rostock** ⓫, once the center of eastern Germany's shipbuilding industry. On the last day pay a visit to 🖼 **Stralsund** ⓯, a much smaller but charming medieval town. It serves as a gateway to the most remote part of the Baltic Coast: the island of **Rügen** ⓰. The **Stubbenkammer** ⓴ and the **Königstuhl** there are outstanding chalk cliffs.

If you have
5 days

Devote a morning to the palace at **Ahrensburg** ❻ ☞, just outside Hamburg, and continue on to the cities of **Schleswig** ❹ and 🖼 **Flensburg** ❶. When you finish exploring Flensburg the next day, head to medieval 🖼 **Lübeck** ❼ to overnight. After seeing Lübeck, visit **Wismar** ❽ before spending the night in 🖼 **Schwerin** ❾. On the fourth day, after a tour of the Schweriner lakes and the Schweriner Schloss, continue your eastward journey via **Bad Doberan** ❿ and Kühlungsborn, a top beach resort. The little Molli train pulled by a steam locomotive connects the resort and Bad Doberan. Spend the late afternoon and night in 🖼 **Rostock** ⓫ and at the beach resort at **Warnemünde** ⓬. On the fifth day explore the medieval port of 🖼 **Stralsund** ⓯.

If you have
8 days

Spend your first day and night in 🖼 **Flensburg** ❶ ☞ and the next in the romantic fishing town of 🖼 **Husum** ❷. On the third morning take the train onto the island of 🖼 **Sylt** ❸. You may find it more economical to leave your car at the Niebüll train embarkment and use bikes, buses, or a rental car on the island. On your fourth day visit **Schleswig** ❹ and **Kiel** ❺ on your way to 🖼 **Lübeck** ❼. From Lübeck head east to **Wismar** ❽ and 🖼 **Schwerin** ❾. The sixth day you can sightsee around 🖼 **Rostock** ⓫ and shop in **Ribnitz-Damgarten** ⓭, the center of Germany's amber industry. If you don't find a souvenir here, you might be luckier in **Ahrenshoop** ⓮, a small coastal village that was once an artists' colony. Spend your sixth night in 🖼 **Stralsund** ⓯ and your seventh day and night on the island of 🖼 **Rügen** ⓰. A visit to Vorpommern wouldn't be complete without a trip to **Greifswald** ㉒, the last of the medieval Hanseatic towns on eastern Germany's coastline. If you still have time on this eighth day, drive to **Wolgast** and over the causeway to **Usedom Island** ㉔.

Flensburg

☞ ❶ *182 km (114 mi) north of Hamburg.*

Germany's northernmost city is known for its superb beer, Flensburger Pils, and the lovely marshland in the surrounding area. For centuries people in this border region between Denmark and Germany have lived more or less peacefully, except when distant empires clashed over their land. Locals have a laid-back, dry-humored attitude, and the mixed Danish-German heritage is reflected in the culture and food. The 87,000 residents of the area are nicknamed *Nordlichter* (northern lighters), a reference to the fact that the region is plagued (in fall and winter) by a lack of sunlight due to fog and rain.

Most of Flensburg has retained its special small-town charm, with red-brick warehouses, Gothic churches, half-timber houses, and cobblestone squares. Many of the city's landmarks are off the streets **Holm, Grosse Strasse,** and **Norderstrasse,** which wind their way through the city center to the waterfront. Around the picturesque **Südermarkt,** the Old City's South Market, are several typical commercial warehouses.

The **St. Nikolai-Kirche** (St. Nicholas Church), named for the patron saint of sailors, was built in 1390. The church's real attraction is hidden inside: one of the most stunning Renaissance organ facades in Germany. ✉ *Nikolaikirchhof* ☎ *0461/8400–4011* 💰 *Free* 🕙 *Mon.–Sat. 8–7, Sun. 11–5.*

The **Museumsberg Flensburg** (Flensburg Museum Mountain), a unique complex of four museums, reveals the rich diversity of crafts, art, and scientific developments in an otherwise rural area. In addition to a collection of local art nouveau furniture and tapestries, the **Heinrich-Sauermann-Haus** also exhibits art from the Middle Ages to the present. The museum even houses several original living rooms from North German island farms of the 17th and 18th centuries. Paintings by local artists of the 19th and 20th centuries are hung in the **Hans-Christiansen-Haus.** Some of the more interesting pieces are by Emil Nolde, Ernst Barlach, and Erich Heckel, all of whom were fascinated by the special and at times mysterious light and atmosphere of North Germany's marshlands. ✉ *Museumsberg* ☎ *0461/852–956* 💰 *€3.50* 🕙 *Apr.–Oct., Tues.–Sun. 10–5; Nov.–Mar., Tues.–Sun. 10–4.*

The **Nordermarkt** (North Market) is surrounded by old alleyways such as the **Rote Strasse,** which is lined by redbrick warehouses now converted into galleries, restaurants, and pubs. The marketplace also preserves a reminder of medieval justice: at a small arcade you can see the metal neck ring used publicly to humiliate people convicted of certain crimes.

The **Schiffahrtsmuseum** (Maritime Museum) is in the old customs warehouse and can be spotted from far away thanks to the wooden masts of the old sailing vessels lying at anchor in the museum's harbor. The museum itself tells the story of the sea trade that made Flensburg prosperous in the Middle Ages and sent the city's sons as far away as Greenland and the West Indies. A special **Rum-Museum** explains how the city traded and manufactured some of Germany's finest rum. ✉ *Museumsberg* ☎ *0461/852–970* 💰 *€3.50* 🕙 *Apr.–Oct., Tues.–Sun. 10–5; Nov.–Mar., Tues.–Sun. 10–4.*

The chief residence of the dukes of Schleswig-Holstein, **Schloss Glücksburg,** lies 14 km (9 mi) northeast of Flensburg. Built in 1582–87, the

14

Beaches Beaches stretch all along the coast of the North Sea and the Baltic. Virtually all these sandy beaches are clean and safe, sloping gently into the water, which is equally gentle and calm. Vacationers pack the seaside resorts during the high season (July and August). Be aware that water temperatures even in August rarely exceed 20°C (65°F). The busiest beaches are at Westerland (Sylt island), Bansin (Usedom Island), Binz (Rügen Island), Ostseebad Kühlungsborn, and Warnemünde. The most beautiful beaches are at Timmendorf on Poel Island (you can drive there from Wismar or take a White Fleet boat); Kap Arkona (reachable only on foot); and Hiddensee Island, off Rügen. The more remote coves can be found at Kampen on Sylt, at the Ahrenshoop Weststrand, on the Darss Peninsula; at Nienhagen (near Warnemünde); and the Grosser Jasmunder Bodden, on Rügen Island to the west of Lietzow.

There's a *Kurtaxe* (entrance fee) of €1.50–€5 for most beaches; the fees on Sylt average €3 per entry. Some beaches allow nude bathing. In German it's known as *Freikörperkultur* (literally "free body culture"), or FKK for short. The most popular of these bare-all beaches are on Sylt island, at Nienhagen, and Prerow (on Darss).

Churches Throughout the region medieval churches with red-and-white facades are prime examples of the German redbrick Gothic style. In Mecklenburg-Vorpommern even the smallest village proudly boasts a redbrick church, and the cathedrals in cities such as Wismar and Stralsund testify to the region's prosperous past as Hanseatic seaports. Note how many churches are named after the sailors' patron saint, St. Nikolai.

On the Menu The restaurants in both coastal states serve mostly seafood such as *Scholle* (flounder) or North Sea *Krabben* (shrimp), often with fried potatoes, eggs, and bacon. Mecklenburg specialties to look for are *Mecklenburger Griebenroller*, a custardy casserole of grated potatoes, eggs, herbs, and chopped bacon; *Mecklenburger Fischsuppe,* a hearty fish soup with vegetables, tomatoes, and sour cream; *Gefüllte Ente* (duck with bread stuffing); and *Pannfisch* (fish patty). A favorite local nightcap since the 17th century is *Grog,* a strong blend of rum, hot water, and local fruits.

bright-white Glücksburg, like many other palaces of the period, was completely surrounded by water. It's also known as the cradle of European high nobility, as the six children of Christian IX, king of Denmark and duke of Schleswig, were married to different European royal families. The palace museum showcases paintings, sculptures, furniture, and porcelain, mostly from the 17th century. ⊠ *Glücksburg, off B-199* ☎ *04631/2213 or 04631/2243* ⊕ *www.schloss-gluecksburg. de* ☞ *€4.50* ☽ *Apr.–Sept., daily 10–6; Oct., Tues.–Sun. 10–6; Nov.–Mar., weekends 10–5.*

Where to Stay & Eat

★ ¢–$ ✕**Schwarzer Walfisch.** The Black Whale has been cooking up fish since 1751, and its house and dining hall are protected monuments. Especially recommendable is the *Walfischteller* (salmon, fried cod, North Sea shrimp, an egg sunny-side up, and fried potatoes). Such dishes are best washed down with the dark local beer on tap. ✉*Angelburgerstr. 44* ☎*0461/13525* ⊛ *Reservations essential* ▭ *No credit cards* ☉ *Closed Tues.*

★ $$ ✕▥**Alter Meierhof Vitalhotel.** Outside Flensburg, on an inlet of the Baltic Sea, this former dairy farm is now a luxurious hotel. Guests come primarily to pamper themselves with massages, mud packs, beauty treatments, and special baths. Rooms are fairly spacious and furnished with reproductions of 19th-century furniture. You can watch the chefs at work in the restaurant ($–$$), which focuses on fresh, international fish dishes. ✉ *Uferstr. 1, D–24960 Glücksburg* ☎ *04631/61990* ▤ *04631/ 619–999* ⊕ *www.alter-meierhof.de* ⇄ *45 rooms, 9 suites* ⌂ *Restaurant, room service, in-room data ports, in-room safes, minibars, cable TV, pool, health club, hot tub, massage, sauna, steam room, beach, bicycles, bar, babysitting, dry cleaning, laundry service, meeting room, free parking, some pets allowed (fee), no-smoking rooms* ▭ *No credit cards* ◯▮ *BP.*

$ ▥**Mercure Hotel Flensburg.** Part of the upscale German Mercure hotel chain, this modern hotel is a rather somber-looking building whose appeal is its proximity to the harbor. Reserve a room on one of the upper floors and you'll enjoy a wonderful view. All rooms are fairly spacious. ⊠ *Norderhofenden 6–9, D–24937* ☎ *0461/84110* 🖷 *0461/841–1299* 🛏 *91 rooms, 4 suites* ⚤ *Minibars, cable TV, sauna, bar, meeting room, parking (fee), some pets allowed (fee), no-smoking rooms; no a/c* ⊟ *AE, DC, MC, V* 🍽 *BP.*

Shopping

A rather exclusive antiques shop, **Borring-Antik** (⊠ Speicherlinie 42 ☎ 0461/807–9540), sells primarily 19th-century furniture, fine porcelain, and cutlery.

Holm-Passage (⊠ Holm 39 ☎ 0461/21955), the only shopping mall in the city's historic downtown area, has many upscale fashion and specialty stores.

Husum

❷ *45 km (28 mi) southeast of Flensburg, 158 km (98 mi) northeast of Hamburg.*

The town of Husum is the epitome of northern German lifestyle and culture. Immortalized in a poem as the "gray city upon the sea" by its famous son, Theodor Storm, Husum is in fact a popular vacation spot in summer. Its wonderful, deserted beaches and proximity to Sylt and the Danish border make it a perfect place to relax.

The central **Marktplatz** (market square) is bordered by 17th- and 18th-century buildings, including the historic Rathaus (Town Hall), which houses the tourist-information office. The best impression of Husum's beginnings in the mid-13th century is found south of the Marktplatz, along **Krämerstrasse**; the **Wasserreihe**, a narrow and tortuous alley; and **Hafenstrasse**, right next to the narrow **Binnenhafen** (city harbor).

The most famous house on Wasserreihe is the **Theodor-Storm-Haus**, where writer Theodor Storm (1817–88) lived between 1866 and 1880. It's a must if you're interested in German literature or if you want to gain insight into the life of the few well-to-do people in this region during the 19th century. The small museum includes the poet's living room and a small *Poetenstübchen* (poets' parlor), where he wrote many of his novels, including the famous *Schimmelreiter* (*The Rider on the Gray Horse*). All of the rooms, the furniture, and many of the writer's belongings are original. ⊠ *Wasserreihe 31* ☎ *04841/666–270* ⊕ *www.storm-gesellschaft. de* 🎟 *€2.50* 🕐 *Apr.–Oct., Tues.–Fri. 10–5, Mon. and Sun. 2–5, Sat. 11–5; Nov.–Mar., Tues., Thurs., and Sat. 2–5.*

Despite Husum's remoteness amid the stormy sea, wide marshes, and dunes, the city used to be a major seaport and administrative center. The **Schloss vor Husum** (Palace of Husum), originally built as a Renaissance castle in the late 16th century, was transformed in 1752 by the dukes of Gottorf into a redbrick baroque country palace. ⊠ *Professor-Ferdinand-Tönnies-Allee* ☎ *04841/897–3130* 🎟 *€2.50* 🕐 *Mid-Mar.–Oct., Tues.–Sun. 11–5.*

Where to Stay & Eat

★ **$$-$$$** ✕▦ **Romantik-Hotel Altes Gymnasium.** In a former redbrick high school behind an orchard of pear trees, you'll find a surprisingly elegant country-style hotel. The rooms are spacious, with wood-panel floors and modern office amenities. The restaurant Eucken ($$) serves game (from its own hunter) and German country cooking such as *Rücken vom Salzwiesenlamm mit Kartoffel-Zucchini-Rösti* (salted lamb back with potato and zucchini hash browns). The hotel's huge health and indoor pool area helps you forget the often bad weather in this region. ✉ *Süderstr. 6, D–25813* ☎ *04841/8330* 🖷 *04841/83312* 🌐 *www.altesgymnasium.de* ⇨ *66 rooms, 6 suites* ♨ *2 restaurants, room service, in-room data ports, in-room safes, minibars, cable TV, indoor pool, gym, health club, massage, sauna, bicycles, bar, babysitting, dry cleaning, laundry service, free parking, some pets allowed (fee), no-smoking rooms; no a/c* ⊟ *AE, DC, MC, V* ⦿ *BP.*

Sylt

❸ *44 km (27 mi) northwest of Husum, 196 km (122 mi) northwest of*
Fodor'sChoice *Hamburg.*
★

Sylt is a long, narrow island (38 km [24 mi] by as little as 222 yards) of unspoiled beaches and marshland off the western coast of Schleswig-Holstein and Denmark. Famous for its clean air and white beaches, Sylt is the hideaway for the jet set of Germany. They come for the secluded beaches and the exclusiveness provided by the island's inaccessibility. The island is a mecca for windsurfers, who rely on constant strong winds.

Wattwanderungen (walking in the Watt, the shoreline tidelands) is a popular activity here, whether on self-guided or guided tours. The small villages with their thatch-roof houses, the beaches, and the nature conservation areas make Sylt the most enchanting German island, rivaled only by Rügen.

The island's major town is **Westerland,** which is not quite as expensive as Kampen but more crowded. An ugly assortment of modern hotels lines an undeniably clean and broad beach. Each September windsurfers meet for the Surf Cup competition off the **Brandenburger Strand,** the best surfing spot.

If you are looking for privacy, detour to the village of **List,** on the northern tip of Sylt, or to **Archsum** or **Hörnum.** The last is on the southernmost point of the island and, like List, has a little harbor and a lighthouse.

Kampen
9 km (6 mi) northeast of Westerland.

The island's unofficial capital is Kampen, which is the main destination for the wealthier crowd. Redbrick buildings or shining white thatch-roof houses spread along the coastline. The real draw—apart from the fancy restaurants and chic nightclubs—are the beaches.

One of the island's best-known features is the **Rotes Kliff** (Red Cliff), a dune cliff on the northern end of the Kampen beaches, which turns an eerie dark red when the sun sets.

The **Naturschutzgebiet Kampener Vogelkoje** (Birds' Nest Nature Conservation Area) was built in the mid-17th century and once served as a mass trap for wild geese. Today it serves as a nature preserve for wild birds. ⊠ *Lister Str., Kampen* ☎ *04651/871–077* 🎫 *€1.70* ☉ *Apr.–Oct., Tues.–Sun. 10–4.*

For a glimpse of the rugged lives of 19th-century fishermen, visit the small village of **Keitum** to the south and drop in on the **Altfriesisches Haus** (Old Frisian House), which preserves an old-world peacefulness in a lush garden setting. The house also documents a time when most seamen thrived on extensive whale hunting. ⊠ *Am Kliff 13, Keitum* ☎ *04651/ 31101* 🎫 *€2.20* ☉ *Apr.–Oct., daily 10–5.*

The 800-year-old church of **St. Severin** was built on the highest elevation in the region. Its tower once served the island's fishermen as a beacon. Strangely enough, the tower also served as a prison until 1806. Today the church is a popular site for weddings. ⊠ *Keitum* ☎ *04651/31713* 🎫 *Free* ☉ *Apr.–Oct., tours Mon. and Thurs. at 5; Nov.–Mar. at 4.*

The small **Sylter Heimatmuseum** (Sylt Island Museum) tells the centuries-long history of the island's seafaring people. It presents traditional costumes, tools, and other gear from fishing boats and tells the stories of prominent islanders such as Uwe Jens Lornsen, who fought for Sylt's independence. ⊠ *Am Kliff 19, Keitum* ☎ *04651/31669* 🎫 *€2.20* ☉ *Apr.–Oct., weekdays 10–5, weekends 11–5; Nov.–Mar., Tues.–Fri. 1–4.*

Where to Stay & Eat

★ $–$$$$ ✕ **Sansibar.** Sansibar is one of the island's most popular restaurants. The cuisine includes seafood and fondue with fish or scampi, served with any one of more than 800 wines. To get a table even in the afternoon, you must reserve well in advance. ⊠ *Strand, Rantum-Süd, Rantum* ☎ *04651/964–646* ⚠ *Reservations essential* ▭ *AE, V.*

$–$$ ✕ **Dorfkrug Rotes Kliff.** The Dorfkrug has fed the island's seafaring inhabitants since 1876. Enjoy meals such as *Steinbuttfilet* (halibut fillet) or *Gebratener Zander* (fried perch fillet) in a homey setting where the walls are covered in traditional blue-white Frisian tiles. ⊠ *Braderuper Weg 3, Kampen* ☎ *04651/43500* ▭ *AE, MC* ☉ *Closed Mon.*

★ $$$$ ✕🏨 **Dorint Söl'ring Hof.** The latest newcomer to the upscale hotel scene of Sylt is this luxurious resort set in a white, thatch-roof country house *on* the dunes: the view from most of the rooms is magnificent—with some luck you may even spot frolicking harbor porpoises. The brightly furnished rooms are spacious, covering two floors, and equipped with a fire place. The real attraction here, however, is the restaurant ($$$$), where renowned chef Johannes King creates delicious German-Mediterranean fish dishes. The hotel is in quiet Rantum, at the southeast end of the island. ⊠ *Am Sandwall 1, D–25980 Sylt-Rantum* ☎ *04651/836–200* 🖷 *04651/836–2020* ⊕ *www.dorint.de* 🛏 *11 rooms, 4 suites* ⚐ *Restaurant, room service, in-room data ports, in-room safes, minibars, cable TV with movies, health club, massage, sauna, spa, steam room, beach, bar, lounge, babysitting, dry cleaning, laundry service, concierge, meeting room, free parking, no-smoking rooms; no a/c* ▭ *AE, DC, MC, V* ❙◎❙ *BP.*

$$$ ✕▥ **Hotelrestaurant Jörg Müller.** The old thatch-roof farmhouse hotel has
Fodor'sChoice a handful of lovely rooms combining Frisian-style designs with classi-
★ cal elegance. A wing added three years ago has modern rooms that lack
the intimate interior of the historic house but have luxurious bath-
rooms, and each has a balcony or terrace. The restaurant Pesel serves
local fish dishes, whereas the upscale main restaurant offers a high-qual-
ity blend of international and Mediterranean cuisine. ✉ *Süderstr. 8,
D–25980 Westerland* ☎ *04651/27788* 🖷 *04651/201–471* ⊕ *www.
hotel-joerg-mueller.de* ↘ *19 rooms, 4 suites* ⌂ *2 restaurants, room
service, in-room safes, minibars, cable TV, hot tub, sauna, steam room,
bar, dry cleaning, laundry service, free parking, some pets allowed (fee),
no-smoking rooms; no a/c* ▭ *AE, DC, MC, V* ¶◎¶ *BP.*

★ **$$–$$$** ▥ **Ulenhof Wenningstedt.** The Ulenhof, one of Sylt's loveliest old thatch-
roof apartment houses, is a quiet alternative to the busier main resorts
in Kampen and Westerland. The Ulenhof has two buildings 750 yards
away from the beach in Wenningstedt. The larger apartments, for up
to three persons, are a good deal. A separate bathing facility offers a
huge wellness area with two saunas, a pool, and a *Tecaldarium*, a
Roman bathhouse. ✉ *Sachsenring 14, D–25996 Wenningstedt* ☎ *04651/
94540* 🖷 *04651/945–431* ⊕ *www.ulenhof.de* ↘ *35 apartments* ⌂ *Cable
TV, indoor pool, health club, hot tub, massage, sauna, steam room, free
parking, no-smoking rooms; no a/c* ▭ *No credit cards* ¶◎¶ *BP.*

★ **$$** ▥ **Witthüs-Apparthotel.** The tiny hotel is situated in a historic thatched
roof house at Wennigstedt and is a good and very reasonably priced al-
ternative to similar hotels on the island. It offers suites with fully
equipped kitchens, and separate living and bedrooms. Most of the
rooms have been carefully furnished in bright yellows and reds, creating a homely Scandinavian ambiance. When making a reservation, try
for the maisonette suite just beneath the roof: There's nothing more romantic than being lulled to sleep by the soothing whistles of the North
Sea winds. ✉ *Alte Dorfstr. 9, D–25996 Wenningstedt* ☎ *04651/98910*
🖷 *04651/985–633* ⊕ *www.witthues-sylt.de* ↘ *8 rooms, 10 suites*
⌂ *Cable TV, sauna, free parking, some pets allowed (fee), no-smoking
rooms; no a/c* ▭ *No credit cards* ¶◎¶ *BP.*

Nightlife & the Arts

The nightspots in Kampen are generally more upscale and quite expensive
compared to the pubs and clubs of Westerland. One of the most classic clubs on Sylt is the **Club Rotes Kliff** (✉ Alte Dorfstr., Kampen ☎ 04651/
43400), a bar and dance club that attracts a hip crowd of all ages. The
Compass (✉ Friedrichstr. 42, Westerland ☎ 04651/23513) is not as
trendy as the typical Sylt disco. The mostly young patrons, however, create a cheerful party atmosphere on weekend nights.

Schleswig

④ *37 km (23 mi) south of Flensburg, 114 km (71 mi) north of Hamburg.*

Schleswig-Holstein's oldest city is also one of its best-preserved examples of a typical North German town. Once the seat of the dukes of
Schleswig-Holstein, it has not only their palace but also ruins left by the
area's first rulers, the Vikings. Those legendary and fierce warriors from

Scandinavia brought terror (but also commerce) to northern Germany between 800 and 1100. Under a wide sky, Schleswig lies on the Schlei River in a landscape of freshwater marshland and lakes, making it a good departure point for bike or canoe tours.

The fishing village comes alive along the **Holm,** an old settlement with tiny and colorful houses. The windblown buildings give a good impression of what villages in northern Germany looked like 150 years ago. Relax in one of the cafés or further inspect the city's history at the **Städtisches Museum** (Municipal Museum). In this typical noble country palace of the late 17th century, you can explore Schleswig's history from the Stone Age onward. ⊠ *Günderothscher Hof, Friedrichstr. 9–11* ☎ *04621/ 936–820* 🎫 *€3* ☉ *Tues.–Sun. 10–5.*

The impressive baroque **Schloss Gottorf,** dating from 1703, is the state's largest secular building and once housed the ruling family. It has been transformed into the **Schleswig-Holsteinisches Landesmuseum** (State Museum of Schleswig-Holstein) and holds a collection of art and handicrafts of northern Germany from the Middle Ages to the present, including paintings by Lucas Cranach the Elder. Among the museum's archaeological exhibits are ancient mummified corpses retrieved from nearby swamps. ⊠ *Schloss Gottorf* ☎ *04621/8130* ⊕ *www.schloss-gottorf.de* 🎫 *€6* ☉ *Apr.–Oct., daily 10–6; Nov.–Mar., Tues.–Fri. 10–4, weekends 10–5.*

The most thrilling museum in Schleswig, the **Wikinger-Museum Haithabu** (Haithabu Viking Museum), is at the site of a Viking settlement. This was the Vikings' most important German port, and the boats, gold jewelry, and graves they left behind are displayed in the museum. ⊠ *Haddeby* ☎ *04621/8130* ⊕ *www.uni-kiel.de/museen* 🎫 *€3* ☉ *Apr.–Oct., daily 9–5; Nov.–Mar., Tues.–Sun. 10–4.*

Where to Stay & Eat

$–$$ ✕ **Stadt Flensburg.** This small restaurant in a city mansion that dates back to 1699 serves mostly fish from the Schlei River. Fishermen living on the Holm will have caught your dinner. The food is solid regional fare such as *Zanderfilet* (perch fillets) or *Gebratene Ente* (baked duck). The familial, warm atmosphere and the local dark tap beers more than make up for the simplicity of the setting. Reservations are advised. ⊠ *Lollfuss 102* ☎ *04621/23984* ☰ *AE, DC, MC, V* ☉ *Closed Wed.*

$–$$ 🏨 **Ringhotel Strandhalle Schleswig.** A modern hotel overlooking the small yacht harbor and the Schlei, this establishment has surprisingly low rates and a good value for its many services. The rooms are furnished in timeless dark furniture, and all have cable television. If you plan to stay a couple of days, ask about the special weekend packages that include nightly four-course meals and other extras. ⊠ *Strandweg 2, D–24837* ☎ *04621/ 9090* 📠 *04621/909–100* ⊕ *www.hotelstrand-halle.de* ➥ *25 rooms* ⚭ *Restaurant, in-room safes, minibars, cable TV, pool, boating, bicycles, meeting room, free parking, some pets allowed (fee), no-smoking rooms; no a/c* ☰ *AE, DC, MC, V* ⦿ *BP.*

Shopping

The tiny **Keramik-Stube** (⊠ *Rathausmarkt* ☎ *04621/24757*) offers craft work and beautiful handmade pottery. It's the ideal place to buy a gift.

The best place to buy tea is **Teekontor Hansen** (✉ Kornmarkt 3 ☎ 04621/ 23385). Try the *Schliekieker,* a very strong blend of different teas.

Kiel

❺ *53 km (33 mi) southeast of Schleswig, 130 km (81 mi) north of Hamburg.*

The sleepy state capital Kiel is known throughout Europe for its annual *Kieler Woche,* a festival and regatta that attracts hundreds of sailing boats from around the world. Despite the many wharves and industries concentrated in Kiel, the **Kieler Föhrde** (Bay of Kiel) has remained mostly unspoiled. Unfortunately, this cannot be said about the city itself. Because of Kiel's strategic significance during World War II—it served as the main German submarine base—the historic city, founded more than 750 years ago, was completely destroyed. Kiel's buildings are mostly modern, and its attraction lies in its outlying beaches, parks, and small towns.

At the **Kieler Hafen** (Kiel Harbor), Germany's largest passenger shipping harbor, you can always catch a glimpse of one of the many ferries leaving for Scandinavia from the **Oslokai** (Oslo Quay). In the background you can spot some of the shipbuilding wharves and—in the Kiel Bay— sometimes even a German submarine charting its way home.

The **Schifffahrtsmuseum** (Maritime Museum), housed in a hall of the old fish market, includes two antique fishing boats. In the past, fishing was Kiel's primary industry. ✉ *Wall 65* ☎ *0431/901–3428* ⊕ *www.kiel.de/ schiffahrtsmuseum* 🎟 *€1* ⊗ *Mid-Apr.–mid-Oct., daily 10–6; mid-Oct.–mid-Apr., Tues.–Sun. 10–5.*

A grim reminder of a different marine past is exhibited at the **U-Boot-Museum** (Submarine Museum) in Kiel-Laboe. The vessels of the much-feared German submarine fleet in World War I were mostly built and stationed in Kiel, before leaving for the Atlantic where they attacked American and British supply convoys. Today the submarine U995 serves as a public viewing model of a typical German submarine. The 280-foot-high **Marineehrenmal** (Marine Honor Memorial), in Laboe, was built in 1927–36. All German submarine personnel are required to salute when passing the memorial. You can reach Laboe via ferry from the Kiel harbor or take B–502 north. ✉ *Strandstr. 92, Kiel-Laboe* ☎ *04343/42700* 🎟 *Memorial €2.80, museum €3* ⊗ *Mid-Apr.–mid-Oct., daily 9:30–6; mid-Oct.–mid-Apr., daily 9:30–4.*

One of northern Germany's best (though small) collections of modern art can be found at the **Kunsthalle zu Kiel** (Kiel Art Gallery), which specializes in Russian art of the 19th and early 20th centuries, German expressionism, and contemporary international art. The collections include paintings, prints, and sculptures. ✉ *Düsternbrooker Weg 1* ☎ *0431/ 880–5756* ⊕ *www.kunsthalle.uni-kiel.de* 🎟 *€5* ⊗ *Tues. and Thurs.–Sun. 10–6, Wed. 10–8.*

Two attractive beach towns close to Kiel, **Laboe** and **Strande**, are crowded with sun-loving Kielers on summer weekends. Both retain their fishing-village appeal, and you can buy fresh fish directly from the boats in the harbor. Most fishermen here still smoke the fish on board, preparing, for example, the famous *Kieler Sprotten,* a small, salty fish somewhat like sardines. Though you can get to Laboe and Strande by car, it's more fun to catch a ferry leaving from Kiel.

Where to Stay & Eat

$–$$$$ ✕ **Quam.** Locals who dine out aren't looking for old-fashioned fish dishes (that's why there isn't a good, traditional fish restaurant in town); they prefer international preparations of fish from all over the world. The stylish Quam, its yellow walls and dimmed lights paying homage to Tuscany, serves international cuisine, including fish specialties from Germany, Italy, France, and Japan, to a mostly young, very chic crowd. The menu changes frequently. ✉ *Düppelstr. 60* ☎ *0431/85195* ☒ *Reservations essential* ⊟ *AE* ⊗ *Closed Sun. No lunch.*

¢–$ ✕ **Feld.** The buzz here is not the food itself, even though the steak, fish, and Asian dishes are formidable, but rather the stylish crowd, lounging on black leather chairs in the bar or dining at the white linen–covered tables. But don't worry about overblown attitudes—service is considered to be the nicest in town, and Sunday brunch feels like a relaxed get-together with old friends. ✉ *Feldstr. 111–113* ☎ *0431/806–0428* ☒ *Reservations essential* ⊟ *No credit cards* ⊗ *Closed Mon. No lunch.*

$$ ✕▥ **Hotel Kieler Yachtclub.** This traditional hotel provides standard yet elegant, newly refurbished rooms in the main building and completely new, bright accommodations in the Villentrakt. The restaurant ($$$) serves mostly fish dishes; in summer try to get a table on the terrace. The club overlooks the Kieler Föhrde. ✉ *Hindenburgufer 70, D–24105* ☎ *0431/ 88130* 🖷 *0431/881–3444* ⊕ *www.hotelkieleryachtclub.de* ➘ *55 rooms, 2 suites* ⊘ *Restaurant, room service, minibars, cable TV, bar, dry cleaning, laundry service, meeting room, free parking, some pets allowed (fee), no-smoking rooms; no a/c* ⊟ *AE, DC, MC, V* ▯◯▮ *BP.*

Nightlife & the Arts

Despite its medium size (250,000 inhabitants), the city has a thriving nightlife. One of the many chic and hip bars is the **Hemingway** (✉ Alter Markt ☎ 0431/96812). A college crowd goes to **Traumfabrik** (✉ Grasweg 19 ☎ 0431/544–450) to eat pizza, watch a movie, or dance (Friday is best for dancing). The popular bar, the Nachtcafé, has a basement disco, **Velvet** (✉ Eggerstedtstr. 14 ☎ 0431/95550).

Ahrensburg

▶ ❻ *25 km (16 mi) northeast of Hamburg.*

One of Schleswig-Holstein's major attractions is within a Hamburg suburb. The romantic, 16th-century **Schloss Ahrensburg** (Ahrensburg Castle) lies within lush parkland on the bank of the Hunnau. The white-washed brick, moated Renaissance castle stands much as it did when first constructed by Count Peter Rantzau. Its interior has had several remodelings, the first after financier Carl Schimmelmann purchased the estate in 1759.

Furniture and paintings, most dating from the early 19th century, fine porcelain, and exquisite crystal are exhibited on the two museum floors. On the grounds stands a simple 16th-century church; the west tower

CloseUp
7-DAY TOUR OF THE HANSEATIC CITIES

FOUNDED IN THE *12th century, the Hanseatic League was one of the most powerful economic and political alliances of the middle ages. Though it is thought of as a league of cities, it was really an alliance of merchant associations; each city had its own association; these groups came together to form the league. Cities from around Europe came together as part of this association. At the height of its power, in the 14th and 15th centuries, it had a virtual trade monopoly over most of Northern Europe.*

The wealth acquired by the Hanseatic League remains evident to this day in the architecture and cultural legacies of such cities as Bremen, Hamburg, Lübeck, Wismar, and Rostock. A driving tour of these cities takes you along ancient trade routes to medieval market squares and centuries-old taverns and guild halls. One week will give you ample time to see everything without feeling rushed.

Spend your first day and night in the Free and Hanseatic City of Bremen. Wander through the historic Schnoor quarter to admire the tiny gabled houses and cobblestone streets. Allow some time at the Marktplatz to take in its magnificent surroundings: St. Peter's Cathedral, which dates back to the 11th century; the stone statue of Charlemagne's knight, Roland, which was erected in 1404; and the 17th-century Renaissance facade of the Rathaus. ⇨ Bremen in Chapter 12 for more city highlights.

On your second day, take A–27 north to Bremerhaven where you can explore Germany's largest maritime museum, the Deutsches Schifffartsmuseum (⇨ Bremerhaven in Chapter 12). Continue on A–27 to Cuxhaven where you can have lunch, then take B–73 into Hamburg.

Plan to spend two nights in Hamburg. On the first afternoon, explore the Old City, which is centered around the neo-Renaissance Rathaus. Start your next day with a boat tour of Hamburg's enormous harbor. Spend the afternoon exploring more tranquil waters, the Alster Lake in the heart of the city. ⇨ Chapter 13 for complete coverage of the Free and Hanseatic City of Hamburg.

On your fourth day, take A–1 to Lübeck, "Queen of the Hanseatic League," and the best place to see some of the wealth the league garnered. The entire Old Town is a UNESCO World Heritage Site. As you wander the tiny streets, look for child-size, covered alleyways that lead to inner courtyards and walkways. Be sure to sample some of the famous Lübecker Marzipan at the Niederegger shop across from the Rathaus. ⇨ Lübeck in this chapter for more information.

On your fifth morning take B–105 to Wismar, also a UNESCO World Heritage Site. After exploring the Old Town, stop for lunch at Alter Schwede. Though it only became a seaman's tavern in 1878, the building itself dates back to 1380 and is the oldest building on the Marktplatz. ⇨ Wismar in this chapter for additional information.

Leave Wismar in the early afternoon and take A–20 to Rostock. For a relaxed finish to your week's journey, spend your last two nights just north of Rostock in Warnemünde, a seaside resort town with a charming village and beautiful white beach. You can easily drive to Rostock to see its 13th-century Rathaus and 17th-century St. Mary's Church, and to explore the pedestrian-only Kröpelinerstrasse. ⇨ Rostock and Warnemünde in this chapter for additional information.

was a later addition, and baroque alterations were made in the 18th century. The church is nestled between two rows of 12 almshouses, or *Gottesbuden* (God's cottages). ⊠ *On bank of the Hunnau* ☎ *04102/42510* ⊕ *www.ahrensburg.de* 🎫 *€3.50* ⊙ *Apr.–Sept., Tues.–Sun. 11–5; Oct.–Mar., Tues.–Thurs. and weekends 11:30–3:30.*

Lübeck

❼ 38 km (24 mi) northeast of Ahrensburg, 60 km (37 mi) southeast of Kiel,
Fodor'sChoice 56 km (35 mi) northeast of Hamburg.
★

The ancient core of Lübeck, one of Europe's largest Old Towns dating from the 12th century, was a chief stronghold of the Hanseatic merchant princes. But it was the roving Heinrich der Löwe (King Henry the Lion) who established the town and, in 1173, laid the foundation stone of the redbrick Gothic cathedral. The town's famous landmark gate, the **Holstentor,** built between 1464 and 1478, is flanked by two round, squat towers and serves as a solid symbol of Lübeck's prosperity as a trading center.

In the **Altstadt** (Old Town), proof of Lübeck's former position as the golden queen of the Hanseatic League is found at every step. More 13th- to 15th-century buildings stand in Lübeck than in all other large northern German cities combined, which has earned the Altstadt a place on UNESCO's register of the world's greatest cultural and natural treasures. The **Rathaus,** dating from 1240, is among the buildings lining the arcaded Marktplatz, one of Europe's most striking medieval market squares. It has been subjected to several architectural face-lifts that have added Romanesque arches, Gothic windows, and a Renaissance roof. ⊠ *Breitestr. 64* ☎ *0451/122–1005* 🎫 *Guided tour in German €2.56* ⊙ *Tour weekdays at 11, noon, and 3.*

The impressive redbrick Gothic **Marienkirche** (St. Mary's Church), which has the highest brick nave in the world, looms behind the Rathaus. ⊠ *Marienkirchhof* ☎ *0451/397–700* ⊙ *Nov.–Feb., daily 10–4; Mar. and Oct., daily 10–5; Apr.–Sept., daily 10–6.*

The **Buddenbrookhaus–Günter Grass-Haus,** two highly respectable-looking mansions, are devoted to two of Germany's most prominent writers, Thomas Mann (1875–1955) and Günter Grass (born 1927). The older mansion is named after Mann's saga *Buddenbrooks.* Mann's family once lived here, and it's now home to the **Heinrich und Thomas Mann Zentrum** (Heinrich and Thomas Mann Center). This museum documents the lives and works of two of the most important German writers of the 20th century. A tour and video in English are offered.

Near the museum is the second mansion, which houses the newly opened **Günter Grass-Haus** (Günter Grass House), devoted to Germany's most famous living writer and most recent German winner of the Nobel prize for literature (1999). Changing cultural and literary exhibits are also shown here. ⊠ *Mengstr. 4 and Glockengiesserstr. 21* ☎ *0451/122–4190* ⊕ *www.buddenbrookhaus.de* 🎫 *€6.50, valid for both houses; €4.10, and 3.50 for single museum* ⊙ *Apr.–Oct., daily 10–6; Nov. and Dec., daily 10–5; Jan.–Mar., daily 11–4.*

Take a look inside the entrance hall of the Gothic **Heiligen-Geist-Hospital** (Hospital of the Holy Ghost). It was built in the 14th century by the town's rich merchants and is still caring for the infirm. ⊠ *Am Koberg* ☎ *0451/122–2040* ☞ *Free* ⏱ *Apr.–Sept., Tues.–Sun. 10–5; Oct.–Mar., Tues.–Sun. 10–4.*

Construction of the **Lübecker Dom** (Lübeck Cathedral), the city's oldest building, began in 1173. Both the Dom and the Marienkirche present frequent organ concerts, a real treat in these magnificent redbrick Gothic churches. ⊠ *Domkirchhof* ☎ *0451/74704* ⏱ *Mar.–Oct., daily 10–6; Nov.–Feb., daily 10–3.*

Where to Stay & Eat

$$$–$$$$ ✕ **Wullenwever.** Culinary critics say this restaurant set a new standard of dining sophistication for Lübeck. It's certainly one of the most attractive establishments in town, with dark furniture, chandeliers, and oil paintings on pale pastel walls. In summer tables fill a quiet flower-strewn courtyard. ⊠ *Beckergrube 71* ☎ *0451/704–333* ♨ *Reservations essential* ▭ *AE, DC, V* ⏱ *Closed Sun. and Mon. No lunch.*

★ **$–$$$** ✕ **Schiffergesellschaft.** Women weren't allowed in the Schiffergesellschaft (Mariners' Society) from its opening in 1535 until 1870. Today mixed company sits in church-style pews at long 400-year-old oak tables. At each end of the pew is a sculpted coat of arms of a particular city. Shipowners had their set trading routes, and they each had their own pew and table. A good meal here is the *Ostseescholle* (plaice), fried with bacon and served with potatoes and cucumber salad. ⊠ *Breitestr. 2* ☎ *0451/76776* ▭ *MC, V.*

★ **$$–$$$** ✕▥ **SAS Radisson Senator Hotel Lübeck.** Close to the famous Holstentor, this ultramodern hotel, with its daring architecture, still reveals a North German heritage: the redbrick building, with its oversize windows and generous, open lobby, mimics an old Lübeck warehouse. When making a reservation, ask for a (larger) Business Class room, whose price includes a breakfast. A big plus are the very comfortable beds, which are large by German standards. The Nautilo restaurant ($$–$$$) serves light Mediterranean cuisine. ⊠ *Willy-Brandt-Allee 6, D–23554* ☎ *0451/1420* 🖶 *0451/142–2222* ⊕ *www.radissonsas.de* ↳ *217 rooms, 7 suites* △ *2 restaurants, room service, in-room data ports, minibars, cable TV with movies, pool, health club, hair salon, massage, sauna, spa, bar, babysitting, dry cleaning, laundry service, concierge, meeting room, parking (fee), some pets allowed (fee), no-smoking rooms* ▭ *AE, DC, MC, V.*

$ ✕▥ **Ringhotel Jensen.** Only a stone's throw from the Holstentor, this hotel is close to all the main attractions and faces the moat surrounding the Old Town. It's family run and very comfortable, with modern rooms, mostly decorated with bright cherrywood furniture. Though small, the guest rooms are big enough for two twin beds and a coffee table and come with either a shower or a bath. ⊠ *An der Obertrave 4–5, D–23552* ☎ *0451/71646* 🖶 *0451/73386* ⊕ *www.hotel-jensen.de* ↳ *41 rooms, 1 suite* △ *Restaurant, cable TV, parking (fee), some pets allowed (fee); no a/c* ▭ *AE, DC, MC, V* ❙❉❙ *BP.*

$$ ▥ **Kaiserhof.** The most comfortable hotel in Lübeck consists of two early 19th-century merchants' houses linked together, retaining many of the original architectural elements. It's a five-minute walk from the cathedral. The spacious bedrooms all have a restful, homey ambience, and the quietest of them overlook the garden at the back. A marvelous breakfast is included in the room cost. ⊠ *Kronsforder Allee 11–13, D–23560* ☎ *0451/703–301* 🖷 *0451/795–083* ⊕ *www.kaiserhof-luebeck.de* 🛏 *58 rooms, 6 suites* ♿ *Room service, in-room safes, minibars, cable TV, pool, sauna, bar, free parking, some pets allowed (fee); no a/c* ⊟ *AE, DC, MC, V* ⊙ *BP.*

★ $ 🏨 **Hotel zur Alten Stadtmauer.** This historic town house in the heart of the city has been converted into a family-operated hotel hideaway. Two floors house small, modest, well-kept guest rooms. Comfortable beds, bright birchwood furniture, a quiet setting, and a great (not to mention nutritious) German breakfast buffet make this a perfect choice for budget travelers yearning for romance. ⊠ *An der Mauer 57, D–23552* ☎ *0451/73702* 🖷 *0451/73239* ⊕ *www.hotelstadtmauer.de* 🛏 *24 rooms, some with bath* ♿ *TV, parking (fee), no-smoking rooms; no a/c* ⊟ *AE, DC, MC, V* ⊙ *BP.*

The Arts

Contact the **Musik und Kongresshallen Lübeck** (⊠ Willy-Brandt-Allee 10, D–23554 ☎ 0451/790–400) for schedules of the myriad concerts, operas, and theater performances in Lübeck.

In summer try to catch a few performances of the **Schleswig-Holstein Music Festival** (mid-July–late August), which features orchestras composed of young musicians from more than 25 countries. Some concerts are held in the Dom or the Marienkirche; some are staged in barns in small towns and villages. Each year between 1986 and 1989, Leonard Bernstein conducted the festival orchestra on a site where cows and chickens are normally fed. For exact dates and tickets, contact **Schleswig-Holstein Konzertorganisation** (⊠ Kartenzentrale Kiel, Postfach 3840, D–24037 Kiel ☎ 0431/570–470 🖷 0431/570–4747).

Shopping

Local legend has it that marzipan was invented in Lübeck during the great medieval famine. According to the story, a local baker ran out of grain for bread and, in his desperation, began experimenting with the only four ingredients he had: almonds, sugar, rose water, and eggs. The result was a sweet almond paste known today as marzipan. Though the story is more fiction than fact (it is generally agreed that marzipan's true origins lie in the Middle East), Lübecker Marzipan, a designation that has been trademarked, is now considered among the best in the world. Lübeck's most famous marzipan maker, **Konditorei-Café Niederegger** (⊠ Breitestr. 89 ☎ 0451/530–1126 ⊕ www.niederegger.de), sells the delicacy molded into a multitude of imaginative forms. The Niederegger shop, located across from the Rathaus, has a cozy café at the back and a small, free marzipan museum upstairs.

The city's largest downtown mall, **Holstentor-Passage** (⊠ An der Untertrave 111 ☎ 0451/704–425), is next to the Holstentor and is filled with stores selling clothing or home accessories.

WESTERN MECKLENBURG

This long-forgotten Baltic Coast region, pinned between two sprawling urban areas—the state capital of Schwerin, in the west, and Rostock, in the east—is thriving again. Despite its perennial economic woes, this part of Germany, and Schwerin in particular, has attracted many businesses, which suggests a light at the end of the tunnel. Though the region is close to the sea, it's made up largely of seemingly endless fields of wheat and yellow rape and a dozen or so wonderful lakes. "When the Lord made the Earth, He started with Mecklenburg," wrote native novelist Fritz Reuter.

Wismar

★ ❽ *60 km (37 mi) east of Lübeck on Rte. 105.*

The old city of Wismar was one of the original three sea-trading towns, along with Lübeck and Rostock, that banded together in 1259 to combat Baltic pirates. From this mutual defense pact grew the great and powerful private trading bloc, the Hanseatic League, which dominated the Baltic for centuries. The wealth generated by the Hanseatic merchants can still be seen in Wismar's ornate architecture.

★ The **Marktplatz** (Market Square), one of the largest and best preserved in Germany, is framed by patrician gabled houses. Their style ranges from redbrick late Gothic through Dutch Renaissance to 19th-century neoclassical. In 1922 filmmaker Friedrich Wilhelm Murnau used the tortuous streets of Wismar's Old Town in his expressionist horror film classic, *Nosferatu.* The square's **Wasserkunst,** the ornate pumping station done in Dutch Renaissance style, was built between 1580 and 1602 by the Dutch master Philipp Brandin. Not only was it a work of art, it supplied the town with water until the mid-19th century.

The **Alter Schwede** (Old Swede), a seamen's tavern since 1878, has entertained guests ranging from sailors to the Swedish royal family. Dating from 1380, it's the oldest building on the Marktplatz and is easily identified by its stepped gables and redbrick facade. ⊠ *Am Markt 19–22* ☎ *03841/283–552.*

The ruins of the **Marienkirche** (St. Mary's Church) with its 250-foot tower, bombed in World War II, lie just behind the Marktplatz; the church is still undergoing restoration. At noon, 3, and 5, listen for one of 14 hymns played on its carillon.

The **Fürstenhof** (Princes' Court), home of the former dukes of Mecklenburg, stands next to the Marienkirche. It's an early 16th-century Italian Renaissance structure with touches of late Gothic. The facade is a series of fussy friezes depicting scenes from the Trojan War. The **St. Georgen zu Wismar** (St. George's Church), another victim of the war, is next to the Fürstenhof. One of Northern Germany's biggest Gothic churches, built between 1315 and 1404, it has been almost completely restored to its former glory. Though the simple interior is not particularly intriguing,

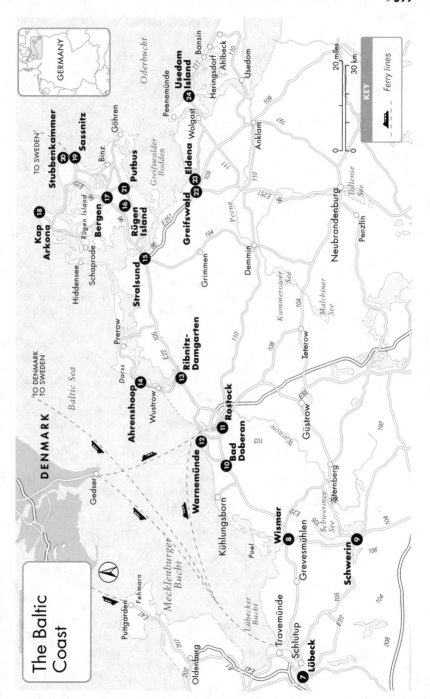

The Baltic Coast

the spiral towers and many architectural details on the facade are an intriguing sight.

The city's turbulent history is chronicled at the **Stadtgeschichtliches Museum Wismar Schabbellhaus** (Museum for City History), located in one of North Germany's oldest Renaissance buildings, the Schabbellhaus (1569–71). Exhibits present the medieval past of the city and focus on the Swedish occupation during the Thirty Years' War. Included are fine paintings, scrimshaw art, and paintings, whose origins (Australia and New Zealand) testify to the extensive trade links Wismar once had. ⊠ *Schweinsbrücke 8* ☎ *03841/282–350* ⊕ *www.schabbellhaus.de* 🖼 *€2* ☾ *May–Oct., Tues.–Sun. 10–8; Nov.–Apr., Tues.–Sun. 10–5.*

The late-Gothic **St. Nikolaikirche** (St. Nicholas's Church), with a 120-foot-high nave, was built between 1381 and 1487. A remnant of the town's long domination by Sweden is the additional altar built for Swedish sailors. ⊠ *Marktpl.* ☎ *03841/210–143* ☾ *Apr.–May, Mon.–Sat. 10–12:30 and 1:30–4; June–Sept., Mon.–Sat. 10–12:30 and 1:30–5; Oct.–Mar., Mon.–Sat. 10–noon and 1:30–5.*

If you have an hour to spare, wander among the jetties and quays of the port, a mix of the medieval and the modern. **To'n Zägenkrog**, a seamen's haven decorated with sharks' teeth, stuffed seagulls, and maritime gear, is a good pit stop along the harbor. ⊠ *Ziegenmarkt 10* ☎ *03841/282–716.*

Where to Stay & Eat

★ **$–$$$** ✕ **Alter Schwede.** Regarded as one of the most attractive, authentic taverns on the Baltic—and correspondingly busy—this eatery focuses not only on Mecklenburg's game and poultry dishes, such as the traditional *Mecklenburger Ente* (Mecklenburg duck), filled with baked plums, apples, raisins, and served with red cabbage and potatoes, but also on new North German cuisine such as *Lachsfilet im Bierteig gebacken auf Hummersauce, mit Brokkoli und Kartoffelgratin* (salmon baked in beer dough, served with lobster sauce, broccoli, and potato gratin). ⊠ *Am Markt 19–22* ☎ *03841/283–552* ▱ *AE, MC, V.*

$–$$ ✕▦ **Citypartner Hotel Alter Speicher.** This small and very personal family-owned hotel is behind the facade of an old merchant house in the downtown area. Some of the rooms may be tiny, but their size contributes to the warm and cozy atmosphere. The lobby and restaurants are decorated with wooden beams and panels. The main restaurant ($$–$$$$) primarily serves game, but it also prepares regional dishes. ⊠ *Bohrstr. 12–12a, D–23966* ☎ *03841/211–746* 🖶 *03841/211–747* ⊕ *www. hotel-alter-speicher.de* ❥ *70 rooms, 3 suites, 2 apartments* ☐ *Restaurant, café, in-room safes, minibars, cable TV, gym, sauna, bar, meeting room, parking (fee), some pets allowed (fee), no-smoking rooms; no a/c* ▱ *DC, MC, V* ❧ *BP.*

★ **$$** ✕▦ **Seehotel Neuklostersee.** Set at the dreamy Naun Lake, this country hotel is a hidden gem just 15 km (9 mi) east of Wismar. The redbrick farmhouse and old thatch-roof barn comprise an upscale yet casual hotel. Each room has a different design (the owners are acclaimed Berlin interior designers), with white walls and terra-cotta tiles. There's a fine restaurant ($) serving German-Italian seafood on a terrace. A sauna at the lake and a beach invite you to relax; a health club was added in 2004. ⊠ *Seestr. 1, D–23992 Nakenstorf* ☎ *038422/25445* 🖷 *038422/25630* ⊕ *www.seehotel-neuklostersee.de* ⮩ *11 rooms, 1 suite, 1 apartment* ⚐ *Restaurant, in-room data ports, cable TV, sauna, beach, boating, bicycles, hiking, horseback riding, free parking, some pets allowed (fee), no-smoking rooms; no a/c* ▤ *MC* ❙◎❙ *BP.*

$$ ⌂ **Steigenberger–Hotel Stadt Hamburg.** This first-class hotel hides behind a rigid gray facade dating back to the early 19th century. The interior is surprisingly open and airy, with skylights and a posh lobby. The rooms have elegant cherrywood art deco–style furnishings. Downstairs, the Bierkeller, a cavernous 17th-century room with vaulted ceilings, is a trendy nightspot. Ask for special package deals such as the *Joker-Wochenende*, which includes two nights, a four-course dinner, a sightseeing tour or boat trip on the Baltic Sea, and a bottle of champagne—all for €178 per person. ⊠ *Am Markt 24, D–23966* ☎ *03841/2390* 🖷 *03841/239–239* ⊕ *www.wismar.steigenberger.de* ⮩ *104 rooms, 3 suites* ⚐ *Restaurant, café, minibars, cable TV, sauna, meeting room, some pets allowed (fee), no-smoking floor; no a/c* ▤ *AE, DC, MC, V* ❙◎❙ *BP.*

The Arts

At the **Niederdeutsche Bühne** (⊠ Philipp-Müllerstr. 5 ☎ 03841/705–501), plays in German and operas are performed regularly; concerts occasionally take place.

Schwerin

★ ❾ *32 km (20 mi) south of Wismar on Rte. 106.*

Schwerin, the second-largest town in the region after Rostock and the capital of the state of Mecklenburg-Vorpommern, is worth a trip just to visit its giant island palace. On the edge of Lake Schwerin, the recently restored **Schweriner Schloss** once housed the Mecklenburg royal family. The original palace dates from 1018 but was enlarged by Henry the Lion when he founded Schwerin in 1160. Portions of it were later modeled on Chambord, in the Loire Valley. As it stands now, the palace is surmounted by 15 turrets, large and small, and is reminiscent of a French château. The part of it that's neo-Renaissance in style are its many ducal staterooms, which date from between 1845 and 1857.

North of the main tower is the **Neue Lange Haus** (New Long House), built between 1553 and 1555 and now used as the **Schlossmuseum.** The Communist government restored and maintained the fantastic opulence of this rambling, 80-room reminder of an absolutist monarchy—and then used it to board kindergarten teachers in training. A fifth of the rooms are now used for state government offices. Antique furniture, objets d'art, silk tapestries, and paintings are sprinkled throughout the salons (the throne room is particularly extravagant), but of special interest are the ornately patterned and highly burnished inlaid wooden floors and wall panels. The parkland contains many beautiful and rare species of trees. Sandstone replicas of Permoser sculptures adorn the boulevards. ⊠ *Lennéstr. 1* ☎ *0385/525–2927* ⊕ *www.museum-schwerin.de*

⌑ €4 ⊙ *Mid-Apr.–mid-Oct., Tues.–Sun. 10–6; mid-Oct.–mid-Apr., Tues.–Sun. 10–5.*

The **Alte Garten** (Old Garden), the town's showpiece square, was the setting of military parades during the years of Communist rule. It's dominated by two buildings: the ornate neo-Renaissance state theater, constructed in 1883–86; and the **Staatliches Museum** (State Museum), which houses an interesting collection of paintings by Max Liebermann and Lovis Corinth, plus an exhibition of Meissen porcelain. ⊠ *Alter Garten 3* ☎ *0385/59580* ⊕ *www.museum-schwerin.de* ⌑ €3 ⊙ *Mid-Apr.–mid-Oct., Wed.–Sun. 10–6, Tues. 10–8; mid-Oct.–mid-Apr., Wed.–Sun. 10–5, Tues. 10–8.*

The **Dom**, a Gothic cathedral, is the oldest building (built 1222–48) in the city. The bronze baptismal font is from the 14th century; the altar was built in 1440. Religious scenes painted on its walls date from the Middle Ages. Sweeping views of the Old Town and lake await those with the energy to climb the 219 steps to the top of the 320-foot-high cathedral tower. ⊠ *Am Dom 4* ☎ *0385/565–014* ⊙ *Tower and nave May–mid-Oct., Mon.–Sat. 10–4, Sun. noon–4; mid-Oct.–Apr., weekdays 11–2, Sat. 11–4, Sun. noon–3.*

☾ The **Mecklenburgisches Volkskundemuseum** (Mecklenburg Ethnology Museum) is a living-history museum representing traditional work and farm life in Germany. Children and history buffs in particular will enjoy wandering through the 17 preserved buildings, which include a blacksmith's shop dating from 1736, a village school from the 19th century, and a traditional fire station. You can watch demonstrations of the tools. ⊠ *Alte Crivitzer Landstr. 13, 6 km (4 mi) south of Schwerin* ☎ *0385/ 208–410* ⌑ €2.50 ⊙ *May–Oct., Tues.–Sun. 10–6.*

A visit to Schwerin wouldn't be complete without one of the **Weisse Flotte** boat tours of the lakes—there are seven in the area. A trip to the island of Kaninchenwerder, a small sanctuary for more than 100 species of water birds, is an unforgettable experience. Boats for this 1½-hour standard tour depart from the pier adjacent to the Schweriner Schloss. ⊠ *Anlegestelle Schlosspier* ☎ *0385/557–770* ⊕ *www.weisse-flotte-schwerin. de* ⌑ €9.50 ⊙ *Apr.–Oct., daily 10–5:30.*

Where to Stay & Eat

★ **$–$$** ✕ **Weinhaus Uhle.** One of the most traditional and popular eateries in Schwerin, this restaurant is named after the wine merchant who opened the restaurant back in 1740. The newer *Weinbistro* (wine bistro) offers primarily German wine tasting and a small menu (mostly cheese plates or soups such as lobster cream soup). In the restaurant, regional specialties and international mixed grills are served in a rustic setting, accompanied by a piano player on Friday and Saturday nights. ⊠ *Schusterstr. 13–15* ☎ *0385/562–956* ▭ *AE, MC, V.*

★ **$** ✕▥ **Alt-Schweriner Schankstuben.** A small family-owned restaurant and hotel, the Schankstuben extends standard but very personal service with emphasis on Mecklenburg tradition. The hotel is within three old houses in the historic downtown district. Its restaurant ($–$$) serves local dishes. The guest rooms are small but bright and furnished with simple pine furniture. ⊠ *Schlachtermarkt 9–13, D–19055* ☎ *0385/592–530* 🖷 *0385/ 557–4109* ⊕ *www.alt-schweriner-schankstuben.de* ⮢ *16 rooms* ⟐ *Restaurant, café, cable TV, meeting room, free parking, some pets allowed (fee), no-smoking rooms; no a/c* ☰ *AE, MC, V* ⦿| *BP.*

★ **$$** 🏨 **Hotel Niederländischer Hof.** The city's most elegant hotel has a 4½-star rating as a result of its luxurious interior, decorated in a classicist style; its romantic, airy rooms; the impeccable service; and, of course, the fine nouvelle cuisine à la Mecklenburg (mostly seafood dishes). All this is tucked inside a late-19th-century historic mansion located on old Schwerin's Pfaffenteich. ⊠ *Karl-Marx-Str.12–13, D–19055* ☎ *0385/591–100* 🖷 *0385/5911–0999* ⊕ *www.niederlaendischer-hof.de* ⮢ *27 rooms, 6 suites* ⟐ *Restaurant, room service, in-room safes, minibars, cable TV, dry cleaning, laundry service, meeting room, free parking, some pets allowed (fee), no-smoking rooms; no a/c* ☰ *AE, DC, MC, V* ⦿| *BP.*

★ **$$** 🏨 **Sorat-Hotel Speicher am Ziegelsee.** This hotel is a fine example of how creative thinkers are giving some of eastern Germany's old and run-down industrial buildings new life. Towering high above the old harbor district, the Speicher am Ziegelsee was built within a deserted redbrick wheat warehouse dating to 1939. The hotel's spacious rooms and apartments are decorated with natural materials and earthy tones and have all the amenities of a modern, first-class hotel. ⊠ *Speicherstr. 11, D–19055* ☎ *0385/50030* 🖷 *0385/500–3111* ⊕ *www.speicher-hotel.de* ⮢ *59 rooms, 20 apartments* ⟐ *Restaurant, room service, kitchenettes, cable TV, gym, hot tub, massage, sauna, steam room, bar, dry cleaning, laundry service, meeting room, free parking, some pets allowed (fee), no-smoking floor; no a/c* ☰ *AE, DC, MC, V* ⦿| *BP.*

Nightlife & the Arts

The **Mecklenburgisches Staatstheater** (⊠ Am Alten Garten ☎ 0385/ 53000) stages German drama and opera. In June check out the **Schlossfestspiele** for open-air drama or comedy performances.

The **Mexxclub** (⊠ Klöresgang 2 ☎ No phone) is the city's hottest dance club, featuring house and soul DJs who attract a stylish young crowd every Saturday night.

Shopping

Antiques and bric-a-brac that have languished in cellars and attics since World War II are still surfacing throughout eastern Germany, and the occasional bargain can be found. The best places to look in Schwerin are on and around **Schmiedestrasse, Schlossstrasse,** and **Mecklenburgstrasse.**

Bad Doberan

🔟 *60 km (37 mi) east of Wismar on Rte. 105, 90 km (56 mi) northeast of Schwerin.*

★ Bad Doberan is home to the meticulously restored redbrick **Doberaner Münster** (monastery church), one of the finest of its kind in Germany. It was built by Cistercian monks between 1294 and 1368 in the northern German Gothic style, with a central nave and transept. The main altar dates from the early 14th century; its highlight is a 45-foot-tall cross. ⊠ *Klosterstr. 2* ☎ *038203/16439* 🎫 *€1, tours €1.50* ⊙ *May–Sept., Mon.–Sat. 9–6,*

Sun. noon–6; Mar., Apr., and Oct., Mon.–Sat. 9–4, Sun. noon–4; Nov.–Feb., Tues.–Fri. 9–noon and 2–4, Sat. 9–4, Sun. noon–4. Tours Apr.–Sept., Mon.–Sat. at 11, 2, and 3; Oct.–Mar., Mon.–Sat. at 2 and 3.

No visit to this part of the country would be complete without a ride on *Molli*, a quaint steam train that has been chugging up and down a 16-km (10-mi) narrow-gauge track between Bad Doberan and the nearby beach resorts of **Heiligendamm** and **Kühlungsborn** since 1886. The train was nicknamed after a little local dog that barked its approval every time the smoking iron horse passed by. At the start of the 45-minute journey the engine and its old wooden carriages make their way through the center of Bad Doberan's cobble streets. In summer *Molli* runs 13 times daily between Bad Doberan and Kühlungsborn. ⊠ *Mecklenburgische Bäderbahn Molli, Küstenbus GmbH* ☎ *038203/4150* ⊕ *www. molli-bahn.de* ✉ *Same-day round-trip €9* ◷ *From Bad Doberan: May–Sept., daily 8:36–6:45; Oct.–Apr., daily 8:35–4:40.*

Where to Stay & Eat

¢–$ ✕ **Weisser Pavillon.** Here's a mixed setting for you: a 19th-century Chinese pagoda–type structure in an English-style park. Come for lunch or high tea; regional specialties are featured. In summer the café closes at 10 PM. ⊠ *Auf dem Kamp* ☎ *038203/62326* ▭ *No credit cards.*

★ $$ ✕▣ **Hotel Friedrich-Franz-Palais.** Built in 1793 for a Mecklenburg duke, this whitewashed hotel has accommodated guests for more than 200 years. Completely restored and renovated, each room exudes old-world elegance with modern comforts. The small restaurant ($–$$$) mostly serves fresh fish and game in a setting ideal for a candlelight dinner. ⊠ *Am Kamp, D–18209* ☎ *038203/63036* ▤ *038203/62126* ⊕ *www.friedrich-franz-palais.de* ➯ *40 rooms, 2 suites, 3 apartments* ⟁ *Restaurant, café, room service, minibars, cable TV, sauna, bicycles, free parking, some pets allowed (fee), no-smoking rooms; no a/c* ▭ *AE, DC, MC, V* ⦸ *BP.*

$$$$ ▣ **Kempinski Grand Hotel.** The small beach resort of Heiligendamm has
FodorsChoice regained its prewar reputation as a getaway for Berlin's up-and-com-
★ ing crowd. The opening of the Kempinski Grand Hotel, arguably the finest first-class hotel on the Baltic Coast, in spring of 2003, is the latest bit of evidence that this is indeed the case. Nestled in five meticulously restored, gleaming white structures on a secluded beach, the Kempinski offers timelessly furnished rooms decorated in soft colors, and exudes an almost Californian Bel Air charm. There are endless activities offered, and the spa area is breathtaking. ⊠ *Grand Hotel at Heiligendamm, D–18209 Heiligendamm* ☎ *038203/7400* ▤ *038203/740–7474* ⊕ *www.kempinski.com* ➯ *225 rooms, 119 suites* ⟁ *Restaurant, room service, in-room data ports, minibars, cable TV with movies, indoor-outdoor pool, health club, massage, sauna, spa, beach, bar, babysitting, dry cleaning, laundry service, concierge, meeting rooms, parking (fee), some pets allowed (fee), no-smoking floor* ▭ *AE, DC, MC, V* ⦸ *BP.*

Rostock

⑪ *14 km (9 mi) east of Bad Doberan on Rte. 105.*

Rostock, the biggest port and shipbuilding center of the former East Germany, was founded around 1200. Of all the Hanseatic cities, the once-thriving Rostock suffered the most from the dissolution of the League in 1669. The GDR (German Democratic Republic) reestablished Rostock as a major port, but since reunification, port work has been cut in half and, though ferries come from Gedser (Denmark) and Trelleborg (Sweden), there's little traffic. The biggest local annual attraction is Hanse Sail, a week of yacht racing held in August.

Because it was home to wartime armament factories, the city suffered severe bombings, but much of the Old Town's core has been rebuilt. The main street, the pedestrians-only **Kröpelinerstrasse,** begins at the old western gate, the Kröpeliner Tor. Here you'll find the finest examples of the late-Gothic and Renaissance houses of rich Hanse merchants. The triangular **Universitätsplatz** (University Square), commemorating the founding of northern Europe's first university here in 1419, is home to Rostock University's Italian Renaissance–style main building, finished in 1867.

At the **Neuer Markt** (Town Square) you'll immediately notice the architectural potpourri of the **Rathaus.** Basically 13th-century Gothic with a baroque facade, the town hall spouts seven slender, decorative towers that look like candles on a peculiar birthday cake. Historic gabled houses surround the rest of the square.

Four-century-old **St. Marienkirche** (St. Mary's Church), the Gothic architectural prize of Rostock, boasts a bronze baptismal font from 1290 and some interesting baroque features, notably the oak altar (1720) and organ (1770). Unique is the huge astronomical clock dating from 1472; it has a calendar extending to the year 2017. ⊠ *Am Ziegenmarkt* ☎ *0381/492–3396* ⊗ *Nov.–May, Mon.–Sat. 10–12:30 and 2–4, Sun. 11–noon; June–Oct., Mon.–Sat. 10–5, Sun. 11–noon.*

☺ The **Schifffahrtsmuseum** (Maritime Museum) traces the history of shipping on the Baltic and displays models of ships, which especially intrigue children. It's just beyond the city wall, at the old city gateway, Steintor. ⊠ *August-Bebel-Str. 1* ☎ *0381/252–060* ⊠ *€3* ⊗ *Tues.–Sun. 10–5.*

☺ The **Zoologischer Garten** (Zoological Garden) has one of the largest collections of exotic animals and birds in northern Germany. This zoo is particularly noted for its polar bears, some of which were bred in Rostock. If you're traveling with children, a visit is a must. ⊠ *Rennbahnallee 21* ☎ *0381/20820* ⊕ *www.zoo-rostock.de* ⊠ *€8* ⊗ *Nov.–Mar., daily 9–4; Apr.–Oct., daily 9–7.*

Where to Stay & Eat

$$ ✕ **Restaurant & Bar Silo 4.** Rostock's latest culinary venture is proof that eastern Germany can do sleek and modern. Located at the top of an office tower on the waterfront, this innovative restaurant offers spectacular views of the river along with a fun and interesting approach to Asian-fusion cuisine. The menu consists of a list of ingredients and seasonings. Guests choose what they like and then leave it to the experts in the kitchen to work their magic. Don't leave without taking a peek at the designer bathrooms and the funky upstairs bar. ⊠ *Am Strande 3d* ☎ *0381/458–5800* ⊕ *www.silo4.de* ▭ *AE, DC, MC, V* ⊗ *No lunch; closed Mon.*

★ **$-$$** ✕ **Zur Kogge.** Looking like the cabin of some ancient sailing vessel, the oldest sailors' beer tavern in town serves mostly fish. Order the *Mecklenburger Fischsuppe* (fish soup) if it's on the menu. *Grosser Fischteller,* consisting of three kinds of fish—depending on the day's catch—served with vegetables, lobster and shrimp sauce, and potatoes is also a popular choice. ⊠ *Wokrenterstr. 27* ☎ *0381/493–4493* ⚲ *Reservations essential* ▤ *DC, MC, V.*

¢–$ ✕ **Petrikeller.** Once you've crossed the threshold to the Petrikeller, you'll be in the medieval world of the Hanseatic merchants, seamen, and wild pirates such as Klaus Störtebecker. The restaurant's motto, "*Wer nicht liebt Wein, Weib und Gesang bleibt ein Narr sein Leben lang*" (He who doth not love wine, woman and song will be a fool his whole life long), a quote from Martin Luther no less, sets the tone for the giddy atmosphere, hearty food, and live music on weekend nights. ⊠ *Harte Str. 27* ☎ *0381/455–855* ▤ *No credit cards* ☉ *Closed Mon. No lunch.*

$$ ▥ **Courtyard by Marriott.** A 19th-century mansion, this hotel is a genuine part of Rostock's historic Old Town. It provides smooth service, and the modern rooms are tastefully decorated. Despite its downtown location, it's a quiet place to stay. A breakfast buffet is included in the room rate. ⊠ *Schwaansche/Kröpeliner Str., D–18055* ☎ *0381/49700* 🖷 *0381/497–0700* ⊕ *www.marriott.com* ⏋ *150 rooms, 2 suites* ⚲ *Restaurant, room service, minibars, cable TV with movies, gym, sauna, bar, dry cleaning, laundry service, meeting room, parking (fee), some pets allowed (fee), no-smoking floor; no a/c* ▤ *AE, DC, MC, V* ⑩ *BP.*

★ **$$** ▥ **Steigenberger–Hotel zur Sonne Rostock.** With more than 200 years of history behind it, the "zur Sonne," located within the Old Town, is one of the best hotels in Rostock. Guests here relax and enjoy the Hanseatic mansion's maritime atmosphere, impeccable service, and modern rooms. When making a reservation, ask for one of the weekend offers and a top-floor room, cozily fitted under the eaves. ⊠ *Neuer Markt 2, D–18055* ☎ *0381/49730* 🖷 *0381/497–3351* ⊕ *www.rostock.steigenberger.de* ⏋ *103 rooms, 21 suites* ⚲ *Restaurant, café, cable TV, massage, sauna, bar, meeting room, parking (fee), some pets allowed (fee), no-smoking rooms; no a/c* ▤ *AE, DC, MC, V* ⑩ *BP.*

Nightlife & the Arts

The summer season brings with it a plethora of special concerts, sailing regattas, and parties on the beach. The **Volkstheater** (⊠ Patriotischer Weg 33 ☎ 0381/381–4600) presents plays and concerts. **Farellis** (⊠ Grubenstr. 6 ☎ 0381/490–7100) is a disco that appeals to all ages.

Shopping

Echter Rostocker Doppel-Kümmel und -Korn, a kind of schnapps made from various grains, is a traditional liquor of the area around Rostock. Fishermen have numbed themselves to the cold for centuries with this 80-proof beverage; a bottle costs €8–€11.

Warnemünde

⑫ *14 km (9 mi) north of Rostock on Rte. 103.*

Warnemünde is a quaint seaside resort town with the best hotels and restaurants in the area, as well as 20 km (12 mi) of beautiful white beach.

It's been a popular summer getaway for families in eastern Germany for years. Children enjoy climbing to the top of the town landmark, a 115-foot-high **Leuchtturm** (lighthouse), dating from 1898; on clear days it offers views of the coast and Rostock Harbor. Inland from the lighthouse is the yacht marina known as **Alter Strom** (Old Stream). Once the entry into the port of Warnemünde, it now has bars, cozy restaurants, and specialty shops.

Where to Stay & Eat

¢–$ ✕ **Fischerklause.** Sailors have stopped in at this restaurant's bar since the turn of the 20th century. The smoked fish sampler, served on a lazy Susan, is delicious, and the house specialty of fish soup is best washed down with some Rostocker Doppel-Kümmel schnapps. An accordionist entertains the crowd on Friday and Saturday evenings. ⊠ *Am Strom 123* ☎ *0381/52516* ⌖ *Reservations essential* ▤ *AE, DC, MC, V.*

$–$$ ▦ **Hotel Neptun.** The 19-story concrete-and-glass Neptun is an eyesore on the outside, but inside it has the redeeming qualities of an upscale hotel. Every one of the neatly decorated rooms has a sea view and a balcony. The hotel's Spa Arkona is one of eastern Germany's finest fitness and sauna clubs. ⊠ *Seestr. 19, D–18119* ☎ *0381/7770* 🖷 *0381/54023* ⊕ *www.hotel-neptun.de* ⤵ *340 rooms, 5 suites* ⌖ *4 restaurants, café, room service, in-room safes, minibars, cable TV, saltwater pool, health club, hair salon, sauna, spa, boating, bicycles, 2 bars, dance club, babysitting, dry cleaning, laundry service, meeting room, parking (fee), some pets allowed (fee), no-smoking rooms; no a/c* ▤ *AE, DC, MC, V* ❙◯❙ *BP.*

$ ▦ **Hotel Germania.** At the harbor entrance and only one block from the beach and the Alter Strom promenade, this small hotel's location alone makes it a good choice. All rooms are tastefully decorated and include a TV. With so many good eateries nearby you won't mind that there's no hotel restaurant. ⊠ *Am Strom 110–111, D–18119* ☎ *0381/519–850* 🖷 *0381/519–8510* ⊕ *www.germania-warnemuende.de* ⤵ *18 rooms* ⌖ *Minibars, cable TV, bar, parking (fee), some pets allowed (fee); no a/c* ▤ *AE, DC, MC, V* ❙◯❙ *BP.*

$ ▦ **Landhotel Ostseetraum.** This family-owned hotel, in a thatched-roof farmhouse outside Warnemünde, expertly blends modern style with rural architecture. The recently refurbished apartments all feature a kitchenette, and separate sitting or living areas. The standard rooms are smaller—some have a maritime flair with dark, heavy but modern furniture and large beds; others, which are even smaller, have a country feel with bright pinewood furnishings. The hotel is 500 yards from the beach. ⊠ *Stolteraaweg 34b, D–18119 Warnemünde-Diedrichshagen* 🖷 *0381/51719* ⊕ *www.ostseetraum.de* ⤵ *18 rooms* ⌖ *Restaurant, cable TV, free parking, some pets allowed (fee); no a/c* ▤ *AE, MC, V* ❙◯❙ *BP.*

Sports & the Outdoors

FISHING Fishing is a rapidly expanding leisure industry in the area. Every port along the coast now has small boats for rent, and some boatmen will lead you to the shoals. For information on equipment, contact the **Rostock tourist office** (☎ 0381/403–0500) for **Warnemünder Hafen** (Warnemünde Harbor).

Nightlife

In Warnemünde nearly all the seaside hotels and resorts, down to the smallest, have dances almost nightly during the summer months. The pubs in marina **Alter Strom** are fun gathering places. The **Skybar** (⊠ Seestr. 19, 19th fl. of Neptun Hotel ☎ 0381/7770) is open until 3 AM. Roof access gives you the chance to sit under the stars and watch ship lights twinkle on the sea.

Ribnitz-Damgarten

> ⑬ *30 km (19 mi) northeast of Warnemünde, 26 km (16 mi) east of Rostock on Rte. 105.*

Ribnitz-Damgarten is the center of the amber (in German, *Bernstein*) business, unique to the Baltic Coast. Amber is a yellow-brown fossil formed from the sap of ancient conifers and is millions of years old. Head for a beach and join the locals in the perennial quest for amber stones washed up among the seaweed. If you want to test what you find on the beach, know that only true amber will float in a glass of water stirred with 2 teaspoons of salt. In the **Deutsches Bernsteinmuseum** (German Amber Museum), which adjoins the main factory, you can see a fascinating exhibit of how this precious "Baltic gold" is collected from the sea and refined to make jewelry. The museum has pieces of amber that are between 35 and 50 million years old. The biggest lump of raw amber ever harvested from the sea weighed more than 23 pounds. ⊠ *Im Kloster 1–2* ☎ *03821/2931* ⊕ *www.bernsteinmuseum.info* 🖃 *€4.50* ⊙ *Apr.–Oct., daily 9:30–6; Nov.–Mar., Wed.–Sun. 9:30–5.*

Shopping

You can buy amber jewelry, chess figures, and ornate jewelry boxes in the **Bernsteinmuseum** (⊠ Im Kloster 1–2 ☎ 03821/2931). The jewelry, often designed with gold and silver as well as amber, costs from €51 to €513. Fossils are often embedded in the stone—a precious find.

VORPOMMERN

The best description of this region is found in its name, which simply means "before Pomerania." This area, indeed, seems trapped between Mecklenburg and the authentic, old Pomerania farther east, now part of Poland. Although Vorpommern is not the dull, monotonous backwater it's made out to be, its tundralike appearance, pine barrens, heaths, and dunes are not typical tourist draws, either. Its very remoteness ensures an unforgettable view of unspoiled nature, primarily attracting families and young travelers.

Ahrenshoop

> ⑭ *75 km (47 mi) north of Ribnitz-Damgarten.*

Ahrenshoop is typical of the seaside villages on the half-island of **Darss**. This curved finger of land was once three islands that became one from centuries of shifting sand. In the late 19th century painters from across

Germany and beyond formed an art colony here. Continue toward Prerow to get back to the mainland, but be sure to stop at the 17th-cen-
tury seamen's church on the edge of town.

Since 1966 much of Darss has been a nature reserve, partly to protect
the ancient forest of beech, holly, and juniper. The island's best beach
is the **Weststrand** (West Beach), a broad stretch of fine white sand that
is free of auto traffic and most development.

Where to Stay & Eat

$–$$$ ✕ **Café Namenlos.** In an old, thatch-roof beach house dating back to 1912,
Café Without a Name specializes in local game and fish dishes. Entrées
such as *Mecklenburgische Hausente* (Mecklenburg duck filled with ap-
ples, raisins, and red cabbage) are served on rustic tables that fit in with
the old tile oven and a low ceiling supported by wooden beams. ⊠ *Am
Schifferberg 2* ☎ *038220/606–105* ▤ *AE, MC, V.*

★ **$–$$** ✕▥ **Elisabeth von Eicken.** The art nouveau villa of the late local painter
Elisabeth von Eicken is a popular hotel and restaurant choice for so-
phisticated travelers. The rooms are small but individually designed in
minimalist styles and adorned with modern art. The airy restaurant
($$–$$$) is undoubtedly one of the best on the Baltic Sea coast. Dishes
feature local fish—such as pike, trout, or perch—prepared with fresh
spices and herbs rather than the usual heavy sauces. The wine list is
exquisite. ⊠ *Dorfstr. 39, D–18347 Ahrenshoop* ☎ *038220/6990*
🖷 *038220/69924* ⊕ *www.elisabeth-von-eicken.de* ⇥ *6 rooms* ⌂ *Restaurant, room service, in-room data ports, minibars, cable TV, babysitting,
dry cleaning, free parking, some pets allowed (fee), no-smoking rooms;
no a/c* ▤ *No credit cards* ⍦⊙⍦ *BP.*

Stralsund

⑮ *59 km (37 mi) east of Ahrenshoop, 42 km (26 mi) east of Ribnitz-
Damgarten on Rte. 105.*

Although much of it had been industrialized, this jewel of the Baltic has
retained its historic city center and parts of its 13th-century defensive
wall. The wall was built following an attack by the Lübeck fleet in 1249.
In 1815 the Congress of Vienna awarded the city, which had been under
Swedish control, to the Prussians.

The **Alter Markt** (Old Market Square) has the best local architecture, ranging from redbrick Gothic through Renaissance to baroque. Most buildings were rich merchants' homes, notably the late-Gothic **Wulflamhaus,**
with 17 ornate, steeply stepped gables. Stralsund's architectural masterpiece, however, is the 14th-century **Rathaus,** considered by many to
be the finest secular example of redbrick Gothic. Its open corridors reduced wind pressure on the tall facade.

The treasures of the 13th-century Gothic **St. Nikolaikirche** (St. Nicholas's
Church) include a 15-foot-high crucifix from the 14th century, an astronomical clock from 1394, and a famous baroque altar. ⊠ *Alter Markt*
☎ *03831/297–199* ⊙ *Apr.–Sept., Mon.–Sat. 10–5, Sun. 11–noon and
2–4; Oct.–Mar., Mon.–Sat. 10–noon and 2–4, Sun. 11–noon and 2–4.*

The **Katherinenkloster** (St. Catherine's Monastery) is a former cloister; 40 of its rooms now house two museums: the famed Deutsches Meeresmuseum, and the Kulturhistorisches Museum.

The **Kulturhistorisches Museum** (Cultural History Museum), exhibits diverse artifacts from more than 10,000 years of this coastal region's history. Highlights include a toy collection and 10th-century Viking gold jewelry found on Hiddensee. You'll reach the museums by walking along Ossenreyerstrasse through the Apollonienmarkt on Mönchstrasse. ⊠ *Kulturhistorisches Museum, Mönchstr. 25–27* ☎ *03831/28790* ⊠ *€3* ⊙ *Tues.–Sun. 10–5.*

🌣 The Stralsund aquarium of Baltic Sea life is part of the three-floor **Deutsches Meeresmuseum** (German Sea Museum), which also displays the skeletons of a giant whale and a hammerhead shark, and a 25-foot-high chunk of coral. ⊠ *Katharinenberg 14–20, entrance on Mönchstr.* ☎ *03831/ 26500* ⊕ *www.meeresmuseum.de* ⊠ *€4.50* ⊙ *Oct.–Mar., daily 10–5; June–Sept., daily 10–6.*

The monstrous **St. Marienkirche** (St. Mary's Church) is the largest of Stralsund's three redbrick Gothic churches. With 4,000 pipes and intricate decorative figures, the magnificent 17th-century Stellwagen organ (played only during Sunday services) is a delight to see and hear. The view from the church tower of Stralsund's old city center is well worth climbing the 349 steps to the top. ⊠ *Neuer Markt, entrance at Bleistr.* ☎ *03831/ 293–529* ⊠ *Tour of church tower €2* ⊙ *May–Oct., weekdays 9–6, weekends 10–noon; Nov.–Apr., weekdays 10–noon, 2–6, weekends 10–noon.*

Where to Stay & Eat

★ **¢–$$** ✕ **Wulflamstuben.** This restaurant is on the ground floor of Wulflamhaus, a 14th-century gabled house on the old market square. Steaks and fish are the specialty; in late spring or early summer, get the light and tasty *Ostseeflunder* (grilled plaice), fresh from the North Sea. In winter, the hearty *Stralsunder Aalsuppe* (Stralsund eel soup) is a must. ⊠ *Alter Markt 5* ☎ *03831/291–533* ⚠ *Reservations essential* ▭ *AE, DC, MC, V.*

¢–$ ✕ **Zum Alten Fritz.** It's worth the trip here just to see the rustic interior and copper brewing equipment. Good, old German beer and ale of all shades are the main focus. In summer the beer garden gets somewhat rambunctious. ⊠ *Greifswalder Chaussee 84–85, at B–96a* ☎ *03831/ 255–500* ▭ *MC, V.*

★ **$$–$$$** 🏨 **Dorint im HanseDom.** This ultramodern hotel, part of Germany's Dorint chain, makes up for a lack of historic ambience with winning amenities and great hospitality at an unbeatable price. The high-rise hotel doesn't look very appealing at first glance, but the spacious rooms (featuring many extras such as a baby bed, satellite TV, and a work desk) are furnished in bright colors and ensure a most pleasant stay. The biggest attraction, the hotel's Vital Spa, is a huge wellness facility and one of the best complexes to be found in northern Germany. ⊠ *Grünhofer Bogen, D–18437* ☎ *03831/37730* 🖷 *03831/377–3100* ⊕ *www. dorint.de* 🛏 *106 rooms, 8 suites* ⚹ *Restaurant, room service, in-room safes, minibars, cable TV, 5 pools (4 indoor), sauna, spa, bar, dry cleaning, laundry service, meeting rooms, parking (fee), some pets allowed (fee), no-smoking rooms* ▭ *AE, DC, MC, V* ⦿ *BP.*

★ **$$** ⊞ **Hotel zur Post.** This redbrick hotel is a great deal for travelers who want to enjoy a homey yet first-class ambience. It's on the market square near the Old Town. The hotel's interior is a thoughtful mix of traditional North German furnishings and modern design. ⊠ *Am Neuen Markt, Tribseerstr. 22, D–18439* ☎ *03831/200–500* 🖷 *03831/200–510* ⊕ *www.hotel-zur-post-stralsund.de* ⟿ *104 rooms, 2 suites, 8 apartments* ⌂ *Restaurant, room service, in-room safes, minibars, cable TV, sauna, bar, dry cleaning, laundry service, meeting room, parking (fee), some pets allowed (fee), no-smoking rooms; no a/c* ⊟ *AE, V* ⍾ *BP.*

$ ⊞ **Norddeutscher Hof.** Don't let the weathered facade fool you; this hotel was completely renovated a few years ago. Unfortunately, the lobby and restaurant were not as tastefully redecorated as the guest rooms. Still, you get the basics at a fair price. ⊠ *Neuer Markt 22, D–18439* ☎ *03831/293–161* 🖷 *03831/287–939* ⊕ *www.nd-hof.de* ⟿ *13 rooms* ⌂ *Cable TV, free parking, some pets allowed (fee); no a/c* ⊟ *AE, MC, V* ⍾ *BP.*

$ ⊞ **Schlosspark-Hotel Hohendorf.** Set among the lovely marshlands north of Stralsund and now an elegant country hotel, the historic Schloss Hohendorf was designed by famous Prussian architect Karl Friedrich Schinkel in the late 18th century. Stralsund, the island of Rügen, and all beaches are easily accessibly by car. The rooms are on the small side, but their plush carpets, carved beds, and fine furniture try to re-create the old world elegance that was typical for this kind of rural palace. ⊠ *Hohendorf, D–18445 Hohendorf at Stralsund* ☎ *038323/2500* 🖷 *038323/25061* ⊕ *www.schlosspark-hotel-hohendorf.de* ⟿ *43 rooms, 8 suites* ⌂ *Restaurant, outdoor café, room service, cable TV, massage, sauna, bicycles, babysitting, dry cleaning, laundry service, meeting rooms, some pets allowed (fee); no a/c* ⊟ *AE, MC, V* ⍾ *BP.*

Nightlife

Bar Hemingway (⊠ Tribseerstr. 22 ☎ 03831/200–500) lures a thirtysomething clientele with the best cocktails in town. A young crowd dances at **Fun und Lollipop** (⊠ Grünhofer Bogen 11–14 ☎ 03831/399–039). For a genuine old harbor *Kneipe* (tavern), head to the **Kuttel Daddeldu** (⊠ Hafenstr. on Hafeninsel ☎ 03831/299–526).

Shopping

Buddelschiffe (ships in a bottle) are a symbol of the magnificent sailing history of this region. They look easy to build, but they aren't, and they're quite delicate. Expect to pay more than €70 for a 1-liter bottle. Also look for *Fischerteppiche* (fisherman's carpets). Eleven square feet of these traditional carpets take 150 hours to create, which explains why they're meant only to be hung on the wall—and why they cost from €260 to €1,200. They're decorated with traditional symbols of the region, such as the mythical griffin.

Rügen Island

🔟 *4 km (2½ mi) northeast of Stralsund on Rte. 96.*

Fodor'sChoice
★

Rügen's diverse and breathtaking landscapes have inspired poets and painters for more than a century. Railways in the mid-19th century brought the first vacationers, and many of the grand mansions and villas on the island date from this period. The island's main route runs between the **Grosser Jasmunder Bodden** (Big Jasmund Inlet), a giant sea inlet, and a smaller expanse of water, the **Kleiner Jasmunder Bodden** (Little Jasmund Inlet Lake), to the port of Sassnitz. You're best off staying at any of the island's four main vacation centers—Sassnitz, Binz, Sellin, and Göhren.

Bergen

⑰ *34 km (21 mi) northeast of Stralsund on Rte. 96.*

Bergen, the island's administrative capital, was founded as a Slavic settlement some 900 years ago. The **Marienkircke** (St. Mary's Church) has geometric murals dating back to the late 1100s and painted brick octagonal pillars. The pulpit and altar are baroque. Outside the front door and built into the church facade is a grave from the 1200s.

off the beaten path　　**HIDDENSEE –** Off the northwest corner of Rügen is a smaller island called Hiddensee. The undisturbed solitude of this sticklike island has attracted such visitors as Albert Einstein, Thomas Mann, Rainer Maria Rilke, and Sigmund Freud. As Hiddensee is an auto-free zone, leave your car in Schaprode, 21 km (13 mi) west of Bergen, and take a ferry. Vacation cottages and restaurants are on the island.

Kap Arkona

⑱ *21 km (13 mi) northwest of Stubbenkammer.*

Kap Arkona has a lighthouse marking the northernmost point in eastern Germany, and you can see the Danish island of Moen from a restored watchtower next door. The blustery sand dunes of Kap Arkona are a nature lover's paradise.

Sassnitz

⑲ *25 km (16 mi) northeast of Bergen on Rte. 96.*

From Sassnitz, where ferries run to Sweden, walk into **Jasmund Nationalpark** (⊕ www.nationalpark-jasmund.de) to stare in awe at the Königstuhl cliffs. For information about the park, contact the Sassnitz tourist office.

⑳ Ten kilometers (6 mi) north of Sassnitz are the twin chalk cliffs of Rügen's main attraction, the **Stubbenkammer** headland, on the east coast of the island. From here you can best see the much-photographed chalk cliffs called the **Königstuhl,** rising 351 feet from the sea. A steep trail leads down to a beach.

en route　　Near the town of Binz is the **Jagdschloss Granitz,** a hunting lodge built in 1836 by Karl Friedrich Schinkel. It stands on the highest point of East Rügen and offers a splendid view in all directions from its lookout tower. It also has an excellent hunting exhibit. ⊠ *Binz* ☎ *038393/2263* 🖃 *€3* ☽ *May–Sept., daily 9–6; Oct.–Apr., Tues.–Sun. 10–4.*

Putbus
㉑ *59 km (37 mi) southeast of Kap Arkona, 8 km (5 mi) south of Bergen.*

The heart of the community is the **Circus,** a round central plaza dating back to the early 19th century. The immaculate white buildings surrounding the Circus give the city its nickname, Weisse Stadt (White City). In summer the blooming roses in front of the houses (once a requirement by the ruling noble family of Putbus) are truly spectacular.

Lovers of old watches and clocks should not miss the tiny **Uhrenmuseum Putbus,** where watchmaker Franz Sklorz showcases a historic collection of more than 600 clocks, watches, musical gadgets, and more. You might catch him at work. ⊠ *Alleestr. 13* ☎ *038301/60988* ⊡ *€3* ⊙ *Apr.–Nov., daily 10–6; Dec.–Mar., daily 11–4.*

From Putbus you can take a ride on the 90-year-old miniature steam train, the **Rasender Roland** (Racing Roland), which runs 24 km (16 mi) to Göhren, at the southeast corner of the Rügen. Trains leave hourly; the ride takes 70 minutes one way. ⊠ *Binzer Str. 12* ☎ *038301/8010* ⊕ *www.rasender-roland.de* ⊡ *€8* ⊙ *Apr.–Oct., daily 5:30* AM*–10:15* PM *from Putbus. Nov.–Mar., same hrs but trains depart only every 2 hrs.*

Where to Stay & Eat
★ **$-$$** ✕ **Nautilus.** The quirky maritime interior is reminiscent of Captain Nemo's fantasy ship, *Nautilus.* An odd mixture of ship and submarine paraphernalia, the Nautilus is jammed with equipment ranging from a deep-diving suit to a periscope. Traditional island food offerings include *Pfefferhering mit Bratkartoffeln* (pepper herring with home fries). ⊠ *Neukamp, Putbus* ☎ *038301/830* ⊟ *AE, MC, V* ⊙ *Closed Mon.*

$$-$$$ ✕🏠 **Hotel Kurhaus Binz.** The grand old lady of the Baltic Sea, the neoclassicist 19th-century Kurhaus Binz, is reviving the splendor of times past, when Binz was called the Nice of the North. The five-star Kurhaus is right on the beach, with a breathtaking sea view in most of the spacious and elegantly furnished rooms. The huge Egyptian-theme spa and wellness area is a real treat. Of the two restaurants, the Kurhaus-Restaurant is the better choice—it serves traditional seafood but adds exotic touches with special fusion-cuisine events. ⊠ *Strandpromenade 27, D–18609 Binz-Rügen* ☎ *038393/6650* 🖷 *038393/665–555* ⊕ *www. tc-hotels.de* ⇱ *106 rooms, 20 suites* ⅋ *2 restaurants, room service, in-room data ports, minibars, cable TV with movies, indoor-outdoor pool, health club, massage, sauna, spa, beach, bar, cabaret, babysitting, dry cleaning, laundry service, concierge, meeting rooms, parking (fee), some pets allowed (fee), no-smoking floor* ⊟ *AE, DC, MC, V* ⧊⧉ *BP.*

$-$$ ✕🏠 **Hotel Godewind.** Two hundred yards from the beaches of Hiddensee that have so inspired writers, this small hotel offers food and lodging at very reasonable prices. In addition, the hotel rents small cottages and apartments around the island, which are a good value if you intend to stay for more than a few days. Godewind's restaurant ($$) is known on the island for its regional dishes. ⊠ *Süderende 53, D–18565 Vitte-Hiddensee* ☎ *038300/6600* 🖷 *038300/660–222* ⊕ *www.hotelgodewind. de* ⇱ *23 rooms, 19 cottages* ⅋ *Restaurant, some pets allowed (fee); no a/c, no room TVs* ⊟ *No credit cards* ⧊⧉ *BP.*

★ **$$** ✕🏨 **Vier Jahreszeiten.** This first-class beach resort is a sophisticated blend of historic seaside architecture and modern elegance. Behind the ornamental white facade, the hotel boasts spacious rooms, decorated with 19th-century reproduction furniture, as well as more-secluded apartments. A great plus is the nearly 6,000-square-foot spa and wellness center, one of the best in Mecklenburg-Pomerania. ⊠ *Zeppelinstrasse 8, D–18609 Binz-Rügen* ☎ *038393/500* 🖷 *038393/50430* ⊕ *www.jahreszeiten-hotels.de* ➝ *69 rooms, 7 suites, 77 apartments* ⚷ *3 restaurants, room service, in-room data ports, minibars, cable TV with movies, indoor-outdoor pool, health club, massage, sauna, spa, bar, babysitting, dry cleaning, laundry service, concierge, meeting rooms, parking (fee), some pets allowed (fee), no-smoking floor* ⊟ *AE, DC, MC, V* ℍ *BP.*

$$ 🏨 **Hotel Loev.** The Loev, set in a great white building at the promenade in Binz, looks very much like a Victorian seaside resort. The spacious rooms are quite modern, with dark-wood furniture, thick carpets, and a wonderful view of the sea. ⊠ *Hauptstr. 20–22, D–18609 Binz-Rügen* ☎ *038393/390* 🖷 *038393/39444* ⊕ *www.loev.de* ➝ *74 rooms, 4 apartments* ⚷ *2 restaurants, in-room safes, minibars, cable TV, gym, sauna, bar, parking (fee), some pets allowed (fee); no a/c* ⊟ *AE, MC, V* ℍ *BP.*

★ **$** 🏨 **Hotel Villa Granitz.** The little town of Baabe claims to have Rügen Island's most beautiful beach. This mostly wooden mansion is a small and quiet retreat for those who want to avoid the masses in the island's other resorts. All rooms are spacious and have a large terrace or balcony; pastel colors (a soft white and yellow) add to the tidy, fairy-tale look of the building. The apartments have small kitchenettes. ⊠ *Birkenallee 17, D–18586 Baabe* ☎ *038303/1410* 🖷 *038303/14144* ⊕ *www.villa-granitz.de* ➝ *44 rooms, 8 suites, 12 apartments* ⚷ *Refrigerators, cable TV, dry cleaning, laundry service, free parking, some pets allowed (fee), no-smoking rooms; no a/c* ⊟ *No credit cards* ℍ *BP.*

★ **$** 🏨 **Villa Seestern.** This cozy yet stately mansion is just a stone's throw from the beach. Many of the simply but contemporarily furnished rooms are a true bargain, on account of both the low rates and the terrific views from the private balconies. Equally inviting is the Fisch-Brasserie Seestern, with a pierlike extension leading to the water. ⊠ *Mühlenstr. 5, D–18546 Sassnitz* ☎ *038392/33257* 🖷 *038392/36765* ➝ *14 rooms* ⚷ *Restaurant, cable TV, free parking, some pets allowed (fee), no-smoking rooms; no a/c* ⊟ *MC* ℍ *BP.*

Shopping

At the end of the 19th century, 16 pieces of 10th-century Viking jewelry were discovered on the Baltic coastline (presently housed in the Kulturhistorisches Museum in Stralsund). Gold and silver replicas of the **Hiddensee Golden Jewelry** are a great souvenir, and their distinctive patterns are found in shops on Rügen Island and on Hiddensee Island.

Water Sports

Equipment for windsurfing, sailing, surfing (although the waves here are modest), and pedal-boat riding is available for hire at the beach resorts. If you have difficulty locating what you want, contact the local tourist offices. The best-protected area along the coast for sailing is **Grosser Jasmunder Bodden**, a huge bay on Rügen Island. Boats for the bay can be hired at Lietzow and Ralswiek.

Greifswald

㉒ *64 km (40 mi) southeast of Putbus, 32 km (20 mi) southeast of Stralsund on Rte. 96.*

Greifswald is the birthplace of two great German artists—Caspar David Friedrich (1774–1840), the painter of German romanticism, and Wolfgang Koeppen (1906–96), one of the country's most important postwar novelists. Last in the string of Hanseatic ports on the Baltic Coast, Greifswald lost some of its prominence during the 19th century, when larger ships couldn't negotiate the shallow Ryck River leading to the sea. Three churches shape the silhouette of the city. The 13th-century **Dom St. Nikolai** (St. Nicholas's Cathedral), at the start of Martin-Luther-Strasse, is a neo-Gothic and Romantic church with an impressive view from its 300-foot-high tower. ⊠ *Domstr.* ☎ *03834/2627* ⊴ *Free* ☉ *May–Oct., Mon.–Sat. 10–4, Sun. 10:30–1; Nov.–Apr., Mon.–Sat. 11–3, Sun. 11:30–1.*

The 14th-century **Marienkirche** (St. Mary's Church), the oldest surviving church in Greifswald, has remarkable 60-foot-high arches and a striking four-corner tower. ⊠ *Friedrich-Loeffler-Str. 68 at Brüggstr.* ☎ *03834/2263* ☉ *June–Nov., weekdays 10–5.*

Splendid redbrick Gothic houses border the **Marktplatz.** The medieval Rathaus, rebuilt in 1738–50 following a fire, was modified during the 19th century and again in 1936. Its heavy doors bear a quote from Bertolt Brecht.

The **Pommersches Landesmuseum** (Pommeranian State Museum) showcases the development of European romantic painters and focuses on works by Caspar David Friedrich such as *Ruine Eldena im Riesengebirge* (Eldene Ruins in the Riesengebirge) and *Greifswalder Marktplatz* (Greifswald Market Square). Other works of art in the gallery include Dutch painters of Friedrich's time. ⊠ *Mühlenstr. 15* ☎ *03834/83120* ⊕ *www.pommersches-landesmuseum.de* ⊴€3 ☉ *May–Oct., Tues.–Sun. 10–6; Nov.–Apr., Tues.–Sun. 10–5.*

㉓ In the suburb of **Eldena** stand the ruins of a 12th-century Zisterzenserkloster (Cistercian monastery). The Gothic monastery was made famous in a painting by Caspar David Friedrich (now at Schloss Charlottenburg's Gallery of Romanticism in Berlin).

Where to Stay & Eat

$ ✕▥ **Alter Speicher.** Its broad selection of delectable grilled items and its wine list have brought this comfortable steak and fish restaurant ($–$$$) regional renown. It also offers small but modern guest rooms; all have private baths. The Alter Speicher is on the edge of the old city center. ⊠ *Rossmühlenstr. 25, D–17489* ☎ *03834/77700* 🖷 *03834/777–077* ⊕ *www.alter-speicher.de* ➳ *14 rooms* ⚖ *Restaurant, cable TV, free parking, some pets allowed (fee); no a/c* ⊟ *MC, V* ⎛◎⎠ *BP.*

$ ▥ **Best Western Hotel Greifswald.** The rooms' decor—curtains, bedspreads, and lamp shades covered in stripes and flowers—stands out from the American southwestern–style palette and patterns common in chain hotels of this region. The hotel's plainly modern design isn't atmospheric, but there are modern amenities, a convenient location, and a

helpful staff. ⌧ *Hans-Beimler-Str. 1–3, D–17491* ☎ *03834/8010*
🖷 *03834/801–100* ⊕ *www.bestwestern-hotel-greifswald.de* 🛏 *51
rooms, 4 apartments* ⚥ *Restaurant, room service, minibars, cable TV,
gym, hair salon, sauna, bar, meeting room, free parking, some pets allowed (fee), no-smoking rooms; no a/c* ▤ *AE, DC, MC, V* ¶ⓞ¶ *BP.*

$ 🖭 **Hotel Maria.** The facilities at this small hotel are clean and up-to-date,
and the friendly service is what you'd hope for from a family-owned
place. The hotel is right on the harbor; the terrace is the perfect place
to linger over a drink while watching the panorama of sailboats. ⌧ *Dorfstr. 45, D–17493* ☎ *03834/841–426* 🖷 *03834/840–136* ⊕ *www.hotel-
maria.de* 🛏 *10 rooms, 1 suite, 1 apartment* ⚥ *Restaurant, cable TV,
free parking, some pets allowed; no a/c* ▤ *MC, V* ¶ⓞ¶ *BP.*

Usedom Island

❷④ On its seaboard side, 40-km-long (25-mi-long) **Usedom Island** has almost
32 km (20 mi) of sandy shoreline and a string of resorts. Much of the
island's untouched landscape is a nature preserve that provides refuge
for a number of rare birds, including the giant sea eagle, which has a
wingspan of up to 8 feet. Even in the summer this island is more or less
deserted and is ready to be explored by bicycle. Bikes can usually be rented
for around €4–€6 a day and about €30 a week.

Wolgast
32 km (20 mi) southeast of Greifswald on Rte. 109, then Rte. 111.

Wolgast is at the causeway that crosses to the island of Usedom. The
bridge closes at times to allow boats to pass through, so if you have time
to spare, Wolgast has some worthwhile sights. **Rathausplatz** (Town Hall
Square) holds a baroque Rathaus and a mid-17th-century half-timber
house known as the Kaffeemühle (Coffee Mill). The **Kaffeemühle**, far from
just serving coffee, contains a charming local history museum.
⌧ *Rathauspl. 6* ☎ *03836/203–041* 🖾 *€3* ⊙ *June–Aug., Tues.–Fri.
10–6, weekends 10–4; Sept.–May, weekdays 10–5, Sat. 10–2.*

The massive redbrick Gothic **St. Petri Kirche** (St. Peter's Church) sits on
the highest point of the Old Town. The church has copies of Holbein's
series of paintings, *Totentanz* (Dance of Death). ⌧ *Kirchpl. 7* ☎ *03836/
202–269* 🖾 *Tower €1.60* ⊙ *May–Oct., weekdays 10–12:30 and 1:30–5.*

Navigating and parking a car can be tricky on these small streets. You
might want to rent a bike at **Fahrrad-Pank** (⌧ *Bahnhofsstr. 42* ☎ *03836/
202–652).*

Peenemünde
16 km (10 mi) north of Wolgast.

At the northern end of Usedom Island is Peenemünde, the launch site
of the world's first jet rockets, the V1 and V2, developed by Germany
toward the end of World War II and mostly fired at London. You can
view these rockets as well as models of early airplanes and ships at the
extensive **Historisch-Technisches Informationszentrum** (Historical-Techni-
cal Information Center), housed in a former army power plant. The ethics
of scientific research are also examined. One exhibit covers the secret

underground plants where most of the rocket parts were assembled and where thousands of slave laborers died. Explanation of the exhibits in English are available. ✉ *Im Kraftwerk* ☎ *038371/5050* 🎫 *€5* 🕐 *Apr.–Oct., Tues.–Sun. 9–6; Nov.–Mar., Tues.–Sun. 10–4.*

Ahlbeck

46 km (29 mi) southeast of Peenemünde on Rte. 111.

Ahlbeck, one of the best resorts on Usedom and the island's main town, has an attractive 19th-century wooden pier with a restaurant. Ahlbeck's promenade is lined with brightly painted turn-of-the-20th-century villas, many of which are now small hotels. If you stroll along the beach to the east, you'll arrive at the Polish border. Bike along the shaded seaside pathway to the other nearby resorts, Heringsdorf and Bansin. **Fahrradverleih Willerts** (✉ Lindenstr. 88 ☎ 038378/30092) rents bikes year-round. **Fahrradverleih Oberländer** (✉ Am Bahnhof 1 ☎ 038378/31684) rents bikes at the train station. In Bansin, **Fahrradverleih SG Medizin Bansin** (✉ Waldstr. 5, at Bansin tennis courts ☎ 038378/22529) rents bikes between April and November.

Where to Stay & Eat

¢–$$ ✕ **Seebrücke.** Perched on pilings over the Baltic, the Sea Bridge is in the historic center of Ahlbeck. The emphasis is on seafood such as *Ahlbecker Fischkartoffeln*, hearty potatoes served with smoked trout fillets, but also includes other choices like tender fillet of lamb. You can also take in the view over coffee and a delectable piece of cake. ✉ *Dünenstr., Ahlbeck* ☎ *038378/28320* 🍴 *AE, MC, V* 🕐 *Closed Jan.*

¢–$ ✕ **Café Asgard.** A visit here is a step back into the 1920s, when this restaurant first opened its doors. You'll dine amid silk wallpaper, potted plants, crisp white napery, and fresh flowers. The Asgard is open all day, so you can stop by between mealtimes for a homemade pastry. ✉ *Strandpromenade 15, Bansin* ☎ *038378/29488* 🍴 *No credit cards.*

$$–$$$ ✕📷 **Romantik Seehotel Ahlbecker Hof.** This first-class resort lacks the coziness of Usedom's other hotels but is undoubtedly one of the region's best and has been meticulously restored to imperial glamour. The baths in the guest rooms are luxurious, and there's a fantastic wellness-and-pool area. A real draw is the hotel's *Kleopatrabad,* a Turkish steam bath. The restaurant ($$$–$$$$) serves some of the finest seafood along the Baltic coastline. ✉ *Dünenstr. 47, D–17419 Ahlbeck* ☎ *038378/620* 🖨 *038378/62100* 🌐 *www.seetel.de* 🛏 *45 rooms, 24 suites* ♿ *Restaurant, room service, in-room safes, minibars, cable TV, 18-hole golf course, pool, gym, hair salon, massage, sauna, Turkish bath, bicycles, bar, dry cleaning, laundry service, meeting room, parking (fee), some pets allowed (fee); no a/c* 🍴 *AE, MC, V* 🍽 *BP.*

$$ ✕📷 **Ringhotel Ahlbeck Ostseehotel.** Generations of families have stayed at this snug, if slightly dated, hotel spread in four 19th-century villas each with a different name: Strandschloss, Möwe, Ostseeresidenz, and Ostseehotel, on Ahlbeck's promenade. Rooms are airy but modestly furnished, and most have a view of the sea. The restaurant ($–$$$) serves hearty, though standard, local dishes. ✉ *Dünenstr. 41, D–17419 Ahlbeck* ☎ *038378/600* 🖨 *038378/60100* 🌐 *www.ostseehotel.de* 🛏 *86 rooms, 32 apartments* ♿ *Restaurant, room service, cable TV, pool, sauna, bi-*

cycles, bar, parking (fee), some pets allowed (fee), no-smoking rooms; no a/c ▤ AE, MC, V ⃝ BP.

$ ✕▦ **Romantik Strandhotel Atlantic.** This small but elegant hotel once served as an intimate summer retreat for Berlin's rich and beautiful. Owing to the 40 years of separation, this tradition came to an end. But today, the upscale restaurant ($$–$$$$) and the lavishly decorated guest rooms—all with venerable 19th-century glamour—have once again made this hotel one of the island's best (and most coveted). ✉ *Strand-promenade 18, D–17429 Bansin* ☎ *038378/605* 🖷 *038378/60600* ⊕ *www.romantikhotels.com* ⤷ *24 rooms, 2 suites* ⚴ *Restaurant, room service, in-room safes, minibars, bicycles, bar, pub, dry cleaning, laundry service, meeting room, parking (fee); no a/c* ▤ *AE, MC, V* ⃝ *BP.*

SCHLESWIG-HOLSTEIN & THE BALTIC COAST A TO Z

To research prices, get advice from other travelers, and book travel arrangements, visit www.fodors.com.

AIR TRAVEL

The international airport closest to Schleswig-Holstein is in Hamburg. For an eastern approach to the Baltic Coast tour, use Berlin's Tegel Airport.

BOAT & FERRY TRAVEL

The Weisse Flotte (White Fleet) line operates ferries linking the Baltic ports, as well as short harbor and coastal cruises. Boats depart from Warnemünde, Zingst (to Hiddensee), Sassnitz, and Stralsund. In addition, ferries run from Stralsund and Sassnitz to destinations in Sweden, Denmark, Poland, and Finland.

Scandlines operates ferries between Sassnitz and the Danish island of Bornholm as well as Sweden.

🚩 **Scandlines** ☎ 01805/72263–54637 ⊕ www.scandlines.de. **Weisse Flotte** ☎ 0180/321–2120 central phone, 03831/268–138 for Warnemünde, 03831/26810 for Stralsund, 038392/57854 for Sassnitz, 0385/557–770 for Schwerin.

BUS TRAVEL

Local buses link the main train stations with outlying towns and villages, especially the coastal resorts. Buses operate throughout Sylt, Rügen, and Usedom islands.

CAR RENTAL

🚩 **Avis** ✉ Willy-Brandt-Allee 6, Lübeck ☎ 0451/71611 ✉ Grubenstr. 29, Rostock ☎ 0381/202–1170 ✉ Wittenburgerstr. 120, Schwerin ☎ 0385/761–000 ✉ Am Flughafen, Westerland, Sylt ☎ 04651/23734. **Hertz** ✉ Willy-Brandt-Allee 1, Lübeck ☎ 0451/702–250 ✉ Röverzhagener Chaussee 5, Rostock ☎ 0381/683–065 ✉ Schwerinerstr. 31, Wismar ☎ 03841/703–259 ✉ Bremsweg 1, Schwerin ☎ 0385/487–5555. **InterrentEuropcar** ✉ Esso-Station am Bahnhof Westerland, Sylt ☎ 04651/7178.

CAR TRAVEL

The two-lane roads (Bundesstrassen) along the coast can be full of traffic during June, July, and August. The ones leading to Usedom Island can be extremely log-jammed, as the causeway bridges have scheduled closings to let ships pass. Using the Bundesstrassen takes more time, but these often tree-lined roads are by far more scenic than the Autobahn.

Sylt island is 196 km (122 mi) from Hamburg via Autobahn A–7 and Bundesstrasse 199 and is ultimately reached via train. B–199 cuts through some nice countryside, and instead of A–7 or B–76 between Flensburg, Schleswig, and Kiel, you could take the slow route through the coastal hinterland (B–199, 203, 503). Lübeck, the gateway to Mecklenburg-Vorpommern, is 56 km (35 mi) from Hamburg via A–1. B–105 leads to all sightseeing spots in Mecklenburg-Vorpommern. From Stralsund, Route 96 cuts straight across Rügen Island, a distance of 51 km (32 mi). From Berlin take A–11 and head toward Prenzlau for B–109 all the way to Usedom Island, a distance of 162 km (100 mi). A causeway connects the mainland town of Anklam to the town of Usedom, on Usedom Island.

TOURS

Although tourist offices and museums have worked to improve the quality and amount of English-language literature about this area, English-speaking tours are infrequent and must be requested ahead of time through the local tourist office. Because most tours are designed for groups, there's usually a flat fee of €20–€30. Towns currently offering tours are Lübeck, Stralsund, and Rostock. Schwerin has two-hour boat tours of its lakes.

Tours of Old Lübeck depart daily from the tourist offices on the Alter Markt between mid-April and mid-October and on weekends only from mid-October to mid-April. Harbor and coastal cruises also operate from Lübeck; contact the Lübeck tourist office for details.

Many of the former fishermen in these towns give sunset tours of the harbors or shuttle visitors between neighboring towns. This is a unique opportunity to ride on an authentic fishing boat. In Flensburg, Kiel, Rostock, and on Sylt, cruise lines make short trips through the respective bays and/or islands off the coast, sailing even as far as Denmark and Sweden. Inquire at the local tourist office about companies and times, as well as about fishing-boat tours.

TRAIN TRAVEL

Train travel is much more convenient than bus travel in this area. Sylt, Kiel, Lübeck, Schwerin, and Rostock have InterCity train connections to either Hamburg, Berlin, or both.

A north–south train line links Schwerin and Rostock. An east–west route connects Kiel, Hamburg, Lübeck, and Rostock, and some trains continue through to Stralsund and Sassnitz, on Rügen Island. Train service between the smaller cities of former East Germany is generally much slower than in the west.

Trains are the *only* way to access Sylt, which is connected to the mainland via the train causeway Hindenburgdamm. Deutsche Bahn will transport you and your car from central train stations at Dortmund, Düsseldorf, Hamburg, Stuttgart, and Frankfurt directly onto the island. In addition, a daily-shuttle car train leaves Niebüll roughly every 30 minutes from 5:20 AM to 8:45 PM (Friday and Sunday until 9:35 PM). There are no reservations on this train.

Villages and towns on Usedom island are linked by the Usedomer Bäderbahn, whose trains operate between Ahlbeck and Peenemünde as well as between Zinnowitz and Züssow on the mainland. For day excursions, taking the train makes sense to avoid the heavy summertime traffic.
🚆 **Niebüll shuttle car train** ☎ 04651/22561. **Usedomer Bäderbahn** ☎ 038378/27132 ⊕ www.ubb-online.de.

VISITOR INFORMATION

The regional tourism board for the Baltic Coast is the TOURBU-Zentrale, Landesfremdenverkehrsverband Mecklenburg-Vorpommern. When writing to any information office, address your letter to "Touristeninformation" and then add the city's name.

🚆 Baltic Coast Information **Bad Doberan** ✉ Goethestr. 1, D-18209 ☎ 038203/91530 🖶 038203/62154 ⊕ www.m-vp.de. **Greifswald** ✉ Schuhhagen 22, D-17489 ☎ 03834/521-380 🖶 03834/521-382 ⊕ www.greifswald.de. **Lübeck** ✉ Breite Str. 62 ☎ Beckergrube 95, D-23552 ☎ 0451/122-1909, 0451/122-8109 for cruises 🖶 0451/122-5419 ⊕ www.luebeck.de. **Rostock-Warnemünde** ✉ Neuer Markt 3, D-18055 ☎ 0381/548-000 🖶 0381/381-2601 ⊕ www.rostock.de. **Rügen Island** ✉ Tourismusverband Rügen, Am Markt 4, D-18528 Bergen ☎ 03838/80770 🖶 03838/254-440 ⊕ www.ruegen.de. **Sassnitz** ✉ Seestr. 1, D-18546 ☎ 038392/5160 🖶 038392/51616 ⊕ www.sassnitz.de. **Schwerin** ✉ Am Markt 10, D-19055 ☎ 0385/592-5212 🖶 0385/555-094 ⊕ www.schwerin.de. **Stralsund** ✉ Alter Markt 9, D-18439 ☎ 03831/24690 🖶 03831/246-949 ⊕ www.stralsund.de. TOURBU-**Zentrale, Landesfremdenverkehrsverband Mecklenburg-Vorpommern** ✉ Pl. der Freundschaft 1, D-18059 Rostock ☎ 0381/403-0500 🖶 0381/403-0555 ⊕ www.tmv.de. **Usedom Island** ✉ Tourismusverband Insel Usedom e.V., Bäderstr. 4, D-17459 Seebad Ückeritz ☎ 038375/23410 🖶 038375/23429 ⊕ www.usedom.de. **Wismar** ✉ Stadthaus, Am Markt 11, D-23966 ☎ 03841/19433 🖶 03841/251-3090 ⊕ www.wismar.de.

🚆 Schleswig-Holstein Information **Flensburg** ✉ Amalie-Lamp-Speicher, Speicherlinie 40, D-24937 ☎ 0461/23090 🖶 0461/17352 ⊕ www.flensburg.de. **Husum** ✉ Grossstr. 27, D-25813 ☎ 04841/89870 🖶 04841/898-790 ⊕ www.husum.de. **Kampen** ✉ Kurverwaltung, Hauptstr. 12, D-25999 ☎ 04651/46980 🖶 04651/469-860 ⊕ www.kampen.de. **Kiel** ✉ Sophienblatt 30, D-24103 ☎ 0431/679-100 🖶 0431/679-1099 ⊕ www.kiel.de. **Schleswig** ✉ Plessenstr. 7, D-24837 ☎ 04621/24878 🖶 04621/981-619 ⊕ www.schleswig.de. **Westerland** ✉ Strandstr. 33 ✉ Stephanstr. 6, Postfach 1260, D-25969 ☎ 04651/9980 🖶 04651/998-6000 ⊕ www.westerland.de.

BERLIN

15

Updated by
Christina
Knight

SINCE THE FALL OF THE IRON CURTAIN, no city in Europe has seen more development and change. Two Berlins that had been separated for 40 years struggled to meld into one, and in the scar of barren borderland between them sprang government and commercial centers that have become the glossy spreads of travel guides and architecture journals. After successfully uniting its own east and west, Berlin will play a pivotal role in a European Union that has undertaken the same task.

But even as the capital thinks and moves forward, history is always tugging at its sleeve. Between the wealth of neoclassical and 21st-century buildings, there are constant reminders, both subtle and stark, of the events of the 20th century. For every new embassy and relocated corporate headquarters, a church stands half-ruined, a synagogue is under 24-hour guard, and an empty lot remains where a building either crumbled in World War II or went up in dynamite as East Germany cleared a path for its Wall. In the chillier months, the scent of coal wafts through the trendy neighborhoods of Kreuzberg and Friedrichshain, where young residents who fuel the cultural scene heat their unrenovated apartments with coal ovens.

Much of what's new in Berlin is firmly rooted to history. A popular city view is from the stunning glass cupola atop the Reichstag, a 1999 crown upon an 1894 parliament building. The short walk from the Reichstag to the pristinely restored Brandenburg Gate, open only to pedestrians and bicyclists since 2002, passes a simple fence hung with white, wooden crosses. These are in memory of East Germans who were killed while trying to cross the Wall that ran between the gate and the Reichstag. One block south of the Brandenburg Gate and to be completed in May 2005 is a vast landscape of concrete stelae that make up the national Holocaust memorial, known as the Memorial to the Murdered Jews of Europe.

Compared to other German cities, Berlin is quite young and, ironically, began as two separate entities more than 760 years ago. The Spree River divided the slightly older Cölln on Museum Island from the fishing village Berlin. By the 1300s, Berlin was prospering thanks to its location at the intersection of important trade routes. After the ravages of the Thirty Years' War, Berlin rose to power as the seat of the Hohenzollern dynasty. The Great Elector Friedrich Wilhelm, in the almost 50 years of his reign (1640–88), touched off a renaissance by supporting such institutions as the Academy of Arts and the Academy of Sciences. Later, Frederick the Great (1712–1786) made Berlin and Potsdam his glorious centers of the enlightened yet autocratic Prussian monarchy.

In 1871, Prussia, ruled by the "Iron Chancellor" Count Otto von Bismarck, unified the many independent German states into the German Empire. Berlin maintained its status as capital for the duration of the German Empire (1871–1918), through the post–World War I Weimar Republic (1919–33), and also through Hitler's so-called Third Reich (1933–45). The city's golden years were the Roaring '20s, when Berlin, the energetic, modern, and sinful counterpart to Paris, became a center for the cultural avant-garde. World-famous writers, painters, and artists met here while the impoverished bulk of its 4 million inhabitants lived

15

If you have 2 days

Start in western, downtown Berlin by visiting the stark shell of the Kaiser-Wilhelm-Gedächtniskirche. Catch the double-decker public Bus 100 (in front of the Zoo railway station) and get a seat on top. The entire scenic ride through the park Tiergarten, past the Reichstag, along Unter den Linden, and around Alexanderplatz shows you the prime attractions in Berlin before doubling back again. Save a good amount of time and energy for the museums on Museum Island and the newly opened German History Museum. You can take a break with German cakes and coffee in the Opernpalais on Unter den Linden. The next day visit the dome of the Reichstag (to beat possible long lines, arrive at 8:20 AM or come in the early evening) and Potsdamer Platz, a study in urban renewal and modern architecture. Whatever order you do it in, walk along Ebertstrasse between the sights, as it takes you past the Brandenburg Gate and the Memorial to the Murdered Jews of Europe. Behind the showy corporate and commercial buildings of Potsdamer Platz is the Gemäldegalerie and Neue Nationalgalerie, two outstanding fine arts museums. From Potsdamer Platz it's also a 10-minute walk to the Topography of Terror, a free, open-air exhibit on the organizations of the SS and the Gestapo, their crimes, and their victims. The site is bordered by a remaining stretch of the Berlin Wall. Spend one evening meandering the smaller streets around Hackescher Markt in Mitte.

If you have 3 days

Follow the two-day itinerary above. After viewing the Topography of Terror, continue on to the Mauermuseum Haus am Checkpoint Charlie, which is open until 10 PM. On your third day, round out the sights and eras of history you've seen by visiting the royals' apartments in Schloss Charlottenburg and the lovely gardens behind it. After touring the palace, hop the U-7 subway from Richard-Wagner-Platz to Adenauerplatz. Head east and browse the most elegant of the Kurfürstendamm boutiques within old city mansions. Turn left on Bleibtreustrasse to reach the cafés and restaurants in the fashionable, but casual Savignyplatz area. Spend one evening at a variety show, perhaps at Chämeleon Varieté or Bar Jeder Vernunft.

If you have 5 days

A five-day visit allows you to spread the sights out at your leisure, linger at cafés, and dip into shops that catch your eye as you please. Follow the three-day itinerary above, then begin your fourth day in the district of Kreuzberg. See if the current exhibits at the Martin-Gropius-Bau interest you, or visit the Jüdisches Museum, where the architecture by Daniel Libeskind is a main draw. Before sunset, ride up to the observatory floor of Berlin's highest structure, the Berliner Fernsehturm (Television Tower). Spend your last day either visiting Potsdam, particularly the summer-palace grounds of Schloss Sanssouci, or cruising the Spree River and its canals on a three-hour boat tour. Narrations by the captains are in German, but you do get amazing views of the city and can quaff beer or coffee and snack as you go.

in heavily overpopulated quarters. This "dance on the volcano," as those years of political and economic upheaval have been called, came to a grisly and bloody end after January 1933, when Adolf Hitler became chancellor. The Nazis made Berlin their capital but ultimately failed to remodel the city into a silent monument to their power. By World War II's end, 70% of the city lay in ruins, with more rubble than in all other German cities combined.

Along with the division of Germany after World War II, Berlin was partitioned into American, British, and French zones in the west and a Soviet zone in the east. By 1947 Berlin had become one of the cold war's first testing grounds. The three western-occupied zones gradually merged, becoming West Berlin, while the Soviet-controlled eastern zone defiantly remained separate. Peace conferences repeatedly failed to resolve the question of Germany's division, and in 1949 the Soviet Union established East Berlin as the capital of its new puppet state, the German Democratic Republic (GDR). The division of the city was cruelly finalized in concrete in August 1961, when the East German government constructed the Berlin Wall, which separated families and friends.

For nearly 30 years Berlin suffered under one of the greatest geographic and political anomalies of all time, a city split in two by a concrete wall—its larger western half an island of capitalist democracy surrounded by an East Germany run by hard-line Communists. With the Wall relegated to the souvenir pile of history (most of it was recycled but it's still being sold off chip by chip to tourists), visitors can now appreciate the qualities that mark the city as a whole. Its particular charm has always lain in its spaciousness, its trees and greenery, and its anything-goes atmosphere. Moreover, the really stunning parts of the prewar capital are in the historic eastern part of town, which has grand avenues, monumental architecture, and museums that house world treasures. Berlin's further progress has been delayed by the city's bankruptcy. In 2001, the city-owned state bank nearly went bankrupt and forced the city government to resign. A staggering US$3 billion bank debt incurred by risky real estate deals in East Germany now has to be paid by the state. Unemployment in 2004 hit 19%, a level not seen since the 1930s.

Berlin is known for having the most international group of inhabitants in Germany, and its bristly natives are just as famous. Berliners' brash, witty, no-nonsense attitudes come across well with their piquant dialects. Whatever the bad press their bad moods might earn them, everyone knows Berlin is a city of "*Herz mit Schnauze*" (a big heart hidden behind every big mouth).

EXPLORING BERLIN

Berlin is laid out on an epic scale—western Berlin alone is four times the size of the city of Paris. When the city-state of Berlin was incorporated, it swallowed towns and villages far beyond the downtown area. Of its 12 boroughs, the five of most interest to visitors are Charlottenburg-Wilmersdorf in the west; Tiergarten (a district of the Mitte borough) and Kreuzberg in the center; Mitte, the historic core of the city

Eat Like a Local

Top-end restaurants can easily import their fresh ingredients from other European countries, but some also rely on the farmers close to home. Surrounding this city is the rural state of Brandenburg, whose name often comes before *Ente* (duck) on a menu. In spring, *Spargel*, white asparagus from Beelitz, is all the rage, showing up in soups and side dishes. Berlin's most traditional four-part meal is *Eisbein* (pork knuckle), always served with sauerkraut, puréed peas, and boiled potatoes. Other old-fashioned Berlin dishes include *Rouladen* (rolled stuffed beef), *Spanferkel* (suckling pig), *Berliner Schüsselsülze* (potted meat in aspic) and *Hackepeter* (ground beef). Since Berlin became the capital again in 1999, restaurants have increasingly offered other regional German cuisine to feed those who followed the federal government here from their home state.

15

Stands near subway stations sell spicy *Currywurst,* a chubby frankfurter served with tomato sauce made with curry and pepper. Turkish food is an integral part of the Berlin diet. On almost every street you'll find narrow storefronts selling *Döner kebab* (grilled lamb or chicken served with salad in a flat-bread pocket).

Museums

Visiting museums is a bargain in Berlin. At the world-class state museums, children under 16 receive free admission and a €6–€8 entrance fee for adults includes a free audio guide. All state museums are free during the four hours before closing on Thursday. With the moving of the Egyptian Museum from Charlottenburg to Museum Island in April 2005, the famous bust of Queen Nefertiti and other parts of the Egyptian collection joins the island's Greek and Roman antiquities, as well as superb monuments of Greek, Persian, and Roman architecture. The private Flick Collection, the most important and largest collection of contemporary art in the world, has begun a seven-year residency at the state museum Hamburger Bahnhof, which has doubled in size as a result. Berlin's other new collection is the Helmut Newton Stiftung, located just behind the central Zoo Station. The late fashion photographer Helmut Newton donated his works to the city of his birth shortly before his death in 2004.

Culture & Cocktails

Berlin is the only European city without official closing hours, so you can stretch your drinks until the wee hours of the morning without fear of a last call. Eastern districts Mitte, Prenzlauer Berg, and Friedrichshain have unusual, impromptu venues for parties and bars. The posher scenes tend to be in the west. Dance clubs don't get going until about 12:30 AM, but parties labeled "after-work" start as early as 8 PM for professionals looking to socialize during the week. Culture abounds between three opera houses, one of the world's leading philharmonic orchestras, innovative German theaters, and cabaret and variety shows.

in the eastern part of town; and Prenzlauer Berg in the northeast. South-west Berlin has lovely escapes in the secluded forests and lakes of the Grunewald area.

Many of the 16 Staatliche Museen zu Berlin (state museums of Berlin) are world-renowned and offer several ticket options (children under 17 are welcomed free of charge). A single ticket ranges €4–€8. An all-day pass (*Tageskarte*) to all state museums costs €10. The SchauLust Museen ticket (€12) allows entrance to all state museums plus many others for three consecutive days. State museums tend to cluster near one another and usually a single entrance ticket grants admission to all museums in that area. These areas include Charlottenburg (€6), Dahlem (€4), the Kulturforum (including the out-of-the-way Hamburger Bahnhof, €6), and Museum Island (€8). All these entrance tickets are for the permanent exhibitions and include an audio guide; special exhibits cost extra. State museums are free on Thursday during the last four hours of operation.

Numbers in the text correspond to numbers in the margin and on the Berlin map.

Kurfürstendamm & Western Downtown Berlin

Ku'damm is the easy-to-pronounce nickname for Kurfürstendamm, a broad, tree-lined boulevard that stretches for 3 km (2 mi) through the heart of western downtown. It developed in the late 19th century as wealthy Berliners moved out to the "New West." Shoppers are the lifeforce of the boulevard, with enough energy and euros to support the local boutiques on the quieter side streets, too. Out-of-towners take it easy at Ku'damm's sidewalk tables as Berliners bustle by with a purpose.

a good walk

The more elegant blocks of **Kurfürstendamm** ❶ ▶ lie east of Leibnizstrasse, where a solid block of haute couture shops in city mansions lead off a commercial strip that gives way to more affordable and sometimes mundane shops. Many bus lines serve the boulevard, so you can choose where to start your stroll, or if using the U-bahn, take the U-15 to Uhlandstrasse. The multimedia museum **Story of Berlin** ❷ lies within the shopping center Ku-damm-Karree near the corner of Uhlandstrasse. You can't miss it for the airplane wing exhibited outside. This was once part of a "Raisen bomber," a U.S. air force DC-3 that supplied Berlin during the Berlin Airlift in 1948 and '49. Continue two blocks west and turn right on Bleibtreustrasse, a street peppered with local stores and eateries. After passing under the S-bahn tracks, turn right into a pedestrian alley. Gift shops, eateries, and bookstores nest within the S-bahn's redbrick viaduct. To the left is Savignyplatz, a green square surrounded by cafés. Grolmanstrasse leads off in a diagonal to the right and will return you to the intersection of Ku'damm and Uhlandstrasse. Walk east on Ku'damm four long blocks toward the jagged steeple of the **Kaiser-Wilhelm-Gedächtniskirche** ❸ on Breitscheidplatz. Its ruined belltower stands as a reminder of World War II. The steps around this symbol of war's destructiveness was once a prime hangout in West Berlin.

Breitscheidplatz separates the church from the dowdy Europa Center mall. At the mall's Budapester Strasse entrance on the left, you'll find the **Tourist Info-Center** ❹. Opposite the tourist office is the Asian-style Elefantentor (Elephant Gate), the main entrance to the **Zoologischer Garten** ❺, western Berlin's zoo and aquarium. Walk back along Budapester Strasse, passing the ruined belltower and the bus and taxi stands at Zoo Station. After walking under the train trestle, turn right onto quiet Jebenstrasse. On the left side is the **Helmut Newton Stiftung** ❻, which exhibits the photography of native Berliner Helmut Newton. The museum opened in 2004, five months after the star photographer's death.

TIMING Allowing for at least one pop into a store, this walk will take about 50 minutes. Set aside three hours for the admirable zoo and aquarium—it has the most species in Europe. The Ku'damm is most crowded on Saturday, since stores are not open on Sunday.

What to See

❻ **Helmut Newton Stiftung.** The inheritance that brought the most honor to Berlin in 2004 consisted of 1,000 photographs from native son Helmut Newton (1920–2004), who had pledged the collection to the city months before his unexpected death. The man who defined fashion photography in the 1960s through 1980s was an apprentice to Yva, a Jewish fashion photographer in Berlin in the 1930s. Newton fled Berlin with his family in 1938 and his mentor was killed in a concentration camp. The photographs, now part of the state museum collection, will be shown on a rotating basis in the former art library behind the train station Zoologischer Garten. ⊠ *Jebenstr. 2, Western Downtown* ☎ *030/266–2951* ⊕ *www.smpk.de* ☒ *€6* ☉ *Tues.–Sun. 10–6* Ⓤ *Zoologischer Garten (U-bahn and S-bahn).*

★ ❸ **Kaiser-Wilhelm-Gedächtniskirche** (Kaiser Wilhelm Memorial Church). A dramatic reminder of World War II's destruction, the ruined bell tower is all that remains of the once massive church, which was completed in 1895 and dedicated to the emperor, Kaiser Wilhelm I. The Hohenzollern dynasty is depicted inside in a gilded mosaic, whose damage, like that of the building, will not be repaired. The exhibition revisits World War II's devastation throughout Europe. On the hour, the tower chimes out a melody composed by the last emperor's great-grandson, the late Prince Louis Ferdinand von Hohenzollern.

In stark contrast to the old bell tower (dubbed the Hollow Tooth), are the adjoining Memorial Church and Tower, designed by the noted German architect Egon Eiermann in 1959–61. These ultramodern octagonal structures, with their myriad honeycomb windows, have nicknames as well: the Lipstick and the Powder Box. Brilliant, blue stained-glass from Chartres dominates the interiors. Church music and organ concerts are presented in the church regularly. ⊠ *Breitscheidpl., Western Downtown* ☎ *030/218–5023* ⊕ *www.gedaechtniskirche.com* ☒ *Free* ☉ *Old Tower Mon.–Sat. 10–4, Memorial Church daily 9–7* Ⓤ *Zoologischer Garten (U-bahn and S-bahn).*

need a break? Forget the fast-food options at Zoo Station. Instead, follow the train tracks to the back of the taxi and bus queues, where you'll enter Tiergarten and within 100 meters come upon the best hideaway in

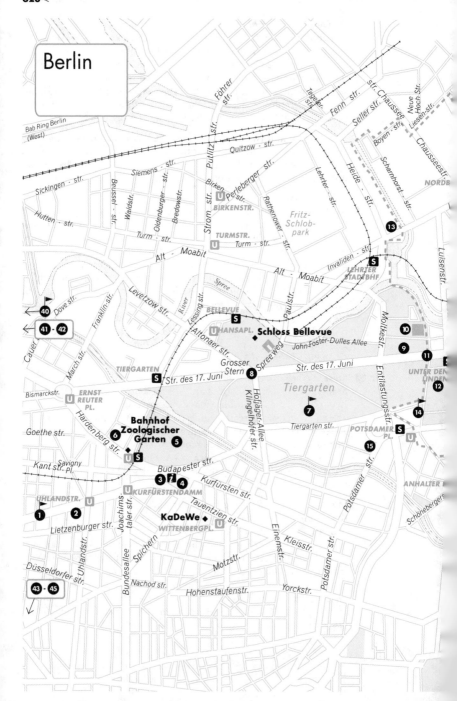

Kurfürstendamm & Western Downtown Berlin ▼

Helmut Newton Stiftung **6**

Kaiser-Wilhelm-Gedächtniskirche **3**

Kurfürstendamm **1**

The Story of Berlin **2**

Tourist Info-Center **4**

Zoologischer Garten . . . **5**

Tiergarten & the Government District ▼

Brandenburger Tor . . . **11**

Denkmal für die Ermordeten Juden Europas **12**

Hamburger Bahnhof, Museum für Gegenwart-Berlin **13**

Reichstag **10**

Siegessäule **8**

Sowjetisches Ehrenmal **9**

Tiergarten **7**

Potsdamer Platz & Kreuzberg ▼

Jüdisches Museum **19**

Kulturforum **15**

Martin-Gropius-Bau . . **16**

Mauermuseum-Museum Haus am Checkpoint Charlie **18**

Sony Center **14**

Topographie des Terrors **17**

Mitte: Unter den Linden to Alexanderplatz ▼

Alexanderplatz **34**

AquaDom & Sea Life Berlin **29**

Bebelplatz **23**

Berliner Dom **28**

Berliner Fernsehturm . **33**

Berliner Rathaus **31**

Deutsches Historisches Museum **25**

Friedrichstrasse **21**

Gendarmenmarkt **22**

Märkisches Museum **35**

Museumsinsel **26**

Neue Wache **24**

Nikolaiviertel **32**

Schlossplatz **27**

St. Marienkirche **30**

Unter den Linden **20**

Mitte's Scheunenviertel & Prenzlauer Berg ▼

Dokumentationszentrum Berliner Mauer **36**

Hackesche Höfe **38**

Kulturbrauerei **39**

Neue Synagoge **37**

Palaces, Parks & Museums in Outer Berlin ▼

Ägyptisches Museum **41**

Bildungs- und Gedenkstätte Haus der Wannsee-Konferenz . . **45**

Dahlemer Museen **43**

Grunewald **44**

Museum Berggruen . . . **42**

Schloss Charlottenburg **40**

KEY

▶ Start of walk

🇮 Tourist information

Ⓤ U-Bahn

Ⓢ S-Bahn

the area: **Schleusen Krug** (⊠ Tiergarten, Western Downtown ☎ 030/313–9909). In warmer weather you can order at the window and sit in the beer garden or on the back patio, watching pleasure ships go through the lock. Inside is a casual restaurant with a changing daily menu.

► ❶ **Kurfürstendamm.** This busy thoroughfare began as a riding path in the 16th century. The elector Joachim II of Brandenburg used it to travel between his palace on the Spree River and his hunting lodge in the Grunewald. The Kurfürstendamm (Elector's Causeway) was transformed into a major route in the late 19th century, thanks to the initiative of Bismarck, Prussia's Iron Chancellor.

Even in the 1920s, the Ku'damm was still relatively new and by no means elegant; it was fairly far removed from the old heart of the city, which was Unter den Linden in Mitte. The Ku'damm's prewar fame was due mainly to the rowdy bars and dance halls, which studded much of its length and its side streets. Almost half of its 245 late-19th-century buildings were completely destroyed in the 1940s, and the remaining buildings were damaged in varying degrees. As in most of western Berlin, what you see today is either restored or newly constructed. Some of the 1950s buildings have been replaced by high-rises, in particular at the corner of Kurfürstendamm and Joachimstaler Strasse.

🕑 ❷ **The Story of Berlin.** Eight hundred years of the city's history, from the first settlers casting their fishing poles to Berliners heaving sledgehammers at the Wall, are conveyed through hands-on exhibits, film footage, and multimedia devices in this unusual venue. The sound of footsteps over broken glass follows your path through the exhibit on the "*Kristallnacht*" pogrom, and to pass through the section on the Nazis' book-burning on Bebelplatz, you must walk over book bindings. Many original artifacts are on display, such as the stretch Volvo that served as Erich Honnecker's state carriage in East Germany. The eeriest relic is the 1974 nuclear shelter, which you can visit by guided tour on the hour. Museum placards are also in English. ⊠ *Ku'damm Karree, Kurfürstendamm 207–208, Western Downtown* ☎ *030/8872–0100* ⊕ *www.story-of-berlin.de* 🔂 *€9.30* ☽ *Daily 10–8; last entry at 6* Ⓤ *Uhlandstrasse (U-bahn).*

❹ **Tourist Info-Center.** Berlin Tourismus Marketing's main tourist office is hidden at the back of the Europa Center, a neon-lit shopping and business complex. This is the largest of the three info-centers, and staff can book tickets to performances and hotel rooms for you. There's a large selection of free leaflets and a larger section of souvenirs to buy. ⊠ *Budapester Str., Western Downtown* ☎ *030/250–025* ⊕ *www.berlin-tourist-information.de* ☽ *Mon.–Sat. 10–7, Sun. 10–6* Ⓤ *Zoologischer Garten (U-bahn and S-bahn).*

★ 🕑 ❺ **Zoologischer Garten** (Zoological Gardens). Germany's oldest zoo opened in 1844 and today holds more species than any other zoo in Europe. Home to more than 14,000 animals belonging to 1,500 different species, the zoo has been successful at breeding rare and endangered species. A baby gorilla, rhinocerous, camel, hippo, and kiwi bird arrived in early

2004. A baby elephant is due in summer 2005. Check the feeding times posted to watch creatures such as seals, apes, hippos, crocodiles, and pelicans during their favorite time of day. The animals' enclosures are designed to resemble their natural habitats, though some structures are ornate, such as the 1910 Arabian-style Zebra house. Pythons, frogs, turtles, invertebrates, and Komodo Dragons are part of the three-floor aquarium. ⊠ *Hardenbergpl. 8 and Budapester Str. 34, Western Downtown* ☎ *030/254–010* ⊕ *www.zoo-berlin.de* ⊠ *Zoo or aquarium €10, combined ticket €15* ☉ *Zoo Nov.–Feb., daily 9–5; Mar., daily 9–5:30; Apr.–Sept., daily 9–6:30; Oct., daily 9–6; aquarium daily 9–6* Ⓤ *Zoologischer Garten (U-bahn and S-bahn).*

Tiergarten & the Government District

The Tiergarten, a bucolic 630-acre park with lakes, meadows, and wide paths, is the "green lung" of Berlin. In the 17th century it served as the hunting grounds of the Great Elector. Now it's Berliners' backyard for sunbathing and barbecuing. Berlin's most fertile grounds for modern architecture—the government district, Potsdamer Platz, and the embassy district—ring the park from its eastern to southern edges. Many of the embassies have exhibitions open to the public, and Germany's parliament convenes beneath one of the city's most popular attractions: the glass dome of the Reichstag. Bordering Tiergarten and the government district is the meticulously restored Brandenburger Tor, the unofficial symbol of the city, and the national Holocaust memorial.

a good walk

Berlin's peaceful **Tiergarten** ➐ ☞ begins within 150 meters of the train station, Zoologischer Garten. Keep the elevated train tracks to your left, passing the zoo on your right. The path bends at the beer garden and café Schleusen Krug, and is bordered on one side by the grass-banked Landwehr canal, and on the other by the zoo's aviaries. Take the footbridge onto Lichtensteinallee, passing the larger beer garden, Café am Neuen See, on your left and the Spanish embassy on the right. The tree-lined path continues straight to the park's traffic circle Grosser Stern (Big Star), where five roads meet. The **Siegessäule** ➑ column provides a lookout from the center of the rotary.

Follow the Spreeweg Road past an oval, charcoal-color government building. Erected in 1998 and powered by solar-energy panels, it was the first new building built by the federal government in Berlin. Next door to it is Schloss Bellevue, built in 1785 and today the residence of Germany's president. Continue east along John-Foster-Dulles Allee, keeping the Spree River in sight on your left. When the riverside path diverges from the main street, keep to the street and take the last path that cuts away from it in a diagonal to the right (Eichenallee). Eichenallee crosses the path Grosse Querallee and continues until it exits at Strasse des 17. Juni, the street that bisects the park. Ahead is the Brandenburger Tor, and on the left across Entlastungsstrasse is the **Sowjetisches Ehrenmal** ➒. The Soviet tanks at this war memorial were two that helped defeat the Nazis during the Battle of Berlin. That West Berliners renamed the street in front of it Strasse des 17. Juni was rather controversial. The name honors the uprising of East Berlin workers in 1953 that was quashed by Soviet tanks.

Head toward the famous gate, but before reaching it, cut through the park to the left to reach the **Reichstag** ⑩. The German Empire's old parliament building has housed the federal parliament since the government returned to Berlin in 1999. Now return to the mighty **Brandenburger Tor** ⑪, probably the most significant icon of German triumph and defeat. In front of the gate is Pariser Platz. On its north side is the Dresdner Bank, the French embassy, and a Starbucks. To the south is the DZ bank designed by Frank O. Gehry. Step in the foyer to see the monstrous, fish-like construction thrusting forth from the back of its atrium. Next door, the historic facade of the prestigious Akademie der Künste (Academy of Arts) is visible behind a modern glass front. At the traditional address of "Unter den Linden No. 1," (now Unter den Linden No. 77) stands the rebuilt Hotel Adlon Berlin, the meeting point of Europe's elite.

Follow Ebertstrasse south from the Brandenburger Tor and cross Behrenstrasse. On what had been the empty borderland of the Berlin Wall system is an expansive Holocaust memorial, **Denkmal für die Ermordeten Juden Europas** , which was 10 years in the making. The next sight is one of Europe's largest museums of contemporary art. The **Hamburger Bahnhof, Museum für Gegenwart–Berlin** ⑬ is in the Tiergarten area, but requires a bus ride. Bus 248 (marked "Richtung U Leopoldplatz) stops on Ebertstrasse close to the Holocaust memorial. It comes every 20 minutes and the ride to Heidestrasse/Invalidenstrasse takes just 10 minutes. The museum is on Invalidenstrasse, a short walk from the corner of Heidestrasse.

TIMING   A leisurely walk from Zoo Station through the Tiergarten to the Brandenburger Tor and the Reichstag will take 90 minutes. To spend a little more time photographing and also visiting the Holocaust memorial, you can count on two hours. The line to visit the dome of the Reichstag varies in length with tourist seasons and school vacations. If the line is down the Reichstag's steps and bending around its driveway, expect a 45-minute wait. The Hamburger Bahnhof, Museum für Gegenwart–Berlin isn't ideally located, but Bus 248 does reach it quickly from the Holocaust memorial and from Platz der Repubik, where the Reichstag stands. A quick way to get roughly the same city impressions is by Bus 100. It starts in the bus queue outside Zoo Station and makes several stops in the western downtown and Tiergarten areas. You can leave and reboard the bus whenever you like.

What to See

★ ⑪   **Brandenburger Tor** (Brandenburg Gate). Once the pride of imperial Berlin and the city's premier landmark, the Brandenburger Tor was left in a desolate no-man's-land when the Wall was built. Since the Wall's dismantling, the stone gateway has become the scene of the city's Unification Day and New Year's Eve parties. After a painstaking renovation, the gate is now open only to pedestrians. This is the sole remaining gate of 14 built by Carl Langhans in 1788–91, designed as a triumphal arch for King Frederick Wilhelm II. Its virile classical style pays tribute to Athens's Acropolis. The quadriga, a chariot drawn by four horses and driven by the Goddess of Victory, was added in 1794. Troops paraded through the gate after successful campaigns—the last time in 1945, when victorious Red Army troops took Berlin. The upper part of the gate, together with its chariot and Goddess of Peace, was destroyed in the war. In 1957 the original molds were discovered in West Berlin, and a new quadriga was cast in copper and presented as a gift to the people of East Berlin. A small outpost of the tourist office is on the south side of the gate. ⊠ *Pariser Pl., Tiergarten* Ⓤ *Unter den Linden (S-bahn).*

⓬ Denkmal für die Ermordeten Juden Europas (Memorial to the Murdered Jews of Europe). This Holocaust memorial, a project whose stirrings date back to 1988, will be realized in May 2005. Designed by American architect Peter Eisenman, the place of remembrance is a grid of 2,700 concrete stelae of varying heights, planted into sloping ground. The memorial can be entered from all sides, and offers no prescribed path. Information, facts, and all known names of the approximately 6 million Jews who were killed in the Holocaust are found in an underground information center. This site was chosen not because its grounds were a setting of the Holocaust, but because the grounds are so near the center of the German federal government. ⊠ *At Ebertstr. and Behrenstr., Tiergarten* ⊕ *www.holocaust-mahnmal.de* Ⓤ *Unter den Linden (S-bahn).*

★ ⓭ Hamburger Bahnhof, Museum für Gegenwart–Berlin (Museum of Contemporary Art). The best place to survey Western art after 1960 is in this light-filled remodeled train station. The modern wing is worth a visit itself for its interplay of natural sunlight, glass, and steel. In 2004 the museum doubled its exhibition space to accommodate a seven-year loan of the Flick Collection, the largest and most valuable collection of contemporary art in the world. The 2,000 works will rotate, but you're bound to see some by Bruce Naumann, Rodney Graham, and Pipilotti Rist. The permanent collection includes installations by German artists Joseph Beuys and Anselm Kiefer as well as paintings by Andy Warhol, Cy Twombly, Robert Rauschenberg, and Robert Morris. Works of Marcel Duchamp and Marcel Broodthaers are exhibited on the second floor. ⊠ *Invalidenstr. 50–51, Tiergarten* ☎ *030/3978–3412* ⊕ *www.smpk.de* 🎫 *€6* ☉ *Tues.–Fri. 10–6, weekends 11–6* Ⓤ *Zinnowitzer Str. (U-bahn), Lehrter Bahnhof (S-bahn).*

★ ⓳ Reichstag (Parliament Building). After last meeting here in 1933, the Bundestag, Germany's federal parliament, returned to its traditional seat in the spring of 1999. British architect Sir Norman Foster lightened up the gray monolith with a glass dome, which quickly became one of the city's main attractions: you can circle up a gently rising ramp while taking in the rooftops of Berlin and the parliamentary chamber below. At the base of the dome is an exhibit on the Reichstag's history, in German and English.

Completed in 1894, the Reichstag housed the imperial German parliament and later served a similar function during the ill-fated Weimar Republic. On the night of February 28, 1933, the Reichstag burned down under mysterious circumstances, an event that provided the Nazis with a convenient pretext for outlawing all opposition parties. It was rebuilt but again badly damaged in 1945. The graffiti of the victorious Russian soldiers can still be seen on some of the walls in the hallways. The building is surrounded by ultramodern new federal government offices, such as the boxlike **Bundeskanzleramt** (German Federal Chancellery), nicknamed the *Waschmaschine* (washing machine) by Berliners. Built by Axel Schultes, it's one of the few new buildings in the government district by a Berlin architect. Behind the cube and extending across the Spree River is the **Kanzlergarten** (Chancellor Garden). Visit the Reichstag in the early morning or evening to avoid the longest lines. To attend a scheduled talk or tour, fax a request as many weeks or months in advance as possible (two months in advance is advised). ⊠ *Reichstag, Pl. der Republik 1, Tiergarten* ☎ *030/2273–2152 or 030/2273-5908* 🖷 *030/2273–0027* ⊕ *www.bundestag.de* 🕾 *Free* ☉ *Daily 8 AM–midnight; last admission 10 PM* ☉ *Reichstag dome closes for 1 wk 4 times a yr* Ⓤ *Unter den Linden (S-bahn).*

❽ Siegessäule (Victory Column). The 227-feet-high granite, sandstone, and bronze column has a splendid view of Berlin. It was erected in front of the Reichstag in 1873 to commemorate Prussia's military successes and then moved to the Tiergarten in 1938–39. You have to climb 285 steps up through the column to reach the observation platform, but the view is rewarding. The gold-tipped canons striping the column are those the Prussians captured from the French in the Franco-Prussian War. ⊠ *Am Grossen Stern, Tiergarten* ☎ *030/391–2961* 🕾 *€2.20* ☉ *Nov.–Mar., daily 9:30–5:30; Apr.–Oct., weekdays 9:30–6, weekends 9:30–7:30; last admission ½ hr before closing* Ⓤ *Tiergarten (S-bahn), Bellevue (S-bahn).*

❾ Sowjetisches Ehrenmal (Soviet Memorial). Built immediately after World War II, this monument stands as a reminder of the Soviet victory over the shattered German army in Berlin in May 1945. The Battle of Berlin was one of the deadliest on the European front. A hulking bronze statue of a soldier stands atop a marble plinth taken from Hitler's former Reichkanzlei (headquarters). The memorial is flanked by what are said to be the first two T-34 tanks to have fought their way into the city. ⊠ *Str. des 17. Juni, Tiergarten* Ⓤ *Unter den Linden (S-bahn).*

▶ **❼ Tiergarten** (Animal Garden). For Berliners the quiet greenery of the 630-acre Tiergarten is a beloved oasis, with some 23 km (14 mi) of footpaths, playgrounds, and a beer garden. In summer the park becomes the embodiment of multicultural Berlin: Turkish families gather in the meadows for spicy barbecues, children play soccer, and gay couples sunbathe. The inner park's 6½ acres of lakes and ponds were landscaped by garden architect Joseph Peter Lenné in the mid-1800s. On the shores of the lake in the southwest part, you can relax at the **Café am Neuen See** (⊠ Lichtensteinallee), a café and beer garden. Off the Spree River and bordering the Kanzleramt (Chancellory) is the **Haus der Kulturen der Welt** (⊠ House of the World Cultures, John-Foster-Dulles Allee 10 ☎ 030/397–870 ⊕ www.hkw.de ☉ Tues.–Sun. 10–9), referred to as the "pregnant oyster" for its design. Thematic exhibits and festivals take place here. Ⓤ *Unter den Linden (S-bahn), Tiergarten (S-bahn), Zoologischer Garten (S-bahn and U-bahn).*

Potsdamer Platz & Kreuzberg

The once-divided capital is rejoined on this square, which was Berlin's inner-city center and Europe's busiest plaza before World War II. Bombings and the wall system left this area a sprawling, desolate lot, where tourists in West Berlin could climb a wooden platform to peek into East Berlin's deathstrip. After the Wall fell, Sony, the former Daimler-Benz, Asea Brown Boveri, and other companies made a rush to build their headquarters on this prime real estate. In the mid-1990s Potsdamer Platz became Europe's largest construction site. Today's modern complexes of red sandstone, terra-cotta tiles, steel, and glass have made it a city within a city. The subtle reminder that this was an empty plot for nearly 50 years is a line of cobblestones that traces the path of the Wall on the west side of Stresemannstrasse.

A few narrow streets cut between the hulking modern architecture, which includes two high-rise towers that are part of the headquarters of debis, the software subsidiary of DaimlerChrysler. The debis center was designed by star architect Renzo Piano. The round atrium of the Sony Center is the closest rendering of a traditional square in terms of being used as a public meeting point. You'll notice more shoppers and moviegoers than businesspeople. Farther down Potsdamer Strasse are the state museums and cultural institutes of the Kuturforum.

Not far from modern Berlin is the hot spot of the Cold War, Checkpoint Charlie. This border crossing manned by the Soviets and Americans lay between West Berlin's Kreuzberg district and East Berlin's Mitte district. It was reserved for non-Germans. All that remains where Soviet and American tanks had a tense stand-off in October 1961 are a replica guardhouse and signage, plus the cobblestones marking the old border.

Kreuzberg is one of the liveliest districts in Berlin. A largely Turkish population lives cheek-by-jowl with a variegated assortment of political radicals and bohemians of all nationalities. There are few attractions here, but it's a great place to people-watch or to sun yourself at a sidewalk café.

a good walk

The Potsdamer Platz U- and S-bahn stations drop you at the edge of the area; follow Neue Potsdamer Strasse to the **Sony Center** ⓮ ▶, one of the city's most striking new buildings. It's surrounded by an entertainment complex with plenty of eateries. Follow Potsdamer Strasse westward, and in 10 minutes you'll reach the **Kulturforum** ⓯, a complex that includes the Philharmonic, state museums, and the state library. Head back toward the S-bahn station, and turn right on Stresemannstrasse. The Wall ran along the current sidewalk and you'll see where it turned at Niederkirchnerstrasse. Cobblestones in the pavement mark the Wall's path. Follow it.

Niederkirchnerstrasse is yet another strip of German history with one sight after the other: the old Preussischer Landtag, the seat of Berlin's parliament, faces the museum **Martin-Gropius-Bau** ⓰, which is next to the barren landscape where the Nazi's SS headquarters stood, now an exhibit called the **Topographie des Terrors** ⓱. Bordering the cellar remains is one of the few sections of the Wall that still stand. Opposite the wall is the enormous former Luftwaffeministerium—the Air Force Ministry of the Third Reich. Today it's home to the federal finance ministry. Cross Wilhelmstrasse and continue east on Zimmerstrasse until you reach the corner of Friedrichstrasse. The border-crossing Checkpoint Charlie was here, and oversize photographs of a young Soviet and American soldier still face their opposing super-power's sector. Just to the right on Friedrichstrasse, gripping stories of the Wall, refugees, and spies are told in the mouthful of a museum named **Mauermuseum-Museum Haus am Checkpoint Charlie** ⑱. From here, round the corner to continue east on Kochstrasse, the newspaper district of the early 20th century. Turn right on Markgrafenstrasse to reach the **Jüdisches Museum** ⑲, Germany's largest museum of Jewish culture. The way to the museum is signposted in maroon.

TIMING The sights are close to one another until you set off for the Jüdisches Museum. In 30 minutes you can take in the architecture at Potsdamer Platz and reach the Kulturforum complex for a look from the outside. To retrace your steps and reach the Topographie des Terrors will take 20 minutes. Owing to its small size and popularity, you may experience a wait or slow line at "the Checkpoint Charlie museum" if you visit any time other than the early morning or evening. Monday is a popular day for both it and the Jüdisches Museum since the state museums are closed that day.

What to See

⑲ **Jüdisches Museum** (Jewish Museum). The history of Germany's Jews from the Middle Ages through today are chronicled here, from explanations of religious traditions to exhibits on prominent historical figures and the evolution of laws regarding Jews' participation in civil society. An attraction in itself is the highly conceptual building, which was designed by Daniel Libeskind (the architect now redeveloping the World Trade Center site). Various physical "voids" represent the loss German society faces because of the Holocaust, and a portion of the exhibits document the Holocaust as well. You can expect to spend three hours here. Devote more time to the second floor if you're already familiar with basic aspects of Judaica, which makes up much of the third floor. ✉ *Lindenstr. 9–14, Kreuzberg* ☎ *030/3087–85681* ⊕ *www.jmberlin.de* ✉ *€5* ◷ *Mon. 10–10, Tues.–Sun. 10–8* Ⓤ *Kochstr. (U-bahn).*

⑮ **Kulturforum** (Cultural Forum). This unique ensemble of museums, galleries, and the Philharmonic Hall was long in the making. The first designs were submitted in the 1960s and the last building completed in
★ 1998. The **Gemäldegalerie** (Picture Gallery) reunites formerly separated collections from East and West Berlin. It's one of Germany's finest art galleries and has an extensive selection of European paintings from the 13th to the 18th century. Seven rooms are reserved for paintings by German masters, among them Dürer, Cranach the Elder, and Holbein. A special collection has works of the Italian masters—Botticelli, Titian, Giotto, Lippi, and Raphael—as well as paintings by Dutch and Flemish masters of the 15th and 16th centuries: Van Eyck, Bosch, Brueghel the Elder, and van der Weyden. The museum also holds the world's second-largest Rembrandt collection. ✉ *Matthäikirchpl. 4, Tiergarten* ☎ *030/266–2951* ⊕ *www.smpk.de* ✉ *€6* ◷ *Tues., Wed., Fri.–Sun. 10–6, Thurs. 10–10* Ⓤ *Potsdamer Pl. (U-bahn and S-bahn).*

Steps away from the Gemäldegalerie are two examples of ultramodern architecture. The **Kunstbibliothek** (Art Library; ✉ Matthäikirchpl. 4,

Tiergarten ☎ 030/266–2951 ⊕ www.smpk.de ☜ €6 ⊙ Tues.–Fri. 10–6, weekends 11–6; reading room Mon. 2–8, Tues.–Fri. 9–4) contains art posters, a costume library, ornamental engravings, and a commercial art collection. The **Kupferstichkabinett** (Drawings and Prints Collection; ⊠ Matthäikirchpl. 4, Tiergarten ☎ 030/266–2951 ⊕ www.smpk. de ☜ €6 ⊙ Tues.–Fri. 10–6, weekends 11–6) has occasional exhibits, which include European woodcuts, engravings, and illustrated books from the 15th century to the present (highlights of its holdings are pen-and-ink drawings by Dürer and drawings by Rembrandt). You can request to see one or two drawings in the study room. Another building displays paintings dating from the late Middle Ages to 1800.

Inside the **Kunstgewerbemuseum** (Museum of Decorative Arts) are European arts and crafts from the Middle Ages to the present. Among the notable exhibits are the Welfenschatz (Welfen Treasure), a collection of 16th-century gold and silver plates from Nürnberg, as well as ceramics and porcelains. *⊠ Matthäikirchpl. 4, Tiergarten ☎ 030/266–2902 ⊕ www.smpk.de ☜ €6 ⊙ Tues.–Fri. 10–6, weekends 11–6.*

★ The glass-box **Neue Nationalgalerie** (New National Gallery) was designed by Bauhaus member Mies van der Rohe and completed in 1968. On view even from the outside are changing installations by contemporary artists. Main exhibitions are below ground. Highlights of the 20th-century collection of paintings, sculptures, and drawings are the works by Otto Dix, Ernst Ludwig Kirchner, and Georg Grotz. These German expressionists will make room for a special exhibition come March or May 2005. *⊠ Potsdamer Str. 50, Tiergarten ☎ 030/266–2951 ⊕ www.smpk.de ☜ €6 ⊙ Tues., Wed., and Fri. 10–6, Thurs. 10–10, weekends 11–8.*

The mustard-yellow complex that resembles a great tent belongs to the **Philharmonie** (☎ 030/2548–8156), home to the renowned Berlin Philharmonic Orchestra since 1963. The Philharmonie and the smaller Chamber Music Hall adjoining it were designed by Hans Scharoun. There's a free tour of the Philharmonie daily at 1 PM. Across the parking lot from the Philharmonie, the **Musikinstrumenten-Museum** (Musical Instruments Museum) has a fascinating collection of keyboard, string, wind, and percussion instruments. These are demonstrated during an 11 AM tour on Saturday, which closes with a 20-minute Wurlitzer organ concert. *Museum ⊠ Tiergartenstr. 1, Tiergarten ☎ 030/2548–1129 ☜ €3, tour €2 ⊙ Tues.–Fri. 9–5, weekends 10–5.*

The **Staatsbibliothek** (National Library; ⊠ Postdamer Str. 33 ☎ 030/ 2660 ☜ €.50 ⊙ Weekdays 9–9, Sat. 9–7) is one of the largest libraries in Europe and was one of the Berlin settings in Wim Wender's 1987 film, *Wings of Desire.*

⑯ **Martin-Gropius-Bau.** This magnificent exhibition hall dates back to 1877 and once housed Berlin's Arts and Crafts Museum. Its architect, Martin Gropius, was the uncle of Walter Gropius, the Bauhaus architect who also worked in Berlin. Since 1980, the international, changing exhibits on art and culture have been among Berlin's most attention-grabbing. The Berlin Wall once stood between the museum and the Preussischer Landtag (now the Berlin Senate) across the street. *⊠ Niederkirchner-*

str. 7, Kreuzberg ☎ *030/2548–6112* ⊕ *www.gropiusbau.de* 🖾 *Varies with exhibit* ⊙ *Wed.–Mon. 10–8* Ⓤ *Kochstr. (U-bahn), Potsdamer Pl. (U-bahn and S-bahn).*

★ ⑱ **Mauermuseum-Museum Haus am Checkpoint Charlie.** Just steps from the famous crossing point between the two Berlins, the Wall Museum—House at Checkpoint Charlie tells the story of the Wall, and even more riveting, the stories of those who escaped through, under, and over it. The homespun museum reviews the events leading up to the Wall's construction and with original tools and devices, plus recordings and photographs, shows how East Germans escaped to the West (one of the most ingenious contraptions was a miniature submarine). Exhibits about human rights and paintings interpreting the Wall round out the experience. Come early or late in the day to avoid the multitudes dropped off by tour buses. Monday can be particularly crowded as well. ⊠ *Friedrichstr. 43–45, Kreuzberg* ☎ *030/253–7250* ⊕ *www.mauermuseum.com* 🖾 *€9.50* ⊙ *Daily 9 AM–10 PM* Ⓤ *Kochstr. (U-bahn).*

need a break?
Try your best to conjure up an image of the Wall from a window seat at **Café Adler** (⊠ Friedrichstr. 206, Kreuzberg ☎ 030/251–8965), which once bumped right up against it. The quality fare is inexpensive and the soups are particularly delicious. Breakfast is served until 5 PM.

off the beaten path
ORANIENSTRASSE – The spine of life in the Kreuzberg district has mellowed from hard-core to funky since reunification. When Kreuzberg literally had its back against the Wall, West German social outcasts, punks, and the radical left made this old working-class street their territory. Since the 1970s the population has become largely Turkish, and many of yesterday's outsiders have turned into successful owners of shops and simple eateries. The hooligans seeking to provoke the police during the annual May 1st demonstrations have left this street in favor of the side streets in the neighborhood. Ⓤ *Görlitzer Bahnhof (U-bahn), Kottbusser Tor (U-bahn).*

▶ ⑭ **Sony Center.** This light glass-and-steel construction wraps around a spectacular circular forum. Topping it off is a tentlike structure meant to emulate Mount Fuji. The architectural jewel, designed by German-American architect Helmut Jahn, is one of the most stunning public spaces of Berlin's new center, filled with restaurants, cafés, movie theaters, apartments, and the European headquarters of Sony. The one reminder of more glorious days gone by is the old **Kaisersaal** (Emperor's Hall), held within a very modern glass enclosure. The hall originally stood 50 yards away in the Grand Hotel Esplanade (built in 1907) but was moved here lock, stock, and barrel. Its restored interior houses a restaurant.

Within the center the **Filmmuseum Berlin** (⊠ Potsdamer Str. 2, Tiergarten ☎ 030/300–9030 ⊕ www.filmmuseum-berlin.de 🖾 €6 ⊙ Tues.–Sun. 10–6, Thurs. 10–8) presents the history of moviemaking with eye-catching displays. The texts are also in English. Memorabilia includes personal belongings of Marlene Dietrich and sketches and costumes of fantasy and science fiction films.

JOINING EAST & WEST

N 1989 THE TELEVISED IMAGES of jubilant Berliners cheering atop the Wall stunned the world. Both West and East Berliners were euphoric, embracing one another with mutual bewilderment and curiosity. The two city administrations managed to successfully integrate, but in the years since, East and West Berliners still move largely in their own respective circles.

Though once a hot sociopolitical issue, the Mauer in den Köpfen ("Wall in the minds") is no longer a topic of people's conversations. Instead, a sort of post-reunification hangover lingers throughout the city. In the mid-1990s close to 50,000 Berliners moved between the east and west halves of the city, enough to change the look of some neighborhood turfs. Prenzlauer Berg and Mitte, two historic and proud East Berlin districts, are now flooded by transplanted yuppies and dinks (double-income, no-kids couples). The new arrivals are often not West Berliners, but West Germans and young European and English-speaking expatriates. In Prenzlauer Berg, once a poor area where East German punks lived, gentrification has pushed rents beyond the resources of even many young professionals.

The extensive city reorganization of January 2001 reduced the number of city districts in Berlin from 23 to 12 and in the process revealed lingering prejudices. Suddenly, western Kreuzberg and eastern Friedrichshain are one district; the same holds true for western Tiergarten and eastern Mitte, as well as for Prenzlauer Berg, Pankow, and Weissensee. In this last case, the administrative reform turned into a hilarious Provinzposse (local farce) when 10,000 people, mostly westerners living in Prenzlauer Berg, protested adopting the former Socialist district name of Pankow. A compromise was reached, and the district's title now consists of three names and a number.

In the civic arena, western conventions were often chosen over eastern ones. An East Berlin design that has gained wide appreciation is the figure that appears on the crosswalk traffic lights. The Ampelmännchen ("little street-light man") wears a wide-brim hat and walks with an animated gait. He's won over all Berliners and thus has held his ground in most of East Berlin. He's even become one of the most lucrative Berlin souvenir icons—he adorns coffee cups, key chains, and there's even candy made in his image.

The days of Ostalgie (nostalgia for the East) memorabilia parties—enjoyed by both East and West Berliners—that affectionately poked fun at the symbols of the eastern regime are long gone, but East Germany's iconography and "fashion" have reemerged as trendy. This campy perspective is not without controversy. Mayor Klaus Wowereit has stressed the importance of remembering that East Germany was a dictatorship, after all. Even the East German Olympic-medal ice-skater Katarina Witt drew criticism for wearing the uniform of the FDJ (Free German Youth) while hosting the TV special "DDR Show," which looked back on the years of the German Democratic Republic. Still, the biggest German film hit of 2003 was the comedy and drama Good Bye Lenin!, which is set in East Berlin in 1989–90, just after the Berlin Wall fell. While the East is embracing all things West, a young man does his best to hide the winds of change from his devout Socialist mother, who is recovering from a coma and knows nothing of the Wall's fall. His best lie was explaining why West Germans were moving into their apartment building: they were disillusioned with capitalism and had chosen to emigrate to the Communist East.

★ ⑰ **Topographie des Terrors** (Topography of Terror). Within the cellar-prison remains of the Nazis' Reich Security Main Office (which was comprised of the SS, SD, and Gestapo), photos and documents explain the police and intelligence organizations that planned and executed Nazi crimes against humanity. The fates of both perpetrators and victims are included in the free, open-air exhibit. Within a humble trailer, you can leaf through books and copies of official documents. Pick up a free audio guide here before viewing the exhibit. ⊠ *Niederkirchnerstr. 8, Kreuzberg* ☎ *030/2548–6703* ⊕ *www.topographie.de* ⊠ *Free* ☉ *Oct.–Apr., daily 10–5; May–Sept., daily 10–8.*

off the beaten path

TÜRKENMARKT (Turkish Market) – On Tuesday and Friday from noon to 6:30 you can find the country's best selection of Arab and Turkish foods on the Maybachufer lining the southern bank of the Landwehrkanal. The bohemian café on the Kottbusser bridge, Ankerklause, or those on Paul-Lincke-Ufer, on the opposite bank, are great places for a coffee break and local color. ⊠ *Maybachufer Neukölln* Ⓤ *Kottbusser Tor (U-bahn), Schönlein Str. (U-bahn).*

Mitte: Unter den Linden to Alexanderplatz

The Mitte (Middle) district is where Berlin first began as two fishing villages separated by the Spree River. Throughout its 760-year-plus history it has served as a seat of government for Prussian kings, German emperors, the Weimar Republic, Hitler's Third Reich, the communist German Democratic Republic, and since 1999, for reunited Germany. Treasures once split between East and West Berlin museums are also reunited on Museum Island, a UNESCO World Heritage site.

The historic boulevard Unter den Linden proudly rolls out Prussian architecture and world-class museums. Its major cross-street is Friedrichstrasse, which was revitalized in the mid-1990s with car showrooms (including Bentley, Bugatti, and Volkswagen) and upscale malls. At its eastern end, Unter den Linden turns into Karl-Liebknecht-Strasse, which leads to vast Alexanderplatz, where eastern Berlin's handful of skyscrapers are dwarfed beneath the city's most visible landmark, the Berlin TV tower.

a good walk

Layers of history seem to be laid out solely for your convenience on this walk. Leading away from the Brandenburger Tor and Pariser Platz is **Unter den Linden** ㉒ ⌐, the elegant eastern counterpart to Kurfürstendamm. On the boulevard's long procession, you'll pass several parliamentary offices and consulates, among them the Russian embassy. Turn right at **Friedrichstrasse** ㉑, passing the Volkswagen showroom and other fancy storefronts. After two blocks, turn left at Französische Strasse to reach **Gendarmenmarkt** ㉒, one of Europe's finest early-19th-century plazas.

Bordering the east side of the square, Markgrafenstrasse leads north to Behrenstrasse, where **Bebelplatz** ㉓ is just steps away to the right. Surrounding it is an architectural ensemble begun in the mid-18th century under Frederick the Great. The square opens onto Unter den Linden, which you should cross to reach the **Neue Wache** ㉔ and the pale pink and newly restored **Deutsches Historisches Museum** 25. Looking back across the street, you'll have a better view of the sculpture-topped Crown Prince's Palace, a baroque-style building originally constructed in 1732 for Crown Prince Friedrich (later Frederick the Great). The Deustches Historisches Museum borders the Spree River, which splits around **Museumsinsel** 26, the island where one of Berlin's two medieval settlements began. Several bridges connect to the island; the grandest is Schinkel's Schloss Brücke, completed in 1824 and lined with statues depicting young heroes guided by the godesses Nike, Athena, and Iris. The vast empty lot on the right is **Schlossplatz** 27, the site of the Hohenzollern palace that the East German government detonated in 1950. More attention-grabbing is the dilapidated former parliament building of the German Democratic Republic on its eastern edge, and opposite it, the enormous **Berliner Dom** 28.

After the Schloss Bruke, Unter den Linden becomes Karl-Liebknecht-Strasse. Past the Berliner Dom and Marx-Engels-Forum, the next cross street is Spandauer Strasse. To the left behind a small entranceway is the new aquarium, **AquaDom & Sea Life Berlin** 29, to the right is a pedestrian square that holds the 13th-century **St. Marienkirche** 30, the Neptune Fountain, and the redbrick **Berliner Rathaus** 31. The city hall is at the border of the **Nikolaiviertel** 32, Berlin's small medieval quarter out of which rises the twin spires of the St. Nikolaikirche. Soaring considerably higher is the concrete column of the **Berliner Fernsehturm** 33, the TV tower planted at the end of the pedestrian square. Across the square is the transportation hub and perennial demonstration ground, the scruffy and clearly socialist-era **Alexanderplatz** 34. Give your feet a break and hop the U-2 line to reach the city's history museum, **Märkisches Museum** 35 (the subway stop is named for it). To reach the redbrick building, walk back along Wallstrasse in the direction the train came from.

TIMING   If you don't look closely at any museums or highlights, you could ramble this route in two hours. To speed your procession down Unter den Linden, you can hop one of the three bus lines that each make five stops between Friedrichstrasse and Alexanderplatz. The state museums off Unter den Linden are closed on Monday.

What to See

34 **Alexanderplatz.** This bleak square, bordered by the train station, the Galeria Kaufhof department store, and the 40-story Park Inn hotel, once formed the hub of East Berlin. German writer Alfred Döblin dubbed it the "heart of a world metropolis" (text from his 1929 novel *Berlin Alexanderplatz* is written on a building across the northeastern side of the square). Today, it's a basic center of commerce and the occasional demonstration. The unattractive modern buildings are a reminder not just of the results of Allied bombing but also of the ruthlessness practiced by East Germans when they demolished what remained. A famous meeting point in the south corner is the World Time Clock (1969), which even keeps tabs on Tijuana.

29 **AquaDom & Sea Life Berlin.** The SeaLife group has aquariums Europe-wide, each with its own focus on local marine life. In Berlin, the tanks

begin with the Spree River, move on to Berlin's lakes, and then take you on a course from fresh- to saltwater. Waterfront city scenes and cobblestones are part of the decor, which gradually gives way to starfish-petting beds, overhead tanks, and a submarinelike room. The last darkened environment emulating a rocky coastline gets dramatic when rains come down and thunder and lightning crashes. Plaques for kids and adults are in English, as well as German. Don't come looking for sharks, shows, or colorful tropical fish: the most exotic creatures here are perhaps the tiny sea horses and spotted rays. The aquarium opened in December 2003 and its finale is a state-of-the-art elevator—a two-level glass one that brings you through a silo-shape fish tank to the exit. Young children love this place, but the timed wait for the elevator can be frustrating for all ages. ⊠ *Spandauer Str. 3, Mitte* ☎ *030/992–800* ⊕ *www.sealife.de* ✉ *€13.50* ☉ *Daily 10–6* Ⓤ *Hackescher Markt (S-bahn).*

➋ **Bebelplatz.** After he became ruler in 1740, Frederick the Great personally planned the buildings surrounding this square. The area received the nickname *Forum Fridericianum*, or Frederick's Forum. A music lover, Frederick's first priority was the **Staatsoper Unter den Linden** (State Opera). Berlin's lavish, prime opera house was completed in 1743 by the same architect that built Sanssouci in Potsdam, Georg Wenzelaus von Knobelsdorff. Daniel Barenboim is maestro of the house. ⊠ *Unter den Linden 7, Mitte* ☎ *030/2035–4555* ⊕ *www.staatsoper-berlin.de* ☉ *Box office weekdays 11–7, weekends 2–7; reservations by phone Mon.–Sat. 10–8, Sun. 2–8* Ⓤ *Französische Str. (U-bahn).*

The green patina dome belongs to **St. Hedwigskathedrale** (St. Hedwig's Cathedral). Begun in 1747, it was modeled after the Pantheon in Rome and was the first Catholic church built in resolutely Protestant Berlin since the 16th-century Reformation. It was Frederick the Great's effort to appease Prussia's Catholic population after his invasion of Catholic Silesia (then Poland). A treasury lies inside. ⊠ *Bebelpl., Mitte* ☎ *030/ 203–4810* ✉ *Free* ⊕ *www.hedwigs-kathedrale.de* ☉ *Weekdays 10–5, Sun. 1–5* ☞ *Tours (€1.50) available in English, call ahead* Ⓤ *Französische Str. (U-bahn).*

Running the length of the west side of Bebelplatz, the former royal library is now part of **Humboldt-Universität** (⊠ Unter den Linden 6, Mitte ☎ 030/20930), whose main campus is across the street on Unter den Linden. The university building was built in 1766 as a palace for Prince Heinrich, the brother of Frederick the Great. With its founding in 1810, the university moved in. The fairy-tale collecting Grimm brothers studied here, as did political philosophers Karl Marx and Friedrich Engels. Albert Einstein taught physics from 1914 to 1932, when he left Berlin for the United States. On May 10, 1933, Joseph Goebbels, the Nazi minister for propaganda and "public enlightenment," organized one of the nationwide book-burnings on Bebelplatz. The books, thrown on a pyre by Nazi officials and students, included works by Jews, pacifists, and Communists. In the center of Bebelplatz, a modern and subtle memorial marks where 20,000 books went up in flames.

off the beaten path

EAST SIDE GALLERY – This 1-km (½-mi) stretch of concrete went from guarded border to open-air gallery within three months. East Berliners breached the wall on November 9, 1989, and between February and June of 1990, 118 artists from around the globe created unique works of art on the longest remaining section of the Berlin Wall. Much of the paint is now peeling and many panels have been vandalized by graffiti. One of the best-known works, by Russian artist Dmitri Vrubel, depicts Brezhnev and Honnecker (the former East German leader) kissing, with the caption "My God. Help me survive this deadly love." The stretch along the Spree Canal runs between the Warschauer Strasse S- and U-bahn station and Ostbahnhof. The redbrick Oberbaumbrücke (an 1896 bridge) at Warschauer Strasse makes that end more scenic. ⊠ *Mühlenstr., Friedrichshain* Ⓤ *Warschauer Str. (U-bahn and S-bahn), Ostbahnhof (S-bahn).*

㉘ Berliner Dom (Berlin Cathedral). A church has stood here since 1536, but this enormous version dates from 1905, making it the largest 20th-century Protestant church in Germany. The royal Hohenzollerns worshiped here until 1918, when Kaiser Wilhelm II abdicated and left Berlin for Holland. The massive dome wasn't restored from World War II damage until 1982; the interior was completed in 1993. The climb to the dome's outer balcony is made easier by a wide stairwell, plenty of landings with historic photos and models, and even a couple of chairs. The more than 80 sarcophagi of Prussian royals in the crypt are significant, but to less-trained eyes, can seem uniformly dull. Every Sunday service includes communion. ⊠ *Am Lustgarten 1, Mitte* ☎ *030/2026–9136* ⊕ *www.berlinerdom.de* 🎟 *€5* ☉ *Apr.–Sept., Mon.–Sat., 9–8, Sun. noon–8; Oct.–Mar., Mon.–Sat. 9–7, Sun. noon–7* Ⓤ *Alexanderpl. (S-bahn and U-bahn), Hackescher Markt (S-bahn).*

㉝ Berliner Fernsehturm (Berlin TV Tower). Finding Alexanderplatz is no problem: just head toward the 1,198-foot-high tower piercing the sky. It was completed in 1969 and is not accidentally 710 feet higher than western Berlin's broadcasting tower and 98 feet higher than the Eiffel Tower. You can get the best view of Berlin from the tower's observation level; on a clear day you can see for 40 km (25 mi). One floor above, the city's highest restaurant rotates for your panoramic pleasure. Make reservations in advance and stick to the German dishes. ⊠ *Panoramastr. 1a, Mitte* ☎ *030/242-3333* ⊕ *www.berlinerfernsehturm.de* 🎟 *€6.80* ☉ *Nov.–Feb., daily 10 AM–midnight; Mar.–Oct., daily 9 AM–1 AM; last admission ½ hr before closing* Ⓤ *Alexanderpl. (S-bahn and U-bahn).*

㉛ Berliner Rathaus (Berlin Town Hall). Nicknamed the Rotes Rathaus (red town hall) for its redbrick design, the town hall was completed in 1869. Its most distinguishing features are its neo-Renaissance clocktower and frieze that depicts Berlin's history up to 1879 in 36 terra-cotta plaques, each 6 meters long. Climb the grand stairwell to view the coat of arms hall and a few exhibits. ⊠ *Jüdenstr. 1 at Rathausstr. 15, Mitte* ☎ *030/ 90260* 🎟 *Free* ☉ *Weekdays 9–6* Ⓤ *Alexanderpl. (S-bahn and U-bahn).*

㉕ Deutsches Historisches Museum (German History Museum). This museum is composed of two buildings. The magnificent pink, baroque Prussian arsenal (Zeughaus) was constructed between 1695 and 1730 and is the oldest building on Unter den Linden. At this writing, it was scheduled to reopen after years-long renovations in autumn 2004. Topical rooms are interspersed between the chronological exhibits. The granite and glass Pei-Bau addition behind it, designed by I. M. Pei, holds temporary exhibits. ⊠ *Unter den Linden 2, Mitte* ☎ *030/203–040* ⊕ *www.dhm.de* ▨ *€6* ☉ *Daily 10–6.*

㉑ Friedrichstrasse. No other street in eastern Germany has changed as dramatically as Friedrichstrasse. The once-bustling 5th Avenue of prewar Berlin has risen from the rubble of war and Communist neglect to recover its glamour of old.

Heading south on Friedrichstrasse, you'll pass various office buildings, including the **Lindencorso** and the **Rosmarin-Karree,** which are worth a look for their architecture, luxury car showrooms, and fancy shops. The jewel of this street is the **Friedrichstadtpassagen,** a gigantic complex of three buildings praised for their completely different designs. An underground mall of shops and eateries connects the buildings. At the corner of Französische Strasse a daring building, designed by French architect Jean Nouvel, houses the French department store **Galeries Lafayette** (⊠ Französische Str. 23 ☎ 030/209–480). In the center is a steel-and-glass funnel surrounded by four floors of merchandise.

㉒ Gendarmenmarkt. Anchoring this large square are the beautifully reconstructed 1818 **Schauspielhaus,** one of Berlin's main concert halls (now called the Konzerthaus), and the **Deutscher Dom and Französischer Dom** (German and French cathedrals). The Französischer Dom contains the **Hugenottenmuseum** (⊠ Gendarmenmarkt 5, Mitte ☎ 030/229–1760 ▨ €2 ☉ Tues.–Sat. noon–5, Sun. 11–5), with exhibits charting the history and art of the French Protestant refugees—the Huguenots—who were expelled from France at the end of the 17th century by King Louis XIV. Their energy and commercial expertise did much to help boost Berlin during the 18th century. Guide materials are in German, French, and English.

The **Deutscher Dom** (⊠ Gendarmenmarkt 1, Mitte ☎ 030/2273–0431 ▨ Free ☉ Sept.–May, Wed.–Sun. 10–6, Tues. 10–10; June–Aug., Wed.–Sun. 10–7, Tues. 10–10) holds an extensive exhibition on the emergence of the parliamentary system in Germany since the late 1800s, sponsored by the German parliament. Leadership and opposition in East Germany are also documented. An English-language audio guide covers a portion of the exhibits on the first three floors. Floors four and five have temporary exhibitions with no English text or audio.

㉟ Märkisches Museum (Brandenburg Museum). This redbrick attic includes exhibits on the city's theatrical past, its guilds, its newspapers, and the March 1848 revolution. Paintings capture the look of the city before it crumbled in World War II. The fascinating collection of mechanical musical instruments is demonstrated on Sunday at 3 PM. ⊠ *Am Köllnischen Park 5, Mitte* ☎ *030/240–020* ⊕ *www.stadtmuseum.de* ▨ *€4, instrument demonstration €2* ☉ *Tues.–Sun. 10–6.*

26 **Museumsinsel** (Museum Island). On the site of one of Berlin's two orig-
FodorśChoice inal settlements, this unique complex of four state museums is an ab-
★ solute must. The **Alte Nationalgalerie** (Old National Gallery, entrance
on Bodestrasse) houses an outstanding collection of 18th-, 19th-, and
early-20th-century paintings and sculptures. Works by Cézanne, Rodin,
Degas, and one of Germany's most famous portrait artists, Max Liebermann, are part of the permanent exhibition. Its **Galerie der Romantik**
(Gallery of Romanticism) collection has masterpieces from such 19th-
century German painters as Karl Friedrich Schinkel and Caspar David
Friedrich, the leading members of the German Romantic school. The
Altes Museum (Old Museum, entrance at Am Lustgarten), a red marble, neoclassical building abutting the green Lustgarten, designed by
Schinkel in 1830, was the first building to be purposefully erected to
serve as a museum. It's home to everyday utensils from ancient Greece
as well as vases and sculptures from the 6th to 4th centuryBC. Etruscan
art is its highlight, and there are a few examples of Roman art. Antique
sculptures, clay figurines, and bronze art of the **Antikensammlung** (Antiquities Collection) are also housed here; the other part of the collection is in the Pergamonmuseum.

Even if you think you aren't interested in the ancient world, make an
exception for the **Pergamonmuseum** (entrance on Am Kupfergraben),
one of the world's greatest museums. The museum's name is derived
from its principal display, the Pergamon Altar, a monumental Greek temple discovered in what is now Turkey and dating from 180 BC. The altar
was shipped to Berlin in the late 19th century. Equally impressive is the
gateway of Miletus and the Babylonian processional way in the Asia
Minor department. ⊠ *Entrance to Museumsinsel: Am Kupfergraben,
Mitte* ☎ *030/209–5577 Museumsinsel, 030/2090–5560* ⊕ *www.smpk.
de* ⬛ *€8 for all Museum Island museums* ☉ *Pergamonmuseum Fri.–Wed.
10–6, Thurs. 10–10; Alte Nationalgalerie Tues.–Sun. 10–6, Thurs.
10–10; Altes Museum Tues.–Sun. 10–6.*

24 **Neue Wache.** (New Guardhouse). One of many Berlin constructions by
19th-century architect Karl Friedrich Schinkel, this building served as
both the Royal Prussian War Memorial (honoring the dead of the
Napoleonic Wars) and the royal guardhouse until the Kaiser abdicated
in 1918. In 1931 it became a memorial to those who fell in World War
I. Badly damaged in World War II, it was restored in 1960 by the East
German state and rededicated as a memorial for the victims of militarism
and fascism. After unification it regained its Weimar Republic appearance and was inaugurated as Germany's central war memorial. Inside
is a copy of Berlin sculptor Käthe Kollwitz's *Pietà,* showing a mother
mourning over her dead son. The inscription in front of it reads, TO THE
VICTIMS OF WAR AND TYRANNY.

32 **Nikolaiviertel** (Nicholas Quarter). This tiny quarter of cobblestone streets
grew up around Berlin's oldest parish church, the medieval, twin-spire
St. Nikolaikirche (St. Nicholas's Church), dating from 1230. The adjacent Fischerinsel (Fisherman's Island) area was the heart of Berlin 750
years ago and retains some of its medieval character. At Breite Strasse
you'll find two of Berlin's oldest buildings: No. 35 is the **Ribbeckhaus,**

the city's only surviving Renaissance structure, dating from 1624, and No. 36 is the early baroque **Marstall,** built by Michael Matthais between 1666 and 1669. Life goes on here, and the area is filled with stores, cafés, and restaurants. ⊠ *Church: Nikolaikirchpl., Mitte* ☎ *030/240–020* ⊕ *www.stadtmuseum.de* ☒ *€1.50* ◷ *Tues.–Sun. 10–6* Ⓤ *Alexanderpl. (S-bahn and U-bahn).*

㉗ Schlossplatz. One of the biggest cultural debates in Berlin is whether to rebuild a portion of the Hohenzollern palace that stood here from the 15th century, or save the country and city some 6.7 million euros. The East German government detonated the war-damaged palace for ideological reasons in 1950. Some 60 plaques describe the history of the palace, and you can also see some tiled cellar remains.

The question of reconstructing even the facade of the glorious palace that had 1,200 rooms has pitted Prussian fans against those nostalgic for the German Democratic Republic, whose gutted former parliament building, the **Palace of the Republic,** wastes away on this empty lot's edge. The building (built 1976) had to be cleared of asbestos, and its intended demolition has been stalled by costs and questions of cultural significance.

At Schlossplatz's south end is the brick-and-glass **Staatsrat** (State Senate), where East German dictator Eric Honnecker worked. The stone portal to this building was one of the few parts of the palace that the East German government preserved. It's believed that it was from this portral that Karl Liebknecht attempted to declare a Soviet-style republic after the Kaiser abdicated in November 1918. Irony upon irony, this former Communist building now houses Germany's first private business school. ⊠ *Mitte* Ⓤ *Hackescher Markt (S-bahn).*

㉚ St. Marienkirche (St. Mary's Church). This medieval church, one of the finest in Berlin, is worth a visit for its late-Gothic, macabre fresco *Der Totentanz* (*Dance of Death*). A tour highlights the fresco on Monday and Tuesday at 1 PM. Daily tours take place at 2 PM. ⊠ *Karl-Liebknecht-Str. 8, Mitte* ☎ *030/242–4467* ☒ *Free* ◷ *Apr.–Sept., Mon.–Sat. 10–6, Sun. noon–6; Oct.–Mar., Mon.–Sat. 10–4, Sun. noon–4. Organ recital Sat. 4:30* Ⓤ *Alexanderplatz, Hackescher Markt (S-bahn).*

need a break? The **Opernpalais** (⊠ Unter den Linden 5, Mitte ☎ 030/202–683), next to the opera house and within the former Crown Princesses Palace, is home to a bar, a restaurant, and a café famous for its selection of 40 cakes and pies, plus other sweet treats.

★ ▶ ⑳ Unter den Linden. The name of this historic Berlin thoroughfare means "under the linden trees"—and as Marlene Dietrich once sang, "As long as the old linden trees still bloom, Berlin is still Berlin." Imagine Berliners' shock when Hitler decided to fell the trees in order to make the boulevard more parade-friendly. The grand boulevard began as a riding path that the royals used to get from their palace to their hunting grounds (now Tiergarten). Lining it now are linden trees planted after World War II, embassies and consulates, cafés and shops, a university, museums, and an opera house. The famous landmark at its end at Tiergarten is the Brandenburger Tor.

Mitte's Scheunenvierte & Prenzlauer Berg

The hip scene of Mitte, the historic core of Berlin, is best experienced in the narrow streets and courtyard mazes of the Scheunenviertel (Barn Quarter), which also encompasses the former Spandauer Vorstadt (Jewish Quarter)—the streets around and to the west of Oranienburger Strasse. Some streets are lined with hip shops, bars, and eateries while others look empty and forlorn. During the second half of the 17th century, artisans, small businessmen, and Jews moved into this area at the encouragement of the Great Elector, who sought to improve his financial situation through their skills. As industrialization intensified, the quarter became poorer, and in the 1880s many East European Jews escaping pogroms settled here.

Northeast of Mitte, the old working-class district of Prenzlauer Berg used to be one of the poorest sections of Berlin. In socialist East Germany, the old (and mostly run-down) tenement houses attracted the artistic avant-garde, who transformed the area into a refuge for alternative lifestyles. The renovated area is now highly desirable and full of young couples with baby in tow. Despite Berlin's blight of graffiti on the 19th-century buildings, the stucco decorations, balconies with wrought-iron parapets, and cobblestone streets evoke a time when handicrafts and small shops flourished.

a good tour

From the Bernauer Strasse U-bahn station, turn left on Bernauer Strasse, and when you reach Strelitzer Strasse, cut to the path that runs parallel to the sidewalk. This path through the former border zone will lead you to a modern chapel. This replaced the church that the East Germans detonated in order to have clear sightlines in the deathstrip. The path continues to the memorial and museum **Dokumentationszentrum Berliner Mauer** 36 ▶. Follow the Wall that still stands to Gartenstrasse, and hop on a southbound S-bahn at Nordbahnhof. Exit one stop later at Oranienburger Strasse, the center of the old Jewish Quarter (Spandauer Vorstadt) and today full of restaurants and bars. You can't miss the gilded cupola of the **Neue Synagoge** 37, which is open to the public and well protected by armed police officers. Before reaching it, peek into the shops of the courtyard Heckmann Höfe on the same side of Oranienstrasse. From here take Krausnickstrasse to Grosse Hamburger Strasse, once the hub of life in Jewish Berlin. In 1941–42 at the home at Nos. 25–26, Nazis assembled Berlin's last 50,000 Jews to be transported to concentration camps. Of the oldest Jewish cemetery in the city, which dated to 1672, only the green lawn and a few gravestones mark what the Nazis destroyed. The Sophienkirche nearby was the first Protestant church built in the Spandauer Vorstadt (1712). Grosse Hamburger Strasse leads back to Oranienburger Strasse. Turn left on Oranienburger Strasse, following it as it curves into Rosenthaler Strasse and the entrance to the **Hackesche Höfe** 38, an art deco warehouse complex. From the nearby Hackescher Markt station, take any S-bahn heading east one stop to Alexanderplatz. Follow the signs for the long transfer to the U-2 line. Take this line in the direction of Pankow, getting off at Eberswalder Strasse in Prenzlauer Berg. One block to your left down Danziger Strasse and a half-block right on Knaackstrasse brings you to the fringe-arts and culture center

Kulturbrauerei ㊲, an old brewery and a typical example of late-19th-century industrial architecture. This is a good neighborhood in which to scout drinks or dinner. For local flavor, follow Sredzkistrasse to the east, or turn north up Knaackstrasse to cross onto Lychener Strasse.

TIMING If you want to indulge in the art galleries or relax at any of the many cafés along the way, reserve a full day for Mitte and Prenzlauer Berg. It's also possible to take in all spots along the tour within four hours.

What to See

㉟ **Dokumentationszentrum Berliner Mauer** (Berlin Wall Memorial Site). This site combines memorials and a museum and research center on the Berlin Wall. The division of Berlin was particularly heart-wrenching on Bernauer Strasse, where neighbors and families on opposite sides of the street were separated overnight. The Reconciliation Chapel, completed in 2000, replaced the community church dynamited by the Communists in 1985. The church had been walled into the "death strip" and was seen as a hindrance to patrolling it. A portion of the Wall remains on Bernauer Strasse and an installation meant to serve as a memorial unfortunately only confuses those wondering what the border once looked like. For a wealth of images and information, head into the museum, where German-speakers can even hear radio broadcasts from the time the Wall was erected. ✉ *Bernauer Str. 111, Wedding* ☎ *030/464–1030* ⊕ *www.berliner-mauer-dokumentationszentrum.de* ☒ *Free* ۩ *Wed.–Sun. 10–5* Ⓤ *Bernauer Strasse (U-bahn).*

★ ㊳ **Hackesche Höfe** (Hacke Warehouses). Built in 1905–07, this series of eight connected courtyards is the finest example of art nouveau industrial architecture in Berlin. Most buildings are covered with glazed white tiles, and additional Moorish mosaic designs decorate the main courtyard off Rosenthaler Strasse. Galleries, boutiques, restaurants, the variety theater Chamäleon Varieté, a drama stage, and a movie theater populate the spaces once occupied by ballrooms, a poets society, and a Jewish girls' club. ✉ *Rosenthaler Str. 40–41 and Sophienstr. 6, Mitte* ☎ *No phone* ⊕ *www.hackesche-hoefe.com* Ⓤ *Hackescher Markt (S-bahn).*

need a break?

Within the first courtyard of Hackesche Höfe **Anatre Feinkost** (✉ Rosenthaler Str. 40–41, Mitte ☎ 030/2838–9915) uses top-quality ingredients for its Mediterranean sandwiches and pastas. The mozzarella is the best in Berlin.

off the beaten path

JÜDISCHER FRIEDHOF (Jewish Cemetery) – More than 150,000 graves make this peaceful retreat in Berlin's Weissensee district Europe's largest Jewish cemetery. The grounds and tombstones are in excellent condition—a seeming impossibility, given its location in the heart of the Third Reich. To reach the cemetery, take Tram 2, 3, 4, 23, or 24 from Hackescher Markt to Albertinenstrasse and head south on Herbert-Baum-Strasse. At the gate you can get a plan from the attendant. The guidebook is in German only. ☎ *030/925–3330* ۩ *Apr.–Oct., Sun.–Thurs. 8–5, Fri. 8–3; Nov.–Mar., Sun.–Thurs. 8–4, Fri. 8–3.*

42 **Kulturbrauerei** (Culture Brewery). The redbrick buildings of the old Schultheiss brewery are now occupied by a multicinema, galleries, pubs, a club, and a concert venue that make up a fringe-arts and entertainment nexus. Parts of the brewery were built in 1842. Around the turn of the 20th century the complex was expanded to include the main brewery of Berlin's famous Schultheiss beer, then the largest brewery in the world. The buildings are completely restored, though no beer is brewed here now. Come Christmastime, a market includes an ice rink and children's rides. ⊠ *Schönhauser Allee 36–39 and Knaackstr. 97, Prenzlauer Berg* Ⓤ *Eberswalder Str. (U-bahn).*

need a break?

For coffee and cake or Berliner Kindl, Potsdamer Rex, or Paulaner Hefeweizen on tap, stop by **Restauration 1900** (⊠ Husemannstr. 1, Prenzlauer Berg ☎ 030/442–2494). It's one of the few popular cafés and restaurants from socialist times still in business today. It sits on the now prime real estate of Kollwitzplatz.

37 **Neue Synagoge** (New Synagogue). This meticulously restored landmark, built between 1859 and 1866, is an exotic amalgam of styles, the whole faintly Middle Eastern. Its bulbous, gilded cupola stands out in the skyline. When its doors opened, it was the largest synagogue in Europe, with 3,200 seats. The synagogue was damaged on November 9, 1938 (*Kristallnacht*—Night of the Broken Glass), when Nazi looters rampaged across Germany, burning synagogues and smashing the few Jewish shops and homes left in the country. Destroyed by Allied bombing in 1943, it wasn't until the mid-1980s that the East German government restored it. The effective exhibit on the history of the building and its congregants includes fragments of the original architecture and furnishings. Sabbath services are held in a modern addition. ⊠ *Oranienburger Str. 28–30, Mitte* ☎ *030/8802–8316* ⊕ *www.cjudaicum.de* ⊠ *€3, €4.60 including special exhibits; tour €1.50, German only* ⊗ *Sept.–Apr., Sun.–Thurs. 10–6, Fri. 10–2; May–Aug., Tues.–Thurs. 10–6, Mon. and Sun. 10–8, Fri. 10–5. Tours Wed. at 4, Sun. at 2 and 4. Cupola Apr.–Sept.* Ⓤ *Oranienburger Str. (U-bahn), Oranienburger Tor (S-bahn).*

Palaces, Parks & Museums in Outer Berlin

The city's outlying areas abound with palaces, lakes, and museums set in lush greenery. Central to the former West Berlin but now a western district of the united city, Charlottenburg was once an independent and wealthy city that only became a part of Berlin in 1920. It holds the baroque Charlottenburg Palace and several important museums. The vast Grunewald (forest) covers most of southwestern Berlin; it's an ideal spot for hiking or for relaxing on one of the lake's islands. Some of the city's most intriguing museums are in the well-to-do neighborhood of Dahlem.

a good tour

Begin at the museums of **Schloss Charlottenburg** ④ ▶ and the adjacent **Ägyptisches Museum** ④ and **Museum Berggruen** ④. To get there, take the U-bahn to Richard-Wagner-Platz (U–7). From the station, look for the dome of the palace and follow Otto-Suher-Allee northwest toward it.

The four **Dahlemer Museen** ④ lie south of Charlottenburg in the neighborhood of Dahlem. To reach them from Richard-Wagner-Platz, take the U–7 in the direction of Rudow until you reach the stop Fehrbelliner Platz. Change trains here and take the U–1 in the direction of Krumme Lanke to Dahlem-Dorf. The trip from the palace to the museums takes about 45 minutes.

After placard reading, it's time for the great outdoors in the **Grunewald** ㊹. From the Dahlem Museums it's a short ride on the U–1 to the Krumme Lanke station, from which you should walk to the S-bahn station Mexikoplatz. Board the S–1 (in the direction of Wannsee) and get off at the Nikolassee or Wannsee station. If you want to continue to the Grunewald station, change to the S–7 (direction Friedrichstrasse) at Nikolassee. Each of these stations serves as a starting point for hour-long hikes through the greenbelt of the Grunewald and Wannsee lakes. A grim reminder of the area's past is the **Bildungs- und Gedenkstätte Haus der Wannsee-Konferenz** ㊺, an old villa where the Holocaust was planned. From the Wannsee S-bahn station the Haus der Wannsee-Konferenz can be reached on Bus 114.

TIMING   Because of travel distances, you will need at least one full day for these attractions; spend the morning at Schloss Charlottenburg and the Dahlem Museums and the rest of the day in the Grunewald area.

Sights to See

㊶ **Ägyptisches Museum** (Egyptian Museum). Until April 2005, the east guardhouse and residence of Prussian king Friedrich I's bodyguard is housing works that trace Egypt's history from 4000 BC and include some of the best-preserved mummies outside Cairo. Then, the first piece to move to the Altes Museum on Museum Island will be the exquisite portrait bust of Queen Nefertiti. The 3,300-year-old sculpture will be joined by the rest of the collection in September 2005. The Altes Museum's ground floor will host the Egyptian Museum until it relocates to the Neue Museum in 2009. ✉ *Schlossstr. 70, Charlottenburg* ☎ *030/3435–7311* ⊕ *www.smpk.de* 🖙 *€6* ☉ *Daily 10–6.*

㊺ **Bildungs- und Gedenkstätte Haus der Wannsee-Konferenz** (Wannsee Conference Memorial Site). The lovely lakeside setting of this Berlin villa belies the unimaginable Holocaust atrocities planned here. This elegant edifice hosted the fateful conference held on January 20, 1942, at which Nazi leaders and German bureaucrats, under SS leader Reinhard Heydrich, planned the systematic deportation and mass extinction of Europe's Jewish population. Today this so-called *Endlösung der Judenfrage* ("final solution of the Jewish question") is illustrated with an exhibition that documents the conference, and more extensively, the escalation of persecution against Jews, and the Holocaust itself. Upstairs is a research center with source materials in English. From the S-bahn station Wannsee, take Bus 114. Allow at least two hours for a visit. ✉ *Am Grossen Wannsee 56–58, Zehlendorf* ☎ *030/805–0010* ⊕ *www.ghwk. de* 🖙 *Free* ☉ *Daily 10–6* Ⓤ *Wannsee (S-bahn).*

㊸ **Dahlemer Museen** (Dahlem Museums). This complex of four museums includes the **Ethnologisches Museum** (Ethnographic Museum) as well as museums for Indian, East Asian, and early European art. It's internationally known for its art and artifacts from Africa, Asia, the South Seas, and the Americas. The large collection of Mayan, Aztec, and Incan ceramics and stone sculptures should not be missed. ⊠ *Lansstr. 8, Zehlendorf* ☎ *030/830–1438* ⊕ *www.smpk.de* 💷 *€4* ☉ *Tues.–Fri. 10–6, weekends 11–6* Ⓤ *Dahlem-Dorf (U-bahn).*

❹❹ Grunewald. Together with its Wannsee lakes, this splendid forest is the city's most popular retreat. In good weather Berliners come out in force, swimming, sailing their boats, tramping through the woods, and riding horseback. In winter a downhill ski run and even a ski jump operate on the modest slopes of Teufelsberg Hill. Excursion steamers ply the water wonderland of the Wannsee and the Havel River. Ⓤ *Grunewald (S-bahn).*

★ ❹❷ Museum Berggruen. This small modern art museum focuses on Matisse, Picasso, and Klee. Heinz Berggruen, a businessman who left Berlin in the 1930s, collected the excellent paintings. He narrates portions of the free audio guide, sharing anecdotes about how he came to acquire pieces directly from the artists, as well as his opinions of the women portrayed in Picasso's portraits. ⊠ *Schlossstr. 1, Charlottenburg* ☎ *030/ 3269–5815* ⊕ *www.smpk.de* 💷 *€6* ☉ *Tues.–Sun. 10–6* Ⓤ *Sophie-Charlotte-Pl. (U-bahn), Richard-Wagner-Pl. (U-bahn).*

> **off the beaten path**
>
> **PFAUENINSEL** (Peacock Island) – Prussian king Friedrich Wilhelm II whisked his mistresses away to this small island oasis on the Great Wannsee. **Schloss Pfaueninsel,** the small white palace, erected in 1794 according to the ruler's plans—and in accordance with the taste of the era—was built as a fake ruin. The simple building looks strangely cartoonlike; it's easy to imagine it appearing in a White Castle commercial. In the early 19th century, garden architect Joseph Peter Lenné designed an English garden on the island, which ultimately became western Berlin's favorite summer getaway. From the Wannsee S-bahn station, take Bus 216 (leaving every 20 minutes) and then a ferry. ⊠ *Pfaueninselchaussee, Zehlendorf* ☎ *030/ 8058–6830* ⊕ *www.spsg.de* 💷 *€3, ferry service €1* ☉ *Palace Apr.–Oct., Tues.–Sun. 10–5; Ferry to Pfaueninsel year-round* Ⓤ *Wannsee (S-bahn).*

SACHSENHAUSEN GEDENKSTÄTTE (Sachsenhausen Memorial) – The only concentration camp near the Third Reich capital was established in 1936. It held prisoners from every nation in Europe, including British officers, Joseph Stalin's son, and 12,000 Soviet prisoners-of-war who were systematically murdered here. The work camp had held approximately 200,000 prisoners and it can be estimated that 50,000 died here. Between 1945 and 1950 the Soviets used the site as a prison, where malnutrition and disease claimed the lives of 20% of the inmates. The East German government made the site a concentration camp memorial in April 1961. A few original facilities remain; the barracks, which hold exhibits, are reconstructions. To reach Sachsenhausen, take the S-bahn 1 to Oranienburg, the last stop. The ride will take 45–50 minutes. From the station it's a 25-minute walk (follow signs), or you can take a taxi or Bus 804 in the direction of Malz. Oranienburg is 35 km (22 mi) north of Berlin. ✉ *Str. der Nationen 22, Oranienburg* ☎ *03301/200–200* ⊕ *www.gedenkstaette- sachsenhausen.de* ✉ *Free, audio guide* €2.50 ☉ *Mid-Mar.–mid- Oct., Tues.–Sun. 8:30–6; mid-Oct.–mid-Mar., Tues.–Sun., 9–4:30; last admission ½ hr before closing* Ⓤ *Oranienburg (S-bahn).*

▶ ⑳ **Schloss Charlottenburg** (Charlottenburg Palace). A monumental reminder of imperial days, this showplace served as a city residence for the Prussian rulers. The gorgeous palace started as a modest royal summer residence in 1695, built on the orders of King Friedrich I for his wife, Sophie-Charlotte. In the 18th century Frederick the Great made a number of additions, such as the dome and several wings designed in the rococo style. By 1790 the complex had evolved into a massive royal domain that could take a whole day to explore. Behind heavy iron gates, the Court of Honor—the front courtyard—is dominated by a baroque statue of the Great Elector on horseback. ✉ *Luisenpl., Charlottenburg* ☎ *030/320–911* ⊕ *www.spsg.de* ✉ *A Tageskarte (day card) for* €7 *covers admission for all bldgs., excluding tour of Altes Schloss baroque apartments; a 2-day* €12 *card covers all palace sights in Berlin area, except Sanssouci.*

The **Altes Schloss** (Nering-Eosander-Bau; ☎ 030/3209–1440 ✉ €8 with tour; €2 for upper floor only ☉ Tues.–Fri. 9–5, weekends 10–5) is the main building with the ground-floor suites of Friedrich I and Sophie-Charlotte. Paintings include royal portraits by Antoine Pesne, a noted court painter of the 18th century. A guided tour visits the Oak Gallery, the early-18th-century palace chapel, and the suites of Friedrich Wilhelm II and Friedrich Wilhelm III, furnished in the Biedermeier style. Tours leave every hour on the hour from 9 to 4. The upper floor has the apartments of Friedrich Wilhelm IV, a silver treasury, and Berlin and Meissen porcelain. It can be seen on its own.

The **Neuer Flügel** (New Wing; ☎ 030/3209–1454 ✉ €5 ☉ Tues.–Fri. 10–6, weekends 11–6), where Frederick the Great once lived, is also called the Knobbeldorff-Flügel. The 138-foot-long Goldene Galerie (Golden Gallery) was the palace's ballroom. West of the staircase are Frederick's rooms, in which his extravagant collection of works by Watteau, Chardin, and Pesne is displayed. An audio guide is included in the admission.

The park behind the palace was laid out in the French baroque style beginning in 1697 and was transformed into an English garden in the early 19th century. In it stand the Schinkel Pavilion and the **Belvedere teahouse** (☎ 030/3209–1412 ✉ €2 ☉ Nov.–Mar., Tues.–Fri. noon–4, weekends noon–5; mid-Apr.–Oct., daily 10–5), which overlooks the lake and the Spree River and holds a collection of Berlin porcelain.

The **Museum für Vor- und Frühgeschichte** (Museum of Pre- and Early History; ☎ 030/326–7480 ✉ €6 ☉ Tues.–Fri. 9–5, weekends 10–5) traces the evolution of mankind from 1 million BC to AD 1,000. It's opposite Klausener Platz (to the left as you face the palace).

need a break? Between visits to the museums clustering around Schloss Charlottenburg, give your feet a rest in the country-kitchen room of the **Kleine Orangerie** (✉ Spandauer Damm 20, Charlottenburg ☎ 030/322–2021 ⊙ Tues.–Fri. 9–5, weekends 10–5), next door to the palace. The breakfast is a good deal. There's also atrium and outdoor seating.

WHERE TO EAT

Neighborhood stalwarts continue the frequent tradition of serving residents from morning to night with a mix of German and international cuisine. Other than at high-end restaurants, Berlin is known for curt or slow service.

The most common food for meals on-the-go are *Wursts* (sausages). Currywurst, a pork sausage served with a mildly curried ketchup, is local to Berlin. Even more popular are Turkish *Döner* stands.

WHAT IT COSTS In Euros				
$$$$	**$$$**	**$$**	**$**	**¢**
AT DINNER over €25	€20–€25	€15–€19	€11–€14	under €10

Restaurant prices are per person for a main course at dinner.

Charlottenburg

$$$$ ✕ **Alt Luxemburg.** This popular restaurant creates an intimate setting with 19th-century-style furniture, wrought-iron lamps, and wonderfully attentive service. Working behind the stove since 1982, owner and chef Karl Wannemacher has used only the freshest ingredients for his modern German dishes. Lobster is always in some form on the menu, be it a salad or the divine lobster lasagna. Entrée options might include rolled saddle of rabbit in coffee sauce. You can order à la carte or opt for a four-course meal for €65. ✉ *Windscheidstr. 31, Charlottenburg* ☎ *030/ 323–8730* ▤ *AE, DC, MC, V* ⊙ *Closed Sun. No lunch* ⓤ *Charlottenburg (S-bahn), Wilmersdorfer Str. (U-bahn).*

★ **$$$$** ✕ **Ana e Bruno.** Most of the guests here are making an evening out of the four- and eight-course meals. This Berlin classic is expensive but exudes a warm and homey atmosphere thanks to the hospitality of the owners, Bruno and Ana. Don't expect hearty home cooking, though: the chef favors a low-calorie reinterpretation of Mediterranean cuisine and prefers fresh vegetables and salads over pasta. The four-course meals are €67; the eight-course, €99. ✉ *Sophie-Charlotten-Str. 101, Charlottenburg* ☎ *030/325–7110* ✍ *Reservations essential* ▤ *AE* ⊙ *Closed Sun. and Mon. No lunch* ⓤ *Westend (S-bahn).*

★ **¢–$** ✕ **Engelbecken.** The beer coasters are trading cards of the Wittelsbach dynasty in this relaxed, but high-quality restaurant serving dishes from Bavaria and the Alps. Classics like Wienerschnitzel, goulasch, or grilled saddle steak are made of "bio" meat and vegetable products, meaning that even the veal, lamb, and beef are the tasty results of organic and

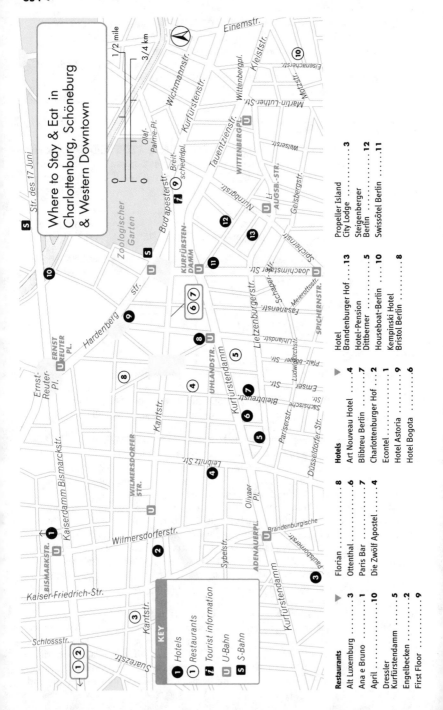

Where to Stay & Eat in Charlottenburg, Schöneburg & Western Downtown

KEY

- ① Hotels
- ① Restaurants
- 🛈 Tourist information
- Ⓤ U-Bahn
- Ⓢ S-Bahn

Restaurants

Alt Luxemburg	**3**
Ana e Bruno	**1**
April	**10**
Dressler Kurfürstendamm	**5**
Engelbecken	**2**
First Floor	**9**
Florian	**8**
Ottenthal	**6**
Paris Bar	**7**
Die Zwölf Apostel	**4**

Hotels

Art Nouveau Hotel	**4**
Blibtreu Berlin	**7**
Charlottenburger Hof	**2**
Econtel	**1**
Hotel Astoria	**9**
Hotel Bogota	**6**
Hotel Brandenburger Hof	**13**
Hotel-Pension Dittberner	**5**
Houseboat-Berlin	**10**
Kempinski Hotel Bristol Berlin	**8**
Propeller Island City Lodge	**3**
Steigenberger Berlin	**12**
Swissôtel Berlin	**11**

humane upbringing. The room is like a dine-in art gallery, but in warm weather, reserve a sidewalk table. With its corner position facing a park bordering Lake Lietzensee, Engelbecken is one of the loveliest open-air dining spots in town. ⊠ *Witzlebenstr. 31, Charlottenburg* ☎ *030/615–2810* ▤ *MC, V* ⊗ *No lunch Mon.–Sat.* Ⓤ *Sophie-Charlotte-Pl. (U-bahn).*

Western Downtown

$$$$ ✕ **First Floor.** Few hotel-restaurants become a sensation, but this award-winning one is outstanding, even if it doesn't shake the hotel-restaurant look with its carpeting and heavy drapes. Chef Matthias Buchholz prepares French cuisine like a native. Occasionally the menu turns to German roots, with *Müritzlammrücken in Olivenkruste mit Bohnenmelange* (Müritz lamb back in olive crust, served with green beans). The four-course menu costs €66.50. If you're a wine connoisseur, ask sommelier Herr Tietz for a look at the caveau that holds more than 800 red wines. ⊠ *Hotel Palace, Budapester Str. 42, Western Downtown* ☎ *030/2502–1020* ⚑ *Reservations essential* ▤ *AE, DC, MC, V* ⊗ *No lunch Sat.* Ⓤ *Wittenbergpl (U-bahn).*

$$–$$$ ✕ **Paris Bar.** Just off the Ku'damm, this trendy restaurant attracts a polyglot clientele of film stars, artists, entrepreneurs, and executives to whom food plays second fiddle to socializing. Meals can be ordered until 1 AM. The cuisine, including such delights as Jacques oysters and lamb chops with Provençal herbs, is reliably French. ⊠ *Kantstr. 152, Western Downtown* ☎ *030/313–8052* ▤ *AE.*

$–$$$ ✕ **Dressler.** Both in its cuisine and in its service, Dressler is a mixture of French brasserie culture and German down-to-earth reliability. Accordingly, the dishes are conceived for a wide range of palates: oysters on the half-shell, duck with red cabbage, or cod with Pommery mustard sauce, for example. The menu changes according to season. Of the two (very similar) Dressler establishments, the one on Kurfürstendamm is livelier, with a genuinely French atmosphere. Reservations are advised. ⊠ *Kurfürstendamm 207/208, Western Downtown* ☎ *030/883–3530* ⊠ *Unter den Linden 39, Mitte* ☎ *030/204–4422* ▤ *AE, DC, MC, V.*

★ $–$$$ ✕ **Florian.** South German, Franconian comfort cuisine makes this a home away from home for transplants to northern Berlin. You won't find *Kirchweihbraten* (marinated pork with baked apples and plums) anywhere else in town. *Nürnberger Rostbratwurst* (small pork sausages) and *Maultaschen* (vegetable- or fish-filled pasta pockets in broth) are other southern specialties. The menu changes daily, and you can choose which type of *Knoedel* (dumpling) you'd like to accompany your meal, such as duck or oxtail in port wine. Florian's other strong draw is its warm, relaxed atmosphere and people-watching opportunities. The kitchen is open until 1 AM, and smaller dishes are available until 2 AM. ⊠ *Grolmanstr. 52, Western Downtown* ☎ *030/313–9184* ▤ *MC, V* ⊗ *No lunch* Ⓤ *Savignyplatz (S-bahn).*

★ $$ ✕ **Ottenthal.** This intimate restaurant with white tablecloths and a checkerboard floor is the city cousin of the Austrian village of Ottenthal, which delivers up the wines, pumpkinseed oil, and organic ingredients on the menu. The curiosity-arousing combinations might be pike-perch with lobster sauce and pepper–pine nut risotto, or venison medallions with vegetable-potato-strudel, red cabbage, and rowanberry sauce. The Wienerschnizel doesn't end and the pastas and strudel are homemade. Tables lined in two rows allow you to peek at what you might order. For one of the best meals for your money in Berlin, Ottenthal is a particularly good choice on Sunday evening, when most of Berlin's finer restaurants are closed. ⊠ *Kantstr. 153, Charlottenburg* ☎ *030/313–3162* ⊟ *AE, DC, MC, V* ☉ *No lunch* Ⓤ *Zoologischer Garten (S-bahn and U-bahn).*

¢–$$ ✕ **Die Zwölf Apostel.** Both of the "Twelve Apostles" are known for their stimulating settings and their great stone-oven pizzas named for Jesus's disciples. The Savignyplatz location in Charlottenburg never closes and offers a winter garden and outdoor dining. In Mitte, eyes are often riveted to the frescoed, vaulted ceilings that rumble as trains pass overhead. In each, garlands of garlic are hung along the wall. Pizzas are discounted weekdays noon–4 and on Monday evening you can eat your fill of pie and pasta for €9.99. Fish and meat dishes round out the menus of these spacious and lively spots. ⊠ *Bleibtreustr. 49, Charlottenburg* ☎ *030/312–1433* Ⓤ *Savignypl. (S-bahn)* ⊠ *Georgenstr. 2, Mitte* ☎ *030/201–0222* Ⓤ *Friedrichstr. (S-bahn and U-bahn)* ⊟ *No credit cards.*

Schöneberg

¢–$ ✕ **April.** There's a back room dressed with white tablecloths, but most regulars pick a place in the front where there's art nouveau light fixtures, stuccowork, and a street view. It's a relaxed bistro and the service can be sluggish, but the consistently delicious meals are very reasonably priced. The menu has a mix of Italian, French, and German cooking and a kids' section. The only lackluster items are the thin-crust Alsatian pizzas (*Pfannkuchen*). The generous *Vorspeisenteller* (selection of five appetizers) might include bresaola over arugula, grilled vegetables, and shrimp tempura. The restaurant is near Winterfeld Platz. ⊠ *Winterfeldstr. 56, Schöneberg* ☎ *030/216–8869* ⊟ *No credit cards* Ⓤ *Nollendorfpl. (U-bahn).*

Kreuzberg

$–$$ ✕ **Abendmahl.** The exquisite vegetarian and fish preparations here prove that an inexpensive meal doesn't have to leave you hungry. Hearty creations have playful names such as *Flammendes Inferno* (Flaming Inferno), a fish curry whose spiciness means business. The campy desserts are particularly over the top, like *Whatever Happened to Simone de Beauvoir?* (part of the Deadly Ice Creams series). Healthy eaters such as Wim Wenders and Nina Hagen are among the artsy crowd frequenting the small restaurant. ⊠ *Muskauer Str. 9, Kreuzberg* ☎ *030/612–5170* ⊟ *No credit cards* ☉ *No lunch* Ⓤ *Görlitzer Bahnhof (U-bahn).*

★ ¢–$ ✕ **Grossbeerenkeller.** This cellar restaurant, with its massive, dark-oak furniture and decorative antlers, is undoubtedly one of the most "German" taverns in town. With rare, old-fashioned Berlin hospitality, owner and bartender Ingeborg Zinn-Baier presents such popular dishes as *Hoppel-Poppel* (an omelettelike dish of smoked and pickled pork, eggs, home fries, onions, and herbs), *Kasseler Nacken mit Grünkohl* (boiled salt-pork

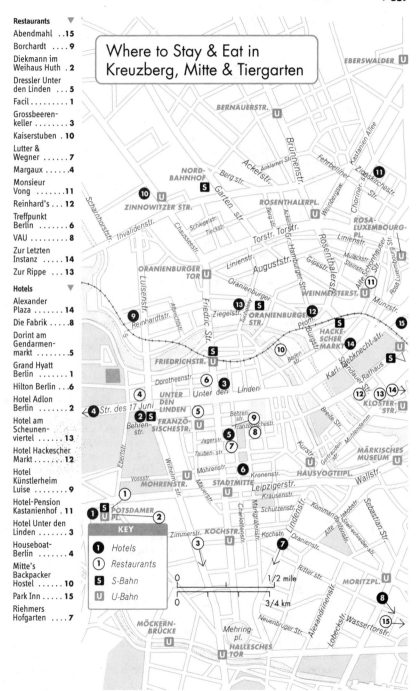

Where to Stay & Eat in
Kreuzberg, Mitte & Tiergarten

KEY

- **①** *Hotels*
- **①** *Restaurants*
- **S** *S-Bahn*
- **U** *U-Bahn*

meat with green cabbage), and Nürnberger sausages. Her fried potatoes are famous. The restaurant opens at 4 PM weekdays and in summer you can sup in the simple courtyard. ☒ *Grossbeerenstr. 90, Kreuzberg* ☎ *030/ 251–3064* 🖃 *No credit cards* ☯ *Closed Sun. No lunch.*

Mitte

★ $$$$ ✕ **Kaiserstuben.** This 16-seat dining room is secreted on the second floor of a palace dating to 1753. In this quiet escape, the only sounds you'll hear are soft conversation and music—the kitchen is on another part of the floor. The cuisine balances regional heritage with French influences. Entrées on the small à la carte menu might include roasted turbot with rice noodles and coconut-ginger sauce or poached veal saddle with truffle risotto. The four-course meal runs about €45. After your dinner, move to the Tadjikistan tea room on the other side of the "palace." Once you've removed your shoes, you're free to recline on pillows while sipping tea from a samovar. ☒ *Am Festungsgraben 1, Mitte* ☎ *030/2061–0548* 🖃 *AE, MC, V* ☯ *Closed Sun. and Mon. No lunch.*

$$$$ ✕ **Margaux.** Michael Hoffman's eclectic cuisine comes with a touch of French influence and plenty of imports. The local asparagus hails from Beelizt; the line-caught Atlantic fish once swam off France; and somehow salt arrives from the Himalayas. Menus run from four to eight courses, and any dinner should be complemented with wine—the sommelier is happy to help you choose one from a list of almost 400 vintages. Above the black marble floor, pillars lined with backlit alabaster, upholstered chairs in russet and mustard, and paintings with bold strokes of color keep the urban design warm. ☒ *Unter den Linden 78, entrance on Wilhelmstr., Mitte* ☎ *030/2265–2611* ⌓ *Reservations essential* 🖃 *AE, DC, MC, V* ☯ *No lunch Sun.*

$$$$ ✕ **VAU.** Trendsetter VAU defined hip in the Mitte district years ago, and
Fodor'sChoice   remains a favorite even as it ages. The excellent German fish and game
   ★   dishes prepared by chef Kolja Kleeberg have earned him endless praise and awards. Daring combinations include *Ente mit gezupftem Rotkohl, Quitten, und Maronen* (duck with selected red cabbage, quinces, and sweet chestnuts) and *Steinbutt mit Kalbbries auf Rotweinschalotten* (turbot with veal sweetbread on shallots in red wine). A four-course menu costs €78; a six-course, €115. A lunch entrée is a bargain at €12. The cool interior was designed by one of Germany's leading industrial architects. ☒ *Jägerstr. 54/55, Mitte* ☎ *030/202–9730* ⌓ *Reservations essential* 🖃 *AE, DC, MC, V* ☯ *Closed Sun.*

★ $–$$$$ ✕ **Borchardt.** The menu changes daily at this fashionable celebrity meeting place. The high ceiling, plush maroon benches, art nouveau mosaic (discovered during renovations), and marble columns create the impression of a 1920s café. The cuisine is high-quality French-German, including several dishes with fresh fish, veal, and some of Berlin's best (and most tender) beef classics. New in 2004 is the Kobe beef. There's a three-course €50 prix-fixe menu as well. ☒ *Französische Str. 47, Mitte* ☎ *030/ 2038–7110* ⌓ *Reservations essential* 🖃 *AE, MC, V.*

★ $–$$$ ✕ **Lutter & Wegner.** One of the city's oldest vintners (*Sekt*, German champagne, was first conceived here in 1811 by actor Ludwig Devrient), Lutter & Wegner has returned to its historic location off Gendarmenmarkt. The dark wood-panel walls, parquet floor, and multitude of rooms takes you back to 19th-century Vienna. The cuisine is mostly Austrian with superb game dishes in winter and, of course, a Wiener schnitzel with lukewarm potato salad. The *Sauerbraten* (marinated pot roast) with red cabbage was named best in Germany in 2003. In the Weinstube, meat and cheese plates are served until 3 AM. ⊠ *Charlottenstr. 56, Mitte* ☎ *030/ 2029–5417* ☲ *AE, MC, V.*

\$–\$\$ ✕ **Reinhard's.** Friends meet here in the Nikolaiviertel to enjoy the carefully prepared entrées and to sample spirits from the amply stocked bar, all served by friendly, tie-wearing waiters. The honey-glaze breast of duck, *Adlon,* is one of its specialties. If you just want to hug the bar but find no room, don't despair; head two doors down to Italian Marcellino's (under the same management). ⊠ *Poststr. 28, Mitte* ☎ *030/242–5295* ⚑ *Reservations essential* ☲ *AE, DC, MC, V.*

¢–\$ ✕ **Treffpunkt Berlin.** This smoky, side-street "meeting point" is easily overlooked, but down-to-earth Berliners fill its bar stools and cluster of tables. The servers are gracious to non–German speakers and will make sure you eat the *Sol Ei* (hard-boiled egg), a dying breed of Berlin snack, in the correct manner: scoop out the yolk, fill the crevice with the condiments delivered, and replace the yolk. Aside from the Berlin specialties, the kitchen cooks up a spicy goulash. This is one of the few inexpensive restaurants with character near Friedrichstrasse and the attractions of Unter den Linden. ⊠ *Mittelstr. 55, Mitte* ☎ *030/204–1819* ☲ *No credit cards* Ⓤ *Friedrichstr. (S-bahn and U-bahn).*

★ ¢–\$ ✕ **Zur Letzten Instanz.** Established in 1621, Berlin's oldest restaurant resides in a forgotten nest of medieval streets, but German tourists do find it and then disperse among the warren of rooms. The small menu points to Berlin's most traditional dish and the specialty: *Eisbein* (pork knuckle). Napoléon is said to have sat alongside the tile stove, Mikhail Gorbachev sipped a beer here in 1989, and Chancellor Gerhard Schröder treated French president Jacques Chirac to a meal here in 2003. Actor Jack Nicholson took in its humble atmosphere while attending the Berlinale festival in 2004. Service can be erratic, though always friendly. ⊠ *Waisenstr. 14–16, Mitte* ☎ *030/242–5528* ⚑ *Reservations essential.* ☲ *AE, DC, MC, V* Ⓤ *Klosterstr. (U-bahn).*

¢–\$ ✕ **Zur Rippe.** This popular place in the Nikolaiviertel serves wholesome food in an intimate setting of oak paneling and ceramic tiles. Specialties include the platter of *Kasseler, Ribbchen, und Eisbein* (cured pork, ribs, and pig knuckle), and a herring casserole. ⊠ *Poststr. 17, Mitte* ☎ *030/ 242–4248* ☲ *AE, DC, MC, V* Ⓤ *Alexanderplatz (S-bahn).*

¢ ✕ **Monsieur Vuong.** Filling this hip eatery are people who share a love for Vietnamese cuisine from Saigon and the Mekong Delta. It's also an incredibly convenient place to meet before hitting Mitte's nightlife, or for slipping in just a few calories before wiggling into the wares of neighboring boutiques. Inevitably, the same steamy dishes and soups, such as *goi bo* (spicy beef salad), land on each low table, as there's only five items and two specials on offer. The menu changes every two days but you can always finish with an artichoke or jasmine tea. ⊠ *Alte Schönhauser Str. 46, Mitte* ☎ *030/3087–2643* ⚑ *Reser-*

vations not accepted ⊟ *No credit cards* ⊘ *No lunch Sun.* Ⓤ *Rosenthaler Str. (U-bahn).*

Tiergarten

★ **$$$$** ✕ **Facil.** Secreted above the hubbub of Potsdamer Platz is this temple-like oasis for the senses. On a fifth-floor terrace planted with bamboo and leafy trees, there are no city views, yet light pours in through the glass walls and retractable glass ceiling. Young chef Michael Kempf earned a Michelin star in November 2003. His changing menu might include veal shank with spiny lobster, a smoked swordfish carpaccio, or ox cheek with truffeled leek purée. Four-course dinners are €75. At lunch, everything on the menu is €12. ⊠ *Hotel Madison, Potsdamer Str. 3, Tiergarten* ☎ *030/5900–51234* ⊜ *Reservations essential* ⊟ *AE, DC, MC, V* ⊘ *Closed weekends* Ⓤ *Potsdamer Pl. (S-bahn and U-bahn).*

$–$$ ✕ **Diekmann im Weinhaus Huth.** Berlin restaurateur Diekmann was one of the first to bring affordable, quality French cuisine to the city in the 1980s and his second restaurant resides in this historic house, the only one in Potsdamer Platz that survived the war and the Wall. The dining room of white-tableclothed tables in arrow-straight rows also has a patio overlooking a whimsical Robert Rauschenberg sculpture. The menu changes, but regularly has coq au vin, half-duck, and crepes Suzette. The raw oysters are a good deal, as is the lunch menu. ⊠ *Alte Potsdamer Str. 5, Tiergarten* ☎ *030/2529–7524* ⊟ *AE, MC, V.*

WHERE TO STAY

Berlin, a city of 3.4 million people, is ambitiously adding more hotels by the month, even surpassing New York City for number of hotel rooms. Despite the city's floundering economy, luxury hotels are in bloom. The Ritz-Carlton that opened on Potsdamer Platz in January 2004 extends a welcoming nod to budget-conscious locals in its brasserie, where all entrées are under €18. In the same week the Ritz debuted, a posh Marriott opened within a red carpet's reach.

The least expensive accommodations are available in local pensions, hostels with attractive double rooms, or through private room agency arrangements. Internet services like Expedia can sometimes book a room at a five-star hotel in Berlin for half the normal price, even in summer. Hotels listed here as **$$$$** often come down to a **$$** level on weekends or during low-demand times. Compared to old European cities such as Paris or London, most hotel rooms in Berlin are large, and many are part of chains that allow for less individual character. Ibis and Mercure are European chains that have several locations in Berlin.

Year-round business conventions and tourism peaks during the summer and Christmastime, meaning you should make reservations well in advance. If you arrive without reservations, consult hotel boards at airports and train stations, which show hotels with vacancies; or go to the tourist office in the Europa Center for help with reservations. Moderately priced pensions and small hotels are common in western districts such as Charlottenburg, Schöneberg, and Wilmersdorf.

WHAT IT COSTS In Euros				
$$$$	**$$$**	**$$**	**$**	**¢**
FOR 2 PEOPLE over €200	€160–€200	€120–€160	€60–€120	under €60

Hotel prices are for two people in a standard double room, including tax and service.

Charlottenburg

★ **$–$$** 🏨 **Art Nouveau Hotel.** The owners' discerning taste in antiques, color combinations, and even televisions (designed by Philip Starke) make this B&B-like pension a pleasure to live in. Rooms share an elegant simplicity, but each has a prize piece, such as a handcarved 18th-century Chinese dresser or a chandelier from the Komische Opera's set of *Don Carlos*. Several rooms are hung with a single large black-and-white photo by Sabine Kačunko. The apartment building shows its age only in the antique wood elevator, high stucco ceilings, and an occasionally creaky floor. You can serve yourself tea or coffee in the breakfast room throughout the day, and you can mix your own drinks at the honor bar. Your friendly English-speaking hosts are Mr. and Mrs. Schlenzka. ⊠ *Leibnitzstr. 59, Charlottenburg, D–10629* ☎ *030/327–7440* 🖷 *030/3277–4440* ⊕ *www.hotelartnouveau.de* 🛏 *19 rooms, 3 suites* ⌂ *Breakfast room, in-room data ports, cable TV, lounge, bar, dry cleaning, laundry service, Internet, meeting rooms, some pets allowed (fee), no-smoking; no a/c* ⊟ *AE, MC, V* ⏐◎⏐ *CP* Ⓤ *Adenauerpl. (U-bahn).*

$–$$ 🏨 **Econtel.** Keep an eye on the Web site for special rates that dip as low as €55 a night. Within walking distance of the Spree River and Charlottenburg Palace, the hotel is also just two stops on Bus X9 from Zoo Station. Families fit in well, most imaginatively in the Mickey Mouse rooms with bunk beds. A crib and children's toilet are available free of charge. Business travelers appreciate the wireless Lan. All the rooms are spotless and have a homey feel. The 68.9-foot breakfast buffet spread (€13) could delay your sightseeing. ⊠ *Sömmeringstr. 24–26, Charlottenburg, D–10589* ☎ *030/346–810* 🖷 *030/3468–1163* ⊕ *www.econtel. de* 🛏 *205 rooms* ⌂ *Restaurant, in-room safes, cable TV, bar, babysitting, dry cleaning, laundry service, meeting room, parking (fee), some pets allowed (fee), no-smoking rooms; no a/c* ⊟ *AE, MC, V* Ⓤ *Mierendorffpl. (U-bahn).*

$–$$ 🏨 **Propeller Island City Lodge.** Make like Alice and fall down the rabbit hole, but in this wildly eccentric accommodation you can choose from 32 Wonderlands (read the Web site carefully before picking which pill to pop). Multitalented artist Lars Stroschen is responsible for each one-of-a-kind, handcrafted furnishing. Theatrical settings such as the Upside Down and Flying Bed rooms predominate, but there are tamer abodes, like the monastic Orange and Temple rooms. Only children get to inhabit the Gnome Room, which keeps out anyone over 4′8″. This creative getaway serves breakfast (€7) but is not service-oriented; reception is open 8 AM–noon only. ⊠ *Albrecht-Achilles-Str. 58, Charlottenburg, D–10709* ☎ *030/891–9016 8 AM–noon, 0163/256–5909 noon–9 PM* 🖷 *030/8928–721* ⊕ *www.propeller-island.de* 🛏 *31 rooms, 1 suite 26 with bath* ⌂ *Breakfast room, in-room data ports, some kitchenettes, some* *pets allowed, no-smoking rooms; no room phones, no TV in some rooms, no a/c ⊟ MC, V Ⓤ Adenauerpl. (U-bahn).*

$ 🏠 **Charlottenburger Hof.** No-fuss travelers will find great value in this

Fodor's Choice low-key hotel. The variety of rooms, all brightened by sunlight and pri-

★ mary-color schemes with prints by Kandinsky, Miró, and Mondrian, can accommodate travelers whether they be friends, couples, or families. All rooms have computers with free Internet access, and amenities include hair dryers. The 24-hour restaurant serves healthy dishes and draws locals, too. The Ku'damm is a 10-minute walk and the bus to and from Tegel Airport stops a block away. ⊠ *Stuttgarter Pl. 14, Charlottenburg, D–10627* ☎ *030/329–070* 🖷 *030/323–3723* ⊕ *www.charlottenburger-hof.de* ⇖ *46 rooms* ⌂ *Restaurant, in-room safes, cable TV, lounge, laundry facilities, laundry service, Internet, meeting rooms, parking (fee), some pets allowed (fee), no-smoking rooms; no a/c ⊟ AE, MC, V Ⓤ Charlottenburg (S-bahn).*

Western Downtown

$$$$ 🏠 **Hotel Brandenburger Hof.** The foyer of this turn-of-the-20th-century

Fodor's Choice mansion is breathtaking with its soaring white Doric columns, but once

★ past these you'll find luxurious minimalism. Days and nights revolve around the beloved Japanese garden in the atrium courtyard. You can breakfast and sip afternoon tea at the sun-soaked tables bordering it, or in the evening, sit and listen to the tinkling of ivories. To either side is Quadriga, where between courses of classic French cuisine, guests lean back in cherrywood chairs by Frank Lloyd Wright. Furnishings in the guest rooms include pieces by Corbusier and Mies van der Rohe. Complementing the clean, timeless Bauhaus style are ikebana floral arrangements. This Relais & Chateaux hotel features Asian silk cosmetic treatments in the spa, overseen by the smiling Mrs. Brüder. ⊠ *Eislebener Str. 14, Western Downtown, D–10789* ☎ *030/214–050* 🖷 *030/2140–5100* ⊕ *www.brandenburger-hof.de* ⇖ *78 rooms, 4 suites* ⌂ *Restaurant, in-room data ports, minibars, cable TV, piano bar, library, massage, spa, steam room, meeting rooms, parking (fee) no-smoking rooms; no a/c ⊟ AE, DC, MC, V Ⓤ Augsburger Str. (U-bahn).*

$$$–$$$$ 🏠 **Kempinski Hotel Bristol Berlin.** Destroyed in the war and rebuilt in 1952, the "Kempi" is a historic Berlin classic with a great view of the Ku'damm scene from its restaurant. Tradition is personified in repeat guests and longtime employees. All rooms and suites are luxuriously decorated and have marble bathrooms. Perks include wireless LAN for Internet surfing, and a steam room and dry sauna. Children under 12 stay for free if they share their parents' room. The best shopping is at the hotel's doorstep, and it has some fine boutiques of its own. ⊠ *Kurfürstendamm 27, Western Downtown, D–10719* ☎ *030/884–340* 🖷 *030/883–6075* ⊕ *www.kempinskiberlin.de* ⇖ *301 rooms, 52 suites* ⌂ *2 restaurants, room service, in-room data ports, minibars, cable TV with movies and video games, pool, gym, hair salon, massage, sauna, bar, lobby lounge, shops, babysitting, dry cleaning, laundry service, concierge, business services, meeting rooms, parking (fee), some pets allowed (fee), no-smoking rooms ⊟ AE, DC, MC, V Ⓤ Uhlandstr. (U-bahn).*

$$$-$$$$ ▣ **Steigenberger Berlin.** This exemplary hotel is very central, only steps from the Ku'damm, but remarkably quiet. Little things that can make your day are the umbrella on loan, extra-large towels, double sinks, and 24-hour room service. Bathrobes and a keyboard to access the Internet through the TV are available upon request; there's also wireless LAN. The sixth-floor Executive Club rooms include late check-out, ironing and shoe-shine service, and a lounge where complimentary breakfast and afternoon tea are served. Louis, the hotel's esteemed restaurant, is probably the only one in town fusing Japanese and Italian cuisine. ⊠ *Los-Angeles-Pl. 1, Western Downtown, D–10789* ☎ *030/21270* 🖷 *030/212–7799* ⊕ *www.berlin.steigenberger.de* ⇆ *386 rooms, 11 suites ⌂ 2 restaurants, room service, in-room data ports, in-room safes, minibars, cable TV with movies and video games, pool, massage, sauna, piano bar, babysitting, dry cleaning, laundry service, concierge, Internet, business center, meeting room, parking (fee), some pets allowed, no-smoking floor* ▤ *AE, DC, MC, V* Ⓤ *Augsburgerstr. (U-bahn), Kurfürstendamm (U-bahn).*

★ $$$-$$$$ ▣ **Swissôtel Berlin.** This ultramodern hotel excels with its reputable Swiss hospitality—from accompanying guests to their floor after check-in to equipping each room with an iron, an umbrella, and a Lavazza espresso machine that preheats the cups. Beds are specially designed to avoid allergens and provide maximum comfort. After using the wireless LAN, you can store and recharge your laptop in the room safe (the safe also charges cell phones). The firm that built the unusual round building housing the hotel also designed the sleek interior, which features original artworks by Marcus Lupertz. The biggest advantage here may be the location at the corner of Ku'damm and Joachimsthaler Strasse. Rooms have sound-proof windows, and the nightly view of the bright city lights is fantastic. ⊠ *Augsburger Str. 44, at Joachimsthaler Strasse, Western Downtown, D–10789* ☎ *030/220–100* 🖷 *030/2201–02222* ⊕ *www.swissotel.com* ⇆ *291 rooms, 25 suites ⌂ Restaurant, room service, in-room data ports, in-room safes, minibars, cable TV with movies and video games, health club, hot tub, massage, sauna, bar, babysitting, dry cleaning, laundry service, concierge, Internet, business services, meeting rooms, parking (fee), some pets allowed (fee), no-smoking floors* ▤ *AE, DC, MC, V.*

★ $$-$$$$ ▣ **Bleibtreu Berlin.** Opened in 1995, Berlin's first design hotel is as fresh and enchanting as ever. Rooms are simple and serene, with untreated oak, polished stone handles, and neutral shades. The eye-teasing stimulation lies in the terra-cotta–tile courtyard that is secreted from the street, but still in front of the hotel. You can sip drinks at its 7-meter-long table, which is covered in shiny blue ceramic shards and rests on a bed of glass pebbles. A tall chestnut tree lends shade. To reinvigorate after shopping at the nearby boutiques, help yourself to the free items in your minifridge or slip into the herbal steam bath. ⊠ *Bleibtreustr. 31, Western Downtown, D–10707* ☎ *030/884–740* 🖷 *030/8847–4444* ⊕ *www.bleibtreu. com* ⇆ *60 rooms ⌂ Restaurant, deli, room service, cable TV, in-room data ports, in-room fax, in-room safes, minibars, bar, massage, steam room, dry cleaning, laundry service, meeting room, no-smoking floor; no a/c* ▤ *AE, DC, MC, V* Ⓤ *Uhlandstr. (U-bahn).*

$$ ⊡ **Hotel Astoria.** You'll be well attended to in this small, privately owned and run hotel. Each room in the simple 1898 building is different and renovations are diligently made every year. When making a reservation, state whether you'd like a bathtub or shower and ask about weekend specials or package deals for longer stays. The fifth-floor rooms have air-conditioning for an extra charge. The location is good for exploring the Ku'damm area, and the side street makes for a wonderful stroll (use a room umbrella if it's raining). Internet use is free in the lobby and wireless LAN is planned for late 2004. ⊠ *Fasanenstr. 2, Western Downtown, D–10623* ☎*030/312–4067* 🖷*030/312–5027* ⊕*www.hotelastoria. de* 🖙 *31 rooms, 1 suite* ♨ *Room service, in-room data ports, in-room safes, minibars, cable TV with movies, bar, dry cleaning, laundry service, Internet, parking (fee), some pets allowed; no a/c in some rooms* 🖃 *AE, DC, MC, V* Ⓤ *Uhlandstr. (U-bahn), Zoologsicher Garten (U-bahn and S-bahn).*

★ **$** ⊡ **Hotel Bogota.** Fashion photography and hall lamps remind guests of the artists and designers who lived in this apartment house beginning in 1911. Each basic room is different, but they all share dated elements such as olive rotary phones, or sherbet combinations of bright red carpeting and mango-color walls. At bedside, you'll find both a Bible and a *Teaching of Buddha*. Triples and quads can be set up in these mostly high-ceiling rooms, children stay for free, and a warm breakfast is included. Doubles that have a shower but share a toilet with a second room range from €64–€84. Ask for a fourth-floor room. Special offers may be available in winter and for stays beginning on a Sunday night. Though the receptionist has a clipped manner, Bogota is a friendly hotel, as its 2001 award from Berlin recognized. ⊠ *Schlüterstr. 45, Western Downtown, D–10707* ☎ *030/881–5001* 🖷 *030/883–5887* ⊕ *www.hotelbogota.de* 🖙*120 rooms, 60 with bath* ♨ *Breakfast room, lounge, no-smoking rooms; no TV in some rooms, no a/c* 🖃 *AE, DC* ⍟ *BP* Ⓤ *Uhlandstr. (U-bahn).*

★ **$** ⊡**Hotel-Pension Dittberner.** For traditional Berlin accommodations, this third-floor pension (with wooden elevator) run by Frau Lange since 1958 is the place to go. Close to Olivaer Platz and next to the Ku'damm, the turn-of-the-20th-century house shows its age, but the huge rooms are wonderfully furnished with antiques, plush stuffed sofas, and artwork selected by Frau Lange's husband, a gallery owner. The high ceilings have stucco work, and some rooms have balconies. The pension received Berlin's "Most Friendly Hotel" award in 2002. ⊠ *Wielandstr. 26, Western Downtown, D–10707* ☎ *030/884–6950* 🖷 *030/885–4046* 🖙 *21 rooms, 1 suite* ♨ *Breakfast room, cable TV, laundry service, concierge, some pets allowed; no a/c* ⍟ *CP* 🖃 *No credit cards* Ⓤ *Adenauerpl. (U-bahn).*

Kreuzberg

$$ ⊡ **Riehmers Hofgarten.** The appeal of this late-19th-century apartment house with a leafy courtyard is its location in a lively neighborhood marked by the streets Mehringdamm and Bergmannstrasse. The richly decorated facade hints that 100 years ago the aristocratic officers of Germany's imperial army lived here. Rooms with low-lying beds are spartanly modern, quiet, and functional. Downstairs is a light-filled lounge and restaurant. In less than five minutes you can reach the subway that speeds you to Mitte and the Friedrichstrasse train station. ⊠ *Yorckstr. 83, Kreuzberg, D–10965* ☎ *030/7809–8800* 🖶 *030/7809–8808* ⊕ *www. riehmers-hofgarten.de* ⟿ *22 rooms* ⛁ *Restaurant, room service, in-room data ports, cable TV, bar, laundry service, parking (fee), some pets allowed (fee), no-smoking rooms; no a/c* ☰ *AE, MC, V* ⍾ *CP* Ⓤ *Mehringdamm (U-bahn).*

¢–$ 🖼 **Die Fabrik.** Near Kreuzberg's and Friedrichshain's alternative nightlife scene and a five-minute walk from the subway, this former factory building—solar powered—is perfect for those who place a priority on mixing with the local scene. Though this is a backpacker stop, basic double rooms and suites with carpeting and metal lockers are also available. To connect to the Internet, insert a euro into the computer at reception. Downside: there are no private bathrooms. Upside: there's a small courtyard with plants and the café is good. Four doubles have a washbasin and double prices drop to €42–€56 between November and February. ⊠ *Schlesische Str. 18, Kreuzberg, D–10997* ☎ *030/611–7116* 🖶 *030/618–2974* ⊕ *www.diefabrik.com* ⟿ *48 rooms without bath* ⛁ *Café, Internet; no a/c, no room phones, no room TVs* ☰ *No credit cards* Ⓤ *Schlesisches Tor (U-bahn).*

Mitte

$$$$ 🖼 **Dorint am Gendarmenmarkt.** Built before the wall came tumbling down, this luxurious lodging has maximized that era's minimalist look. In the formerly austere conference room, the designers added an illuminated glass floor that made it a masterpiece. The spa tucked under the mansard roof is suffused with light, thanks to the new angled windows. Make sure to request one of the compact rooms that the staff cheekily calls "love boxes." Everything folds away or slides to the side to make the most of the small space. The best part is you'll have one or two balconies overlooking Gendarmenmarkt, one of the city's most stunning squares. ⊠ *Charlottenstr. 50–52, Mitte, D–10117* ☎ *030/203–750* 🖶 *030/2037–5100* ⊕ *www.dorint.com* ⟿ *70 rooms, 22 suites* ⛁ *Restaurant, room service, in-room data ports, in-room safes, minibars, cable TV, health club, massage, sauna, spa, steam room, laundry services, Internet, business services, meeting room* ☰ *AE, DC, MC, V* Ⓤ *Französische Str. (U-bahn).*

★ $$$$ 🖼 **Grand Hyatt Berlin.** Europe's first Grand Hyatt is *the* address for entourages attending the Berlinale Film Festival in February. Stylish guests feel at home with a minimalist, Feng Shui–approved design that combines Japanese and Bauhaus elements. Large guest rooms (they start at 406 square feet) have cherrywood furniture and bathrooms that include fog-free shaving mirrors and tubs from which water can overflow onto the marble floor. You'll get a wonderful view of Potsdamer Platz from the top-floor swimming pool. The restaurant and bar, Vox, whets guests' appetites for its international and Asian cuisine with a "show kitchen." ⊠ *Marlene-Dietrich-Pl. 2, Mitte, D–10785* ☎ *030/2553–1234* 🖶 *030/ 2553–1235* ⊕ *www.berlin.grand.hyatt.com* ⟿ *325 rooms, 17 suites* ⛁ *2 restaurants, café, room service, in-room data ports, in-room safes, minibars, room TVs with movies and video games, pool, gym, massage, sauna, spa, bar, babysitting, dry cleaning, laundry service, concierge, business* *services, meeting room, parking (fee), some pets allowed (fee), no-smoking floor* ⊟ *AE, DC, MC, V* Ⓤ *Potsdamer Pl. (U-bahn and S-bahn).*

$$$$ ⚏ **Hotel Adlon Berlin.** Aside from its prime setting on Pariser Platz, the allure of the government's unofficial guesthouse is its almost mythical predecessor. Until its destruction during the war, the Hotel Adlon was considered Europe's ultimate luxury resort. Rebuilt in 1997, the hotel's elegant rooms are furnished in 1920s style with cherrywood trim, myrtle-wood furnishings, brocade silk bedspreads, and big bathrooms in black marble. Book a suite for a Brandenburger Tor view. Sipping coffee in the lobby of creamy marble and limestone makes for good people-watching, so much so that the armrests show wear. Sparkling new are the expanded spa and wellness areas, as well as wireless LAN. After meetings at the nearby Reichstag or Chancellory, relax with a meal at Lorenz Adlon—the restaurant was crowned with a Michelin star in 2003. ⊠ *Unter den Linden 77, Mitte, D–10117* ☎*030/22610* 🖷*030/2261–2222* ⊕ *www.hotel-adlon.de* 🛏 *264 rooms, 121 suites* ⚱ *3 restaurants, room service, in-room data ports, in-room safes, minibars, cable TVs with movies and video games, pool, hair salon, health club, massage, sauna, spa, bar, lobby lounge, shops, babysitting, dry cleaning, laundry service, concierge, business services, meeting room, parking (fee), some pets allowed (fee), no-smoking floor* ⊟ *AE, DC, MC, V.*

$$$$ ⚏ **Hilton Berlin.** Old-fashioned elegance reigns in rooms with striped wallpaper, gold-frame watercolors, and large art deco desks. If you can't open your window to a view of Gendarmentmarkt, you can at least see the square from the breakfast room, where the spread (€21!) is delectable. Executive-floor guests enjoy a private lounge for breakfast and drinks, as well as late checkout privileges. Wireless LAN is available throughout the hotel. The state-of-the-art spa offers Ayurvedic massage and hot stone treatments. Other places to relax are the moodily lit Trader Vic's restaurant and Mai Tai bar. ⊠ *Mohrenstr. 30, Mitte, D–10117* ☎ *030/20230* 🖷 *030/2023–4324* ⊕ *www.hilton.com* 🛏 *589 rooms, 16 suites* ⚱ *4 restaurants, 2 cafés, room service, in-room data ports, minibars, cable TV with movies and video games, pool, gym, hair salon, massage, sauna, spa, 2 bars, shops, babysitting, dry cleaning, laundry service, concierge, business services, meeting room, parking (fee), some pets allowed (fee), no-smoking rooms* ⊟ *AE, DC, MC, V.*

$$$–$$$$ ⚏ **Westin Grand Hotel.** The service sometimes lacks a genuine first-class approach, but the setting and architecture of this grand hotel make it a preferred choice among American travelers. The neoclassical pink-marble lobby, with its soaring six-story atrium, has polished brass accents, stuccowork, and richly decorated wallpaper. Standard rooms are tastefully decorated in muted tones; bathrooms have large tubs. ⊠ *Friedrichstr. 158–164, Mitte, D–10117* ☎ *030/20270* 🖷 *030/2027–3419* ⊕ *www.westin.com/berlin* 🛏 *323 rooms, 35 suites* ⚱ *2 restaurants, room service, in-room data ports, minibars, room TVs with movies and video games, pool, hair salon, hot tub, sauna, bar, lobby, lounge, shops, babysitting, laundry service, concierge, business services, convention center, meeting room, parking (fee), some pets allowed (fee), no-smoking floor* ⊟ *AE, DC, MC, V.*

$$–$$$$ ⊞ **Alexander Plaza.** A modern refitting of this mercantile building compliments the original mosaic floor, tiled walls, and stairwells of stone, iron, and stuccowork. The hotel welcomes a mostly European, trendy clientele. The business center offers Internet access, and for €280, you can get one of the executive suites, which have pride of place in the four turrets. The hotel's entranceway has an exhibit on the significant Jewish history of the area. Automatic glass doors to the street reveal the landmarks of the Hackescher Markt train station, the TV tower, and St. Marienkirche. ⊠ *Rosenstr. 1, Mitte, D–10178* ☎ *030/240–010* 🖶 *030/2400–1777* ⊕ *www.hotel-alexander-plaza. com* ⤶ *84 rooms, 8 suites △ Restaurant, room service, cable TV, in-room data ports, minibars, gym, massage, sauna, bar, babysitting, dry cleaning, laundry service, concierge, business services, Internet, meeting rooms, parking (fee), some pets allowed (fee), no-smoking floors* ▤ *DC, MC, V.*

$$–$$$ ⊞ **Hotel Hackescher Markt.** Amid the nightlife around the Hackescher Markt, this hotel provides discreet and inexpensive first-class services. Unlike those of many older hotels in eastern Berlin, rooms here are spacious and light and furnished with wicker chairs and floral patterns in an English cottage style. In winter, you'll appreciate the under-floor heating in your bathroom, and in summer, you can enjoy a coffee in the small courtyard. The staff is friendly and attentive. Guests can use the gym of the Alexander Plaza hotel nearby. Wireless LAN is available in the bar area. ⊠ *Grosse Präsidentenstr. 8, Mitte, D–10178* ☎ *030/ 280–030* 🖶 *030/2800–3111* ⊕ *www.hotel-hackescher-markt.de* ⤶ *28 rooms, 3 suites △ Room service, in-room safes, minibars, cable TV, bar, babysitting, dry cleaning, laundry service, parking (fee), some pets allowed (fee), no-smoking floor; no a/c* ▤ *DC, MC, V* Ⓤ *Hackescher Markt (S-bahn).*

$–$$$ ⊞ **Park Inn.** A bird's-eye view of Berlin and a location above a main transportation hub are the draws of this 40-story high-rise. Rooms have a cabinlike feel with low furnishings and narrow desks. The frosted glass walls in the bathrooms are a nice touch; not-so-usual amenities include a coffeemaker and an ironing board. The street-scene atmosphere is that of a mall, but you're very close to the museums along Unter den Linden and the neighborhoodlike streets of Mitte and Prenzlauer Berg. The casino on the 37th floor is open until 3 AM. ⊠ *Alexanderpl., Mitte, D–10178* ☎ *030/23890* 🖶 *030/2389–4305* ⊕ *www.parkinn.com* ⤶ *994 rooms, 12 suites △ 2 restaurants, snack bar, in-room data ports, minibars, cable TV with movies, gym, massage, sauna, bar, casino, babysitting, dry cleaning, laundry service, concierge, business services, meeting rooms, parking (fee), some pets allowed (fee), no-smoking floor; no a/c in some rooms* ▤ *AE, DC, MC, V.*

$–$$ ⊞ **Hotel Unter den Linden.** Within walking distance of Berlin's best attractions, this hotel's inexpensive room and parking rates are jaw-dropping. The well-kept rooms are somewhat small, but you'll have plenty of opportunity to stretch your legs at the nearby Friedrichstrasse shops and Unter den Linden's grand landmarks. You can also hop on the sightseeing bus that stops outside. For the best view of this central corner, join the mostly middle-age and older clientele in the restaurant. Drink machines on each floor replace minibars, and there's the quaint novelty of an ironing room. Wireless LAN is available on the ground floor. ✉ *Unter den Linden 14, Mitte, D–10017* ☎ *030/238–110* 🖷 *030/ 2381–1100* ⊕ *www.hotel-unter-den-linden.de* ➲ *331 rooms* ⚘ *Restaurant, room service, in-room data ports, cable TV, bar, dry cleaning, laundry service, meeting rooms, parking (fee), no-smoking rooms* ⚑ *CP* ⊟ *AE, DC, MC, V* Ⓤ *Friedrichstr. (S-bahn and U-bahn).*

★ **$$** 🖵 **Hotel Künstlerheim Luise.** This hotel's name, which means "home for artists," suggests little more than a bohemian commune, but nothing could be farther from the truth. The Künstlerheim is one of Berlin's most original boutique hotels, with each fantastically creative room in the 1825 house or new wing—facing the Reichstag—styled by a different German artist. Memorable furnishings range from a suspended bed and airplane seats to a gigantic sleigh bed and a free-standing, podlike shower with multiple nozzles. A lavish breakfast buffet in the neighborhing restaurant costs €7. The hotel is a stretch from the Friedrichstrasse train stations, but a convenient bus line stops outside the hotel. ✉ *Luisenstr. 19, D–10117* ☎ *030/284–480* 🖷 *030/2844–8448* ⊕ *www.kuenstlerheim-luise.de* ➲ *44 rooms, 40 with bath, 2 suites* ⚘ *Restaurant, in-room data ports, cable TV, dry cleaning, laundry service, some pets allowed, no-smoking rooms; no a/c in some rooms, no TV in some rooms* ⊟ *AE, DC, MC, V.*

$ 🖵 **Hotel-Pension Kastanienhof.** The rooms in this small hotel in a 19th-century tenement house are simply furnished but spacious and equipped with amenities usually found only in more expensive hotels. An elevator serves the four floors. The Kastanienhof is an excellent deal for those bent on exploring the hip nightlife in Prenzlauer Berg and Mitte. ✉ *Kastanienallee 65, Prenzlauer Berg, D–10119* ☎ *030/443–050* 🖷 *030/ 4430–5111* ⊕ *www.hotel-kastanienhof-berlin.de* ➲ *34 rooms, 2 suites* ⚘ *In-room safes, cable TV, bicycles, bar, meeting room, parking (fee), no-smoking rooms; no a/c* ⊟ *AE, MC, V.*

$ 🖵 **Hotel am Scheunenviertel.** This simply furnished but well-kept small hotel offers personal service and a wonderful breakfast buffet. The biggest advantage is its location near the nightlife and restaurants of the old Jewish neighborhood around the Neue Synagogue. All rooms have dark carpeting and white walls, and are on the second floor. The drawback is that it can be noisy. ✉ *Oranienburger Str. 38, Mitte, D–10117* ☎ *030/282–2125* 🖷 *030/282–1115* ⊕ *www.hotelas.com* ➲ *18 rooms* ⚘ *In-room data ports, cable TV, parking (fee), some pets allowed (fee); no a/c* ⊟ *AE, DC, MC, V* ⚑ *CP* Ⓤ *Oranienburger Tor (U-bahn), Oranienburger Str. (S-bahn).*

¢ 🖵 **Mitte's Backpacker Hostel.** Accommodations are simple but creative in this orange-painted hostel, and service goes the extra mile, with cheap bike rentals, free city maps, ticket services, and ride-sharing arrangements. Rooms—from doubles to girls-only sleepaways—are individually decorated. The location is convenient for both sightseeing and nightlife—in the evening you can opt to stay in for happy hour or a film. ✉ *Chauseestr. 102, Mitte, D–10115* ☎ *030/2839–0965* 🖷 *030/ 2839–0935* ⊕ *www.backpacker.de* ➲ *4 double rooms, 2 with bath; 2 singles, 4 quads, 1 triple, 9 dorm rooms* ⚘ *Kitchen, bicycles, bar, lounge,*

Internet, laundry facilities, travel services; no a/c, no room phones, no room TVs ⊟ *AE, MC, V.*

Tiergarten

★ ¢ ⊞ **Houseboat-Berlin.** It's rare to wake up in a city and watch water gently flowing one foot beneath your floor-to-ceiling window. Tiny as the bare-bone cabins are, being near the great outdoors of Tiergarten is the point. This houseboat community is also near civilization: an S-bahn stop and fun weekend flea market are a minute's walk away, and shops and restaurants 10 minutes farther. Two can snuggle on the small beds, and you can stretch out on the common-room couch or at its long wooden table. Bedding costs €7 during your stay; drinking water is included. Make reservations by e-mail. ⊠ *Strasse des 17. Juni, houseboat 5, Tiergarten, D–10623* ☎ *No phone or fax* ⊕ *www.houseboat-berlin. com* ⟿ *5 rooms* ♦ *Kitchenette, lounge; no a/c, no room phones, no room TVs, no kids, no smoking* ⊟ *No credit cards* ☉ *Closed late Oct.–mid-Mar.* Ⓤ *Tiergarten (S-bahn).*

NIGHTLIFE & THE ARTS

The Arts

Today's Berlin has a tough time living up to the reputation it gained from the film *Cabaret*. In the 1920s it was said that in Berlin, if you wanted to make a scandal in the theater, you had to have a mother committing incest with *two* sons; one wasn't enough. Political gaffes are now the prime comic material for Berlin's cabarets. Even if nightlife has toned down since the 1920s and '30s, the arts and the avant-garde still flourish. Detailed information about events is covered in the *Berlin Programm,* a monthly tourist guide to Berlin arts, museums, and theaters. The magazines *Tip* and *Zitty,* which appear every two weeks, provide full arts listings (in German). For listings in English, consult the *Ex-Berliner,* a monthly, or *Berlin Kalendar,* published six times a year by the city's tourism office.

The **Berlin Festival Weeks** (Kartenbüro ⊠ Schaperstr. 24, D–10719 Berlin ☎ 030/254–890 ≣ 030/2548–9111 ⊕ www.berlinerfestspiele.de), held annually from late August through September or early October, include concerts, operas, ballet, theater, and art exhibitions. For information and reservations, write **Berliner Festspiele.**

If your hotel can't book a seat for you or you can't make it to a box office directly, go to a ticket agency. Surcharges are 18–23 percent of the ticket. **Showtime Konzert- und Theaterkassen** (⊠ KaDeWe, Tauentzienstr. 21, Western Downtown ☎ 030/217–7754 ✉ Wertheim, Kurfürstendamm 181, Western Downtown ☎ 030/882–2500) has offices within the major department stores. The **Theaterkasse Centrum** (⊠ Meinekestr. 25, Western Downtown ☎ 030/882–7611) is a small agency but employs a very informed and helpful staff. The **Hekticket offices** (⊠ Karl-Liebknecht-Str. 12, off Alexanderpl., Mitte ☎ 030/2431–2431 ✉ At Zoo-Palast, Hardenbergstr. 29d, Western Downtown ☎ 030/230–9930) offers discounted and last-minute tickets.

Concerts

Among the major symphony orchestras and orchestral ensembles in Berlin is one of the world's best, the Berliner Philharmonisches Orchester, which resides at the **Philharmonie mit Kammermusiksaal** (⊠ Herbert-von-Karajan-Str. 1, Tiergarten ☎ 030/2548–8132 or 030/2548–8301). The Kammermusiksaal is dedicated to chamber music. Free guided tours take place daily at 1 PM.

The beautifully restored hall at **Konzerthaus Berlin** (⊠ Schauspielhaus, Gendarmenmarkt, Mitte ☎ 030/2030–92101 or 030/2030–92102) is a prime venue for classical music concerts. The Rundfunk Symphonie orchestra performs here as well as at the Philharmonie. A wide range of performances take the stage at the **Universität der Künste** (University of Arts; ⊠ Hardenbergstr. at Fasanenstr., Charlottenburg ☎ 030/3185–2374). The box office is open Tuesday–Friday 3–6:30, and Saturday 11–2.

Dance, Musicals & Opera

Berlin's three opera houses also host guest productions and companies from around the world. Vladimir Malakhov, a principal guest dancer with New York's American Ballet Theatre, is a principal in the Staatsballett Berlin as well as its director. The company jetés their classic and modern productions between the Deutsche Oper in the west and the Staatsoper in the east. Of the 17 composers represented in the repertoire of **Deutsche Oper Berlin** (⊠ Bismarckstr. 35, Charlottenburg ☎ 030/343–8401), Verdi is the most presented. Most of the operas are sung in German at the **Komische Oper** (⊠ Behrenstr. 55–57, Mitte ☎ 030/4799–7400 or 01805/304–168). On the day of the performance, discount tickets are sold at the box office on Unter den Linden 41. The small and alternative **Neuköllner Oper** (⊠ Karl-Marx-Str. 131–133, Neukölln ☎ 030/6889–0777) has showy, fun performances of long-forgotten operas as well as humorous musical productions. Though renovated twice after bombings, the **Staatsoper Unter den Linden** (⊠ Unter den Linden 7, Mitte ☎ 030/2035–4555 ⊕ www.staatsoper-berlin.de) dates to 1743, when Frederick the Great oversaw productions. Maestro Daniel Barenboim oversees a repertoire of many Wagner and Strauss operas. Tickets can be as inexpensive as €7.

Sasha Waltz (born 1963) is the heir apparent to the still cutting-edge dance-theater choreographer Pina Bausch. Waltz's modern dance troupe takes to the enormous stage of the **Schaubühne am Lehniner Platz** (⊠ Kurfürstendamm 153, Western Downtown ☎ 030/890–023).

New musicals with German themes are occasionally staged at the **Schiller-Theater** (⊠ Bismarckstr. 110, Charlottenburg ☎ 0800/248–9842). The late-19th-century **Theater des Westens** (⊠ Kantstr. 12, Western Downtown ☎ 030/882–2888), one of Germany's best musical theaters, features musicals such as *Les Misérables*.

In a white tentlike home beyond the ruined facade of Anhalter Bahnhof, the future of bankrupt **Tempodrom** (⊠ Askanischer Pl. 4, Kreuzberg ☎ 030/6110–1313) is uncertain. It normally features pop and rock stars such as Annie Lennox. Modern-dance performances as well as experimental music and electronic and multimedia art are presented at the **Podewil** (✉ Klosterstr. 68–70, Mitte ☎ 030/2474–9777). The **Tanzfabrik** (✉ Möckernstr. 68, Kreuzberg ☎ 030/786–5861) is still Berlin's best venue for young dance talents and the latest from Europe's avant-garde. **Hebbel am Ufer** (✉ Stresemann Str. 3, Kreuzberg ☎ 030/2590–0427) consists of three venues within a five-minute walk of one another. Fringe theater, international modern dance, and solo performers share its stages.

Film

International and German movies are shown in the big theaters on Potsdamer Platz, and around the Ku'damm. If a film isn't marked "OF" or "OV" (*Originalfassung*, or original version) or "OmU" (original with subtitles), it's dubbed. Previews often run for 25 minutes, so don't worry if you're late. In February, theaters around Berlin host the **Internationale Filmfestspiele** (⊕ www.berlinale.de), or Berlinale, a 10-day international festival at which the Golden Bear award is bestowed on the best films, directors, and actors. Individual tickets are first sold three days prior to a film's screening. Film buffs should purchase the season pass or accept shut-outs and third-choice films after hour-long waits at ticket outlets.

On a hard-to-find dead-end street, **Babylon** (✉ Dresdnerstr. 126, Kreuzberg ☎ 030/6160–9693) often shows English-language films undubbed. You can reach Bablyon by cutting through a building overpass off Adalbertstrasse, near the Kottbusser Tor U-bahn station. Mainstream U.S., British, and other foreign productions are screened in their original versions at the sleek **CineStar im Sony Center** (✉ Potsdamer Str. 4, Tiergarten ☎ 030/2606–6400). Tuesday and Thursday are discount evenings.

Documentary films, international films in their original language, and German arthouse films are shown at **Hackesche Höfe** (✉ Rosenthaler Str. 40–41, Mitte ☎ 030/283–4603). There's no elevator to this top-floor moviehouse, but you can recover on the wide banquettes in the lounge.

Theater

Theater in Berlin is outstanding, but performances are usually in German. The exceptions are operettas and the (nonliterary) cabarets. The theater most renowned for both its modern and classical productions is the **Deutsches Theater** (✉ Schumannstr. 13a, Mitte ☎ 030/2844–1221 or 030/2844–1225). It has an excellent studio theater next door, the **Kammerspiele,** which has evolved as a thrilling playground for the country's most promising young directors, writers, and actors. The rebellious actors at the **Schaubühne am Lehniner Platz** (✉ Kurfürstendamm 153, Western Downtown ☎ 030/890–023), once the city's most experimental stage, have somewhat mellowed but are still up to great performances.

The excellent **Berliner Ensemble** (✉ Bertolt Brecht-Pl. 1, Mitte ☎ 030/2840–8155) is dedicated to Brecht and works of other international playwrights. The **Hebbel Theater** (✉ Stresemannstr. 29, Kreuzberg ☎ 030/2590–0427) showcases international theater and modern dance troupes in three venues. The **Renaissance-Theater** (✉ Hardenbergstr. 6, Charlottenburg ☎ 030/312–4202) shows German productions of international-hit dramatic plays. The **Volksbühne am Rosa-Luxemburg-Platz**

(✉ Rosa-Luxemburg-Pl., Mitte ☎ 030/247–6772 or 030/247–7694) is unsurpassed for its aggressively experimental style, and Berliners often fill its 750 seats. The unusual building was reconstructed in the 1950s using the original 1914 plans. The program changes daily, and the name of the day's play is posted on a large banner outside the theater.

For children's theater head for the world-famous **Grips Theater** (✉ Altonaer Str. 22, Tiergarten ☎ 030/3974–7477), whose musical hit *Linie 1,* about life in Berlin viewed through the subway, is just as appealing for adults.

In a blackbox theater, the **Friends of Italian Opera** (✉ Fidicinstr. 40, Kreuzberg ☎ 030/691–1211 ⊕ www.thefriends.de) presents dramas and comedies from England, Scotland, and the United States.

Variety Shows, Comedy & Cabaret

Berlin's variety shows can include magicians, circus performers, musicians, and classic cabaret stand-ups. Intimate and intellectually entertaining is **Bar Jeder Vernunft** (✉ Schaperstr. 24, Wilmersdorf ☎ 030/883–1582), which is housed within a glamorous tent and includes the American entertainer Gayle Tufts on its calendar. Within the Hackesche Höfe, the **Chamäleon Varieté** (✉ Rosenthaler Str. 40–41, Mitte ☎ 030/282–7118) is the most affordable and offbeat variety venue in town. You don't need to understand German to enjoy the Mitternacht (midnight) show. Europe's largest variety show takes place at the **Friedrichstadtpalast** (✉ Friedrichstr. 107, Mitte ☎ 030/2326–2326), a glossy showcase for revues, famous for its female dancers. The **Wintergarten Varieté** (✉ Potsdamer Str. 96, Tiergarten ☎ 030/2500–8888) pays romantic homage to the old days of Berlin's original variety theater in the 1920s.

Social and political satire has a long tradition in cabaret theaters. The **BKA–Berliner Kabarett Anstalt** (✉ Mehringdamm 34, Kreuzberg ☎ 030/202–2007) features not only guest performances by Germany's leading young comedy talents but also *Chanson* vocalists. Eastern Berlin's traditional cabaret is the **Distel** (✉ Friedrichstr. 101, Mitte ☎ 030/204–4704). The **Grüner Salon** (✉ Freie Volksbühne, Rosa-Luxemburg-Pl., Mitte ☎ 030/2859–8936) is one of Berlin's hip venues for live music, cabaret, dancing, and drinks. The programs change almost daily. The **Stachelschweine** (✉ Europa Center, Breitscheidpl., Western Downtown ☎ 030/261–4795), Berlin's most traditional and oldest cabaret, carries on tradition with biting wit and style. **Die Wühlmäuse** (✉ Pommernallee 2–4, off Theodor-Heus-Pl., Charlottenburg ☎ 030/3067–3011), owned by one of Germany's most popular TV comedians, features mostly comedy.

Nightlife

Berlin's nightspots are open to the wee hours of the morning, but if you stay out after 12:45 Monday–Thursday or Sunday, you'll have to find a night bus line or the last S-bahn to get you home. On Friday and Saturday, most subway lines run every 15 to 20 minutes throughout the night. Clubs often switch the music they play nightly, so their crowds and popularity can vary widely. Though club nights are driven by the DJ name, the music genres are written in English in listing magazines.

The happening places in western Berlin are around Savignyplatz in Charlottenburg, Nollendorfplatz and Winterfeldplatz in Schöneberg, Ludwigkirchplatz in Wilmersdorf, and along Oranienstrasse and Wienerstrasse in Kreuzberg, as well as Lützowplatz in Tiergarten. In Mitte most of the action radiates off Rosenthaler Platz and the Hackesche Höfe. Kastanienallee and Helmholzplatz are the hubs in Prenzlauer Berg.

Clubs and bars in downtown western Berlin tend to be dressier and more conservative; the scene in Kreuzberg, Prenzlauer Berg, Mitte, and Friedrichshain is laid-back, alternative, grungy, and only occasionally stylish. For the latest information on Berlin's bustling house, electro, and hip-hop club scene, pick up *(030)*, a free weekly.

Bars

In Germany the term *Kneipen* is used for down-to-earth bars that are comparable to English pubs. You'll know where to order a three-ingredient cocktail when you spot a lengthy drink menu, which many bars offer guests in the same manner restaurants do.

The most elegant bars and lounges are in western downtown Berlin, and though not frequented by Berliners, Berlin's four-star hotels provide stylish, seductive settings. The cocktail menu is the size of a small guidebook at **Bar am Lützowplatz** (⊠ Am Lützowpl. 7, Tiergarten ☎ 030/262-6807), where an attractive, professional crowd lines the long blond-wood bar. The Grand Hotel Esplanade's **Harry's New-York Bar** (⊠ Am Lützowufer 15, Tiergarten ☎ 030/2547–88633) is the best hotel bar in town. In good weather, you can sit outside and watch moneyed guests make their entrance into the hotel. A pianist entertains Monday–Saturday. Old-world **E. & M. Leydicke** (⊠ Mansteinstr. 4, Schöneberg ☎ 030/216-2973) is a must for out-of-towners. The proprietors operate their own distillery and have a superb selection of sweet wines and liqueurs. Shabby **Kumpelnest 3000** (⊠ Lützowstr. 23, Tiergarten ☎ 030/261–6918) has a reputation as wild as its carpeted walls. It's the traditional last stop of the evening, and both gays and heteros mingle on the tiny dance floor. There's no tap beer and the Caipirinhas are among the better mixed drinks.

A mature crowd who wants to concentrate on conversation and appreciating outstanding cocktails heads to **Green Door** (⊠ Winterfeldstr. 50, Schöneberg ☎ 030/215–2515), a Schöneberg classic with touches of kitsch that lighten the mood. Now the oldest posh bar in Mitte, marble-lined **Newton** (⊠ Charlottenstr. 57, Mitte ☎ 030/2029–5421) flaunts Helmut Newton's larger-than-life photos of nude women across its walls. Upstairs is a cigar lounge. Subterranean **Lola Lounge** (⊠ Rosa-Luxemburg-Str. 17, Mitte ☎ 030/2759–4430) discreetly heralds the arrival of the "see and be seen set" in the former East. Make a reservation to avoid a wait for a seat. The low stools at center stage are circled by a canvas top like a sultan's tent. The overall design is seductive down to the sink the men's and women's bathroom share. The lounge is closed Sunday throughTuesday.

Groups of friends fill the tables, battle at foozball tables, and dance in the small back room at **August Fengler** (⊠ Lychner Str. 11, Prenzlauer

Berg ☎ 030/4435–6640). On weekends the place is packed, but fun. Sitting canalside on a deckchair at **Freischwimmer** (✉ Vor dem Schlesischen Tor 2a, Kreuzberg ☎ 030/6107–4309) is perfect for warm nights, but heat lamps and an enclosed section make a cozy setting on cool ones, too. To get here, walk five minutes south of the Schlesisches Tor subway station and turn left down a path after the gas station. It opens at 6 PM during the week in winter; and 12 PM in warm months. Year-round, weekends begin at 11 AM.

Casinos

On Potsdamer Platz, **Spielbank Berlin** (✉ Marlene-Dietrich-Pl. 1, Tiergarten ☎ 030/255–990 ⊕ www.spielbank-berlin.de) is Berlin's posher casino. You can try your luck at roulette tables, three blackjack tables, and slot machines from 2 PM to 3 AM. The **Casino Berlin** (✉ Alexanderpl., Mitte ☎ 030/2389–4113 ⊕ www.casino-berlin.de) is located on the 37th floor of the Park Inn. It's worth blowing a few euros for the view.

Clubs

Perhaps the only nonmainstream club in western Berlin, **Big Eden** (✉ Kurfürstendamm 202, Western Downtown ☎ 030/882–6120) points the way with a huge, flashing red-and-white sign. Curving booths and huge cushions are perfect for taking in the one-man shows or revues that sometimes usher in the evening. Many nights are gay parties, and others feature rhythm and bass or electro-trash. The decor is an eyeful of mirrors and tube lighting.

More like a lounge than a club, **Delicious Doughnuts** (✉ Rosenthaler Str. 9, Mitte ☎ 030/283–3021) has a small dance floor and its layout is fairly conducive for mingling.

Thursday through Saturday, the docked boat **Hoppetosse** (✉ Eichenstr. 4, Treptow ☎ 030/4171–5437) rocks steady to reggae and dancehall, house, techno, or hip-hop. Just south of Kreuzberg, it's a bit out of the way, but you get a fantastic Spree Canal view from either the lower-level dance floor or the top deck.

The tiered, white chill-out area is much larger than the dance floor at **90 Grad** (✉ Dennewitzstr. 37, Tiergarten ☎ 030/2300–5954), but the resident DJ could pack more dancers onto the floor if only the doormen weren't so particular. German MTV has held DJ battles here and Hollywood stars dropped by several times in 2004. The place really gets going around 2 AM. **Bastard** (✉ Kastanienallee 7–9, Prenzlauer Berg ☎ 030/448–5688), the club next to the beer garden Prater, presents bands before dancers work off their energy with indie music and Brit pop. **Sage-Club** (✉ Köpenicker Str. 78, Mitte ☎ 030/278–9830) is the most popular of Berlin's venues for young professionals who dance to hip-hop, house, and some techno. On some nights it can be tough getting past the man with the "by invitation only" list.

Gay & Lesbian Bars

Berlin is unmistakably Germany's gay capital, and many Europeans come to partake in the diverse scene, which is concentrated in Schöneberg (around Nollendorfplatz) and Kreuzberg. Check out the magazines

Siegessäule, (030), and *Sergej* (free and available at the places listed below as well as at many other locations around town).

Close to Wittenbergplatz, the dance club **Connection** (✉ Fuggerstr. 33, Schöneberg ☎ 030/218–1432) provides heavy house music and lots of dark corners. The decor and the energetic crowd at **Hafen** (✉ Motzstr. 18, Schöneberg ☎ 030/211–4118) make it ceaselessly popular and a favorite singles mixer. At 4 AM people move next door to Tom's Bar, open until 6 AM. A gay thirtysomething crowd frequents the upscale **Lenz** (✉ Eisenacher Str. 3, Schöneberg ☎ 030/217–7820).

You can get extensive information on gay life, groups, and events at **Mann-O-Meter** (✉ Bülowstr. 106, Schöneberg ☎ 030/216–8008). Talks are held in the café, which has a variety of books and magazines. It's open weekdays 3–11, Saturday 3–10. If you don't bump up against any eye candy at tiny **Roses** (✉ Oranienstr. 187, Kreuzberg ☎ 030/615–6570) there's always the furry red walls and kitschy paraphernalia to admire. It opens at 10 PM. **Schwuz** (✉ Mehringdamm 61, Kreuzberg ☎ 030/693–7025) consists of two dance floors underneath the laid-back café Melitta Sundström. Eighties music and house are the normal fare.

Jazz Clubs
A-Trane Jazzclub (✉ Bleibtreustr. 1, Charlottenburg ☎ 030/313–2550 ⊕ www.a-trane.de), on the corner of Pestalozzistrasse, also has nights for electronic jazz, Afro-Cuban music, and "the art of duo." With no columns to obstruct your view, you can see young German artists almost every night at **B-Flat** (✉ Rosenthaler Str. 13, Mitte ☎ 030/280–6349). The Wednesday jam sessions focus on free and experimental jazz. On Sunday, dancers come for tango night. Snacks are available. **Quasimodo** (✉ Kantstr. 12a, Charlottenburg ☎ 030/312–8086 ⊕ www.quasimodo.de), the most established and popular jazz venue in the city, has a college town pub feel in its basement. Seats are few.

SPORTS & THE OUTDOORS

Biking
Bike paths are generally marked by red pavement or white markings on the sidewalks. Be careful when walking on bike paths or crossing them. Many stores that rent or sell bikes carry the Berlin biker's atlas. **Fahrradstation** (✉ Bergmannstr. 9, Kreuzberg ☎ 030/215–1566 ✉ Rosenthaler Str. 40–41, Mitte ☎ 030/2838–4848 ⊕ www.fahrradstation.de) rents bikes for €15 per day, €25 for three days. Bring ID and call for its other locations. **Fahrrad Vermietung Berlin** (✉ Kurfürstendamm 236, Western Downtown ☎ 030/261–2094) rents black bikes with baskets that it keeps in front of the Marmorhaus movie theater, opposite the Gedächtniskirche. Rates are €10 a day, and you must leave either a €50 deposit or ID as security. Call the Allgemeiner **Deutscher Fahrrad-Club** (✉ ADFC, Brunnenstr. 28, Prenzlauer Berg ☎ 030/448–4724 ⊕ www.adfc-berlin.de) for information and rental locations.

Jogging
The Tiergarten is the best place for jogging in the downtown area. Run down the paths parallel to Strasse des 17. Juni and back, and you'll have

covered 8 km (5 mi). Joggers can also take advantage of the grounds of Charlottenburg Palace, 3 km (2 mi) around. For longer runs, make for the forest Grunewald.

Swimming

There are public pools throughout the city. For full listings ask at the tourist office. The lakes Wannsee, the Halensee, and the Plötzensee all have beaches that get crowded during summer weekends. The huge, lakeside park **Strandbad Wannsee** (⌧ Wannseebad-weg 25, Zehlendorf ☎ 030/803–5612) attracts as many as 40,000 Berliners to its fine, sandy beach on summer weekends. The **Olympia-Schwimmstadion** (⌧ Olympischer Pl., Charlottenburg ☎ 030/3081–3249 Ⓤ Olympiastadion (U-bahn) was made for the 1936 Olympic games and includes a separate area for three diving platforms. The **Blub Badeparadies lido** (⌧ Buschkrugallee 64, Neuköulln ☎ 030/606–6060 Ⓤ Grenzallee (U-bahn) has indoor and outdoor pools, a sauna garden, hot whirlpools, and a solarium. A 1½-hour card costs €8.20–€9.20; to include the sauna landscape costs extra.

SHOPPING

What's fashionable in Berlin is creative, bohemian style, so designer labels have less appeal here than in Hamburg, Düsseldorf, or Munich. Young people seem to spend more money on cell phone cards than clothing.

Shopping Districts

Charlottenburg

Although Ku'damm is still touted as the shopping mile of Berlin, many shops are ho-hum retailers. The best stretch for exclusive fashions, such as Bruno Magli, Hermès, and Jil Sander, are the three blocks between Leibniz Strasse and Bleibtreustrasse. For home furnishings, gift items, and unusual clothing boutiques, follow this route off Ku'damm: Leibniz Strasse to Mommsenstrasse to Bleibtreustrasse, then on to the ring around Savignyplatz. Fasanenstrasse, Knesebeckstrasse, Schlüterstrasse, and Uhlandstrasse are also fun places to browse.

Ku'damm ends at Breitscheidplatz but the door-to-door shopping continues along Tauentzienstrasse, which, in addition to international retail stores, offers Europe's largest department store, the upscale Kaufhaus des Westens, or KaDeWe.

Mitte

The finest shops in historic Berlin are along Friedrichstrasse, including the French Galeries Lafayette department store. Nearby, Unter den Linden has just a few souvenir shops and a Meissen ceramic showroom. Smaller clothing and specialty stores populate the Scheunenviertel. The area between Hackescher Markt, Weinmeister Strasse, and Rosa-Luxemburg-Platz alternates pricey independent designers with groovy secondhand shops. Neue Schönhauser Strasse curves into Alte Schönhauser Strasse and both streets are full of stylish casual wear. Art galleries along Gipsstrasse and Sophienstrasse round out the mix.

Department Stores & Arcades

The smallest and most luxurious department store in town, **Department Store Quartier 206** (⊠ Friedrichstr. 71, Mitte ☎ 030/2094–6240) offers primarily French women's and men's designer clothes, perfumes, and home accessories. Intimate and elegant, **Galeries Lafayette** (⊠ Französische Str. 23, Mitte ☎ 030/209–480) carries almost exclusively French products, including designer clothes, perfume, and all the produce you might need for preparing haute cuisine at home. Anchoring Alexanderplatz, **Galeria Kaufhof** (⊠ Alexanderpl. 9, Mitte ☎ 030/247–430 ⊕ www.kaufhof.de) is the most successful branch of the German chain.

The largest department store in Europe, classy **Kaufhaus des Westens** (KaDeWe; ⊠ Tauentzienstr. 21, Western Downtown ☎ 030/21210 ⊕ www.kadewe.de) surpasses even London's Harrods. It has a grand selection of goods on seven floors, as well as food and deli counters, champagne bars, beer bars, and a winter garden on its two upper floors. Its wealth of services includes fixing umbrellas and repairing leather and furs. Similar to an American mall, the three-tiered **Potsdamer Platz Arkaden** (⊠ Alte Potsdamer Str. 7, Tiergarten ☎ 030/255–9270) has shops such as Benetton, Esprit, and Eddie Bauer and reputedly the best gelato café in Berlin. All the upscale shops on the four floors of **Stilwerk** (⊠ Kantstr. 17, Charlottenburg ☎ 030/315–150 ⊕ www.stilwerk.de/berlin) cater to stylish home furnishings and accessories.

The elegant **Uhland-Passage** (⊠ Uhlandstr. 170, Western Downtown) has leading-name stores as well as cafés and restaurants. **Wertheim** (⊠ Kurfürstendamm 181, Western Downtown ☎ 030/883–8152) is neither as big nor as attractive as KaDeWe but offers a large selection of fine wares.

Gift Ideas

All the books, maps, and souvenirs focus on the city at **Berlin Story** (⊠ Unter den Linden 10, Mitte ☎ 030/2045–3842), which is even open on Sunday. Fine porcelain is still produced by **Königliche Porzellan Manufaktur** (⊠ Kurfürstendamm 27, Western Downtown ☎ 030/886–7210 ⊠ Unter den Linden 35, Mitte ☎ 030/206–4150 ⊠ Factory salesroom, Str. des .17 Juni, Tiergarten ☎ 030/3900–9215), the former Royal Prussian Porcelain Factory, also called KPM. You can buy this delicate handmade, hand-painted china at KPM's two stores, but it may be more fun to visit the factory salesroom, which also sells seconds at reduced prices. Kitschy props, costumes, and imitation antiques from the Komische Oper and other theaters are on sale at **Kunstsalon** (⊠ Unter den Linden 41, Mitte ☎ 030/2045–0203).

Puppenstube im Nikolaiviertel (⊠ Propststr. 4, Mitte ☎ 030/242–3967) is the ultimate shop for any kind of (mostly handmade) dolls, including designer models as well as old-fashioned German dolls. It's for collectors, not kids. Tucked under the elevated train tracks, **Scenario** (⊠ Savignypassage, Bogen 602, Western Downtown ☎ 030/312–9199) sells stationery articles, gifts of any kind, and a lot of leather wares and jewelry. The designs here are modern. In the homey setting of **Wohnart**

Berlin (⊠ Uhlandstr. 179–180, Western Downtown ☎ 030/882–5252) you can imagine how the stylish European furnishings, lamps, housewares, or stationery items might suit your own pad.

Specialty Stores

Antiques

Not far from Wittenbergplatz lies Keithstrasse, a street full of antiques stores. Eisenacher Strasse, Fuggerstrasse, Kalckreuthstrasse, Motzstrasse, and Nollendorfstrasse—all close to Nollendorfplatz—have many antiques stores of varying quality. Another good street for antiques is Suarezstrasse, between Kantstrasse and Bismarckstrasse. Other antiques stores are found under the tracks from Friedrichstrasse station east to Universitätsstrasse, open Monday and Wednesday–Sunday 11–6.

On weekends from 10 to 5, the lively **Berliner Trödelmarkt und Kunstmarkt** (Berlin Flea and Art Market) on Strasse des 17. Juni swings into action. The flea-market stands are nearer the Tiergarten S-bahn station; the handicrafts begin past the Charlottenburg gates. **Villa Grisebach** (⊠ Fasanenstr. 25, Western Downtown ☎ 030/885–9150 ⊕ www.villa-grisebach.de), one of the city's most classic arts and antiques auction houses, also hosts exhibitions and special events at which you can buy paintings.

Jewelry

Bucherer (⊠ Kurfürstendamm 26a, Western Downtown ☎ 030/880–4030 ⊕ www.bucherer.de) carries fine handcrafted jewelry, watches, and other stylish designer accessories. German designers featured at **Klaus Kaufhold** (⊠ Kurfürstendamm 197, Western Downtown ☎ 030/8847–1790) share a philosophy of sleek minimalism. Rubber and diamond rings and matte platinum and diamond pieces are conscious understatements.

Men's Clothing

For guys who envy the diversity of wares offered to gals, **Boyz 'R' Us** (⊠ Maassenstr. 8, Schöneberg ☎ 030/2363–0640) is your chance to grab a pink-gingham shirt or spangled turquoise top. Patterned jeans and loud tartan pants make this store a magnet for gay and straight clubbers. The most sought-after German label here is Kresse Hamburg. Handmade and timeless shoes and brogues, mostly from England, Austria, and Hungary, are sold at **Budapester Schuhe** (⊠ Kurfürstendamm 199, Western Downtown ☎ 030/881–1707 ⊠ Friedrichstr. 81, Mitte ☎ 030/2038–8110). The gentlemen's outfitter **Mientus** (⊠ Wilmersdorfer Str. 73, Western Downtown ☎ 030/323–9077 ⊠ Kurfürstendamm 52, Western Downtown ☎ 030/323–9077) stocks Armani, Versace Classic, and Boss and has an in-house tailor. The Wilmersdorfer Strasse location offers free parking for customers.

Women's Clothing

The designs of **Anette Petermann** (⊠ Bleibtreustr. 49, Western Downtown ☎ 030/323–2556) are a delight of Berlin haute couture. Roses are her trademark; you'll find fabric buds sewn into pinstripe jackets or taffeta stoles. Crushed organza evening wear or functional wool and fur are popular with local celebrities. The creations of Berlin's top avant-garde designer, **Claudia Skoda** (⊠ Alte Schönhauser Str. 35, Mitte ☎ 030/280–

7211), are mostly for women, but there's also men's knitwear. The flagship store of German designer **Jil Sander** (⊠ Kurfürstendamm 185, Western Downtown ☎ 030/886–7020) carries her complete line of understated clothing. **Peek und Cloppenburg** (⊠ Tauentzienstr. 19, Western Downtown ☎ 030/212–900), or "P and C," stocks women's, men's, and children's clothes on five floors. Don't miss the Joop! designer store on the top floor and the international designer department in the basement.

SIDE TRIP FROM BERLIN

A trip to Berlin wouldn't be complete without paying a visit to Potsdam and its park, which surrounds the Prussian palaces Neue Palais and Sanssouci. This separate city, which was in East Germany, can be reached within a half hour from Berlin's Zoo Station.

Potsdam

Potsdam still retains the imperial character it earned during the many years it served as a royal residence and garrison quarters. The Alter Markt and Neuer Markt show off stately Prussian architecture, and both are easily reached from the main train station by any tram heading into the town center. Karl Friedrich Schinkel designed the Alter Markt's domed **Nikolaikirche.** In front of it stands an Egyptian obelisk erected by Schloss Sanssouci architect von Knobelsdorff. A gilded figure of Atlas tops the tower of the old **Rathaus,** built in 1755. The region's history museum, the **Haus der Brandenburg-Preussischen Geschichte,** is in the royal stables of the Neuen Markt. ⊠ *Schlossstr. 1* ☎ *0331/201–3949* 🎫 *Varies* ◷ *Daily 10–6.*

The center of the small **Holländisches Viertel** (Dutch Quarter) is an easy walk north along Friedrich-Ebert-Strasse to Mittelstrasse. Friedrich Wilhelm I built the settlement in 1732 to entice Dutch artisans who could support the city's rapid growth. Few Dutch came, and the gabled, mansard-roof brick houses were largely used to house staff. Stores and restaurants inhabit the buildings now, and the area is Potsdam's most visited.

need a break? Fine coffee blends and rich cakes are offered at the **Wiener Restaurant-Café** (⊠ Luisenpl. 4 ☎ 0331/967–8314), an old-style European coffeehouse on the way to the Grünes Gitter entrance to Sanssouci. A favorite cake here is the *Sanssouci-Torte.*

Prussia's most famous king, Friedrich II—Frederick the Great—spent more time at his summer residence, **Schloss Sanssouci,** than in the capital of Berlin. Its name means "without a care" in French, the language Frederick cultivated in his own private circle and within the court. Some experts believe Frederick actually named the palace "Sans, Souci," which they translate as "with and without a care," a more apt name; its construction caused him a lot of trouble and expense and sparked furious rows with his master builder, Georg Wenzeslaus von Knobelsdorff. His creation nevertheless became one of Germany's greatest tourist attractions. The palace lies on the edge of Park Sanssouci, which includes various buildings and palaces with separate admissions and hours.

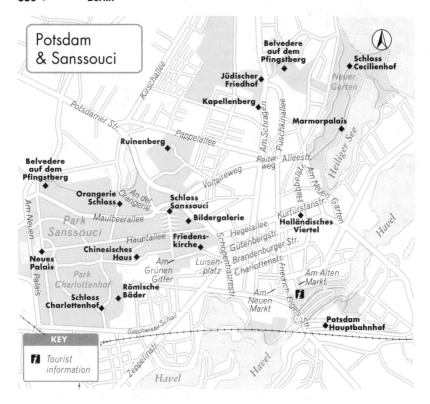

Executed according to Frederick's impeccable French-influenced taste, the palace, built between 1745 and 1747, is extravagantly rococo, with scarcely a patch of wall left unadorned. Leading up to the building is an unusual formal terrace where wine was once cultivated. To the west of the palace are the **Neue Kammern** (New Chambers; ☎ 0331/969–4206 ✉ €2, guided tour €3 ⊘ Apr.–mid-May, weekends 10–5; mid-May–mid-Oct., Tues.–Sun. 10–5), which housed guests of the king's family after its beginnings as a greenhouse. Just east of Sanssouci Palace is the **Bildergalerie** (Picture Gallery; ☎ 0331/969–4181 ✉ €2 ⊘ Mid-May–mid-Oct., Tues.–Sun. 10–5), with expensive marble from Siena in the main cupola. The gallery displays Frederick's collection of 17th-century Italian and Dutch paintings, including works by Caravaggio, Rubens, and Van Dyck. ✉ Park Sanssouci ☎ 0331/969–4200 or 0331/969–4201, 0331/969–4204 for recorded information ⊕ www.spsg.de ✉ Guided tour €8, park free ⊘ Apr.–Oct., Tues.–Sun. 9–5; Nov.–Mar., Tues.–Sun. 9–4.

The **Neues Palais** (New Palace), a much larger and grander palace than Sanssouci, stands at the end of the long, straight avenue that runs through Sanssouci Park. It was built after the Seven Years' War (1756–63), when Frederick loosened the purse strings. It's said he wanted to demonstrate that the state coffers hadn't been depleted too severely by the long conflict. The Neues Palais has much of interest, including an indoor grotto hall with walls and columns set with shells, coral, and other aquatic decor. The upper apartments of royalty contain paintings by 17th-century Italian masters. A good English guide can be borrowed with a deposit. ⊠ *Strasse am Neuen Palais, Sanssouci* ☎ *0331/969–4255* ⊕ *www. spsg.de* ⌚ *Guided tour €6* ⊙ *Apr.–Oct., Sat.–Thurs. 10–5.*

Schloss Charlottenhof stands on its own grounds in the southern part of Sanssouci Park. After Frederick the Great died in 1786, the ambitious Sanssouci building program ground to a halt, and the park fell into neglect. It was 50 years before another Prussian king, Friedrich Wilhelm IV, restored Sanssouci's earlier glory. He engaged the great Berlin architect Karl Friedrich Schinkel to build this small palace for the crown prince. Schinkel gave it a classical, almost Roman appearance, and he let his imagination loose in the interior, too—decorating one of the rooms as a Roman tent, with its walls and ceiling draped in striped canvas.

Between the Sanssouci palaces are later additions to the park. In 1836 Friedrich Wilhelm IV built the **Römische Bäder** (Roman Baths; ☎ 0331/ 969–4224 ⌚ €2 ⊙ Mid-May–mid-Oct., Tues.–Sun. 10–5). The **Orangerieschloss und Turm** (☎ 0331/969–4280 ⌚ Guided tour €3, tower only €1 ⊙ Palace and tower open mid-May–mid-Oct., Tues.–Sun. 10–5; tower only open Apr.–mid-May, weekends 10–5) was completed in 1860; its two massive towers linked by a colonnade evoke an Italian Renaissance palace. Today it houses 47 copies of paintings by Raphael. The **Chinesisches Teehaus** (Chinese Teahouse; ☎ 0331/969–4222 ⌚ €1 ⊙ Mid-May–mid-Oct., Tues.–Sun. 10–5) was erected in 1757 in the Chinese style, which was all the rage at the time. Completed in 1848, the Italianate **Friedenskirche** (Peace Church; ⌚ Free ⊙ May–Oct., daily) houses a 12th-century Byzantine mosaic taken from an island near Venice. ☎ *0331/ 969–4228* ⌚ *Guided tour €4* ⊙ *Mid-May–mid-Oct., Tues.–Sat. 10–5.*

need a break?

Halfway up the park's Drachenberg Hill, above the Orangerie, stands the curious **Drachenhaus** (Dragon House), modeled in 1770 after the Pagoda at London's Kew Gardens and named for the gargoyles ornamenting the roof corners. It now houses a popular café.

Resembling a rambling, half-timber country manor house, **Schloss Cecilienhof** (Cecilienhof Palace) was the final addition to Sanssouci Park. It was built for Crown Prince Wilhelm in 1913, on a newly laid-out stretch of the park, called the New Garden, which borders the Heiliger See. It was here that the Allied leaders Truman, Attlee, and Stalin hammered out the fate of postwar Germany at the 1945 Potsdam Conference. From Sanssouci you can reach the New Garden with any tram or bus going toward the Neuer Garten station. ☎ *0331/969–4244* ⊕ *www.spsg.de* ⌚ *Guided tour €5; tour of prince's private rooms €2* ⊙ *Apr.–Oct., Tues.–Sun. 9–5; Nov.–Mar., Tues.–Sun. 9–4. Tours of prince's rooms at 11 and 2.*

On a hill near Schloss Cecilienhof, the palacelike **Belvedere auf dem Pfingstberg** was built in 1849–52 as an observation platform for the royals. Farther down the hill is the simple **Pomonatempel** (⊙ Easter–Oct., weekdays 3–6), the first building built by Karl Friedrich Schinkel (1801).

✉ *Am Pfingstberg* ☎ *0331/2701972* ⊕ *www.spsg.de* 🎫 *€3.50* ⊙ *Mar. and Nov., weekends 10–4; Apr., May, and Sept., daily 10–6; June–Aug., daily 10–8; Oct., daily 10–4.*

Where to Stay & Eat

★ **$$–$$$** ✕ **Juliette.** In a city proud of its past French influences, the highly praised French cuisine here is delivered to your table by French waiters, no less. The intimate restaurant at the edge of the Dutch Quarter has old-fashioned brick walls and a fireplace. The menu offers dishes such as rack of lamb, wild hare pie with hot peppered cherries, and a starter plate of four foie gras preparations. Its wine list of 120 French vintages is unique in the Berlin area. Potsdam's proximity to the Babelsberg film studios assures regular appearances by those shooting there. ✉ *Jägerstr. 39* ☎ *0331/270–1791* ▭ *AE, DC, MC, V.*

$$ ▦ **Hotel am Luisenplatz.** This intimate hotel conceals a warm, upscale elegance and friendly, personal service behind a somber-looking facade. The large rooms are decorated in dark blue and red—and all have a bathtub. The biggest draw, however, is the hotel's location, which offers a spectacular view of historic Luisenplatz and its restored Prussian city mansions. ✉ *Luisenpl. 5, D–14471* ☎ *0331/971–900* 🖷 *0331/971–9019* ⊕ *www.hotel-luisenplatz.de* 🛏 *22 rooms, 3 suites* ⚭ *In-room data ports, in-room safes, minibars, cable TV, dry cleaning, laundry service, Internet, meeting room, parking (fee), some pets allowed, no-smoking rooms; no a/c* ▭ *AE, DC, MC, V* ✵ *CP.*

$$ ▦ **Steigenberger Maxx Hotel Sanssouci Potsdam.** The terrace of this fine hotel overlooks the palace and park of Sanssouci. The Maxx, a slimmeddown and casual version of the luxurious Steigenberger chain, offers spacious, movie-theme rooms (complete with Hollywood and Babelsberg vintage photos and memorabilia) with terra-cotta floors and rattan furniture. A nice plus is the free transportation card for Berlin and Potsdam for the duration of your stay. The hotel restaurant serves international dishes, including those of the Brandenburg region. ✉ *Allee nach Sanssouci 1, D–14471* ☎ *0331/90910* 🖷 *0331/909–1909* ⊕ *www.steigenberger. de* 🛏 *133 rooms, 4 suites* ⚭ *Restaurant, in-room data ports, minibars, cable TV, massage, sauna, steam room, bicycles, bar, shops, babysitting, dry cleaning, laundry service, meeting room, parking (fee), some pets allowed (fee), no-smoking floor; no a/c* ▭ *AE, DC, MC, V.*

Potsdam A to Z

Potsdam is virtually a suburb of Berlin, 20 km (12 mi) southwest of the city center and a half-hour journey by car, bus, or regional train (RE 1). The S-7 line of the S-bahn takes about 40 minutes from Zoo Station. City traffic is heavy, so a train journey is recommended. The most effortless way to visit Potsdam and its attractions is to book a tour with one of the big Berlin operators.

BOAT TRAVEL   Six-hour tours to Potsdam and Werder Island ("Excursion to Werder") leave Berlin's Wannsee S-bahn station at 11 AM (April–September, Tuesday–Sunday). A round-trip ticket costs €14.

🛈 **Stern- und Kreisschiffahrt** ☎ 030/536–3600 ⊕ www.sternundkreis.de.

BUS TRAVEL   From Berlin there's regular service from the bus station at the Funkturm on Messedamm 8 (U–1 U-bahn: Kaiserdamm). From Spandau (U–7 U-bahn: Rathaus Spandau), take Bus 638 to Potsdam. From Potsdam's train station, Bus 695 goes to Sanssouci and makes stops all around its park.

CAR TRAVEL   From central Berlin take Potsdamer Strasse south until it becomes Route 1 and then follow the signs to Potsdam. A faster way is taking the high-way from Funkturm through Zehlendorf to Potsdam.

TOURS   All major sightseeing companies (⇨ Tours *in* Berlin A to Z) offer three-to four-hour tours of Potsdam and Sanssouci for €28. April through October the Potsdam Tourist Office offers a 3½-hour bus tour includ-ing a walk through Sanssouci for €26; a 1½-hour bus tour of the city alone is €15. Both tours are offered in English and German.

TRAIN TRAVEL   From Berlin, take the S-bahn 7 or 1 line, or the RE 1 train to Potsdam Hauptbahnhof. From the Potsdam train station, take Tram 90, 92, or 95 into the city, or Bus 695 to Sanssouci. You could also transfer to the RE 21 train (marked "Wustermark") to reach the station Park Sanssouci, which is close to the Neues Palais.

VISITOR INFORMATION   The Potsdam tourist office has information on tours, attractions, and events and also reserves hotel rooms for tourists. It's open daily.
🚩 **Potsdam Tourist Office** ✉ Touristenzentrum am Alten Markt, Friedrich-Ebert-Str. 5, Postfach 601220, D-14467 Potsdam ☎ 0331/275-580 🖷 0331/275-5829 ⊕ www. potsdam.de.

BERLIN A TO Z

To research prices, get advice from other travelers, and book travel ar-rangements, visit www.fodors.com.

AIR TRAVEL TO & FROM BERLIN

Major airlines serve western Berlin's Tegel Airport after a first stop at a major European hub (such as Frankfurt). Massive Tempelhof Airport is an example of fascist architecture and is used by smaller airlines for flights within Europe. Eastern Berlin's Schönefeld Airport is about 24 km (15 mi) outside the downtown area and is used principally by charter and low-budget airlines. The three airports share a central phone number.
🚩 **Central airport service** ☎ 0180/500-0186 ⊕ www.berlin-airport.de.

AIRPORTS & TRANSFERS

Tegel Airport is 6 km (4 mi) from the downtown area. The express X9 airport bus runs at 10-minute intervals between Tegel and Bahnhof Zo-ologischer Garten (Zoo Station), the center of western Berlin. From here you can connect to bus, train, or subway. The trip takes 25 minutes; the fare is €3.10, or an additional €1 if you already have a regular metro or bus ticket. Alternatively, you can take Bus 128 to Kurt Schumacher Platz or Bus 109 to Jakob Kaiser Platz and change to the subway, where your bus ticket is also valid. Expect to pay about €14 for a taxi from the airport to the western downtown area. If you rent a car at the air-port, follow the signs for the Stadtautobahn into Berlin. The Halensee exit leads to Kurfürstendamm.

Tempelhof is linked directly to the city center by the U–6 subway line. From Schönefeld a free express shuttle bus leaves every 10–15 minutes for the nearby S-bahn station. The system is a bit clumsy here. You can buy a ticket (AB zone) from an S-bahn platform vending machine to get you into town. This ticket is also good for the Airport Express train, which runs about every half hour from a track that has no vending machine. Look for a small dark blue sign for Airport Express at the foot of the stairs leading to its platform. Bus 171 also leaves Schönefeld every 20 minutes for the Rudow subway station. A taxi ride from the Schönefeld Airport takes about 40 minutes and will cost around €28. By car, follow the signs for Stadtzentrum Berlin.

BUS TRAVEL TO & FROM BERLIN

BerlinLinien Bus is the only intra-Germany company serving Berlin. Gullivers Reisen serves foreign destinations. Make reservations for either through ZOB-Reisebüro, or buy your ticket at its office at the central bus terminal, the Omnibusbahnhof. A more central place to buy bus tickets is Mitfahrzentrale, a tiny, busy office that also arranges car ride shares. Only EC credit cards and cash are accepted.

🚍 **Mitfahrzentrale** ✉ U-2 Pankow-bound platform, Zoologischer Garten subway station Western Downtown ☎ 030/19440 ⊙ Weekdays 9-8 PM, weekends 10-6 PM ⊕ www. mfzoo.de. **ZOB-Reisebüro** ✉ Zentrale Omnibusbahnhof, Masurenallee 4-6 at Messedamm, Charlottenburg ☎ 030/301-0380 for reservations ⊙ Weekdays 6-7:30 PM, weekends 6-3 PM ⊕ www.berlinlinienbus.de.

CAR RENTAL

🚗 **Avis** ✉ Tegel Airport, Reinickendorf ☎ 030/4101-3148 ✉ Tempelhof Airport, Kreuzberg ☎ 030/6951-2340 ✉ Budapester Str. 43, at Europa Center, Western Downtown ☎ 030/230-9370. **Europcar** ✉ Tegel Airport, Reinickendorf ☎ 030/417-8520 ✉ Kurfürstenstr. 101-104, Schöneberg ☎ 030/235-0640 ✉ Zentrale Omnibusbahnhof, Messedamm 8, Charlottenburg ☎ 030/306-9590. **Hertz** ✉ Tegel Airport, Reinickendorf ☎ 030/4170-4674 ✉ Budapester Str. 39, Western Downtown ☎ 030/261-1053. **Sixt** ✉ Tegel Airport, Reinickendorf ☎ 030/4101-2886 ✉ Nürnberger Str. 65, Western Downtown ☎ 030/4101-2886 ✉ Kaiserdamm 40, Charlottenburg ☎ 030/411-7087 ✉ Leipziger Str. 104, Mitte ☎ 030/4101-2886.

CAR TRAVEL

Berliners are known to be reckless drivers, so exploring the city by car can be extremely frustrating for out-of-towners. Rush hour is stop-and-go. It's best to leave your car at the hotel and take the public transit system. Daily parking fees at hotels can go up to €18 per day. Vending machines in the city center dispense timed tickets to display on your dashboard. Thirty minutes cost €.50.

DISABILITIES & ACCESSIBILITY

All major S- and U-bahn stations have elevators, and most buses have hydraulic lifts. Check the public transportation maps or call the Berliner Verkehrsbetriebe. The Service-Ring-Berlin e.V. runs a special bus service for travelers with physical disabilities. Though hotels can often make the arrangement, you can call the Verband Geburts- und anderer Behinderter e.V. to borrow a wheelchair (donations are accepted).

🚹 **Berliner Verkehrsbetriebe** ☎ 030/19449 ⊕ www.bvg.de. **Service-Ring-Berlin e. V** ☎ 030/859–4010. **Verband Geburts- und anderer Behinderter e.V** ☎ 030/341–1797.

EMBASSIES
⇨ Embassies *in* Smart Travel Tips.

EMERGENCIES
Pharmacies in Berlin offer late-night service on a rotating basis and display a schedule with shop addresses on their doors. The American Hotline serves English-speakers in need of medical, legal, or counseling referrals.

🚹 **Police** ☎ 030/110. **Ambulance** ☎ 030/112. **Pharmacy** ☎ 030/11880. **Emergency poison assistance** ☎ 030/19240. **American Hotline** ☎ 0177/814–1510.

ENGLISH-LANGUAGE MEDIA
The Ex-Berliner (€2) is an English-language monthly that includes cultural, arts, and nightlife listings. The weekly *New Berlin* (€1.50) is a summary of restaurants, sights, club nights, and hostels.

BOOKS 🚹 **Books in Berlin** ⊠ Goethestr. 69, Charlottenburg ☎ 030/313–1233. **Dussmann Kulturkaufhaus** ⊠ Friedrichstr. 90, Mitte ☎ 030/2025–2410. **Hugendubel** ⊠ Tauentzienstr. 13, Western Downtown ☎ 030/214–060. **Marga Schoeller Bücherstube** ⊠ Knesebeckstr. 33, Western Downtown ☎ 030/881–1112.

LODGING
PRIVATE ROOMS
& APARTMENTS
German and European travelers often use rooming agents, and Americans on a budget should consider it, too (apartments start at €200 per month). In Berlin, double rooms with shared bathrooms in private apartments begin around €36. Wohn-Agentur Freiraum is an English-speaking agency that has its own guesthouse with rooms and apartments. All of its private room listings are in the Kreuzberg district.

🚹 **Wohn-Agentur Freiraum** ⊠ Wiener Str., Kreuzberg ☎ 030/618–2008 🖨 030/618–2006 ⊕ www.freiraum-berlin.com.

TAXIS
The base rate is €2.50, after which prices vary according to a complex tariff system. Figure on paying around €8 for a ride the length of the Ku'damm. If you've hailed a cab on the street and are taking a short ride of less than 2 km (1 mi), ask the driver as soon as you start off for a special fare (€3) called *Kurzstreckentarif*. There's no additional fee if you call a cab by phone. You can also get cabs at taxi stands or order one by calling. U-bahn employees will call a taxi for passengers after 8 PM.

Students operate *Velotaxis*, a rickshaw service system, along Kurfürstendamm, Friedrichstrasse, and Unter den Linden; and in Tiergarten. Just hail one of the cabs on the street or look for the VELOTAXI-STAND signs along the boulevards mentioned. The fare is €2.50 for up to 1 km (½ mi), €2.50 for a tour between sightseeing landmarks (for example, Europa Center to the Brandenburger Tor), and €7.50 for 30 minutes of travel. Velotaxis operate April–October, daily 1–8.

🚹 **Taxis** ☎ 030/210-101, 030/210-202, 030/443-322, or 030/261-026.

TOURS

The easiest and most inexpensive way to orient yourself within West and East Berlin's downtown areas is a ride on public bus lines No. 100 or 200, which run between Zoo Station and Alexanderplatz (No. 100) and between Zoo Station, Potsdamer Platz, Alexanderplatz, and Prenzlauer Allee (No. 200), stopping at almost all major sightseeing spots on the way.

BOAT TOURS   Tours of downtown Berlin's Spree and Landwehr canals give you up-close and unusual views of sights such as Charlottenburg Palace, the Reichstag, and the Berliner Dom—bring plenty of film. Tours usually depart twice a day from several bridges and piers in Berlin, such as Schlossbrücke in Charlottenburg, Hansabrücke in Tiergarten, Kottbusser Brücke in Kreuzberg, Potsdamer Brücke, and Haus der Kulturen der Welt in Tiergarten. Drinks, snacks, and wursts are available during the narrated trips. Reederei Riedel offers three inner-city trips that range from €6 to €14.

A tour of the Havel Lakes (which include Tegeler See and Wannsee) is the thing to do in summer. Trips begin at the Greenwich Promenade in Tegel (U-bahn: Tegel). From Tegel, you can sail on either the whale-shape vessel *Moby Dick* or the *Havel Queen,* a Mississippi-style boat, and cruise 28 km (17 mi) through the lakes and past forests (Stern- und Kreisschiffahrt). Tours can last from one hour to seven and cost between €10 and €14. There are 20 operators.

🚢**Reederei Bruno Winkler** ☎030/349-9595. **Reederei Riedel** ☎030/693-4646. **Stern-und Kreisschiffahrt** ☎ 030/536-3600 ⊕ www.sternundkreis.de.

BUS TOURS   Four companies (Berliner Bären, Berolina Berlin-Service, Bus Verkehr Berlin, and Severin & Kühn) jointly offer city tours on yellow, double-decker City Circle buses, which run every 15 or 30 minutes, depending on the season. The full-circuit runs two hours as does the recorded narration listened to through headphones. For €18 you can jump on and off at the 14 stops. The bus driver sells tickets. During the warmer months, the last circuit leaves at 4 PM from the corner of Rankestrasse and Kurfürstendamm. Most companies have tours to Potsdam. Severin & Kühn also runs all-day tours to Dresden and Meissen.

The Stadtrundfahrtbüro Berlin offers a 2½-hour tour (€15) and 1¾-hour tour (€12) at 11, 2, and 3:45. A guide narrates in both German and English. The bus departs from Kurfürstendamm 236, at the corner of Rankestrasse.

🚌 **Berliner Bären Stadtrundfahrten** (BBS) ✉ Seeburgerstr. 19b, Charlottenburg ☎ 030/3519-5270 ⊕ www.sightseeing.de. **Berolina Berlin-Service** ✉ Kurfürstendamm 220, at Meinekestr., Western Downtown ☎ 030/8856-8030 ⊕ www.berolina-berlin.com. **Bus Verkehr Berlin** (BVB) ✉ Kurfürstendamm 225, Western Downtown ☎ 030/683-8910 ⊕ www.bvb.net. **Severin & Kühn** ✉ Kurfürstendamm 216, Western Downtown ☎ 030/880-4190 ⊕ www.severin-kuehn-berlin.de. **Stadtrundfahrtbüro Berlin** ✉ Kurfürstendamm 236, Western Downtown ☎ 030/2612-001 ⊕ www.stadtrundfahrtbuero-berlin.de.

WALKING TOURS   In addition to their "Discover Berlin" tour, Berlin Walks offers tours such as "Third Reich" sites and historic "Jewish Life," as well as trips to Potsdam and the concentration camp Sachsenhausen. When not leading city highlights tours, Insider Tours offers a pub crawl and bike tour. Brit Terry

Brewer's firsthand accounts of divided and reunified Berlin are a highlight of the "Brewer's Best of Berlin" tour (€10), which can run from 6 to 10 hours. He and his team also conduct tours of Potsdam and many of its palaces. Tours cost from €9 to €15. Printable discount coupons may be available on the tour operators' Web sites.

StattReisen's weekend tours cost approximately €8. Tours include "Jewish History" and "Prenzlauer Berg Neighborhoods" and are in German; English tours are offered upon request.

🏳 **Berlin Walks** ☎ 030/301-9194 ⊕ www.berlinwalks.com. **Insider Tours** ☎ 030/692-3149 ⊕ www.insidertour.com. **"Brewer's Best of Berlin"** ☎ 030/9700-2906 ⊕ www.brewersberlin.com. **StattReisen** ✉ Malplaquetstr. 5, Wedding ☎ 030/455-3028 ⊕ www.stattreisen.berlin.de.

TRANSPORTATION AROUND BERLIN

The city has one of the most efficient public-transportation systems in Europe, a smoothly integrated network of subway (U-bahn) and suburban (S-bahn) train lines, buses, and trams (in eastern Berlin only). Get a map from any information booth. Don't be afraid to try to figure out the bus schedules posted—a bus can often cut the most direct path to your destination. From Sunday through Thursday, U-bahn trains stop around 12:45 AM and S-bahn trains stop by 1:30 AM. All-night bus and tram service operates seven nights a week (indicated by the letter N next to route numbers). On Friday and Saturday night, most S- and U-bahn lines run all night.

Most visitor destinations are in the broad reach of the fare zones A and B. Both the €2 ticket (fare zones A and B) and the €2.60 ticket (fare zones A, B, and C) allow you to make a one-way trip with an unlimited number of changes between trains, buses, and trams.

If you are just making a short trip, buy a *Kurzstreckentarif*. It allows you to ride six bus stops or three U-bahn or S-bahn stops for €1.20. The best deal if you plan to travel around the city extensively is the *Tageskarte* (day card for zones A and B), for €5.60, good on all transportation until 3 AM. (It's €6 for all three zones.) A 7-*Tage-Karte* (seven-day ticket) costs €23.40 and allows unlimited travel for fare zones A and B; €29 buys all three fare zones. The Berlin WelcomeCard (sold by EurAid, BVG offices, the tourist office, and some hotels) entitles one adult and three children between 6 and 14 to three days of unlimited travel in the ABC zones for €21, and includes admission and tour discounts.

Tickets are available from vending machines at U-bahn and S-bahn stations. Look for rib-high red or yellow machines that time-validate tickets. If you're caught without a ticket or with an unvalidated one, the fine is €40. Some stations have intercom stands through which you can ask for travel advice. The Berliner Verkehrsbetriebe also answers calls day and night. There's a BVG-information office on Hardenbergplatz, directly in front of the Zoo train station. Questions about S-bahn connections can be answered by S-bahn Berlin GmbH.

Information about transportation methods between Berlin and the out-lying state of Brandenburg is provided by the region's central transit au-thority, the VBB.

◪ Berliner Verkehrsbetriebe ☎ 030/19449 ⊕ www.bvg.de. **S-Bahn Berlin GmbH** ☎ 030/297-4333 ⊕ www.s-bahn-berlin.de. **VBB** ✉ Hardenbergpl. 2, Western Down-town ☎ 030/2541-4141 ⊕ www.vbbonline.de.

TRAVEL AGENCIES

Sharing the same space as Deutsche Bahn in the Zoologischer Garten train station is EurAide, which serves English-speaking travelers. It can book your long-distance train tickets and inform you about local Berlin tours. It's closed on weekends and the entire month of January.

◪ EurAide ✉ Hardenbergpl., Western Downtown ⊕ www.euraide.com ☉ Weekdays 9-12:30, 1:30-5.

VISITOR INFORMATION

The main information office of Berlin Tourismus Marketing is in the Eu-ropa Center, a short walk from Zoo Station. The other two branches are in the south wing of the Brandenburg Gate and at the base of the Fernsehn Turm (TV tower) at Alexanderplatz and are open daily 10–6. The tourist information centers have longer hours April–October. To request mate-rials before your trip, write Berlin Tourismus Marketing GmbH.

The tourist office publishes the *Berlin Kalender* (€1.60) six times a year and *Berlin Buchbar* (free) two times a year. Both are written in German and English. The office and Berlin's larger transportation offices (BVG) sell the WelcomeCard (€21) that grants three days of free transporta-tion and 25%–50% discounts at museums and theaters (it does not in-cluded the state museums).

Staatliche (state) museums are free on Thursday during the last four hours of operation. A free audio guide is included at all state museums. The MD Infoline provides comprehensive information about all of Berlin's museums, exhibits, and theme tours.

◪ Berlin Tourist Info Center ✉ Budapester Str. 45, Western Downtown ☎ 030/250-025 ☉ Mon.-Sat. 10-7, Sun. 10-6 ✉ Berlin Tourismus Marketing GmbH, Am Karls-bad 11, D-10785 Berlin ☎ No phone 🖷 030/2500-2424 ⊕ www.berlin-tourist-information.de. **MD Infoline** ☎ 030/9026-99444 ⊕ www.mdberlin.de ☉ Weekdays 9-4, weekends 9-1. **Staatliche Museen zu Berlin** ☎ 030/266-2951 operator, 030/2090-5555 recorded information ⊕ www.smpk.de.

SAXONY, SAXONY-ANHALT & THURINGIA

16

Updated by
Jürgen
Scheunemann

THE EASTERN STATES of Saxony, Saxony-Anhalt, and Thuringia have a great many secrets in store and some gems of German culture. An old-world state of mind exists here, the likes of which you will never find in West Germany. Communism never penetrated the culture here as deeply as the American influence did in West Germany. The German Democratic Republic (GDR, commonly referred to by its German acronym—DDR) clung to its German heritage, proudly preserving connections with such national heroes as Luther, Goethe, Schiller, Bach, Handel, Wagner, and the Hungarian-born Liszt. Towns in the regions of the Thüringer Wald (Thuringian Forest) or the Harz Mountains—long considered the haunt of witches—are drenched in history and medieval legend.

East Germans rebuilt extensively after bombings devastated most of their cities during World War II. Though you will see eyesores of industrialization and stupendously bland housing projects, most historic centers were restored to their old glamour. Some of Europe's most famous palaces and cultural wonders—the Zwinger and Semperoper in Dresden, the Wartburg at Eisenach, the Schiller and Goethe houses in Weimar and Jena, as well as Luther's Wittenberg—await the traveler here.

Traditional tourist sights aside, East Germany is also worth visiting precisely because it still *is* in transition. In 1989 the resolute people of Leipzig, with their now legendary *Montagsdemonstrationen* (Monday demonstrations) through the streets of their proud city, startled the East German regime and triggered the peaceful revolution. A year later the initiative for unification came as much from the West as it did from the East, and the "Wall" finally came down. This is not the end of the story, however. Both the East and West are still struggling with problems caused by the sudden unification of their country. In the former East Germany, the closing of factories and a shrunken welfare system have left many jobless; in the former West, people are burdened by additional taxes imposed to help rebuild the East.

Though economic woes still haunt parts of the eastern region, a class of young entrepreneurs has transformed such cities as Leipzig and Dresden with a wave of start-up businesses. This is particularly impressive when you consider this upswing in light of the past. When the GDR was communism's "Western Front," it was largely isolated from Western ideas. Saxony's Dresden area, in particular, was nicknamed Tal der Ahnungslosen (Valley of the Know-Nothings), as residents there couldn't receive Western television or radio signals.

The three states described here survived under a harsh political regime and have now embarked on a mostly promising future. Eastern Germany used to move very slowly, but today, the pace of cities such as Leipzig and Dresden has overtaken that of their West German counterparts.

Exploring Saxony, Saxony-Anhalt & Thuringia

These three states cover the southeastern part of the former East Germany, and some of the old and now run-down industrial towns will remind you of its communist past. But Germany's most historically important cities are here, and reconstruction programs are slowly restor-

Numbers in the text correspond to numbers in the margin and on the Saxony, Saxony-Anhalt, and Thuringia, Leipzig, and Dresden maps.

16

If you have
3 days

Spend your first day and night in ⊡ **Dresden** ❶–❶⓮ ▶, with its impressive Zwinger complex and fine museums. Set out the next afternoon for **Meissen** ⑰, to see how its famous porcelain is produced. Continue northwest to spend the next two nights in ⊡ **Leipzig** ⑳–㉞, where Bach once resided.

If you have
5 days

Spend your first day and night in ⊡ **Dresden** ❶–❶⓮ ▶. Finish taking in its splendors in the morning and continue to **Meissen** ⑰, stopping long enough for a visit to the porcelain factory, before ending the day in ⊡ **Leipzig** ⑳–㉞. On the third day, head north to the birthplace of Martin Luther and the Reformation, **Wittenberg** ㉟. An indirect route then takes you to the old Harz Mountain towns of **Quedlinburg** ㊳, **Wernigerode**, and **Goslar** ㊴, the unofficial capital of the Harz region. Drive south to ⊡ **Eisenach** ㊶, and prowl through the Wartburg Castle, where Luther translated the Bible in hiding. The final stops are **Erfurt** ㊷, a city of towers that mostly managed to escape wartime bombing, and ⊡ **Weimar** ㊸, where you might want to peek into its most famous hotel, the charming and luxurious Elephant.

If you have
7 days

Your first day and night should be fully devoted to the various sights in ⊡ **Dresden** ❶–❶⓮ ▶. The next day, explore the **Sächsische Schweiz** ⑮, a mountainous region south of the city. Depending on how long you hiked through the mountains, you should still have enough time to drive to the Polish-border town of ⊡ **Görlitz** ⑯. Spend the night there and travel to **Meissen** ⑰, and then follow a northern route on A–14 autobahn to ⊡ **Leipzig** ⑳–㉞, spending the rest of the day there. Leave enough time in Leipzig for visits to its outstanding museums, including the Grassimuseum complex and the Museum der Bildenden Künste. On your fourth and fifth days, from Leipzig drive back to the sights at **Halle** ㊲ before touring the old towns of **Wittenberg** ㉟ and **Quedlinburg** ㊳. You can spend the nights in any of the Harz towns and venture into the mountains for some fresh air. The sixth day is best spent at the Wartburg in **Eisenach** ㊶, which can be reached by following either the country roads or the autobahn from the Harz Mountains toward the south. From there, proceed to **Erfurt** ㊷ and ⊡ **Weimar** ㊸. Spend your last day either in both cities or concentrate fully on the culture and museums in Weimar. If time permits, also detour to **Jena** ㊹ and **Gera** ㊺.

ing them. Dresden is promoting its reputation as the "Florence on the River Elbe," and just downstream, Meissen has undergone an impressive face-lift. Weimar, one of the Continent's old cultural centers, and Leipzig, in particular, have washed off their grime and almost completely restored their historic city centers.

About the Restaurants

Enterprising young managers and chefs are beginning to establish themselves in the East, so look for new and mostly small restaurants along the way. Some successfully blend nouvelle German cuisine with such regional specialties as *Thüringer Sauerbraten mit Klössen* (roast corned beef with dumplings), spicy *Thüringer Wurst* (sausage), *Bärenschinken* (cured ham), *Harzer Köhlerteller mit Röstkartoffeln* (charcoal-grilled meat with fried potatoes), *Harze Käse* (a strong-smelling cheese), and *Moskgauer Bauerngulasch mit Klump* (goulash with dumplings).

About the Hotels

All major hotel chains are present in the larger cities, most of them within beautifully restored mansions. Smaller and family-run hotels often combine a good restaurant with fairly good accommodations. In an effort to further improve tourism, most big hotels offer special (weekend) or activity-oriented packages that aren't found in the western part of the country.

During the trade fairs and shows of the **Leipziger Messe,** particularly in March and April, most Leipzig hotels increase their prices.

WHAT IT COSTS In Euros					
	$$$$	**$$$**	**$$**	**$**	**¢**
RESTAURANTS	over €25	€21–€25	€16–€20	€9–€15	under €9
HOTELS	over €225	€175–€225	€100–€175	€50–€100	under €50

Restaurant prices are per person for a main course at dinner. Hotel prices are for two people in a standard double room, including tax and service.

Timing

Winters in this part of Germany can be cold, wet, and dismal, so unless you plan to ski in the Harz Mountains or the Thüringer Wald, visit in late spring, summer, or early autumn. Avoid Leipzig at trade-fair times, particularly in March and April.

SAXONY

The people of Saxony, a once almost-forgotten corner of Germany near the Czech and Polish borders, identify themselves more as Saxon than German, and their somewhat indecipherable dialect is the target of endless jokes and puns. However, Saxon pride is rebuilding three cities magnificently: Dresden and Leipzig—the showcase cities of eastern Germany—and the smaller town of Görlitz, on the Neisse River. If you make your way toward Dresden from Freiberg, you can follow the Freital road, or first cut north to the Elbe River and the enchanting little city of Meissen.

Dresden

▶ *205 km (127 mi) south of Berlin.*

Saxony's capital city sits in baroque splendor on a wide sweep of the Elbe River, and its proponents are working with German thoroughness to recapture the city's old reputation as the "Florence on the River Elbe." Its yellow and pale-green facades are enormously appealing, and their

Trains & Steamers

Eastern Germany is a treasure house of old steam-driven tractors, factory engines, train engines, and riverboats, many lovingly restored by enthusiasts. Deutsche Bahn (German Railways) regularly runs trains from the years 1899–1930 on a small-gauge line that penetrates deep into the Saxon countryside and the Fichtelberg Mountains. In Saxony-Anhalt you can ride the steam-powered narrow-gauge Brockenbahn to the Harz Mountains' highest point. The world's largest and oldest fleet of paddle steamers (Weisse Flotte) plies the Elbe. Eight old steamers (all of them under historic preservation orders) and two reconstructed ships cruise the Elbe, following the Saxon Wine Route as far as the Czech Republic.

16

Sports & the Outdoors

You can canoe on the Elbe, Gera, and Saale rivers and seldom see another paddler. Contact the tourist office in Dresden, Gera, or Halle for rental information.

Hiking is good in the Harz Mountains, particularly around Thale and Wittenberg. Maps and guides to bicycle and walking trails are available in most hotels and bookstores. The Thale and Wernigerode tourist offices and the Wittenberg District Rural Information Office have great resources. Braunlage, in the Harz, offers good family skiing.

The elevated, dense Thuringian Forest is a popular holiday destination in summer and winter. Its center is Suhl, the administrative heart of an area where every 10th town and village is a spa or mountain resort. The region south of Erfurt, centering on Oberhof, has comfortable hotels and full sports facilities.

Wine & Vineyards

Saxony has cultivated vineyards for more than 800 years and is known for its dry red and white wines, among them Müller-Thurgau, Weissburgunder, Ruländer, and the spicy Traminer. The Sächsische Weinstrasse (Saxon Wine Route) follows the course of the Elbe River from Diesbar-Seusslitz (north of Meissen) to Pirna (southeast of Dresden). Meissen, Radebeul, and Dresden have upscale wine restaurants, and wherever you see a green seal with the letter S and grapes depicted, good local wine is being served. Most of the hotels and restaurants reviewed in this chapter have their own wine cellars.

---

mere presence is even more overwhelming when you compare what you see today with photographs of Dresden from February 1945, after an Allied bombing raid destroyed the city overnight. Dresden was the capital of Saxony as early as the 15th century, although most of its architectural masterpieces date from the 18th century and the reigns of Augustus the Strong and his son, Frederick Augustus II.

Though some parts of the city center still look as if they're stuck halfway between demolition and construction, the present city is an enormous

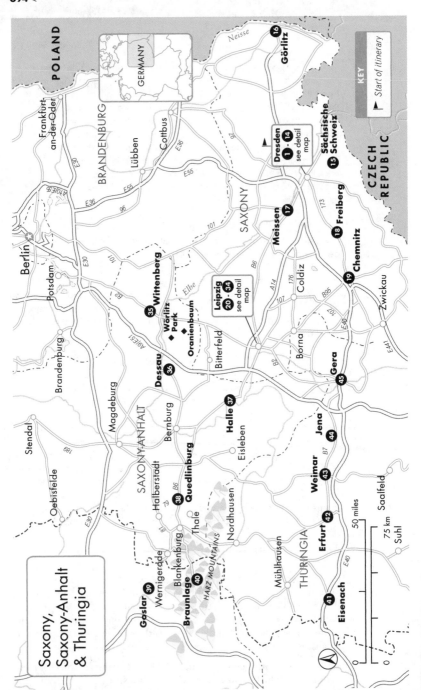

Saxony, Saxony-Anhalt & Thuringia

POLAND

GERMANY

BRANDENBURG

CZECH REPUBLIC

SAXONY

SAXONY-ANHALT

THURINGIA

HARZ MOUNTAINS

KEY

▲ Start of itinerary

Berlin
Potsdam
Frankfurt-an-der-Oder
Brandenburg
Stendal
Oebisfelde
Magdeburg
Lübben
Cottbus
Wittenberg **35**
Wörlitz Park
Oranienbaum
Dessau **36**
Bitterfeld
Bernburg
Borna
Halle **37**
Eisleben
Halberstadt
Quedlinburg **38**
Thale
Nordhausen
Mühlhausen
Suhl
Saalfeld
Goslar **39**
Wernigerode
Blankenburg
Braunlage **40**
Eisenach **41**
Erfurt **42**
Weimar **43**
Jena **44**
Gera **45**
Leipzig **20 – 34**
see detail map
Dresden **1 – 14**
see detail map
Görlitz **16**
Sächsische Schweiz **15**
Meissen **17**
Freiberg **18**
Chemnitz **19**
Zwickau
Coldiz

Elbe
Neisse

50 miles
75 km

tribute to Dresdeners' skills and dedication. The resemblance of today's riverside to Dresden cityscapes painted by Canaletto in the mid-1700s is remarkable. Unfortunately, the war-inflicted gaps in the urban landscape in other parts of the city are too big to be closed anytime soon.

a good walk

It's easy to cover the downtown area of Dresden on foot. From the main railway station (which has adequate parking), you'll first have to cross a featureless expanse surrounded by postwar high-rises to reach the old part of the city. Pick up any materials you like at the tourist-information office on pedestrians-only Pragerstrasse (No. 8).

Buildings representing several centuries of architecture border the **Altmarkt ❶ ►**. At the square's southeast side, take a look at the **Kreuzkirche ❷** before heading east on Wilsdruffer Strasse to the **Stadtmuseum Dresden im Landhaus ❸** with its historic exhibits. Continue east toward Pirnaischer Platz, and make a sharp left turn onto Landhausstrasse, which connects to Dresden's historic heart, the Neumarkt (New Market). On your left is the baroque **Frauenkirche ❹**, rising up from rubble. On the other side of the Neumarkt behind the church, off Brühlsche Gasse, stands the impressive **Albertinum ❺**, which has one of the world's leading art galleries. If you leave the Albertinum by the Brühlsche Terrasse exit, you'll find yourself on what was once known as the Balcony of Europe, a terrace high above the Elbe, carved from a 16th-century stretch of the city fortifications. From the terrace, a breathtaking vista of the Elbe River and the Dresden skyline opens up. From here, you can detour to **Schloss Pillnitz** and its museum. Back at the Neumarkt, you'll see the **Johanneum ❻** on its northwestern corner. The historic building is part of the former palace that now houses a transportation museum. The outside wall of the Johanneum has a unique porcelain-tile painting of a royal procession; walk along the wall, and at the end of the street you'll reach the **Residenzschloss ❼**, which is still under reconstruction.

Next, walk a short distance north on any of the small paths from the Neumarkt, crossing Augustusstrasse in the direction of Terrassenufer. Cross Schlossplatz and then turn left, where you'll encounter Sophienstrasse. If you turn left, you can't miss Saxony's largest church, the **Katholische Hofkirche ❽**. Just opposite the church on the Theaterplatz is the architecturally wondrous **Semperoper ❾**, one of Europe's finest opera houses. Theaterplatz has as its centerpiece a proud equestrian statue of King Johann, who ruled Saxony when Gottfried Semper was at work. Don't be misled by Johann's confident pose in the saddle—he was terrified of horses and never learned to ride. Five minutes south of the Semperoper is the world-famous **Zwinger ❿**, a richly decorated baroque palace with an entrance off Ostra-Allee. From the Zwinger, walk north, crossing the Elbe River on the **Augustusbrücke ⓫**, and then turn left on Grosse Meissner Strasse. You'll pass the **Japanisches Palais ⓬**, a baroque-classicist palace, on your left before crossing Albertplatz to reach **Königstrasse ⓭**, one of Dresden's most beautiful, historic little streets. To get a further glimpse of Dresden's magnificent past, cross Albertplatz and continue down Bautzener Strasse to **Pfund's Molkerei ⓮**, an old dairy specialty shop.

TIMING A full day is sufficient for a quick tour of historic Dresden, but if you plan to explore any of the museums, such as the Zwinger, or take a guided tour of the Semperoper, you'll need more than a day. Allow at least two hours each for the Zwinger, the Johanneum, and the Albertinum. In summer, schedule some time to relax in one of the cafés along the Elbe River. Take note that in winter and early spring, it can get quite windy on the wide, open squares.

What to See

❺ **Albertinum.** This massive, imperial-style building houses Dresden's leading art museum, one of the world's great galleries. The Albertinum is named after Saxony's King Albert, who between 1884 and 1887 converted a royal arsenal into a suitable setting for the treasures he and his forebears had collected. The upper story of the Albertinum, accessible from the Brühlsche Terrasse, houses 19th- and 20th-century paintings and sculptures in the **Gemäldegalerie Neue Meister** (Gallery of Modern Masters). Permanent exhibits include outstanding works by German masters of the 19th and 20th centuries (Caspar David Friedrich's haunting *Das Kreuz im Gebirge* is here) and French Impressionists and Postimpressionists.

Next door is the **Skulpturensammlung** (Sculpture Collection), which includes ancient Egyptian and classical works and examples by Giovanni da Bologna and Adriaen de Vries. ⊠ *Am Neumarkt, Brühlsche Terrasse* ☎ *0351/491–4619* ⊕ *www.skd-dresden.de* 🎫 *€6, including Gemälde-galerie Neue Meister, Grünes Gewölbe, Münzkabinett (coin collection), and Skulpturensammlung* ☉ *Tues.-Sun. 10–6.*

▶ **❶ Altmarkt** (Old Market Square). Although dominated by the nearby un-appealing Kulturpalast (Palace of Culture), a concrete leftover from the 1970s, the broad square and its surrounding streets are the true center of Dresden. The square's colonnaded beauty (from the Stalinist-era architecture of the early 1950s) survived the disfiguring efforts of city planners to turn it into a huge outdoor parking lot. The rebuilt **Rathaus** (Town Hall) is here, as well as the yellow-stucco, 18th-century Landhaus, which contains the Stadtmuseum Dresden im Landhaus.

⓫ Augustusbrücke (Augustus Bridge). This bridge, which spans the river in front of the Katholische Hofkirche, is the reconstruction of a 17th-century baroque bridge blown up by the SS shortly before the end of World War II. The bridge was restored and renamed for Georgi Dimitroff, the Bulgarian Communist accused by the Nazis of instigating the Reichstag fire; after the fall of communism the original name, honoring Augustus the Strong, was reinstated.

> **off the beaten path**
>
> **DEUTSCHES HYGIENE-MUSEUM DRESDEN –** This unique museum (even in a country with a national tendency for excessive cleanliness) relates the history of public health and often features special art exhibits. ⊠ *Lingnerpl. 1* ☎ *0351/48460* ⊕ *www.dhmd.de* 🎫 *€2.50* ☉ *Tues.–Fri. 9–5, weekends 10–6.*

❹ **Frauenkirche** (Church of Our Lady). Germany's greatest Protestant
Fodor's Choice church was reduced to jagged ruins after the infamous February 1945
★ Allied bombing raid during World War II. The once-mighty baroque church was so sturdily built that it had withstood a three-day bombardment during the Seven Years' War. A painstaking reconstruction of the Frauenkirche is under way; its sandstone facade has now been completely restored, and a new golden cross is shining above the new cupola. It's hoped that it can be reconsecrated by the year 2006, the 800th anniversary of the founding of Dresden. The church has also evolved as a symbol of German-British reconciliation. The golden church cross (worth US$400,000) was donated to the building by a British foundation. Daily tours of the church's completed sections and the construction site start at entrance F of the church (northern facade). Try to avoid the always-crowded weekend tours. ⊠ *An der Frauenkirche* ☎ *0351/ 498–1131* ⊕ *www.frauenkirche-dresden.org* 🎫 *Free, donation requested* ☉ *Daily 10–4, tour every hr. Call for dates and times of English-language tours.*

⓬ **Japanisches Palais** (Japanese Palace). This baroque palace was built in 1715–1733 to hold Augustus the Strong's collection of fine china. One of the city's most magnificent buildings, it features Asian architectural elements such as porticos and courtyard statues as well as a roof reminiscent of a pagoda. Today, the palace houses the **Museum für Völkerkunde** (Museum of Ethnology; ☎ *0351/814–4586*) and the **Museum**

für Vorgeschichte (Prehistoric Museum; ☎ 0351/814–450). Those who have already visited similar museums in Berlin may wish to skip these, though special exhibits may make them worth your while. ⊠ *Palaispl. 11* ⊕ *www.archsax.sachsen.de* ✉ *Prehistoric Museum €2, Museum of Ethnology €6* ⊙ *Prehistoric Museum Mon.–Sun. 10–6; Museum of Ethnology Tues.–Sun. 10–5.*

❻ Johanneum. At one time the royal stables, this 16th-century building now houses the **Verkehrsmuseum** (Transportation Museum), a collection of historical conveyances, including vintage automobiles and engines. The former **stable exercise yard,** behind the Johanneum and enclosed by elegant Renaissance arcades, was used during the 16th century as an open-air festival ground. A ramp leading up from the courtyard made it possible for royalty to reach the upper story to view the jousting below without having to dismount. More popular even than jousting in those days was *Ringelstechen,* a risky pursuit in which riders at full gallop had to catch small rings on their lances. Horses and riders often came to grief in the narrow confines of the stable yard.

On the outside wall of the Johanneum is a remarkable example of **Meissen porcelain art:** a Meissen tile mural of a royal procession, 336 feet long. More than 100 members of the royal Saxon house of Wettin, half of them on horseback, are represented on the giant mosaic of 25,000 porcelain tiles, painted in 1904–07 after a design by Wilhelm Walther. The Johanneum is reached by steps leading down from the Brühlsche Terrasse. ⊠ *Am Neumarkt at Augustusstr. 1* ☎ *0351/86440* ⊕ *www. verkehrsmuseum.sachsen.de* ✉ *€3* ⊙ *Tues.–Sun. 10–5.*

❽ Katholische Hofkirche (Catholic Court Church). The largest church in Saxony is also known as the Cathedral of St. Trinitatis. Frederick Augustus II (reigned 1733–63) brought architects and builders from Italy to construct a Catholic church in a city that had been the first large center of Lutheran Protestantism (like his father, Frederick Augustus II had to convert to Catholicism to be eligible to wear the Polish crown). Inside, the treasures include a beautiful stone pulpit by the royal sculptor Balthasar Permoser and a painstakingly restored 250-year-old organ said to be one of the finest ever to come from the mountain workshops of the famous Silbermann family. In the cathedral's crypt are the tombs of 49 Saxon rulers and a relic containing the heart of Augustus the Strong. Owing to restoration work, the cathedral's opening hours may vary. ⊠ *Schlosspl.* ☎ *0351/484–4712* ✉ *Free* ⊙ *Weekdays 9–5, Sat. 10–5, Sun. noon–4:30.*

⓭ Königstrasse (King Street). The grand estates lining this historic boulevard attest to Dresden's bygone wealth. The street itself was once an important thoroughfare of a residential quarter founded by Augustus the Strong in the mid-18th century. Some of the meticulously restored buildings house restaurants, shops, and art galleries in their lovely open courtyards. ⊠ *Between Grosse Meissner Str. and Albertpl.*

❷ Kreuzkirche (Cross Church). Soaring high above the Altmarkt, the richly decorated tower of the baroque Kreuzkirche dates back to 1792. The city's main Protestant church is still undergoing postwar restoration, but the tower and church hall are open to the public. A famous boys' choir, the Kreuzchor, performs here regularly (check Web site or call for scheduled concerts). ⊠ *Altmarkt* ☎ *0351/439–390* ⊕ *www.dresdner-kreuzkirche.de* ⛟ *Tower €1* ☉ *Nov.–Feb., weekdays 10–4, Sun. noon–4; Mar.–Oct., daily 10–5.*

⑭ **Pfund's Molkerei** (Pfund's Dairy Shop). This decorative 19th-century shop has been a Dresden institution since 1880 and offers a wide assortment of cheese and other goods. The shop is renowned for its intricate tile mosaics on the floor and walls. Pfund's is also famous for introducing pasteurized milk to the industry; it invented milk soap and specially treated milk for infants as early as 1900. ⊠ *Bautzener Str. 79* ☎ *0351/808–080* ⊕ *www.pfunds.de* ☉ *Mon.–Sat. 10–6, Sun. 10–3.*

off the beaten path

RADEBEUL – Follow the road along the north bank of the Elbe to Meissen. The small town of Radebeul, on the way, is a mecca for fans of westerns. Radebeul is the birthplace of Germany's well-loved novelist Karl May, who wrote popular, convincing westerns without once visiting America. A museum here explains just how he did it. ⊠ *Karl-May-Str. 5* ☎ *0351/837–300* ⊕ *www.karl-may-museum.de* ⛟ *€5* ☉ *Mar.–Oct., Tues.–Sun. 9–5:30; Nov.–Feb., Tues.–Sun. 10–3:30.*

SCHLOSS PILLNITZ (Pillnitz Palace) – This romantic baroque palace, once a summer retreat for King Augustus the Strong, was built in 1720–22 and is surrounded by a landscaped garden and two smaller palaces, the Wasserpalais and the Bergpalais. Both buildings were designed in Germany's late baroque faux-Chinese pagoda style. Today, they house the **Kunstgewerbemuseum,** which showcases baroque furniture and crafts as well as modern design. To get to Schloss Pillnitz, take Tram 10 from the central train station toward Striesen, exit there and continue with Tram 12 (to Schillerplatz), change there again, and take Bus 83 to Pillnitz. ⊠ *Kleinzschachwitz* ☎ *0351/261–3201* ⊕ *www.skd-dresden.de* ⛟ *€4* ☉ *Bergpalais May–Oct., Tues.–Sun. 10–6; Wasserpalais, May–Oct., Wed.–Mon. 10–6.*

❼ **Residenzschloss** (Dresden City Royal Palace). Restoration work is still under way (scheduled for completion in 2006) behind the Renaissance facade of this former royal palace, much of which was built between 1709 and 1722. Some of the finished rooms in the **Georgenbau** host historical exhibitions, among them an excellent one on the reconstruction of the palace itself. The palace's main gateway, the Georgentor, has an enormous statue of the fully armed Saxon count George. From April through October, the palace's old **Hausmannsturm** (Hausmann Tower) offers a wonderful view of the city and the Elbe River.

But the main attraction is the world-famous **Grünes Gewölbe** (Green Vault) which was returned to the palace, its original location, last year (prior to that, it had been housed in the Albertinum). In 2006 it will be moved into its original rooms in the palace. Named after a green room in the palace of Augustus the Strong, it contains an exquisite collection of unique objets d'art fashioned from gold, silver, ivory, amber, and other precious and semiprecious materials. Among the crown jewels is the world's largest "green" diamond, 41 carats in weight, and a dazzling group of tiny gem-studded figures called *Hofstaat zu Delhi am Geburtstag des Grossmoguls Aureng-Zeb* (The Court at Delhi during the Birthday of the Great Mogul Aureng-Zeb). The unwieldy name gives a false idea of the size of the work, dating from 1708; some parts of the tableau are so small they can be admired only through a magnifying glass. Somewhat larger and less delicate is the drinking bowl of Ivan the Terrible, perhaps the most sensational artifact in this extraordinary museum.

The palace now also houses the **Kupferstichkabinett** (Museum of Prints and Drawings) with more than 500.000 pieces of art spanning several centuries. Changing exhibits present masterworks by Albrecht Dürer, Peter Paul Rubens, and Jan van Eyck, but also 20th-century art by Otto Dix, Edvard Munch, and Ernst Ludwig Kirchner as well as East European art and some Southeast Asian prints.

Two equally impressive collections, the **Münzkabinett** (Coin Museum), and the **Rüstkammer** (Armory), will be moving back to the palace sometime in 2006.

⊠ *Schlosspl.* ☎ *0351/491–4619* 🗓 *€6, for all museums and collections at palace* ☉ *Wed.–Mon. 10–6.*

★ ❾ **Semperoper** (Semper Opera House). One of Germany's best-known and most popular theaters, this magnificent opera house saw the premieres of Richard Wagner's *Rienzi, Der Fliegende Holländer,* and *Tannhäuser,* and Richard Strauss's *Salome, Elektra,* and *Der Rosenkavalier.* The Dresden architect Gottfried Semper built the house in 1838–41 in Italian Renaissance style, then saw his work destroyed in a fire caused by a careless lamplighter. Semper had to flee Dresden after participating in a democratic uprising, so his son Manfred rebuilt the theater in the neo-Renaissance style you see today. Even Manfred Semper's version had to be rebuilt after the devastating bombing raid of February 1945. On the 40th anniversary of that raid—February 13, 1985—the Semperoper reopened with a performance of *Der Freischütz,* by Carl Maria von Weber, another artist who did much to make Dresden a leading center of German music and culture. Even if you're no opera buff, the Semper's lavish interior can't fail to impress. Velvet, brocade, and well-crafted imitation marble create an atmosphere of intimate luxury (it seats 1,323). Guided tours of the building are offered throughout the day, depending on the opera's rehearsal schedule. Tours begin at the entrance to your right as you face the Elbe River. ⊠ *Theaterpl. 2* ☎ *0351/491–1496* ⊕ *www.semperoper.de* 🗓 *Tour €5* ☉ *Tours usually weekdays at 1:30, 2, and 3, weekends at 10.*

❸ **Stadtmuseum Dresden im Landhaus** (Dresden City Museum at the Country Mansion). The city's small but fascinating municipal museum tells the ups and downs of Dresden's turbulent past—from the dark Middle Ages to the bombing of Dresden in February 1945. There are many peculiar exhibits on display, such as an American 250-kg bomb and a stove made from Allied bomb casing. ✉ *Wilsdruffer Str. 2* ☎ *0351/656–480* ⊕ *www.stadtmuseum.dresden.de* ⌨ *€2.50* ⊙ *Sat.–Tues. and Thurs. 10–6, Wed. 10–8; closed Wed. during Oct.–Apr.*

❿ **Zwinger** (Bailey). Dresden's magnificent baroque showpiece is entered
Fodor'sChoice by way of the mighty Kronentor (Crown Gate), off Ostra-Allee. Augustus
★ the Strong hired a small army of artists and artisans to create a "pleasure ground" worthy of the Saxon court on the site of the former bailey, part of the city fortifications. The artisans worked under the direction
of the architect Matthäus Daniel Pöppelmann, who came reluctantly out
of retirement to design what would be his greatest work, begun in 1707
and completed in 1728. Completely enclosing a central courtyard filled
with lawns, pools, and fountains, the complex is made up of six linked
pavilions, one of which boasts a carillon of Meissen bells, hence its name:
Glockenspielpavillon.

The Zwinger is quite a scene—a riot of garlands, nymphs, and other
baroque ornamentation and sculpture. Wide staircases beckon to gal-
leried walks and to the romantic Nymphenbad, a coyly hidden courtyard where statues of nude women perch in alcoves to protect them from
a fountain that spits unexpectedly. The Zwinger once had an open view
of the riverbank, but the Semper Opera House now closes in that side.
Stand in the center of this quiet oasis, where the city's roar is kept at
bay by the outer wings of the structure, and imagine the court festivities held here.

The **Sempergalerie** (Semper Gallery), in the northwestern corner of the
complex, was built to house portions of the royal art collections. It contains the world-renowned Gemäldegalerie Alte Meister (Old Masters
Gallery). The Zwinger Palace complex also contains a porcelain collection,
a zoological museum, and the Staatlicher Mathematisch-Physikalischer
Salon, which displays old scientific instruments.

Among the priceless paintings in the Sempergalerie collection are works
by Dürer, Holbein, Jan van Eyck, Rembrandt, Rubens, van Dyck, Hals,
Vermeer, Raphael (*The Sistine Madonna*), Titian, Giorgione, Veronese,
Velázquez, Murillo, Canaletto, and Watteau. On the wall of the entrance
archway you'll see an inscription in Russian, one of the few amusing
reminders of World War II in Dresden. It reads, in rhyme: "Museum
checked. No mines. Chanutin did the checking." Chanutin, presumably,
was the Russian soldier responsible for checking one of Germany's
greatest art galleries for anything more explosive than a Rubens nude.
☎ *0351/491–4619* ⊕ *www.staatl-kunstsammlungen-dresden.de* ⌨ *€6*
⊙ *Tues.–Sun. 10–6.*

The Zwinger's **Porzellansammlung** (Porcelain Collection; ☎ *0351/491–*
4619 ⌨ *€5* ⊙ *Tues.–Sun. 10–6*), stretching from the curved gallery that
adjoins the Glockenspielpavillon to the long gallery on the east side, is
considered one of the best of its kind in the world. The focus, naturally,
is on Dresden and Meissen china, but there are also outstanding examples
of Japanese, Chinese, and Korean porcelain. The **Rüstkammer** (Armory; ☎ *0351/491–4619* ⌨ *€3* ⊙ *Tues.–Sun. 10–6*) holds medieval
and Renaissance suits of armor and weapons. The **Naturhistorische Samm-**

lung (Natural History Collection; ☎0351/495–2503 ⬚€3 ⏰Tues.–Sun. 10–6) has a small but very interesting collection of natural history exhibits, including skeletons of wild animals that once roamed the Elbe Valley. The **Staatlicher Mathematisch-Physikalischer Salon** (State Mathematics and Physics Salon; ☎0351/491–4660 ⬚€3 ⏰Tues.–Sun. 10–6) is packed with rare and historic scientific instruments. ✉ *Zwinger entrance, Ostra–Allee.*

Where to Stay & Eat

$–$$ ✕ **Marcolinis Vorwerk.** This old villa with a picturesque garden is frequented by a hip, young crowd with a taste for fine wine. The restaurant–art gallery serves Italian dishes with an original spin on meat dishes, such as veal chops served with blue cheese, or chicken baked in a honey-nut crust. In summer, terrace dining provides a spectacular view of Dresden's skyline and the Elbe River. ✉ *Bautzner Str. 96* ☎ *0351/899–6356* ▣ *AE, DC, MC, V* ⏰ *No lunch weekdays.*

★ $ ✕ **Sophienkeller.** One of the liveliest restaurants in town re-creates an 18th-century beer-cellar in the basement of the Taschenberg Palace. Waitresses wear period costumes, and the furniture and porcelain are as rustic as the food is traditional, including the typically Saxon *Gesindeessen* (rye bread, pan-fried with mustard, slices of pork, and mushrooms, baked with cheese). The Sophienkeller is popular with larger groups; you might have to wait if you're a party of three or fewer. ✉ *Taschenbergpalais, Taschenberg 3* ☎ *0351/497–260* ▣ *AE, DC, MC, V.*

¢–$ ✕ **Ballhaus Watzke.** One of the city's oldest microbreweries, the Ballhaus Watzke offers a great panorama view of Dresden from outside the historic downtown area. Several different beers are on tap (you can even help brew one). The extensive menu is made up of mostly hearty local dishes and also has a great variety of Saxon desserts. In summer, the beer garden is open for seating. ✉ *Koetzschenbroderstr. 1* ☎ *0351/852–920* ▣ *AE, MC, V.*

¢–$ ✕ **Ristorante Bellotto im Italienischen Dörfchen.** The name of the restaurant refers to the fact that this historic building on the bank of the Elbe once housed Italian craftsmen. They were brought to Dresden to work on the Hofkirche. Today the lavishly restored, colorful rooms offer a warm welcome. Choose between the beer tavern, café, or shady garden for a mostly Saxon menu. The Bellotto restaurant upstairs serves upscale Italian cuisine. ✉ *Theaterpl. 3* ☎ *0351/498–160* ▣ *AE, DC, MC, V.*

$$$ ✕▨ **Hotel Bülow-Residenz.** One of the most intimate first-class hotels in East Germany, the Bülow-Residenz is in a baroque palace built in 1730 by a wealthy Dresden city official. Each spacious room is tastefully decorated with thick carpets and mostly dark, warm cherrywood furniture and has individual accents and modern amenities. In summer the verdant courtyard is a romantic setting for dinner. The Carousel restaurant ($$$$) holds Saxony's sole Michelin star and serves a large variety of sophisticated fish and game dishes. ✉ *Rähnitzg. 19, D–01097* ☎ *0351/80030* ▤ *0351/800–3100* ⊕ *www.buelow-residenz.de* ➲ *25 rooms, 5 suites ⌙ Restaurant, room service, in-room safes, minibars, cable TV with movies, bar, babysitting, dry cleaning, laundry service, concierge, meeting room, parking (fee), some pets allowed (fee), no-smoking floor; no a/c in some rooms* ▣ *AE, DC, MC, V.*

★ **$$$$** **Kempinski Hotel Taschenbergpalais Dresden.** Destroyed in wartime bombing but now rebuilt, the historic Taschenberg Palace—the work of the Zwinger architect Matthäus Daniel Pöppelmann—is Dresden's premier address and the last word in luxury, as befits the former residence of the Saxon crown princes. Rooms are as big as city apartments, although suites earn the adjective *palatial;* they are all furnished with bright elm-wood furniture and have several phone lines, as well as fax machines and data ports. ✉ *Taschenberg 3, D–01067* ☎ *0351/49120* 🖷 *0351/491–2812* 🌐 *www.kempinski-dresden.de* *188 rooms, 25 suites* *4 restaurants, room service, in-room data ports, in-room safes, minibars, cable TV with movies, pool, hair salon, massage, sauna, bar, shops, babysitting, dry cleaning, laundry service, concierge, business services, meeting room, parking (fee), some pets allowed (fee), no-smoking rooms* 💳 *AE, DC, MC, V.*

$$–$$$ **artotel Dresden.** The artotel keeps the promise of its rather unusual name. It's all modern, designed by Italian interior architect Denis Santachiara and decorated with more than 600 works of art by Dresden-born painter and sculptor A. R. Penck. It's definitely a place for the artsy crowd; you might find the heavily styled rooms a bit much. The Kunsthalle Dresden and its exhibits of modern art are right next door. Apart from offering art, the hotel's rooms and service have genuine first-class appeal at slightly better prices. ✉ *Ostra-Allee 33, D–01067* ☎ *0351/49220* 🖷 *0351/492–2777* 🌐 *www.artotels.de* *155 rooms, 19 suites* *2 restaurants, room service, in-room data ports, minibars, cable TV, gym, massage, sauna, bar, babysitting, dry cleaning, laundry service, concierge, business services, meeting room, parking (fee), some pets allowed (fee), no-smoking rooms* 💳 *AE, DC, MC, V* 🍽 *BP.*

$$ **Hotel Elbflorenz.** This centrally located hotel lives up to Dresden's somewhat presumptuous nickname *Elbflorenz,* or Florence on the River Elbe, thanks to its first-class service and stylish ambience. The Italian-designed rooms are bathed in red and yellow tones and sit alongside a garden courtyard. There's a fine sauna and relaxation area, and the hotel's restaurant, Quattro Cani della Citta, serves delicious Italian seafood and other specialties. ✉ *Rosenstr. 36, D–01067* ☎ *0351/86400* 🖷 *0351/864–0100* 🌐 *www.hotel-elbflorenz.de* *212 rooms, 15 suites* *Restaurant, café, in-room data ports, in-room safes, minibars, cable TV, hair salon, gym, sauna, bar, children's programs (from infancy to age 14), concierge, meeting room, parking (fee), some pets allowed (fee), no-smoking rooms* 💳 *AE, DC, MC, V* 🍽 *BP.*

$$ **Rothenburger Hof.** One of Dresden's smallest and oldest luxury hotels, the historic Rothenburger Hof opened in 1865 and is only a few steps away from the city's sightseeing spots. A highlight is the dining room, which gives you some insight as to how Dresden's wealthy wined and dined 150 years ago. The rooms are not very large, but they're comfortable and nicely decorated with furniture that looks antique but, in fact, is reproduction. ✉ *Rothenburger Str. 15–17, D–01099* ☎ *0351/81260* 🖷 *0351/812–6222* 🌐 *www.dresden-hotel.de* *26 rooms, 13 apartments* *Room service, minibars, cable TV, pool, health club, sauna, bar, dry cleaning, laundry service, meeting room, parking (fee), no-smoking rooms; no a/c* 💳 *AE, MC, V* 🍽 *BP.*

$$ 🏨 **Schlosshotel Dresden-Pillnitz.** On the grounds of Schloss Pillnitz (Pillnitz Palace), this small hotel allows you to enjoy the countryside without getting too far from the city. The beautifully restored mansion is run by the Zepp family, who extend extremely personal service. The airy rooms are decorated with bright colors and timeless, elegant country furniture. Just a few hundred yards from the hotel is a pier where Elbe River cruises depart. The spa Vitalzentrum zum goldenen Apfel is a short walk away. ⊠ *August-Böckstiegel-Str. 10, D–01326* ☎ *0351/26140* 📠 *0351/261–4400* 🌐 *www.schlosshotel-pillnitz.de* 🛏 *42 rooms, 3 suites* ⚫ *Restaurant, minibars, cable TV, bar, dry cleaning, laundry service, meeting rooms, free parking, some pets allowed (fee), no-smoking floor; no a/c* ⊟ *AE, MC, V* ¶⊙¶ *BP.*

Nightlife & the Arts

Dresdeners are known for their industriousness and very efficient way of doing business, but they also know how to spend a night out. Most of Dresden's pubs, bars, and *Kneipen* are in the **Äussere Neustadt** district and along the buzzing **Münzgasse** (between Frauenkirche and Brühlsche Terrasse). Folk and rock music are regularly featured at **Bärenzwinger** (⊠ Brühlscher Garten ☎ 0351/495–1409). One of the best bars in town is the groovy and hip **Aqualounge** (⊠ Louisenstr. 56 ☎ 0351/810–6116). The name of the **Planwirtschaft** (⊠ Louisenstr. 20 ☎ 0351/801–3187) ironically refers to the Socialist economic system and attracts an alternative crowd. The hip dance club **Dance Factory** (⊠ Bautzner Str. 118 ☎ 0351/802–0066) is in an old Stasi garrison. The **Motown Club** (⊠ St. Petersburger Str. 9 ☎ 0351/487–4150) attracts a young and stylish crowd.

The opera in Dresden regained its international reputation when the **Semper Opera House** (Sächsische Staatsoper Dresden; ⊠ Theaterpl. 📧 Evening box office, Abendkasse, left of main entrance ☎ 0351/491–1705) reopened in 1985 following an eight-year reconstruction. Tickets are reasonably priced but also hard to come by; they're often included in package tours. Try your luck at the evening box office about a half hour before the performance. If that doesn't work, take one of the opera-house tours.

Dresden's fine **Philharmonie Dresden** (Philharmonic Orchestra Dresden; ⊠ Kulturpalast am Altmarkt ☎ 0351/486–6286) takes center stage in the city's annual music festival, from mid-May to early June. In addition to the annual film festival in April, open-air **Filmnächte am Elbufer** (Elbe Riverside Film Nights; ⊠ Am Königsufer, next to the State Ministry of Finance ☎ 0351/899–320) take place on the bank of the Elbe from late June to late August.

May brings an annual international Dixieland **jazz** festival, and the Jazz Autumn festival follows in October. Jazz musicians perform most nights of the week at the friendly, laid-back **Tonne Jazz Club** (⊠ Waldschlösschen, Am Brauhaus 3 ☎ 0351/802–6017).

Shopping

Dresden is almost as famous as Meissen for its porcelain. It's manufactured outside the city in **Freital,** where there's a showroom and shop, Sächsische Prozellan-Manufaktur Dresden (⊠ Bachstr. 16, Freital ☎ 0351/

647–130), open weekdays 9–5. Within Dresden you'll find exquisite Meissen and Freital porcelain at the department store **Karstadt** (✉ Prager Str. 12 ☎ 0351/490–6833). The **Kunststube am Zwinger** (✉ Hertha-Lindner-Str. 10–12 ☎ 0351/490–4082) sells wooden toys and the famous Saxon *Rächermännchen* (Smoking Men) and *Weihnachtspyramiden* (Christmas Lights Pyramids) manufactured by hand in the Erzbirge Mountains.

Sächsische Schweiz

⓯ *42 km (26 mi) southeast of Dresden.*

True mountain climbers may smile at the name of the Sächsische Schweiz (Saxon Switzerland), the mountainous region southeast of Dresden. The highest summit is a mere 633 feet, but the scenery in this region, a mixture of cliffs, gorges, and small canyons, certainly has drama. The stone formations are at least 100 million years old and are leftovers from the Elbe River's sandstone deposits. In time, the soft stone was sculpted by wind and water into grim but fantastic-looking tall columns of stone.

The **Nationalpark** covers 97 square km (37 square mi) of the region. Thanks to its inaccessibility, Saxon Switzerland is home to game and many other wild animals (such as the lynx), which are otherwise extinct in Germany. The park is divided into two parts, which can be explored by foot, either following marked routes or by registering with the park rangers for guided tours. To reach the park from Dresden, drive southeast on B–172 toward Pirna, or take the S-bahn from the central train station to Königsstein or Bad Schandau; both towns are served by buses and minitrains. The train ride itself takes close to an hour. ✉ *Nationalpark-und Forstamt Sächsische Schweiz, An der Elbe 4, D–01814 Bad Schandau* ☎ *035022/90060* ⊕ *www.nationalpark-saechsische-schweiz.de* 🎫 *Free* ☉ *Free guided walking tours mid-Apr.–Oct., Mon. at 10 AM at Bad Schandau; Tues. at 10 AM at Kurort Rathen; Wed. at 10:20 AM at Hinterhermsdorf; Thurs. at 10 AM at Wehlen. Call for exact meeting points.*

Görlitz

⓰ *60 km (38 mi) northeast of Dresden, 265 km (165 mi) southeast of Berlin.*

Quiet, narrow cobblestone alleys and late-medieval and Renaissance structures make Görlitz one of the most charming finds in eastern Germany. Once a major commercial hub between Dresden and Wroclaw, Germany's easternmost city fell into small-town oblivion after World War II, which left the city almost completely intact.

A vivid reminder of the city's wealthy past is the richly decorated Renaissance homes and warehouses on the **Obermarkt** (Upper Market). During the late Middle Ages the most common merchandise here was cloth, which was bought and sold from covered wagons and the first floors of many buildings. On **Verrätergasse** (Traitors' Alley), off the Obermarkt, is the **Peter-Liebig-Haus,** where the city's cloth makers secretly met in 1527 to plan a rebellion against the city council. Their plans were uncovered, and the plotters were hanged. The initials of the first four words of their meeting place, *Der verräterischen Rotte Tor* (The treacherous gang's gate), are inscribed above the door.

The **Städtische Kunstsammlung** (Municipal Art Collection) has two locations. The massive **Kaisertrutz** (Emperor's Fortress) once protected the western city gates and now houses late-Gothic and Renaissance art from the area around Görlitz. The **Barockhaus Neissestrasse** mostly displays 17th- to 19th-century furniture and art. ⊠ *Kaisertrutz, Am Obermarkt* ⊠ *Barockhaus Neissestrasse, Neissestr. 30* ☎ *03581/671–351* ⊠ *€3.50* ⊙ *Tues.–Thurs., weekends 10–5, Fri. 10–8; Kaisertrutz closed Nov.–Apr.*

The city's oldest section surrounds the **Untermarkt** (Lower Market), whose most prominent building is the **Rathaus.** Its winding staircase is as peculiar as the statue of the goddess of justice, whose eyes—contrary to European tradition—are not covered. The corner house on the square, the **Alte Ratsapotheke** (Old Council Pharmacy), has a sundial on the facade (painted in 1550) based on the 12 signs of the zodiac.

The **Schlesisches Museum** (Silesian Museum) is housed in the magnificent Schönhof building, one of Germany's oldest *Patrizierhäuser* (grand mansion of the city's ruling business and political elite, the Patricians). The museum showcases the history—primarily 17th–19th century—and art of formerly German Silesia. ⊠ *Untermarkt 4* ☎ *03581/87910* ⊕ *www.schlesisches-museum.de* ⊠ *€1* ⊙ *Tues.–Sun. 10–5.*

The **Karstadt** department store, off busy Marienplatz, dates to 1912–13 and is Germany's only original art nouveau department store. The main hall has a colorful glass cupola and several stunning freestanding staircases. ⊠ *An der Frauenkirche 5* ☎ *03581/4600.*

Perched high above the river is the **Kirche St. Peter und Paul** (St. Peter and Paul Church), one of Saxony's largest late-Gothic churches, dating to 1423. The real draw of the church is its famous organ, built in 1703 by Eugenio Casparini. Its full and deep sound can be heard during guided tours (which must be prearranged by phone). ⊠ *Bei der Peterkirche 5* ☎ *03581/409–590* ⊠ *Free* ⊙ *Mon.–Sat. 10:30–4, Sun. 11:30–4; guided tours Thurs. and Sun. at noon.*

off the beaten path

KULTURINSEL EINSIEDEL – This handcrafted amusement park is a delightful wonderland of ships, forts, games, and mazes. Kids descend into tunnels and can choose between various routes that lead to surprising places. This topsy-turvy world is mirrored in the Expressionist-like design of the outdoor stage, restaurant, and covered buildings. A family entry price includes a credit toward snacks. ⊠ *Zentendorfer Str., Zentendorf, 17 km (11 mi) north of Görlitz* ☎ *035891/4910* ⊕ *www.kulturinsel.de* ⊠ *€4.50* ⊙ *Mar.–Oct., daily 10–6.*

Where to Stay & Eat

$ ✕ **Le Trou Normand.** Behind the thick walls of a historic baroque building, this charming little restaurant serves the cuisine of northern France. The wine list is impressive, the atmosphere is friendly and familial, the menu changes monthly. ⊠ *Untermarkt 13* ☎ *03581/417–037* ▤ *MC, V* ⊙ *Closed Mon. Oct.–Mar.*

★ **$$** ✕🖭 **Romantik-Hotel Tuchmacher.** The city's best hotel is also its most modern accommodation in antique disguise. In a mansion dating to 1528, guest rooms with wooden floors and thick ceiling beams are sparsely furnished with modern dark-cherrywood furniture. The colorful ceilings may remind you of Jackson Pollock paintings, but they are original ornaments from the Renaissance. The Schneider-Stube ($–$$$) serves traditional Saxon dishes. All room prices include a luxurious breakfast buffet. ⊠ *Peterstr. 8, D–02826* ☎ *03581/47310* 🖷 *03581/473–179* ⊕ *www.tuchmacher.de* ⇆ *42 rooms, 1 suite* ⌂ *Restaurant, room service, minibars, cable TV, gym, sauna, bar, dry cleaning, laundry service, meeting room, free parking, some pets allowed (fee), no-smoking rooms; no a/c* ⊟ *AE, DC, MC, V* ⧖ *BP.*

Meissen

🟑 *25 km (16 mi) northwest of Dresden.*

This romantic city on the Elbe River is known the world over for its porcelain, bearing the trademark crossed blue swords. The first European porcelain was made in this area in 1708, and in 1710 the Royal Porcelain Workshop was established in Meissen, close to the local raw materials.

The story of how porcelain came to be produced in Meissen reads like a German fairy tale: The Saxon elector Augustus the Strong, who ruled from 1694 to 1733, urged his court alchemists to find the secret of making gold, something he badly needed to refill a state treasury depleted by his extravagant lifestyle. The alchemists failed to produce gold, but one of them, Johann Friedrich Böttger, discovered a method for making something almost as precious: fine hard-paste porcelain. Already a rapacious collector of Oriental porcelains, Prince August put Böttger and a team of craftsmen up in a hilltop castle—Albrechtsburg—and set them to work.

The **Albrechtsburg,** where the story of Meissen porcelain began, sits high above Old Meissen, towering over the Elbe River far below. The 15th-century castle is Germany's first truly residential one, a complete break with the earlier style of fortified bastions. In the central *Schutzhof,* a typical Gothic courtyard protected on three sides by high rough-stone walls, is an exterior spiral staircase, the **Wendelstein,** a masterpiece of early masonry hewn in 1525 from a single massive stone block. The ceilings of the castle halls are richly decorated, although many date only from a restoration in 1870. Adjacent to the castle is an early Gothic cathedral. It's a bit of a climb up Burgstrasse and Amtsstrasse to the castle, but a bus runs regularly up the hill from the Marktplatz. ☎ *03521/47070* ⊕ *www.albrechtsburg-meissen.de* 🖭 *€3.50, €5 with tour* ☉ *Mar.–Oct., daily 10–6; Nov.–Jan. 9 and Feb., daily 10–5.*

A set of porcelain bells at the late-Gothic **Frauenkirche** (Church of Our Lady), on the central Marktplatz, was the first of its kind anywhere when installed in 1929. Nearby the Frauenkirche is the **Alte Brauerei** (Old Brewery), which dates to 1569 and is graced by a Renaissance gable. It now houses city offices.

The city's medieval past is recounted in the museum of the **Franziskanerkirche** (St. Francis Church), a former monastery. ✉ *Heinrichspl. 3* ☎ *03521/458–857* 🎟 *€2.50* ⏲ *Daily 11–5.*

The **Staatliche Porzellan–Manufaktur Meissen** (Meissen Porcelain Works) outgrew its castle workshop in the mid-19th century and today is on the southern outskirts of town. One of its buildings has a demonstration workshop and a museum whose Meissen collection rivals that of the Porcelain Museum in Dresden. ✉ *Talstr. 9* ☎ *03521/468–700* 🌐 *www.meissen.de* 🎟 *Museum €4.50; workshop €3, including guided tour; combined ticket €5* ⏲ *May–Oct., daily 9–6; Nov.–Apr., daily 9–5.*

Near the porcelain works is the **Nikolaikirche** (St. Nicholas Church; ✉ Neumarkt 29), which holds the largest set of porcelain figures ever crafted (8¼ feet) and also has remains of early Gothic frescoes.

Where to Stay & Eat

★ **$–$$** ✕ **Restaurant Vincenz Richter.** Tucked away in a yellow wooden-beam house, this historic restaurant has been painstakingly maintained by the Richter family since 1873. The dining room is adorned with rare antiques, documents, and medieval weapons, as well as copper and tin tableware. Guests can savor the exquisite dishes on the Saxon-German menu, while sampling the restaurant's own personally produced white wine; a bottle of the Riesling is a real pleasure. *Meissener Kapitelberg.* ✉ *An der Frauenkirche 12* ☎ *03521/453–285* 💳 *AE, MC, V* ⏲ *Closed Mon. No lunch, no dinner Sun.*

$ ✕ **Domkeller.** Part of the centuries-old complex of buildings ringing the town castle, this ancient and popular hostelry is the best place to enjoy fine wines and hearty German dishes in Meissen. It's also worth a visit for the sensational view of the Elbe River valley from its large dining room and tree-shaded terrace. ✉ *Dompl. 9* ☎ *03521/457–676* 💳 *AE, DC, MC, V.*

$$ ✕🏨 **Mercure Parkhotel Meissen.** This art nouveau villa on the bank of the Elbe sits across from the hilltop castle. Although most of the luxuriously furnished and appointed rooms are in the newly built annexes, try for one in the villa—and for an unforgettable experience book the *Hochzeitssuite* (wedding suite), on the top floor (€203 a night), for its stunning view. The restaurant serves nouvelle cuisine in a dining room ($$) with original stained glass and elegantly framed doors. ✉ *Hafenstr. 27–31, D–01662* ☎ *03521/72250* 📠 *03521/722–904* 🌐 *www.mercure.de* 🛏 *92 rooms, 5 suites* 👍 *Restaurant, room service, in-room data ports, minibars, cable TV, gym, hot tub, massage, sauna, bar, babysitting, dry cleaning, laundry service, meeting room, parking (fee), some pets allowed (fee), no-smoking rooms; no a/c* 💳 *AE, DC, MC, V* 🍽 *BP.*

The Arts

Meissen's cathedral, the **Dom** (✉ Dompl. 7 ☎ 03521/452–490), has a year-long music program, with organ and choral concerts every Saturday during the summer. Regular **concerts** (☎ 03521/47070) are held at the Albrechtsburg castle, and in early September the *Burgfestspiele*—open-air evening performances—are staged in the castle's romantic courtyard.

Shopping

Meissen porcelain can be bought directly from the **Staatliche Porzel-lan–Manufaktur Meissen** (✉ Talstr. 9 ☎ 03521/468–700) and in every china and gift shop in town. To wine connoisseurs, the name *Meissen* is associated with vineyards producing top-quality wines much in demand throughout Germany—try a bottle of Müller-Thurgau, Weissburgunder, or Goldriesling. They can be bought from the producer **Sächsische Winzer-ergenossenschaft Meissen** (✉ Bennoweg 9 ☎ 03521/780–970).

Freiberg

⓲ *40 km (25 mi) south of Meissen.*

Once a prosperous silver-mining community, Freiberg has two picturesque Gothic town squares, the Obermarkt (Upper Market), and the Untermarkt (Lower Market). The late-Gothic cathedral, with its Golden Gate, constructed in 1230, has a richly decorated interior and a Silbermann organ dating from 1711.

The **Stadt- und Bergbaumuseum** (City and Mining Museum), on central Domplatz, vividly describes the history of silver mining in and around Freiberg. ✉ *Am Dom 1* ☎ *03731/20250* 🖾 *€3* ☉ *Tues.–Sun. 10–5.*

The **Sächsisches Lehr- und Besucherbergwerk** (Saxon Educational and Visitors' Mine), outside the city, offers a unique glimpse into silver and ore mining from the early 19th century until today. Visitors are guided through two restored mines, the Reiche Zeche (Rich mine) and the Alte Elisabeth (Old Elisabeth mine). ✉ *Fuchsmühlenweg* ☎ *03731/394–571* 🖾 *€12.50, no children under 12 years* ☉ *Reiche Zeche tours weekdays at 9:30; May–Sept., Sat. 8, 11, and 2; Oct.–Apr., 1st Sat. of month at 8, 11, and 2; Alte Elisabeth tours May–Sept., weekdays at 1, Sat. at 10 and 2, Sun. at 11.*

> **en route** Take the winding Freital Valley road (follow B–173, and then take the country road in Oberschöna toward Frankenstein) west to Chemnitz. You'll pass through the village of **Frankenstein** on the way. It has no relation to Mary Shelley's fictional scientist-baron, but there are some ancient castle ruins in the vicinity.

Chemnitz

⓳ *35 km (22 mi) west of Freiberg, 80 km (50 mi) southeast of Leipzig.*

On older maps Chemnitz may appear as Karl-Marx-Stadt, an appellation imposed on the city in 1953 to remind the East German working community of the man who really started it all. In 1990 the inhabitants, free to express a choice, overwhelmingly voted to restore the original name. Badly damaged during World War II, Chemnitz has been revived as a center of industry and culture.

Chemnitz's main visual attraction is its 12th-century **Rote Turm** (Red Tower; ✉ Off Strasse der Nationen) in the center of the city. The **Altes Rathaus** (Old Town Hall; ✉ Marktpl.), dating from 1496–98, incorporates a variety of styles from many reconstructions. Outside the city museum (which is not particularly interesting) on Theaterplatz is a group of 250-million-year-old **petrified tree trunks,** unique in Europe and oddly resembling a modern work of sculpture.

The **Kunstsammlungen Chemnitz im König-Albert-Museum** (Chemnitz Art Collection at the King Albert Museum) boasts some 80,000 paintings and sculptures, spanning centuries of European art, from Romanticism to French impressionism and the German 20th-century expressionist movement known as *Die Brücke* (The Bridge). One of the most famous members of this lattermost movement, Karl Schmidt-Rotluff (1884–1976), was born in the neighboring vicinity, and the museum houses the world's second-largest collection of his paintings. ⊠ *Theaterpl.* ☎ *0371/488–4424* ☑ *€5* ☉ *Tues.–Sun. noon–7.*

Where to Stay & Eat

$$ ✕▦ **Günnewig Hotel Chemnitzer Hof.** This city-center hotel was built in 1930 in early Bauhaus style, in which ornamentation was discarded in favor of abstract design (it's now on the National Historic Register). The spacious rooms are furnished with fine veneers and attractive shades of blue. The restaurant Opera ($–$$) serves international dishes and has an extensive menu of local fish. ⊠ *Theaterpl. 4, D–09111* ☎ *0371/6840* ☐ *0371/676–2587* ⊕ *www.guennewig.de* ↪ *98 rooms, 3 apartments* ዽ *Restaurant, room service, in-room safes, minibars, cable TV, sauna, bar, dry cleaning, laundry service, meeting room, parking (fee), some pets allowed (fee), no-smoking rooms; no a/c* ⊟ *AE, DC, MC, V* ⦿ *BP.*

$ ✕▦ **Adelsberger Parkhotel Hoyer.** The first hotel built in Chemnitz after reunification has a modern, graceful exterior and elegant, comfortable guest rooms. The apartments under the steeply sloping eaves are particularly attractive, especially where sunlight streams through large dormer windows. The restaurant's (¢–$) royal-blue-and-white furnishings are flooded with light from floor-to-ceiling bay windows. The imaginative menu includes hearty Saxon specialties. ⊠ *Wilhelm-Busch-Str. 61, D–09127* ☎ *0371/773–303* ☐ *0371/773–377* ⊕ *www.adelsberger-parkhotel.de* ↪ *23 rooms, 3 suites* ዽ *Restaurant, room service, minibars, cable TV, gym, sauna, babysitting, dry cleaning, laundry service, meeting room, free parking, some pets allowed (fee); no a/c* ⊟ *AE, MC, V* ⦿ *CP.*

---

en route B–95 leads to Leipzig, but for a scene out of World War II, detour at Borna, taking 176 to **Colditz.** A pretty river valley holds the town whose name still sends a chill through Allied veterans. During the war the Germans converted the town's massive, somber castle into what they believed would be an escape-proof prison for prisoners regarded as security risks. But many managed to flee, employing a catalog of ruses that have since been the stuff of films and books. The castle is now a home for the elderly, but the courtyards and some of the installations used during the war can be visited. You can continue to Leipzig via 107 to the autobahn.

Leipzig

80 km (50 mi) northwest of Chemnitz, 32 km (20 mi) southeast of Halle.

With a population of about 500,000, Leipzig is the second-largest city in East Germany (after Berlin) and has long been a center of printing and bookselling. Astride major trade routes, it was an important market town in the Middle Ages, and it continues to be a trading center, thanks to the *Leipziger Messe* (trade and fair shows) throughout the year that bring together buyers from East and West.

Those familiar with music history associate Leipzig with the great composer Johann Sebastian Bach (1685–1750), who was organist and choir director at the Thomaskirche, and the 19th-century composer Richard Wagner, who was born here in 1813.

World War II left little of old Leipzig intact. Restoration conveys touches of the city's Renaissance character and art nouveau flair, although some of the newer buildings (notably the university's skyscraper tower) distort the perspective and proportions of the old city.

a good walk

Start your tour of downtown Leipzig at the gigantic **Hauptbahnhof** ⓴ ☞, the city's main train station and premier shopping mall. Cross the broad expanse of Willy-Brandt-Platz to walk south on Goethestrasse. On your left you'll see the modern **Opernhaus** ㉑, whose socialist facade is a sad contrast to the magnificent old architecture of the Hauptbahnhof. Turn right onto Grimmaischestrasse and after a short walk turn right onto Nikolaistrasse, where you can visit the **Nikolaikirche** ㉒. As you return south, Nikolaistrasse turns into Universitätstrasse, where the rather unappealing **Leipziger Universitätsturm** ㉓ looms above every other building in the city center. On its east side, the tower faces the vast Augustusplatz; across this square stands the **Neues Gewandhaus** ㉔, home of the city's renowned orchestra. Return north to Grimmaischestrasse and walk west; on your left you'll pass by the **Mädlerpassage** ㉕, one of the city's finest shopping arcades, which dates to the turn of the 20th century. Continue a bit farther west, and just off the street on your right is the market square, the **Markt** ㉖, with the old town hall and its museum devoted to Leipzig's past. Not far away, off the narrow Barfussgässchen, is the **Museum zum Arabischen Kaffeebaum** ㉗, a coffeehouse and museum devoted to the bitter bean. From here it's just a five-minute walk northeast to the Sachsenplatz with the newly built, ultramodern **Museum der Bildenden Künste** ㉘, the city's leading art gallery. Continue west on to the **Museum in der Runden Ecke** ㉙, a special exhibition about East Germany's secret police, the Stasi. Take the Dittrichring to **Thomaskirche** ㉚, where Johann Sebastian Bach once worked as choirmaster. Opposite the church is the **Bach-Museum im Bach-Archiv Leipzig** ㉛. Following Thomasgasse eastwards, the street name will change to Grimmaischestrasse, you'll reach the **Grassimuseum** ㉜, Leipzig's grand historic museum center, in about 10 minutes.

After a stop here you can take a streetcar (No. 15 to Meusdorf) from Johannisplatz to the **Völkerschlachtdenkmal** ㉝, a huge memorial to the battle that marked the beginning of Napoléon's final defeat in 1815.

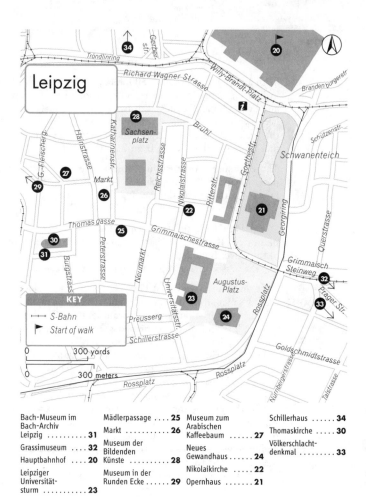

Leipzig

For another side trip, take streetcar No. 6 to the **Schillerhaus** ㉞, once the home of German poet and playwright Friedrich Schiller.

TIMING It's possible to walk around the downtown area in just about three hours and still stop at some of the sights mentioned above. The churches can be inspected in less than 20 minutes each. But if you're interested in German history and art, you'll need perhaps two full days so you can spend a whole day just visiting the museums. The Völkerschlachtdenkmal is perfect for a half-day side trip.

What to See

off the beaten path

BOTANISCHER GARTEN (Botanical Garden) – This set of splendid open-air gardens and greenhouses incorporates Germany's oldest university botanical garden, which dates from 1542. The journey to the Botanischer Garten stop takes about 15 minutes on Tram 2 or 21 (get off at the Johannisallee stop). ⊠ *Linnestr. 1* ☎ *0341/973–6850* ☒ *Gardens free, greenhouses €3* ☉ *Gardens Nov.–Feb., daily 9–4; Mar, Apr., and Oct., daily 9–6; May–Sept., daily 9–8. Greenhouses Nov.–Feb., daily 9–4; Mar., Apr., and Oct., daily 9–6; May–Sept., daily 9–8, greenhouse hrs can vary according to events. Butterfly house May–Oct., daily 10–6.*

㉛ **Bach-Museum im Bach-Archiv Leipzig.** (Bach Museum at the Bach Archives Leipzig). The Bach family home, the old Bosehaus, stands opposite the Thomaskirche and is now a museum devoted to the composer's life and work. Musical instruments on display date to Bach's time. The exhibits are in German only; an English-language guide can be purchased in the shop. ⊠ *Thomaskirchhof 16* ☎ *0341/91370* ☒ *€3, €6 with guided tour* ☉ *Daily 10–5.*

㉜ **Grassimuseum.** This major cultural venue is a fine example of German art deco and was restored and modernized by British star architect David Chipperfield in 2003–05. The building, dating to 1925–29, houses three important museums, which will be gradually reopened in summer and fall 2005. The **Museum für Kunsthandwerk** (Museum of Arts and Crafts; ☎ 0341/213-3719 ⊕ www.grassimuseum.de ☒ €4 ☉ Tues. and Thurs.–Sun. 10–6, Wed. 10–8) showcases works from Leipzig's and East Germany's proud tradition of handicrafts such as exquisite porcelain, fine tapestry art, and modern Bauhaus design.

The **Museum für Völkerkunde** (Ethnological Museum; ☎ 0341/213–3719 ⊕ www.grassimuseum.de ☒ €2 ☉ Tues.–Fri. 10–6, weekends 10–5) presents arts and crafts from all continents and various era, including a thrilling collection of Southeast Asian antique art. The **Musikinstrumentenmuseum** (Musical Instruments Museum; ☎ 0341/687–0795 ⊕ www.uni-leipzig.de/museum/musik ☒ €3 ☉ Tues.–Sun. 11–5) showcases musical instruments, mostly from the Renaissance, including the world's oldest clavichord, constructed in 1543 in Italy. There are also spinets, flutes, and lutes. Sample sounds of these instruments can be heard while looking at them. ⊠ *Johannispl. 5–11.*

▶ ⑳ **Hauptbahnhof.** With 26 platforms, Leipzig's main train station is Europe's largest. It was built in 1915, and while a protected monument, modern commerce rules its bi-level shopping mall (the Promenaden). Many of the shops and eateries stay open until 10 PM. ✉ *Willy-Brandt-Pl.* ☎ *0341/141–270 for mall, 0341/9968–3275 for train station.*

㉓ **Leipziger Universitätsturm** (Leipzig University Tower). Towering over Leipzig's city center is this 470-foot-high structure, which houses administrative offices and lecture rooms. Some of the University of Leipzig students have dubbed it the Jagged Tooth. Students were also largely responsible for changing the university's name, replacing its postwar title, Karl Marx University, with the original one. The **Augustusplatz** spreads out below the university tower like a space-age campus.

㉕ **Mädlerpassage** (Mädler Mall). This shopper's paradise is Leipzig's finest arcade, where the ghost of Goethe's Faust lurks in every marble corner. Goethe set one of the scenes of *Faust* in the famous Auerbachs Keller restaurant, at No. 2. A bronze group of characters from the play, sculpted in 1913, beckons you down the stone staircase to the restaurant. A few yards away is a delightful art nouveau bar called Mephisto, done in devilish reds and blacks. ✉ *Grimmaische Str.*

㉖ **Markt.** Leipzig's showpiece is its huge, old market square. One side is occupied completely by the Renaissance town hall, the **Altes Rathaus,** which houses the **Stadtgeschichtliches Museum,** where Leipzig's past is well documented. ✉ *Markt 1* ☎ *0341/965–130* 💶 *€2.50* ⊙ *Tues.–Sun. 10–6.*

★ ㉘ **Museum der Bildenden Künste** (Museum of Fine Arts). In 2004 the city's leading art gallery reopened in an ultramodern, cubelike complex at the exact location of the original, historic museum which was destroyed by Allied bombing. The museum has more than 2,700 paintings representing everything from the German Middle Ages to contemporary American art; one of its finest collections focuses on Cranach the Elder. ✉ *Sachsenpl.* ☎ *0341/216–990* ⊕ *www.leipzig.de/museum_d_bild_kuenste.htm* 💶 *€2.50, free 2nd Sun. of month* ⊙ *Tues. and Thurs.–Sun. 10–6, Wed. 1–8.*

★ ㉙ **Museum in der Runden Ecke** (Museum in the Round Corner). This building once served as the headquarters of the city's secret police, the dreaded *Staatssicherheitsdient.* The exhibition, *Stasi—Macht und Banalität* (Stasi—Power and Banality), not only presents the offices and surveillance work of the Stasi but also shows hundreds of documents revealing the magnitude of its interests in citizens' private lives. The material is written in German, but the items and the atmosphere still give an impression of how life under such a regime might have felt. ✉ *Dittrichring 24* ☎ *0341/961–2443* ⊕ *www.runde-ecke-leipzig.de* 💶 *Free, €3 with tour in English, by appointment only* ⊙ *Daily 10–6.*

㉗ **Museum zum Arabischen Kaffeebaum** (Arabic Coffee Tree Museum). This museum and café–restaurant tells the fascinating history of coffee culture in Europe, particularly in Saxony. The café is one of the oldest on the Continent and once proudly served coffee to such luminaries as Lessing, Schumann, Goethe, and Liszt. The museum features many paintings, Arabian coffee vessels, and coffeehouse games. It also explains the basic principles of roasting coffee. ✉ *Kleine Fleischerg. 4* ☎ *0341/123–4294* 💶 *Free* ⊙ *Daily 11–7, free tour Tues. at 11.*

㉔ Neues Gewandhaus (New Orchestra Hall). In the shadow of the Leipziger Universitätsturm is the glass-and-concrete home of the city orchestra, one of Germany's greatest. Kurt Masur is a former director and Herbert Blomstedt is currently at the helm. Owing to the world-renowned acoustics of the concert hall, a tone resonates here for a full two seconds. ⊠ *Augustuspl. 8* ☎ *0341/127–0280.*

★ **㉒ Nikolaikirche** (St. Nicholas Church). This church with its undistinguished facade was center stage during the demonstrations that helped bring down the Communist regime. Every Monday for months before the government collapsed, thousands of citizens gathered in front of the church chanting, *"Wir sind das Volk"* ("We are the people"). Inside is a soaring Gothic choir and nave. Note the unusual patterned ceiling supported by classical pillars that end in palm tree–like flourishes. Luther is said to have preached from the ornate 16th-century pulpit. ⊠ *Nikolaikirchhof* ☎ *0341/960–5270* ☎ *Free* ☉ *Mon.–Sat. 10–6; Sun. services at 9:30, 11:15, and 5.*

㉑ Opernhaus (Opera House). Leipzig's stage for operas was the first postwar theater to be built in Communist East Germany. Its solid, boxy style is the subject of ongoing local controversy. ⊠ *Opposite Gewandhaus, on north side of Augustuspl.*

㉞ Schillerhaus (Schiller House). This small country residence was, for a time, the home of the German poet and dramatist Friedrich Schiller. While staying here in 1785, Schiller wrote parts of his *Don Carlos* and the first draft of his world-famous *Ode an die Freude* (Ode to Joy). Documenting the 18th-century country lifestyle, the small museum contains period furniture, personal items, and other objects. To reach the Schillerhaus, take streetcar Line 6, 20, or 24 to Menckestrasse or Fritz-Seger-Strasse. ⊠ *Menckestr. 42* ☎ *0341/566–2170* ☎ *€2* ☉ *Apr.–Oct., Tues.–Sun. 10–6; Nov.–Mar., Wed.–Sun. 10–4.*

㉚ Thomaskirche (St. Thomas's Church). Bach was choirmaster at this Gothic church for 27 years, and Martin Luther preached here on Whitsunday 1539, signaling the arrival of Protestantism in Leipzig. Originally the center of a 13th-century monastery, the tall church (rebuilt in the 15th century) now stands by itself. Bach wrote most of his cantatas for the church's famous boys' choir, the *Thomanerchor,* which was founded in the 13th century; the church continues as the choir's home as well as a center of Bach tradition.

Fodor'sChoice ★

The great music Bach wrote during his Leipzig years commanded little attention in his lifetime, and when he died, he was given a simple grave, without a headstone, in the city's Johannisfriedhof (St. John Cemetery). It wasn't until 1894 that an effort was made to find where the great composer lay buried, and after a thorough, macabre search his coffin was removed to the Johanniskirche. That church was destroyed by Allied bombs in December 1943, and Bach subsequently found his final resting place in the church he would have selected: the Thomaskirche. You can listen to the famous boys' choir during the *Motette,* a service with a special emphasis on choral music.

Bach's 12 children and the infant Richard Wagner were baptized in the early 17th-century font; Karl Marx and Friedrich Engels also stood before this same font, godfathers to Karl Liebknecht, who grew up to be a revolutionary as well. ⊠ *Thomaskirchhof, off Grimmaischestr.* ☎ *0341/ 960–2855* ⊕ *www.thomaskirche.org and www.thomanerchor.com* ⊠ *Free, Motette €1* ⊙ *Daily 9–6; Motette, Fri. at 6 PM, Sat. at 3.*

㉝ Völkerschlachtdenkmal (Memorial to the Battle of the Nations). On the city's outskirts, Prussian, Austrian, Russian, and Swedish forces stood ground against Napoléon's troops in the Battle of the Nations of 1813, a prelude to the French general's defeat two years later at Waterloo. An enormous, 300-foot-high monument erected on the site in 1913 commemorates the battle. Despite its ugliness, the site is well worth a visit, if only to wonder at the lengths—and heights—to which the Prussians went to celebrate their military victories and to take in the view from a windy platform (provided you can climb the 500 steps to get there). The Prussians did make one concession to Napoléon in designing the monument: a stone marks the spot where he stood during the three-day battle. An exhibition hall explains the history of the memorial. The memorial can be reached via Streetcar 15 or 21 (leave the tram at the Probstheida station). ⊠ *Prager Str.* ☎ *0341/878–0471* ⊠ *€3* ⊙ *Nov.–Apr., daily 10–4; May–Oct., daily 10–6; tour daily at 10:30, 1:30, and 2:30.*

Where to Stay & Eat

★ **$$–$$$** ✕ **Kaiser Maximilian.** Leipzig's best Mediterranean restaurant serves inventive Italian and French dishes in a setting dominated by high, undecorated walls and black, leather seats. The Maximilian is known for its pasta and fish dishes such as *Schwarze Lachstortelloni im Safransud* (black salmon tortelloni cooked in saffron juice). ⊠ *Neumarkt 9–19* ☎ *0341/998–6900* ⊕ *www.kaiser-maximilian.de* ⌔ *Reservations essential* ⊟ *AE, MC, V.*

★ **¢–$$$** ✕ **Auerbachs Keller.** The most famous of Leipzig's restaurants consists of an upscale, international gourmet restaurant and another restaurant specializing in hearty Saxon fare. It has been around since 1530, and Goethe immortalized one of the several vaulted historic rooms in his *Faust.* The menu features regional dishes from Saxony, mostly hearty, roasted meat recipes. There's also a good wine list. ⊠ *Mädlerpassage, Grimmaische Str. 2–4* ☎ *0341/216–100* ⌔ *Reservations essential* ⊟ *AE, MC, V* ⊙ *Mon.*

$–$$ ✕ **Barthels Hof.** The English-language menu at this restaurant explains not only the cuisine but the history of Leipzig as well. Waitresses wear traditional *Trachten* dresses, but the rooms are quite modern. The restaurant is popular with locals, especially for breakfast. ⊠ *Hainstr. 1* ☎ *0341/141–310* ⊟ *AE, MC, V.*

★ **$–$$** ✕ **Thüringer Hof.** One of Germany's oldest restaurants and pubs (dating back to 1454) served its hearty Thuringian and Saxon fare to Martin Luther and the likes—who certainly had more than a mere pint of the beers on tap here. The menu in the reconstructed, cavernous and always buzzing dining hall doesn't exactly offer gourmet cuisine but rather an impressively enormous variety of game, fish, and bratwurst dishes. The Thuringian sausages (served with either sauerkraut and potatoes or onions and mashed potatoes) and the famous Thuringian *Sauerbraten* (beef marianted in a sour essence) are a must. ⊠ *Burgstr. 19* ☎ *0341/ 994–4999* ▤ *AE, MC, V.*

★ **¢–$$** ✕ **Zill's Tunnel.** The "tunnel" refers to the barrel-ceiling ground-floor restaurant, where foaming glasses of excellent local beer are served with a smile. The friendly staff will also help you decipher the Old Saxon descriptions of the menu's traditional dishes. Upstairs there's a larger wine restaurant with an open fireplace. ⊠ *Barfussgässchen 9* ☎ *0341/960–2078* ▤ *AE, MC, V.*

¢–$ ✕ **Apels Garten.** This elegant little restaurant in the city center pays homage to nature with landscape paintings on the wall, floral arrangements on the tables, and fresh produce on the imaginative menu. In winter the wild-duck soup with homemade noodles is an obligatory starter; in summer try the *Räucherfischsuppe* (smoked fish soup)—you won't find another soup like it in Leipzig. ⊠ *Kolonnadenstr. 2* ☎ *0341/960–7777* ▤ *AE, MC, V* ☽ *No dinner Sun.*

¢–$ ✕ **Paulaner Restaurant Hutter Culinaria.** Munich's Paulaner Brewery returned to its Leipzig subsidiary of prewar times and transformed the building into a vast complex, with restaurants, a banquet hall, a café, and a beer garden. There's something here for everyone, from intimate dining to noisy, Bavarian-style tavern-table conviviality. The food, such as *Schweinshaxen mit Sauerkraut* (salty pork with sauerkraut), is a mix of Bavarian and Saxon. The Paulaner beer is a perfect accompaniment. ⊠ *Klosterg. 3–5* ☎ *0341/211–3115* ▤ *AE, DC, MC, V.*

$$$ ▥ **Hotel Fürstenhof Leipzig.** The city's grandest hotel is inside the renowned
Fodor'sChoice Löhr-Haus, a revered old mansion. The stunning banquet section is the
★ epitome of 19th-century grandeur, with red wallpaper and black serpentine stone; the bar is a lofty meeting area under a bright glass cupola. Rooms are spacious and decorated with cherrywood designer furniture. ⊠*Tröndlin-ring 8, D–04105* ☎ *0341/1400* 🖷 *0341/140–3700* ⊕ *www. luxurycollection.com* ⇆ *80 rooms, 12 suites* ⬧ *Restaurant, room service, in-room data ports, in-room safes, minibars, cable TV with movies, pool, gym, massage, sauna, spa, bar, piano bar, babysitting, dry cleaning, laundry service, concierge, business services, meeting room, parking (fee), some pets allowed (fee), no-smoking floors* ▤ *AE, DC, MC, V.*

$$–$$$ ▥ **Westin Leipzig.** Although the hotel's service is outstanding, the high-rise edifice and its accommodations lack true atmosphere. Rooms, however, offer every luxury, including bathrooms with marble floors and walls and full air-conditioning. The owners have included a Japanese restaurant and garden. The hotel is convenient to the main train station. ⊠ *Gerberstr. 15, D–04105* ☎ *0341/9880* 🖷 *0341/988–1229* ⊕ *www. westin.com/leipzig.com* ⇆ *447 rooms, 27 suites* ⬧ *3 restaurants, room service, in-room data ports, in-room safes, minibars, cable TV with movies, pool, gym, hair salon, massage, sauna, spa, bowling, bar, shops, babysitting, dry cleaning, laundry service, concierge, business services, meeting room, parking (fee), some pets allowed (fee), no-smoking rooms* ▤*AE, DC, MC, V* ⦿ *BP.*

$$ ▥ **Park Hotel-Seaside Hotel Leipzig.** A few steps from the central train station, the Park Hotel is primarily geared to the business traveler. The modern rooms may lack some individuality and are definitely not designed for romantic weekends, but the warm service and exceptional bathrooms and swimming-pool area make for a pleasant stay. The Orient Express restaurant, a reconstruction of the famous 19th-century train, is another plus. ✉ *Richard-Wagner-Str. 7, D–04109* ☎ *0341/98520* 🖶 *0341/985–2750* ⊕ *www.seaside-hotels.de* 🛏 *281 rooms, 9 suites* ⚲ *Restaurant, room service, in-room safes, minibars, cable TV, health club, hot tub, sauna, bar, babysitting, dry cleaning, laundry service, concierge, meeting room, parking (fee), some pets allowed (fee), no-smoking floor; no a/c* ▭ *AE, DC, MC, V* ⦿| *BP.*

$$ ▢ **Renaissance Leipzig Hotel.** One of the largest hotels in the city, the Renaissance Leipzig is popular with business travelers because of its quiet atmosphere. It has large, elegant rooms—with fashionable bathrooms in dark marble. When making a reservation, ask for a room on the Club Floor: for about €12 a day you get access to the Club Lounge. The hotel's restaurant serves light nouvelle German cuisine. The Renaissance is in the heart of old Leipzig, a perfect spot from which to explore the city on foot. ✉ *Grosser Brockhaus 3, D–04103* ☎ *0341/12920* 🖶 *0341/129–2800* ⊕ *www.renaissancehotels.com* 🛏 *295 rooms, 61 suites* ⚲ *Restaurant, room service, in-room data ports, minibars, cable TV, pool, gym, massage, sauna, bar, dry cleaning, laundry service, concierge, business services, meeting room, parking (fee), some pets allowed (fee), no-smoking floor* ▭ *AE, DC, MC, V* ⦿| *BP.*

$ ▢ **Ringhotel Adagio Leipzig.** The quiet Adagio, tucked away behind the facade of a 19th-century city mansion, is centrally located between the Grassimuseum and the Neues Gewandhaus. All rooms are individually furnished; when making a reservation, ask for a "1920s room," which features the style of the Roaring '20s and bathtubs almost as large as a whirlpool. ✉ *Seeburgstr. 96, D–04103* ☎ *0341/216–699* 🖶 *0341/960–3078* ⊕*www.hotel-adagio.de* 🛏 *30 rooms, 1 suite, 1 apartment* ⚲ *Cable TV, dry cleaning, laundry service, meeting room, parking (fee), some pets allowed (fee), no-smoking rooms; no a/c* ▭ *AE, DC, MC, V* ⦿| *CP.*

Nightlife & the Arts

The *Kneipenszene* (pub scene) of Leipzig is centered on the **Drallewatsch** (a Saxon slang word for "going out"), the small streets and alleys around Grosse and Kleine Fleischergasse. A magnet for young people is the **Moritzbastei** (✉ Universitätsstr. 9 ☎ 0341/702–590), reputedly Europe's largest student club, with bars, a disco, a café, a theater, and a cinema. Nonstudents are welcome. One of the city's top dance clubs is the hip **Spizz Keller** (✉ Markt 9 ☎ 0341/960–8043). The **Tanzpalast** (✉ Dittrichring ☎ 0341/960–0596), in the august setting of the *Schauspielhaus* (city theater), attracts a thirtysomething crowd. The upscale bar, pub, and restaurant **Weinstock** (✉ Markt 7 ☎ 0341/1406–0606) is in a Renaissance building and offers a huge selection of good wines. A favorite hangout among the city's business elite is the **Schauhaus** (✉ Bosestr. 1 ☎ 0341/960–0596), a stylish bar serving great cocktails.

The **Neues Gewandhaus** (✉ Augustuspl. 8, D–04109 ☎ 0341/127–0280 ⊕ www.gewandhaus.de), a controversial piece of architecture, is home to an undeniably splendid orchestra. Tickets to concerts are very difficult to obtain unless you reserve well in advance and in writing only.

Sometimes spare tickets are available at the box office a half hour before the evening performance. Leipzig's annual music festival, **Music Days,** is in June.

One of Germany's most famous cabarets, the **Leipziger Pfeffermühle** (⊠ Thomaskirchhof 16 ☎ 0341/960–3196), has a lively bar off a courtyard opposite the Thomaskirche. On pleasant evenings the courtyard fills with benches and tables, and the scene rivals the indoor performance for entertainment. The variety theater **Krystallpalast** (⊠ Magazinstr. 4 ☎ 0341/140–660 ⊕ www.krystallpalast.de) features a blend of circus, vaudeville, and comedy not to be missed.

The **Gohliser Schlösschen** (⊠ Menckestr. 23 ☎ 0341/589–690), a small rococo palace outside Leipzig's center, frequently holds concerts. It's easily reached by public transportation: take streetcar No. 20 or No. 24 and then walk left up Poetenweg; or take streetcar No. 6 to Menckestrasse. Daytime tours can be arranged for groups.

Shopping

Small streets leading off the Markt attest to Leipzig's rich trading past. Tucked in among them are glass-roof arcades of surprising beauty and elegance, including the wonderfully restored **Specks Hof, Barthels Hof, Jägerhof,** and the **Passage zum Sachsenplatz.** Invent a headache and step into the *Apotheke* (pharmacy) at Hainstrasse 9—it is spectacularly art nouveau, with finely etched and stained glass and rich mahogany. For more glimpses into the past, check out the antiquarian-book stores of the nearby **Neumarkt Passage.**

The **Hauptbahnhof** (⊠ Willy-Brandt-Pl.) offers more than 150 shops, restaurants, and cafés. All shops are open Monday through Saturday 9:30 AM–10 PM, and many shops are also open on Sunday, with the same hours. Thanks to the historic backdrop, it's one of the most beautiful and fun shopping experiences in East Germany.

SAXONY-ANHALT

The central state of Saxony-Anhalt is a region rich in natural attractions. In the Altmark, on the edge of the Harz Mountains, fields of grain and sugar beets stretch to the horizon. In the mountains themselves are the deep gorge of the Bode River and the stalactite-filled caves of Rubeland. The songbirds of the Harz are renowned, and though pollution has taken its toll, both the flora and the fauna of the Harz National Park (which encompasses much of the region) are coming back. Atop the Brocken, the Harz's highest point, legend has it that witches convene on Walpurgis Night (the night between April 30th and May 1st).

Saxony-Anhalt's Letzlinger Heide (Letzling Heath), another home to rare birds and animals, is one of Germany's largest tracts of uninhabited land. The Dübener Heide (Düben Heath), south of Wittenberg, has endless woods of oaks, beeches, and evergreens that are wonderful to explore by bike or on foot. In and around Dessau are magnificent parks and gardens.

Architecturally, Saxony-Anhalt abounds in half-timber towns and Romanesque churches. Quedlinburg has both the oldest half-timber house in Germany and the tomb of Germany's first king, 10th-century Henry I. In Dessau, the Bauhaus School pointed the world to modern architecture and design just before the start of World War II. Music has thrived in Saxony-Anhalt as well. Among its favorite sons are the composers Georg Philipp Telemann, of Magdeburg; Georg Friedrich Handel, of Halle; and in modern times Kurt Weill, of Dessau. And it was in Wittenberg that Martin Luther nailed his 95 Theses to a church door.

Wittenberg

 107 km (62 mi) southwest of Berlin, 67 km (40 mi) north of Leipzig.

Protestantism was born in the little town of Wittenberg (officially called Lutherstadt-Wittenberg). In 1508 the fervent, idealistic young Martin Luther, who had become a priest only a year earlier, arrived to study and teach at the new university founded by Elector Frederick the Wise. Nine years later, enraged that the Roman Catholic Church was pardoning sins through the sale of indulgences, Luther posted his 95 Theses attacking the policy on the door of the Castle Church.

Martin Luther is still the center of attention in Wittenberg, and sites associated with him are marked with plaques and signs. You can see virtually all of historic Wittenberg on a 2-km (1-mi) stretch of Collegienstrasse and Schlossstrasse that begins at the railroad tracks and ends at the Schlosskirche (Castle Church).

In a small park where Weserstrasse meets Collegienstrasse, the **Luthereiche** (Luther Oak) marks the spot where in 1520 Luther burned the papal bull excommunicating him for his criticism of the Church. The present oak was planted in the 19th century.

Fodor'sChoice

★

Within **Lutherhalle** (Luther Hall) is the Augustinian monastery where Martin Luther lived both as a teacher-monk and later, after the monastery was dissolved, as a married man. Today it's a museum dedicated to Luther and the Reformation. Visitors enter Lutherhalle through a garden and an elegant door with a carved stone frame; it was a gift to Luther from his wife, Katharina von Bora. Inside the much-restored structure is the monks' refectory, where works of Luther's contemporary, the painter Lucas Cranach the Elder, are displayed. The room that remains closest to the original is the dark, wood-panel Lutherstube. The Luthers and their six children used it as a living room, study, and meeting place for friends and students. Prints, engravings, paintings, manuscripts, coins, and medals relating to the Reformation and Luther's translation of the Bible into the German vernacular are displayed throughout the house. ⊠ *Collegienstr. 54* ☏ *03491/42030* ⊕ *www.martinluther.de* 🖅 *€5* ⊗ *Apr.–Oct., daily 10–6; Nov.–Mar., Tues.–Sun. 10–5.*

In the elegantly gabled Renaissance **Melanchthonhaus** (Melanchthon House), the humanist teacher and scholar Philipp Melanchthon corrected Luther's translation of the New Testament from Greek into German. Luther was hiding in the Wartburg in Eisenach at the time, and as each section of his manuscript was completed it was sent to Melanchthon for approval. (Melanchthon is a Greek translation of the man's real name, Schwarzerdt, which means "black earth"; humanists routinely adopted such classical pseudonyms.) The second-floor furnishings have been painstakingly re-created after period etchings. ⊠ *Collegienstr. 60* ☎ *03491/403–279* ⊕ *www.martinluther.de* ⊠ *€2.50* ☉ *Apr.–Oct., Mon.–Sun. 10–6; Nov.–Mar., Tues.–Sun. 10–5.*

From 1514 until his death in 1546, Martin Luther preached two sermons a week in the twin-tower **Stadtkirche St. Marien** (Parish Church of St. Mary). He and Katharina von Bora were married here (Luther broke with monasticism in 1525 and married the former nun). The altar triptych by Lucas Cranach the Elder includes a self-portrait, as well as portraits of Luther wearing the knight's disguise he adopted when hidden away at the Wartburg; Luther preaching; Luther's wife and one of his sons; Melanchthon; and Lucas Cranach the Younger. Also notable is the 1457 bronze baptismal font by Herman Vischer the Elder. On the church's southeast corner you'll find a discomforting juxtaposition of two Jewish-related **monuments**: a 1304 mocking caricature called the Jewish Pig, erected at the time of the expulsion of the town's Jews, and, on the cobblestone pavement, a contemporary memorial to the Jews who died at Auschwitz. ⊠ *Kirchpl.* ☎ *03491/404–415* ⊠ *€1.50, including tour* ☉ *May–Oct., Mon.–Sat. 10–5, Sun. 11:30–5; Nov.–Apr., Mon.–Sat. 10–4, Sun. 11:30–4.*

Two statues are the centerpiece of the **Marktplatz** (market square): an 1821 statue of Luther by Johann Gottfried Schadow, designer of the quadriga and Victory goddess atop Berlin's Brandenburg Gate, and an 1866 statue of Melanchthon by Frederick Drake. Their backdrop is the handsome white High Renaissance **Rathaus** (Town Hall). Gabled Renaissance houses containing shops line part of the square. ⊠ *Markt 26* ☎ *03491/421–720* ⊠ *€2* ☉ *Apr.–Oct., Tues.–Sun. 9–6; Nov.–Mar., Tues.–Sun. 10–5.*

The **Cranachhaus** is believed to have been the first home, in town, of Lucas Cranach the Elder, the court painter, printer, mayor, pharmacist, and friend of Luther's. His son, the painter Lucas Cranach the Younger, was born here. Some of the interior has been restored to its 17th-century condition. It's now a gallery showing an exhibition about the life and work of Cranach. ⊠ *Markt 4* ☎ *03491/420–190* ⊠ *€3* ☉ *May–Oct., Mon.–Sat. 10–5, Sun. 1–5; Nov.–Apr., Tues.–Sat. 10–5, Sun. 1–5.*

Renaissance man Lucas Cranach the Elder, probably the wealthiest man in Wittenberg in his day, lived in two different houses during his years in town. In a second **Cranachhaus,** near the Schlosskirche (Castle Church), he not only lived and painted but also operated a print shop, which has been restored, and an apothecary. The courtyard, where it's thought he did much of his painting, remains much as it was in his day. Children attend the **Malschule** (drawing school) here. ⊠ *Schlossstr. 1* ☎ *03491/ 410–919* ⊠ *Free* ☉ *Mon.–Thurs. 8–4, Fri. 8–3.*

In 1517 the indignant Martin Luther affixed to the doors of the **FodorśChoice** **Schlosskirche** (Castle Church) his 95 Theses attacking the Roman Catholic ★ Church's policy of selling indulgences. Written in Latin, the theses might have gone unnoticed had not someone—without Luther's knowledge—translated them into German and distributed them. In 1521 the Holy Roman Emperor Charles V summoned Luther to Worms when Luther refused to retract his position. It was on the way home from his confrontation with the emperor that Luther was "captured" by his protector, Elector Frederick the Wise, and hidden from papal authorities in Eisenach for the better part of a year. Inside the church, simple bronze plaques mark the burial places of Luther and Melanchthon. ✉ *Schlosspl.* ☎ *03491/402–585* 🎟 *€1.50* ☉ *May–Oct., Mon.–Sat. 10–5, Sun. 11:30–5; Nov.–Apr., Mon.–Sat. 10–4, Sun. 11:30–4.*

Where to Stay & Eat

¢–$$ ✕ **Schlosskeller.** At the back of the Schlosskirche, this restaurant's four dining rooms are tucked away in a basement with 16th-century stone walls and barrel-vaulted ceilings. The kitchen specializes in German dishes, such as *Schlosskellerpfanne* (pork fillets with fried potatoes, tomatoes, and pepper bells). ✉ *Schlosspl. 1* ☎ *03491/480–805* 🖃 *AE, MC, V.*

★ ¢–$ ✕ **Luther-Schenke.** Dressed in costumes of Luther's day, waiters serve the beer and dishes that the reformer might have eaten—roast boar and pigs' knuckles with sauerkraut—as well as such fare as salsa, pasta, lamb, or chicken roasted on a spit. The brick-vaulted beer cellar has a laid-back ambience. ✉ *Markt 2* ☎ *03491/406–592* 🖃 *AE, DC, MC, V.*

$$ 🏨 **Best Western Stadtpalais Wittenberg.** In an old city mansion just a few steps from the Lutherhaus, this hotel offers modern style and high-quality service. The elegant lobby and upscale rooms may suggest high prices, but the rates are more than reasonable. The best deals are the special executive double rooms, which are 330 square feet and have many extras. The rooms lack creativity, but their shiny new look and the quality furniture make up for the blandness. ✉ *Collegienstr. 56–57, D–06886* ☎ *03491/4250* 🖨 *03491/425–100* ⊕ *www.stadtpalais-bestwestern.de* ⇘ *78 rooms ⚐ Restaurant, minibars, cable TV, sauna, steam room, bar, babysitting, dry cleaning, laundry service, meeting room, parking (fee), some pets allowed (fee), no-smoking rooms; no a/c in some rooms* 🖃 *AE, DC, MC, V* ⍐ *BP.*

$ 🏨 **Hotel Grüne Tanne.** Four hundred years ago a knight's estate stood on the land occupied today by this cozy country hotel. A hostelry since 1871, the Grüne Tanne is a starting place for walks and bicycle and horseback rides into the countryside. Rooms are fairly basic and somewhat outdated but very clean and comfortable. The two suites with a separate living-room area make for a romantic stay. A shuttle service goes to the Wittenberg train station. ✉ *Am Teich 1, D–06896 Wittenberg/Reinsdorf* ☎ *03491/6290* 🖨 *03491/629–250* ⊕ *www.gruenetanne.de* ⇘ *40 rooms, 1 apartment, 2 suites ⚐ Restaurant, cable TV, sauna, free parking, some pets allowed (fee); no a/c* 🖃 *AE, DC, MC, V* ⍐ *BP.*

en route From Wittenberg take B–187 west for 13 km (8 mi); then turn onto B–107 south for 8 km (5 mi) to Wörlitz. Leopold III Friedrich Franz of Anhalt-Dessau loved gardens and sought to create a garden kingdom in his lands. He had **Wörlitz Park** laid out between 1765 and 1802, largely in the naturalistic English style. It was the first such garden created in central Europe, with meadowlands, a lake, canals, woods, rocks, and grottoes. You can walk or bicycle the 42 km (26 mi) to Dessau through the park.

From Wörlitz continue another 5 km (3 mi) on B–107 to the **Oranienbaum-Park.** Leopold enlarged his garden kingdom by incorporating Oranienbaum—a 17th-century baroque palace—and adding an English-Chinese garden with a tea house as well as a pagoda inspired by the one in England's Kew Gardens. After visiting Oranienbaum, go west on the road that becomes B–185 in Dessau.

On B–185, 9 km (5½ mi) outside Dessau, you'll come to Mosigkau and its 18th-century late-baroque **Schloss Mosigkau** (Mosigkau Palace). Prince Leopold of Anhalt-Dessau commissioned the palace for his favorite daughter, Anna Wilhelmine. When she died, she left the property to an order of nuns. They immediately tore up the formal grounds to make an English-style park, and after a post–World War II attempt to restore the original baroque appearance, money and enthusiasm ran out. The palace itself, however, was always well maintained. Only a quarter of the rooms can be visited, but they include one of Germany's very few baroque picture galleries. Its stucco ceiling is a marvel of rococo decoration, a swirling composition of pastel-color motifs. ☒ *Knobelsdorffallee 3, Dessau* ☎ *0340/521–139* ☐ *Palace €4.50, including tour; gardens free* ☉ *Apr. and Oct., Tues.–Sun. 10–5; May–Sept., Tues.–Sun. 10–6.*

Dessau

⓶ *35 km (22 mi) southwest of Wittenberg.*

The name *Dessau* is known to every student of modern architecture. In 1925–26 architect Walter Gropius set up his highly influential Bauhaus school of design here. Gropius hoped to replace the dark and inhumane tenement architecture of the 1800s with standardized yet spacious and bright apartments. His ideas and methods were used in building 316 villas in the city's Törten section in the 1920s.

For a contrast to the no-nonsense Bauhaus architecture, look at downtown Dessau's older buildings, including the Dutch baroque **Georgkirche** (St. George's Church; ☒ Georgenstr. 15), built in 1712.

★ Architectural styles that would influence the appearance of such cities as New York, Chicago, and San Francisco were conceived in the **Bauhaus Building.** The architecture school is still operating, and the building can be visited. Other structures designed by Gropius and the Bauhaus architects, among them the Meisterhäuser, are open for inspection off Ebertallee and Elballee. ☒ *Gropiusallee 38* ☎ *0340/650–8251* ⊕ *www.bauhaus-dessau.de* ☐ *€4* ☉ *Daily 10–6. Meisterhäuser Nov.–mid-Feb., Tues.–Sun. 10–5; mid-Feb.–Oct., Tues.–Sun. 10–6.*

Halle

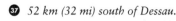 *52 km (32 mi) south of Dessau.*

This 1,000-year-old city, built on the salt trade, has suffered from the shortfalls of Communist urban planning; the hastily built residential area, Halle-Neustadt, was cynically nicknamed Hanoi. Yet the Old City has an unusual beauty, particularly its spacious central marketplace, the **Markt,** and its five distinctive sharp-steepled towers.

Of the four towers belonging to the late-Gothic **Marienkirche** (St. Mary's Church), two are connected by a vertiginous catwalk bridge. Martin Luther preached in the church, and George Friedrich Handel (Händel in German), born in Halle in 1685, was baptized at its font. He went on to learn to play the organ beneath its high, vaulted ceiling. The Markt's fifth tower is Halle's celebrated **Roter Turm** (Red Tower; ⊠ Markt), built between 1418 and 1506 as an expression of the city's power and wealth. It houses a carillon and the local tourist office.

The **Marktschlösschen** (Market Palace), a late-Renaissance structure just off the market square, has an interesting collection of historical musical instruments, some of which could have been played by Handel and his contemporaries. ⊠ *Marktpl. 13* ☎ *0345/202–9141* 🖼 *Free* ☉ *Weekdays 10–7, weekends 10–6.*

Handel's birthplace, the **Händelhaus,** is now a museum devoted to the composer. The entrance hall displays glass harmonicas, curious musical instruments perfected by Benjamin Franklin in the 1760s. ⊠ *Grosse Nikolaistr. 5* ☎ *0345/500–900* 🖼 *€2.60, free Thurs.* ☉ *Fri.–Wed. 9:30–5:30, Thurs. 9:30–7.*

The **Moritzburg** (Moritz Castle) was built in the late 15th century by the archbishop of Magdeburg after he claimed the city for his archdiocese. The typical late-Gothic fortress, with a dry moat and a sturdy round tower at each of its four corners, was a testament to Halle's early might, which vanished with the Thirty Years' War. Prior to World War II the castle contained a leading gallery of German Expressionist paintings, which were ripped from the walls by the Nazis and condemned as "degenerate." Some of the works are back in place at the **Staatliche Galerie Moritzburg,** together with some outstanding late-19th- and early-20th-century art. You'll find Rodin's famous sculpture *The Kiss* here. ⊠ *Friedemann-Bach-Pl. 5* ☎ *0345/212–590* ⊕ *www.moritzburg.halle.de* 🖼 *€4* ☉ *Tues. 11–8:30, Wed.–Sun. 10–6.*

Halle's only early Gothic church, the **Dom** (cathedral) stands about 200 yards southeast of the Moritzburg. Its nave and side aisles are of equal height, a common characteristic of Gothic church design in this part of Germany. ⊠ *Dompl. 3* ☎ *0345/202–1379* 🖼 *Free* ☉ *June–Oct., Mon.–Sat. 2–4.*

The former archbishop's home, the 16th-century **Neue Residenz** (New Residence), houses the **Geiseltalmuseum** and its world-famous collection of fossils dug from brown coal deposits in the Geisel Valley near

Halle. ⊠ *Dornstr. 5* ☎ *0345/552–6135* 🖅 *Free* ☉ *Weekdays 9–noon and 1–5; every 2nd and 4th weekend 9–1.*

The salt trade on which Halle built its prosperity is documented in the **Technisches Halloren- und Salinemuseum** (Technical Mine Museum). A replica salt mine shows the salt-mining process, and the exquisite silver goblet collection of the Salt Workers' Guild is on display. The old method of evaporating brine from local springs is sometimes demonstrated. The museum is on the south side of the Saale River (cross the Schiefer Bridge to get there). ⊠ *Mansfelderstr. 52* ☎ *0345/202–5034* 🖅 *€2.10* ☉ *Tues.–Sun. 10–5.*

Where to Stay & Eat

$–$$$ ✕ **Restaurant Mönchshof.** Hearty German fare in hearty portions is served in high-ceiling, dark-wood surroundings. Lamb from Saxony-Anhalt's Wettin region and venison are specialties in season, but there are always fish and crisp roast pork on the menu. The wine list is extensive, with international vintages. ⊠ *Talamstr. 6* ☎ *0345/202–1726* ▭ *AE, DC, MC, V.*

$ ✕🖫 **Ankerhof Hotel.** A tollhouse once stood here beside the saltworks, and some of the hotel's unique features are reminiscent of this past. All rooms are decorated individually, and most have wooden beams under the ceiling, naked stone walls, and heavy furniture made from exquisite wood. The hotel's Saalkahn restaurant ($–$$) serves both regional and international dishes, such as *Anhaltinischer Krustenbraten mit Sauerkraut und Klössen* (Anhaltine roasted pork with crust, served with sauerkraut and potato dumplings). ⊠ *Ankerstr. 2a, D–06108* ☎ *0345/232–3200* 🖷 *0345/232–3219* ⊕ *www.ankerhofhotel.de* ⋅❄ *49 rooms, 1 suite* ₰ *2 restaurants, in-room safes, minibars, cable TV, health club, sauna, bowling, free parking, some pets allowed (fee), no-smoking rooms; no a/c* ▭ *AE, DC, MC, V* ⊙ *BP.*

$$ 🖫 **Kempinski Hotel Rotes Ross.** Behind a 265-year-old facade in the city center, this friendly, well-equipped modern hotel has a certain old-fashioned elegance. There's a modern wing, however, that lacks the old-world atmosphere of the original main building. ⊠ *Leipziger Str. 76, D–06108* ☎ *0345/29220* 🖷 *0345/2334–3699* ⊕ *www.kempinski.com* ⋅❄ *89 rooms, 1 suite* ₰ *Restaurant, room service, in-room safes, minibars, cable TV with movies, health club, hot tub, sauna, Weinstube, babysitting, dry cleaning, laundry service, concierge, convention center, meeting room, parking (fee), some pets allowed (fee), no-smoking rooms* ▭ *AE, DC, MC, V.*

The Arts

The city of Händel's birth is of course an important music center. Halle is famous for its opera productions, its orchestral concerts, and particularly its choirs. For schedules, prices, and reservations of opera performances staged at the city's renowned **Opernhaus,** call 0345/5110–0355. The city's main orchestra, the **Philharmonisches Staatsorchester Halle** (State Philharmonic Orchestra; ⊠ Kleine Brauhausstr. 26 ☎ 0345/221–3000 for concert information and tickets), performs at the Konzerthalle. The annual **Händel Festival** (☎ 0345/5009–0222) takes place in the first half of June, and two youth-choir festivals occur in May and October.

en route

To reach Quedlinburg in the Harz, you can take E–49 directly, or take a somewhat longer route via E–80 to **Eisleben** first. Martin Luther came into and out of this world here. Both the square Franconian house with the high-pitched roof that was his birthplace and the Gothic patrician house where he died are open to the public as are, on request, the Petri-Pauli Kirche (Church of Sts. Peter and Paul), where he was baptized, and the Andreaskirche (St. Andrew's Church), where his funeral was held. From Eisleben take B–180 north to join with E–49 to Quedlinburg.

Quedlinburg

68 *79 km (49 mi) northwest of Halle.*

This medieval Harz town has more half-timber houses than any other town in Germany: more than 1,600 of them line the narrow cobblestone streets and squares. The town escaped World War II unscathed, and in GDR days, though not kept up, Quedlinburg was treasured, so it remains much as it was centuries ago. Today it's a UNESCO World Heritage Site.

For nearly 200 years Quedlinburg was a favorite imperial residence and site of imperial diets, beginning with the election in 919 of Henry the Fowler (Henry I), as the first Saxon king of Germany. It became a major trading city and a member of the Hanseatic League, equal in stature to Köln.

The Altstadt (Old Town) is full of richly decorated half-timber houses, particularly along Mühlgraben, Schuhof, the Hölle, Breitestrasse, and Schmalstrasse. Notable on the **Marktplatz** are the Renaissance **Rathaus** (Town Hall), with a 14th-century statue of Roland signifying the town's independence, and the baroque 1701 Haus Grünhagen. Street and hiking maps and guidebooks (almost all in German) are available in the information office at the Rathaus. ⊠ *Markt 2* ☎ *03946/90550* ☒ *Free* ⊙ *Mon.–Sat. 9–3.*

The oldest half-timber house in Quedlinburg, built about 1310, is the **Ständerbau Fachwerkmuseum,** a museum of half-timber construction. ⊠ *Wordg. 3* ☎ *03946/3828* ☒ *€2.50* ⊙ *Nov.–Mar., Fri.–Wed. 10–4; Apr.–Oct., Fri.–Wed. 10–5.*

Placed behind half-timber houses so as not to affect the town's medieval feel is the sophisticated, modern **Lyonel Feininger Gallery.** When the art of American-born painter Lyonel Feininger, a Bauhaus teacher in both Weimar and Dessau, was declared "decadent" by the Hitler regime in 1938, the artist returned to America. Left behind with a friend were engravings, lithographs, etchings, and paintings. The most comprehensive Feininger print collection in the world is displayed here. ⊠ *Finkenherd 5a* ☎ *03946/2238* ⊕ *www.feininger-gallery.de* ☒ *€6* ⊙ *Apr.–Oct., Tues.–Sun. 10–6; Nov.–Mar., Tues.–Sun. 10–5.*

Quedlinburg's largely Renaissance castle buildings perch on top of the Schlossberg (Castle Hill), with a terrace overlooking woods and valley. The grounds include the **Schlossmuseum** (Castle Museum), which has exhibits on the history of the town and castle, artifacts of the Bronze Age, and the wooden cage in which a captured 14th-century robber baron was put on public view. Restored 17th- and 18th-century rooms give an impression of castle life at that time. ⊠ *Schlossberg 1* ☎ *03946/2730* ⊡ *€3* ⊗ *Daily 10–6.*

The simple, graceful **Stiftskirche St. Servatius** (Collegiate Church of St. Servatius) is one of the most important and best-preserved 12th-century Romanesque structures in Germany. Henry I and his wife, Mathilde, are buried in its crypt. The renowned Quedlinburg Treasure of 10th-, 11th-, and 12th-century gold and silver and bejeweled manuscripts is also kept here (what's left of it). In Nazi days SS leader Heinrich Himmler made the church into a shrine dedicated to the SS, insisting that it was only appropriate, since Henry I was the founder of the first German Reich. ⊠ *Schlossberg 1* ☎ *03946/709–900* ⊡ *€3* ⊗ *May–Oct., Tues.–Fri. 10–6, Sat. 10–4, Sun. noon–6; Nov.–Apr., Tues.–Sat. 10–4, Sun. noon–4.*

Where to Stay & Eat

$ ✕⌂ **Hotel Zum Bär.** There are stuffed bears in the hall and a bear motif in the maroon stair carpet of this 250-year-old half-timber hostelry, which has views out onto the marketplace. The French provincial furniture is painted white and gold. Careful detail has gone into the interior decorating, and no two rooms are alike. The restaurant is known for its filling local dishes. ⊠ *Markt 8–9, D–06484* ☎ *03946/7770* 🖷 *03496/700–268* ⊕ *www.hotelzumbaer.de* ➳ *50 rooms, 1 suite* ♿ *Restaurant, minibars, free parking, some pets allowed (fee); no a/c* ▭ *No credit cards* ⑪*❘ BP.*

$–$$ ✕⌂ **Romantik Hotel Theophano.** This 1668 baroque half-timber merchant's house was the seat of the tanners' guild in the 18th century, a restaurant-coffeehouse in the early 20th century, and a domestic linen store until the Communists "deprivatized" the business. Now restored with care, its elegant rooms have country antiques. The vault-ceiling restaurant ($–$$$) serves such dishes as Harz trout and local wild boar. ⊠ *Markt 13–14, D–06484* ☎ *03946/96300* 🖷 *03946/963–036* ⊕ *www. hoteltheophano.de* ➳ *22 rooms* ♿ *Restaurant, cable TV, free parking, some pets allowed (fee); no a/c, no-smoking rooms* ▭ *AE, MC, V* ⑪*❘ BP.*

★ $ ✕⌂ **Hotel Zur Goldenen Sonne.** Rooms in this baroque half-timber inn are furnished in a pleasing, rustic fashion. The cozy restaurant ($–$$) offers such Harz fare as venison stew with plum sauce and potato dumplings as well as smoked ham in apricot sauce. ⊠ *Steinweg 11, D–06484* ☎ *03946/96250* 🖷 *03946/962–530* ⊕ *www. hotelzurgoldenensonne.de* ➳ *27 rooms* ♿ *Restaurant, minibars, cable TV, free parking, some pets allowed (fee), no-smoking rooms; no a/c* ▭ *AE, MC, V* ⑪*❘ BP.*

en route The most scenic way to go from Quedlinburg to Braunlage is via Blankenburg, with its hilltop castle, and Wernigerode, 28 km (20 mi) away. Half-timber **Wernigerode** has a colorful twin-tower Rathaus on the marketplace, and the neo-Gothic castle above it is a starting point for walks in the Harz. Also departing from this town is the steam-power narrow-gauge **Harzequerbahn,** which takes passengers to the heights (3,745 feet) of the Brocken. From Wernigerode take B–244 south 10 km (6 mi) to Elbingerode; then turn onto B–27 west and continue another 17 km (10 mi) along mountain roads through spruce forests to Braunlage.

Goslar

39 *48 km (30 mi) northwest of Quedlinburg.*

Goslar, the lovely, unofficial capital of the Harz region, is one of Germany's oldest cities and is known for the medieval glamour expressed in the fine Romanesque architecture of the Kaiserpfalz, an imperial palace of the German Empire. Thanks to the deposits of ore close to the town, Goslar was one of the country's most wealthy hubs of trade during the Middle Ages. In this town of 46,000 today, time seems to have stood still among the hundreds of well-preserved (mostly typical northern German half-timber) houses that were built during the course of seven centuries. The town has been declared a UNESCO World Heritage site.

Despite Goslar's rapid decline after the breakup of the medieval German empire, the city—thanks to its ore deposits—maintained all the luxury and worldliness born of economic success. The **Rathaus** with its magnificent **Huldigungssaal** (Hall of Honor) dates to 1450 and testifies to the wealth of Goslar's merchants. ⊠ *Markt 1* ☎ *05321/704–241* 🖼 *€2* ⊙ *Daily 11–4.*

★ The impressive **Kaiserpfalz**, set high above the historic downtown area, dates to the early Middle Ages. It once was the center of German imperial glory, when emperors held their regular diets here. Among the rulers who frequented Goslar were Heinrich III (1039–1056) and his successor, Heinrich IV (1056–1106), who was also born in Goslar. You can visit an exhibit about the German medieval kaisers who stayed here, inspect the small chapel where the heart of Heinrich III is buried (the body is in Speyer), or view the beautiful ceiling murals in the Reichssaal (Imperial Hall). ⊠ *Kaiserbleek 6* ☎ *05321/311–9693* 🖼 *€4.50* ⊙ *Apr.–Oct., daily 10–5; Nov.–Mar., daily 10–4.*

The source of the town's riches is outside the city in the **Erzbergwerk Rammelsberg**, the world's only silver mine that was in continuous operation for more than 1,000 years. It stopped operating in 1988, but you can inspect the many tunnels and shafts of the old mine. ⊠ *Bergtal 19* ☎ *05321/7500* ⊕ *www.rammelsberg.de* 🖼 *€10, including tour* ⊙ *Daily 9–6; tours given as needed 9:30–4:30.*

Where to Stay & Eat

$$ ✕🏨 **Kaiserworth-Hotel und Restaurant.** Hidden behind the reddish-brown walls of a 500-year-old house, the seat of medieval tailors and merchants, this hotel offers small but bright, pleasantly furnished rooms. The front rooms have windows on the medieval city market. The restaurant ($–$$$) offers reliable German food. ⊠ *Markt 3, D–38640* ☎ *05321/7090* 🖨 *03521/709–345* ⊕ *www.kaiserworth.de* 🛏 *66 rooms* ♿ *Restaurant, room service, cable TV, babysitting, dry cleaning, laundry service, meeting room, parking (fee), some pets allowed (fee), no-smoking rooms; no a/c* ▭ *AE, DC, MC, V* 🍴 *BP.*

Braunlage

🔟 *34 km (21 mi) south of Goslar.*

One of the oldest winter-sports centers in central Germany, Braunlage gets snow from December to March and is the best spot for skiing in the Harz. In spring, summer, and fall, hiking on mountain trails is a favorite pastime, and the bald top of the Brocken offers a 16-km (10-mi) walk. In the days of a divided Germany, this small resort was little more than 2 km (1 mi) from the border. Guesthouses, restaurants, and ski shops are everywhere. A year-round attraction is the indoor skating rink.

Where to Stay & Eat

★ **$–$$** ✕⌂ **Romantik Hotel Zur Tanne.** Built in 1725, this is one of the oldest buildings in Braunlage. Most rooms have balconies and banquette corners. The historic house connects to a modern annex, and a less expensive guesthouse on the outskirts of the village opens out to forest and mountains. When making a reservation, ask for a room in the Bachhaus building. Diners can choose between hearty mountain dishes or lighter fare in the upscale Zur Tanne restaurant ($–$$$). ⊠ *Herzog-Wilhelm-Str. 8, D–38700* ☎ *05520/93120* 🖷 *05520/3992* ⊕ *www.romantikhotels.com/braunlage* 🛏 *19 rooms, 3 suites* 🍴 *Restaurant, room service, in-room safes, minibars, cable TV, health club, massage, sauna, steam room, babysitting, dry cleaning, laundry service, meeting room, free parking, some pets allowed (fee), no-smoking rooms; no a/c* ☰ *V* |◎| *CP.*

Sports & the Outdoors

SKIING Many cross-country trails (lighted at night for after-dark skiing) wind their way through the evergreen forests of Braunlage. Alpine skiers have five ski slopes and a ski jump. The jump was closed until the Wall fell—because the bottom of it was in the GDR. For Alpine skiing, a cable car rises to the top of the 3,237-foot-high Wurmberg. It has three ski lifts. There are also toboggan runs, horse-drawn sleigh rides, ski instruction, and equipment rentals. Contact the tourist office for more information.

THURINGIA

The tiny state of Thuringia is one of Germany's most historic regions, with a rich cultural past still present in small villages, medieval cities, and country palaces throughout the hilly countryside. In the 14th century traders used the 168-km (104-mi) Rennsteig ("fast trail") through the dark depths of the Thuringian Forest, and cities such as Erfurt, Eisenach, and Gera evolved as major commercial hubs. Today the forests and the Erzgebirge Mountains are a remote paradise for hiking and fishing. The city of Weimar is one of Europe's old cultural centers, and the short-lived German democracy, the Weimar Republic, was established here in 1918. Already a prime vacation spot during Communist times, Thuringia boomed when it attracted investors after reunification.

Eisenach

41 *126 km (79 mi) south of Braunlage, 95 km (59 mi) northeast of Fulda (nearest ICE rail station).*

When you stand in Eisenach's ancient market square, it's difficult to imagine this half-timber town as an important center of the East German automobile industry. Yet this is where trabis and wartburgs (very tiny, noisy, and cheaply produced cars, which are now collector's items) were made. The cars were named after the famous castle that broods over Eisenach, atop one of the foothills of the Thuringian Forest, the Wartburg. Today, West German automaker Opel is continuing the automobile tradition. The GM company built one of Europe's most modern car-assembly lines on the outskirts of Eisenach.

Fodor'sChoice Begun in 1067 (and expanded through the centuries), the mighty **Wart-**
★   **burg** has hosted a parade of German historical celebrities. Hermann I (1156–1217), count of Thuringia and count palatine of Saxony, was a patron of the poets Walther von der Vogelweide (1170–1230) and Wolfram von Eschenbach (1170–1220). Legend has it that this is where Walther von der Vogelweide, the greatest lyric poet of medieval Germany, prevailed in the celebrated *Minnesängerstreit* (minnesinger contest), which is featured in Richard Wagner's *Tannhäuser.*

Within the castle's stout walls, Frederick the Wise (1486–1525) shielded Martin Luther from papal proscription from May 1521 until March 1522, even though he did not share the reformer's beliefs. Luther completed the first translation of the New Testament from Greek into German while in hiding, an act that paved the way for the Protestant Reformation. You can peek into the simple study in which Luther worked.

Frederick was also a patron of the arts. Lucas Cranach the Elder's portraits of Luther and his wife are on view in the castle, as is a very moving sculpture, the *Leuchterengelpaar* (Candlestick Angel Group), by the great 15th-century artist Tilman Riemenschneider. The 13th-century great hall is breathtaking; it's here that the minstrels sang for courtly favors. Don't leave without climbing the belvedere for a panoramic view of the Harz Mountains and the Thuringian Forest. ☎ 03691/77073 ⊕ *www. wartburg-eisenach.de* ✉ *€6.50, including guided tour* ☉ *Nov.–Feb., daily 9–3:30; Mar.–Oct., daily 8:30–5.*

The **Lutherhaus,** in downtown Eisenach, has many fascinating exhibits illustrating the life of Luther, who lived here as a student. ✉ *Lutherpl. 8* ☎ 03691/29830 ✉ *€2.50* ☉ *Apr.–Oct., daily 9–5; Nov.–Mar., daily 10–5.*

Johann Sebastian Bach was born in Eisenach in 1685. The **Bachhaus** has exhibits devoted to the entire lineage of the musical Bach family and includes a collection of historical musical instruments. ✉ *Frauenplan 21* ☎ 03691/79340 ⊕ *www.bachhaus.de* ✉ *€4* ☉ *Daily 10–6.*

Composer Richard Wagner gets his due at the **Reuter-Wagner-Museum,** which has the most comprehensive exhibition on Wagner's life and work outside Bayreuth. Monthly concerts take place in the old **Teezimmer** (tearoom), a hall with wonderfully restored French wallpaper.

The Erard piano, dating from the late 19th century, is occasionally rolled out. ⊠ *Reuterweg 2* ☎ *03691/743–293* 🎟 *€3* 🕐 *Tues.–Sun. noon–5, Thurs. 3–8.*

At Johannesplatz 9, look for what is said to be the **narrowest house** in East Germany, built in 1890; its width is just over 6 feet, 8 inches; its height, 24½ feet; and its depth, 34 feet.

Where to Stay & Eat

★ **$$** ✕🏨 **Steigenberger Hotel Thüringer Hof.** Enter the lobby of this historic 16th-century mansion, admire its huge chandelier and wooden stairways, set foot on the luxurious carpets, and you'll be instantly transported to the Middle Ages. Traditional Thuringian hospitality and the professional service one has grown to expect of the Steigenberger hotels make this establishment the town's hotel gem, while the upscale Galerie restaurant, serving international and local dishes with an accent on fish recipes, is one of the better restaurants to be found in Eisenach. ⊠ *Karlspl. 11, D–99817* ☎ *03691/280* 🖷 *03691/28190* ⊕ *www.steigenberger.de* 🛏 *127 rooms, 1 suite* ♿ *Restaurant, room service, in-room data ports, minibars, cable TV, gym, massage, sauna, bar, dry cleaning, laundry service, concierge, business services, meeting room, parking (fee), some pets allowed (fee), no-smoking floor* ☰ *AE, DC, MC, V* ⦿❙ *BP.*

$ ✕🏨 **Hotel Glockenhof.** At the base of Wartburg Castle, this former church-run hostel has blossomed into a handsome hotel, cleverly incorporating the original half-timber city mansion into a modern extension. The excellent restaurant ($–$$) has been joined by a brasserie. ⊠ *Grimmelg. 4, D–99817* ☎ *03691/2340* 🖷 *03691/234–131* ⊕ *www. glockenhof.de* 🛏 *38 rooms, 2 suites* ♿ *2 restaurants, room service, cable TV, meeting room, parking (fee), some pets allowed (fee), no-smoking rooms; no a/c* ☰ *AE, MC, V* ⦿❙ *BP.*

★ **$$$$** 🏨 **Hotel auf der Wartburg.** In this castle hotel, where Martin Luther, Johann Sebastian Bach, and Richard Wagner were guests, you'll get a splendid view over the town and the countryside. The standard of comfort is above average, and antiques and Oriental rugs mix with modern furnishings. The hotel runs a shuttle bus to the rail station and parking lot of the Wartburg. ⊠ *Wartburg, D–99817* ☎ *03691/7970* 🖷 *03691/ 797–100* ⊕ *www.wartburghotel.de* 🛏 *35 rooms* ♿ *Restaurant, room service, in-room safes, minibars, cable TV, dry cleaning, laundry service, meeting room, free parking, some pets allowed (fee), no-smoking rooms; no a/c* ☰ *AE, DC, MC, V* ⦿❙ *BP.*

Erfurt

㊷ *55 km (34 mi) east of Eisenach.*

The city of Erfurt emerged from World War II relatively unscathed, and with most of its innumerable towers intact. The city's highly decorative and colorful facades are easy to admire on a walking tour. Downtown Erfurt is a photographer's delight, with narrow, busy ancient streets dominated by a magnificent 14th-century Gothic cathedral, the Mariendom. The **Domplatz** (Cathedral Square) is bordered by houses dating from the 16th century. The pedestrian-zone **Anger** is also lined with restored Renaissance houses. The **Bartholomäusturm** (Bartholomew Tower), the base of a 12th-century tower, holds a 60-bell carillon.

On weekends, you can take an old-fashioned horse-drawn open-carriage tour of Erfurt's Old Town center. Tours leave from the Tourist-Information office. ✉ *Tourist-Information, Benediktsplatz 1* ⊙ *Apr.–Dec., weekdays at 1, weekends 11 and 1; Jan.–Mar., weekends 11 and 1.*

★ The **Mariendom** (St. Mary's Cathedral) is reached by a broad staircase from the expansive Cathedral Square. Its Romanesque origins (foundations can be seen in the crypt) are best preserved in the choir's glorious stained-glass windows and beautifully carved stalls. The cathedral's biggest bell, the Gloriosa, is the largest free-swinging bell in the world. Cast in 1497, it took three years to install in the tallest of the three sharply pointed towers, painstakingly lifted inch by inch with wooden wedges. No chances are taken with this 2-ton treasure; its deep boom resonates only on special occasions, such as Christmas and New Year's. ✉ *Dompl.* ☎ *0361/646–1265* 🎫 *Tour €2.50* ⊙ *May–Oct., weekdays 9–5, Sat. 9–4:30, Sun. 2–4; Nov.–Apr., Mon.–Sat. 10–11:30 and 12:30–4, Sun. 1–4.*

The Gothic church of **St. Severus** has an extraordinary font, a masterpiece of intricately carved sandstone that reaches practically to the ceiling. It's linked to the cathedral by a 70-step open staircase.

Behind the predominantly neo-Gothic Rathaus you'll find Erfurt's most outstanding attraction spanning the Gera River, the **Krämerbrücke** (Shopkeepers' Bridge). This Renaissance bridge, similar to the one in Florence, incorporates shops and homes. Built in 1325 and restored in 1967–73, the bridge served for centuries as an important trading center. Today, antiques shops fill the majority of the timber-frame houses built into the bridge, some dating from the 16th century. The area around the bridge, crisscrossed with old streets lined with picturesque and often crumbling homes, is known as **Klein Venedig** (Little Venice) because of the recurrent flooding it endures.

The young Martin Luther spent his formative years in the **St. Augustin Kloster** (St. Augustine Monastery; ✉ Gotthardstr.), which is now a seminary. Erfurt's interesting local-history museum is in a late-Renaissance house, **Zum Stockfisch.** ✉ *Johannesstr. 169* ☎ *0361/655–5644* 🎫 *Museum €3* ⊙ *Tues.–Sun. 10–6.*

Where to Stay & Eat

¢–$$$ ✕ **Paganini im Gildehaus.** This Italian restaurant in one of the city's oldest (and most beautiful) historic mansions serves a wide variety of both basic country cooking and complex fish dishes. In summer the restaurant opens its beer garden, where Thuringian specialties are served, but the focus is on Italian cooking, whose quality is far better than that of the German dishes. The chef, after all, is Italian. ✉ *Fischermarkt 13–16* ☎ *0361/643–0692* 🍽 *AE, DC, MC, V.*

¢–$$ ✕ **Faustus Restaurant.** In the heart of historic Erfurt the stylish Faustus defines fine Thuringian dining. This restaurant is in an old mansion, with both an inviting summer terrace and a bright, airy dining room. An after-dinner drink at the superb bar is an absolute must. ✉ *Wenigermarkt 5* ☎ *0361/540–0954* 🍽 *AE, DC, MC, V.*

¢–$ ✕ **Dasdie.** Wolfgang Staub's Dasdie combines restaurant, bistro, bar, cabaret stage, and dance floor under one roof, so you can dine here (for less than €11), return later (or simply hang loose at the bar) for a show, and end the evening with a dance. The food is hit-or-miss, but the place is always lively and prices are low. Make sure to call ahead about schedules and programs. ✉ *Marstallstr. 12* ☎ *0361/551–166* ▭ *No credit cards.*

$ ✕▥ **Radisson SAS Hotel Erfurt.** Since the SAS group gave the ugly highrise Kosmos a face-lift, the socialist-realist look of the GDR years no longer intrudes on Hotel Erfurt. The hotel underwent several renovations, and the rooms now have bright, modern colors and fabrics (including leather-upholstered furniture). The Classico restaurant ($–$$) serves mostly local dishes and is one of Erfurt's best. ✉ *Juri-Gagarin-Ring 127, D–99084* ☎ *0361/55100* 🖷 *0361/551–0210* ⊕ *www. radissonsas.com* ⇦ *282 rooms, 3 suites* ⚷ *Restaurant, room service, minibars, cable TV, gym, sauna, spa, bar, babysitting, dry cleaning, laundry service, meeting room, car rental, parking (fee), some pets allowed (fee), no-smoking floor* ▭ *AE, DC, MC, V* ▥ *BP.*

Weimar

❹❸ *21 km (13 mi) east of Erfurt.*

Sitting prettily on the Ilm River between the Ettersberg and Vogtland hills, Weimar occupies a place in German political and cultural history completely disproportionate to its size (population 63,000). It's not even particularly old by German standards, with a civic history that started as late as 1410. By the early 19th century the city had become one of Europe's most important cultural centers, where poets Goethe and Schiller wrote, Johann Sebastian Bach played the organ for his Saxon patrons, Carl Maria von Weber composed some of his best music, and Franz Liszt was director of music, presenting the first performance of *Lohengrin* here. In 1919 Walter Gropius founded his Staatliches Bauhaus here, and behind the classical pillars of the National Theater, the German National Assembly drew up the constitution of the Weimar Republic, the first German democracy. After the collapse of the Weimar government, Hitler chose the little city as the site for the first national congress of his Nazi party. On the outskirts of Weimar the Nazis built—or forced prisoners to build for them—the infamous Buchenwald concentration camp.

Much of Weimar's greatness is owed to the widowed countess Anna Amalia, whose home, the **Wittumspalais** (Wittum Mansion), is surprisingly modest. In the late 18th century the countess went talent hunting for cultural figures to decorate the glittering court her Saxon forebears had established. Goethe was one of her finds, and he served the countess as a counselor, advising her on financial matters and town design. Schiller followed, and he and Goethe became valued visitors to the countess's home. Within this exquisite baroque house you can see the drawing room in which she held soirées, complete with the original cherrywood table at which the company sat. The east wing of the house contains a small museum that's a fascinating memorial to those cultural gatherings. ✉ *Am Theaterpl.* ☎ *03643/545–377* ▱ *€3.50* ☉ *Nov.–Mar., Tues.–Sun. 10–4; Apr.–Oct., Tues.–Sun. 9–6.*

A statue on **Theaterplatz,** in front of the National Theater, shows Goethe placing a paternal-like hand on the shoulder of the younger Schiller. Goethe spent 57 years in Weimar, 47 of them in a house two blocks south of Theaterplatz that has since become a shrine for millions of visitors. The Fodor'sChoice **Goethe Nationalmuseum** (Goethe National Museum) consists of several ★ houses, including the **Goethehaus,** where Goethe lived. It shows an exhibit about life in Weimar around 1750 and contains writings that illustrate not only the great man's literary might but his interest in the sciences, particularly medicine, and his administrative skills (and frustrations) as minister of state and Weimar's exchequer. You'll see the desk at which Goethe stood to write (he liked to work standing up) and the modest bed in which he died. The rooms are dark and often cramped, but an almost palpable intellectual intensity seems to illuminate them. ✉ *Frauenplan 1* ☎ *03643/545–320* ⊕ *www.weimar-klassik.de* 🖃 *€6* ⊙ *Nov.–Mar., Tues.–Sun. 9–4; Apr.–Oct., Tues.–Sun. 9–6.*

The **Schillerhaus,** a green-shutter residence and part of the Goethe National Museum, is on a tree-shaded square not far from Goethe's house. Schiller and his family spent a happy, all-too-brief three years here (he died here in 1805). Schiller's study is tucked underneath the mansard roof, a cozy room dominated by his desk, where he probably completed *Wilhelm Tell.* Much of the remaining furniture and the collection of books were added later, although they all date from around Schiller's time. ✉ *Schillerstr. 17* ☎ *03643/545–350* ⊕ *www.weimar-klassik.de* 🖃 *€3.50* ⊙ *Nov.–Mar., Wed.–Mon. 9–4; Apr.–Oct., Wed.–Mon. 9–6.*

Goethe's beloved **Gartenhaus** (Garden House) is a modest country cottage where he spent many happy hours, wrote much poetry and began his masterly classical drama *Iphigenie.* It's set amid meadowlike parkland on the bank of the River Ilm. Goethe is said to have felt very close to nature here, and you can soak up the same rural atmosphere on footpaths along the peaceful little river. ✉ *Goethepark* ☎ *03643/545–375* ⊕ *www.weimar-klassik.de* 🖃 *Cottage €3* ⊙ *Nov.–Mar., Wed.–Mon. 10–4; Apr.–Oct., Wed.–Mon. 9–6.*

Goethe and Schiller are buried in the **Historischer Friedhof** (Historic Cemetery), a leafy cemetery where virtually every gravestone commemorates a famous citizen of Weimar. Their tombs are in the vault of the classical-style chapel. The cemetery is a short walk past Goethehaus and Wieland Platz. 🖃 *Goethe-Schiller vault €2* ⊙ *Nov.–Mar., Wed.–Mon. 10–1 and 2–4; Apr.–Oct., Wed.–Mon. 9–1 and 2–6.*

On the central town square, at the **Herderkirche** (two blocks east of Theaterplatz), you'll find the home of Lucas Cranach the Elder. Cranach lived here during his last years, 1552–53. Its wide, imposing facade is richly decorated and bears the coat of arms of the Cranach family. It now houses a modern art gallery. The Marktplatz's late-Gothic **Herderkirche** (Herder Church) has a large winged altar started by Lucas Cranach the Elder and finished by his son in 1555.

★ Weimar's 16th-century **Stadtschloss,** the city castle, is around the corner from the Herderkirche. It has a finely restored classical staircase, a festival hall, and a falcon gallery. The tower on the southwest projection dates from the Middle Ages but received its baroque overlay circa 1730. The **Kunstsammlung** (art collection) here includes several works by Cranach the Elder and many early-20th-century pieces by such artists as Böcklin, Liebermann, and Beckmann. ⊠ *Burgpl. 4* ☎ *03643/545–930* ⊕ *www.kunstsammlungen-weimar.de* ⊠ *€4.50* ⊙ *Apr.–Oct., Tues.–Sun. 10–6; Nov.–Mar., Tues.–Sun. 10–4.*

The city is proud of the **Neues Museum Weimar** (New Museum Weimar), eastern Germany's first museum exclusively devoted to contemporary art. The building, dating from 1869, was carefully restored and converted to hold collections of American minimalist and conceptual art and works by German installation artist Anselm Kiefer and American painter Keith Haring. In addition, it regularly presents international modern art exhibitions. ⊠ *Weimarpl. 5* ☎ *03643/545–930* ⊕ *www. kunstsammlungen-weimar.de* ⊠ *€3* ⊙ *Apr.–Oct., Tues.–Sun. 10–6; Nov.–Mar., Tues.–Sun. 10–4.*

off the beaten path

SCHLOSS BELVEDERE (Belvedere Palace) – Just 8 km (5 mi) south of Weimar is the lovely 18th-century, yellow-stucco Belvedere Palace, which once served as a hunting and pleasure castle; today you'll find a baroque museum and an interesting collection of coaches and other historic vehicles inside. The formal gardens were in part laid out according to Goethe's concepts. ⊠ *Belvedere Allee* ☎ *03643/545–962* ⊕ *www.weimar-klassik.de* ⊠ *€3.50* ⊙ *Apr.–mid-Oct., Tues.–Sun. 10–6; mid-Oct.–Nov., Tues.–Sun. 10–4:30.*

GEDENKSTÄTTE BUCHENWALD – In the Ettersberg Hills just north of Weimar is a blighted patch of land that contrasts cruelly with the verdant countryside that so inspired Goethe: Buchenwald, one of the most infamous Nazi concentration camps. Sixty-five thousand men, women, and children from 35 countries met their deaths here through forced labor, starvation, disease, and gruesome medical experiments. Each is commemorated by a small stone placed on the outlines of the barracks, which have long since disappeared from the site, and by a massive memorial tower. Besides exhibits, tours are available. To reach Buchenwald, you can take the public bus (No. 6), which leaves every 10 minutes from Goetheplatz in downtown Weimar. The one-way fare is €1.25. ☎ *03643/4300* ⊕ *www.buchenwald.de* ⊠ *Free* ⊙ *May–Sept., Tues.–Sun. 9:45–5:15; Oct.–Apr., Tues.–Sun. 8:45–4:15.*

Where to Stay & Eat

¢–$ ✕ **Ratskeller.** This is one of the region's most authentic town hall–cellar restaurants. Its whitewashed, barrel-vaulted ceiling has witnessed centuries of tradition. At the side is a cozy bar, where you can enjoy a prepandial drink beneath a spectacular art nouveau skylight. The delicious sauerbraten and the famous bratwurst (with sauerkraut and mashed potatoes) are the highlights of the Thuringian menu. If venison is in season, try it—likewise the wild duck or wild boar in red-wine sauce. ⊠ *Am Markt 10* ☎ *03643/850–573* ⊟ *MC, V.*

¢–$ ✕ **Scharfe Ecke.** Thuringia's traditional *Knödel* (dumplings) are at their best here, but be patient—they're made to order and take 20 minutes. The *Klösse* are salty and less dense than the Knödel and come with just about every dish, from roast pork to venison stew, and the wait is well worth it. The ideal accompaniment to anything on the menu is one of the three locally brewed beers on tap. ⊠ *Eisfeld 2* ☎ *03643/202–430* ▤ *AE, DC, MC, V* ☾ *Closed Mon.*

¢–$ ✕ **Sommer's Weinstuben und Restaurant.** The city's oldest pub and restaurant, a 130-year-old landmark in the center of Weimar, is still going strong. The authentic Thuringian specialties and huge *Kartoffelpfannen* (potato pans) with fried potatoes and various kinds of meat are prepared by the 5th generation of the Sommer family and are as tasty as ever. Add to that the superb wine list with some rare vintages from local vineyards and the romantic courtyard, and your Weimar experience will be perfect. ⊠ *Humboldtstr. 2* ☎ *03643/400–691* ▤ *No credit cards* ☾ *Closed Sun. No lunch.*

$$$–$$$$ 🏨 **Hotel Elephant.** The historic Elephant, dating from 1696, is famous
Fodor'sChoice for its charm—even through the Communist years. Book here (well in
★ advance), and you'll follow the choice of Goethe, Schiller, Herder, Liszt (after whom the hotel bar is named)—and Hitler—all of whom were guests. Behind the sparkling white facade are comfortable modern rooms decorated in beige, white, and yellow in a timeless blend of art deco and Bauhaus styles. A sense of the past is ever present. ⊠ *Markt 19, D–99423* ☎ *03643/8020* 🖷 *03643/802–610* ⊕ *www. luxurycollection.com* 🛏 *94 rooms, 5 suites* ⚐ *2 restaurants, room service, in-room safes, minibars, cable TV, piano bar, dry cleaning, laundry service, meeting room, parking (fee), some pets allowed (fee), no-smoking rooms; no a/c* ▤ *AE, DC, MC, V* ¶◎¶ *BP.*

$$–$$$ ✕🏨 **Grand Hotel Russischer Hof.** This historic, classicist hotel, once a
Fodor'sChoice hallmark of the European nobility and intellectual society, continues
★ to be a luxurious gem in the heart of Weimar—it's one of eastern Germany's finest hotels. Tolstoy, Liszt, Schumann, Turgenev, and others once stayed at this former Russian city palace, whose (partly historic) rooms are decorated today with antique French tapestries, linens, and furniture. The service is impeccable. The atmosphere is casual yet serene and elegant. The restaurant Anastasia ($$) serves fine Austrian-Thuringian cuisine. ⊠ *Goethepl. 2, D–99423* ☎ *03643/7740* 🖷 *03643/ 774–840* ⊕ *www.russischerhof.com* 🛏 *119 rooms, 6 suites* ⚐ *Restaurant, room service, in-room safes, minibars, cable TV with movies, bar, babysitting, dry cleaning, laundry service, concierge, meeting room, parking (fee), some pets allowed (fee), no-smoking floor* ▤ *AE, DC, MC, V.*

$ 🏨 **Amalienhof VCH Hotel.** Book far ahead to secure a room at this friendly little hotel central to Weimar's attractions. The building opened in 1826 as a church hostel. Double rooms are furnished with first-rate antique reproductions; public rooms have the real thing. ⊠ *Amalienstr. 2, D–99423* ☎ *03643/5490* 🖷 *03643/549–110* ⊕ *www.vch.de* 🛏 *23 rooms, 9 apartments* ⚐ *Cable TV, free parking, some pets allowed (fee); no a/c, no-smoking rooms* ▤ *AE, MC, V* ¶◎¶ *CP.*

Nightlife

Weimar's lively after-dark scene is focused on piano bars and nightclubs around the Marktplatz such as **Shakespeares** (✉ Windischenstr. 4–6 ☎ 03643/901–285), a Bauhaus-style bar and restaurant.

Jena

㊹ *26 km (16 mi) east of Weimar.*

This charming 800-year-old valley town is overlooked by barnacle cliffs and lies right on the River Saale. Blessed with a fair share of sunshine, it's one of Thuringia's cheeriest towns and home to one of Germany's oldest and most renowned universities. The academic institution dates back to 1558 and, in the 19th century, attracted some of the nation's greatest minds, including Schiller, Goethe, and Fichte. Jena has also thrived as an industrial hub thanks to Zeiss Optikwerke, one of the world's premier high-tech glass and optics manufacturers.

It was in Jena that Germany's two most prominent writers, the romantic Friedrich Schiller, and the less flowery Johann Wolfgang von Goethe, met and became friends. You can educate yourself on the great thinker's most varied interests at the **Goethe-Gedenkstätte.** Goethe lived and worked here as a writer, scientist, and Prussian minister. ✉ *Fürstengraben 26* ☎ *03641/949–009* 🖼 *€1* ☉ *Apr.–Oct., Wed. 11–3.*

The lovely **Schiller's Gartenhaus** (Schiller's Garden house) is Schiller's last remaining residence, where he lived while working as a Jena university professor. The tiny *Gartenzinne,* an annex to the main building, served as the writer's study. It's here that he penned some of Germany's most celebrated plays such as *Wallenstein, Maria Stuart,* and *The Maid of Orleans.* ✉ *Schillergäschen* ☎ *03641/931–188* 🖼 *€2* ☉ *Apr.–Oct., Tues.–Sun. 11–3; Nov.–Mar., Tues.–Sat. 11–3.*

For those wanting to see history a bit more in focus, there's the Zeiss Corporation's **Optisches Museum** (Optical Museum). Exhibits include microscopes, binoculars, telescopes, and spectacles from throughout the ages. The informative facility also houses a more futuristic-looking holographic art collection. Zeiss's latest breakthroughs and inventions can be seen in action at the **Zeiss Planetarium** (✉ Am Planetarium 5 ☎ 03641/885–488). The mind-boggling, artificial night sky jeweled by thousands of stars is not to be missed. Call for program times and details. ✉ *Carl-Zeiss-Pl. 12* ☎ *03641/443–165* 🖼 *€5 museum; €6 planetarium; €9 combined ticket* ☉ *Tues.–Fri. 10–4:30, Sat. 11–5.*

Gera

㊺ *37 km (23 mi) east of Jena.*

Once a princely residence and center of a thriving textile industry, the city has largely been rebuilt since World War II. Gera had often been compared with old Vienna, although today you have to search long and hard to discover any striking similarities between the German provincial town and the Habsburg capital. Keep an eye out for the ornate and beautifully restored facades on some of the houses that hint at Gera's rich past.

Although the palace, in which prince-electors once held court, was destroyed in the final weeks of World War II and never rebuilt, the palace's 16th-century **Orangerie** still stands in the former Küchengarten in the suburb of Untermhaus. It's an imposing semicircular baroque pavilion, irreverently dubbed the Roast Sausage by the people of Gera, and now houses the **Kunstsammlung**, the city's official art gallery. ⊠ *Küchengartenallee 4* ☏ *0365/ 832–2147* ✉ *€2.50* ☉ *Tues. 1–8, Wed.–Fri. 10–5, weekends 10–6.*

Gera's real claim to fame is artist Otto Dix (1891–1969). The residence where the satirical Expressionist painter was born is now known as the **Otto-Dix-Haus** (Otto Dix House). It has a gallery of his work and a permanent exhibition on his life. ⊠ *Mohrenpl. 4* ☏ *03643/832–4927* ✉ *€2.50; €3.50, including Orangerie* ☉ *Tues. 1–8, Wed.–Fri. 10–5, weekends 10–8.*

Don't leave Gera without checking out the **Marktplatz.** The Renaissance buildings surrounding it were restored with rare care. The 16th-century **Rathaus** has a vividly decorated entrance and a vaulted cellar restaurant. Note the weird angles of the lower-floor windows; they follow the incline of the staircase winding up the interior of the building's picturesque 185-foot-high tower.

SAXONY, SAXONY-ANHALT & THURINGIA A TO Z

To research prices, get advice from other travelers, and book travel arrangements, visit www.fodors.com.

AIR TRAVEL

It's easiest, and usually cheapest, to fly into Berlin and rent a car from there. However, Dresden Flughafen is about 10 km (6 mi) north of Dresden, and Leipzig's Flughafen Leipzig-Halle is 12 km (8 mi) northwest of the city.

🛫 **Dresden Flughafen** ☏ 0351/881-3360 ⊕ www.dresden-airport.de. **Flughafen Leipzig-Halle** ☏ 0341/224-1155 ⊕ www.leipzig-halle-airport.de.

BUS TRAVEL

Long-distance buses travel to Dresden and Leipzig. Bus service within the area is infrequent and mainly connects with rail lines. Check schedules carefully at central train stations or call the service phone number of Deutsche Bahn at local railway stations.

CAR RENTALS

Cars can be rented at Dresden's and Leipzig's airports and train stations and through all major hotels. Be aware that you are not allowed to take rentals into Poland or the Czech Republic.

🚗 **Avis** ⊠ Dresden Airport, Dresden ☏ 0351/881-4600 ⊠ Friedrichstr. 24, Dresden ☏ 0351/496-9613 ⊠ Torgauer Str. 231, Leipzig ☏ 0341/259-580 ⊠ Leipzig-Halle Airport, Leipzig ☏ 0341/224-1804 ⊠ Hauptbahnhof, Willy-Brandt-Allee 6, Leipzig ☏ 0341/ 961-1400 ⊠ Schomburgkstr. 4, Leipzig ☏ 0341/448-4316 ⊕ www.avis.de. **Hertz**

✉ Dresden Airport, Dresden ☎ 0351/881-4580 ✉ Antonstr. 39, Dresden ☎ 0351/452-630 ✉ Leipzig-Halle Airport, Leipzig ☎ 034204/14317 ✉ Hauptbahnhof, Willy-Brandt-Pl. 5 Reisezentrum, Leipzig ☎ 0341/212-5867 ⊕ www.hertz.de. **Europcar** ✉ Dresden Airport, Dresden ☎ 0351/881-4590 ✉ Hauptbahnhof, Dresden ☎ 0351/877-320 ✉ Leipzig-Halle Airport, Leipzig ☎ 034204/7700 ✉ Wittenberger Str. 19, Leipzig ☎ 0341/904-440 ✉ Hauptbahnhof, Leipzig ☎ 0341/141-160 ⊕ www.europcar.de. **Sixt** ✉ Dresden Airport, Dresden ☎ 01805/262-525 ✉ Hilton Hotel, An der Frauenkirche 5, Dresden ☎ 0351/490-5781 ✉ Hamburger Str. 36-38, Dresden ☎ 0351/495-4105 ✉ Leipzig-Halle Airport, Leipzig ☎ 0341/224-1869 ✉ Löhrstr. 2, next to Fürstenhof Hotel, Leipzig ☎ 01805/252-525 ⊕ www.sixt.de.

CAR TRAVEL

Expressways connect Berlin with Dresden (A–13) and Leipzig (A–9). Both journeys take about two hours. A–4 stretches east–west across the southern portion of Thuringia and Saxony.

A road-construction program in eastern Germany is ongoing, and you should expect traffic delays on any journey of more than 300 km (186 mi). The Bundesstrassen throughout eastern Germany are narrow, tree-lined country roads, often jammed with traffic. Roads in the western part of the Harz Mountains are better and wider.

TRAIN TRAVEL

The fastest and most inexpensive way to explore the region is by train. All cities are connected by a network of trains and some—Dresden and Meissen, for example—by commuter trains. Slower D- and E-class or InterRegio trains link smaller towns. From Dresden a round-trip ticket to Chemnitz costs about €21 (a 1½-hour journey one-way); to Görlitz, €31 (a 1½-hour ride). Trains connect Leipzig and Halle or Erfurt and Eisenach within 40 minutes, and tickets cost around €10 each way. The train ride between Erfurt and Gera (1½ hours) costs €12.40 one-way.

TOURS

BOAT TOURS Viking K–D has two luxury cruise ships on the Elbe River. It operates a full program of cruises of up to eight days in length, from mid-April until late October, that go from Hamburg as far as Prague. All the historic cities of Saxony and Thuringia are ports of call—including Dresden, Meissen, Wittenberg, and Dessau. For details *see* Cruise Travel *in* Smart Travel Tips.

Weisse Flotte's historic paddle-steam tours depart from and stop in Dresden, Meissen, Pirna, Pillnitz, Königsstein, and Bad Schandau. Besides tours in the Dresden area, boats also go into the Czech Republic. For more information contact the Sächsische Dampfschiffahrt.

🚩 **Sächsische Dampfschiffahrt** ✉ Hertha-Lindner-Str. 10, D-01067 Dresden ☎ 0351/866-090 ⊕ www.saechsische-dampfschiffahrt.de.

BUS TOURS Dresden bus tours (in German and English, run by the Dresdner Verkehrsbetriebe) leave from Postplatz (daily at 10, 11:30, and 3); the Stadtrundfahrt Dresden bus tours (also in German and English), leaving from Theaterplatz/Augustusbrücke (April–October, daily 9:30–5 every 30 minutes; November–March, daily 10–3, every hour), stop at most sights.

Guided bus tours of Leipzig (in English and German) run April–October, daily 1:30; November and March, Monday–Thursday 10:30, Friday–Sunday 1:30; December–February, Friday and Sunday 10:30 and Saturday 1:30. Tours leave opposite the tourist information office on Richard-Wagner-Strasse 1.

🚌 **Dresdner Verkehrsbetriebe AG** ☎ 0351/857-2201 ⊕ www.dvbag.de. **Stadtrundfahrt Dresden** ☎ 0351/8995-650 ⊕ www.stadtrundfahrt.com.

CANOE & PADDLE TOURS
Tour operators and boat-rental companies can be found throughout the region. One of the largest operators is Saale-Unstrut-Tours, which runs canoe tours on the Rivers Saale and Unstrut. In Dresden, contact the Kanuverein Laubegast e.V., an association that offers canoe rentals and guided tours on the Elbe River. For canoe rental and tours on the Elbe River starting near Meissen, try Sachsenboote Marlies Trepte.

🚣 **Kanuverein Laubegast e.V** ✉ Laubegaster Ufer 35, Dresden ☎ 0351/252-5613. **Saale-Unstrut-Tours** ✉ Campingplatz Blütengrund, D-06618 Naumburg ☎ 03445/202-051. **Sachsenboote Marlies Trepte** ✉ Niedermuschützer Str. 20, D-01665 Zehren ☎ 035247/51215.

TRAIN TOURS
In Saxony, two historic narrow-gauge trains still operate on a regular schedule. Both the *Lössnitzgrundbahn*, which connects Ost-Radebeul-Ost and Radeburg, as well as the *Weisseritzelbahn*, which operates between Freital-Hainsberg and Kurort Kipsdorf, are perfect for taking in some of Saxony's romantic countryside and Fichtelberg Mountains. A two-way ticket is between €6.60 and €10.70, depending on the length of the ride. For schedule and information contact Deutsche Bahn's regional Dresden office.

The famous steam locomotive *Harzquerbahn* connects Nordhausen-Nord with Wernigerode and Gernerode in the Harz Mountains. The most popular track of this line is the *Brockenbahn,* a special narrow-gauge train transporting tourists to the top of northern Germany's highest mountain. For schedule and further information contact the Harzer Schmalspurbahnen GmbH.

🚂 **Lössnitzgrundbahn** ☎ 0351/4616-563-684. **Harzer Schmalspurbahnen GmbH** ✉ Bahnhof Westerntor, Friedrichstr. 151, Wernigerode ☎ 03943/5580 or 03943/558-343 ⊕ www.hsb-wr.de.

WALKING TOURS
A walking tour of Leipzig (in English) sets off from the tourist office May–September, daily 1:30; October–April, Saturday 1:30 and Sunday 10:30.

TRAVEL AGENCIES

Information on travel and tours to and around East Germany is available from most travel agents. Most Berlin tourist offices carry brochures about travel in East Germany.

🏢 **Berolina Berlin-Service** ✉ Meinekestr. 3, D-10719 Berlin ☎ 030/8856-8030. **Reiseland American Express** ✉ Willy-Brandt-Pl. 5, D-04109 Leipzig ☎ 0341/961-7373 ✉ Dohnaer Str. 246, D-01239 Dresden ☎ 0351/288-1109 ⊕ www.americanexpress.de.

VISITOR INFORMATION

Most of the region's larger cities offer special tourist (exploring) cards such as the Dresdencard, Hallecard, Leipzigcard, and Weimarcard, which include discounts at museums, concerts, hotels, and restaurants or special sightseeing packages for up to three days. For details, call the cities' tourist information offices. State tourism offices may have more English-language resources than the tourist offices of smaller towns.

🗗 State Tourist Offices **Saxony-Anhalt** (Sachsen-Anhalt) ✉ Am Alten Theater 6, D-39104 Magdeburg ☎ 0391/567-7080 🖷 0391/567-7081 ⊕ www.sachsen-anhalt.de. **Thuringia** (Thüringen) ✉ Weimarische Str. 45, D-99099 Erfurt ☎ 0361/37420 🖷 0361/374-2299 ⊕ www.thueringen-tourismus.de.

🗗 Lower Saxony Tourist Offices **Braunlage** ✉ Elbingeröder Str. 17, D-3700 ☎ 05520/19433 or 05520/93070 🖷 05520/930-720 ⊕ www.braunlage.de. **Goslar** ✉ Tourist-Information, Markt 7, D-38640 ☎ 05321/78060 🖷 05321/780-644 ⊕ www.goslarinfo.de.

🗗 Saxony Tourist Offices **Chemnitz** ✉ City-Management und Tourismus GmbH Chemnitz, Bahnhofsstr. 6, D-09111 ☎ 0371/19433 🖷 0371/690-6830 ⊕ www.chemnitz.de. **Dresden** ✉ Tourist-Information, Prager Str. 10, D-01069 ☎ 0351/491-920 🖷 0351/4919-2116 ⊕ www.dresden-tourist.de. **Freiberg** ✉ Fremdenverkehrsamt Freiberg, Obermarkt 24, D-09599 ☎ 03731/273-266 🖷 03731/273-260 ⊕ www.freiberg.de. **Görlitz** ✉ Tourist-Information, Obermarkt 29, D-02826 ☎ 03581/47570 🖷 03581/475-727 ⊕ www.goerlitz.de. **Leipzig** ✉ Leipzig Tourist Service e.V., Richard-Wagner-Pl. 1, D-04109 ☎ 0341/710-4260 🖷 0341/710-4301 ⊕ www.leipzig.de. **Meissen** ✉ Tourist-Information Meissen, Markt 3, D-01662 ☎ 03521/41940 🖷 03521/419-419 ⊕ www.meissen.de.

🗗 Saxony-Anhalt Tourist Offices **Dessau** ✉ Tourist-Information Dessau, Zerbster Str. 2c, D-06844 ☎ 0340/204-1442 🖷 0340/204-1142 ⊕ www.dessau.de. **Halle** ✉ Tourist-Information, Marktpl., D-06108 ☎ 0345/472-330 🖷 0345/472-3333 ⊕ www.halle-tourist.de. **Quedlinburg** ✉ Tourismus-Marketing GmbH, Markt 2, D-06484 ☎ 03946/905-624 🖷 03946/905-629 ⊕ www.quedlinburg.de. **Thale** ✉ Tourist-Information, Rathaustr. 1, D-06502 ☎ 03947/2597 🖷 03947/2277 ⊕ www.thale.de. **Wernigerode** ✉ Tourist-Information, Nikolaipl. 1, D-38855 ☎ 03943/633-035 🖷 03943/632-040 ⊕ www.wernigerode.de. **Wittenberg** ✉ Tourist-Information, Schlosspl. 2, D-06886 Wittenberg ☎ 03491/498-610 🖷 03491/498-611 ⊕ www.wittenberg.de. **Wittenberg District Rural Information Office** ✉ Mittelstr. 33, D-06886 ☎ 03491/402-610 🖷 03491/405-857. **Wörlitz** ✉ Wörlitz-Information, Neuer Wall 103, D-06786 ☎ 034905/21704 🖷 034905/20216 ⊕ www.woerlitz.de.

🗗 Thuringia Tourist Offices **Eisenach** ✉ Eisenach-Information, Markt 2, D-99817 ☎ 03691/79230 🖷 03691/792-320 ⊕ www.eisenach-tourist.de. **Erfurt** ✉ Tourist-Information, Benediktspl. 1, D-99084 ☎ 0361/66400 🖷 0361/664-0290 ⊕ www.erfurt-tourist-info.de. **Freiberg** ✉ Fremdenverkehrsamt Freiberg, Obermarkt 24, D-09599 ☎ 03731/273-266 🖷 03731/273-260 ⊕ www.freiberg.de. **Gera** ✉ Gera-Information, Ernst-Toller-Str. 14, D-07545 ☎ 0365/800-7030 🖷 0365/830-4481 ⊕ www.gera-tourismus.de. **Suhl** ✉ Tourist-Information Suhl, Kongresszentrum, Friedrich-König-Str. 7, D-98527 ☎ 03681/720-052 🖷 03681/720-052 ⊕ www.suhl.com. **Weimar** ✉ Tourist-Information Weimar, Markt 10, D-99421 ☎ 03643/24000 or 03643/19443 🖷 03643/240-040 ⊕ www.weimar.de.

UNDERSTANDING GERMANY

GERMANY AT A GLANCE

Fast Facts

Name in local language: Deutschland
Capital: Berlin
National anthem: *Das Lied der Deutschen (The Song of the Germans)*
Type of government: Federal republic
Administrative divisions: 16 states
Independence: January 18, 1871 (German Empire unification); U.K., U.S., U.S.S.R., and France formally relinquished rights to post-WWII zones on March 15, 1991
Constitution: October 3, 1990
Legal system: Civil law system with indigenous concepts; judicial review of legislative acts in the Federal Constitutional Court
Suffrage: 18 years of age; universal
Legislature: Bicameral parliament consists of the Federal Assembly (603 seats; elected by popular vote under a system combining direct and proportional representation; a party must win 5% of the national vote or three direct mandates to gain representation; members serve four-year terms) and the Federal Council (69 votes; state governments are directly represented by votes; each has 3 to 6 votes depending on population and are required to vote as a block)
Population: 82.4 million
Population density: 611 people per square mi
Median age: Female 42.8, male 39.9
Life expectancy: Female 81.6, male 75.5
Infant mortality rate: 4.2 deaths per 1,000 live births
Literacy: 99%
Language: German (official)
Ethnic groups: German 91.5%; other 6.1%; Turkish 2.4%
Religion: Protestant 34%; Roman Catholic 34%; unaffiliated and other 28.3%; Muslim 3.7%
Discoveries & inventions: Printing press with moveable type, aka "Gutenberg Press" (1440), globe (1492), Bunsen burner (1855), contact lenses (1887), diesel engine (1892), X-ray (1895), Geiger counter (1912), electron microscope (1931), ballistic missile (1944)

German diligence is actually endurance.

Franz Grillparzer

Geography & Environment

Land area: 349,223 square km (134,836 square mi), slightly smaller than Montana
Coastline: 2,389 km (1,484 mi) along North Sea, Baltic Sea
Terrain: Lowlands in north, uplands in center, Bavarian Alps in south; highest point: Zugspitze 9,721 feet
Natural resources: Arable land, coal, copper, iron ore, lignite, natural gas, nickel, potash, salt, timber, uranium
Natural hazards: Flooding
Environmental issues: Emissions from coal-burning utilities and industries contribute to air pollution; acid rain, resulting from sulfur dioxide emissions, is damaging forests; pollution in the Baltic Sea from raw sewage and industrial effluents from rivers in eastern Germany; hazardous waste disposal

Economy

Currency: Euro
Exchange rate: €.81 = $1
GDP: €1.8 trillion ($2.16 trillion)
Per capita income: €18,529 ($22,670)
Inflation: 1.2%
Unemployment: 9.8%
Work force: 41.9 million; services 63.8%; industry 33.4%; agriculture 2.8%
Major industries: Cement, chemicals, coal, electronics, food and beverages, iron, machine tools, machinery, shipbuilding, steel, textiles, vehicles
Agricultural products: Barley, cattle, cabbages, fruit, pigs, potatoes, poultry, sugar beets, wheat
Exports: $608 billion

Major export products: Chemicals, foodstuffs, machinery, metals, textiles, vehicles
Export partners: France 10.7%; U.S. 10.3%; U.K. 8.4%; Italy 7.3%; Netherlands 6.1%; Austria 5.1%; Belgium 4.8%; Spain 4.6%; Switzerland 4.2%
Imports: $487.3 billion
Major import products: Chemicals, foodstuffs, machinery, metals, textiles, vehicles
Import partners: France 9.5%; Netherlands 8.2%; U.S. 7.7%; U.K. 6.5%; Italy 6.4%; Belgium 5.2%; Austria 4%; China 4%

Political Climate

Germany's entrance into the European Union was not smooth, leaving political fallout that has been difficult to overcome. Unemployment rose to its highest postwar levels and cutbacks in benefits, which were necessary to meet requirements for the euro, were met with strikes and protests. In 2001,

Chancellor Gerhard Schröderís support for the United States invasion of Afghanistan strained his coalition. Schröder opposed the U.S.-led war in Iraq in 2003, but disagreement between the Social Democrats and the Greens continued to slow the political agenda.

Did You Know?

• Germany is the world's largest recycler of paper. Almost 80% gets reused, compared to about 35% in the U.S.

• Germany routinely submits more patent applications than any other European country.

• Between the world wars, Germany's inflation was so high that $1 equaled more than 4,000,000,000,000 German Marks.

• There are 13 breeds of dogs that people are not allowed to breed or sell in Germany because they are labeled "attack dogs." Twenty-nine other breeds are considered potential attack dogs and must be muzzled when walked.

• In 1916, Germany became the first country to institute Daylight Savings Time.

• Munich's Oktoberfest was officially named the world's largest beer festival in 1999, when 7 million people consumed a record 1.5 million gallons of beer in 11 beer tents standing on a site as large as 50 football fields.

• German citizens are required to pay special taxes on their dogs.

• Many holiday customs originated in Germany, including the Christmas Tree and the Easter Bunny.

CHRONOLOGY

ca. 5000 BC   Indo-Germanic tribes settle in the Rhine and Danube valleys

ca. 2000–800 BC   Distinctive German Bronze Age culture emerges, with settlements ranging from coastal farms to lakeside villages

ca. 450–50 BC   Salzkammergut people, whose prosperity is based on abundant salt deposits (in the area of upper Austria), trade with Greeks and Etruscans; Salzkammerguts spread as far as Belgium and have first contact with the Romans

9 BC–AD 9   Roman attempts to conquer the "Germans"—the tribes of the Cibri, the Franks, the Goths, and the Vandals—and are only partly successful; the Rhine becomes the northeastern border of the Roman Empire (and remains so for 300 years)

212   Roman citizenship is granted to all free inhabitants of the empire

ca. 400   Pressed forward by Huns from Asia, such German tribes as the Franks, the Vandals, and the Lombards migrate to Gaul (France), Spain, Italy, and North Africa, scattering the empire's populace and eventually leading to the disintegration of central Roman authority

486   The Frankish kingdom is founded by Clovis; his court is in Paris

497   The Franks convert to Christianity

Early Middle Ages

776   Charlemagne becomes king of the Franks

800   Charlemagne is declared Holy Roman Emperor; he makes Aachen capital of his realm, which stretches from the Bay of Biscay to the Adriatic and from the Mediterranean to the Baltic. Under his enlightened patronage there is an upsurge in art and architecture—the Carolingian renaissance

843   The Treaty of Verdun divides Charlemagne's empire among his three sons: West Francia becomes France; Lotharingia becomes Lorraine (territory to be disputed by France and Germany into the 20th century); and East Francia takes on, roughly, the shape of modern Germany

911   Five powerful German dukes (of Bavaria, Lorraine, Franconia, Saxony, and Swabia) establish the first German monarchy by electing King Conrad I; Henry I (the Fowler) succeeds Conrad in 919

962   Otto I is crowned Holy Roman Emperor by the pope; he establishes Austria—the East Mark. The Ottonian renaissance is marked especially by the development of Romanesque architecture

Middle Ages

1024–1125   The Salian dynasty is characterized by a struggle between emperors and the Church that leaves the empire weak and disorganized; the great Romanesque cathedrals of Speyer, Trier, and Mainz are built

1138–1254   Frederick Barbarossa leads the Hohenstaufen dynasty; there is temporary recentralization of power, underpinned by strong trade and Church relations

1158   Munich, capital of Bavaria, is founded by Duke Henry the Lion; Henry is deposed by Emperor Barbarossa, and Munich is presented to the House of Wittelsbach, which rules it until 1918

1241   The Hanseatic League is founded to protect trade; Bremen, Hamburg, Köln, and Lübeck are early members. Agencies are soon established in London, Antwerp, Venice, and along the Baltic and North seas; a complex banking and finance system results

mid-1200s   The Gothic style, exemplified by the grand Köln Cathedral, flourishes

1349   The Black Death plague kills one-quarter of the German population

Renaissance & Reformation

1456   Johannes Gutenberg (1400–68) prints the first book in Europe

1471–1553   Renaissance flowers under influence of painter and engraver Albrecht Dürer (1471–1528); Dutch-born philosopher and scholar Erasmus (1466–1536); Lucas Cranach the Elder (1472–1553), who originates Protestant religious painting; portrait and historical painter Hans Holbein the Younger (1497–1543); and landscape-painting pioneer Albrecht Altdorfer (1480–1538). Increasing wealth among the merchant classes leads to strong patronage of the revived arts

1517   The Protestant Reformation begins in Germany when Martin Luther (1483–1546) nails his 95 Theses to a church door in Wittenberg, contending that the Roman Church has forfeited divine authority through its corrupt sale of indulgences. Luther is outlawed, and his revolutionary doctrine splits the Church; much of north Germany embraces Protestantism

1524–30   The (Catholic) Habsburgs rise to power; their empire spreads throughout Europe (and as far as North Africa, the Americas, and the Philippines). Erasmus breaks with Luther and supports reform within the Roman Catholic Church. In 1530 Charles V (a Habsburg) is crowned Holy Roman Emperor; he brutally crushes the Peasants' War, one in a series of populist uprisings in Europe

1545   The Council of Trent marks the beginning of the Counter-Reformation. Through diplomacy and coercion, most Austrians, Bavarians, and Bohemians are won back to Catholicism, but the majority of Germans remain Lutheran; persecution of religious minorities grows

Thirty Years' War

1618–48   Germany is the main theater for the Thirty Years' War. The powerful Catholic Habsburgs are defeated by Protestant forces, swelled by disgruntled Habsburg subjects and the armies of King Gustav

Adolphus of Sweden. The bloody conflict ends with the Peace of Westphalia (1648); Habsburg and papal authority are severely diminished

Absolutism & Enlightenment

1689   Louis XIV of France invades the Rhineland Palatinate and sacks Heidelberg. At the end of the 17th century, Germany consolidates its role as a center of scientific thought

1708   Johann Sebastian Bach (1685–1750) becomes court organist at Weimar and launches his career; he and Georg Friederic Handel (1685–1759) fortify the great tradition of German music. Baroque and, later, rococo art and architecture flourish

1740–86   Reign of Frederick the Great of Prussia; his rule sees both the expansion of Prussia (it becomes the dominant military force in Germany) and the spread of Enlightenment thought

ca. 1790   The great age of European orchestral music is raised to new heights with the works of Joseph Haydn (1732–1809), Wolfgang Amadeus Mozart (1756–91), and Ludwig van Beethoven (1770–1827)

early 1800s   Johann Wolfgang von Goethe (1749–1832) is part of the Sturm und Drang movement, which leads to Romanticism. Painter Caspar David Friedrich (1774–1840) leads early German Romanticism. Other luminary cultural figures include writers Friedrich Schiller (1759–1805) and Heinrich von Kleist (1777–1811); and composers Robert Schumann (1810–56), Hungarian-born Franz Liszt (1811–86), Richard Wagner (1813–83), and Johannes Brahms (1833–97). In architecture, the severe lines of neoclassicism become popular

Road to Nationhood

1806   Napoléon's armies invade Prussia; it briefly becomes part of the French Empire

1807   The Prussian prime minister Baron vom und zum Stein frees the serfs, creating a new spirit of patriotism; the Prussian army is rebuilt

1813   The Prussians defeat Napoléon at Leipzig

1815   Britain and Prussia defeat Napoléon at Waterloo. At the Congress of Vienna, the German Confederation is created as a loose union of 39 independent states, reduced from more than 300 principalities. The Bundestag (national assembly) is established at Frankfurt. Already powerful Prussia increases its territory, gaining the Rhineland, Westphalia, and most of Saxony

1848   The "Year of the Revolutions" is marked by uprisings across the fragmented German Confederation; Prussia expands. A national parliament is elected, taking the power of the Bundestag to prepare a constitution for a united Germany

1862   Otto von Bismarck (1815–98) becomes prime minister of Prussia; he is determined to wrest German-populated provinces from Austro-Hungarian (Habsburg) control

1866   Austria-Hungary is defeated by the Prussians at Sadowa; Bismarck sets up the Northern German Confederation in 1867. A key figure in Bismarck's plans is Ludwig II of Bavaria. Ludwig—a political simpleton—lacks successors, making it easy for Prussia to seize his lands

1867   Karl Marx (1818–83) publishes *Das Kapital*

1870–71   The Franco-Prussian War: Prussia lays siege to Paris. Victorious Prussia seizes Alsace-Lorraine but eventually withdraws from all other occupied French territories

1871   The four south German states agree to join the Northern Confederation; Wilhelm I is proclaimed first kaiser of the united Empire

Modernism

1882   The Triple Alliance is forged between Germany, Austria-Hungary, and Italy. Germany's industrial revolution blossoms, enabling it to catch up with the other great powers of Europe. Germany establishes colonies in Africa and the Pacific

ca. 1885   Daimler and Benz pioneer the automobile

1890   Kaiser Wilhelm II (rules 1888–1918) dismisses Bismarck and begins a new, more aggressive course of foreign policy; he oversees the expansion of the navy

1890s   A new school of writers, including Rainer Maria Rilke (1875–1926), emerges. Rilke's *Sonnets to Orpheus* give German poetry new lyricism

1905   Albert Einstein (1879–1955) announces his theory of relativity

1906   Painter Ernst Ludwig Kirchner (1880–1938) helps organize *Die Brücke,* a group of artists who, along with *Der Blaue Reiter,* create the avant-garde art movement Expressionism

1907   Great Britain, Russia, and France form the Triple Entente, which, set against the Triple Alliance, divides Europe into two armed camps

1914–18   Austrian archduke Franz-Ferdinand is assassinated in Sarajevo. The attempted German invasion of France sparks World War I; Italy and Russia join the Allies, and four years of pitched battle ensue. By 1918 the Central Powers are encircled and must capitulate

Weimar Republic

1918   Germany is compelled by the Versailles Treaty to give up its overseas colonies and much European territory (including Alsace-Lorraine to France) and to pay huge reparations to the Allies; Kaiser Wilhelm II repudiates the throne and goes into exile in Holland. The tough terms leave the new democracy (the Weimar Republic) shaky

1919 The Bauhaus school of art and design, the brainchild of Walter Gropius (1883–1969), is born. Thomas Mann (1875–1955) and Hermann Hesse (1877–1962) forge a new style of visionary intellectual writing

1923 Germany suffers runaway inflation. Adolf Hitler's Beer Hall Putsch, a rightist revolt, fails; leftist revolts are frequent

1925 Hitler publishes *Mein Kampf* (My Struggle)

1932 The Nazi party gains the majority in the Reichstag (parliament)

1933 Hitler becomes chancellor; the Nazi "revolution" begins. In Berlin, Nazi students stage the burning of more than 25,000 books by Jewish and other politically undesirable authors

Nazi Germany

1934 President Paul von Hindenburg dies; Hitler declares himself Führer (leader) of the Third Reich. Nazification of all German social institutions begins, spreading a policy that is virulently racist and anticommunist. Germany recovers industrial might and rearms

1936 Germany signs anticommunist agreements with Italy and Japan, forming the Axis; Hitler reoccupies the Rhineland

1938 The *Anschluss* (annexation): Hitler occupies Austria. Germany occupies the Sudetenland in Czechoslovakia. *Kristallnacht* (Night of Broken Glass), in November, marks the Nazis' first open and direct terrorism against German Jews. Synagogues and Jewish-owned businesses are burned, looted, and destroyed in a night of violence

1939–40 In August Hitler signs a pact with the Soviet Union; in September he invades Poland; war is declared by the Allies. Over the next three years, there are Nazi invasions of Denmark, Norway, the Low Countries, France, Yugoslavia, and Greece. Alliances form between Germany and the Baltic states

1941–45 Hitler launches his anticommunist crusade against the Soviet Union, reaching Leningrad in the north and Stalingrad and the Caucasus in the south. In 1944 the Allies land in France; their combined might brings the Axis to its knees. In addition to the millions killed in the fighting, more than 6 million Jews and other victims die in Hitler's concentration camps. Germany is again in ruins. Hitler kills himself in April 1945. East Berlin and what becomes East Germany are occupied by the Soviet Union

The Cold War

1945 At the Yalta Conference, France, the United States, Britain, and the Soviet Union divide Germany into four zones; each country occupies a sector of Berlin. The Potsdam Agreement expresses the determination to rebuild Germany as a democracy

1946 East Germany's Social Democratic Party merges with the Communist Party, forming the SED, which would rule East Germany for the next 40 years

1948 The Soviet Union tears up the Potsdam Agreement and attempts, by blockade, to exclude the three other Allies from their agreed zones in Berlin. Stalin is frustrated by a massive airlift of supplies to West Berlin

1949 The three Western zones are combined to form the Federal Republic of Germany; the new West German parliament elects Konrad Adenauer as chancellor (a post he held until his retirement in 1963). Soviet-held East Germany becomes the Communist German Democratic Republic (GDR)

1950s West Germany, aided by the financial impetus provided by the Marshall Plan, rebuilds its devastated cities and economy—the *Wirtschaftswunder* (economic miracle) gathers speed. The writers Heinrich Böll, Wolfgang Koeppen, and Günter Grass emerge

1957 The Treaty of Rome heralds the formation of the European Economic Community (EEC); West Germany is a founding member

1961 Communists build the Berlin Wall to stem the outward tide of refugees

1969–74 The vigorous chancellorship of Willy Brandt pursues *Ostpolitik,* improving relations with Eastern Europe and the Soviet Union and acknowledging East Germany's sovereignty

mid-1980s The powerful German Green Party emerges as the leading environmentalist voice in Europe

Reunification

1989 Discontent in East Germany leads to a flood of refugees westward and to mass demonstrations; Communist power collapses across Eastern Europe; the Berlin Wall falls

1990 In March the first free elections in East Germany bring a center-right government to power. The Communists, faced with corruption scandals, suffer a big defeat but are represented (as Democratic Socialists) in the new, democratic parliament. The World War II victors hold talks with the two German governments, and the Soviet Union gives its support for reunification. Economic union takes place on July 1, with full political unity on October 3. In December, in the first democratic national German elections in 58 years, Chancellor Helmut Kohl's three-party coalition is reelected

1991 Nine months of emotional debate end on June 20, when parliamentary representatives vote to move the capital from Bonn— seat of the West German government since 1949—to Berlin, the capital of Germany until the end of World War II

1998   Helmut Kohl's record 16-year-long chancellorship of Germany ends with the election of Gerhard Schröder. Schröder's Social Democratic Party (SPD) pursues a coalition with the Greens in order to replace the three-party coalition of the Christian Democratic Union, Christian Social Union, and Free Democratic Party

1999   The Bundestag, the German parliament, returns to the restored Reichstag in Berlin on April 19. The German federal government also leaves Bonn for Berlin, making Berlin capital of Germany again

1999–2003   For the first time since 1945, the German army (the Bundeswehr) is deployed in combat missions in the former Yugoslavia and Afghanistan

2000   Hannover hosts Germany's first world's exposition, EXPO 2000, the largest ever staged in the 150-year history of the event

VOCABULARY

	English	German	Pronunciation
Basics			
	Yes/no	Ja/nein	yah/nine
	Please	Bitte	**bit**-uh
	Thank you (very much)	Danke (vielen Dank)	**dahn**-kuh (**fee**-lun-dahnk)
	Excuse me	Entschuldigen Sie	ent-**shool**-de-gen zee
	I'm sorry.	Es tut mir leid.	es toot meer lite
	Good day	Guten Tag	**goo**-ten tahk
	Good bye	Auf Wiedersehen	auf **vee**-der-zane
	Mr./Mrs.	Herr/Frau	hair/frau
	Miss	Fräulein	**froy**-line
Numbers			
	1	ein(s)	eint(s)
	2	zwei	tsvai
	3	drei	dry
	4	vier	fear
	5	fünf	fumph
	6	sechs	zex
	7	sieben	**zee**-ben
	8	acht	ahkt
	9	neun	noyn
	10	zehn	tsane
Days of the Week			
	Sunday	Sonntag	**zone**-tahk
	Monday	Montag	**moan**-tahk
	Tuesday	Dienstag	**deens**-tahk
	Wednesday	Mittwoch	**mit**-voah
	Thursday	Donnerstag	**doe**-ners-tahk
	Friday	Freitag	**fry**-tahk
	Saturday	Samstag/ Sonnabend	**zahm**-stakh/ **zonn**-a-bent
Useful Phrases			
	Do you speak English?	Sprechen Sie Englisch?	**shprek**-hun zee **eng**-glish?
	I don't speak German.	Ich spreche kein Deutsch.	ich **shprek**-uh kine doych

Please speak slowly.	Bitte sprechen Sie langsam.	**bit**-uh **shprek**-en-zee **lahng**-zahm
I am American/ British	Ich bin Amerikaner(in)/ Engländer(in)	ich bin a-mer-i-**kahn**-er(in)/ **eng**-glan-der(in)
My name is . . .	Ich heiße . . .	ich **hi**-suh
Where are the restrooms?	Wo ist die Toilette?	vo ist dee twah-**let**-uh
Left/right	links/rechts	links/rechts
Open/closed	offen/geschlossen	O-fen/geh-**shloss**-en
Where is . . .	Wo ist . . .	**vo** ist
the train station?	der Bahnhof?	**dare bahn-hof**
the bus stop?	die Bushaltestelle?	**dee booss-hahlt-uh-**shtel-uh
the subway station?	die U-Bahn-Station?	dee oo-bahn-**staht**-sion
the airport?	der Flugplatz?	dare **floog**-plats
the post office?	die Post?	dee **post**
the bank?	die Bank?	dee **banhk**
the police station?	die Polizeistation?	dee po-lee-tsai-**staht**-sion
the Hospital?	das Krankenhaus?	dahs **krahnk**-en-house
the telephone	das Telefon	**dahs te-le-fone**
I'd like . . .	Ich hätte gerne . . .	ich **het**-uh gairn . . .
a room	ein Zimmer	ein **tsim**-er
the key	den Schlüssel	den **shluh**-sul
a map	eine Stadtplan	I-nuh **staht**-plahn
a ticket	eine Karte	I-nuh cart-uh
How much is it?	Wieviel kostet das?	**vee-feel cost**-et dahs?
I am ill/sick	Ich bin krank	ich bin krahnk
I need . . .	Ich brauche . . .	ich **brow**-khuh
a doctor	einen Arzt	**I-nen** artst
the police	die Polizei	dee po-li-**tsai**
help	Hilfe	**hilf-uh**
Stop!	Halt!	**hahlt**
Fire!	Feuer!	**foy**-er
Look out/Caution!	Achtung!/Vorsicht!	**ahk**-tung/for-zicht

Dining Out

A bottle of . . .	eine Flasche . . .	I-nuh **flash**-uh
A cup of . . .	eine Tasse . . .	I-nuh **tahs**-uh
A glass of . . .	ein Glas . . .	ein glahss
Ashtray	der Aschenbecher	dare **Ahsh**-en-bekh-er
Bill/check	die Rechnung	dee **rekh**-nung

Do you have . . .?	Haben Sie . . .?	**hah**-ben zee
I am a vegetarian.	Ich bin Vegetarier(in)	ich bin ve-guh-**tah**-re-er
I'd like to order . . .	Ich möchte . . . bestellen	ich **mohr**-shtuh . . . buh-**shtel**-en
Menu	die Speisekarte	dee **shpie**-zeh-car-tuh
Napkin	die Serviette	dee zair-vee-**eh**-tuh

MENU GUIDE

English	German

General Dining

English	German
Side dishes	Beilagen
Extra charge	Extraaufschlag
When available	Falls verfügbar
Entrées	Hauptspeisen
(not) included	. . .(nicht) inbegriffen
Depending on the season	je nach Saison
Lunch menu	Mittagskarte
Desserts	Nachspeisen
at your choice	. . . nach Wahl
at your request	. . . nach Wunsch
Prices are . . .	Preise sind . . .
Service included	*inklusive Bedienung*
Value added tax included	*inklusive Mehrwertsteuer (Mwst.)*
Specialty of the house	Spezialität des Hauses
Soup of the day	Tagessuppe
Appetizers	Vorspeisen
Is served from . . . to . . .	Wird von . . . bis . . . serviert

Breakfast

English	German
Bread	Brot
Roll(s)	Brötchen
Eggs	Eier
Hot	heiß
Cold	kalt
Jam	Konfitüre
Milk	Milch
Orange juice	Orangensaft
Scrambled eggs	Rühreier
Bacon	Speck
Fried eggs	Spiegeleier
Lemon	Zitrone
Sugar	Zucker

Soups

English	German
Stew	Eintopf
Chicken soup	Hühnersuppe
Potato soup	Kartoffelsuppe
Liver dumpling soup	Leberknödelsuppe
Onion soup	Zwiebelsuppe

Methods of Preparation

Blue (boiled in salt and vinegar)	Blau
Baked	Gebacken
Fried	Gebraten
Steamed	Gedämpft
Grilled (broiled)	Gegrillt
Boiled	Gekocht
Sauteed	In Butter geschwenkt
Breaded	Paniert
Raw	Roh

When ordering steak, the English words "rare, medium, (well) done" are used and understood in German.

Fish and Seafood

Eel	Aal
Oysters	Austern
Trout	Forelle
Flounder	Flunder
Prawns	Garnelen
Halibut	Heilbutt
Herring	Hering
Lobster	Hummer
Scallops	Jakobsmuscheln
Cod	Kabeljau
Crab	Krabbe
Salmon	Lachs
Mackerel	Makrele
Mussels	Muscheln
Squid	Tintenfisch
Tuna	Thunfisch

Meats

Veal	Kalb(s)
Lamb	Lamm
Beef	Rind(er)
Pork	Schwein(e)

Cuts of Meat

Example: For "Lammkeule" see "Lamm" (above) + ". . . keule" (below)

breast	. . . brust
leg	. . . keule
liver	. . . leber
tenderloin	. . . lende
kidney	. . . niere
rib	. . . rippe

Meat patty	Frikadelle
Meat loaf	Hackbraten
Ham	Schinken

Game and Poultry

Duck	Ente
Pheasant	Fasan
Chicken	Hähnchen (Huhn)
Deer	Hirsch
Rabbit	Kaninchen
Venison	Reh
Pigeon	Taube
Turkey	Truthahn
Quail	Wachtel

Vegetables

Eggplant	Aubergine
Cauliflower	Blumenkohl
Beans	Bohnen
green	*grüne*
white	*weiße*
Peas	Erbsen
Cucumber	Gurke
Cabbage	Kohl
Lettuce	Kopfsalat
Asparagus, peas and carrots	Leipziger Allerlei
Corn	Mais
Carrots	Mohrrüben
Peppers	Paprika
Mushrooms	Pilze
Celery	Sellerie
Asparagus (tips)	Spargel(spitzen)
Tomatoes	Tomaten
Onions	Zwiebeln

Condiments

Vinegar	Essig
Garlic	Knoblauch
Horseradish	Meerettich
Oil	Öl
Mustard	Senf
Artificial sweetener	Süßstoff
Cinnamon	Zimt
Sugar	Zucker
Salt	Salz

Cheese

Mild	Allgäuer Käse, Altenburger (goat cheese), Appenzeller, Greyerzer, Hüttenkäse (cottage cheese), Quark, Räucherkäse (smoked cheese), Sahnekäse (creamy), Tilsiter, Ziegekäse (goat cheese).
Sharp	Handkäse, Harzer Käse, Limburger.
curd	frisch
hard	hart
mild	mild

Fruits

Apple	Apfel
Orange	Apfelsine
Apricot	Aprikose
Blueberry	Blaubeere
Strawberry	Erdbeere
Raspberry	Himbeere
Cherry	Kirsche
Grapefruit	Pampelmuse
Raisin	Rosine
Grape	Weintraube
Banana	Banane
Pear	Birne

Drinks

with/without ice	mit/ohne Eis
with/without water	mit/ohne Wasser
straight	pur
brandy	. . . geist
liqueur	. . . likör
Mulled claret	Glühwein
Caraway-flavored liquor	Kümmel
Fruit brandy	Obstler

When ordering a Martini, you have to specify "gin (vodka) and vermouth," otherwise you will be given a vermouth (Martini & Rossi).

Beer and Wine

non-alcoholic	Alkoholfrei
A dark beer	Ein Dunkles
A light beer	Ein Helles
A mug (one quart)	Eine Maß
Draught	Vom Faß
Dark, bitter, high hops content	Altbier
Strong, high alcohol content	Bockbier (Doppelbock, Märzen)

Wheat beer with yeast	Hefeweizen
Light beer, strong hops aroma	Pils(ener)
Wheat beer	Weizen(bier)
Light beer and lemonade	Radlermaß
Wines	Wein
Rosé wine	Rosëwein
Red wine	Rotwein
White wine and mineral water	Schorle
Sparkling wine	Sekt
White wine	Weißwein
dry	herb
light	leicht
sweet	süß
dry	trocken
full-bodied	vollmundig

Non-alcoholic Drinks

Coffee	Kaffee
decaffeinated	*koffeinfrei*
with cream/sugar	*mit Milch/Zucker*
black	*schwarz*
Mineral water	Mineralwasser
carbonated/non-carbonated	*mit/ohne Kohlensäure*
juice	*. . . saft*
(hot) Chocolate	(heiße) Schokolade
Tea	Tee
iced tea	*Eistee*
herb tea	*Kräutertee*
with cream/lemon	*mit Milch/Zitrone*

INDEX

NOTES

NOTES

NOTES

NOTES

NOTES

NOTES

NOTES

NOTES

FODOR'S KEY TO THE GUIDES

America's guidebook leader publishes guides for every kind of traveler.
Check out our many series and find your perfect match.

FODOR'S GOLD GUIDES
America's favorite travel-guide series offers the most detailed insider reviews of hotels, restaurants, and attractions in all price ranges, plus great background information, smart tips, and useful maps.

COMPASS AMERICAN GUIDES
Stunning guides from top local writers and photographers, with gorgeous photos, literary excerpts, and colorful anecdotes. A must-have for culture mavens, history buffs, and new residents.

FODOR'S CITYPACKS
Concise city coverage in a guide plus a foldout map. The right choice for urban travelers who want everything under one cover.

FODOR'S EXPLORING GUIDES
Hundreds of color photos bring your destination to life. Lively stories lend insight into the culture, history, and people.

FODOR'S TRAVEL HISTORIC AMERICA
For travelers who want to experience history firsthand, this series gives in-depth coverage of historic sights, plus nearby restaurants and hotels. Themes include the Thirteen Colonies, the Old West, and the Lewis and Clark Trail.

FODOR'S POCKET GUIDES
For travelers who need only the essentials. The best of Fodor's in pocket-size packages for just $9.95.

FODOR'S FLASHMAPS
Every resident's map guide, with dozens of easy-to-follow maps of public transit, restaurants, shopping, museums, and more.

FODOR'S CITYGUIDES
Sourcebooks for living in the city: thousands of in-the-know listings for restaurants, shops, sports, nightlife, and other city resources.

FODOR'S AROUND THE CITY WITH KIDS
Up to 68 great ideas for family days, recommended by resident parents. Perfect for exploring in your own backyard or on the road.

FODOR'S HOW TO GUIDES
Get tips from the pros on planning the perfect trip. Learn how to pack, fly hassle-free, plan a honeymoon or cruise, stay healthy on the road, and travel with your baby.

FODOR'S LANGUAGES FOR TRAVELERS
Practice the local language before you hit the road. Available in phrase books, cassette sets, and CD sets.

KAREN BROWN'S GUIDES
Engaging guides—many with easy-to-follow inn-to-inn itineraries—to the most charming inns and B&Bs in the U.S.A. and Europe.

SEE IT GUIDES
Illustrated guidebooks that include the practical information travelers need, in gorgeous full color. Thousands of photos, hundreds of restaurant and hotel reviews, prices, and ratings for attractions all in one indispensable package. Perfect for travelers who want the best value packed in a fresh, easy-to-use, colorful layout.

OTHER GREAT TITLES FROM FODOR'S
Baseball Vacations, The Complete Guide to the National Parks, Family Vacations, Golf Digest's Places to Play, Great American Drives of the East, Great American Drives of the West, Great American Vacations, Healthy Escapes, National Parks of the West, Skiing USA.